TUGENDHAT AND CHRISTIE

# THE LAW OF PRIVACY AND THE MEDIA

THIRD EDITION

*Edited by*

N A MOREHAM

SIR MARK WARBY

*Consultant Editors*

SIR MICHAEL TUGENDHAT

IAIN CHRISTIE

OXFORD

UNIVERSITY PRESS

OXFORD
UNIVERSITY PRESS

Great Clarendon Street, Oxford, OX2 6DP,
United Kingdom

Oxford University Press is a department of the University of Oxford.
It furthers the University's objective of excellence in research, scholarship,
and education by publishing worldwide. Oxford is a registered trade mark of
Oxford University Press in the UK and in certain other countries

Second Edition published in 2011
Third Edition published in 2016

Impression: 1

Published in the United States of America by Oxford University Press
198 Madison Avenue, New York, NY 10016, United States of America

British Library Cataloguing in Publication Data
Data available

Library of Congress Control Number: 2015958367

ISBN 978–0–19–968574–5

Printed and bound by
CPI Group (UK) Ltd, Croydon, CR0 4YY

# TUGENDHAT AND CHRISTIE
# THE LAW OF PRIVACY AND THE MEDIA

# FOREWORD

Misuse of private information was recognized as a new cause of action in *Campbell v MGN*.[1] In *Google Inc v Vidal-Hall*[2] it was held to be a tort. The emergence of a new tort, otherwise than by statute, is a very rare event in English law. That it happened in this case is all the more striking because of the statements of so distinguished a judge as Megarry V-C, in *Malone v Metropolitan Police Commissioner*. In that case the question was whether the plaintiff had a cause of action for having his telephone tapped by the police without any trespass upon his land. He said[3] that

> 'where Parliament has abstained from legislating on a point that is plainly suitable for legislation, it is indeed difficult for the court to lay down new rules of common law or equity that will carry out the Crown's treaty obligations, or to discover for the first time that such rules have always existed…I can do no more than express a hope, and offer a proleptic welcome to any statute on the subject…., I would have thought that in any civilised system of law the claims of liberty and justice would require that telephone users should have effective and independent safeguards against possible abuses.'

In relation to that, and other types, of privacy claim, Parliament did subsequently legislate.[4] But, notwithstanding a number of proposals that it legislate in relation to misuse of private information, Parliament chose not to do so.

When, in *Campbell* in 2004, judges nevertheless did recognise the misuse of private information as a cause of action, this was the occasion of bitter criticism of judges by the press. Parliament and others have confirmed that there was no foundation for this criticism of the judges.[5]

This unsuccessful press campaign nevertheless did great damage to the public interest. It cast doubt on the values of human rights generally in the minds of ordinary citizens. They are the electorate in our democracy. As Professor Feldman has said: 'Ordinary citizens…must internalize the values of individual and group rights, because democracy can be reconciled with respect for rights only if the

---

[1] [2004] UKHL 22, [2004] 2 AC 457.
[2] [2015] EWCA Civ 311.
[3] [1979] Ch 344 379, 381A.
[4] Interception of Communications Act 1985 (following *Malone v United Kingdom* (1984) 7 EHRR 14) and the Protection from Harassment Act 1997.
[5] Culture, Media and Sport Committee - Second Report Press standards, privacy and libel, 9 February 2010.

people who participate in political decision-making, however remotely, exercise their powers in the light of people's rights.'[6]

The tort of misuse of private information is now firmly established in English law. So, the scope of this tort, and of related torts, such as the statutory tort of harassment (to which Dr Moreham has devoted a new chapter in this edition), is wide enough to afford the effective remedy for invasions of privacy that was previously lacking. In 2003 the House of Lords had foreshadowed this saying 'There are a number of common law and statutory remedies of which it may be said that one at least of the underlying values they protect is a right of privacy'. They were referring to defamation and other ancient causes of action discussed in this book.[7]

If respect for private life had not been a principle which was already recognised in English law, the UK would not have accepted to be bound by Art 8 of the European Convention. What had been lacking is not recognition of the principles at stake, but, the specific means by which English law might give an effective remedy for infringements of these principles.

The judicial oath includes to 'do right to all manner of people after the laws and usages of this realm…'. When the law is clear, all that is normally necessary for judges to do right, is for them to apply the law correctly to the true facts. When the law is not clear, or where judges feel constrained by the law from doing what they believe to be right (as Megarry V-C made clear was his position in *Malone*), then it may be difficult or impossible for judges to do to some people what those judges believe to be right. It is of the first importance that such situations should be avoided if at all possible. It is to be hoped that such situations will not arise in the future, whether or not the Human Rights Act 1998 remains in its present form, or is repealed and replaced.

The law of privacy, and the law of freedom of expression generally, are branches of the law which are less well known amongst some practitioners and judges than some other branches of the law of tort. The right answers to the legal problems posed are often ones which seem counter-intuitive to those unfamiliar with the subject. These branches of the law are also ones on which, very often, advice has to be given, and decisions made, with very little time for reflection or research. It is therefore vital that there should be the clear and up-to-date exposition of the law which is now to be found in this third edition.

The third edition includes a substantial body of new case law. These are cases decided, not only in England, but also in numerous other jurisdictions, both in the UK, and in common law and civil law countries. Amongst its other qualities, this book represents an outstanding example of the valuable use to which comparative

---

[6] *Civil Liberties and Human Rights in England and Wales*, 2nd ed, OUP 2002, 1089.
[7] *Wainwright v Home Office* [2003] UKHL 53 [2004] 2 AC 406 para 18.

law can be put. The participation of specialist foreign law contributors is a notable feature of this book.

Together with my colleagues in chambers at 5RB, I practised in the field of breach of confidence from the early 1970s. For over thirty years I was privileged to contribute as a barrister to the development of that law, and to the emergence of the new tort of misuse of private information. As a judge I had the further privilege of developing that law in the many cases which are discussed and noted in this third edition.

It is a great honour for me that, following my retirement from the Bench, this book still bears my name. I have not written anything new in this edition. That fact enables me to give to all those who have written new material for this edition, in particular to Dr Nicole Moreham, and Sir Mark Warby, the praise that they deserve for producing such an outstanding legal text. Dr Moreham first studied this subject as a PhD student at Cambridge, and has since earned the well-deserved reputation as one of the leading scholars of privacy. Warby J will no doubt have many opportunities to apply and develop the law from the bench.

I would also like to express my thanks to all who have contributed to this, and earlier, editions in other capacities. Not least amongst these are Chris Rycroft and others at the publishers, Oxford University Press. They had the foresight to accept for publication the proposal for a book on the law of privacy at a time when other law publishers saw no need for such a book.

Michael Tugendhat
*Inner Temple*
*October 2015*

# PREFACE

It was a bold move when this book was first published in 2002 to write a book called *The Law of Privacy and the Media*. The impact of measures like the Human Rights Act 1998, the Data Protection Act 1998, and the Protection from Harassment Act 1997 was only just beginning to be felt and debate continued about what place privacy had in the common law. By bringing together into one volume the different facets of privacy protection, *The Law of Privacy and the Media* was therefore something of a foretoken. It showed what might lie ahead if academics and judges seized the gauntlet and recognized privacy as a fully-fledged legal right.

Now, just thirteen years later, the gauntlet has been seized. The tort of misuse of private information is an established part of the common-law landscape, harassment legislation has been harnessed in the fight against intrusion and publication of private information, and the importance of data protection legislation and European data directives is finally coming to be fully understood. Similar developments are occurring abroad: New Zealand and Ontario have recognized new torts of intrusion into seclusion; Australian judges continue to push the boundaries of breach of confidence; and recommendations for privacy reform abound.

Public awareness of privacy issues has also dramatically increased since 2002. The launch of the second edition coincided with the so-called 'super-injunction' furore in the UK press, an impassioned debate about the propriety of granting anonymized injunctions to public figures wanting to keep discreditable information out of the public eye. Then came the gradual revelation of the scale of telephone hacking at News Group Newspapers and, latterly MGN Ltd. The resulting parliamentary inquiries, prosecutions, civil cases, and of course the Leveson Inquiry into the Culture, Practices and Ethics of the Press have raised public awareness of media privacy issues like never before.

Alongside these exposés has been the explosion in the use of 'new media' and portable digital devices, especially the smartphone. The ability of ordinary individuals to obtain and widely circulate private material is now a part of our daily reality. This democratization of mass communication not only brings fresh challenges for the law, it has re-defined our understanding of the media. This book is no longer just about newspapers, broadcasters, and their related news sites; blogs and social networking sites are also now an unavoidable part of the media landscape.

So how does the third edition of *Tugendhat & Christie: The Law of Privacy and the Media* respond to these changes? The most conspicuous change is the addition of two new chapters. The first—'Harassment by Publication'—examines the burgeoning use of harassment legislation to protect against the disclosure of private material, particularly on the internet. The second—'Privacy, the Internet, and Social Media'—discusses the law relating to 'new media', including practical ways to address internet trolling and to get material taken down from the web. To make way for this new discussion, chapters on the protection of journalistic sources and special issues relating to the publication of personal information have been removed and key parts of their content integrated into other chapters.

Other chapters from the second edition are retained but their content is updated and invariably much changed. Chapter 14, on the privacy codes, now includes discussion of the Independent Press Standards Organisation, the self-regulatory press body formed in the aftermath of the Leveson Inquiry. Chapter 7 discusses the implications of *Google Spain*, the so-called 'right to be forgotten' case in which search engines were held to be data controllers for the purpose of European data protection legislation. And the remaining chapters—including those on breach of confidence and misuse of private information—address the great many developments in case law and legislation that have taken place since 2011. Indeed, this new edition contains more than 350 new cases, including more than 250 from the United Kingdom alone.

All that said, some things about this topic remain the same. Many of the fundamental questions about what privacy is and why and how it should be protected transcend the vagaries of technological development or public scandal. Like Warren and Brandeis writing in the Harvard Law Review in 1890, we are still seeking to refine 'the principle which may be invoked to protect the privacy of the individual from invasion either by the too enterprising press, the photographer, or the possessor of any other modern device for recording or reproducing scenes or sounds'. Many of the concepts that we use to identify that principle—dignity, autonomy, intimacy, and privacy itself—remain the same. This book talks about those issues too.

It is difficult to predict what challenges might arise for the law of privacy while this edition of the book is in print. Whatever they are, it is hoped that the ensuing pages will provide a sound understanding of existing law and principles to help guide the way through.

Nicole Moreham
October 2015

# ACKNOWLEDGEMENTS

The publication of the third edition of this book marks a turning point in several ways. Above all, this is the first edition which has not involved a substantial editorial contribution from Sir Michael Tugendhat. Between the last edition and this one he has retired from the Bench and, understandably, stood back from the task of preparing this manuscript. Despite this, he has found the time to provide valuable insights, as ever. And we believe that much remains of the stamp of his scholarship, erudition, and humanity, which made the first edition such a success.

So many of the decisions we cite in this edition are those of Sir Michael that it is hard to imagine that will not be the case. The modern law of privacy and the media owes so much to his conscientious and scrupulous policing of the sometimes foggy boundaries between privacy and freedom of expression. In the hope that this edition might be a fitting tribute to his enormous contribution to this area of our law, we dedicate it to him and—appropriately, we hope—his family. His own views on whether we have achieved something acceptable will be found in the Foreword which he has kindly agreed to provide for this edition.

Secondly, we say farewell to Iain Christie as an Editor. Iain, the other founding editor, has also moved on, in his case to become a Board Member of IMPRESS—The Independent Monitor for the Press—while remaining Secretary of the Civil Mediation Council. He has therefore joined Sir Michael as a Consultant Editor. We thank Iain for his significant writing and editorial contribution to the creation of this work, and to its second edition.

Thirdly, the cover and title pages of this new edition properly reflect the fact that its main progenitor is now Nicole Moreham, without whose tireless efforts it would not have seen the light of day—at least, not this side of 2018. Her primary role reflects the fact that I have moved to the Bench which—though many would query this—has left me less, not more time to devote to this work. It is fitting, anyway, that the academic input should have taken a more prominent role at this point in the book's evolution.

Our thanks are due to Duncan McLachlan, research assistant at the law faculty at Victoria University of Wellington for his hugely valuable assistance with finalizing the text. His work was invariably thorough, careful, and, despite the need to fit it around a busy university schedule, cheerfully provided. We are also indebted to Tom McKenzie for his research assistance with aspects of Chapter 5 and to Marcin Betkier, a PhD candidate at Victoria, for his careful work on the final proofs.

In addition, we as editors and the authors of Chapter 15 all wish to thank Daithí MacSíthigh of Newcastle University for his characteristic generosity in agreeing to review this new chapter in draft and for providing a series of perceptive and useful observations.

This remains, however, not an academic treatise but a practitioner's textbook. That makes the input of so many of my former colleagues at 5RB especially valuable. The practitioner's insight is an enormously important part of this work, and I am delighted that so many have allowed themselves to be inveigled, induced, persuaded, cajoled or—let us admit it—dragooned into making a contribution. There are no fewer than five new contributors from 5RB this time. The white heat of adversarial argument, and reflection before and after the contest, do help forge the law.

We have again been fortunate in the quantity and quality of input from practitioners and academics in other jurisdictions for their contributions to Chapter 3, which we continue to regard as a valuable source of comparative law. The individuals involved are so numerous that we have found it best to list them in the Contributors section of the book. Interested readers will find a list of some of the most distinguished names in their field. On the editors' behalf I must express our warm thanks to all of them for the time and effort they have put in, to share their expertise with our readers.

At OUP, we must thank Gemma Parsons, and Emma Taylor, for their roles in nudging us towards the completion of this edition. If we have not always met their deadlines, and we have not, I apologize on behalf of us all but pay tribute to their progress-chasing skills and enthusiasm. Others whom we would like to acknowledge by name are: the Royal Society of New Zealand for funding (via the Rutherford Discovery Fellowship) Nicole Moreham's teaching buy-out and the valuable services of Duncan McLachlan, Tom McKenzie, and Marcin Betkier; Professor ATH Smith of Victoria University of Wellington; Tim Smith, for his sound legal judgment and unfailing practical and moral support; and Ann Kenrick for her tolerance, and her ability to encourage when the will to carry on was flagging.

Finally, we owe a debt to all those who practise in this field of law—as academics or practitioners—for their continued dedication to the task of ensuring that the vital rights that compete for attention in this important field of law are weighed up in a principled and effective way.

Mark Warby
Royal Courts of Justice, Strand, London WC2
October 2015

# CONTENTS—SUMMARY

# CONTENTS

## II PUBLICATION OF PERSONAL INFORMATION

## III COMMERCIAL RIGHTS AND INTRUSION

## IV JUSTIFICATIONS AND DEFENCES

## VI  THE ACTION

## VII  PRIVACY REGULATION

## VIII PRIVACY, THE INTERNET, AND SOCIAL MEDIA

# TABLE OF CASES

## EUROPEAN COMMISSION AND COURT OF HUMAN RIGHTS

## EUROPEAN COURT OF JUSTICE

## FOREIGN

### Australia

## Austria

## Canada

## New Zealand

# TABLE OF ADJUDICATIONS
# OF THE MEDIA REGULATORS

# TABLE OF LEGISLATION

## UK STATUTORY INSTRUMENTS

### FOREIGN LEGISLATION

**Australia**

**Canada**

# TABLE OF INTERNATIONAL TREATIES
# AND CONVENTIONS

# LIST OF CONTRIBUTORS

## Editors

Dr Nicole Moreham
Sir Mark Warby

## Consultant Editors

Sir Michael Tugendhat
Iain Christie

## Contributors

Nigel Abbas
Professor Tanya Aplin
Jonathan Barnes
Stephen Bate
Godwin Busuttil
Adèle Garrick
Felicity McMahon
Dr Nicole Moreham
Richard Munden
Matthew Nicklin QC
Richard Parkes QC
Justin Rushbrooke QC
Julian Santos
Victoria Shore
Adam Speker
Chloe Strong
Yuli Takatsuki
Sir Mark Warby
Gervase de Wilde
Adam Wolanski

# Foreign Law Contributors

*United States*

**Robert Balin** Davis Wright Tremaine LLP, New York; and **Chloe Strong** 5RB, Gray's Inn, London

*Ireland*

**Dr Eoin Carolan** Senior Lecturer, University College Dublin

*New Zealand*

**Dr Nicole Moreham** Associate Professor, Victoria University of Wellington

*Australia*

**Megan Richardson** Professor, University of Melbourne; and **Michael Rivette** Barrister, Chancery Chambers, Melbourne

*Canada*

**Dr Barbara von Tigerstrom** Professor, University of Saskatchewan

*South Africa*

**Iain Currie** Advocate, Johannesburg Bar

*Scotland*

**Roddy Dunlop QC** Axiom Advocates, Edinburgh

*Germany*

**Richter am Landgericht Björn Raap** Judge of the Aurich District Court

*France*

**Dr Eva Steiner** Senior Lecturer and the Director of the LLB in English Law and French Law, King's College London

# Part I

## SOURCES AND PRINCIPLES OF PRIVACY LAW

# 1

## CONTEXT AND BACKGROUND

*Adam Wolanski and Victoria Shore*

## A. Introduction

The law of privacy has come a long way since the Human Rights Act 1998 (HRA) **1.01**
came into force in October 2000. Before then, the prevailing view was that there
was no right to privacy at common law[1] and that it had 'so long been disregarded
here that it can be recognised only by the legislature'.[2] Instead, indirect, piecemeal
protection of privacy was afforded through existing causes of action where the facts

---

[1] *Kaye v Robertson* [1991] FSR 62, CA; applied in *Khorasandjian v Bush* [1993] QB 727, CA.
[2] *Kaye* (n 1) 71 (Legatt LJ). Similar remarks were made by Buxton LJ in *Secretary of State for the Home Dept v Wainwright* [2001] EWCA Civ 2081, [2002] QB 1334 [94]: 'It is thus for Parliament to remove, if it thinks fit, the barrier to the recognition of a tort of breach of privacy that is at present erected by *Kaye v Robertson* and *Khorasandjian*.'

of individual cases permitted it.[3] Despite judicial dicta leaving the question open,[4] this appears to have remained the position at least until the HRA came into force.[5]

**1.02**  At the time of entry into force of the HRA, the House of Lords confirmed in *Wainwright v Home Office*[6] that English law does not recognize a general tort of invasion of privacy. Some gaps in the existing law could be filled by judicious development of an existing principle,[7] others only by legislation.

**1.03**  The HRA itself was a substantial gap-filler in that it provided (via the operation of ss 6 and 7) a statutory remedy against public authorities for breaches of Convention rights, including an infringement of rights under Article 8 of the European Convention on Human Rights (ECHR).[8] In two important cases following the implementation of the HRA the courts considered the extent to which Convention rights indirectly affected the traditional causes of action with respect to the protection of privacy between individuals: that is, whether the Act had 'horizontal effect'. By virtue of s 6(3) HRA, courts and tribunals are public authorities for the purposes of the HRA. Even in the absence of facts giving rise to a direct claim under one or more of the ECHR Articles, there is an obligation on the courts to develop the common law in conformity with the protection afforded by the ECHR. In *Campbell v MGN Ltd*,[9] the House of Lords recognized that while the HRA could not create new causes of action between individuals 'if there is a relevant cause of action, the court as a public authority must act compatibly with both parties' Convention rights'. Further, the House held in *Campbell* that where the invasion is occasioned by wrongful disclosure of personal information, 'the essence of the tort is better encapsulated now as misuse of private information'.[10] In *Douglas v Hello! Ltd*, Sedley LJ observed at [133] that subsection (4) of Article 12 HRA 'puts beyond

---

[3] The Court of Appeal in *Kaye* (n 1) itself contemplated that flashlight photography of an unwilling subject could in certain circumstances constitute a battery: 68 (Glidewell LJ). In *Hellewell v Chief Constable of Derbyshire* [1995] 1 WLR 804, Laws J stated at 807 that 'the law would protect what might reasonably be called a right of privacy, although the name accorded to the cause of action would be breach of confidence'.

[4] See *eg R v Khan (Sultan)* [1997] AC 558, 571 (Lord Browne-Wilkinson) and 582–83 (where Lord Nolan left open 'the important question whether the present, piecemeal protection of privacy has now developed to the extent that a more comprehensive principle can be seen to exist').

[5] On 2 October 2000. The remarks of Buxton LJ cited at n 2, although expressed to be a view of the 'present' state of the law must be read subject to his Lordship's comment at [74] that the current case was not the place in which to resolve the issue of whether the HRA is itself the legislation which arguably creates a private law right to privacy. However, in *Douglas v Hello! Ltd* [2001] QB 967, Sedley LJ observed at [111] that, even without the impact of the HRA, equity and the common law had reached a point where the courts were 'in a position to respond to an increasingly invasive social environment by affirming that everybody has a right to some private space'.

[6] [2003] UKHL 53, [2004] 2 AC 406. The facts of the case pre-dated entry into force of the HRA but Lord Hoffmann's remarks are of general application.

[7] *Wainwright* (n 6) [18].

[8] Convention for the Protection of Human Rights and Fundamental Freedoms (the European Convention on Human Rights) (Rome, 4 November 1950; TS 71 (1953); Cmd 8969).

[9] [2004] UKHL 22, [2004] 2 AC 457.

[10] *Campbell* (n 9) [14] (Lord Nicholls).

question the direct applicability' of Article 10 ECHR 'as between one private party to litigation and another—in the jargon, its horizontal effect'. At a later stage in the same case, it was explicitly recognized that confidence and misuse of private information had become separate and distinct wrongs.[11]

The position now arrived at, therefore, is that insofar as informational privacy is **1.04** concerned English law has an established and rapidly developing law of privacy under which it is able to give effect to its obligations under the Convention. As this aspect of privacy is the one that most concerns the media it is the primary focus of this book.

This chapter first briefly explains the wider context in which developments in the **1.05** law of privacy have taken place. Section B introduces the various common-law causes of action which have historically been used to protect privacy in English law and considers their limitations. Section C contains an account of pre-HRA protections of privacy in common law and equity, with Section D assessing the impact of the HRA on media cases involving Articles 8 and 10. Section E considers the broader statutory framework for the protection of privacy and Section F briefly considers the Media Codes. The chapter concludes in Section G by reference to the position of 'new media'.

## B. Privacy Controversy and Reform

The absence of any general right to privacy in English common law or statute has **1.06** been the subject of much debate over the years and, in spite of recent developments in informational privacy protection, that debate continues. From time to time the government has established specific bodies to consider whether the law in this area should be reformed by the implementation of a statutory right to privacy. For example, the question was considered in detail following the publication in 1990 of the Calcutt Report and again in 1993 after the publication of Sir David Calcutt's Review of Press Self Regulation. In the Review, Sir David concluded that the existing self-regulation regime had failed and recommended, amongst other things, that the government give further consideration to the implementation of a new tort of infringement of privacy. Some limited reforms of the Press Complaints Commission followed. The Culture Media and Sports Select Committee also published a review in 2008 which again highlighted shortcomings in the self-regulation regime, but did not recommend the introduction of a new statutory tort.

A full analysis of the various reviews and the proposals they put forward and the **1.07** political impetus behind such reforms can be found in the previous editions of this work. Since publication of the last edition, these issues have come to the fore once

---

[11] [2007] UKHL 21, [2008] 1 AC 1 [255] (Lord Nicholls).

again thanks to the phone-hacking scandal involving the now defunct *News of the World* and other British newspapers published by News International. Employees of the newspaper were revealed to have engaged in phone hacking, police bribery, and exercising improper influence in the pursuit of publishing stories. As a result, in July 2011, Prime Minister David Cameron announced a public inquiry to investigate the culture, practices and ethics of the press chaired by Lord Justice Leveson. The Leveson Inquiry published its *Report on Part 1 of the Inquiry* on 29 November 2012.

**1.08**  The Inquiry and its specific recommendations are discussed in detail in Chapter 14. Despite the trenchant criticisms made in the Report of the activities of certain sectors of the media, the Inquiry was not asked to consider whether there was a need for a statutory law of privacy, and there appears to be no prospect that such legislation will be enacted in the near future. However, as a consequence of the Report a new press watchdog was established by Royal Charter on 3 November 2014, 'the Recognition Panel'. This fully independent body was incorporated to consider whether any newly-established self-regulators of the press meet the recognition criteria recommended by the Leveson Report and subsequently included within the Royal Charter. At the time of writing it seems unlikely that most UK media publishers will sign up to any regulator approved by the Panel. Instead several media organizations have stated their intention to subscribe to the new independent regulator, the Independent Press Standards Organisation (IPSO). Several of the broadsheet newspapers, including the *Financial Times, The Independent* and *The Guardian* have indicated they will not take part in IPSO. The *Financial Times* joins *The Guardian* in establishing its own independent complaints system. The decision by the press not to sign up to an approved regulator could have significant implications for those media organizations which choose not to participate in the approved regulatory scheme: under the Crime and Courts Act 2013 such organizations may be liable to pay aggravated and exemplary damages in litigation resulting from the publication of news-related material.[12]

## C.  Pre-HRA Protections of Privacy in Common Law and Equity

### (1)  Introduction

**1.09**  The misuse of private information action, which was first recognized in *Campbell v MGN Ltd* and *Douglas v Hello! Ltd*,[13] is the closest thing English law has to

---

[12]  ss 39–42. Some industry lawyers have argued that these provisions are incompatible with Art 10. See *eg* <inforrm.wordpress.com/2013/03/22/briefing-note-on-exemplary-damages-and-costs-gill-phillips>.

[13]  See nn 9–11, and text thereto.

a free-standing right to privacy. The decision in *Campbell* makes it clear that, despite courts' attempts to shoe-horn Convention requirements into the traditional action for breach of confidence, the traditional three-part *Coco v Clark* analysis is no longer apposite in cases where personal information is concerned. The HRA requires a different approach. Those developments are discussed in Chapter 5. The focus of this section is on those causes of action which provided piecemeal protection to the right to privacy before enactment of the HRA and which continue to provide incidental protection in areas where misuse of private information does not apply.

## (2) Trespass and Wrongful Interference with Goods

Before the invention of photography and telegraphy individuals could usually **1.10** control the dissemination of information about themselves by controlling access to their home and correspondence. These have always been protected by the law of trespass. The right to own property, protected in England by the tort of trespass, is so fundamental to Western traditions of human dignity that dignity is rarely referred to. But 'the common law has always recognised a man's house as his castle',[14] and the connotation of the word 'castle' speaks for itself: property in land and papers promotes autonomy.

The tort of trespass to land will provide a right of action for invasion of privacy but, **1.11** as discussed at 10.47 *et seq*, the action has considerable limitations. The main limitation on the protection afforded to privacy by the tort of trespass is the requirement that there be physical interference with land or property. Observation from a neighbouring property or public place will not give rise to a cause of action; nor will observation from a reasonable height above a property. In *Bernstein v Skyviews and General Ltd*,[15] Griffiths J held that the rights of an owner in the air space above his land are restricted to such height as is necessary for the ordinary use and enjoyment of his land and that 'there is no law against taking a photograph, and the mere taking of a photograph cannot turn an act which is not a trespass into the plaintiff's air space into one that is a trespass'.[16]

Further, liability for trespass can only arise if the victim is the legal occupier whose **1.12** property is physically interfered with.[17] And unless there is actual damage to the

---

[14] S Warren and L Brandeis, 'The Right to Privacy' (1890) 4 Harvard L Rev 193, 220; *R (Bright) v Central Criminal Court* [2001] 1 WLR 662, 680; and see the *Report of the Committee on Privacy* (Cmnd 5012, 1972) (Chairman: Kenneth Younger) (Younger Report) para 289.

[15] [1978] QB 479. Baron Bernstein of Leigh objected to an offer to sell him an aerial photograph of his estate taken by the defendant without his knowledge or consent.

[16] *Bernstein* (n 15) 483.

[17] *Hickman v Maisey* [1900] 1 QB 752. The owner of papers, including the recipient of a letter, has sufficient property in it to sue for wrongful interference with goods and obtain substantial damages: *Oliver v Oliver* (1861) 142 ER 748; *Thurston v Charles* (1905) 21 TLR 659; *R v IRC, ex p Rossminster* [1980] AC 952.

land, damages are likely to be unsatisfactory unless exemplary or aggravated, and the remedy is an empty one where no injunction can be obtained.[18]

**1.13** An attempt to merge the requirements of the torts of trespass to the person with those of the tort of intentional infliction of emotional harm[19] and privacy was rejected by the House of Lords in *Secretary of State for the Home Dept v Wainwright*.[20] Under the *Wilkinson v Downton* principle, a person may sue where he or she has been caused physical harm (including psychiatric injury) by a wilfully committed act or statement calculated to cause physical harm. The claimants, a mother and son, were invasively strip-searched for drugs on a prison visit in 1997 in breach of the Prison Rules. Both were humiliated and distressed and the son developed post-traumatic stress disorder. At first instance it had been held that trespass to the person, consisting of wilfully causing a person to do something to him or herself that infringed his or her right to privacy, had been committed against both claimants. In addition, trespass to the person, consisting of wilfully causing a person to do something calculated to cause him or her harm, had been committed against the second claimant (as well as a battery).

**1.14** The Court of Appeal allowed the Home Office's appeal against the finding of trespass, dismissed the first claimant's claim and limited the second claimant's award to recovery for damages for battery. Lord Hoffmann later expressed complete agreement with Buxton LJ's observations in the Court of Appeal[21] that *Wilkinson v Downton* has nothing to do with trespass to the person.

### (3) Nuisance

**1.15** In certain circumstances an action in nuisance will lie in respect of interference with a person's enjoyment of his or her land where trespass would not. As Griffiths J said in *Bernstein v Skyviews*:[22]

> If a plaintiff were subject to the harassment of constant surveillance of his house from the air, accompanied by the photographing of his every activity, I am far from saying that the court would not regard such a monstrous invasion of his privacy as an actionable nuisance for which they would give relief.

The taking of a single photograph would not, however, constitute an actionable nuisance.

**1.16** Persistent watching and besetting may also be a nuisance[23] as may persistent telephoning, if it amounts to a substantial and unreasonable interference with a

---

[18] Younger Report (n 14) para 85.
[19] Established in English law by the case of *Wilkinson v Downton* [1897] 2 QB 57. See further *Rhodes v OPO* [2015] UKSC 32, [2015] 2 WLR 1373. For further discussion of the *Wilkinson v Downton* tort, see 10.56 *et seq.*
[20] *Wainwright*, HL (n 6).
[21] *Wainwright*, CA (n 2) [67]–[72].
[22] *Bernstein* (n 15) 484.
[23] *Lyons & Sons v Wilkins* [1899] 1 Ch 255.

person's use and enjoyment of land.[24] But the scope of the protection afforded to privacy by the tort of nuisance is restricted by the fact that an action only lies at the suit of a person with a right to the land affected. Although this category includes persons in actual possession, whatever their legal right to be there, a mere licensee on the land (for example, a person using a gym or dining in a restaurant) has no right to sue.[25]

### (4) Breach of Confidence

Prior to the recognition of the new cause of action for 'misuse of personal informa-    **1.17** tion' an action for breach of confidence was the closest in substance to an action for invasion of privacy through the disclosure of personal information.[26] The relationship between the two interests was expressly recognized in judicial dicta prior to the enactment of the HRA. For example, in *Hellewell v Chief Constable of Derbyshire*[27] Laws J stated:

> If someone with a telephoto lens were to take from a distance and with no authority a picture of another engaged in some private act, his subsequent disclosure of the photograph would, in my judgment, as surely amount to a breach of confidence as if he had found or stolen a diary in which the act was recounted and proceeded to publish it. In such a case, the law would protect what might reasonably be called a right of privacy, although the name accorded to the cause of action would be breach of confidence.

Many years earlier, the leading case of *Prince Albert v Strange* was argued and    **1.18** decided on the basis of protecting a property right in etchings of the Queen and Prince Albert, as well as on the basis of a breach of confidence, even though the motive for the proceedings was obviously the protection of their privacy.[28] Privacy was essential to the decision whether or not to grant an injunction. Lord Cottenham said: 'In the present case, where privacy is the right invaded, the postponing of the injunction would be equivalent of denying it altogether.'[29] Lord Cottenham did not comment on the reasons for valuing privacy, but Vice-Chancellor Knight Bruce had explained why he regarded it as important. He noted that 'pain inflicted in point of

---

[24] It may also be an offence under the Telecommunications Act 1984, s 43(1)(b). See 1.80 and 10.07–10.20 for the effect of the Protection from Harassment Act 1997.

[25] *Hunter v Canary Wharf Ltd* [1997] UKHL 14, [1997] AC 655. For further discussion of nuisance in the context of physical privacy, see 10.60.

[26] The Younger Committee on Privacy described it as offering 'the most effective protection of privacy in the whole of our existing law': (n 14) [87]. See also, *Campbell v MGN Ltd* [2002] EWCA Civ 1373, [2003] QB 633 [70] and, in the House of Lords decision in the same case (n 9), Lord Nicholls [14], Lord Hope [125] and Lord Carswell [171]. See also the observations of the Court of Appeal in *Douglas v Hello! Ltd* [2005] EWCA Civ 595, [2006] QB 125 [82].

[27] *Hellewell* (n 3) 807.

[28] *Prince Albert v Strange* (1849) 2 De G & Sm 652, 668–9, 695, 698; 64 ER 293, 300, 312–13; 1 H & TW 1, 12–14, 23.

[29] *Prince Albert* (n 28) 1 H & TW 1, 26; 47 ER 1312.

sentiment or imagination is not always disregarded in Courts of Justice' and gave as examples 'calumny' and 'trespass accompanied by…oppression or…affront'.[30]

**1.19** The ability of the law of confidence to protect private information has been enhanced in recent years by a willingness of the courts to find that the second of the action's three requirements—that the information was 'imparted in circumstances importing an obligation of confidence'[31]—may be inferred where the information is obviously confidential. In other words where it is clear that information has the necessary quality of confidence about it (which means the first requirement is satisfied), it will be easier to conclude that a person in receipt of such information, even a third party, is bound by a duty of confidence. The limitation of the breach of confidence action is therefore that it does not cover information which is private but not obviously confidential nor information which is already in the public domain. The third requirement for an action for breach of confidence to succeed, that there must be an unauthorized use (or, on an application for an injunction, threatened use) of the information, has traditionally emphasized that the right relates to disclosure of information and not the obtaining of it. This again restricts the action's utility in the privacy domain. However, the Court of Appeal held in *Imerman v Tchenguiz* that a breach of confidence is committed when a defendant, without the authority of the claimant, 'examines, makes, retains or supplies to a third party' copies of documents whose contents are (or ought to have been) appreciated by the defendant to be confidential.[32] The significance of this change and the extent to which the traditional action for breach of confidence may still be relied on to protect privacy are discussed in Chapters 10 and 4 respectively.

### (5) Defamation and Malicious Falsehood

**1.20** Libel protects a person against humiliation and unjust discrimination. It protects the individual and society from the making of choices on a factual basis which is false. Privacy also protects the individual against humiliation and unjust discrimination. It protects the individual and society from the making of choices on a factual basis which is true but irrelevant. If libel is necessary to protect the reputation that a person has in the minds of *right*-thinking members of society generally, then privacy is necessary to protect the reputation a person has in the minds of *wrong*-thinking members of society.[33]

---

[30] *Prince Albert* (n 28) 1 H & TW 1, 26; 47 ER 1312.
[31] *Coco v A N Clark (Engineers) Ltd* [1969] RPC 41, 47 (Megarry J).
[32] [2010] EWCA Civ 908, [2011] Fam 116 [69]. The case is considered controversial for its encroachment into the Hildebrand principle long-established in family law.
[33] See 2.83–2.87. Examples of discrimination, and even injury, suffered by persons about whom disclosures had been made are given in the Younger Report (n 14) paras 161–5] and 171 (a woman had her property vandalized and was subject to harassment after a newspaper reported that she practised witchcraft in private; and a county council could not arrange foster care for a child after publicity). Feldman includes honour and reputation amongst the list of interests at the core of privacy: D Feldman, 'Privacy-related Rights and Their Social Value' in P Birks (ed), *Privacy and Loyalty* (Clarendon Press 1997) 21.

The link between protection of privacy and of reputation is made by the two inter-  **1.21**
ests being included together in Article 12 of the Universal Declaration of Human
Rights.[34] The link can also be seen from the principles which justify protection of
reputation, as expressed by Lord Nicholls:

> Reputation is an integral and important part of the dignity of the individual. It also
> forms the basis of many decisions in a democratic society which are fundamental to
> its well-being: whom to employ or work for, whom to promote, whom to do busi-
> ness with or to vote for…it should not be supposed that protection of reputation
> is a matter of importance only to the affected individual and his family. Protection
> of reputation is conducive to the public good. It is in the public interest that the
> reputation of public figures should not be debased falsely. In the political field, in
> order to make an informed choice, the electorate needs to be able to identify the
> good as well as the bad. Consistently with these considerations, human rights con-
> ventions recognise that freedom of expression is not an absolute right. Its exercise
> may be subject to such restrictions as are prescribed by law and are necessary in a
> democratic society for the protection of the reputations of others.[35]

Many of these reasons for protecting against the dissemination of false information apply equally to protection against the dissemination of true, but private,
information.

As long ago as 1930 the Court of Appeal recognized that the law of defamation  **1.22**
could provide a remedy for interests which are now more closely associated with a
right to privacy. In *Tolley v JS Fry & Sons Ltd*[36] the claimant, a well-known amateur
golfer, complained about a newspaper advertisement which appeared without his
consent for a brand of chocolate which contained a caricature of him and a verse
implying that he endorsed the product. Greer LJ said that the defendants had 'acted
in a manner inconsistent with the decencies of life and in doing so they were guilty
of an act for which there ought to be a legal remedy'.[37] The remedy was afforded in
defamation by holding that readers would have understood Tolley to have allowed
his portrait to be used for advertising purposes for gain and reward, and thereby to
have engaged in conduct unworthy of his status as an amateur golfer.[38]

A similar contrivance was relied on to provide a partial remedy in *Kaye v*  **1.23**
*Robertson*,[39] where the claimant complained of being photographed and

---

[34] See also 2.83–2.87.
[35] *Reynolds v Times Newspapers Ltd* [2001] 2 AC 127, 201. Fleming also notes that '[p]erhaps
the closest affinity to some aspects of the right of privacy is found in the law of libel. Though libel
and slander are primarily concerned with reputation—an interest in relations with others—they
incidentally also safeguard the individual's sense of honour and self-respect': J Fleming, *The Law of
Torts* (9th edn, Thomson Reuters 1998) 664 and see generally ch 8.
[36] [1931] AC 333.
[37] [1930] 1 KB 467, CA, 478.
[38] This case was described by the Younger Committee on Privacy as 'the nearest the law of defamation ever came to protecting 'privacy' as such': (n 14) app 1, para 5. It is also an early example of
the Court providing a remedy for use of a celebrity's image or likeness placing him in a false light,
which is a recognized aspect of the law of privacy in the US. See further 2.40–2.46 and 3.73–3.79.
[39] *Kaye* (n 1).

interviewed by a tabloid journalist as he lay in hospital recovering from head injuries. The Court accepted that the claimant had not been fit to give informed consent to the interview or the photography. The Court of Appeal upheld an interlocutory injunction to prevent the newspaper publishing any article suggesting that the claimant had so consented, on the basis that to do so would amount to a malicious falsehood.[40] This was not, however, an effective remedy, as publication of the article went ahead without implying that the claimant had consented, which arguably only served to draw attention to the harm done.

1.24 *Kaye v Robertson*[41] is a case in which more than one privacy right was involved. There was the intrusion into the hospital, and there was a publication of information. To grant a remedy for the former would have required development of the laws of trespass or harassment. The publication of information about the claimant was only partly remedied by reliance on the tort of malicious falsehood and could, perhaps, have been better protected by recognition that the law of confidentiality did not require personal information to have been imparted to the defendant.

1.25 Reviewing the development of privacy law in *Douglas v Hello! Ltd*, the Court of Appeal described *Kaye v Robertson* as a case in which the potential for the law of confidence to protect private information that was not recorded in a document was not appreciated.[42] The analysis of the modern law in *Douglas*[43] lends strong support to the view which others have expressed: if the facts of *Kaye v Robertson* were to recur today, relief would be granted in the law of confidence, or misuse of private information, and the relief would be more extensive and effective than that which was granted in *Kaye*.[44]

1.26 It is now firmly established that Article 8 protects the right to reputation, as part of the right to respect for private life.[45] However, there are two major limitations in

---

[40] The requirements for which are that the defendant maliciously published false words about the claimant calculated to cause him pecuniary damage. In respect of damage the Court said in *Kaye* (n 1) 68: 'Mr Kaye... has a potentially valuable right to sell the story of his accident and his recovery when he is fit enough to tell it. If the defendants are able to publish the article they proposed, or anything like it, the value of this right would in my view be seriously lessened...' Thus, although the case is notorious for asserting the absence of a right to privacy in English law, the Court recognized that control of publicity is a right which the law should protect.

[41] *Kaye* (n 1).

[42] *Douglas* (n 26) [62].

[43] *Douglas* (n 26) [118].

[44] Note, however, that absent publication the invasion suffered in *Kaye* (n 1) was of the type experienced in *Wainwright* (n 6), namely a physical interference with private space and dignity and, as it was occasioned by a news organization and not a public authority, there would be no direct action under the HRA.

[45] See *Radio France v France* (2005) 40 EHRR 706; *Cumpana v Romania* (2005) 41 EHRR 41; *Pfeifer v Austria* (2007) 48 EHRR 175; *Petrina v Romania* App no 78060/01 (ECtHR, 14 October 2008); *Karakó v Hungary* (2011) 52 EHRR 36; *Europapress Holding DOO v Croatia* App no 25333/06 (ECtHR, 22 October 2009), [2010] EMLR 10; *Petrenco v Moldova* App no 20928/05 (ECtHR, 20 March 2010), [2011] EMLR 5; *Greene v Associated Newspapers Ltd* [2004] EWCA Civ 1462, [2005] QB 972; *Axel Springer AG v Germany* (2012) 55 EHRR 6; *Re Guardian News & Media Ltd, HM Treasury v Ahmed* [2010] UKSC 1, [2010] 2 AC 697.

the protection of privacy afforded by the tort of defamation.[46] The first is that justification is a complete defence, so that the publication of true but private facts about an individual is not actionable. In *Charleston v News Group Newspapers Ltd*,[47] for example, an unsuccessful attempt was made to use defamation to protect a portrait image after the defendants published, without consent, a false image of the plaintiffs' faces on a pornographic image of other people's bodies. The claim failed because the text made clear that the image was false.[48]

The second is that the words complained of must be defamatory of the claimant, **1.27** so that publication of them is likely to lower his or her reputation in the estimation of right-thinking members of society.[49] This is not always the case with publication of private personal information, though in some circumstances the effect might be to make others shun and avoid the claimant.[50] These issues are explored in further detail in Chapter 8.

## (6) Privilege of Witnesses

At common law nobody can be compelled to give any information except as a wit- **1.28** ness in court. Even witnesses are protected by privileges which are regarded as protecting privacy. Lord Mustill explained the motives underpinning various forms of the right to silence, including the privilege against self-incrimination, to become embedded in English law, emphasizing the link between privacy and liberty, in the sense of autonomy:

> The first is a simple reflection of the common view that one person should so far as possible be entitled to tell another person to mind his own business. All civilised states recognise this assertion of personal liberty and privacy. Equally, ... few would dispute that some curtailment of liberty is indispensable to the stability of society; and indeed in the United Kingdom today our lives are permeated by enforceable duties to provide information on demand, created by Parliament and tolerated by the majority, albeit in some cases with reluctance. Secondly, there is a long history of reaction against abuses of judicial interrogation. The Star Chamber and the Council had the power to administer the oath and to punish recusants;[51]

---

[46] See ch 8 for further discussion of privacy and false facts.

[47] [1995] UKHL 6, [1995] 2 AC 65.

[48] *Charleston* (n 47) 74.

[49] In addition, since the enactment of the Defamation Act 2013, an imputation is only defamatory if it has caused, or is likely to cause, serious harm to the reputation of the claimant, an additional hurdle

[50] This latter element is not required in an action for malicious falsehood. In neither cause of action will the court grant an injunction unless satisfied that the claimant will succeed at trial: *Bonnard v Perryman* [1891] 2 Ch 269, CA; *William Coulson and Sons v James Coulson and Co* [1887] 3 TLR 46; *Herbage v Times Newspapers Ltd* (CA, 30 April 1981). Thus, although the Court of Appeal in *Kaye* (n 1) also held that if the proposed publication was arguably libellous, that was not enough. The Court concluded, however, that a malicious falsehood would inevitably occur if the original publication had gone ahead.

[51] For the development of the right to silence from the struggles for freedom, including freedom of thought, conscience, and religion in the sixteenth and seventeenth centuries see *Bishopsgate Investment v Maxwell* [1993] Ch 1, 17.

and literally to press confessions out of those under interrogation...although the misuse of judicial interrogation is now only a distant history, it seems to have left its mark on public perceptions of the entire subject: and indeed not just public perceptions, for in the recent past there have been several authoritative and eloquent judicial reminders of the abuses of our former inquisitorial system and of the need to guard against their revival.[52]

**1.29**  A separate protection of witnesses was to be found in the rule that husband and wife were not competent to give evidence against each other. One of the considerations supporting that rule was recognized to be 'to guard the security and confidence of private life, even at the risk of an occasional failure of justice'.[53] This rule was an important influence upon the development in *Duchess of Argyll v Duke of Argyll* of the law of confidentiality in relation to communications between spouses.[54] This is an example of the transfer of a policy of public law into the development of a private law cause of action.[55]

### (7) Privacy and Necessity

**1.30**  Other circumstances in which a right of control over the dissemination of information has been given by the common law for reasons of necessity include matters relating to a person's health. In a case involving infectious disease, Rose J expressed the principle as follows:

> Confidentiality is of paramount importance to such patients, including doctors...If it is breached, or if the patients have grounds for believing that it may be or has been breached they will be reluctant to come forward for and to continue with treatment...If the actual or apprehended breach is to the press that reluctance is likely to be very great. If treatment is not provided or continued the individual will be deprived of its benefit and the public are likely to suffer from an increase in the rate of the spread of the disease. The preservation of confidentiality is therefore in the public interest.[56]

**1.31**  Legal professional privilege is similarly justified. Lord Taylor CJ summarized it:

> The principle...is that a man must be able to consult his lawyer in confidence, since otherwise he might hold back half the truth. The client must be sure that what he tells his lawyer in confidence will never be revealed without his consent. Legal professional privilege is thus much more than an ordinary rule of evidence, limited in its application to the facts of a particular case. It is a fundamental condition on which the administration of justice as a whole rests.[57]

---

[52]  *R v Director of Serious Fraud Office, ex p Smith* [1993] 1 AC 1, 31.

[53]  *Rumpling v DPP* [1964] AC 814, HL, 841, 857. See also *Russell v Russell* [1924] AC 687, 725 for the justification of this rule in family proceedings on grounds of decency and 'invasion of the privacy of the marriage chamber'.

[54]  *Argyll (Duchess) v Argyll (Duke)* [1967] Ch 302, 322–30.

[55]  'For the need to preserve confidential communications between husband and wife to be a reason for a rule of the law necessarily establishes to my mind that the preservation of those communications inviolate is an objective of public policy': *Argyll* (n 54) 324.

[56]  *X v Y* [1988] 2 All ER 648, 656.

[57]  *R v Derby Magistrates' Court, ex p B* [1996] AC 487, 507.

The necessity principle is applied to disclosure of the correspondence between **1.32** informants and the police and other bodies for the purpose of preventing or expos-ing crime and other wrongdoing: 'Unless this immunity exists many persons, reputable or disreputable, would be discouraged from communicating all they know.'[58] It is also extended, although with greater qualification, to a journalist's sources and other materials, for the purpose of promoting freedom of expression. Bingham LJ has adopted the description a 'gross invasion of privacy' for orders compelling a journalist to disclose documents.[59] Judge LJ has emphasized the link between privacy rights of journalists (in their communications with their sources) and their rights of freedom of expression and later explained:

> Legal proceedings directed towards the seizure of the working papers of an individ-ual journalist, or the premises of the newspaper or television programme publish-ing his or her reports, or the threat of such proceedings, tends to inhibit discussion. When a genuine investigation into possibly corrupt or reprehensible activities by a public authority is being investigated by the media, compelling evidence is nor-mally needed to demonstrate that the public interest would be served by such pro-ceedings. Otherwise, to the public disadvantage, legitimate inquiry and discussion and 'the safety valve of effective investigative journalism'—the phrase used in a different context by Lord Steyn in *R v Secretary of State for the Home Department, ex p Simms*[60]—would be discouraged, perhaps stifled.[61]

The necessity principle is also implicit in the rule (applied mainly in the public law **1.33** context) that information given for one purpose should not be used for another purpose.[62] Prior to entry into force of the Human Rights Act 1998, the adequacy of public law protection of private information was questioned, because the court in judicial review proceedings did not start with a presumption that an interfer-ence with Article 8(1) is illegitimate and in need of powerful justification.[63] With the development of new technology it came to be appreciated that the necessity principle should be extended to data stored by computer.[64] Abuse of personal data has commonly been practised in totalitarian states. Data protection gives to indi-viduals a statutory right to control the circulation of data about themselves.[65] As

---

[58]  *R v Lewes Justices, ex p Home Secretary* [1973] AC 388, 413; *D v NSPCC* [1978] AC 171, 219.

[59]  *R v Lewes Crown Court, ex p Hill* (1991) 93 Cr App R 60, 66–7.

[60]  [2000] 2 AC 115, 131.

[61]  *Bright* (n 14) 681. For other examples of privacy promoting freedom of expression see Feldman, 'Privacy-related Rights and Their Social Value' (n 33) 24 and E Berendt, 'Privacy and freedom of speech' in A Kenyon and A Richardson (eds), *New Dimensions in Privacy Law: International and Comparative Perspectives* (Cambridge University Press 2006) 11.

[62]  *R v Chief Constable of North Wales Police, ex p Thorpe* [1999] QB 396; *Elliott v Chief Constable of Wiltshire* (1996) TLR 693; *Harman v Secretary of State for the Home Dept* [1983] AC 280, 308 (where Lord Keith said: 'Discovery constitutes a very serious invasion of the privacy and confidentiality of a litigant's affairs'), 311 (Lord Scarman refers to 'the individual citizen's right to privacy'), and 323 (Lord Roskill); *Marcel v Commissioner of Police for the Metropolis* [1992] Ch 225, CA, 262.

[63]  D Feldman, 'Information and Privacy' in J Beatson and Y Cripps (ed), *Freedom of Information and Freedom of Expression* (Oxford University Press 2000) 322.

[64]  The Younger Report (n 14) paras 54 and 619, and see generally ch 7.

[65]  Directive 95/46/EC of the European Parliament and of the Council of 24 October 1995 on the protection of individuals with regard to the processing of personal data and on the free movement

such it has been seen as a right recognized in the ECHR at Article 8 and in the International Covenant on Civil and Political Rights (ICCPR) at Article 17. In this context the right has been described as 'a fundamental democratic ideal'.[66]

### (8) The Family Court's Jurisdiction in Respect of Children and Vulnerable Adults

**1.34** The Family Court has long exercised power to restrict publicity about children who are under its protective jurisdiction. Following cases such as *Bensaid v UK*[67] the Family Court has also shown itself prepared to make orders protecting the private and family lives of vulnerable relatives of such children. In *A Local Authority v A*[68] an application for reporting restrictions was made by a mother for an order preventing reports of her arrest on suspicion of murdering two of her children. While the application was rejected, the Court accepted it had jurisdiction to make such an order on the basis not just of the potentially damaging effects of such reports on the surviving child, but also because of the vulnerable state of the mother.

**1.35** The House of Lords has confirmed that in cases where a child's private life is concerned this power now extends in principle to making orders restricting the reporting of criminal proceedings in open court which might harm the child, even if the child is not a party or a witness, or the subject of the publication.[69] In *In re S* the House of Lords stated that such orders would be exceptional in practice. However, such orders have been made. [70]

### (9) Criminal Law

**1.36** Criminal offences relating to intrusion into physical privacy are discussed in Chapter 10. While the vast majority of criminal offences relevant to privacy are now prescribed by statute, a common law offence of relevance to the media is illustrated by *Attorney General's Reference (No 5 of 2002)*.[71] A police officer was prosecuted for conspiracy to commit the common-law offence of misconduct in public office, by supplying confidential information to persons not entitled to receive it, who were alleged to include journalists.[72] The offence featured in many prosecutions of

---

of such data [1995] OJ L281/31, Recital (10); *Thorpe* (n 62) 429 ('although the convictions of the applicants had been in the public domain, the police, as a public authority, could only publish that information if it was in the public interest to do so'); UK *Report of the Committee on Data Protection* (Cmnd 7341, 1978) (Chairman: Sir Norman Lindop) para 2.04.

[66] R Wacks, 'Privacy in Cyberspace: Personal Information, Free Speech, and the Internet' in Birks (ed) (n 33) 109.

[67] [2001] 33 EHRR 10.

[68] [2011] EWHC 1764 (Fam), [2012] 1 FLR 239.

[69] *In Re S (A Child)* [2004] UKHL 47, [2005] 1 AC 593.

[70] See eg *A Local Authority v W, L, W, T and R (by the Children's Guardian)* [2005] EWHC 1564 (Fam), [2006] 1 FLR 1.

[71] [2004] UKHL 40, [2005] 1 AC 167.

[72] In certain of the criminal trials arising out of phone hacking at the *News of the World* the defendants were charged with conspiracy offences under the Criminal Law Act 1977.

journalists in the second decade of the twenty-first century, where the allegation was that public officials had been bribed to misuse the powers of their office.

## D. The Impact of the Human Rights Act 1998

The enactment of the HRA was probably the most significant development in the **1.37** history of privacy protection in England and Wales. The HRA came into force in the United Kingdom in October 2000. Its aim was to 'give further effect' under English law to the rights contained in the ECHR. The Act provides a remedy for breach of a Convention right under domestic law, thereby obviating the need to seek redress before the European Court of Human Rights (ECtHR).

In particular, the Act makes it unlawful for any public body to act in a way which is **1.38** incompatible with the Convention, unless the wording of any other primary legislation provides no other choice. It thereby requires courts and tribunals to interpret legislation, as far as possible, in a way which is compatible with Convention rights and also imposes upon the same judicial bodies a requirement to take account of any decision, judgment or opinion of the Strasbourg Court.

Among the rights 'incorporated'[73] into English law by the HRA is the qualified **1.39** right to respect for private and family life, one's home, and correspondence.[74] Article 8 provides:

**Right to respect for private and family life**
1. Everyone has the right to respect for his private and family life, his home and his correspondence.
2. There shall be no interference by a public authority with the exercise of this right except such as is in accordance with the law and is necessary in a democratic society in the interests of national security, public safety or the economic well-being of the country, for the prevention of disorder or crime, for the protection of health or morals, or for the protection of the rights and freedoms of others.

The significance of this development should not be underestimated: for the first time a general positive right to privacy was enshrined in an English Act of Parliament.

The oft-competing, qualified right to receive opinions and information and the **1.40** right to express them are also enshrined within the Act under s 10, which provides:

**Freedom of expression**
1. Everyone has the right to freedom of expression. This right shall include freedom to hold opinions and to receive and impart information and ideas without

---

[73] The word is used advisedly. The rights set out in sch 1 to the HRA are not made part of English law: rather the HRA provides a mechanism for enforcing those rights in English courts and for obtaining remedies for their violation.

[74] Art 8 ECHR. The full text of Art 8 is set out in Appendix B (available at <http://www.5rb.com/publication/the-law-of-privacy-and-the-media>).

interference by public authority and regardless of frontiers. This Article shall not prevent States from requiring the licensing of broadcasting, television or cinema enterprises.

2. The exercise of these freedoms, since it carries with it duties and responsibilities, may be subject to such formalities, conditions, restrictions or penalties as are prescribed by law and are necessary in a democratic society, in the interests of national security, territorial integrity or public safety, for the prevention of disorder or crime, for the protection of health or morals, for the protection of the reputation or rights of others, for preventing the disclosure of information received in confidence, or for maintaining the authority and impartiality of the judiciary.

**1.41**  The impact of this legislation is still being felt fifteen years later and continues to be a matter of some controversy.[75] The entry into force of the Act was cited soon afterwards by one judge of the Court of Appeal in *Douglas v Hello! Ltd*[76] as giving 'the final impetus to the recognition of a right of privacy in English law'.[77]

**1.42**  However, the House of Lords subsequently held that English law does not recognize any general principle of 'invasion of privacy' from which the conditions of liability in a particular case can be deduced.[78] Furthermore, the enactment of the HRA has been said to weaken the argument in favour of a general tort of invasion of privacy to fill gaps in the existing remedies.[79] The absence of a general tort of invasion of privacy should be distinguished, however, from the extension and renaming of the old action for breach of confidence. Certain types of breach of confidence, where an invasion of privacy is occasioned by wrongful disclosure of personal information, are now more accurately and indeed are commonly described as actions for 'misuse of private information'.[80]

**1.43**  Like most rights, a right to privacy is not absolute. Under the Convention, limitations on its enjoyment may be imposed providing they are in accordance with the law and necessary in a democratic society in pursuit of one of a number of legitimate aims, which include the protection of the rights and freedoms of others. The right most frequently invoked to justify an invasion of privacy in the media context is the right to freedom of expression which is itself recognized as a positive right in Article 10 ECHR. More significantly, the main purpose of Article 8 is to prevent arbitrary interference with the exercise of the right

---

[75] At the time of writing, the Conservative Party is proposing to repeal the HRA as promised in its 2015 election manifesto.

[76] [2001] QB 967, CA.

[77] *Douglas* (n 76) [111] (Sedley LJ). However, in *Wainwright* (n 2) [78]–[79], Buxton LJ described Sedley LJ's view of the process as one of 'judicial development of the common law, with the Convention acting as, at most, a catalyst for that development'. This, he said, was an attractive prospect but one that would be contrary to authority and about which there were 'serious difficulties of principle'.

[78] *Wainwright* (n 6) [19].

[79] *Attorney General's Reference* (n 71) [34].

[80] *Campbell* (n 9) [14] (Lord Nicholls).

to respect for private life by a public authority.[81] With the possible exception of some public service broadcasters,[82] media organizations are not themselves 'public authorities' which owe a direct duty to act compatibly with Convention rights. However, by virtue of the court's position as a public authority within the meaning of s 6 of the Act, together with the positive obligations inherent in the notion of 'respect' in Article 8,[83] the right to respect for private life must be given effect even in actions between private individuals.[84]

Under s 2 HRA the court is required to take into account any relevant Strasbourg **1.44** jurisprudence[85] in determining a question that has arisen in connection with a Convention right.[86] For a detailed account of guidance given by Strasbourg institutions on the application of Article 8 in cases of alleged media intrusion into private life, see Chapter 3.

## (1) Margin of Appreciation

The various decisions of the ECtHR are not always easy to reconcile and largely **1.45** turn on their own facts. In each case the court will have regard to the reasons given by the national courts for granting or refusing relief, as the case may be, and make

---

[81] *Botta v Italy* (1998) 26 EHRR 241, para 33. For a fuller discussion of the scope of Art 8 see 3.13–3.39.

[82] Whose position is considered at 1.57–1.65.

[83] See *eg X and Y v Netherlands* (1985) 8 EHRR 235 and 3.20.

[84] Although this has been said not to give rise to a new cause of action of invasion of privacy: *Venables* (n 32). Brooke LJ in *Douglas* (n 5) [91] questioned whether the absence of Art 1 ECHR from the list of Convention rights in sch 1 to the Human Rights Act 1998 affects the extent of the positive duty under English law. Article 1 provides: 'The High Contracting Parties shall secure to everyone within their jurisdiction the rights and freedoms defined in section I of this Convention' and has occasionally been relied on by the European Court to support the notion of positive obligation. All these remarks must now be seen in the light of the developments in *Campbell* (n 9). See further 3.37–3.39 and 5.02–5.13.

[85] This includes judgments, decisions, declarations, and advisory opinions of the Court, opinions and decisions of the (now defunct) Commission, and decisions of the Committee of Ministers.

[86] The House of Lords has indicated that Strasbourg jurisprudence should normally be followed: *R (Alconbury Developments Ltd) v Secretary of State for the Environment, Transport and the Regions* [2001] UKHL 23, [2003] 2 AC 295 [26] per Lord Slynn: 'In the absence of some special circumstances it seems to me that the courts should follow any clear and constant jurisprudence of the European Court of Human Rights. If it does not do so there is at least a possibility that the case will go to that court which is likely in the ordinary course to follow its own constant jurisprudence.' In *Boyd v Army Prosecuting Authority* [2002] UKHL 31, [2003] 1 AC 734, however, the House of Lords declined to follow Strasbourg jurisprudence (*Morris v UK* (2002) 34 EHRR 1253) which it considered had been wrongly decided because of a lack of awareness of the full facts: see Lord Bingham at [12]. Where there is conflicting House of Lords and Strasbourg authority, the lower courts are bound by the rule of precedent to follow the House of Lords authority: *Kay v Lambeth London Borough Council* [2006] UKHL 10, [2006] 2 AC 465. The effect of this is that lower courts have to follow authorities that have already been declared to breach the Convention by the European Court: see *R (GC) v Commissioner of Police of the Metropolis* (DC, 16 July 2010) following House of Lords authority on retention of biometric samples which was found to be in breach of Art 8 by the European Court in *S v UK* (2009) 48 EHRR 50, granting permission for a leapfrog appeal to the Supreme Court.

its own assessment of whether those reasons were relevant and sufficient to justify the interference concerned. In assessing the proportionality of any measures taken it will have regard to the totality of the sanctions imposed and the effect of any invasion of privacy on the victim. In cases concerning the balancing of rights between private entities (as is the case with most, if not all, media invasions of privacy) the court will also stress the significance of the doctrine of margin of appreciation. This doctrine allows the court to take into account the fact that the Convention will be interpreted differently in different Member States. Judges are obliged to take into account the cultural, historic and philosophical differences between Strasbourg and the nation in question. The doctrine is applied at its widest when the court is considering a state's positive obligations.

**1.46**   Thus, in *Tammer v Estonia*[87] the ECtHR had regard to the margin of appreciation in finding that the conviction of a journalist for insulting a former political aide and the imposition of a fine equivalent to ten days' income did not amount to a disproportionate interference with his right to freedom of expression under Article 10. The applicant had published an interview with the former aide's would-be biographer in which he described her as a marriage-wrecker and child-deserter because of an affair she had had some seven years previously with the former prime minister of Estonia whom she subsequently married. The court noted[88] that the impugned remarks related to the former aide's private life and could not be justified by considerations of public interest, despite evidence of her continued political involvement. The fact that she herself intended to put these details into the public domain in her forthcoming memoirs did not justify the use of the actual words chosen.

**1.47**   Similarly, in *Hachette Filipacchi Associates v France*[89] the ECtHR found that the national courts had not strayed outside their margin of appreciation by ordering the publishers of *Paris-Match* to publish an apology to the family of Claude Erignac, the Prefect of Corsica, for publishing a two-page colour photograph of the scene showing his dead body taken moments after his assassination. Although it was a matter on which opinions could reasonably differ (as shown by the dissenting opinions of Judge Louciades and Judge Vajic), the majority held that the measure taken, being the least possible sanction that could have been imposed, was not a disproportionate interference with the publisher's right to freedom of expression, given the distress the publication caused to the victim's family, coming so soon after his murder and funeral. The Court also took into account the fact that the family had expressly objected to use of the photograph.[90]

---

[87]   (2003) 37 EHRR 43.
[88]   *Tammer* (n 87) [66]–[68].
[89]   (2009) 49 EHRR 23.
[90]   *Standard Verlags GmbH v Austria (No 2)* App no 21277/05 (ECtHR, 4 September 2009) is a further example of the Strasbourg Court finding in favour of the national authorities on the basis of the margin of appreciation. A newspaper owner complained of a violation of his Art 10 rights in

In *Mosley v UK*[91] the ECtHR concluded that, largely as a consequence of the 'wide   **1.48**
margin of appreciation in determining the steps to be taken to ensure compliance
with the Convention', Article 8 does not require a legally binding requirement
of pre-notification of publication in the press of private information. The Court
emphasized 'the importance of a prudent approach to the State's positive obligations to protect private life in general and of the need to recognise the diversity
of possible methods to secure its respect'.[92] It went on: 'the notion of "respect" in
Article 8 is not clear-cut, especially as far as the positive obligations inherent in that
concept are concerned: bearing in mind the diversity of the practices followed and
the situations obtaining in the Contracting States, the notion's requirements will
vary considerably from case to case'.[93]

The concept of margin of appreciation has developed at the international level in   **1.49**
order to give Member States a certain latitude in the way they give effect to their
obligations under the Convention. The dangers of directly transferring this principle to the application of Convention rights under the HRA in the domestic context
has been pointed out by several commentators.[94] Nevertheless, a similar concept
of a 'discretionary area of judgment' has developed under the Act, at least as far as
review of decisions by public authorities is concerned, where the degree of scrutiny
of an administrative decision is dependent on the context.[95]

The difference with a right to privacy in respect of an individual's relations with   **1.50**
the media is that this essentially concerns an aspect of private law where the only
act of a public authority (save that of the court making the decision) is the failure
of Parliament to legislate.[96] In fulfilling their duty under the HRA to develop the
common law compatibly with the Convention right to respect for private life, however, the English courts are guided by the decisions of the ECtHR.[97] It remains the
case that a general right to privacy in the private law sphere is neither required nor
prohibited by the Convention. In striking the proper balance, therefore, the courts

---

respect of an article which speculated on the state of the federal president's marriage and alleged
extra-marital relations of his wife (a high-ranking public official) with another leading politician.
The Strasbourg Court concluded that the rumours speculated about the private and family lives of
those involved and did not contribute to a debate of public interest.

  [91] (2011) 53 EHRR 30, [2012] EMLR 1.

  [92] *Mosley* (n 91) [107].

  [93] *Mosley* (n 91) [108].

  [94] See *eg* R Singh, M Hunt, and M Demetriou, 'Is there a role for the "Margin of Appreciation"
in national law after the Human Rights Act?' [1999] EHRL Rev 15.

  [95] *R (Daly) v Secretary of State for the Home Dept* [2001] UKHL 26, [2001] 2 AC 532; *R v A (No 2)*
[2001] UKHL 25, [2002] 1 AC 45. See also *R (Mahmood) v Secretary of State for the Home Dept*
[2001] 1 WLR 840; *R (Samaroo) v Secretary of State for the Home Dept* [2001] UKHRR 1150.

  [96] A challenge on these grounds under the HRA is expressly prohibited under s 6(3) and (6).

  [97] To the extent that a court is required to interpret any applicable primary or secondary legislation in this field it must read and give effect to it, so far as it is possible to do so, in a way which is
compatible with Convention rights: s 3 HRA. If that cannot be done then the higher courts are
empowered to declare such legislation incompatible with a Convention right: s 4 HRA. On the
distinction between 'interpreting' and 'legislating' see *R v A (No 2)* (n 101) [44]–[45] (Lord Steyn).

are likely to be guided by decisions of the European Court.[98] Domestic courts will also continue to look to comparative jurisprudence from jurisdictions with more developed laws of privacy and the principles on which such laws are based. These aspects are considered in Chapters 3, 4 and 5.

**1.51** The increasing involvement of the European Court in the detailed balancing between Articles 8 and 10 (and consequent weakening of the doctrine of margin of appreciation) owed itself largely to a new approach first enunciated in *Hatton v UK*.[99] In a now familiar passage subsequently adopted in media cases the Court there held for the first time:

> Whatever analytical approach is adopted—the positive duty or an interference—the applicable principles regarding justification under Article 8(2) are broadly similar. In both contexts, regard must be had to the fair balance that has to be struck between the competing interests of the individual and of the community as a whole. In both contexts the State enjoys a certain margin of appreciation in determining the steps to be taken to ensure compliance with the Convention. Furthermore, even in relation to the positive obligations flowing from Article 8(1), in striking the required balance the aims mentioned in Article 8(2) may be of a certain relevance.[100]

**1.52** It is important to remember that this case concerned the very different context of the failure of the UK authorities to prevent night flights which disturbed the sleep of local residents during take-off and landing at Heathrow airport (which is a private enterprise). It can be seen that in that context the precise status of the airport authority as a public or private body was not that significant. By adopting the same approach in the context of the media, however, the traditional distinction between a state's negative duty not to interfere arbitrarily with private life and its positive obligation[101] to ensure respect for it has broken down still further, both as a matter of domestic and European law.

**1.53** The significance of this development should not be underestimated. In his dissenting opinion in *Hatton* at first instance, Sir Brian Kerr described the approach laid out by the majority as 'a wholly new test'.[102] It is now, however, accepted in all cases concerning the balancing of rights between private individuals, including the disclosure of personal information by the media. In *von Hannover v Germany*,[103]

---

[98] The Court has stated, in the context of Art 10, that it 'does not consider it desirable, let alone necessary, to elaborate a general theory concerning the extent to which the Convention guarantees should be extended to relations between private individuals per se': *Vgt Verein Gegen Tierfabriken v Switzerland* (2002) 34 EHRR 4, para 46.

[99] App no 36022/97, both by the Chamber Judgment (2002) 34 EHRR 1 and the Grand Chamber Judgment (2003) 36 EHRR 51.

[100] *Hatton* (n 99), para 96 in the Chamber Judgment and para 98 in the Grand Chamber.

[101] A positive obligation under human rights law denotes a State's obligation to engage in an activity to secure the effective enjoyment of a right, as opposed to a negative obligation merely to abstain from human rights violations.

[102] The development was even more remarkable given the Court's remarks in *Vgt Verein Gegen Tierfabriken* (n 98) [46].

[103] *von Hannover v Germany (No 1)* (2005) 40 EHRR 1, [2004] EMLR 21 [57].

where the photographs complained of were all published by private enterprises, the Court reiterated that the positive obligation under Article 8 involved the adoption of measures designed to secure respect for private life even in the sphere of the relations of individuals between themselves and stated:

> The boundary between the State's positive and negative obligations under this provision does not lend itself to precise definition. The applicable principles are, nonetheless, similar. In both contexts regard must be had to the fair balance which has to be struck between the competing interests of the individual and of the community as a whole; and in both contexts the State enjoys a certain margin of appreciation.

The same approach was followed in *Karhuvaara and Iltalehti v Finland*[104] and in *Craxi (No 2) v Italy*[105] and became firmly accepted in the Court's jurisprudence. In the latter case, the European Court held that the state was under a positive obligation to prevent disclosure to the press of private information contained in court records. The documents concerned were transcripts of private telephone conversations which had been intercepted by the police for the purposes of the prosecution of the applicant, a former prime minister of Italy, for corruption. That duty extended to a requirement to carry out effective inquiries into the causes of the leak after it had occurred.[106] **1.54**

There are difficulties in importing this approach into the private law sphere. In *Craxi* for example, in a partly dissenting opinion, Judge Zagrebelsky noted that this was the first occasion on which the Court had extended the positive obligation under Article 8 to include a requirement to carry out an effective investigation into its possible breach, a duty which had previously been restricted to alleged breaches of Articles 2 and 3. He pointed out that where that investigation might require, as here, disclosure of a journalist's source, it was difficult to see how it could be effective without breaching Article 10. **1.55**

For a period of time the decisions of the Court in this field appeared to be increasingly proscriptive.[107] However, the decisions of the Grand Chamber in *Axel Springer v Germany* and *Von Hannover v Germany (No 2)*,[108] concerning the balancing of privacy of public figures and freedom of expression, suggest that the Court may have tilted the balance back in favour of national authorities' own careful weighing of the relevant facts 'with the advantage of their knowledge and their continuous contact with the social and cultural reality of their country'.[109] In *Animal Defenders International v UK*,[110] a case concerning the prohibition on political advertising, **1.56**

---

[104] (2005) 41 EHRR 51, para 42.
[105] (2004) 38 EHRR 995.
[106] *Craxi* (n 105), paras 74–5.
[107] *eg, von Hannover (No 1)* (n 103).
[108] *Axel Springer* (n 45); *Von Hannover (No 2)* (2012) 55 EHRR 15.
[109] *Axel Springer* (n 45), minority judgment of Judge Lopez Guerra, on behalf of five dissenting judges.
[110] (2013) 57 EHRR 21, [2013] EMLR 28.

the Court noted that '[t]here is a risk that by developing the notion of positive obligations to protect the rights under articles 8–11...one can lose sight of the fundamental negative obligation of the state to abstain from interfering'.[111]

### (2) Media Organizations as Public Authorities

**1.57**   During the passage of the Human Rights Bill through Parliament public service broadcasters such as the BBC and Channel 4 were cited as examples of bodies which were or would be likely to be considered public authorities within the meaning of s 6 HRA.[112] If that were the case then such media organizations would be susceptible to actions brought under s 7 HRA and would owe direct duties to individuals to respect their right to private life under Article 8, interference with which could only be justified in accordance with the strict necessity test under Article 8(2). This would put them in a markedly different position to other private media organizations (such as the print media) which are entitled to rely on their own right to freedom of expression in any claim brought against them, which would have to be under an existing cause of action other than the HRA.

**1.58**   There are arguments based on public funding and statutory obligations which support this government's view. There are, however, contrary indications. The focus is the issue of whether a body is sufficiently public to engage the responsibility of the State.[113] Convention rights can only be relied on in any legal proceedings (or proceedings under the Act against a public authority can only be brought) by persons, non-governmental organizations, or groups of individuals who would qualify as 'victims' within the meaning of the Convention.[114] In Strasbourg the

---

[111] *Animal Defenders International* (n 110), para 12, joint dissenting judgment of Judges Ziemele, Sajo, Kalaydjiyeva, Vucininc, and De Gaetano.

[112] See Lord Williams, Minister of State at the Home Office, *Hansard*, HL (series 6) vol 583, col 1309 (3 November 1997) and Jack Straw, Home Secretary, *Hansard*, HC (series 6), vol 314, col 411 (17 June 1998). The former contrasted the position of 'other commercial organisations, such as private television stations, [which] might well not be public authorities'. See also *BKM Ltd v BBC* [2009] EWHC 3151 (Ch) in which the judge simply says that 'BKM brought this application to restrain broadcast [of residents of a care home for the elderly]...in order to protect the right of the home's residents to privacy and family life under the Human Rights Act' ([7]). No mention is made of a claim for breach of confidence or misuse of private information but it is unclear whether the judge was applying Art 8 directly or simply applying the requirements of the misuse of private information action (*ie* the need to balance privacy and freedom of expression interests) without making explicit mention of the cause of action.

[113] As the Home Secretary said, *Hansard*, HC (series 6) vol 314, col 433 (17 June 1998). See also the remarks of the Lord Chancellor in *Hansard*, HL (series 6) vol 583, col 808: 'In developing our proposals in [s] 6 we have opted for a wide-ranging definition of public authority. We have created a correspondingly wide liability. That is because we want to provide as much protection as possible for the rights of individuals *against the misuse of power by the state* within the framework of a Bill which preserves parliamentary sovereignty' (emphasis added). Note, however, that the Court of Appeal has rejected the notion that the term 'public authority' in s 6 is so ambiguous or obscure as to allow reference to *Hansard* as an aid to construction: *Aston Cantlow and Wilmcote with Billesly Parochial Church Council v Wallbank* [2001] EWCA Civ 713, [2002] Ch 51 [29].

[114] s 7(1) and (7) HRA and Art 34 ECHR. In arriving at the conclusion that s 6 HRA was intended to replicate, as far as possible, the test that Strasbourg would apply in determining whether

two categories are mutually exclusive: the same organization cannot both be liable for a violation of the Convention and have standing to bring a complaint.[115] Both Channel 4 and the BBC have lodged applications in Strasbourg.[116] In the BBC cases the Commission expressly left open the question of whether it had standing, assuming that it did for the purposes of declaring the applications inadmissible on other grounds. In the Channel 4 case the issue was addressed in respect of the National Union of Journalists which had brought a complaint based on the same facts[117] but the point was not taken against Channel 4. It might be supposed that in any of these cases the Commission would have declared that the applicants were themselves public authorities and therefore lacking status to bring proceedings if the matter was as clear as it seemed to the promoters of the Human Rights Bill.

No cases involving the BBC or Channel 4 since entry into force of the HRA have **1.59** conclusively decided the point but there are some indications in the way those cases have been handled that would appear to confirm that the broadcasters are not to be treated as core public authorities within the meaning of s 6. In various cases where applications have been made to prevent the broadcast of programmes which would allegedly interfere with the right to privacy of the applicants, the broadcasters have been permitted to rely on Convention rights of their own under Article 10. In

---

the responsibility of the state was engaged, the House of Lords in *Aston Cantlow* [2003] UKHL 37, [2004] 1 AC 546 adopted precisely the analysis set out in this paragraph. Relying on s 7 HRA, Art 34 ECHR, and the Strasbourg authorities cited in the next footnote, the Court endorsed the view that, as far as 'core' or 'standard' public authorities are concerned, a body cannot both be under a duty to act compatibly with Convention rights under the HRA and seek to invoke them against others: see Lord Nicholls [6]–[8], Lord Hope [44]–[52], Lord Hobhouse [87], and Lord Roger [158]–[160].

[115] *Ayuntamiento de M v Spain* (1991) 68 DR 209, 215: Any 'authority which exercises public functions' will be excluded from the definition of victim. See also *Rothenthurm Commune v Switzerland* (1988) 59 DR 251. The position under the HRA may be different. In *London Regional Transport Ltd v Mayor of London* [2001] EWCA Civ 1491, [2003] EMLR 4 [60] (a case where all four parties to the proceedings were public authorities) Sedley LJ was of the view that the status of the defendants (who were relying on Art 10) may not matter 'since private individuals will in principle enjoy the same protection'. The argument that the defendants could not rely on Convention rights precisely because they were not private individuals would, in any event, have been met by Sedley LJ's view that 'the illegality created by s 6 seems to me to be independent of the individualised provision for bringing or defending proceedings contained in s 7, and to carry one straight to the judicial obligation created by s 8(1) to make such order as the court considers just and appropriate in relation to any unlawful act of a public authority'. In other words, the proceedings were treated as if they were brought by the Mayor of London and Transport for London on behalf of the people of London and the status of the defendants as public authorities was merely incidental. In *Aston Cantlow* (n 113) [33], however, the Court of Appeal (of which Sedley LJ was a member) noted that it was in order to locate the state 'which stands distinct from persons, groups and nongovernmental organisations' (*ie* those that can claim to be a victim under s 7) that the concept of 'public authority' is used in s 6.

[116] *BBC v UK* (1996) 21 EHRR CD 93; *BBC Scotland, McDonald, Rodgers and Donald v UK* (1997) 25 EHRR CD 179; *Channel 4 Television Ltd v UK* (1988) 10 EHRR 503.

[117] *Hodgson, Woolf Productions and National Union of Journalists v UK* (1988) 10 EHRR 503. The applications were joined for the admissibility decision. The NUJ was found not to satisfy the victim test. That position was reversed in respect of the NUJ, in *Wilson and NUJ v UK* App no 30668/96 (ECtHR, 2 July 2002), in which the European Court found a violation of Art 11 in respect of the applicant union and individual.

*Leeds City Council v Channel Four Television Corp*[118] the Court founded its authority under its inherent jurisdiction and did not rule out the possibility of a cause of action for breach of confidence, then proceeded to weigh up the respective rights of the parties as required by *Re S*.[119] In *T (by her litigation friend the Official Solicitor) v BBC*[120] the precise nature of the Court's jurisdiction was not made clear but may be assumed to be the same. Had either case been brought under s 7 HRA it is to be assumed that the broadcaster would not have been able to rely on Convention rights but merely be required to justify its interference with the applicant's rights under Article 8(2).[121]

**1.60**  The closest a court has come to treating a broadcaster like a public authority is in the Court of Appeal's judgment in *R (ProLife Alliance) v BBC*.[122] In that case a political party challenged the refusal by the BBC and the other terrestrial broadcasters[123] to broadcast a graphic anti-abortion party election broadcast. The broadcasters defended their actions on the grounds of taste, decency, and offensiveness to which they had to have regard under their respective codes of practice.[124] The proceedings were brought against the BBC only by way of judicial review to which the BBC accepted it was amenable. It would appear, however, that the Court was also treating the BBC as a public authority within the meaning of s 6 HRA. Thus, in the context of political speech at election time, the Court considered that its duty was 'to decide for itself whether this censorship was justified'[125] and concluded that it was not. The broadcaster's margin of discretion was reduced almost to vanishing point and a strict necessity test applied.

**1.61**  As it did before the Court of Appeal, the BBC accepted for the purposes of its appeal to the House of Lords in *ProLife*[126] that it was a public authority, without making any wider concession as to its status in different contexts. However, the House of Lords took a view of its role on judicial review of the BBC's decision not to broadcast the party election broadcast that was quite different from that of the Court of Appeal. In according to the broadcaster a much greater degree of deference than the Court below, it appears that the direct application of s 6 HRA to the BBC did not add much of substance to the review.

---

[118]  (2007) 1 FLR 678. Curiously the applicant in this case, which is definitely a core public authority, was allowed to rely on Convention rights under Art 8. It did so, however, on the same basis as *London Regional Transport* (n 122), namely on behalf of others whom it represented.

[119]  *In re S (A child)* (n 69).

[120]  [2007] EWHC 1683 (QB), (2008) 1 FLR 281.

[121]  In *Sugar v BBC* [2012] UKSC 4, [2012] 1 WLR 439, Lord Brown at [94] appeared to presume that the BBC was a 'public authority' capable of interfering in the claimant's Art 10 rights.

[122]  [2002] EWCA Civ 297, [2002] 3 WLR 1080.

[123]  ITV, Channel 4, and Channel 5.

[124]  BBC Producer's Guidelines, ch 6; and ITV Programme Code, s 1, respectively.

[125]  *ProLife* (n 122) [37] (Laws LJ).

[126]  *R (ProLife Alliance) v BBC* [2003] UKHL 23, [2004] 1 AC 185.

It is debatable whether this case is authority for the proposition that the BBC **1.62** is a public authority for all purposes under the HRA. Where the proceedings are brought by way of judicial review it may not matter much for most practical purposes whether the body also owes a direct duty to act compatibly with Convention rights. But it should be noted that in this case there was a general requirement for the broadcasters to transmit party election broadcasts.[127] In this specific context, therefore, they were carrying out a public service function where there would be good reason for treating all of them as public authorities. The position could well be different where the broadcast relates to journalistic, artistic, or literary material.[128]

If state broadcasters are found to be public authorities for the purpose of HRA, then **1.63** useful guidance on the degree of latitude to be afforded to them as decision-makers might be found in in Laws LJ's dissenting judgment in *International Transport Roth GmbH v Secretary of State for the Home Department*[129] which was cited with apparent approval by Lord Walker in *ProLife* (although *International Transport* did not involve a media organization). His judgment sets out the principles governing the approach that will be adopted, with particular focus on the varying degree of deference that is due to the various sources of powers to which the broadcasters must have regard.[130]

However, these principles still leave a great deal of uncertainty which can only be **1.64** resolved on the facts of a particular case. Perhaps the most that can be said is, as Lord Walker concluded in *ProLife*,[131] that the Court's task is 'to review the decision with an intensity appropriate to all the circumstances of the case'.[132]

There would be much merit in an approach under the HRA whereby all media **1.65** organizations (whether print or broadcast) owed the same duty to respect the right to private and family life of those about whom they disclose personal information in their publications or broadcasts and were, in turn, able to rely to the same extent on Convention rights, such as the right to freedom of expression.[133] In any event,

---

[127] Deriving from the Broadcasting Act 1990, s 36 in the case of ITV, Channel 4, and Channel 5; and Art 12(4) proviso (i) of the *Royal Charter for the Continuance of the British Broadcasting Corporation* (Cm 3284, 1996) in the case of the BBC.

[128] The Freedom of Information Act 2000 gives the BBC special status in pt IV of sch 1, in that it is a public authority for some purposes but not for others.

[129] [2002] EWCA Civ 158, [2003] QB 728 [376]–[378].

[130] *International Transport Roth GmbH* (n 145) [136].

[131] *ProLife* (n 126) [139].

[132] For an example of the application of these principles in the context of a restriction on the exercise of freedom of expression, see *British American Tobacco v Secretary of State for Health* [2004] EWHC 2493 (Admin).

[133] One possible solution would be to adopt the approach taken in the Freedom of Information Act 2000. The list of 'public authorities' to which the obligations under that Act apply are set out in sch 1. The same formulation appears in respect of the BBC and Channel 4: both are defined as public authorities but only 'in respect of information held for purposes other than journalism, art or literature'. This has the effect of putting the public service broadcasters in the same position in

it would seem that the traditional distinction between the public and private law aspects of rights under Articles 8 and 10 is breaking down.[134] The position of the media regulators as public authorities (which led directly to the introduction of s 12 HRA) is considered in Chapter 14.

## E. Other Legislative Protections for Privacy and Confidentiality

**1.66**  Privacy interests in personal information have received an increasing degree of protection through legislation, most of it potentially applicable to media activities. For a long while the development of this protection was piecemeal, sometimes resulting from particular narrow issues catching the popular or political imagination.[135] The result is that there now exists a miscellany of statutory provisions which confer a degree of privacy on specific classes of personal information. There are provisions applying to the full range of media activities, from news-gathering to internal processing of information to publication. But these provisions fall into no overall pattern, and in some instances there is overlap.[136]

**1.67**  Equally, there is no discernible pattern to the remedies provided for. Most statutes make breach of their restrictions a criminal offence or a contempt of court, but do not provide for any civil right of action.[137] Relatively few provide for rights of action enforceable in the courts. To a large extent it is still fair to say, as the Younger Committee observed over forty years ago, that 'a number of statutory provisions

---

respect of these categories of information as the independent broadcasters and press which are not listed as public authorities. Pre-HRA cases have been decided on the assumption that the BBC does enjoy rights under Art 10: *R v BSC, ex p BBC* [2001] QB 885 [18]; *Kelly v BBC* [2001] Fam 59, 79–89. In *R v BBC, ex p Referendum Party* [1997] EMLR 605, 623 the Court left open the question whether a party election broadcast was a governmental function, while recording at 622 that 'the traditional view of it is that [the BBC] does not exercise a governmental function'. In *West v BBC* (QBD, 10 June 2002) the Court was invited to restrain a broadcast identifying a paedophile on the ground that the BBC, as a public authority, was bound by Art 3. It declined to do so, on the basis that the claimant would be less likely to succeed on that basis than on the alternative claim in confidentiality.

[134]  See the cases following the European Court's decision in *Hatton v UK* (2003) EHRR 28 (Grand Chamber) referred to 1.53 *et seq*.

[135]  An example is the Protection from Harassment Act 1997, introduced primarily to deal with concerns about 'stalking'. For discussion of legislative protection against intrusion into physical privacy see 10.04–10.45.

[136]  See *eg* the overlap between the Protection from Harassment Act 1997, s 1 and the Criminal Justice and Police Act 2001, s 42 (discussed at 1.80 and 10.21–10.24), and N A Moreham, 'Protection Against Intrusion in English Legislation' in N Witzleb, D Lindsay, M Paterson and S Rodrick (eds), *Emerging Challenges in Privacy Law: Comparative Perspectives* (Cambridge University Press 2014).

[137]  The question of whether civil claims might in some instances be fashioned on the basis of criminal statutes is considered at 1.91–1.94. A notable case in point is *Rickless v United Artists* [1988] QB 40 where the Dramatic and Musical Performers' Protection Act 1958 was construed to give a private right to performers to prevent the use of film images of their performances without their consent.

give some protection to privacy but since few of them are designed for that purpose they rarely provide a satisfactory remedy'.[138]

There is, however, more recent legislation which gives some general protection to privacy. The impact of Article 8 ECHR has already been discussed (and is the subject of further analysis in Chapter 5). Other major modern statutes which provide protection to privacy interests generally, and are of particular importance to the media, are the Data Protection Act 1998 (DPA)[139] and the Freedom of Information Act 2000 (FIA). Most of these legislative measures are discussed in greater detail in the chapters which follow. The aim of this section is to provide an overview of the scope of these overlapping statutes as well as to touch upon certain legislative provisions relevant to media activities. The section concludes with a brief discussion of the extent to which it may be argued that civil remedies should be granted to enforce statutory prohibitions even where no civil remedy is expressly provided for.  **1.68**

### (1) The Copyright, Designs and Patents Act 1988

Copyright is capable of conferring a measure of privacy on private documents. The relationship between the two concepts was recognized in *Williams v Settle*,[140] where the plaintiff recovered damages for the unauthorized publication of private photographs, the copyright of which was vested in him. Upholding the award of £1,000 punitive damages by the Court at first instance, Sellers LJ commented that the publication was:  **1.69**

> A flagrant infringement of the right of the plaintiff, and it was scandalous conduct and in total disregard not only of the legal rights of the plaintiff regarding copyright but of his feelings and his sense of family dignity and pride. It was an intrusion into his life, deeper and graver than an intrusion into a man's property.

Although copyright protects only the form and not the substance of, or ideas contained in, a copyright work, the newsworthy element of a literary, artistic or, more often, photographic work may indeed lie in its particular form. What is more, in the case of photographs and films commissioned for private and domestic purposes the law provides an explicit privacy right,[141] which lasts so long as copyright subsists in the work.[142] Infringement of these rights may be restrained by injunction, and remedied by damages (which may include 'additional' damages) or an account of profits.  **1.70**

*Rocknroll v News Group Newspapers Ltd*[143] was a case in which an individual sought to enforce privacy rights through a claim in copyright. The claimant successfully  **1.71**

---

[138] Younger Report (n 14) app I, para 34.

[139] Extending and enhancing privacy protection initially given under the Data Protection Act 1984.

[140] [1960] 1 WLR 1072, CA, decided under the Copyright Act 1956.

[141] Copyright Designs and Patents Act 1988, s 85.

[142] Copyright Designs and Patents Act 1988, s 86(1).

[143] [2013] EWHC 24 (Ch).

obtained an interim injunction to restrain the republication of private information contained within photographs taken of him on the grounds of a threatened breach of privacy. His application for the injunction on the basis of an alleged breach of copyright was not separately analysed in detail; Briggs J was willing to grant the injunction solely on the basis of breach of privacy but indicated that an injunction to restrain republication of the photographs themselves (as opposed to a description of the information contained within them) would also have been justified on the basis of the threatened breach of copyright. The topic of privacy, copyright, and moral rights is considered in detail in Chapter 9.

### (2) The Data Protection Act 1998

**1.72** This Act contains the most comprehensive privacy provisions now affecting the media. It is of general application to those who 'process' 'personal data' outside the purely domestic sphere. It imposes controls on such processing, and sanctions for breach of those controls. There is little doubt that the media's dealings with information are affected by the Act.[144] 'Process' encompasses virtually anything which can be done with data, including publication; 'personal data' includes any information relating to an identifiable living person provided only that it is, or is intended to be, processed on a computer or part of a 'relevant filing system'. This includes a manual system, provided that it is structured so that specific information relating to a particular individual is readily accessible.[145]

**1.73** The processing of eight categories of 'sensitive personal data' is subject to additional controls under the Act. This is one of a number of statutory 'checklists' to which resort may be had to identify those types of information to be regarded as private in nature and those which may be deserving of protection from disclosure.[146] The Act includes, in s 32, a specific but limited exemption for the media. The sanctions available under the Act include compensation, which can include compensation for distress whether or not actual damage has been suffered.[147] In addition, orders are available for rectifying, blocking, erasure, or destruction of records. An action may be brought before the court for such remedies and (subject to restrictions) for

---

[144] In *Campbell* (n 26) the Court of Appeal confirmed at [97]–[107] that 'where the data controller is responsible for the publication of hard copies that reproduce data that has previously been processed by means of equipment operating automatically, the publication forms part of the processing and falls within the scope of the [Data Protection] Act'. There was no appeal against this finding when the case went to the House of Lords.

[145] The Act was extended to cover all unstructured data held by a public authority on 1 January 2005, when s 1(1) of the 1998 Act was amended by the FIA. The term 'personal data' was considered by the Court of Appeal in *Durant v Financial Services Authority* [2003] EWCA Civ 1746, [2004] FSR 28, and given a narrow interpretation. But see now *Edem v Information Commissioner* [2014] EWCA Civ 92 [18]–[22], explaining *Durant*.

[146] Other helpful statutory 'checklists' are to be found in the Local Government Act 1972 and the Employment Rights Act 1996. The controls on surveillance contained in the Regulation of Investigatory Powers Act 2000 are also a useful reference point.

[147] *Vidal-Hall v Google Inc* [2015] EWCA Civ 311, [2015] 3 WLR 409.

an injunction. The DPA also creates offences of gaining illicit access to data. These important provisions are examined in detail in Chapter 7.

### (3) The Freedom of Information Act 2000

This Act has been widely used by the media for news-gathering purposes since its **1.74** main provisions entered into force on 1 January 2005. Section 1 of the Act grants 'any person' extensive rights to know[148] about 'information' which is recorded in some form,[149] and which is held by a 'public authority'.[150] These rights are not in any way dependent on the identity or motives of the applicant for information. However, the Act contains a substantial number of exemptions from the rights of access for which it provides, and the classes of exempt information include 'personal data' of the applicant and other personal data the disclosure of which would breach the DPA.[151] Also exempted is information obtained by the public authority from another person (including another public authority) if 'disclosure of the information to the public by the public authority...would constitute a breach of confidence actionable by that or any other person'.[152] The privacy of journalistic material is recognized in the Act. While the BBC, Channel 4, and S4C are subject to the Act, this is only in respect of 'information held for purposes other than those of journalism, art or literature'.[153]

### (4) Statutory Offences of Relevance to the Media

#### (a) Publishing leaked information

Like the Freedom of Information Act, the legislation providing for public access to **1.75** meetings and documents of local authorities contains exemptions for personal information. The Local Government Act 1972 contains a list[154] of fifteen classes of (mostly) personal information which may be withheld from the public, and provides for the withholding of 'confidential information'.[155] Regulations made under the Local

---

[148] The rights are, on making a request, '(a) to be informed in writing by the public authority whether it holds information of the description specified in the request, and (b) if that is the case, to have that information communicated to the person requesting it': s 1(1) FIA.

[149] s 84 FIA (interpretation).

[150] The term 'public authority' covers a wide range of national, regional, and local bodies, including quangos and a large number of individuals holding public office: see s 3(1) and sch 1 FIA.

[151] s 40 FIA. 'Personal data' has the same meaning as in the DPA. Hence, the adoption of a narrow interpretation of 'personal data' as in *Durant* (n 145) would mean that the exemptions in s 40 FIA is correspondingly narrower.

[152] s 41 FIA. There are similar exemptions from access under the Local Government Act 1972.

[153] sch 1, pt VI FIA. The Act does not apply to material held to any significant degree for journalistic purposes. It does not matter whether the journalistic purpose is the dominant one: *BBC v Sugar (No 2)* [2012] UKSC 4, [2012] 1 WLR 439. See also *Kennedy v Charity Commissioner* [2014] UKSC 20, [2014] 2 WLR 808, in which the Supreme Court held (by a majority) that the FIA is compatible with Art 10.

[154] Local Government Act 1972, sch 12A.

[155] Local Government Act 1972, s 100A(2), (3). Provisions for withholding exempt or confidential information are in ss 100A(4), 100B(2), 100C(1)(a), 100D(4).

Government Act 2000 provide a separate and more restrictive regime in relation to public access to meetings of local authority executives, and information about such meetings.[156]

**1.76**  Leaks of personal information by a governmental or other state source may be in breach not only of the source's duties as an employee but also of a specific statutory duty of non-disclosure. Provisions of this kind are too numerous to list but examples are to be found in the Abortion Act 1967,[157] the Taxes Management Act 1970,[158] the Rehabilitation of Offenders Act 1974,[159] the Race Relations Act 1976,[160] and the Telecommunications Act 1984.[161] Such provisions are not uniform. Two features are common, however: the imposition of a duty of non-disclosure, and criminal sanctions for breach of that duty. Sometimes the duties are so expressed as to prohibit disclosure by 'any person', so that a journalist publishing the information in question would commit the offence.[162] More commonly, the duties and sanctions are expressed to apply to those who obtain information officially; in other words to media sources.[163] It is conceivable that in such a case a journalist might be prosecuted for inciting, procuring, aiding, or abetting such an offence[164] although, outside the context of national security, no examples are known and, in the context of the Official Secrets Act 1989, the Court of Appeal has said that a prosecution of the media for incitement would only be justified in an extreme case on the facts.[165]

---

[156] Local Authorities (Executive Arrangements) (Access to Information) (England) Regulations 2000, SI 2000/3272, as amended by SI 2002/716 and SI 2006/69.

[157] The Abortion Regulations 1991, SI 1991/449, reg 5, as amended by SI 2002/887, prohibit unauthorized disclosure of information which medical practitioners are required to provide about terminations. Section 2(3) of the 1967 Act makes it an offence wilfully to contravene or fail to comply with the requirements of the regulations.

[158] s 6, and sch 1, requiring Commissioners, Inspectors, Collectors, and other officers to make solemn declarations on taking office that 'I will not disclose any information received by me in the execution of [my] duties, except…' for certain specified purposes.

[159] s 9, making unauthorized disclosure by officials of information about spent convictions an offence.

[160] s 52, imposing prohibitions on disclosure of information given to the Commission for Racial Equality (superseded in October 2007 by the Equality and Human Rights Commission).

[161] s 45, prohibiting disclosure of the contents of any message transmitted by a public telecommunications system, and about the use made of telecommunications services.

[162] An example is Electronic Communications Act 2000, s 4 which provides that, subject to exceptions, 'no information which (a) has been obtained under or by virtue of the provisions of this Part and (b) relates to the private affairs of any individual or to any particular business shall, during the lifetime of that individual or so long as that business continues to be carried on, be disclosed without the consent of that individual or the person for the time being carrying on that business'.

[163] *eg*, the offence created by Race Relations Act 1976, s 52(2) is disclosure 'by the Commission or by any person who is or has been a Commissioner, additional Commissioner or employee of the Commission'. The offence under Telecommunications Act 1984, s 45 is intentional disclosure by 'a person engaged in the running of a public telecommunications system'.

[164] A prosecution for theft of the information would not be possible; information is not 'property' capable of being stolen for the purposes of the Theft Acts: *Oxford v Moss* (1978) 68 Cr App R 183.

[165] *R v Shayler* [2001] EWCA Crim 1977, [2001] 1 WLR 2206 [96]. The House of Lords, in dismissing the applicant's appeal, did not comment on this observation: [2002] UKHL 11, [2003] 1 AC 247.

As for civil proceedings, it will naturally be of powerful assistance to a person seeking to establish a claim for breach of confidence against the media to show that the information came to the media in breach of a statutory non-disclosure provision. In some circumstances a claim for breach of statutory duty may be possible.[166]

### (b) 'Chequebook journalism'

A number of prosecutions took place in the second decade of the twenty-first century in which journalists were accused of paying public officials for information.[167] The charge commonly laid was the common law crime of misconduct in a public office, though there were some charges under the Prevention of Corruption Act 1916. That Act was repealed and replaced by the Bribery Act 2010, which prohibits payments to public and private sector officers and employees to induce them to perform otherwise than in accordance with the reasonable expectations of their employers. This is a broad prohibition, capable of application to a range of journalistic activities, some at least of which would be considered justified in the public interest. There is no public interest defence, but the exercise of the discretion whether to prosecute is governed by Guidance issued by the Director of Public Prosecutions on assessing the public interest in media cases.[168]

**1.77**

### (c) Surveillance

The monitoring and recording by the media of messages and communications is subject to the Wireless Telegraphy Act 1949 and the Regulation of Investigatory Powers Act 2000 (RIPA). The 1949 Act creates two offences which can be summarized as (i) using wireless telegraphy apparatus to find out about messages, whether wireless or not, and (ii) disclosing information obtained by anyone in this way.[169] RIPA makes unauthorized interception of the public post or telecommunications and of private telecommunications an offence, and also makes most such interceptions actionable at the suit of the sender, recipient, or intended recipient.[170] While RIPA's short title might imply otherwise, these provisions apply not only to the conduct of public authorities but also to private persons such as journalists who may intercept the communications of others. RIPA also contains extensive provisions regulating surveillance.[171] These are concerned with authorization of official surveillance, but provide a reference point when considering the propriety of intrusion by non-government bodies such as the media.

**1.78**

---

[166] See 1.91–1.94.

[167] These included charges laid as the result of a police inquiry named Operation Elveden.

[168] <http://www.cps.gov.uk/legal/d_to_g/guidance_for_prosecutors_on_assessing_the_public_interest_in_cases_affecting_the_media_/> issued on 13 September 2012.

[169] Wireless Telegraphy Act 1949, s 5(b)(i) and (ii). These provisions and the possibility, raised in *Francome v Mirror Group Newspapers Ltd* [1984] 1 WLR 892, CA, that a civil claim might be based upon them, are further discussed at 1.93.

[170] s 1.

[171] pt II, ss 26–48.

**1.79** A variety of provisions of the criminal law have been relied on to prosecute journalists for offences arising out of the phone hacking affair. In the main the journalists alleged to have improperly intercepted voicemail messages while working for the *News of the World* at the relevant time were prosecuted for conspiracy to intercept communications without lawful authority pursuant to s 1 of the Criminal Law Act 1977.

*(d) 'Doorstepping'*

**1.80** The media practice of confronting an individual for an interview outside his home or office may fall foul of s 42 of the Criminal Justice and Police Act 2001, by which doorstepping can be an offence if carried on in contravention of a police requirement to desist.[172] Doorstepping could also be contrary to the Protection from Harassment Act 1997 which prohibits the pursuit of a 'course of conduct' which a person knows or ought to know amounts to harassment of another.[173] Both criminal sanctions and civil remedies are available.[174] In addition, however, the concept of harassment under the 1997 Act is capable of applying to publication; the Court of Appeal has held that repeated newspaper publications may, in exceptional circumstances, amount to harassment and be actionable under the Act.[175] The 1997 Act is also considered in Chapters 6 and 10.

*(e) Information disclosed in legal proceedings*

**1.81** Private and personal information and documents may come to the media as a result of their involvement, or the involvement of a source, in legal proceedings. If such material has been obtained through a process of compulsory disclosure in the proceedings then it is protected by duties of non-disclosure imposed by either primary or secondary legislation unless and until the information enters the public domain in the course of the proceedings. It will be a contempt of court for the party to use or disclose it otherwise than for the proceedings.[176] A journalist or publisher knowingly participating in such use or disclosure could face contempt proceedings.[177]

---

[172] See also the prohibitions on intimidation, harassment and persistent pursuit in cl 3 of the IPSO Editors' Code and at Appendix G(iii) (available at <http://www.5rb.com/publication/the-law-of-privacy-and-the-media>).

[173] s 1(1). Harassing includes alarming a person or causing a person distress; a course of conduct must involve conduct on at least two occasions; conduct includes speech: s 7. See further, chs 6 and 10.The PHA is set out in full at Appendix C (available at <http://www.5rb.com/publication/the-law-of-privacy-and-the-media>).

[174] See further 6.04.

[175] *Thomas v News Group Newspapers Ltd* [2001] EWCA Civ 1233, [2002] EMLR 4.

[176] In the criminal context, restrictions on disclosure of 'unused material' are imposed on the accused by the Criminal Procedure and Investigations Act 1996, s 17; and s 18 makes contravention a contempt. In civil proceedings, disclosures are protected by CPR 31.22 (documents provided by way of disclosure), CPR 32.12 (information in witness statements), and CPR 34.12 (information from an examination about assets other than at trial) and further information under pt 18 may be protected by direction of the court: CPR 18.2. In each case contempt proceedings are the sanction. These provisions are further discussed at 13.70–13.71 and 13.177–13.179.

[177] See *Home Office v Harman* [1983] AC 1 (albeit that decision would be different on its facts today). See further 13.127.

Non-party access to information about proceedings which is held on court files is **1.82** restricted by the Civil Procedure Rules. These do not permit a general roving search[178] but a journalist or other non-party who is able to identify specific documents may be allowed to inspect them, even after a settlement, where they have been read or referred to in open court.[179]

In a significant development the Court of Appeal has held that where documents have **1.83** been placed before a judge and referred to in the course of proceedings (whether civil or criminal), the default position is that the media should be permitted to have access to those documents on the open justice principle.[180]

*(f) Restrictions on reports of crime and the courts*

Victims and alleged victims of rape offences are afforded lifetime anonymity by the **1.84** Sexual Offences (Amendment) Act 1976.[181] It is a criminal offence to identify a victim once the relevant allegation has been made. No provision is made for civil sanctions.[182] Similar anonymity for victims of a variety of other sexual offences is provided for by the Sexual Offences (Amendment) Act 1992.[183] The Act does not however provide the court with a power protecting victims of sexual crime by anonymizing defendants who have been named in open court.[184] The Rehabilitation of Offenders Act 1974 entitles most criminal convicts[185] 'to be treated for all purposes in law' as if they had not committed the crime[186] once a specified rehabilitation period of not more than ten years has elapsed. The main effects of rehabilitation set out in the Act are rights not to disclose convictions in answer to questions.[187] Publication of a spent conviction

---

[178] *Dian AO v David Frankel and Mead (A Firm)* [2004] EWHC 2662 (Comm), [2005] 1 WLR 2951.

[179] *Re Guardian Newspapers Ltd* [2004] EWHC 3092 (Ch), [2005] 1 WLR 2965 (also known as *Chan U Seek v Alvis Vehicles Ltd*).

[180] *R (ex P Guardian News and Media) v (1) City of Westminster Magistrates Court (2) Government of the United States* [2012] EWCA Civ 420, [2013] QB 618.

[181] s 4(1)(a). The offences covered are rape, attempted rape, aiding abetting counselling and procuring, incitement, conspiracy, and burglary with intent to rape. Male rape is also covered. In November 2002 the House of Commons Home Affairs Select Committee recommended that consideration be given to the grant of anonymity to those accused of sex crimes: *HC Select Committee for Home Affairs Second Report* (HC Paper (2002–03) no 83) para 45. The Home Office was unconvinced: see its Response of March 2003 (Cm 5787), para gg. The rights of victims were however extended.

[182] But see 1.91–1.94.

[183] s 1. The offences include indecent assaults on men and women, buggery, various offences of procurement and unlawful intercourse, incest, and attempts and conspiracy to commit such acts: s 2. Anonymity for victims was extended to a wide variety of other sexual crimes with effect from 1 May 2004. The crimes include voyeurism, indecent exposure, engaging in or causing sexual activity with children, and numerous other offences involving children. This is by virtue of amendments to the Sexual Offences (Amendment) Acts of 1976 and 1992 made by s 139 of and sch 6, paras 20 and 31 to the Sexual Offences Act 2003, which created many of the offences in question.

[184] *R (Press Association) v Cambridge Crown Court* [2012] EWCA Crim 2434, [2013] 1 WLR 1979.

[185] The main exceptions being those who have been sentenced to life imprisonment, or to prison or youth custody, detention in a young offender institution, or corrective training for more than 30 months: s 5.

[186] Or been charged with, or prosecuted for, or convicted or sentenced for it: s 4(1).

[187] s 4(1)–(3).

is not a crime nor civilly actionable as such under the Act. However, malicious publication is made actionable as a libel.[188]

**1.85** The confidentiality of jury deliberations is protected by the Contempt of Court Act 1981 by which it is a contempt to obtain, disclose, or solicit details of those deliberations.[189]

**1.86** The privacy of children involved in any proceedings in adult courts may be protected by directions under the Youth Justice and Criminal Evidence Act 1999 prohibiting their identification or the publication of a picture of them.[190] In youth courts prohibitions on identification until adulthood of children concerned in the proceedings are automatic.[191] There is power to give directions prohibiting identification of children involved in any form of civil proceedings,[192] and automatic restrictions in certain specific kinds of civil proceedings.[193] Other provisions, too numerous to list here, either protect or confer on the courts power to protect those involved in legal proceedings from publicity.[194]

### (5) Statutory Protections for Journalists/News-gatherers/Relevant to the Media

#### (a) Whistle-blowing

**1.87** Information from an employee about perceived wrongdoing within his or her organization may be a source of important news stories. Workers who blow the whistle in the public interest are now protected by the Employment Rights Act

---

[188] s 8(5).

[189] Contempt of Court Act 1981, s 8.

[190] Youth Justice and Criminal Evidence Act 1999, ss 45 (anonymity until adulthood) and 45A (lifetime anonymity, under certain conditions). For the convoluted legislative history of these provisions and those mentioned in nn 191 and 192 see *Aitken v DPP* [2015] EWHC 1079 (Admin) [3]–[9].

[191] Children and Young Persons Act 1933, s 49 as amended by the Youth Justice and Criminal Evidence Act 1999. Anonymity can be dispensed with by the court. For the duration of the protection see n 192.

[192] Children and Young Persons Act 1933, s 39 as amended by the Criminal Justice and Courts Act 2015. The previous version of this provision was held to confer power to grant anonymity until adulthood only: *JC v Central Criminal Court* [2014] EWHC 1041 (Admin), [2014] 1 WLR 3697, aff'd [2014] EWCA Civ 1777. It appears that the same is true of s 49 of the 1933 Act (n 191). The position in criminal matters was changed with effect from 13 April 2015 by s 45A of the Youth Justice and Criminal Evidence Act 1999, which was added by the Criminal Justice and Courts Act 2015. In civil matters the position at the time of writing appears to be that lifetime anonymity cannot be granted under s 39: see *Aitken* (n 190).

[193] Administration of Justice Act 1960, s 12(1); Magistrates' Courts Act 1980, s 71; Children Act 1989, s 97(2).

[194] *eg* Judicial Proceedings (Regulation of Reports) Act 1926, s 1 which concerns divorce and related proceedings; Youth Justice and Criminal Evidence Act 1999, s 46 provides a power to restrict reports about certain adult witnesses in criminal proceedings. In *R v ITN* [2013] EWCA Crim 773, [2014] 1 WLR 199 the Court of Appeal held that the court has jurisdiction to make an order under s 46 where the name of a witness was common knowledge but publication of photographs of her and her children would have led to her identification which would have affected the quality of her evidence at trial.

1996 from action by their employers.[195] In particular, the Act makes void any contractual provision which would preclude what it calls a 'protected disclosure'.[196] This means a disclosure in good faith, to an appropriate person or persons, of one or more of six specified kinds of information, about criminal or civil misconduct; risks to justice, health, or the environment; or cover-ups of such matters.[197] Private, personal information could well fall within the scope of these provisions. If a worker's disclosure of such information to the media was a 'protected disclosure' then it would be reasonable to assume that the media would avoid liability for publishing it. By the same token, an attempt by the media to justify on public interest grounds the publication of a whistle-blowing story would be likely to fail if the worker's own disclosure failed to satisfy the statutory criteria for protection.[198] The scheme of the relevant provisions is such that disclosure to the public generally appears to be regarded as a measure of last resort needing clear justification.[199]

### (b) Privacy of journalistic material

The identity of confidential media sources is given qualified protection by s 10 of the **1.88** Contempt of Court Act 1981. This entitles a publisher or journalist to withhold the identity of 'the source of information contained in a publication for which he is responsible' and prohibits the court from ordering disclosure unless that is 'necessary in the interests of justice or national security or for the prevention of disorder or crime'. Journalistic material generally has exemption from the access rights under the DPA and, where this is otherwise applicable, the FIA.[200] Journalistic material also has special status under the Police and Criminal Evidence Act 1984[201] which

---

[195] pt IVA (ss 43A–L) and s 103A, all inserted by the Public Interest Disclosure Act 1998. The Public Interest Disclosure Act's requirement for a disclosure to be in good faith was removed by s 18 of the Enterprise and Regulatory Reform Act 2013: the good faith requirement was replaced with a power to reduce damages by 25% where a protected disclosure was made in bad faith.

[196] s 43J.

[197] s 43B.

[198] Such an unsuccessful attempt was made in the context of a dispute over the disclosure of research data on the internet in *Imutran Ltd v Uncaged Campaigns Ltd* [2001] 2 All ER 385, [2001] EMLR 21, HC. See Sir Andrew Morritt V-C [22].

[199] The first port of call is the employer, or other person whom the worker believes to have legal responsibility over the matter in question: s 43C. This would cover, for instance, disclosure to the police in a case of alleged crime or to a regulator such as the Animal Procedures Committee in *Imutran* (n 198). Another possible course short of media publication which is contemplated by the Act is disclosure to a legal adviser: s 43D. For other disclosures the first in the list of factors to which regard is to be had is 'the identity of the person to whom disclosure is made': s 43G(3)(a).

[200] s 32 DPA. The FIA applies in qualified form to the BBC, Channel 4, and S4C. Where the access rights do apply, the identities of sources may be withheld if they do not consent and it is 'reasonable' to withhold their identities: s 7(4) DPA. In *Durant* (n 145) the Court of Appeal was wary of attempting to devise any principles of general application on the reasonableness test in s 7(4). It felt that everything depended on the circumstances, and that the Court should limit itself to a review of the data controller's decision rather than assuming the role of primary decision-maker or 'second guessing' data controllers' decisions.

[201] There are two categories. First, 'journalistic material' generally, which means 'material acquired or created for the purposes of journalism' which is 'in the possession of a person who

exempts all such material from the general power to enter and search premises under a search warrant[202] and imposes specific 'access conditions' which must be established to the satisfaction of a circuit judge before the police can have access to any of it.[203]

**1.89**  A similar procedure governs access to journalistic material under the Terrorism Act 2000[204] but there are important differences which give the police easier access.[205] Moreover, while the anti-terrorism legislation has recently undergone substantial reform it remains a criminal offence for a person not promptly to inform a police officer of his or her knowledge or suspicion, based on information gained in the course of his or her work, that another person is funding or providing various forms of financial assistance for terrorism, and the grounds for such knowledge or suspicion.[206] It is also an offence to 'interfere with' material knowing or suspecting that it is likely to be relevant to a current or prospective terrorist investigation, a provision which could, it seems, affect the destruction of journalistic material.[207] Finally, if a media organization possesses information the disclosure of which would infringe s 5 of the Official Secrets Act 1989[208] then it is a criminal offence not to hand it over to a government official when requested to do so.[209]

**1.90**  Section 38B of the Terrorism Act 2000[210] adds a further criminal offence of failing without reasonable excuse to disclose information which a person knows or believes might be of material assistance in preventing an act of terrorism or

---

acquired or created it for the purposes of journalism'. This is amongst the categories designated in the Act as 'special procedure material', access to which requires the permission of a circuit judge. Secondly, 'journalistic material' which is held in confidence. This is amongst the categories designated as 'excluded material'. Access to excluded material can only be given under Police and Criminal Evidence Act 1984 if the circuit judge is satisfied that another Act allows access to it, and that this is appropriate.

[202]  Police and Criminal Evidence Act 1984, s 117.

[203]  Police and Criminal Evidence Act 1984, sch 1, paras 1–2. These provisions were analysed, and their stringency emphasized, in *Bright* (n 14).

[204]  sch 5, pt 1.

[205]  In particular, application may be made under sch 5 to the Terrorism Act 2000 without notice to the respondent, and excluded or special procedure material may be seized even if no other Act allows this.

[206]  Terrorism Act 2000, s 19(1)–(2). There is however a defence of 'reasonable excuse' for non-disclosure: s 19(3). In the course of parliamentary debates it was said on behalf of the government that it saw this as an important safeguard for journalists, given that protecting sources was 'clearly an important principle for journalists, particularly those working in this difficult area': *Hansard*, HL (series 6), vol 613, col 653 (23 May 2000) (Lord Bassam of Brighton).

[207]  Terrorism Act 2000, s 39(2) and (4). Again, though, this is subject to a defence (among others) of 'reasonable excuse'.

[208]  Some personal information may fall within these provisions. They cover not only government secrets as to security and intelligence, defence, and international relations but also any information the disclosure of which 'impedes the prevention or detection of offences' (s 4(2)(iii)) and any information obtained by official interception of communications, or about such interception (s 4(3)(a)).

[209]  Official Secrets Act 1989, s 8(4).

[210]  Inserted by Anti-Terrorism, Crime and Security Act 2001, s 117.

in securing the apprehension, prosecution, or conviction of a person for terrorist acts. Unlike the offence under s 19, this crime is not limited to information obtained in the course of employment. It applies even if the information is acquired overseas.

## (6) Sanctions and Remedies

Leaving aside the DPA, the majority of the statutes mentioned above provide only for **1.91** criminal sanctions. In such cases the question may arise as to whether an injunction can be obtained, or a claim for damages pursued, for breach of the statutory prohibition. Could damages and/or an injunction be obtained, for example, in respect of actual or threatened breaches of the anonymity provisions of the Sexual Offences (Amendment) Acts? These state that where a relevant allegation has been made:

> ...neither the name nor address, and no still or moving picture, of that person shall, during that person's lifetime...be published in England and Wales in a written publication available to the public...if it is likely to lead members of the public to identify that person as the person against whom the offence is alleged to have been committed.[211]

On conventional principles, an action for breach of statutory duty may be available **1.92** where, as a matter of construction, it appears that the 'statutory duty was imposed for the protection of a limited class of the public and that Parliament intended to confer on members of that class a private right of action for breach of the duty'.[212] This was the basis upon which the County Court of Melbourne (Victoria) found for a claimant in a claim for breach of statutory duty against a broadcaster who identified her as a rape victim. [213]

Provisions such as those of the Sexual Offences (Amendment) Act 1976 would **1.93** certainly appear designed to protect a limited class of victims of crime. However, a parliamentary intention to protect a class is not enough; it must be shown that Parliament intended to afford a civil right of action.[214] Discerning whether this is so is not generally easy. While the Law Commission long ago proposed a simple, general presumption in favour of a civil right of action whenever a statute does not expressly exclude one,[215] this has never been acted upon. It may be that a breach of the duty not to identify a victim of certain sexual offences is actionable according to the tests for discerning parliamentary intent which have been developed by the courts.[216]

---

[211] Sexual Offences (Amendment) Act 1976, s 4(1)(a).

[212] *X (Minors) v Bedfordshire County Council* [1995] 2 AC 633, 732; *Rickless v United Artists* (n 137).

[213] *Jane Doe v Australian Broadcasting Corp* [2007] VCC 281.

[214] *Pickering v Liverpool Daily Post and Echo Newspapers Ltd* [1991] 2 AC 370; *R v Deputy Governor of Parkhurst Prison, ex p Hague* [1992] 1 AC 58, 170–1 (Lord Jauncey).

[215] Law Commission, *The Interpretation of Statutes* (Law Com No 21, 1969) para 38 and app A(4).

[216] Amongst the relevant factors are the remedies, if any, expressly provided for by the statute and the adequacy of alternative remedies whether administrative or at law, together with certain policy considerations.

The Court of Appeal has held it arguable that electronic eavesdropping on a telephone conversation in breach of s 5 of the Wireless Telegraphy Act 1949 amounts to an actionable breach of statutory duty.[217] However, the established tests have attracted understandable criticism for their inconsistency and the discretion they permit the courts.[218]

**1.94**  In the context of privacy statutes the single most important canon of statutory interpretation is, arguably, the one provided for by s 3 HRA, that 'so far as it is possible to do so, primary legislation and subordinate legislation must be read and given effect in a way which is compatible with the Convention rights' which, of course, include the privacy rights under Article 8. If some aspect of the Convention right to 'respect for … private and family life … home and correspondence' under Article 8 is protected by a particular statute which does not exclude a civil remedy then, it might be argued, a court which refused to grant a civil remedy for breach of the statute would be acting incompatibly with a Convention right, in breach of s 6 HRA. Such reasoning could be applied to the anonymity provisions mentioned above, and quite possibly to other statutory prohibitions.

## F. The Media Codes

**1.95**  Running alongside the legislative and common law provisions relating to privacy are the Codes of Practice which apply to the media. These consist of the Ofcom Broadcasting Code to which broadcasters are required to adhere as a condition of their licences and in relation to the press the Editors' Code of Practice of the Independent Press Standards Organisation, a voluntary code to which members of the press commit themselves. IPSO was established in the wake of Lord Justice Leveson's recommendations and replaced the Press Complaints Commission. The BBC has additional responsibilities under its Editorial Guidelines. The relevant provisions of those codes relating to privacy are considered in Chapter 14 together with the adjudications made under them and the powers of the bodies which implement them. Study of these codes is important not least because of the interrelationship between them and the legal framework for the protection of privacy by virtue of s 12(4) HRA which requires a court to have particular regard to the terms of any relevant privacy code when considering whether to grant any relief which might affect the exercise of the right to freedom of expression and the publication of any journalistic, literary, or artistic material.

---

[217] *Francome* (n 176) 896–7 (Sir John Donaldson MR), 901–2 (Stephen Brown LJ).
[218] G Williams, 'The Effect of Penal Legislation in the Law of Tort' (1960) 23 MLR 233.

## G. Privacy, the Internet, and Social Media

The authors of Chapter 15 have tackled the particular legal problems created by the **1.96** ascendancy of social media. While the existing media industry codes of practice may apply to online versions of print and broadcast material if they would otherwise come within the regulator's remit, they do not apply to the various other forms of new media which have sprung up in recent years. These include citizen blogs, Twitter, and social networking sites such as Facebook which are of increasing concern as regards infringements of a right to privacy.

Unless the specific publication complained about is made by a journalist or media **1.97** organization which is amenable to the jurisdiction of Ofcom, the BBC, or IPSO a victim must have recourse to the law in the ordinary way. As such the 'new media' are largely unregulated although the legislative and common law provisions considered in the previous sections will apply as appropriate. The legal means by which the court seeks to protect individuals against unwarranted infringements of privacy online are the same as those it deploys in other situations: there is as yet no civil cause of action directed specifically to online wrongdoing.

The criminal law may have a particular role in protecting individuals from **1.98** the deleterious consequences of online activity. On 20 June 2013 the Director of Public Prosecutions published *Guidelines on prosecuting cases involving communications sent via social media.*[219] The guidelines make specific reference to the provisions of s 1 of the Malicious Communications Act 1988 (sending an electronic communication which conveys a threat), and s 127 of the Communications Act 2003 (sending a message of a menacing character by means of a public telecommunications network).

As for civil remedies, misuse of private information, breach of confidence, copy- **1.99** right, data protection, defamation, and human rights and anti-discrimination legislation all have a role to play, but the tort of harassment under the Protection from Harassment Act 1997 appears to have a special place in the armoury. A more detailed consideration of these issues, as well as the changes brought about by the implementation of the Defamation Act 2013 and the accompanying Defamation (Operators of Websites) Regulations 2013 is contained in Chapter 15.

---

[219] <http://www.cps.gov.uk/legal/a_to_c/communications_sent_via_social_media/>.

# 2

## THE NATURE OF
## THE PRIVACY INTEREST

*N A Moreham*

## A. Introduction

**2.01** It has often been said that privacy is an elusive concept which defies precise definition. It has been used to protect interests as diverse as the right to the confidentiality of one's correspondence to the right to access abortion services or to have one's post-operative transgender identity recognized. Conceptions of what is private also differ from one individual to another—what one person will be happy to post on Facebook, another will regard as an intimate secret.

**2.02** This chapter will suggest, however, that privacy does have a core Anglo-Commonwealth meaning. There is also much consensus on why it is important: scholars and judges consistently refer to privacy's role in promoting dignity, autonomy, relationships, and well-being. Understanding these two issues—what privacy is and why it is important—is necessary if lawyers are meaningfully to assess the formulation of a legal privacy right, compensate its breach effectively and balance it properly against other competing interests. Drawing on English authorities, foreign decisions and academic thought, this chapter will therefore identify the key components of the privacy interest and explain why they are worthy of protection.

Before turning to those questions, it is important to note that this book is about **2.03** 'privacy' and its impact on the media, and not the broader concept of 'private life' protected by Article 8 of the European Convention on Human Rights (ECHR). Although the two concepts overlap to a considerable degree, they are not the same. As the European Commission acknowledged in the early decision of *X v Iceland*:

> For numerous Anglo-Saxon and French authors the right to respect for 'private life' is the right to privacy, the right to live, as far as one wishes, protected from publicity...however, the right to respect for private life does not end there. It comprises also, to a certain degree, the right to establish and to develop relationships with other human beings, especially in the emotional field for the development and fulfilment of one's own personality.[1]

Since this decision, the right to private life has been held by the European Court of Human Rights (ECtHR) to encompass, amongst other things, physical and psychological integrity, autonomy, and identity.[2] The fact that 'private life' is a significantly broader concept than 'privacy' means that interests which fall within the English conception of privacy will almost certainly be part of an individual's private life. The inverse does not, however, apply. Protection of privacy without more will not cover all of the multifarious interests covered by the ECHR right to private life. Some of those interests, therefore, fall beyond the scope of this work.

# B. The Scope of the Privacy Interest

Anglo-Commonwealth conceptions of privacy usually equate privacy with the **2.04** ability to avoid unwanted observation, exposure, or publicity. They are narrower than the liberty-based constitutional privacy right developed in the United States (which famously extends to interests like the right to access contraceptives and abortion services)[3] and the right to respect for private life in the ECHR (which includes, *inter alia*, identity rights and environmental rights such as a right to be free from excessive noise pollution).[4] In contrast to these broad decisional rights, Anglo-Commonwealth privacy rights are about restricting access to private information and to the physical self.

The equation of privacy with an ability to avoid unwanted observation, exposure, **2.05** and publicity was articulated as early as 1848 in the seminal case of *Prince Albert v Strange*. In that case, Knight Bruce V-C described the unauthorized publication

---

[1] *X v Iceland* App no 6825/74, (1976) 5 DR 86, 87.
[2] See 3.15–3.36.
[3] See eg *Roe v Wade* 410 US 113, 93 S Ct 705 (1973) 727 and *Griswold v Connecticut* 381 US 479, 85 S Ct 1678 (1965) 1682.
[4] See 3.15–3.36.

of etchings which Prince Albert had made for his own and his family's private amusement as:

> ...an intrusion—an unbecoming and unseemly intrusion...offensive to that inbred sense of propriety natural to every man—if intrusion, indeed, fitfully describes a sordid spying into the privacy of domestic life—into the home (a word hitherto sacred among us).[5]

**2.06**  The same idea was echoed by Lord Mustill 153 years later when he said in *R v Broadcasting Standards Commission, ex p BBC* that:

> To my mind the privacy of a human being denotes at the same time the personal 'space' in which the individual is free to be itself, and also the carapace, or shell, or umbrella, or whatever other metaphor is preferred, which protects that space from intrusion. An infringement of privacy is an affront to the personality, which is damaged both by the violation and by the demonstration that the personal space is not inviolate.[6]

'Space', here, is clearly meant both physically and metaphorically; it is the mental space to 'be oneself' as well as the physical space which makes up the home and other places of retreat.[7] Intrusion and retreat also feature clearly in Tipping J's definition of privacy in the leading New Zealand decision, *Hosking v Runting*. He says that:

> Privacy is potentially a very wide concept; but, for present purposes, it can be described as the right to have people leave you alone if you do not want some aspect of your private life to become public property. Some people seek the limelight; others value being able to shelter from the often intrusive and debilitating stresses of public scrutiny...It is of the essence of the dignity and personal autonomy and well-being of all human beings that some aspects of their lives should be able to remain private if they so wish. Even people whose work, or the public nature of whose activities make them a form of public property, must be able to protect some aspects of their lives from public scrutiny.[8]

Similar ideas of restricting access to one's private sphere, particularly to private information about oneself, can be seen throughout breach of confidence, misuse of private information, and data protection cases in England, Australia, Canada and New Zealand.[9]

**2.07**  This retreat-focused conception of privacy enjoys considerable academic support. It is most commonly expressed by scholars by reference to an individual's ability to restrict access to him or her self by others. For example, Ruth Gavison defines

---

[5] *Prince Albert v Strange* (1848) 2 De G & SM 652, 698; 64 ER 293, 313.

[6] [2001] QB 885 [48].

[7] The decision itself concerned secret filming of sales assistants inside a Dixons electronics store. The Court of Appeal upheld the Broadcasting Standards Commission's decision that the filming was a breach of privacy.

[8] *Hosking v Runting* [2005] 1 NZLR 1, CA [238]–[239].

[9] For further discussion see chs 3, 4, 5, and 7.

privacy as 'a limitation of others' access to an individual' which is lost whenever a person finds out about, pays attention to, or gets close enough to a person to touch or observe a person through the normal use of the senses.[10] Ernest van den Haag defines privacy as the exclusive access of a person to a realm of his or her own and says that it entitles a person to exclude others from watching, utilizing, or invading his or her private realm.[11] More recently, Kirsty Hughes has argued that 'the right to privacy should be understood as a right to respect for [behavioural] barriers, and that an invasion of privacy occurs when Y (the intruder) breaches a privacy barrier used by X (the privacy-seeker) to prevent Y from accessing X'.[12]

There is also widespread academic agreement that privacy implies choice. Most **2.08** proponents of the 'access' definition therefore include an element of voluntariness in their definitions. For example, James Rachels, and Eoin Carolan and Hilary Delany, see privacy as a *control* over, respectively, 'access to us and to information about us'[13] and 'the access which others have to the different dimensions of that individual's privacy'.[14] Others reject the idea that privacy should be equated with control but nonetheless stress the importance of making the privacy definition sub-jective. For example, Chris Hunt says that privacy refers to an individual's 'claim to be free from unwanted sensorial access' in relation to information and activities which are 'intimate', 'personal' or about which one feels acutely sensitive;[15] Kirsty Hughes says that 'an invasion of privacy occurs when Y (the intruder) breaches a privacy barrier used by X (the privacy-seeker) to prevent Y from accessing X';[16] and this author, Moreham, has argued elsewhere that privacy should be defined as 'freedom from *unwanted* access' or as a state of 'desired "inaccess"'.[17]

---

[10] R Gavison, 'Privacy and the Limits of the Law' (1979) 89 Yale LJ 421, 428–33.

[11] E van den Haag, 'On Privacy' in J Pennock and J Chapman (eds), *Privacy* (NOMOS Vol XIII, Atherton Press 1971) 149.

[12] K Hughes, 'A Behavioural Understanding of Privacy and its Implications for Privacy Law' (2012) 75 MLR 806, 810.

[13] J Rachels, 'Why Privacy is Important' (1975) 4 Phil & Publ Aff 323, 326.

[14] H Delany and E Carolan, *The Right to Privacy: A Doctrinal and Comparative Analysis* (Thomson Round Hall 2008) 25. See also C Fried, 'Privacy' (1968) 77 Yale LJ 475, 482 (defines privacy as 'the *control* we have over information about ourselves'); and H Gross, 'Privacy and Autonomy' in Pennock and Chapman (n 11) 169 and 'The Concept of Privacy' (1967) 42 NYULR 34, 35–6 (defines privacy as '*control* over acquaintance with one's personal affairs by the one enjoying it').

[15] C Hunt, 'Conceptualizing Privacy and Elucidating its Importance: Foundational Considerations for the Development of Canada's Fledgling Privacy Tort' (2011) 37 Queen's LJ 167, 201.

[16] Hughes (n 12) 810.

[17] N A Moreham, 'Privacy in the Common Law: A Doctrinal and Theoretical Analysis' (2005) 121 LQR 628, 636 (emphasis added). See also M Weinstein, 'The Uses of Privacy in the Good Life' in Pennock and Chapman (n 11) 94 (defines privacy as a condition of *voluntary* limitation of com-munication to or from certain others with respect to specified information of 'perceived good'); S Benn, 'Privacy, Freedom and Respect for Persons' in Pennock and Chapman (n 11) 3–4 (says that the right to privacy includes a claim 'not to be watched, listened to, or reported upon *without leave*, and not to have public attention focused upon one uninvited' (emphasis added)); and H Fenwick and G Phillipson, *Media Freedom under the Human Rights Act* (Oxford University Press 2006) 663. But compare Gavison (n 10) 427 (she says that in order '[t]o be nonpreemptive, privacy must not depend on choice').

**2.09**   Where access-based definitions have been criticized it is usually because they are insufficiently broad to capture the decisional, liberty-based decisions which the United States courts treat as part of the privacy interest.[18] Thus, American academic, Daniel Solove, criticizes Gavison's access definition as 'too narrow' because it excludes 'invasions into one's private life by harassment and nuisance and the government's involvement in decisions regarding one's body, health, sexual conduct, and family life'.[19] However, Gavison deliberately excluded these things,[20] and those seeking to capture a narrower, retreat-based conception of privacy regard this as an advantage. Thus, Chris Hunt argues that because Gavison's access definition 'necessarily excludes "substantive" or "decisional" privacy claims', she avoids the 'over breadth of the "right to be alone" conception, which conflates privacy with liberty'.[21] Definitions based on unwanted access are, therefore, broad enough to include unwanted surveillance, intrusion into the home, interference with communications and technology, and the revelation of intimate secrets or images (all of which have been treated as part of the privacy interest by Anglo-Commonwealth courts and lawmakers) without also including decisional-autonomy.[22]

### (1) Informational Privacy

**2.10**   The next question is *what kind of access* will breach a person's privacy? This section will suggest that the answer—that privacy is breached by unwanted access to personal *information* or to the *physical self*—helps us identify the two core components of the privacy interest.

### (a) Unwanted dissemination of private information or material about a person

**2.11**   There is almost universal consensus amongst judges, lawmakers, and commentators that the right to privacy includes protection against the dissemination of private information or material. Most legal redress for breach of privacy focuses on this aspect of the privacy interest. The ECtHR recognizes that the collection and storage of information can interfere with the right to respect for private life in Article 8 ECHR;[23] the Data Protection Act 1998 is aimed at 'the regulation of the processing of information relating to individuals, including the obtaining, holding use or disclosure of such information';[24] and, as its label suggests, the misuse of private information action identified by the House of Lords in *Campbell v MGN Ltd*

---

[18]   See 2.04.

[19]   D Solove, 'Conceptualizing Privacy' (2002) 90 Cal L Rev 1087, 1105.

[20]   Gavison (n 10) 436–40.

[21]   Hunt (n 15) 190. See also Delany and Carolan (n 14) 7–8. Solove himself declines to adopt the 'right to be let alone' definition seeing it as 'rather broad and vague' (n 19) 1102. He prefers a 'pragmatic' approach drawing on Ludwig Wittgenstein's notion of 'family resemblances' (n 19) 1096–9.

[22]   It should be stressed again here that this chapter is concerned with a definition of 'privacy' and not of the broader concept of private life in Art 8 ECHR (see 2.03).

[23]   See 3.26–3.28.

[24]   The Data Protection Act 1998, short title. See generally ch 7.

protects against the disclosure of private information.[25] Overseas, United States and New Zealand courts have expressly recognized torts of giving unreasonable publicity to another's private life[26] and disclosure of personal information is protected under Article 9 of the French Civil Code and Articles 1 and 2 of the German Basic Law.[27] The privacy of communications is also expressly protected in s 14 of the South African Constitution and specific legislation in the Canadian provinces of British Columbia, Saskatchewan, Manitoba, and Newfoundland.[28] There is little doubt, then, that courts and lawmakers regard the protection of private information as a core part of the privacy interest.

Almost all commentators agree that unwanted access to personal information is a **2.12** breach of privacy. Samuel Warren and Louis Brandeis's famous call for recognition of a right to be 'let alone' stressed the individual's need to keep certain personal information from the world at large.[29] In his oft-cited definition, Alan Westin also described privacy as 'the claim of individuals, groups, or institutions to determine for themselves, when, how, and to what extent information about them is communicated to others'.[30] And Ruth Gavison says 'a loss of privacy occurs as others obtain information about an individual',[31] noting that this is not a novel claim.[32] This judicial and academic consensus reflects societal instincts about the nature of the privacy interest. Most people, it is suggested, would regard the unwanted dissemination of intimate information about their health, sexual activities, fantasies, financial position, home life, and relationships as a breach of privacy. Likewise, most people regard their correspondence—whether it is communicated by post, email, internet, or telephone—as private.

The relevance to the media of legal rules about the dissemination of private infor- **2.13** mation needs hardly to be stated. Any limit on what can be disseminated will affect the media's operation. If the media are unable to publish private material about a person, then its ability to report on him or her will inevitably be affected. A good understanding of when information will and will not be private is, therefore, of vital

---

[25] [2004] UKHL 22, [2004] 2 AC 457.

[26] For the US position, see Restatement (Second) of Torts § 652D (1977), adopted and promulgated by the American Law Institute, and 3.44–3.84. For the New Zealand position, see *Hosking* (n 8) and 3.98–3.103.

[27] See further 3.152–3.176.

[28] See, respectively, 3.132 and 3.119.

[29] S Warren and L Brandeis, 'The Right to Privacy' (1890) 4 Harvard L Rev 193.

[30] A Westin, *Privacy and Freedom* (Atheneum 1967) 7.

[31] Gavison (n 10) 428.

[32] Gavison (n 10) 429. See also, T Gerety, 'Redefining Privacy' (1977) 12 Harv CR–CLL Rev 233; J Wagner DeCew, 'The Scope of Privacy in Law and Ethics' (1986) 5 L and Phil 145; H Gross, 'The Concept of Privacy' (1967) 42 NYULR 34; R Wacks, *Personal Information: Privacy and the Law* (Clarendon Press 1989) and *Privacy and Media Freedom* (Oxford University Press 2013); W Parent, 'A New Definition of Privacy for the Law' (1983) 12 Phil & Publ Aff 269, 305; D Solove, 'A Taxonomy of Privacy' (2006) 154 U Pa L Rev 447; and Hunt (n 15). But compare R Parker, 'A Definition of Privacy' (1974) 27 Rutg L Rev 275.

importance both to the media and those seeking protection from their attention. Much of this book is devoted to that issue in both the English and comparative contexts.

### (b) When will information be private?

**2.14** The fact that private information should be accorded some protection is unlikely to be disputed either by those developing privacy laws or those, like the media, who are subject to them. Much more difficult is the question of *what* information should be regarded as private. A substantial part of this book looks at how courts and lawmakers have answered that question. It is also useful, however, to consider the issue in more general terms.

**2.15** **A broad subjective approach**   When defining privacy at a theoretical level, many commentators take a broad approach to the concept of private information. For example, consistent with her view that privacy should be a 'neutral' concept, Ruth Gavison argues that privacy is lost whenever a person finds out *any* information about another.[33] For most commentators, however, Gavison's insistence on objectivity makes the definition too wide; they focus instead on the subjective desires of the subject. Thus, Charles Fried suggests that privacy is lost whenever *control* over information about oneself is lost.[34] Similarly, Alan Westin describes privacy as 'the claim of individuals, groups, or institutions to determine for themselves, when, how, and to what extent information about them is communicated to others'.[35] On these authors' approaches, the subject's own attitudes determine whether information should be regarded as private. Neither attempts to limit the nature of private information to particular types or categories of material.

**2.16** These broad subjective definitions reflect the fact that attitudes to personal information differ from person to person. While one person will keep medical affairs completely private, others will talk about them to anyone who will listen. Equally, some people will laugh openly about their indebtedness while others would regard the same information as deeply private. This inherent subjectivity makes it difficult to identify characteristics which all private information has in common.[36] Broad subjective definitions avoid this problem by eschewing the attempt.

**2.17** Although it might accurately describe the theoretical privacy interest, this broad subjective approach does have its limitations. First, these definitions do not tell us, even on a theoretical level, how to determine what an individual's subjective desires are. As Kirsty Hughes says, in order to take the privacy analysis further, 'we

---

[33] Gavison (n 10) 425–8.
[34] Fried (n 14) 482–3.
[35] Westin (n 30) 7. See also, Moreham (n 17) 636–9 where this author argues that the definition of privacy must include desire as an element.
[36] See further, Moreham (n 17) 641–2.

need to know how a desire for privacy is manifested'.[37] Further analysis of people's attitudes and behaviours is required.[38] Second, as even their proponents acknowledge, broad subjective definitions cannot, on their own, form the basis of a legal privacy right. An action which enabled the individual to claim breach of privacy simply because he or she did not want the information disclosed would obviously be intolerably broad.[39] Some kind of objective check or other limitation mechanism is therefore necessary.

**Reasonable expectation of privacy**   One way to translate a broad, subjective   **2.18** approach into the legal context is to add an objective check to determine when information should be regarded as private. Courts often do this by introducing a 'reasonable expectation of privacy' test. Thus, for example, the first step in establishing liability for misuse of private information in England is to show that the claimant had a reasonable expectation of privacy in respect of the information in question.[40] The first requirement of the New Zealand privacy tort is also that the claimant establish '[t]he existence of facts in respect of which there is a reasonable expectation of privacy'.[41]

The reasonable expectation of privacy test can be seen, at least in part, as short-   **2.19** hand for whether, in a given situation, the protection of privacy is consistent with prevailing social norms.[42] It has the advantage of being flexible and responsive to change, thereby avoiding the arbitrariness associated with more prescriptive approaches. It also allows courts to consider a broad range of factors when assessing what information is private. These go beyond the nature of the information in question and include steps the claimant took (or failed to take) to keep the information private. Hughes has argued that, if applied appropriately, the reasonable expectation of privacy test allows courts to ask, both whether the scenario was one in which there was or should be an objectively recognized social norm that privacy should be respected and, if not, what steps the claimant took to protect his or her privacy through the use of physical and/or behavioural barriers. A reasonable expectation of privacy can be established on either analysis.[43]

---

[37]  Hughes (n 12) 810.

[38]  Kirsty Hughes argues that individuals use three behavioural mechanisms to obtain or maintain privacy—physical barriers (which include things such as walls, doors, hedges, locks and safes), behavioural barriers (such as verbal or non-verbal cues), and normative rules (Hughes (n 12) 812). Daniel Solove also argues that the 'limited-access conceptions do not tell us the substantive matters for which access would implicate privacy' (Solove (n 19) 1104) and Chris Hunt argues that the 'desired inaccess' definition includes situations where inaccess is desired for some reason other than privacy (Hunt (n 15) 195).

[39]  See *eg* Gavison (n 10) 440–41; and Moreham (n 17) 643.

[40]  See *eg Campbell* (n 25) [21] and ch 5. This position was reaffirmed by the majority of the Supreme Court *Re JR38's application for Judicial Review* [2015] UKSC 42, [2015] 3 WLR 155.

[41]  *Hosking* (n 8) at [117], [249]. See further, 3.98–3.99.

[42]  *eg* Kirsty Hughes argues that application of the test in the misuse of privacy context is shaped largely around the judicial recognition of social norms (Hughes (n 12) 827–8).

[43]  Hughes (n 12) 824.

**2.20** The reasonable expectation of privacy test is not, however, without disadvantages. First, although the test is essentially an appeal to prevailing social attitudes about when privacy *should* be protected, because it refers to a claimant's reasonable expectations, liability can be taken to depend on whether privacy is likely to be respected in a particular situation. This problem is exemplified by the Supreme Court of California's decision in *Schulman v W Productions Ltd*.[44] In that case, the Court held that a woman did not suffer an actionable breach of privacy when a television crew filmed her being attended by paramedics at the scene of a serious road accident because 'for journalists to attend and record the scenes of accidents and rescues is in no way unusual or unexpected'.[45] In contrast, she could have an objectively reasonable expectation of privacy inside a rescue helicopter because the Court was 'aware of no law or custom permitting the press to ride in ambulances or enter hospital rooms during treatment without the patient's consent'.[46] Whether the claimant had an objectively reasonable expectation of privacy therefore depended on whether the media usually respected an individual's privacy in the situations in question. This means that:

> ...whether or not there is a breach of privacy is determined by reference to the practices of privacy interferers *themselves*—once an intrusive practice becomes sufficiently widespread to be 'in no way unusual or unexpected' (be it videoing people in ambulances, bugging Narcotics Anonymous meetings, or spying on people in public toilets) then claimants will have no action for breach of privacy if it occurs. It follows that there is a strong argument for shifting the focus of the English privacy action away from the claimant's *expectations* of privacy and on to his or her *desires*.[47]

**2.21** Secondly, some commentators argue that courts applying the reasonable expectation of privacy test take account of factors which should in fact be considered when privacy rights are balanced against other interests. According to the Court of Appeal in the important decision of *Murray*:

> ...the question whether there is a reasonable expectation of privacy is a broad one, which takes account of all the circumstances of the case. They include the attributes of the claimant, the nature of the activity in which the claimant was engaged, the place at which it was happening, the nature and purpose of the intrusion, the absence of consent and whether it was known or could be inferred, the effect on the claimant and the circumstances in which and the purposes for which the information came into the hands of the publisher.[48]

---

[44] *Schulman v Group W Productions Inc* 955 P 2d 469 (Cal 1998).
[45] *Schulman* (n 44) 490.
[46] *Schulman* (n 44) 490.
[47] Moreham (n 17) 647. Kirsty Hughes agrees that '[t]he role of normative barriers must reach beyond merely a consolidation of the status quo' (Hughes (n 12) 814; see also 828–32). See also D Solove, 'Fourth Amendment Pragmatism' (2010) 51 Boston College L Rev 1511, 1524; and E Barendt, 'A Reasonable Expectation of Privacy: A Coherent or Redundant Concept?' in A Kenyon (ed), *Comparative Defamation and Privacy Law* (Cambridge University Press) (forthcoming).
[48] *Murray v Express Newspapers plc* [2008] EWCA Civ 446, [2009] Ch 481 [36].

Commentators argue, though, that factors such as the purpose of the intrusion, the harm caused,[49] and attributes such as the claimant's status as a public figure or person who has courted publicity,[50] should not bear on a court's assessment of whether the information is private. Otherwise, the test can end up requiring a claimant to disprove a defence, 'when the burden should be on the defendant to show that the claim is a spurious one, or that the privacy claim is outweighed by the definition's interest in freedom of expression'.[51]

Third, the reasonable expectation of privacy test does not, on its own, provide **2.22** a ready-made list of what is and is not private. This, some detractors have suggested, creates uncertainty about its application: the social mores underpinning the test are difficult to identify and subject to change.[52] This can perhaps be ameliorated over time by the emergence of categories of information which are likely to be treated as private. For example, Eady J noted in *Author of a Blog v Times Newspapers Ltd* that successful cases in the English courts had concerned matters of 'a strictly personal nature concerning, for example, sexual relationships, mental or physical health, financial affairs, or the claimant's family or domestic arrangements'.[53] While not determinative, these categories do provide some guidance. But Eric Barendt argues that this reliance on categories of information which is usually private obviates the need for the reasonable expectation of privacy test altogether. He says:

> The continued existence of the [reasonable expectation of privacy] test is tolerable, only because it is almost always a ritual incantation; courts decide that information about, say, the claimant's health, or family or sexual relationship, is covered by ECHR, art 8, because it is clearly or obviously private, without seriously considering whether it is information in respect of which he had a reasonable expectation of privacy.[54]

Indeed, Barendt questions whether an objective check on the privacy action is **2.23** necessary at all, arguing that there is no comparable check in the definition of 'personal data' in the Data Protection Act 1998 nor in the law of defamation or right to freedom of expression.[55] A better approach, he says, would be to rely on a 'non-triviality' or 'seriousness' test to exclude trivial or frivolous claims and for 'privacy law [to] provide…a broad list of categories of private information'.[56]

**Identifying categories of private information**  An alternative approach to iden- **2.24** tifying what information is private is, therefore, to identify categories or types of

---

[49] See Hughes (n 12) 828.
[50] Barendt (n 47).
[51] Barendt (n 47).
[52] See eg Barendt (n 47) and Solove (n 47) 1522–4.
[53] *Author of a Blog v Times Newspapers Ltd* [2009] EWHC 1358 (QB) [9].
[54] Barendt (n 47).
[55] Barendt (n 47).
[56] Barendt (n 47).

information which should be regarded as private. An oft-cited judicial attempt at categorization is Gleeson CJ's observation in the Australian High Court case of *Lenah v Game Meats* that '[c]ertain kinds of information about a person, such as information relating to health, personal relationships, or finances, may be easy to identify as private'.[57] Eady J's list in *Author of a Blog v Times Newspapers Ltd*, just outlined, could also provide a useful starting point.[58] Eric Barendt argues that the ideal would be for Parliament to determine what types of information should be regarded as private for the purposes of a disclosure of private facts tort, to revise it from time to time, and to draft the list non-exhaustively so that 'there is room for an argument that material not on the list should be protected as private'.[59]

**2.25**  A list-based approach to identifying private information has the advantage of promoting certainty. It might well be easier for an editor, blogger, or media lawyer to determine whether something falls within a particular category of private information—sexual information, information about family life, information about finances, for example—than it is to determine whether the person had a reasonable expectation of privacy. Like the other options, however, it has its drawbacks. The first difficulty lies with working out what categories of private information should be on any list. As argued above, what is private to one person will not necessarily be private to another. As a result, people will not always agree about the types of information which should be regarded as private. For example, s 2 of the Data Protection Act 1998 includes in its list of 'sensitive personal data' (which enjoy special privacy protection under the Act), a person's racial or ethnic origin, political opinions, religious beliefs, membership of a trade union, the commission of a criminal offence or the proceedings for such an offence. None of these matters is included in the lists provided Gleeson CJ in *Lenah* nor by Eady J in *Author of a Blog*.[60]

**2.26**  Even if consensus could be reached on the *types* of information which should be regarded as private, it would still be difficult to work out what information falls within each category. If it is too rigidly applied, a categorical approach can lead to arbitrary results. The fact that one person has a sexually-transmitted infection and that another person has a cold could both be described as medical information. However, where the former is highly intimate private information, the latter is unlikely to be regarded as private at all. A rigid rule which said that 'all medical information is private' would provide insufficient scope to distinguish between these very different pieces of information.[61] Likewise, the fact that a man has a

---

[57] *Australian Broadcasting Corp v Lenah Game Meats Pty Ltd* (2001) 208 CLR 199 [42] (cited with approval by Lord Hope in *Campbell* (n 25) [93]–[94]). Baroness Hale also said in *Campbell* that: 'It has always been accepted that information about a person's health and treatment for ill-health is both private and confidential' ([145]).

[58] See *Author of a Blog* (n 53) [9] and 2.22.

[59] Barendt (n 47).

[60] See, respectively, 2.24 and 2.22.

[61] See further, Moreham (n 17) 641–3.

wife and child, that the child was educated in a particular way, and that he has another secret illegitimate child are all matters of family life. A test which simply says 'family life is private' or even, to add Barendt's limitation, 'non-trivial information about family life is private', does not, obviously provide the analytical tools to differentiate between these different types of information. As a result, there is a risk that relatively unimportant (but not necessarily 'trivial') information will be protected because it happens to fall within a category. Conversely, private information falling outside the categories might not be protected, because it does not.

Finally, an approach which relies too heavily on the categorization of information **2.27** risks ignoring other factors which have an important bearing on whether information is private. In particular, if courts focus exclusively on the subject matter of the information, they might give insufficient weight to the way in which the information was communicated by the defendant. There is a significant difference, for example, between the disclosure of a photograph and the disclosure of a description. A bluntly-applied list approach would also provide insufficient scope to consider the claimant's own behaviour in respect of the information, in particular the degree to which he or she has sought or failed to seek privacy for the matter in question.[62]

**A combined approach?** None of the three approaches to identifying private **2.28** information—a broad subjective approach, the reasonable expectation of privacy test, or identifying categories of private information—is without difficulties. The best approach might therefore be to combine elements of all three approaches when identifying private information. These might include the claimant's manifest desires in respect of the information, social mores concerning its protection, the nature of the misuse in question, and the nature of the information. Examination of the type or category of information would form an important, though not necessarily determinative, part of this analysis. The current reasonable expectation of privacy test might well be sufficiently flexible to accommodate these various factors within it. Or it could be that some other test—perhaps one focusing on the claimant's desire for inaccess—would be better. Either way, it is important that all relevant factors are considered when assessing whether information is private.

### (2) Physical Privacy: Protection against Interference with the Physical Self

It is a widely-held view that, as well as private information, a comprehensive pri- **2.29** vacy right must protect physical privacy. 'Physical privacy' refers to freedom from unwanted access to the physical self, rather than to private information about oneself. It includes, in particular, freedom from unwanted watching, listening, recording, photographing, and filming of one's private activities. Paradigmatic examples of interferences with physical privacy include individuals bugging their tenants;

---

[62]  Kirsty Hughes stresses the importance of this factor (Hughes (n 12) 824–8).

spying on people in toilets, showers or changing rooms; or intercepting people's telephone calls.[63]

### (a) Recognition of the importance of physical privacy

**2.30**  There is strong academic support for recognition of the physical aspect of the privacy interest. For example, Ruth Gavison identifies as 'typical' breaches of privacy:

> ...the collection, storage, and computerization of information; the dissemination of information about individuals; peeping, following, watching, and photographing individuals; intruding or entering 'private' places; eavesdropping, wiretapping, reading of letters; drawing attention to individuals; and forced disclosure of information.[64]

Consistently with this, she divides 'limitation of "access"' (which she says is the essence of the privacy interest) into three components: secrecy, anonymity, and solitude.[65] Both 'anonymity' (which is lost when someone pays attention to another) and 'solitude' (which is lost when one person obtains physical access to another by becoming sufficiently proximate to a person to be able to perceive him or her with the normal use of the senses),[66] protect the physical privacy interest. Other commentators also stress the importance of freedom from unwanted observation and encroachment. For example, Ernest van den Haag defines privacy as the exclusive access of a person to a realm of his or her own and says that it entitles a person to exclude others from watching, utilizing, or invading his or her private realm.[67] Judith Wagner DeCew also says that an individual's privacy is diminished when another gains physical proximity to him or her, for example by observing his or her body, behaviour, or interactions; by entering into a home under false pretences; or 'even by a move from a single-person office to a shared one'.[68] This author, Moreham, has also argued that there are two types of overlapping but distinct privacy interference: the misuse of private information (informational privacy) and unwanted sensory access (physical privacy):

> The principal objection in the informational privacy cases is to the fact that someone is *finding out* something about you against your wishes...The second category— physical privacy—is all about unwanted access to the physical self. The interference in these cases is *sensory*: the intruder interferes with your physical privacy by watching, listening to or otherwise sensing you against your wishes.[69]

---

[63]  See *eg*, respectively, *Amati v City of Woodstock, Illinois* 829 F Supp 998 (ND Ill 1993); *Harkey v Abate* 346 NW 2d 74 (Mich App 1983); *C v Holland* [2012] 3 NZLR 672 (HC); *Benitez v KFC National Management* 714 NE 2d 1002 (Ill App 2 Dist 1999); and *Rhodes v Graham* 37 SW 2d 46 (1931).

[64]  R Gavison, 'Privacy and the Limits of the Law' (1979) 89 Yale LJ 421, 436. See also Daniel Solove's broad taxonomy in 'A Taxonomy of Privacy' (n 32).

[65]  Gavison (n 64) 428.

[66]  Gavison (n 64) 428–33.

[67]  van den Haag (n 11).

[68]  DeCew (n 32) 156.

[69]  N A Moreham, 'Beyond Information: Physical Privacy in English Law' (2014) 73 CLJ 350, 354. See also N A Moreham, 'Liability for Listening: Why Phone Hacking is an Actionable Breach of Privacy' (2015) 8 JML (forthcoming) Many academics divide the concept along similar lines

As with informational privacy it seems that these many expressions of support for **2.31** recognition of physical privacy accord with people's instincts about what privacy is. Most people, it is suggested, would regard being spied on in their bedroom, having their intimate bodily functions observed, their personal telephone conversations recorded, or their house broken into as a breach of privacy irrespective of whether there was any subsequent publication of the material obtained. Indeed, in the Supreme Court of California case of *Schulman v Group W Productions Inc*, Werdeger J held that it is the intrusion tort which 'best captures the common understanding of an "invasion of privacy"' and 'is most clearly seen as an affront to individual dignity'.[70] Academic, Tom Gerety, agrees. He says, physical intrusion 'brings us to the core of our expectations and intuitions about privacy and hence of our rights to it'.[71]

Commentators also argue that because of the importance of physical privacy, a **2.32** concept of privacy which focused exclusively on the disclosure of private information would fail to protect privacy comprehensively. This is well-illustrated by Robert Parker's hypothetical example of an astronaut in a space capsule having all his bodily functions monitored through electrodes sending information to ground control on Earth. As Parker says, although ground control knows more about the astronaut's bodily functions than he does, we can still imagine the astronaut switching off a television camera monitoring the inside of the capsule so that he can 'have a little privacy' when going to the toilet. But the astronaut does not turn off the camera to restrict ground control's access to information about his bodily functions—they know all there is to know already. Instead, he is seeking physical privacy—he does not want ground control to *see* him using the toilet.[72]

It follows that an action focused entirely on informational privacy would fail prop- **2.33** erly to recognize one aspect of the privacy interest. As Raymond Wacks says:

> What is essentially in issue in cases of intrusion is the frustration of the legitimate expectations of the individual that he should not be seen or heard in circumstances where he has not consented to or is unaware of such surveillance. The quality of the information thereby obtained, though it will often be of an intimate nature, is not the major objection.[73]

If privacy is to be protected comprehensively both informational and physical privacy, therefore, need to be protected.

---

including (in addition to those cited elsewhere in this section) R Mulheron, 'A Potential Framework for Privacy? A Reply to *Hello!*' (2006) 69 MLR 679, 696–701; Hunt (n 15) 201; R Wacks, *Privacy and Media Freedom* (Oxford University Press 2013) ch 6; and Hughes (n 12) 810–1.

[70] *Schulman* (n 44) 489.

[71] Gerety (n 32) 265.

[72] Parker (n 32) 281.

[73] R Wacks, *Personal Information: Privacy and the Law* (Clarendon Press 1989) 248. See also Wacks (n 69) 120–2; 186–219; and 245–8.

### (b) Legal recognition of physical privacy

**2.34**  Although they still enjoy less protection than informational privacy, there is increasingly widespread legal recognition of physical privacy interests. The most significant common law protection is the well-established United States tort of intrusion into solitude or seclusion. It is described in § 652B of the Restatement (Second) of Torts as meaning that:

> One who intentionally intrudes, physically or otherwise, upon the solitude or seclusion of another or his private affairs or concerns, is subject to liability to the other for invasion of his privacy, if the intrusion would be highly offensive to a reasonable person.[74]

The Restatement explains that liability does not depend on publication of material about the claimant.[75] Instead, an intrusion can be effected physically (when the defendant forces his or her way into an individual's hotel room or insists over the individual's objection on entering his or her home, for example) or by the use of the senses, either with or without mechanical aids (for example, by using binoculars to look through the upstairs windows of a person's house or tapping telephone wires). Consistently with this, United States courts have upheld claims against defendants who, *inter alia*, bug their tenants;[76] spy on people in toilets or changing rooms; [77] or intercept people's telephone calls.[78]

**2.35**  Physical privacy is also being increasingly recognized in Commonwealth courts. For example, in the New Zealand decision of *C v Holland*, a first instance judge declined to strike out a claim against a man who had surreptitiously filmed his female flatmate in the shower, observing that recognition of a tort of intrusion into seclusion was 'entirely compatible with, and a logical adjunct to, the *Hosking* tort of wrongful publication of private facts'.[79] The tort of intrusion into seclusion has also been recognized by the Ontario Court of Appeal which, in *Jones v Tsige*, awarded damages against a bank clerk who accessed (but did not disseminate) the banking records of her partner's former wife on 174 separate occasions.[80] Four other Canadian states have broad statutory privacy torts which extend to situations where a defendant looks at, listens to or records others against their wishes.[81]

---

[74]  Restatement (Second) of Torts § 652B (1977).

[75]  Restatement (n 74) § 652B(b).

[76]  See *Amati v City of Woodstock* (n 63).

[77]  See, respectively, *Harkey v Abate* (n 63) and *Benitez v KFC* (n 63).

[78]  *Rhodes v Graham* (n 63).

[79]  *C v Holland* (n 63) at [75]. The case subsequently settled.

[80]  *Jones v Tsige*, 2012 ONCA 32, 108 OR (3d) 241. See also *Leung v Shanks*, 2013 ONSC 4943, 231 ACWS (3d) 540 and 3.122–3.129.

[81]  See eg *Malcolm v Fleming*, 2000 Carswell BC 1316 (SC); *LAM v JELI*, 2008 BCSC 1147, 170 ACWS (3d) 674; *Lee v Jacobson* (1992) 87 DLR (4th) 401, 31 ACWS (3d) 329 (BCSC); and *Watts v Klaemt* 2007 BCSC 662, [2007] BCWLD 4106. Discussed further at 3.119–3.120.

This increasing support for recognition of physical privacy interests is consistent with **2.36** recommendations of various law reform bodies. For example, in 2014 the Australian Law Reform Commission recommended the enactment of a new statutory tort protecting against both the misuse of private information, and intrusion into seclusion 'such as by physically intruding into the plaintiff's private space or by watching, listening to or recording the plaintiff's private activities or private affairs'.[82] The New South Wales Law Commission has also observed that there are two 'elemental situations' that call for privacy protection in private law: 'those in which the defendant has disclosed private information about the plaintiff ("information privacy"), and those in which the defendant has intruded on the plaintiff's solitude, seclusion or private affairs ("seclusion")'.[83] Similar observations have been repeatedly made in England and Wales.[84]

Further, although there is still no specific protection of physical privacy in English **2.37** law, there is increasing recognition of its importance. These developments are discussed in detail in Chapter 10. Any enhancement of physical privacy protections would obviously have a significant impact on the news-gathering activities of the media in England and Wales. Recording people's conversations, photographing or filming them surreptitiously, pursuing them for an interview, or sometimes even obtaining unauthorized access to private spaces, are legitimate investigative reporting techniques. Any developments in this area must therefore be accompanied by defences protecting legitimate news-gathering activities. Again, these issues are discussed in Chapter 10.

## C. Privacy-related Interests

This chapter has so far suggested that the two core components of privacy are **2.38** informational privacy and physical privacy. The focus of this book will be on English protection of those two interests. There are, however, a number of other

---

[82] Australian Law Reform Commission, *Serious Invasions of Privacy in the Digital Era,* Report No 123 (2014) para 5.15 and Recommendation 5-1.

[83] New South Wales Law Commission, *Invasion of Privacy,* Report No 120 (2009) para 4.3. See Law Commission (NZ), *Invasion of Privacy: Penalties and Remedies—Review of the law of privacy Stage 3* (NZLC R113, 2010).

[84] *eg,* the 1970 Justice Report proposed criminal sanctions against the use of electronic surveillance devices and civil liability for 'any substantial and unreasonable infringement of any person's privacy' (Justice (British Section of the International Commission of Jurists), *Privacy and the Law* (Chairmen: M Littman and P Carter-Ruck) (Stevens & Sons Ltd 1970) 41–2; the 1972 Younger Committee recommended criminal sanctions for unlawful surveillance and the creation of a 'new tort of unlawful surveillance by device' (Younger Committee, *Report of the Committee on Privacy* (Cmnd 5012, 1972) (Chairman: K Younger) para 53); and in 1990 the Calcutt Committee recommended criminal sanctions against entering private property for the purpose of obtaining personal information, placing bugging devices on private property, or photographing or recording the voices of a person on private property and injunctive relief against publication of any material so obtained (Calcutt Committee, *Report of the Committee on Privacy and Related Matters* (Cm 1102, 1990) (Chairman: D Calcutt, QC) paras 17.8–17.9).

interests associated with the concept of privacy. For example, Daniel Solove includes in his four-part taxonomy of activities that 'create privacy problems'[85] invasions (decisional interference and intrusion), information collection (surveillance and interrogation), information processing (aggregation, identification, insecurity, secondary use, and exclusion), and information dissemination (breach of confidence, disclosure, blackmail, appropriation, distortion, exposure, and increased accessibility).[86] William Prosser's famous taxonomy of the American tort of breach of privacy (which was adopted in the Second Restatement)[87] also divides privacy into four separate interests: '[p]ublic disclosure of embarrassing private facts about the plaintiff'; '[i]ntrusion upon the plaintiff's seclusion or solitude, or into his private affairs'; '[p]ublicity which places the plaintiff in a false light in the public eye'; and '[a]ppropriation, for the defendant's advantage, of the plaintiff's name or likeness'.[88]

**2.39**    As has already been argued, the Anglo-Commonwealth concept of privacy is less expansive than understandings of privacy in the United States. So far, tortious and legislative liability in the Anglo-Commonwealth has focused on protection against private information and intrusion into solitude and seclusion.[89] However, given the impact of Prosser's taxonomy on the development of the common law, the other two aspects of his conception of privacy—false light and misappropriation of name and likeness—will both be briefly considered here and in ensuing chapters.

### (1) False Light

**2.40**    The Restatement describes the false light tort in the following terms:

> One who gives publicity to a matter concerning another that places the other before the public in a false light is subject to liability to the other for invasion of his privacy, if
> a. the false light in which the other was placed would be highly offensive to a reasonable person, and
> b. the actor had knowledge of or acted in reckless disregard as to the falsity of the publicised matter and the false light in which the other would be placed.[90]

Prosser and the Restatement provide numerous examples of the sorts of activity which would be actionable under this tort. They include making use of an honest taxi driver's image to illustrate an article on the practices of dishonest taxi drivers, including an innocent person's photograph in a 'rogues' gallery' of convicted

---

[85]  D Solove, *Understanding Privacy* (Harvard University Press 2008) 102.
[86]  Solove (n 85) 104. He stresses that inclusion of a particular activity within the taxonomy does not automatically imply that legal redress should follow (Solove (n 85) 102).
[87]  Restatement (n 74) ch 28A. Prosser was a Reporter for the Restatement.
[88]  W Prosser, 'Privacy' (1960) 48 Cal L Rev 383, 389. See also Restatement (n 74) § 652A.
[89]  Although four Canadian states have also recognized a statutory right to privacy which includes using the name or likeness of a person without consent in advertising or promotion (see 3.119–3.120).
[90]  Restatement (n 74) § 652E.

criminals, falsely attributing an inferior poem to a renowned poet, and 'publicity falsely attributing to the plaintiff some opinion or utterance' such as a fictitious advertising testimonial.[91] According to the Restatement, the tort protects an individual's interest 'in not being made to appear before the public in an objectionable false light or false position, or in other words, otherwise than as he is'.[92] Both sources also stress that the defendant's actions need not give rise to liability in defamation although the false light must be something which would be objectionable to an ordinary, reasonable person.[93]

Although it is the least prominent of the four American torts,[94] the false light **2.41** action enjoys some support amongst academic commentators. Daniel Solove includes 'harms of inaccuracy' in his taxonomy of privacy problems. He says that, like disclosure, 'distortion' (which he defines as the 'manipulation of the way a person is perceived and judged by others... [which] involves the victim being inaccurately characterized') involves 'the spreading of information which affects the way society views a person... [that] can result in embarrassment, humiliation, stigma and reputational harm'.[95] Other commentators agree that the false light tort plays an important role in allowing an individual to 'define himself' in public and to 'exercise a legitimate right to be shown to the public as he is' even when the objectionable statement is not defamatory.[96] For example John Wigmore stated in 1916 that, 'I am entitled to be judged in public by my actual opinions and utterances. To have false ones ascribed to me is an injury to my feelings of self respect. And that is the injury against which I am entitled to be protected.'[97]

Advocates for the tort also maintain that non-defamatory false statements can have **2.42** a significant adverse impact on people's well-being and self-perception. In particular, they can force individuals to discuss matters which should have remained private. For example, referring to the actual case of an athlete credited with wartime heroics which he did not perform, American commentator Nathan Ray says that the athlete might 'be forced to endure the enmity of his comrades, the embarrassment of having to admit details of his undistinguished service, and self-imposed withdrawal from feelings of guilt or shame'.[98]

---

[91] See Prosser (n 88) 398–9 and Restatement (n 74) § 652E and, for further discussion, 3.73–3.79. The action is said to have made its first appearance in 1816 when it was relied on by Lord Byron to prevent circulation of an inferior poem which was being attributed to him: see Prosser (n 88) 398.

[92] Restatement (n 74) § 652E.

[93] Prosser (n 88) 400; and Restatement (n 74) § 652E(b).

[94] Discussed at 3.44–3.84.

[95] Solove (n 85) 160.

[96] N Ray, 'Let There Be False Light: Resisting the Growing Trend Against an Important Tort' (1999–2000) 84 Minn L Rev 713, 749.

[97] J Wigmore, 'The Right Against False Attribution of Belief or Utterance' (1916) 4 Kentucky LJ 3, 8.

[98] Ray (n 96) 749, referring to the case of *Spahn v Julian Messner Inc* 21 NY 2d 124, 233 NE 2d 840 (NY 1967).

**2.43**  It is suggested, however, that most Anglo-Commonwealth lawyers would intuitively regard the interests at stake in the American false light cases as affecting reputation, not privacy. The objection to being included in a 'rogues' gallery', depicted in a photograph of dishonest taxi drivers, or having one's name associated with an inferior artistic work (to use the examples of false light provided by the Restatement) is that it suggests that one is a rogue, dishonest, or an inferior artist. These interests are reputational. Indeed, Prosser himself acknowledged that the interest protected by the false light tort is 'clearly that of reputation, with the same overtones of mental distress as in defamation'.[99] Raymond Wacks agrees that a person's objection in false light cases is not:

> ...about the mere fact of unwanted publicity nor about the disclosure of intimate facts, but about the fact that the world has received a misleading impression of him. This is the domain of defamation. And even if the plaintiff's reputation is unimpaired by the publicity he is given, it is difficult to see in what sense his *privacy* has been invaded.[100]

**2.44**  Reputation is one of the interests protected by the right to respect for private life in Article 8 ECHR. However, as Wacks's quotation suggests, in the domestic English law, it is protected principally by actions such as defamation, malicious falsehood, and passing off.[101] Further, although the action for the disclosure of private information provides some protection against the disclosure of damaging true information and, in some limited circumstances, the disclosure of false facts, English courts have been cautious to preserve the boundaries between privacy and defamation. Thus, in *Terry v Persons Unknown*, Tugendhat J said that since 'the nub' of the application before him was 'a desire to protect what is in substance reputation', the claimant's injunction claim should be determined by reference to the rule in *Bonnard v Perryman* (the stricter defamation standard) even though it was pleaded in breach of confidence and privacy.[102]

**2.45**  Tugendhat J's desire to retain the distinction between privacy and reputation is consistent with Prosser's own concerns about the scope of the false light tort. He said:

> There has been a good deal of overlapping of defamation in the false light cases, and apparently either action, or both, will very often lie. The privacy cases do go considerably beyond the narrow limits of defamation, and no doubt have succeeded in affording a needed remedy in a good many instances not covered by the other

---

[99]  Prosser (n 88) 400.

[100]  R Wacks, *The Protection of Privacy* (Sweet & Maxwell 1980) 171 (original emphasis). Bruce McKenna also argues that '[p]rotection of a reputation interest is inconsistent with the concept of privacy': B McKenna, 'False Light: Invasion of Privacy?' (1979–80) 15 Tulsa LJ 113, 119. Although see 2.83–2.87.

[101]  *eg*, an amateur golfer, who was depicted without his knowledge or consent in a newspaper advertisement for a Fry's chocolate bar, successfully sued in defamation arguing that the advertisement implied that he had compromised his reputation and status as an amateur golfer (*Tolley v JS Fry & Sons Ltd* [1931] AC 333).

[102]  *Terry v Persons Unknown* [2010] EWHC 119 (QB) [123]. See also ch 8.

tort. It is here, however, that one disposed to alarm might express the greatest concern over where privacy may be going. The question may well be raised, and apparently still is unanswered, whether this branch of the tort is not capable of swallowing up and engulfing the whole law of public defamation; and whether there is any false libel printed, for example in a newspaper, which cannot be redressed upon the alternative ground. If that turns out to be the case, it may well be asked, what of the numerous restrictions and limitations which have hedged defamation about for many years, in the interest of freedom of the press and the discouragement of trivial and extortionate claims? Are they of so little consequence that they may be circumvented in so casual and cavalier a fashion?[103]

It is suggested, then, that in spite of recognition of 'reputation' as part of the **2.46** Article 8 right to private life, 'accuracy harms' do not fall squarely within Anglo-Commonwealth conceptions of privacy. Even if there were judicial sympathy in England and Wales for pro-false light arguments, it seems unlikely that a false light tort would be the vehicle for addressing them. The lines between defamation and privacy can, however, be somewhat blurred. The relationship between the two actions, and between privacy and reputation more generally, is therefore discussed at length in Chapter 8.

## (2) Misappropriation of Name and Likeness

The final tort in William Prosser's four-part taxonomy protects against the misap- **2.47** propriation of name and likeness. The Restatement (Second) of Torts defines it succinctly, saying that '[o]ne who appropriates to his own use or benefit the name or likeness of another is subject to liability to the other for invasion of his privacy'.[104] The Corpus Juris Secundum expands further, explaining that the tort gives an individual 'an exclusive right to control the commercial value and exploitation of his name, picture, likeness or personality and to prevent others from exploiting that value without permission or from unfairly appropriating that value for their commercial benefit'.[105] The classic case, it continues, is one in which a person's name or image is used without consent 'to advertise the defendant's product, or to accompany an article sold, to add lustre to the name of a corporation, or for other business purposes'.[106]

In the earliest misappropriation cases, the tort was used by claimants who wished **2.48** to avoid publicity altogether. For example, in *Roberson v Rochester Folding Box Co*[107]

---

[103] Prosser (n 88) 400–401. The Australian Law Commission has also said that it is 'questionable whether… placing a person in a false light… [is] properly characterised' as an invasion of privacy and that attacks upon the reputation are 'better left to the law of defamation': see Australian Law Reform Commission, *For Your Information: Australian privacy law and practice*, Report No 108 (2008) para 74.120. See also Australian Law Reform Commission (n 82) paras 5.67–5.73 and New South Wales Law Commission (n 83) para 4.5.

[104] Restatement (n 74) § 652C.

[105] 'Right of Privacy and Publicity' in *Corpus Juris Secundum* (1994), vol 77, 539 [40].

[106] Prosser (n 88) 402. See in the Canadian context *Aubry v Éditions Vice-Versa Inc* [1998] 1 SCR 591, 157 DLR (4th) 577.

[107] 171 NY 538, 64 NE 442 (NY Ct of Apps 1902).

(in which the misappropriation tort was supported in a powerful dissent), a private citizen objected to her photograph appearing on many thousands of boxes of flour without her consent. Similarly, in *Pavesich v New England Life Insurance Co*[108] (in which the *Roberson* dissent was adopted) the objection was to an insurance advertisement which featured a private individual's photograph and an entirely fabricated quotation in which he purportedly endorsed the defendant's policies.

**2.49** In both these cases, the claimants' principal objection was to the mental or spiritual upset which the unwanted exposure caused. In *Roberson*, Gray J noted that the defendant's unauthorized use of her image had 'greatly humiliate[d] her, by the scoffs and jeers of persons who have recognised her face upon these advertisements, and her good name has been attacked'.[109] The claimant suffered a 'severe nervous shock' as a result.[110] Gray J continued that:

> ...for that complete personal security which will result in the peaceful and wholesome enjoyment of one's privileges as a member of society there should be afforded protection, not only against the scandalous portraiture and display of one's features and person, but against the display and use thereof for another's commercial purposes or gain. The proposition is, to me, an inconceivable one that these defendants may, unauthorisedly, use the likeness of this young woman upon their advertisement as a method of attracting widespread public attention to their wares, and that she must submit to the mortifying notoriety, without right to invoke the exercise of the preventive power of a court of equity.[111]

The Court in *Pavesich* similarly stressed human interests at stake in the claim, focusing particularly on the assault on the claimant's liberty which the publication entailed:

> The knowledge that one's features and form are being used for such a purpose, and displayed in such places as such advertisements are often liable to be found, brings not only the person of an extremely sensitive nature, but even the individual of ordinary sensibility, to a realisation that his liberty has been taken away from him; and, as long as the advertiser uses him for these purposes, he cannot be otherwise than conscious of the fact that he is for the time being under the control of another, that he is no longer free, and that he is in reality a slave, without hope of freedom, held to service by a merciless master; and if a man of true instincts or even of ordinary sensibilities, no one can be more conscious of his enthrallment than he is.[112]

**2.50** These non-publicity cases fit comfortably with the access-based Anglo-Commonwealth conception of privacy being advanced in this chapter. The interests at stake in *Roberson* and *Pavesich*—dignity, autonomy, and emotional well-being—are much

---

[108] 69 LRA 101, 50 SE 68 (SC Ga 1905).
[109] *Roberson* (n 107) 448.
[110] *Roberson* (n 107) 448.
[111] *Roberson* (n 107) 450. These dicta were expressly adopted in *Pavesich* (n 108) 78.
[112] *Pavesich* (n 108) 80.

like those interfered with by a breach of physical or informational privacy (discussed above). As one American commentator has observed:

> In a societal context in which unauthorized commercial appropriation of a personality is seen as an invasion, causing shame, discomfort, or irritation, rather than economic loss, it is not unreasonable for such an appropriation to be considered part of the 'privacy' interest.[113]

However, in modern times, the typical misappropriation case is unlikely to be **2.51** brought by an individual objecting to the commercial use of his or her image in any circumstances. Instead, the claimant will probably be a celebrity who is unhappy either with the quality of the publicity in question, the defendant's failure to pay for it, or both.[114] In these cases, the misappropriation tort is often seen to be protecting a right to publicity, preventing unjust enrichment through the unauthorized exploitation of an individual's goodwill or the reputation associated with his or her name or likeness, often developed 'through the investment of time, effort and money'.[115] In this context, it is more difficult to see the misappropriation tort as protecting a core privacy interest as defined in this chapter. As James Treece says:

> When a celebrity has consented to prior advertising uses of his name or photograph in connection with similar products his chances for recovery based on injury to sensibilities should diminish. Such a plaintiff can hardly complain of a substantial encroachment on his right to privacy—a significantly diminishing and injurious subjection to the public gaze. Furthermore, his consent to earlier advertisements precludes an argument that the mere appearance of his personality in an advertisement injures his self-esteem. In reality the injury to sensibilities concept does not normally meaningfully apply when a person routinely permits advertising uses of his name or picture. Any anger or outrage that he might feel hardly flows from the shock of confronting his likeness in an advertisement. Rather, his injury takes the form of diminished income. The harm resides not in the use of his likeness but in the user's failure to pay.[116]

Prosser agrees that:

> It seems sufficiently evident that appropriation is quite a different matter from intrusion, disclosure of private facts, or a false light in the public eye. The interest protected is not so much a mental as a proprietary one, in the exclusive use of the plaintiff's name and likeness as an aspect of his identity.[117]

---

[113] S Halpern, 'The Right of Publicity: Commercial Exploitation of the Associative Value of Personality' (1986) 39 Vanderbilt L Rev 1199, 1205.

[114] See D Dobbs, *The Law of Torts* (West Group 2000) 1198 (he says that the cases usually involve 'public figures who do not seek privacy but on the contrary seek out opportunities for public exposure and who wish to use their name, likeness, voice or other aspects of "identity" as a property to be sold').

[115] 'Right of Privacy and Publicity' (n 105) [40].

[116] J Treece, 'Commercial Exploitation of Names, Likeness, and Personal Histories' (1973) 51 Texas L Rev 637, 641.

[117] Prosser (n 88) 406. The Restatement also says that 'although the protection of [the individual's] personal feelings against mental distress is an important factor leading to a recognition of the rule, the right created by it is in the nature of a property right...': Restatement (n 74) § 652C. For other similar observations see R Wacks (ed), *Privacy: The International Library of Essays in Law and Legal Theory. Privacy: Volume II* (Dartmouth Publishing 1993) xiii; Dobbs (n 114) 1199; Australian Law Reform Commission (n 103) paras 74.120–74.123 and Australian Law Reform Commission (n 82) paras 5.67–5.73.

**2.52**   English courts have so far declined to recognize a character or image right protecting a celebrity's name or image and seem to have limited enthusiasm for doing so.[118] They have, however, acknowledged the commercial value of image and personality rights and are willing, in some circumstances, to use other causes of action such as breach of confidence to protect it.[119] Further, even without express recognition of image rights, the misuse of private information action enhances celebrities ability to control when and in what terms images of them appear in the media.[120] Incidental image rights can therefore impact on the activities of the media. They are discussed in greater detail at 9.89 *et seq.*

## D. Rationales for Privacy Protection

**2.53**   In 1765, the Court in *Entick v Carrington* held, for the first time, that the search of the claimant's home and private papers was unlawful. The plaintiff objected to the search on the grounds that when the messengers:

> ...broke open the doors to the rooms, the locks...the boxes, chests, drawers, etc...and read over, pryed into, and examined all the private papers, books, etc of the plaintiff...the secret affairs, etc of the plaintiff became wrongfully discovered and made public...[121]

The decision was based on the property rights of the claimant and justified by reference to the theories of John Locke. The claimant's rights were said to flow from the right of property which was, in turn, understood to be a right existing in the state of nature, by reason and scripture alike. Thus, the judgment says:

> The great end, for which men entered into society, was to secure their property. That right is preserved sacred and incommunicable in all instances where it has not been taken away or abridged by some public law for the good of the whole...By the laws of England, every invasion of private property, be it ever so minute, is a trespass. No man can set his foot upon my ground without my license.[122]

**2.54**   The rationales for protecting the privacy of a person's home and correspondence have moved on since then. Privacy is now seen to promote numerous interests that

---

[118]  See *Douglas v Hello! Ltd* [2007] UKHL 21, [2008] 1 AC 1 [285], [293].

[119]  Lord Walker suggests in *Douglas* (n 118) [285] that the claimants' 'claims come close to claims to a "character right" protecting a celebrity's name and image'. But compare Lord Hoffmann [124] and Lord Nicholls [253].

[120]  See eg *Murray v Big Pictures* [2008] EWCA Civ 446 and *Weller v Associated Newspapers Ltd* [2014] EWHC 1163 (QB).

[121]  *Entick v Carrington* (1765) 19 Howell's State Trials 1029, 2 Wils KB 275.

[122]  *Entick* (n 121). The reasoning corresponds to John Locke's second treatise in *Two Treatises of Government* (first published 1689, Macmillan 1960) 321–2, paras 87–9. It should be noted, however, that this passage does not appear in the Wilson report in the English Reports. In that version, Lord Camden is quoted as saying that, 'our law holds the property of every man so sacred, that no man can set his foot upon his neighbour's close without his leave' (2 Wils KB 275, 291).

are regarded as essential for human flourishing in a Western liberal democracy. They include individual dignity and autonomy; the development and maintenance of relationships; the promotion of health and well-being; and protection against the judgment of others. Understanding these reasons for protecting privacy is a vital pre-requisite for protecting the interest appropriately: both the formulation of the privacy action and the balancing of privacy against other interests require a sound under-standing of the reasons why it is important.

### (1) Protection of Dignity

The relationship between privacy and dignity is widely recognized by judges and com-mentators alike. For example, in *Campbell v MGN Ltd*, Lord Hoffmann observed that human rights law has identified private information 'as something worth protecting as an aspect of human autonomy and dignity'.[123] In *Douglas v Hello! Ltd*, Lord Walker said that the law's protection of the confidentiality of individuals' private lives is 'based on the high principle of respect for human autonomy and dignity'.[124] The ECtHR has also held that, '[t]he very essence of the Convention is respect for human dignity and human freedom'.[125]   **2.55**

Commentators also recognize that privacy and dignity are closely related. In their celebrated article on the American law, Warren and Brandeis describe the interests protected by privacy as 'spiritual'[126] and as closely connected with an individual's 'inviolate personality'.[127] American academics Jeffrey Reiman and Stanley Benn identify the protection of dignity as the principal reason why privacy is important[128] and Harry Kalven agrees that privacy is 'deeply linked' to individual dignity and the needs of human existence.[129] In the doctrinal context, Peter Cane has identified privacy as a 'dignitary tort'[130] and in his response to William Prosser's fragmentary   **2.56**

---

[123] [2004] UKHL 22, [2004] 2 AC 457 [50]. See also [51]. Baroness Hale also acknowledged that privacy interferences harm both the 'moral' and 'physical' integrity of the claimant ([157]) and Lord Nicholls said that '[a] proper degree of privacy is essential for the well-being and development of an individual' ([12]).

[124] *Douglas* (n 118) [275]. See also *Associated Newspapers Ltd v HRH Prince of Wales* [2006] EWCA Civ 1776, [2008] EMLR 4 [70]; *Mosley v News Group Newspapers Ltd* [2008] EWHC 1777 (QB), [2008] EMLR 20 [7] and [214]; and, in the New Zealand context, *Hosking v Runting* (n 8) at [239] and *Brooker v Police* [2007] 3 NZLR 91 (SC) at [182] and [252].

[125] *Pretty v UK* (2002) 35 EHRR 1, para 65; see also para 61.

[126] S Warren and L Brandeis, 'The Right to Privacy' (1890) 4 Harvard L Rev 193, 197.

[127] Warren and Brandeis (n 126) 205.

[128] See S Benn, 'Privacy, Freedom and Respect for Persons' in Pennock and Chapman (n 11) 1–13; and J Reiman, 'Privacy, Intimacy and Personhood' (1976) 6 Phil & Publ Aff 26, 39. See also D Feldman, 'Secrecy, Dignity or Autonomy? Views of Privacy as a Civil Liberty' (1994) 47 Curr Legal Prob 4, 54–58 (especially 55).

[129] H Kalven Jr, 'Privacy in Tort Law: Were Warren and Brandeis Wrong?' (1966) 31 L and Contemp Prob 326, 326. See also N A Moreham, 'Why is privacy important? Privacy, Dignity and the Development of the New Zealand Breach of Privacy Tort' in J Finn and S Todd (eds), *Law, Liberty, Legislation* (Lexis Nexis 2008) 231.

[130] P Cane, *The Anatomy of Tort Law* (Hart 1997) 71–4.

analysis of United States tort law,[131] Edward Bloustein argues that the coherence of privacy lies in the fact that all privacy interferences are 'an affront to dignity':

> ...just as we may regard [assault, battery, or false imprisonment] as offences 'to the reasonable sense of personal dignity,' as offensive to our concept of individualism and the liberty it entails, so too should we regard privacy as a dignitary tort. Unlike many other torts, the harm caused is not one which may be repaired and the loss suffered is not one which may be made good by an award of damages. The injury is to our individuality, to our dignity as individuals, and the legal remedy represents a social vindication of the human spirit thus threatened rather than a recompense for the loss suffered.[132]

### (a) Evolution of the concept of dignity

**2.57** The concept of 'dignity' referred to in these cases and articles refers to the idea that there is an inherent value in all human beings.[133] This concept of dignity is reflected in the Preamble to the Universal Declaration of Human Rights which states that:

> Whereas recognition of the inherent dignity and of the equal and inalienable rights of all members of the human family is the foundation of freedom, justice and peace in the world...[134]

**2.58** The use of the word 'dignity' to refer to the relative positions of human and non-human beings can be traced to Pico della Mirandola, who wrote a Latin text in the fifteenth century which came to be known as *On the Dignity of Man*. Pico links the dignity of man with reason and the moral law. In a translation of one of Pico's works, Thomas More identified '[t]he nature and dignity of man' as one of twelve reasons for avoiding wrongdoing.[135] Blaise Pascal wrote to the same effect:

> Thought constitutes the very essence of humanity...So our whole dignity consists in thought...So let us work at thinking well: that is the basis of morality.[136]

**2.59** The belief that humans enjoyed free will, and had moral duties, was derived in these early times from religious belief. Specifically, the belief was based on the creation narrative in the book of Genesis and the Gospels, which included the command to 'Love thy Neighbour'. By the eighteenth century the idea that such rights existed was held to be 'self-evident', or a matter of intuition, although in 1776 it was still said that men were 'endowed by their Creator' with these rights.[137]

---

[131] See Prosser (n 88).
[132] E Bloustein, 'Privacy as an Aspect of Human Dignity: An Answer to Dean Prosser' (1964) 39 NYULR 962, 1002–03 (see also 1000–07).
[133] Paras 2.57–2.60 were written by Sir Michael Tugendhat for the second edition of this book.
[134] Adopted and proclaimed by the United Nations General Assembly Res 217A (III) (10 December 1948).
[135] Sir Thomas More, *The Complete Works of Thomas More* (Yale University Press 1997) vol 1, 109.
[136] B Pascal, *Pensées: Contradiction de L'Homme, sa Grandeur* (Everyman Library 1956) 97, cited by Conor Gearty, *Can Human Rights Survive?* (Cambridge University Press 2006) 30.
[137] Declaration of Independence (US 1776).

In 1785, Immanuel Kant set out a new basis for the derivation of duties. He argued **2.60** that the scriptural command to love our neighbour cannot of itself create a moral duty; a duty must be deduced by reason and arise from free will.[138] Kant offered instead a secular basis for moral duties and human rights[139] and took human dignity (*Würde*) as a given. He said:

> ...the human being and in general every rational being *exists* as an end in itself, *not merely as a means* to be used by this or that will at its discretion; instead he must in all his actions, whether directed to himself or to other rational beings, always be regarded *at the same time as an end*...[Rational beings], therefore, are not merely subjective ends, the existence of which as an effect of our action has a worth for us, but rather *objective ends*, that is, beings the existence of which is in itself an end, and indeed one such that no other end, to which they would serve *merely* as a means, can be put in its place, since without it nothing of *absolute worth* would be found anywhere.[140]

This principle—that one should respect the intrinsic value of all persons and seek, **2.61** insofar as possible, to further their ends as well as one's own—demands that one should '[a]ct that you use humanity, whether in your own person or in the person of any other, always at the same time as an end, never merely as a means'.[141] To use a person simply as a means to one's ends—to make money, to titillate, to entertain— is to fail to accord sufficient respect to that individual's inherent value as a person.

### (b) Dignity and privacy: modern theoretical accounts

Many theorists argue that the entitlement to respect which Kant identified—the **2.62** right to be treated as an 'end' and not simply as a 'means'—underpins the modern privacy interest. For example, Stanley Benn argues that the 'general principle of privacy' is grounded upon a more general 'principle...of respect for persons' which he explains in the following terms:

> To *conceive* someone as a person is to see him as actually or potentially a chooser, as one attempting to steer his own course through the world, adjusting his behaviour as his apperception of the world changes, and correcting course as he perceives his errors. It is to understand that his life is for him a kind of enterprise, like one's own...To *respect* someone as a person is to concede that one ought to take account of the way in which his enterprise might be affected by one's own decisions. By the principle of respect for persons, then, I mean the principle that every human being, insofar as he is qualified as a person, is entitled to this minimal degree of consideration.[142]

The objection that a person has been treated as a means to another's ends can **2.63** be raised in almost any situation where one party interferes with the privacy of

---

[138] I Kant, *Groundwork of the Metaphysics of Morals* (Mary Gregor tr, Cambridge University Press 1996) 4:399, 4:409.

[139] However, some commentators who support the idea of human rights regard the idea of human dignity as unclear and controversial: M Ignatieff, *Human Rights as Politics and Idolatory* (Princeton University Press 2001) 54; Gearty (n 136) 10: 'neither religion nor reason has the hold that each once had'.

[140] Kant (n 138) 4:399, 4:428 (original emphasis).

[141] Kant (n 138) 4:399, 4:429.

[142] Benn (n 128) 8–9. See also Reiman (n 128) 39.

another. This includes the media. A journalist who discloses personal information against another's wishes or intrudes when a person wishes to be left alone is inevitably prioritizing his or her own wishes over the subject's. The journalist might be acting for a high minded reason (like serving the public interest) or a self-interested one (like increasing his or her prestige or revenue) but either way he or she is claiming the right to decide whether and how the information is disclosed. Hyman Gross argues that the subject in these situations is 'humiliated' and 'shamed', not just because of what others learn about him or her, but because someone other than the individual is determining what will be done with what is learnt.[143]

**2.64**  Although dignity is implicated in all privacy intrusions, the claimant's dignitary claims will be stronger if the defendant intrudes upon a particularly intimate aspect of private life, for example by disseminating footage of a person engaged in sexual activity, exercising bodily functions, or suffering severe grief or trauma. A breach of privacy might also be a particular affront to dignity if the defendant is intruding on the claimant to serve his or her own personal ends rather than the public interest. A wide range of factors therefore need to be considered when striking a balance between privacy and other competing interests.

### (2) Autonomy

**2.65**  A second reason for protecting privacy, commonly identified by English courts alongside dignity, is the promotion of individual autonomy. As outlined in 2.55, Lord Hoffmann identified the relationship between privacy and dignity and autonomy in *Campbell*,[144] as did Lord Walker in *Douglas v Hello! Ltd*.[145] In *Douglas v Hello! Ltd*, Sedley LJ also referred to privacy as 'a legal principle drawn from the fundamental value of personal autonomy'[146] and, in *Campbell*, Lord Nicholls held that privacy 'lies at the heart of liberty in a modern state'.[147]

**2.66**  Autonomy is recognized as a core aspect of the broader right to respect for private life in Article 8 ECHR. According to the ECtHR 'the notion of personal autonomy is an important principle underlying the interpretation of [Convention] guarantees'[148] and confers on individuals 'the ability to conduct one's life in a manner of one's own choosing':[149]

> The very essence of the Convention is respect for human dignity and human freedom. Without in any way negating the principle of sanctity of life under the

---

[143] H Gross, 'Privacy and Autonomy' in Pennock and Chapman (n 11) 177.
[144] *Campbell* (n 123) [50]–[51]. See also *Associated Newspapers* (n 124) [70].
[145] *Douglas* (n 118) [275]. See also Eady J in *Mosley* (n 124) [214].
[146] *Douglas v Hello! Ltd* [2000] EWCA Civ 353, [2001] QB 967 [126].
[147] *Campbell* (n 123) [12].
[148] *Goodwin v UK* (2002) 35 EHRR 18, para 90; and *I v UK* (2003) 36 EHRR 53, para 70. See also *Pretty v UK* (n 125), para 61; and *Van Kück v Germany* (2003) 37 EHRR 51, para 69.
[149] *Pretty* (n 125) para 62.

Convention, the Court considers that it is under Article 8 that notions of the quality of life take on significance.[150]

A similar approach has been adopted in domestic Human Rights Act 1998 cases where 'autonomy' has often been equated with self-determination.[151] In *R (Pretty) v DPP*, for example, four of their Lordships accepted that 'the guarantee under article 8 prohibits interference with the way in which an individual leads his life'.[152]

English courts have yet to articulate what 'autonomy' means in the narrower **2.67** context of privacy rights. If, as suggested in Section B 'privacy' in the Anglo-Commonwealth is about the ability to protect a zone of inaccessibility, then it only protects autonomy in some circumstances. More particularly, it protects a right to determine whether and in what circumstances others have access to one's physical body and private affairs. Cobb J uses 'liberty' in this sense in the American misappropriation case of *Pavesich v New England Life Insurance Co*:

> Liberty includes the right to live as one will, so long as that will does not interfere with the rights of another or of the public. One may desire to live a life of seclusion; another may desire to live a life of publicity; still another may wish to live a life of privacy as to certain matters, and of publicity as to others. One may wish to live a life of toil, where his work is of a nature that keeps him constantly before the public gaze, while another may wish to live a life of research and contemplation, only moving before the public at such times and under such circumstances as may be necessary to his actual existence. Each is entitled to a liberty of choice as to his manner of life, and neither an individual nor the public has a right to arbitrarily take away from him this liberty.[153]

If one substitutes the word 'liberty' for 'autonomy', this passage seems to articulate the way in which 'privacy' (as opposed to the broader concept of 'private life') promotes autonomy in English legal thinking.

Many commentators argue though that the relationship between privacy and **2.68** autonomy is not just about respect for individual choice; it also promotes autonomous thought and action. They argue that by allowing individuals to retreat from the observation of others, privacy creates a zone where people can be free from concern about the judgment of others, 'be themselves', and think and act in accordance with their own ideas and principles. The underlying premise of this argument

---

[150] *Pretty* (n 125) para 65.

[151] Lord Hope expressly referred to 'self-determination' in *R (Pretty) v DPP* [2001] UKHL 61, [2002] 1 AC 800 [100]; and also *R (Purdy) v DPP* [2009] UKHL 45, [2009] 3 WLR 403 [36]. See also *Montgomery v Lanarkshire Health Board (Scotland)* [2015] UKSC 11, [2015] 2 WLR 768 [80].

[152] *R (Pretty)* (n 151) [61] (Lord Steyn). See also [23] (Lord Bingham) and [100] (Lord Hope). See in addition *R (Purdy)* (n 151) and *Wood v Commissioner of the Metropolis* [2009] EWCA Civ 414, [2009] 4 All ER 951 [20] (Laws LJ).

[153] *Pavesich* (n 108) 70. See also *Hosking* (n 8) at [239] (Tipping J says, '[i]t is of the essence of the dignity and personal autonomy and well-being of all human beings that some aspects of their lives should be able to remain private if they so wish').

is that unwanted observation and/or dissemination of information about a person has an inhibiting effect. This is, in turn, said to mean that people will only feel free to 'be themselves' in a zone from which observers can be legitimately excluded: we 'need a sanctuary or retreat, in which we can drop the mask, desist for a while from projecting on the world the image we want to be accepted as ourselves, an image that may reflect the values of our peers rather than the realities of our natures'.[154] So, if people are denied the opportunity to escape the chilling effect of unwanted observation, they will have little scope for independent thought or action:

> The man who is compelled to live every minute of his life among others and whose every need, thought, desire, fancy or gratification is subject to public scrutiny, has been deprived of his individuality...Such an individual merges with the mass. His opinions, being public, tend never to be different; his aspirations, being known, tend always to be conventionally accepted ones.[155]

Conversely, privacy allows people to learn to be autonomous by enabling them to express and act on their own principles in a protected environment:

> [Although] the man who is truly independent—the autonomous man...has the strength of mind to resist the pressure to believe with the rest, and has the courage to act on his convictions...For the rest of us, the freedom we need is the freedom to be something else—to be ourselves, to do what we think best, in a small, protected sea, where the winds of opinion cannot blow us off course. We cannot learn to be autonomous save by practising independent judgment.[156]

**2.69** As with dignity, the autonomy of the claimant will always be a factor to be weighed against the competing freedom of expression interests of the media and other defendants. Publications which reveal private information about people will inevitably undermine their ability to choose what is revealed about them. As with dignity, however, the more serious and intrusive the privacy interference, the greater will be the interference with the claimant's autonomy.

### (3) Freedom of Expression

**2.70** Discussion of the relationship between privacy and freedom of expression usually focuses on the tension between them. Such tension inevitably arises when one party asserts a privacy right in order to stop another from obtaining or disseminating information about him or her. However, privacy can also facilitate freedom of expression both at an individual and societal level.

---

[154] Benn (n 128) 24–5. See also Gross (n 143) 173; R Gavison, 'Privacy and the Limits of the Law' (1979) 89 Yale LJ 421, 450. As long ago as 1890, Warren and Brandeis observed, '[t]he intensity and complexity of life, attendant upon advancing civilisation, have rendered necessary some retreat from the world' (Warren and Brandeis (n 126) 196).

[155] Bloustein (n 132) 1003. See also S Jourard, 'Some Psychological Aspects of Privacy' (1966) 31 L and Contemp Prob 307, 308–9.

[156] Benn (n 128) 25–6. See also Gavison (n 154) 450 ('societies should enable all, not only the exceptional, to seek moral autonomy'); A Westin, *Privacy and Freedom* (Atheneum 1970) 34; and P Freund, 'Privacy: One Concept or Many?' in Pennock and Chapman (n 11) 182, 195.

## (a) Individual freedom of expression

On an individual level, privacy is said to promote freedom of expression by ena-  **2.71**
bling people to engage in creative individual pursuits free both from distraction
and 'the inhibitive effects that arise from close physical proximity with another
individual'.[157] Privacy can therefore promote those kinds of activities—writing,
painting, drawing, composing, *etc*—which may require some kind of retreat from
the world.[158] It also gives people a chance to practise: by 'insulating the individual against ridicule and censure at early stages of grouping and experimentation',
privacy allows us to have 'some abortive attempts' before going public with our
efforts.[159] Without this, it is claimed, we would 'dare less...and only do what we
thought we could do well'.[160]

Some also argue that privacy enhances individual freedom of expression by provid-  **2.72**
ing a space in which people can access reading and visual materials without fear
of sanction or disapproval.[161] An individual might be more inclined to explore
alternative religious ideas, for example, if he or she is able to do so away from the
scrutiny of other members of his or her religious community.

## (b) Promoting societal discourse

Privacy is often said to serve the wider societal interest of promoting free and open  **2.73**
discourse. The concept of an open democratic society sustained by freedom of
expression presupposes independent-minded individuals:[162] 'freedom of expression would lose much of its value if... [people] had nothing unique, creative or controversial to express'.[163] So if, as many commentators suggest, privacy is necessary
for the development of autonomous thinking, it is also a vital aspect of open, democratic society. Privacy is also said to encourage the expression of a diverse range of
opinions. This is because individuals who have the chance to test new, radical, or
potentially unpopular ideas in a protected environment might, '[a]fter a period of
germination...be more willing to declare their unpopular views in public'.[164]

**Facilitating uninhibited communication**   Privacy also promotes free, uninhib-  **2.74**
ited communication by ensuring that people can use communication channels
without interception or observation. This argument is well-illustrated in the United

---

[157]  Gavison (n 154) 446–7.
[158]  Gavison (n 154) 447.
[159]  Gavison (n 154) 448.
[160]  Gavison (n 154) 448.
[161]  See eg E Barendt, 'Privacy and freedom of speech' in A Kenyon and M Richardson (eds),
*New Dimensions in Privacy Law: International and Comparative Perspectives* (Cambridge University
Press 2006).
[162]  See eg Westin (n 156) 34 and the discussion of autonomy from 2.65–2.69.
[163]  D Craig, *Privacy and Employment Law* (Hart 1999) 25. See also C Hunt, 'Conceptualizing
Privacy and Elucidating its Importance: Foundational Considerations for the Development of
Canada's Fledgling Privacy Tort' (2011) 37 Queen's LJ 167, 216–17.
[164]  Gavison (n 154) 450. See also Westin (n 156) 34; and Craig (n 163).

States Supreme Court case of *Bartnicki v Vopper*.[165] The case concerned a radio journalist's broadcast of an intercepted mobile telephone conversation between two union officials. A majority of the Supreme Court held that the officials' privacy concerns were overridden by the public interest in the material. Rehnquist CJ dissented, however, arguing that the journalists' actions in fact undermined freedom of expression. He said that the majority decision 'diminishes, rather than enhances, the purposes of the First Amendment, thereby chilling the speech of the millions of Americans who rely upon electronic technology to communicate each day'.[166] People who fear that their mobile phone conversations or other communications will be intercepted are less likely to use them freely.

**2.75** The fact that media intrusion can chill individual speech was also recognized by the Californian Court of Appeal in *Miller v National Broadcasting Company*.[167] The California Court of Appeal (Second District) said that permitting news-gatherers to have unauthorized access to private premises (in this case as part of an ambulance 'ride-along') 'might have extraordinarily chilling implications for all of us; instead of a zone of privacy protecting our secluded moments, a climate of fear might surround us instead'.[168] The interrelationship between privacy and freedom of expression has also been acknowledged in the context of prisoners' correspondence. In Convention jurisprudence, the right to communicate with those outside the prison system is protected as part of the right to 'private life' and 'correspondence' in Article 8, even though it also involves freedom of expression interests protected in Article 10.[169] It is widely recognized that failure to protect the privacy of individuals' communications with one another can therefore 'lead overall to a loss of free speech'.[170]

**2.76** Privacy also promotes free and uninhibited communication in the context of particular kinds of relationships. Of particular relevance to the media is the protection afforded to journalists' sources. The free flow of information is greatly enhanced if whistle-blowers and other informants can, in appropriate cases, share information with journalists without fear of exposure.

### (4) Intimacy and Relationships

**2.77** As its relationship with freedom of expression illustrates, privacy is not simply about cutting oneself off from others. Many commentators emphasize privacy's

---

[165] 532 US 514, 121 S Ct 1753 (2001).
[166] *Bartnicki* (n 165) 1769. See discussion of the case in Barendt (n 161).
[167] 232 Cal Rptr 668, 187 Cal App 3d 1463 (Cal App 2 Dist 1986).
[168] *Miller* (n 167) 1493.
[169] See *eg Klamecki v Poland (No 2)* (2004) 39 EHRR 7, paras 137–40; *Natoli v Italy* (2003) 37 EHRR 49, paras 40–6; *AB v Netherlands* (2003) 37 EHRR 48, paras 81–8; *Petra v Romania* (2001) 33 EHRR 5, paras 36–9; *Giovine v Italy* (2003) 36 EHRR 8, paras 24–6; and *Szuluk v UK* (2010) 50 EHRR 10, para 43.
[170] Barendt (n 161).

importance in protecting intimate and social interaction within delineated social spheres. For example, David Feldman says that privacy:

> ...express[es] the fact that, in modern Western societies...individuals live their lives in a number of different social spheres, which interlock, and in each of which they have different responsibilities, and have to work with people in relationships of varying degrees of intimacy...Typically, while we mark off each sphere from the others, we individually have relatively little privacy as against people operating in our sphere for the purposes of that sphere.[171]

Such 'spheres' can involve varying degrees of closeness, ranging from the inti- **2.78** macy of family or sexual relationships to the wider sociability of clubs or religious groups.[172] Within all such groups, however, privacy enables individuals to act as they think appropriate for that context without having to worry about judgment or observation of those outside it. Thus, James Rachels says it enables one to:

> ...behave with certain people in the way that is appropriate to the sort of relationship we have with them, without at the same time violating our sense of how it is appropriate to behave with, and in the presence of, others with whom we have a different kind of relationship.[173]

This ability to engage more or less exclusively with chosen intimates is seen by **2.79** some to be a necessary precondition of intimacy and friendship. Fried argues that intimacy (which he says both friendship and love require, in different degrees) is the sharing of information about one's actions, beliefs, or emotions which one does not share with all. Thus, by conferring the right not to share information, 'privacy creates the moral capital which we spend in friendship and love'.[174]

Others argue that the ability to share information and experiences exclusively **2.80** with those with whom one feels particularly comfortable—a freedom which privacy confers—is necessary for the formation and maintenance of relationships. This is because, 'we do not find it as easy to express our feelings for one another spontaneously [and] to produce the same kind of mutually sensitive and responsive relations, in full view of a nonparticipant third party'.[175] Rachels illustrates this by imagining a conversation between two close friends. As he says, if the friends were joined by a casual acquaintance then the character of the group would change and conversation about intimate matters would no longer be appropriate. If the friends could never be alone (because there were always casual acquaintances or strangers intruding) then they would have to either carry

---

[171] D Feldman, 'Secrecy, Dignity or Autonomy? Views of Privacy as a Civil Liberty' (1994) 47 Curr Legal Prob 4, 51. See also Fried (n 14) 485.

[172] Feldman (n 171) 51.

[173] J Rachels, 'Why Privacy is Important' (1975) 4 Phil & Publ Aff 323, 330–1. See also Hunt (n 163) 213–16.

[174] Fried (n 14) 484.

[175] Benn (n 128) 20. Thomas Nagel makes a similar point about sexual activity: T Nagel, 'Concealment and Exposure' (1998) 30 Phil & Publ Aff 3, 19.

on as close friends do, thereby 'violating their sense of how it is appropriate to behave around casual acquaintances or strangers', or avoid doing or saying anything which they thought inappropriate before a third party.[176] This latter course would mean that 'they could no longer behave with one another in the way that friends do and further that, eventually, they would no longer *be* close friends'.[177] The same would be true, says Rachels, of more intimate relationships such as husband and wife. Others have made similar observations in respect of wider social relationships with, for example, acquaintances, extended family members, work mates, and members of the community.[178]

**2.81** The relationship between privacy and relationships is implicitly recognized in the many cases where breach of confidence or misuse of private information actions have been used to protect claimants against disclosure of details of intimate relationships. For example, in *Duchess of Argyll v Duke of Argyll*, Ungoed-Thomas J held that the 'confidential nature of the relationship [between spouses] is of its very essence and so obviously and necessarily implicit in it that there is no need for it to be expressed'.[179] Detailed disclosures about sexual or intimate relationships have also been held to breach privacy,[180] as have disclosures about social occasions such as weddings and family outings.[181] This is consistent with the ECtHR's view that the Convention right to respect for private life includes 'the right to establish and to develop relationships with other human beings, especially in the emotional field for the development and fulfilment of one's own personality'[182] and that '[r]espect for private life must... [therefore] comprise to a certain degree the right to establish and develop relationships with other human beings'.[183]

## (5) Health and Well-being

**2.82** As courts have consistently acknowledged, a breach of privacy can cause an individual distress and upset. Such distress is in large part caused by the interference with dignity, autonomy, and relationships discussed above, but preservation of health and well-being can also be seen as an independent reason for privacy interests. Psychologists have established links between unwanted surveillance and ill

---

[176] Rachels (n 173) 330.

[177] Rachels (n 173) 330 (original emphasis).

[178] See Feldman (n 171); and Freund (n 156) 195–6.

[179] [1967] 1 Ch 302, 322.

[180] See *eg Mosley* (n 124); and *Theakston v Mirror Group Newspapers Ltd* [2002] EWHC 137 (QB) (esp [59] and [60]).

[181] See *eg Douglas* (n 118); *Murray v Express Newspapers plc* [2008] EWCA Civ 446, [2009] Ch 481; and *Weller v Associated Newspapers Ltd* [2014] EWHC 1163 (QB).

[182] *X v Iceland* App no 6825/74 (1976) 5 DR 86, 87 (a decision of the European Commission on Human Rights). See also *Botta v Italy* (1998) 26 EHRR 241, para 32; *Rotaru v Romania* App no 28341/95 (2000) 8 BHRC 449, para 43; *Pretty v UK* (n 125) para 61; and *Peck v UK* (2003) 36 EHRR 719, para 57.

[183] *Niemietz v Germany* (1992) 16 EHRR 97, para 29.

health[184] and commentators stress the importance of privacy in facilitating relaxation and emotional release. As Westin says, 'individuals can sustain roles only for reasonable periods of time, and no individual can play indefinitely, without relief, the variety of roles that life demands'; privacy is therefore important because it gives people 'a chance to lay their masks aside for rest'.[185] Privacy is also seen as important for the natural expression of strong or intimate feeling, particularly at times of loss, shock or sorrow.[186]

## (6) Freedom from Judgment/Discrimination

Private activities which are neither unlawful nor harmful can result in disap-  **2.83**
proval or sanction from other members of society. Some commentators therefore argue that privacy has an important role to play in shielding people who engage in unpopular activities from unjustified discrimination and/or hostility. As discussed above, freedom from censure can help promote autonomous action[187] but it is also seen to be important for its own sake. As David Feldman says:

> People ought to tolerate, if not respect, choices which we make in those circles of life to which they are not privy. Although privacy is sometimes regarded as a poor substitute for toleration, being a protection against being watched over by the intolerant rather than an assertion of the wrongfulness of intolerance, they actually go together inseparably. A right to privacy represents an institutional limit on people's capacity to make one suffer from the intolerance.[188]

In other words, as Gavison puts it, 'privacy permits individuals to do what they would not do without it for fear of an unpleasant or hostile reaction from others'.[189] This is said to be particularly important where, although the information would not lower the claimants in the minds of 'right-thinking people', it would engender hostility in a significant minority. The ability to suppress information about one's homosexuality was often used to exemplify this argument in the past.

By conferring this ability to hide things about one's character that others might  **2.84**
disapprove of, privacy provides incidental protection for reputation. A man who restrains the media from publishing information about his sado-masochistic sexual activities, for example, will prevent friends, associates and the wider public from taking account of those activities when forming their impression of him.

---

[184] See *eg* M Smith et al, *Electronic Performance Monitoring and Job Stress in Telecommunications Jobs* (Department of Industrial Engineering and the Communications Workers of America University of Wisconsin, Madison 1990).
[185] Westin (n 156) 35.
[186] See Westin (n 156) 35–6; and Nagel (n 175) 19–20. For discussion of the impact of intense media interest at times of grief see N A Moreham and Y Tinsley, 'Grief Journalism, Physical Intrusion, and Loss: The Pike River Coal Mine Disaster' in A T Kenyon (ed), *Comparative Defamation and Privacy Law* (Cambridge University Press) (forthcoming).
[187] See 2.68–2.69.
[188] Feldman (n 171) 57–8. See also Gross (n 143) 177.
[189] Gavison (n 154) 451.

Regardless of whether privacy protection was intended to protect it, the individual's reputation is thereby preserved; by saying that something is nobody else's business, courts prevent others from considering it when deciding what they think of the person. As Feldman explains:

> A person is entitled to protect his or her dignity, including both self respect and the esteem of others, from assault on the basis of activities which are nobody else's business. Saying that certain areas of life, or types of activity, are nobody else's business certainly asserts that other people have no right to know what is going on, but also goes a good deal further. In particular, it asserts that the activity in question should be regarded as being irrelevant to the esteem in which a person is held by those who, in other spheres of life, enter into relationships (whether business or social) with us.[190]

Richard Posner puts it less sympathetically: 'privacy as the concealment of discreditable facts about oneself... is a method... of enhancing reputation'.[191]

**2.85** The idea that privacy can be used to protect reputation is not without difficulty. As discussed in the context of the false light tort above, Anglo-Commonwealth courts and commentators are cautious about using privacy to protect reputation.[192] Indeed, one of the arguments raised against privacy protection is that it enables individuals to protect reputations that they do not deserve. Posner expresses this argument in strong terms:

> Much of the demand for privacy... concerns discreditable information, often information concerning past or present criminal activity or moral conduct at variance with a person's professed moral standards. And often the motive for concealment is... to mislead those with whom he transacts. Other private information that people wish to conceal, while not strictly discreditable, would if revealed correct misapprehensions that the individual is trying to exploit, as when a worker conceals a serious health problem from his employer or a prospective husband conceals his sterility from his fiancée.[193]

**2.86** It is important to note though that privacy can only be said to protect reputation in situations where the private information in question is in some way discreditable. Reputation is not affected in situations, such as those in *Douglas v Hello! Ltd*,[194] *Murray v Express Newspapers plc*,[195] *Weller v Associated Newspapers Ltd*[196] or *von Hannover v Germany*,[197] where the claimant is not doing anything embarrassing or shameful but simply wants to be left alone.

---

[190] Feldman (n 171) 57.
[191] R Posner, 'Privacy, secrecy, and reputation' (1979) 28 Buffalo L Rev 1, 11.
[192] See 2.43–2.46.
[193] R Posner, 'The right of privacy' (1978) 12 Georgia L Rev 393, 399. See also Posner (n 191) 11–12.
[194] *Douglas* (n 146) (photographs of the claimants' wedding).
[195] *Murray* (n 181) 446 (photographs of the claimant being wheeled in a pushchair on an Edinburgh street).
[196] *Weller* (n 181) (photographs of a family trip to a café).
[197] (2005) 40 EHRR 1.

Further, even in cases involving discreditable information, the extent to which **2.87**
privacy enables individuals to 'mislead' in the way that Posner describes depends
on the operation of the public interest defence. If an individual engages in activity which is unlawful or harmful to others, media defendants will usually be able
to show that its disclosure is in the public interest. Courts also recognize that the
media are entitled to 'set the record straight' if a celebrity or other public figure
has misled the public about his or her private character.[198] As Lord Denning MR
said in *Woodward v Hutchins*, '[i]f the image which they fostered was not a true
image, it is in the public interest that it should be corrected'.[199] Courts have also
recognized that a defendant might be entitled to provide private information to an
interested party (such as the spouse of an adulterer) even if the information is not
to be disclosed to the public at large.[200] There is recognition then that matters in
which the public or a person's acquaintances have a legitimate interest should not
be held to be none of their business. This goes at least some way towards addressing
Posner's concerns.

---

[198] *Woodward v Hutchins* [1977] 1 WLR 760. See also *Campbell* (n 123) and *A v B plc* (n 141).
However, note *Campbell v MGN Ltd* [2002] EWCA Civ 1373, [2003] QB 663 [41].
[199] *Woodward* (n 198) 764.
[200] See *eg SKA v CRH* [2012] EWHC 766 (QB); and *BUQ v HRE* [2012] EWHC 774 (QB).

# 3

# PRIVACY IN EUROPEAN, CIVIL, AND COMMON LAW

*N A Moreham and Tanya Aplin*

## A. Introduction

**3.01** The purpose of this chapter is to examine some of the external sources that influence the shape and scope of the protection of privacy in English law. Those influences are diverse. They include the jurisprudence of the European Court of Human Rights (ECtHR) and other institutions of the Council of Europe, European Union instruments, international human rights obligations, foreign common law jurisdictions, and European civil law. All of these sources form part of the multifaceted context in which English privacy protections are developing.

**3.02** This chapter explains that context, first, by identifying the content of the United Kingdom's international obligations and examining the scope of privacy protection in the European Convention on Human Rights (ECHR).[1] Secondly, it includes

---

[1] Convention for the Protection of Human Rights and Fundamental Freedoms (European Convention on Human Rights) (Rome, 4 November 1950; TS 71 (1953); Cmd 8969).

a brief overview of the shape and scope of privacy protection in the United States, Ireland, New Zealand, Australia, Canada, South Africa, Scotland, Germany, and France. All of these sources provide important context in which to understand recent English developments—the traditions they build on, the influences they are shaped by, and developments that English law might yet embrace.

## B. The Protection of Privacy in Relevant International Instruments

The right to privacy is protected in a number of international instruments to which **3.03** the United Kingdom is a party.

### (1) The United Nations

The first formal declaration of fundamental rights to include a right of privacy was **3.04** the Universal Declaration of Human Rights 1948.[2] The United Kingdom was an original signatory to the Declaration and it is therefore a source of English privacy law. Article 12 provides that:

> No one shall be subject to arbitrary interference with his privacy, family, home, or correspondence, nor to attacks on his honour or reputation. Everyone has the right to protection of the law against such interference.

The Declaration was intended to set out what the Preamble refers to as 'a common **3.05** understanding of . . . rights and freedoms', that is to say principles that were already recognized by the signatories. The explanation for all the rights, including privacy, given in the Preamble is 'the inherent dignity . . . of all members of the human family'. The Universal Declaration had been preceded by a number of unofficial drafts, which also recognized a right to privacy, mostly by reference to the sanctity of the home and correspondence, without explicitly mentioning personal information.

In addition, Article 17 of the International Covenant on Civil and Political Rights **3.06** (ICCPR) provides:

(1) No one shall be subjected to arbitrary or unlawful interference with his privacy, family, home or correspondence, nor to unlawful attacks on his honour and reputation.
(2) Everyone has the right to the protection of the law against such interference or attacks.

Although the United Kingdom is a party to the ICCPR it does not accept the right of individual petition to the Human Rights Committee.[3] This means that its

---

[2] Adopted and proclaimed by the United Nations General Assembly Res 217A (III) (10 December 1948).
[3] The UN body charged with supervising the implementation of the Covenant, based in Geneva.

provisions are not directly enforceable against the United Kingdom at the instigation of an individual before an international tribunal. Nor is the Covenant
incorporated into English domestic law. Along with the Universal Declaration,
therefore, its status is that of any other international instrument ratified by the
United Kingdom, namely that it has no direct effect in the courts of this country
but may be relied on as representative of generally accepted international norms
and as an aid to interpretation.[4]

### (2) Protection of Privacy in the European Union

**3.07** The most important area relating to privacy in which the institutions of the
European Union provide source material for the United Kingdom is in relation to
data protection. Directive 95/46/EC on the Protection of Individuals with regard
to the processing of Personal Data and on the free movement of such data[5] is a
comprehensive privacy code insofar as it prescribes the conditions for regulation
of personal data within the Union.[6] The Directive is of direct effect in Member
States and is implemented in the United Kingdom through the Data Protection
Act 1998.[7] These important instruments, together with the relevant jurisprudence
of the European Court of Justice (ECJ) on the application of the Directive, are
considered in Chapter 7.

**3.08** Beyond that, the European Union also influences the English law of privacy more
generally. The right to privacy is a general principle of European Union law[8] and

---

[4] This is because a state is presumed to act compatibly with its international obligations. Other
UN Conventions which guarantee rights to certain classes of individuals also contain specific
provisions safeguarding privacy: see *eg* Art 16 of the Convention on the Rights of the Child (20
November 1989, 1577 UNTS 3).

[5] Directive 95/46/EC of the European Parliament and of the Council of 24 October 1995 on the
protection of individuals with regard to the processing of personal data and on the free movement
of such data [1995] OJ L281/31. The Directive is set out in full in Appendix D (available at <http://
www.5rb.com/publication/the-law-of-privacy-and-the-media>).

[6] Directive 95/46/EC, Art 1(1) provides that 'Member States shall protect the fundamental
rights and freedoms of natural persons, and in particular their right to privacy with respect to the
processing of personal data'.

[7] See Joined Cases C-468/10 and C-469/10 *ASNEF v Administración del Estado* [2012] 1 CMLR 48,
[55] where the CJEU ruled Art 7(f) of Directive 95/46/EC had direct effect. The European Commission
has proposed comprehensive reform of EU data protection law in the form of a Regulation on the
protection of individuals with regard to the processing of personal data and on the free movement of
such data (General Data Protection Regulation), COM/2012/011 and also a Proposed Directive on the
protection of individuals with regard to the processing of personal data by competent authorities for
the purposes of prevention, investigation, detection or prosecution of criminal offences or the execut-
ing of criminal penalties, and the free movement of such data, COM/2012/010. See the Explanatory
Memorandum to the Proposed Regulation and also the Communication 'Safeguarding Privacy in a
Connected World: A European Data Framework for the 21st Century', COM/2012/09. On 12 March
2014, an overwhelming majority of the European Parliament voted in support of the proposals. A common agreement from the Council is awaited and expected to occur by the end of 2015.

[8] Art 6(3) of the Treaty on the European Union states that fundamental rights in the ECHR and
the constitutional traditions of Member States 'shall constitute general principles of the Union's
law'. Unfortunately, the EU's proposed accession to the ECHR has been stalled because the CJEU

EU institutions are guided in their interpretation of that right by the ECHR and the jurisprudence of the Strasbourg Court made under it.[9]

More specifically, the Charter of Fundamental Rights of the European Union[10] **3.09** puts human dignity at the forefront of the rights protected. The Preamble to the Charter provides:

> Conscious of its spiritual and moral heritage, the Union is founded on the indivisible, universal values of human dignity, freedom, equality and solidarity; it is based on the principles of democracy and the rule of law. It places the individual at the heart of its activities, by establishing the citizenship of the Union and by creating an area of freedom, security and justice.[11]

Article 7 of the Charter (in terms reminiscent of Article 8(1) ECHR) provides:

> Everyone has the right to respect for his or her private and family life, home and communications.[12]

Article 8 of the Charter (which does not have a parallel in the ECHR) provides:

> 1. Everyone has the right to the protection of personal data concerning him or her.
> 2. Such data must be processed fairly for specified purposes and on the basis of the consent of the person concerned or some other legitimate basis laid down by law. Everyone has the right of access to data which has been collected concerning him or her, and the right to have it rectified.
> 3. Compliance with these rules shall be subject to control by an independent authority.

The Charter is addressed to the institutions of the European Union and has no **3.10** independent application outside the Union. For it to be engaged the issue under review must be within the scope of EU law. The obligation on the United Kingdom to comply with the Charter is not apparently affected by Protocol 30 to the Charter.[13] The Charter was intended to be a showcase of existing rights and the Explanations to the Charter show the derivation of each right and principle within it.

---

has ruled that the draft agreement providing for such accession is incompatible with EU law: see Opinion 2/13 of the CJEU (Full Court) 18 December 2014.

[9] Under Art 52(3) of the Charter of Fundamental Rights of the European Union, rights that correspond to rights in the ECHR must be given the same meaning although greater protection can be given. Moreover, Art 6(2) of the Treaty on the European Union provides that the EU will itself become a party to the ECHR.

[10] Originally solemnly declared as a non-binding instrument at the Nice Summit on 7 December 2000, the Charter is now part of the Lisbon Treaty which entered into force on 1 December 2009. The Lisbon Treaty is implemented into UK law by the EU (Amendment) Act 2008.

[11] Art 1 provides: 'Human dignity is inviolable. It must be respected and protected.'

[12] Art 52(1) of the Charter recognizes that there can be limitations on the exercise of the rights and freedoms where they are 'provided for by law' and 'only if they are necessary and genuinely meet objectives of general interest recognised by the Union or the need to protect the rights and freedoms of others'.

[13] See Joined Cases C-411/10 and C-493/10 *NS v Secretary of State for the Home Department and ME v Refugee Applications Commissioner* [2013] QB 102, [118]–[122].

However, by giving the Charter the status of a treaty it may now be relied on directly in cases which fall within its remit.[14]

**3.11**  Prior to the Treaty of Lisbon, the lack of binding legal effect of the Charter meant that it played a limited role in EU law for the first nine years of its existence.[15] However, since the Treaty of Lisbon entered into force, we have seen Charter fundamental rights feature more prominently in the reasoning of the ECJ. A striking example of this is *Digital Rights Ireland*,[16] where the Grand Chamber of the ECJ held that Directive 2006/24 (on the retention of data generated or processed in connection with the provision of publicly available electronic communications services or of public communications networks and amending Directive 2002/58/EC)[17] was invalid because of its incompatibility with Articles 7 and 8 of the Charter.[18] In the context of interpreting Regulation 2252/2004 on standards for security features and biometrics in passports and travel documents issued by Member States[19] the ECJ found that respect for a person's name was a constituent element of Article 7 of the Charter, such that Member States that chose to include the birth name of a passport holder alongside his or her forenames and surnames had to distinguish clearly between these different names so as to avoid confusion about identity.[20] The Court has also recognized that the protection of professional secrets falls with Articles 7 and 8 of the Charter.[21]

**3.12**  In *Google Spain*,[22] the ECJ frequently invoked a data subject's fundamental rights under Articles 7 and 8 of the Charter to give a broad interpretation to Directive 95/46/EC.[23] In this case, the Court held that information location activities of a search engine involved 'processing of personal data' within Article 2(b) and that the operator of the search engine was a 'controller' within the meaning of Article 2(d). Further, 'the processing was carried out in the context of the activities

---

[14]  This is particularly likely to be relevant to data protection law since most national laws on data protection now derive from the EU directive.

[15]  S Douglas-Scott, 'The European Union and Human Rights after the Treaty of Lisbon' (2011) 11 HRL Rev 645, 651.

[16]  Joined Cases C-293/12 and C-594/12 *Digital Rights Ireland Ltd v Minister for Communications, Marine and Natural Resources; Proceedings brought by Kärntner Landesregierung* [2014] 3 WLR 1607.

[17]  [2006] OJ L105/54.

[18]  For a discussion see T Ojanen, 'Privacy is more than just a seven-letter word: the Court of Justice of the European Union sets constitutional limits on mass surveillance' (2014) ECL Rev 528.

[19]  [2004] OJ L385/1, as amended by Regulation 444/2009 [2009] OJ L142/1 and corrigendum [2009] OJ L188/127.

[20]  Case C-101/13 *U v Stadt Karlsruhe* [2015] 1 CMLR 29, paras 48–51.

[21]  Case C-450/06 *Varec SA v Belgium* [2008] 2 CMLR 24, paras 47–48; Case T-345/12R *Akzo Nobel NV v European Commission* [2013] 4 CMLR 12; Case T-462/12R *Pilkington Group Ltd v European Commission* [2013] 5 CMLR 20, paras 44–5. To the extent that Art 7 of the Charter refers to 'home' this includes business premises: see Case T-410/09 *Almamet v European Commission* [2013] 4 CMLR 24, para 23.

[22]  Case C-131/12 *Google Spain SL v Agencia Española de Protección de Datos* [2014] QB 1022 [32]–[33].

[23]  *Google Spain* (n 22) paras 38, 53, 58, 66, 68, 80–1, and 97.

of an establishment of the controller on the territory of the Member State' within the meaning of Article 4(1)(a) because Google Inc had set up a subsidiary in Spain to 'promote and sell, in that member state, advertising space offered by the search engine which serves to make the service offered by that engine profitable'.[24] According to the Court, the operator of the search engine was obliged to remove from the list of search results relating to a person's name, links to web pages published by third parties and relating to that person, thereby recognizing the 'right to be forgotten'.[25]

### (3) The European Convention on Human Rights

The third source of English privacy law, the ECHR, was negotiated within the **3.13** Council of Europe in 1949 and 1950, at a time when negotiations in the United Nations for a covenant based on the Universal Declaration of Human Rights were making no progress. As recognized in the Preamble to the Convention, the rights guaranteed, including the right to privacy, are the rights stated in the Universal Declaration.[26] Article 8 provides:

(1) Everyone has the right to respect for his private and family life, his home and his correspondence.
(2) There shall be no interference by a public authority with the exercise of this right except such as is in accordance with the law and is necessary in a democratic society in the interests of national security, public safety or the economic well-being of the country, for the prevention of disorder or crime, for the protection of health or morals, or for the protection of the rights and freedoms of others.

Since 1966, the United Kingdom has accepted the right of individual petition **3.14** under Article 34[27] allowing individuals who allege that their rights have been violated to bring an application before the international tribunals based in Strasbourg.[28] Since 2 October 2000, the substantive rights under the Convention

---

[24] *Google Spain* (n 22) para 55.

[25] *Google Spain* (n 22) para 88. For a discussion of the *Google Spain* case see E Frantziou, 'Further Developments in the Right to be Forgotten: the European Court of Justice's Judgment in Case C-131/12, *Google Spain, SL, Google Inc v Agencia Espanola de Proteccion de Datos*' (2014) 14 HRL Rev 761. Note that Max Mosley is attempting to enforce his right to be forgotten under the UK Data Protection Act 1998 in relation to still images from video footage capturing his sexual activities. The High Court dismissed Google's application to strike out the claim/obtain summary judgment, Mitting J finding that it was 'a viable claim which raises questions of general public interest, which ought to proceed to trial': see *Mosley v Google Inc* [2015] EWHC 59 (QB), [2015] EMLR 11 [53].

[26] The Members of the Council of Europe 'resolved...to take the first steps for the collective enforcement of certain of the Rights stated in the Universal Declaration': ECHR, Preamble.

[27] Prior to entry into force of Protocol 11 on 1 November 1998 this was an optional mechanism under Art 25 ECHR. Acceptance of the right of individual petition is now a compulsory requirement for all states parties to the Convention.

[28] Prior to entry into force of Protocol 11 applications were first considered by the European Commission of Human Rights which gave a non-binding ruling on admissibility and merits and were only subsequently referred to the European Court at the instigation of the state, as far as the United Kingdom was concerned, for a binding judgment. Since 1 November 1998 applications have gone straight to one of the Chambers of the Court which gives a binding judgment and only in 'exceptional

have been directly enforceable in courts in the United Kingdom in accordance with the terms of the Human Rights Act 1998 (HRA), although prior to this date the courts were increasingly having regard to the Convention and the decisions of the European Commission and Court of Human Rights in their judgments.[29] For both these reasons the Convention has achieved a special status in English law and is by far the most significant influence in the development of the law of privacy in this jurisdiction. The jurisprudence of the Strasbourg institutions therefore deserves detailed consideration as the English courts continue to develop their own body of case law in this area.

### (a) *The scope of 'private life' in Article 8*

**3.15** The right to respect for private life is an amorphous and broad one, extending well beyond narrow Anglo-Saxon conceptions of the right to privacy. The ECtHR has acknowledged that 'private life' extends beyond the 'right to privacy, the right to live, as far as one wishes, protected from publicity',[30] but beyond that merely says that it is 'a broad term not susceptible to exhaustive definition'.[31] It has however made several broad statements about the nature of the interest.

**3.16** 'Private life', says the Court, includes 'activities of a professional or business nature',[32] the 'right to establish and develop relationships with other human beings and the outside world',[33] 'a zone of interaction of a person with others, even in a public context',[34] the 'physical and psychological integrity of a person',[35] the 'right to … personal development', [36] and 'the right to establish details of their identity as individual human beings'.[37] In a number of cases, the Court has also asked whether the applicant had a 'reasonable expectation' of protection and respect for private life in the circumstances of the case.[38] Interests as diverse as the right to live a traveller lifestyle, to change one's name, and to be free from environmental pollution, as

---

cases' is the application referred to the Grand Chamber for a re-hearing. The request for a second-tier judgment may be made by either party but will only be granted in cases which raise a serious question affecting the interpretation or application of the Convention or a serious issue of general importance: Art 43.

[29] See generally M Hunt, *Using Human Rights Law in English Courts* (Hart 1997).

[30] *X v Iceland* App no 6825/74, (1976) 5 DR 86, 87.

[31] *Peck v UK* (2003) 36 EHRR 719, para 57. See also *Niemietz v Germany* (1993) 16 EHRR 97, para 29; *Pretty v UK* (2002) 35 EHRR 1, para 61; and *PG and JH v UK* App no 44787/98 (ECtHR, 25 September 2001) para 56.

[32] *Niemietz v Germany* (n 31) para 29. See also *Peck v UK* (n 31) para 57; *Rotaru v Romania* App no 28341/95 (ECtHR, 4 May 2000) para 43; *Amann v Switzerland* (2000) 30 EHRR 843, para 65.

[33] *Peck v UK* (n 31) para 57. See also *X v Iceland* (n 30) 87; *Rotaru v Romania* (n 32) para 43; and *Amann v Switzerland* (n 32) para 65.

[34] *Peck v UK* (n 31) para 57 and *von Hannover v Germany* (2005) 40 EHRR 1, para 50.

[35] *Pretty v UK* (n 31) para 61.

[36] *Peck v UK* (n 31) para 57. See also *X v Iceland* (n 30) 87.

[37] *Goodwin v UK* (2002) 35 EHRR 18, para 90. See also *Pretty v UK* (n 31) para 61.

[38] See eg *Halford v UK* (1997) 24 EHRR 523, para 45; *von Hannover v Germany* (n 34) para 51; *Perry v UK* (2004) 39 EHRR 3, para 37; and *Copland v UK* (2007) 45 EHRR 37, para 42.

well as more traditional 'privacy' rights such as protection against dissemination of personal information and images, therefore all fall within it.

Despite its amorphous nature, it is suggested that five sub-categories of private-life **3.17** interest can be identified from within the Article 8 jurisprudence. They are the right, first, to be free from interference with physical and psychological integrity; secondly, to be free from unwanted access to and collection of information; thirdly, to be free from serious environmental pollution; fourthly, to be free to develop one's identity; and fifthly, the right to live one's life in the manner of one's choosing.[39]

**The structure of Article 8**  Article 8 imposes two sorts of obligation: a 'negative' **3.18** obligation to avoid interfering with any of the rights outlined in Article 8(1) unless the conditions in Article 8(2) are satisfied and a 'positive' obligation to take active steps to protect individuals' private lives, particularly against interference by others. The Court's approach to Article 8 cases depends on which kind of obligation is at stake.

*Negative obligations*  Where negative obligations are concerned, the Court asks **3.19** two questions: has there been an interference with one of the rights specified in Article 8(1) and, if so, was the interference justified under Article 8(2)? In order to satisfy Article 8(2), the interfering measure must satisfy three requirements. First, it must be 'in accordance with the law', which means that the interference must have been made in accordance with a national law[40] which is compatible with the rule of law.[41] The measure must, secondly, be shown to have served one of the 'legitimate aims' specified in Article 8(2)—namely the interests of national security; public safety; economic well-being; the prevention of disorder or crime; or the protection of health, morals, or the rights and freedoms of others. Thirdly, the measure must be 'necessary in a democratic society'. This means that there must be a '"pressing social need" for the interference',[42] the establishment of which will depend, *inter alia*, on whether the measure was proportionate.[43] Member States are

---

[39] The analysis of the private-life interest set out in this paragraph, and the discussion which follows, is based on the articulation of the Court's principles in N A Moreham, 'The Right to Respect for Private Life in the European Convention on Human Rights: A Re-examination' [2008] 1 EHRL Rev 44.

[40] 'Law' in this context includes judge-made or unwritten law (see *eg Sunday Times v UK* (1979) 2 EHRR 245, para 47; and *Malone v UK* (1985) 7 EHRR 14, para 66) as well as statutes (see *Klass v Germany* (1980) 2 EHRR 214, para 43) and non-statutory regulations (see *eg Golder v UK* (1975) 1 EHRR 524, para 45). However, it does not include non-binding directions such as Home Office guidelines: *Khan v UK* (2001) 31 EHRR 45, para 27.

[41] This means that it 'must provide a measure of legal protection against arbitrary interference by public authorities with the rights safeguarded by paragraph 1 of Article 8': *Segerstedt-Wiberg v Sweden* (2007) 44 EHRR 2, para 76.

[42] *Dudgeon v UK* (1982) 4 EHRR 149, para 51. See also *Handyside v UK* (1976) 1 EHRR 737, para 48 and *Sunday Times v UK* (n 40) para 59.

[43] Proportionality is not expressly mentioned in the Convention but has been clearly recognized in the case law; see *eg Handyside v UK* (n 42) para 49 and *Leander v Sweden* (1987) 9 EHRR 433, para 58.

accorded a 'margin of appreciation' when determining what is necessary in their particular societies.[44]

**3.20** *Positive obligations*   Member States also have a positive obligation to protect individuals' private lives, particularly against interference by others. This is because:

> ...while the essential object of Article 8 is to protect the individual against arbitrary interference by the public authorities, it does not merely compel the State to abstain from such interference: in addition to this negative undertaking, there may be positive obligations inherent in an effective respect for private or family life. These obligations may involve the adoption of measures designed to secure respect for private life even in the sphere of the relations of individuals between themselves.[45]

**3.21** Unlike the negative obligation cases, the focus in positive obligation cases is not on the precise requirements of Article 8(1)–(2) but on a broader inquiry into whether Article 8(1) is 'applicable'[46] and a fair balance has been struck between the competing interests involved in the case.[47] The Court has however stressed that similar principles apply to both positive and negative obligations. In both situations, 'regard must be had to the fair balance which has to be struck between the general interest and the interests of the individual; and in both contexts the State enjoys a certain margin of appreciation'.[48] So, although a state cannot rely expressly on Article 8(2) to justify a breach of a positive obligation, the considerations listed therein will have a 'certain relevance' when determining whether a 'fair' balance has been struck.[49]

**3.22** **The five categories**   It is suggested that five distinct categories of interest can be identified from within the 'private-life' decisions.[50]

**3.23** *Category 1: Freedom from interference with physical and psychological integrity*   The Court has consistently observed that the right to respect for 'private life' includes 'the physical and psychological integrity of a person'.[51] A variety of different

---

[44] *Handyside v UK* (n 42) para 48 and *Sunday Times v UK* (n 40) para 59.

[45] *Van Kück v Germany* (2003) 37 EHRR 51, para 70. See also *von Hannover* (n 34) para 57; *McGinley and Egan v UK* (1999) 27 EHRR 1, para 98; *Stubbings v UK* (1997) 23 EHRR 213, paras 61–2 and *Airey v Ireland* (1980) 2 EHRR 305, para 32.

[46] See *eg Guerra v Italy* (1998) 26 EHRR 357, para 57; and *Taşkin v Turkey* (2006) 42 EHRR 50, paras 111–15 (although note that the Court does not always address the question of applicability separately).

[47] See eg *Lopez Ostra v Spain* (1995) 20 EHRR 277, para 51.

[48] *Van Kück v Germany* (n 45) para 71. See also *von Hannover v Germany* (n 34) para 57; *Rees v UK* (1987) 9 EHRR 56, para 37; *Gaskin v UK* (1990) 12 EHRR 36, para 42; *Hatton v UK* (2003) 37 EHRR 28, para 119 and *Mosley v UK* (2011) 53 EHRR 20, paras 106–11.

[49] *Rees v UK* (n 48) para 37. The Court there said that Art 8(2) 'refers in terms only to "interferences" with the right protected by the first paragraph in other words is concerned with the negative obligations flowing therefrom'. See also *Gaskin v UK* (n 48) para 42 and *Lopez Ostra v Spain* (n 47) para 51.

[50] These five categories are drawn from Moreham (n 39). More detailed analysis of each category can be found in that article.

[51] See eg *YF v Turkey* (2004) 39 EHRR 34, para 33 and *Pretty v UK* (n 31) para 61.

interferences fall within this part of the private-life interest. They include the right to be free from physical assault[52] (including forced medical procedures),[53] forced bodily exposure,[54] unjustified search of one's home[55] or place of work,[56] unjustified interception of one's conversations through use of bugging devices[57] or telephone taps,[58] unwarranted videoing of one's activities even in public and semi-public places,[59] and the unwarranted dissemination of images of oneself.[60] The right to reputation has also been held to form part of a person's 'psychological integrity' (along with his or her 'personal identity') and therefore to fall within the scope of 'private life'.[61] However, in later decisions, reputation has been held to engage Article 8 only where the factual allegations 'were of such a seriously offensive nature that their publication had an inevitable direct effect on the applicant's private life'[62] or where the attack on a person's reputation attained 'a certain level of seriousness' such as to cause prejudice to the enjoyment of private life.[63] Subsequent cases provide an inconsistent picture about whether and how such a threshold needs to be met.[64] It has been argued, however, that the

---

[52] See *eg X and Y v Netherlands* (1986) 8 EHRR 235 (failure to provide criminal sanction against the rape of a 16-year-old handicapped girl) and *MC v Bulgaria* (2005) 40 EHRR 20 (failure to sanction effectively the offence of 'date rape').

[53] See *eg YF v Turkey* (n 51); *Jalloh v Germany* (2007) 44 EHRR 32; *Storck v Germany* (2005) 43 EHRR 96; *Glass v UK* (2004) 39 EHRR 15.

[54] *Wainwright v UK* (2007) 44 EHRR 40.

[55] See *eg Keegan v UK* (2007) 44 EHRR 33; *Sallinen v Finland* (2007) 44 EHRR 18; *Buck v Germany* (2006) 42 EHRR 21; *Funke v France* (1993) 16 EHRR 297.

[56] *Niemietz v Germany* (n 31) para 29.

[57] See *eg Wood v UK* App no 23414/02 (ECtHR, 16 November 2004); *Allan v UK* (2003) 36 EHRR 12; *Khan v UK* (n 40) para 35; *PG and JH v UK* (n 31) para 60.

[58] See *eg Huvig v France* (1990) 12 EHRR 528, para 25; *Halford v UK* (n 38) paras 43–6, 52; *Doerga v Netherlands* (2005) 41 EHRR 4, para 43; *Kopp v Switzerland* (1999) 27 EHRR 91, para 50; *Amann v Switzerland* (n 32) para 44.

[59] See *Allan v UK* (n 57) para 35 (breach of Art 8 to video a person in his or her prison cell or waiting area); *Peck v UK* (n 31) paras 57–9; *Perry v UK* (n 38) paras 37–8.

[60] *Perry v UK* (n 38); *Peck v UK* (n 31); *Sciacca v Italy* (2006) 43 EHRR 20; *von Hannover v Germany* (n 34).

[61] *Pfeifer v Austria* (2007) 48 EHRR 175, para 35, was the first case to explain that reputation falls within 'private life' because reputation 'forms part of his or her personal identity and psychological integrity'. Earlier cases had recognized reputation as an aspect of private life, but without any explanation as to why this was so: see *Radio France v France* (2005) 40 EHRR 29, para 31; *Chauvy v France* (2005) 41 EHRR 610, para 70; and *Cumpana v Romania* (2005) 41 EHRR 41, para 91. Later cases have reiterated that reputation is connected to psychological integrity: see *Axel Springer AG v Germany* (2012) 55 EHRR 6, para 83; *Somesan v Romania* App no 45543/04 (ECtHR, 19 November 2013) paras 23, 29 and *Putistin v Ukraine* App no 16882/03 (ECtHR, 21 November 2013) para 32.

[62] *Karako v Hungary* (2011) 52 EHRR 36, para 23.

[63] *Axel Springer AG v Germany* (n 61) para 83.

[64] Cases that have applied a threshold test include: *Popovski v Former Yugoslav Republic of Macedonia* App no 12316/07 (ECtHR, 31 October 2013) para 88; *Pauliukiene v Lithuania* App no 18310/06 (ECtHR, 5 November 2013) para 44 and *Lavric v Romania* App no 22231/05 (ECtHR, 14 January 2014). Cases that have not obviously applied a threshold test include: *Somesan v Romania* (n 61); *Putistin v Ukraine* (n 61); and *Cârstea v Romania* App no 20531/06 (ECtHR, 28 October 2014). In *Re Guardian News and Media* [2010] 2 AC 697 [39]–[42] Lord Rodger struggled to reconcile *Karako* (n 62) with earlier Strasbourg decisions and to make sense of the threshold test.

threshold *is* applicable and that the seriousness of the attack on reputation acts as a proxy for assessing whether harm to private life has occurred.[65]

**3.24**  It is accepted that Member States 'may consider it necessary to resort to [search] measures in order to obtain physical evidence of certain offences'.[66] However, Article 8(2) will only be satisfied if the search measures taken were 'proportionate'. This means, first, that the 'relevant legislation and practice must afford adequate and effective safeguards against abuse'[67] and that the interference in question must have been proportionate to the aim pursued.[68]

**3.25**  Once the 'in accordance with the law' hurdle is cleared, states also enjoy a 'certain discretion' under Article 8(2) in determining the conditions under which any system of surveillance is to be operated.[69] The Court has accepted that surveillance is often 'necessary in a democratic society' for the prevention of crime and 'highly sophisticated forms of espionage and by terrorism'[70] but insists that a measure will only be 'necessary in a democratic society' if 'there exist adequate and effective guarantees against abuse'.[71]

**3.26**  *Category 2: The collection and disclosure of information*  The second category of private life cases concerns the right to be free from unwanted informational access. This aspect of the Article 8 right includes the unjustified collection and storage of information, the release of personal materials, and the interception of correspondence. In particular, the Court has held that it is a breach of Article 8(1) to collect information by surveilling a person's home, workplace, or prison cell;[72] to intercept or monitor mail or telecommunications;[73] or to seize an applicant's diaries or memoirs.[74]

**3.27**  Authorities can also breach Article 8(1) by storing information relating to an applicant's private life (including fingerprints, DNA profiles or cellular samples)[75] on a

---

[65] See T Aplin and J Bosland, 'The Uncertain Landscape of Article 8 of the ECHR: The Protection of Reputation as a Fundamental Human Right?' in A Kenyon (ed), *Comparative Defamation and Privacy Law* (Cambridge University Press) (forthcoming).

[66] *Buck v Germany* (n 55) para 45. In this case there was a breach of the right to 'home' and not 'private life' but the dicta appear to apply equally in both contexts.

[67] *Funke v France* (n 55) para 56. See also *Chappell v UK* (1989) 12 EHRR 1, paras 58–66 and *Buck v Germany* (n 55) paras 45–6.

[68] *Buck v Germany* (n 55) para 45.

[69] *Klass v Germany* (n 40) para 49. See also *Leander v Sweden* (n 43) para 59.

[70] *Klass v Germany* (n 40) para 48. See also *Leander v Sweden* (n 43) para 59.

[71] *Klass v Germany* (n 40) para 50. See also *Leander v Sweden* (n 43) para 60 and *Segerstedt-Wiberg v Sweden* (n 41) para 88.

[72] See 3.23 and nn 55, 56 and 59 respectively.

[73] See *Klass v Germany* (n 40) para 41; *Taylor-Sabori v UK* (2003) 36 EHRR 17, para 18 (the interception of pager messages); *PG and JH v UK* (n 31) para 42 (telephone 'metering'); *Copland v UK* (n 38) paras 41–2 (monitoring telephone and internet usage).

[74] See *Smith and Grady v UK* (1999) 29 EHRR 493 and *Yankov v Bulgaria* (2005) 40 EHRR 36.

[75] *S v UK* (2009) 48 EHRR 50, paras 73–5 and 84. '[T]he state's systematic collection and storage in retrievable form even of public information [such as presence at a public demonstration] about an individual is an interference with private life': see *R (Catt) v Commissioner of Police of the*

secret police register or national security file, using that information, and/or refusing to allow the applicant to refute it.[76] This systematic collection and storage of information will breach Article 8(1) even if the information in question is publicly available[77] and/or is not of a particularly sensitive or personal nature.[78]

The dissemination of information about a person (such as images of the person[79] or transcripts of his or her telephone conversations)[80] is also a breach of Article 8(1) that needs to be justified under Article 8(2). **3.28**

*Category 3: Protection of one's living environment* The right to live free from serious environmental pollution—the third aspect of the right to respect for private life—does not fit neatly into traditional concepts of 'privacy' nor with other aspects of the 'private-life' interest protected under Article 8. Although there is no explicit right in the Convention to a clean and quiet environment,[81] the Court has acknowledged that: **3.29**

> ...severe environmental pollution may affect individuals' well-being and prevent them from enjoying their homes in such a way as to affect their private and family life adversely, without, however, seriously endangering their health.[82]

Member States have therefore breached their obligations under Article 8 by failing to prevent a waste treatment plant (which was operating without a licence) from causing noise pollution and emitting toxic fumes in a residential area,[83] failing to provide information about the risks associated with the operation of a local chemical factory,[84] failing to prevent private bar and club operators from causing noise pollution in a residential area,[85] and failing to enforce a domestic judgment annulling a permit which authorized the use of hazardous substances in a gold-mining operation.[86] **3.30**

*Category 4: Identity* The Court has consistently recognized that 'aspects of an individual's physical and social identity'[87] and the 'right to identity and personal development'[88] are protected by the right to respect for private life. A number of **3.31**

---

*Metropolis* [2015] UKSC 9, [2015] AC 1065 [6] (per Lord Sumption with whom Lord Neuberger agreed). See also Lady Hale [47], Lord Mance [58] and Lord Toulson [60].

[76] *Leander v Sweden* (n 43) para 48 and *Rotaru v Romania* (n 32) para 46.

[77] *Rotaru v Romania* (n 32) paras 42–4 and *Segerstedt-Wiberg v Sweden* (n 41) paras 72–3.

[78] *Amann v Switzerland* (n 32) para 70.

[79] See 3.23 and n 60.

[80] *Craxi v Italy (No 2)* (2004) 38 EHRR 47, paras 60–84.

[81] See *Hatton v UK* (n 48) para 96 and *Kyrtatos v Greece* (2005) 40 EHRR 16, para 52.

[82] *Lopez Ostra v Spain* (n 47) para 51. See also, *Guerra v Italy* (n 46) para 60; *Hatton v UK* (n 48) para 96; and *Taşkin v Turkey* (n 46) para 113.

[83] *Lopez Ostra v Spain* (n 47) paras 44–58.

[84] *Guerra v Italy* (n 46) paras 56–60.

[85] *Moreno Gómez v Spain* (2005) 41 EHRR 40, paras 53–63. However, compare *Kyrtatos v Greece* (n 81) para 54.

[86] *Taşkin v Turkey* (n 46) paras 111–26.

[87] See *Pretty v UK* (n 31) para 61 and *Van Kück v Germany* (n 45) para 69.

[88] *Bensaid v UK* (2001) 33 EHRR 10, para 47. See also *Odievre v France* (2004) 38 EHRR 43, para 29 and *Peck v UK* (n 31) para 57.

interests fall within this category. These include the right to information about one's parents and early development,[89] which includes an obligation to resolve paternity disputes efficiently and accurately so as to avoid 'prolonged uncertainty' as to 'personal identity' on the part of children.[90] Indignity associated with the type of social or medical care that is provided by the state to those who are physically incapacitated has been treated as conflicting with ideas of self and personal identity.[91] Reputation has also been held to form part of a person's 'personal identity' (as well as his or her 'psychological integrity')[92] and professional activities that impact on the construction of one's social identity may also fall within 'private life'.[93]

**3.32**   Recognition of one's sexual and cultural identity is also part of an applicant's private life. The Court has held that Member States have an obligation to recognize the new gender of post-operative transsexuals[94] and to facilitate, at least to some extent, the pursuit of a traditional traveller lifestyle.[95] The Court has held that a surname is an important part of an individual's personal identity and that rules requiring married women to change it[96] or preventing married men from changing it can breach Article 8.[97]

**3.33**   *Category 5: Personal autonomy*   The final aspect of the right to respect for private life is the right to live autonomously. The Court recognizes that '[t]he very essence of the Convention is respect for human dignity and human freedom'[98] and that 'the notion of personal autonomy is an important principle underlying the interpretation of its guarantees'.[99] All interferences with private life will affect autonomy to some extent, but autonomy and human freedom are central to cases concerning the right to develop sexual and familial relationships and to exercise control over one's health and medical treatment.

---

[89] *Gaskin v UK* (n 48) para 36. See also *MG v UK* (2003) 36 EHRR 3, paras 27–8; *Shofman v Russia* (2007) 44 EHRR 35; and *Znamenskaya v Russia* (2007) 44 EHRR 15. Although compare *Odievre v France* (n 88) and *Kroon v Netherlands* (1995) 19 EHRR 263, para 40.

[90] *Mikulić v Croatia* App no 53176/99 (ECtHR, 7 February 2002) paras 56–66.

[91] *McDonald v UK* App no 4241/12 (ECtHR, 20 May 2014).

[92] See *Pfeifer v Austria* (n 61) para 35, and 3.36.

[93] *Martínez v Spain* [2014] ELR 467, para 110.

[94] *I v UK* (2003) 36 EHRR 53, para 57 and *Goodwin v UK* (n 37) paras 77 and 89–93. See also *B v France* (1992) 16 EHRR 1; *Grant v UK* (2007) 44 EHRR 1 and *Van Kück v Germany* (n 45) paras 78–84. Because being able to express one's identity (*eg*, as a homosexual, a traveller or a post-operative transsexual) often depends on one's ability to live one's life in a manner of one's choosing, these interests also overlap with the right to live autonomously which will be discussed in the next section.

[95] See *Connors v UK* (2005) 40 EHRR 9, para 84 and *Chapman v UK* (2001) 33 EHRR 18, para 73.

[96] *Unal Tekeli v Turkey* (2006) 42 EHRR 53.

[97] *Burghartz v Switzerland* (1994) 18 EHRR 101.

[98] *Pretty v UK* (n 31) para 65.

[99] *Goodwin v UK* (n 37) para 90 and *I v UK* (n 94) para 70. See also *Pretty v UK* (n 31) para 61 and *Van Kück v Germany* (n 45) para 69.

*Autonomy in relationships*  The Convention right to respect for private life includes **3.34** 'the right to establish and to develop relationships with other human beings, especially in the emotional field for the development and fulfilment of one's own personality'.[100] This right includes the right to engage in homosexual activities.[101] In the familial context, deportation measures which disrupt familial and other relationships can also breach the right to respect for private life[102] (although they are usually dealt with under the Article 8 right to respect for family life).[103] The right to end spousal relationships also enjoys some protection under Article 8.[104]

*Medical autonomy*  The right to private life has also been breached where appli- **3.35** cants have been forced to undergo medical procedures[105] or where they have unsuccessfully sought information about health risks to which they have been exposed.[106] Applicants have also argued, with limited success, that it is a breach of Article 8 to deny access to certain medical procedures. First, the Court has held that private life 'incorporates the right to respect for both the decisions to become and not to become a parent'.[107] However, the United Kingdom was held not to have breached its positive obligations by adopting an absolute rule that either party to IVF treatment could withdraw consent up to the point at which the embryos were implanted[108] or by denying a woman, whose husband was in prison for murder, access to artificial insemination facilities.[109]

In *Brüggeman and Scheuten v Germany*, the European Commission of Human Rights **3.36** also rejected the argument that restrictions on the circumstances in which the applicants could abort unwanted pregnancies after twelve weeks interfered with their private lives.[110] In *Pretty v UK*, the Court held that it was 'not prepared to exclude' the possibility that sanctions preventing the applicant from choosing to avoid what she considered 'an undignified and distressing end to her life' were an interference with Article 8(1).[111]

---

[100]  *X v Iceland* (n 30) 87. See also *Botta v Italy* (1998) 26 EHRR 241, para 32; *Rotaru v Romania* (n 32) para 43; *Pretty v UK* (n 31) para 61; *Peck v UK* (n 31) para 57; *Niemietz v Germany* (n 31) para 29.

[101]  See *eg Dudgeon v UK* (n 42) paras 40–1; *ADT v UK* (2001) 31 EHRR 33; *Norris v Ireland* (1989) 13 EHRR 186; *Modinos v Cyprus* (1993) 16 EHRR 485; *BB v UK* (2004) 39 EHRR 30.

[102]  *Slivenko v Latvia* (2004) 39 EHRR 24, paras 96–7. See also *Jakupovic v Austria* (2004) 38 EHRR 27, paras 18–33 and *Radovanovic v Austria* (2005) 41 EHRR 6, para 28 (the deportation of family members was held to be a breach of both 'private life' and 'family life').

[103]  See *eg Mokrani v France* (2005) 40 EHRR 5; *Yildiz v Austria* (2003) 36 EHRR 32; and *Yilmaz v Germany* (2004) 38 EHRR 23.

[104]  A refusal to grant legal aid for judicial separation proceedings was held to contravene the positive obligation to make available the means of separating from one's husband: see *Airey v Ireland* (n 45) paras 32–3.

[105]  See 3.23 and n 53.

[106]  *McGinley and Egan v UK* (n 45) para 101 and *Roche v UK* (2006) 42 EHRR 30, para 162.

[107]  *Evans v UK* (2008) 46 EHRR 34, para 71.

[108]  *Evans* (n 107) paras 83–92.

[109]  *Dickson v UK* (2007) 44 EHRR 21, paras 26–40.

[110]  (1981) 3 EHRR 244. The applicants claimed that the restrictions compelled them to renounce sexual intercourse, apply methods of contraception, or carry out a pregnancy against their will: para 50.

[111]  *Pretty v UK* (n 31) para 67.

The sanctions were, however, held to be necessary in a democratic society for the protection of others.

### (b) Article 8 in English private law

**3.37** The impact of Article 8 on English private law has been significant. The rights contained in the ECHR—including the Article 8 right to respect for private life—were incorporated into English domestic law on 2 October 2000 via the HRA. Even in the lead-up to its enactment, there was considerable debate about whether and how the Act would have 'horizontal effect'; in other words, whether (and if so how) it would apply to disputes between citizens, as opposed to disputes between citizens and the state.[112] The Act was not intended to have a general direct horizontal effect,[113] which means that it was not intended to impose 'duties directly upon a private body to abide by its provisions' and to make breach of such duties directly actionable.[114] But s 2 HRA requires the courts to 'have regard' to the jurisprudence of the Strasbourg Court when applying domestic law, and s 6 provides that it is 'unlawful for a public authority to act in a way which is incompatible with a Convention right', s 6(3) making it absolutely clear that the courts are public authorities for these purposes. The combined effect of these provisions is that the HRA can have an impact on disputes between citizens.

**3.38** Nowhere has the 'horizontal effect' of the Act been felt more keenly than in the development of the law of breach of confidence, the principal vehicle through which privacy has been protected in English law.[115] At common law, there was no free-standing right to privacy, and no cause of action that could be employed to vindicate privacy-type rights.[116] There was, however, an action in breach of confidence that could be used to protect, for example, information obtained in the course of a confidential relationship (whether business or domestic). As discussed in Chapter 5, that action was progressively expanded and in *Campbell v MGN Ltd* the House of Lords held that a new action had emerged from within it.[117] That new

---

[112] Sir William Wade QC, 'Horizons of Horizontality' (2000) 16 LQR 217; G Phillipson, 'The Human Rights Act, "Horizontal Effect" and the Common Law: A Bang or a Whimper?' (1999) 62 MLR 824; M Hunt, 'The "Horizontal Effect" of the Human Rights Act' [1998] Public Law 423.

[113] See Sir Richard Buxton, 'The Human Rights Act and Private Law' (2000) 116 LQR 48, citing at n 36 a statement from the speech of the Lord Chancellor, Lord Irvine, to that effect. Although compare Wade (n 112).

[114] Phillipson (n 112) 826.

[115] See D Feldman in D Feldman (ed), *English Public Law* (2nd edn, Oxford University Press 2009) 847. Indeed, Feldman goes so far as to say that breach of confidence is 'the only area in which the Convention rights appear to have had this sort of influence'. See also J Wright, 'A Damp Squib? The impact of section 6 HRA on the common law: horizontal effect and beyond' [2014] Public Law 289, 294: 'With the exception of the development of privacy of information and (to a lesser extent) defamation, the HRA itself has had remarkably little influence on the development of private common law.'

[116] *Wainwright v Home Office* [2003] UKHL 53, [2004] 2 AC 406. See also ch 1.

[117] [2004] UKHL 22, [2004] 2 AC 457. See also the significant decisions of *Douglas v Hello! Ltd* [2001] QB 967 and *A v B plc* [2002] EWCA Civ 337, [2003] QB 195 [11] and discussion at 5.02 *et seq.*

action—misuse of private information—required examination of the comparative importance of Convention rights (Article 8 (private life) and Article 10 (freedom of expression)), analysis of the justifications for interfering with these rights, and then an application of the proportionality test to each.[118] This 'balancing exercise', which has been applied in numerous decisions since,[119] is 'treated as analogous to the exercise of a discretion'[120] and encapsulates the essence of the misuse of private information tort.[121] Thus, while *Campbell* did not explicitly resolve the debate concerning horizontal effect, the House of Lords clearly applied 'some sort of indirect horizontal effect for Art 8'.[122]

As indicated above, the precise nature of the 'indirect' horizontal effect of the **3.39** HRA has been controversial. Opinions have ranged across the spectrum from 'full indirect' horizontal effect (meaning that courts are obliged to create new causes of action between private individuals to give effect to their Convention rights),[123] to 'strong' indirect horizontal effect,[124] to 'weak' indirect horizontal effect,[125] to no horizontal effect at all.[126] The *Campbell* decision dismisses the extreme positions, with Baroness Hale remarking that '[t]he [Act] does not create any new cause of action between private persons'[127] and the House obviously recognizing some kind of indirect horizontal effect. But questions still remain about whether courts are obliged to develop common law compatibly with Convention rights and if so, in what circumstances.[128]

---

[118] *Campbell* (n 117) [141] where Baroness Hale stated that the parties agreed with this approach, as set out in *Re S (A Child(* [2003] EWCA Civ 963, [2004] Fam 43 [54]–[60]. In *Re S (A Child)* [2004] UKHL 47, [2005] 1 AC 593 [17] Lord Steyn (with whom the other members of the House agreed) approved of this approach.

[119] See *eg McKennitt v Ash* [2006] EWCA Civ 1714, [2008] QB 73 and *Lord Browne of Madingly v Associated Newspapers Ltd* [2007] EWCA Civ 295, [2008] QB 103.

[120] *AAA v Associated Newspapers Ltd* [2013] EWCA Civ 554 [8].

[121] See *Google Inc v Vidal-Hall* [2015] EWCA Civ 311, [2015] 3 WLR 409 [21], [43] recognizing that the tort of misuse of private information was distinct from equitable breach of confidence, where this had particular relevance to the rules relating to service out of the jurisdiction.

[122] J Morgan, 'Privacy in the House of Lords, Again' (2004) 120 LQR 563, 565.

[123] Wade (n 112). See also J Morgan, 'Questioning the "True Effect" of the Human Rights Act' (2002) 22 LS 259; and D Beyleveld and S Pattinson, 'Horizontal Applicability and Horizontal Effect' (2002) 118 LQR 623.

[124] *ie* a duty to interpret and apply existing law so as to achieve compatibility: see Hunt (n 112).

[125] *ie* courts must take account of Convention values in their common law adjudication: see Phillipson (n 112).

[126] Buxton (n 113).

[127] *Campbell* (n 117) [132].

[128] The position may well be that, 'courts must develop the common law compatibly with the Convention, but only where such development can be achieved by "incremental" development' as argued in G Phillipson and A Williams, 'Horizontal Effect and the Constitutional Constraint' (2011) 74 MLR 878, 878–9. But contrast Wright (n 115) 295 who argues that where a cause of action (such as defamation) engages Convention rights 'the court must act compatibly with those rights', but 'if a cause of action does not exist, there can be no *requirement* to develop the common law, for the simple reason that ECHR rights are exigible against the state and ECHR jurisprudence consistently refrains from directing states regarding which arm of the state is require to provide the remedy'.

## (4) Other Instruments of the Council of Europe

**3.40**  On 23 January 1970 the Consultative Assembly of the Council of Europe adopted a resolution containing a declaration on mass communication media and human rights, in which privacy was defined as follows:

> The right to privacy consists essentially in the right to live one's own life with a minimum of interference. It concerns private, family and home life, physical and moral integrity, honour and reputation, avoidance of being placed in a false light, non-revelation of irrelevant and embarrassing facts, unauthorised publication of private photographs, protection against unjustifiable or unreasonable spying and prying, protection against misuse of private communications, protection from disclosure of information given or received by the individual confidentially.[129]

Paragraph C7 of the Resolution provides:

> ...The right to privacy afforded by Article 8 of the Convention on Human Rights should not only protect an individual against interference by public authorities, but also against interference by private persons or institutions, including the mass media.[130]

**3.41**  A more detailed resolution on the right to privacy was adopted by the Consultative Assembly in 1998 in the aftermath of the death of Diana, Princess of Wales. Resolution 1165 (1998)[131] calls on Member States to adopt various measures including passing legislation to enable victims to claim compensation for invasion of privacy, and to render editors, journalists, and photographers liable for invasions of privacy for which they are responsible. The United Kingdom might be regarded as having complied with this requirement by the passing of the HRA which received royal assent in the same year that the resolution was passed. The general standards set out in the resolution have been cited with approval in domestic decisions.[132]

**3.42**  Other Council of Europe instruments contain specific provisions relating to privacy and the media in certain contexts. For example Recommendation (2003) 13 on the provision of information through the media in relation to criminal proceedings contains the following principle at point 8:

> *Protection of privacy in the context of on-going criminal proceedings*
> The provision of information about suspects, accused or convicted persons or other parties to criminal proceedings should respect their right to protection of privacy in accordance with Article 8 of the Convention. Particular protection should be

---

[129] Resolution 428 (1970), para C2, available at <http://assembly.coe.int/nw/xml/XRef/Xref-XML2HTML-EN.asp?fileid=15842&lang=en>.

[130] A provision repeated in Resolution 1165 adopted by the Assembly on 26 June 1998 (24th sitting), para 12.

[131] Available at <http://semantic-pace.net/?search=KjoqfGNvcnBlc19uYW1lX2VuOiJPZmZpZY2lhbCBkb2N1bWVudHMi&lang=en>.

[132] See *eg A v B plc* (n 117) [11(xii)] where Lord Woolf described paras 6–12 of the resolution as providing 'useful guidance of a general nature' on the 'difficult issue of finding the right balance' between privacy and freedom of expression.

given to parties who are minors or other vulnerable persons, as well as to victims, to witnesses and to families of suspects, accused and convicted. In all cases, particular consideration should be given to the harmful effect which the disclosure of information enabling their identification may have on the persons referred to in this Principle.

# C. Privacy in Other Common Law (and Mixed) Jurisdictions

Privacy protection in foreign common law jurisdictions forms an important part of the context in which English privacy developments are occurring. Relevant developments will be discussed throughout the chapters of this book. This section is designed to provide brief overviews of the scope of privacy protection in the United States, Ireland, New Zealand, Australia, Canada, and South Africa. **3.43**

## (1) United States

### (a) Introduction

Nearly 125 years ago,[133] Boston lawyers Samuel Warren and Louis Brandeis, in their pioneering Harvard Law Review article, called for creation of a free-standing common law right of privacy.[134] Courts responded, and by the early 1900s privacy law was born in America.[135] **3.44**

As developed over the last century, and now set forth in the *Restatement (Second) of Torts*,[136] privacy law in America has crystallized into four distinct and well-recognized torts: (1) publication of intimate private facts; (2) unwarranted intrusion upon seclusion; (3) false light (a relative of defamation); and (4) commercial misappropriation of name or likeness (also called the right of publicity).[137] Of these four torts, it is the first two—the 'private facts' claim and the 'intrusion upon seclusion' claim—that most resemble the privacy right that has more recently developed under English law and jurisprudence from the ECtHR. It is these two privacy torts that will be discussed in greatest detail in this chapter. **3.45**

---

[133] This section was written by Chloe Strong of 5RB, Gray's Inn, London and Robert Balin of Davis Wright Tremaine LLP in New York.

[134] S Warren and L Brandeis, 'The Right to Privacy' (1890–91) 4 Harvard L Rev 193.

[135] *Pavesich v New England Life Ins Co*, 50 SE 68 (Ga 1905) is often cited as the first American decision to expressly recognize a right of privacy by that name, though the Georgia Supreme Court cited even earlier decisions by American courts that—if not using the 'right of privacy' moniker—nonetheless extended protection to privacy interests.

[136] Restatement (Second) of Torts (1977), vol 3, adopted by the American Law Institute. The Restatements of the Law are a set of treatises on legal subjects that, while not binding, seek to inform judges and lawyers about general common law principles in the US.

[137] Restatement (n 136) § 652A–652E.

**3.46**   Unlike Article 8 ECHR, the US Constitution does not establish a 'privacy' right that may be invoked by privacy claimants in civil tort litigation.[138] Instead, in America, privacy torts are created by state law—either state common law or state statutes or, in some cases, by state constitutions. This fact highlights two important aspects of privacy law in America.

**3.47**   First, not all of the 50 US states recognize all four privacy torts (or define them identically); and, as a result, privacy protection may vary from state to state. For example, New York (historic home of America's publishing industry) recognizes only a statutory claim for non-consensual use of a person's name or likeness for advertising or trade (NY Civil Rights Law § 50–51), and New York courts have repeatedly held that other than this narrow statutory prohibition there is no common law right of privacy in New York.[139] In contrast, California (the home of America's entertainment industry, where many celebrities reside) recognizes all four privacy torts and, not surprisingly, provides strong protection to privacy rights.[140] Thus, in America, the location where an alleged breach of privacy takes place may well determine whether a claimant has a viable claim.[141] Second, and equally important, because privacy torts in America are created by state law and have no federal constitutional pedigree, they are necessarily subordinate to the First Amendment to the US Constitution, which guarantees freedom of speech and of the press.[142] As discussed further on in this section, First Amendment protections for news

---

[138] The US Supreme Court has recognized that certain provisions of the federal Constitution do implicitly create a penumbra of 'privacy' rights in relation to governmental conduct—*eg*, restrictions on a woman's reproductive and contraceptive decisions, or unreasonable searches and seizures in the home, *eg Griswold v Connecticut*, 381 US 479, 484 (1965) (Douglas J). But American courts have consistently observed that this federal constitutional right of privacy applies only to government intrusion, and may not be invoked by tort claimants in invasion of privacy litigation against the press or other private-party defendants, eg *Polin v Dun & Bradstreet, Inc,* 768 F2d 1204, 1207 (10th Cir 1985); *Rosenberg v Martin*, 478 F2d 520, 524 (2d Cir 1973); *Hall v Post*, 323 NC 259, 262, 372 SE 2d 711, 713 (NC 1988). Also J McCarthy, *The Rights of Publicity and Privacy* (Clark Boardman Callaghan 2014) § 5:56, 523–8 (citing cases).

[139] *Messenger v Gruner and Jahr Printing and Publ'g*, 94 NY2d 436, 441 (2000). Also *Cain v Hearst Corp*, 878 SW 2d 577, 578 (Tex 1994) (recognizing the torts of 'intrusion upon seclusion' and 'publicity given to private facts', but declining to recognize a 'false light' tort).

[140] 5 Witkin, Summary of Cal Law Torts (9th edn 1988) 674–93, § 580–94. For other state examples see McCarthy (n 138) § 1:24, 43 n 2 (listing states that recognize all four privacy torts).

[141] As of 2013, forty-one states in America have recognized the 'private facts' tort, and four have rejected the doctrine; forty-two states have recognized the 'intrusion upon seclusion' tort, while two have rejected it; forty-four states have recognized a 'commercial misappropriation/right of publicity' claim, and six states have not had the opportunity to rule on the issue; and thirty-four states have recognized the 'false light' privacy tort, and ten have rejected it. R Trager, J Russomanno, S Dente Ross, A Reynolds, *The Law of Journalism and Mass Communication* (4th edn, CQ Press College 2014) 237. In this regard, while many cases discussed in this chapter come from Californian courts, those decisions should not be taken as representing the protection offered to privacy rights across the United States.

[142] Under American principles of federalism, the provisions of the federal US constitution (including the First Amendment) are accorded supremacy over state law, regardless of whether that state law is created by common law, statute, or state constitution. See US Constitution, Art 6, cl 2 ('Supremacy Clause').

reporting on matters of public concern play an important role in defining and limiting privacy claims in America.

**Generally only living individuals may sue**    Privacy is generally considered a per-    **3.48** sonal right in American jurisprudence. Accordingly, only a living individual may assert a claim for publication of intimate private facts, intrusion upon seclusion, or false light. In most states, estates may not bring these privacy claims on behalf of the dead. Similarly, since companies, associations, unions, and other groups do not have personal rights, they too are typically barred in most states from bringing any of these three privacy claims. In many states commercial misappropriation (or right of publicity) claims are also limited to living individuals, though some states do permit commercial misappropriation claims to be brought by estates, businesses, and other organizations.[143]

### (b) Publication of intimate private facts

**Nature and scope of the wrong**    While the formulation of a 'private facts' claim    **3.49** may vary slightly from state to state, generally a defendant who publishes truthful private facts about a person will be held liable if revelation of those facts would be 'highly offensive to a reasonable person' and 'is not of legitimate concern to the public'.[144] The private facts tort is designed to protect against revelations of personal information so intimate and so unwarranted as to outrage the community's notions of decency.[145]

**Extent of publication**    Actionable 'publication' of private facts requires 'communi-    **3.50** cation to the public at large'.[146] For example, in *Grinenko v Olympic Panel Products*, an employer's disclosure of details regarding an employee's sexual assault to two of the employee's colleagues was deemed not to constitute 'publication' within the meaning of the tort.[147] By contrast, dissemination of intimate facts in mass media or on-line to the world at large will almost certainly constitute publication.

**Reasonable expectation of privacy**    As its name connotes, the private facts    **3.51** tort also requires that the facts publicized by the defendant be truly 'private, secluded, or secret'[148] such that there can be said to be a reasonable expectation

---

[143] Restatement (n 136) § 652I ('Except for the appropriation of one's name or likeness, an action for invasion of privacy can be maintained only by a living individual whose privacy is invaded') and cmts a–c; Trager et al (n 141) 237.

[144] Restatement (n 136) § 652D ('One who gives publicity to a matter concerning the private life of another is subject to liability to the other for invasion of privacy if the matter publicized is of a kind that (a) would be highly offensive to a reasonable person and (b) is not of legitimate concern to the public').

[145] *Sidis v F-R Pub Corp*, 113 F2d 806, 809 (2d Cir 1940), *cert denied*, 311 US 711 (1940).

[146] *Grinenko v Olympic Panel Prods*, 2008 WL 5204743, at 7 (WD Wash Dec 11, 2008).

[147] *Grinenko* (n 146); *Roe v Heap*, 2004-Ohio-2504, para 60 (Ohio Ct App) (sending email containing private facts regarding a boy to a handful of diving club officials deemed insufficient to constitute 'public disclosure').

[148] *Ramsey v Georgia Gazette Pub Co*, 164 Ga App 693, 695 (Ga Ct App 1982).

of privacy with respect to them. Private facts have been held to include intimate medical information,[149] details about sexual relations[150] as well as concealed information regarding a person's change of sexual identity.[151] Even the fact that a woman had cosmetic plastic surgery was held by one court to be private where she kept the surgery secret, telling only her family and very intimate friends.[152] In contrast, information that is already available to the public will not be protected as a private fact, nor does an individual have a reasonable expectation of privacy in respect of matters that are 'plainly visible' to members of the public.[153]

**3.52** *Information in public records*  Publication of intimate facts contained in open court proceedings and public records will not give rise to a private facts claim. This is not only because there is no reasonable expectation of privacy in that which has already been revealed, but also because of First Amendment protections for news reporting on judicial and governmental proceedings. The US Supreme Court has repeatedly held that, under the First Amendment, 'if a newspaper lawfully obtains truthful information about a matter of public significance then state officials may not constitutionally punish publication of the information, absent a need...of the highest order'.[154] Applying this principle, in *Cox Broadcasting Corp v Cohn*,[155] the Supreme Court ruled that the First Amendment barred a private facts claim arising from publication of the name of a seventeen-year-old rape/murder victim obtained from a publicly-available indictment since the information was 'open to public inspection'.[156] Following

---

[149] Restatement (n136) § 652D cmt b (listing as private facts 'many unpleasant or disgraceful or humiliating illnesses'); *White v Twp of Winthrop*, 128 Wash App 588, 594 (2005) (holding it to be a jury question whether plaintiff's seizure disorder constituted a humiliating illness 'one would not wish announced in the newspaper').

[150] Restatement (n 136) § 652D cmt b ('Sexual relations, for example, are normally entirely private matters').

[151] *Diaz v Oakland Tribune Inc*, 139 Cal App 3d 118, 132, 188 Cal Rptr 762 (1983) (plaintiff's sex change was a private (and therefore protectable) fact, where the plaintiff took positive steps to conceal her sex change, including changing her name, driver's licence, school records, and social security records).

[152] *Vassiliades v Garfinckel's, Brooks Bros*, 492 A 2d 580, 588 (DC 1985). However, obvious cosmetic surgery would not be deemed private: *Sandler v Calcagni*, 565 F Supp2d 184, 198 (D Me 2008), in which the Court held that information published about the plaintiff's plastic surgery was not private because 'cosmetic surgery on one's face is by its nature exposed to the public eye'.

[153] *eg*, in *Jaubert v Crowley Post-Signal, Inc*, 375 So 2d 1386, 1391 (La 1979), the Court held that a newspaper's publication of photographs showing the exterior of the plaintiff's unkempt home was not actionable as a disclosure of private facts because the home was plainly visible from the public street. Also *Moreno v Hanford Sentinel, Inc*, 172 Cal App 4th 1125, 1130, 91 Cal Rptr 3d 858, 862 (2009), in which facts published by a local newspaper were not deemed to be private since the plaintiff had originally posted those facts on a social networking site.

[154] *Smith v Daily Mail Publ'g Co*, 443 US 97, 103 (1979). Also *Bartnicki v Vopper*, 532 US 514, 528 (2001).

[155] 420 US 469 (1975).

[156] *Cox* (n 155) 496 ('the First and Fourteenth Amendments will not allow exposing the press to liability for truthfully publishing information released to the public in official court records'). Also *Florida Star v BJF*, 491 US 524 (1989) (even though state statute prohibited reporting the names of rape victims, the First Amendment barred a negligence claim against the newspaper for publishing

*Cox*, lower courts have consistently held that '[t]he First Amendment[]...do[es] not permit the [defendant] to be held liable in damages for accurately publishing a document contained in a court record open to the public'.[157]

**Newsworthiness** Since lack of a legitimate public interest is a required element of **3.53** the private facts tort, US courts have repeatedly held that where the published private facts relate to a matter of legitimate public concern (or, in American parlance, are 'newsworthy'), this serves as 'a complete bar to liability'.[158] Moreover, this bar to liability for publication of newsworthy truthful information is not only a common law limitation, but is compelled by First Amendment principles as well.[159]

While English law also takes into consideration whether publication of private **3.54** facts furthers a legitimate public interest, the relative weight that English and US courts accord to free expression rights in privacy litigation highlights a fundamental distinction between the two countries' approaches to such claims; a difference that flows in part from their different constitutional charters.

*Newsworthiness bars private facts claims* Under the ECHR, both the right to pri- **3.55** vate life (Article 8) and freedom of expression (Article 10) are recognized as fundamental rights. Neither right has priority over the other, and both rights must be balanced in determining the outcome of English privacy claims.[160]

In contrast, while long protected under American common law, privacy simply **3.56** does not have the same constitutionally-protected status as does free speech under the First Amendment. As a result, if an American court finds that publication of

---

the name of a rape victim disclosed in a police report made available by the sheriff's department to a reporter).

[157] *Uranga v Federated Publ'ns, Inc*, 138 Idaho 550, 556, 67 P3d 29 (2003), *cert denied*, 540 US 940 (2003). Also *Green v CBS Inc*, 286 F3d 281 (5th Cir 2002) a case in which a mother, who claimed during court proceedings that her husband had sexually abused their daughter, sued the defendants for publicizing the allegations in a television programme. The court affirmed dismissal of the private facts claim on the grounds that (1) the sexual abuse allegations were stated in open court, (2) no court order was sought to protect the child's anonymity, and (3) the daughter's name and likeness were a matter of public record and therefore not private.

[158] *Shulman v Group W Prods, Inc*, 18 Cal 4th 200, 215, 74 Cal Rptr 2d 843 (1998). Indeed, in their article inviting adoption of a common law right of privacy, Warren and Brandeis ((n 134) 214) noted as their very first limiting principle that '[t]he right to privacy does not prohibit any publication of matter which is of public or general interest'. Also Restatement (n 136) § 652B, cmt d ('The common law has long recognized that the public has a proper interest in learning about many matters. When the subject matter of the publicity is of legitimate public concern, there is no invasion of privacy').

[159] Restatement (n 136) § 652D, cmt d (newsworthiness bar to private facts claim 'has now become a rule not just of the common law of torts, but of the Federal Constitution as well') (citing *Cox* (n 155)); *Prince v Out Publishing, Inc*, No. B140475, 2002 WL 7999, at 8, 30 Media L Rep 1269 (Cal Ct App, Jan 3, 2002) ('newsworthiness is a constitutional defence to, or privilege against, liability for publication of truthful [private] information'); *Virgil v Time, Inc*, 527 F2d 1122, 1129 (9th Cir 1975) (newsworthiness defence 'is one of constitutional dimension delimiting the scope of the tort'), *cert denied*, 425 US 998 (1976).

[160] *Re S (A Child)* [2004] UKHL 47, [2005] 1 AC 593 [17]; *Ferdinand v MGN Ltd* [2011] EWHC 2454 (QB) [61].

private facts relates to a matter of legitimate public concern (*ie* is newsworthy), that serves as a First Amendment (as well as a common law) privilege mandating dismissal of the privacy claim.[161] In other words, 'under the federal Constitution [in America] newsworthiness is a complete bar to liability, rather than merely an interest to be balanced against private…interests'.[162]

**3.57**  *Broad definition of newsworthiness*  Newsworthiness in the United States is not limited to 'news' in the narrow sense of just reports of current events involving issues of public debate. 'It also extends to the use of names, likenesses or facts in giving information to the public for [the] purposes of education, amusement, or enlightenment, when the public may reasonably be expected to have a legitimate interest in what is published.'[163] Thus 'the constitutional guarantees of freedom of expression apply with equal force to the publication whether it be a news report or an entertainment feature'.[164]

**3.58**  American courts also typically give 'considerable deference' to the editorial judgments of reporters and editors.[165] US courts require that, for the newsworthiness privilege to apply, there must be a 'logical nexus' between publication of the private facts at issue and a matter of legitimate public concern.[166] But, sensitive to the need to avoid unconstitutional interference with editorial judgment, American courts have frequently stated that 'it is not for a court or a jury to say how a particular story is best covered'.[167]

---

[161]  *eg, Nobles v Cartwright,* 659 NE2d 1064, 1075 (Ind Ct App 1995), in which it was said that '[i]f a matter is determined to be of legitimate public interest, the disclosure or publication of information about that matter is said to be privileged under the First Amendment'; *Prince,* 2002 WL 7999, at 9: '[t]he newsworthiness defence applies to bar plaintiff's cause of action for invasion of privacy based on publication of private facts'.

[162]  *Shulman* (n 158) 227.

[163]  Restatement (n 136) § 652D cmt j.

[164]  *Gill v Hearst Publ'g Co,* 40 Cal 2d 224, 229, 253 P2d 441 (1953), in which the Court held there to be no privacy claim arising from a magazine photo showing a couple embracing at the Los Angeles Farmers' Market.

[165]  *Shulman* (n 158) 224.

[166]  *Shulman* (n 158) 224. Also *Cinel v Connick,* 15 F3d 1338, 1346 (5th Cir 1994) ('substantially related'); *Ross v Midwest Commc'ns, Inc,* 870 F2d 271, 274 (5th Cir 1989) ('logical nexus'); *Gilbert v Medical Econ Co,* 665 F2d 305, 308 (10th Cir 1981) ('substantial relevance'); *Haynes v Alfred A Knopf, Inc,* 8 F3d 1222, 1233 (7th Cir 1993) (facts 'germane' to story). In *Bonome v Kaysen,* 17 Mass L Rep 695, 32 Media L Rep 1520 (Mass Super Ct 2004), for example, the defendant was the well-known author of the autobiographical book, *Girl, Interrupted* (on which a film was also based). In another autobiographical book she described intimate details of her sexual relationship with the plaintiff. Although his name and other identifying features were changed, he was clearly still recognizable to his family and friends. The court dismissed the private facts claim on the basis that, although the details fell 'squarely within the sphere of private life' and the defendant was portrayed in a highly offensive light, the plaintiff nonetheless had a First Amendment right to tell her own story and her sexual relationship with the plaintiff was logically connected to her story.

[167]  *Shulman* (n 158) 225. Also *Howard v Des Moines Register & Tribune Co,* 283 NW 2d 289, 302 (Iowa 1979): 'In determining whether an item is newsworthy courts cannot impose their own views about what should interest the public'; *Heath v Playboy Enters,* 732 FSupp 1145, 1149, n 9 (SD Fla 1990): '[T]he judgment of what is newsworthy is primarily a function of the publisher, not the courts'; *Glickman v Stern,* 19 Media L Rep 1769, 1776 (Sup Ct NY C'ty 1991): 'It is well-settled that

Nonetheless, 'newsworthiness' is not simply that which sells newspapers, and **3.59** American courts often 'struggle' to define the circumstances under which the newsworthiness privilege applies.[168] California courts, for example, have developed a three-part test to determine newsworthiness, which examines: (1) the social value of the private facts published, (2) the depth of the intrusion into alleged private facts, and (3) the extent to which the plaintiff has voluntarily consented to a position of public notoriety (*ie* is a voluntary public figure).[169] 'Where the publicity is so offensive as to constitute a morbid and sensational prying into private lives for its own sake, it serves no legitimate public interest and is not deserving of protection.'[170]

*Public figures*  The plaintiff's degree of public prominence will invariably affect **3.60** the newsworthiness of published information—with public officials and celebrities typically receiving less protection than private plaintiffs in private facts cases.[171] That said, 'even people who voluntarily enter the public sphere retain a privacy interest in the most intimate details of their lives'.[172] Additionally, the smaller zone of privacy for public figures does not necessarily apply to those linked with them. In *Hood v National Enquirer*,[173] for example, a private facts claim against the *National Enquirer* was allowed to go to the jury because the newspaper had published information regarding the financial affairs of actor Eddie Murphy's illegitimate son and the son's mother in a story about the financial support he provided to them. While the Court accepted that the plaintiffs were related to a celebrity and therefore of some newsworthiness, the specific facts of their private financial affairs were not necessarily of sufficient newsworthiness to justify publication nor was their inclusion required to tell the story.

---

courts will not endeavour to supplant the editorial judgment of the media in determining what is "newsworthy" or of "public interest"'.

[168] *Shulman* (n 158) 215–6 ('It is in the determination of newsworthiness—in deciding whether published or broadcast material is of legitimate public concern—that courts must struggle most directly to accommodate the conflicting interests of privacy and press freedom').

[169] *Kapellas v Kofman*, 1 Cal 3d 20, 36, 81 Cal Rptr 360 (1969); *Virgil v Sports Illustrated*, 424 FSupp 1286, 1288 (SD Cal 1976).

[170] *Diaz* (n 151) 767. Also Restatement (n 136) § 652D, cmt h.

[171] *Eastwood v Superior Court*, 149 Cal App 3d 409, 422, 198 Cal Rptr 342 (1983) ('a celebrity has relinquished "a part of his right of privacy to the extent that the public has a legitimate interest in his doings, affairs or character"') (citation omitted); *Michaels v Internet Enter Group, Inc*, 5 FSupp2d 823, 840 (CD Cal 1998) ('Michaels's voluntary assumption of fame as a rock star throws open his private life to some extent'); Restatement (n 136) § 652D, cmt h ('permissible publicity to information concerning voluntary or involuntary public figures is not limited to the particular events that arouse the interest of the public'). At least one court has taken the view that any person who engages in a pursuit or occupation which calls for the approval or patronage of the public submits his or her private life to substantial scrutiny by those whose approval or patronage is sought: *Ramsey* (n 148) 696.

[172] *Michaels* (n 171) 840.

[173] No: BC 088691 (Cal Ct App Mar 10, 1995) (unpublished opinion), *cert denied*, 516 US 1009 (1995).

**3.61**   *The effect of the passage of time on newsworthiness*   American courts have also grappled with the question of whether the passage of time can transform something that was previously newsworthy into something that is not. Some older California cases accepted this principle. For example, in *Briscoe v Reader's Digest*,[174] the California Supreme Court held that a man convicted of a truck hijacking eleven years earlier could pursue a private facts claim over a magazine article discussing his criminal acts since he was a rehabilitated offender and current discussion of his past crime was no longer necessarily newsworthy. *Briscoe*, however, was decided before the US Supreme Court's decision in *Cox Broadcasting v Cohn* (discussed at 3.52), which held that the First Amendment bars imposing liability on the press for truthfully reporting facts obtained from public court records. Following *Cox*, the California Supreme Court overruled *Briscoe*, holding that 'courts are not freed, by the mere passage of time, to impose sanctions on the publication of truthful information that is obtained from public official court records'.[175]

*(c)  Intrusion upon seclusion*

**3.62**   **Nature and scope of the wrong**   Whereas the publication of private facts tort focuses on speech (*ie* publication of embarrassing private facts), the intrusion upon seclusion tort is concerned with conduct. Specifically with respect to the press, intrusion liability arises from overt acts in the news-gathering process (hence the common reference to intrusion as a 'news-gathering tort'). The intrusion tort focuses on the means of obtaining private information rather than on the information actually gained. Of the four privacy torts, it perhaps best epitomizes the 'right to be left alone'.[176]

**3.63**   The core of the intrusion tort is the offensive prying into the private domain of another. It prohibits unconsented-to physical intrusions into traditionally recognized private spaces (such as the home or a hospital room) as well as unwarranted sensory intrusions (such as eavesdropping, wiretapping, or surreptitious recording) into private areas, matters, and conversations.[177] To prevail, the claimant must establish that he or she had an 'objectively reasonable expectation of privacy' in

---

[174]  4 Cal 3d 529, 93 Cal Rptr 866 (1971).

[175]  *Gates v Discovery Commc'ns*, 34 Cal 4th 679, 694, 21 Cal Rptr 3d 663 (2004). Since *Cox*, other courts have likewise held that the passage of time does not negate the newsorthiness of (or First Amendment protection for) reports on past crimes and court proceedings. *Eg*, *Uranga* (n 157) 556: 'There is no indication that the First Amendment provides less protection to historians than to those reporting current events'; *Romaine v Kallinger*, 109 NJ 282, 293, 537 A2d 284, 300 (1988): 'courts after *Cox Broadcasting* have found a privilege to disseminate matters contained in public court records despite the passage of a significant period of time'.

[176]  *Cooley on Torts* (2nd edn 1888) 29.

[177]  Restatement (n 136) § 652B cmt B. Also *Carter v Superior Ct of San Diego C'ty*, 30 Med L Rptr 1193, 2002 WL 27229, at 6 (Cal Ct App Jan 10, 2002), *petition for review denied*, 2002 Cal LEXIS 2491 (Cal 2002), in which the Court held that the claimant who had been filmed while receiving medical treatment in a hospital emergency room adequately pleaded that he was 'in a zone of physical and sensory privacy and he had a reasonable expectation of privacy'.

the place, conversation, or data source,[178] and that the intrusion would be 'highly offensive to a reasonable person'.[179] Annoying conduct will not suffice.[180] If the plaintiff establishes intrusion liability against the media, he or she will be able to recover for the intrusion even if the photograph, recording, or private information is not published.

Acts of actionable intrusion have been held to include unlawfully recording conver-   **3.64**
sations ('wiretapping'), the use of hidden cameras, 'ride-alongs' (where, for example, a news camera crew, without consent, accompanies the police in the raiding of a suspected criminal's house or paramedics attending to an injured person),[181] and information gained through false pretences.[182] The concept of intrusion is akin to the tort of trespass inasmuch as it often involves a physical or mechanical invasion (by way of surreptitious audio or video surveillance) into a private sphere.

*No 'newsworthiness' bar to intrusion claims*   Importantly, unlike the publication of   **3.65**
private facts tort (where 'newsworthiness' is both an element of the tort and serves as a complete bar to a claim under First Amendment principles), the fact that a reporter secures newsworthy material through commission of an intrusion tort does not generally serve as a defence to intrusion claims.[183] As one court has explained, '[t]he reason for the difference is simple: the intrusion tort, unlike that for publication of private facts, does not subject the press to liability for the contents of its publication'.[184] Rather than focusing on speech or publications by the press (which are protected by the First Amendment), the intrusion tort is only concerned with conduct.

---

[178] *Shulman* (n 158) 231–2.

[179] Restatement (n 136) § 652B ('One who intentionally intrudes, physically or otherwise, upon the solicitude or seclusion of another or his private affairs or concerns, is subject to liability to the other for invasion of his privacy, if the intrusion would be highly offensive to a reasonable person').

[180] In *Dempsey v National Enquirer*, 702 FSupp 927 (D Me 1988), for example, it was held that persistent attempts to photograph a pilot who had fallen out of a commercial aeroplane were not actionable, since although the photographer had visited his house, driven past his house for 45 minutes, and made inquiries at a restaurant, he did not go beyond the front door of the pilot's house and the restaurant was open to the public.

[181] For example, in *Miller v Nat'l Broad Co*, 187 Cal App 3d 1463, 232 Cal Rptr 668 (1986), in which a film crew entered the plaintiffs' home uninvited and filmed paramedics administering emergency medical care to the plaintiff husband, the Court held that the plaintiffs could pursue claims for intrusion upon seclusion and trespass.

[182] McCarthy (n 138) § 590–2, pp 659–70 (discussing cases).

[183] *Deitman v Time Inc*, 449 F2d 245, 249 (9th Cir 1971): 'The First Amendment has never been construed to accord newsmen immunity from torts or crimes committed during the course of newsgathering. The First Amendment is not a license to trespass, to steal, or to intrude by electronic means into the precincts of another's home or office.' More broadly, the US Supreme Court has ruled that the press in its news-gathering activities receives no special First Amendment protection or exemption from generally applicable laws that govern conduct: *Cohen v Cowles Media Co*, 501 US 663, 669 (1991).

[184] *Shulman* (n 158) 240. Also M Nimmer, 'The Right to Speak from *Time* to *Time*' (1968) 56 Cal L Rev 935, 957: 'Intrusion does not raise First Amendment difficulties since its perpetration does not involve speech or other expression.'

**3.66** Therefore, while intrusion and private facts claims may often be brought together, they are analysed by US courts in a very different way. For example, the well-known case of *Shulman v Group W Productions*[185] concerned the filming and television broadcast of footage of emergency medical personnel attending a mother and son who were seriously injured in a road accident. Without the patients' knowledge or consent, the film crew placed a microphone on a nurse to capture her private medical conversations with the mother, and entered and filmed within a helicopter ambulance transporting the patients to hospital. The California Supreme Court dismissed the plaintiffs' claim for publication of private facts, holding that the subject matter of the television broadcast—automobile accidents and emergency response procedures—was of 'legitimate public concern' and that '[t]he challenged material was...substantially relevant to the newsworthy subject matter of the broadcast'.[186] However, the Court ruled that, with respect to recording the mother's private conversation with the nurse and filming in the helicopter ambulance, the plaintiffs had stated a claim for intrusion upon seclusion that they could present to a jury. Significantly, the Court stated that, unlike the private facts claim (where the newsworthiness of the broadcast story served as a complete First Amendment bar), 'the fact that a reporter may be seeking "newsworthy" material does not in itself privilege' what would otherwise be an actionable intrusion upon seclusion.[187]

**3.67** *Newsgathering motive may be relevant*   While newsworthiness is not generally a defence to intrusion upon seclusion claims, the defendant's motive to gather news is not completely irrelevant. The US Supreme Court has generally observed that 'without some protection for seeking out the news, freedom of the press could be eviscerated'.[188] Accordingly, even though newsworthiness does not of itself bar intrusion claims, some courts, in deciding whether a reporter's alleged intrusion is 'highly offensive to a reasonable person' (a required element of the tort), will take into consideration 'the extent to which the intrusion was, under the circumstances, justified by the legitimate motive of gathering the news'.[189] In *Shulman v Group W Productions* for example, the Court noted that, in deciding whether a challenged intrusion is 'highly offensive' (and hence actionable):

> At one extreme, 'routine...reporting techniques,' such as asking questions of people with information ('including those with confidential or restricted information') could rarely, if ever, be deemed an actionable intrusion. (*Nicholson v. McClatchy Newspapers, supra*, 177 Cal.App.3d at p. 519; accord, *Wolfson v. Lewis* (E.D.Pa. 1996) 924 F.Supp. 1413, 1417.) At the other extreme, violation of well-established legal areas of physical or sensory privacy-trespass into a home or tapping a personal telephone line, for example—could rarely, if ever, be justified by a reporter's need to

---

[185] *Shulman* (n 158).
[186] *Shulman* (n 158) 227, 229.
[187] *Shulman* (n 158) 240.
[188] *Branzburg v Hayes*, 408 US 665, 681 (1972).
[189] *Shulman* (n 158) 236–7.

get the story. Such acts would be deemed highly offensive even if the information sought was of weighty public concern.[190]

**Spatial limitation on 'reasonable expectation of privacy'**   In stark contrast to   **3.68** developing English and EU privacy law principles, US law imposes a spatial limitation on the 'zone of privacy' protected by the intrusion tort. As a result, a great deal of material which would pass the privacy threshold of Article 8 in English and ECtHR case law, would simply not be deemed private in the United States.

American courts have frequently held that merely photographing a person (whether   **3.69** a public or private figure) in a public place, even if done surreptitiously, is not an actionable intrusion, 'since he is not then in seclusion, and his appearance is public and open to the public eye'.[191] For example, in the case of *Prince v Out Publishing*,[192] the plaintiff brought an intrusion claim based on publication of photographs showing him dancing naked from the waist up at a private dance club in Los Angeles, which was attended by at least 1,000 people. Affirming the lower court's dismissal of the suit, the Californian Court of Appeal ruled that the plaintiff simply could not establish an 'objectively reasonable expectation of seclusion or solitude in the place' necessary for an intrusion claim. The party was open to all members of the public who purchased a ticket, and the plaintiff was dancing in full view of those who attended.[193]

Similarly, in *Wilkins v National Broadcasting Co*,[194] the Court held that the plain-   **3.70** tiff had no reasonable expectation of privacy, and hence no actionable intrusion claim, where undercover reporters surreptitiously videotaped their conversation with him, which could be overheard by others, at a lunch meeting held at an outside patio table at a restaurant open to the public. This 'public space' limitation on the intrusion tort is applied even if the person's presence or activities in public might otherwise be embarrassing. For example, in *US v Vasquez*,[195] the Court held that videos of female patients entering and leaving an abortion centre were not actionable since they were taken on a public street, and 'no one walking in this area could have a legitimate expectation of privacy'.[196] In short, unlike the much

---

[190] *Shulman* (n 158) 237 (quoting, in part, *Nicholson v McClatchy Newspapers*, 177 Cal App3d 509, 519, 223 Cal Rptr 58 (1986)).

[191] Restatement (n 136) § 652B, cmt b (Illustrations). Also McCarthy (n 138) § 5:88 (citing cases); *Stonum v US Airways, Inc*, 83 F Supp2d 894, 906 (SD Ohio 1999): 'Photographing an individual in plain view of the public eye does not constitute an invasion of privacy.'

[192] 2002 WL 7999, 30 Media L Rptr 1289 (Cal Ct App Jan 3, 2002).

[193] *Prince* (n 192) 8. In a factually similar English case, *Rocknroll v News Group Newspapers* [2013] EWHC 24 (Ch), the claimant, who was married to the actress Kate Winslet, brought a privacy claim over photographs taken at a private party, some of which showed him partially naked. The photographs could be viewed by approximately 1,500 'friends' that he had on Facebook. In contrast to the outcome in *Prince*, the English High Court held that the claimant had a reasonable expectation of privacy in respect of the photographs and that his Art 8 rights were 'plainly engaged'.

[194] 71 Cal App 4th 1066, 1080, 84 Cal Rptr 2d 329 (1999).

[195] 31 F Supp2d 85 (D Conn 1998).

[196] *US v Vasquez* (n 195) 91. Compare *Campbell* (n 117) [124] (per Lord Hope) (publication of a photograph showing Naomi Campbell on a public street outside a drug addiction therapy clinic

broader Article 8 principles that extend an individual's expectations of privacy into public settings, American courts have consistently held that the press 'is subject to no liability for giving further publicity to that which plaintiff leaves open to the public eye'.[197]

**3.71** In contrast, if the press invades a truly secluded conversation or space (such as film-ing in an emergency ward without consent, peeping through bedroom windows, or exceeding the authority granted to enter certain premises by the owner), liability for intrusion typically follows. For example, in *Webb v CBS Broadcasting Inc*,[198] where the plaintiffs alleged that a television camera crew used a telephoto lens to secretly videotape them swimming in their backyard pool, which was surrounded by a seven-foot high privacy fence, the Court held that the plaintiffs had adequately pleaded an intrusion claim.

**3.72** Ultimately, whether the plaintiff has a reasonable expectation of privacy in a par-ticular place or conversation will be very much dependent on the facts of each case, with courts sometimes applying different doctrinal approaches to situations involv-ing 'limited privacy'. Some US courts have held for example that plaintiffs lack a reasonable expectation of privacy in what might be traditionally thought of as 'semi-private settings', for instance backstage at a hotel performance space.[199] By contrast, other American courts have held that privacy is a relative, not absolute, concept. This principle of 'limited privacy recognizes that although an individual may be visible or audible to some limited group of persons, the individual may nonetheless expect to remain secluded from other persons and particularly from the world at large'.[200] Thus, for example in *Sanders v American Broadcasting Co*,[201] the California Supreme Court ruled that an employee could have a reasonable expectation of pri-vacy from undercover news filming of his conversations at his private workplace even though he could be overheard by other co-workers in the vicinity.[202]

---

constituted a 'gross interference with her right to respect for her private life') and *Murray v Big Pictures (UK) Ltd* [2008] EWCA Civ 446, [2009] Ch 481 [57] (holding it at least arguable that JK Rowling's infant son had a reasonable expectation of privacy in respect of photographs of him being pushed down a public street in a pram).

[197] *Machleder v Diaz*, 801 F2d 46, 59 (2d Cir 1986) (citation omitted).

[198] *Webb v CBS Broad Inc*, 2009 WL 1285836, at 3 (ND Ill May 7, 2009).

[199] *People for Ethical Treatment of Animals v Berosini*, 111 Nev 615, 635, 895 P2d 1269 (1995) (plaintiff lacked reasonable expectation of privacy in backstage location at Stardust Hotel, a location where the defendant had 'every right to be' and 'the filming was of a subject that could be seen and heard by any number of persons'); *M&R Inv Co v Mandarino*, 103 Nev 711,719, 748 P2d 488 (1987) (dismissing an intrusion claim on grounds that a man who disguised himself and counted cards in a privately-run casino had no reasonable expectation of privacy in his appearance inside the casino).

[200] *Med Lab Mgmt Consultants v American Broad Cos, Inc*, 306 F3d 806, 815 (9th Cir 2002).

[201] 20 Cal 4th 907, 85 Cal Rptr 2d 909 (1999).

[202] Although note that this is not necessarily the view held by all states in relation to what is deemed 'private', *eg Kemp v Block*, 607 FSupp 1262, 1264 (D Nev 1985) (no reasonable expectation of privacy in recording of plaintiff and co-worker arguing in loud voices in an instrument shop at a workplace where two other mechanics were present and other mechanics went in and out of the room during the argument).

## (d) False light

According to the Restatement (Second) of Torts,[203] the elements of the false light **3.73**
tort are as follows:

### 652E. Publicity Placing Person in False Light

One who gives publicity to a matter concerning another that places the other
before the public in a false light is subject to liability to the other for invasion of
his privacy, if
(a) the false light in which the other was placed would be highly offensive to a
reasonable person, and
(b) the actor had knowledge of or acted in reckless disregard as to the falsity of the
publicized matter and the false light in which the other would be placed.

As discussed more fully below (at 3.78), it is unsettled whether all false light claimants must establish that the defendant acted with knowledge of falsity or reckless
disregard for the truth (that is, prove 'actual malice'), or whether this actual malice
requirement is limited to false light suits brought by public officials and public
figures. State courts are divided on the question, with courts in some states holding
that private figures need only prove negligence to recover for false light invasion of
privacy.[204]

The false light action is recognized in about thirty-four states including **3.74**
California, which, however, requires the dismissal of false light claims where
they are asserted along with traditional libel claims based on the same facts.[205]
About ten states, including New York, Ohio, Texas, and Minnesota, have
decided that the tort will not be recognized as part of the common law of the
state.[206]

False light claims in the United States have arisen in three general categories: **3.75**
embellishment (where false material is added to a news feature story or other

---

[203] Restatement (n 136).

[204] For examples of decisions in which courts have required private figure false light claimants to
show actual malice, see *Zeran v Diamond Broadcasting*, 203 F 3d 714, 719–20 (10th Cir 2000) and
*Welling v Weinfeld*, 113 Ohio St3d 464, 472 (Ohio 2007). By contrast see the decision in *Russell
v Thomson Newspapers Inc*, 842 P2d 896, 907 (Utah 1992), in which the Supreme Court of Utah
refused to apply the actual malice standard to a false light claim brought by a private figure and,
instead, applied a negligence standard.

[205] *McClatchy Newspapers v Superior Court* 189 Cal App 3rd 961, 234 Cal Rptr 702 (1987).

[206] The first state to reject false light was North Carolina: *Renwick v News and Observer* 312
SE 2d 405, 10 Med L Rptr 1443 (NC 1984). The *Renwick* majority noted the 'overlapping' with
defamation remedies, that 'false light need not necessarily be defamatory light', and the tension
already existing between the First Amendment and these torts. The New York Court of Appeals
has held that New York has 'no common law of privacy', noting that the legislature has rejected
bills to codify the four privacy torts (*Howell v New York Post*, 81 NY 2d 115, 122–3 (1993)) and
that New York's narrow privacy statute (New York Civil Rights Law, ss 50–1) creates only a claim
for commercial misappropriation (known in many states as right of publicity) and does not provide
for false light actions. Florida's Supreme Court has also refused to recognize the tort because it
lacks the First Amendment safeguards present in defamation actions (see *Jews for Jesus v Rapp*, 997
So 2d 1098 (Fla 2008)).

publication, thereby placing someone in a false light),[207] distortion (where material concerning a person is used in a distorted manner rendering it highly offensive),[208] and fictionalization (where fiction includes references to real people either as disguised characters or as themselves).[209] The common element in all three of the above categories is the person's objection to the manner in which he or she has been portrayed. The objection is to being made to appear in an unflattering light through either words or pictures, or a combination of both.

**3.76** False light can be difficult to distinguish from actions in defamation and the two causes of action are very often brought together. However, as in the tort of malicious falsehood, the falsity in false light need not necessarily be defamatory (although it must be highly offensive to a reasonable person). And, while defamation protects against injury to reputation, false light protects against emotional distress. Significant misrepresentations of a plaintiff's character or activities may therefore give rise to a claim in false light if they are highly offensive.[210]

**3.77** **Limitations** Even though false light claims are often brought to avoid common law defences or privileges applicable to defamation claims, where the two causes of action rely upon the same publication or circumstances of publication, most US courts have applied the same defences or privileges to the false light part of the claim.[211] In most states, the courts have held that the same statute of limitations should apply to both libel and false light claims. Attempts to bring a false light claim where the libel claim is statute-barred usually fail on that basis.[212]

**3.78** **Disagreement over whether private figures must show actual malice** There remains an open question whether actual malice is a required element of a false

---

[207] *Spahn v Julian Messner*, 18 NY 2d 324 (1966), 21 NY 2d 124 (1967) in which a famous baseball player was wrongly described as a war hero in a biography of his life. The court found that the material was infected with deliberate and substantial falsification. Also *Sinatra v Wilson*, 2 Med L Rptr 2008 (SDNY 1977).

[208] *Solano, Jr v Playgirl Inc* 292 F 3d 1078 (9th Cir 2002) where the Ninth Circuit reinstated an actor's false light claim in respect of a magazine cover which conveyed the false impression that he had posed and consented to publication of nude photographs of himself in a pornographic magazine. The court held there was sufficient evidence of malice to allow the claim to proceed. See also *Palmisano v Modernismo Publications*, 98 AD 2d 953, 470 NYS 2d 196 (NYAD 1983) (which held that the use of a photograph without consent in an advertisement in a homosexual magazine, with fictionalized thoughts attributed to the plaintiff, was actionable) and *Mayers v Michaels*, 9 Med L Rptr 1484 (Sup Ct NY Co 1983).

[209] Where real people appear as characters in fictional works, the cases have been inconsistently decided. Compare *Sliwa v Highgate Pictures*, 7 Med L Rptr 1386 (Sup Ct NY Co 1981), with *Taylor v ABC*, 82 Civ 6977, SDNY (1985). Where the real people are clearly public figures or the events portrayed are matters of public concern, false light claims are generally dismissed: J Goodale (ed), *Communications Law 2000* (Practicing Law Institute 2000) vol 3, 970.

[210] *Godbehere v Phoenix Newspapers Inc*, 162 Ariz 335, 783 P2d 781 (1990).

[211] *Holbrook v Chase*, 12 Med L Rptr 1732 (Id Dist Ct, 4th Dist 1986); *Jensen v Times Mirror*, 634 F Supp 304, 12 Med L Rptr 2137, reconsidered, 647 F Supp 1525, 13 Med L Rptr 2160 (D Conn 1986).

[212] *eg Swan v Boardwalk Regency Corp*, 969 A 2d 1145 (NJ Super AD, 2009).

light claim brought by a plaintiff who is a private individual, as opposed to a public figure. A caveat to § 652E states:

> The Institute takes no position on whether there are any circumstances under which recovery can be obtained under this Section if the actor did not know of or act with reckless disregard as to the falsity of the matter publicized and the false light in which the other would be placed but was negligent in regard to these matters.[213]

This caveat was put in place because of the unsettled state of First Amendment **3.79** law on the issue. In *Time, Inc v Hill*,[214] the Supreme Court held that the First Amendment requires a showing of actual malice in all false light cases brought by private individuals where the challenged publication involves 'matters of public interest'.[215] The ruling in *Hill*, however, was placed into question when the Supreme Court subsequently held in *Gertz v Robert Welch, Inc*,[216] that a private individual alleging defamation against a media defendant need not prove actual malice to satisfy the First Amendment, even when the publication in suit relates to a matter of public interest. In *Gertz*, the Court ruled that where the plaintiff in a defamation action is a private individual, states may decide for themselves the appropriate level of fault that must be shown, so long as the states did not impose liability without fault. The Supreme Court has not yet resolved whether the *Gertz* rule should also apply to false light claims brought by private individuals. Thus, in *Cantrell v Forest City Publishing Co*,[217] the Supreme Court left open the question of whether, in view of *Gertz*, 'a State may constitutionally apply a more relaxed standard of liability [than 'actual malice'] for a publisher or broadcaster of false statements injurious to a private individual under a false light theory of invasion of privacy, or whether the constitutional standard announced in *Time, Inc v Hill* applies to all false light cases'.[218] About ten states have since held that *Gertz* limits the actual malice requirement to false light claims by public figures (and that private figures may recover on a lesser showing of negligence), but fourteen states have followed *Hill* and required actual malice for all false light claims as a matter of state law.

---

[213] Restatement (n 136).

[214] 385 US 374 (1967).

[215] *Time, Inc* (n 214) 387–8. In *Hill*, members of the Hill family, who had been held hostage by escaped convicts, alleged that a *Life* magazine article—in reviewing a fictionalized play that was loosely based on their ordeal—placed them in a false light by erroneously suggesting that the fictionalized scenes of brutality in the play represented the Hill family's actual experience. Even though the Hills were private individuals, not public officials or public figures, the Supreme Court ruled that they nonetheless had to prove actual malice (not mere negligence) to prove their false light claim because the *Life* article concerned a matter of public interest.

[216] 418 US 323, 340 (1974).

[217] 419 US 245 (1974).

[218] *Cantrell* (n 217) 348.

## (e) Misappropriation of name or likeness

**3.80**  The tort of misappropriating name or likeness (or 'right of publicity') creates a right to control the use of one's own name, image, voice, signature, or any other distinguishing characteristic that identifies a particular person. Even by the 1960s, the tort of misappropriation protecting this interest had 'bulked rather large in the law of privacy'.[219]

**3.81**  The Restatement (Second) of Torts,[220] § 652C states that:

> One who appropriates to his own use or benefit the name or likeness of another is subject to liability to the other for invasion of privacy.

**3.82**  The right of publicity is protected in part under federal law by way of the Lanham Act which essentially sets forth the structure of US trade marks law and prevents 'the unauthorized use of a celebrity's identity... [through] the misuse of a trademark, *ie* a symbol or device such as visual likeness, vocal imitation, or other uniquely distinguishing characteristic which is likely to confuse consumers as to the plaintiff's sponsorship or approval of the product'.[221] The right of publicity is also protected through the common law of individual states or state statute or both.[222] The courts have drawn a distinction between the unauthorized use of a person's image or likeness which infringes the person's right to privacy and the use which affects the person's right to exploit and control his or her own image (commercial misappropriation). The latter is seen by some states as a property right which can be owned and assigned by both individuals and corporations and which will survive the death of the celebrity.[223]

**3.83**  Publicity rights will usually be of concern only to a person whose name or likeness has a commercial value. In these cases, the issue is not preserving or protecting a person's secret information but controlling his or her public persona, and because of this it has sometimes been seen as a proprietary and not a privacy right.[224] In the United States, the law allows a person 'an exclusive right to control the commercial value and exploitation of his name, picture, likeness or personality and to prevent others from exploiting that value without permission or from unfairly appropriating that value for their commercial benefit'.[225] The tort seeks to prevent unjust

---

[219]  W Prosser 'Privacy' (1960) 48 Cal L Rev 383, 401.

[220]  Restatement (n 136).

[221]  *Waits v Frito-Lay Inc*, 978 F 2d 1093, 1106–10 (9th Cir 1992), a case in which a food company used a singer whose voice resembled the distinctive gravelly tones of the singer/actor Tom Waits in one of its commercials. Waits sued and was awarded US$2.5 million damages.

[222]  See *eg* ss 50–1 of the New York Civil Rights Law which provides that the name or likeness (including the voice) of a living person for 'advertising purposes or for the use of trade' requires the written consent of the person.

[223]  *PETA v Bobby Berosini Ltd*, 895 P 2d 1269, 23 Med L Rptr 1961 (Nev 1995); California Civil Code, s 990(b), amended in 1985 to give statutory protection to, *inter alia*, the voice of a deceased celebrity.

[224]  R Wacks, *Personal Information, Privacy and the Law* (2nd edn, Clarendon Press 1993) 38.

[225]  'Right of privacy and publicity' Corpus Juris Secundum (1994), vol 77, 539, para 40.

enrichment through the unauthorized exploitation of a person's goodwill or the reputation which a person develops in his or her name or likeness, often 'through the investment of time, effort and money'.[226]

The Supreme Court has stated that the First Amendment is not a bar to the **3.84** recovery of damages for an infringement of a person's publicity rights, although First Amendment considerations will need to be balanced against any individual's rights.[227] Exceptions to the right of publicity have been held to apply in cases where the use of the claimant's name or likeness is newsworthy and/or is incidental to the main purpose of the publication or broadcast in question. Thus, a claim relating to the use of a six-second extract from the claimant's television show (*The Sandy Kane Comedy Show!*) in a satirical television show (*Comedy Central*) was dismissed because the item was found to be newsworthy (being for the purposes of entertainment and amusement).[228] Use of the clip in the show's introduction and in the commercials for the show were protected incidental uses.[229]

## (2) Ireland

### (a) *The development of a constitutional right to privacy*

In Ireland,[230] the right to privacy is protected by various means. Privacy is a **3.85** protected value under the Press Council and Press Ombudsman system.[231] The European Convention on Human Rights Act 2003 gives legal effect to the right to private life under Article 8 ECHR.

However, the primary basis for the enforcement of privacy interests in Ireland **3.86** remains its status as a constitutional right. Limited protection for individual privacy is provided by the Article 40.5 guarantee of the inviolability of the dwelling.[232] In addition, however, the courts have recognized and developed a free-standing right to privacy. This was first established in *McGee v Attorney General*[233] where the Supreme Court, in reliance on Ireland's unenumerated rights doctrine, under which the courts may derive specific rights from the general guarantee of 'personal

---

[226] 'Right of privacy and publicity' (n 225).

[227] *Zacchini v Scripps-Howard Broadcasting Co* 433 US 562 (1977).

[228] *Kane v Comedy Partners*, 2003 US Dist LEXIS 18513, 32 Med L Rptr. 1113 (SDNY 2003), aff'd, 98 Fed Appx 73 (2d Cir 2004). The plaintiff claimed, *inter alia*, breach of copyright and misappropriation under the New York Civil Rights Law, s 51.

[229] *Kane* (n 228).

[230] This section on Ireland was written by Dr Eoin Carolan, Senior Lecturer, University College Dublin.

[231] E Nagle, 'Keeping its Own Counsel? The Irish *Press Council*, Self-regulation and Media Freedom' (2009) 20 Ent L Rev 93.

[232] 'Article 40.5 ... assures the citizen that his or her privacy, person and security will be protected against all comers': *People (DPP) v O'Brien* [2012] IECCA 68 (Hardiman J). See also *Damache v DPP* [2012] IESC 11.

[233] [1974] IR 284.

rights' contained in Article 40.3.1 of Bunreacht na hEireann (the Constitution of Ireland)[234] recognized a right of marital privacy. As Budd J explained:

> Whilst the 'personal rights' are not described specifically, it is scarcely to be doubted in our society that the right to privacy is universally recognised and accepted with possibly the rarest of exceptions...[235]

In *Norris v Attorney General*[236] Henchy and McCarthy JJ (dissenting) sought to expand the *McGee* right to marital privacy into a more general privacy right. These judgments strongly influenced Hamilton P's subsequent ruling in *Kennedy v Ireland*[237] that the tapping of telephones by the state breached the affected individuals' right to privacy. This decision has removed any lingering uncertainty over the recognition by the Irish constitutional order of an individual right to privacy.

### (b) Scope of the constitutional right to privacy

**3.87** The Irish courts favour a broad conception of privacy which emphasizes its connection with dignitary values. In *Norris*, Henchy J described privacy as a right which 'inhere[s] in the individual personality of the citizen in his capacity as a vital human component of the social, political and moral order posited by the Constitution'.[238] This understanding of privacy as a social right was reiterated by Hanna J in *Caldwell v Mahon*,[239] where he observed that the right to privacy is a continuum which extends beyond the purely personal.

> This confirms that the Irish right to privacy does not apply only to the inaccessible or the exclusive. It protects the individuality and autonomy of the citizen in his personal and social life and can therefore apply to many areas of activity, albeit with differing degrees of force.[240]

**3.88** The result is that the right to privacy has a relatively broad field of application under Irish law. Most notably, the right applies to third parties. This reflects the fact that the horizontal application of constitutional rights has been a long-standing feature of Irish constitutional jurisprudence.[241] Arguments that the right to privacy could only give rise to an action in damages against public bodies were rejected by the High Court in *Herrity v Associated Newspapers*.[242] Dunne J concluded that 'a breach of the constitutional right to privacy is actionable against a private person

---

[234] See the seminal decision in *Ryan v Attorney General* [1965] IR 313.
[235] [1974] IR 284, 322.
[236] [1984] IR 36.
[237] [1987] IR 587.
[238] These dicta have frequently been cited with approval. See *eg Foy v An t-Ard Chláraitheoir* [2002] IEHC 116; *Re a Ward of Court (No 2)* [1996] 2 IR 79; *Desmond v Glackin (No 2)* [1993] 3 IR 67; *Fleming v Ireland* [2013] IESC 19.
[239] [2006] IEHC 86.
[240] H Delany and E Carolan, *The Right to Privacy* (Thomson Round Hall 2008) 38.
[241] See *eg Meskell v CIE* [1973] IR 121; *Parsons v Kavanagh* [1990] 1 ILRM 1; *Conway v INTO* [1991] 2 IR 305.
[242] [2008] IEHC 249.

or entity' and awarded damages against the defendant for unlawfully recording the plaintiff's telephone conversations.

The High Court held in *Digital Rights Ireland v Minister for Communications*[243]   **3.89** that corporate entities are entitled to rely on the constitutional guarantee of privacy. The courts had previously found that the right to privacy applied to an individual's business affairs.[244] While this has been described as at the 'outer reaches of and at the furthest remove from the core personal right to privacy',[245] it has also been successfully invoked to justify orders restraining publication of individual's banking affairs.[246] However, a strong argument has been made that to confer a right to privacy upon companies themselves would be inconsistent with the constitutional conception of privacy as an autonomy value.[247]

Despite an earlier ruling in *Atherton v DPP*[248] that the right to privacy was not   **3.90** engaged by surveillance of the individual's home where any of the actions under surveillance were potentially visible to the public, more recent decisions of the High Court appear to accept that the right to privacy is capable of applying to conduct which occurs in public or quasi-public places. In *Cogley v RTE*[249] and *Sinnott v Carlow Nationalist*,[250] the right to privacy was held to have been engaged, respectively, by the secret recording of individual patients in the quasi-public environment of a nursing home, and by the publication of a photograph of a Gaelic football match in which the plaintiff's genitalia could be seen. However, Kearns P cautioned in *Hickey v Sunday Newspapers* that, while he would not say 'there will never be occasions where a person photographed in a public place can successfully invoke privacy rights', his 'intuitiv[e] feel[ing] is that a right of privacy is less easily established in public places'.[251]

### (c) Constitutional restrictions on the right to privacy

Hamilton P commented in *Kennedy v Ireland*[252] that the right to privacy 'may be   **3.91** restricted by the constitutional rights of others, by the requirements of the common good and is subject to the requirements of public order and morality'.[253] Limiting

---

[243] (HC, 5 May 2010).

[244] *Hanahoe v Hussey* [1998] 3 IR 69.

[245] *Caldwell v Mahon* [2007] 3 IR 542. This was endorsed by McGovern J in *Slattery v Friends First* [2013] IEHC 136 where he reserved his position on whether an actionable ground of privacy in business dealings could be derived from the Constitution.

[246] *McKillen v Times Newspapers* [2013] IEHC 150; *O'Brien v RTE* (21 May 2015).

[247] See A O'Neill, *The Constitutional Rights of Companies* (Thomson Round Hall 2007) ch 15.

[248] [2005] IEHC 429, discussed in E Carolan, 'Stars of Citizen CCTV—Video Surveillance and the Right to Privacy in Public Places' (2006) 28 Dublin ULJ 326.

[249] [2005] 4 IR 79.

[250] (HC, 30 July 2008).

[251] [2011] 1 IR 228, 247.

[252] [1987] IR 587.

[253] *Kennedy* (n 252) 592. Quoted in *Re a Ward of Court (No 2)* [1996] 2 IR 79, 125; *O'T v B* [1998] 3 IR 321, 348; *Haughey v Moriarty* [1999] 3 IR 1, 58; *Re Ansbacher (Cayman) Ltd* [2002] 2 ILRM 491, 502; *Caldwell v Mahon* [2006] IEHC 86, 3–4; *Gray v Minister for Justice, Equality and Law*

considerations include the exigencies of the common good,[254] the public interest,[255] and public order and morality.[256] These grounds have 'been referred to but rarely considered by the Irish courts'.[257] However, there are two specific constitutional provisions that have given rise to a greater degree of litigation.

**3.92** **Public administration of justice** Article 34.1 of the Constitution requires that justice be administered in public. This was held in *Irish Times Ltd v Ireland*[258] to require that court proceedings be open to the media so as to facilitate full public scrutiny of the administration of justice. The Irish courts have consistently rejected attempts to prohibit or restrain the reporting of court proceedings by reference to the private affairs of the parties.[259] They have also asserted an inherent jurisdiction to depart from a statutory prohibition on publicity and allow media access or coverage in exceptional cases, such as the death of a child in care.[260]

**3.93** **Freedom of expression** Freedom of expression is guaranteed by Article 40.6.1(i) of the Constitution. The general relationship between the right to privacy and the media's freedom of expression has been considered in a small number of Irish cases. In *M v Drury*,[261] O'Hanlon J expressed the view that, in light of the 'strongly-expressed guarantees in favour of freedom of expression' in the Constitution, the courts would only be required to intervene to protect a plaintiff's right to privacy in 'extreme cases'. However, in *Cogley v RTE*,[262] Clarke J favoured a more evenly weighted approach. Clarke J indicated that a media publication might be prohibited where it infringed the right to privacy and did not feature matters of legitimate public interest. He also accepted, however, that prior restraints were traditionally granted only in 'unusual circumstances and after careful scrutiny'.

**3.94** In her more recent decision in *Herrity*, Dunne J appeared to reiterate the more traditional view. She observed that '[t]here is a hierarchy of constitutional rights and as a general proposition, I think that cases in which the right to privacy will prevail

---

*Reform* [2007] IEHC 52, 18; *National Maternity Hospital v Information Commissioner* [2007] IEHC 113, 25. See also *Trent v Commissioner of An Garda Siochana* [1999] IEHC 84, 27; *Cogley v RTE* [2005] 4 IR 79, 90; *Domican v Axa Insurance Ltd* [2007] IEHC 14, 10.

254 *Bailey v Flood* (SC, 14 April 2000) 3 (Denham J).
255 *National Maternity Hospital v Information Commissioner* [2007] IEHC 113, 25.
256 *Norris v AG* [1984] IR 36.
257 Delany and Carolan (n 240) 63.
258 [1998] 1 IR 359, 382.
259 *Re R Ltd* [1989] IR 126; *Claimant v Board of St James Hospital* (HC, 10 May 1989); *Roe v Blood Transfusion Service Board* [1996] 3 IR 67; *MCD v Liberty Syndicate Management Ltd* (HC, 5 March 2007); *Doe v Revenue Commissioners* [2008] IEHC 5; *McKeogh v John Doe 1* [2012] IEHC 95; *DF v Garda Commissioner* [2013] IEHC 5. The Constitution provides for the possibility of statutory exceptions. See *eg* s 45(1) of the Courts (Supplemental Provisions) Act 1961 (restricting reporting of matrimonial matters, cases of lunacy, matters involving minors, and proceedings involving disclosure of a secret manufacturing process).
260 *HSE v McAnespie* [2012] 1 IR 548.
261 [1994] 2 IR 8.
262 [2005] 4 IR 79.

over the right to freedom of expression may well be few and far between'.[263] This was cited with approval by Kearns P in *Hickey*. There, the Court, relied heavily on the New Zealand decision of *Hosking v Runting* (see 3.98) in holding that the publication of photographs of a child and his parents following the registration of his birth did not constitute a breach of privacy. The Court referred to a number of factors, including the public location and public nature of the function being carried out, but was most influenced by the mother's prior engagement with a journalist regarding the birth.[264]

*(d) The action for breach of privacy under Irish law*

Considerable uncertainty still exists as to the precise parameters of the action for breach of privacy under Irish law. Although the number of actions for breach of privacy initiated in Ireland appears to have increased in recent years, many actions are settled or initiated in the Circuit Court where it is extremely rare for a written decision to be delivered. This means that the Superior Courts have had little opportunity to clarify the nature of Ireland's privacy laws.  **3.95**

However, it would appear, as suggested by the academic commentary in this area,[265] that actions for damages may be successfully brought as a constitutional tort for breach of privacy. Damages have been awarded against individuals, media organizations, and public authorities[266] for various forms of interference with the right to privacy. In *K v Independent Star*,[267] Hedigan J dismissed a claim arising from media reporting of a rape trial which unintentionally facilitated the identification of the victim in her locality on the basis that damages would only be awarded where there had been a deliberate, conscious, and unjustified violation of the right to privacy. This need to establish a deliberate and conscious breach as a prerequisite to the award of damages seems inconsistent, however, with the approach applied to damages claims in relation to the alleged breach of other constitutional rights.  **3.96**

It is unclear when injunctive relief will be available to restrain publication of material where that may infringe an individual's right to privacy. The Irish courts have traditionally been reluctant, in keeping with common law, constitutional and ECHR principles, to permit prior restraints. However, in *Cogley*, Clarke J suggested that different considerations may apply in the privacy context:  **3.97**

> [T]he balancing exercise which . . . the court must engage in is not one which would arise at all in circumstances where the underlying information sought to be disclosed was of a significantly private nature and where there was no, or no significant, legitimate public interest in its disclosure. In such a case (for example where the information intended to be disclosed concerned the private life of a public

---

263  *Herrity* (n 242) [63].
264  *Hickey* (n 251).
265  Delany and Carolan (n 240) 342–3.
266  *Gray v Minister for Justice* [2007] IEHC 52.
267  [2010] IEHC 500.

individual in circumstances where there was no significant public interest of a legitimate variety in the material involved) it would seem to me that the normal criteria for the grant of an interlocutory injunction should be applied. In such cases it is likely that the balance of convenience would favour the grant of an interlocutory injunction on the basis that the information, once published, cannot be unpublished. It is also likely, in such cases, that damages would not be an adequate means of vindicating the right to privacy of the individual.[268]

More recently, the High Court in *O'Brien v RTE*[269] granted an order restraining publication of the relationship between a high-profile businessman and a state entity in respect of debts owed by him. In so doing, the Court suggested (but did not decide) that *Cogley* may permit the application of a lower threshold[270] for the grant of an interlocutory injunction restraining expression that applies in matters not involving claims of privacy or confidentiality.

### (3) New Zealand

#### (a) Tort of wrongful publication of private facts

**3.98** In 2004, a majority of the New Zealand Court of Appeal recognized a tort of wrongful publication of private information in the case of *Hosking v Runting*.[271] *Hosking* (the facts of which bear a striking resemblance to the English case of *Murray v Express Newspapers plc*)[272] concerned an attempt by a television presenter and his former wife to restrain publication of photographs of their two young children being wheeled down a busy Auckland shopping street in a pushchair. The claimants maintained that the photographs breached the children's privacy and, given the celebrity status of the first plaintiff, potentially jeopardized their safety. All five judges agreed that there was no breach of privacy in the circumstances (primarily because the photographs were of an innocuous event which took place in public) but three of the five nonetheless held that there was a tort of breach of privacy in New Zealand.

**3.99** In the more widely cited of the two majority judgments, Gault P and Blanchard J held that the tort has two requirements: first, the 'existence of facts in respect of which there is a reasonable expectation of privacy' and, secondly, 'publicity given to those private facts that would be considered highly offensive to an objective reasonable person'.[273] A defence of legitimate public concern was also recognized, as was the

---

[268] *Cogley* (n 262) 95.
[269] 21 May 2015.
[270] *O'Brien* (n 269) [61].
[271] [2005] 1 NZLR 1, CA. This section is written by N A Moreham.
[272] *Murray* (n 196).
[273] *Hosking v Runting* [2005] 1 NZLR 1, CA [117]. The focus of the highly offensive publicity requirement was not on offensiveness in its usual sense but on the plaintiff's ability to prove that the breach of privacy caused real 'harm', 'distress', or 'humiliation': [128]. For discussion calling into question the desirability of the highly offensive publicity requirement, see N A Moreham, 'Why is Privacy Important? Privacy, Dignity and the Development of the New Zealand Breach of Privacy Tort' in J Finn and S Todd (eds), *Law Liberty, Legislation* (LexisNexis 2008) 231.

need to ensure that the tort does not create an unjustified interference with freedom of expression interests protected by the New Zealand Bill of Rights Act 1990.[274]

*Hosking* followed a number of High Court decisions in which the tort of wrong- **3.100** ful publication had been applied[275] but neither the existence nor the form of the *Hosking* tort has been affirmed by the Supreme Court. In *Rogers v Television New Zealand*[276] (the only case in which the Supreme Court has considered the matter), two of their Honours applied Gault P and Blanchard J's test from *Hosking* but expressly declined to approve it[277] and Elias CJ (with whom Anderson J concurred) stressed that the Court of Appeal 'did not purport to establish the limits of the tort in all circumstances'.[278] Particular doubt was cast on the desirability of the second limb of the *Hosking* test.[279] Elias CJ held that the Court should 'reserve its position on the view...that the tort of privacy requires not only a reasonable expectation of privacy but also that publicity would be "highly offensive"'.[280] This echoes the views of Tipping J, the third member of the *Hosking* majority, who preferred that 'the question of offensiveness be controlled within the need for there to be a reasonable expectation of privacy'.[281]

### (b) Tort of intrusion into seclusion

The New Zealand High Court has also recognized a tort of intrusion into seclusion **3.101** in the case of *C v Holland*.[282] In that case, the defendant used a video camera to film his flatmate through a hole in the ceiling while she was having a shower. The claimant sued for damages and proceedings were brought to establish the preliminary issue of 'whether invasion of privacy of this type, without publicity or the prospect of publicity, is an actionable tort in New Zealand'.[283] Whata J held that it was, regarding the tort of intrusion into seclusion as:

> ...entirely compatible with, and a logical adjunct to, the *Hosking* tort of wrongful publication of private facts. They logically attack the same underlying wrong, namely unwanted intrusion into a reasonable expectation of privacy.[284]

---

[274] *Hosking* (n 273) [129]–[130].
[275] See *eg Bradley v Wingnut Films* [1993] 1 NZLR 415 and *Tucker v News Media Ownership Ltd* [1986] 2 NZLR 716.
[276] [2008] 2 NZLR 277, SC.
[277] *Rogers* (n 276) [99] (McGrath J) and [144] (Anderson J).
[278] *Rogers* (n 276) [23].
[279] *Rogers* (n 276) [25] (Elias CJ). See also [144] (Anderson J). Similar reservations can be gleaned from the judgment of Young P in the Court of Appeal decision in *Rogers v Television New Zealand* [2007] 1 NZLR 156, CA [122].
[280] *Hosking* (n 273) [256]. He continued that if 'offensiveness' is to be included as a requirement then a 'substantial' level of offence should be required rather than a 'high' level as Gault P and Blanchard J suggested: [256].
[281] See further, Moreham (n 273) 231.
[282] *C v Holland* [2012] NZHC 2155. The tort was also applied in *Faesenkleot v Jenkin* [2014] NZHC 1637. *Holland* is usefully discussed by T McKenzie in 'The New Intrusion Tort: The News Media Exposed' (2014) 45 VUWLR 79.
[283] *C v Holland* (n 282) [1].
[284] *C v Holland* (n 282) [75].

**3.102** The New Zealand tort of intrusion into seclusion has four main requirements:

(a) an intentional and unauthorised intrusion;
(b) into seclusion (namely intimate personal activity, space or affairs);
(c) involving an infringement of a reasonable expectation of privacy; and
(d) that is highly offensive to a reasonable person.[285]

The last two elements, Whata J observed, are also required by the tort of wrongful publication to private facts (as set out in *Hosking v Runting*) and he therefore said that the boundaries of that tort will apply to the intrusion tort where they are relevant.[286] He also said that a legitimate public concern in the information may provide a defence to the privacy claim.[287] 'Information' in this context appears to refer to any material gathered in the course of the intrusion.

### (c) Legislative protections

**3.103** Unlike freedom of expression, privacy is not directly protected in the New Zealand Bill of Rights Act 1990,[288] and the Privacy Act 1993 (which provides protections similar to the English Data Protection Act 1998) does not apply to 'any news medium' engaged in 'news activities'.[289] Piecemeal privacy protection is, however, to be found in legislation such as the Crimes (Intimate Covert Filming) Amendment Act 2006, which creates an offence of making an 'intimate visual recording';[290] the Broadcasting Act 1989, which obliges broadcasters to maintain standards consistent with 'the privacy of the individual'[291] and empowers the Broadcasting Standards Authority to enforce that obligation (which it does by applying a comprehensive set of 'Privacy Principles'); the Harassment Act 1997, which protects against harassment; and the Harmful Digital Communications Act 2015 which is designed to deter, prevent, and mitigate harm caused to individuals by digital communications (including harm caused by serious privacy breaches) and to provide victims of harmful digital communications with a quick and efficient means of redress. In the second stage of a review of privacy protection, the New Zealand Law Commission also recommended civil and criminal protection against the use of visual surveillance, tracking, and interception devices.[292]

---

[285] *C v Holland* (n 282) [94].
[286] *C v Holland* (n 282) [96]. See also discussion of *Hosking* at 3.98–3.100.
[287] *C v Holland* (n 282) [96].
[288] Although a measure of protection is provided by s 21 which protects citizens against unreasonable search and seizure.
[289] Privacy Act 1993, s 2(1).
[290] Crimes (Intimate Covert Filming) Amendment Act 2006, s 216H.
[291] Broadcasting Act 1989, s 4(1)(a).
[292] See New Zealand Law Commission, *Invasion of Privacy: Penalties and remedies: Review of the law of privacy stage 3* (Law Com No 113, 2010).

## (4) Australia

### (a) No general statutory privacy law

In Australia[293] there is no general statutory prohibition on invasions of privacy. **3.104** Although there are statutory bills/charters of rights now in one Australian state[294] and one territory,[295] both providing for the right to privacy (modelled on the International Covenant on Civil and Political Rights), these appear to be (or at least have been treated as) directed primarily at actions of legislators and public authorities. The limited protections of personal data available under Commonwealth, state, and territory statutes either do not extend to or, as in the case of the Commonwealth Privacy Act 1988 (Cth), specifically exempt media organisations engaged in journalism.[296]

The Australian, New South Wales, and Victorian Law Reform Commissions **3.105** recommended statutory causes of action in privacy in reports published between 2009 and 2010,[297] and the Australian Law Reform Commission followed up with further recommendations for a statutory tort (in rather different terms from its earlier recommendations) in a report published in 2014.[298] To date none of these recommendations have led to legislation. In the meantime, protection of privacy vis-à-vis the media by and large currently falls under the common law.

### (b) No common law cause of action: piecemeal protection

The relevant common law causes of action available to protect privacy in Australia **3.106** are piecemeal and historically developed, and the suggestion that a specific cause of action for invasion of privacy should be recognized has been resisted by Australian courts at the highest level. In *Australian Broadcasting Corp v Lenah Game Meats Pty Ltd*,[299] the High Court refused to accept that ABC's proposed broadcast of video footage showing possums being stunned and killed at the plaintiff's abattoir (the

---

[293] This section was written by Megan Richardson, Professor of Law, Melbourne Law School, The University of Melbourne, and Michael Rivette, Barrister, Chancery Chambers, Melbourne. Thanks to Karin Clark, Senior Fellow, Melbourne Law School and Moira Paterson, Associate Professor, Law Faculty, Monash University, Melbourne for valuable assistance and advice.

[294] Charter of Human Rights and Responsibilities Act 2006 (Vic).

[295] Human Rights Act 2004 (ACT).

[296] Privacy Act 1988 (Cth), s 7B(4)—and small business operators and individuals acting in a non-business capacity are further exempted under ss 6C and 7B(1) of the Act. The Act has been the subject of an extensive review by the Australian Law Reform Commission, which has recommended changes to both the small business and journalism exemptions (removing the first and modifying the second): Australian Law Reform Commission, *For Your Information: Australian privacy law and practice* (ALRC Report 108, 2008) chs 39 and 42. To date, although some of the ALRC's other recommendations for updating the Privacy Act have been moved on, these recommendations have not.

[297] Australian Law Reform Commission (n 298) paras 74.70–74.76; New South Wales Law Commission, *Invasion of Privacy* (Law Comm No 120, 2009); Victorian Law Reform Commission, *Surveillance in Public Places* (VLRC Report 18, 2010) ch 7.

[298] Australian Law Reform Commission, *Serious Invasions of Privacy in the Digital Era* (ALRC Report 123, 2014).

[299] (2001) 208 CLR 199.

videotape having been surreptitiously obtained by animal rights activists) gave rise to a cause of action in privacy. As Gleeson CJ said, '[i]f the activities filmed were private, then the law of breach of confidence is adequate to cover the case'.[300] (The plaintiff having conceded the information was not confidential, breach of confidence was not argued.) The possibility of a privacy cause of action being developed in a future case was not ruled out by the High Court and there has been some scholarly support.[301] However, so far there is minimal authority for the development.

*(c) Flexible use of common law causes of action*

**3.107** On the other hand, Australian courts seem to be prepared to offer flexible protection to privacy under the common law, especially through a broad treatment of the equitable doctrine of breach of confidence.

**3.108** **Breach of confidence** So, for instance, in *Lenah* it was accepted that breach of confidence is not limited to situations where information is imparted in confidence to a confidant who stands in a 'relationship' of confidence with the confider, but may also extend to 'the activities of eavesdroppers and the like',[302] with references also made to the possibility of a range of remedies including constructive trusts in appropriate cases.[303] Moreover, in *Giller v Procopets*[304] the Victorian Court of Appeal accepted that the plaintiff, who had made out a claim for breach of confidence against her former partner who showed or sought to show private video footage of their engagement in sexual activity to members of her family, her community, and her employer, could have damages of $40,000 for 'mere distress'.[305]

---

[300] *Lenah* (n 299) [39]. Compare also Gummow and Hayne JJ [123].

[301] See *eg* D Lindsay, 'Protection of Privacy under the General Law following *ABC v Lenah Game Meats*: Where to Now?' [2002] 9 Privacy L and Policy Reporter 101; D Butler, 'A Tort of Invasion of Privacy in Australia' (2005) 29 Melbourne UL Rev 339.

[302] *Lenah* (n 299) [123] (Gummow and Hayne JJ). See also Gleeson CJ [34], citing Laws J in *Hellewell v Chief Constable of Derbyshire* [1995] 1 WLR 804, 807. Note, however, that although Gleeson CJ included from Laws J that '[i]t is, of course, elementary that, in all such cases, a defence based on the public interest would be available' (making reference also to the implied freedom of political communication in the Australian Constitution), Gummow J has taken a narrower view of the 'defence': *Corrs Pavey Whiting and Byrne v Collector of Customs (Vic)* (1987) 14 FCR 434, 451–6.

[303] *Lenah* (n 299) [102]–[103] (Gummow and Hayne JJ); see also Callinan J [297].

[304] (2009) 24 VR 1.

[305] *Giller* (n 304) [418] (Neave JA) (Maxwell P and Ashley JA concurring), citing *Campbell* (n 117) and *Douglas* (n 117) as 'high authority'. The decision was made under the particular terms of the Supreme Court Act 1986 (Vic) but Neave JA in the leading judgment intimated that equitable compensation could equally be awarded ((n 304) [233]). The Australian Law Reform Commission in its Report on *Serious Invasions of Privacy in the Digital Era* (n 298) ch 13, has recommended that there be statutory clarification of the power of courts to award distress damages in all Australian jurisdictions. However, in the recent Western Australian case of *Wilson v Ferguson* [2015] WASC 15, where photographs and videos of the plaintiff showing her 'naked or partially naked and, in some cases, engaging in sexual activities' were posted on the defendant's Facebook page, breach of confidence was claimed and upheld, and without resort to the language of the Supreme Court Act 1935 (WA), equitable compensation in the amount of $48,000 was awarded including $35,000 for distress on the basis that 'the approach taken in *Giller* is an appropriate incremental adaptation of an established equitable principle to accommodate the nature, ease and extent of electronic communications in contemporary Australian society': [82].

This liberal treatment of breach of confidence arguably explains why the Court saw **3.109** no need to accept an action in privacy to give relief to the plaintiff.[306] The defendant, Procopets, sought to obtain special leave to appeal to the High Court but the application was denied on the basis that the papers filed 'raise no question of law on which, if special leave were granted, an appeal could enjoy any real prospects of success'.[307]

That the media may be susceptible to breach of confidence claims is also shown **3.110** by the earlier Victorian case of *Jane Doe v Australian Broadcasting Corp*,[308] where Hampel J in the County Court found the plaintiff's confidence had been breached after ABC published her identity as a rape victim (in breach of the Judicial Proceedings Reports Act 1958 (Vic)) and awarded, *inter alia*, $25,000 distress damages.[309]

**Other causes of action**    As to other developing actions, breach of a tort of harass- **3.111** ment was the conclusion of Skoien J in the Queensland District Court stalking case of *Grosse v Purvis*,[310] which was premised on a pattern of behaviour of such seriousness that 'an ordinary person should not reasonably be expected to endure it'.[311] This emerging tort might extend to conduct of the media that is extreme and repeated.[312]

Another possible source of development is the tort of intentional infliction of emo- **3.112** tional harm.[313] In *Giller*, Maxwell P thought it sufficient that there was an intention to cause distress which is in fact caused,[314] although Ashley JA disagreed[315] and Neave JA left the issue open.[316] Negligence may also be relied on in certain cases, as in *Doe*, although there the defendant's breach of the statute was a particular consideration.[317]

---

[306] See *Giller* (n 304) [447]–[452] (Neave JA) (Maxwell CJ concurring) and cf [167]–[168] (Ashley JA).

[307] *Procopets v Giller* [2009] HCASL 187.

[308] [2007] VCC 281. The case was settled on appeal.

[309] In addition to $85,000 for 'psychiatric injury' (post-traumatic stress disorder). Hampel J also found violation of a tort of privacy: *Jane Doe* (n 308) [157]–[164]. However, this aspect of the judgment was not approved by the Court of Appeal (a court of higher authority than the County Court) in *Giller* (n 304).

[310] [2003] Australia Torts Rep 81-706.

[311] *Grosse* (n 310) [450]–[451], citing Todd, 'Protection of privacy' in N Mullany (ed), *Torts in the Nineties* (LBC Information Services 1997) 174, 200–04. See also *Lenah* (n 299) [123], Gummow and Hayne JJ noting 'what may be a developing tort of harassment' as a potential source of privacy protection. Note also that the Australian Law Reform Commission has recommended that if a privacy tort is not enacted, the states and territories should enact a statutory tort of harassment: see *Serious Invasions of Privacy in the Digital Era* (n 298) ch 15.

[312] Skoien J also found that the defendant had invaded the plaintiff's privacy (*Grosse* (n 310) [444]), but (again) contrast *Giller* (n 304).

[313] Based on *Wilkinson v Downton* [1897] 2 QB 57.

[314] *Giller* (n 304) [24], [34]–[36], accepting *Wainwright* (n 116) [44] (Lord Hoffman).

[315] *Giller* (n 304) [164]–[166].

[316] *Giller* (n 304) [471]–[478].

[317] *Jane Doe* (n 308) [92].

**3.113** Thus it seems that there is a variety of torts that may be drawn on where breach of confidence does not provide a complete response to the violation (or violations) of privacy alleged—in particular where the gravamen centres around the intrusive character of conduct rather than (or going beyond) the personal character of information being published.

### (d) Miscellaneous statutory provisions

**3.114** Also worth noting are the statutory prohibitions on stalking and surveillance activities which may apply to the media, for instance the Victorian Surveillance Devices Act 1999 and New South Wales Surveillance Devices Act 2007.[318] Both the Victorian and Australian Law Reform Commissions have noted the relevance of these types of legislation schema to the protection of privacy and made recommendations for their modernization.[319] Further, the recent Victorian sexting legislation[320] represents an effort to deal with one type of contemporary conduct (namely electronic distribution of intimate images) on a *sui generis* basis.

### (5) Canada

### (a) Overview

**3.115** In Canada,[321] privacy is protected by the Canadian Charter of Rights and Freedoms,[322] legislation, and, in some instances at least, under the common law. The province of Quebec is unique in having its own Charter of Human Rights and Freedoms,[323] which explicitly provides for the right to 'respect for...private life'[324] as well as to 'the safeguard of...dignity, honour, and reputation'.[325] In a case involving publication of a photograph of the complainant without her consent,

---

[318] The New South Wales Surveillance Devices Act 2007 (one of the more modern of the surveillance devices statutes) was invoked by the Australian Communications Media Authority in its inquiry into radio station Today FM's conduct in relation to the recording and broadcasting of a telephone call made between two of the station's presenters posing as Queen Elizabeth and Prince Charles and two hospital staff at King Edward VII Hospital in London, where the Duchess of Cambridge was an inpatient being treated for acute morning sickness. The legality of the Authority's preliminary conclusion that the radio station in recording and broadcasting a private telephone call without consent contravened the Act and thereby breached a condition of its licence has been upheld by the High Court: see *Australian Communications and Media Authority v Today FM (Sydney) Pty Ltd* [2015] HCA 7.

[319] Victoria Law Reform Commission's Report on *Surveillance in Public Places* (n 297); Australian Law Reform Commission, *Serious Invasions of Privacy in the Digital Era* (n 298) ch 14.

[320] Summary Offences Act 1966 (Vic), s 41DA (distribution of intimate image) and 41DB (threats to distribute intimate image), as inserted by the Crimes Amendment (Sexual Offences and Other Matters) Act 2014.

[321] This section was written by Dr Barbara von Tigerstrom, Professor, University of Saskatchewan.

[322] Canadian Charter of Rights and Freedoms, pt I of the Constitution Act 1982, being sch B to the Canada Act 1982 (UK) 1982, c 11.

[323] Quebec Charter of Human Rights and Freedoms, RSQ, c C-12.

[324] Quebec Charter of Human Rights (n 323) s 4.

[325] Quebec Charter of Human Rights (n 323) s 5.

the right to respect for private life was found by the Supreme Court of Canada to include the right to control the use made of one's image.[326]

Unlike the Quebec Charter, the Canadian Charter of Rights and Freedoms applies only to the government,[327] not to the actions of private persons. It does not expressly include a right to privacy, but both s 7 ('the right to life, liberty, and security of the person')[328] and s 8 ('the right to be secure against unreasonable search or seizure')[329] have been applied to protect reasonable expectations of privacy.[330] Government organizations at the federal, provincial, and local levels are also subject to legislation that governs the collection, use, and disclosure of personal information by government bodies and rights of access to government information.[331]    **3.116**

In addition, the federal government and several provinces[332] have enacted privacy legislation covering the private sector. The Personal Information Protection and Electronic Documents Act (PIPEDA),[333] enacted in 2000, gives legal force, with some modifications, to the Canadian Standards Association Model Code for the Protection of Personal Information.[334] PIPEDA generally applies to personal information collected, used, or disclosed by organizations in the course of commercial activities,[335] but not solely 'for journalistic, artistic or literary purposes'.[336] Complaints regarding alleged breaches of PIPEDA can be made to the Privacy Commissioner of Canada, who has the authority to investigate and issue a report with findings and recommendations.[337] Further recourse is available to the Federal Court, which can make binding orders and award damages.[338] The former Privacy Commissioner recommended a series of reforms to PIPEDA, including stronger enforcement powers and provisions requiring mandatory notification of breaches to the Privacy Commissioner and affected persons.[339] A bill    **3.117**

---

[326] *Aubry v Éditions Vice Versa Inc* [1998] 1 SCR 591, (1998) 157 DLR (4th) 577.

[327] Canadian Charter of Rights and Freedoms (n 322) s 32.

[328] Canadian Charter of Rights and Freedoms (n 322) s 7.

[329] Canadian Charter of Rights and Freedoms (n 322) s 8.

[330] *R v O'Connor* [1995] 4 SCR 411, (1995) 130 DLR (4th) 235; *Hunter v Southam Inc* [1984] 2 SCR 145, 11 DLR (4th) 641.

[331] See *eg* the Privacy Act, RSC 1985, c P-21; Access to Information Act, RSC 1985, c A-1.

[332] Personal Information Protection Act, SBC 2003, c 63; Personal Information Protection Act, SA 2003, c P-6.5; Act respecting the protection of personal information in the private sector, RSQ c P-39.1.

[333] SC 2000, c 5.

[334] CAN/CSA-Q830-96.

[335] PIPEDA, SC 2000, c 5, s 4(1)(a). It also applies to personal information about the organization's employees if the organization is a federally regulated undertaking or business, such as radio broadcasting, banking, or air transportation: s 4(1)(b).

[336] PIPEDA, SC 2000, c 5, s 4(2)(c).

[337] PIPEDA, SC 2000, c 5, ss 11–13.

[338] PIPEDA, SC 2000, c 5, ss 14–16.

[339] Office of the Privacy Commissioner of Canada, *The Case for Reforming the Personal Information Protection and Electronic Documents Act* (May 2013), available at <http://www.priv.gc.ca/parl/2013/pipeda_r_201305_e.pdf>.

amending the Act to implement some of these recommendations was introduced in Parliament and passed in 2015.[340]

**3.118** In a decision released in November 2013, the Supreme Court of Canada declared the province of Alberta's private sector privacy law, the Personal Information Protection Act,[341] to be invalid.[342] The challenge to the Act arose in the context of a labour dispute, during which the union had posted on its website images of individuals crossing the picket line. Several of those individuals complained to the Alberta Information and Privacy Commissioner and the Commissioner's adjudicator decided that the union's collection, use, and disclosure of information violated the Act. The union then applied for judicial review, arguing that the Act's provisions infringed the right to freedom of expression, protected by s 2(b) of the Canadian Charter of Rights and Freedoms. The Supreme Court of Canada agreed, holding that to the extent that the Act prevented the collection, use, and disclosure of information for legitimate labour relations purposes, it unjustifiably violated freedom of expression. As a result, the Court declared the Act to be invalid, suspending the declaration of invalidity for one year to allow the legislature sufficient time to consider necessary amendments to the legislation. An amended Act was passed in 2014, adding new sections dealing with collection, use, and disclosure of personal information by trade unions.[343]

### (b) Statutory causes of action

**3.119** Four provinces—British Columbia,[344] Saskatchewan,[345] Manitoba,[346] and Newfoundland[347]—have statutes that establish a cause of action for violations of privacy. These statutes provide that it is a 'tort, actionable without proof of damage, for a person wilfully and without claim of right, to violate the privacy of another person'.[348] The tort includes using the name or likeness of a person without consent in advertising or promotion,[349] or using letters or other personal

---

[340] Bill S-4, An Act to Amend the Personal Information Protection and Electronic Documents Act and to make a consequential amendment to another Act, 41st Parl, 2014 (received Royal Assent in 2015); see also Bill C-475, An Act to Amend the Personal Information Protection and Electronic Documents Act (order-making power), 41st Parl, 2014 (defeated at second reading).

[341] SA 2003, c P-6.5.

[342] *Alberta (Information and Privacy Commissioner) v United Food and Commercial Workers, Local 401* [2013] 3 SCR 733, 2013 SCC 62.

[343] Personal Information Protection Amendment Act, SA 2014, c 14.

[344] Privacy Act, RSBC 1996, c 373.

[345] Privacy Act, RSS 1978, c P-24.

[346] Privacy Act, CCSM, c P125.

[347] Privacy Act, RSNL 1990, c P-22.

[348] Privacy Act, RSBC 1996, c 373, s 1(1); Privacy Act, RSS 1978, c P-24, s 2; Privacy Act, RSNL 1990, c P-22, s 3(1). Manitoba's statute uses the language of 'substantially, unreasonably, and without claim of right': Privacy Act, CCSM, c P125, s 2(1).

[349] Privacy Act, RSBC 1996, c 373, s 3; Privacy Act, RSS 1978, c P-24, s 3(c); Privacy Act, CCSM, c P125, s 3(c); Privacy Act, RSNL 1990, c P-22, s 4(c).

documents without consent.[350] The remedies that may be awarded include damages, injunctions, accounting for profits, or delivery of articles or documents.[351] Defences include consent, lawful authority, or in the case of publication, public interest, fair comment, or privilege according to the law of defamation.[352]

In *Hollinsworth v BCTV*,[353] the plaintiff had undergone a surgical procedure for **3.120** baldness and consented to the procedure being videotaped by the clinic for educational purposes. Part of the video, with the plaintiff's face fully visible and identifiable, was later broadcast by BCTV as part of a television programme. The Court awarded compensatory and exemplary damages against the clinic and its owner under the Privacy Act, but found that BCTV had acted reasonably in relying on the (false) assurances of the clinic's representative that consent for use of the videotape had been granted.[354]

### (c) Common law causes of action

Damages may also be awarded in negligence or breach of contract for violations **3.121** of privacy.[355] Contractual obligations were also at issue in *Calgary Regional Health Authority v United Western Communications Ltd*,[356] where a nurse disclosed confidential details about abortions being performed at the applicant's hospital to a news magazine. In view of the fact that the information had been obtained in 'flagrant breach'[357] of the nurse's employment contract and that its publication could put individuals' safety at risk, the Court enjoined the publisher from disclosing the information. Under the circumstances, the privacy and safety rights of the doctors and hospital staff outweighed any public interest in disclosure.[358]

Canadian judicial decisions have expressed mixed views on whether an independ- **3.122** ent common law tort of invasion of privacy exists in Canada, with some courts expressing doubt on this point,[359] while others have taken the opposite position or at least left open the possibility.[360] A significant decision of the Ontario Court of

---

[350] Privacy Act, RSS 1978, c P-24, s 3(d); Privacy Act, CCSM, c P125, s 3(d); Privacy Act, RSNL 1990, c P-22, s 4(d).

[351] Privacy Act, RSS 1978, c P-24, s 7; Privacy Act, RSNL 1990, c P-22, s 6; Privacy Act, CCSM, c P125, s 4(1). The British Columbia legislation does not specify the remedies available.

[352] Privacy Act, RSBC 1996, c 373, s 2; Privacy Act, RSS 1978, c P-24, s 4; Privacy Act, CCSM, c P125, s 5; Privacy Act, RSNL 1990, c P-22, s 5.

[353] (1996) 34 CCLT (2d) 95, BCSC; aff'd (1998) 113 BCAC 304, BCCA.

[354] *Hollinsworth* (n 353) (BCCA) [31].

[355] *Peters-Brown v Regina District Health Board* [1996] 1 WWR 337, para 17; aff'd [1997] 1 WWR 638, CA.

[356] (1999) 242 AR 173, QBD.

[357] *Calgary* (n 356) para 17.

[358] *Calgary* (n 356) para 16.

[359] See *eg Hung v Gardiner* [2002] BCSC 1234, para 110; aff'd [2003] BCCA 257, (2003) 227 DLR (4th) 282; *Bingo Enterprises Ltd v Plaxton* (1986) 26 DLR (4th) 604, Man CA, para 17 (Monnin CJM), and para 22 (Twaddle JA); *Lord v Canada (Attorney General)* 2000 BCSC 750, para 16; *Euteneier v Lee* (2005) 260 DLR (4th) 145, para 63.

[360] See *eg Ontario (Attorney General) v Dieleman* (1994) 117 DLR (4th) 449, paras 542–64; *Savik Enterprises v Nunavut (Commissioner)* 2004 NUCJ 4; *Somwar v McDonald's Restaurants of*

Appeal in 2012, *Jones v Tsige*, recognized the existence of the tort of 'intrusion on seclusion' as a form of breach of privacy.[361] Jones and Tsige were both employees of the same bank; they did not know each other or work together but Tsige had become involved with Jones' former husband. Over the course of four years, Tsige accessed information about Jones' personal bank accounts using her workplace computer but not for any legitimate work-related purpose.[362] Tsige apologized and was disciplined by her employer, then was sued by Jones for invasion of privacy and breach of fiduciary duty (though the latter claim was dismissed at trial).[363] The judge at first instance held that Jones had no cause of action for invasion of privacy.[364] This decision was reversed by the Ontario Court of Appeal, which held that an independent tort of 'intrusion upon seclusion' should be recognized and was made out in this case.[365]

**3.123**    Justice Sharpe, writing for a unanimous court, reviewed the earlier cases, finding that 'there has been no definitive statement from an appellate court' in Canada on whether there was a common law right of action for intrusion upon seclusion, and that the judge below had erred in considering an earlier Ontario Court of Appeal decision[366] as a binding authority on this point. After reviewing the key authorities from several common law jurisdictions, as well as the protection of privacy under the Canadian Charter of Rights and Freedoms and international human rights instruments, Sharpe JA concluded that all of these justified the recognition of an action for intrusion upon seclusion. He also considered the framework of relevant federal and provincial legislation, and disagreed with the trial judge's conclusion that these excluded or displaced a common law tort; none of the legislation showed an intent to displace the common law or provided a private right of action to individuals for breach of privacy.[367]

**3.124**    To define the elements of the tort, Sharpe JA drew on American law and set out the following 'key features of this cause of action':

> ...first, that the defendant's conduct must be intentional, within which I would include reckless; second, that the defendant must have invaded, without lawful justification, the plaintiff's private affairs or concerns; and third, that a reasonable person would regard the invasion as highly offensive causing distress, humiliation or anguish. However, proof of harm to a recognized economic interest is not an element of the cause of action.[368]

---

*Canada Ltd* (2006) 263 DLR (4th) 752, paras 22, 31; *Shred-Tech Corp v Viveen* [2006] OJ No 4893, Ont SCJ, para 30; *Nitsopoulos v Wong* (2008) 298 DLR (4th) 265, Ont SCJ, para 19.

[361]    2012 ONCA 32.
[362]    *Jones* (n 361) para 4.
[363]    *Jones* (n 361) paras 6–7, 9.
[364]    *Jones v Tsige* 2011 ONSC 1475.
[365]    *Jones* (n 361) para 92.
[366]    *Euteneier v Lee* (2005) 260 DLR (4th) 145.
[367]    *Jones* (n 361) paras 49–51. Ontario is not one of the provinces with a statutory tort of invasion of privacy (see 3.119).
[368]    *Jones* (n 361) para 71.

Finally, he considered how damages should be assessed in cases where there was **3.125** no pecuniary loss. Referring to earlier cases and guidance on this point in the Manitoba Privacy Act,[369] Sharpe JA summarized the following factors as being relevant to determining damage awards:

1. the nature, incidence and occasion of the defendant's wrongful act;
2. the effect of the wrong on the plaintiff's health, welfare, social, business or financial position;
3. any relationship, whether domestic or otherwise, between the parties;
4. any distress, annoyance or embarrassment suffered by the plaintiff arising from the wrong; and
5. the conduct of the parties, both before and after the wrong, including any apology or offer of amends made by the defendant.[370]

It was suggested that the damages awarded, where there is no pecuniary loss, should be 'modest but sufficient to mark the wrong that has been done' and the range should be up to $20,000, absent exceptional circumstances where additional aggravated and punitive damages are warranted.[371]

Applying the law to the case at hand, Sharpe JA held that Tsige had committed the **3.126** tort of intrusion on seclusion, since her actions were intentional and without lawful justification, and invaded Jones' private affairs in a way that would be 'highly offensive to a reasonable person and caused distress, humiliation or anguish'.[372] Damages were assessed at the mid-point of the range ($10,000), since the conduct was deliberate and repeated, in a context of emotional domestic relationships, but there had been no public embarrassment or harm to Jones' interests and Tsige had apologized.

To date, *Jones v Tsige* has been applied or considered in several cases, both within **3.127** Ontario and in other provinces. In one 2013 Ontario case, the judge held that the tort of intrusion upon seclusion had not been made out by the claimant, because on the facts as established at trial, the defendant had only faxed some documents containing the claimant's personal information to a third party who had a legal right to read them; the defendant himself had not read the documents.[373] In another case, damages in the amount of $7,500 were awarded where the plaintiff's personal information was improperly accessed by her ex-boyfriend's new partner and disclosed to the ex-boyfriend.[374] A class proceeding recently certified in Ontario raises the novel questions of an employer's vicarious liability for deliberate intrusions by

---

[369] Privacy Act, CCSM, c P125, s 4.
[370] *Jones* (n 361) para 87.
[371] *Jones* (n 361) para 87.
[372] *Jones* (n 361) para 89.
[373] *Ludmer v Ludmer* 2013 ONSC 784, aff'd 2014 ONCA 827.
[374] *McIntosh v Legal Aid Ontario* 2014 ONSC 6136.

its employee and the availability of damages for intrusion upon seclusion where resulting pecuniary loss suffered by the plaintiffs has already been compensated.[375]

**3.128** The status of the tort of intrusion upon seclusion remains uncertain outside Ontario. A series of decisions in the province of British Columbia, both before and after *Jones v Tsige*, have rejected the existence of a common law tort supplementing the statutory tort under the Privacy Act.[376] In Newfoundland, where a statutory tort also exists, the question remains open.[377] Courts in New Brunswick[378] and Nova Scotia[379] have declined to decide whether the tort exists in those provinces. In the Nova Scotia decision, the Court accepted that a claim could be made in that province for intrusion on seclusion, but noted that considering the tort in that case (where the violation involved publication of personal information in newspaper reports and blogs) would require the Court to decide what weight should be given to freedom of expression in deciding such claims—a point which had not been argued.[380] This question was explicitly left open by the Ontario Court of Appeal in *Jones v Tsige*, where it was stated that the protection of privacy 'will have to be reconciled with, and even yield to' competing claims, foremost of which were 'claims for the protection of freedom of expression and freedom of the press'.[381]

**3.129** How the Canadian courts approach this reconciliation will be one key area to follow in the years to come. Another will be the extent to which the other elements of invasion of privacy also come to be recognized as valid common-law causes of action.[382] Finally, it appears that the question of the common-law tort's relationship to statutory remedies may not have been entirely settled by the decision in *Jones*. Although that decision held that a common-law claim should be recognized regardless of federal and provincial legislation that also deals with privacy issues, subsequent litigation has revisited the question as to whether a claim can be brought when the individual has other remedies available in a statutory scheme.[383]

---

[375] *Evans v Bank of Nova Scotia* 2014 ONSC 2135 (certification of class proceeding against bank where bank employee improperly accessed and disclosed customers' personal information, leading to some of them being victims of identity theft and fraud).

[376] *Hung v Gardiner* 2002 BCSC 1234, aff'd 2003 BCCA 257; *Demcak v Vo* 2013 BCSC 899; *Ari v Insurance Corp of British Columbia* 2013 BCSC 1308; *Ladas v Apple Inc* 2014 BCSC 1821.

[377] *Hynes v Western Regional Integrated Health Authority* 2014 CanLII 67125 (NLTD).

[378] *Avery v Canada (Attorney General)* 2013 NBQB 152 (unnecessary to decide because conduct was legally justified).

[379] *Trout Point Lodge Ltd v Handshoe* 2012 NSSC 245 (damages awarded for the alternative claim of defamation).

[380] *Trout* (n 379) para 78.

[381] *Jones* (n 361) para 73.

[382] Sharpe JA had adopted the four-part articulation of invasion of privacy from American jurisprudence (including intrusion on seclusion as well as public disclosure of embarrassing facts, publicity placing the plaintiff in a false light, and appropriation of the plaintiff's name or likeness), and limited his consideration to the category of intrusion on seclusion: *Jones* (n 361) paras 18–21.

[383] See *eg Hopkins v Kay* 2015 ONCA 112.

## (6) South Africa

### (a) Tort law

South Africa,[384] a mixed legal system, inherits its private law from the continental **3.130** tradition rather than English law. Accordingly, South African law has long recognized a right to privacy as an independent personality right that is a component of the Roman legal concept of 'dignitas' and that is protected by a tortious action to remedy the breach of a personality right—the *actio iniuriarum*.[385] The breach of a person's right to privacy occurs when there is an unlawful and intentional acquaintance with private facts by outsiders contrary to the determination and will of the person whose right is infringed, such acquaintance taking place by an intrusion or by disclosure.[386]

There are two elements to unlawfulness: the infringement must be subjectively **3.131** contrary to an individual's will and must also be objectively unreasonable in the sense of being contrary to the general sense of justice of the community, as perceived by the court.[387] Apart from wrongfulness, intention is required to establish a breach of privacy.[388] Intention is presumed once wrongful infringement of privacy has been established by the plaintiff; the defendant must then rebut the presumption.[389] Defendants may justify a breach of privacy on one or more grounds. In the case of media defendants the most relevant ground of justification is that there is a public interest in the private information.[390]

### (b) The Constitution

Section 14 of the Constitution[391] entrenches a right to privacy in the following terms: **3.132**

**Privacy**

14. Everyone has the right to privacy, which includes the right not to have—
(a) their person or home searched;
(b) their property searched;

---

[384] This section was written by Iain Currie, Advocate, Johannesburg Bar.

[385] *Bernstein v Bester NO* [1996] (2) SA 751 (CC) para 68. J Neethling, JM Potgieter, and PJ Visser, *Neethling's Law of Personality* (2nd edn, Lexis Nexis 2005) 217–20.

[386] Neethling, Potgieter, and Visser (n 385) 221.

[387] *Financial Mail v Sage Holdings* 1993 (2) SA 451 (A) at 462G; Neethling, Potgieter and Visser (n 385) 221.

[388] Neethling, Potgieter, and Visser (n 385) 252.

[389] Neethling, Potgieter, and Visser (n 385) 253, citing *Kidson v SA Associated Newspapers* 1957 (3) SA 461 (W), 468–9.

[390] *Financial Mail* (n 387) 462–3. See *eg MEC for Health, Mpumulanga v M-Net* [2002] 6 SA 714 (T) (broadcast of 'hidden camera' video material showing alleged mistreatment of patients in public hospital a violation of privacy; broadcast however justified on ground of public interest); *Greeff v Protection 4U h/a Protect International* [2012] 6 SA 392 (GNP) (no public interest in publication of video of incident involving Springbok rugby team engaged in demeaning rituals during training camp).

[391] Constitution of the Republic of South Africa, 1996. Its immediate predecessor, the interim Constitution (Constitution of the Republic of South Africa, Act 200 of 1993) also contained a right to privacy in s 13. The interim Constitution was in force between April 1994 and February 1997.

(c) their possessions seized; or

(d) the privacy of their communications infringed.

Section 14 is part of the Bill of Rights and is therefore binding on the state in the negative sense that it may not legislate or conduct itself to infringe the right to privacy and in the positive sense that the state must promote the right to privacy.[392] The right is also binding in the 'horizontal' dimension, principally as a result of the courts' obligation to develop the common law in accordance with the Bill of Rights.[393] Despite this, following the *NM* decision of the Constitutional Court[394] (considered in 3.135), in the absence of a challenge to the constitutionality of the common law, or an argument for its development, most privacy litigation in the horizontal dimension entails a straightforward employment of the common-law action for breach of privacy.

**3.133** The South African Constitutional Court has delivered several judgments on the constitutional right to privacy. These deal with legislation prohibiting the possession of indecent or obscene photographs[395] and child pornography,[396] the criminal law prohibition of sodomy,[397] legal compulsion to attend and give evidence at an insolvency inquiry,[398] powers of inspection to enforce the regulation of pharmaceutical manufacture and distribution,[399] the criminalization of prostitution[400] and consensual sexual relations of children.[401] The right has also been invoked in challenges to search and seizure powers in the context of the investigation of crime,[402] the regulation of gambling,[403] the control of money laundering,[404] and customs and revenue.[405]

**3.134** The Court's interpretation of the constitutional right to privacy is a mixture of US and European privacy jurisprudence. On the one hand, the Court has emphasized that the roots of the right lie in the value of human dignity.[406] On the other hand,

---

[392] Constitution (n 391) s 7(2).

[393] Constitution (n 391) s 39(2). The right might also be directly invoked by private litigants in appropriate cases: s 8(2).

[394] *NM v Smith* [2007] 5 SA 250 (CC).

[395] *Case v Minister of Safety and Security* [1996] 3 SA 617 (CC).

[396] *De Reuck v Director of Public Prosecutions (Witwatersrand Local Division)* [2004] 1 SA 406 (CC).

[397] *National Coalition for Gay and Lesbian Equality v Minister of Justice* [1999] 1 SA 6 (CC).

[398] *Bernstein v Bester NO* (n 385).

[399] *Mistry v Interim National Medical and Dental Council of South Africa* [1998] 4 SA 1127 (CC).

[400] *S v Jordan* [2002] 6 SA 642 (CC) (no significant privacy interests in the act of prostitution).

[401] *Teddy Bear Clinic for Abused Children v Minister of Justice and Constitutional Development* [2014] 2 SA 168 (CC) (legislation imposing criminal liability on children under age of sixteen for consensual sexual conduct unjustifiably infringes children's rights to human dignity and privacy).

[402] *Investigating Directorate: Serious Economic Offences v Hyundai Motor Distributors (Pty) Ltd* [2001] 1 SA 545 (CC).

[403] *Magajane v Chairperson, North West Gambling Board* [2006] 5 SA 250 (CC).

[404] *Estate Agency Affairs Board v Auction Alliance (Pty) Ltd* [2014] 3 SA 106 (CC).

[405] *Gaertner v Minister of Finance* [2014] 1 SA 442 (CC).

[406] *S v Jordan* (n 400) para 81.

the Court has defined the right, along US lines, as protecting an actual (or subjective) expectation of privacy that society is prepared to recognize as reasonable.[407]

The decisions just mentioned all deal with the 'vertical' aspect of the right to privacy, **3.135** involving challenges to legislation or to state conduct. In *NM*, the Constitutional Court was invited for the first time to consider the question of the correspondence of the *iniuria* of breach of privacy with the constitutional right to privacy.[408] A chapter of a biography of an opposition politician disclosed the names of three women who had been involved in a controversial drug trial as well as the fact that they were HIV-positive. The common-law action for breach of privacy requires a defendant to have acted intentionally or knowingly. There is no liability for a merely negligent or innocent breach of privacy. The High Court found that the disclosure in this case was not intentional and that the defendants were accordingly not liable for a negligent breach of privacy.[409]

On appeal to the Constitutional Court, it was argued on behalf of the plaintiffs **3.136** that the recognition of a constitutional-level right to privacy required reconsideration of this rule. A similar rule in the common law of defamation had been overturned by the South African courts since the advent of the Constitution, creating liability for negligent publication of defamatory material by media defendants. The same development, so the argument went, should take place for breach of privacy, creating a delict of negligent breach of privacy. A majority of the Constitutional Court decided the case without deciding this question, preferring to leave the question whether the 'age-old' approach of the common law needed reconsideration to a future, more 'appropriate', case.[410]

Some indication of what the Court might hold in such a future case is given in **3.137** a minority decision in the case. O'Regan J set out a reformulated standard of breach of privacy applicable to the publication of private fact by media defendants, understood as 'professional and commercial purveyors of information'.[411] Before publishing private material without the consent of the data subject, editors and journalists must 'ask the question: is the publication of this information, although it is private information, nevertheless reasonable in the circumstances?'[412]

### (c) Data protection

Data protection legislation was enacted in 2013. The Protection of Personal **3.138** Information Act 4 of 2013 aims to regulate comprehensively the processing of

---

[407] *Bernstein v Bester NO* (n 385) para 67.
[408] *NM v Smith* (n 394).
[409] *NM v Smith* [2005] 3 All SA 457 (W).
[410] *NM v Smith* (CC) (n 394) para 57. The majority was able to avoid the argument by holding that the defendants had in fact acted intentionally, understood as a standard of recklessness as to the probable outcome of a course of action.
[411] *NM v Smith* (n 394) para 181.
[412] *NM v Smith* (n 394) para 178.

personal information. It does so by requiring the processing of personal information to be fair and lawful and specifying a set of general principles of fair and lawful
processing. These principles are enforceable as legislative rights at the instance of
the data subject, with the assistance of an independent authority: the Information
Regulator. The principles restrict the processing of personal information by the
person who controls it, including obligations not to disclose it to third parties
without the knowledge or consent of the data subject. They also entail obligations
of transparency when personal information is processed. This entails that personal
information should, in principle, be collected directly from the data subject rather
than from third parties. If it is necessary for it to be collected by indirect means, the
data subject should be made aware that this is taking place.

**3.139** The Act exempts professional journalists who are subject to a binding code of conduct. There is limited protection of privacy in the current codes—the South African
Press Code and the Broadcasting Complaints Authority Codes of Conduct—and
these will need updating. There is also a general exclusion of processing of personal
information 'for the purpose of journalistic, literary or artistic expression to the
extent . . . necessary to reconcile, as a matter of public interest, the right to privacy
with the right to freedom of expression'.[413]

## D. Privacy in Civil Law

### (1) Scotland

#### (a) Traditional common law rights

**3.140** It might be said that Scots law[414] is more disposed to recognize, at common law, a
general right to privacy that seems to be the case elsewhere in the United Kingdom.
The law of England has of course conclusively rejected any such right arising at
common law.[415] However, Scots law, based on Roman law, might encompass a
claim for breach of privacy as part of the *actio iniuriarum*. Thus in 1936, in the case
of *Robertson v Keith*,[416] a Bench of seven judges considered a claim for damages
following on the decision of a Chief Constable to set up surveillance to observe the
home of the pursuer (*ie* the claimant) because he suspected that one of his officers
was concealing himself there and refusing to return to duty. The Court had little difficulty in comprehending this as *prima facie* wrongful. Lord Justice Clerk
Aitchison said:

> I do not doubt that to set and maintain a police watch upon the house of a citi-
> zen, in circumstances that attract public attention and give rise to suspicion in the

---

[413] Protection of Personal Information Act 4 of 2013, s 7.
[414] This section was written by Mr Roddy Dunlop, QC, Axiom Advocates, Edinburgh.
[415] *Wainwright v Home Office* [2004] 2 AC 406.
[416] 1936 SC 29.

public mind, may, if done without just cause, amount to an invasion of the liberty of the citizen as truly and effectively as if the citizen were subjected to physical restraint. But whether in any case it is an unlawful invasion of liberty must depend upon the circumstances of the particular case.[417]

In more modern, post-ECHR times, Lord Bonomy considered an argument, **3.141** based on *Robertson* and on Article 8 rights, that a pursuer in a claim for personal injuries had suffered actionable wrong as a result of surveillance conducted on behalf of the defender for the purposes of discrediting his claims of disability.[418] On the question of a free-standing, common-law right to privacy, Lord Bonomy was not prepared to rule it out, saying:

> Of course it does not follow that, because a specific right to privacy has not so far been recognised, such a right does not fall within existing principles of the law. Significantly my attention was not drawn to any case in which it was said in terms that there is no right to privacy . . . Counsel for the defender submitted that the *actio iniuriarum* provides redress only where deliberate conduct involves an attack on personality for an unlawful purpose. Examples were insulting and abusive behaviour, harassment or stalking, which was seen as an attack on the honour of another, beating another man's slave, which was an insult to the honour of the owner, and intruding into another's home for an unlawful purpose. It may, however, be only a short step from an assault on personality of the nature of an insult to the dignity, honour or reputation of a person, causing hurt to his feelings, to deliberate conduct involving unwarranted intrusion into the personal or family life of which the natural consequence is distress.[419]

Accordingly, an interesting question arises as to whether or not Scots law has, for **3.142** some time prior to the introduction of the HRA, recognized a right to privacy. However, this discussion is likely to prove academic given the evolution in England of a cause of action, based on breach of confidence, designed to protect Article 8 rights. Such an evolution is easily recognized by a Scots lawyer. Scots law has for many years acknowledged that certain species of confidential information are entitled to protection. This was seen in circumstances of some notoriety in *Duke of Argyll v Duchess of Argyll*.[420] There, the House of Lords was required to consider an attempt, in the course of an action for divorce, to obtain an order from the court requiring the production of the wife's diary which, it was said, would contain details of an illicit affair.

The Lord Ordinary (*ie* the judge at first instance), on the grounds of confiden- **3.143** tiality, refused to allow the diary to be recovered. On appeal, the Inner House (*ie* the Scottish appeal court) ruled that, by agreeing to a proof (or trial) on averments which included an admission by the wife that she kept a diary, the wife had

---

[417] *Robertson v Keith* (n 416) 48. The case is discussed by Lord Kilbrandon in 'The Law of Privacy in Scotland' (1971) 2 Cambrian L Rev 35, 42–3.

[418] *Martin v Mcguiness* 2003 SLT 1424.

[419] *Martin v Mcguiness* (n 418) [28]–[29].

[420] 1962 SC (HL) 88.

waived any question of confidentiality. That point was then appealed to the Lords, who held, unanimously, that there was no question of confidentiality having been waived, and that accordingly production of the diary would not be ordered. In so ruling, the Lords affirmed a long-standing line of authority[421] that diary entries are entirely private and entitled to a high degree of protection under the law of Scotland.

**3.144**  Those proceedings were, of course, followed by further litigation in England, in which the Duke of Argyll was prohibited by injunction from disclosing details of his former wife's infidelity, again on the grounds of confidence.[422] The injunction was sought in England because the threatened publication (by the *People* newspaper) would originate in England, but there is no reason to suppose that any different result would have been obtained from a Scottish court: while the decision of Ungoed-Thomas J in *Duchess of Argyll* was doubted in certain respects by Lady Paton in the more recent case of *Nicol v Caledonian Newspapers Ltd*,[423] there was no criticism of the decision so far as it depended on a common law duty of confidence.

*(b) The impact of the Human Rights Act 1998*

**3.145**  Equally, there can be little doubt that the Scottish courts will adopt a similar approach to those in England following the advent of the HRA. There have already been several cases where Scottish courts have asserted that domestic Scots law is Article 8 compliant.[424] Further, and of more direct relevance, there have been two cases in which an interim interdict (the equivalent to an interim injunction) has been sought under express reliance on Article 8 rights, and opposed under express reliance on Article 10. The first of these was *X v BBC*,[425] in which interim interdict was granted such as to restrain the broadcasting of a television programme relating to the operation of Glasgow Sheriff Court. One of the participants in the programme contended that the broadcast would infringe her Article 8 rights, to such an extent that she threatened suicide. The temporary judge granted interim interdict, following the law regarding Article 8 in its domestic context as explained by the Lords in *Campbell v MGN Ltd*.[426]

**3.146**  A contrary result was arrived at in *Response Handling Ltd v BBC*.[427] There, a company operating call centres sought interim interdict preventing the BBC from broadcasting a programme investigating bank account and credit card fraud, which featured video footage obtained covertly in the pursuers' premises by an

---

[421] Notably *Creasey v Creasey* 1931 SC 9.
[422] *Argyll (Duchess) v Argyll (Duke)* [1967] Ch 302.
[423] 2003 SLT 109.
[424] *Narden Services Ltd v Inverness Retail and Business Park Ltd* 2008 SLT 621; *HM Advocate v Murtagh* 2009 SLT 1060.
[425] 2005 SLT 796.
[426] *Campbell* (n 117).
[427] 2008 SLT 51.

undercover reporter, in express breach of a confidentiality clause. Interim interdict was refused, the Lord Ordinary having undertaken the balancing test between the competing Article 8 and Article 10 interests and having ruled that it could not be said to be 'likely' that the pursuers would succeed at proof. The test for interim interdict as set out in s 12(3) HRA, as explained by the Lords in *Cream Holdings Ltd v Banerjee*,[428] was thus not met.

Article 8 was again relied upon, this time in judicial review proceedings, in *Potter v Scottish Ministers*. There, a prisoner sought judicial review of a policy of the Scottish Prison Service to attach a pre-recorded message to all outgoing telephone calls, informing the recipient that the call was coming from a prison and might be the subject of surveillance. The petitioner complained that this breached Article 8. That complaint was initially upheld,[429] but overturned on appeal[430] with the Inner House holding that, in considering the complaint, one also had to take into account the Article 8 rights of recipients of phone calls from prisoners. The case ended up proceeding to an evidential hearing, after which it was held[431] that recipients of phone calls originating in Scottish prisons had a legitimate expectation of privacy, and their Article 8 rights would be infringed were they not informed of the surveillance to which the calls might be subjected; and moreover that there was evidence of a pressing need to protect victims of domestic abuse and violence from unwanted calls. Accordingly, Lord Matthews took the view that there was no interference with Article 8(1); but that even if there was such interference was justified under Article 8(2). **3.147**

In each of these cases, the Court has borrowed heavily from English jurisprudence on the incorporation of Article 8 rights into domestic law, and it is now unlikely that there will be any material divergence between the law of Scotland and that of England in this area. Indeed, any doubt in that regard was surely removed by the unanimous views expressed in the Supreme Court in *A v BBC (Secretary of State for the Home Department intervening)*.[432] **3.148**

### (c) Procedural differences from England and Wales

The main difference between Scots law and that of England and Wales may, accordingly, lie in procedure rather than in substantive law. In matters of procedure, significant differences do exist. In particular, the practice which has developed in England relating to interim non-disclosure orders,[433] which are capable of binding persons not party to the litigation, has no analogue north of the border. **3.149**

---

428 [2004] UKHL 44, [2005] 1 AC 253.
429 2007 SLT 363.
430 2007 SLT 1019.
431 2010 SLT 779.
432 [2014] UKSC 25, [2014] 2 WLR 1243 [46]–[48].
433 *Practice Guidance (Interim Non-disclosure Orders)* [2012] 1 WLR 1003.

**3.150**  Scots law requires an identifiable and identified defender before an action may be commenced. The English procedure of allowing an action against 'persons unknown' would not be permitted in Scotland. While it is permissible to raise proceedings against persons whose names are not known, there must be an identifiable defender upon whom a summons may be served.[434] Moreover, Scots law does not recognize the concept of transferred injunctions. The law of England, of course, holds that anyone who becomes aware of the granting of an injunction is bound not to contravene the same. That was established in the course of the *Spycatcher* litigations in the late 1980s, and in particular by *Attorney General v Newspaper Publishing plc*.[435]

**3.151**  In the Scottish incarnation of the *Spycatcher* dispute,[436] the Inner House held that purported interdict of 'any other person having notice of said interlocutor' was incompetent, because it was contrary to the principles of the law of Scotland that the court should make a prohibition order against persons who had no knowledge that it was being sought. When that case reached the House of Lords,[437] Lord Keith of Kinkel, giving the leading speech, indicated he could find no error in the approach of the Inner House, though he did not specifically comment on this point of competency. Lord Jauncey noted the point but indicated he did not feel it necessary to address it. Accordingly, the position rests with the decision of the Inner House in *Lord Advocate v Scotsman*, and on that basis it is not competent in Scotland to seek an order which would be effective against persons who are not parties to the litigation but who come to have notice of that order. Reporting restrictions can, of course, be sought,[438] and such restrictions are effective against non-parties, but interdicts prohibiting disclosure of private material require to be directed against the person(s) whom it is feared will so disclose. Obviously, in certain cases, identification of such parties can be very difficult. Whether Scots procedure can demonstrate the elasticity required to tackle the problem of anonymous disclosure via the internet remains to be seen.

### (2) Germany

**3.152**  German[439] courts did not explicitly acknowledge a right to privacy before the German Basic Law (*ie* the German constitution) came into force in 1949.[440] Although it stipulates

---

[434]  *Kay v Morrison's Representatives* 1984 SLT 175; *McLaren v Procurator Fiscal* 1992 SLT 844.

[435]  [1988] Ch 333.

[436]  *Lord Advocate v The Scotsman Publications Ltd* 1988 SLT 490.

[437]  *Lord Advocate* (n 436).

[438]  *eg* under s 11 of the Contempt of Court Act 1981; cf *A v BBC* (n 432).

[439]  This section is written by Richter am Landgericht Björn Raap, LLM (VUW), Judge of the Aurich District Court.

[440]  Cases concerning the law of privacy were decided by referring to other legal actions; see RGZ 45, 170 (*Bismarck case*); see also K Zweigert and H Kötz, *Introduction to Comparative Law* (3rd edn, Oxford University Press 1998) 688–9; B Markesinis and H Unberath, *The German Law of Torts: A Comparative Treatise* (4th edn, Hart 2002) 76.

an extensive catalogue of fundamental rights, the Basic Law does not explicitly include a right to privacy.[441] However, the German Federal Constitutional Court has held that Article 1, which guarantees the inviolability of human dignity, and Article 2, which among other fundamental rights comprises the right to a free development of the personality, nonetheless create a 'general personality right'.[442]

The right to personality is therefore an unwritten fundamental right which includes  **3.153**
the right of the individual to reputation and to the free development of his or her personality. It also ensures that every individual has ownership of the information disclosed and spread about him or her, be it his or her image, his or her spoken or written word, or details about his or her private life.[443] It reflects the principles of dignity and autonomy and protects a person from commercial exploitation whether of image, name, or voice.

The German Basic Law, and particularly its catalogue of fundamental rights, only  **3.154**
binds state authorities and does not have a direct effect on private law.[444] However, since the 1950s, German superior courts have held that the 'general personality right' creates corresponding protection for personality interests in private law.[445] Ever since, courts have recognized fundamental rights in civil cases, and a significant proportion of these cases have concerned the horizontal effect of the right to privacy.

The resolution of privacy disputes in German civil law invariably involves con-  **3.155**
sideration of the balance to be struck between an individual's privacy interests and conflicting fundamental rights. Typically, the conflict is between the 'general personality right' and the categories of expression that the German Basic Law protects in Article 5,[446] which include the freedom to express and disseminate one's opinion; freedom of the press, radio, and TV broadcasting; freedom of free speech; and artistic freedom.

Both the German Federal High Court and the German Federal Constitutional  **3.156**
Court stress that the weighing up of competing fundamental rights has to be made

---

[441] Zweigert and Kötz (n 440) 688. A Ohly, A Lucas-Schloetter, and H Beverley-Smith, 'Artistic freedom versus privacy—a delicate balance: The *Esra* case analysed from a comparative law perspective' [2008] Intl Rev Intell Prop and Competition L 526, 528.

[442] See also Zweigert and Kötz (n 440) 690.

[443] R Youngs, *English, French and German Comparative Law* (Routledge-Cavendish 1998) 277–78.

[444] See G Wagner, 'Comparative Tort Law' in M Reimann and R Zimmermann (eds), *The Oxford Handbook of Comparative Law* (Oxford University Press 2006) 1003, 1020–23.

[445] German Federal Constitutional Court, BVerfGE 7, 198, 205; 101, 361, 388; German Federal High Court, BGHZ 13, 334, 338.

[446] Zweigert and Kötz (n 440) 691–2; Ohly, Lucas-Schloetter, and Beverley-Smith (n 441) 529; K von Bassewitz, 'Hard times for paparazzi: Two landmark decisions concerning privacy rights stir up the German and English media' [2004] Intl Rev Intell Prop and Competition L 642, 644.

on a case-by-case basis.[447] However, German superior courts have nonetheless repeatedly applied the following guiding principles:[448] (1) the distribution of false facts is not protected by the Basic Law;[449] (2) truthful facts can be distributed as long as they contribute to the formation of opinion and are not intimate or confidential; (3) value judgments are extensively protected by Article 5 German Basic Law and their restriction requires proof of a *substantial* competing third party interest or *substantial* reasons of public interest interests (which corresponds broadly with the English concept of the 'public interest').

### (a) The influence of Strasbourg

**3.157**  The German law of privacy and the judgments of German superior courts are increasingly influenced by the jurisprudence of the ECtHR. This influence is continually evident in the development of German case law, especially the well-known *Caroline* case. The *Caroline* case concerned the publication of surreptitiously taken photographs of Princess Caroline of Monaco. The photographs showed the Princess in public places undertaking obviously private activities such as dining with her partner at a restaurant or on outings with her children. Princess Caroline sought redress in the national courts, claiming that publication of the photographs infringed her right to privacy.[450] On appeal, the Federal Constitutional Court weighed up the Princess's 'general personality right' with the freedom of the press and partially granted her claim.[451] The Court stated that even when acting in the public arena, there are situations where celebrities have a reasonable expectation of privacy. The Court held that photographs taken of celebrities in a 'secluded place' might be actionable even though the respective place was in the public arena, *eg* at the corner of a restaurant. The judges held that photographs taken from a considerable distance may indicate a reasonable expectation of privacy.[452] Additionally, the Court pointed out that a celebrity's expectation of privacy deserves particular protection in cases where the press release of photographs involves the depiction of a celebrity's children. It ruled that the parent-child relationship is particularly sensitive and deserves special protection, irrespective of it being acted out in the private or the public arena.[453] Therefore, Princess Caroline's appeal was partially granted with regard to those pictures showing herself together with her children.

---

[447] See *eg Caroline Case* German Federal Constitutional Court, BVerfGE 101, 361, 384; German Federal High Court, *Mascha S* case, Judgment of 5 November 2013—VI ZR 304/12 and *Günther J* case, Judgment of 29 April 2014-VI ZR 137/13.

[448] Compare Palandt, *Bürgerliches Gesetzbuch* (74th edn, Verlag CH Beck 2015) § 823 BGB, 1380–1; Ohly, Lucas-Schloetter and Beverley-Smith (n 441) 529.

[449] See *eg* German Federal High Court, *IM Christoph* case, Judgment of 11 December 2012-VI ZR 314/10.

[450] German Federal High Court, BGH Z 131, 332.

[451] German Federal Constitutional Court, BVerfGE 101, 361.

[452] German Federal Constitutional Court, BVerfGE 101, 361, 395.

[453] German Federal Constitutional Court, BVerfGE 101, 386; the Court refers to Art 6 of the German Basic Law which stipulates the state's obligation to protect the family; see also *Mascha S* case (n 447) and *Günther J* case (n 447).

Even though the *Caroline* case considerably enhanced celebrities' right of privacy  **3.158**
under German law, in *von Hannover v Germany*, the ECtHR criticized the domestic courts' approach to privacy protection and held that it does not adequately
protect the personality rights of public figures.[454] The ECtHR held that the distinctions the domestic courts drew between different types of public figure and
different types of places were in practice too vague for an individual to know in
advance what kind of public figure he or she was and, more importantly, whether
he or she was in a protected sphere at any given time. The judges said:

> As a figure of contemporary society *'par excellence'* [the applicant] cannot—in the
> name of freedom of the press and the public interest—rely on protection of her pri-
> vate life unless she is in a secluded place out of the public eye and, moreover, succeeds
> in proving it (which can be difficult). Where that is not the case, she has to accept that
> she might be photographed at almost any time, systematically, and that the photos
> are then very widely disseminated even if, as was the case here, the photos and accom-
> panying articles relate exclusively to details of her private life. In the Court's view, the
> criterion of spatial isolation, although apposite in theory, is in reality too vague and
> difficult for the person concerned to determine in advance. In the present case merely
> classifying the applicant as a figure of contemporary society *'par excellence'* does not
> suffice to justify such an intrusion into her private life.[455]

The ECtHR did not, however, repeat these criticisms in the second *Caroline* case,  **3.159**
*von Hannover v Germany (No 2)*, thanks to a change of approach by German
domestic courts.[456] This case concerned three pictures released by German
magazines between 2002 and 2004. Two of the pictures were taken of Princess
Caroline and her husband while walking on a public street in a popular ski resort
in Switzerland. The first picture was published in connection with an article concerning the poor health of Princess Caroline's father, the late Prince Rainier. The
second was published alongside a written report on the Princess's winter holiday.
The third picture showed the Princess and her husband sitting in a public chairlift
in an Austrian skiing area and was accompanied by a report about an upcoming
ball in Monaco. On appeal, the German Federal High Court partially granted
the Princess's claim that the defendant should refrain from further publication of
the pictures.[457] The judges held that, even if considered in connection with the
accompanying articles, the second and third pictures did not make a significant
contribution to the formation of public opinion. However, the first picture was
different. The publication of that picture had to be assessed in connection with the
article about the health of Prince Rainier, who was an important figure in contemporary society. The Court held that the illness of the reigning Prince of Monaco
constituted an event of general public interest. The press were allowed to include

---

[454] *von Hannover v Germany (Caroline case)* (2005) 40 EHRR 1, 25, paras 67 and 74; von
Bassewitz (n 446) 646–8; see also G Wagner in Reimann and Zimmermann (n 444) 1021.
[455] *von Hannover* (n 454) paras 74–5.
[456] [2012] ECHR 228, para 126.
[457] German Federal High Court, Judgment of 6 March 2007-VI ZR 51/06.

in reports of this important information a picture of Princess Caroline in a public place even though she was obviously on private business when it was taken. This decision was approved on appeal by the Federal Constitutional Court.[458] The ECtHR also upheld it. In *von Hannover v Germany (No 2)*, it explicitly held that the German superior courts had, in response to criticism of the first *Caroline* judgment, implemented adequate protections of the Article 8 right to respect for private life.[459]

**3.160** That conclusion was endorsed in *Axel Springer v Germany* which the ECtHR handed down on the same day as *von Hannover v Germany (No 2)*.[460] In this case, the applicant was the publisher of a widely disseminated daily German newspaper. In 2004 and 2005 the newspaper published two articles concerning a popular German actor who was well known for playing the role of a police superintendent in a famous TV series. The first publication was a front-page report about the arrest of the actor at the Oktoberfest in Munich for the possession of cocaine. In the second publication the actor's confession in court was reported. The publication of both articles contained several photographs of the actor. The actor successfully sued the publishing house and obtained an interim injunction prohibiting further publication of the articles and photographs. In the main proceedings, the judges once again upheld the actor's claim and held that his right to privacy outweighs the public interest in information about the case.[461] The judges of the Hamburg High Court pointed out that the charges against the actor were minor because of the small quantity of drugs found in his possession. Therefore, the Court reasoned, the criminal proceedings would not have been reported but for the celebrity of the accused and, accordingly, were not of particular public interest.

**3.161** In contrast to *von Hannover v Germany (No 1)*, where German privacy protections were seen to be too restrictive, in *Axel Springer v Germany* they were held to be too expansive. As in *von Hannover v Germany (No 2)*,[462] the ECtHR emphasized the essential role played of the press in a democratic society and held that press freedom extends to a right to exaggerate or even provoke.[463] Even though the ECtHR approved of the German courts' general approach to privacy, the judges held that the German courts have not given sufficient weight to the extensive scope of the freedom of the press. The Court pointed out that the arrest of the actor and the subsequent criminal procedures were of public interest since the arrest took place in in the public arena of the Munich Oktoberfest. This was the

---

[458] German Federal Constitutional Court, Order of 26 February 2008-1 BVR 1602/07.

[459] *von Hannover v Germany (No 2)* (n 456) para 126.

[460] *Axel Springer AG v Germany* (2012) 55 EHRR 6, paras 107, 110.

[461] The final decision in this case was decided by the Hamburg High Court. Further appeals of the publishing house to the German Federal High Court and the German Federal Constitutional Court were not permissible by German procedural law.

[462] *von Hannover v Germany (No 2)* (n 456) para 102.

[463] *Axel Springer AG v Germany* (n 460) paras 79–81.

more so since the actor was popular for his role as a police superintendent, whose mission was law enforcement and crime prevention.[464]

In *von Hannover v Germany (No 2)* and the *Axel Springer* case the ECtHR applied **3.162** and established seven guiding principles that have to be taken into account when weighing up the freedom of expression and of a free press against an individual's right to privacy.[465] These are: (1) the contribution of the released information to a debate of general interest; (2) the degree of popularity of the person concerned and the subject matter of the revelations; (3) the prior conduct of the person concerned as regards the public and the media: had the claimant him or herself revealed private information to the public and therefore actively sought the limelight in the past?; (4) the method by which the concerned information was obtained by the media; (5) the validity and accuracy of the publication; (6) the form and content of the released information and the consequences of the release; (7) the gravity of the sanction imposed on the applicant. The application of these principles can be observed in several recent German Federal High Court cases.[466] This highlights the ongoing, and increasing, influence of the ECtHR's law of privacy jurisdiction on contemporary German case law.

### (3) France

#### (a) Informational privacy

French law[467] on informational privacy is referred to as *protection du secret de la* **3.163** *vie privée* to distinguish it from other types of personality rights included in the concept of *la vie privée*, and from the concept of autonomy expressed in the phrase *la liberté de la vie privée*.

The French Constitution of 22 August 1795 had recognized only the limited pri- **3.164** vacy right that '[e]very citizen's home is an inviolable asylum' (subject to serious qualifications).[468] During the nineteenth and twentieth centuries, French law developed various piecemeal personality rights, including at an early stage the right to control one's image.[469] Later, in 1970, the right to respect for private life was formalized first in the new Article 9 of the French Civil Code. This states no

---

[464] *Axel Springer AG v Germany* (n 460) para 99.
[465] *Axel Springer AG v Germany* (n 460) paras 89–95; *von Hannover v Germany (No 2)* (n 456) paras 108–13.
[466] See *eg Mascha S* case (n 447); *Günther J* case (n 447); *Sächsische Korruptionsaffäre* case, Judgment of 17 December 2013-VI ZR 211/12.
[467] This section was written by Dr Eva Steiner, King's College London. The law discussed in this section is also addressed in E Steiner, 'The new president, his wife and the media: Pushing away the limits of privacy law's protection in France?' (2009) 13.1 Electronic J of Comparative L.
[468] É Picard, 'The right to privacy in French law' in B Markesinis (ed), *Protecting Privacy* (Oxford University Press 1999) 49.
[469] Picard (n 468) 50; P Kayser, *La Protection de la Vie Privée par le Droit* (3rd edn, Economica 1995) 217, paras 118–22.

more than that '[e]veryone has the right to respect for his private life', a wording borrowed from Article 8(1) ECHR.

**3.165** When France ratified the ECHR in 1974 (and later accepted the right of individual petition in 1981) the Convention became directly applicable in domestic law. Although the right to privacy is not referred to as such in the text of the French Constitution, in 1995 it was ascribed constitutional value by the French Constitutional Court as a corollary of the principle of individual freedom recognized by Article 2 of the Declaration of the Rights of Man and the Citizen 1789, and Articles 2 and 66 of the Constitution itself.[470]

**3.166** Within the terms of the Civil Code, Article 9, everyone, whether or not he or she is in the public eye, has the right to respect for his or her private life.[471] This principle has by now become very well established and French judges do not hesitate to make a reference to it when necessary and appropriate. Thus, according to French courts, 'everyone, regardless of rank, birth, wealth and present or future role in society, is entitled to respect to his/her private life'. However, the long tradition that French politicians never had to worry about the French press reporting their intimate life came under serious attack following the huge media coverage in 2011 of the rape case scandal involving the former French head of the International Monetary Fund, D Strauss-Kahn, and, more recently, the publication by the magazine *Closer* of photographs showing French President F Hollande leaving his alleged mistress's Paris apartment in January 2014.[472]

**3.167** The Civil Code provides for specific remedies which include the possibility of an interim injunction to restrain any publication of private information, the seizure of any offending publication, the award of damages, and the publication of the judgment given against the newspaper or magazine. Any intrusion into someone else's private life is also an offence under Article 226-1 of the New Criminal Code 1994. Anyone found guilty in this respect is liable to a term of one year's imprisonment and/or a fine to a maximum of €45,000.

*(b) Image rights*

**3.168** Under Article 9 of the French Civil Code, protection of privacy has always included not only disclosure of what have been perceived as elements of a person's private life but also the unauthorized taking of photographs of people and their publication, as well as 'false light' presentation. In this respect, it should be pointed out that public figures in France have a considerable degree of control over how their image is used by the media. Thus, there is no right in France to use the picture of a public figure for a purpose or in a manner which differs from the one

---

[470] Decision 94-352DC, 18 January 1995; also, Decision 99-416 DC, 23 July 1999.
[471] See 3.164.
[472] Although the President decided not to sue *Closer*, in January 2014 his alleged mistress was seeking from the magazine €50,000 in damages and €4,000 in legal costs in a Paris court.

which was originally agreed and, further, there is no right to distort the manner in which an individual interviewed has chosen to project his or her image or express his or her opinion.[473]

In addition, the fact that a celebrity or a politician is presumed to have given his or her tacit consent for the taking and publication of photographs in the carrying out of his or her public activities or official duties does not permit the use of these pictures for commercial purposes. A celebrity or politician's absolute and exclusive right to control his or her own image is reaffirmed in the 2008 *Sarkozy and Bruni Tesdeschi v Ryanair* judgment where the budget airline was ordered to pay damages to President Sarkozy and his new wife for using their picture in an advertisement without their consent.[474] **3.169**

It has to be noted here that in France public figures and celebrities are afforded better protection than ordinary individuals who are not generally successful in their attempt to protect their image in similar circumstances. In recent cases where pictures of individuals have been taken, either to cover an event or to illustrate books or magazines, the courts have decided that, unless there has been a breach of their right to 'human dignity', the public interest to be informed and freedom of expression should prevail over their right to privacy.[475] **3.170**

### (c) Balancing privacy and freedom of expression

Article 9 of the Civil Code has generated a very important body of case law. Today, French courts are attempting to strike a balance between the freedom of the press and the people's right to know on the one hand, and, on the other hand, the individual's right to respect for private life.[476] **3.171**

Generally, French courts approach the balancing exercise required in this area in the light of two principles: **3.172**

   (1) There is no hierarchy between the competing rights involved. All have the same normative value.

---

[473] A classic illustration is Paris, 13 February 1971, *Société des Publications et Société Marie-Claire Albums v JP Belmondo* JCP 1971 II 16774. More recently, see Civ 1, 30 May 2000, D 2001, Somm 1989 (the case of rock singer J Hallyday).

[474] TGI Paris, 5 February 2008, JCP 2008, Act 117. There are two precedents to *Ryanair* in respect of French presidents, one is TGI Paris, 4 April 1970 JCP 1970 II 16328 (photograph of President Pompidou on board a motor boat which was used to advertise that brand of boat); the other is TGI Nancy, 15 October 1976 JCP 1977 II 18526 (where the picture of President Giscard D'Estaing was used as a figure appearing on a card game).

[475] Thus, the picture of a victim of a terrorist attack can be published without her consent as long as there is no interference with her dignity (Cass Civ 1, 20 February 2001, D 2001, 1199); the same applies to the picture of a victim of a road traffic accident (Civ 2, 4 November 2004, D 2005, Jur 696; JCP 2004 10186) and to the publication of an artistic book showing the pictures of individuals taken on the street (TGI Paris, 9 May 2007 and 25 June 2007, D 2008, 57).

[476] For a recent typical illustration, see TGI Nanterre, 22 November 2012 where the Court draws a distinction between a marriage of a celebrity which falls within the field of the public right to be informed and a mere intent to marry which belongs to the sphere of privacy.

(2) All measures taken in the balancing process must be proportionate to the aim pursued.

**3.173**  More specifically, freedom of the press and freedom of expression must prevail when there is a public interest to be informed of a current event (*fait d'actualité*) or when the fact against which the privacy issue is raised is capable of contributing to a 'debate of general interest'. This latter notion is borrowed from the Strasbourg jurisprudence and has been assimilated in French case law quite recently.[477] Although this notion overlaps with *fait d'actualité*, it does not necessarily need to be a current event.

**3.174**  However, privacy will override press freedom and freedom of expression when the disclosure either concerns the 'intimacy of private life' or when intrusion was made in complete disregard to 'human dignity'.[478] This latter notion was first raised by the French Constitutional Court in 1994 when asked to review the legislation on bioethics.[479] It is today encapsulated in Article 16 of the French Civil Code and has been used widely by the courts in the context of personal rights, including the right to privacy. Human dignity has never been clearly defined but encompasses any degrading or humiliating treatment of an individual by the media. Recent cases refer in addition to the level of distress caused by possible disclosure.[480]

**3.175**  The scope of the notion of 'intimacy' was further tested in a 2013 Paris Court of Appeal decision where the plaintiffs claimed that a book soon to be published had infringed their private right to intimacy by outing them as homosexuals.[481] Here, the Court had to decide whether the public right to be informed—since one of the partners was a prominent member of the far-right National Front party known for its conservative views on family law—came before the respect to private life. At the time, it was pointed out by some commentators that the fact that high-ranking members of the National Front party were themselves homosexual was one of the reasons for the National Front not to support the massive marches against the government proposal to legalize gay marriage in 2013. Taking on board these considerations, the Paris Court operated a fine distinction between the two

---

[477] See *von Hannover v Germany* (n 454) paras 60, 76: according to the ECtHR, the 'debate of general interest' was the decisive factor in balancing the protection of private life against freedom of expression. In France, see the case of *Express-Expansion v J Copin* Civ 1, 24 October 2006, Bull Civ I, 437, D 2006 IR 2754. Here, in order to keep its readership abreast of current influential networking chains in France, a magazine published a list of local councillors belonging to Freemason guilds. The Court decided that such disclosure was a legitimate contribution to 'a debate of general interest'.

[478] See also 3.170.

[479] DC 94-343-344, 27 July 1994.

[480] See TGI Paris, 12 February 1998, upheld on appeal on 24 February 1998 and in the Court of Cassation in December 2000 concerning the murder in Corsica of a French high ranking police officer whose lifeless body photograph was published in the French magazine *Paris Match*. The ECtHR, to which the case was referred, further decided that there was no violation of Art 10 ECHR on freedom of expression in this case: *Hachette, Filipacchi v France* (2009) 49 EHRR 23.

[481] CA Paris, 19 December 2013, JCP, 2014, 13.

partners involved in the case by ruling that for the partner who was not involved in the politics of the party the right to intimacy should prevail over public interest; however, as far as the other person was concerned, the Court stated that there was a right for the public to be informed of his sexual orientation in view of his political responsibilities. In so doing the Court assumed that the sexual orientation of a political figure had an influence on the political decisions he or she makes in the name of the party. This ruling contrasts with the line of previous precedents where such revelations would have amounted to a breach of privacy rights.

### (d) The right to be forgotten

French law further recognizes the principle of compassion in a 'right to be forgot- **3.176** ten'. This right is increasingly under threat from the capacity of the memories of modern computers to preserve indefinitely personal data and the results of processing of the data. This can interfere with the right to be forgotten (*droit à l'oubli*), which can be regarded as a natural right, grounded in the idea that people's pasts should not crush them by making them lose their sense of freedom nor by preventing them from reforming themselves. In order to address these concerns and strengthen the protection of personal data online, the French Secretary of State in charge of the digital economy introduced in 2010 two codes (charters) of good practice, one being specifically about 'the right to be forgotten on social networks and search engines'.[482] These codes were signed by a number of representatives of social networks, service providers, and search engines committed to safeguarding internet users' right to consent to data processing.[483] These commitments have been seen by the French government as a starting point for further legislation and future international agreements in this area.

---

[482] 13 October 2010, *Charte du droit à l'oubli numérique dans les sites collaboratifs et moteurs de recherche.*
[483] However, Facebook and Google were not signatories to these codes.

# Part II

## PUBLICATION OF PERSONAL INFORMATION

# 4

## BREACH OF CONFIDENCE

*Justin Rushbrooke QC and Adam Speker*

## A. Introduction

This chapter is concerned with claims for what is commonly known as breach **4.01** of confidence. Until quite recently, reliance on the cause of action for breach of confidence has been one of the two main ways in which claims to protect or vindicate privacy have been pursued in English law. The other, much less significant in practice,[1] is reliance on statutory rights such as those afforded by the Data Protection Act 1998. Today, as a result of the House of Lords' decisions in

---

[1] Possibly because of the restrictions on the availability of interim injunctions (as to which see 7.116) and possibly because data protection law does not appear in any other respect to be more advantageous to claimants than breach of confidence.

149

*Campbell v MGN Ltd* [2] and *Douglas v Hello! Ltd*,[3] it is possible to differentiate between two different kinds of claim: (i) traditional breach of confidence actions;[4] and (ii) claims for misuse of private information.[5] The first of these kinds of claim will be discussed in this chapter. The second, misuse of private information, is a cause of action which has developed in the present century originating in, becoming separate and distinct from, breach of confidence.[6] It will be addressed separately in Chapter 5.

**4.02**   It is the cause of action for misuse of private information that will be of most relevance in the majority of privacy cases involving the media. Nevertheless, it is important for practitioners and others interested in privacy law to recognize that in some factual situations causes of action for breach of confidence, traditional or hybrid, and for misuse of private information may coexist, and that in certain situations the older-established cause of action may be easier to establish, or may reinforce the newer cause of action. Moreover, the boundaries of the causes of action are not immutable but may change to reflect changes in society, technology, and business practice.[7] In addition, although the Court of Appeal said in *A v B plc* that authorities relating to the action for breach of confidence prior to the coming into force of the Human Rights Act 1998 (HRA) 'are largely of historic interest only',[8] courts will still find it necessary in developing both the laws of confidence and misuse of personal information to have regard to the existing structure of the law and to proceed incrementally, as was suggested in the Court of Appeal in *Douglas v Hello! Ltd*.[9]

---

[2] [2004] UKHL 22, [2004] 2 AC 457.

[3] [2007] UKHL 21, [2008] 1 AC 1.

[4] Including the 'hybrid' confidence action involving personal information where, as the House of Lords said in *Douglas* (n 3) the claim depends on the commercial value of the confidential information in question: see 4.07 and 4.25.

[5] Where, as explained in *Campbell* (n 2), there is no need for a duty to exist and the true basis of the action is the protection of personal autonomy and dignity: see [13]–[15] (Lord Nicholls) and [48]–[50] (Lord Hoffmann).

[6] As Lord Nicholls said in *Douglas* (n 3) [255], we now have 'two distinct causes of action, protecting two different interests: privacy, and secret ("confidential") information. It is important to keep these two distinct.'

[7] *Douglas v Hello! Ltd* [2001] QB 967 [165] (Keene LJ) and *Secretary of State for the Home Dept v Wainwright* [2001] EWCA Civ 2081, [2002] QB 1334 [39], [42] (Mummery LJ). In 2012, Lord Neuberger MR observed that 'it is probably fair to say that the extent to which privacy is to be accommodated within the law of confidence as opposed to the law of tort is still in the process of being worked out': *Phillips v News Group Newspapers Ltd* [2012] EWCA Civ 48, [2013] 1 AC 1 [48] (Lord Neuberger MR).

[8] *A v B plc* [2002] EWCA Civ 337, [2003] QB 195 [9]. It should be noted that the specific context in which the Court of Appeal made these remarks was that of over-citation of authority on urgent interim injunction applications.

[9] *Douglas* (n 7).

## B. The Cause of Action for Breach of Confidence: An Overview

### (1) Origins and Development

The modern English law of confidence is considered to have its origins in the mid-  **4.03**
nineteenth-century case of *Prince Albert v Strange*.[10] Prince Albert obtained an
injunction restraining the defendant from publishing a catalogue of private etchings made by Queen Victoria and Prince Albert. Lord Cottenham LC held that
the evidence showed:

> ...that the catalogue and the descriptive and other remarks therein contained,
> could not have been compiled or made, except by means of the possession of the
> several impressions of the said etchings surreptitiously and improperly obtained.
> To this case no answer is made...If then, these compositions were kept private,
> except as to some...sent to [B] for the purposes of having certain impressions
> taken, the possession of the defendant...must have originated in a breach of trust,
> confidence, or contract, in [B] or some person in his employ taking more impres-
> sions than were ordered, and retaining the extra number.[11]

Although this case concerned private matters, until relatively recently the law  **4.04**
of confidence had mainly developed in the commercial sphere, protecting trade
secrets and business information rather than *personal* private information. Most
cases depended on express or implied contractual duties.[12] For years the potential of the law of confidence for protecting privacy lay largely unrecognized, even
neglected.[13] However, in the last few decades of the twentieth century and the
early years of the twenty-first, there was an increasing recognition of the important role which the law of confidence could play in the protection of personal
privacy.[14] The doctrine of confidentiality proved to be extremely flexible, and has

---

[10] (1849) 2 De G & Sm 652, 64 ER 293; (1849) 1 Mac & G 25, 41 ER 1171, CA. In *Douglas*
Lindsay J described *Prince Albert's case* as 'a case as to personal confidence but in which authorities
on commercial confidence are cited': [2003] EWHC 55 (Ch), [2003] 2 All ER 996 [181]. The Court
of Appeal in the same case said that the information was 'personal, not commercial, although the
defendant intended to make money out of it': *Douglas v Hello! Ltd* [2005] EWCA Civ 595, [2006]
QB 125 [54].

[11] *Prince Albert v Strange* (1849) 41 ER 1171, 1178–9. *Prince Albert's case* might even be considered the first privacy case, since although the relationship of 'trust, confidence or contract' was necessary to bind the defendant's conscience, it is questionable whether the nature of the information
protected was truly 'confidential' in the modern sense.

[12] *Attorney General v Observer Ltd* [1990] 1 AC 109, 281 and *Thomas v Farr plc* (2007) ICR 932,
(2007) IRLR 419. The protection of confidential business information is considered at 4.34 and
4.57–4.61.

[13] *Kaye v Robertson* [1990] FSR 62, CA; *Bryan v MGN Ltd* (HC, 1992, Latham J).

[14] See the discussion of Lord Hoffmann in 'Mind your own business', Goodman Lecture 22 May
1996, referred to by Sedley LJ in *Douglas* (n 7) [136] and by Butler-Sloss P in *Venables v News Group
Newspapers Ltd* [2001] Fam 430 [41]. Recent developments were in fact foreshadowed long before
these decisions: see 1.17–1.18.

been held capable of protecting from publication or other misuse a variety of kinds of personal information, including information about an individual's medical condition, marital life, sexual relationships, private conversations, and other activities out of public view.[15]

**4.05** After the HRA came into force the courts initially sought to perform their duty not to act inconsistently with Convention rights by 'absorbing' the values enshrined in the Convention into the established cause of action for breach of confidence.[16] It came to be recognized, however, that this was not an entirely comfortable process: the established framework of the cause of action for breach of confidence was not wholly suitable for the protection of all kinds of personal or private information. Nor was it a wholly apt vehicle for the implementation of the right to respect for private life guaranteed by Article 8. So by 2004 the House of Lords was moved to declare, in *Campbell v MGN Ltd*, that the law had 'shaken off' the need to prove the existence of a duty of confidence.[17] In a parallel development, the House declared Convention rights to be the foundation of its jurisdiction to protect privacy.[18] The judgment of the European Court of Human Rights (ECtHR) in *von Hannover v Germany*[19] confirmed a positive obligation on Member States to protect one individual from an unjustified invasion of private life by another individual, and this was recognized as requiring further development of domestic law.[20] In 2007 it was acknowledged by the House of Lords that such development had led to the creation of a new cause of action, labelled as misuse of private information, separate and distinct from 'traditional' breach of confidence.[21]

**4.06** This has not meant that traditional breach of confidence has ceased to play a role in privacy cases involving the media. The Court of Appeal has repeatedly made clear that where, on long-established principles, a duty of confidence arises from a confidential relationship, that is important to, and may be decisive for, a claim for misuse of private information. In *McKennitt v Ash* the Court held that once it

---

[15] See 5.33 *et seq* for detailed discussion of the types of information which may be protected in confidence.

[16] *A v B plc* (n 8) [4]; *Campbell* (n 2) [17].

[17] *Campbell* (n 2) [14].

[18] *In re S (A Child)* [2004] UKHL 47, [2005] 1 AC 593 [22]–[23], which involved both direct (vertical) and indirect (horizontal) application of the HRA.

[19] (2005) 40 EHRR 1.

[20] *Douglas* (n 10) [50]–[53].

[21] *Douglas* (n 3) [255]. The House had until that point expressly disavowed the creation of a new cause of action: see *Campbell* (n 2) [86] (Lord Hope), [132]–[134] (Lady Hale). The Court of Appeal had loyally adopted this approach: see *eg Douglas* (n 10) [53]; *McKennitt v Ash* [2006] EWCA Civ 1714, [2008] 1 QB 73 [8(ii)]. In *Phillips v News Group Newspapers Ltd* [2012] UKSC 28, [2013] 1 AC 1 [29] Lord Walker described the law of confidence as having become 'bifurcated' inasmuch as its protection extended to private information of a personal nature as well as commercial information. In *Vidal-Hall v Google Inc* [2015] EWCA Civ 311, [2015] 3 WLR 409 the Court of Appeal upheld Tugendhat J's finding that the new cause of action for misuse of private information was a tort for the purposes of CPR PD 6B para 3.1(9).

was recognized that the duty of confidence relied on by the claimant arose from the relationship between them (rather than the nature of the information) the case 'reverts to a more elemental enquiry into breach of confidence in its traditional understanding of that expression'.[22] In *HRH Prince of Wales v Associated Newspapers Ltd* the information again derived from a confidential relationship, this time one of employment. The Court held that to approach the case by reference to the criteria specified in *Campbell* was an oversimplification; if the information was confidential in character, 'there are in this action all the elements of a claim for breach of confidence under [the old] law'.[23] The public interest in the observance of duties of confidence, the fact the information was disclosed in breach of such a duty, and that the publisher knew this, all added weight to the claim.[24] In *Browne v Associated Newspapers Ltd* the Court cited these cases and reiterated that a previous relationship of confidence was of considerable importance in answering the question whether the claimant had a reasonable expectation of privacy in respect of particular facts.[25]

In addition, there emerged from the *Douglas* litigation a hitherto unrecognized **4.07** subcategory of breach of confidence claim which has been labelled 'hybrid' breach of confidence, where commercial confidentiality attaches to personal information whether or not it is also private. The House of Lords by a majority affirmed the validity of a breach of confidence claim by the publishers of *OK!* magazine, who had bought exclusive rights to photographic images of the Douglases' wedding, against the publishers of *Hello!*, who had published unauthorized photographs. This claim, the majority considered, was 'not concerned with the protection of privacy' or Convention rights; the fact that the information was about the Douglases' personal life was irrelevant.[26] It was 'simply information of commercial value'.[27] The House approved the trial judge's analysis of the claim as a conventional claim for remedies for breach of confidence in which the commercially valuable confidential information happened to be information of a private nature over which the Douglases had sufficient control to impose duties of confidence.[28]

---

[22] *McKennitt* (n 21) [15] (Buxton LJ).

[23] [2006] EWCA Civ 1776, [2008] Ch 57 [25], [28].

[24] *HRH Prince of Wales* (n 23) [66]–[69], [74].

[25] [2007] EWCA Civ 295, [2008] 1 QB 103 [25]–[26]. See further 5.148–5.151.

[26] *Douglas* (n 3) [118] (Lord Hoffmann).

[27] *Douglas* (n 3) [120].

[28] See further 4.25 and 4.84. Note that this concept may cause difficulties in the context of s 72 of the Senior Courts Act 1981, which removes the privilege against self-incrimination in respect of civil claims for (*inter alia*) infringement of rights pertaining to intellectual property. The Supreme Court has construed s 72(5), which includes within the definition of intellectual property 'any . . . technical or commercial information or other intellectual property', in such a way as to exclude private information of a personal nature, while recognizing that there may be some difficult borderline cases: see *Phillips v News Group Newspapers Ltd* (n 21) [29], [31].

## (2) Juridical Basis

**4.08**  A duty of confidence may arise expressly or impliedly by contractual or other agreement, or may be imposed by law. The juridical nature of the wrong has been the subject of considerable academic and judicial debate.

### (a) Contract

**4.09**  It is common for terms to be included in employment contracts and commercial agreements which restrict the disclosure of confidential information. Even in the absence of an express term an employee is bound by an implied term of good faith to his or her employer not to use or disclose for the duration of his or her employment confidential information gained in the course of that employment, and has certain more limited post-employment obligations. Contracts may similarly be used to protect personal information. In this context normal contractual principles, such as those governing the construction of terms, apply, though there are some important differences between the rules applicable to commercial and those relevant to personal information.[29]

### (b) Equity

**4.10**  An obligation of confidence, express or implied, can and often does arise at common law independently of contractual terms:

> The law on this subject does not depend on any implied contract. It depends on the broad principle of equity that he who has received information in confidence shall not take unfair advantage of it. He must not make use of it to the prejudice of him who gave it without obtaining his consent.[30]

The obligation arising in equity has often been said to be based on conscience: if the conscience of a reasonable person in the defendant's position would be affected by the conduct or threatened conduct in question the defendant comes under a duty of confidence.[31]

### (c) Tort, or sui generis

**4.11**  Equity is not the only juridical basis apart from contract which has been suggested for claims in confidence. The majority view has been that breach of confidence is an equitable cause of action, but there is some confusion in the authorities, and in particular the more recent ones, as to whether it is a tort[32] or whether it is *sui*

---

[29]  See further at 4.57–4.61.

[30]  *Seager v Copydex Ltd* [1967] 1 WLR 923, 931 (Lord Denning MR). See also *Moorgate Tobacco Co Ltd v Philip Morris Ltd* (1984) 156 CLR 414; *Imerman v Tchenguiz* [2010] EWCA Civ 908, [2011] Fam 116.

[31]  See *eg R v Dept of Health, ex p Source Informatics Ltd* [2001] QB 424, CA [31]; *WB v H Bauer* [2002] EMLR 145 [30]; *Douglas* (n 10), Lindsay J, cited with approval by Lord Hoffmann in the House of Lords: *Douglas* (n 3) [114]. The 'conscience test' is discussed at 4.154–4.155.

[32]  For a more detailed discussion see R Toulson and C Phipps, *Confidentiality* (3rd edn, Sweet & Maxwell 2012) ch 2, and T Aplin et al (eds), *Gurry on Breach of Confidence* (2nd edn, Oxford University Press 2012) ch 4.

*generis.*[33] Several of the leading recent authorities refer to it as a tort[34] but the point does not appear to have been argued in any of these cases. In *Douglas*, the Court of Appeal specifically considered the issue and thought otherwise.[35]

### (d) The significance of the issue

The authorities on the categorization of breach of confidence are difficult to reconcile. **4.12** It might be thought that in practice classification is unimportant, and that the difference between tort and equitable duty is largely one of terminology. However, the nature and extent of available remedies,[36] as well as defences,[37] may in principle be affected by this question, as may the appropriate court in which to bring a claim.[38] The question may also be of practical importance in considering the applicable law in publications with an international dimension.[39] If it is not a tort, *Dicey, Morris and Collins* suggest that the applicable law may be the law of the country where enrichment occurs.[40] This would be likely to raise difficult questions, and could lead to multiple applicable laws in cases where individuals in different jurisdictions are involved.

It is possible that categorization depends on the precise kind of wrong at issue. It **4.13** may be that traditional breach of confidence cases and 'hybrid' claims are properly viewed as grounded in equitable doctrines,[41] and that judicial references to a 'tort'

---

[33] See *Gurry on Breach of Confidence* (n 32) para 4.09: 'the action for breach of confidence is *sui generis* in nature and . . . it is difficult to confine the action exclusively within one conventional jurisdictional category'.

[34] See *eg Douglas*, CA (n 7) [117], [123] (Sedley LJ); *Venables* (n 14) [30], [44] (Butler-Sloss P); *Campbell* (n 2) [15] (Lord Nicholls). See also the discussion in *Giller v Procopets* (2008) 79 IPR 489 (Supreme Court of Victoria).

[35] See 13.86. An earlier edition of *Clerk and Lindsell on Torts* supported the tort analysis, but the 20th edition concludes at para 28-03 that the most favoured basis for the action to date is that of an equitable principle of good faith. See also *Imerman v Tchenguiz* (n 30) where the Court of Appeal regarded claims based on confidentiality as equitable. The Court of Appeal has now held in *Vidal-Hall v Google Inc* (n 21) that misuse of private information is a tort for the purposes of CPR PD 6B para 3.1(9). See further n 41.

[36] *eg* whether exemplary damages are available (as to which see the discussion of *Mosley v News Group Newspapers Ltd* at 12.134, and the statutory provisions discussed at 12.135), or whether an account of profits can be ordered, or a constructive trust imposed on property acquired in breach of confidence. For a detailed discussion of the current state of breach of confidence relating to trade secrets, particularly on when it is appropriate to grant an injunction and the limits of the 'springboard' doctrine, see *Vestergaard Frandsen A/S v Bestnet Europe Ltd* [2010] FSR 2 [27]–[96] (Arnold J) (rvsd in part on other grounds [2011] EWCA Civ 424; Court of Appeal upheld by Supreme Court [2013] UKSC 31, [2013] 1 WLR 1556).

[37] *eg* expiry of the limitation period: 11.219 *et seq.*

[38] See 13.66 *et seq.*

[39] See 13.82 *et seq.* See also *Vidal-Hall v Google Inc* (n 21).

[40] L Collins et al (eds), *Dicey, Morris and Collins on the Conflict of Laws* (15th edn, Sweet & Maxwell 2012) paras 34-091–34-092; but see 13.86. There are also potential complications in commercial confidence cases, arising from the 'Rome II' regulation, as to which see C Wadlow, 'Trade secrets and the Rome II Regulation on the law applicable to non-contractual obligations' [2008] EIPR 309.

[41] In *Kitetechnology BV v Unicor GmbH Plastmaschinen* [1995] FSR 765, 777–8, breach of confidence was held not to be a tort, but it was treated as analogous to a tort in *Seager v Copydex (No 2)* [1969] 1 WLR 809 and *Dowson & Mason Ltd v Potter* [1986] 1 WLR 1419: see *Vestergard Frandsen*

of breach of confidence are best explained by the fact that the cases in question were staging points on the journey towards the creation of the separate, new cause of action in tort for misuse of private information.[42]

### (3) Essential Elements of Traditional Breach of Confidence

**4.14**  In order to establish a cause of action for traditional breach of confidence, apart from contract, three elements are normally required:

(1)  that the information has the necessary quality of confidence about it
(2)  that the information has been imparted in circumstances importing an obligation of confidence
(3)  that there has been an unauthorized use [or a misuse] of the information.[43]

**4.15**  These elements, and the further question of whether it is necessary to show detriment to the confider are each discussed briefly in the next nine paragraphs, and considered in more detail in later sections of this chapter, to which cross-references are given in the footnotes.

*(a) Information having the quality of confidence*[44]

**4.16**  **Inaccessibility in the public domain**  The quality of confidence is not easy to define, and there is no clearly established set of rules for determining whether any given type of information satisfies this requirement. It is generally considered, however, that if information is to be the subject of a claim to confidentiality it must be inaccessible, and not in the public domain.[45]

**4.17**  **Other criteria**  Otherwise, certain classes of information have been authoritatively established to be of a confidential character, and a smaller number are established to be non-confidential.[46] It has been said of personal information that the answer to the question whether it is private will usually be obvious,[47] but this does

---

*A/S* (n 36) [19] (Arnold J). In *Douglas* the Court of Appeal had under consideration both the misuse of private information and what Lindsay J described, with the approval of the Court of Appeal (n 10 [34]), as a 'hybrid kind of commercial confidence'. The latter may be closer to an image right rather than the protection of genuinely private information.

[42]  See 4.05 for an account of the journey.

[43]  *Coco v AN Clark (Engineers) Ltd* [1969] RPC 41, 47, approved in *Attorney General v Observer Ltd* (n 12) 168 (Lord Griffiths) and unanimously by the House of Lords in *Douglas* (n 3) [307]. This is 'the conventional starting point for considering the nature and scope of the duty of confidentiality': *Source Informatics* (n 31) [14] (Simon Brown LJ). For a recent summary of the breach of confidence principles see Arnold J's judgment in *Force India Formula One Team Ltd v 1 Malaysia Racing Team SDN BHD* [2012] EWHC 616 (Ch), [2012] RPC 29 [215]–[224] (aff'd [2013] EWCA Civ 780, [2013] RPC 36). As to what constitutes sufficient misuse in the context of personal information as opposed to trade secrets, see *Imerman v Tchenguiz* (n 30). The authorities also consider but do not decide whether there is a fourth element: that the misuse of the information must be to the detriment of the confider: see the cases cited at n 394.

[44]  Discussed in detail at 4.63–4.91.

[45]  See 4.65 and 11.43 *et seq.*

[46]  For discussion of types of information that are capable of protection, see 5.28 *et seq.*

[47]  *A v B plc* (n 8) [11(vii)].

not necessarily answer the question whether it is confidential.[48] In any event, where the answer is not obvious a number of criteria can be identified in the case law, which may be used to determine whether particular information has a confidential quality.[49]

**Collections of data**   These may have a value and a status as confidential in their **4.18** own right, even if the individual items are all drawn or collected from the public domain. As Megarry J said in *Coco v AN Clark (Engineers) Ltd*:[50]

> Something that has been constructed solely from materials in the public domain may possess the necessary quality of confidentiality: for something new and confidential may have been brought into being by the application of the skill and ingenuity of the human brain. Novelty depends on the thing itself, and not upon the quality of its constituent parts.[51]

For a collection to acquire the quality of confidence however there must be some application of human skill, some selection. A list of public domain materials created by a mechanical and non-selective process is unlikely to qualify.[52]

*(b) Imparted in circumstances importing an obligation of confidence*[53]

**Information confided to a person**   In *Coco v A N Clark (Engineers) Ltd* Megarry J **4.19** held that an equitable obligation of confidence will be imposed 'if the circumstances are such that any reasonable man standing in the shoes of the recipient of the information would have realised that upon reasonable grounds the information was being given to him in confidence'.[54] The obligation has mostly arisen from a relationship between the two parties, the confider and the confidant, which demands that the latter respect the confidentiality of information imparted to him by the former. In more recent years, however, the courts have moved away from the need to establish a prior confidential relationship. This development was noted with approval by the European Commission of Human Rights.[55]

**Confidence imposed by the circumstances of receipt**   It is clear now that 'impart- **4.20** ing' in this context should not be read restrictively. A duty can arise from a communication made by someone other than the claimant, perhaps accidentally, or

---

[48] Decisions such as *A v B plc* (n 8) may need to be treated with some caution, being decided before the recognition of misuse of private information as a separate cause of action, and in a period where the boundaries between confidentiality and privacy were somewhat blurred.

[49] See 4.66–4.102.

[50] *Coco* (n 43) 47. See also *Saltman Engineering v Campbell Engineering* [1948] 65 RPC 203, 215 (Lord Greene MR).

[51] For the application of a similar principle in respect of personal information see *Green Corns Ltd v Claverley Group Ltd* [2005] EWHC 958 (QB), [2005] EMLR 748.

[52] *Ocular Sciences Ltd v Aspect Vision Care Ltd* [1997] RPC 289, 374 (Laddie J). Cf *Inline Logistics v UCI Logistics* (HC, 31 July 2000, Ferris J, aff'd [2002] RPC 32, CA).

[53] Discussed in detail at 4.114–4.145.

[54] *Coco* (n 43) 48.

[55] *Winer v UK* App no 10871/84, (1986) 48 DR 154; *Spencer (Earl and Countess) v UK* App nos 28851/95 and 28852/95 (1998) 25 EHRR CD 105.

merely from acquisition. In the *Spycatcher* case Lord Goff put the law on a broader footing when he stated that:

> ...a duty of confidence arises when confidential information comes to the knowledge of a person (the confidant) in circumstances where he has notice, or is held to have agreed, that the information is confidential, with the effect that it would be just in all the circumstances that he should be precluded from disclosing the information to others.[56]

This formulation, explained Lord Goff, was deliberately adopted so as to capture situations such as those 'beloved of law teachers', in which a confidential document is found in the street.

**4.21** **Confidence imposed to protect a human right** The President of the Family Division further developed the common law to treat as confidential information identifying the notorious murderers of James Bulger. She held not only that no pre-existing relationship was required to give rise to an obligation of confidentiality, but also that an injunction may be granted, even against the whole world, to restrain the disclosure of personal information if it is necessary to do so to protect another human right.[57] That decision and those that followed it[58] are probably best seen as points on the way to the new wrong of misuse of personal information which is discussed in the next chapter.[59]

### (c) Unauthorized use/misuse of the information

**4.22** **The conscience test** To determine whether confidential information has been misused it is necessary to know the nature and scope of the duty of confidence that the confider owed to the claimant in respect of it.[60] The *Coco v Clark* test for the creation of the duty[61] gives no guidance as to its scope.[62] The conventional and well-established test for the scope of the duty is whether the confidant's conscience would or should be troubled by the particular disclosure at issue. That test was reaffirmed by the Court of Appeal in *Source Informatics*[63] after an extensive review of the case law, and remains authoritative although it, in its turn, has been criticized

---

[56] *Attorney General v Observer Ltd* (n 12) 281. In *Campbell* (n 2) [48] Lord Hoffmann referred to this statement as 'now firmly established'.

[57] The President held that the rights under Arts 2 and 3 ECHR prevailed over the right to freedom of expression guaranteed by Art 10 but that the right to respect for private life guaranteed by Art 8 is also capable of prevailing over freedom of speech in an appropriate case: see *Venables* (n 14) [48]–[51].

[58] *eg A v B plc* (n 8).

[59] See 5.02–5.10 for discussion of the emergence of the new wrong. *OPQ v BJM* [2011] EWHC 1059 (QB), [2011] EMLR 23 provides a more recent example of a *contra mundum* injunction being issued to protect the claimant's and his family's Art 8 rights in the context of an old-fashioned breach of confidence claim.

[60] See the detailed discussion at 4.151–4.156.

[61] Set out at 4.19.

[62] *Smith Kline and French Laboratories (Australia) Ltd v Secretary to the Dept of Community Services and Health* [1990] FSR 617, 637–8, cited in *Source Informatics* (n 31) [24].

[63] *Source Informatics* (n 31).

for its vagueness and it has been suggested that Convention jurisprudence provides a better model.[64] In *A v B plc*, the Court of Appeal proposed a form of reasonableness test,[65] but again that may best be seen as a stage in the development of the separate wrong of misuse of private information which is considered in Chapter 5.

**The 'springboard' doctrine** The use of confidential information as a 'spring- **4.23** board' to the obtaining of other information is regarded as 'unauthorised use' because it allows one party to obtain an improper advantage over another and would be, accordingly, enjoined.[66] So if a claimant proves that there was an initial acquisition of confidential information the burden of proof shifts to the defendant to show that other information ultimately obtained and used was obtained completely independently of the confidential source.[67]

*(d) Detriment*

There is discussion in the case law as to whether detriment to the claimant is also a **4.24** necessary element of the cause of action for breach of confidence.[68] Detriment to the public interest is certainly required in cases about government secrets; and has been held to be a requirement of a hybrid breach of confidence claim. In breach of confidence relating to purely personal information the position is less clear, though there are indications that in most cases the overriding of personal autonomy can be considered a sufficient detriment.[69]

## (4) Hybrid Breach of Confidence

The *Coco v Clark* analysis[70] applies where a claim for hybrid breach of confidence **4.25** is advanced,[71] but in this context the 'quality of confidence' may be conferred on particular information because of its commercial value rather than its intrinsic character. The majority of the House of Lords in *Douglas v Hello! Ltd* (Lord Hoffmann, Baroness Hale, and Lord Brown) considered that the information at issue was confidential because it was 'information of commercial value over which the Douglases had sufficient control to enable them to impose an obligation of confidence'.[72] This view prevailed over that of the minority (Lords Nicholls and Walker), who considered that the case on breach of confidence 'must stand or fall

---

[64] *London Regional Transport Ltd v Mayor of London* [2001] EWCA Civ 1491, [2003] EMLR 4 [58] (Sedley LJ), discussed at 4.155–4.156.

[65] *A v B plc* (n 8) [11(x)].

[66] *Terrapin Ltd v Builder's Supply Co Ltd* [1960] RPC 128; *Seager v Copydex Ltd* (n 30); *QBE Management Services (UK) Ltd v Dymoke* [2012] EWHC 80 (QB), [2012] IRLR 458 [8].

[67] See *Spencer (Earl and Countess) v UK* (n 55).

[68] See n 394.

[69] See 4.36, 4.160–4.165 as regards personal information. As to government secrets, see 4.41–4.42; as to hybrid breach of confidence, see *Douglas*, CA (n 10) [118].

[70] See 4.14.

[71] *Douglas* (n 3) [111]–[113], [117] (Lord Hoffmann).

[72] *Douglas* (n 3) [124] (Lord Hoffmann). See also [117]–[120], and Lady Hale at [302], [307], and Lord Brown at [355].

on the ground of a right to short-term confidentiality for a trade secret' and that 'the confidentiality of any information must depend on its nature not on its market value'.[73]

### (5) The Position of Third Parties

#### (a) *Those acquiring information from a confidant or by some other means*[74]

**4.26** A duty of confidence is, as a general rule, imposed on a third party who acquires information knowing it to be subject to a duty of confidence, and an injunction may lie against any third party acquiring confidential information from a confidant on the ground that 'equity gives relief against all the world, including the innocent, save only a bona fide purchaser for value without notice'.[75] These principles will affect media organs which obtain information from one of the parties to a relationship subject to a duty of confidence. The position will usually be the same even if the information is acquired without the intervention of a party under a duty of confidence, as long as its confidential character is sufficiently obvious—to take one example, where the media organization acquires a photograph of the claimant holding a confidential document which (unbeknown to him or her) can be magnified to reveal its contents.[76]

**4.27** Whether the media will always be liable for financial remedies where they disclose information so acquired is not clear. In general, it appears that a third party acting in breach of confidence will not be held so liable unless shown to have acted dishonestly (in the equitable sense of 'not acting as an honest person would in the circumstances').[77] The Court of Appeal has held that this limitation does not apply to the new version of breach of confidence which has become the civil wrong of misusing private information,[78] but it may nonetheless be arguable that the principle, or something like it, may apply to a claim for traditional breach of confidence.[79]

#### (b) *Those on notice of injunctions against others*[80]

**4.28** If a third party is put on notice of an interim injunction granted against another to protect a confidence that notice may, and usually will, suffice to place the third party under a duty of confidence. Separately, and in addition, it may well be a contempt of court for the third party to publish material which is the subject of the

---

[73] *Douglas* (n 3) [295], [299]. For a critical academic analysis see G Black, '*OK!* for some: *Douglas v Hello!* in the House of Lords' (2007) 11 Edinburgh L Rev 402.

[74] See 4.137–4.143.

[75] Per Nourse LJ in *Attorney General v Observer Ltd* (n 12).

[76] For the reasons given in 4.20.

[77] *Thomas v Pearce* [2000] FSR 718, CA; see also 4.139–4.140.

[78] *Campbell v MGN Ltd* [2002] EWCA Civ 1373, [2003] QB 633 [66]–[70]. The House of Lords did not deal directly with this question, but agreement with the Court of Appeal's view is implicit in all the speeches.

[79] See 4.139–4.140.

[80] See 4.144–4.147.

order. It is a serious offence against justice itself for a newspaper or media organization to take action which would destroy the confidentiality that the court was seeking to protect by granting the injunction.[81]

### (6) Answers, Defences, and Justifications

In summary, the possible answers to claims for traditional breach of confidence, **4.29** often described as 'defences', include consent, waiver, that the information is in the public domain, that the restraint which the claimant seeks to enforce is an unlawful restraint of trade or otherwise contrary to public policy, and that disclosure is justified in the public interest. All of these are considered in detail in Chapter 11. It may be strictly more accurate to describe 'the public domain' not as a defence but as a factor which precludes the existence of a cause of action,[82] and it has been described[83] as a 'limiting principle'. However, for convenience, but with this note of caution, 'public domain' is dealt with only briefly in this chapter and in more detail in Chapter 11 at 11.43 *et seq.*

### (7) Remedies

The equitable remedy of an injunction is, for obvious reasons, the one most often **4.30** sought in confidence actions, but damages (in lieu of an injunction as well as by way of compensation for past breaches)[84] or, in principle, an account of profits are also available. Remedies are considered in Chapter 12.

## C. Classification of Confidential Information

Breach of confidence has traditionally been concerned with protecting four main **4.31** classes of information: trade secrets, personal confidences, government information, and artistic and literary confidences.[85] The paragraphs which follow consider briefly each of these four categories, starting with government information.

### (1) Government Information

The law of confidence has been used on occasion by central government to pre- **4.32** vent, or attempt to prevent, the disclosure of government secrets. That the law of confidence applies to government secrets was established in the *Crossman Diaries*

---

[81] *Attorney General v Newspaper Publishing Ltd* [1988] Ch 333, CA, 374. The same is probably not true of a permanent injunction. See further 4.146–4.147.

[82] See *eg Gurry on Breach of Confidence* (n 32) para 5.14. See also 11.43.

[83] By Lord Goff, in *Attorney General v Observer Ltd* (n 12) 282.

[84] Chancery Amendment Act 1858 (Lord Cairns' Act); see the discussion in Toulson and Phipps (n 32) paras 9-037 *et seq.*

[85] See *eg Source Informatics* (n 31) [31] (Simon Brown LJ).

case, *Attorney General v Jonathan Cape Ltd*,[86] where the information at issue was the detail of cabinet discussions. The law of confidence has since been applied to governmental information on a number of occasions, most notably in the *Spycatcher* case[87] and in *Attorney General v Blake*,[88] where the information was about the workings of the secret services and included actual or alleged intelligence information.

**4.33** Although the law of confidence clearly applies to information of this nature it is also clear that the applicable legal principles differ significantly from those which apply in private law cases: 'when equity protects government information it will look at the matter through different spectacles' from those used in cases about private information.[89] The differences are discussed below.[90]

### (2) Commercial, Trade, and Business Information

**4.34** This is the class of case in which confidentiality issues have most often been litigated. A wide range of kinds of commercial information has been held to be capable of protection as confidential. The archetypal case is the customer list, which was the subject of the claim in the well-known case of *Robb v Green*.[91] Other examples include technical secrets such as production drawings for a machine[92] or other information about manufacturing methodology;[93] business and trading information such as a company's manufacturers and suppliers, and prices paid;[94] other financial secrets such as unpublished company accounts;[95] and information which is disclosed or comes into being in the course of an arbitration.[96] The list is in principle unlimited. As the Court of Appeal said in *Faccenda Chicken Ltd v Fowler*, it is impossible to provide an exhaustive list of matters which will qualify for

---

[86] [1976] 1 QB 752, 769–70 (Lord Widgery CJ), where he rejected the contention that the principles developed in *Prince Albert's case* and subsequent authorities were applicable only between private parties.

[87] *Attorney General v Observer Ltd* (n 12).

[88] [2001] 1 AC 268.

[89] *Commonwealth of Australia v John Fairfax & Sons Ltd* (1980) 147 CLR 39, 151–2, Mason J, cited with approval by the House of Lords in *Attorney General v Observer Ltd* (n 12) 258, Lord Keith; 270, Lord Griffiths; and 283, Lord Goff.

[90] See 4.39–4.44.

[91] [1895] 2 QB 1, [1895] 2 QB 315, CA.

[92] *Microtherm Electrical Co Ltd v Percy* [1956] RPC 272, [1957] RPC 207, CA.

[93] *Saltman* (n 50).

[94] *Thomas Marshall v Guinle* [1979] Ch 227.

[95] *X Ltd v Morgan-Grampian (Publishers) Ltd* [1991] 1 AC 1.

[96] Including 'any documents prepared for and used in the arbitration, or disclosed or produced in the course of the arbitration, or transcripts, or notes of the evidence in the arbitration or the award ... [and] what evidence had been given by any witness': *Dolling Baker v Merrett* [1990] 1 WLR 1205, 1213, (Parker LJ). See also *Hassneh Insurance Co of Israel v Steuart; J v Mew* [1993] 2 Lloyd's Rep 243 (Colman J). See generally on the topic of arbitrations and confidentiality, Toulson and Phipps (n 32) ch 22.

protection: all depends on the circumstances.[97] Criteria for determining whether information is confidential, many drawn from the commercial authorities, are considered in paras 4.63–4.102.

### (3) Literary and Artistic Confidences

In a number of cases the courts have applied the law of confidence to the use and  **4.35** disclosure of artistic and literary works. The cases fall into two broad categories. In one are cases concerning information ultimately intended for public performance, sale, or display such as the plot of a play,[98] an idea for a television series,[99] political diaries,[100] and watercolour drawings.[101] In cases of this kind the claimant's interest is usually of a commercial nature. The other category of case has concerned works created for purely private use and enjoyment such as the private letters in the late eighteenth-century case of *Thompson v Stanhope*,[102] the etchings the subject of *Prince Albert v Strange*,[103] the physician's diary in the nineteenth-century case of *Wilson v Wyatt*,[104] and the travel journals in the twenty-first-century case of *HRH Prince of Wales v Associated Newspapers Ltd*.[105] In these cases the interest to be protected is a privacy interest.

### (4) Personal Information

It has been said that equity will intervene whenever a person's private affairs are  **4.36** liable to be exposed, regardless of whether that exposure would cast a creditable or a scandalous light on the person.[106] Until the later years of the twentieth century the cases in which this principle had been applied in practice were relatively few, and its boundaries uncertain, but the 1990s and the early years of the twenty-first century saw a major expansion in the use of the law of confidence as a means of protecting personal information. It is now clear that

---

[97] [1987] Ch 117, 136–7. For further examples up to 1984, see *Gurry on Breach of Confidence* (n 32) 90–7.

[98] *Gilbert v Star Newspaper Co Ltd* (1894) 11 TLR 4 where an injunction was granted to restrain the defendants from publishing the plot of W S Gilbert's comic opera *His Excellency* which was due to open a few days later.

[99] *Talbot v General Television Corp Pty Ltd* [1981] RPC 1; *Fraser v Thames Television Ltd* [1984] 1 QB 44.

[100] *Times Newspapers Ltd v Mirror Group Newspapers Ltd* [1993] EMLR 443, CA; *Ashdown v Telegraph Group Newspapers Ltd* [2001] EWCA Civ 1142, [2002] Ch 149.

[101] *Tuck v Priester* (1887) 19 QBD 48, (1887) 19 QBD 629, CA.

[102] (1774) Amb 737, 27 ER 476.

[103] *Prince Albert* (n 11).

[104] 1820, unreported. Referred to in *Prince Albert* (n 11) and *Argyll (Duchess) v Argyll (Duke)* [1967] 1 Ch 302, 319–20. The diary entries related to the health of King George II.

[105] *HRH Prince of Wales* (n 23).

[106] *Gurry on Breach of Confidence* (1st edn, Oxford University Press 1984) 13, citing *Prince Albert* (n 11) (Knight-Bruce V-C): 'A man may employ himself in private in a manner very harmless, but which, disclosed to society, may destroy the comfort of his life, or even his success in it. Everyone, however, has a right, I apprehend, to say that the produce of his private hours is not more liable to

both the law of confidence and the new cause of action for misuse of private information are in principle capable of application to a wide range of types of personal information.

**4.37** It is also clear that the criteria to be applied when considering the application of these two causes of action are different in kind. The first question in a misuse of private information case is whether the claimant enjoys in respect of the information at issue a reasonable expectation of privacy.[107] Even though some have suggested this will often be an easy question to answer,[108] the same is not necessarily true when it comes to the different questions of whether the information is of a confidential character, and subject to a duty of confidence.[109] These questions will often enough have to be answered by reference to principle or authority, or both. For that reason it is helpful to examine both the criteria for confidentiality which have emerged from the authorities, and the subcategories or kinds of personal information that have been held to be confidential in nature. Both these aspects of the matter are considered below.[110]

### (5) The Significance of Classification

**4.38** Classification of the information the subject of a confidence claim can affect the legal principles that apply to the particular claim. The nature of the information at issue and how it is acquired and held may also, without altering the principles, affect the way those principles should be applied to the specific case. Information which someone wants to protect will not necessarily fall neatly or completely within just one of the four classes considered above. It may be necessary to consider to which class or classes the information properly belongs before determining what principles should be applied in determining any claims made in respect of its use or disclosure.

---

publication without his consent, because the publication must be creditable or advantageous to him, than it would be in opposite circumstances.'

107 See 5.14.

108 *A v B plc* (n 8) [11(vii)] citing dicta of Gleeson CJ in *Australian Broadcasting Corp v Lenah Game Meats Pty Ltd* (2001) 185 ALR 1 [42]: 'Certain kinds of information about a person such as information relating to health, personal relationships, or finances, may be easy to identify as private; as may certain kinds of activity which a reasonable person, applying contemporary standards of morals and behaviour, would understand to be meant to be unobserved.'

109 One example of information held to be (arguably) private but which might well not qualify as confidential is afforded by *Murray v Express Newspapers Ltd* [2008] EWCA Civ 446, [2009] Ch 481, which concerned an image of the infant claimant in his pushchair in a public street. In *Weller v Associated Newspapers Ltd* [2014] EWHC 1163 (QB), [2014] EMLR 24 Dingemans J held, at trial, that photographs of the children of a well-known musician taken on the street in California and published on a newspaper website were a misuse of private information. Private addresses, available in the public domain, might afford another example.

110 For criteria for confidentiality see 4.63 *et seq*. Because of the unavoidable overlap between the categories of personal information which may be confidential and those considered private for the purposes of the Convention-based wrong of misuse of private information, the authorities on the kinds of information capable of protection by each means are collected and considered once, in 5.34 *et seq*.

## (a) The principles differ where government secrets are concerned

**Confidentiality and the public domain**    As discussed in more detail in Chapter 11,[111]    **4.39**
it is a general requirement of the law of confidence that the information which the
claimant seeks to protect be inaccessible, and not available in the public domain.
This is certainly the case in respect of commercial and business information, but
the position may differ in respect of personal information. In that context, confidentiality may survive quite extensive publicity. Certainly, a claim for misuse of
private information can in principle survive mass publication.

When it comes to government secrets, however, quite limited disclosure can destroy    **4.40**
confidentiality. Thus, when the former secret serviceman Peter Wright published
a book containing allegedly confidential intelligence and other secret information
derived from his government work, it was assumed that the intelligence would
quite quickly be picked up by hostile states. The information was no longer, in any
relevant sense, secret.[112]

**The need to prove harm to the public interest**    A public body seeking to protect    **4.41**
a government secret must show that the publication has caused or will cause detriment to the public interest, which is at least a reversal of the usual onus of proof.[113]
A risk of embarrassment to the claimant is plainly not enough, or even relevant, as
grounds for a claim where government secrecy is concerned:

> It may be a sufficient detriment to the citizen that disclosure of information relat-
> ing to his affairs will expose his actions to public discussion and criticism. But it
> can scarcely be a relevant detriment to the government that publication of material
> concerning its actions will merely expose it to public discussion and criticism ... the
> court will determine the government's claim to confidentiality by reference to the
> public interest. Unless disclosure is likely to injure the public interest, it will not
> be protected.[114]

Put another way, a governmental claimant must show not only that the disclo-    **4.42**
sure in question was or would be a breach of confidence but also that 'the public
interest requires that the publication be restrained and ... that there are no other
facts of the public interest contradictory of and more compelling than that
relied upon'.[115] The logic of this reasoning must, it is suggested, apply equally to

---

[111] See 11.43 *et seq.*

[112] See *Attorney General v Observer Ltd* (n 12) 267 (Lord Brightman), 290 (Lord Goff).

[113] Ordinarily, the onus of proving that disclosure is in the public interest lies on the defendant.
Proof of detriment may not even be required in commercial cases or those concerned with personal
information. See the discussion at 4.160–4.165.

[114] *Attorney General v Observer Ltd* (n 12) 258 (Lord Keith), citing with approval *Commonwealth
of Australia v John Fairfax & Sons Ltd* (n 89).

[115] *Attorney General v Jonathan Cape Ltd* (n 86) 770, (Lord Widgery CJ). By the application
of these principles the government's claim to an injunction in *Lord Advocate v The Scotsman
Publications Ltd* [1990] 1 AC 812 failed. The government conceded that the memoirs in question
contained nothing damaging to national security, and its claim that an injunction could be supported on the basis that publication would cause injury to morale and confidence in the British

local or regional public sector bodies, and to public sector agencies as it does to central government.[116]

**4.43** **The impact of the Human Rights Act 1998** Public bodies have no Convention rights of their own, so that unlike a private individual they cannot rely on such rights to found or bolster a claim asserting confidentiality in governmental secrets. Moreover, as has been pointed out by Sedley LJ, s 6 HRA means that a claim by a public body to enforce confidentiality must be tested directly against Article 10 of the European Convention on Human Rights (ECHR); for a public body to seek to prevent free speech by a claim to secrecy which could not be justified under Article 10(2) would be unlawful.[117]

**4.44** **The Freedom of Information Act** Although the Convention does not create a duty to disclose or guarantee a general right of access to information,[118] most public bodies are subject to the provisions of the Freedom of Information Act 2000. This imposes positive duties to disclose information, and thereby to make it public, on request. It is suggested that no public body subject to the Act of 2000 could enforce a duty of confidence in respect of information which, on a proper analysis, it would be bound to disclose in response to a freedom of information request. The imposition or enforcement of such a duty would be contrary to the public policy which the Act is designed to implement.[119]

### (b) Information both governmental and commercial

**4.45** Public bodies often undertake or fund or direct the performance of functions which have a clear commercial flavour and which, if carried out by private-sector organizations, would demand a certain level of commercial confidentiality for their successful performance. When a public body seeks to protect information on the grounds of commercial confidentiality it will be necessary to consider

---

intelligence services was held unarguable. See also *Attorney General v Times Newspapers Ltd* [2001] EWCA Civ 97, [2001] 1 WLR 885.

[116] As suggested by Toulson and Phipps (n 32) paras 5-013–5-014.

[117] *London Regional Transport Ltd* (n 64) [59]–[61].

[118] The issue of whether the Convention conferred a positive right to receive information was reviewed by the Supreme Court in *Kennedy v Information Commissioner* [2014] UKSC 20, [2014] 2 WLR 808. The majority held that the recent developments in Strasbourg's case law were not sufficient to justify a departure from the principle clearly established in a series of Grand Chamber decisions that Art 10 did not impose a freestanding positive general duty of disclosure on public authorities. At the time of writing this edition, however, Mr Kennedy's complaint to the ECtHR and application for it to be referred to the Grand Chamber is outstanding; see also the subsequent decision in *Guseva v Bulgaria* [2015] ECHR 171 which suggests that the European Court is moving towards the recognition of such a positive general duty, at least where public interest journalism is concerned.

[119] An argument to this effect was raised at first instance by the defendant in *HRH Prince of Wales* (n 23). It was rejected, but on the facts of the case rather than as a matter of principle: see [105], [113] (Blackburne J). See also n 139 and text to that note. For the Convention jurisprudence on access to information see 3.31 (nn 89 and 90) and 3.35 (n 106). For further discussion of a possible principle that confidence does not protect information required by law to be made public, see 4.101–4.102.

whether the claim is subject to the rule that requires proof of detriment to the public interest.[120] It will also be necessary to determine whether there is any—and if so, what—genuine commercial interest in protecting the information and, if so, to identify it and evaluate its importance when weighed against the competing rights of others under Article 10 and otherwise. This will not always be an easy task, as illustrated by the *London Regional Transport* case.[121]

**4.46** The task will sometimes be complicated further by one or more of two additional factors. First, the dividing line between the governmental and the commercial can be blurred, and tends to shift and alter with changes of public policy and in the organization of the public sector, such as 'contracting out' of service delivery. Extensive public law litigation since the entry into force of the HRA has explored the boundaries of the 'state' for the purposes of enforcing Convention rights, and in particular Article 8 rights.[122]

**4.47** Secondly, a private individual or organization may have their own rights of confidentiality in respect of information which has, for commercial purposes, been shared with government. It would appear to be possible in theory at least for concurrent claims to confidentiality in the same information to be advanced by a public body and a private company or individual, and for the fate of such claims to differ because of the different approach to the claims which the different status of the claimants would dictate.

### (c) Information both governmental and personal

**4.48** **Personal records of governmental information** Some information may have both governmental and personal or private characteristics, and the dividing line can be unclear. For example, a personal diary of a minister or senior civil servant may contain records of private meetings undertaken in an official capacity which include not only details of diplomatic negotiations but also the writer's own reflections, thoughts, and feelings on the matter.[123] Such thoughts and feelings may be of a work-related nature, and may have been passed on to others in the course of official business, or they may be of a personal and private nature. It may be hard to label or categorize particular information, and a given sentence or paragraph might in principle fall into more than one of the categories identified above. Such cases raise the question of whether the court should apply the principles applicable to governmental information or those relating to personal information.

---

[120] See 4.41–4.42.

[121] *London Regional Transport* (n 64), and see the discussion at 4.154–4.156.

[122] See *eg Poplar Housing and Regeneration Community Association v Donoghue* [2002] EWCA Civ 595, [2002] QB 48; *R (Heather) v Leonard Cheshire Foundation* [2002] EWCA Civ 366, [2002] 2 All ER 936; *YL v Birmingham City Council* [2007] UKHL 27, [2008] 1 AC 95.

[123] cf the travel journals of HRH Prince of Wales which were the subject of his breach of confidence claim against the *Mail on Sunday* (n 23).

**4.49**  Authority, such as it is, suggests that information embodied in a diary, journal, or similar record which is created for private use and limited disclosure to friends will be treated as confidential personal information in respect of which the author can impose on others a duty of confidence, even if the information has been created in the course of or in relation to official duties undertaken at public expense, and includes a substantial amount of information about those official duties which either is public knowledge or would properly be made public knowledge if a request for it were made.[124] It may be that in cases of this kind there can exist two separate rights of confidence, one possessed by the individual concerned and one by the state, and that the outcome of claims to enforce such rights could be different because of the differing approach of the law to such cases.

**4.50**  **Government records of personal information**  Governments and other public bodies, of course, hold vast reserves of personal information, collated and organized at some expense for the purposes of facilitating public administration. This gives rise to two separate questions: first, whether government may have rights of confidence in respect of such information; secondly, what duties of confidence government owes to those from, or in respect of, whom it has obtained such information.

**4.51**  *Government rights*  Personal information put together for public purposes will often have value not only for those purposes but also in commercial terms. This is especially true of collections of information. Collections, as already noted, can have a confidential character even if the individual items of information are all in the public domain.[125] The freedom of public bodies to exploit personal information by sale or for other commercial purposes is tightly circumscribed by the duties they owe to individuals under the Data Protection Act, and by duties of confidence imposed on them by statute and by equity.[126] Nevertheless, some such collections are commercially exploited by government, the prime example being the electoral roll.[127] No example is known of a public body taking action to protect alleged rights of confidence of its own in respect of personal information it has collected, but on the face of it the requirements of hybrid breach of confidence could be met in such a case.

**4.52**  *Government duties*  Where personal information is obtained by an arm or agency of the state, a duty of confidentiality will often be owed by the public body to the person to whom the information relates. A duty not to misuse personal information may exist in law whenever such information is acquired by a state agency.[128]

---

[124]  See generally the *HRH Prince of Wales* case (n 23).

[125]  See 4.18.

[126]  Considered at 4.53–4.54.

[127]  That is, a version of the electoral roll which contains only information that the individuals listed have agreed should be contained in a saleable list. The option to avoid inclusion on such a list was legislated for following the decision in *R (Robertson) v City of Wakefield Metropolitan Borough Council* [2001] EWHC 915 (Admin), [2002] QB 1052.

[128]  'Where in the course of performing its public duties, a public body (such as a police force) comes into possession of information relating to a member of the public, being information not generally available and potentially damaging to that member of the public if disclosed, the body

The precise nature of this duty may be open to debate. The authorities canvass a number of bases for it including public law, the HRA, a duty of care,[129] and an equitable duty of confidence. It is possible, of course, that particular circumstances could give rise to a duty owed under more than one of these heads. The nature and scope of the duty may well differ according to the legal basis on which it is imposed so that, for instance, there could be a public law duty not to disclose information which is not confidential in character.[130]

Not all personal information obtained by the state will necessarily be of a confi- **4.53** dential nature, such as to found a claim in traditional breach of confidence. Some of it at least may be in the public domain, as is the case with the published version of the electoral roll. Where the information is confidential in nature, however, it is suggested that in most if not all cases the public body which has acquired it will owe a duty of confidence to the person who has provided it, or to whom it relates, whatever other rights may be in play. There is clear authority that a duty of confidence will be owed by a state agency which acquires information through the use of compulsory powers.[131] Most of the numerous statutes which provide for the acquisition by the state of personal information impose an express duty of confidence on the officials who receive such information.[132] In cases where there is no statutory provision and no compulsion it is likely that a duty of confidence will come into existence pursuant to the circumstantial test laid down in the *Spycatcher* case.[133]

---

ought not to disclose such information save for the purpose of and to the extent necessary for the performance of its public duty or enabling some other public body to perform its public duty': *R v Chief Constable of North Wales Police, ex p Thorpe* [1999] QB 396, 409–10 (Lord Bingham CJ). Such disclosure should only be made if there is a 'pressing need', and after careful examination of the merits of the individual case: *R v A Local Authority and Police Authority in the Midlands, ex p LM* [2000] 1 FLR 612, approved in *R(A) v Hertfordshire County Council* [2001] EWCA Civ 2113 [24], [29], [31]. See also *Butler v Board of Trade* [1971] Ch 680 (information obtained by Official Receiver), *R v Birmingham City Council, ex p O* [1983] 1 AC 578 (social services files held by a local authority), *Hellewell v Chief Constable of Derbyshire* [1995] 1 WLR 804 (photo of suspect) and *Bunn v BBC* [1998] 3 All ER 552 (confession statement to police). In *Mitchell v News Group Newspapers Ltd; Rowland v Mitchell* [2014] EWHC 879 (QB) the Court refused applications for non-party disclosure concerning witness statements made to the police in circumstances where an equitable obligation of confidence was owed and the third parties were not respondents to the application.

[129] It has been said, for example, that there is a duty 'to take reasonable care to avoid unnecessary disclosure to the general public of the information which [an informant] had given to the police': *Swinney v Chief Constable of Northumbria Police (No 2), The Times*, 26 May 1999 (Jackson J). See also *Swinney v Chief Constable of Northumbria Police (No 1)* [1997] QB 464, CA.

[130] A public body may have two distinct types of duty: (1) a public law duty, including a duty not to act in contravention of Art 8 ECHR and (2) a private law duty of confidence. The two will not always coexist, and breach of a public law duty will not necessarily amount to a breach of confidence in private law. As Lord Woolf MR said in *R v Chief Constable of North Wales Police, ex p Thorpe* (n 128) 429: 'The issue here is not the same as it would be in private law. The fact that the applicants' convictions had been in the public domain did not mean that the police as a public authority were free to publish information about their previous offending absent any public interest in this being done.' See also *Preston Borough Council v McGrath* [2000] TLR 401, CA.

[131] See *eg Norwich Pharmacal Co v Customs and Excise Commissioners* [1974] AC 133.

[132] For examples, see 1.75.

[133] See 4.20.

**4.54**  Duties of the kinds discussed above would not necessarily preclude the state agency from disclosing such information to another person or body with a proper interest in receiving it, where there was an overriding public interest in the information being passed on.[134] The public body must make a judgment, taking account of the private interests at stake, but if it reasonably concludes that disclosure is appropriate it is entitled to disclose.[135]

**4.55**  **The position of the media**  The existence of the duties discussed in the previous paragraphs means that disclosure of private or personal information by a public body to the media will require clear and cogent justification.[136] If there is none, then any subsequent use and disclosure of such information by the media may be actionable by the individual concerned as a breach of a duty of confidence owed by the media to him or her. This would be on the basis that the media have acquired the information knowing it to have been provided to the public body in circumstances importing a duty of confidence.[137] This will often be so where the media acquire confidential personal information from a state source by means of a leak. However, leaks do not inevitably amount to wrongful disclosures in breach of confidence. It is conceivable that a public body may on occasion be unduly cautious with personal information, as has sometimes been suggested.[138] It may be the case that information is leaked which ought properly to have been made the subject of official disclosure.[139]

**4.56**  Of course, the opposite is also a possibility: the state may wrongly make official disclosure of information which it ought to have kept confidential. If so, the individual concerned may have a claim against the public authority for breach of confidence and possibly in other causes of action.[140] In principle, it would seem that

---

[134] See *Butler v Board of Trade* (n 128) 690, and *Re A Company's Application* [1989] Ch 477, 482.

[135] 'If the police come into possession of confidential information which, in their reasonable view, in the interests of public health or safety, should be considered by a professional or regulatory body, then the police are free to pass that information to the regulatory body...in each case a balance has to be struck between competing public interests...the primary decision as to disclosure should be made by the police': *Woolgar v Chief Constable of Sussex Police* [2000] 1 WLR 25, 36–7 (Kennedy LJ); see also *Thorpe* (n 128).

[136] Though it may be justified, *eg* under statutory powers to promote the prevention of crime.

[137] See 4.26. However, although journalists have no special status in law, the activity of journalism does. The Strasbourg jurisprudence gives the greatest protection to the type of speech that is directed towards informing debate. It was not necessarily a breach of confidence on the part of a journalist either to read a leaked document or to publish it: *Commissioner of Police of the Metropolis v Times Newspapers Ltd* [2011] EWHC 2715 (QB), [2014] EMLR 1 [122]–[136].

[138] Media organizations have faced reluctance from police, hospitals, and other public bodies to release personal information about victims of crime or accidents for fear of claims being made against the authorities. It may be that such fears have been prompted more by concerns about the Data Protection Act 1998 than the common law of confidence, but the law of confidence is capable of applying in such cases.

[139] This was arguably the case in respect of at least some of the extensive information about MPs' expenses claims which was published by the *Daily Telegraph* during 2009, at a time when freedom of information claims for disclosure of such information were still working their way through the legal system.

[140] *eg* under the Data Protection Act or the HRA. See 4.47 and 4.51.

the media would be susceptible to a claim for an injunction in respect of personal information wrongly disclosed to it by a state agency. There would, however, be an argument available that a media organization that acted in good faith in publishing under such circumstances should not be subject to any claim for monetary remedies.[141]

### (d) *The principles are different for commercial and personal confidences*

Claims to confidentiality in business information are different in nature from confidence claims about personal information, raising different issues. Confidentiality in business information protects rights which are merely economic and akin to property. Confidentiality in personal information may involve the protection of an individual's economic rights but also protects human dignity and autonomy. These differences may in individual cases affect whether, and if so in what way, legal principles established in the commercial context should be applied.[142] An example is the way in which the application of the public domain doctrine differs according to whether the confidence interest at stake is personal or commercial.[143] *Douglas v Hello! Ltd* indicated further that categorization of the information can have an important impact on the remedies available, such as the grant of an interim injunction.[144]

**4.57**

### (e) *Information which is both personal and commercial*

**Separating claims**    As Sedley LJ observed in *Douglas v Hello! Ltd*, there is no bright line between the personal and the commercial.[145] In some cases, as in *Douglas* itself, the same information may have both commercial and personal private value to the same people. This may often be the case where celebrities are concerned.[146] The history of the *Douglas* litigation and the points made in the previous paragraph suggest that in such cases it will probably be best to analyse the personal and commercial claims separately. Now that misuse of private information has emerged as a cause of action separate and distinct from breach of confidence, it may be that in most cases a claimant's interest in protecting his or her private life is best advanced by framing a claim in misuse of private information, with a breach of confidence claim, where available, being reserved for or relied on primarily to advance any claims of a commercial nature.

**4.58**

---

[141] See 4.139–4.140 and 11.33.

[142] Simon Brown LJ indicated as much in the *Source Informatics* case (n 31) [33]–[34].

[143] See 11.54.

[144] *Douglas* (n 7). See ch 12 for a more detailed analysis of Remedies.

[145] *Douglas* (n 7) [143].

[146] Even where overlaps of this kind do not exist, there may be no clear line to draw between the private and business life of an individual. In *Niemietz v Germany* (1992) 16 EHRR 97 the ECtHR considered a businessman's or professional's office to come within the concept of 'home' life as protected by Art 8(1). For further discussion of the Art 8 rights of businesses see 13.28–13.42.

**4.59** **Separate complainants** Sometimes claims in respect of both commercial and personal confidentiality may be available on the same facts, but to different persons. *Douglas* again furnishes an example. The couple pursued the personal claims, while the commercial claim was pursued by OK! Ltd. Other examples can be drawn from the world of business. Most businesses hold collections of personal and private information about individuals[147] and both commercial and private interests may exist simultaneously in respect of such data. The business may have a commercial interest in the utility of the collection as a business tool, and rights of commercial confidentiality in respect of the collection.[148] At the same time, the individuals concerned may have personal interests in controlling the dissemination of particular items of information about them, and a right to object to disclosure.[149] In these situations too the separate rights will need to be disentangled and analysed separately, to ensure that the appropriate principles are applied to any claims which are pursued. This may not always be straightforward, especially if the commercial and personal interests are intertwined.

**4.60** **Absent complainants** The task of analysis may be complicated if some of those who complain of an actual or threatened breach of confidence are not themselves before the court asserting rights. In *Imutran Ltd v Uncaged Campaigns Ltd*[150] the claimants successfully sought an injunction restraining the defendants from publishing information alleged to be confidential, which included names and addresses and other details of individuals involved in controversial animal-research projects. The claimants asserted not only that disclosure would breach commercial confidentiality but also that it would, by providing information to animal-rights activists, expose staff to risks to health and life. The impact with which the claimants were directly concerned was the impact on their business. The individuals whose identities were sought to be protected were not parties. The injunction was granted.

**4.61** It has now become accepted practice in cases of this nature and others for the court to take into account the private-life rights of non-parties.[151] This is clearly proper, given the duty imposed on the court by s 6 HRA. There can, however, be a degree of awkwardness about the process, which requires clarity of analysis and caution lest the rights of non-parties be advanced as cover for unstated claims by the actual

---

[147] *eg* regarding employees, or customers, or suppliers, or for marketing purposes.

[148] Even if all the individual elements of the data set are in the public domain: see 4.18.

[149] Although here there would be doubt whether a right of confidence as traditionally understood could be maintained if all the information about the particular individual was in the public domain. As to the public domain doctrine, see 4.65 and 1.43 *et seq*.

[150] [2001] EWHC Ch 31, [2001] EMLR 21.

[151] See *eg Green Corns Ltd* (n 51); *CC v AB* [2006] EWHC 3083 (QB), [2007] EMLR 312; *Ambrosiadou v Coward* [2010] EWHC 1794 (QB), [2010] 2 FLR 1775 approved on this point by the Court of Appeal [2011] EWCA Civ 409, [2011] EMLR 21; *OPQ v BJM* (n 59); *Goodwin v News Group Newspapers Ltd* [2011] EWHC 1437 (QB), [2011] EMLR 27; *K v News Group Newspapers Ltd* [2011] EWCA Civ 439, [2011] 1 WLR 1827 (taking into account the rights of children). See also 5.111 and 13.49.

claimants.[152] It would seem hard to justify seeking relief in reliance on third party rights if the rights asserted were not Convention rights but, say, separate commercial rights.

### (f) Artistic and literary confidences

As indicated by the examples given above,[153] this is a class of case in which the **4.62** information at issue may include either or both of the personal and private, and the commercial. Again, it is likely that the approach of the court will be guided by its identification of the nature of the interest at stake. Cases where the information is personal and meant for purely private disclosure may fit best into the new cause of action for misuse of private information, even if they also satisfy the requirements of traditional breach of confidence. Such cases may more readily justify permanent injunctive relief than those where the information is intended for public disclosure for profit. Cases involving disclosures for profit may fall to be treated either as traditional or hybrid breach of confidence claims. A claim in confidentiality, and injunctive relief on that basis, is likely to be available only for a period of time, pending publication. It may be that at a trial the purely commercial interests in protecting information of this kind could on appropriate facts be satisfied by a monetary award alone. Further, as discussed in Chapter 9, a claim for copyright infringement will often be a candidate in a case of this kind, and may afford relief as effective, or more so, than a claim for breach of confidence.

## D. Criteria for Confidentiality

### (1) Introduction

Where parties have agreed by an express contract to characterize a particular class **4.63** of personal information as confidential, that will in general suffice to identify it as such.[154] If, as in most media cases, there is no contract, then a claimant will need to establish by other means that the information in issue has 'the necessary quality of confidence about it'.[155] It has been recognized that the quality of confidence is an elusive one: 'It is far from easy to state in general terms what is confidential information or a trade secret.'[156] The fact that the information is inaccessible and not in

---

[152] See the observations of Mann J in *BKM Ltd v BBC* [2009] EWHC 3151 (Ch) [7] and [13] (injunction to prevent broadcast of undercover footage of elderly in care home refused after balancing Art 10 and Art 8 rights); see also 13.49, and the discussion at 13.148–13.151 of reliance on third-party rights and the caution with which the court may approach such reliance. Whatever the position as regards injunctive relief, it is obvious that a claimant cannot be awarded damages for wrongs suffered by third parties: *Abbey v Gilligan* [2013] EWHC 3217 (QB), [2013] EMLR 12 [41] (Tugendhat J).

[153] At 4.35.

[154] *Tuck v Priester* (1887) 19 QBD 48, (1887) 19 QBD 629, CA.

[155] *Saltman* (n 50) 215, Lord Greene MR; *Coco v Clark* (n 43) 47, Megarry J.

[156] *Thomas Marshall v Guinle* (n 94) 248, Megarry V-C.

the public domain is generally recognized as a requirement of any valid claim in breach of confidence. Beyond that, there are some kinds of personal information which are now authoritatively classified as confidential in character.[157] The criteria by which that classification is arrived at have, however, received relatively little analysis, and in a case concerned with information outside one of the established classes it will be important to consider the applicable principles in order to determine whether information has the necessary quality of confidence.

**4.64**   A variety of criteria can be distilled from the authorities. In this section these criteria are considered, with particular reference to their applicability to private information and the media.[158] Since it is in the commercial sphere that the courts have mainly dealt with confidence cases, it is from that sphere that most of the authorities cited are drawn. However, reasons are identified for qualifying or modifying criteria relevant in that sphere, and additional factors are identified which it is suggested are relevant to the question whether personal information is confidential in character.

### (2) Inaccessibility: Not in the Public Domain

**4.65**   It is a firmly established doctrine that information which has entered the public domain is not confidential. 'Something which is public property and public knowledge cannot per se provide any foundation for breach of confidence.'[159] 'Once [information] has entered what is usually called the public domain...then, as a general rule, the principle of confidentiality can have no application to it.'[160] There is a clear contrast to be drawn here with the tort of misuse of private information, which is concerned not just with information or secrets, but also with protection against intrusion: the concept of public domain is recognized as a more flexible concept, and the law will in an appropriate case restrain publication in the mass media even if the information is readily available on the internet, as it did in the case of Ryan Giggs prior to his being named in Parliament. Chapter 11 contains detailed discussion of the public domain doctrine, with particular emphasis on its application to personal information.[161]

---

[157] See 5.28 *et seq.*

[158] While the Law Commission, *Breach of Confidence* (Law Com No 110, Cmnd 8388 1981) para 2.11, considered that the same principles should govern confidentiality whether in a commercial or industrial setting or otherwise, there are some principles which, it is suggested, are inapplicable in privacy. It is obvious in any event that the weight to be given to the different criteria may vary according to the setting.

[159] *Coco v Clark* (n 43) 47, Megarry J, citing Lord Greene MR in *Saltman* (n 50) 214. See also Lord Buckmaster in *O Mustad and Son v Dosen (Note)* [1964] 1 WLR 109, 111: 'The secret, as a secret, had ceased to exist'; but note the helpful discussion of 'relative confidentiality' in *Force India Formula One Team Ltd v 1 Malaysia Racing Team SDN BHD* (n 43) [218]–[223] (Arnold J).

[160] *Attorney General v Observer Ltd* (n 12) 282 (Lord Goff).

[161] See 11.43 *et seq.* As to Giggs' case, see *CTB v News Group Newspapers Ltd* [2011] EWHC 1326 (QB) [20]–[24] (Eady J); see also *Goodwin v News Group Newspapers Ltd* (n 151) [85]–[86] (Tugendhat J).

## (3) Factors Indicating that Personal Information is Confidential

### (a) Intimate or other confidential subject matter

This can be a crucial factor where personal information is concerned, and may **4.66** be enough to confer *prima facie* confidentiality on the information.[162] The court will have regard to the degree to which the information at issue concerns intimate aspects of the claimant's personal life.[163] For example, '[t]o most people the details of their sexual lives are high on their list of those matters which they regard as confidential'[164] and information in correspondence 'on private matters such as their feelings for each other' has been held to be a prime candidate for protection.[165] More generally, it has been held that '[i]n the ordinary way, those who participate in sexual or personal relationships may be expected not to reveal private conversations or activities'.[166]

The list of classes of 'sensitive personal data' contained in s 2 of the Data Protection **4.67** Act 1998[167] may assist in identifying other types of especially intimate and private information, albeit the 1998 Act is designed to give effect to rights of privacy rather than confidentiality. Reference may also be made to other statutory lists of confidential personal information.[168] That is not to say, however, that personal information will only qualify as confidential if it concerns an especially intimate subject matter. For instance, the Court in *Prince Albert v Strange*[169] paid little attention to what the etchings depicted. Similarly, in *Argyll (Duchess) v Argyll (Duke)*,[170] the subject matter of the parties' private photographs was not regarded as crucial to the determination of whether they were confidential.

### (b) Believed by the confider to be confidential

In the commercial context, the following criteria for the identification of confiden- **4.68** tial information have been proposed: (i) the party claiming confidentiality must believe that the release of the information would be injurious to him or her[171] or

---

[162] See *eg Venables* (n 14).

[163] See *Dudgeon v UK* (1982) 4 EHRR 149, para 152 and *Douglas*, CA (n 7) [169] (Keene LJ).

[164] *Stephens v Avery* [1988] 1 Ch 449, 454 (Sir Nicholas Browne-Wilkinson V-C).

[165] *Maccaba v Lichtenstein* [2005] EMLR 109 [4] (Gray J).

[166] *Mosley v News Group Newspapers Ltd* [2008] EWHC 1777 (QB), [2008] EMLR 20 [105] (Eady J). This observation was part of the reasoning leading to his conclusion, at [108], that he would be prepared to hold that the newspaper's informant had committed an 'old fashioned breach of confidence' in disclosing details of the claimant's sado-masochistic party. However, in neither *Mosley* nor *Stephens* (n 164) was the question of consent in issue. Where sexual conduct is immoral or unlawful, disclosure of such activity is not necessarily an actionable breach of confidence: see the discussion in *AVB v TDD* [2014] EWHC 1442 (QB) [71]–[78] (Tugendhat J).

[167] See ch 7 and Appendix E (available at <http://www.5rb.com/publication/the-law-of-privacy-and-the-media>).

[168] Such as the Local Government Act 1972 for which see 1.75.

[169] *Prince Albert* (n 11).

[170] *Argyll* (n 104).

[171] The relevance of the damage which disclosure would cause is considered at 4.90–4.91.

advantageous to his or her rivals or others; (ii) he or she must believe that the information is confidential; (iii) these beliefs must be reasonable; and (iv) the matter is to be judged in the light of the usages and practices of the particular trade or industry concerned.[172]

*(c) Stipulated by the confider to be confidential*

**4.69**   A non-contractual stipulation that information is, or is to be treated as, confidential will not be conclusive, but may be an important factor in determining whether the information is indeed confidential in nature. In general, 'if something is expressly said to be confidential, then it is much more likely to be so held by the courts'.[173] This is a factor recognized in the commercial-confidence cases. If an employer impresses upon an employee the confidentiality of certain information then, while this is not sufficient of itself, it provides evidence which may help in determining whether or not the information can properly be regarded as a trade secret.[174]

**4.70**   Similarly, in the context of personal information, one party to a personal relationship may stipulate that certain information he or she discloses is confidential,[175] or a person may give notice granting access to a private event on express terms as to confidentiality,[176] and this will provide an important, albeit not conclusive, indication that information about the event is confidential in character. Other instances of stipulations would be the marking of a letter as 'Confidential', stating that a conversation should be 'strictly between ourselves', or agreement to abide by rules of anonymity and confidentiality imposed by a therapy programme such as Narcotics Anonymous.

*(d) Protected by controlling access*

**4.71**   A person may take steps which implicitly indicate his or her belief that particular information is confidential, and a desire to keep it so. Such belief and desire could be demonstrated by limiting access to the information by means, for instance, of secure storage, requiring access by means of a secret password or combination. Such measures have been recognized as relevant in commercial cases[177] and in a

[172] *Thomas Marshall* (n 94) 248 (Sir Robert Megarry V-C).

[173] *Barrymore v News Group Newspapers Ltd* [1997] FSR 600, 603 (Jacob J). Cf *Abbey* (n 152) [59], Tugendhat J, where an email with a limited circulation was held to attract no right of confidentiality or privacy for its sender (as opposed to the company by whom he was engaged as a consultant, which was not a claimant in the action) despite carrying the wording 'DO NOT circulate this PLEASE!!!'.

[174] See *Faccenda Chicken Ltd* (n 97); see also the detailed discussion in *Force India Formula One Team Ltd* (n 43) [225]–[238] (Arnold J).

[175] As was alleged to be the case in *Stephens* (n 164).

[176] As in *Douglas* (n 10). See also *Creation Records Ltd v News Group Newspapers Ltd* [1997] EMLR 444.

[177] '[T]he fact that the circulation of certain information is restricted to a limited number of individuals may throw light on the status of the information and its degree of confidentiality': *Faccenda Chicken* (n 97) 138 (Neill LJ). Similarly, in *Lansing Linde v Kerr* [1991] 1 WLR 251, CA, 260 Staughton LJ identified as one criterion in determining whether information was a trade secret that 'the owner must limit the dissemination of it or at least not encourage or permit widespread publication'.

personal-information case it has been said there is 'a powerful case for saying that *any* information stored on a computer to which access is password-protected may be regarded as confidential, irrespective of its actual content, by virtue of that fact alone'.[178] Other measures which would indicate information is being treated as confidential in character would be locking away a diary or other document, locking doors, shutting curtains, seeking out a secluded place to conduct a conversation or liaison, or otherwise attempting to exclude prying eyes, ears, or other methods of observation.

### (e) Created or imparted in confidential circumstances

If there are neither express nor implied indications of confidentiality then other circumstances may indicate that information is confidential. In commercial cases involving employees one relevant factor is the nature of the employment and whether it is one in which confidential material is habitually handled.[179] Corresponding examples in the case of personal information are cases where personal information is imparted to a professional such as a doctor, lawyer, accountant, or financial adviser. The information so imparted will readily be regarded as confidential in nature.[180]   **4.72**

Outside these well-recognized cases of professional confidants, it will be relevant to consider whether the information was created or imparted in circumstances where few had access to it, whether or not any particular measures were taken to ensure that this should be so. The number of people involved in the creation of the information, and the location at which it comes into being or is imparted will be relevant factors; for example, whether it is created by one person or two, whether it takes place in a private home, a private room, or in a public place.[181] Seclusion is relevant, though not conclusive.[182] Thus, if information is noted down or recorded by a single individual in a diary or notebook, or if it arises from a private occasion at home when few others are present, these factors will tend to support an argument that it is confidential in character.   **4.73**

### (f) Regarded as confidential by a reasonable confidant

The court may have regard to the belief which would be held by a reasonable person in the position of the person to whom information is imparted, or whether his or   **4.74**

---

[178] *Imerman v Tchenguiz* [2009] EWHC 2023 (QB), [2010] FLR 735, [27] (Eady J) (emphasis in original). This is not necessarily the case, however: *Mars v Teknowledge Ltd* [2000] FSR 138 [33] (Jacob J); and the Court of Appeal in *Tchenguiz* did not appear to go quite so far as the judge, despite holding that '[c]onfidentiality is not dependent upon locks and keys or their electronic equivalents': (n 30) [79].

[179] *Faccenda Chicken* (n 97) 137.

[180] See 5.146–5.151.

[181] See *eg A v B plc* [2001] 1 WLR 2341 (Jack J).

[182] See *Campbell v Frisbee* [2002] EWHC 328 (Ch), [2002] EMLR 31 [38] (Lightman J) (not commented upon when the case went to the Court of Appeal).

her conscience would be affected by an appreciation of the confidentiality of the information. Sir Robert Megarry V-C suggested that the court may employ the concept of the reasonable man, so that if the circumstances are such that any such person 'would have realised that upon reasonable grounds the information was being given to him in confidence' this should suffice to impose a duty.[183] Similarly, Cross J in considering the appropriate test for breach of confidence, advanced a test of what 'any man of average intelligence and honesty' would think of the propriety of using the information for his new employer's benefit.[184] It has been said of the confidant that 'the touchstone by which to judge the scope of his duty and whether or not it has been fulfilled is his own conscience, no more and no less'.[185] It may well be appropriate to import similar approaches into the assessment of whether information is confidential in character.

*(g) Recognizable by the court as confidential*

**4.75** On occasion judicial instinct has been relied on. In *Argyll (Duchess) v Argyll (Duke)*, Ungoed-Thomas J was not deterred from recognizing confidentiality in the various marital communications and information under consideration by the fact that the court was 'not already provided with fully developed principles, guides, tests, definitions and the full armament for judicial decision. It is sufficient that the court recognises that the communications are confidential, and their publication within the mischief which the law as its policy seeks to avoid, without further defining the scope and limits of the jurisdiction.'[186] Similarly, in *WB v H Bauer Publishing Ltd*, Eady J noted with apparent approval arguments to the effect that information as to the claimant's involvement in criminal proceedings on serious charges (of rape) had 'nothing inherently confidential' about it.[187]

---

[183] *Coco v Clark* (n 43) 48, Megarry J. What may be seen as a similar approach was adopted in *Pollard v Photographic Co* (1889) 40 Ch D 345, where North J implied a contractual term that prints of photographs commissioned by the plaintiff would be appropriated only to the plaintiff's use.

[184] *Printers and Finishers Ltd v Holloway* [1965] RPC 239, 256. In *Commissioner of Police of Metropolis* (n 137) Tugendhat J considered at [103]–[114] that while conscience denoted an objective standard of right and wrong, and was not the equivalent of a personal judgment or preference, there was a subjective element whereby a person should not be held to have acted unconscionably unless his or her decision was unreasonable. The courts should give a generous interpretation to what a reasonable person might believe to be right or wrong or it risked making the law an instrument for enforcing unity of thought.

[185] *Source Informatics* (n 31) [31] (Simon Brown LJ).

[186] *Argyll* (n 104) 330F.

[187] *WB* (n 31) [23]. See also [31]. The observation may highlight one important difference between confidence and privacy. Involvement in criminal proceedings, however serious, is 'sensitive personal data' for the purposes of the Data Protection Act 1998. See 7.24. In *Hannon v News Group Newspapers* [2014] EWHC 1580 (Ch), [2015] EMLR 1 Mann J refused to strike out claims in breach of confidence and misuse of private information where the facts and circumstances of arrests were published in a newspaper. The judge held that the Strasbourg authority relied upon by the defendant, *Axel Springer AG v Germany* (2012) 55 EHRR 6, did not support an absolute right of the press to have, and to publish, the fact and circumstances of an arrest. The right to report an arrest is fact sensitive: [87], [96]. In *PNM v Times Newspapers Ltd* [2014] EWCA Civ 1132, [2014] EMLR 30 Sharp LJ (giving the lead judgment of the court) said at [68] that 'at a time before these matters were mentioned at the trial, the information that the Claimant had been arrested (and other

## (h) Form or medium

In some cases the form or medium in which information is recorded or conveyed **4.76** may provide an indication as to how it should be treated. Like other classes of confidential information, personal information may be recorded and conveyed in a variety of forms and media, and there is no rule or principle which excludes information in any particular form or medium from protection.[188] Relief has been granted to protect confidentiality in personal information conveyed orally,[189] in writing,[190] or recorded in visual images, whether still or moving.[191] Information in digital electronic forms is equally capable of protection.[192] However, the form in which the information is recorded is far from irrelevant. There may be some kinds of document which deserve *prima facie* protection on account of their form alone. Examples would include a private diary, or a personal letter.[193]

In addition some media, such as film or photographs, may convey information **4.77** about a particular event which differs in substance from that which is or can be conveyed through another medium, such as written or spoken words. For this reason there may be cases where confidence can be claimed in relation to the former, though it could not be claimed in relation to the latter.[194] In *Service Corp*

---

information) was private information which engaged the Claimant's rights under Art 8'. However, on the facts in *PNM* the position changed once the information was disclosed in open court. The Court of Appeal upheld the judge below, Tugendhat J, that it was not a misuse of private information to identify the claimant by name as having been arrested and released without charge following an investigation into allegations of child sex grooming and prostitution once his name had been mentioned in open court. Although Tugendhat J recorded that the application for an injunction had been brought under breach of confidence and misuse of private information no consideration was given to whether the fact that the claimant had been arrested and released without charge was confidential information; rather the application proceeded on the basis that his Art 8 rights were engaged. The Supreme Court has given PNM permission to appeal.

[188] See *Gurry on Breach of Confidence* (n 32) para 5.10, providing examples, mainly drawn from commercial cases, of the wide range of forms in which confidential information has been held to reside.

[189] eg *Francome v Mirror Group Newspapers Ltd* [1984] 1 WLR 892 (telephone); *A v B plc* (HC, 30 April 2001) (oral confession of an affair); and *A v B plc* (n 181), a further decision of Jack J in the same case, dated 10 September 2001.

[190] eg *W v Egdell* [1990] Ch 359 and *Cornelius v de Taranto* [2002] EMLR 112, CA, both cases of psychiatric reports; *Thompson* (n 102) (letters).

[191] Photographic images were protected in *Shelley Films Ltd v Rex Features Ltd* [1994] EMLR 134, and film in *Nicholls v BBC* [1999] EMLR 791. In *Douglas* (n 7) [71] Brooke LJ, citing the *Shelley Films* case, said: 'It is well settled, then, that equity may intervene to prevent the publication of photographic images taken in breach of an obligation of confidence.' Keene LJ said, 'I reject without hesitation the submission . . . that [breach of confidence] cannot encompass photographs of an event . . . There is no reason why these photographs inherently could not be the subject of a breach of confidence': *ibid*, [165].

[192] *Imerman v Tchenguiz* (n 178).

[193] For letters, see *Maccaba* (n 165). For diaries, see *HRH Prince of Wales* (n 23) and *Imerman v Tchenguiz*, CA (n 30) [88].

[194] See *Douglas* (n 7) [165]: 'The photographs conveyed to the public information not otherwise truly obtainable, that is to say, what the event and its participants looked like . . . The same result is not obtainable through the medium of words alone, nor by recollected drawings with their inevitable inaccuracy.' See also [138] (Sedley LJ).

*International plc v Channel Four Television Corp Ltd* Lightman J held the distinction between conveying information by words and by pictures to be one without a difference.[195] Later cases have taken a different approach. In *Hyde Park Residence Ltd v Yelland* Jacob J remarked '[a] picture says more than a thousand words'.[196] In *Theakston v MGN Ltd*[197] the medium of the confidential information made a crucial difference. Ouseley J restrained publication of photographs depicting the claimant's activities in a brothel, but not the same information conveyed by them in the form of the prostitutes' narrative account of what happened.[198]

**4.78**   It has further been held that a tape recording of a private conversation may have a status of its own, separate and distinct from that deserved by the information contained in or revealed by the tape. In *D v L*[199] the Court of Appeal held that 'the publication of a covert tape recording of a private conversation involves a breach of confidence'.[200] Referring to the observations of the Court on the interim appeal in *Douglas v Hello! Ltd*[201] it was said that the same principle was applicable:

> Just as a photograph can make a greater impact than an account of the matter depicted by that photograph, so the recorded details of the very words of a private conversation can make more impact, and cause more embarrassment and distress, than a mere account of the conversation in question.[202]

**4.79**   It has to be recognized that analysis of the authorities discussed above is not assisted by the fact that, with the exception of *Service Corp*, they were all decided in the period when the courts were expanding the scope of breach of confidence and developing what has become the civil wrong of misuse of private information. It does, however, seem that there are two key questions when considering the relevance of the form or medium in which information is recorded. One is whether the form affects the informational content, and this can clearly be relevant to the issue of whether the information has a confidential character. The second key question is whether the form affects the impact on the claimant of an unauthorized disclosure. This will be relevant to a claim for misuse. Whether it is relevant, or weighty, so far as breach of confidence is concerned, is perhaps less clear.[203]

*(i) Qualities of the information*

**4.80**   **Novel, original, unique**   In the commercial sphere it appears that ingenuity is not a requirement of confidentiality; very simple ideas are capable of being protected as

---

[195]   [1999] EMLR 83, 90.
[196]   [1999] EMLR 654, 662. Note that Keane LJ made the same observation in *Douglas* (n 7) [165].
[197]   [2002] EMLR 398.
[198]   *Theakston* (n 197) [77]–[79]. The decision was made on an interim application.
[199]   [2003] EWCA Civ 1169, [2004] EMLR 1.
[200]   *D v L* (n 199) [34] (Lord Phillips MR).
[201]   *Douglas* (n 7).
[202]   *D v L* (n 199) [24].
[203]   The damage which disclosure might do is discussed at 4.90–4.91.

confidential.[204] On the other hand, if information can be shown affirmatively to be ingenious, or novel, original, or unique then this will count in favour of its classification as confidential.[205] Originality has, indeed, been identified as a requirement of confidentiality in an idea for a television series.[206] Ingenuity, novelty, and originality are difficult and probably inappropriate labels to apply to most types of personal information which might be in issue in a privacy claim. However, uniqueness may well be a factor in favour of classifying personal information as confidential. Indeed, it might more easily be said of the details of a person's private life and behaviour than of an industrial design that such information is unique.

### Not trivial, but useful or valuable

*Triviality*   It is well established that information will not be regarded as hav-   **4.81** ing the necessary quality of confidence if it is 'trivial tittle-tattle',[207] 'perfectly useless',[208] or 'pernicious nonsense…utterly absurd'.[209] This 'triviality' doctrine may on occasion be of importance in commercial cases, which is the context in which it has mainly found expression.[210] However, it has been said to be irrelevant in cases concerned with government intelligence or counter-intelligence secrets, where it is extremely difficult for outsiders to determine what is or is not trivial.[211] It remains unclear to what extent the triviality doctrine has a significant role to play in confidence cases concerning personal information and the media.

Media stories do sometimes contain personal information of doubtful utility   **4.82** which could be said to be mere tittle-tattle or gossip, and it does appear that triviality is, in principle, a factor limiting the scope of confidentiality. Sexual matters seem, however, most unlikely to be treated as trivial. When, in *Stephens v Avery*, a

---

[204] See *Gurry on Breach of Confidence* (n 32) para 5.55 and *Cranleigh Precision Engineering Ltd v Bryant* [1965] 1 WLR 1293, 1310, Roskill J. In *Coco v Clark* (n 43) 47, Megarry J went so far as to say that '[t]he simpler an idea, the more likely it is to need protection'.

[205] In *Terrapin Ltd v Builders' Supply Co Ltd* [1960] RPC 128, 134 Lord Evershed MR clearly regarded 'the novelty of [the] idea' in question as important, and saw the 'eulogistic language' of the defendants' brochure as evidence which supported the proposition that it was 'something new if it were workable'. See also *Cranleigh Precision Engineering* (n 204) 1310, where Roskill J emphasized as an important point in favour of the plaintiff's claim to confidentiality in features of their swimming pool design the fact that the defendants had described those features as 'a new development in pool design' and 'unique'. In *Coco v Clark* (n 43) 47, Megarry J clearly regarded novelty and ingenuity as relevant factors when considering information put together from materials in the public domain: 'something new and confidential may have been brought into being by the skill and ingenuity of the human brain. Novelty depends on the thing itself and not upon the quality of its constituent parts.'

[206] *Fraser* (n 99) 66, Hirst J, citing *Talbot* (n 99).

[207] *Coco v Clark* (n 43) 48.

[208] *McNicol v Sportsman's Books* (1930) McG GC 116 where an injunction was refused on this ground. 'It is obvious that, as a general proposition, a duty of confidence will not be imposed so as to protect useless information': *Attorney General v Observer Ltd* (n 12) 149 (Scott J).

[209] *Church of Scientology v Kaufman* [1973] RPC 635, 658 (Goff J).

[210] See the cases cited in the previous three notes.

[211] See *Attorney General v Observer Ltd* (n 12) 284 (Lord Goff). See also the observations of Lord Donaldson MR to similar effect in the same case in the Court of Appeal at 180.

newspaper seeking to make 'wholesale revelation of the sexual conduct of an individual' argued that the information was trivial, Sir Nicholas Browne-Wilkinson V-C was unconvinced. He expressed 'the gravest doubt' whether this could 'properly be described as "trivial" tittle-tattle'.[212] The twenty-first century decisions suggest that only information of the most banal kind is likely to be held to lack the requisite quality of confidence.

**4.83** In *Mills v News Group Newspapers Ltd*, the relative triviality of the personal information (the claimant's address) counted in the balance against the grant of an injunction against a newspaper in confidence.[213] However, triviality was just one factor in the decision.[214] In *Campbell v MGN Ltd* the Court of Appeal found that publication of details of the claimant's attendance at Narcotics Anonymous was 'not, in context, sufficiently significant to amount to a breach of duty owed to her'.[215] A minority of the House of Lords agreed,[216] but the majority disagreed, taking the view that disclosure could cause the claimant harm by disrupting her treatment and contributing to her sense of having been betrayed by a confidant.[217] In *McKennitt v Ash* the Court of Appeal approved the trial judge's rejection of some of the claimant's complaints on grounds that the disclosure was anodyne and hence did not cross the threshold.[218] The dismissed complaints were, however, of a fairly minor kind, and the judge also upheld complaints in respect of '[e]ven relatively trivial details' regarding the claimant's home life on account of 'the traditional sanctity accorded to hearth and home'.[219] In *Lady Archer v Williams* an argument that the matters in issue were trivial tittle-tattle was dismissed,[220] although they included not only 'details about the claimant's home life' but also 'any incident or conversation concerning any member of the claimant's family, guest, visitor or member of her staff which occurred in the claimant's home'.[221]

---

[212] *Stephens* (n 164) 454.

[213] [2001] EMLR 957 [33]. The claimant, a model who had become publicly associated with Sir Paul McCartney (whom she later married), sought an injunction to restrain publication of her private address.

[214] Among other factors to which the Court attached weight were the fact that 'the evidence which [the claimant] puts forward for a real risk [of damage] is very slight' and the fact that some information about her address was likely to come into the public domain. See *Mills* (n 213) [34]–[35].

[215] *Campbell* (n 78) [58]. See also [53].

[216] *Campbell* (n 2) [25]–[27], [70]–[71].

[217] *Campbell* (n 2) [98], [119], [146], [153], [165].

[218] *McKennitt* (n 21) [12].

[219] See the first-instance decision [2005] EWHC 3003 (QB), [2006] EMLR 10, *eg* [132], [134], [139], [141], [145], [149], dismissing complaints about disclosure of passing references to friendships with men, shopping trips, the state of relations between the claimant and the defendant's friends, and similar matters; cf [135] upholding complaints in respect of the relatively trivial details. See also *Lord Browne v* (n 25) [33], where the Court of Appeal rejected the notion that a trivial piece of information could never be regarded as private: a detailed examination of all the circumstances was required, and the nature of the relationship within which information was imparted might be 'of considerable importance' in answering this question.

[220] [2003] EWHC 1670 (QB), [2003] EMLR 38 [67] (Jackson J).

[221] *Lady Archer* (n 220) [34]–[35].

*Value* Where commercial information is concerned one consideration relevant **4.84**
to whether it is confidential is whether it is of 'commercial or industrial value';[222]
evidence that information has value in the sense that people are prepared to pay for
it will assist in demonstrating that it is confidential.[223] It is clearly open to argument
in a personal information case that if a media organization believes its readers or
audience will pay to acquire the information that should count in favour of a claim
to confidentiality. If a media organization has itself bought the information, that
argument would appear to be the stronger. The latter point was specifically relied
on by both the trial judge and the House of Lords in *Douglas v Hello! Ltd*. Lindsay J
held that the competition between *Hello!* and *OK!* for exclusivity, and 'that each
was ready to pay so much for it', both pointed to 'the commercial confidentiality
of coverage of the event', and the majority in the House of Lords agreed, Lord
Hoffmann observing that '[p]rovided one keeps one's eye firmly on the money, and
why it was paid, the case is, as Lindsay J held, quite straightforward'. [224]

**Detailed and identifiable** Considerable emphasis is laid in the commercial-  **4.85**
confidence cases on the need for information to be specific, detailed, and readily
identifiable if it is to be treated as confidential, and on the linked requirement that
a claimant must identify with precision just what is alleged to be confidential.[225]
Similar requirements have been identified in relation to artistic or literary ideas.[226]
In a number of cases concerning personal information, a distinction has been
drawn between information constituted by a particular fact about an individual
and information comprising the detail or the 'colour' of that fact.

In *Theakston v MGN Ltd* Ouseley J, in considering whether to grant the claim-  **4.86**
ant injunctive relief, distinguished information as to the fact that he had visited a
brothel from the detail of what went on when he was there.[227] In *Campbell v MGN
Ltd*, the claimant's success at trial and in the House of Lords was predicated on the
drawing of a distinction between the fact that the claimant was a drug addict having therapy to cure her of her addiction (the disclosure of which was admitted to
be legitimate, given her previous lies about it) and the 'detail' that she had attended
Narcotics Anonymous to that end, and what she had done there.[228] These cases

---

[222] See *Coco v Clark* (n 43) 48.
[223] *Potters Ballotini Ltd v Weston-Baker* [1977] RPC 202, 206 (Lord Denning MR). See also
*Exchange Telegraph Co Ltd v Central News Ltd* [1897] 2 Ch 48, 53 (Stirling J).
[224] *Douglas* (n 10) [197] (Lindsay J); *Douglas*, HL (n 3) [117].
[225] In *Smith Kline and French Laboratories (Australia) Ltd* (n 62) 639, Gummow J held that this
was one of the elements of a cause of action in confidence. See the discussion in Toulson and Phipps
(n 32) paras 3-085 *et seq*.
[226] 'To succeed in his claim the plaintiff must establish ... that the content of the idea was clearly
identifiable, original, of potential commercial attractiveness and capable of being realised in actual-
ity. With these limitations, I consider there is no basis for Mr Harman's fears that authors' freedom
to develop ideas will be unduly stifled': *Fraser* (n 99) 66 (Hirst J).
[227] *Theakston* (n 197) [75].
[228] [2002] EWHC 499 (QB), [2002] EMLR 617 (Morland J); (n 2) (HL). Cf the rejection of
some of the complaints in *McKennitt v Ash* on the grounds that they were too general to give rise to

demonstrate, in line with traditional confidence principles, the importance for claimants of identifying with specificity the information of which they wish, and more importantly are entitled, to restrain publication.

**4.87** One of the main reasons for these requirements is the need, in the commercial context, to ensure that confidence claims are not exploited so as to oppress ex-employees or otherwise prevent fair competition. For this reason it is necessary clearly to distinguish a trade secret, in which confidentiality may exist, from information which may be carried in the head of an ex-employee as stock-in-trade, as to which no confidence claim can be maintained.[229] These considerations are less relevant, if relevant at all, in confidence cases where personal information is concerned. A second reason for the above requirements may be more relevant in cases of personal information. This is the need to avoid a prohibition on the disclosure of information which is not confidential because it is already in the public domain.[230]

**4.88** In this context, the degree of detail contained in the personal information at issue may be an important factor in establishing its confidentiality. For instance, it has been suggested that while information which merely indicates that an entertainer has had a homosexual relationship with a particular individual may not be confidential if the entertainer's sexual orientation has already been disclosed by him, 'when one goes into detail ... one has crossed the line into breach of confidence'.[231] An alternative means of resolving this problem has been adopted in more recent cases: the use of a 'public domain' proviso to any injunction, approved by the court.[232]

**4.89** A third reason for the requirements mentioned above is the cardinal rule that any injunction granted by the court must be in clear terms which tell the defendant

---

a reasonable expectation of privacy, and lacked precision: see decision of Eady J (n 219) [147]–[149], [153], approved by the Court of Appeal (n 21) [12]. Precise identification of personal confidential material may, however, sometimes be disproportionate and unnecessary, particularly where the circumstances of disclosure suggest the totality will be confidential and the quantity of information is large, *eg* where electronic data is concerned: see *Tchenguiz v Imerman* (n 30) [78] Lord Neuberger MR.

[229] See *eg Faccenda Chicken Ltd* (n 97) 136, Neill LJ; *Lock v Beswick* [1989] 1 WLR 1268, 1273–4, Hoffmann J.

[230] See *eg Under Water Welders and Repairers Ltd v Street and Longthorne* [1968] RPC 498, 506–7, Buckley LJ.

[231] *Barrymore* (n 173) 603, Jacob J, where the judge observed, *obiter*, that it 'may well be the case [that] ... merely to disclose that [the claimant] had had a particular partner would be to add nothing new'. See now *Hutcheson (previously 'KGM') v News Group Newspapers Ltd* [2011] EWCA Civ 808, [2012] EMLR 2, where the Court of Appeal upheld Eady J's decision to reject the applicant's application to restrain the defendant from publishing the fact that he had a second family known only to a few people.

[232] The proviso excludes from the scope of the injunction information that is already in the public domain or enters the public domain otherwise than as a result of a breach of the order. See cl 15 of the *Practice Guidance: Interim Non-Disclosure Orders* [2012] 1 WLR 1003 for the recommended wording, and the discussion at 12.78 and 13.123.

precisely what may and may not be done.[233] This proved a stumbling block when an injunction was sought in confidence to restrain the unauthorized advance disclosure of extracts from Lady Thatcher's diaries. The Court refused the injunction on the grounds, among others, that no satisfactory injunction could be framed.[234] It may be, however, that a public domain proviso of the kind mentioned above will suffice to resolve this problem also in many cases.

*(j) The damage which disclosure might do*

This is most obviously a factor which will influence the court's decision whether **4.90** to grant an injunction, especially at the interim stage.[235] However, the nature and extent of the damage which might be caused by disclosure of information can also be a criterion in deciding the prior question of whether it is confidential in nature. Amongst the criteria for the identification of confidential information which Sir Robert Megarry V-C proposed in *Thomas Marshall v Guinle* were that the party claiming confidentiality must believe that release of the information would be injurious to him, and his belief must be reasonable.[236] The point has featured little in subsequent commercial case law, but appears to be of some importance in confidence cases concerning personal information.

The hallmarks of breaches of personal confidence include particular kinds of **4.91** damage, quite distinct from the damage caused to businesses by disclosures of commercial information. These have been said to include distress and injury to feelings caused by the loss of control over personal information;[237] intrusion into the private space, with consequent feelings of affront to the personality; and damage to the sensibilities from the public exposure of inward feelings.[238] As Toulson and Phipps have pointed out, 'in the case of misuse of confidential information relating to personal matters... the law is intended to protect personal feelings'.[239] Similarly, it may be argued that in assessing whether personal information is of a confidential character the nature and extent of the damage which its disclosure would cause is a useful criterion, and this approach appears to have informed the House of Lords' decision to restore the judgment in favour of the claimant in *Campbell v MGN Ltd*.[240]

---

[233] See *Potters Ballotini* (n 223) 206 (Lord Denning MR).

[234] *Times Newspapers Ltd* (n 100). See esp 448 (Leggatt LJ). See also *O v A* [2015] UKSC 32, [2015] 2 WLR 1373 [78]–[79].

[235] See *eg Mills* (n 213) [35].

[236] *Thomas Marshall* (n 94) 248.

[237] *Cornelius v de Taranto* [2001] EMLR 6 [79]–[80]. Morland J's decision was appealed without affecting this point: [2001] EWCA Civ 1511, [2002] EMLR 12.

[238] *R v Broadcasting Standards Commission, ex p BBC* [2001] 1 QB 885 [48] Lord Mustill.

[239] Toulson and Phipps (n 32) para 9-044. However, feelings are not the only or even necessarily the main interest that is protected: see ch 2.

[240] *Campbell* (n 2) [119], [124], Lord Hope and [157]–[158], Lady Hale.

### (4) Factors Negating Confidentiality

#### (a) Falsity

**4.92** It has been the conventional view that there can be no claim to confidentiality in false information.[241] It seems that the existence of some inaccuracies will not rob personal information of an otherwise confidential character.[242] It would, however, appear to remain the case in respect of true, or traditional, breach of confidence that complete falsity is inconsistent with confidentiality.[243] It is, indeed, hard to see how the *Coco v Clark* analysis can be comfortably applied to information the essence of which is false.

**4.93** On the other hand, it is clear that the mere fact that personal information which has been published is false cannot of itself be a defence to a claim based on Article 8. The Strasbourg Court has held that the publication of false and defamatory statements about private life engages Article 8.[244] It has also been said in the Court of Appeal that falsity is irrelevant in deciding whether private information is entitled to be protected,[245] and injunctive relief against the publication of falsehoods about private life has been granted on the basis of misuse of private information.[246] Protection against the dissemination of false facts about private life is addressed in detail in Chapter 8.[247]

#### (b) Public knowledge

**4.94** Proof that the information at issue is in the public domain, in the sense that it has already been disclosed to such an extent that it can no longer be considered secret, will in principle lead to the failure of a claim in confidentiality, though this will not necessarily follow in respect of a claim for misuse of private information.[248]

---

[241] See eg *Khashoggi v Smith* (1980) 124 SJ 149, CA. The proposition was apparently accepted without question in the commercial confidence case of *Interbrew SA v Financial Times Ltd* [2002] EWCA Civ 274, [2002] 2 Lloyd's Rep 229 [38].

[242] *Campbell* (n 228) (Morland J). The Court of Appeal differed on the facts, rather than the principle: see n 243. See also Eady J in *Beckham v Gibson* (QBD, 29 April 2005) and *McKennitt* (n 21) [78].

[243] See *Interbrew* (n 241) and *Campbell*, CA (n 78) [57] where the Court, reversing the judge's decision, expressed the view that, contrary to his finding, the inaccuracies covered 'a substantial proportion' of the allegedly confidential detail. The falsity issue was barely touched on in the decision of the House of Lords, but Lord Hope's *obiter* remarks at [102] are in line with the principle suggested in the text. In *McKennitt* (n 21) it was observed by Buxton LJ at [79] that a confidence claim in respect of false information where the nub of the complaint was the falsity would face objections in terms of abuse of process. However, in *Hannon* (n 187) Mann J declined to strike out claims brought in breach of confidence and misuse of private information where it was contended the actions should have been brought in defamation. Mann J cautioned against applying what was said in a general way in *McKennitt* to developing privacy jurisprudence: [36].

[244] *Cumpana and Mazare v Romania* (2005) 41 EHRR 14, para 91, Grand Chamber (citing *Chauvy v France* (2005) 41 EHRR 29, para 70).

[245] *McKennitt* (n 21) [79] (Buxton LJ) and [85]–[86] (Longmore LJ). See also *Hannon* (nn 187 and 243).

[246] See eg *Beckham v Gibson* (n 242).

[247] See in particular 8.71–8.73 .

[248] See the discussion at 11.43 *et seq.*

There is a limited number of other situations in which the court has declined to rec-  **4.95**
ognize information as having a confidential character. These are briefly discussed
at 4.96 to 4.102. Some of them are not easy to distinguish from cases in which
a claim for breach of confidence may be met by the justifications or defences of
public interest or 'just cause or excuse'. Those are dealt with separately and in more
detail in Chapter 11.

*(c) Public record*

In ruling on issues of 'public domain' in various contexts the courts have fre-  **4.96**
quently drawn a distinction between information being accessible to the public,
for instance on a website, and information being common knowledge as a matter of
fact.[249] It is, in general, only proof of the latter that will sustain a claim that information is in the public domain. There is nevertheless a body of authority which
suggests that there are circumstances in which information which the law requires
to be accessible to the public will not be treated as confidential in nature, regardless of the extent to which the public actually knows it. Such authorities frequently
speak in terms of 'public domain' but may be explicable on the basis of principles
of public policy quite distinct from the rationale that underlies the ordinary public
domain doctrine.

**Information about public legal proceedings**  Many court proceedings, though  **4.97**
conducted in public, receive no public attention at all. Information, otherwise
secret, may be disclosed in circumstances where, as a matter of fact, very few come
to know it. As has been observed, under modern English civil procedure 'there
may be a degree of unreality in the proposition that the material documents in
the case have (in practice as well as in theory) passed into the public domain'.[250]
Nevertheless, the ordinary rule is that the press can report everything that took
place in open court and that 'strong rule' could only be displaced in unusual or
exceptional circumstances.[251]

Information on publicly accessible court records has been held to fall outside the  **4.98**
scope of litigation privilege, because it lacks confidentiality; but it would seem
that the inadvertent inclusion of information claimed to be confidential in a statement of case will not deprive it of that character, at least in the absence of evidence
that it has in fact been inspected by the public.[252] In *Elliott v Chief Constable of
Wiltshire* Sir Richard Scott V-C held the proposition that the claimant's criminal

---

[249] See 11.48.
[250] *SmithKline Beecham Biologicals SA v Connaught Laboratories Inc* [1999] 4 All ER 498, 512
(Lord Bingham CJ).
[251] *PNM v Times Newspapers Ltd* (n 187) applying *Re S (A Child)* (n 18).
[252] Compare *Goldstone v Williams* [1899] 1 Ch 47 with *Orr-Adams v Bailey* [2013] EWPCC 30,
where the allegedly confidential information was mistakenly included in an Annex to Particulars of
Claim (Miss Recorder Amanda Michaels at [43]–[47]).

convictions were confidential information to be 'absurd'.[253] In *Bunn v BBC* it was held sufficient to rob information about a statement made to police of its otherwise confidential character that a judge had read the statement to himself at a public hearing.[254] In neither of these cases did the Court consider the actual extent of public knowledge of the information in question to be significant.[255] In *D v L* the Court of Appeal appears to have taken a similar approach, finding certain information to be non-confidential because it had been 'revealed in evidence and made the subject of a finding in the judgment'.[256]

**4.99**  It is also relevant to note that none of the 'public domain' exceptions to the restrictions on the collateral use of documents or information disclosed by compulsion in legal proceedings[257] depends on the extent of actual public knowledge of the information. Mere mention of a document in court serves to release a document from the bar on collateral use imposed by the rules of procedure. These exceptions have been created to give effect to the public interest in freedom of expression, as recognized under Article 10(1) ECHR: the 'public domain' exception to the implied undertaking in civil proceedings was first introduced as part of a settlement of proceedings before the European Commission of Human Rights in which it had been alleged that the then English law was incompatible with Article 10.[258]

**4.100**  One court, referring to the second edition of this book, has concluded that there is indeed an absolute or near-absolute rule of law that once information is disclosed in open court it cannot thereafter be considered confidential, even if nobody outside the case has come to know of it.[259] The court observed that:

> The preponderance of English authority supports the view that once material has been read or referred to in open court, it enters the public domain. It seems to me that there is a need for a clear and simple rule on this point, which reflects the principle of open justice, and which can be overridden, if at all, only in exceptional circumstances where the interests of justice so require.... The touchstone, in my

---

[253] (1996) TLR 693, 694. The claim for breach of confidence was struck out on this ground. This principle would appear to apply even to convictions that are spent under the Rehabilitation of Offenders Act 1974: see *L v Law Society* [2008] EWCA Civ 811, the Master of the Rolls at [24]–[25]; *XJO v XIM* [2011] EWHC 1768 (QB), where Eady J appeared to doubt that there could be a reasonable expectation of privacy in relation to a spent conviction; see also 5.73.

[254] [1998] 3 All ER 552, 557. It is not clear from the judgment whether the judge read the statement aloud or silently.

[255] In *Elliott* (n 253), Sir Richard Scott V-C acknowledged that the information was relatively inaccessible but said that since the convictions had been announced in open court 'they were therefore in the public domain'. See also *WB v H Bauer* (n 31) and *PNM v Times* (n 187)

[256] *D v L* (n 199) [19] Waller LJ and see, to similar effect, [34(iii)], Lord Phillips MR.

[257] CPR 31.22(1) and Criminal Procedure and Investigations Act 1996, s 17(3).

[258] See *SmithKline Beecham* (n 250) 506–7, Lord Bingham CJ.

[259] *Commissioners for Her Majesty's Revenue and Customs v Banerjee* [2009] EWHC 1229 (Ch), [2009] EMLR 24 (Henderson J).

view, is whether the hearing in question is held in public, not whether it is in fact attended by any member of the public.[260]

On this basis, it would seem that a media defendant may be able to defeat a claim in confidence by proving such disclosure, without the need to prove the extent of publicity given to it. That said, the discussion of the issue in the subsequent case of *Ambrosiadou v Coward*[261] provides grounds for suggesting that the position may be more nuanced than this, and that confidentiality in certain information may not be lost 'at a stroke' by the mere mention of a document in court, especially in circumstances where the Court is under an obligation to protect the Article 8 rights of third parties such as children.

**Information required by law to be public**    There may be a more general public    **4.101**
policy principle that information which the law requires to be made public will not be protected by the law of confidentiality. This is the position in the United States, where the law precludes an action for invasion of privacy in respect of accurate disclosure of information contained in public records, regardless of the extent of actual public knowledge.[262] The Calcutt Committee on Privacy, writing in 1990, saw merit in excluding from the ambit of personal information to be protected by a privacy law 'any material . . . required by law to be registered, recorded or otherwise available to public inspection'.[263]

There is some support in the authorities for such an approach. In *Initial Services v*    **4.102**
*Putterill* the Court of Appeal held it arguable that information was not confidential in nature because, although not in fact a matter of public knowledge or actually a matter of public record, it was required by law to be placed on a public register.[264] That said, the Calcutt Committee's views have not been reflected in any legislation. It might also be argued that an absolute rule permitting the use and disclosure of information drawn from, or contained in public records would be hard to reconcile with the scheme of the Data Protection Act 1998.

---

[260] *Banerjee* (n 259) [38]. See also *Crossley v Newsquest (Midlands South) Ltd* [2008] EWHC 3054 (QB) [58]–[59], where Eady J held that a proposed amendment to pursue a confidence and privacy claim in respect of reports of information disclosed in open court was unarguable.

[261] [2010] EWHC 1794 [20]–[21] and [29]–[31] (Eady J). On appeal, the Court of Appeal gave brief guidance on how to ensure that a hearing took place in public while confidential information referred to did not enter the public domain: see [2011] EMLR 21 [52] (Master of the Rolls) and [54] (Leveson LJ).

[262] Restatement of the Law, Second, Torts (1977) § 652S; the US Supreme Court decisions in *Cox Broadcasting Corp v Cohen* 420 US 469, 494–5 (1975); *Landmark Communications Inc v Virginia* 435 US 829, 849, 3 Media L Rep (BNA) 2153 (1978) and the decision of the Supreme Court of Iowa in *Howard v Des Moines Register and Tribune Co* (1979) 283 NW 2d 289, 5 Media L Rep (BNA) 1667. See also R Sack, *Sack on Defamation* (4th edn, Practising Law Institute 2010) para 12.4.5.5 [C]–[E], in which this US law principle is analysed.

[263] *Report of the Committee on Privacy and Related Matters* (Cm 1102, 1990), chairman David Calcutt QC, para 12.17.

[264] [1968] 1 QB 396, CA, 406, Lord Denning MR. The information concerned an allegedly unlawful restrictive trade practice.

# E. The Duty of Confidence

## (1) When Will Duties of Confidence be Imposed?

### (a) Express contract

**4.103** Express restrictions on the disclosure of personal information are often found in contracts between public figures and third parties.[265]

### Principles

**4.104** *Jurisdiction* The basis of the jurisdiction in these cases is contract, not confidence.[266] The jurisdiction to enforce a contractual duty of confidence is based on the principle that equity will intervene to enforce the parties' bargain.[267] Subject to s 12 HRA,[268] this approach is appropriate even when the claimant is seeking injunctive relief to enforce the duty at the interim stage, at least where no sensible attack can be made on the validity of the covenant.[269]

**4.105** *Parties and consideration* The claimant must show that the undertaking is binding on the person who gave it.[270] If the undertaking is contained in a deed, no consideration is necessary. If there is no deed, the court may well locate sufficient consideration or contractual intention in order to render the undertaking enforceable as a contract. In *Adams v Attridge*,[271] for example, Buckley J considered it arguable that a written undertaking given by a former chauffeur of the Spice Girls pop group was enforceable on the basis that (among other things) the undertaking was required before the chauffeur actually commenced driving for the group.

**4.106** *Scope and duration* The scope and duration of a contractual duty of confidence depend, in the first place, on the proper construction of the contract. The duty to maintain secrecy must be shown to extend to the facts in question. Thus, in *Barrymore v News Group Newspapers Ltd*[272] it was argued on behalf of the defendant publishers that the covenant did not catch events that occurred before the agreement was entered into.[273] If the covenant is appropriately drawn, the protection it confers may

---

[265] *eg Attorney General v Barker* [1990] 3 All ER 257, CA: former employee of Royal Household; *Barrymore* (n 173): former sexual partner of well-known entertainer; *Adams v Attridge* (HC, 8 October 1998, Buckley J): former chauffeur to pop group Spice Girls; *Campbell v Frisbee* [2002] EWCA Civ 1374, [2003] EMLR 3: personal assistant to celebrity model.
[266] See *Attorney General v Barker* (n 265) 259, 261–2.
[267] *Doherty v Allman* (1878) 3 App Cas 709, 720.
[268] See further 12.02 *et seq* for discussion of the general impact of s 12.
[269] *Attorney General v Barker* (n 265) 262, Nourse LJ.
[270] Celebrity confidentiality agreements are often made by or with companies representing the individuals concerned.
[271] *Adams* (n 265).
[272] *Barrymore* (n 173).
[273] The argument failed on the facts: *Barrymore* (n 173) 602.

extend beyond matters that are by nature truly confidential.[274] The protection may be cast so as to endure beyond the termination of the contractual relationship.[275]

*Enforceability* Confidentiality covenants will be enforced, it has been said, unless **4.107** the covenant can be attacked for obscurity, illegality, or on other public policy grounds.[276] The doctrine of restraint of trade usually has no role to play, and covenants to keep personal matters confidential are routinely upheld at the interim stage.[277] It may be that even if the confidant accepts the repudiation of a contract of service or for services, the enforceability of any covenant for confidentiality is unaffected.[278]

**Limitations** The fact that an obligation of confidence is contractual does not **4.108** necessarily vest it with some special status arising from the sanctity of freedom of contract. An undertaking not to disclose matters of legitimate public interest may be insufficient consideration to support a contract and, if the matters are such that in the public interest they ought to be disclosed, an undertaking not to disclose them will not be enforced.[279] The reasonableness or otherwise of the covenant at the time the contract was entered into may be a factor in ascertaining the scope of a contractual duty; so too whether or not it would be reasonable to enforce it in the light of events that have occurred.[280]

More generally, it may be that the limitations which equity imposes on the **4.109** enforceability of a duty of confidence, and Article 10 considerations, both apply to a contractual duty. The ECtHR has held that Article 10 applies to employment contracts, at least for those employed in the public sector.[281] A contractual

---

[274] See *eg R v Her Majesty's Attorney General for England and Wales* [2003] UKPC 22, [2003] EMLR 24 where, following damaging disclosures by serving members of the SAS, the Ministry of Defence considered it necessary to restrict by contract the disclosure of any information by serving members 'relating to the work of, or in support of, the United Kingdom Special Forces', without prior authorization. See also, however, 4.108–4.109.

[275] As Jackson J held to be the case in respect of the employee's contract in *Lady Archer v Williams* (n 220) [48].

[276] *Attorney General v Barker* (n 265) 260, Lord Donaldson MR. See, however, 4.108–4.109.

[277] This is not to say, however, that contractual obligations will always be upheld. Art 10 may apply, as do considerations of public interest and, possibly, reasonableness: see 4.108.

[278] This was the conclusion of Lightman J in *Campbell v Frisbee* (n 182) [21]–[22], following Morritt LJ in *Rock Refrigeration Ltd v Jones* [1997] 1 All ER 1. However, the Court of Appeal considered the issue unsuitable for summary determination, finding that the effect of repudiation on duties of confidence was not clearly established: n 265 [34].

[279] See *Chitty on Contracts* (31st edn, Sweet & Maxwell 2012) vol 1, para 16-005 and cases there cited at nn 23, 24.

[280] *Dunford and Elliott v Johnson and Firth Brown* [1978] FSR 143, 148.

[281] *Grigoriades v Greece* (1997) 27 EHRR 464, para 45; *Vogt v Germany* (1995) 21 EHRR 205, 43–5. See, however, the contrasting approach of the New Zealand Court of Appeal in *Attorney General for England and Wales v R* [2002] 2 NZLR 91, in which it was held that the right to freedom of expression in the New Zealand Bill of Rights Act 1990 (which was considered to be of like effect to Art 10 ECHR) had no bearing on the construction of a confidentiality contract between a soldier and his former employer, the Ministry of Defence. It was, however, one of the factors which led the Court to refuse injunctive relief.

restriction must satisfy the requirements of Article 10(2) or it will not be enforced, at least not by injunction.[282] The Court of Appeal has held that the same approach to enforcement should be adopted, regardless of whether the duty arose under contract or otherwise.[283] There are, however, previous and subsequent authorities at first instance and in the Court of Appeal which take a different view, and cast doubt on this proposition. These cases suggest that a duty assumed under contract carries more weight than a duty not buttressed by express agreement.[284] The weight of authority now appears to favour the slightly different approach, that in conducting a balancing exercise in a case where the duty of confidence is contractual the court should give weight to the wider public interest that exists in upholding express agreements to maintain confidentiality.[285]

**4.110** **Shortcomings** An obvious shortcoming of the contractual basis for protecting privacy is that contractual obligations do not bind third parties. The tort of inducing breach of contract is not a reliable means of preventing disclosure at the hands of third parties, given the restricted circumstances in which that tort would apply in the present context.[286] However, where the relationship between the parties also gives rise to a duty of confidence in equity, third parties may be restrained more readily.[287]

### (b) The equitable duty of confidence

**4.111** **Basic principles** If the confidential character of the information in question is established, a duty of confidence will arise if the second of the three criteria identified in *Coco v Clark*[288] is satisfied: if the information has been communicated in circumstances 'importing an obligation of confidence'.[289] This classic formulation is the starting point, but has to be read in the light of the broader formulation of the law of confidence by Lord Goff in *Spycatcher*, emphasizing the particular importance of the circumstances of acquisition.[290]

---

[282] See *London Regional Transport Ltd* (n 64).

[283] *London Regional Transport* (n 64) [46] (Robert Walker LJ).

[284] In *Attorney General v Barker* (n 265) 259, Lord Donaldson MR drew a clear distinction between a contractual and equitable duty of confidence, the former being habitually enforced. In *Campbell v Frisbee* it was held at first instance that an express obligation of confidence may be given added weight due to the nature of the relationship, *eg* a confidential agency: (n 182) [41], [42]. The Court of Appeal in the same case ((n 265) [22]) held it arguable that an express contractual duty carries more weight, and referred to the contrasting observations of Lord Donaldson in *Barker* and Walker LJ in *London Regional Transport*. In *Attorney General v Parry* [2004] EMLR 223 Lewison J considered it 'well arguable' that an express duty should carry more weight that an implied duty.

[285] See *McKennitt* (n 21) and *HRH Prince of Wales* (n 23).

[286] See further *Gurry on Breach of Confidence* (n 32) paras 2.120–2.124, 4.36.

[287] See 4.137–4.143.

[288] *Coco* (n 43) 47. See 4.14.

[289] *Coco* (n 43) 47. See also *Saltman* (n 50).

[290] *Attorney General v Observer Ltd* (n 12) 281, quoted in 4.20.

It is also necessary to consider in this context the extent to which more recent **4.112** developments in the law, by which the new wrong of misuse of private information has come into being, have affected the underlying principles of traditional breach of confidence. It has been clear, at least since the Court of Appeal's decision on the final appeal in *Douglas v Hello! Ltd*, that where private information is concerned a claim in respect of its misuse may succeed without proof that the defendant acquired the information in circumstances importing a duty of confidence; in other words, where the second *Coco v Clark* criterion is not met.[291] It is sufficient to show that the claimant had a reasonable expectation of privacy in respect of the information.[292]

It is suggested, however, that it does not follow that the second limb of the *Coco* **4.113** test has disappeared. Rather, as the House of Lords recognized in disposing of the final *Douglas* appeal, it can now be acknowledged that two separate and distinct causes of action exist, protecting separate and distinct interests, and with different requirements.[293] It should follow that it is no longer necessary to shoehorn cases of misuse of private information into the established cause of action for breach of confidence, or to bend or cast aside the established rules and principles of that cause of action to accommodate claims which are aimed at the protection of information which is private but not secret. In the discussion which follows, therefore, the focus will be on 'traditional breach of confidence'. More recent authorities concerned with misuse of private information will be considered in Chapter 5.

**'Circumstances importing a duty of confidence'**  The identification of circum- **4.114** stances surrounding the acquisition of information which will 'import' a duty of confidence upon the recipient is not a straightforward matter. Attempting to elaborate on this aspect of the law, Megarry J himself resorted to the concept of the reasonable man. If a reasonable person in the defendant's shoes would have realized the information was given in confidence then a duty would be imposed.[294]

This formulation offers some guidance, but without identifying particular circum- **4.115** stances which would give rise to such a realization in the mind of the reasonable person. A number of categories of relevant circumstance can be identified, how- ever. It may be that these can compendiously be described as circumstances in which the recipient of the information can be said to be on notice of circumstances giving rise to a reasonable expectation of confidentiality, or secrecy, of some degree.

---

[291] 'Megarry J in *Coco v AN Clark* identified two requirements for the creation of a duty of confidence. The first was that the information be confidential in nature and the second was that it should have been imparted in circumstances importing a duty of confidence. As we have seen, it is now recognised that the second requirement is not necessary if it is plain that the information is confidential, and for the adjective "confidential" one can substitute the word "private"': *Douglas* (n 10) [83] (Lord Phillips MR).

[292] Per Lord Phillips MR, *Douglas* (n 10) [50]–[82].

[293] See 4.01 (n 6).

[294] See passage cited from *Coco v Clark* in 4.74.

**4.116** **A confidential relationship** It is often the case that parties to a relationship are taken implicitly to have assumed an obligation to maintain the secrecy of information received in the course of that relationship. The possible relationships are many. As Toulson and Phipps point out:

> It would be impossible to compile a list of all relationships likely to give rise to duties of confidentiality. They include agents; trustees; partners; directors and employees; professional people; holders of public and private offices; people in close personal relationships; and many others.[295]

However, it would be wrong to treat all information passing between parties to a relevant relationship as impressed with a duty of confidence. For the purposes of an equitable duty of confidence, the information must be confidential.

**4.117** *Professional contracts and relationships* In *Tournier v National Provincial and Union Bank of England*,[296] Scrutton LJ applied to the relationship between banker and customer the principle that the court will imply terms if they must 'necessarily have been in the contemplation of the parties to the contract'. Applying this principle he had no doubt that 'it is an implied term of a banker's contract with his customer that the banker shall not disclose the account, or transactions relating thereto, of his customer except in certain circumstances'.[297] The scope of the duty in any particular situation may differ according to the exact nature of the relationship.[298] Examples of other professional relationships involving the disclosure of personal information include doctors,[299] accountants,[300] and solicitors.[301] The extent of the duty is never absolute, but qualified. There are countervailing public interests that may require disclosure in many if not all such relationships.[302]

**4.118** *Transactions* The very nature of a transaction may give rise not only to a contractual duty on the part of the party to whom personal information is disclosed but also, or alternatively, to an equitable duty of confidence not to use the information otherwise than for the purposes permitted under the contract. Examples of this type of case are *Prince Albert v Strange*[303] and *Pollard v Photographic Co.*[304] A more

---

[295] Toulson and Phipps (n 32) para 3-008.
[296] [1924] 1 KB 461.
[297] *Tournier* (n 296) 480–1.
[298] *Tournier* (n 296) Bankes LJ, 475. But see R Pattenden, *The Law of Professional–Client Confidentiality* (Oxford University Press 2003), where it is submitted that when information is imparted in the course of, or generated by, a professional relationship that the client has expressly or impliedly stipulated should be confidential or which is so by custom and usage, it is unnecessary to look beyond the traditional indicia of confidentiality.
[299] *W v Egdell* (n 190).
[300] *Weld-Blundell v Stephens* [1919] 1 KB 520.
[301] *Re Van Laun, ex p Chatterton* [1907] 2 KB 23, 29.
[302] See *W v Egdell* (n 190). In *AVB v TDD* (n 166) Tugendhat J applied this principle to the relationship between a prostitute and her client.
[303] *Prince Albert* (n 11).
[304] (1889) 40 Ch D 344.

recent example of this type of case was *A v B, C and D*[305] where an injunction was granted restraining the defendant publishers from publishing sexually explicit photographs of the claimant in circumstances where the publishers had derived copyright title from the photographer, but where the photographer had (on the claimant's case) agreed not to disseminate the photographs beyond a limited class of persons without her consent. Some transactions, such as prostitution, have however left the courts with some uncertainty about the legitimate expectations of the purchaser as to confidentiality.[306]

*Fiduciary relationships*  A duty of confidence may arise where one party owes the other the special obligations of a fiduciary. However, not all fiduciaries owe the same duties in all circumstances. The crucial question is whether a duty of confidence arises in the course of a particular fiduciary relationship. Often it does, as in the case of employer and employee.[307] However, the fact that a person owes a duty of confidence does not of itself create a duty of loyalty, a duty which can be wider than a duty of confidence and capable of affecting the use to which information can lawfully be put.[308]  **4.119**

*Non-contractual relationships generally*  A duty of confidence with respect to personal information will arise in the context of other relationships not underpinned by a contract. The relationships include or may include husband and wife, family relations, lovers, and any other relationship (commercial, domestic, or otherwise) between two persons where one person confides confidential information to another or where confidential information is generated as a result of the relationship. In such cases, it must be asked whether the principles identified by Lord Goff in *Spycatcher* and in the second limb of *Coco v Clark* serve to impose the duty of confidence.  **4.120**

Circumstances held by the Court of Appeal in *D v L* to impose a duty of confidence in respect of recordings of private conversations in the context of a personal relationship included the fact that these 'were being taken secretly, related to private matters being discussed in a private conversation and were taped without the consent of [the claimant]'.[309]  **4.121**

The extent to which the courts will protect the confidentiality of information generated by a relationship depends on the nature of the relationship and of the disclosure. Confidential information arising in the context of a marriage is likely to be afforded a high degree of protection; outside marriage, the general approach is likely to be that the more permanent the relationship the greater the protection  **4.122**

---

[305] (HC, 2 March 2001) (Mackay J).
[306] See *eg Theakston v MGN Ltd* (n 197) [64]; *AVB v TDD* (n 166).
[307] See the discussion as to the relationship between fiduciary obligations and duties of confidence in *Gurry on Breach of Confidence* (n 32) paras 9.127–9.142; *Bristol and West v Mothew* [1998] Ch 1; *Attorney General v Blake* (n 88) 454.
[308] *Arklow Investments Ltd v Maclean* [2000] 1 WLR 594.
[309] *D v L* (n 199) [26] (Waller LJ).

that will be afforded to it. A distinction is also to be drawn between disclosure by a third party without the consent of either party to a relationship and a situation where one of the parties to a relationship seeks to make the disclosure. In the latter case, that party's right to freedom of expression will carry weight.[310] Where the disclosure is made by a stranger to the relationship, either party to it may be in a stronger position to protect the confidentiality of the relationship, depending on the nature of the disclosure.[311]

**4.123**  **An express stipulation**  Personal information may be imparted with an express but non-contractual stipulation of confidence. Express notice will commonly create a duty of confidence in equity. Thus, in *Stephens v Avery*, the claimant's case that she had impressed on the first defendant the confidentiality of the information concerning her lesbian relationship with a third party was held sufficient, assuming it to be true, to establish the duty of confidence. The court rejected submissions that merely saying that information was given in confidence was insufficient to impose a duty, and that a pre-existing confidential relationship, such as employer and employee, was necessary.[312]

**4.124**  **No pre-existing relationship: notice of a requirement of confidence**  Persons who have no pre-existing relationship with the complainant can become bound by a duty of confidence with respect to personal information in a variety of circumstances. Generally, these can be comprehended within Lord Goff's general guidance in *Spycatcher*,[313] that a duty of confidence is capable of arising where a person comes into possession of information in circumstances where that person actually knows—or is fixed by law with knowledge of, or ought as a reasonable person to know—that the claimant wishes to keep that information confidential. This approach has been confirmed in *Douglas v Hello! Ltd* and in subsequent cases such as *Venables v News Group Newspapers Ltd* and *A v B plc*.[314]

**4.125**  *Unauthorized photography*  The cases of breach of confidence involving no pre-existing relationship have included unauthorized photography, examples of which are *Shelley Films Ltd v Rex Features Ltd*,[315] *Creation Records Ltd v News Group Newspapers Ltd*,[316] and *Douglas v Hello! Ltd*. In the *Creation Records* case the claimant relied in part on security measures taken to prevent unauthorized photography and on the fact that the photographer must have behaved surreptitiously in order to obtain the shots, the inference being that he knew that photography was not permitted. Lloyd J once again pressed into service the reasonable man from *Coco v*

---

[310] See *A v B plc* (n 8) [11(xi)]; although it will not necessarily prevail: see *eg Donald v Ntuli* [2010] EWCA Civ 1276, [2011] 1 WLR 294.
[311] *Stephens* (n 164).
[312] *Stephens* (n 164) 456.
[313] *Attorney General v Observer Ltd* (n 12) 281, cited at 4.20.
[314] *Venables* (n 8)[11(ix)].
[315] *Shelley Films Ltd* (n 191).
[316] [1997] EMLR 444.

*Clark*, so as to fix the photographer with an arguable duty of confidence.[317] A similar approach was ultimately adopted in *Douglas v Hello! Ltd.*

In *Shelley Films*, the presence or absence of notices forbidding photography was **4.126** not considered essential for a duty to arise. Further, the unauthorized taking of a photograph by telephoto lens of a person engaging in conduct of a private nature would be likely to fix the photographer with a duty of confidence.[318] This approach is entirely consistent with the second factor necessary to found a claim in confidence identified by Megarry J in *Coco v Clark*, namely that the information has been imparted in circumstances importing an obligation of confidence. Courts have noted that photography can be particularly intrusive.[319]

It would be wrong to say that unauthorized photography will necessarily give rise to **4.127** a duty of confidence on the part of a photographer. The mere fact that a celebrity or other person makes it clear that they do not want photographs taken of themselves does not necessarily mean that a duty of confidence will be imposed if photographs are taken. The existence of a duty will depend on all the circumstances of the case. In *Douglas v Hello! Ltd* the private nature of the occasion was an important factor in giving rise to the duty.[320]

*Information obtained by trespass*    There is a range of situations in which a person **4.128** may acquire confidential information as a result of a trespass.[321] Trespass as such gives rise to no rights to restrain use of the information acquired.[322] Its relevance is that the trespasser will be at risk of being subject to a duty of confidence.[323] The person who could maintain a claim in trespass will not always be the person who would want protection from a threatened invasion of privacy. A guest in hotel grounds may want to prevent publication of photographs of her sunbathing topless taken from within the hotel grounds but would have no property right which had been infringed. Nonetheless, the trespass would again be highly significant in the context of the notice imputed to the photographer.[324] Indeed, whether the photographs were taken from within or outside the hotel property would not matter much for the purposes of deciding whether or not a duty of confidence existed. The important point is that the guest (as opposed to the photographer) is on private property.

---

[317] *Creation Records* (n 316) 453.
[318] *Hellewell v Chief Constable of Derbyshire* (n 128) 807, Laws J, cited with approval by the Court of Appeal in *Douglas* (n 7) [166].
[319] See *Theakston* (n 197) [78]; *R v Loveridge* [2001] EWCA Crim 973; *R v Broadcasting Standards Commission, ex p BBC* (n 238).
[320] *Douglas* (n 7) [71]. See *R (Wood) v Commissioner of Police of the Metropolis* [2009] EWCA Civ 414, [2010] 1 WLR 123 considering the position where the police take photographs of individuals on the street and store them.
[321] eg *Franklin v Giddins* [1978] QR 72: technique of propagation embodied in stolen bud-wood trees.
[322] *Kaye v Robertson*, CA (n 13) 69, applied in *Service Corp International plc* (n 195) 90 (Lightman J).
[323] See eg *Shelley Films Ltd* (n 191).
[324] cf *Holden v Express Newspapers Ltd* (HC, 7 June 2001) (Eady J).

**4.129** *Eavesdropping* Some authorities suggest that where a public medium is used to convey confidential information, it may be very difficult to impose the requisite duty of confidence on a third party who comes by the information. For example, it has been said that it would not be a breach of confidence to decode a coded message placed in the personal columns of *The Times*.[325] There is of course a difference between overhearing and eavesdropping. However, even the latter may be difficult to restrain in confidence, depending on the circumstances. In *Malone v Commissioner of Police for the Metropolis*[326] Megarry J dismissed a claim seeking a declaration that tapping of the plaintiff's telephone by the police was unlawful. One of the grounds relied on was confidence. It was held that a person using a medium such as the telephone must be taken to assume the inherent risk of being overheard. The judge used the analogy of two neighbours talking over the garden wall, who run the risk of having their conversation overheard by the unseen neighbour.

**4.130** Similar reasoning would appear to have underlain the decision in *Shepherd v News Group Newspapers Ltd*,[327] where directors of Newcastle United Football Club who, in public bars, had boasted to undercover *News of the World* reporters about their sexual exploits, were not able to establish that their disclosures were made in circumstances importing an obligation of confidence. Their application for an injunction was refused.

**4.131** *Surveillance and 'snooping'* In *Francome v Mirror Group Newspapers Ltd*,[328] however, the Court of Appeal did not follow the approach taken in *Malone*. The tapping of the telephone line of the claimant jockey was held to give rise to an arguable duty of confidence. The telephone-tapping was not conducted by or on behalf of the police, and was arguably a criminal offence under s 5 of the Wireless Telegraphy Act 1949. Fox LJ considered that the reasoning in *Malone* did not apply to eavesdropping by private persons.[329]

**4.132** The law now requires the police to follow specified procedures in order to legitimate telephone-tapping, in the light of the decision of the ECtHR in *Malone v UK*.[330] Secret methods of obtaining information about communications were regulated by the Interception of Communications Act 1985,[331] and now by the Regulation

---

[325] See *BBC Enterprises Ltd v Hi-Tech Xtravision Ltd* [1990] FSR 217, 237 (Scott J). In *Mars UK Ltd* (n 178) [33] Jacob J held that a person who decrypts something in code is not necessarily to be taken as receiving information in confidence.

[326] [1979] Ch 344.

[327] Ch, 20 March 1998, Lindsay J. Cf the decision of Rimer J in *Y v A Newspaper Group* (HC, 18–20 September 1996).

[328] [1984] 1 WLR 892.

[329] *Francome* (n 328) 900.

[330] (1984) 7 EHRR 14.

[331] See *R v Sargent* [2001] UKHL 54, [2003] 1 AC 347, where it was held that evidence obtained through tapping by a telephone engineer in breach of Interception of Communications Act 1985, s 1(1) was inadmissible in a criminal trial.

of Investigatory Powers Act 2000 (RIPA). Where such acquisition is authorized under RIPA, it will be hard to invoke the law of confidence. Acquisition which involves an offence under RIPA or s 5 of the Wireless Telegraphy Act 1949[332] is more likely to give rise to a breach of confidence. There are also arguments that, at least in relation to s 5, a claimant may have a right of action if special damage is suffered by breach of the Act which is particular to him.[333] However, all will depend on the circumstances.

Where 'snooping' techniques are used which fall outside statutory controls, either **4.133** because no electronic means are used or because the means used are not caught by the statutes, recourse should be had to the basic principles identified by Lord Goff in *Spycatcher* and Megarry J in *Coco v Clark*. In *A v B plc* the bugging of someone's home or the use of other surveillance techniques were given as obvious examples of intrusions into privacy capable of giving rise to liability in an action for breach of confidence, unless the intrusion could be justified.[334] Moreover, there does not seem to have been any suggestion in any of *The News of the World* or *Mirror* phone-hacking claims that intercepting and listening to voicemail messages was not an actionable breach of confidence. In *Phillips v News Group Newspapers Ltd* it was accepted that the claimant's voicemail messages contained commercially confidential information.[335]

*Equity and 'improper or surreptitious' acquisition*   The cases discussed above in   **4.134** which a duty of confidence was held to exist may be seen as examples of surreptitious acquisition of information. There is a well-established jurisdiction in equity which was explained by Swinfen Eady LJ in *Ashburton v Pape* as follows: 'The principle upon which the Court of Chancery has acted for many years has been to restrain the publication of confidential information improperly or surreptitiously obtained or of information imparted in confidence which ought not to be divulged.'[336]

The decision in *Ashburton* is good law but the authorities differ as to the extent to   **4.135** which the decision was based on privilege, as opposed to confidence.[337] However, if there has been surreptitious or improper conduct on the part of the recipient of the information, it is likely that he will be treated as having sufficient knowledge or notice of the confidentiality of the information.[338] In *A v B plc*, it was held that

---

[332] As amended by s 73(1) RIPA. See further 10.35 (n 73).

[333] See *Gouriet v Union of Post Office Workers* [1978] AC 435, referred to in *Francome* (n 328) 897.

[334] *A v B plc* (n 8) [11(xi)].

[335] *Phillips* (n 21).

[336] [1913] 2 Ch 469, 474.

[337] See *eg Goddard v Nationwide Building Society* [1987] 1 QB 670; *Webster v James Chapman & Co* [1989] 3 All ER 939; *A v B* [2000] EMLR 1007. In *Istil Group Inc v Zahoor* [2003] EWHC 165 (Ch), [2003] 2 All ER 252 the Court carefully analysed the authorities and concluded that the Court of Appeal in *Lord Ashburton v Pape* was applying the law of confidence: see [74] (Lawrence Collins J).

[338] See Toulson and Phipps (n 32) para 3-044.

'the fact that the information is obtained as a result of unlawful activities does not mean that its publication should necessarily be restrained by injunction on the grounds of breach of confidence…[but] the fact that unlawful means have been used to obtain the information could well be a compelling factor when it comes to exercising discretion'.[339]

**4.136** *'Innocent' acquisition* Cases on the gathering of confidential information by surreptitious means are sometimes contrasted with what may be described as 'innocent' acquisition of confidential information. However, the question always is whether the recipient obtained the information in circumstances importing an obligation of confidence. There is no reason in principle why a person who merely witnesses a private act or transaction should not be fixed with a duty of confidence, if that person's acquisition of the information is or should be recognized as unintended and unauthorized by the claimant. Whereas the acquisition of documents might be innocent, reading their contents could fix the reader with a duty of confidence.[340]

### (c) Equitable duties on the media and other third party recipients

**4.137** **General principles** A third party who receives confidential information with knowledge that it has been disclosed in breach of an equitable duty of confidence will generally assume a duty of confidence towards the original confider.[341] The justification for this is obvious and was set out by Lord Griffiths in *Spycatcher*:

> If this was not the law the right would be of little practical value: there would be no point in imposing a duty of confidence in respect of the secrets of the marital bed if newspapers were free to publish those secrets when betrayed to them by the unfaithful partner in a marriage.[342]

**4.138** There is however no absolute rule. The position of third parties may vary widely according to the circumstances of the case, depending on whether injunctive relief is practical, and whether the third party should be restrained as a matter of fair dealing.[343] For present purposes, there are three main situations of relevance. The first is where the third party acquires the knowledge from the person who owes the duty, the confidant. Typical media cases in this class are where an employee

---

[339] *A v B plc* (n 8) [11(x)].

[340] *English and American Insurance Ltd v Herbert Smith* [1988] FSR 232.

[341] *Attorney General v Observer Ltd* (n 12).

[342] *Attorney General v Observer Ltd* (n 12) 268.

[343] *Attorney General v Observer Ltd* (n 12) 272, Lord Griffiths: 'The position of a third party who receives information that has been published in breach of confidence will vary widely according to the circumstances of the case…Each case will depend upon its own facts and the decision of the judge as to whether or not it is practical to give injunctive protection and whether the third party should, as a matter of fair dealing, be restrained or, to use the language of the equity lawyer, whether the conscience of the third party is affected by the confidant's breach of duty. There is certainly no absolute rule even in the case of a breach of a private confidence that a third party who receives the confidential information will be restrained from using it.'

discloses an employer's personal secrets, or a partner to a personal relationship 'kisses and tells'. The second is where knowledge is acquired from the confider. The third is where the information is acquired from another source, or in another way.

**Acquisition from the confidant**    In general, the position of the third-party recipi-    **4.139**
ent of confidential information may depend on whether an injunction is sought, or some other remedy is sought after disclosure or use of the information. While an injunction may be granted in advance, some financial remedies will not be granted unless the defendant is shown to have acted dishonestly in the sense explained in *Royal Brunei Airlines v Tan*.[344] In sum, this means 'not acting as an honest man would in the circumstances...an objective standard'.[345] In these cases, the dishonesty usually becomes relevant to the use made of the information, although the circumstances of the receipt are highly material to the honesty or otherwise of any subsequent use.

If applied to media cases the dishonesty requirement would call for the court to    **4.140**
ask a question on these lines: 'would the honest reporter, editor, or director [as the case may be] have done this in these circumstances?'[346] In *Campbell v MGN Ltd*, however, the Court rejected the argument that the claimant had to show that the defendant on receiving the confidential information was dishonest in publishing what it did. Morland J stated that the true question was whether the defendant was clothed in conscience with a duty of confidentiality.[347] The House of Lords in the same case unanimously accepted that where there is some public interest in disclosure the media do not have an absolute duty to strike the right balance, but have a reasonable degree of latitude in deciding whether and if so what to publish.[348] The outer limits of that latitude remain to be established but there is some authority which suggests that honest belief in the legitimacy of publication may play a role.[349]

**Acquisition from the confider**    In this second type of case, the confider will often    **4.141**
have the opportunity of preserving the confidentiality of the information, because it is he or she who puts the third party on notice of that confidentiality. These situations arise where the third party first acquires the information without guilty knowledge. There is no reason why 'after-acquired' notice should prevent a duty arising, so that a subsequent publication or other use of the information would be

---

[344] [1995] 2 AC 378. *Tan* was concerned with the test for accessory liability for breach of trust. The application of these principles to cases of breach of confidence was proposed in the 1st edition of Toulson and Phipps, *Confidentiality* (Sweet & Maxwell 1996) paras 7-02–7-03, endorsed by the Court of Appeal in *Thomas v Pearce* (n 77) and applied in *ABK Ltd v Foxwell* [2002] EWHC 9 (Ch). See also *Satnam Investments Ltd v Dunlop Heywood & Co Ltd* [1999] FSR 722, CA, 742–4.

[345] *Tan* (n 344) 389, Lord Nicholls. This includes turning a blind eye: *Thomas* (n 77).

[346] cf the test approved by the Court of Appeal in *Thomas* (n 77): 'what the honest estate agent would do in these circumstances'.

[347] *Campbell* (n 228) [40.2].

[348] *Campbell* (n 2) [28]–[29], [63]–[65], [112], [143], [169].

[349] See the detailed discussion in *Commissioner of Police for the Metropolis v Times Newspapers Ltd* (n 137) [94]–[212], Tugendhat J. More generally, 11.119, 11.173, 11.176 *et seq*.

a breach of confidence.[350] In this type of situation the third party may be able to raise defences based on a relevant change in position.[351]

**4.142**　**Other means of acquisition**　The case law has demonstrated that there is a wide range of circumstances in which the courts are willing to impose a duty of confidence on media organizations even where there has been no breach of confidence by a confidant or other third person. The most extreme case so far is *Venables v News Group Newspapers Ltd*,[352] where Butler-Sloss P considered it appropriate to develop the law of confidence so as to impose a direct duty of confidence not only on the defendant news organizations but also on persons not party to the litigation with respect to the whereabouts and personal appearances of the killers of James Bulger. The duty was justified so as to give proper effect to the claimants' rights under Articles 2 and 3 ECHR, namely their right to life and protection from inhuman and degrading treatment or punishment. The President doubted whether it would have been appropriate to create any direct duty, had the claimants only been seeking to protect their Article 8 rights.

**4.143**　In *Mills v News Group Newspapers Ltd*[353] Lawrence Collins J considered it inappropriate to restrain by interim injunction publication of the celebrity claimant's new address although the Court did say that restraining a newspaper from publishing the address of a person would be appropriate where there was a risk of death or injury. The case did not decide that no direct duty of confidence was placed on the defendant publishers, merely that in the circumstances no injunction should be granted. As Butler-Sloss P made clear in the *Venables* case,[354] subjecting a media organization to a direct duty was consistent with the broad guidelines given by Lord Goff in *Spycatcher*.[355] The Court of Appeal reaffirmed this in *A v B plc*.[356]

*(d) Those given notice of an injunction against others*

**4.144**　Solicitors acting for claimants in confidence cases against media defendants, or where the subject matter of the claim is of interest to the media, commonly serve third-party media organizations or give them notice that an injunction has been obtained.[357] Service or notification does not of itself make the third-party organization subject to the injunction, but can have two effects.

---

[350] *Prince Albert* (n 11); see also *Printers and Finishers Ltd* (n 184) 253.

[351] See 11.26 *et seq*.

[352] *Venables* (n 14).

[353] *Mills* (n 213). See also *Mahmood v BBC* [2014] EWHC 4207 (QB) [11] and [2014] EWCA Civ 1567 where the Court of Appeal refused permission to appeal.

[354] *Venables* (n 14) [81].

[355] *Attorney General v Observer Ltd* (n 12) 281. Cf *West v BBC* (QBD, 10 June 2002, Ouseley J).

[356] *A v B plc* (n 8)[11(ix)–(x)].

[357] The position is now governed by the *Practice Guidance: Interim Non-Disclosure Orders* (n 232), which requires amongst other things that a claimant give advance notice of an application for an interim injunction to any third party whom it is intended to notify of an injunction once obtained. Other issues arising from such service or notification, and the prospect of it, are discussed at 13.118 and 13.140–13.42.

**The media may come under a duty of confidence**  The principles discussed  **4.145**
above[358] mean that notice of the existence of information in respect of which a person claims a right of confidentiality, coupled with notice that a court has decided to
uphold that claim, will ordinarily have the effect of imposing a duty of confidence
on the person given notice. This will be so in the case of an interim injunction.
The case for such a conclusion where the injunction is permanent is, of course,
stronger still.

### Disclosure may be a contempt of court

*Interim injunctions*  Where, on notice of an interim injunction granted to pro-  **4.146**
tect confidentiality, a person publishes information knowing the publication will
serve to destroy the confidentiality which the injunction was designed to protect,
the person will be in contempt of court. The reason is that the publisher will
have acted, with relevant knowledge, in such a way as to defeat or undermine
the court's purpose of protecting the alleged confidence pending a final decision
on whether it should be protected.[359] However, third parties served with such
injunctions have rights to apply to the court to vary or discharge the order.[360]
Further, the standard of proof for contempt is the criminal one and an application to commit for contempt of court may fail either because the requisite *mens
rea* has not been established, or because only minimal use has been made of the
prohibited material,[361] or because the use made is not shown to have destroyed
the confidentiality which the injunction was intended to protect.[362]

*Final injunctions*  It may be that the *Spycatcher* contempt doctrine described in  **4.147**
the previous paragraph does not apply where the injunction is a final order, as its
underlying rationale is inapplicable.[363] At the conclusion of an action a claimant
wishing to harness the law of contempt to protect rights of confidence against
persons who are not named as defendants in his or her action has two alternative
means of doing so. The first is an injunction against the world, which has direct

---

[358] At 4.26–4.27, 4.137–4.143.

[359] *Attorney General v Newspaper Publishing plc* (n 81). In *Attorney General v Greater Manchester
Newspapers Ltd* [2001] TLR 688 the paper was fined £30,000 for a publication held to have infringed
the injunction granted by the President of the Family Division in *Venables* (n 14) which prohibited
publications likely to lead to the identification of James Bulger's murderers. The newspaper had not
been formally notified, but was on notice of the injunction.

[360] See *Imutran Ltd* (n 150) 398 (Sir Andrew Morritt V-C). See now para 17 of the model form
of Interim Non-Disclosure Order annexed to the *Practice Guidance: Interim Non-Disclosure Orders*
(n 232), which expressly provides that anyone affected by any of the restrictions in the Order has
the right to apply to vary or discharge it.

[361] *Attorney General v Newspaper Publishing* (n 81).

[362] *Attorney General v Punch Ltd* [2001] QB 1028, CA.

[363] *Jockey Club v Buffham* [2002] EWHC 1866 (QB), [2003] QB 462 (Gray J) citing *Attorney
General v Punch Ltd* (n 362). On the appeal from the latter decision ([2002] UKHL 50, [2003] 1
AC 1046) the House did not address the issue. However, in *Hutcheson v Popdog Ltd* [2011] EWCA
Civ 1580, [2012] 1 WLR 782 Lord Neuberger MR observed at [26], with the agreement of his fel-
low judges, that it could not 'be safely assumed' that the *Spycatcher* principle did not apply to final
injunctions.

effect against anyone notified of its terms. The second is an injunction against persons unknown, which takes effect against those who fit the description given in the order, once they are notified. These forms of order are discussed in Chapters 12 and 13.

### (2) Who Can Sue for Breach of Confidence?

**4.148** The claimant must, of course, be a person with a right of confidence enforceable against the defendant. Rights of confidentiality are, however, not necessarily confined to a single person, firm, or company; two or more persons may share a right of confidence,[364] or have concurrent rights.[365]

### (a) Concurrent rights

**4.149** This may arise, for example, where an organization holds confidential records of its own, containing information confidential to an individual, the disclosure of which would be injurious to each of them.[366] Alternatively, two or more persons concerned in the same private and confidential activity may each have a right enforceable against a third party.[367] At the same time, one of those persons may owe a duty of confidence to the other.[368] In situations such as these it may be that one person can exploit his or her own rights of confidence to secure effective protection for the rights and interests of another. Another situation of this kind would be a case where a management company providing services to a celebrity is able to enforce contractual duties owed by an employee, to preserve secrecy in respect of the celebrity's affairs.

### (b) Duties but no rights

**4.150** The fact that one person owes a duty to protect the confidential information of a second does not, however, give the first person a right to sue a third party for wrongful disclosure of that information. The person who makes a claim in confidence must be a person with a right to confidentiality. A person holding another's confidential information may be a confidant who owes duties of confidence in respect of it, but has no rights to enforce such confidentiality against third parties.

---

[364] As discussed in *Murray v Yorkshire Fund Managers Ltd* [1998] 1 WLR 951.

[365] See *eg Ashworth Hospital Authority v MGN Ltd* [2001] 1 WLR 515, CA, [52] (affirmed, [2002] UKHL 29, [2002] 1 WLR 2033): patient and hospital with concurrent interests and rights in preserving confidentiality of the patient's medical records.

[366] *Ashworth* (n 365). That decision is authority that 'institutions can be proper claimants in respect of the rights of those entrusted to their care': *Green Corns Ltd* (n 51) [51].

[367] See the first-instance decision in *Douglas* (n 10) [187], asserting a right of co-ownership. The Court of Appeal disagreed with this conclusion: (n 10) [118], [119], [122]–[137]. It did so on the basis that the right in question depends on a duty rather than being a proprietary right. The Court did not, however, directly address the question of concurrent rights of confidence.

[368] *eg* in *Ashworth Hospital Authority* (n 365) the hospital owed the patient a duty of confidence in respect of the same patient records. In *Douglas,* no doubt the couple owed each other duties of confidence in respect of the relevant information.

Thus it was that the Court of Appeal held that a public relations consultant to the Greek government had no right to prevent *The Sunday Times* from publishing extracts from one of his reports. The newspaper owed no duty to him. The appropriate claimant would have been the Greek government.[369] Similarly, where solicitor–client confidences are concerned, it is the client and not the solicitor who is entitled to make a claim alleging breach of confidence against a third party.[370]

### (3) What Will Amount to a Breach of Duty?

A claimant in a breach of confidence claim must show that there has been an unauthorized use/misuse of relevant information; or in a *quia timet* claim, that there is a threat of misuse. To identify what is a misuse it is necessary to identify the nature, scope, and duration of the duty of confidence.    **4.151**

### (a) Breach of contractual duties

Where there is a contract, the scope of the duty and the question of whether it has been broken will be determined by the pertinent express or implied terms. If the duty arises in the context of a fiduciary relationship, special considerations may affect the scope and content of the duty.[371]    **4.152**

### (b) Breach of equitable duties

**Use for a collateral purpose**   It is well established that confidential information may be imparted for a limited purpose and that, if so, use for another purpose is likely to be a breach of duty. In *Barrymore v News Group Newspapers Ltd* Jacob J was considering whether details of a sexual relationship were confidential. He stated: 'The information about the relationship is for the relationship and not for a wider purpose. It is well established that in many cases the law will spell out a duty of confidence when information is given for a limited purpose.'[372] Similarly, in *D v L*[373] the Court of Appeal held that equity would impose on a person secretly recording a private conversation for a justified purpose an obligation not to use the recording for any other purpose. It seems, however, that use for an unauthorized purpose will not necessarily amount to a breach of confidence.[374]    **4.153**

---

[369] *Fraser v Evans* [1969] 1 QB 349, followed in *Abbey* (nn 152 and 370).
[370] *Nationwide Building Society v Various Solicitors (No 2)* (HC, 30 March 1998) (Blackburne J). See also *CHC Software Care Ltd v Hopkins and Wood* [1993] FSR 241, 251; *Murray* (n 364); *Apps v Weldtite Products Ltd* [2001] FSR 703. In *Abbey* (n 152) Tugendhat J held that the newspaper defendants did not owe the claimant any duty of confidence in respect of emails sent and received by him in his capacity as consultant to a company which contained no information that was personal to him, since he was acting merely as an agent for the company in sending and receiving the emails.
[371] *SmithKline and French Laboratories (Australia) Ltd* (n 62) 637.
[372] *Barrymore* (n 173) 602. See also *Bunn v BBC* (n 128) 556: statements to police under caution.
[373] *D v L* (n 199) [26].
[374] In *Source Informatics* (n 31) Simon Brown LJ at [52]–[53] approved the notion that use beyond a specified limited use would not necessarily amount to unfair use or misuse.

**4.154**  **Unconscionable behaviour**  As Brooke LJ stated in *Douglas v Hello! Ltd*:

> For a very long time the judges of the Court of Chancery exercised an equitable
> jurisdiction to restrain freedom of speech in circumstances in which it would be
> unconscionable to publish private material. If information is accepted on the basis
> that it will be kept secret, the recipient's conscience is bound by that confidence,
> and it will be unconscionable for him to break his duty of confidence by publishing
> the information to others.[375]

This test of what the reasonable man's conscience would dictate was reaffirmed by
the Court of Appeal in *R v Dept of Health, ex p Source Informatics Ltd*,[376] after an
extensive review of the authorities.[377]

**4.155**  This test was subsequently considered by the Court of Appeal in *London Regional
Transport Ltd v Mayor of London*,[378] where it had been applied at first instance by
Sullivan J.[379] Both Robert Walker and Sedley LJJ considered the judge's approach
unobjectionable, but the latter stated that conscience was not the determining factor in every case, and suggested it was an unreliable indicator as to when an obligation should prevent disclosure, at least where considerations of public interest had
to be weighed against rights of confidence. Sedley LJ said the key lay elsewhere, in
a test of proportionality.

**4.156**  **Disclosure disproportionate**  In the *London Regional Transport* case,[380] where
rights of confidence had to be balanced against public interest considerations,
Sedley LJ suggested the key to determination of whether disclosure would be a
breach of confidence lay in the concept of proportionality and the proper weighing of the competing public interests at play so as to strike the balance required
by Article 10(2).[381] Questions as to the scope of a duty of confidence may be theoretically distinct from situations where a person under a duty of confidence may

---

[375] *Douglas* (n 7) [65].

[376] '[T]he one clear and consistent theme emerging from all these authorities is this: the confidant is placed under a duty of good faith to the confider and the touchstone by which to judge the
scope of his duty and whether or not it has been fulfilled or breached is his own conscience: no more
and no less': *Source Informatics* (n 31) [41], Simon Brown LJ. See also *Vestergaard Frandsen A/S v
Bestnet Europe Ltd* [2013] UKSC 31, [2013] 1 WLR 1556, Lord Neuberger MR at [22]: 'After all, an
action in breach of confidence is based ultimately on conscience.'

[377] In particular, dicta of the Federal Court of Australia in *SmithKline and French Laboratories
(Australia) Ltd* (n 62) 649–50.

[378] *London Regional Transport* (n 64).

[379] Sullivan J had discharged an injunction restraining publication of a redacted version of a
report by accountants Deloitte and Touche on private–public partnership (PPP) arrangements for
the London Underground Transport system: [2001] EWHC 637 (Admin).

[380] *London Regional Transport* (n 64).

[381] *London Regional Transport* (n 64) [58] (Sedley LJ): 'Whilst [the conscience test] has the impri-
matur of high authority, I can understand how difficult it is to give useful advice on the basis of
it.' See generally, *London Regional Transport* (n 64) [57]–[59]. A similar approach was taken in
the context of proposed use by media defendants of confidential material in the public interest in
*Commissioner of Police for the Metropolis* (n 137) where Tugendhat J reviewed the authorities in some
detail.

have just cause or excuse for breaking the confidence.[382] However, the decision in *London Regional Transport* shows the difficulty of keeping the two areas separate.

**Responsibility for publication**    In *Douglas v Hello! Ltd* the Court of Appeal held    **4.157**
that there was a good arguable case that the author of a photograph is as much a joint wrongdoer, responsible for its publication in breach of confidence, as an author of a written piece would be jointly liable with its publishers in a suit for libel.[383] Sir Andrew Morritt V-C reached similar conclusions in relation to others alleged to be involved in the publication of the photographs.[384] Chapter 11 discusses further the application in confidence and privacy of the common-law principles as to responsibility for publication, and the statutory defences and exemptions available for those who publish in ignorance of the claimant's rights.[385]

### (c) Duration of the duty of confidence

The duration of a contractual duty of confidence will be affected by the status    **4.158**
of the information and the terms of the contract.[386] Generally, where there is a contractual or other relationship from which the duty of confidence originates, the duty is capable of surviving termination of the relationship depending on the circumstances.[387] A full discussion on that topic falls outside the scope of this book.[388] In general, however, an obligation of confidence is capable of lasting for as long as the information is confidential. Information of a commercial nature will cease to be confidential, and the duty to keep it confidential will disappear, when it enters the public domain. The same is true of a duty to maintain the confidentiality of personal information,[389] although the position is different in respect of a privacy claim for misuse of private information.[390]

**Death**    Whether an equitable obligation of confidence relating to personal infor-    **4.159**
mation will survive the death of the confider is uncertain. There is no clear authority on the point. Some authorities tend to suggest that in general the duty will cease on death,[391] but it has been held arguable that a duty of medical confidentiality survives.[392] A claim for breach of confidence arising during the lifetime of the confider will survive, it is suggested, and pass to his or her personal representatives

---

[382] See also *Dunford and Elliott* (n 280) and *Webster* (n 337) 944.
[383] *Douglas* (n 7) [33] (reversing Laddie J).
[384] *Douglas v Hello! Ltd* [2003] EMLR 601 [72].
[385] See 11.32–11.42.
[386] See *Faccenda Chicken Ltd* (n 97). The obligation may not cease upon repudiation: n 277.
[387] See *Bolkiah (Prince Jefri) v KPMG (a firm)* [1999] 2 AC 222.
[388] See *Gurry on Breach of Confidence* (n 32) ch 12.
[389] *Gunn-Russo v Nugent Care Society* [2001] EWHC Admin 566, [2002] 1 FLR 1, in which Scott Baker J said, in relation to adoption records at [52]: 'a duty of confidentiality should cease if the information loses the quality of confidence, whether through the passage of time, loss of secrecy or other circumstances'.
[390] See *R v BCC, ex p Granada Television Ltd* [1995] EMLR 163 and, more generally, 11.44 *et seq.*
[391] See *Rickless v United Artists* [1988] QB 40; *Gunn-Russo* (n 389); and 13.20–13.21.
[392] See the discussion at 13.22.

pursuant to the Law Reform (Miscellaneous Provisions) Act 1934.[393] However, it must be doubtful whether an injunction would be available in such circumstances.

### *(d) Is detriment to the claimant necessary?*

**4.160** There has been much debate in the case law and in academic writings as to whether detriment to the confider is a necessary element of the cause of action for breach of the equitable duty of confidence, but so far the question is unresolved.[394] The Court of Appeal has held that detriment is required in a 'hybrid' breach of confidence case.[395] In 'ordinary' traditional breach of confidence cases involving personal information it is however strongly arguable that it is enough that the claimant has a legitimate interest in protecting the particular information from disclosure and that the defendant has acted or threatens to act contrary to that interest.[396]

**4.161** In *Spycatcher* Lord Keith gave the example of the donor to a charity who wished to remain anonymous. Disclosure of his identity would not cast the donor in an unfavourable light and yet Lord Keith considered that the donor would surely be in a position to restrain disclosure. He also considered that it would suffice if the confider preferred not to have the information disclosed; he would not have to show that disclosure would be harmful in a positive way.[397] Although these observations were *obiter* such an approach has the persuasive support of the Australian judge Gummow J[398] (albeit also *obiter*) and of the authors Toulson and Phipps.[399]

**4.162** It may be argued, however, that this approach needs refinement lest it should give excessive protection to privacy interests. There is perhaps a danger that English law might set the threshold for proof of breach of confidence too low, unduly restricting media freedom by extending the boundaries of what is regarded as confidential, while requiring defendants to show a public interest justification for the disclosure of even relatively unimportant personal information. Lord Griffiths

---

[393] See 13.24.

[394] See *eg Coco v Clark* (n 43) 48; *Attorney General v Observer Ltd* (n 12) 255–6, 270, 281–2; *Source Informatics* (n 31) [16], [35].

[395] *Douglas*, CA (n 10) [118].

[396] See *Ashworth Hospital Authority* (n 365); cf *West v BBC* (n 355). In *Imerman v Tchenguiz* (n 30) the Court of Appeal held that it was a breach of confidence to obtain, to examine and/or to copy another person's private financial documents: no further misuse was necessary to found a cause of action, and the owner would be entitled to an injunction to prevent further reading or copying as well as to enforce the return or destruction of the documents and any copies. Cf *Abbey* (n 152), where Tugendhat J held that a journalist who received and read confidential material for the purposes of considering whether or not to publish it in the public interest would not thereby commit an actionable wrong; and *Commissioner of Police for the Metropolis* (n 137).

[397] *Attorney General v Observer Ltd* (n 12) 256.

[398] 'The obligation of confidence is to respect the confidence, not merely to refrain from causing detriment to the plaintiff... To look into a related field, when has equity said that the only breaches of trust to be restrained are those that would prove detrimental to the beneficiaries?': *SmithKline and French Laboratories (Australia) Ltd* (n 62) 664.

[399] By the same token, if the claimant had no legitimate interest in preventing disclosure the claim would fail for want of the necessary quality of confidence: see Toulson and Phipps (n 32) para 3-166.

in *Spycatcher* recognized this as a possible problem in holding that 'detriment or potential detriment to the confider' was a necessary constituent of a claim for breach of confidence. The reason he gave was that 'the remedy had been fashioned to protect the confider not to punish the confidant, and there seems little point in extending it to the confider who has no need of the protection'.[400] In *Campbell v MGN Ltd* it was held at first instance that detriment was a necessary ingredient to the cause of action in confidence and that the requirement had been made out. Viewed objectively, the newspaper's disclosures relating to the claimant's treatment for drug abuse were likely to have an adverse effect on her attendance at meetings of Narcotics Anonymous.[401]

**'Offensiveness'** The English post-HRA jurisprudence in the period when breach **4.163** of confidence was mutating has included much discussion of a possible threshold requirement of 'offensiveness'. In *Campbell* Morland J adopted at first instance the test of 'whether disclosure…would be highly offensive to a reasonable person of ordinary sensibilities'. The judge drew this test from dicta in the High Court of Australia's decision in the *Lenah Game Meats* case,[402] which appeared to have at least the implicit approval of the Court of Appeal in *A v B plc*.[403] The origins of the test lie further back, in the work of the US jurist Dean Prosser. The Court of Appeal in *Campbell* took a similar approach to Morland J, while doubting the utility of the adjective 'highly'.[404]

The majority of the House of Lords took the view that 'this particular formu- **4.164** lation should be used with care', and that courts should guard against using it as a touchstone for whether a *prima facie* breach of confidence has occurred, as it more properly goes to the separate issue of proportionality.[405] Parts of Lord Hope's speech[406] can nevertheless be read[407] as approving offensiveness as part of the threshold test, and the House appeared to approve the New Zealand Court of Appeal's decision in *Hosking v Runting*, which identified as the second requirement of a successful claim 'publicity…that would be considered highly offensive to an objective reasonable person'.[408] However, the Court of Appeal in *Murray v Express Newspapers plc* distinguished *Hosking* and held that the English law test, as determined by their Lordships in *Campbell*, is not the same.[409]

---

[400] *Attorney General v Observer Ltd* (n 12) 270.
[401] *Campbell* (n 228) [40.1]–[40.3].
[402] *Lenah Game Meats* (n 108) [42].
[403] *A v B plc* (n 8) [11(vii)].
[404] *Campbell*, CA (n 78) [48]–[51], [54].
[405] *Campbell*, HL (n 2) [21]–[22], Lord Nicholls. See also, to like effect, Lord Hope at [94]–[96], Lady Hale [135]–[137] and Lord Carswell, [166].
[406] See esp [92] and [99].
[407] As the Court of Appeal observed in *Murray* (n 109) [29].
[408] *Hosking v Runting* [2005] 1 NZLR 1 [117], cited in *Murray* (n 109) [48].
[409] *Murray* (n 109) [51]–[52].

**4.165** In the light of the authorities discussed in the last two paragraphs it would be hard to argue now that offensiveness is a requirement of the cause of action for misuse of private information, let alone a requirement of a claim for traditional breach of confidence. However, the related question of triviality could in principle form part of an analysis of whether the particular circumstances give rise to a reasonable expectation of (in a confidence case) secrecy or (in a misuse case) privacy. Offensiveness, or the degree of harm which could be caused by disclosure, are clearly relevant to the stage of the analysis at which the court considers whether a duty of confidence has been broken or, in the context of misuse, whether the proportionality assessment favours imposing liability on the defendant.

# 5

## MISUSE OF PRIVATE INFORMATION

*Sir Mark Warby, Adèle Garrick, and Chloe Strong*

## A. Introduction

This chapter is concerned with the cause of action known as misuse of private **5.01** information.[1] The cause of action, though closely related to traditional breach of confidence, is separate and distinct from it, and protects different interests.[2] It is claims for misuse that are likely to be of greatest significance in most media privacy cases, but practitioners should not overlook the fact that there are overlaps between this and traditional breach of confidence.[3]

---

[1] The nomenclature derives from Lord Nicholls' speech in *Campbell v MGN Ltd* [2004] UKHL 22, [2004] 2 AC 457 [14].

[2] The cause of action protects privacy as distinct from secrecy: *Douglas v Hello! Ltd* [2007] UKHL 21, [2008] 1 AC 1 [255] (Lord Nicholls).

[3] See 5.12.

# B. Overview of the Cause of Action

### (1) Origins, Nature, and Development

#### (a) *The European Convention on Human Rights as a catalyst*

**5.02**   At common law, there was no free-standing right to privacy, and no cause of action that could be employed to vindicate privacy-type rights.[4] The civil wrong of misuse of private information emerged gradually as a new cause of action over a period of years following the entry into force of the Human Rights Act 1998 (HRA), which incorporated into domestic law the European Convention on Human Rights (ECHR). Article 8 ECHR protects the right to respect for private and family life, home and correspondence and Article 10 protects the right to freedom of expression. The advent of the HRA required the courts to 'grapple with...how to afford protection to "privacy rights" under article 8 of the Convention, in the absence...of a common law tort of invasion of privacy'.[5]

#### (b) *Horizontal effect of the Human Rights Act 1998*

**5.03**   The rights in Articles 8 and 10 ECHR are expressed in terms that protect only against interference by a public authority: they have 'vertical effect' between the state and the citizen. Even before the HRA came into force, there was 'enormous academic interest' in the extent to which the Convention, via the HRA, had 'horizontal effect', between private persons.[6] Would it enable the creation of new causes of action between individuals based directly on the Convention rights? Or would it, less dramatically but nevertheless significantly, influence the development of existing private law causes of action?[7] Certainly, the Act was not intended to have a general direct horizontal effect.[8]

**5.04**   The Court of Appeal first discussed the question of horizontal effect in *Douglas v Hello! Ltd*, where the claimants sought, ultimately unsuccessfully, to prevent publication of unauthorized photographs of their wedding.[9] Brooke LJ expressed the 'dilemma' in this way:[10]

> On the one hand, Article 8(1) of the Convention appears to create a right, exercisable against all the world, to respect for private and family life. On the other hand, Article 8(2) of the Convention...and the general philosophy of both the Convention

---

[4]   *Wainwright v Home Office* [2003] UKHL 53, [2004] 2 AC 406.
[5]   *Google Inc v Vidal-Hall* [2015] EWCA Civ 311, [2015] 3 WLR 409 [18], [2015] 3 WLR 409.
[6]   *Doherty v Birmingham City Council* [2008] UKHL 57, [2009] 1 AC 367 [99]. For citations see 3.37, n 112.
[7]   See 3.37, n 112 and A Lester and D Pannick, 'The Impact of the Human Rights Act on Private Law: The Knight's Move' (2000) 116 LQR 380.
[8]   See M Hunt, 'The "Horizontal Effect" of the Human Rights Act' (1998) Public Law 423, 438; Sir Richard Buxton, 'The Human Rights Act and Private Law' (2000) 116 LQR 48.
[9]   *Douglas v Hello! Ltd* [2001] QB 967 (CA) [110] (Sedley LJ).
[10]   *Douglas* (n 9) [82] (Brooke LJ).

and the Act (namely that these rights are enforceable only against public authorities), all appear to water down the value of the right created by Article 8(1).

While resolution of this difficult issue was not strictly necessary in *Douglas v Hello!*, **5.05** Sedley LJ described the HRA and the common law as 'run[ning] in the same channel' by virtue of ss 2 and 6.[11] Section 6 HRA makes it unlawful for the court to act incompatibly with a Convention right, and s 2 requires the courts to 'have regard' to the jurisprudence of the European Court of Human Rights (ECtHR) when applying domestic law. Keene LJ added cautiously that the courts' duty to act compatibly with the Convention 'arguably includes their activity in interpreting and developing the common law'.[12] This was the beginning of recognition that the combined effect of these provisions is that the HRA can have an impact on the resolution by the courts of purely private disputes between citizens.[13]

### (c) Positive obligation

The Court of Appeal in *Douglas v Hello!* identified two other factors that touch on **5.06** the issue of the horizontal effect of Article 8. First, further support for the horizontal effect of the HRA can be found in the positive obligation of the state,[14] recognized by the ECtHR in *von Hannover v Germany* and consistently since, to protect one individual from an unjustified invasion of private life by another individual.[15] The positive obligation arises from the framing of Article 8(1): 'It provides that everyone has the right to "respect" for certain things and in some circumstances a state can "respect" them only by taking positive action.'[16]

### (d) Relevance of privacy codes

Second, Brooke LJ noted that the HRA provides that, in making decisions whether **5.07** to grant relief that might affect freedom of expression, the court must have regard to 'any relevant privacy code'.[17] At the time the HRA was passed, the Press Complaints Commission (PCC) Code of Practice stated that: 'Everyone is entitled to

---

[11] *Douglas* (n 9) [111].

[12] *Douglas* (n 9) [166]. See also [91] (Brooke LJ). See further N A Moreham, '*Douglas and others v Hello! Ltd*—the Protection of Privacy in English Private Law' (2001) 64 MLR 767, 767–70; Hunt (n 8) 440–3.

[13] In the contemporaneous academic debate, frequent reference was made to the dissenting judgment of Kreigler J of the South African Constitutional Court in *Du Plessis v De Klerk* 1996 SA 850, 871 for the proposition that, while the Convention did not directly affect the relationship between private individuals, it did affect 'all law', including that which applied to such persons and disputes between them. See *eg* Lester and Pannick (n 7) 384; Hunt (n 8) 434–35.

[14] See *Douglas* (n 9) [83]–[85] (Brooke LJ); Lester and Pannick (n 7).

[15] *von Hannover v Germany* (2005) 40 EHRR 1, para 57. This point has since been reiterated in eg *Mosley v UK* (2011) 53 EHRR 30, para 106; *von Hannover v Germany (No 2)* (2012) 55 EHRR 15, para 98; *Jalbă v Romania* App no 43912/10 (ECtHR, 18 February 2014) para 27.

[16] *R (T) v Chief Constable of Greater Manchester Police (Liberty intervening)* [2014] UKSC 35, [2014] 3 WLR 96 [23], citing *Marckx v Belgium* (1979) 2 EHRR 330. See also *Ageyevy v Russia* App no 7075/10 (ECtHR, 18 April 2013) para 219.

[17] s 12(4)(b) HRA. *Douglas* (n 9) [92]–[95] (Brooke LJ). See also *Campbell* (n 1) [111] (Lord Hope), [159] (Baroness Hale).

respect for his or her private and family life, home, health and correspondence.'[18] The wording was drawn largely from the Convention. Section 12(4)(b) might therefore be taken as an indication that Parliament intended that the HRA should operate horizontally, at least in the particular sphere of media intrusion into privacy.[19] The IPSO Editors' Code of Practice, successor to the PCC Code, retains this language, with an additional reference to digital communications.[20]

### (e) Extending breach of confidence

**5.08** When asked in *Douglas v Hello! Ltd* to protect individuals against the wrongful disclosure of private information, the Court of Appeal sought to fulfil its duty not to act incompatibly with Convention rights by extending the established law of breach of confidence.[21] The Court recognized for the first time the existence of a 'right to personal privacy', conceiving of this as a development of the confidence action, for which the HRA and Convention principles provided 'the final impetus'.[22] It was not suggested that a new cause of action based solely on the HRA should be, or was, developed in that case.[23] It came to be seen domestically[24] and elsewhere,[25] however, that 'shoehorning' privacy claims into breach of confidence was a rather artificial and unsatisfactory solution.[26]

### (f) A new cause of action

**5.09** The decisive breakthrough was the decision of the House of Lords in *Campbell v MGN Ltd*.[27] The House of Lords held that in the context of private information the law of confidence had 'firmly shaken off' the limiting constraint of the need for an initial confidential relationship,[28] and that 'the essence of the tort is better encapsulated now as misuse of private information'.[29] The courts were ultimately driven to recognize that this was not just a question of nomenclature but that the mutation of breach of confidence had brought into being a new and separate cause of action, something eventually acknowledged by the House of Lords in 2007.[30]

---

[18] cl 3(i).

[19] *Douglas* (n 9) [92]–[95] (Brooke LJ).

[20] cl 2(i). The PCC was replaced by the Independent Press Standards Organisation (IPSO) in September 2014. IPSO now has responsibility for enforcing the Editors' Code of Practice amongst its members.

[21] *A v B plc* [2002] EWCA Civ 337, [2003] QB 195 [4].

[22] *Douglas* (n 9) [111] (Sedley LJ). See also [166] (Keene LJ).

[23] Moreham (n 12) 769.

[24] See *eg Douglas v Hello! Ltd* [2005] EWCA Civ 595, [2006] QB 125 [53]. See also *McKennitt v Ash* [2006] EWCA Civ 1714, [2008] QB 73 [8(iii)].

[25] In *Hosking v Runting* [2005] 1 NZLR 1, CA [42], Gault P and Blanchard J of the Court of Appeal of New Zealand reviewed the then state of English law and said, 'it seems then that there are now in English law two quite distinct versions of the tort of breach of confidence'.

[26] *Douglas* (n 24) [53].

[27] *Campbell* (n 1).

[28] *Campbell* (n 1) [14] (Lord Nicholls).

[29] *Campbell* (n 1).

[30] *Douglas* (n 2) [255] (Lord Nicholls). See also *Google Inc v Vidal-Hall* (n 5) [18]–[43]. For more discussion of the emergence of the new cause of action see 4.03–4.07.

In *Campbell*, Lord Nicholls also felt able to set to one side the 'controversial ques-  **5.10**
tion' of horizontal effect in reaching the conclusion that:

> The values embodied in articles 8 and 10 are as much applicable in disputes
> between individuals or between an individual and a non-governmental body
> such as a newspaper as they are in disputes between individuals and a public
> authority.[31]

Lord Hoffmann was unable to see any logical ground on which an individual
should enjoy less protection against another private individual than against the
state, in respect of the publication of private information.[32] Although, these observations were arguably not part of the *ratio* of the decision,[33] the cause of action for
misuse of private information has continued to develop in a form that determines
the parties' rights by direct reference to Articles 8 and 10.

### (g) Nature of the cause of action

The cause of action for misuse of private information embodies the values  **5.11**
enshrined in Articles 8 and 10 ECHR, operates between private individuals,
and is of a rights-based character.[34] As Lord Hoffmann explained in *Campbell*,
the focus is upon protecting an individual's privacy as an aspect of 'human
autonomy and dignity—the right to control the dissemination of information about one's private life and the right to the esteem and respect of other
people'.[35]

The misuse action is distinct from breach of confidence, which is designed to pro-  **5.12**
tect confidential information or secrecy. There is, however, overlap between the
misuse of private information and breach of confidence actions. Many factual situations may give rise to viable claims in both causes of action;[36] a misuse claim may
be reinforced by a claim for breach of confidence; and the authorities relating to
breach of confidence may have relevance to the newer cause of action.[37] Misuse of
private information action is also distinct from defamation although in a limited
class of cases, the two will overlap. The relationship between misuse and defamation is discussed in Chapter 8.

---

[31] *Campbell* (n 1) [17].
[32] *Campbell* (n 1) [50].
[33] In *Douglas* (n 24) [50]–[53], the Court of Appeal observed that the contention that the HRA
gave the Convention 'full, direct horizontal effect' had been rejected by the House of Lords in
*Wainwright* (n 4) and *Campbell* (n 1).
[34] *Campbell* (n 1) [17]–[18] (Lord Nicholls). In *Hosking* (n 25) [42], the New Zealand Court of
Appeal said that the new 'version' of breach of confidence that had emerged in the English jurisprudence, 'reflects more the impact of a developing rights-based approach'.
[35] *Campbell* (n 1) [50]–[51]. See further 5.26.
[36] *eg McKennitt* (n 24); *Associated Newspapers Ltd v HRH Prince of Wales* [2006] EWCA Civ
1776, [2008] Ch 57; *Abbey v Gilligan* [2012] EWHC 3217 (QB), [2013] EMLR 12.
[37] *Imerman v Tchenguiz* [2010] EWCA Civ 908, [2011] Fam 116 [65]–[67] and 4.06 and 4.37.

*(h) Juridical nature*

**5.13**   As the new cause of action has developed it has frequently been referred to as a tort.[38] Its juridical nature was considered in detail for the first time in *Google Inc v Vidal-Hall*, where, for the purposes of service out of the jurisdiction, the Court of Appeal held misuse of private information to be a tort rather than an equitable cause of action.[39] The characterization of the action may have a number of significant ramifications as regards, for example, jurisdiction, remedies, and applicable law.[40]

## (2)  Essential Elements of the Cause of Action

**5.14**   A new methodology has been developed to determine whether actual or threatened conduct amounts to a misuse of private information. It requires assessing whether Article 8 is engaged and, if so, whether Article 10 is also engaged. If both rights are engaged, the court will conduct a balancing exercise to determine which should yield in the particular case. A cause of action for misuse of private information will exist whenever:

>   (a) the particular information at issue engages Article 8 by being within the scope of the claimant's private or family life, home, or correspondence; and
>   (b) the conduct or threatened conduct of the defendant is such that, upon a pro-portionality analysis of the competing rights under Articles 8 and 10, it is determined that it is necessary for freedom of expression to give way.[41]

*(a) Is the information private?*

**5.15**   *A reasonable expectation of privacy*   The 'touchstone' of when information concerns private life so as to engage Article 8 is whether the person concerned has a reasonable expectation of privacy in respect of the information.[42] This will be made out where it is shown that 'the person publishing the information knows or ought to know that there is a reasonable expectation that the information in question will be kept [private]'.[43] If this is not established, that is the end of the case.[44] The assessment of whether a person has a reasonable expectation of privacy is an objective one which involves consideration of all the circumstances.[45]

---

[38]   See, *eg*, the citations in the text to nn 29 and 73.

[39]   *Google Inc v Vidal-Hall* (n 5).

[40]   See 13.62 (jurisdiction), 13.89 (choice of law).

[41]   *Campbell* (n 1) [137] (Baroness Hale); *McKennitt* (n 24) [11]; *HRH Prince of Wales* (n 36); *Murray v Express Newspapers plc* [2008] EWCA Civ 446, [2009] Ch 481 [27].

[42]   *Campbell* (n 1) [21] (Lord Nicholls), a position reaffirmed by the majority in *Re JR38's Application for Judicial Review* [2015] UKSC 42, [2015] 3 WLR 155.

[43]   *Campbell* (n 1) [134] (Baroness Hale). In view of Lord Nicholls' observations (text to n 29), the term 'private' has been substituted for Baroness Hale's use of the word 'confidential'.

[44]   *McKennitt* (n 24) [11].

[45]   See 5.21.

## (b) Balancing competing rights

Articles 8 and 10 each express a fundamental right which there is a 'pressing social **5.16** need' to protect, but equally each is qualified to the extent necessary and proportionate in order to accommodate the other.[46] Article 8(2) recognizes that there are occasions where the intrusion into private life is necessary for the protection of the rights and freedoms of others. Similarly, Article 10(2) recognizes there are occasions when protection of the rights of others may make it necessary for freedom of expression to give way.

When both these rights are engaged, a difficult question of proportionality may **5.17** arise.[47] In conducting this exercise, neither the Article 8 nor Article 10 right has automatic priority.[48] As Baroness Hale explained in *Campbell*, when two Convention rights are in play, 'the proportionality of interfering with one has to be balanced against the proportionality of restricting the other'.[49] The basic approach involves:

> ...looking first at the comparative importance of the actual rights being claimed in the individual case; then at the justifications for interfering with or restricting each of those rights; and applying the proportionality test to each.[50]

This dual application of the proportionality test has been dubbed 'the ultimate **5.18** balancing test'.[51] It has been increasingly recognized that the rights relevant to this ultimate balancing exercise may include rights other than Articles 8 and 10, and the rights of persons other than the claimant and defendant. If, overall, the balance falls on the side of the claimant, the court will then consider what remedies, if any, should be ordered.[52]

## (3) The Cause of Action at the Interim Injunction Stage

Section 12 HRA provides a 'statutory steer' for the court at the interim injunction **5.19** stage,[53] which is so important in many media privacy cases. The court must consider, in addition to the matters already identified:

(1) whether there is evidence from which the court can infer that the defendant intends to publish particular information or a particular class of information—it is impermissible to grant a speculative injunction;[54]

---

[46] *Campbell* (n 1) [140] (Baroness Hale), also [55] (Lord Hoffmann); *Re W (Children) (Identification: Restrictions on Publication)* [2005] EWHC 1564 (Fam), [2006] 1 FLR 1 [53], later adopted in *Clayton v Clayton* [2006] EWCA Civ 878, [2006] Fam 83 [58] (Sir Mark Potter P).
[47] *Campbell* (n 1) [20] (Lord Nicholls).
[48] *Campbell* (n 1) [113] (Lord Hope).
[49] *Campbell* (n 1) [140] (Baroness Hale)
[50] *Campbell* (n 1) [141] (Baroness Hale); *Re W* (n 46) [53].
[51] *Re S (A Child) (Identification: Restrictions of Publication)* [2004] UKHL 47, [2005] 1 AC 593 [17] (Lord Steyn).
[52] See ch 12 for remedies.
[53] *Hutcheson (previously 'KGM') v News Group Newspapers Ltd* [2011] EWCA Civ 808, [2012] EMLR 2 [35].
[54] *Lord Browne of Madingley v Associated Newspapers Ltd* [2007] EWCA Civ 295, [2008] QB 103 [64]–[65].

(2) whether the applicant has shown, in accordance with s 12(3) HRA, that he is likely[55] to succeed at trial in establishing that publication should not be allowed—this usually requires the court to come to a provisional conclusion on the merits.[56]

## C. When is there a Reasonable Expectation of Privacy?

### (1) The Court's Approach to the Question

#### (a) An objective test

**5.20** The underlying question in all cases is whether the information is private.[57] There must be some interest of a private nature that the claimant wishes to protect.[58] It is clear that the reasonable expectation of privacy must be one possessed by the particular claimant in respect of the particular information at issue.[59] This is an objective question.[60] The court will give separate consideration to different items or classes of information.[61] In some cases it will be obvious whether a reasonable expectation of privacy exists;[62] in others, the decision will be far from straightforward.[63]

**5.21** All the circumstances of the case are to be considered in assessing whether there is a reasonable expectation of privacy.[64] In *Murray v Express Newspapers plc*, the Court of Appeal said the factors to be taken into account include:

> the attributes of the claimant, the nature of the activity in which the claimant was engaged, the place at which it was happening, the nature and purpose of the intrusion, the absence of consent and whether it was known or could be inferred, the effect on the claimant and the circumstances in which and the purposes for which the information came into the hands of the publisher.[65]

---

[55] In the sense explained in *Cream Holdings Ltd v Banerjee* [2004] UKHL 44, [2005] 1 AC 253. See 12.46–12.50 for further discussion of this issue.

[56] *X v Persons Unknown* [2006] EWHC 2783 (QB), [2007] EMLR 10 [44]–[45].

[57] *Campbell* (n 1) [92] (Lord Hope).

[58] *Campbell* (n 1) [92], citing *A v B plc* (n 21) [11(vii)].

[59] This follows from the formulation adopted by Lord Nicholls in *Campbell* (text to n 42). See also *Lord Browne* (n 54) [32]; *Goodwin v News Group Newspapers Ltd* [2011] EWHC 1437 (QB), [2011] EMLR 27 [87].

[60] *Murray* (n 41) [35].

[61] eg *Trimingham v Associated Newspapers Ltd* [2012] EWHC 1296 (QB), [2012] 4 All ER 717 [288].

[62] *Campbell* (n 1) [92] (Lord Hope); *A v B plc* (n 21)[11](vii).

[63] *CDE v MGN Ltd* [2010] EWHC 3308 (QB), [2011] 1 FLR 1524 [2].

[64] *Murray* (n 41) [35]. Also *Lord Browne* (n 54) [33], where the Court of Appeal said 'a detailed examination of all the circumstances on a case by case basis' is required. It is also necessary to focus on 'the underlying value or collection of values which article 8 is designed to protect': *JR38* (n 42) [97].

[65] *Murray* (n 41) [36].

This list of factors is self-evidently not exhaustive. The broad and open-textured approach prescribed by the Court of Appeal has the virtue of permitting the court to take account of the almost infinite variety of factual situations in which a person may assert a right to claim protection of his or her Article 8 right to respect for private life. The approach prescribed by *Murray* has, however, the weakness of affording relatively scant guidance as to the weight to be accorded to particular circumstances, or the likely outcome of the court's assessment.[66]

The post-HRA authorities so far suggest that there are four factors that tend to weigh **5.22** heavily in the court's decision as to whether the claimant enjoys a reasonable expectation that information will be kept private:

(1)  the nature of the information or activity;
(2)  the form in which the information is kept;
(3)  the effect on the claimant of its disclosure or other use; and
(4)  the attributes of the claimant.

The following paragraphs describe the scope and aims of Article 8;[67] consider the **5.23** authorities on the four factors just identified;[68] and explore other circumstances relevant to the assessment of whether a reasonable expectation of privacy exists,[69] using the non-exhaustive list from *Murray*[70] as a template. The extent to which the information is available to the public, and the passage of time, are other factors that will have weight; both are discussed in Chapter 11.[71]

## (2)  The Continued Influence of Article 8(1)

### (a)  Relevance of Strasbourg authorities

To identify the content of the Article 8 right that the action for misuse of private **5.24** information is designed to protect, and to ascertain the applicable rules of English law, the courts must look to the jurisprudence of the ECtHR. Section 2 HRA requires the English courts to 'take into account' the jurisprudence of the ECtHR when resolving questions about Convention rights.[72] Moreover, Articles 8 and 10 are 'the very content of the domestic tort that the English court has to enforce'.[73] Article 8 and Strasbourg

---

[66]  For a critique, suggesting that some of these factors are really relevant to the second stage, see K Hughes, 'A Behavioural Understanding of Privacy' (2012) 75 MLR 806, 828.

[67]  See 5.24–5.27.

[68]  See 5.28–5.83 (nature of the information); 5.84–5.103 (form of the information); 5.104–5.113 (effect of disclosure); 5.114–5.126 (attributes of the claimant).

[69]  See 5.127–5.153.

[70]  *Murray* (n 41) [36], set out at 5.21.

[71]  See 11.59 (the 'fade factor') and 11.61–11.62 (public domain).

[72]  s 2(1) HRA. This does not mean Strasbourg decisions prevail over domestic ones; the duty to take into account is subject always to compliance with the rules of precedent of English law: *Kay v Lambeth LBC* [2006] UKHL 10, [2006] 2 AC 465; *R (Purdy) v DPP* [2009] UKHL 45, [2010] 1 AC 345 [34]–[39] (Lord Hope).

[73]  *McKennitt* (n 24) [11]. For a discussion of 'applying' Convention rights in practice see G Phillipson and A Williams, 'Horizontal Effect and Constitutional Restraint' (2011) 74 MLR 878.

jurisprudence accordingly have considerable impact on the assessment by the domestic courts of whether a reasonable expectation of privacy exists.

**5.25** It should be noted, however, that there are differences between the way the domestic court assesses whether a claim for misuse of private information is made out and the approach taken by the ECtHR in assessing whether there has been a violation of Article 8. For example, in recent cases, the Strasbourg Court has approached the question whether Article 8 is engaged in a manner akin to a threshold inquiry antecedent to the balancing exercise,[74] whereas the English court's assessment of whether a reasonable expectation of privacy exists incorporates factors that the ECtHR considers in balancing the competing rights.[75]

### (b) The nature of the interests protected

**5.26** An important aspect of the Article 8(1) right that must be borne in mind by courts when applying the broad objective test is the nature of the protection that Article 8 is designed to afford. That includes the specific matters listed in Article 8, including family life, home, and correspondence, as well as those matters that fall within the overall aims of Article 8, including securing human dignity and autonomy.[76] The ECtHR cases establish that the concept of private life, while incapable of precise or exhaustive definition:

> includes a person's physical and psychological integrity; the guarantee afforded by Article 8 of the Convention is primarily intended to ensure the development, without outside interference, of the personality of each individual in his relations with other human beings.[77]

To keep these underlying interests in mind is likely to be of assistance when considering whether it is reasonable to expect information to be kept private.[78]

### (c) A right to respect

**5.27** A second aspect which it is suggested may be significant is that the Article 8(1) right is not only qualified by Article 8(2); it is an inherently qualified right. In *M v Secretary of State for Work and Pensions*, Lord Walker pointed out that Article 8(1), uniquely, affords a right to 'respect' for privacy rather than an absolute right.[79] This

---

[74] *von Hannover (No 2)* (n 15) paras 95–9 (concerning private life), paras 108–13 (criteria relevant to balancing exercise).

[75] *Hutcheson* (n 53) [36]–[39], where the Court of Appeal rejected as 'semantic' the question whether the English courts are required to give separate consideration to first, whether Art 8 is engaged *and*, second, whether there is a reasonable expectation of privacy before moving on to the ultimate balancing test. See also Hughes (n 66).

[76] See 5.11. For fuller discussion in the domestic context of the core interests protected by Art 8: *R (Wood) v Commissioner of Police of the Metropolis* [2009] EWCA Civ 414, [2010] 1 WLR 123 [16]–[22] (Laws LJ) and 3.22–3.36.

[77] *von Hannover* (n 15) para 50.

[78] *Hutcheson* (n 53) [24].

[79] *M v Secretary of State for Work and Pensions* [2006] UKHL 11, [2006] 2 AC 91 [83]; *Wood* (n 76) [22] (Laws LJ).

feature of Article 8(1) has given rise to a threshold so that trivial misuses of private information are not actionable.[80] It also, it is suggested, gives a measure of recognition to the interactive nature of a democratic society, and the fact that, in such a society, it may be neither possible nor desirable to seek to accord individuals complete autonomous control over information that relates to them.[81] For example, the court may in due course come to regard the Article 8 right to self-development of an individual as qualified by the rights of others to develop their own personalities, in part, by absorbing information about other individuals. The ECtHR has reiterated, however, that the notion of 'respect' does not compromise the principle that Article 8 'must be interpreted in such a way as to guarantee...rights that are practical and effective' rather than 'theoretical or illusory'.[82]

### (3) The Nature of the Information or Activity

#### (a) Preliminary matters

The nature of the information is plainly of considerable if not prime importance. **5.28** The Court of Appeal said in *Douglas v Hello! Ltd* that '[t]he nature of the information, or the form in which it is kept,[83] may suffice to make it plain' that it is private information.[84] The nature of the information accordingly requires 'careful consideration'.[85]

**Information relating to the claimant**    The information must in general relate in **5.29** some way to the claimant,[86] for otherwise it is hard to see how it can impact on his or her right to respect for private life.[87] In *Lady Archer v Williams*, the claimant was denied protection in respect of the details of conversations that did not relate to the claimant, her family, staff, or the defendant's duties as the claimant's personal assistant.[88] In *OPO v MLA*,[89] the claimant sought to prevent his father publishing an autobiography including details of the father's history of sexual abuse and his ongoing mental health problems. The Court of Appeal upheld the conclusion of Bean J that there was no cause of action in misuse of private information because

---

[80] Triviality in the context of misuse is further discussed at 5.154–5.158. For triviality in the context of breach of confidence see 4.81–4.83.

[81] *O'Halloran v UK* (2008) 46 EHRR 21 (concurring opinion of Judge Borrego Borrego).

[82] *Mitkus v Latvia* App no 7259/03 (ECtHR, 2 October 2012) para 127.

[83] See 5.84–5.103 for the significance of this factor.

[84] *Douglas* (n 24) [83].

[85] *Hutcheson* (n 53) [26].

[86] There have been some exceptions, *eg Green Corns Ltd v Claverley Group Ltd* [2005] EWHC 958 (QB), [2005] EMLR 31 (see 5.62, 5.126, 5.171).

[87] This is an important difference between misuse of private information and breach of confidence. Under the latter, a claimant may sue in respect of information relating to third parties: *AVB v TDD* [2014] EWHC 1442 (QB) [80].

[88] *Lady Archer v Williams* [2003] EWHC 1670 (QB), [2003] EMLR 38 [50]. For reasons that are not clear, this approach was not carried through in the court's ruling in respect of the diaries kept by the defendant; the entire contents of these were protected.

[89] *OPO v MLA* [2014] EWCA Civ 1277, [2015] EMLR 4.

the information belonged to the defendant, notwithstanding that publication of the information would affect the claimant.[90] It has yet to be decided whether information that relates to the claimant can be the subject of a misuse claim even if effectively anonymized.[91]

**5.30** **The information need not be true** While the traditional action for breach of confidence requires the information in question to be true,[92] Article 8 is engaged irrespective of whether the private information is true or false.[93] In most claims for misuse of private information, the essence of the wrong will lie in the communication of information which is in substance true, and which has been presented as true by the defendant. Case law indicates that where, despite its accuracy, a publication could nevertheless be interpreted in different ways, the court will determine its meaning for the purpose of a misuse of private information claim.[94] When doing so, the court will consider the meaning that the information would communicate to an ordinary reasonable reader, even if there is a risk that some of the audience will not be so fair-minded.[95]

**5.31** **False information** The falsity of private information may nevertheless have some relevance. It may be necessary for a claimant to adduce evidence that private information is untrue where a defendant seeks to show that its disclosure was in the public interest. The reason is that there will not be a public interest in the disclosure of false information about private life.

**5.32** Privacy claims brought solely or predominantly in relation to information said to be false require special scrutiny. At the interim injunction stage, if there is reason to believe that the essence of a privacy claim is false information damaging to reputation—in other words, 'defamation in disguise'[96]—the rule against prior restraint in defamation may have to be surmounted.[97] This was one reason for the

---

[90] *OPO* (n 89) [32], [35], [38]–[47] (Arden LJ, with whom the other members of the Court agreed.)

[91] Discussed at 5.55–5.58.

[92] See 4.92.

[93] *McKennitt* (n 24) [78]–[80]; *AMM v HXW* [2010] EWHC 2457 (QB) [14]; 4.93.

[94] *Re Guardian News and Media Ltd* [2010] UKSC 1, [2010] 2 AC 697 [60], [66]; *Trimingham* (n 61) [297]; *PNM v Times Newspapers Ltd* [2014] EWCA Civ 1132, [2014] EMLR 30 [35]–[38].

[95] In *PNM* (n 94) Sharp LJ held that the effect of disclosing the fact of the claimant's arrest for alleged child sex offences was more limited than had been argued on his behalf because 'most members of the public understand the presumption of innocence and are able to distinguish between the position of someone who has been (merely) arrested, someone who has been charged, and someone who has been convicted of a criminal offence'. The other members of the Court agreed. Cf the approach taken in defamation: A Mullis and R Parkes (eds), *Gatley on Libel and Slander* (12th edn, Sweet & Maxwell 2013) para 3.16.

[96] *Ambrosiadou v Coward* [2010] EWHC 1794 (QB), [2010] 2 FLR 1775 [55]. In the context of breach of confidence, *Viagogo Ltd v Myles* [2012] EWHC 433 (Ch) [81]: 'the court does need to be astute to consider what is the nub or gist of the application'.

[97] The rule in *Bonnard v Perryman* [1891] 2 Ch 269, CA and its implications for misuse are discussed at 8.50–8.84 and 12.25, 12.45.

failure of the injunction application in *Terry v Persons Unknown*.[98] The relationship between defamation and misuse of private information is discussed in Chapter 8.

### (b) A review of the authorities

A review of particular classes of information follows, drawing on various strands of authority in an attempt to identify classes of information capable of being regarded as private in nature. Reference will be made to Strasbourg decisions,[99] and English case law. Reference is also made to the law of data protection and to cases from the law of breach of confidence, which serve, among other things, as an extension of Chapter 4.  **5.33**

**A cautionary note**   Any such review must be read with some obvious but important warnings in mind. There are dangers in generalizations[100] and it will always be necessary to look at the circumstances of the case. Further, the criteria for confidentiality and privacy in English law are different. It is only the ECtHR authorities, and those domestic cases decided since the HRA came into force, that can be regarded as authoritative as to the scope of the reasonable expectation of privacy.[101] For these reasons, the attempt has been made to deal separately with the individual categories of authority.  **5.34**

Subject to those warnings, it is suggested that the breach of confidence pre-HRA and foreign authorities are instructive. The review set out in this chapter, taken as a whole, shows that, although certain classes of information are likely to be readily recognized as intrinsically private, others can give rise to real difficulties.  **5.35**

### Information about health

*Confidentiality*   A wide range of information relating to an individual's physical or mental health and medical treatment has long been recognized as capable of protection in confidence.[102] In *X v Y*, the plaintiffs obtained a permanent injunction restraining publication of information contained in hospital records that identified individual doctors as suffering from HIV and AIDS.[103]  **5.36**

---

[98]   *Terry (previously 'LNS') v Persons Unknown* [2010] EWHC 119 (QB), [2010] EMLR 16 [123].

[99]   See 5.24–5.25.

[100]   *Mosley v News Group Newspapers Ltd* [2008] EWHC 1777 (QB), [2008] EMLR 20 [98].

[101]   Although data protection law, grounded as it is in Art 8 considerations, is also of significance for the misuse wrong.

[102]   *Argyll (Duchess) v Argyll (Duke)* [1967] Ch 302, 319–20 where the unreported case of *Wilson v Wyatt* (1820) is discussed. In *Wilson*, Lord Eldon took the view that the contents of a physician's diary relating to the state of health of King George III was confidential. In *Argyll*, the disclosure by the defendant in a newspaper article of the nature of her ex-husband's medication was described as a 'serious breach of confidence' (331). Also *R v Dept of Health, ex p Source Informatics* [2001] QB 424, CA [13] where Simon Brown LJ referred to the 'undoubted duty of confidentiality' a pharmacist owes to those to whom he dispenses medical prescriptions.

[103]   *X v Y* [1988] 2 All ER 648, QB. Also *H (A Healthcare Worker) v Associated Newspapers Ltd* [2002] EWCA Civ 195, [2002] EMLR 23 where it was accepted by the defendant that information tending to identify H as a healthcare worker suffering from HIV was confidential. The key issue was whether the identity of the health authority where H worked and his medical specialty constituted such information.

In *W v Egdell*, a case concerning the disclosure by a doctor of a psychiatric report on an individual, there was no dispute that the content of the report was confidential.[104]

**5.37** *Privacy* There is ample Strasbourg authority for the proposition that the privacy of information about health lies at the heart of the protection afforded by Article 8.[105] In the post-HRA era, the English courts too have considered it beyond dispute as a general proposition that a person's health is a private matter.[106] Personal information about individuals derived from medical records, reports, or interviews, whatever the purpose for which they were prepared or conducted, is both confidential and private.[107] Information as to 'physical or mental health or condition' is also one of the classes of sensitive personal data listed as deserving special protection in s 2 of the Data Protection Act 1998 (DPA).[108]

**5.38** In *Campbell*, the House of Lords held that details of the claimant's therapy for her drug addiction related to the condition of her physical and mental health, and the treatment she was receiving for it, and was therefore private and confidential information.[109] The privacy of medical information was accepted by the Court of Appeal in *McKennitt v Ash*, which involved information about the state of the claimant's health, made worse by fragility associated with bereavement.[110] In *Cooper v Turrell*, the Court held there to be a reasonable expectation of privacy in information concerning a past misdiagnosis and the claimant's description of the symptoms he was presently experiencing.[111]

**5.39** *Limitations* The fact the information relates to the health or medical history of the claimant is not necessarily determinative. In *Spelman v Express Newspapers Ltd*, the claimant, a young sportsman, was refused an interim injunction to prohibit publication of the information related to his use of banned performance-enhancing substances.[112] In particular, there may be no reasonable expectation

---

[104] *W v Egdell* [1990] Ch 359, CA. Also *Cornelius v de Taranto* [2001] EWCA Civ 1511, [2002] EMLR 6; *Ashworth Hospital Authority v MGN Ltd* [2001] 1 WLR 515, CA; *Mersey Care NHS Trust v Ackroyd* [2003] EWCA Civ 663, [2003] EMLR 36.

[105] *Z v Finland* (1998) 25 EHRR 371, paras 95–6; *I v Finland* (2009) 48 EHRR 31, para 38. For the interests underlying this protection: *Varapnickaitė-Mazylienė v Lithuania* App no 20376/05 (ECtHR, 17 January 2012) para 44; *Mitkus v Latvia* (n 82) para 133.

[106] *McKennitt* (n 24) [23]; *Australian Broadcasting Corp v Lenah Game Meats Pty Ltd* (2001) 208 CLR 199 [42].

[107] *Venables v News Group Newspapers Ltd* [2001] Fam 430. For a discussion of the privacy of medical correspondence: *R (Szuluk) v Governor of Full Sutton Prison* [2004] EWCA Civ 1426. But see the public law case of *R (WXYZ) v Secretary of State for Health* [2014] EWHC 1532 (Admin) which indicates that not all information held by a health service provider will necessarily engage Art 8 if it does not relate to a person's medical history.

[108] s 2(e) DPA.

[109] *Campbell* (n 1) [53] (Lord Hoffmann), [146]–[147] (Baroness Hale).

[110] *McKennitt* (n 24).

[111] *Cooper v Turrell* [2011] EWHC 3269 (QB).

[112] *Spelman v Express Newspapers Ltd* [2012] EWHC 355 (QB), discussed at 5.154.

that anonymized information will not be used,[113] and harmless disclosures of trivial information about health may not breach privacy.[114]

### Information about sexual life and relationships

*Confidentiality*    In *Argyll v Argyll*, it was held that details about a married cou-    **5.40**
ple's sex life, including extramarital adulterous affairs, were confidential.[115] In *Stephens v Avery*, Sir Nicholas Browne-Wilkinson V-C held that information relating to the sex lives of lesbian partners was confidential: 'to most people the details of their sexual lives are high on their list of those matters which they regard as confidential'.[116] Jacob J came to the same conclusion with regard to information about a male homosexual relationship in *Barrymore v News Group Newspapers Ltd*, observing that when people kiss and later one of them tells, the second person is almost certainly breaking a confidential arrangement.[117]

*Privacy*    Personal sexuality is 'an extremely intimate aspect of a person's private    **5.41**
life'.[118] In *PG v UK*, the ECtHR held that 'gender identification,...sexual orientation and sexual life are important elements of the personal sphere protected under Article 8'.[119] Information as to 'sexual life' is also classed as 'sensitive personal data' in s 2(f) DPA.

There are numerous general statements from English courts to the effect that    **5.42**
sexual behaviour is an aspect of private life that is high on the list of matters to be protected by Article 8.[120] This does not, however, mean that information about a person's sexual activities will invariably be protected.[121] Although some relationships are more likely to be protected than others,[122] the courts have protected information about sexual life relating to a wide variety of relationships.[123] Numerous injunctions have been granted to protect information relating to the fact or details of adultery.[124] The current view appears to be that all sexual relationships will engage Article 8, although abusive, criminal, or grossly offensive sexual

---

[113] See 5.55 *et seq.*

[114] See 5.156.

[115] *Argyll* (n 102). This point was conceded in *Lady Archer* (n 88), as was Lady Archer's right to claim confidentiality in respect of the sexual relationships of any of her children.

[116] *Stephens v Avery* [1988] Ch 449, 454. The Court of Appeal adopted this in *Lord Browne* (n 54) [85], which related to information obtained through a homosexual relationship.

[117] *Barrymore v News Group Newspapers Ltd* [1997] FSR 600 (Ch).

[118] *Douglas* (n 9) [168] (Keene LJ), discussing *Dudgeon v UK* (1982) 4 EHRR 149.

[119] *PG v UK* (2008) 46 EHRR 51 [56]. For a different opinion in the context of the Employment Tribunal, see *X v Y* [2004] EWCA Civ 662, [2004] ICR 1634.

[120] *Mosley* (n 100) [99]–[100]; *Contostavlos v Mendahun* [2012] EWHC 850 (QB) [25]; *Lenah Game Meats* (n 106) [42] (Gleeson CJ).

[121] *Ferdinand v MGN Ltd* [2011] EWHC 2454 (QB) [56].

[122] *A v B plc* (n 21) [43], approving Ouseley J's observation in *Theakston v MGN Ltd* [2002] EWHC 137 (QB), [2002] EMLR 398 [59]–[60].

[123] Whatever the relationship, there is still a need to identify the information as being private. See 5.154–5.158.

[124] See *eg CC v AB* [2006] EWHC 3083 (QB), [2007] EMLR 11; *AMM v HXW* (n 93); *CTB v News Group Newspapers Ltd* [2011] EWHC 1232 (QB); *K v News Group Newspapers Ltd* [2011]

activity is possibly excepted.[125] In *Mosley v News Group Newspapers Ltd*, Eady J held that 'clandestine recording of sexual activity on private property must be taken to engage Article 8'.[126]

**5.43** *Sexual orientation* Although the protection of Article 8 encompasses sexual orientation,[127] it will not do so if this is a public fact. In *Trimingham v Associated Newspapers Ltd*, Tugendhat J held that the claimant, who had previously been married to a man, had been in a civil partnership with a woman, and had not attempted to keep her sexual identity private, had no reasonable expectation her bisexuality would be kept private.[128]

**5.44** *Bare fact of a sexual relationship* The fact that details of a sexual relationship are confidential or private does not necessarily mean that the mere fact of a sexual relationship (unorthodox or otherwise) is such.[129] In *Goodwin v News Group Newspapers Ltd*, Tugendhat J said:

> sooner or later [a] relationship is likely to come to light... There are few things that people are more sensitive to than signs that two other people are in a relationship. It is rarely realistic for partners in a relationship to expect that the bare fact of their relationship will remain confidential between the two of them for a long or indefinite period.[130]

Whether there is a reasonable expectation of privacy in the bare fact of a relationship requires consideration of the circumstances,[131] including the extent to which the relationship was conducted openly or publicly.[132] It is unlikely that the fact of marriage or civil partnership will be private, seeing as such relationships have a public aspect.[133] By contrast, in *Lord Browne*, the Court of Appeal said that the ambit of privacy might extend to a relationship that was conducted openly among a limited circle of friends or acquaintances.[134] In *K v News Group*, it was held that the fact that a relationship between colleagues had become known to other employees did not prevent there being a reasonable expectation of privacy.[135]

---

EWCA Civ 439, [2011] 1 WLR 1827; *MJN v News Group Newspapers Ltd* [2011] EWHC 1192 (QB); *NEJ v Wood* [2011] EWHC 1972 (QB).

[125] See 5.45.
[126] *Mosley* (n 100) [104].
[127] See 5.41.
[128] *Trimingham* (n 61) [292]–[294], where the Court held it unarguable that the claimant's bisexuality was private when she had married a man and later gone through a civil partnership ceremony with a woman.
[129] eg *Lord Browne* (n 54); *Donald v Ntuli* [2010] EWCA Civ 1276, [2011] 1 WLR 294; *Hutcheson* (n 53). Tugendhat J considered the reasons for this distinction in *Goodwin* (n 59) [93]–[99].
[130] *Goodwin* (n 59) [102]. See 11.59 on another aspect of the effects of time passing.
[131] *Goodwin* (n 59) [91].
[132] *CTB v News Group* (n 124) [23]; *EWQ v GFD* [2012] EWHC 2182 (QB).
[133] *Trimingham* (n 61); *Lillo-Stenberg v Norway* App no 13258/09 [2014] ECHR 59.
[134] *Lord Browne* (n 54) [61]; see 11.61–11.62 on when information will be so well-known as to be considered public rather than private.
[135] *K v News Group* (n 124). As to relationships in the workplace, see 5.132.

*Unlawful or immoral conduct*    The main theoretical limitation to the protection    **5.45**
of detailed information about sexual life is where the information relates to unlawful sexual conduct.[136] In addition, there cannot be a reasonable expectation of privacy in sexual activity that is abusive or amounts to sexual harassment.[137] Another
possible limitation relates to non-criminal conduct so 'grossly immoral' as to debar
the claimant from the law's protection.[138] Such arguments were however dismissed
in *Mosley v News Group*, in which the subject matter of the privacy claim concerned
sadomasochist group sex sessions for which payment was exchanged.[139]

### Information about family life

*Confidentiality*    A child's parents and caregivers owe a duty to the child to keep    **5.46**
confidential information about his or her background, care, upbringing, and
education.[140]

*Privacy*    Information about an individual's life and experiences with his or her    **5.47**
family, both within and outside the home, is capable of being the subject of a
reasonable expectation of privacy. In *A Local Authority v A Mother*, Baker J held
that information about the lifestyle within a household and the circumstances of
the children's upbringing clearly related to aspects of 'family life which in most
cases are kept shielded from the public gaze'.[141] Publication in the media of photographs of a very young mother said to have had a child with a 13-year-old boy
was held to engage Article 8.[142] In *Murray*, the Court of Appeal held that it was
an arguable infringement of Article 8 to publish photographs of a child on a family outing in a public place, and in *AAA v Associated Newspapers Ltd* and *Weller v
Associated Newspapers Ltd*, damages were awarded for such publications.[143] These
cases make clear that, particularly where children are involved, no clear line can be
drawn between family activities in the home and routine family outings such as a visit
to the shops.[144] In *AMP v Persons Unknown*, the claimant obtained an interim injunction to prevent further distribution on the internet of photographs of her family and
friends that had been stored on her mobile phone.[145]

---

[136] *Mosley* (n 100) [110]–[119]. Compare *Laskey v UK* (1997) 24 EHRR 39 with *ADT v UK* (2001) 31 EHRR 33.

[137] *BUQ v HRE* [2012] EWHC 774 (QB) [61] (alleged sexual harassment in the workplace); *Mosley* (n 100) [100] as to exploitation of the young or vulnerable.

[138] *Stephens v Avery* (n 116) 453.

[139] *Mosley* (n 100). The approach taken in *Mosley* and *Lord Browne* (n 54), which involved a homosexual relationship, can be contrasted with that of Garland J in the pre-HRA case of *M v Mackenzie* (HC, 18 January 1988). He found there was no confidence in information derived from a 'transient' homosexual relationship.

[140] *Re Z (A Minor) (Identification: Restrictions on Publication)* [1997] Fam 1, CA, 25.

[141] *A Local Authority v A Mother* [2011] EWHC 1764 (Fam), [2012] 1 FLR 239 [64].

[142] *Re Stedman* [2009] EWHC 935 (Fam), [2009] 2 FLR 852 (the Alfie Patten paternity case).

[143] *Murray* (n 41); *AAA v Associated Newspapers Ltd* [2012] EWHC 2103 (QB), [2013] EMLR 2; *Weller v Associated Newspapers Ltd* [2014] EWHC 1163 (QB), [2014] EMLR 24. Compare *Hosking* (n 25) where the New Zealand Court of Appeal decided differently a case on similar facts in *Murray*.

[144] See 5.130–5.131.

[145] *AMP v Persons Unknown* [2011] EWHC 3454 (TCC).

**5.48** *Care proceedings* The Article 8 rights of a child who is the subject of a Child Protection Case Conference are engaged, as are the rights of the adults involved.[146] A father's intention to involve his daughter, who had been the subject of care proceedings, in the making of a film or to involve her more widely in his campaigning and media activities engaged her welfare interests and infringed her Article 8 rights.[147]

**5.49** *Paternity* In *AAA*, Nicola Davies J readily accepted that 'the paternity of [a] young child is a matter which engages her rights pursuant to Article 8'.[148] Similarly, the ECtHR has found that the fact a child is adopted comes within the notion of private life.[149] It has been suggested that, as with sexual relationships, there is a difference between the publication of details about a parental or family relationship and the bare fact of its existence, and it may be less likely that there is a reasonable expectation of privacy in relation to the latter.[150] Different considerations seem to apply, however, to relationships willingly entered into between consenting adults and family relationships, which are not a matter of choice. Particular considerations arise where young children are involved.[151]

### Information about the home

**5.50** *Address* Whether disclosure of a person's address would represent a misuse of private information is likely to depend on whether there are circumstances that render the individual's location confidential, or evidence of a risk of harm, such as harassment or intrusion,[152] that would flow from its disclosure. In *Mills v News Group Newspapers Ltd*, a celebrity failed to obtain an injunction to prevent *The Sun* publishing information that tended to reveal the address of her new home.[153] There was insufficient evidence of any risk to her personal safety if the information were published. In its third *von Hannover* decision, the ECtHR, although accepting that Article 8 was engaged, dismissed the Princess's complaint relating to publication of details about and photographs of a holiday home that her family had visited.[154] By contrast, in *AM v News Group Newspapers Ltd*, the claimant obtained an injunction prohibiting publication of his address or any photograph or video likely to identify his address. There had been a considerable media presence at the claimant's home because he was the landlord of a property that was the bail address for a suspected terrorist.[155]

---

[146] *W v Westminster City Council* [2005] EWHC 102 (QB), [2005] 4 All ER 96.
[147] *Clayton* (n 46).
[148] *AAA* (n 143) [113].
[149] *Ageyevy* (n 16) para 193.
[150] *SKA v CRH* [2012] EWHC 2236 (QB) [16].
[151] *AAA* (n 143) [115] and 5.166–5.168 for the particular considerations that apply where the claimant is a child.
[152] Discussed further at 5.61–5.62.
[153] *Mills v News Group Newspapers Ltd* [2001] EMLR 41.
[154] *von Hannover v Germany (No 3)* App no 8772/10 (ECtHR, 19 September 2013).
[155] *AM v News Group Newspapers Ltd* [2012] EWHC 308 (QB). Also *Green Corns* (n 86) (discussed at 5.62).

*Inside the home*   A very well-known married couple obtained an injunction **5.51** restraining publication in a tabloid newspaper of unauthorized photographs of the interior of their new home.[156] The couple's reason for seeking the injunction was not just concern about an invasion of their privacy, but also fear that the security of their home would be compromised by the publication, particularly when they had been subjected to threats and their young son was at risk of being kidnapped.[157]

At first instance in *McKennitt v Ash*, the judge protected as private and confidential **5.52** a description of a person's home.[158] He explained:

> [Home] is one of the matters expressly addressed in Article 8(1) of the Convention as entitled to 'respect'. Correspondingly, there would be an obligation of confidence. Even relatively trivial details would fall within this protection simply because of the traditional sanctity accorded to hearth and home. To describe a person's home, the décor, the layout, the state of cleanliness, or how the occupiers behave inside it, is generally regarded as unacceptable. To convey such details, without permission, to the general public is almost as objectionable as spying into the home with a long distance lens and publishing the resulting photographs.[159]

**Information about other activities in private places**   Generally, information **5.53** about individuals' conduct in a private place is clearly capable of being confidential and private. Intimate information about sexual conduct or information about activities within the home, discussed in previous sections,[160] are the most obvious examples. There will be other acts carried out by individuals in private in respect of which the individual has a reasonable expectation of privacy.[161] In *Rocknroll v News Group Newspapers Ltd*, the claimant sought to prevent publication of photos showing him partially naked at a fancy dress party.[162] Briggs J said:

> First and foremost, the photographs show the claimant in the company of his family and friends at a private party on private premises. Not least because of his partial nakedness they show him behaving in a manner in which he would be entirely unlikely to behave in public.[163]

*Limitations*   The apparent limitations on this aspect of the Article 8 right are where the **5.54** information concerns acts that are revealed in open court[164] to be 'grossly immoral'[165]

---

[156] *Beckham v MGN Ltd* (HC, 23 June 2001), (QB, 28 June 2001).
[157] Also *Nicholls v BBC* [1999] EMLR 791, CA; *Venables* (n 107).
[158] *McKennitt v Ash* [2005] EWHC 3003 (QB), [2006] EMLR 10. The decision was unaffected by the subsequent appeal.
[159] *McKennitt* (n 158) [135], approved by the Court of Appeal (n 24) [21]–[22].
[160] See 5.40–5.44 and 5.50–5.52 respectively.
[161] *McKennitt* (n 24).
[162] *Rocknroll v News Group Newspapers Ltd* [2013] EWHC 24 (Ch).
[163] *Rocknroll* (n 162) [12].
[164] See 5.133–5.138.
[165] As discussed in 5.46.

or objectively trivial.[166] But it may depend upon where and in what circumstances the information was imparted or acquired.[167]

### Anonymized information and identifying information

**5.55** *Anonymized information* The authorities in breach of confidence have so far held that if information is anonymized, so that the identity of the person who is the subject of that information cannot be detected, disclosure will not amount to an infringement of the subject's rights. The Court of Appeal has accordingly held that disclosure by pharmacists of information contained in anonymized patients' prescription forms without patients' consent was not a breach of confidence or of privacy.[168] This is clearly also the case in data protection law, the ambit of which is expressly limited to information relating to a living individual.[169] To date, the same approach has been applied in misuse of private information claims.[170]

**5.56** A more difficult situation arises where anonymized information is published, but there is a risk of 'jigsaw' identification because of information already known to some people or already in the public domain.[171] The development of the law of privacy has led to an increase in publications in which private information is disclosed, but the person to whom it relates is not named or otherwise identified. So, for example, a newspaper published allegations that a named woman had had an affair with a Premier League footballer, but the player was not named.[172] Where the claimant is able to show that the publication in fact made him or her identifiable to some, despite any efforts by the defendant to avoid this, such as pixelation of an image,[173] it could be held that any requirement of identifiability would be satisfied.[174] This would be consistent with the position in the law of defamation.[175]

**5.57** A further scenario is that a claimant may become identifiable at a later time, as a result of information acquired, by a later publication or otherwise, after the

---

166 See 5.154–5.158.

167 *McKennitt* (n 24) [18]–[22]; *Lord Browne* (n 54) [29].

168 *Source Informatics* (n 102). Also *Common Services Agency v Scottish Information Commissioner* [2008] UKHL 47, [2008] 1 WLR 1550, where the issue was whether disclosure of 'barnardised' medical data would infringe patients' rights. The case was argued and decided on the footing that anonymization would achieve this.

169 s 1 DPA.

170 The same approach has been taken in New Zealand: *Andrews v Television NZ Ltd* [2009] 1 NZLR 220 (HC) [52]–[60].

171 *JIH v News Group Newspapers Ltd* [2011] EWCA Civ 42, [2011] 1 WLR 1645 [40].

172 *CTB* (n 124). Also *NEJ* (n 124).

173 See the New Zealand case of *Andrews* (n 170).

174 In *Varapnickaitė-Mazylienė v Lithuania* (n 105), the ECtHR held that Art 8 was not violated by publication of an article that included medical information about the applicant but which did not identify the applicant or her son. Judges Pinto de Albuquerque and Keller dissented on the basis that, in their opinion, there was a risk of 'jigsaw' identification based on information that the applicant had already disclosed to the public.

175 See generally Mullis and Parkes (n 95) paras 7.2–7.4. Note that, in the context of defamation, one exception to the general rule is where a person is wrongly identified as the subject of a statement because he or she is a 'look-alike': *O'Shea v MGN Ltd* [2001] EMLR 40, QB.

contested disclosure. Again, the position in defamation indicates an appropriate approach: a defendant will be liable if it is responsible for both the original disclosure and publication of the additional information that enabled identification.[176]

There may be situations where an exception to any requirement of identifiability **5.58** would be appropriate. In *R v Broadcasting Standards Commission, ex p BBC*, Lord Mustill said that 'an infringement of privacy is an affront to the personality, which is damaged both by the violation and by the demonstration that personal space is not inviolate'.[177] Neither aspect of the 'affront' so described is obviously dependent on the communication to a third person of the identity of the individual whose privacy has been violated. It might therefore be open to a court to hold that identification is not necessary in situations where the affront suffered does not depend on the observer's ability to identify the person. For example, dissemination of an image showing intimate body parts would likely be regarded as inherently humiliating or affronting.[178]

*The preservation of anonymity* Linked with the issue of whether the disclosure of **5.59** anonymous information can amount to a breach of confidence or misuse of private information[179] is that of whether matter which serves to identify a person, and thus to connect him or her with other facts or events, can itself be confidential or private. Can the law of confidence or privacy protect anonymity? The authorities make clear that it can, depending mainly on the nature of the other information to which identification would point.

*Confidentiality* The law of confidence can in principle be used to prevent the **5.60** disclosure of the private, undisclosed identity of those who perform public acts or services, or have become involved in public events, even if those acts reflect well on the person concerned. As Lord Keith observed in *Spycatcher*:

> The anonymous donor of a very large sum to a very worthy cause has his own reasons for wishing to remain anonymous, which are unlikely to be discreditable. He should surely be in a position to restrain disclosure in breach of confidence of his identity in connection with the donation.[180]

*Risk of harm* The Australian case of *G v Day* is an example of a class of case in **5.61** which this principle has been used to prevent the disclosure of information about an individual's appearance or identity where such disclosure, coupled with other information, might lead to him or her being put at risk of physical harm.[181] In *G v Day*, a police informant, who feared for his personal safety if he was publicly

---

[176] Whether because the defendant itself made both publications, or can be said to have somehow brought them about.
[177] *R v Broadcasting Standards Commission, ex p BBC* [2001] QB 885, CA [48].
[178] The effect of disclosure is discussed further at 5.104–5.113.
[179] Discussed at 5.55–5.58.
[180] *Attorney General v Observer Ltd* [1990] 1 AC 109, HL, 256.
[181] *G v Day* [1982] 1 NSWLR 24, SC.

identified as such, was granted an injunction restraining the media from publishing this information.[182]

**5.62** *Post-HRA authority* In *Venables v News Group Newspapers Ltd*, Butler-Sloss P granted an injunction *contra mundum* preventing publication of information about the appearance, the new identities, or the whereabouts of the now adult murderers of James Bulger, such was the evidence of the threat to their safety.[183] In *Green Corns Ltd v Claverley Group Ltd*, an injunction was granted to restrain publication of information that would identify troubled youths who were being housed by a charity.[184] The risk of harm to the clients was a significant factor in the decision.

**5.63** It is to be supposed, however, that a causal connection between the publication complained of and any harm suffered by the claimant would also be necessary to found an award of damages.[185] The Youth Justice and Criminal Evidence Act 1999, s 46 gives the court power to make a 'reporting direction' restricting reports that identify an adult as a witness in criminal proceedings.[186] There is automatic anonymity for alleged victims of sexual crimes.[187]

**5.64** *Limitations* In *Author of a Blog v Times Newspapers Ltd*, the Court held that the identity of a police officer who was the author of a publicly accessible blog was not confidential, and nor did he have a reasonable expectation of privacy.[188] It should be noted, however, that the premise for this decision, that the author's identity could be ascertained from public sources, later proved to be false; the journalist had identified him from a hacked email account.[189]

**5.65** **Appearance** The law of breach of confidence has for a long time been deployed to prevent unauthorized disclosure of information about a person's appearance, at least in a particular place or at a particular time. Information

---

[182] Also *Nicholls* (n 157); *Swinney v Chief Constable of Northumbria Police Force* [1997] QB 464, CA.

[183] *Venables* (n 107). In *West v BBC* (HC, 10 June 2002), the Court held that *Venables* required the claimant to establish 'the existence of a real and immediate risk' of infringement of his rights under Arts 2 or 3. Similar *contra mundum* orders were made in *X, A Woman Formerly known as Mary Bell v SO* [2003] EWHC 1101 (Fam), [2003] EMLR 37; *Carr v News Group Newspapers Ltd* [2005] EWHC 971 (QB).

[184] *Green Corns* (n 86).

[185] See 12.80 *et seq* on damages generally.

[186] *Family of Derek Bennett v Officers 'A' and 'B'* [2004] EWCA Civ 1439, [2005] UKHRR 44; *R v Lord Saville of Newdigate, ex p B (No 2)* [2000] 1 WLR 1855, CA; *Re ITN* [2013] EWCA Crim 773, [2014] 1 WLR 199.

[187] Sexual Offences (Amendment) Act 1992, s 1.

[188] *Author of a Blog v Times Newspapers Ltd* [2009] EWHC 1358 (QB), [2009] EMLR 22. Also *BBC v HarperCollins Publishers Ltd* [2010] EWHC 2424 (Ch), [2011] EMLR 6, where an application for an interim injunction preventing publication of the identity of an anonymous television character failed because the information had lost its confidential nature.

[189] L O'Carroll, 'Leveson attacks "utterly misleading" Times court statement' *The Guardian* (London, 15 March 2012), available at <http://www.theguardian.com/media/2012/mar/15/leveson-attacks-times-court-statement>.

about a person's appearance may also engage Article 8, for appearance is held to be a unique and primary attribute of one's personhood.[190] Such claims have primarily arisen in relation to photographs, which are discussed in greater detail below.[191]

**Political opinions**    Political opinions are one of the kinds of information clas-    **5.66**
sified as 'sensitive personal data' by s 2 DPA. Often, such opinions will be made public by the individual concerned, and for that reason it may be argued that an individual does not enjoy any reasonable expectation of privacy in respect of them.[192] Where personal data is collected and retained by public authorities, how-ever, Article 8 will be engaged.[193] Such collection and retention in retrievable form is an interference with Article 8 which must be prescribed by law and proportionate to the legitimate aim pursued.[194]

If political opinions are expressed only privately they may well enjoy protection. In    **5.67**
the *HRH Prince of Wales* case, the fact that the claimant's journals disclosed poten-tially controversial expressions of political views by the heir to the throne was held by the Court of Appeal to be a matter worthy of consideration at the 'balancing' stage of the analysis, rather than in considering the question whether he enjoyed a reasonable expectation of privacy.[195]

### Information about knowledge of or involvement in crime

*Confidentiality*    Up to the point that matters have been aired in open court,[196]    **5.68**
the court has found that under certain circumstances a person is entitled to keep confidential his knowledge of or involvement in criminal or alleged crimi-nal conduct. In *Marcel v Commissioner of Police of the Metropolis*, Sir Nicholas Browne-Wilkinson V-C held that 'private information obtained under com-pulsory powers cannot be used for purposes other than those for which the powers were conferred'.[197] This principle also applies if the relevant information

---

[190] *Weller* (n 143) [152]; *Reklos v Greece* App no 1234/05 (ECtHR, 15 January 2009), [2009] EMLR 16 [40]; *von Hannover (No 2)* (n 15) [96]; *Lillo-Stenberg v Norway* (n 133) [26].

[191] See 5.85–5.91.

[192] This was the view of the Divisional Court in *Catt v Commissioner of Police of the Metropolis* [2012] EWHC 1471 (Admin), [2012] HRLR 23 where Gross LJ observed at [36] that 'the essential nature of such activity is that it is of a public nature. Indeed, its very object is to make others aware of his views and the causes to which he lends his support.' Also [69] (Irwin J). But see nn 193, 194. For the effect of making information public see also 11.21–11.23, 11.63.

[193] *R (Catt) v Association of Chief Police Officers of England, Wales and Northern Ireland* [2013] EWCA Civ 192, [2013] 1 WLR 3305 [30]–[31], reversing *Catt* (n 192).

[194] *R (Catt) v Association of Chief Police Officers of England, Wales and Northern Ireland* [2015] UKSC 9, [2015] AC 1065, reversing the Court of Appeal (n 193) on the issue of whether the interference was justified.

[195] *HRH Prince of Wales* (n 36) [45]. At the 'balancing' stage, this factor was held to make only a 'minimal' contribution to providing the public with information on the claimant's political conduct: [72].

[196] See 5.133–5.138.

[197] *Marcel v Commissioner of Police of the Metropolis* [1992] Ch 225, CA, 237.

is not in fact obtained by the use of compulsory powers, but under the threat of them.[198]

**5.69** Information imparted in the context of criminal investigation or proceedings may be confidential even if no compulsion has been used or threatened to obtain it. There is substantial public interest in an accused person being able to make full disclosure in a statement to the police without fear of it being used for extraneous purposes.[199] In *Bunn v BBC*, Lightman J held that the statement of an accused under caution was given subject to an obligation of confidence binding on the police and all those into whose hands it subsequently fell, which precluded its use for any purpose save those for which it was provided.[200]

**5.70** 'Unused' prosecution material disclosed to criminal defendants is treated as confidential.[201] In *Taylor v Director of the Serious Fraud Office*, the House of Lords held that such 'unused' material was subject to an implied undertaking at common law not to use it for collateral purposes.[202] Their Lordships observed that such an undertaking was necessary in order to ensure that the privacy and confidentiality of those who made (and those who were mentioned in) statements as a result of a criminal investigation was not invaded any more than was absolutely necessary for the purposes of justice.[203] Such information has now been given statutory protection as 'confidential'.[204]

**5.71** As for 'used' prosecution material, there is no such statutory designation.[205] The Court of Appeal has held, in *Mahon v Rahn*, that there is no implied undertaking at common law.[206] That decision, however, predated *Taylor* and the reasoning of the House of Lords in the later case arguably supports the conclusion that such material is to be treated as confidential at common law and subject to an implied undertaking.[207]

**5.72** *Privacy* Among the categories of 'sensitive personal data' specified in s 2 DPA is information relating to the data subject's 'commission or alleged commission . . . of

---

[198] *Re Barlow Clowes Gilt Managers Ltd* [1992] Ch 208, Ch, 217.

[199] *Tchenguiz v Director of the Serious Fraud Office* [2014] EWHC 4199 (Comm) [3], [18].

[200] *Bunn v BBC* [1998] 3 All ER 552, Ch. Also *Hellewell v Chief Constable of Derbyshire* [1995] 1 WLR 804, QB which concerned an attempt to restrain use of a 'mugshot' photograph that the police provided to shopkeepers to try to combat shoplifting.

[201] Criminal Procedure and Investigations Act 1996, s 17; 5.135.

[202] *Taylor v Director of the Serious Fraud Office* [1999] 2 AC 177, HL.

[203] *Taylor* (n 202) 210–12, 220. But see n 205.

[204] Criminal Procedure and Investigations Act 1996, s 17.

[205] When proposing protection for unused material under the Criminal Procedure and Investigations Bill, the government expressed the view that it would be inappropriate to impose a like statutory duty for material relied on by the prosecution.

[206] *Mahon v Rahn* [1998] QB 424, CA. Also *Mahon v Rahn (No 2)* [2000] 1 WLR 2150, CA [187].

[207] In *Taylor* (n 202) the House of Lords did not rule on the existence or otherwise of an implied undertaking in respect of used material, but expressed its disapproval of the line of reasoning which led the Court of Appeal in *Mahon (No 2)* (n 206) to find there was no such undertaking.

any offence' and as to 'any proceedings for any offence committed or alleged to have been committed by him, the disposal of such proceedings, or the sentence of any court to such proceedings'.[208] There are statutory restrictions on the publication of some information (for instance, the names of alleged rape victims) and some proceedings (for instance, those involving children in the Family Division).[209]

*Convictions and acquittals*   The notion that convictions could be confidential was **5.73** described by Sir Richard Scott V-C as 'absurd'.[210] The post-HRA authorities make clear that, in general, the principle of open justice permits the free reporting of criminal trials and the proper identification of those who have been convicted and sentenced, and also those who have been acquitted.[211] Once information has been disclosed in public (for instance, in open court[212]) the position appears to be that there is no reasonable expectation of privacy, unless a conviction is spent or, possibly, the information has otherwise receded in to the past.[213] There is, however, jurisdiction, exercisable in the High Court, to grant injunctive relief to prohibit publication of the identities of individuals accused and convicted of criminal offences.[214]

In both *X (A Woman Formerly known as Mary Bell) v SO*[215] and *R (Ellis) v Chief* **5.74** *Constable of Essex Police*[216] the Court proceeded on the assumption that information about criminal convictions is capable of protection as private. It may be that the better view is that while in general criminal convictions are not confidential or private there will be rare cases where additional circumstances or features of a case require them to be so. For instance, the injunction granted in the *Mary Bell* case protected the identity of the claimant in order to protect the Article 8 rights of her child.[217]

---

[208] s 2(g)–(h) DPA; *R (Ellis) v Chief Constable of Essex Police* [2003] EWHC 1321 (Admin), [2003] 2 FLR 566; *Green Corns* (n 86).

[209] Children Act 1989, s 97.

[210] *Elliott v Chief Constable of Wiltshire* (Ch, 20 November 1996) striking out a confidence claim based on a police officer's disclosure of such convictions; *R v Chief Constable of the North Wales Police, ex p Thorpe* [1999] QB 396, CA, where the applicants' criminal convictions were held to be in the public domain; compare *R v A Police Authority, ex p LM* (HC, 6 September 1999) in which a decision by a police authority to disclose past unproven allegations of sex abuse about the applicant was held to have been unlawful.

[211] *Re Guardian News and Media* (n 94); *PNM* (n 94). For a case that appeared to proceed on the basis that details of a violent assault were confidential: *Campbell v Frisbee* [2002] EWCA Civ 1374, [2003] EMLR 3 [7].

[212] See 5.133–5.138 for matters that have been revealed in open court.

[213] See further 11.59 (passage of time) and, in the public law context *R (T) v Chief Constable of Greater Manchester Police* (n 16).

[214] *Re S (A Child)* (n 51); *Re W* (n 46); *Re Trinity Mirror plc (A intervening)* [2008] EWCA Crim 50, [2008] QB 770.

[215] *X, A Woman Formerly known as Mary Bell* (n 183).

[216] *Ellis* (n 208).

[217] *X, A Woman Formerly known as Mary Bell* (n 183). Also *Re W* (n 46). The Court of Appeal in *Re Trinity Mirror* (n 214) [33] acknowledged the sad truth that a person's criminal activities can bring 'misery, shame, and disadvantage' to his or her innocent children, parents, or partner. However, the Court went on to say, 'if the court were to uphold this ruling so as to protect the rights of the defendant's children under Article 8, it would be countenancing a substantial erosion of the

**5.75** *Arrest and suspicion*    At least in the absence of a warrant, an arrest is not a 'judicial' fact and, accordingly, it should not be assumed that an arrest is of so public a nature as a conviction.[218] The question of whether and, if so, when information about a person's arrest will be private has attracted considerable debate.[219] Naming a person who has been arrested may encourage more victims or witnesses to come forward, furthering law enforcement objectives. On the other hand, naming a suspect may cause irreparable damage to the reputation and personal integrity[220] of a person who may not ultimately be charged and who is, in fact, innocent. Similarly, it might give rise to a risk of that person suffering physical harm.

**5.76** In *Re Guardian News and Media Ltd*, the Supreme Court rejected the argument that the fact that persons had been the subject of directions under terrorism law should not be published because, no matter how accurate the reporting of the true facts, members of the public would proceed on the basis that those subject to the orders were in fact terrorists.[221] The Court held that members of the public are 'more than capable of drawing a distinction between mere suspicion and sufficient evidence to prove guilt'.[222] The same approach was applied in *PNM v Times Newspapers Ltd*, where the claimant had been arrested and investigated on suspicion of serious child sex offences but ultimately no charges were laid.[223] In those circumstances, the claimant did not have the benefit of an acquittal to clear his name.

**5.77** The present approach recognizes that whether the fact of arrest is private in a particular case is a highly fact-sensitive question of fact and degree, and a key consideration will be the circumstances, public or otherwise, of arrest.[224] The decision of the ECtHR in *Axel Springer AG v Germany* indicates that, at least where an arrest takes place in public, publication of the circumstances of, and events following, an arrest will not be considered information about private life.[225] In *Hannon v News Group Newspapers Ltd*, Mann J thought a 'potentially key distinction' between two

principle of open justice, to the overwhelming disadvantage of public confidence in the criminal justice system, the free reporting of criminal trials and the proper identification of those convicted and sentenced in them'.

[218] *Hannon v News Group Newspapers Ltd* [2014] EWHC 1580 (Ch), [2015] EMLR 1 [87].

[219] Law Commission, *Contempt of Court: A Consultation Paper* (Law Com CP No 209, 2012); Information Commissioner's Office, *The Information Commissioner's response to the Law Commission's consultation on 'Contempt of Court'* (2013); Treacy LJ and Tugendhat J et al, *Contempt of Court: A Judicial Response to Law Commission Consultation Paper No 209* (2013).

[220] See 5.26.

[221] *Re Guardian News and Media* (n 94). The identities of persons who are subject to control orders which have been the subject of legal proceedings may nonetheless be withheld from the public where identification would infringe privacy and pose a risk of physical harm: *Secretary of State for the Home Dept v AP (No 2)* [2010] UKSC 26, [2010] 1 WLR 1652.

[222] *Re Guardian News and Media* (n 94) [60], although acknowledging that some readers would draw the unjustified inference of guilt.

[223] *PNM* (n 94).

[224] *Hannon* (n 218) [96]; *Axel Springer AG v Germany* (2012) 55 EHRR 6, para 108. As to the place of arrest, see 5.130.

[225] *Axel Springer* (n 224) para 108.

claimants' cases was that, whereas one had been arrested in an aircraft cockpit and taken from it in an unmarked car, the other had been escorted from the cabin of the airplane by police and arrested.[226]

*Cautions and warnings*   The starting point is that a caution or warning is private. **5.78** In the public law case of *R (T) v Chief Constable of Greater Manchester Police*, the Supreme Court held that the claimants' Article 8 rights were infringed by disclosure by the state of the details of past cautions or warnings.[227] Lord Wilson said:

> My receipt of a caution, whenever received, is a sensitive, certainly embarrassing and probably shameful, part of my history, which may have profound detrimental effects on my aspirations for a career; and the unchallengeable fact that I did commit the offence for which I was cautioned makes it no less sensitive but, on the contrary, more sensitive.[228]

### Financial and business information

*Confidentiality*   Financial and business information is commonly protected **5.79** in commercial confidence cases, subject always to the doctrine of restraint of trade.[229] Communications between husband and wife in relation to their business affairs were expressly recognized as confidential in the *Argyll* case.[230] In *John Reid Enterprises Ltd v Pell*, information about Elton John's financial arrangements was treated as confidential.[231] The Court of Appeal in *McKennitt v Ash* upheld the finding of the judge below that information about the singer claimant's contract was imparted under an obligation of confidence.[232]

*Privacy*   Although first impressions may be that business and commercial activi- **5.80** ties are outside Article 8, a reasonable expectation of privacy may exist in relation to information about a person's financial or professional affairs.[233] The Court of Appeal has held family financial affairs to be private.[234] In *Cooper v Turrell*, information obtained by covertly recording a conversation between directors regarding business affairs and legal advice was held to be private.[235]

---

[226] *Hannon* (n 218) [101].
[227] *R (T) v Chief Constable of Greater Manchester Police* (n 16).
[228] *R (T) v Chief Constable of Greater Manchester Police* (n 16) [17].
[229] eg *Cream Holdings Ltd* (n 55); *Northern Rock plc v Financial Times Ltd* [2007] EWHC 2677 (QB); for restraint of trade see 4.29, 4.107.
[230] *Argyll* (n 102) 329–30.
[231] *John Reid Enterprises Ltd v Pell* [1999] EMLR 675, Ch. Also *Lord Levy v Times Newspapers Ltd* (HC, 23 June 2000), and CPR 39.2(3)(c) which identifies 'personal financial matters' as confidential information that may justify a hearing in private.
[232] *McKennitt* (n 24) [24]. Also *Viagogo* (n 96).
[233] *Lord Browne* (n 54) [34]; *Imerman* (n 37); *Ambrosiadou v Coward* [2010] EWCA Civ 1456 [13]–[14]; *Ambrosiadou v Coward* [2011] EWCA Civ 409, [2011] EMLR 21. For the position in respect of tax information: *Inland Revenue Commissioners v National Federation of Self Employed and Small Businesses Ltd* [1982] AC 617, HL, 650–1; *Revenue and Customs Commissioners v Banerjee* [2009] EWHC 1229 (Ch), [2009] 3 All ER 930 [13].
[234] *Lykiardopulo v Lykiardopulo* [2010] EWCA Civ 1315, [2011] 1 FLR 1427.
[235] *Cooper* (n 111).

**5.81** The collection of data relating to a named individual's personal income, with a view to communicating this to third parties, is within the scope of Article 8. It does not matter whether or not the information is sensitive or whether any disadvantage is caused by disclosure.[236] The situation may, however, be different in respect of public figures.[237] In the case of *Fressoz v France*, the ECtHR held that information relating to the salaries of public figures did not form part of their private lives.[238]

**5.82** *Limitations*  In *Lord Browne*, the Court held that it was not for the court to help protect the privacy of a senior executive in relation to the use of corporate information and resources when the effect would be to keep such allegations from those who might ordinarily be expected to exercise supervision.[239] As well, financial affairs raised in open court may no longer be private.[240]

**5.83** **Collections of personal information**  In *Green Corns v Claverley Group*, Tugendhat J held that a person may be entitled to assert confidentiality in a collection of personal information, even if some elements of the combination were, to some degree, in the public domain.[241] Adding to an individual's home address the information that he or she is a child and has a history of mental illness, sexual abuse, and involvement in the commission of crime created a highly sensitive combination to which the court should afford protection.[242]

### (4) The Form in which the Information is Kept

#### (a) Introduction

**5.84** In some authorities the principal focus of the court has been on the form or repository of the information as one likely to contain confidential or private information, rather than on the specifics of the information it actually contains. It has been held that the form in which information is kept may suffice to give rise to a reasonable expectation of privacy.[243] Personal diaries, private correspondence, and conversations on the telephone have all been recognized as forms of information likely to be private.[244] Photographs and information stored on a computer or mobile phone will also attract particular scrutiny.

---

[236] Case C-465/00 *Rechnungshof v Osterreichischer Rundfunk* [2003] ECR I-4989, paras 73–5.

[237] The position of public figures generally is discussed at 5.114–5.120.

[238] *Fressoz v France* (2001) 31 EHRR 2. The reach of the principle is unclear. It may relate solely to publicly funded salaries. The information was in any event required by French law to be available to the public, in one form.

[239] *Lord Browne* (n 54) [52].

[240] *Crossley v Newsquest (Midlands South) Ltd* [2008] EWHC 3054 (QB) [58]–[59]. Also *Revenue and Customs Commissioners v Banerjee* (n 233). For further discussion of disclosure of private matters in open court see 5.133–5.138.

[241] *Green Corns* (n 86).

[242] *Green Corns* (n 86) [81], cf *Mills* (n 153).

[243] *Douglas* (n 24) passage quoted at 5.28.

[244] For discussion of the authorities on the significance of the form in which information is kept in breach of confidence see 4.76–4.79.

## (b) Photographs

**Confidentiality**   In the nineteenth century, the law of breach of confidence was   **5.85**
used to prevent unauthorized publication of etchings created by Queen Victoria
and Prince Albert featuring their children's appearances and other images of private and domestic life,[245] and of portrait photographs commissioned for private
use. The rationale of these cases is arguably that an individual's appearance or
image in a private place is confidential and so he or she should be able to control
how it is used.[246]

**Privacy**   The law of misuse of private information has developed rapidly in respect   **5.86**
of the publication of photographs, which can be said to contain information about
an individual's appearance[247] or conduct. Article 8 rights are particularly likely
to be engaged by publication of or a threat to publish photographs,[248] which 'can
be much more intrusive and informative than words'.[249] In *Douglas v Hello! Ltd*,
the Court of Appeal said, in the context of surreptitiously taken photographs at a
wedding:

> Special considerations attach to photographs in the field of privacy. They are not
> merely a method of conveying information that is an alternative to verbal descrip-
> tion. They enable the person viewing the photograph to act as a spectator, in some
> circumstances voyeur would be the more appropriate noun, of whatever it is that
> the photograph depicts. As a means of invading privacy, a photograph is particu-
> larly intrusive. This is quite apart from the fact that the camera, and the telephoto
> lens, can give access to the viewer of the photograph to scenes where those pho-
> tographed could reasonably expect that their appearances or actions would not be
> brought to the notice of the public.[250]

The same underlying principles and concerns apply, probably even more strongly,
to video recordings.[251]

The ECtHR's first *von Hannover* decision set a very low threshold, finding that pho-   **5.87**
tographs of quite ordinary events in a person's life may engage Article 8.[252] Later
decisions of the ECtHR and the domestic courts indicate, however, that whether
there is a reasonable expectation of privacy will depend on the circumstances,[253]

---

[245] *Prince Albert v Strange* (1849) 1 Mac & G 25, 41 ER 1171; (1849) 2 De Gex & Sm 652, 64 ER
293, CA and commentary thereon in *Argyll* (n 102) 318–19.

[246] See 5.53–5.54 addressing the issue of information concerning private acts.

[247] See 5.65.

[248] *Rocknroll* (n 162) [28].

[249] *Terry* (n 98) [55]. Also *Ferdinand* (n 121) [101]; *Contostavlos* (n 120) [25]; *Weller* (n 143) [63].

[250] *Douglas* (n 24) [84]. This builds upon a line of confidentiality jurisprudence starting with the
dicta of Laws J in *Hellewell* (n 200).

[251] *Mosley* (n 100) concerned information that had been recorded on a video camera, as did
*Contostavlos* (n 120).

[252] *von Hannover* (n 15).

[253] Compare *Douglas* (n 2) with *Lillo-Stenberg* (n 133) where the ECtHR held there was no
reasonable expectation of privacy in respect of photographs of parts of a wedding that took place
in public view.

including the nature of the activity depicted in the images.²⁵⁴ In *Campbell*, Baroness Hale doubted that a photograph of the claimant going out for a pint of milk would engage Article 8.²⁵⁵

**5.88**  Although there is no hard-and-fast line to be drawn between photographs taken of a claimant in a public place and in a private place,²⁵⁶ the claimant's location is another significant factor in determining whether he or she has a reasonable expectation he or she will not be photographed, or that the resulting images will not be published. It is also relevant whether a photographer has 'targeted' the individual whose image has been taken in a public place.²⁵⁷ In *Campbell*, Lord Hope drew a distinction between showing a scene of a street where a passer-by may have his or her photograph published by chance, which would not ordinarily engage Article 8, and photographs taken in public deliberately, in secret and with a view to publication.²⁵⁸

**5.89**  **Examples of images protected**  Injunctions have been granted in confidence or misuse of private information to prevent the publication of family photographs of an actress and her young children;²⁵⁹ sexually explicit photographs and video of pop singers;²⁶⁰ unauthorized photographs of a television actress walking around topless in a hotel garden;²⁶¹ photographs taken of a television presenter in a brothel;²⁶² and CCTV images of a couple having sex in a nightclub.²⁶³ It has been held to be a misuse of private information to publish photographs of a model leaving a Narcotics Anonymous meeting;²⁶⁴ photographs and a video of the head of Formula 1 participating in sadomasochistic sex sessions;²⁶⁵ and banal photographs of young children in public places.²⁶⁶

---

²⁵⁴ Discussed at 5.36 *et seq.*
²⁵⁵ *Campbell* (n 1) [154]. As to triviality, see 5.154–5.158.
²⁵⁶ See 5.130–5.131.
²⁵⁷ *Murray* (n 41) [57].
²⁵⁸ *Campbell* (n 1) [122]–[123] (Lord Hope). Although note the decision of the Supreme Court of Canada in *Aubry v Les Éditions Vice-Versa Inc* [1998] 1 SCR 591 (referred to by Lord Hope), in which it was held that the claimant was entitled to restrain the publication of a photograph of her sitting on the steps of a public library. See also *Murray* (n 41) [50]; *Weller* (n 143) [171].
²⁵⁹ *W v W* (HC, 22 February 2001). Also *AMP v Persons Unknown* (n 145) which involved photographs of family and friends, amongst other things.
²⁶⁰ *A v B* (QBD, 2 March 2001); *Contostavlos* (n 120); *AMP v Persons Unknown* (n 145); *ABK v KDT* [2013] EWHC 1192 (QB).
²⁶¹ *Holden v Express Newspapers Ltd* (QB, 7 June 2001).
²⁶² *Theakston* (n 122).
²⁶³ *Jagger v Darling* [2005] EWHC 683 (Ch). Bell J granted an injunction holding that Ms Jagger, who was filmed on CCTV having sex, had a reasonable expectation of privacy and there was no proper basis to sell the footage to a tabloid newspaper.
²⁶⁴ *Campbell* (n 1).
²⁶⁵ *Mosley* (n 100).
²⁶⁶ *AAA* (n 143); *Weller* (n 143); *Murray* (n 41) (where strike out of such a claim was refused); *Re Stedman* (n 142); *Re A* (Fam, 15/16 June 2001).

**Examples of images not protected**  By contrast, Sir Elton John failed in an  **5.90**
attempt to obtain an injunction in 2006 to restrain publication of photographs
of him taken in the street outside his home.[267] In *Trimingham*, it was held that a
photograph showing the claimant on the day of her civil partnership did not communicate any significant information in respect of which there was a reasonable
expectation of privacy.[268] The claimant had previously used a cropped version of
the image as her Facebook profile picture and had also given it to a journalist to
illustrate an article related to her work.

**Mere taking or retention of a photograph or recording**  In *Mosley v News Group*,  **5.91**
Eady J considered that the very fact of clandestine recording may be regarded as
an unacceptable infringement of Article 8 rights.[269] It is, however, the public disclosure or misuse of images that will, in most media cases, engage Article 8. In the
public law case of *R (C) v Commissioner of Police of the Metropolis*, the long-term
retention of photographs by the police, without further use, was held to engage
Article 8.[270]

### (c) Correspondence

**Confidentiality**  The court has protected the confidentiality of private corre-  **5.92**
spondence since at least the late eighteenth century.[271] It is clearly established that,
as a starting point, the contents of private letters are to be regarded as subject to
a duty of confidentiality owed by the recipient to the writer.[272] Internal memoranda have also been considered confidential in two cases: in the first a memorandum written by a journalist to her editor,[273] in the second an internal company
memorandum.[274]

**Privacy**  Correspondence is explicitly protected by Article 8. In *Maccaba v*  **5.93**
*Lichtenstein*, Gray J accepted that as a starting point 'correspondence between
A and B on private matters such as their feelings for each other would be a prime
candidate for protection'.[275] In *Copland v UK*, the ECtHR considered that emails
(including personal email use at work) were included within private life for the
purpose of Article 8.[276] Similarly, in *Imerman v Tchenguiz*, the Court of Appeal

---

[267] *John v Associated Newspapers Ltd* [2006] EWHC 1611 (QB), [2006] EMLR 27.
[268] *Trimingham* (n 61).
[269] *Mosley* (n 100) [17]. This issue is discussed further at 10.77 *et seq.*
[270] *R (C) v Commissioner of Police of the Metropolis (Liberty intervening)* [2012] EWHC 1681 (Admin), [2012] 1 WLR 3007. See also *Reklos v Greece* (n 190), where the taking of the photo was considered to be an interference: see 5.124.
[271] *Thompson v Stanhope* (1774) Amb 737, 27 ER 476.
[272] *Philip v Pennell* [1907] 2 Ch 577, Ch; *Haig v Aitken* [2001] Ch 110, Ch.
[273] *Beloff v Pressdram Ltd* [1973] 1 All ER 241, Ch.
[274] *Lion Laboratories Ltd v Evans* [1985] QB 526, CA.
[275] *Maccaba v Lichtenstein* [2004] EWHC 1579 (QB), [2005] EMLR 6 [4]. Also *McKennitt* (n 24) [76].
[276] *Copland v UK* (2007) 45 EHRR 37.

held that emails concerned with an individual's private life, including his personal financial and business affairs, were within the scope of Article 8.[277] In principle, text messages are another example of 'correspondence' within Article 8.[278]

**5.94** It has, however, been suggested that correspondence is not categorically entitled to protection nor its contents 'inherently private'.[279] The nature of the information contained in the correspondence will accordingly be relevant.[280]

### (d) Telephone conversations

**5.95** **Confidentiality** In *Malone v Metropolitan Police Commissioner*, Sir Robert Megarry V-C thought that a telephone user takes 'such risks of being overheard as are inherent in the system'. He could not see how a duty of confidence was imposed on those who overheard a telephone conversation 'whether by tapping or otherwise'.[281] In the *Francome* case, however, Sir John Donaldson MR described this as a 'surprising proposition' and restrained the publication of tapped telephone conversations between a jockey and his wife.[282]

**5.96** **Privacy** The ECtHR has held that telephone conversations, although not expressly included in Article 8, are within the scope of 'correspondence' and 'private life'.[283] It has held telephone-tapping of private conversations to infringe Article 8.[284] In *D v L*, the respondent made secret recordings of her conversations, in person rather than over the telephone, with the appellant.[285] Lord Phillips MR observed that, 'on the face of it, publication of a covert tape recording of a private conversation involves a breach of confidence'.[286] It is suggested that it would likewise involve a misuse of private information.

### (e) Voicemail

**5.97** **Phone hacking** The phone hacking scandal of 2006 onwards led to a large number of claims for breach of confidence and misuse of private information against News Group Newspapers Ltd, the publisher of the now-defunct *News of the World*.[287] It was alleged that the publisher's employees or agents had gained unauthorized access to

---

[277] *Imerman* (n 37) [76]–[77].

[278] *Ferdinand* (n 121) [55]; *ABK* (n 260), which involved photos sent by text message.

[279] *Abbey* (n 36) [37]–[39].

[280] See N A Moreham, 'Beyond Information: Physical Privacy in English Law' (2014)] 73 CLJ 350, 372.

[281] *Malone v Metropolitan Police Commissioner* [1979] Ch 344, Ch 376.

[282] *Francome v Mirror Group Newspapers Ltd* [1984] 1 WLR 892, CA, 895. It might be that the difference in view was due to developing expectations of telephone users; there was a time when overhearing was not unusual given party lines and crossed wires.

[283] *Drakšas v Lithuania* App no 36662/04 (ECtHR, 31 July 2012) para 52.

[284] *Halford v UK* (1997) 24 EHRR 523; *Ludi v Switzerland* (1992) 15 EHRR 173; *Copland* (n 276). In the context of interference with prisoners' rights to use the telephone, see *R (Taylor) v Governor of HM Prison Risley* [2004] EWHC 2654 (Admin).

[285] *D v L* [2003] EWCA Civ 1169, [2004] EMLR 1.

[286] *D v L* (n 285) [34].

[287] According to media reporting, there were 24 claims pending when News Group Newspapers made its first admissions of liability on 8 April 2011: J Robinson, 'News of the World phone hacking

the voicemail inboxes of individuals' mobile phones and, in some cases, that this had enabled publication of stories about the private lives of the claimants or others. None of the claims against News Group Newspapers Ltd for phone-hacking ever came to trial but it has been held that where a person's voicemail messages are intercepted, 'there must be a strong presumption that at least some of the information contained in the messages will be confidential',[288] although 'there will often be some messages which contain confidential information and some which do not'.[289] It can be inferred from this that the fact that the information was stored on a private voicemail system, and was obtained by hacking, is not enough on its own to establish confidentiality.[290]

Subsequent to the News Group cases, similar claims were made against MGN Ltd, **5.98** publisher of the *Mirror* titles. The publisher's application to strike out or for summary judgment on some claims was dismissed.[291] A number of cases were selected for trial as test cases,[292] and determined in May 2015, when Mann J awarded total of £1.2 million to eight claimants.[293] Phone hacking may also give rise to criminal liability.[294]

### (f) *Personal diaries and journals*

**Confidentiality**   In *Spycatcher*, one of the paradigms used by Lord Goff to illus-   **5.99** trate when the law would impose a duty of confidence on a third-party recipient of confidential information was 'where an obviously confidential document, such as a private diary, is dropped in a public place, and is then picked up by a passer-by'.[295] In the *HRH Prince of Wales* case, the Court of Appeal said this of the confidentiality of the Prince's travel journals:

> They were set out in a journal in his own hand. They were seen by his staff, who were under an express contractual obligation to treat their content as confidential.

---

victims get apology from Murdoch' *The Guardian* (London, 11 April 2011), available at <http://www.theguardian.com/media/2011/apr/08/phone-hacking-victims-apology-news>.

[288] *Coogan v News Group Newspapers Ltd* [2012] EWCA Civ 48, [2012] 2 WLR 848 [55].

[289] *Coogan* (n 288) [53].

[290] See Moreham (n 280) 372.

[291] *Gulati v MGN Ltd* [2013] EWHC 3392 (Ch).

[292] *Various v MGN Ltd* [2014] EWHC 3655 (Ch); 'Case Preview: Various Claimants v MGN Ltd, Mirror phone hacking trial to begin on Monday, 2 March 2015' *Inforrm Blog* (1 March 2015), available at <inforrm.wordpress.com/2015/03/01/case-preview-various-claimants-v-mgn-ltd-mirror-phone-hacking-trial-to-begin-on-monday-2-march-2015/>.

[293] *Gulati v MGN Ltd* [2015] EWHC 1482 (Ch).

[294] See 1.78–1.79 and 10.35 *et seq*. In July 2012, eight individuals were charged with offences relating to phone hacking. On 4 July 2014, the former *News of the World* editor, Andy Coulson, three journalists, and the private investigator Glenn Mulcaire were sentenced to terms of imprisonment (two of them suspended) for conspiracy to intercept communications in the course of their transmission, without lawful authority: 'Phone hacking: full list of charges' *The Guardian* (London, 24 July 2012), available at <http://www.theguardian.com/uk/2012/jul/24/phone-hacking-charges>; 'Hacking trial: the verdicts' *BBC* (London, 4 July 2014), available at <http://www.bbc.co.uk/news/uk-27145187>.

[295] *Attorney General v Observer* (n 180) 281. Also *Hellewell* (n 200) 807; *Lifely v Lifely* [2008] EWCA Civ 904.

They were sent to selected recipients under cover of a letter signed by Prince Charles in an envelope marked 'private and confidential'. The journals were paradigm examples of confidential documents.[296]

**5.100 Privacy** The handwritten journals in the *HRH Prince of Wales* case were also protected as private,[297] as were the contents of diaries in *Lady Archer v Williams*.[298] In the former case, the Court of Appeal went on to emphasize the importance of form, when assessing whether information is private, saying:

> It is not easy in this case, as in many others, when concluding that information is private to identify the extent to which this is because of the nature of the information, the form in which it is conveyed and the fact that the person disclosing it was in a confidential relationship with the person to whom it relates. Usually, as here, these factors form an interdependent amalgam of circumstances. If, however, one strips out the fact of breach of a confidential relationship, and assumes that a copy of the Journal had been brought to the Newspaper by someone who had found it dropped in the street, we consider that its form and content would clearly have constituted it private information entitled to the protection of Article 8(1) as qualified by Article 8(2).[299]

**5.101 Limitations** The nature of the information will be relevant.[300] Some information about others contained in diaries, letters, or conversations may not be capable of protection.[301] Information of a trivial nature,[302] or information which is identical to that which is already in the public domain,[303] may not qualify as either confidential or private, just because it happens to be recorded in a private diary or journal.

**5.102 Impropriety** It may be that letters or conversations involving misconduct will fall outside the scope of any reasonable expectation of privacy. It has been held that an expectation on the claimant's part that the contents of unsolicited love letters he had written to a married woman should be kept private was not a reasonable one.[304]

### (g) Computers and mobile phones

**5.103** There will be a *prima facie* reasonable expectation of privacy in respect of information stored on a personal computer[305] or mobile phone,[306] which often contain the same kind of information as a personal diary or journal. This may be so even

---

[296] *HRH Prince of Wales* (n 36) [35].
[297] *HRH Prince of Wales* (n 36).
[298] *Lady Archer* (n 88).
[299] *HRH Prince of Wales* (n 36) [36].
[300] Different kinds of information are discussed at 5.36 *et seq.*
[301] *Lady Archer* (n 88) [50], discussed at 5.29.
[302] See 5.155.
[303] See 11.43 *et seq.*
[304] *Maccaba* (n 275).
[305] *L v L* [2007] EWHC 140 (QB), [2007] 2 FLR 171; *Imerman* (n 37).
[306] *AMP* (n 145) [27].

where there is no restriction, physical or otherwise, on access to the computer.[307] But again, the nature of the information obtained and/or disclosed will still be relevant.[308]

### (5) The Effect of Disclosure

In deciding whether there is a reasonable expectation of privacy, the court will **5.104** take into account the likely effect of disclosure on the claimant and others. The court will be on guard, however, against using a test of whether publication would be 'offensive' or 'highly offensive' to a reasonable person, because this is a stricter standard than whether a reasonable expectation of privacy exists.[309]

### (a) Audience and extent of disclosure

The court will give separate consideration to the different persons or classes of **5.105** persons to whom disclosure has been made or is threatened. Different considerations will arise depending on whether the actual or threatened publication is to those who already know the information,[310] to those with a particular interest in the information, or to the public at large.[311] Even in cases where it may not be reasonable to expect that information will be kept absolutely private, it may be reasonable to expect that it will not be disclosed in the press. This may affect the terms of any injunction granted. For example, the injunction granted in *Donald v Ntuli* to prevent publication of details about a sexual relationship included an exception permitting the claimant to discuss the relationship 'with any family member or close friend'.[312]

Although in the public law context there have been cases successfully brought **5.106** based on the wrongful retention of private information, even without disclosure,[313] the question of what will amount to misuse in the civil context has not been considered in detail. Cases to date have primarily concerned general publication or intended publication by the media and, in this context, a triviality threshold has been applied, so that the cause of action is not likely to be made out where disclosure is relatively harmless.[314] There may be some situations where it would nevertheless be right to hold that personal information has been misused, even though publication was limited or even if it was never disseminated.

---

[307] *Imerman* (n 37) [79].

[308] *Imerman* (n 37) [77]. See Moreham (n 280).

[309] *Campbell* (n 1) [22] (Lord Nicholls). See the discussion of 'offensiveness' at 4.163–4.165.

[310] *eg*, if the only persons who would be able to identify that the claimant was the subject of the information already knew the information, the effect of disclosure would be minimal.

[311] *BUQ* (n 137) [34]; and *SKA* (n 150) [31], both citing *Lord Browne* (n 54).

[312] *Donald* (n 129). Also *CC* (n 124) [35]; *BUQ* (n 137), where the injunction did not prevent disclosure to the officers or employees of the company that controlled the corporate group in which the parties had been employed or, by subsequent agreement, to the claimant's wife.

[313] *eg Wood* (n 76).

[314] Discussed at 5.155–5.157.

### (b) Medium of disclosure

**5.107**  Strasbourg jurisprudence suggests that the medium of disclosure will likewise be relevant. In the second *von Hannover* decision, the ECtHR observed that 'the publication of a photo may amount to a more substantial interference than a written article'.[315] The Court has also acknowledged that 'the audiovisual media have often a much more immediate and powerful effect than the print media'[316] and that the internet poses a particular risk to the right to respect for private life.[317]

### (c) The claimant's attitude

**5.108**  The claimant's own fortitude and attitude are relevant to assessing the effect of disclosure. In *Terry v Persons Unknown*, Tugendhat J had regard to the degree to which the claimant considered the information to be sensitive, and the robustness of his personality.[318] Such attributes are not, however, determinative and do not necessarily mean that a robust person who is 'able to look after himself and give "as good as he gets"' is not entitled to seek the court's protection in respect of information that is genuinely private.[319]

### (d) Embarrassment, distress, and other emotional harm

**5.109**  Some misuses of private information are likely to cause readily recognizable types of harm for which judges will frequently make awards of compensation. These include feelings of embarrassment, distress, or humiliation at the fact that others have come to know information that the person concerned did not intend to be known to the public. In *Weller*, the teenaged complainant gave evidence that she had felt shocked, threatened, and embarrassed by the taking and publication of photographs.[320] Where there is no mention of any personal distress resulting or likely to result from disclosure, this may indicate that the claimant is motivated to protect his or her reputation or business interests.[321] Where the effect complained of is to the claimant's reputation, it must be of a sufficiently serious nature before Article 8 will be engaged.[322]

---

[315]  *von Hannover (No 2)* (n 15) para 113. See 5.129.

[316]  *Mosley v UK* (n 15) [115].

[317]  *Węgrzynowski v Poland* App no 33846/07 (ECtHR, 16 July 2013) para 58. See ch 15.

[318]  *Terry* (n 98) [95], [127]. See also *Ferdinand* (n 121) [59]; *Price v Powell* [2012] EWHC 3527 (QB).

[319]  *KGM v News Group Newspapers Ltd* [2010] EWHC 3145 (QB) [32]. On appeal, the claimant effectively discounted his own claim to privacy, seeking to rely primarily on the effect publication would have on his family: *Hutcheson* (n 53). The relevance of effect on third parties is considered at 5.113. For the effect on children see 5.121–5.123.

[320]  *Weller* (n 143) [162]–[163].

[321]  *Terry* (n 98) [95]; *YXB v TNO* [2015] EWHC 826 (QB) [61(iii)].

[322]  *Re Guardian News and Media* (n 94) [40]–[42]. The protection of reputation by the misuse action is fully discussed in ch 8.

## (e) Intrusion or harassment

Where publication is more likely than not to result in 'intrusive and distressing **5.110** press coverage', this will be relevant, but the court is unlikely to be willing to speculate as to what may happen.[323] In *AM v News Group*, where an injunction was granted preventing publication of information that would identify the claimant or his address, the judge acknowledged that his order was made with a view to preventing interference with the claimant's Article 8 right by intrusion or harassment, rather than preventing disclosure of inherently sensitive information.[324] By contrast, in *KGM v News Group Newspapers Ltd*, Eady J warned:

> One must not confuse, so it seems to me, the question of whether there is a reasonable expectation of privacy in relation to certain information...with that of whether tabloid publicity would be likely to involve harassment or intrusion in the immediate aftermath. They appear to be distinct issues.[325]

## (f) Other forms of harm

More generally, it seems that an 'intrusion' into the private sphere or demonstra-  **5.111** tion that it is not inviolate may itself be an important factor in assessing whether a particular disclosure is one that interferes with a reasonable expectation of privacy, regardless of whether any particular form of emotional harm is caused.[326]

In *Campbell*, Lord Hoffmann emphasized that the values to which the action for mis-  **5.112** use of private information gives effect are human dignity and autonomy.[327] Baroness Hale identified the risk of damage to 'physical or moral integrity' as a key element in determining whether a reasonable expectation of privacy existed.[328] She held that the text accompanying photographs showing Naomi Campbell going to or having just left a therapy 'added to the potential harm, by making her think that she was being followed or betrayed, and deterring her from going back to the same place again'.[329]

## (g) Effect on third parties

The likely effect of disclosure on the rights of third parties will be relevant to the  **5.113** ultimate balancing test, particularly if they are children.[330]

---

[323] The likely impact of disclosure on claimants and their families was discussed under the label of 'intrusion' in *CTB v News Group Newspapers Ltd* [2011] EWHC 1326 (QB) [23]–[24] and *Goodwin* (n 59) [114]–[118]. The significance of the court's assessment of the likelihood of distressing coverage is illustrated by comparison of *Spelman* (n 112) [83] where Tugendhat J did not think such coverage was likely, with the earlier judgment of *Spelman v Express Newspapers Ltd* [2012] EWHC 239 (QB) [17] and [26], where Lindblom J considered it was.

[324] *AM* (n 155) [3].

[325] *KGM* (n 319) [29].

[326] There have been several cases involving children where relief has been granted in the absence of emotional harm, discussed at 5.123.

[327] *Campbell* (n 1) [50]–[51] cited at 5.11.

[328] *Campbell* (n 1) [157].

[329] *Campbell* (n 1) [155].

[330] See 5.169.

### (6) The Attributes of the Claimant

#### (a) Public figures

**5.114** **Strasbourg** The Strasbourg jurisprudence indicates that 'public figures' may enjoy lesser protection than others,[331] but there is no blanket retraction of protection.[332] There has been a significant shift in Strasbourg's approach to this issue since the decision of the ECtHR in the first *von Hannover* case, which suggested that an individual who happens to be well known to the public, but performs no official public function, will ordinarily have the same rights to privacy as any other individual.[333] In that case, the Court found that publication of banal photographs of Princess Caroline of Monaco going about her daily life in public places engaged her right to privacy under Article 8. As far as public figures were concerned, the Court held that the public's right to know 'in certain special circumstances, can extend to the private life of public figures, particularly where politicians are concerned', but that this principle was inapplicable in the applicant's case.[334]

**5.115** In *von Hannover v Germany (No 2)*, the ECtHR substantially confirmed these principles, but, by contrast, found that the Princess must be regarded as a public figure, regardless of the extent to which she assumed official functions, because she was 'undeniably very well known'.[335]

**5.116** **Who is a public figure?** There has been considerable discussion in the post-HRA authorities about the impact on a person's rights of confidentiality and privacy of his or her status as a 'public figure'. Whether a person is a public figure seems primarily to turn on whether he or she is a role model or holds a position where higher standards of conduct can be rightly expected by the public.[336] This includes those who exercise a public or official function,[337] including 'headmasters and clergymen...politicians, senior civil servants, surgeons and journalists'.[338] The concept also extends to a 'narrow category of persons' not engaged in any public office, such as 'the chairmen of major public companies, and the captains of national sporting teams'.[339] The English

---

[331] *Ageyevy* (n 16) [221] where the ECtHR said that, in contrast to a public figure, a person's 'status as an ordinary person enlarges the zone of interaction which may fall within the scope of private life'; *Mitkus* (n 82) [132].

[332] The ECtHR has affirmed that even a person who is known to the general public may still, in certain circumstances rely on a legitimate expectation of protection of his or her private life: *von Hannover (No 2)* (n 15) para 97.

[333] *von Hannover* (n 15).

[334] *von Hannover* (n 15) para 64, citing *Éditions Plon v France* (2006) 42 EHRR 36, where the information at issue concerned the health of President Mitterand.

[335] See *von Hannover (No 2)* (n 15) paras 110 and 120. See also *Lillo-Stenberg v Norway* (n 133) para 37 where 'well-known performing artists' were held to be public figures even though they had no 'public community functions'.

[336] *A v B plc* (n 21) [11](xii); *Ferdinand* (n 121).

[337] *Spelman* (n 112) [44].

[338] *McKennitt* (n 24) [65].

[339] *Rocknroll* (n 162) [15]. In *Spelman* (n 112) the applicant, who was the son of a Member of Parliament and also played rugby in a national youth team, was held to be a public figure,

authorities have primarily involved celebrities from the worlds of sport, entertainment, and fashion, as opposed to politics or public affairs.[340]

**Persons associated with public figures** '[A] person who might otherwise not **5.117** be a public figure may be treated as such by reason of association with someone who undoubtedly is a public figure.'[341] The claimant in *Trimingham v Associated Newspapers* was not a 'purely private figure' because of her involvement with a Member of Parliament, both professionally, as his press officer, and personally, as his secret mistress.[342] How this factor is approached in cases involving children is discussed later in this chapter.[343]

**Effect on privacy rights** The cases make clear that a person who is a public figure **5.118** has a right to a private life; that his or her status may set some limits on the extent to which it is reasonable for him or her to expect privacy; but that the extent to which his or her ordinary rights are curtailed by their status is limited. In *A v B plc*, where the claimant was a footballer, Lord Woolf said that a public figure:

> ...should recognize that because of his public position he must expect and accept that his actions will be more closely scrutinized by the media. Even trivial facts relating to a public figure can be of great interest to readers and other observers of the media. Conduct which in the case of a private individual would not be the appropriate subject of comment can be the proper subject of comment in the case of a public figure.... The higher the profile of the individual concerned the more likely that this will be the position.[344]

A person's status as a public figure does not, however, constitute a licence to **5.119** publish any and all information about his or her private life.[345] The House of Lords in *Campbell* held that the mere fact that a person is a public figure with a symbiotic relationship with the media does not rob him or her of a right to privacy.[346]

---

and in *McClaren v News Group Newspapers Ltd* [2012] EWHC 2466 (QB), [2012] EMLR 33 [31], the former England manager McClaren was described by Lindblom J as 'undoubtedly a public figure'.

[340] *eg* models (Campbell (n 1), Mills (n 153)), footballers (Flitcroft, whose anonymity was subsequently removed after the successful appeal by the defendant (*A v B plc*, n 21), Ferdinand (n 121)) other figures from sport (Mosley (n 100), McClaren (n 339)), actors (Michael Douglas, Catherine Zeta-Jones (*Douglas* (nn 2, 9, 24)), musicians (Tulisa Contostavlos (n 120), Loreena McKennitt (n 24)), royalty (Prince Charles (n 36), Princess Caroline (n 15)), and businessmen (Browne (n 54), Goodwin (n 59))).

[341] *Abbey* (n 36) [43]: this argument was advanced by counsel for the claimant and not disputed by the defendant or the judge.

[342] *Trimingham* (n 61) [338]. By contrast, in *Rocknroll* (n 162) [15]–[16], neither the claimant's marriage to Kate Winslet, nor his relationship to his uncle Sir Richard Branson placed 'the claimant in the public sphere in his own right'.

[343] See 5.124–5.125.

[344] *A v B plc* (n 21).

[345] *Campbell v MGN Ltd* [2002] EWCA Civ 1373, [2003] QB 633 [40]–[41], qualifying Lord Woolf's statement in *A v B plc* (n 21).

[346] *Campbell* (n 1) [57] (Lord Hoffmann), [120] (Lord Hope).

**5.120**  The nature of the information and the circumstances of the particular case will be important when considering the effect of a person's status as a public figure. In numerous cases, public figures in the sporting and entertainment industries have succeeded in preventing disclosure of information relating to their sexual lives.[347] By contrast, the footballer appointed as captain of the English team after the previous captain was dismissed because of an extra-marital affair failed in a claim for damages for misuse of private information.[348] The information that the replacement captain, who many would see as a role model, had also had an affair legitimately contributed to debate about his suitability for the role and was relevant to correcting a false image.[349]

### (b) Children

**5.121**  Although children do not enjoy a general right to privacy simply because of their age, the substantive privacy rights of children are at least as great as those of adults.[350] Further, children, by virtue of their immaturity and greater vulnerability, may be entitled to protection from publicity where an adult would not be.[351] Clauses 6 and 7 of the IPSO Editors' Code of Practice offer special protection for children.[352]

**5.122**  The significance of the fact that the claimant is a child will depend on the child's age and circumstances. For example, by contrast with *Murray*,[353] which involved 'an infant in a push chair', the claimant in *Spelman* was a 17-year-old who had played sport at an international level and had a 'personality and public profile of his own'.[354] In the latter case, the fact the claimant was a child provided only 'limited support' for the claim.[355] Where, as in *Spelman*, a child is something of a public figure in his or her own right,[356] the considerations discussed earlier in this chapter in relation to public figures will be relevant, although their application could be expected to be modified for children.[357]

**5.123**  **Effect of disclosure**  More recent Strasbourg and English authorities suggest that, where children are involved, a focus on whether disclosure would cause identifiable harm is too narrow. In *Reklos v Greece*, the ECtHR held that photographing a day-old child in a hospital unit and retaining the negatives was a breach of his Article 8 rights, even though the child was unaware of the infringement and suffered no

---

[347]  *AMM* (n 93); *CTB* (n 124); *MJN* (n 124); *TSE v News Group Newspapers Ltd* [2011] EWHC 1308 (QB); *NEJ* (n 124); *K v News Group* (n 124); *Contostavlos* (n 120).

[348]  *Ferdinand* (n 121).

[349]  The contribution that the information will make to a debate of general public interest is primarily relevant to the ultimate balancing exercise: see 11.125, 11.137 *et seq*.

[350]  Discussed at 13.13–13.19.

[351]  *Spelman* (n 112) [53].

[352]  IPSO Editors' Code of Practice (n 20).

[353]  *Murray* (n 41).

[354]  *Spelman* (n 112) [55].

[355]  *Spelman* (n 112) [72].

[356]  *Spelman* (n 112) [67]–[68].

[357]  See 5.114–5.120 on public figures.

tangible harm.[358] In *Murray*, the Court of Appeal held that a child of a famous author arguably had a reasonable expectation of privacy in respect of photographs of him in his pushchair on a public street, although the child was oblivious to the taking and publishing of the photograph and had suffered no distress as a result.[359] A similar approach was adopted in the more recent decisions of *AAA*[360] and *Weller*,[361] both of which involved children of very tender age.

**Impact of parents' status or conduct**   Clause 6 of the IPSO Editors' Code of Practice   **5.124**
states that 'the fame, notoriety or position of a parent or guardian' must not be used as sole justification for publishing details of a child's private life.[362] The rights of a child should not be confused with the actions of a parent, over which the child will usually have no control. Nevertheless, the conduct of a child's parent may affect his or her reasonable expectation of privacy. In *Murray*, the Court of Appeal approved the following account given by Patten J at first instance of how the court should take into account 'the position of [a] child's parents and the way in which the child's life as part of that family has been conducted':[363]

> The question whether a child in any particular circumstances has a reasonable expectation for privacy must be determined by the court taking an objective view of the matter including the reasonable expectations of his parents in those same circumstances as to whether their children's lives in a public place should remain private. Ultimately it will be a matter of judgment for the court with every case depending upon its own facts. The point that needs to be emphasised is that the assessment of the impact of the taking and the subsequent publication of the photograph on the child cannot be limited by whether the child was physically aware of the photograph being taken or published or personally affected by it. The court can attribute to the child reasonable expectations about his private life based on matters such as how it has in fact been conducted by those responsible for his welfare and upbringing.[364]

A child's family context may weigh in favour of or against the existence of a rea-   **5.125**
sonable expectation of privacy. In *Murray*, the claimant's parents had 'repeatedly and consistently taken steps to secure and maintain the privacy' of the claimant.[365] The Court of Appeal said the position could be quite different 'if the parents of a child courted publicity by procuring the publication of photographs of the child in order to promote their own interests'.[366] In *AAA*, the Court of Appeal approved

---

[358] *Reklos* (n 190).
[359] *Murray* (n 41). Recognizing that the New Zealand Court of Appeal took a different view of similar facts in *Hosking* (n 25), the Court of Appeal in *Murray* noted at [53] that, in *Television NZ Ltd v Rogers* [2007] NZSC 91, [2008] 2 NZLR 277, the New Zealand Supreme Court had doubted the correctness of *Hosking* on this point.
[360] *AAA* (n 143).
[361] *Weller* (n 143).
[362] See also the Ofcom Broadcasting Code, para 8.20.
[363] *Murray* (n 41) [37].
[364] *Murray v Express Newspapers plc* [2007] EWHC 1908 (Ch), [2007] EMLR 22 [23].
[365] *Murray* (n 364) [13]. Compare the New Zealand case of *Hosking* (n 25) where a claim in similar circumstances failed.
[366] *Murray* (n 41) [38].

of the judge's analysis at first instance that the conduct of the claimant's mother in disclosing, in an interview and at a social event, the paternity of her daughter had compromised the claimant's reasonable expectation of privacy.[367]

### (c) Corporations and other business entities

**5.126** Whether corporate entities, partnerships, or unincorporated associations have rights in privacy has been little explored in the domestic authorities. A company that ran a residential home for children could obtain an injunction where the principal reason was to protect the Article 8 rights of third-party children.[368] The issue is fully discussed in Chapter 13.

### (7) Other Relevant Circumstances

#### (a) The place at which it was happening

**5.127** **Private places** Individuals are ordinarily entitled to expect that information about their behaviour in their home or another private place is and will remain private.[369] The IPSO Editors' Code of Practice makes clear that it is 'unacceptable' to photograph an individual without his or her consent in 'places where there is a reasonable expectation of privacy'.[370] In *NNN v D1*, the claimant obtained permanent injunctions preventing disclosure of a covert recording of a conversation between him and 'X', which had taken place in the hallway of an apartment building.[371] The judge said:

> … the conversation was conducted between two people who believed themselves to be alone in a private or semiprivate place (the locked entrance hall of X's apartment building). Indeed they held it there precisely because it was more private than X's flat, in which X had visitors. Even if the conversation had at times been conducted in raised voices, they had no reason to suppose that it was being overheard, still less recorded.[372]

**5.128** **Public places generally** The restriction on non-consensual photography in the IPSO Editors' Code of Practice applies to 'public or private places where there is a reasonable expectation of privacy'.[373] Both Strasbourg and English jurisprudence indicates that whether or not there is a reasonable expectation of privacy in relation to conduct in a public place will depend on the circumstances of the case, including the nature of the activity or information.[374]

---

[367] *AAA v Associated Newspapers Ltd* [2013] EWCA Civ 554, approving *AAA* (n 143). The parents' conduct was also considered in *Weller* (n 143).
[368] *Green Corns* (n 86).
[369] *Rocknroll* (n 162), discussed at 5.53.
[370] IPSO Editors' Code of Practice, cl 2.
[371] *NNN v D1* [2014] EWHC B14 (QB).
[372] *NNN* (n 371) [12].
[373] IPSO Editors' Code of Practice, cl 2(iii).
[374] The Court of Appeal surveyed Strasbourg and English authorities in *Catt* (n 193) [7]–[20]. Further discussion can be found in N Moreham, 'Privacy in Public Places' (2006) 65 CLJ 606.

**Strasbourg**   The ECtHR has held that there is 'a zone of interaction of a person with    **5.129**
others, even in a public context, which may fall within the scope of "private life".[375]
The court held in *Peck v UK* that publication in the media of CCTV footage of a man
attempting to commit suicide on a public road engaged his Article 8 rights.[376] In *von
Hannover (No 1)*, the Court held that published photographs of Princess Caroline of
Monaco engaged in various everyday activities were a violation of her Article 8 rights
even though all the photographs, except one at a private beach club, were taken in public places.[377] The ECtHR has since found on two occasions that the Princess's Article 8
rights were, although engaged, not infringed by publication of similar photographs.[378]
In *Lillo-Sternberg v Norway*, the Court held that the claimant's Article 8 rights were
not violated by publication of images of the bride and groom arriving at their wedding
because it had taken place in a popular holiday location that was visible and accessible
to the public.[379]

**The English cases**   In the public law case of *Kinloch v HM Advocate*, the Supreme    **5.130**
Court said:

> A person who walks down a street has to expect that he will be visible to any member
> of the public who happens also to be present. So too if he crosses a pavement and gets
> into a motor car. He can also expect to be the subject of monitoring on closed circuit
> television in public areas where he may go, as it is a familiar feature in places that the
> public frequent.[380]

In *Hannon v News Group*, two claimants sought damages for publication of information about their arrests on an aircraft. One had been arrested in the cockpit, the other
in the passenger cabin. In refusing to strike out the claims, Mann J observed that
the 'rather more public nature' of the events in the latter claimant's case was a factor
relevant to the viability of the action. Although not determining the point, the judge
said that 'an aircraft cabin is no more a private place than the interior of a bus' nor 'very
different from a street with only a limited number of passers-by'.[381]

Despite such considerations, the law of misuse of private information has notably    **5.131**
expanded in protecting against intrusion by publication in the media of photographs
or video recordings, even where the images have been captured in more or less public
places. The photographs of the claimant in the *Campbell* case were taken in a public
place, yet their publication was held by the House of Lords to be actionable.[382] In

---

[375]   *PG v UK* (n 119) [56]; *Gillan v UK* (2010) 50 EHRR 45, para 61.
[376]   *Peck v UK* (2003) 36 EHRR 41.
[377]   *von Hannover* (n 15).
[378]   *von Hannover (No 2)* (n 15); *von Hannover (No 3)* (n 154). The key difference in approach
seems to have come in the balance struck between the Art 8 and Art 10 rights.
[379]   *Lillo-Stenberg* (n 133) paras 42–3.
[380]   *Kinloch v HM Advocate* [2012] UKSC 62, [2013] 2 AC 93 [19].
[381]   *Hannon* (n 218) [101].
[382]   *Campbell* (n 1).

several cases, a reasonable expectation of privacy has been held to exist in respect of photographs taken of children on family outings in public places.[383]

**5.132** **Workplace** A reasonable expectation of privacy may exist in relation to information about events or conduct in a workplace. This may not, however, be the case where the information concerns events or conduct related to the employees' duties or where a reasonable person in the claimant's position would recognize the possibility that disclosure of information may become necessary to resolve a workplace dispute. This is more so if one of the relevant persons is junior to the other.[384] In *Goodwin v News Group*, workplace dynamics were a factor in the judge's decision that there was no reasonable expectation of privacy in the fact of a sexual relationship between the chief executive of the Royal Bank of Scotland and a colleague.[385]

**5.133** **Open court** Where information that is otherwise private or confidential is revealed in open court, the reasonable expectations of the person to whom the information relates are likely to be significantly modified, and it may be that they have no continuing reasonable expectation of privacy in respect of the information.[386] The ordinary rule applicable to both criminal and civil proceedings is that the press may report everything that takes place in open court, and any departure from this principle will require close scrutiny.[387] Procedural measures, such as anonymity, private hearings, and reporting restrictions, are the principal vehicle by which information relevant to court proceedings is protected from publication where that would infringe Article 8.[388]

**5.134** *Criminal proceedings* The jurisprudence of the ECtHR makes clear that a court is obliged to strike a fair balance between the public interest in publicity for court proceedings, and the interest of a party or third person in maintaining confidentiality of personal data.[389] However, the principle of open justice permits free reporting of criminal trials.[390] In *Re BBC*, the House of Lords held that the fact that a defendant was acquitted of rape is not of itself private information the publication of which would be incompatible with his right to privacy.[391] Lord Hope said that

---

[383] *Murray* (n 41) (an application for strike out); *AAA* (n 143); *Weller* (n 143).

[384] *BUQ* (n 137) [63]–[64].

[385] *Goodwin* (n 59) [102]–[103]; cf *K v News Group* (n 124).

[386] The focus is on the information that is disclosed in public court, not the person who is involved in criminal proceedings. A person who is the subject of criminal proceedings does not, for that reason, lose the benefit of Art 8's protection in relation to other areas of his or her life: *Ageyevy* (n 16) [221].

[387] *PNM* (n 94) [21]. Also the pre-HRA case of *Bunn* (n 200); *BUQ* (n 137) [71], and discussion at 4.97–4.100.

[388] See 13.93–13.94, 13.100–13.106.

[389] *Z v Finland* (n 105) paras 94–7.

[390] See 5.133–5.134. For further discussion of the open justice and reporting principles see 11.71, 11.159.

[391] *Re BBC* [2009] UKHL 34, [2010] 1 AC 145.

the principle of open justice permits identification of those who have been acquitted, as it does those who have been convicted and sentenced.[392]

Private information is frequently deployed in criminal proceedings, and this may **5.135** include information about individuals who are neither parties nor witnesses.[393] Rights of confidentiality in respect of a document that has been provided as part of a compulsory disclosure process in litigation[394] may be lost when that document is deployed in public legal proceedings. The statutory restrictions on the use by a defendant of 'unused' material disclosed by the prosecution do not apply 'to the extent that [the information] has been communicated to the public in open court'.[395] This statutory release does not, however, affect 'any other restriction or prohibition on the use or disclosure of an object or information' whether statutory or otherwise.[396] This would appear to leave any other question of confidentiality or privacy for resolution by reference to common law principles. At common law, any private law claim to confidentiality evaporates to the extent that a document has been read aloud to or read by the court or referred to at a public court hearing.[397] The mechanisms for controlling the public disclosure of private information may require tightening if the privacy of non-parties is to receive adequate protection.

*Civil proceedings*   On several occasions, the court has held that when information **5.136** is deployed in a public court in civil proceedings the open justice principle prevails over any reasonable expectation of confidentiality or privacy that might otherwise exist.[398] The Civil Procedure Rules' (CPR) prohibition on collateral use of a document disclosed by compulsion in civil proceedings ceases once the document has been read to or by the court or referred to at a hearing in public,[399] unless the court specifically makes an order restricting or prohibiting the use of the document.[400] This rule places a premium on the making of an application to preserve privacy

---

[392] *Re BBC* (n 391) [6], citing *Re Trinity Mirror* (n 214) [33].

[393] The content of illicit recordings of conversations between the Duke and Duchess of Cambridge became public in March 2014 during the Old Bailey phone-hacking trial: *The Telegraph* (London, 18 March 2014), available at <http://www.telegraph.co.uk/news/uknews/phone-hacking/10705513/Hacking-trial-Phone-message-from-Duke-of-Cambridge-to-Kate-Middleton-intercepted.html>.

[394] See also 5.68–5.71.

[395] Criminal Procedure and Investigations Act 1996, s 17(3).

[396] Criminal Procedure and Investigations Act 1996, s 17(8).

[397] As to civil cases before the CPR, see *Derby v Weldon*, *The Times*, 20 October 1988; *SmithKline Beecham Biologicals SA v Connaught Laboratories Inc* [1999] 4 All ER 498, CA, a decision on RSC Ord 24, r 14A.

[398] *Re LM (Reporting Restrictions; Coroner's Inquest)* [2007] EWHC 1902 (Fam); *Napier v Pressdram Ltd* [2009] EWCA Civ 443, [2010] 1 WLR 934 (a Law Society investigation). Also *Revenue and Customs Commissioners* (n 233); *Crossley* (n 240); *BUQ* (n 137).

[399] CPR 31.22(1)(a).

[400] As permitted by CPR 31.22(2). The corresponding provisions of RSC Ord 24, r 14A were held not to allow restrictions to be imposed after the event: *Derby* (n 397). However, the wording of the current rule seems deliberately drafted so as to permit afterthoughts. The fact that restraints might now be imposed after the event brings into focus the question of whether the public domain doctrine in this context depends on fact and degree, or principle: see 4.97–4.102 and 11.71–11.72.

in the contents of a document before it becomes public. It is also possible for non-parties unwittingly to suffer invasions of privacy by the reading of documents that relate to them which are held by parties to litigation.

**5.137** *Documents referred to in a limited way*   In striking a balance between privacy or confidentiality and open justice, courts quite frequently permit or direct the parties to use discretion in deploying documents in open court, rather than sitting in private. It may be important to distinguish between information the substance and detail of which is actually revealed to the public in open court, and information which is shown to a judge or witness or otherwise conveyed to the court without its details being disclosed to those present as onlookers.[401] Where information is treated in the second of these ways, it cannot be said that secrecy or privacy has been lost as a matter of fact, and it is suggested that a reasonable expectation of privacy may survive.[402] In *Ambrosiadou v Coward*, Eady J decided that although documents that had been filed in court proceedings were 'technically available to public scrutiny' by reason of a hearing and other steps taken in the proceedings, they had not 'in reality' entered the public domain so as to preclude the grant of an injunction.[403]

**5.138** If the document deployed, but not read out, in court is one that a party has disclosed under compulsion, the party or the person to whom it belongs can seek a court order protecting its contents from further dissemination.[404] If a document is put in voluntarily by another party, however, the provisions of the CPR do not control what that party may do with it outside court. That party's freedom to impart the information is controlled by the general law. If the information contained in the document is such that the claimant would otherwise enjoy a reasonable expectation of privacy in respect of it, the mere fact that it has, for example, been mentioned to a judge would not appear to compel a conclusion that the claimant's Article 8 rights evaporate. So, it is suggested, a person may not necessarily be able lawfully to 'launder' confidential or private information into the public domain merely by putting it before a court, even at a public hearing. An attempt to use the court process to launder allegations or information into the public domain in this way may be an abuse of process.[405]

---

[401] Although see the pre-HRA case of *Bunn* (n 200) 557, where the distinction between a document read by the judge and one read to the judge was described as 'artificial today when it is a matter of taste for the individual judge'.

[402] It is of some relevance to this discussion that fair and accurate court reports are privileged from actions for libel, both at common law and by statute, and the position may be similar in privacy: see 11.64, 11.71. A rule that the mere mention of a document in court means that its contents can be reported under privilege could be criticized as unduly favouring open justice over privacy rights. In general, however, that is the law's approach: *BUQ* (n 137).

[403] *Ambrosiadou* (n 96) [56].

[404] Under CPR 31.22(2). See further 13.170–13.172, 13.175.

[405] *CC* (n 124) [55]; *BUQ* (n 137) [69], [73]–[74].

## (b) The nature of the intrusion

The 'nature of the intrusion' was a factor the Court of Appeal in *Murray* mentioned as **5.139** relevant to the existence of a reasonable expectation of privacy, without elaboration.[406] The relevant 'intrusion' is the interference with Article 8, whether by publication or other misuse of private information. As well as the nature of the information, another major aspect of an 'intrusion' which is plainly material to such an assessment is the nature of the use made of the information and, in particular, the nature and extent of the disclosure that is made or threatened.[407] As Laws LJ observed in *R (Wood) v Commissioner of Police of the Metropolis*: 'It is clear that the real vice in *Campbell* (and also the *von Hannover* case…and *Murray*…) was the fact or threat of publication in the media, and not just the snapping of the shutter.'[408]

**Interim injunctions**   A difficulty at the interim injunction stage is that often **5.140** the nature of the intrusion sought to be prevented cannot be known. In *Spelman*, Tugendhat J observed that past publications may indicate what the future may hold,[409] but the court is unlikely to be willing to speculate.

## (c) The purpose of the intrusion

In *Murray*, the Court of Appeal held that the circumstances to be taken into **5.141** account in deciding whether there is a reasonable expectation of privacy include the 'purpose of the intrusion' and 'the purposes for which the material came into the hands of the publisher'.[410] This aspect of the law of misuse of private information remains relatively undeveloped. In *Murray*, the 'purpose' that the Court considered relevant was the defendant's purpose of taking the pictures for commercial use in the media. Distinguishing other authority, the Court held that the pictures had been:

> …taken deliberately, in secret and with a view to their subsequent publication. They were taken for the purpose of publication for profit, no doubt in the knowledge that the parents would have objected to them.[411]

The Court held that a child at least arguably has a reasonable expectation 'that he or she will not be targeted in order to obtain photographs in a public place for publication'.[412]

In subsequent cases, the court has had regard to indications that the defendant may **5.142** be seeking personal gain through blackmail, or seeking to harass the claimant.[413]

---

[406] *Murray* (n 41) [36], quoted at 5.21.
[407] See 5.14.
[408] *Wood* (n 76) [33].
[409] *Spelman* (n 112) [83].
[410] *Murray* (n 41) [36]. For purpose as a factor in evaluating freedom of expression rights see 11.156.
[411] *Murray* (n 41) [50].
[412] *Murray* (n 41) [57]. Also *AAA* (n 143); *Weller* (n 143).
[413] *WXY v Gewanter* [2012] EWHC 496 (QB); *NNN* (n 371); *EWQ* (n 132).

Commercial or unlawful objectives can be contrasted with purposes such as law enforcement or publication in order to contribute to a debate of general public interest.[414]

### (d) The claimant's consent and conduct

**5.143** **Consent** The relevance of consent to the assessment of whether a reasonable expectation of privacy exists is obvious. The central value protected by the Article 8 right is the personal autonomy of every individual.[415] As Laws LJ has put it, 'an individual's personal autonomy makes him—should make him—master of all those facts about his own identity, such as his name, health, sexuality, ethnicity, [and] his own image'.[416] It may be necessary to consider not only whether there has been consent, but the scope of any consent the claimant has given.[417]

**5.144** **Claimant's conduct and attitude** If an individual jealously guards his or her privacy and makes this known that may support his or her claim.[418] A claimant's conduct and attitude may also serve to weaken his or her position. In *Spelman*, Tugendhat J accepted that the claimant's past conduct will be relevant to the existence of a reasonable expectation of privacy.[419] In that case, the relevant conduct was the claimant's participation in sport at a national and international level, which involved submission to requirements that matters relating to his health be disclosed and monitored.[420] It was also taken into account that the claimant had made relevant information available to the public in the past.[421] A claimant's earlier conduct may also be relevant on the basis that, as a result, the claimant could be said to have become a public figure or, where there is a suggestion of hypocrisy, it may be relevant to an argument that disclosure of further information is in the public interest to correct a false image.[422]

**5.145** Consideration of past conduct in this context should not permit reasoning that, because a person has previously revealed, or consented to the publication of, information relating to a 'zone' of his or her private life, he or she has a reduced expectation of privacy in relation to any other information falling within that 'zone'. This argument, which the Court of Appeal rejected in *McKennitt v Ash*,[423] is inconsistent

---

[414] Discussed at 11.125, 11.137 *et seq.*
[415] *Wood* (n 76) [20].
[416] *Wood* (n 76) [21]. Laws LJ went on to explain three qualifications to this protection: [22]–[28].
[417] See *Rocknroll* (n 162), where the claimant had consented to the taking of photographs, but not to the photographs being posted on Facebook or published.
[418] *McKennitt* (n 158) [6]–[8]; and the discussion of *Murray* at 5.125.
[419] *Spelman* (n 112).
[420] *Spelman* (n 112) [69].
[421] *Spelman* (n 112) [84]–[85]. For discussion of the relevance of the fact that information has been made available to the public see 11.43 *et seq.*
[422] *Ferdinand* (n 121). For discussion of the public interest see 11.74 *et seq.*
[423] *McKennitt* (n 24).

with the autonomy that Article 8 seeks to protect.[424] The argument that the absence of prior complaint can be any kind of consent was rejected in *Weller*.[425]

**Defendant's knowledge**   Also relevant is whether the defendant knew or   **5.146**
ought to have inferred the absence of consent.[426] In *Murray*, it was assumed to be true that the defendant knew the parents of the infant claimant objected to any media coverage of the child.[427] In *Weller*, Dingemans J accepted that the defendants, who had purchased images from an agency, were not aware of the circumstances in which the photographs were taken, including that the claimants' father had asked the photographer to leave.[428] Nevertheless, the judge held that the article accompanying the pictures demonstrated the publishers were aware the claimants had not consented to the taking or publication of the photographs.[429]

As *Weller* indicates, this factor could in principle cut the other way: the court will   **5.147**
also take account of matters that the publisher did not know and could not have known about.[430] If a claimant were to behave in such a way that a media organization reasonably formed the impression that the claimant consented to the taking and publication of photographs at a particular time and place, or generally, that could weaken or perhaps even undermine any claim to a reasonable expectation of privacy.

*(e) The circumstances in which the information came into*
*the hands of the publisher*

The relevant considerations in assessing if there is a reasonable expectation of pri-   **5.148**
vacy include 'the circumstances in which [the information] has been imparted or obtained'.[431] If it is evident from the circumstances or manner in which the information is obtained that the claimant had a reasonable expectation of privacy in respect of it, knowledge that it was private information may be imputed to the defendant.[432] If the defendant did not gather the information firsthand, the court will consider the extent that the defendant knew or could have known about the circumstances in which the information was obtained.[433]

---

[424] See 5.11 and 5.26.
[425] *Weller* (n 143) [135].
[426] *Weller* (n 143) [37]–[38].
[427] *Murray* (n 41) [50].
[428] The relevance of how the defendant obtained the information is discussed further at 5.148–5.153.
[429] *Weller* (n 143) [160]–[161], [169].
[430] *Weller* (n 143) [37]–[38].
[431] *Lord Browne* (n 54) [32].
[432] *Imerman* (n 37) [68]. In cases concerned with unauthorized or purloined information 'the primary focus has to be on the nature of the information, because it is the recipient's perception of its confidential nature that imposes the obligation on him': *McKennitt* (n 24) [15].
[433] *Weller* (n 143) [37]–[38], [160]–[161], [169].

**5.149** **Subterfuge or other intrusive means**    Closely connected with the issues of consent[434] is consideration of whether the information was obtained by subterfuge or other illicit or intrusive means.[435] In *Cooper v Turrell*, the claimant obtained damages and an injunction after information about his health, obtained by an unauthorized secret audio recording of a business meeting, was published on the internet.[436] In *NNN v D1*, a permanent injunction was granted to prevent publication of information obtained by surreptitiously recording a conversation that the eavesdropper must have appreciated was private.[437] Information that is obtained surreptitiously may be the subject of a reasonable expectation of privacy, even if the information in question is already public.

**5.150** **The relevance of a pre-existing confidential relationship**    In traditional breach of confidence, the existence of a confidential relationship is a key factor.[438] It is clear law that a cause of action for misuse of private information may arise without the need to establish the existence of an initial confidential relationship.[439]

**5.151** The existence of a relationship may however lead to the conclusion that the person publishing the information knew or ought to have known that there was a reasonable expectation that the information in question would be kept private.[440] The Court of Appeal emphasized in the *HRH Prince of Wales* case that where a confidential relationship exists, it is wrong to analyse a case exclusively by reference to the 'new methodology', and without regard to the importance in the public interest of upholding duties of confidence.[441] In *Lord Browne*, the Court of Appeal summarized the position arrived at in this way:

> The cases make it clear that, in answering the question whether in respect of the disclosed facts the claimant has a reasonable expectation of privacy in the particular circumstances of the case the nature of any relationship between the relevant persons or parties is of considerable potential importance.[442]

**5.152** In *Lord Browne*, the Court was required to consider a number of different categories of information relating to the sexual relationship between the chief executive of BP and his partner. It considered that private discussions between the couple

---

434 See 5.143–5.147.
435 *D v L* (n 285) [23] (Waller LJ), relating to photographs; *Imerman* (n 37) [68].
436 *Cooper* (n 111).
437 *NNN* (n 371).
438 See 4.14.
439 *Campbell* (n 1) [14] (Lord Nicholls); *Douglas* (n 24) [83]; *Lord Browne* (n 54) [24].
440 *Campbell* (n 1) [134] (Baroness Hale).
441 *HRH Prince of Wales* (n 36) [28]–[32], [67]–[68], albeit in the context of the balance to be struck between Arts 8 and 10.
442 *Lord Browne* (n 54) [26]; *McKennitt* (n 24) [23]. For discussion of these issues see N Moreham, 'Breach of Confidence and Misuse of Private Information—How Do the Two Actions Work Together?' (2010) 15 Media & Arts L Rev 265.

in a domestic environment, which included information about business matters, 'could readily be held to be information which the latter knew or ought reasonably to have known was fairly and reasonably to be regarded as confidential or private'.[443] In *BUQ v HRE*, which involved a sexual relationship between colleagues, the 'dual' personal and professional relationships were both relevant to assessing if there was a reasonable expectation of privacy.[444]

It does not follow from the mere fact that a particular item of information was **5.153** imparted in the context of a confidential relationship that the information is necessarily the subject of a reasonable expectation of privacy.[445] To use the example given by the Court of Appeal in *Lord Browne*, such an expectation would not exist, for example, in respect of 'a husband telling his wife that Oxford or Cambridge won the boat race in a particular year'.[446] Rather, 'the test must be applied to each item of information communicated to or learned by the person concerned in the course of the relationship'.[447] In applying the test in this way, however, the nature of the relationship is of considerable importance, so that the mere fact that a piece of information is trivial is not decisive against the existence of a reasonable expectation of privacy.[448]

## (8) The Threshold of Seriousness

The law of misuse of private information is developing something akin to the 'trivi-  **5.154** ality' doctrine that forms part of the law of breach of confidence.[449] This reflects the nature of Article 8(1) as a right to 'respect' for private life: for Article 8 to be engaged, the interference with private life must attain a certain level of seriousness, as the House of Lords held in *M v Secretary of State for Work and Pensions*.[450] The precise nature and extent of this doctrine remain to be worked out. In particular, there is scope for a triviality threshold to operate either in relation to the nature of the information or to the effect of disclosure.[451]

**Trivial interferences unlikely to be actionable**   In *McKennitt v Ash*, the Court of  **5.155** Appeal held that, in rejecting some of the claimant's complaints on the grounds that the information at issue was so banal that it did not attract a reasonable expectation

---

[443] *Lord Browne* (n 54) [34].
[444] *BUQ* (n 137) [63]. Similarly, in *Ambrosiadou* (nn 96, 233) the parties were husband and wife and, at the same time, business partners.
[445] *Lord Browne* (n 54) [29].
[446] *Lord Browne* (n 54) [29].
[447] *Lord Browne* (n 54) [32].
[448] *Lord Browne* (n 54) [33].
[449] *Attorney General v Observer* (n 180) 282 (Lord Goff). Discussed at 4.81–4.83.
[450] *M v Secretary of State for Work and Pensions* (n 79) [83]. See further *R (Gillan) v Commissioner of Police of the Metropolis* [2006] UKHL 12, [2006] 2 AC 307 [28] (Lord Bingham); *Wood* (n 76) [22]–[28] (Laws LJ).
[451] For the effect of disclosure see 5.104–5.113.

of privacy, the trial judge had 'respected the spirit of' the guidance given by the House in *McKennitt*.[452] In *Ambrosiadou v Coward*, Lord Neuberger MR said:

> Just because information relates to a person's family and private life, it will not automatically be protected by the court: for instance, the information may be of slight significance, generally expressed, or anodyne in nature. While respect for family and private life is of fundamental importance, it seems to me that the courts should, in the absence of special facts, generally expect people to adopt a reasonably robust and realistic approach to living in the 21st century.[453]

Lord Neuberger MR approved the finding of Eady J that some information was 'of a trivial nature, of a low level of personal significance, in respect of which the claimant did not really have any expectation of privacy'.[454]

**5.156** **'What harm could it possibly do?'**    Although she was one of the majority who upheld the claim in *Campbell*, Baroness Hale gave examples of information that she considered would not engage Article 8 rights of the claimant, a model, such as 'how she looks if and when she pops out to the shops for a bottle of milk'.[455] Baroness Hale went on to say:

> Not every statement about a person's health will carry the badge of confidentiality or risk doing harm to that person's physical or moral integrity. The privacy interest in the fact that a public figure has a cold or a broken leg is unlikely to be strong enough to justify restricting the press's freedom to report it. What harm could it possibly do?[456]

**5.157**    In the first *von Hannover* case, the ECtHR held intrinsically banal information to be the subject of a reasonable expectation of privacy.[457] Any tension between the Strasbourg and English approaches, however, seems to have been resolved by the ECtHR's decisions in later cases brought by Princess Caroline, in which it has held that there was no infringement of Article 8 by publication of photos of the Princess and her family engaged in everyday activities in public places.[458] A more protective approach may still be applied, particularly in cases involving children.[459]

**5.158**    **Cases involving private and non-private information**    Where a case relates to both private information and information in respect of which there is no

---

[452] *McKennitt* (n 24) [12]. The information included 'passing references to friendships with various men' and 'conversations about record companies': *McKennitt* (n 158) [132], [134], and see [14]–[17] and [19].

[453] *Ambrosiadou* (n 233) [30].

[454] *Ambrosiadou* (n 233) [28]. At first instance it was said the information amounted in essence to 'allegations critical of [the claimant's] behaviour in a business or corporate context': (n 96) [56(4)] (Eady J).

[455] *Campbell* (n 1) [154].

[456] *Campbell* (n 1) [157].

[457] *von Hannover* (n 15); 5.87 and 5.129.

[458] *von Hannover (No 2)* (n 15); *von Hannover (No 3)* (n 154).

[459] *AAA* (n 143); *Weller* (n 143); *Murray* (n 41), where strike-out of such a claim was refused.

expectation of privacy, the approach taken in *Trimingham* indicates that the court will look to see if the private information adds sufficiently to the non-private information to support an action for misuse of private information.[460] In *Trimingham*, Tugendhat J held that references to the claimant wearing Doc Marten boots and having 'a boyish cropped spiky haircut' conveyed 'no meaningful information about her, or no information which is not already disclosed by the reference to her known bisexuality'.[461]

## D. When May Interference be Justified?

### (1) The 'Ultimate Balancing Test'

Where it has been established that there is a reasonable expectation of privacy **5.159** in respect of information, such that a claimant's Article 8 rights are engaged, the court must undertake the 'ultimate balancing test', weighing the claimant's Article 8 rights, the rights of the defendant, and the rights of other individuals concerned, to ascertain which should yield.[462] The Article 10 rights of the defendant (and others) will be most relevant. The Article 8 and 10 rights are of equal value in a democratic society,[463] and s 12(4) HRA does not accord pre-eminence to Article 10.[464] The relationship between Articles 8 and 10 was authoritatively explained by the House of Lords in *Re S (A Child)*:

> First, neither article has *as such* precedence over the other.[465] Secondly, where the values under the two articles are in conflict, an intense focus on the comparative importance of the specific rights being claimed in the individual case is necessary. Thirdly, the justifications for interfering with or restricting each right must be taken into account. Finally, the proportionality test must be applied to each.[466]

The court must give careful consideration to the weight that should be accorded **5.160** to the specific information at issue in the particular case. As Eady J neatly put it in *CDE v MGN Ltd*: 'There are no hard and fast rules. It is a question of weighing the competing Convention rights and forming a judgment on the unique facts of each case.'[467]

---

[460] *Trimingham* (n 61) [305].

[461] *Trimingham* (n 61) [296]–[297].

[462] *Murray* (n 41) [27]; *HRH Prince of Wales* (n 36); *McKennitt* (n 24) [11].

[463] *Campbell* (n 1) [113] (Lord Hope).

[464] *Campbell* (n 1) [111], citing Sedley LJ in *Douglas* (n 9) [137].

[465] In this respect, see *Campbell* (n 1) [55] (Lord Hoffmann), [113] (Lord Hope); *Re BBC* (n 391) [17]. The ECtHR has also taken this approach: *eg Mosley v UK* (n 15) para 111; *von Hannover (No 2)* (n 15) para 106; *Axel Springer* (n 224) para 87.

[466] *Re S* (n 51) [17] (Lord Steyn); *Campbell* (n 1) [140]–[141] (Baroness Hale); *Clayton v Clayton* (n 46) [57]–[58].

[467] *CDE* (n 63) [2].

### (2) The Hierarchy of Article 8 Rights

**5.161**  As Baroness Hale observed in *Campbell*, just as there are undoubtedly different types of speech,[468] '[t]here are different types of private information, some of which are more deserving of protection in a democratic society than others'.[469] Baroness Hale continued:

> The weight to be attached to these various considerations is a matter of fact and degree...The privacy interest in the fact that a public figure has a cold or a broken leg is unlikely to be strong enough to justify restricting the press's freedom to report it.[470]

**5.162**  At a general level, it may safely be said that there is something of a hierarchy of privacy interests and that, as a rule, the more intimate the nature of the information in question, and the closer it lies to the 'core' of the values protected by Article 8, the greater the weight which the court will accord to the information when conducting the balancing exercise.[471] Thus, a claim to privacy in respect of information about health or sexual life is likely to weigh more heavily in the scales than a claim to protect financial information or other information that, although private in character, is intrinsically less intimate.

**5.163**  But it is important not to deal in generalities.[472] Beyond mere classification lies the further task of evaluating the specific information at issue in a given case.[473] As Baroness Hale indicated in the passage cited at 5.161, the privacy interest in some kinds of information about health is less weighty than in others.

### (3) Competing Rights, Freedoms, and Interests

#### (a) Introduction

**5.164**  The protection of privacy rights is a legitimate aim for which freedom of expression may be limited. The claimant will, however, need to persuade the court that the remedy sought, which will inescapably involve an interference with the Article 10 rights of others, is necessary and proportionate for that purpose.

**5.165**  At the same time, the defendant will need to identify a justification for interfering with the Article 8 rights asserted by the claimant. The available justifications are exhaustively listed in Article 8(2). In media privacy cases, it is the 'protection of the rights and freedoms of others' that is most likely to be prayed in aid by defendants, and the rights most likely to be relied on are the Article 10 rights of the defendant to impart and the rights of others to receive information and ideas. Other Convention

---

[468]  See 5.166, 11.133–11.135.
[469]  *Campbell* (n 1) [148].
[470]  *Campbell* (n 1) [157].
[471]  *Dudgeon v UK* (n 118).
[472]  *Re W* (n 46) [53].
[473]  The approach of Nicol J in *Ferdinand* (n 121) provides an example of consideration of the way in which the competing rights are engaged in the circumstances of a particular case.

rights may also come into play, however. These may include not only the Article 8 and 10 rights of media sources, but also on occasion the rights protected by Articles 6 (right to a fair trial) and 9 (freedom of thought conscience and religion). Some cases may engage the public interest, such as public safety or the prevention of crime, mentioned in Article 8(2), or non-Convention rights and freedoms, such as those acquired by contract. These countervailing rights, freedoms, and interests are examined in more detail in Chapter 11.[474]

### (b) The rights of defendants

**Article 10 rights**   It is clear that there are different kinds of speech, some of   **5.166**
which are more deserving of protection in a democratic society than others.[475]
Political speech sits at the top of that list, with speech in Parliament having an exceptionally high value. Other forms of speech recognized as being highly valuable are speech in legal proceedings, speech about paternity and other familial relationships, intellectual and educational speech, and artistic speech and expression. At the other end of the scale is 'vapid tittle-tattle' about celebrities,[476] and blackmailing speech. In between, there is a range of categories to be considered, including speech which exposes wrongdoing, corrects the public record, or holds up to scrutiny the conduct of those in public roles. It needs always to be remembered, however, that categorization is only a starting point for assessment of the comparative value of the specific rights being asserted in the individual case.[477]

**Other rights and interests**   Civil and criminal litigation and the open justice   **5.167**
principle usually involve intrusion into private life interests, and the Article 6 right to a fair trial may come into play as a justification for interfering with privacy rights. Fair trial rights may support the communication of information to a litigant, and the right to a public trial will tend to justify the disclosure of relevant information to the public at large.[478] Article 9, the right to freedom of thought, conscience and religion, may also provide support for critical communications about others' private lives.[479]

### (c) The special position of children

Particular consideration must be given to the rights and interests of a child.[480]   **5.168**
In *K v News Group*, the Court of Appeal adopted as applicable in the misuse of

---

[474]  See 11.106 *et seq.*
[475]  *Campbell* (n 1) [148] (Baroness Hale). See 11.133–11.135 for further discussion of the value attached to different kinds of speech.
[476]  *CC* (n 124) [36].
[477]  See 5.161–5.163.
[478]  Discussed further at 11.159.
[479]  See 11.160.
[480]  As to the effect of childhood on whether a reasonable expectation of privacy exists, see 5.121–5.125.

private information context the approach of the Supreme Court in *ZH (Tanzania) v Secretary of State for the Home Department*:

> It is a universal theme of . . . various international and domestic instruments[481] . . . that, in reaching decisions that will affect a child, a primacy of importance must be accorded to his or her best interests. This is not, it is agreed, a factor of limitless importance in the sense that it will prevail over all other considerations. It is a factor, however, that must rank higher than any other. It is not merely one consideration that weighs in the balance alongside other competing factors. Where the best interests of the child clearly favour a certain course, that course should be followed unless countervailing reasons of considerable force displace them. It is not necessary to express this in terms of a presumption but the primacy of this consideration needs to be made clear in emphatic terms. What is determined to be in a child's best interests should customarily dictate the outcome of cases such as the present, therefore, and it will require considerations of substantial moment to permit a different result.[482]

The decisions in *Weller*[483] and *AAA*[484] both applied this 'primacy' principle.[485] The principle is to be applied even where the risk of adverse publicity arises because of the way in which a parent of the child has chosen to behave.[486]

**5.169**  Indeed, the protection now afforded to children's rights is such that a child's interests may be the deciding factor even where the child is not a party to the case.[487] The consequences of disclosure for children are likely to be given more weight in cases of 'younger or more vulnerable children, or where there is, for example, evidence of particular mental or emotional fragility'.[488] The young age of a child could, however, mean the effects of disclosure are limited, as was the case in *Ferdinand v MGN Ltd*, where the claimant accepted that his children were too young to fully understand the circumstances, being publication of the fact of their father's extramarital affair.[489]

---

[481] The instruments the Supreme Court referred to include the United Nations Declaration of the Rights of the Child (20 November 1959), principle 2; Convention on the Rights of the Child 1577 UNTS 3 (opened for signature 20 November 1989, entered into force 2 September 1990), Art 3.1; European Union Charter of Fundamental Rights, Art 24.

[482] *ZH (Tanzania) v Secretary of State for the Home Dept* [2011] UKSC 4, [2011] 2 AC 166 [46] (Lord Kerr SCJ), adopted in *K v News Group* (n 124) [19].

[483] *Weller* (n 143).

[484] *AAA* (n 143); *AAA* (n 367).

[485] For further applications of the 'primacy' principle see also *Rocknroll* (n 162); *Othman v English National Resistance* [2013] EWHC 1421 (QB).

[486] *K v News Group* (n 124) [18].

[487] *K v News Group* (n 124). For the position of third parties generally, see 5.171–5.175. Note that while a child's interests best interests are often acknowledged as crucial in the balancing exercise where the private information in issue relates to its parents, it seems very unlikely the child itself could ever bring a successful claim for misuse of private information in respect of such information that strictly does not relate to the child: *OPO* (n 89).

[488] *KGM* (n 319) [28], referring to *Ambrosiadou* (n 233). A striking instance of such fragility is provided by *OPO* (n 89). Although the misuse claim failed in that case, this was for reasons unconnected with the potential impact on the child.

[489] *Ferdinand* (n 121) [60].

If the best interests of a child are to be considered, it may be expected that there will **5.170** be expert evidence as to what the child's interests are.[490]

*(d) The rights of third parties*

**Third party rights must be considered**  The process of balancing rival rights will **5.171** often involve the court considering the rights of others who are not parties to the proceedings. Sometimes a claimant will pursue a claim that is, on its face at least, partly for the benefit of non-parties such as the claimant's relatives,[491] or staff,[492] or persons for whom the claimant has a legal responsibility.[493] Whether or not the claimant relies on the rights of others affected, they must be identified and placed on the scales with which the competing rights are being weighed.[494] The rights of third parties cannot be ignored 'on the basis of traditional arguments along the lines of who has a cause of action and who does not'.[495]

**Third party rights may be weighty**  Third party rights may play a powerful role **5.172** in determining the outcome of a case. This is particularly so where a third party is a child, because the same primacy principle that governs the weight to be given to the interests of a child claimant applies to third-party children.[496] But the rights of third parties may not necessarily swing the outcome of the case.[497] As Eady J said in *KGM v News Group*: 'Sometimes, the fallout of publicity on innocent bystanders may be unavoidable.'[498] The quality of the evidence put before the court as to a third party's interests will affect considerably the weight attributed to those interests.[499]

**In support of the claim**  The rights of third parties are most often relied on as **5.173** bolstering the claimant's case, for instance when the privacy interests of the claimant's family members coincide with those of the claimant.[500] In *K v News Group*, the claimant sought to prevent publication of an extra-marital affair. Ward LJ said that weight was to be given not only to the rights of the claimant, but also to the rights of the woman (X) with whom he had an affair, and his wife and children.[501] Both X and the claimant's wife, who was pursuing reconciliation with her husband, were clearly opposed to publicity.[502] Furthermore, it would be inevitable

---

[490] *AAA* (n 143) [114].

[491] *CC* (n 124); *K v News Group* (n 124) (spouses and children); *Donald* (n 129) (children).

[492] *Imutran Ltd v Uncaged Campaigns Ltd* [2001] 2 All ER 385 (employees of a medical research company).

[493] *Green Corns* (n 86) (troubled children in care homes); *BKM Ltd v BBC* [2009] EWHC 3151 (Ch) (adults in care homes).

[494] *CDE* (n 63) [6]; *K v News Group* (n 124) [20]; *CTB* (n 124) [3].

[495] *CDE* (n 63) [7].

[496] See 5.168–5.170; *K v News Group* (n 124). But see n 487 in relation to *OPO*.

[497] *PNM* (n 94).

[498] *KGM* (n 319) [28].

[499] *YXB* (n 321) [61(v)]; and see 13.148–13.151.

[500] *X, A Woman Formerly known as Mary Bell* (n 183); *CC* (n 124); *Ambrosiadou* (nn 96, 233); *Goodwin* (n 59); *PNM* (n 94); *NEJ* (n 124); *CDE* (n 63).

[501] *K v News Group* (n 124) [14].

[502] *K v News Group* (n 124) [16]–[17].

that the children would be harmed by disclosure because it would 'undermine the family as a whole' and expose them to playground ridicule.[503] Ward LJ referred to *Beoku-Betts v Secretary of State for the Home Dept*, where Baroness Hale identified the risk of:

> ...missing the central point about family life, which is that the whole is greater than the sum of its individual parts. The right to respect for the family life of one necessarily encompasses the right to respect for the family life of others, normally a spouse or minor children, with whom that family life is enjoyed.[504]

**5.174** The court will however pay close attention to the source and reliability of evidence as to the rights and interests of family members other than the claimant, and evaluate carefully its proper place in the balancing exercise. Thus, in *A v B plc* the Court of Appeal observed that it was not possible in that case, where no evidence was adduced from A's wife, to reach a conclusion on the harm that would be done to family life; 'the court should not, in our view, assume that it was in the interests of A's wife to be kept in ignorance of A's relationships'.[505] In *SKA v CRH* Tugendhat J found the claimant's evidence of concern for his wife 'particularly unimpressive', noting that 'he does not explain how he claims to know that she does not know', and that:

> Claimants have a tendency to confuse the interests of their wives and partners with their own interests. Even if the wife or partner is truly in ignorance of the relationship which the claimant seeks to keep secret, it does not follow that the court should accept the claimant as being in a position to speak for the best interests of the wife or partner (or children).[506]

**5.175** **In support of the defence**   In support of the argument that freedom of expression should prevail, media defendants are entitled to rely on the Article 10 rights of their audience to receive information. Reliance may also be placed on the Convention rights of individual sources to speak about their own lives.[507] Other, more subtle elements of third parties' rights to privacy and information may be in play, as in *SKA v CRH*, where the claimant sought to prevent publication of the fact that he and the woman with which he was in a long-term extra-marital relationship were expecting twins. Tugendhat J pointed out that Articles 8 and 10 encompass the right of persons to know information about their identity and family. The twins accordingly would have a right to know who their father was and the claimant's older children had rights to know information about their family life.[508]

---

[503] *K v News Group* (n 124) [17].

[504] *Beoku-Betts v Secretary of State for the Home Dept* [2008] UKHL 39, [2009] AC 115 [4]. A similar approach was taken in *Rocknroll* (n 162) [36]–[39].

[505] *A v B plc* (n 21) [43(v)].

[506] *SKA* (n 150) [82]–[83].

[507] *Theakston* (n 122) (Art 10); *A v B plc* (n 21) (Art 10); *Re Angela Roddy (A Minor)* [2003] EWHC 2927 (Fam), [2004] EMLR 8 (Art 8).

[508] *SKA* (n 150) [25] and [81]. Also *CTB* (n 124), where the defendants sought to vary an injunction to permit them to tell the claimant's wife of his extra-marital affair.

# 6

## HARASSMENT BY PUBLICATION

*N A Moreham*

## A. Introduction

The Protection from Harassment Act 1997 (PHA) is becoming an increasingly **6.01** important tool for those seeking to protect their privacy against intrusion by the media and private individuals. The Act was introduced to combat stalking, racial harassment, and disruption from neighbours[1] but 'harassment' is not defined in the Act and its reach is therefore in fact much wider. As will be discussed in Chapter 10, the PHA has the potential to catch a range of media news-gathering activities including persistent photography, trailing, and door-stepping.

Significantly for the media, 'conduct' under the PHA also includes speech[2] and **6.02** courts have held that publishing information about a person—in a newspaper, on the internet, in pamphlets or elsewhere—can amount to harassment under

---

[1] See *Hansard*, HC (series 6) vol 287, cols 781, 783–4 (17 December 1996) and HL (series 6) vol 577, col 917 (24 January 1997).

[2] s 7(4) PHA. The PHA is set out in full in Appendix C (available at <http://www.5rb.com/publication/the-law-of-privacy-and-the-media>.

the Act.[3] Courts have also confirmed on a number of occasions that the PHA gives 'effect to the obligation of the state to prevent interference with the right of individuals to protection of their private lives under ECHR Art 8'.[4] Courts should therefore take account of both Article 8 and 10 when applying it.[5] Claims for harassment by publication are increasingly being brought alongside actions for breach of confidence, misuse of private information, and defamation.[6]

**6.03**  The prohibition of harassment is contained in s 1 PHA. It provides that:

> (1)  A person must not pursue a course of conduct—
> > (a)  which amounts to harassment of another, and
> > (b)  which he knows or ought to know amounts to harassment of the other.
> (1A)[7]  A person must not pursue a course of conduct—
> > (a)  which involves harassment of two or more persons, and
> > (b)  which he knows or ought to know involves harassment of those persons, and
> > (c)  by which he intends to persuade any person (whether or not one of those mentioned above)—
> > > (i)  not to do something that he is entitled or required to do, or
> > > (ii)  to do something that he is not under any obligation to do.
> (2)  For the purposes of this section, the person whose course of conduct is in question ought to know that it amounts to harassment of another if a reasonable person in possession of the same information would think the course of conduct amounted to harassment of the other.
> (3)  Subsection (1) does not apply to a course of conduct if the person who pursued it shows—
> > (a)  that it was pursued for the purpose of preventing or detecting crime,
> > (b)  that it was pursued under any enactment or rule of law or to comply with any condition or requirement imposed by any person under any enactment, or
> > (c)  that in the particular circumstances the pursuit of the course of conduct was reasonable.

**6.04**  A person who pursues a harassing 'course of conduct' in breach of s 1(1) or (1A) is guilty of an offence under s 2 for which he or she can be fined or imprisoned for a maximum of six months.[8] Restraining orders can also be imposed on the defendant

---

[3] See *Thomas v News Group Newspapers Ltd* [2001] EWCA Civ 1233, [2002] EMLR 4.

[4] *Trimingham v Associated Newspapers Ltd* [2012] EWHC 1296 (QB), [2012] 4 All ER 717 [48]. See also *Law Society v Kordowski* [2011] EWHC 3185 (QB), [2014] EMLR 2 [59].

[5] See *eg Levi v Bates* [2015] EWCA Civ 206 [16] and *Hipgrave v Jones* [2004] EWHC 2901 (QB) [21].

[6] See *eg EWQ v GFD* [2012] EWHC 2182 (QB); *Trimingham* (n 4); and *AVB v TDD* [2014] EWHC 1442 (QB).

[7] Inserted by the Serious Organised Crime and Police Act 2005, s 125.

[8] s 2(1)–(2) PHA. Section 4 PHA also creates a separate offence of pursuing a course of conduct which causes another to fear that violence will be used against him or her. As with the s 1 offence, a defendant will be guilty of the offence if he or she knows or ought to know that his or her course of conduct will cause the other so to fear on each of those occasions. A person guilty of an offence under s 4 is liable for a term of imprisonment of up to five years: s 4(4) PHA. The Act also creates specific stalking offences: see ss 2A, 4A PHA and 10.18.

to protect the victim or any other person both on conviction and acquittal.[9] In addition, the victim of an actual or apprehended breach of s 1(1) can bring a civil claim against the harasser. The claimant can apply for damages (including damages for anxiety and financial loss)[10] or an injunction to restrain the harassing conduct, breach of which entitles the victim to apply for the issue of a warrant for the defendant's arrest.[11]

## B. The Requirements of the Protection from Harassment Act 1997

'Harassment' is not defined by the PHA. Section 7 provides that a 'course of con-  **6.05** duct' must involve conduct on at least two occasions;[12] that 'conduct' includes speech;[13] and that 'harassment' includes 'alarming the person or causing the person distress'.[14] Courts have consistently held that the definition of 'harassing a person' in s 7 is 'inclusive not exhaustive' and have therefore provided further explanation of its meaning.[15]

In *Dowson v Chief Constable of Northumbria Police*, Simon J set out six ele-  **6.06** ments which must be established before liability for harassment can be found. He said:

(1) There must be conduct which occurs on at least two occasions,
(2) which is targeted at the claimant [although the Court of Appeal has since held that conduct merely needs to have been targeted at *an* individual][16]
(3) which is calculated in an objective sense to cause alarm or distress, and
(4) which is objectively judged to be oppressive and unacceptable.[17]
(5) What is oppressive and unacceptable may depend on the social or working context in which the conduct occurs.
(6) A line is to be drawn between conduct which is unattractive and unreasonable, and conduct which has been described in various ways: 'torment' of the victim, 'of an order which would sustain criminal liability'.[18]

---

[9]  s 5 (on conviction) and s 5A PHA (on acquittal). For discussion of the requirements of s 5A, see *Smith v R* [2012] EWCA Crim 2566 and *R v Major* [2010] EWCA Crim 3016.

[10]  s 3(2) PHA.

[11]  s 3(3) PHA. Section 3A creates the right to apply for an injunction for harassment under s 1A.

[12]  s 7(3) PHA.

[13]  s 7(4) PHA.

[14]  s 7(2) PHA. 'Alarming' a person and 'causing him or her distress' should be considered disjunctively: *DPP v Ramsdale* [2001] EWHC 106 (Admin), *The Independent*, 19 March 2001 [20].

[15]  See *eg Thomas* (n 3) [29] and *DPP v Ramsdale* [2001] EWHC 106 (Admin), *The Independent*, 19 March 2001 [16].

[16]  See *Levi* (n 5) [55] and 6.11–6.14.

[17]  The first four factors in Simon J's list echo those listed by Owen J in *Green v DB Group Services (UK) Ltd* [2006] EWHC 1898 (QB) [14] (but Owen J said that the conduct must be 'calculated in an objective sense to cause distress' and it must be 'oppressive and unreasonable').

[18]  *Dowson v Chief Constable of Northumbria Police* [2010] EWHC 2612 (QB) [142].

**6.07**  This list of criteria is often relied on as a starting point for discussion of the PHA[19] and it will, loosely, be used in that manner here.

### (1)  Course of Conduct

**6.08**  Section 1(1) and (1A) state that in order to constitute actionable harassment, there must be a 'course of conduct' against either an individual or a group of individuals.[20] Section 7(3) then expressly provides that a course of conduct must involve conduct on more than one occasion. This is consistent with the purpose of the Act which, according to the Court in *R v Miah*, is 'to provide protection and to permit punishment in circumstances where it is not the individual acts or conduct themselves, but their persistence and their impact upon the victim to which regard should be paid'.[21] It follows that when assessing whether harassment has taken place, the court will look at the defendant's conduct as a whole as well as at the nature and impact of each of the defendant's individual acts. Thus, in *Iqbal v Dean Mason Solicitors*, Rix LJ, speaking for the Court of Appeal, approved Burton J's observation in the Court below that:

> It is ... not necessary for there to be alarm caused in relation to each of the incidents relied upon as forming part of the course of conduct. It is sufficient if, by virtue of the course of conduct, the victim is alarmed or distressed.[22]

And, in a similar vein:

> When a defendant, D, walks past a claimant C's door, or calls C's telephone but puts the phone down without speaking, the single act by itself is neutral, or may be. But if that act is repeated on a number of occasions, the course of conduct may well amount to harassment. That conclusion can only be arrived at by looking at the individual acts complained of as a whole. The course of conduct cannot be reduced to or deconstructed into the individual acts, taken solely one by one. So it is with a course of communications such as letters. A first letter, by itself, may appear innocent and may even cause no alarm, or at most a slight unease. However, in the light of subsequent letters, that first letter may be seen as part of a campaign of harassment.[23]

**6.09**  However, in order to establish a 'course of conduct' there must be 'a consistent motive on a consistent course of conduct'.[24] Some kind of nexus between the various harassing activities complained of is therefore required.[25] Courts have held that 'the fewer the occasions and the wider they are spread the less likely it would

---

[19]  Simon J's summary was described as 'a helpful guide to the issues that arise', albeit not 'definitive' in *Crawford v Jenkins* [2014] EWCA Civ 1035 [74].

[20]  s 1(1), (1A) PHA respectively.

[21]  *R v Miah (Mohbub)* [2000] 2 Cr App R (S) 439, 441.

[22]  *Iqbal v Dean Mason Solicitors* [2011] EWCA Civ 123 [49] citing *Kelly v DPP* [2002] EWHC 1428 (Admin), [2003] Crim LR 45 [24].

[23]  *Iqbal* (n 22) [45].

[24]  *Tuppen and Singh v Microsoft Corp Ltd* (QBD, 14 July 2000) 16.

[25]  See *R v Hills* (CA, 4 December 2000) [27].

be that a finding of harassment can reasonably be made'.[26] However, incidents as far apart as a year could constitute a course of conduct, particularly if the behaviour occurred on a certain date such as a religious holiday or a birthday.[27]

Continuous publication of harassing words can be a 'course of conduct' for the **6.10** purposes of the PHA. In *Law Society v Kordowski*, Tugendhat J accepted that naming solicitors on the website 'Solicitors from Hell' was an act of harassment. Having accepted that the defendant would have known that the publications would come to the attention of their subjects on more than one occasion (and on each occasion cause them alarm and distress),[28] he said:

> The publication is an ongoing one on a prominent website; accordingly the distress and alarm caused by the publication will also be continuous. It is reasonable to infer in every case that those posted would suffer such distress and alarm on at least two occasions.[29]

### (2) Targeting an Individual

Although it is not an express requirement of the PHA, courts have held that har- **6.11** assing conduct must be 'targeted at an individual'.[30] This means that it needs to be 'targeted behaviour' in the sense that it is 'aimed at someone, rather than behaviour which merely causes alarm or distress without being aimed at anyone'.[31] As Briggs LJ further explains, in the leading judgment in *Levi v Bates*:

> The value of targeting as a concept is that it excludes behaviour which, however alarming or distressing it may be, is not aimed or directed at anyone. For example, a person may drive his fast sports car on regular occasions through a neighbourhood in a way that causes foreseeable alarm and distress to pedestrians and parents of young children. It may amount to speeding, careless or dangerous driving, but it is not harassment because it is not targeted at anyone at all. The driver is merely selfishly enjoying himself.[32]

But the behaviour need not be targeted at the claimant.[33] Briggs LJ said that he: **6.12**

> ...cannot conceive why Parliament should by implication rather than express words (for there are none) have deliberately excluded from the protection of the Act persons

---

[26] *Lau v DPP* [2000] EWHC 182 (QB), [2000] 1 FLR 799, 801–2 (slapping the complainant while they were in a relationship and threatening her new boyfriend in her presence four months later did not amount to a course of conduct). See also *Hills* (n 25) [27]–[32] (two domestic assaults six months apart were not a course of conduct); *AVB* (n 6) [224]–[228] (events, including emails and messages, nearly a year apart did not form part of a course of conduct but communications within a two-week period did); and *Pratt v DPP* [2001] EWHC 483 (Admin) [11]–[12] there was a (course of conduct where the defendant threw a beaker of water at his wife and then, three months later, chased her around the house, shouting and swearing at her (although the Court said that it was a borderline case)).

[27] *Lau* (n 26) 801–2 and *Hills* (n 25) [27].

[28] *Law Society* (n 4) [61].

[29] *Law Society* (n 4) [64]. See also *Coulson v Reed* [2014] EWHC 3404 (QB) [49]–[50].

[30] *Thomas v News Group Newspapers Ltd* [2001] EWCA Civ 1233, [2002] EMLR 4 [30].

[31] *Levi* (n 5) [27].

[32] *Levi* (n 5) [28].

[33] Simon J therefore 'went a step too far' by suggesting that it did in *Dowson v Chief Constable of Northumbria Police* [2010] EWHC 2612 (QB) [142] set out at 6.06 (*Levi* (n 31) [26]).

who are foreseeably alarmed and distressed by a course of conduct of the targeted type contemplated by the word harassment.[34]

He notes that stalking, for example, can be as alarming or distressing to the target's new partner as it is to the target him or herself: '[w]hy should the law make protection from harassment for the new partner dependent upon the target taking the requisite proceedings?'[35]

**6.13** Harm to the claimant must, however, be foreseeable.[36] This rule is derived from the requirement in s 1(1)(b) that the perpetrator knows or ought to know that the relevant course of conduct amounts to harassment.[37] In order to establish foreseeability, the claimant must be able to show that he or she was 'foreseeably, and directly, harmed by the course of targeted conduct of which complaint is made, to the extent that they can properly be described as victims of it'.[38] The foreseeable harm suffered by the third party will usually, but not necessarily, be alarm and distress.[39]

**6.14** Alarm or distress which a claimant suffers because of sympathy or concern for the target of the defendant's harassment will not be enough to establish a claim.[40] So, a spouse cannot claim simply because he or she is concerned about the effect of the harassment on his or her husband or wife. But the spouse can succeed if, as in *Levi v Bates*, the defendant directed his or her hostile acts towards the couple's shared home. The Court there held that it was an actionable harassment to publish the couple's address and phone number in a column (published in football programme notes) encouraging club supporters to intervene in a business dispute between the defendant and her husband. Briggs LJ said it was plainly foreseeable that publication of the incitement to intervene would cause alarm and distress to Mr Levi's wife, regardless of whether anyone took up the cudgels or not.[41] The class of potential claimants would also extend, 'and be limited to', anyone else whom the defendant knew was living at Mr Levi's home.[42]

---

[34] *Levi* (n 31) [29].

[35] *Levi* (n 31) [30]. See also [55] (Longmore LJ) ('if...a defendant knows or ought to know that his conduct amounts to harassment, he should be liable to the person harassed, even if the conduct is aimed at another person').

[36] *Levi* (n 31) [33]–[34] (Briggs LJ).

[37] *Levi* (n 31) [33].

[38] *Levi* (n 31) [34] (Briggs LJ). See also [52] (Ryder LJ) ('targeting is an objective concept that includes a situation where the conduct complained of is not only intended to harm a particular victim, but would also foreseeably harm another person, because of her proximity to the intended victim').

[39] *Levi* (n 31) [33].

[40] *Levi* (n 31) [33].

[41] *Levi* (n 31) [35].

[42] *Levi* (n 31) [35]. He adds the further qualification that that is 'provided perhaps that they were old enough to pick up the telephone or answer the front door-bell' (*Levi* (n 31) [35]). See also *Trimingham v Associated Newspapers Ltd* [2012] EWHC 1296 (QB), [2012] 4 All ER 717 [271] where Tugendhat J leaves open the possibility that a secondary character to a newspaper story might succeed in a claim for harassment.

### (3) Calculated in an Objective Sense to Cause Alarm or Distress

#### (a) Causing alarm or distress

Section 7 PHA provides that 'harassment' includes 'alarming the person or causing   **6.15**
the person distress'.[43] However, May LJ confirmed in the Court of Appeal judgment in *Majrowski v Guy's and St Thomas's NHS Trust* that 'the fact that a person
suffers distress is not by itself enough to show that the cause of the distress was
harassment'.[44] As discussed at 6.21 *et seq*, the conduct must also meet the requisite
threshold of seriousness. Conversely, Baroness Hale said in the House of Lords'
decision in *Majrowski* that 'conduct might be harassment even if no alarm or distress were in fact caused'.[45]

#### (b) The defendant's knowledge

Section 1(2) provides that a person 'ought to know' that his or her course of con-   **6.16**
duct amounts to harassment of another if 'a reasonable person in possession of the
same information would think the course of conduct amounted to harassment of
the other'. The Court of Appeal has confirmed that whether the defendant 'ought
to have known' that what he or she was doing amounted to harassment is to be
assessed by reference to 'what a reasonable person would think' taking account of
'the information actually in the possession of th[e] defendant'.[46] As the Court of
Appeal held in *Majrowski*:

> The conduct has also to be calculated, in an objective sense, to cause distress...It
> has to be conduct which the perpetrator knows or ought to know amounts to
> harassment, and conduct which a reasonable person would think amounted to
> harassment.[47]

Although the test is an objective one, the attitude of the claimant to the defendant   **6.17**
and his or her conduct is relevant. Thus, in *AVB v TDD*, in which the claimant
argued that an escort had harassed him by taking USB memory sticks and sending messages to his colleagues and family, Tugendhat J said that when assessing
objectively whether a reasonable person would realize that the conduct in question
would cause distress, one must 'tak[e] into account the actual circumstances in
which the conduct occurred'.[48] Since the claimant continued to renew his association with the defendant and deliberately provoked her with his manipulative and
exploitative behaviour, it could not be said that the conduct complained of was
objectively likely to cause him distress.[49]

---

[43] s 7(2) PHA.
[44] *Majrowski v Guy's and St Thomas's NHS Trust* [2005] EWCA Civ 251 [82].
[45] *Majrowski v Guy's and St Thomas's NHS Trust* [2006] UKHL 34, [2007] 1 AC 224 [66].
[46] *R v C (Sean Peter)* [2001] EWCA Crim 1251, [2001] 2 FLR 757 [20] (also reported as *R v SPC* and *R v Colohan*).
[47] [2005] EWCA Civ 251 [82] (May LJ).
[48] *AVB v TDD* [2014] EWHC 1442 (QB) [230].
[49] *AVB* (n 48) [230]–[231]. Tugendhat J had also found that although the claimant was embarrassed by the defendant's disclosures, he was not distressed by them ([230]).

**6.18**  It is also clear that, when deciding whether a person in possession of the same information as the defendant would think the course of conduct amounted to harassment, the court can take account of the personality and previous conduct of the claimant. Thus, in *King v Medical Services International Ltd* HHJ Williams QC said that:

> ...someone who knows of an individual's vulnerability, needs to take that vulnerability into account when considering his conduct. He cannot shelter behind the argument that most people would not be alarmed or distressed if he knows or ought to know that the targeted individual's vulnerability could result in him or her suffering alarm or distress.[50]

Conversely, Tugendhat J held in *Trimingham* that a journalist considering whether repeated descriptions of the claimant's appearance and sexuality would amount to harassment, could reasonably take account of the fact that she was 'tough, a woman of strong character, not likely to be upset by comments or offensive language, a woman who was known to give as good as she got'.[51] Also relevant was the fact that the claimant had sold stories about the personal lives of others to the media in the past.[52] This suggested, said Tugendhat J, that she saw nothing wrong with disclosing to the world at large newsworthy information about the sexual activities of others or information which had been conveyed in private conversations (which is what she complained the defendants had done to her).[53]

### (4) Conduct which is Objectively Judged to be Oppressive and Unreasonable

**6.19**  In *Thomas v News Group Newspapers Ltd*, Lord Phillips MR (speaking for the Court of Appeal) said that:

> 'Harassment' is...a word which has a meaning which is generally understood. It describes conduct targeted at an individual which is calculated to produce the consequences described in section 7 and which is oppressive and unreasonable. The practice of stalking is a prime example of such conduct.[54]

The Court of Appeal has subsequently confirmed that Lord Phillips MR's reference to conduct 'calculated to' cause anxiety and distress means 'that the conduct must be such as is liable to produce those consequences'.[55] The Court of Appeal elaborated further in *Jones v Ruth*, explaining that:

> Harassment means the persistent tormenting or irritation of the victim. It is therefore deliberate conduct which its perpetrator either knows or certainly ought reasonably to be aware has this effect on the complainant. It will therefore usually

---

[50] *King v Medical Services International Ltd* [2012] EWHC 970 (QB) [201].
[51] *Trimingham* (n 42) [252] citing *Banks v Ablex Ltd* [2005] EWCA Civ 173, [2005] ICR 819 [26].
[52] *Trimingham* (n 42) [153].
[53] *Trimingham* (n 42) [153].
[54] *Thomas* (n 30) [30]. See also *Majrowski* (n 44) [82].
[55] *Banks* (n 51) [20]. See further, *Sharma v Jay* [2003] EWHC 1230 (QB) [22] and *Crossland v Wilkinson Hardware Stores Ltd* [2005] EWHC 481 (QB) [75]–[77].

consist of conduct of a kind which Lord Nicholls has described as intensely personal in character between two individuals: [citing *Majrowski* (n 45) [25]] ... This may range from actual physical force or the threat of force to much more subtle but nonetheless intimidating conduct. In each case the defendant will be (or should be) aware of the effect which his conduct is having on the claimant.[56]

Lord Phillips MR also confirmed in *Thomas* that, even though reasonableness is a defence under s 1(3)(c) PHA, the claimant needs to establish that the behaviour was at least arguably unreasonable in the first instance: **6.20**

While [s 1(3)(c)] places the burden of proof on the defendant, that does not absolve the claimant from pleading facts which are capable of amounting to harassment. Unless the claimant's pleading alleges conduct by the defendant which is, at least, arguably unreasonable, it is unlikely to set out a viable plea of harassment.[57]

### (a) Seriousness of the defendant's conduct

Courts have consistently made it clear that a high threshold of seriousness will be needed before a defendant's conduct is found to be 'oppressive and unreasonable'. They have stressed that conduct which amounts to 'harassment' under s 1 gives rise to both criminal and civil liability under the Act. This means that, even in the civil context, the defendant's conduct must be of sufficient gravity to warrant the intervention of the criminal law before it is defined as 'harassment'. In the House of Lords' decision in *Majrowski v Guy's and St Thomas's NHS Trust*, Lord Nicholls said: **6.21**

Courts are well able to separate the wheat from the chaff at an early stage of the proceedings. They should be astute to do so ... [C]ourts will have in mind that irritations, annoyances, even a measure of upset, arise at times in everybody's day-to-day dealings with other people. Courts are well able to recognise the boundary between conduct which is unattractive, even unreasonable, and conduct which is oppressive and unacceptable. To cross the boundary from the regrettable to the unacceptable the gravity of the misconduct must be of an order which would sustain criminal liability under section 2.[58]

Baroness Hale similarly said that '[a] great deal is left to the wisdom of the courts to draw sensible lines between the ordinary banter and badinage of life and genuinely offensive and unacceptable behaviour'.[59] The resulting standard was well-expressed by Pill LJ in *R v Curtis*, where he said:

To harass as defined in the Concise Oxford Dictionary, Tenth Edition, is to 'torment by subjecting to constant interference or intimidation'. The conduct must be unacceptable to a degree which would sustain criminal liability and also must be oppressive.[60]

---

[56] *Jones v Ruth* [2011] EWCA Civ 804 [24].
[57] *Thomas* (n 30) [31]. For discussion of s 1(3)(c), see 6.34–6.35.
[58] *Majrowski* (n 44) [30].
[59] *Majrowski* (n 44) [66].
[60] *R v Curtis* [2010] EWCA Crim 123 [29]. See also *Roberts v Bank of Scotland* [2013] EWCA Civ 882 [28] and *Halcyon House Ltd v Baines* [2014] EWHC 2216 (QB) [268].

**6.22** However, the requirement that the conduct in question be capable of sustaining criminal liability should not be overemphasized. In *Veakins v Kier Islington*, a case concerning 'extraordinary', 'one-sided' victimization in the workplace, the Court of Appeal held that the Recorder below had been wrong to focus primarily on whether a prosecuting authority would have pursued a criminal case and what chance of success such a prosecution would have had.[61] Maurice Kay LJ, with whom Rimer and Waller LJJ concurred, said that although courts have been enjoined to 'keep in mind' the fact that the conduct must be capable of sustaining criminal liability, the primary question is still whether the conduct complained of is 'oppressive and unacceptable' rather than merely unattractive, unreasonable, or regrettable.[62] In *Ferguson v British Gas Trading Co*, Jacob LJ also held that a course of conduct must be grave before it can be labelled harassment but cautioned that:

> ...the fact of parallel criminal and civil liability is not generally, outside the particular context of harassment, of significance in considering civil liability. There are a number of other civil wrongs which are also crimes...It has never been suggested generally that the scope of a civil wrong is restricted because it is also a crime. What makes the wrong of harassment different and special is because, as Lord Nicholls and Lady Hale recognised, in life one has to put up with a certain amount of annoyance: things have got to be fairly severe before the law, civil or criminal, will intervene.[63]

Tugendhat J observed in a similar vein in *Trimingham* that, '[t]he question for me to decide is not whether the CPS would or should prosecute the defendant, but whether Ms Trimingham has proved her claim that the defendant has committed the statutory tort created by the PHA 1997'.[64]

**6.23** The Court of Appeal has also made it clear that courts should not be too quick to assume that conduct is not capable of supporting a claim for criminal harassment. In *Ferguson*, the Court of Appeal unanimously held that it was 'strongly arguable' that the defendant's conduct in bombarding the claimant with unjustified gas bills and threatening her with disconnection and adverse credit reports was sufficiently serious to amount to harassment. Jacob LJ said that it would be 'entirely proper' for a prosecutor such as a Trading Standards Officer to bring criminal proceedings in such a case.[65] Likewise, in *Veakins*, a unanimous Court of Appeal said that:

> The account of victimisation, demoralisation [of the claimant in her workplace] and the reduction of a substantially reasonable and usually robust woman to a state

---

[61] *Veakins v Kier Islington Ltd* [2009] EWCA Civ 1288 [12].

[62] *Veakins* (n 61) [11].

[63] *Ferguson v British Gas Trading Co* [2009] EWCA Civ 46, [2009] 3 All ER 304, [18] (referring to the House of Lords' decision in *Majrowski* (n 44)).

[64] *Trimingham* (n 42) [63].

[65] *Ferguson* (n 63) [19]. The same conclusion was reached in *Roberts v Bank of Scotland* in respect of hundreds of automatically generated telephone calls from call centre workers to the claimant in respect of actual or alleged indebtedness to the bank: see *Roberts* (n 60) [15].

of clinical depression is not simply an account of 'unattractive' and 'unreasonable' conduct (in Lord Nicholl's words) or 'the ordinary banter and badinage of life' (in Baroness Hale's words). It self-evidently crosses the line into conduct which is 'oppressive and unreasonable'. It may be that, if asked, a prosecutor would be reluctant to prosecute but that is not the consideration, which is whether the conduct is 'of an order which would sustain criminal liability'. I consider that, in the event of a prosecution, the proven conduct would be sufficient to establish criminal liability.[66]

He suggested, however, that it will be rare that conduct in the workplace meets the threshold of seriousness required by the Act.[67]

### (b) *The relevance of context*

Whether the line has been crossed between 'unattractive, even unreasonable conduct' and 'conduct which is oppressive and unacceptable'[68] will depend on the context in which it occurs. As Gage LJ said in the lead judgment in *Conn v Sunderland City Council*, '[w]hat might not be harassment on the factory floor or in the barrack room might well be harassment in the hospital ward and vice versa'.[69] The court in that case relied on Lord Nicholls' dicta in *Majrowski v Guy's and St Thomas's NHS Trust*[70] in concluding that two incidents on a building site in which, first, the claimant's foreman became angry and threatened to punch his fist through a window and secondly, became enraged, threatened to give the claimant 'a good hiding', and said that he knew where he lived, were held not to be 'of an order that would sustain criminal liability'.[71]   **6.24**

### (5) Vicarious and Corporate Liability

An employer can be vicariously liable for the harassment meted out to an individual by one of its employees as long as the connection between the harassment and acts that the employee is authorized to do is sufficiently close that the employee can be said to have been 'acting in the course of his employment'.[72]   **6.25**

The House of Lords have also said that it is 'tolerably clear' that although the victim of harassment must be an individual (or, they might have added,   **6.26**

---

[66] *Veakins* (n 61) [15] (referring to the House of Lords' decision in *Majrowski* (n 44)).
[67] *Veakins* (n 61) [17].
[68] *Majrowski* (n 44) [30] (Lord Nicholls).
[69] *Conn v Sunderland City Council* [2007] EWCA Civ 1492, [2008] IRLR 324 [12].
[70] *Majrowski* (n 44) [30].
[71] *Conn* (n 69) [18] (Buxton LJ). See also [15] (Gage LJ) and [19] (Ward LJ).
[72] *Majrowski* (n 44) [10]. Lord Hope ([43]–[44]), Baroness Hale ([64]–[71]), Lord Brown ([81]) and Lord Carswell ([78]) all held that there were persuasive arguments against the imposition of vicarious liability but held that it was plainly contemplated by the Act. See also discussion in *Allen v Chief Constable of the Hampshire Constabulary* [2013] EWCA Civ 967 [13]–[34] (decision striking out the claimant's vicarious liability argument upheld) and *Veakins* (n 61) [1] (vicarious liability conceded by the defendant).

individuals for the purpose of s 1(1A)),[73] the perpetrator of the harassment can be a corporate body.[74] In *Ferguson v British Gas Trading Ltd*, the Court of Appeal declined to strike out an allegation of harassment against a company which bombarded the claimant with threats and demands even though the correspondence was computer-generated and the claimant could not point to anyone who was responsible for, or even aware of, the letters.[75] Successful claims have also been upheld against banks for bombarding customers with letters and/or telephone calls.[76]

### (6) Defences and Exceptions

**6.27** Section 1(3) PHA provides a defence to an action for harassment. It provides that:

> Subsection (1) does not apply to a course of conduct if the person who pursued it shows –
> (a) that it was pursued for the purpose of preventing or detecting crime,
> (b) that it was pursued under any enactment or rule of law or to comply with any condition or requirement imposed by any person under any enactment, or
> (c) that in the particular circumstances the pursuit of the course of conduct was reasonable.

### (a) Preventing or detecting crime

**6.28** A defendant seeking to rely on the defence in s 1(3)(a) must show that there was some objectively rational basis for his or her belief that the conduct in question was necessary for 'the purpose of preventing or detecting crime'. In *Hayes v Willoughby*, which concerned, *inter alia*, persistent, unfounded official complaints of business impropriety, the Supreme Court identified three different approaches to the assessment of the defendant's 'purpose' under s 1(3)(a). The first required the defendant to show that the belief that the course of conduct was necessary for the prevention or detection of crime was *reasonable* (the wholly objective test).[77] The second was that there must 'objectively judged be some rational basis' for the belief (the rationality test).[78] The third merely required that the belief was genuinely held (the wholly subjective test).[79]

---

[73] See further, *Merlin v Cave* [2014] EWHC 3036 (QB) [25], [50].

[74] *Majrowski* (n 44) [19]. See also *Kosar v Bank of Scotland (trading as Halifax)* [2011] EWHC 1050 (Admin) [3]–[10] in which Silber J confirmed that the reference in section 7(5) to 'a person who is an individual' applies only to victims and not perpetrators.

[75] *Ferguson* (n 63) [24]–[45].

[76] See *Bank of Scotland v Johnson* [2013] EWCA Civ 982 and *Roberts* (n 60).

[77] This was the test adopted by Tugendhat J in *KD v Chief Constable of Hampshire, John Hull* [2005] EWHC 2550 (QB), [2005] Police LR 253 [114], at least where the victim's Art 8 rights were at stake.

[78] This was the approach taken by Eady J in *Howlett v Holding* [2006] EWHC 41 (QB) [33].

[79] This was the approach in *EDO MBM Technology Ltd v Axworthy* [2005] EWHC 2490 (QB) [28]–[29].

All the judges in *Hayes* agreed that the wholly objective test is inconsistent with the   **6.29**
language and purpose of the PHA.[80] The majority said this is because, in other provisions of the Act, the test of reasonableness was specifically included. For example, the words 'knows or ought to know' are used in s 1(1)(b) and 'if a reasonable
person would think' included in s 1(2).[81] If Parliament had wanted s 1(3)(a) to be
wholly objective it would, they argue, have used similar language. Further, if the
preventing or detecting crime defence in s 1(3)(a) required reasonableness, it would
be subsumed within the general 'reasonableness' defence in s 1(3)(c).[82] The majority also doubted whether an objective requirement could be workably applied to
public authorities.[83]

The majority also regarded the purely subjective test as unsatisfactory. Lord Sumption   **6.30**
(with whom Lords Neuberger and Wilson agreed) noted that harassment is often
carried out by people who 'will in the nature of things be obsessives and cranks, who
will commonly believe themselves to be entitled to act as they do'.[84] People, he argues,
need protection from such individuals:

> Recent cases in the courts illustrate the propensity of obsessives to engage in con-
> duct which is oppressive enough to constitute harassment, in the genuine belief
> that they are preventing crime... It cannot be the case that the mere existence
> of a belief, however absurd, in the mind of the harasser that he is detecting or
> preventing a possibly non-existent crime, will justify him in persisting in a course
> of conduct which the law characterises as oppressive. Some control mechanism is
> required.[85]

He continues that 'rationality' should be the control mechanism.[86] Rationality,   **6.31**
he says, is a lower standard than 'reasonableness' which is 'an external, objective
standard applied to the outcome of a person's thoughts or intentions'.[87] If 'reasonableness' is the standard, then the question is 'whether a notional hypothetically
reasonable person in [the defendant's] position would have engaged in the relevant

---

[80] *Hayes v Willoughby* [2013] UKSC 17 [11]. The dissenting judge, Lord Reed, agreed with the
majority on this point but solely on the basis that reading a reasonableness requirement into s 1(3)(a)
would render s 1(3)(c) otiose ([24]).

[81] *Hayes* (n 80) [11].

[82] *Hayes* (n 80) [11].

[83] *Hayes* (n 80) [11].

[84] *Hayes* (n 80) [12].

[85] *Hayes* (n 80) [12]–[13]. See also *Brand v Berki* [2014] EWHC 2979 (QB) [44] ('since the test of
knowledge is constructive and objective... [t]he fact that [the defendant] might suffer from a mental
illness is... irrelevant by way of defence').

[86] Lord Mance agreed that some sort of control mechanism, short of reasonableness, is required.
He said that 'the law recognizes looser control mechanisms such as complete irrationality, perversity,
abusiveness or, indeed, in some contexts gross negligence' (*Hayes* (n 80) [22]). He continued that
in the present case it did not matter which of these standards was adopted since 'they all probably
amount to very much the same thing' and it was clear that on any such measure, the defendant's state
of mind took his course of conduct 'outside paragraph (a)' (*Hayes* (n 80) [23]).

[87] *Hayes* (n 80) [14].

conduct for the purpose of preventing or detecting crime'.[88] In contrast, a test of 'rationality':

> ...applies a minimum objective standard to the relevant person's mental processes. It imports a requirement of good faith, a requirement that there should be some logical connection between the evidence and the ostensible reasons for the decision, and (which will usually amount to the same thing) an absence of arbitrariness, of capriciousness or of reasoning so outrageous in its defiance of logic as to be perverse.[89]

All this means that:

> Before an alleged harasser can be said to have had the purpose of preventing or detecting crime, he must have sufficiently applied his mind to the matter. He must have thought rationally about the material suggesting the possibility of criminality and formed the view that the conduct said to constitute harassment was appropriate for the purpose of preventing or detecting it. If he has done these things, then he has the relevant purpose. The court will not test his conclusions by reference to the view which a hypothetical reasonable man in his position would have formed. If, on the other hand, he has not engaged in these minimum mental processes necessary to acquire the relevant state of mind, but proceeds anyway on the footing that he is acting to prevent or detect crime, then he acts irrationally. In that case, two consequences will follow. The first is that the law will not regard him as having had the relevant purpose at all. He has simply not taken the necessary steps to form one. The second is that the causal connection which section 1(3)(a) posits between the purpose of the alleged harasser and the conduct constituting the harassment, will not exist.[90]

**6.32** Rationality is not, said Lord Sumption, a demanding standard: 'it is hard to imagine that Parliament can have intended anything less'.[91] Nonetheless, it was not satisfied in *Hayes* itself. The defendant's vendetta against the claimant was found to have become 'irrational' and 'obsessive', with an unshakable conviction of the claimant's guilt preceding rather than following an objective assessment of the evidence.[92]

**6.33** In his dissenting judgment, Lord Reed agreed with the trial judge that the test in s 1(3)(a) was purely subjective and criticized the imposition of the rationality requirement. His reasons were threefold. First, he said that introducing a requirement of objective rationality requires the court to read in words which Parliament did not use,[93] a step which is, secondly, contrary to the rule that a statute is not normally to be construed as extending criminal liability beyond

---

[88] *Hayes* (n 80) [14].

[89] *Hayes* (n 80) [14]. He is 'not talking about the broader categories of *Wednesbury* unreasonableness, a legal construct referring to a decision lying beyond the furthest reaches of objective reasonableness' ([14]).

[90] *Hayes* (n 80) [15]. The test is said to have the added advantage of applying to private persons the standard already applied to public authorities under public law when they engage in crime detection or prevention activities (*Hayes* (n 80) [15]). See also, *Brand* (n 85) [44] where Carr J questions how the publicity the defendant was seeking for her accusations again the claimants would advance the aim of preventing and detecting crime, given that the police were already investigating the activities about which she was complaining.

[91] *Hayes* (n 80) [15].

[92] *Hayes* (n 80) [16].

[93] *Hayes* (n 80) [26].

the limits that Parliament has made clear in its enactments.[94] Thirdly, he said that criminal liability should not turn on the subtle distinction between what is unreasonable and what is irrational partly because he doubts that a jury would be able to make sense of it: 'I am not convinced that Parliament can have intended that a jury should be expected to understand and apply the sophisticated distinctions which Lord Sumption seeks to draw.'[95] Further, Lord Reed says that from a policy perspective it is understandable why Parliament might wish to exclude from the Act's reach persons genuinely seeking to prevent or detect crime such as, for example, public agencies exercising investigative powers and investigative journalists.[96] Potential liability, he said, might have an inhibiting effect on such people's activities.[97]

### (b) Reasonableness in section 1(3)(c)

In *Thomas v News Group Newspapers Ltd*, the Court of Appeal held that whether **6.34** conduct satisfies the requirements of the reasonableness test in s 1(3)(c) 'will depend upon the circumstances of the particular case'.[98] The test is however an objective one. In *R v C (Sean Peter)*, the Court of Appeal Criminal Division held that:

> As to section 1(3)(c) that, we are satisfied, poses even more clearly [than s 1(2)] an objective test, namely whether the conduct is in the judgment of the jury reasonable. There is no warrant for attaching to the word 'reasonable' or via the words 'particular circumstances' the standards or characteristics of the defendant himself.[99]

Where publication in the press is concerned, whether the conduct was reason- **6.35** able 'does not turn upon whether opinions expressed in the article are reasonably held' but must be determined 'by reference to the right of the press to freedom of expression'[100] which is discussed further at 6.37 *et seq.*

## C. Specific Types of Harassment

### (1) Newspaper Articles as Harassment

As outlined above, s 7 PHA expressly provides that 'conduct', for the purposes **6.36** of the PHA, includes 'speech'. The publication of true or false information about a person, including in newspaper articles, can be harassment for the purposes of s 1(1).

---

[94] *Hayes* (n 80) [27].
[95] *Hayes* (n 80) [28].
[96] *Hayes* (n 80) [29]–[30].
[97] *Hayes* (n 80) [29].
[98] *Thomas v News Group Newspapers Ltd* [2001] EWCA Civ 1233, [2002] EMLR 4 [32].
[99] *R v C (Sean Peter)* [2001] EWCA Crim 1251, [2001] 2 FLR 757 [21] (also reported as *R v SPC* and *R v Colohan*).
[100] *Thomas* (n 98) [32].

*(a)* Thomas v News Group Newspapers Ltd

**6.37** In *Thomas v News Group Newspapers Ltd*, the Court of Appeal held that the publication of articles in the press was capable of amounting to harassment under
the Act.[101] It therefore declined to strike out or dispose summarily of the claimant's argument that the defendant had harassed her by publishing three articles
referring to her as a 'black clerk', criticizing her involvement in a dispute over a
racist comment made by police officers at her place of work, and disclosing her
name and work address. The Court recognized the importance of the defendant's
freedom of expression and said that, even if it has foreseeably caused distress, '[i]n
general, press criticism, even if robust, does not constitute unreasonable conduct
and does not fall within the natural meaning of harassment'.[102] Before press
articles can be held to constitute harassment 'they must be attended by some
exceptional circumstance which justifies sanctions and the restriction on the
freedom of expression that they involve'.[103] Lord Phillips MR held that the test
for whether the articles amount to harassment requires the publisher to consider:

> ...whether a proposed series of articles, which is likely to cause distress to an indi-
> vidual, will constitute an abuse of the freedom of press which the pressing social
> needs of a democratic society require should be curbed.[104]

As for how that test should be applied, he said earlier in the judgment that:

> In general, press criticism, even if robust, does not constitute unreasonable conduct
> and does not fall within the natural meaning of harassment. A pleading, which
> does no more than allege that the defendant newspaper has published a series of
> articles that have foreseeably caused distress to an individual, will be susceptible
> to a strike-out on the ground that it discloses no arguable case of harassment.[105]

**6.38** Circumstances in which newspaper publications will amount to harassment will
be rare but both parties accepted that publication of articles calculated to incite
racial hatred of an individual could amount to harassment under the PHA, recognizing, said the Court, that 'the Convention right of freedom of expression
does not extend to protect remarks directly against the Convention's underlying
values'.[106] Since the claimant was found to have pleaded an arguable case that the
articles did have such an effect, the appeal was unsuccessful.[107]

**6.39** This decision had a significant impact on the scope of the media's potential
liability under the PHA. As long as it was foreseeable that the publicity would
cause the claimant distress and alarm, a media body which disseminated, on
more than one occasion, personal details about the claimant and/or encouraged

---

[101] *Thomas* (n 98) [15].
[102] *Thomas* (n 98) [34].
[103] *Thomas* (n 98) [35].
[104] *Thomas* (n 98) [50].
[105] *Thomas* (n 98) [34].
[106] *Thomas* (n 98) [37].
[107] *Thomas* (n 98) [49].

readers to contact him or her could be liable for harassment.[108] A newspaper could therefore be liable for publishing, as part of a course of conduct, the address of a celebrity who was, or thought she was, particularly vulnerable to stalking (regardless of whether the stalking actually ensued) or for publishing an article criticizing an ordinary member of the public and encouraging readers to contact him. If the claimant can show that the defendant's conduct would amount to an abuse of the freedom of the press which should be curbed in the public interest, then the requirements of the legislation could well be made out.

*(b)* Trimingham v Associated Newspapers Ltd

Since *Thomas*, however, there is no case in which a harassment claim against **6.40** a newspaper has been successfully established.[109] In *Trimingham v Associated Newspapers Ltd*, Tugendhat J found against a claimant who argued that the defendant had harassed her by publishing observations about her sexuality and personal appearance in articles and readers' comments concerning an affair she had with married Cabinet Minister, Chris Huhne, while working as his press officer and in a civil partnership with another woman. The claimant complained that in 57 articles and the readers' comments she was repeatedly referred to as 'bisexual' and/or as having a masculine, ugly appearance, and that these references were offensive, irrelevant, homophobic, and caused her significant distress. She claimed damages, including aggravated damages, and an injunction restraining the defendant from, *inter alia*, publishing photographs of her civil union ceremony, irrelevant references to her sexuality, and claims that she is ugly and masculine in appearance.

Central to Tugendhat J's disposal of the case was the need to ensure that the appli- **6.41** cation of the PHA did not encroach unduly on freedom of expression. He began by citing *Thomas* at some length, concluding that:

> What I understand Lord Phillips to be saying is that, for the court to comply with HRA s.3, it must hold that a course of conduct in the form of journalistic speech is reasonable under PHA 1997 s.1(3)(c) unless, in the particular circumstances of the case, the course of conduct is so unreasonable that it is necessary (in the sense of a pressing social need) and proportionate to prohibit or sanction the speech in pursuit of one of the aims listed in Art 10(2), including, in particular, for the protection of the rights of others under Art 8.[110]

---

[108] See *eg Levi* (n 5) (regarding publication in football programme notes). See also *Thomas* (n 98) [46] where Lord Phillips MR took account of the fact that the defendant published the claimant's name and place of work in concluding that it was at least arguably foreseeable that the publication would lead *Sun* readers to cause the respondent additional stress by addressing hostile letters to her.

[109] Although harassment was established in respect of statements made in football programme notes and in a radio broadcast in *Levi* (n 108).

[110] *Trimingham v Associated Newspapers Ltd* [2012] EWHC 1296 (QB), [2012] 4 All ER 717 [53].

He agreed with Lord Phillips MR that the overarching question is, as outlined above, 'whether a proposed series of articles, which is likely to cause distress to an individual, will constitute an abuse of the freedom of press which the pressing social needs of a democratic society require should be curbed'.[111]

**6.42** Tugendhat J held that Lord Phillips MR's view that 'harassment must not be given an interpretation that restricts the right to freedom of expression'[112] bears on two aspects of the PHA's application: first, the assessment of whether a reasonable person in possession of the same information as the defendant would know that the course of conduct amounted to harassment (for the purpose of establishing liability under s 1(2) and (3)) and second, when considering whether the defendant's conduct was reasonable (for the purpose of the defence in s 1(3)).[113] He explained that 'a reasonable person within the meaning of s 1(2) must be a person who adheres to the values in the Convention'.[114]

**6.43** **Did the defendant's conduct amount to harassment under s 1(2) and (3)?** As well as freedom of expression, Tugendhat J identified a number of other factors which are relevant to an assessment of whether a reasonable person in possession of the same information would have regarded the defendant's conduct as harassment.[115]

**6.44** *The status of the claimant* The first factor Tugendhat J considered was whether the claimant was a public or private figure. He held that there was no dispute that this question was relevant when freedom of expression is at stake[116] and he rejected the claim that Ms Trimingham was a private individual.[117] This is, first, because Ms Trimingham had undertaken work as a press officer for a leading politician. The public therefore 'had an interest in knowing whether they could trust Mr Huhne and Ms Trimingham not to deceive them', especially since 'spin doctors' are not always trusted by the electorate.[118] Secondly, in her private capacity, the claimant had 'take[n] the risk of being mixed up in a political scandal, which her own conduct precipitated'.[119] She must have known that this meant that the scope of her private life would become somewhat more limited.[120] Later, in the judgment he explained that:

> ...discussion or criticism of sexual relations which arise within a pre-existing pro-
> fessional relationship, or of sexual relationships which involves the deception of

---

[111] *Trimingham* (n 110) [54]–[55] citing *Thomas* (n 98) [50].

[112] See *Trimingham* (n 110) [78] citing *Thomas* (n 98) [24] (although the original quotation in *Thomas* continues 'save as this is necessary in order to achieve a legitimate aim').

[113] *Trimingham* (n 110) [78].

[114] *Trimingham* (n 110) [78].

[115] *Trimingham* (n 110) [78].

[116] *Trimingham* (n 110) [93].

[117] *Trimingham* (n 110) [249].

[118] *Trimingham* (n 110) [249].

[119] *Trimingham* (n 110) [249].

[120] *Trimingham* (n 110) [250]. See also [249] ('The public has an interest in knowing how the personal life of a leading politician, especially a Cabinet Minister, is likely to affect, or has affected, the business of government').

a spouse, or a civil partner, or of others with a right not to be deceived, are matters which a reasonable person would not think would be conduct amounting to harassment, and would think was reasonable, unless there are some other circumstances which make it unreasonable.[121]

*The 'personality' of the claimant*   It was not in dispute that, when considering **6.45** whether a journalist ought to know that his or her articles amount to harassment of an individual, the court should consider the 'characteristics of that person which are known to the journalist'.[122] So, it was relevant that the claimant could reasonably be seen by a person in possession of the same information as the defendants to be 'tough, a woman of strong character, not likely to be upset by comments or offensive language, a women who was known to give as good as she got'.[123] As mentioned at 6.18, this conclusion was strengthened by the fact that the claimant had herself sold to the media stories about the personal lives of others in the past, thereby suggesting that she saw nothing wrong with such conduct.[124]

*The meaning of the words complained of*   When considering the effect of a course **6.46** of conduct which consists of speech, a court might have to decide 'what meaning the words convey'.[125] When making that assessment, the court must consider what the defendant knew or ought to have known about the effect of the words on the subject.[126] Tugendhat J confirmed that, in principle, the repeated publication in the media of offensive or insulting words about a person's appearance can amount to harassment.[127] The same applies, *a fortiori*, to references to a person's sexuality:

> I accept [counsel's] general proposition that repeated mocking by a national newspaper of a person by reference to that person's sexual orientation would almost inevitably be so oppressive as to amount harassment. The same is likely to apply to repeated mocking by reference to any of the characteristics which are defined as protected characteristics in the Equality Act 2010, s4, [namely, age; disability; gender reassignment; marriage and civil partnership; pregnancy and maternity; race; religion or belief; sex; sexual orientation] even where the Equality Act 2010 does not apply. That is because of the nature of those characteristics.[128]

---

[121] *Trimingham* (n 110) [262].

[122] *Trimingham* (n 110) [89]. See also 6.18.

[123] *Trimingham* (n 110) [252] citing *Banks v Ablex Ltd* [2005] EWCA Civ 173, [2005] ICR 819 [26].

[124] *Trimingham* (n 110) [153]. He also stressed that '[i]t is all the more important that the court be careful to interpret the PHA 1997 in a manner which is compatible with Art 10, where, as here, it is not alleged that any of the many journalists who wrote the words complained of were personally pursuing a course of conduct which they knew was causing distress to Ms Trimingham' ([90]).

[125] *Trimingham* (n 110) [57].

[126] *Trimingham* (n 110) [57].

[127] *Trimingham* (n 110) [70]. See also [62] where he said that speech referring to a person's sexual orientation, looks, race or other personal characteristics would be capable of causing 'distress', 'harassment', 'insult', 'abuse', and 'ridicule', and therefore of constituting harassment for the purposes of the PHA 1997.

[128] *Trimingham* (n 110) [70].

**6.47**  Applying these arguments to the facts of the case, the judge accepted that the defendant journalists' comments about the claimant's personal appearance and clothing
were insulting and offensive.[129] But, in contrast, he did not accept that the words
'bisexual' and 'lesbian' would have been understood by a reasonable reader to have
been pejorative.[130] He said that the reasonable reader who knew that the claimant had
been living with her civil partner when the affair was conducted would understand
them to refer, not to her sexual orientation as such, but to 'her conduct in deceiving her
civil partner, at the same time as Mr Huhne was deceiving his wife'.[131] He said that the
words 'bisexual' and 'lesbian' were factual words[132] and that it was acceptable to use
them as shorthand labels to remind readers of the back story to the affair.[133]

**6.48**  *Causation*   Although Tugendhat J accepted that the claimant had suffered the
distress described, he was not persuaded that it was caused (nor that the defendant
ought to have known it would be caused) by the course of conduct to which her
claim was directed—namely the repetition of comments about her sexuality and
appearance.[134] He said that a reasonable person in possession of the information
available to the defendant would think that distress would instead be caused by
the publication of true allegations about the affair about which no complaint was
made.[135] Further, he said that the claimant had not adequately distinguished the
effect of the particular words complained of from the effect of the conduct of other
media operators.[136] Tugendhat J therefore did not accept that the defendant ought
to have known that its conduct in relation to that language would be 'sufficiently
distressing to be considered oppressive or amount to harassment'.[137]

**6.49**  **Was the defendant's conduct reasonable for the purposes of s 1(3)(c)?**   As discussed at 6.34, s 1(3)(c) PHA provides that s 1(1) does not apply to a course of
conduct if the person who pursues it shows that 'in particular circumstances the
pursuit of the course of conduct was reasonable'. Tugendhat J noted that the question of whether a reasonable person in the position of the defendant ought to have
known that the words amounted to harassment (s 1(1) and (2)) and whether in the
particular circumstances of the case the course of conduct was reasonable (s 1(3)(c)),
'are closely linked in the present case'.[138] Many of the issues, including those

---

[129]  *Trimingham* (n 110) [255].
[130]  *Trimingham* (n 110) [256].
[131]  *Trimingham* (n 110) [256].
[132]  *Trimingham* (n 110) [255].
[133]  See *Trimingham* (n 110) [256]. Defence witnesses had consistently referred to the practice
of inserting an identifier or tag to remind readers of previous coverage (see [106], [172], [186],
and [216]).
[134]  *Trimingham* (n 110) [252].
[135]  *Trimingham* (n 110) [254]. He found that in so far as the conduct of the defendant had caused
her distress, it was in fact because it had published defamatory but true allegations of that nature
[254]. See also [91]–[92] and [146].
[136]  *Trimingham* (n 110) [253].
[137]  *Trimingham* (n 110) [254].
[138]  *Trimingham* (n 110) [260].

relating to the meaning of the words, their relevance, and freedom of expression, were therefore relevant in both contexts.

*Reference to sexuality not irrelevant*  Tugendhat J did not accept that the fact of the **6.50** claimant's sexuality was irrelevant to the reporting of and reference to the claimant's affair with Mr Huhne. Applying s 1(3), he said that:

> ...if a journalist is criticising a person for deceitful, unprofessional or immoral behaviour in a sexual and public context, it is not of itself unreasonable to refer to that person as homosexual if in fact they are, and it is their sexual conduct which is one of the factors giving rise to the newsworthy events.[139]

Further, he said it is not 'unreasonable to refer to those facts on as many occasions as the substance of the story is repeated and referred to explain subsequent events of public interest'.[140]

*Deception in relationships*  He went on to say, as mentioned at 6.44, that a reason- **6.51** able person would not regard as unreasonable discussion or criticism of sexual relations within a pre-existing professional relationship, or of sexual relationships which involves the deception of a spouse, or a civil partner, or of others unless there are some other circumstances which make it unreasonable.[141] Such discussion is, therefore, neither harassing for the purposes of s 1(1)(1) and (2) nor unreasonable under s 1(3)(c).

*Balance between Article 8 and 10 rights*  One circumstance which might make a **6.52** course of conduct unreasonable for the purposes of s 1(3)(c) is if it is an interference with the Article 8 rights of the claimant.[142] But, in *Trimingham*, the claimant's Article 8 rights had become very limited.[143] This was on account, first, of the fact that she is not a purely private figure and secondly, of her own openness about her sexuality and sexual relationships.[144]

Further, Tugendhat J stressed that the word 'reasonable' in s 1(3)(c) must be inter- **6.53** preted compatibly with the Article 10 right to freedom of expression.[145] The issue he had to decide was whether it was reasonable for the purposes of s 1(3)(c) for the claimant's critics, particularly the defendant, repeatedly to refer to her sexuality, and occasionally to her appearance and other information about her, in the circumstances of this case even though that conduct might offend, shock, or disturb a sector of the population, including Ms Trimingham herself.[146] In holding that

---

[139] *Trimingham* (n 110) [261].

[140] *Trimingham* (n 110) [26].

[141] *Trimingham* (n 110) [262].

[142] *Trimingham* (n 110) [263].

[143] *Trimingham* (n 110) [263].

[144] *Trimingham* (n 110) [263].

[145] *Trimingham* (n 110) [264]. See also [78] and the discussion at 6.34–6.35.

[146] *Trimingham* (n 110) [264]. (The judgment in fact says 'unreasonable' but this appears to be an error.)

it was, Tugendhat J said that pluralism has long been recognized by the European Court of Human Rights to be one of the essential ingredients of a democracy and that pluralism 'requires members of society to tolerate the dissemination of information and views which they believe to be false and wrong',[147] particularly in regard to matters such as sexual conduct where there is no consensus about what is true or right.[148] It follows that 'the law must not penalise the expression of views that may offend, shock or disturb sectors of the population, including, of course, particular individuals (subject to the rights of those individuals under Art 8 and to the application of Art 10(2))'.[149]

**6.54** So, even if the words which the claimant complained of were offensive or insulting, that of itself would not suffice for her to succeed.

> It would be a serious interference with freedom of expression if those wishing to express their own views could be silenced by, or threatened with, claims for harassment based on subjective claims by individuals that they feel offended or insulted. The test for harassment is objective.[150]

Thus, he repeated Lord Phillips MR's observation in *Thomas* that before press publications can be capable of constituting harassment, 'they must be attended by some exceptional circumstance which justifies sanctions and the restriction on the freedom of expression that they involve', and that such circumstances will be rare.[151]

**6.55** *Article 10 and the importance of truth* Earlier in the judgment, Tugendhat J said that it was particularly significant that Ms Trimingham was not pursuing a claim in respect of the central defamatory theme of the articles as they refer to her, namely her involvement in the break-up of Mr Huhne's marriage.[152] As Tugendhat J acknowledged, the same point was emphasized by the judge at first instance and the Court of Appeal in the Northern Irish case of *King v Sunday Newspapers Ltd*. The defendant newspaper in that case had written 29 articles accusing the claimant of being a drug dealer and an accessory to the murder of a journalist, and had disclosed allegedly private information such as the claimant's address, the name of his partner and child, and their religion. Although Weatherup J held that there was a course of conduct targeting the claimant which had, and was calculated to have, the effect of causing distress to the claimant, and that the articles contained some inaccuracies and private material, the defendant's conduct was nonetheless reasonable.[153] This was

---

147 *Trimingham* (n 110) [265].
148 *Trimingham* (n 110) [266].
149 *Trimingham* (n 110) [266].
150 *Trimingham* (n 110) [267].
151 *Trimingham* (n 110) [267] citing *Thomas* (n 98) [35].
152 *Trimingham* (n 110) [91].
153 *King v Sunday Newspapers Ltd* [2010] NIQB 107 [43].

because 'the truth of the central theme of the articles was not an issue in these proceedings'.[154] The Court of Appeal agreed. It said:

> Particularly in light of the fact that the appellant declined to institute defamation proceedings to challenge the correctness of the thrust of the robust allegations of serious criminality made in the articles we conclude that the judge was correct to conclude that the appellant had not made out a case of harassment.[155]

*Taunting or excessive repetition*    Tugendhat J ended his discussion of reasonable-  **6.56** ness by saying that excessive repetition of speech so that, for example, it amounts to taunting can turn an otherwise acceptable course of conduct (including references to one's sexual orientation) into harassment.[156] But that was not the case in *Trimingham*. Although the fact that the claimant was bisexual had been mentioned in some 65 articles and comments about her appearance had also been repeated, in all of these stories the focus of the article was Mr Huhne[157] and related to a news-worthy event in which he was involved.[158] The repetition did not turn the speech (which was otherwise reasonable for the purposes of s 1(3)(c)) into harassment.[159]

**Readers' comments**    In addition to the articles, the claimant in *Trimingham*  **6.57** complained about readers' comments about her appearance and/or sexuality which appeared beneath the defendants' articles on their website, *MailOnline*. She said the comments taunted and lampooned her for being ugly and attacked her in regard to her sexuality and that it would be obvious to any reasonable person that comments of this type would cause the claimant unwarranted distress.[160] She also said that the reactions in the readers' comments were stimulated by the articles written by the journalists.[161] The defendant claimed in response that although some of the readers' comments included insulting observations, it had expressly disassociated itself from readers' comments with a statement on the website.[162] It also said there was no good reason to edit out all comments which were critical of Ms Trimingham nor to think that Ms Trimingham would read the readers' comments section.[163]

---

[154] *King* (n 153) [43]. The defendants were, however, restrained on other grounds from publishing the defendant's place of residence; details of his partner's workplace, family members and religion; details about his child; his partner's identity and a photograph of her (see *King* (n 153) [47], affirmed in *King v Sunday Newspapers Ltd* [2011] NICA 8 [39]).

[155] *King v Sunday Newspapers Ltd* [2011] NICA 8 [38]. For further discussion of the freedom of expression defence, see 6.63–6.68.

[156] *Trimingham* (n 110) [268].

[157] *Trimingham* (n 110) [269].

[158] *Trimingham* (n 110) [272]. Tugendhat J declined to say that it would never be possible for a secondary character in a story to establish harassment and left open the question of whether Ms Trimingham was 'targeted' here ([269]–[272]). For further discussion of targeting, see 6.11–6.14.

[159] *Trimingham* (n 110) [272].

[160] *Trimingham* (n 110) [42].

[161] *Trimingham* (n 110) [45].

[162] *Trimingham* (n 110) [104].

[163] *Trimingham* (n 110) [104].

**6.58** The judge made no decision on those matters. Instead, Tugendhat J rejected the claim relating to readers' comments for the same reasons that he rejected the claim about the newspaper articles.[164] He said that although some of the comments were insulting and offensive and therefore unreasonable in the ordinary meaning of that word, they were not so unreasonable that it was necessary and proportionate to prohibit their publication.[165] He also noted that the complaints related to a very small proportion of the total number of comments and that other comments were in a different tone, including some which were supportive of the claimant.[166]

### (2) Campaigns of Vilification

**6.59** Campaigns of vilification involving the publication of defamatory allegations, indecent images, or private or personal information are increasingly the subject of interim injunctions for harassment.[167] Such claims are often brought alongside claims for misuse of private information or defamation.[168]

### (a) Examples of harassing campaigns of vilification

**6.60** Unsurprisingly, many vilification cases involve publications on the internet. For example, in *R v Debnath*, a woman's obsessive email and internet campaign against a man with whom she had a casual sexual encounter (and his fiancée) was held to amount to harassment.[169] In *Brand v Berki*, a masseuse was held to have harassed celebrity couple, Russell Brand and Jemima Khan, by accusing them of serious criminal offending in the media, in emails to numerous people (including politicians and journalists), and in an online petition.[170] Harassment was also found when a defendant published a website (*Solicitors from Hell*) containing false allegations of wrongdoing against solicitors;[171] a defendant disclosed on the internet (or threatened to disclose) allegations about the private life of a woman connected to a powerful ruling family who owed him money;[172] and a defendant published on the internet (and in leaflets, banners, and emails) allegations of murder against NHS doctors of a baby who died of natural causes.[173]

**6.61** More traditional methods of publication were used in *Howlett v Holding*.[174] In that case, a wealthy businessman was held to have harassed a former local

---

[164] *Trimingham* (n 110) [275].
[165] *Trimingham* (n 110) [275].
[166] *Trimingham* (n 110) [275].
[167] *ZAM v CFW and TFW* [2013] EWHC 662 (QB) [21].
[168] See *eg EWQ v GFD* [2012] EWHC 2182 (QB); *Trimingham* (n 110); and *AVB v TDD* [2014] EWHC 1442 (QB).
[169] *R v Debnath* [2005] EWCA Crim 3472, [2006] 2 Cr App R (S) 25.
[170] *Brand v Berki* [2014] EWHC 2979 (QB).
[171] *Law Society v Kordowski* [2011] EWHC 3185 (QB).
[172] *WXY v Gewanter* [2012] EWHC 496 (QB).
[173] *Petros v Chaudhari* [2004] EWCA Civ 458, [2004] All ER (D) 173. But compare *Crawford v CPS* [2008] EWHC 148 (Admin) [69]–[70] (sending a letter alleging professional misconduct to the claimant's law firm did not contribute to a course of harassment).
[174] *Howlett v Holding* [2006] EWHC 41 (QB).

councillor by arranging for banners to be flown across the sky and for leaflets to be delivered to local households containing derogatory comments about her.[175] Leeds United Football Club and its chairman were also found to have harassed a former director of the club by publishing allegations against him in match programmes, and by broadcasting a radio message saying that the club was looking for him and inviting listeners to ring in with information about his whereabouts.[176]

Tugendhat J held in *Thompson v James and Carmarthenshire County Council* that it **6.62** is not an answer to an allegation of harassment arising from specific blog posts to say that many or most of the other matters posted on the blog are not harassment.[177] A blog can 'be both a contribution to public debate in respect of some of its content, and an ongoing act of harassment *etc* in relation to other parts of its content'.[178]

### (b) Balancing privacy and freedom of expression

As Eady J explained in *Howlett v Holding*, where the claimant's Article 8 right to **6.63** private life comes into conflict with the defendant's Article 10 right to freedom of expression, courts must apply an 'intense focus' to ascertain the comparative importance of the specific rights being claimed (as required by the House of Lords in *Re S (A Child)*).[179]

A court will only grant an injunction restraining campaigns of vilification if it is **6.64** satisfied that the claimant is not attempting to use the law of harassment to circumvent the law on freedom of speech.[180] As Laing J observed in *Merlin v Cave*:

> There is no express indication in the PHA that Parliament intended the provisions of the PHA to abrogate the rights conferred by Article 10, or to change the law of defamation, which is, by necessary implication, involved in any consideration of the scope of the legitimate restrictions which may be placed by a contracting state on the rights conferred by Article 10. Nothing in the PHA indicates that Parliament intended to encroach on the rule in *Bonnard v Perryman* [*ie* that courts should not award an injunction where a defamation defendant intends to plead justification].[181]

---

[175] *Howlett* (n 174).
[176] *Levi* (n 5). See also *Hayes v Willoughby* [2013] UKSC 17 (defendant persistently made baseless complaints of business impropriety to numerous public authorities and sought to discredit the claimant by making other allegations about him and passing on confidential about information about his health).
[177] *Thompson v James and Carmarthenshire County Council* [2013] EWHC 515 (QB) [297].
[178] *Thompson* (n 177) [298].
[179] *Howlett* (n 174) [11]–[14] referring to *Re S (FC) (A Child)* [2004] UKHL 47, [2005] 1 AC 593. See also *Hipgrave v Jones* [2004] EWHC 2901 (QB) [50] and, for further discussion of *Re S* and the 'intense focus', 5.159–5.160.
[180] *ZAM* (n 167) [21]. See also *Crossland v Wilkinson Hardware Stores Ltd* [2005] EWHC 481 (QB) [81] ('In so far as the conduct relied on by a claimant as harassment is speech, the courts must not allow baseless claims to chill the exercise of rights of freedom of expression of employers and others').
[181] *Merlin v Cave* [2014] EWHC 3036 (QB) [39].

**6.65** However, the rule in *Bonnard v Perryman* is not necessarily a complete answer to an application for an interim injunction in the harassment context: there may be cases where an injunction is appropriate even though the harassment consisted of statements which the defendant claims are justified.[182] This will be the case where:

> ...such statements are part of the harassment which is relied on, but where that harassment has additional elements of oppression, persistence or unpleasantness, which are distinct from the content of the statements. An example might be a defendant who pursues an admitted adulterer through the streets for a lengthy period, shouting 'You are an adulterer' through a megaphone. The fact that the statement is true, and could and would be justified at trial, would not necessarily prevent the conduct from being harassment, or prevent a court from restraining it at an interlocutory stage.[183]

Tugendhat J explains why this is in *Law Society v Kordowski*:

> The different causes of action are directed to protecting different aspects of the right to private life. A claim in libel is directed to protecting the right to reputation. The claim in harassment is to protect persons from being subjected to unjustifiable alarm and distress.[184]

**6.66** However, courts must scrutinize very carefully claims that the defendant's conduct is sufficiently oppressive, persistent, or unpleasant to cross the line from acceptable conduct into harassment and must 'ensure that any relief sought, while restraining objectionable conduct, goes no further than is absolutely necessary in interfering with article 10 rights'.[185] Laing J therefore held, in *Merlin*, that the defendant's freedom to raise his concerns about safety at the claimant's theme parks outweighed the claimant's interest in stopping his internet and mass email campaigns against it. In reaching that decision, she stressed the public interest in the safety of theme parks and that the officers of a public listed company are not immune from criticism, even if it is misguided and intemperate.[186] If such criticism is defamatory, she said, the remedy is a claim in defamation.[187]

**6.67** That said, it is rare for a defendant in a vilification case to raise a freedom of expression defence successfully. For example, in *Howlett*, Eady J held that the claimant's right to 'lead a peaceful life and enjoy her privacy' clearly outweighed the defendant's right to express his views by the methods he had chosen.[188] He noted, in reaching that conclusion, that even with the injunction in place the defendant would be free to report any genuinely held concerns about misconduct by the

---

[182] *Merlin* (n 181) [40].
[183] *Merlin* (n 181) [40].
[184] *Law Society* (n 171) [74].
[185] *Merlin* (n 181) [41].
[186] *Merlin* (n 181) [56]. See also cases concerning protests such as *Heathrow Airport v Garman* [2007] EWHC 1957 (QB) [99] and *University of Oxford v Broughton* [2008] EWHC 75 (QB) [35]–[36].
[187] *Merlin* (n 181) [56].
[188] *Howlett* (n 174) [13].

claimant to the appropriate authorities.[189] A similar approach was taken at first instance in *Levi v Bates*, where HHJ Gosnell concluded that the claimant's rights outweighed the defendant's freedom to publish because, 'there was no real public interest in the subject matter and an underlying motive of revenge behind the stories'.[190] Briggs LJ (who delivered the leading judgment in the Court of Appeal) agreed, saying that '[i]ncitement of others to weigh in for the furtherance of a grudge about a private business dispute has nothing whatever to do with free speech'.[191]

Further, in *Thompson v James*, Tugendhat J held that it is 'so obvious as to not need **6.68** stating' that '[f]reedom of expression is not freedom to state matters which the speaker knows to be false and by which she intends to injure another person'.[192] As he said in *ZAM*:

> Freedom of expression is valued, amongst other reasons, because it tends to lead to discovery of the truth...So where a defamatory allegation has been proved to be false (as has happened in the present case) there is no public interest in allowing it to be republished, and a strong public interest in preventing the public from being further misinformed.[193]

### (3) Publication of Intimate Images as Harassment

Publication of intimate images of an individual can also amount to harassment **6.69** under the PHA. In *AMP v Persons Unknown*, the Technology and Construction Court restrained those in possession or control of an intimate photograph of the claimant (which had been taken when her mobile telephone was stolen) from, *inter alia*, uploading or transmitting it on the internet.[194] The relief was granted on the grounds of privacy and harassment. In relation to the harassment claim, Ramsey J held that he was satisfied, on existing evidence, that there had been conduct on at least two occasions; that it was targeted at the claimant; that it was calculated, in an objective sense, to cause alarm or distress; that, judged objectively, the conduct was oppressive and unreasonable in the context in which it occurred; and that the conduct would 'cross the line and be conduct which amounts to harassment, alarm or distress'.[195]

### (4) Blackmail and Other Threats to Publish Private and/or Defamatory Material

Repeatedly threatening to make defamatory allegations or to disclose pri- **6.70** vate information about or images of a person in the media, on the internet, or

---

[189] *Howlett* (n 174) [12].
[190] *Levi v Bates* (Leeds County Court, 7 June 2012) [72].
[191] *Levi* (n 5) [37].
[192] *Thompson* (n 177) [308].
[193] *ZAM* (n 167) [23].
[194] *AMP v Persons Unknown* [2011] EWHC 3454 (TCC).
[195] *AMP* (n 194) [44].

elsewhere, can also amount to harassment. For example, in *CC v AB*, Eady J imposed an (unopposed) interim protection order on a defendant who had made abusive telephone calls and sent abusive emails threatening to expose the celebrity claimant in the media and on the internet after he had an affair with the defendant's wife.[196]

**6.71** These claims often arise in the context of blackmail. For example, in *EWQ v GFD*, Tugendhat J continued an injunction in privacy and harassment against a woman who had repeatedly threatened to inform the claimant's wife, business associates, and the media of their affair unless he paid her very substantial sums of money.[197] She was restrained from communicating with the claimant, visiting his home or business address, and generally from pursing a course of conduct which amounts to harassment under the PHA. Likewise, in *SKA*, a wealthy man in his seventies was granted a permanent injunction (on the grounds of privacy and harassment) restraining a blackmailer from revealing to anyone other than the claimant's wife and children the fact that the claimant was expecting twins with his much younger extra-marital girlfriend.[198] Disclosure (to the claimant's family or anyone else) of photographs, emails, and intimate details of the relationship was also prohibited.[199] In *WXY v Gewanter*, Slade J also confirmed that threats to publish damaging or embarrassing material in order to secure or accelerate payment of a debt can amount to harassment requiring restraint by injunction.[200] The defendant in that case, who had been publishing and threatening to publish personal information about a woman with close connections to a foreign head of state whose family owed him money, was restrained from publishing the relevant information about her, communicating any direct or indirect threat to the claimant to publish the information, and from otherwise harassing her.[201]

**6.72** However, injunctions restraining publication of personal information by potential blackmailers are not always all-inclusive. For example, as mentioned in *SKA*, the interim injunction did not extend to communications informing the claimant's wife and children of the bare fact of the claimant's extra-marital relationship and the twins he and his mistress were expecting.[202] In concluding that the claim was unlikely to succeed at trial, Tugendhat J said that there is a strong argument that the twins would have a right to know who their father is, and that his other children have a right to know that there are other children who might make claims on their father and his money.[203] He was also unpersuaded that it was in the claimant's

---

[196] *CC v AB* [2006] EWHC 3083 (QB), [2007] EMLR 11.
[197] *EWQ v GFD* [2012] EWHC 2182 (QB).
[198] *SKA and PLM v CRH and Persons Unknown* [2012] EWHC 2236 (QB).
[199] *SKA and PLM* (n 198).
[200] *WXY v Gewanter* [2012] EWHC 496 (QB) [69].
[201] *WXY* (n 200).
[202] *SKA and PLM* (n 198).
[203] *SKA and PLM* (n 198) [81].

wife's interests to remain unaware of her husband's deception.[204] In reaching these conclusions, Tugendhat J stressed that it is a normal exercise in freedom of expression for people to talk about one another's lives: '[t]he birth of babies is a normal topic of such conversations, and there is no reason why it should not be. So too with talk about who is in a relationship with whom.'[205]

Courts will take account of the defendant's own conduct when assessing a black-  **6.73** mail claim. In *AVB*, the claimant's harassment claim failed even though the defendant, an escort with whom the claimant had had a relationship of sorts, had, *inter alia*, sent several emails to the claimant's business associates claiming that the defendant owed her money for sexual services. Although Tugendhat J held that the messages were part of a course of conduct, he did not accept that in the particular circumstances of the case, her conduct was objectively likely to cause the claimant distress nor that it was oppressive.[206] Tugendhat J held that he could not ignore the fact that the claimant continued to associate with the claimant in spite of difficulties in the relationship and that he continued to provoke her with his manipulative and exploitative behaviour.[207]

*Threatening to publish false accusations*   Courts considering harassment claims  **6.74** have stressed that there is a public interest in preventing dissemination of false accusations of impropriety. In *ZAM v CFM and TFW*, the claimant obtained a permanent injunction (on the grounds of harassment and defamation) against a defendant who was making false allegations of financial and sexual misconduct to the claimant's associates and threatening to publish to the world at large if his demands were not met.[208] Tugendhat J stressed that:

> . . . in a blackmail case, where the blackmailer is threatening to publish something he knows to be false, or does not believe to be true, there is no public interest in his allegations being disseminated. The public interest is that the blackmailer's allegations should not be published: that is both the public interest that the public should not be misinformed or deceived, and the public interest that victims of blackmail should receive the protection of the courts.[209]

*Anonymity in blackmail proceedings*   Unsurprisingly, the claimants in the black-  **6.75** mail proceedings discussed in this section have all been anonymized. In the final judgment in *ZAM*, Tugendhat J observed that courts dealing with cases of

---

[204] *SKA and PLM* (n 198) [82]–[87]. It is notable that although a wider interim injunction was granted in *EWQ v GFD* [2012] EWHC 2182 (QB), the claimant's former mistress had already sent one message to the claimant's wife informing her of the relationship (although the claimant maintained that he had explained it away as malicious) (see [6] and [34]).

[205] *SKA and PLM* (n 198) [89]. Discussion of whether to award an injunction in this case was couched in terms of reasonable expectations of privacy but the judge did also conclude that there was an actionable harassment (see [1]).

[206] *AVB v TDD* [2014] EWHC 1442 (QB) [230]–[232].

[207] *AVB* (n 206) [231].

[208] *ZAM v CFM and TFW* [2013] EWHC 662 (QB).

[209] *ZAM* (n 208) [102].

blackmail and extortion have long been accustomed to granting anonymity.[210] The court, he said, must adapt its procedures to ensure that it does not provide encouragement or assistance to blackmailers, and does not deter victims of blackmail from seeking justice from the courts.[211] He therefore made the anonymity order part of the final order even though the claim was also brought in defamation and anonymity is unusual in that context.[212] These comments echo observations Tugendhat J. made in his interim injunction decision in *ZAM*, including the statement that:

> …it would frustrate the purpose of the injunctions sought if the claimant's applications had the effect of making public the very allegations in respect of which he is seeking relief by way of injunction…In a case like the present, where there is a strong case for believing there to be an attempt at blackmail, such Orders [for anonymity in accordance with s 6 of the HRA 1998 and Civil Procedure Rule 39.2(4)] are frequently made in respect of both parties. There are strong policy reasons to discourage such conduct, which would be undermined if anonymity was refused.[213]

### (5) Letters

**6.76** Although it is likely to be of limited relevance to media parties, it is noted for completeness that sending abusive or threatening letters to an individual can also amount to harassment under the PHA.[214]

### (6) Damage Need Not be Foreseeable

**6.77** Damages for harassment, including that effected by actual or threatened publication, compensate for distress and injury to feelings.[215] Although a claimant has to show that the defendant knew or ought to have known that his or her conduct amounted to harassment before a claim under the PHA can be made out,[216] he or she does not need to show that the precise loss suffered was foreseeable in order to recover damages for it. The Court of Appeal said in *Jones v Ruth*:

> Conduct of the kind described in s 1 is actionable under s 3 in respect of anxiety or injury caused by the harassment and any financial loss resulting from the harassment. There is nothing in the statutory language to import an additional

---

[210] *ZAM* (n 208) [35].
[211] *ZAM* (n 208) [44].
[212] *ZAM* (n 208) [24]–[52] esp [47].
[213] *ZAM v CFW and TFW* [2011] EWHC 476 (QB) [27].
[214] See *eg Iqbal v Dean Manson Solicitors* [2011] EWCA Civ 123 (letters sent between lawyers representing third parties in legal proceedings); *Baron v CPS* (DC, 13 June 2000) (letters threatening Benefits Agency employees); *Ferguson v British Gas Trading Ltd* [2009] EWCA Civ 46 (letters demanding payment, threatening to cut off gas supply, report the claimant to credit rating agencies, commence legal proceedings); *Bloom v Robinson-Millar* [2013] EWHC 3918 (QB) (letters containing baseless allegations of dishonesty against the claimant's neighbour, a director of the company managing a shared block of flats, sent to a wide range of people); and *Graham v West* [2011] EWHC 4 (QB) (suggestive letters from a former police translator to an Acting Inspector which included suggestions that he was at risk of a fabricated rape complaint).
[215] *ZAM* (n 208) [59].
[216] See 6.16–6.18.

requirement of foreseeability. Nor is the foreseeability of damage the gist of the tort. Section 1 is concerned with deliberate conduct of a kind which the defendant knows or ought to know will amount to harassment of the claimant. Once that is proved the defendant is responsible in damages for the injury and loss which flow from that conduct. There is nothing in the nature of the cause of action which calls for further qualification in order to give effect to the obvious policy objectives of the statute.[217]

The first claimant was therefore able to recover for £28,750 for personal injury and £115,000 for loss of earnings resulting from the defendant's aggressive and intimidating behaviour during a four-year building project on properties adjacent to the claimants' home.

Damages for harassment, including that effected by actual or threatened publication, compensate for distress and injury to feelings.[218] In *WXY v Gewanter*, the parties agreed that it was appropriate to look to the guidance provided in the employment case of *Vento v Chief Constable of West Yorkshire Police* as to the assessment of damages for injury to feelings.[219] Tugendhat J held that three factors made *WXY* a serious case: the fact that the defendant was deliberately putting pressure on the claimant for financial gain; the sensitive and highly personal nature of the information in question; and the fact that its disclosure had the potential to cause the most serious interference with her personal life.[220] He therefore awarded her damages of £24,950 (including £5,000 in aggravated damages), placing the award in the top of the three bands identified in *Vento*.[221] Because the claimant's distress related to both material the claimant had published and material he was threatening to publish, he held that the harassment claim could not be regarded as separate from the misuse of private information claim and thus, that one inclusive damages award should be made.[222]  **6.78**

Where the harassment consists of the publication of defamatory allegations, the harassment may aggravate the damages but should not lead to double counting of the award.[223] Thus, in *ZAM*, the claimant was awarded £120,000 in defamation for false allegations of financial impropriety and sexual offending made to specific individuals and on the internet in breach of an interim injunction.[224] No separate award was made under the PHA although £20,000 was awarded because of the  **6.79**

---

[217] *Jones v Ruth* [2011] EWCA Civ 804 [32].
[218] *ZAM* (n 208) [59].
[219] See *WXY* (n 200) [25] referring to *Vento v Chief Constable of West Yorkshire Police* [2002] EWCA Civ 1871 [65] in which the Court of Appeal identified three broad bands of compensation for injury to feelings.
[220] *WXY* (n 200) [58].
[221] *WXY* (n 200) [59].
[222] *WXY* (n 200) [52]–[53]. See also *Levi* (n 5) (discussed at 6.11–6.14) where the claimant was awarded £6,000.
[223] *ZAM* (n 208) [59].
[224] *ZAM* (n 208) [122].

aggravating factors in the case and to compensate the claimant for the distress and harassment suffered.[225]

## D. Harassment in the Public Order Act 1986

**6.80** Section 4A of the Public Order Act 1986 makes it an offence intentionally to cause a person harassment, alarm, or distress by using threatening, abusive, or insulting words or by displaying any writing, sign, or other visible representation which is threatening, abusive, or insulting.[226] Courts have acknowledged the similarities between s 4A of the Public Order Act 1986 and the offences in the PHA[227] and have established that the offence can be committed by uploading material to the internet.[228] Although theoretically possible, it would be rare for such an offence to be committed by a media defendant.

---

[225] *ZAM* (n 208) [118].

[226] Public Order Act 1986, s 5 creates a similar offence although, since amendment in s 57(2) of the Crime and Courts Act 2013, it applies only to words which are threatening or abusive and is therefore less likely to cover disclosures which breach the victim's privacy.

[227] See *eg AMP v Persons Unknown* (n 194) [42] and *S & D Property Investments Ltd v Nisbet* [2009] EWHC 1726 (Ch) [68].

[228] See *S v CPS* [2008] EWHC 438 (Admin) (Court upheld the conviction of a man who had published an offensively doctored photograph of the claimant on an animal rights website).

# 7

# DATA PROTECTION: BREACH
# OF STATUTORY DUTY

*Jonathan Barnes*

## A. Introduction

This chapter examines the way in which the Data Protection Act 1998 (DPA) **7.01**
protects individual privacy and the challenges the Act presents to the protection
of media and freedom of expression in English law.[1] The Act represents the United
Kingdom's implementation of Directive 95/46/EC,[2] which, as Recital 9 makes
clear, is expressly concerned with the right to privacy and laid down requirements
for Member States to adopt data protection legislation at the national level in order

---

[1] The DPA 1998, which came into force on 1 March 2000, replaced the DPA 1984, which had
little practical application to the media. Extracts from the DPA 1998 are set out in Appendix E
(available at <http://www.5rb.com/publication/the-law-of-privacy-and-the-media>).

[2] [1995] OJ L281/31. Implementation of the Directive throughout the European Union was
intended to give effect in the context of data protection to Art 8 (right to respect for private and fam-
ily life) of the ECHR. It is a striking example of the harmonization of private law among Member
States. The Directive can be relied on as having direct effect: *R (Robertson) v City of Wakefield
Metropolitan Council* [2001] EWHC 915 (Admin), [2002] QB 1052 [17]–[20]. For the effect of
directives in giving rise to rights enforceable against individuals see D Vaughan (ed), *Law of the
European Communities* (Butterworths 1990–2002) vol III, paras 324–327, 330–344, 362–365.
The Directive is set out in full in Appendix D (available at <http://www.5rb.com/publication/
the-law-of-privacy-and-the-media>).

to protect privacy in relation to both computerized and manual files. The words 'privacy' and 'private' in this context mean no more than that information is personal. There is no connotation of *secrecy*. In other words, the terms are used in the same sense as in the expression 'private property', meaning property which is personal, not inaccessible or hidden away. Data protection rights are apt to protect information which is secret. But, like copyright, they are also apt to enable individuals to seek to prevent others exploiting for gain information about an individual which is not secret.[3]

**7.02** The Act is also of direct interest to the media, since for practical purposes all dealings with personal information that are carried out by journalists, whether investigations, news-gathering, editorial activities, or publication, are subject to its provisions.

**7.03** There are a number of areas of data protection that, while potentially of interest to the media (in the sense that they may form the subject matter of current affairs journalism), do not directly affect and regulate the media and their role. For example, the DPA contains detailed provisions concerning the conduct of credit reference agencies, advertising and direct marketing, national security, and historical research. Further, the Act's application to private contractual relationships between many organizations and their employees, and indeed, to the employment market in general, may well affect media organizations in their corporate and employment affairs.[4] However, this chapter concentrates only on the effect the DPA may or will have on the media's function of publishing and broadcasting in the United Kingdom.[5] Criminal liability under the Act is considered briefly at 10.29; regulatory aspects at 14.21–14.31; and particular points concerning remedies are addressed in Chapter 12.

## B. Data Protection

### (1) Control over Personal Information

**7.04** Data protection is a part of the law of privacy, although the word 'privacy' is notably absent from the UK legislation. The privacy rights underpinning data protection are recognized in the main human rights treaties: in the European Convention on Human Rights (ECHR) at Article 8, in the International Covenant

---

[3] *R (Robertson) v City of Wakefield Metropolitan Council* (n 2) and *R (Robertson) v Secretary of State for the Home Dept* [2003] EWHC 1760 (Admin) concerning the use of the electoral roll by commercial organizations; see 7.24.

[4] For general reference see H Grant, R Boardman, and R Jay (eds), *Encyclopedia of Data Protection and Privacy* (Sweet & Maxwell 1988–2015); P Carey, *Data Protection: A practical guide to UK and EU law* (3rd edn, Oxford University Press 2009); R Jay, *Data Protection Law and Practice* (4th edn, Sweet & Maxwell 2012).

[5] See M Tugendhat, 'The Data Protection Act 1998 and the media' in E Barendt and A Firth (eds), *Yearbook of Copyright and Media Law 2000* (Oxford University Press 2000) 115.

on Civil and Political Rights at Article 17, and in the Charter of Fundamental Rights of the European Union at Article 7 (Respect for private and family life) and Article 8 (Protection of personal data). A 'right to data protection' establishes and underpins individuals' rights to control the storage and circulation of data about themselves.[6] Previously individuals had little control in English law over information about themselves in the hands of others except in the limited cases where, for example, public laws or the private laws of confidence, defamation, or copyright applied.[7] The implementation of the Act and its secondary legislation, however, has led to a position that has been described as 'informational self-determination'.[8] This reflects the fact that through the introduction of express statutory rights for data subjects, and statutory obligations on data controllers that in turn create further correlative rights for data subjects, data subjects now enjoy rights of access to, control over, and compensation for the misuse of information held and used by others about them.

### (2) Data Protection and the Article 10 Right to Freedom of Expression—Tension or Conflict?

Freedom of expression itself is mentioned only once in the DPA in the context of the 'media exemption' in s 32.[9] This is surprising, given that the fundamental freedoms protected by the ECHR, and Article 10 in particular, are referred to comprehensively throughout the Directive.[10] By contrast, French law does contain wide exemptions for all processing of data by the media from provisions that might have the effect of limiting the exercise of freedom of expression.[11] When a Member State transposes  **7.05**

---

[6] UK, *Report of the Committee on Data Protection* (Cmnd 7341, 1978), chairman: Sir Norman Lindop, para 2.04.

[7] Where a public authority is required to use information acquired by it only for the performance of a public duty: see *R v Chief Constable of North Wales Police, ex p Thorpe* [1999] QB 396; *Elliott v Chief Constable of Wiltshire* (1996) TLR 693. See also *R v Brentwood Borough Council, ex p Peck* [1998] EMLR 697 on a local authority's decision to hand over to a broadcasting company CCTV footage of a man who was about to attempt suicide; it was the failure of judicial review proceedings in the latter case that led to the European Court of Human Rights finding violations of Arts 8 and 13 in *Peck v UK* (2003) 36 EHRR 41.

[8] I Lloyd, *A Guide to the Data Protection Act 1998* (Butterworth 1998) para 4.6. See also R Wacks, 'Privacy in cyberspace: Personal information, free speech, and the Internet' in P Birks (ed), *Privacy and Loyalty* (Clarendon Press 1997) 93, 109.

[9] As to which see 7.109–7.116.

[10] There is express reference in Art 9 of Directive 95/46/EC and other references in Recitals 1, 10, 17, 33, 37 and Arts 13(g) and 31. In the Consultation Paper (March 1996) para 4.19, the government had stated that a blanket exemption for the press would not be compatible with the Directive, and maintained that view in the White Paper *Data Protection: The government's proposals*, 1 August 1997, para 4.10, while it was recognized that a balance between privacy and the public's right to know had to be struck. Throughout the summer and autumn of 1997 submissions were made by Lord Wakeham on behalf of the then Press Complaints Commission, and by the BBC, Channel 4, and the independent television companies, as well as newspapers and newspaper lawyers. The result was the exemption now found in s 32 which was introduced into the Bill at the last minute, late in 1997: *Hansard* HL (5th Series), vol 585, col 442 (2 February 1998): see 7.111.

[11] French Loi no 78–17 of 6 January 1978. And see Council of Europe, *Data Protection and the Media: Study prepared by the Committee of Experts on Data Protection under the authority of the*

Community law into national law, it must comply with the Convention.[12] Article 10 may therefore be relied on in proceedings based on these obligations independently of the Human Rights Act 1998 (HRA), and perhaps more effectively.[13]

**7.06** In *Campbell v MGN Ltd*[14] the Court of Appeal accepted that the right to freedom of expression referred to in Recital 37 and Article 9 of the Directive must inform the interpretation of the DPA. The Court held[15] that the media exemption in s 32 applies not only to the period before publication, but is of general application. It remains open to question whether this interpretation of s 32 is sufficient to give effect to Article 10 ECHR in relation to data protection, or whether some more general Article 10 defence will have to be recognized. The Court of Appeal stated[16] that, in the absence of s 32, the requirements of the Act would impose restrictions on the media which would radically restrict freedom of the press. The reasoning of the Court of Appeal may therefore imply the need for a defence based on freedom of expression in some cases not covered by s 32. The House of Lords in *Campbell*[17] did not give separate consideration to the claimant's data protection claim.[18]

**7.07** In *Durant v Financial Services Authority*[19] the Court of Appeal accepted that the Directive 'is an important aid to construction of the Act' and that the DPA 'should... be interpreted, so far as possible in the light of, and to give effect to, the Directive's provisions'. The Court held that the Directive's primary objective was to protect an individual's right to privacy, as enshrined in Article 8 ECHR, but recognized[20] the inevitable tension between that objective and the facilitation of

---

European Committee on Legal Co-operation, Council of Europe (1991) para 13, and P Kayser, *La Protection de la Vie Privée par le Droit* (3rd edn, Economica-PUAM 1995) 465.

[12] Case 36/75 *Rutili v Minister of the Interior* [1975] ECR 1219; Case 249/86 *Commission v Germany* [1989] ECR 1263; Case 222/84 *Johnston v Chief Constable of the Royal Ulster Constabulary* [1986] ECR 1651. The Directive itself does not apply to the processing of personal data in the course of an activity which falls outside the scope of Community law. In its White Paper (n 10) paras 1.12, 1.13, 2.21, the government explained that the Bill would nevertheless apply to all activities, whether or not within EU law, in order to avoid the difficulties which would be entailed if there were two statutory regimes. If effect is to be given to that intention, it should follow that Art 10 should be enforceable through both EU law and the HRA whether or not a particular case is within or without the scope of Community law.

[13] The use of EU law to enforce the ECHR was discussed by N Bratza and P Duffy in G Barling (ed), *Practitioners' Handbook of EC Law* (Trenton 1998) 635 and by M Demetriou, 'Using human rights through EC law' [1999] EHRL Rev 484. See Case C-260/89 *Elliniki Radiophonia Tileorassi AE v Dimotiki Etairia Pliroforris and Storious Kouvelas* [1991] ECR I-2925. See also n 2.

[14] *Campbell v MGN Ltd* [2002] EWCA Civ 1373, [2003] QB 633 [97] and [110]–[112].

[15] *Campbell* (n 14) [128].

[16] *Campbell* (n 14) [124].

[17] *Campbell v MGN Ltd* [2004] UKHL 22, [2004] 2 AC 457.

[18] In *Terry (previously 'LNS') v Persons Unknown* [2010] EWHC 119 (QB), [2010] EMLR 16 [73], Tugendhat J observed (without making any relevant finding) that while the DPA might well apply to a newspaper publication, and in particular to an online publication, it would be anomalous if the public interest defence under s 32 required the court to have regard to the reasonable belief of the journalist, but that the same defence under the general law did not.

[19] *Durant v Financial Services Authority* [2003] EWCA Civ 1746, [2004] FSR 28 [3] and [47].

[20] *Durant* (n 19) [4].

the free movement of data. That tension is not so evident in the domestic setting for which the Act provides, in particular in the right of access to personal data with which that case was concerned.

In *Criminal Proceedings against Lindqvist*[21] the Court of Justice of the European **7.08** Union found that the provisions of the Directive do not, in themselves, bring about a restriction which conflicts with the general principles of freedom of expression or other freedoms and rights, enshrined, *inter alia*, in Article 10 ECHR. The Court said it was for the national authorities and courts responsible for applying national legislation implementing the Directive to ensure a fair balance between the rights and interests in question.

While there is an obvious tension between rights to privacy and freedom of expres- **7.09** sion, data protection rights do not necessarily need to be balanced with rights of freedom of expression and the right to receive and impart information. Data protection in fact encourages freedom of expression in a number of ways, and so can give effect to both Articles 10 and 8 at the same time. For example, a data subject's right of access under the Act is a right to receive information.[22] The right to have inaccurate data corrected self-evidently promotes accuracy and so fosters proper discussion and the expression of ideas based on information that is accurate: it is in the public interest to minimize falsehood and inaccuracy, without preventing proper discussion. And this is recognized by the codes of practice that apply to journalists and broadcasters, all of which (already) impose requirements as to accuracy and respect for privacy. Further, one of the main justifications for the making of the Directive is given by Recitals 3 and 5 as the promotion of the free flow of information between Member States.

The European Commission is presently proceeding with plans to implement **7.10** the General Data Protection Regulation to unify data protection law within the European Union. The proposal has met domestic resistance, not least from the UK government on grounds of bureaucracy and cost. Nevertheless a proposed regulation was released on 25 January 2012. This is expected to be adopted in 2015 or early 2016 with enforcement from 2017/18 after a two-year period of transition. Amongst other refinements, the Regulation in its final form may see greater clarity as concerns the conditions required for data subject consent,[23] including specific provision for the withdrawal of consent previously given, and provide an express

---

[21] Case C-101/01 [2004] QB 1014 [90].
[22] The ECtHR has held that access to personal information in certain circumstances is an aspect of the right to respect for private and family life under Art 8: see *eg McMichael v UK* (1995) 20 EHRR 205 (personal social services records) and *McGinley and Egan v UK* (1999) 27 EHRR 1 (medical records). The right to receive information enshrined in Art 10 is restricted to information which others may be willing to impart: *Leander v Sweden* (1987) 9 EHRR 433, para 74. But see *Kenedi v Hungary* App no 31475/05 (ECtHR, 26 August 2009) for possible inroads into this principle.
[23] Art 7.

'right to erasure' requiring data to be deleted where consent for it to be processed has been withdrawn or there is in any event no justification for keeping it.[24]

# C. Data Protection Act 1998

### (1) The Data Protection Act and the Media

**7.11**  Section 17(1) DPA prohibits the processing of personal data by computer (or by any means, if the data in question are assessable data)[25] unless an entry in respect of the data controller is included in the register of data-controller notifications maintained by the Information Commissioner. This process of registration is referred to in the Act as 'notification'.[26] Media organizations, and indeed individual journalists if self-employed or working freelance, will be considered data controllers[27] and so subject to the notification requirements.

**7.12**  More significantly as concerns day-to-day media practice, the Act addresses the processing of personal data in two main ways. First, s 4(4) imposes a statutory duty on data controllers to comply with the Act's data protection Principles in relation to all personal data with respect to which they are the data controller. The first data protection Principle is the most important for present purposes. It requires dealings with personal data to be fair, lawful, and to meet at least one of certain specified conditions. The statutory duty under s 4(4) DPA also encompasses, by reason of the sixth data protection Principle,[28] requirements on the data controller to supply information when a data subject request has been made under s 7, and to comply with a notice given under s 10(1) requiring a data controller to cease, or not to begin, data processing that is likely to cause damage or distress. Secondly, and in addition to the requirement that data controllers comply with the Act's data protection Principles, data subjects are given statutory rights to compensation;[29] to have inaccurate data held about them rectified, blocked, destroyed, or erased;[30] and to invoke the Commissioner's roles of assessment and enforcement.[31]

**7.13**  The DPA 1998's predecessor, the DPA 1984, applied only to computer processing and therefore only affected a media organization where, in the period from the mid-1980s until early 2000, it chose to store data it held on individuals on computer rather than on paper. The now universal use by the media of computers and

---

[24]  Art 17.
[25]  s 17(2) DPA and see 7.37–7.39.
[26]  For detailed discussion of the principles and requirements of notification under the DPA, see Jay (n 4) ch 9. See also D Bainbridge, *Data Protection Law* (2nd edn, XPL 2005).
[27]  See 7.28–7.32.
[28]  sch 1, pt I; see also sch 1, pt II, para 8.
[29]  s 13 DPA. See 7.92–7.99.
[30]  s 14 DPA. See 7.100–7.102.
[31]  ss 40–47 DPA. See 7.103–7.108.

other electronic devices, and the broadening of the DPA 1998 to include many manual files, mean that the current data protection legislation carries very real significance for the media.

The Information Commissioner's website is located at <http://www.ico.org.uk>. **7.14** It contains the Commissioner's present guidance on the Act and its application. Many First Tier Tribunal (Information Rights)[32] decisions are now published independently. Some have also been made available historically at the Information Commissioner's website and in the *Encyclopedia of Data Protection*.[33] In the wake of the report of the Leveson Inquiry and in particular in response to Recommendation 59 (which said that he should prepare good practice guidelines), the Information Commissioner published on 4 September 2014 his good practice advice entitled, 'Data protection and journalism: a guide for the media'.

### (2) Definitions—Data, Parties, Processing, Purposes

*(a) Data*

The definition of 'data' within the Act covers information that may be held in **7.15** five different ways: (a) information that is being processed by means of 'equipment operating automatically in response to instructions given for that purpose' (*ie* by computer); (b) information that is recorded with the intention it should be processed by such equipment; (c) information that is recorded as part of a relevant filing system or with the intention that it should form part of such a system; (d) information that forms part of an accessible record;[34] or (e) information that is recorded information held by a public authority and does not fall within any of the four preceding descriptions.[35]

In *Campbell*[36] the Court of Appeal accepted that the claimant would have had a **7.16** claim for compensation under s 13 DPA for the publication of the fact that she was a drug addict had s 32 not exempted the newspaper publishers. In *Johnson v Medical Defence Union Ltd*[37] and *Smith v Lloyds TSB Bank plc*[38] Laddie J emphasized that since the definition of data in s 1 DPA refers to data which 'is' being processed or recorded, the relevant date for assessing whether particular data are covered by the data subject's access request is the date upon which the request is made. In *Smith*,

---

[32] On 18 January 2010 the former Information Tribunal was abolished and replaced by the First Tier Tribunal (Information Rights) by the Transfer of Tribunal Functions Order 2010, SI 2010/22.

[33] See n 4.

[34] See s 1(1)(a)–(d) DPA. An 'accessible record' means an individual's health, educational, or accessible public record: s 68 DPA.

[35] s 1(1)(e) DPA inserted by Freedom of Information Act 2000, s 68. By s 68(2)(b) 'public authority' has the same meaning as in the Freedom of Information Act 2000; this extension of the definition of 'data' is unlikely to affect media organizations as data controllers.

[36] *Campbell* (n 14) [124].

[37] [2004] EWHC 347 (Ch).

[38] [2005] EWHC 246 (Ch).

Laddie J further rejected at [20]–[28] the contention that any 'pile of documents' could be caught by the s 1 definition on the basis that modern computer scanning techniques could convert such a pile to an accessible computer database.

**7.17** **'Equipment operating automatically in response to instructions given for that purpose'** This means computer systems. Any information processed or held for processing by computer will fall within the Act's definition of 'data'. This will include, for example, the digitally stored form of a photograph taken with a digital camera[39] or notes recorded onto a digital telephone. It will also include pictures and interviews recorded on to disks or other electronic storage media used by journalists. In effect, this means that any material (including photographs) printed in a newspaper, broadcast on television, or published on a website may be covered by the provisions of the DPA.

**7.18** In *Douglas v Hello! Ltd*[40] Lindsay J held that the *Hello!* defendants (who were magazine proprietors and others allegedly involved in the supply for publication by *Hello!* magazine of unauthorized photographs taken at the claimants' wedding) were each data controllers, that the unauthorized pictures represented personal data, and that the publication of them in England was caught by the DPA. The act of publication was itself held to form part of the processing within the scope of the Act. The processing in *Douglas* involved the transmission of the pictures by ISDN line from California to London, the calling up of them on a screen in London, their transmission by ISDN line from London to Madrid, electronic touching up, transmission to the printers, and the printing processes. There was also (unauthorized) publication of the pictures on a *Hello!* website. These findings were not subject to challenge in the Court of Appeal.[41]

**7.19** **Relevant filing system—manual data** This is any set of information relating to individuals to the extent that, although not processed by equipment, the set is structured, either by reference to individuals or by reference to criteria relating to individuals in such a way that specific information relating to a particular individual is readily accessible.[42] The Act gives no further guidance than this. While there are likely to be grey areas, in practice it appears there are four basic characteristics for a relevant filing system:

(1) Set: 'A grouping together of things by reference to a distinct identifier i.e. a set of information with a common theme or element.'[43] There is however

---

[39] See the short discussion in *Douglas v Hello! Ltd* [2001] QB 967, CA [55]–[56].

[40] *Douglas v Hello! Ltd* [2003] EWHC 786 (Ch), [2003] 3 All ER 996 [230]–[231].

[41] *Douglas v Hello! Ltd* [2005] EWCA Civ 595, [2006] QB 125.

[42] s 1(1) DPA.

[43] *Data Protection Act 1998: Legal guidance* (December 2001) para 2.1.1; albeit that publication appears no longer current at the Information Commissioner's website, <http://www.ico.org.uk> and there is instead in the present respect now a part of the website entitled 'FAQs about relevant filing systems'.

no necessary requirement of files being grouped together physically, and a set of information might be dispersed over different locations within one organization.

(2) Structure: The set must be structured in relation either to individuals themselves or to criteria by which individuals can be identified. Obvious examples of such criteria include age, type of job, credit history, shopping habits, and membership of particular organizations.[44]

(3) Specific information: This contrasts the totality of the information an organization may hold about a particular individual with specific items of information that it holds and expects to use. The set must be able to be accessed for such specific information.

(4) Readily accessible: The specific information must be readily accessible within the set and its structure. In practice, this means that a straightforward search within the set and its structure should readily turn up a manual record containing specific information. The Commissioner has previously advised[45] that an organization should assume that any set of manual information referenced to individuals (or criteria relating to individuals) and which is specific to an individual is caught by the Act if it is accessible to someone within the organization on a day-to-day basis. The maintaining of cuttings files by a media organization would be likely to bring the information contained in them within the legislative reach of the Act.

In *Durant*[46] the Court of Appeal concluded that a 'relevant filing system' is limited to a system in which the files are structured or referenced in such a way as clearly to indicate at the outset of the search whether specific information capable of amounting to personal data is held within the system; and which has, as part of its structure or referencing mechanism, a sufficiently sophisticated and detailed means of readily indicating whether and where an individual file's specific criteria about an individual can be located.    **7.20**

In practice, any data in text (or permanent) form, such as in a journalist's notebook, interview note, written research, or draft article should now be considered potentially liable to fall within the Act. Whether it does or not will be very much a question of fact and degree. Notes on the back of an envelope may be unlikely to be caught, but a detailed research note containing names, addresses, sources, and story details may well be.    **7.21**

---

[44] Cases where an unnamed person can be identified for the purposes of defamation include *Morgan v Odhams Press Ltd* [1971] 1 WLR 1239, and are discussed in A Mullis and R Parkes (eds), *Gatley on Libel and Slander* (12th edn, Sweet & Maxwell 2013) ch 7, paras 7.1–7.4.
[45] *Data Protection Act 1998: Legal guidance* (n 43).
[46] *Durant* (n 19) [50].

## (b) Personal data

**7.22** The Act is concerned with personal data. That is data that relate to a living individual who can be identified either from those data alone or from those data in combination with other information in the possession of, or likely to come into the possession of, the data controller.[47] This definition excludes all non-natural persons as well as deceased individuals (and their estates) from the Act's regime. However, where data do relate to a living individual they are in many cases likely to be 'personal data', if only by virtue of a prospective 'jigsaw' analysis. While data are defined by the Act effectively as 'information',[48] the Act specifies under its definition of 'personal data' that this will include any expression of opinion recorded about the individual and any indication of the intentions of the data controller or any other person in respect of that individual.[49] These latter two categories may well be of particular significance to the media, for example where a publication or broadcast programme is centred on opinion or, in a different context, a media organization learns of the intentions of other parties towards its subject.

**7.23** In *Durant*[50] the Court of Appeal held that not all information retrieved from a computer search against an individual's name or unique identifier is personal data within the Act. Auld LJ suggested that two notions may be of assistance: first, whether the information is biographical in a significant sense and, secondly, whether the information has the putative data subject as its focus. In the wake of this decision the European Commission is reported to have written to the UK government expressing certain concerns at the United Kingdom's implementation of Directive 95/46/EC, including the apparently restrictive approach taken in *Durant* to the definition of personal data.[51] The House of Lords in *Common Services Agency v Scottish Information Commissioner*[52] has subsequently suggested, however, that the notions put forward by Auld LJ were limited to the context of the data subject access requests under consideration in *Durant*. Lord Hope in particular stressed that the answer to the problem generally whether or not 'personal data' is in issue must be found in the wording of the definition in s 1(1) DPA, read in the light of the Directive. More recently, in *R (Kelway) v Upper Tribunal (Administrative Appeals Chamber) and Northumbria Police and R (Kelway) v Independent Police Complaints Commission*,[53]

---

[47] s 1 DPA.
[48] See 7.15.
[49] s 1 DPA.
[50] *Durant* (n 19) [27]–[28].
[51] See the brief consideration of this in *Quinton v Peirce* [2009] EWHC 912 (QB) [62]. The European Commission confirmed publicly on 24 June 2010 that it had requested, by a reasoned opinion, that the UK strengthen the powers of its data protection authority, but this confirmation was inconclusive as to precisely which aspects of the UK's implementation of Directive 95/46/EC remain in issue. The UK Ministry of Justice has not commented susbstantively on the Commission's request. Leave to petition the House of Lords out of time in *Durant* was refused in 2005 and an application to the ECtHR alleging a breach of Art 8 was declared inadmissible for being out of time the following year.
[52] [2008] UKHL 47, [2008] 1 WLR 1550 [19]–[22].
[53] [2013] EWHC 2575 (Admin) [49] *et seq*.

HHJ Thornton QC (sitting as a judge of the High Court) held that, as well as the decision in *Durant*, both the Opinion on the Concept of Personal Data (WPO) (promulgated by a working party established under Article 29(1) of the Directive)[54] and the Information Commissioner's Technical Guidance Notes (TGN)[55] provide valuable guidance on the meaning of personal data for the purposes of the DPA.[56] Explaining the relationship between these different sources of guidance, he said:

> ...in a difficult or uncertain case, the decision-maker should apply first the *Durant* test and then the WPO test coupled with the TGN test. Having done so, the decision-maker should see whether the information in question is confirmed to be personal data by an application of the statutory tests. In any but an exceptional case, information identified as personal data by the application of the *Durant*, WPO and TGN tests will also be identified as personal data by a straightforward application of the statutory test since the other three tests are intended to be no more than guidance as to the application of that test.[57]

In *Vidal-Hall v Google Inc* the Court of Appeal considered it at least arguable that an internet user's browser-generated information is personal data for the purposes of the s 1(1) definition.[58]

*(c) Sensitive personal data*

The Act defines a subset of personal data in respect of which specific additional provisions apply. 'Sensitive personal data' are personal data consisting of information as to a data subject's racial or ethnic origin, political opinions, religious beliefs or beliefs of a similar nature, trade union membership, physical or mental health or condition, sexual life, commission or alleged commission of any offence and any related legal proceedings, including the disposal of them or any court sentence.[59] This definition does not include any specific reference to records held as to a data subject's financial position or dealings, nor the holding of a data subject's private or other address.[60] Nevertheless, a large part of what newspapers or broadcasters would want to say about individuals is covered by this definition.[61] The significance of this for the media is in the additional protective measures that sensitive personal data attract.

**7.24**

---

[54] Adopted on 20 June 2007.

[55] Adopted on 21 August 2007.

[56] *Kelway* (n 53) [49].

[57] *Kelway* (n 53) [59].

[58] [2015] EWCA Civ 311, [2015] 3 WLR 409.

[59] s 2 DPA.

[60] In *Robertson* (n 2) [29]–[34], the Court held that the refusal of the defendant council's Electoral Registration Officer to accede to the claimant's request that his name and address on the register should not be supplied to commercial organizations was contrary to Directive 95/46/EC and to Art 8 and Protocol 1, Art 3 ECHR.

[61] In *Campbell v MGN Ltd* [2002] EMLR 617, Morland J held at [87] that information as to the nature and details of the claimant's therapy at Narcotics Anonymous including photographs with captions was clearly information as to her physical or mental health or condition (her drug addiction) and therefore 'sensitive personal data' for the purposes of the Act. The judge considered it immaterial at [85] that the photographs concerned also contained information as to the claimant's racial or ethnic origin, since in her case she had suffered no damage or distress because the

**7.25** It seems that the question of whether a statement concerns sensitive personal data may turn on what the statement means. In *Lord Ashcroft v (1) Attorney-General and (2) Dept for International Development*,[62] Gray J held that it was at least arguable that a reference in a memorandum to the claimant's laundry arrangements would be understood to be a reference to the criminal offence of money laundering, with the result that the memorandum in question could constitute sensitive personal data under s 2(g) DPA. In *R (Ellis) v Chief Constable of Essex Police*[63] it was assumed that a scheme by the police to deter crime by publishing poster images of offenders would engage the sensitive personal data provisions of the DPA, but it was considered that the position under the Act would be the same as under Article 8 itself.

**7.26** There is a comparison to be drawn between this subcategory of personal data under the Act and the Independent Press Standards Organisation's (IPSO) Editors' Code of Practice. Like the Act, the IPSO Editors' Code is influenced by Article 8 ECHR. Indeed, para 2 of the code incorporates the words of Article 8. However, the adjudicated complaints of the Press Complaints Commission (PCC), IPSO's predecessor, made it clear that the concept of privacy in the PCC Code did not include many aspects of 'sensitive personal data' as it is defined under the 1998 Act, for example political opinions and trade union membership. Racial and ethnic origins and the commission of crime are referred to only in restricted circumstances in the IPSO Editors' Code,[64] and certainly not by way of the special categorization employed in the Act. The Ofcom Broadcasting Code, in particular s 8, discloses different areas of emphasis again.[65]

**7.27** Where a journalist's activities are subject both to the DPA and to a press or broadcasting code of practice, the relevant code clearly will not release the journalist from the requirements of the Act. Each code must either be harmonized with the Act, or read subject to it. To that extent, the DPA will override any less stringent media self-regulatory regime. But while data protection is required by Article 8, neither Article 8 nor the Strasbourg jurisprudence is the source for the definition of 'sensitive personal data', nor for the detailed provisions of the Act that apply to it. It is entirely possible that in appropriate circumstances the courts, applying s 3 HRA[66] and having regard to Article 10, will take the view that the requirements of Article 8 are given sufficient effect in the codes and, where possible or necessary, limit the effect of the DPA.

---

photographs disclosed that she is black. However he was keen at [86] to emphasize that he was not ruling out the possibility that images whether photographic or otherwise that disclose, whether from physical characteristic or dress, racial, or ethnic origins could amount to sensitive personal data. These findings were unaffected by the Court of Appeal or House of Lords judgments.

[62] [2002] EWHC 1122 (QB) [30].

[63] [2003] 2 FLR 566 [29].

[64] cll 12 and 9 respectively.

[65] The Code is kept up-to-date at <stakeholders.ofcom.org.uk/broadcasting/broadcast-codes/broadcast-code/>. For further discussion of the IPSO and PCC codes see ch 14.

[66] Which requires, so far as it is possible to do so, primary and subordinate legislation to be read and given effect in a way which is compatible with the Convention rights.

### (d) Data controller and data processor

A data controller is a person who either alone, jointly, or in common with other  **7.28**
persons determines the purposes for which and the manner in which any personal
data are, or are to be, processed.[67] A data controller can be any legal person, that is
to say an individual or an organization such as a company or other incorporated or
unincorporated body. Two or more data controllers may in practice exercise different degrees of control over the pool of data in respect of which they are joint data
controllers. It is quite clear that the existence of one data controller in respect of a
pool of data does not exclude the possibility of there being other data controllers
in respect of the same pool: the test in respect of each potential data controller is
whether he or she determines the purposes for which and the manner in which the
personal data in question are, or are to be, processed.

In *Douglas v Hello! Ltd*[68] the Court of Appeal held that the argument that the sixth  **7.29**
defendant, an American paparazzo who transmitted the unauthorized photo-
graphs down an ISDN line to London, fell within s 5(1)(b) DPA, had a reasonable
prospect of success and should not be struck out, thereby reversing the decision of
Laddie J at first instance. It was at least arguable, they said, that the sixth defendant was a data controller since he was on the pleaded case 'using equipment in
the United Kingdom for processing [the] data otherwise than for the purposes of
transit through the United Kingdom'. This interpretation assimilates liability for
breaches of the statutory torts under the DPA with liability for causing the publication from abroad of a libel which is read in England.

A data processor, in relation to personal data, is any person (other than an employee  **7.30**
of the data controller) who processes data on behalf of the data controller.[69] Media
organizations will inevitably be data controllers in a great deal of their functions.
They will also share control of data with other organizations and individuals who
are themselves data controllers, for example news agencies and freelance journalists. Media organizations will also direct processing of data on their behalf by
employees or agents. Definitional intricacies may arise, for example in the context
of the editorial function.[70] In *Campbell*[71] the Court of Appeal accepted that the

---

[67] s 1(1) DPA. Where any enactment requires the processing of personal data, s 1(4) imposes the
statutory obligation solely on the data controller.
[68] *Douglas v Hello! Ltd* [2003] EMLR 28.
[69] s 1 DPA.
[70] This is the case in libel, where a newspaper editor is often sued although it is universally
accepted that he or she cannot expressly authorize every word printed before it is published. In
*Registrar v Griffin*, Data Prot R, 13 March 1994, the Divisional Court reversed an earlier magistrates' court decision and held that an accountant who entered and held information on his computer provided from his clients was a data 'user' (the equivalent term under the 1984 Act for what
is now defined under the DPA 1998 as a data 'controller') and therefore subject to the requirements
of notification, despite the fact that he was restricted to using the personal data solely for purposes
dictated by his clients, since he controlled the contents of the data and how it was manipulated.
[71] *Campbell* (n 14) [76].

newspaper publishers were a data controller. They also noted that the data controller tended to be equated with the editor, who had been personally responsible for the decisions taken in relation to the content of the articles complained of (albeit not as a data controller in his or her own right).

**7.31**  Where, for example, the media make use of CCTV material[72] provided to them by other organizations or individuals they will be subject to the same obligations to comply with the data protection Principles laid down in the Act as if they had harvested themselves as data controllers any personal data recorded in the material concerned.[73]

**7.32**  In *Google Spain SL, Google Inc v Agencia Espanola de Proteccion de Datos (AEPD), Mario Costeja Gonzalez,* (the 'right to be forgotten' case) the European Court of Justice held that the activity of an internet search engine—finding information published or placed on the internet by third parties, indexing it automatically, storing it temporarily and, finally, making it available to internet users according to a particular order of preference—must be classified as 'processing of personal data' within the meaning of Article 2(b) of the Directive when that information contains personal data.[74] The operator of a search engine must also be regarded as the 'controller' in respect of that processing, within the meaning of Article 2(d) of the Directive. In the subsequent domestic case of *Mosley v Google Inc* (which concerned the continued internet availability of footage of Max Mosley's private sexual activity) Google is recorded as having conceded that it was a data controller for the purposes of the 1998 Act and, in particular in the context of that case, s 10.[75]

*(e)  Data subject*

**7.33**  This is any individual who is the subject of personal data.[76] Guidelines first issued by the Data Protection Registrar[77] indicated that data may be taken to refer to an unnamed individual even though the information contained in the data does not include a name. Guidance to that effect has been maintained to date at the Information Commissioner's website.[78] This position is potentially similar to the tests of identification of and reference to the claimant in a libel claim.[79]

---

[72] See *eg Peck* (n 7) on a local authority's decision to hand over to a broadcasting company CCTV footage of a man who was about to attempt suicide.

[73] Implicit recognition of this position can be found in the BBC Producers' Guidelines, by which producers are advised in relation to acquired CCTV material to consider the issues of privacy, anonymity, and defamation and are warned to apply the same ethical, editorial considerations as if the BBC had recorded the material itself.

[74] Case C-131/12 [2014] QB 1022 [41].

[75] [2015] EWHC 59 (QB), [2015] EMLR 11 [23].

[76] s 1 DPA.

[77] September 1997 revision, p 21, para 10.2.

[78] See Guidelines, ch 3, para 10, available at <http://www.ico.org.uk/for_organisations/data_protection/~/media/documents/library/Data_Protection/Practical_application/the_guide_to_data_protection.pdf>.

[79] See *Gatley on Libel and Slander* (n 44) ch 7.

### (f) Recipients and third parties

A 'recipient' in relation to any personal data means any person to whom the data **7.34** are disclosed, including any person (such as an employee or agent of the data con- troller or of a data processor) to whom they are disclosed in the course of process- ing, except where such disclosure is made in the exercise of any power conferred by law.[80] In the case of the media's data, recipients will include their readers and audiences as well possibly as sources and interviewees. A 'third party' is any per- son other than the data subject, data controller, and any data processor or other person authorized to process data for the data controller or processor (such as their employees or agents).[81]

### (g) Processing

The 1998 Act's definition of 'processing' is all-encompassing: obtaining, recording, **7.35** or holding information or data or carrying out any operation or set of operations on them, including organization, adaptation, alteration, retrieval, consultation, use, disclosure by transmission, dissemination or otherwise making available, alignment, combination, blocking, erasure, or destruction. In short, 'processing' appears to cover any imaginable treatment of information or data, as was reflected by the Information Commissioner's initial guidance on the Act.[82] For example, whenever a journalist obtains information to be put into a database the Principles apply. Equally, they apply whenever a newspaper extracts information from a data- base. This approach can be contrasted with the now superseded definition of 'use' under the 1984 Act, which the House of Lords considered did not include the retrieval of information from a database.[83]

Digital publication will clearly count as 'processing' and the Court of Appeal in **7.36** *Campbell*[84] concluded, with reference to the appellant newspaper as 'data control- lers' within the terms of the DPA 1998, that:

> ...where the data controller is responsible for the publication of hard copies that reproduce data that has previously been processed by means of equipment operat- ing automatically, the publication forms part of the processing and falls within the scope of the Act.

The Court added that:[85]

> ...the definition of processing is so wide that it embraces the relatively ephemeral operations that will normally be carried out by way of the day-to-day tasks, involv- ing the use of electronic equipment, such as the lap-top and the modern printing press, in translating information into the printed newspaper.

---

[80] s 70(1) DPA.
[81] s 70(1) DPA.
[82] *Data Protection Act 1998: Legal guidance* (n 43) para 2.2.
[83] *R v Brown* [1996] AC 543.
[84] *Campbell* (n 14) [107].
[85] *Campbell* (n 14) [123].

*(h) Assessable processing*

**7.37** Section 22 DPA empowers the Secretary of State to specify a particular description of processing as 'assessable processing' if it appears to him or her to be particularly likely (a) to cause substantial damage or substantial distress to data subjects or (b) otherwise significantly to prejudice the rights and freedoms of data subjects.[86]

**7.38** Both the nature of the information being processed and the nature of the processing itself seem to be relevant to an assessment of whether processing should be assessable. Prior to implementation of the Act it was suggested that three kinds of processing might be made assessable, one of these being processing by private investigators.[87] There are obvious similarities between the techniques of investigative journalists and those of private investigators, so that there is clearly the potential for some areas or types of investigative journalism to be held to involve assessable processing.

**7.39** If during the notification process[88] the Commissioner considers that any processing by a data controller is assessable processing then he or she must within ten days of the date of receipt of a notification give a notice to the data controller stating the extent to which the Commissioner believes that the processing is likely or unlikely to comply with the Act.[89] A data controller who conducts assessable processing without completing this notification and notice process is guilty of an offence punishable with a fine.[90] The Act is unclear as to whether the offence is restricted to processing without due notification and notice, or whether it will also extend to processing that the Commissioner has assessed as unlikely to comply with the Act. If the latter, there would at some stage need to be a determination of whether or not the fears underpinning the Commissioner's assessment were justified or not. There is, however, no specific procedure set out in the legislation for this to happen.

*(i) The special purposes*

**7.40** These are one or more of the purposes of journalism, artistic purposes, and literary purposes.[91] These purposes coincide with the conventional functions of the media and so are of particular significance. Having been defined, the 'special purposes' are referred to three further times in the Act and its statutory instruments. First, processing for the 'special purposes' exposes a data controller to a special and extended liability to pay compensation for contravention of the Act

---

[86] s 22(1) DPA. No such specifications have been made.

[87] Home Office Consultation Paper, August 1998.

[88] See 7.11 and n 26.

[89] s 22(2)–(3) DPA, as amended by the Data Protection (Notification and Notification Fees) Regulations 2000, SI 2000/188, para 9.

[90] ss 5 and 60(2) DPA.

[91] s 3 DPA. See *Sugar v BBC* [2012] UKSC 4, [2012] 1 WLR 439 for consideration by the Supreme Court of the scope of 'journalism' in particular for the purposes of this statutory wording. See also the Information Commissioner's 'Data protection and journalism: a guide for the media', 4 September 2014, 29 *et seq.*

even if the contravention in question has not caused the claimant to suffer actual damage.[92] Secondly, s 32 DPA provides the 'media exemption' discussed further below.[93] Thirdly, the Data Protection (Processing of Sensitive Personal Data) Order 2000[94] makes provision concerning the disclosure of sensitive personal information in a media context.

### (3) Section 4(4): Duty to Comply with the Data Protection Principles

The eight Principles are set out in pt I of sch 1 to the Act. The first Principle in particular is broad in scope. Guidance on its interpretation, together with that of the second, fourth, sixth, seventh, and eighth Principles is provided in pt II of the same schedule. **7.41**

#### (a) First Principle—processing to be fair and lawful

**The Principle and its conditions**   Personal data are to be processed fairly and lawfully and, in particular, not to be processed unless, in the case of any personal data, at least one of the conditions in sch 2 to the Act is met and, in the case of sensitive personal data, at least one of the conditions in sch 3 is also met.[95] In *Campbell v MGN Ltd* the judge at first instance found that these requirements are cumulative.[96] **7.42**

Consideration of whether data have been processed fairly and lawfully in the context of publication by a media data controller will only be addressed once a court has come to the conclusion that the s 32 media exemption does not apply, taking account of the fact that the Court of Appeal in *Campbell*[97] held that the exemption applies before, after, and at the moment of publication. Where it applies, s 32 exempts personal data which are processed exclusively for the 'special purposes'[98] of journalism (and literature and art) from any provision of the data protection Principles save the seventh[99] and ss 7 (right of access to personal data), 10 (right to prevent processing likely to cause damage or distress), 12 (rights in relation to automated decision-making), and 14(1)–(3) (rectification, blocking, erasure, and destruction). Three conditions must be satisfied for the exemption to apply. These are:[100] first, that the processing is undertaken with a view to the publication **7.43**

---

[92]   See 7.92.
[93]   See 7.109–7.116.
[94]   SI 2000/417. See further 7.117–7.124.
[95]   sch 1, pt I, para 1 DPA.
[96]   *Campbell* (n 61). This finding was unaffected by the decisions in the Court of Appeal and House of Lords.
[97]   *Campbell* (n 14).
[98]   Defined by s 3 DPA.
[99]   Which requires appropriate technical and organizational measures to be taken against unauthorized or unlawful processing of personal data and against accidental loss or destruction of, or damage to, personal data: sch 1, pt I, para 7 DPA.
[100]   s 32(1)(a)–(c) DPA.

by any person of any journalistic, literary, or artistic material; secondly, that the data controller reasonably believes that, having regard in particular to the special importance of the public interest in freedom of expression, publication would be in the public interest; and thirdly, that the data controller reasonably believes that, in all the circumstances, compliance with that provision is incompatible with the special purposes.

**7.44** In *Murray v Express Newspapers plc*[101] the judge at first instance considered that the reference to 'lawfully' in sch 1, pt I must be construed by reference to the current state of the law in particular in relation to the misuse of confidential information. He noted that the draftsman of the Act did not attempt to give the word any wider or special meaning, and held that the processor of the personal data therefore has the same obligations of confidentiality as would apply but for the Act.

**7.45** *Schedule 2—conditions for the processing of any personal data* The particular conditions set by sch 2 for the fair and lawful processing of any personal data are that the data subject has given his or her consent to the processing,[102] or the processing is necessary for one of a collection of different reasons or purposes.[103] These are that the processing is necessary: in relation to an actual or prospective contract involving the data subject; for compliance with any legal (other than contractual) obligation to which the data controller is subject; in order to protect the vital interests of the data subject;[104] for the administration of justice, the exercise of any statutory, Crown, ministerial, governmental function, or any other function of a public nature exercised in the public interest;[105] or for the purposes of legitimate interests pursued by the data controller or a third party,[106] except where the processing is unwarranted in any particular case by reason of prejudice to the rights and freedoms or legitimate interests of the data subject.[107] It is the last of these conditions that is of greatest significance for the media.

**7.46** **Legitimate interests** Schedule 2, para 6(1) DPA provides for the processing of personal data (but not *sensitive* personal data) where this is necessary for the purposes of legitimate interests pursued by the data controller or by the third party

---

[101] [2007] EWHC 1908 (Ch), [2007] EMLR 22 [72].

[102] sch 2, para 1 DPA and see 7.56–7.57.

[103] Set out at sch 2, paras 2–5 DPA.

[104] The Commissioner has previously given as an example of a life and death situation the disclosure of a data subject's medical history to a hospital casualty department after a serious road accident involving the data subject—*Data Protection Act 1998: Legal guidance* (n 43) para 3.1.1. On this basis, it will be rarely, if ever, that the media finds itself in a position to rely on this justification.

[105] This exception might be available to at least the public service media (and is derived from Art 7(e) of Directive 95/46/EC, not Art 9 which explicitly refers to a media exemption). It is not perhaps clear why any greater protection, though, should be given to public service broadcasters than other journalists. This also raises the issue of the 'public' status of various media organizations (*eg*, under s 6 HRA and the Freedom of Information Act 2000, sch 1, pt VI). See further 1.57–1.65.

[106] As to the 'legitimate interest' of journalism pursued by a media data controller see 7.46–7.49.

[107] sch 2, para 6(1) DPA.

or parties to whom the data are disclosed, except where the processing is unwarranted in any particular case by reason of prejudice to the rights and freedoms or legitimate interests of the data subject. The Secretary of State may by order specify particular circumstances in which this condition is, or is not, to be taken to be satisfied,[108] but that has not happened to date.

This provision appears not to have been derived from the media exemption set out **7.47** in Article 9 of the Directive but from Article 7(f).[109] Journalism may be regarded as a legitimate interest pursued by a data controller.[110]

In *Douglas v Hello! Ltd*[111] Lindsay J found the *Hello!* defendants to have a legitimate **7.48** interest within sch 2, para 6 DPA in publishing their magazine to include coverage of the Douglases' wedding. In particular, he found that the processing the defendants had carried out was illegitimate since it was unwarranted by reason of prejudice to the rights of the data subjects. In so doing, he expressed the questionable view that a finding of prejudice under this provision did not require a general balance between freedom of expression and rights to privacy or confidence, but rather a consideration simply of whether something more than trivial prejudice had arisen to the data subjects' legal rights.

In *Campbell*[112] the judge at first instance found that while publication of the claim- **7.49** ant's drug addiction and the fact that she was having therapy was necessary for the purposes of legitimate interests of the defendant as a newspaper publisher, and was not an unwarranted intrusion into the claimant's right of privacy, it was not necessary to publish the therapy details complained of. All that needed to be published in pursuit of the defendant's legitimate interests were the facts of drug addiction and therapy. Publication of the details of the therapy were therefore an unwarranted intrusion into the claimant's right of privacy and, on the principle of proportionality, the defendant did not pass through the condition 6(1) 'gateway' (even if the therapy details were not 'sensitive personal data').

In *Murray v Express Newspapers plc*,[113] the judge at first instance accepted the **7.50** defendant picture agency's submission that the pursuit of a legitimate business is a legitimate interest for the purposes of sch 2, para 6(1). It is suggested that

---

[108] sch 2, para 6(2) DPA.

[109] 'Member States shall provide that personal data may be processed only if... (f) processing is necessary for the purposes of the legitimate interests pursued by the controller or by the third party or parties to whom the data are disclosed, except where such interests are overridden by the interests for fundamental rights and freedoms of the data subject which require protection under Article 1(1).' See Appendix D (available at <http://www.5rb.com/publication/the-law-of-privacy-and-the-media>).

[110] There are numerous references in the Strasbourg jurisprudence to the important role of the press in a democratic society, *eg Lingens v Austria* (1986) 8 EHRR 407, para 41.

[111] *Douglas* (n 40) [238].

[112] *Campbell* (n 61) [112].

[113] *Murray* (n 101) [76].

the interests of consumers of journalism in receiving information would also be a legitimate interest promoted by this paragraph.

**7.51**   *Schedule 3—conditions for the processing of sensitive personal data*   In the case of sensitive personal data, one of the conditions just listed for the processing of any personal data must be met, but the Act also requires that the data controller also meet one of a further set of additional conditions.[114] These are that the data subject has given his or her explicit consent to the processing of the personal data;[115] the processing is necessary for the exercise or performance of any legal right or obligation by the data controller in connection with employment;[116] the processing is necessary to protect the vital interests of the data subject or another person, and consent cannot be given by or on behalf of the data subject, the data controller cannot reasonably be expected to obtain such consent, or consent has been unreasonably withheld but processing is necessary to protect the vital interests of another person; the processing is carried out in the course of the legitimate activities of a non-profit-making political, philosophical, religious, or trade union body or association which has appropriate safeguards for the rights and freedoms of data subjects and relates only to individuals who are members of the body or association or have regular contact with it; the information contained in the personal data has been made public as a result of steps deliberately taken by the data subject;[117] the processing is necessary for the pursuit of legal proceedings, provision of legal advice, or to establish, exercise, or defend legal rights;[118] the processing is necessary for the administration of justice or the exercise of any statutory, Crown, ministerial, or governmental function;[119] the processing is necessary for medical purposes and is undertaken (confidentially) by a health professional or other such person; the processing is of information as to racial or ethnic origin, is undertaken to enable the promotion or maintenance of equality, and is carried out with appropriate safeguards for the rights and freedoms of data subjects;[120] or the processing is in circumstances specified in an order made by the Secretary of State.

**7.52**   **The 'fair processing code'**   In determining whether personal data are processed fairly, regard is to be had to the method by which they are obtained, including in particular whether any person from whom they are obtained is deceived or misled

---

[114]   These are set out at sch 3, paras 1–10 DPA.

[115]   sch 3, para 1 DPA and see further 7.56–7.57.

[116]   Under para 2(2) the Secretary of State may by order exclude the application of this provision or specify cases in which the condition is not to be regarded as satisfied. No orders have been made.

[117]   See further 7.58–7.61.

[118]   As to the exercise of the legal right to freedom of expression see 7.125.

[119]   sch 3, para 7(1) DPA. Again, here, para 7(2) allows the Secretary of State by order to exclude the application of this paragraph or specify cases in which the condition is not to be regarded as satisfied, but no such orders have been made.

[120]   sch 3, para 9(1) DPA. By para 9(2) the Secretary of State may by order specify circumstances in which such processing is to be taken to be carried out with appropriate safeguards for the rights and freedoms of data subjects. No such orders have been made.

as to the purpose or purposes for which they are to be processed.[121] The problem with this from the media's perspective is that it is sometimes necessary or legitimate for a journalist to mislead a source or data subject in order to obtain accurate information that would otherwise be unobtainable.[122] The IPSO Editors' Code[123] envisages the acquisition of material through misrepresentation or subterfuge in exceptional situations, where it can be justified in the public interest and when the material cannot be obtained by other means.

Data are not to be treated as processed fairly unless the data controller ensures so **7.53** far as practicable that the data subject has, is provided with, or has made readily available to him or her the identity of the data controller and his or her nominated representative, the purpose(s) for which the data are to be processed, and any further information necessary in the specific circumstances to enable the processing to be fair.[124] This requirement is on one view unrealistic and impractically onerous given the familiar and traditional methods employed by journalists (see *eg* the National Union of Journalists' Code of Conduct). It is unclear whether, if a journalist has complied with a relevant press or broadcasting code, he or she will automatically be relieved from strict compliance with these conditions. The fact that in 1995 the Data Protection Tribunal supported the Registrar's earlier view that personal information will not be fairly obtained unless the individual has been informed, before the information is obtained, of the non-obvious purposes for which it is required would suggest not.[125] In the non-media case of *Quinton v Peirce*, which concerned local council election leaflets, Eady J rejected the suggestion that in order to comply with the obligation to be fair, an election candidate should not 'process' information concerning his rival by including it in a leaflet

---

[121] sch 1, pt II, para 1(1) DPA.

[122] *eg* the cases of the then Home Secretary's son trapped into a drugs offence and the directors of a football club enticed into a brothel, discussed in Perri 6, *The Future of Privacy*, vol 1: *Private Life and Public Policy* (Demos 1998) 265. In *R v Thwaites* [2000] EWCA Crim 60, the Court dismissed an appeal against a drugs conviction on the grounds that it was an abuse of process since the conviction had only been obtained as a result of a 'sting' operation carried out by *News of the World* journalists.

[123] cl 10(ii). See Appendix G(iii) (available at <http://www.5rb.com/publication/the-law-of-privacy-and-the-media>).

[124] sch 1, pt II, paras 2(1)(a) and (3) DPA. Where the data have been obtained from a party other than the data subject, the data controller must nevertheless make the same information available to the data subject as near as possible to the time of first processing and/or disclosure to a third party by him or her under para 2(1)(b) and (2). However, and subject to any conditions the Secretary of State may prescribe by order, para 3 relieves a data controller of his or her obligations in the latter respect if the provision of such information to the data subject would involve a disproportionate effort or the data controller is processing the data in compliance with some legal (other than contractual) obligation.

[125] *Innovations (Mail Order) Ltd v Data Protection Registrar* (Case DA/92 31/49/1) 29 September 1993, [30]; *Linguaphone Institute Ltd v Data Protection Registrar* (Case DA/94/31/49/1) 14 July 1995, [14]. In *Data Protection Act 1998: Legal guidance* (n 52) para 3.1.7.3, the Commissioner observed that the more unforeseen the consequences of processing, the more likely it is that the data controller will be expected to provide further information to the data subject.

without notifying the rival in advance.[126] (The proposition was based on sch 1, pt 2, paras 2 and 3 DPA, containing the fair processing code.) He held that it would be absurd to interpret the statute in that way. He said it was plain that the legislature could not have intended to require electoral candidates to give their opponents advance warning each time reference is to be made to them in a document that happens to be computer-generated.[127]

**7.54** Subject to the above exceptions, data are to be treated as fairly obtained if they consist of information obtained from a person who is statutorily authorized or required to supply them.[128] This provides scope for protection of the media where they obtain information, whatever its nature, from statutorily appointed or authorized 'official' sources.

**7.55** In *Murray*[129] the judge at first instance rejected the contention that the covert taking of a photograph of the claimant in his pushchair in a public street without his consent was unfair. He noted that no actual deception was practised and did not consider that the taking of the photograph could be said to be unfair if it was otherwise lawful (as he had held it to be). The judge also considered that the claimant's further objection based on the processing of his sensitive personal data by the taking of the photograph, even if otherwise well-founded, failed since the claimant (or his parents, acting on his behalf) had, by appearing in public, deliberately exposed his own image to the public thus bringing condition 5 of sch 3 into play.

**7.56** **Consent and explicit consent**   The sch 2 conditions that are most obviously relevant to a journalist are consent (personal data) and explicit consent (sensitive personal data) of the data subject, *ie* the person to whom information obtained and to be published relates. The relevant codes[130] already prescribe requirements for journalists to obtain consent from their subjects in particular situations, but the need for consent under the DPA is much wider. The Directive requires that consent be given 'unambiguously' and defines a data subject's consent as 'any freely given specific and informed indication of his wishes by which the data subject signifies his agreement to personal data relating to him being processed',[131] but this definition is not repeated in the Act. It is entirely unclear how the word 'explicit' is to be interpreted in practice, and it is also unclear whether consent, once given, can be withdrawn or overridden or for how long it will remain valid.[132]

---

[126] *Quinton v Peirce* [2009] EWHC 912 (QB), [2009] FSR 17 [93].

[127] *Quinton* (n 126) [93].

[128] sch 1, Pt II, para 1(2) DPA.

[129] *Murray* (n 101) [73]–[81].

[130] Ofcom Broadcasting Code; IPSO Editors' Code. See Appendices G(i) and G(iii) (available at <http://www.5rb.com/publication/the-law-of-privacy-and-the-media>).

[131] Directive 95/46/EC, Arts 7(a) and 2(h).

[132] In *Data Protection Act 1998: Legal guidance* (n 43) para 3.1.5 it was suggested that individuals may be able to withdraw consent depending upon the nature of the consent given and the circumstances of the processing.

In *R v Dept of Health, ex p Source Informatics Ltd*,[133] in relation to medical information, **7.57** the Court of Appeal indicated approval of a submission that: 'for there to be effective consent sufficient information must have been given to the patient about the purpose and extent of the disclosure of confidential personal information: see *Sidaway v Board of Governors of the Bethlem Royal Hospital and the Maudsley Hospital*'.[134] Consent may be signified by conduct.[135] The right to protection of doctor/patient confidences cannot be abridged or eroded by a public authority without good reason.[136] It has been long established under the general law that only informed and explicit patient consent will suffice for the disclosure of personal medical patient data.[137]

**Sensitive personal data and the public domain**   In the case of sensitive personal **7.58** data, if explicit consent has not been obtained then it is sufficient that such information has been made public as a result of steps deliberately taken by the data subject.[138] The word 'deliberately' here is to be compared with the provisions of the Directive, which refer to data that are 'manifestly' made public by the data subject.[139] The reason for this change of wording by the UK legislature is unclear. The preference of the Act for 'deliberately' over 'manifestly' may suggest a subjective approach to the question,[140] as opposed to a consideration of whether in all the circumstances it appeared 'obvious' that the data subject had made information public. The two concepts are quite different: something can be manifestly made public without being deliberately made public, and vice versa. Further, the expression 'steps deliberately taken' begs the question whether what is required is for the data subject simply to have taken deliberate steps, the result of which, intended or not, has been the publication of the information, or whether it is required that in taking the steps in question the data subject actually intended and foresaw that publication should follow. In summary, the change in wording does appear to have omitted from the Act a public domain defence in the case of the processing of sensitive personal data that the Directive intended should be available. The absence of, or restrictions on, a public domain defence is difficult to reconcile with the Strasbourg jurisprudence.[141]

---

[133]  [2001] QB 424, 429.

[134]  [1985] AC 871.

[135]  *O'Brien v Cunard SS Co* (1891) 28 NE 266.

[136]  *Dudgeon v UK* (1981) 4 EHRR 149.

[137]  See *Bowater v Rowley Regis Corp* [1944] KB 476; *Burnett v British Waterways Board* [1973] 1 WLR 700; *Kirkham v Chief Constable of Greater Manchester Police* [1990] 2 QB 283; *Morley v United Friendly Insurance plc* [1993] 1 WLR 996; and *Sarch v Blackburn* (1830) 4 C&P 297.

[138]  sch 3, para 5 DPA.

[139]  Directive 95/46/EC, Art 8(2)(e).

[140]  ie did the data subject as a matter of fact intend and foresee that his actions would lead to publication of the information?

[141]  See *eg Sunday Times Ltd v UK (No 2)* (1991) 14 EHRR 229, 243–4 (the ECtHR accepted in principle that republication of material already in the public domain might be restrained in certain cases where it would do further harm: para 54); *Weber v Switzerland* (1990) 12 EHRR 508, 524–5 (an offence under which the importance of the information and the fact that it was common

**7.59**  The Commissioner's general advice in this area is that data controllers should consider the extent to which the use of personal data by them is or is not reasonably foreseeable by the data subject. To the extent that their use of personal data is not reasonably foreseeable by the data subject, data controllers should ensure that they provide such further information as may be necessary to inform the data subject.[142] In the media context, it is not clear that a journalist would be considered to have met this condition simply because it is obvious to all that the function of a journalist is to publish stories.

**7.60**  These considerations are indeed likely to present difficulties for the media on a practical level. It may not be easy for a journalist to establish consent or that information has entered the public domain as a result of steps deliberately taken by the data subject. For example, if information about a person's sexuality has come into the public domain, but not as a result of any deliberate act of that person, the Act on its face prohibits its republication (which is a further act of processing) without his or her explicit consent. A cautious approach would require journalists to obtain written consent from a data subject every time they intended to publish an item of sensitive personal information. Not only does this seem unrealistic, but a widespread practice of seeking written consents[143] would be likely to prompt requests for copy approval from data subjects, attempts to embargo information, requests for payment, and so on. This would clearly militate strongly against freedom of expression, and is a troubling and difficult area of the legislation.

**7.61**  Whether the difficulties for the media are so acute in the case of public-figure data subjects remains to be seen. In *Lingens v Austria*[144] the European Court of Human Rights (ECtHR) found in the context of Article 10(2) that the limits of acceptable public criticism are 'wider as regards a politician as such than as regards a private individual: unlike the latter, the former inevitably and knowingly lays himself open to close scrutiny of his every word and deed by both journalists and the public at large, and must consequently display a greater degree of tolerance'. It is perhaps arguable on this basis that by volunteering themselves into public life politicians and other public figures must be taken to consent to a degree of prying, or they 'deliberately' put at least certain aspects of their private lives into the public domain.

---

knowledge before the publication was only taken in account at sentencing was held to be inconsistent with Art 10). For the direct effect of a directive see n 2 and n 12.

[142] *Data Protection Act 1998: Legal guidance* (n 43) para 3.1.7.3.

[143] Broadcasters are of course accustomed to obtaining consent to broadcast from studio interviewees, but in any other context journalistic practice has been far less formal.

[144] (1986) 8 EHRR 407, paras 41–42. See also B Markesinis and N Nolte, 'Some comparative reflections on the right of privacy of public figures in private places' in Birks (n 8) 113 and F Schauer, 'Can public figures have private lives?' in E Paul, F Miller, and J Paul (eds), *The Right to Privacy* (Cambridge University Press 2000) 293.

*(b) Second Principle—processing only for specified and lawful purposes*

Personal data is to be obtained only for one or more specified and lawful pur-  **7.62**
poses, and is not to be further processed in any manner incompatible with that
purpose or those purposes.[145] The purpose or purposes for which personal data are
obtained may in particular be specified in a notice given by the data controller to
the data subject or in a notification given by the data controller to the Information
Commissioner pursuant to his or her notification obligations under the Act. In
determining whether any disclosure of personal data by the data controller is compatible with the purpose or purposes for which the data were obtained, regard is to
be had to the purpose or purposes for which the personal data are intended to be
processed by any person to whom they are disclosed.

It will not necessarily be enough for a media organization simply to rely on a general  **7.63**
notification of purposes to the Commissioner under the notification procedure[146] for
compliance under the second Principle. Where information is collected for a specific
purpose in practice it will be prudent to review whether the acquisition is covered
by an organization's general notification, or whether a further specific obligation
of notification either to the Commissioner and/or the data subject in the particular case arises. This will include consideration of the purpose or purposes to which
the data in question are to be put by any person to whom they are to be disclosed.

A cautious view is that a data controller should seek contractual reassurance  **7.64**
from any person to whom such data are disclosed that disclosed data will only
be used within the data controller's own notified purposes, but in the context
of the media it is difficult to see in many situations how this can be a realistic
solution. One area, however, in which media organizations may be advised to
review their personal data disclosures is where they contribute to news-agency
databases: there is no reason in principle why database contribution or subscrip-
tion agreements should not appropriately limit the purposes to which database
information is to be put.

*(c) Third, fourth, and fifth Principles—personal data to be adequate, relevant,*
*and not excessive; accurate; and not to be kept longer than is necessary*

These three Principles taken together amount to an exhortation to all data control-  **7.65**
lers, the media included, to exercise 'good housekeeping' in relation to data they hold.
In the *Google Spain*, the European Court of Justice noted that it is because of these
requirements (as they are expressed in the Directive) that initially lawful processing
of accurate data can become incompatible with the Directive once those data are no
longer necessary for the purposes for which they were collected or processed.[147] On
the Court's analysis, since the data subject may, in the light of his or her fundamental

---

[145]  sch 1, pt I, para 2 and pt II, paras 5(a)–(b) and 6 DPA.
[146]  See n 26.
[147]  *Google Spain* (n 74) [92]–[93].

rights in these respects, request that the information in question no longer be made available to the general public by its inclusion in internet search results, those rights override, as a rule, not only the economic interest of the operator of the search engine but also the interest of the general public in finding that information upon a search relating to the data subject's name.[148] That is, however, not necessarily the case if it appeared, for particular reasons, such as a role played by the data subject in public life, that the interference with his fundamental rights is justified by the preponderant interest of the general public in having, on account of inclusion in the list of results, access to the information in question. It seems, therefore, that *Google Spain* creates some sort of new priority for the third, fourth, and fifth Principles as expressed in the DPA. It is of course a decision made against a particular search engine. But its foundation is the finding that the search engine in question, Google, is a data controller.[149] Given that media organizations will be data controllers in a great deal of their functions (see 7.30), there appears to be no bar in principle to the argument that a similar priority ought to apply in favour of a data subject as against a media organization maintaining publicly, for example by way of a website posting, some stale personal information about the data subject to which he objects.

**7.66** **Third Principle** Personal data should be adequate, relevant, and not excessive in relation to the purpose or purposes for which they are processed.[150] An obvious difficulty here for the journalist is that at the information-gathering stage, when looking for a story, it will be impossible to know what actual data are required and what is excessive.

**7.67** **Fourth Principle** Data should be accurate and, where necessary, kept up to date.[151] This Principle is not to be regarded as contravened by reason of any inaccuracy in personal data where, having regard to the purpose or purposes for which the data were obtained and further processed, the data controller has taken reasonable steps to ensure their accuracy and, if the data subject has notified the data controller of the data subject's view that the data are inaccurate, the data themselves make that clear.[152] In the context of a complaint against a credit reference agency, Davis LJ in *Smeaton v Equifax* emphasized that the fourth Principle does not impose an 'absolute and unqualified' obligation on the data controller to ensure the entire accuracy of data being maintained.[153]

**7.68** The need for a media organization to keep data in relation to a particular broadcast or publication will be open to interpretation on a case-by-case basis. It is unclear whether, or to what extent, a media organization is required to update its data once it has made its broadcast or publication. If inaccurate information has been published,

---

[148] *Google Spain* (n 74) [97].
[149] *Google Spain* (n 74) [41].
[150] sch 1, pt I, para 3 DPA.
[151] sch 1, pt I, para 4 DPA.
[152] sch 1, pt II, para 7 DPA.
[153] *Equifax v Smeaton* [2013] EWCA Civ 108 [80].

for example, there is no indication of the extent to which a media organization is bound by the data protection legislation to amend its story, or publish a correction. In *Quinton v Peirce*[154] the Court was unimpressed with the contention[155] that the defendants as data controllers of the claimant's personal data were under a statutory duty by virtue of ss 4(4) and 70(2) and the fourth data protection Principle to ensure the data's accuracy, suggesting that it is neither necessary nor proportionate to interpret the DPA as conferring on the court the power to order the circulation of a correction if the data controller does not believe he or she has published anything untrue. The judge said that such a scheme could only work in respect of factual statements which could be demonstrated uncontroversially and objectively to be false, but cannot be intended to compel publication of an account of a factual scenario which is capable of being understood in different ways simply because, on one interpretation, it might not be accurate.[156] Subject to the facts of a particular case, however, this apparent exclusion of the possibility of inaccurate data being corrected where the data controller (whether a media organization or otherwise) mistakenly believes them to be accurate runs contrary to the unequivocal terms of the fourth Principle, that data should be accurate and where necessary kept up to date. In particular, the Act does not indicate that the operation of the fourth Principle, in favour of correcting inaccurate data, depends upon the data controller not believing in their accuracy.

**Fifth Principle**   Personal data processed for any purpose or purposes should not be   **7.69** kept for longer than is necessary for that purpose or purposes.[157] There are a number of familiar and competing considerations and media customs relating to the length of time records are kept. On the one hand, for example, there are the media's sensitivity to potential applications for evidence under the Police and Criminal Evidence Act 1984, and desire not to prejudice their confidential sources by retaining information that they might later be ordered to disclose in order to identify them. These may militate against prolonged holding of data. On the other hand, journalists may need to keep records in case litigation arises from a broadcast or publication. The usual time limit for libel claims is one year from publication,[158] but for confidence or misuse of private information claims, and claims for compensation under the DPA,[159] the time limit will typically be six years. These considerations must all now be

---

[154]   *Quinton* (n 51).

[155]   *Quinton* (n 51) [58].

[156]   *Quinton* (n 51) [88].

[157]   sch 1, pt I, para 5 DPA.

[158]   Defamation Act 1996, s 5, incorporating the Limitation Act 1980, ss 4 and 32A. For further discussion of limitation periods, see 11.218 *et seq*. The particular difficulties caused to newspapers by ongoing publication on their internet services when set against the rule in *Duke of Brunswick v Harmer* (1849) 14 QB 185, as affirmed in *Loutchansky v Times Newspapers Ltd (Nos 2, 3, 4, 5)* [2002] QB 783, CA (and see also *Times Newspapers Ltd v UK* App nos 3002/03 and 23676/03, [2009] EMLR 14), may well now be a thing of the past, with the introduction by s 8 of the Defamation Act 2013 of the 'single publication rule' into English law.

[159]   The position is more complicated for claims in confidence and under the DPA where there is ongoing processing: see further 11.218.

taken into account alongside the purpose or purposes for which data were processed in the first place. Additionally, so far as any continuing publication is concerned, particularly in the form for example of a website posting, the *Google Spain* decision discussed at 7.65 is likely to provide fresh impetus to a subject of such publication who objects to it and so insists on his 'right to be forgotten'.

*(d) Sixth Principle—processing in accordance with rights of data subjects*

**7.70**   Personal data should be processed in accordance with the rights of data subjects under the Act.[160] The sixth Principle is contravened if, but only if, the data controller contravenes the statutory rights given to data subjects by ss 7, 10, 11, and 12 of the Act.[161] Sections 11 and 12 concern processing for direct marketing and automated decision-taking, which are unlikely to be of direct concern to the media, but ss 7 ('right of access to personal data') and 10 ('right to prevent processing likely to cause damage or distress') are both potentially significant. These rights are enforceable by application made to the High Court.[162] The power of the court to enforce each right is expressed in the words 'the court may order', indicating that the power of the court is discretionary, not mandatory. Given that the Act contains no general public interest or public domain defences, it may be that it is at the hearing of an application that effect may be given to Article 10 rights of defendants.[163]

**7.71**   **Section 7—right of access**   This section gives an individual a right to be informed by any data controller whether personal data of which that individual is the data subject are being processed by or on behalf of the data controller. If they are, the data subject is entitled to be given by the data controller a description of the personal data of which that individual is the data subject, the purposes for which they are being or are to be processed, and the recipients or classes of recipients to whom they are or may be disclosed. Further, and importantly both for the media and the general public, the individual is entitled to have communicated to him or her in an intelligible form the information constituting any personal data of which the individual is the data subject and any information available to the data controller as to the source of those data.[164] Unless it is impossible, would involve disproportionate effort, or the data subject agrees otherwise, the data controller must supply the information constituting the personal data in permanent form and provide with it any explanation that might be required to render it intelligible to the data subject.[165] The data controller is normally obliged to comply with any request within forty days of it being

---

[160] sch 1, pt I, para 6 DPA.
[161] sch 1, pt II, para 8 DPA.
[162] s 15 DPA and ss 7(9), 10(4), 13, and 14 and see ss 42–4 discussed in 7.103 *et seq.*
[163] cf *Ashdown v Telegraph Group Ltd* [2001] Ch 685, CA.
[164] s 7(1)(a)–(c) DPA.
[165] s 8(2) DPA. Orders made under s 38 DPA exempt personal data of various kinds from the right of access. See Data Protection (Subject Access Modification) (Health) Order 2000, SI 2000/413; Data Protection (Subject Access Modification) (Education) Order 2000, SI 2000/414; Data Protection (Subject Access Modification) (Social Work) Order 2000, SI 2000/415; Data Protection (Miscellaneous Subject Access Exemptions) Order 2000, SI 2000/419 as amended

made.[166] If it fails to do so it may be ordered by the High Court or County Court to do so.[167] It will not however be obliged to comply with a 'repeat' request if the request is identical or similar to a previous one and has been made before a reasonable interval has passed, with regard to be had to the purposes for which the data in question are processed and the frequency with which they are altered.[168]

Notwithstanding the use of the expression 'may order' in s 7(9) as opposed to 'must    **7.72** order' or some other prescriptive form of words, the better view is that a court should only decline to make such an order in exceptional circumstances, where the making of the request amounts to an abuse of process. It is suggested that any lower threshold for denying applicants their statutory rights to personal information held or processed about them would be wrong in principle. However, in *P v Wozencroft*[169] Wilson J declined to make an order for disclosure of documents pursuant to s 7, on the basis of evidence before him to the effect that the documents being sought had never existed. He also, in his discretion under s 14, declined rectification of information held by the data controller, on the basis that the rectification sought (an attempt to amend an opposing party's expert report in previous concluded litigation) was an abuse of the court's process. In *Durant v Financial Services Authority* the Court at first instance declined to make an order under s 7 on the basis the data controller, the FSA, had in fact complied with the request made of it.[170] However, the Court also held that had it concluded that the FSA had failed to comply with the data-access request made of it, it would still in its discretion have declined to make an order. The reasons given were, first, that the information being sought (about himself) could be of no practical value to the applicant. Secondly, the purpose of the DPA is to ensure that records of an inaccurate nature are not kept about an individual, not to fuel a separate collateral argument between the applicant and the data controller or another third party (in that case, Barclays Bank). Thirdly, the Court found that the FSA had acted at all times in good faith. As noted at 7.23, the Court of Appeal took a different approach, holding that the data requested by the applicant did not constitute 'personal data' within the meaning of s 1(1) DPA and he was therefore not entitled to have access to it under s 7.[171]

Where access to the data might disclose the identity of another individual the court    **7.73** should be entitled to ask what legitimate interest the data subject had in obtaining that information, subject to the discretion of the court to order access to a redacted

---

by Data Protection (Miscellaneous Subject Access Exemptions) (Amendment) Order 2000, SI 2000/1865. These relate, amongst other things, to human fertilization and embryology information, information contained in adoption and parental order records and reports, and statements and records of the special educational needs of children.

[166] s 7(8) and (10) DPA.
[167] ss 7(9) and 15(1) DPA.
[168] s 8(3)–(4) DPA.
[169] *P v Wozencroft* [2002] 2 FLR 1118.
[170] Edmonton County Court, 24 October 2002, HHJ Zeidman QC.
[171] *Durant* (n 19) [27]–[28].

version of the data.[172] In *Smith v Lloyds TSB Bank plc*,[173] Laddie J applied the Court of Appeal's analysis in *Durant* in finding that although the claimant was mentioned by name in loan documents created between a lending bank and a company, the documents were not personal to the claimant in a relevant sense and so did not contain his personal data.[174]

**7.74** *Disproportionate effort*   The Information Commissioner has previously expressed the view that what will amount to disproportionate effort for the purposes of the fair processing code is a question of fact to be determined in each and every case.[175] A number of factors may be relevant, including the cost of compliance to the data controller, the time it will take to comply, and the ease of compliance, all set against the perceived benefit to the data subject. These factors should be 'balanced' against the effect on the data subject, or in other words the prejudice he or she will suffer in not being informed about the processing. That said, it is suggested that what s 7 is *not* intended to do is necessarily to import a cost–benefit assessment into every application made under it. In *Elliott v Lloyds Bank TSB*,[176] HHJ Behrens sitting in the Leeds County Court considered that the data controller was only obliged to supply such personal data to the applicant as is found 'after a reasonable and proportionate search'.

**7.75** Data controllers are not obliged to supply any of the requested information unless they have received (from the data subject) a request in writing and any relevant fee.[177] They are also not obliged to comply with a request unless they are supplied with such information as they may reasonably require to satisfy themselves as to the identity of the person making the request and to locate the information sought.[178]

**7.76** *Disclosure of sources*   Where they cannot comply with the request without disclosing information relating to another individual (including the source of the information)[179] who can be identified from that information, or whom the data controller reasonably believes can be identified from that information and any other information which they reasonably believe is likely to be in or to come into the possession of the data subject making the request,[180] data controllers are not obliged to comply with a request unless the other individual has consented or it is reasonable in all the circumstances to comply with the request without the consent of the other individual.[181] 'Reasonableness' in these circumstances requires

---

[172] *Durant* (n 19) [61].

[173] *Smith* (n 38).

[174] In *Common Services Agency* (n 52) the House of Lords appeared reluctant to follow the approach of the Court of Appeal in *Durant*, instead choosing to answer the question of whether personal data was in issue by referring afresh to the DPA definitions and the language of Directive 95/46/EC.

[175] *Data Protection Act 1998: Legal guidance* (n 43) paras 3.1.7.5–3.1.7.6.

[176] *Elliott v Lloyds Bank TSB*, Leeds County Court, 24 April 2012, HHJ Behrens.

[177] The current statutory maximum fee for a straightforward request is £10.

[178] s 7(2)–(3) DPA.

[179] s 7(5) DPA.

[180] s 8(7) DPA.

[181] s 7(4)(a)–(b) DPA.

regard to be had to any duty of confidentiality owed to the other individual, any steps taken by the data controller to seek his or her consent, whether the other individual is capable of giving consent, and any express refusal of consent by the other individual.[182] A data controller is in any event not excused from disclosing as much of the information as he or she can, without disclosing the identity of the other individual concerned, whether by the omission of names or other identifying particulars or otherwise.[183]

The potential identification of sources will be particularly sensitive for the media. There is a clear tension with the Contempt of Court Act 1981, s 10, which itself reflects Article 10.[184] In many cases the media are unlikely to know what information can be supplied without disclosing the identity of a source. This will not depend upon what the media know, but how much or how little the data subject knows or can piece together. The media data controller simply will not know whether or not he or she is supplying the last piece of the jigsaw.[185] However, the ECtHR[186] held that data-subject access provisions in the DPA 1984 fell foul of Article 8, which is one of the reasons for the improved data-subject access rights in the 1998 Act. This threat to the confidentiality of sources coincides with what appears to be a general shift away from absolute protection of sources.[187] **7.77**

*Cuttings service*   On a practical level, the data subject's rights of access could in certain cases be used essentially to obtain a 'cuttings service' from the media for the nominal statutory fee. There is, for example, no objection in principle to a potential claimant in a libel or privacy action or otherwise seeking to enforce his or her statutory rights and so obtain 'pre-action disclosure' through the Act. The Civil Procedure Rules (CPR) pt 31 (Disclosure) contain no prohibition against such a practice. In *Lord Ashcroft v (1) Attorney General and (2) Dept for International* **7.78**

---

[182] s 7(6) DPA.

[183] s 7(5) DPA.

[184] As the ECtHR held in *Goodwin v UK* (1996) 22 EHRR 123, 143. See also *Financial Times Ltd v UK* App no 821/03 (ECtHR, 15 December 2009). On disclosure of sources generally see 1.87–1.90.

[185] See *Attorney General v Guardian Newspapers Ltd (No 2)* [1990] AC 109, 180.

[186] In *Gaskin v UK* (1990) 12 EHRR 36.

[187] This is a consequence both of the development of the so-called *Reynolds* defamation defence, which, if a journalist wishes to rely on it, requires him or her to be candid to a court as to the nature, status, and reliability of sources he or she has used (see eg the difficulties in this respect encountered by the journalists in *Loutchansky v Times Newspapers Ltd (No 4)* [2001] EMLR 898) and also of the procedural rule change introduced by CPR 53.3. This latter provision provides the court with a power to order a defamation defendant to provide further information about the identity of its sources of information, whereas the previous rule, RSC Ord 82 r 6, was an absolute bar to 'interrogatories' on this issue. See also *Ashworth Hospital Authority v MGN Ltd* [2001] 1 WLR 515, where the Court of Appeal upheld the judge's decision to order the newspaper to disclose the identity of the intermediary through whom confidential medical records of a convicted murderer had been passed to it from the hospital; and *Mersey Care NHS Trust v Ackroyd* [2007] EWCA Civ 101, [2008] EMLR 1.

*Development*[188] the claimant 'energetically pursued' personal-data access requests under s 7 DPA and, having thereby obtained 'disclosure' of documents, applied successfully to amend his pleaded case on the basis of them.[189]

**7.79**  In *Johnson v Medical Defence Union Ltd*,[190] the claimant applied for specific disclosure under CPR 31.12 in the context of his ongoing claims under ss 10 and 14 DPA to prevent certain processing of personal data about him; for such data to be rectified, blocked, or destroyed; and under s 13 for financial compensation. The same claimant had earlier applied unsuccessfully for an order under s 7(9) DPA that the defendant respond to a s 7 data-subject access request made by him.[191] Laddie J concluded that the application for disclosure was not disposed of by the fact that the claimant's earlier application under s 7(9) had failed: the machinery of s 7(9), in conjunction with that of s 15(2), was different and separate from the CPR disclosure regime. In particular, s 15(2) DPA contains no general prohibition on a data subject obtaining CPR disclosure in an action where he or she claims relief for breaches of the data protection Principles.

**7.80**  One way in which the Act prevents the data subject's rights of access interfering with the media and its functions is by specifically disapplying the access rights[192] where the media's activity is 'with a view to publication'.[193]

**7.81**  **Section 10—right to prevent processing likely to cause damage or distress**  An individual has a right by notice in writing at any time to require a data controller (at the end of such period as is reasonable in the circumstances) to cease, or not to begin, processing or processing for a specified purpose, or in a specified manner, any personal data in respect of which he or she is the data subject. The data subject can do this on the ground that the processing of those data or their processing for that purpose or in that manner is causing or is likely to cause substantial damage or substantial distress to the data subject or another individual and that damage or distress is or would be unwarranted.[194] It is to be noted that there is no minimum prior notice requirement: the period of time after which the data subject notice may require compliance from the data controller is simply that which is reasonable in the circumstances.

**7.82**  The right does not apply in a number of situations: where the data subject has consented to the processing or if the processing is necessary in relation to an actual or prospective contract concerning the data subject; necessary for compliance with some legal (other than contractual) obligation to which the data controller is

---

[188]  *Ashcroft* (n 62).
[189]  See also the discussion of *P v Wozencroft* and *Durant v Financial Services Authority* at 7.72.
[190]  [2004] EWHC 2509 (Ch), [2005] 1 WLR 750.
[191]  *Johnson* (n 37).
[192]  s 32(2)(b) DPA.
[193]  See further the discussion about s 32 at 7.110–7.116.
[194]  s 10 DPA.

subject; necessary to protect the vital interests of the data subject; or in such other cases as may be prescribed by the Secretary of State by order.[195]

The processing in relation to which the notice is provided may also be exempt **7.83** from the provisions of s 10 if and to the extent that s 32 applies, that is, that it is the processing of personal data only for the special purposes, with a view to the publication by any person of any journalistic, literary, or artistic material; the data controller reasonably believes that, having regard in particular to the special importance of the public interest in freedom of expression, publication would be in the public interest; and the data controller reasonably believes that, in all the circumstances, compliance with s 10 (and therefore the notice given under it) is incompatible with the special purposes.[196] As noted at 7.32, in *Mosley v Google Inc*,[197] Google is recorded as having conceded that in that case it was the data controller for the purposes of s 10, in the light of the *Google Spain* decision.

Where s 10 does apply, the data controller's obligation (once it has received a 'data-  **7.84** subject notice') is to give the individual concerned a written notice within twenty-one days either stating that it has complied with or intends to comply with the data-subject notice or giving its reasons for regarding any aspect of the notice as unjustified and the extent (if any) to which it has complied or intends to comply with it.[198]

If, regardless of the timing of the data controller's written notice in response, the **7.85** court finds the data subject's notice to be justified (in whole or in part) and the data controller has failed to comply with it then the court may order the data controller to take such steps to comply with the notice as the court thinks fit.[199] That could include an order that the data controller ceases to process, or does not begin to process, the data subject's personal data, if the court finds that the requirement of the data subject's notice to that effect is justified.

In the case of a media-organization data controller, however, an application for an **7.86** immediate order under s 10(4) will be frustrated by the operation of s 32(4), where the data controller claims, or it appears to the court, that the personal data in question are being processed only for the special purposes and with a view to the publication by any person of any journalistic, literary, or artistic material which, at the time 24 hours immediately beforehand, had not been published by the data controller. In that event, the court is required to stay any proceedings brought under s 10(4) until such time as either the Information Commissioner determines that

---

[195] s 10(2) DPA, including reference to sch 2, paras 1–4. No orders have been made under this section.
[196] s 32(1) and (2)(c) DPA.
[197] (n 75) [23].
[198] s 10(3) DPA.
[199] s 10(4) DPA.

the special purposes are not engaged[200] or the claim is withdrawn.[201] In *Murray v Express Newspapers plc*[202] the judge at first instance accepted that any application that could have been made by the claimant in that case to prevent the processing of his personal data would have been subject to s 32(4). Therefore, the Court did not accept the claimant's argument that the defendant's failure to notify him of its processing of his personal data by the taking of a photograph deprived him of the ability to prevent such processing.

**7.87** Determining what damage or distress will be necessary to engage s 10 requires the application of the principle of proportionality and the weighing of Article 10 against the data subject's Article 8 rights.

### (e) Seventh Principle—security

**7.88** Appropriate technical and organizational measures are to be taken against unauthorized or unlawful processing of personal data and against accidental loss or destruction of, or damage to, personal data.[203] Having regard to technology and cost, such measures must ensure a level of security appropriate to the harm that might result from unauthorized or unlawful processing or accidental loss, destruction, or damage and the nature of the data to be protected. A data controller must take reasonable steps to ensure the reliability of its employees who have access to personal data, and where a data processor is to carry out processing of personal data on behalf of a data controller the data controller must choose a data processor who gives sufficient security guarantees and take reasonable steps to ensure that the data processor complies with its own security measures. Specifically in this case, the data controller is not to be regarded as complying with the seventh Principle unless he or she has contracted in writing with the data processor that the data processor will act only on his or her instructions and comply with the seventh Principle security measures in its own right.[204] Again, media organizations may wish to review their database contribution arrangements in the light of these requirements.[205]

### (f) Eighth Principle—transfer outside the European Economic Area

**7.89** Personal data are not to be transferred outside the European Economic Area unless the country or territory of destination ensures an adequate level of protection for the rights and freedoms of data subjects in relation to the processing of personal data.[206] An adequate level of protection is one which is adequate in all

---

[200] With reference to s 45 DPA.
[201] s 32(5) DPA.
[202] *Murray* (n 101) [82]–[87].
[203] sch 1, pt I, para 7 DPA.
[204] sch 1, pt II, paras 9–12 DPA.
[205] See 7.64.
[206] sch 1, pt I, para 8 DPA.

the circumstances of the case, having particular regard to the nature of the personal data; the geographical origin of the information in the data and that of its final destination; the purposes for which, and period during which, the data are intended to be processed; the law in force in the country or territory in question; its international obligations and any relevant codes of conduct or other rules; and any security measures taken in respect of the data in the country or territory of destination.[207] The eighth Principle will not apply to any transfer to which the data subject has consented; which is necessary in light of actual or prospective contractual relations concerning the data subject and data controller; which is necessary for reasons of substantial public interest;[208] which is necessary for legal proceedings, legal advice or otherwise for the purposes of establishing, exercising, or defending legal rights;[209] which is necessary to protect the vital interests of the data subject; and which is of personal data on a public register and any conditions subject to which the register is open to inspection are complied with; or is made on terms approved by or that have been authorized by the Information Commissioner in order to ensure adequate safeguards for the rights and freedoms of data subjects.[210]

While the disclosure of data may be evidence of a breach of the obligations as to **7.90** security or transfer, the conclusion that the seventh or eighth Principle has been breached if disclosure has occurred is not automatic. In the context of transfer of data between Member States, the European Court of Justice found in *Lindqvist*[211] that the uploading of personal data by an individual from her computer to an internet host (not in the same country), thus making that data available on the internet generally, was not in itself a transfer of data to a third country within the meaning of Article 25 of the Directive. Further, a court may not permit a free-standing claim based on alleged breach of the seventh or eighth Principles when the crux of a claimant's complaint concerns disclosures that offend the Act's other substantive provisions.[212]

### (4) Further Rights of Data Subjects— Remedies, Orders, and Sanctions

In addition to the rights of access and prevention referred to above in the context **7.91** of the sixth Principle,[213] s 13 DPA introduces a data subject's right to financial compensation for non-compliance with certain requirements by a data controller;

---

[207] sch 1, pt II, para 13 DPA.
[208] sch 4, paras 1–4 DPA. Under para 4(2) the Secretary of State may specify by order circumstances in which this provision does or does not apply. No such orders have been made.
[209] As to which see further 7.125.
[210] sch 4, paras 5–9 DPA.
[211] *Lindqvist* (n 21).
[212] *Ashcroft* (n 62) [27] and [35].
[213] See 7.70–7.87.

s 14 provides for court-ordered rectification, blocking, erasure, or destruction of data in particular circumstances; and ss 42–4 give an individual the right to make a request to the Commissioner to assess whether any provision of the Act has been contravened. Sections 43 and 44 also go further, and entitle the Commissioner to seek further information from the data controller on the Commissioner's own initiative, even if an individual has not made a request for assessment. These further rights, and the sanctions to which they give rise, are now considered in turn.

*(a) Section 13—compensation*

**7.92**  **Section 13**  An individual who suffers damage by reason of any contravention by a data controller of any requirements of the Act is entitled to compensation from the data controller for that damage.[214] According to the scheme of s 13(2) DPA, if the contravention causes distress to be suffered by an individual and the individual also suffers damage by reason of the contravention, or the contravention relates to the processing of personal data for the special purposes,[215] then the individual concerned is entitled to compensation from the data controller for that distress.[216] That was the approach of the trial judge in *Campbell*. In *Johnson v MDU*, Buxton LJ also said that s 13(2)(a) required a claimant to prove pecuniary loss before compensation for distress could be recovered.[217] Patten J also construed the provision in this way when striking out the claim for s 13 compensation in *Murray v Express Newspapers Ltd*[218] although the question was re-opened when the Court of Appeal reinstated the claim generally on appeal.[219] However in *Vidal-Hall v Google Inc*, the Court of Appeal found that s 13(2) had to be disapplied to make s 13 compatible with Article 23 of the Directive (and therefore EU law).[220] This means that compensation is recoverable under s 13(1) for *any* damage suffered as a result of a contravention by a data controller of any of the requirements of the Act. The data controller will though have a defence to such financial claims if it can establish that

---

[214]  s 13(1) DPA. See *Ogle v Chief Constable of Thames Valley Police* [2001] EWCA 598 [14] and [29], where the Court of Appeal, in considering the predecessor to this section under the 1984 Act, distinguished between damage caused by reason of an incorrect entry on a register and other damage. In that case, the Court held that the damage and distress suffered arose from the wrongful arrest of the claimant and not from his discovery of the alleged incompetence in failing to amend his entry on the Police National Computer to reflect the reduction of an earlier driving disqualification after a successful appeal, despite this incorrect entry being the reason for his arrest. See also *Campbell* (n 61) [124] on the need to exclude duplication of damage (in that case caused both by breach of duty of confidence and under the DPA) when assessing compensation.

[215]  *ie* the purposes of journalism, artistic purposes, and literary purposes: see 7.40.

[216]  s 13(2) DPA. In *Campbell* (n 61) [128] the judge considered that 'damage' in s 13(1) and (2)(a) means special or financial damages in contradistinction to distress in the shape of injury to feelings. *Rotaru v Romania* (2000) 8 BHRC 449 supports the view that damages for injury to reputation are recoverable.

[217]  [2007] EWCA Civ 262, (2007) 96 BMLR 99 [77].

[218]  [2007] EWHC 1980 (Ch) [89]–[92].

[219]  [2008] EWCA Civ 446, [2009] Ch 481 [62]–[63].

[220]  (n 58) [105].

it has taken such care as in all the circumstances was reasonably required to comply with the requirement of the Act concerned.[221]

In *Douglas v Hello! Ltd*, Lindsay J found that, although the Douglases had estab- **7.93** lished claims to compensation under s 13 because there had been a breach of the DPA, the DPA claim did not add a separate route to recovery for damage or distress beyond a nominal award. That is because the judge could not see how it could reasonably be said with reference to the wording of s 13 that the damage and distress occasioned to the Douglases was 'by reason of any contravention...of [the] Act'.[222] He said that even if the defendants had asked the claimants for their consent, as required by the Act, and it had been refused, they would still have elected to publish the photographs and the Court of Appeal would still have held that damages would be a sufficient remedy.[223] A comparable approach was taken by the judge at first instance in *Murray v Express Newspapers plc*.[224]

In *Lord Ashcroft v (1) Attorney General and (2) Dept for International Development*[225] **7.94** Gray J interpreted the DPA as containing a free-standing duty on data controllers to comply with the data protection Principles, breach of which sounds in damages under s 13, as does breach of any of the other requirements of the Act. The 1998 Act can be contrasted with the DPA 1984, which (under s 23) only conferred a private law right to damages in respect of the disclosure of documents and not for breach of the Act's principles.[226] Any other breach of the 1984 Act or its principles was found to be a matter for the Information Commissioner, rather than for a damages claim through the courts.[227] The action concerned the leak of personal information about Lord Ashcroft from government files. This can be compared with *Craxi (No 2) v Italy*,[228] in which it was held that a leak of personal information from court files was a breach of Article 8 by the state, as was the subsequent failure to hold an effective investigation.

In *Murray v Express Newspapers plc*[229] the judge at first instance observed that a **7.95** claimant must prove any damage or distress which he or she claims under s 13.

---

[221] s 13(3) DPA. In *Campbell* (n 61) [121] the judge at first instance considered the newspaper which had published photographs of the claimant's attendance at Narcotics Anonymous to have 'utterly failed' to establish a defence under s 13. In that case the editor gave evidence of his opinion that the claimant had lost all right to privacy. The Court of Appeal found the appellant newspaper to be protected by the s 32 exemption in any event. It follows that the data controller cannot, in the language of s 13 of the Act, have been in 'contravention...of any of the requirements of the Act' because the requirements do not *ex hypothesi* apply to the data controller in question, by virtue of the s 32 exemption.
[222] [2003] EWHC 786 (Ch) [239].
[223] *Douglas* (n 40) [239]. So too in *Ellis* (n 63) the Court held that a claim under the DPA added nothing to the claim under Art 8.
[224] *Murray* (n 101) [82]–[88].
[225] *Ashcroft* (n 62) [29].
[226] *Ashcroft* (n 62) [26].
[227] *Ashcroft* (n 62) [26].
[228] (2004) 38 EHRR 995, paras 72–6.
[229] *Murray* (n 101) [88]–[92].

He noted that damage under s 13(1) means ordinary pecuniary loss,[230] and rejected the claimant's contention that damages could be awarded under the Act by reference to the market value of the data which had been misused. He also rejected the claimant's contention that s 13 gives rise to a right to claim damages in connection with a complaint that at the time of the processing the data controller was not registered as such with the Information Commissioner in compliance with s 17 DPA.[231]

**7.96** **An alternative to defamation or malicious falsehood?** Section 13 grants remedies for a statutory tort.[232] The basic conditions for liability under s 13 are (1) that there has been a contravention of a requirement of the Act, and (2) the absence of a defence on the part of the data controller that it has taken reasonable care to comply with the Act. It is therefore not a tort of strict liability. On the other hand, it is easy to see that if a media organization has published or continues to publish something about a data subject that is false or, for example after *Google Spain*,[233] out of date, it may well have an uphill struggle to establish that this was not as a result of some shortcoming in its attempted compliance with the Act. Innocent mistakes are likely to be forgiven, but a failure of systems or practices is likely in many cases to result in liability.[234]

**7.97** It will be noted that this statutory tort comes without a number of the hurdles faced by a claimant in the 'informational' common law torts of defamation and malicious falsehood. For the claimant, a claim under s 13 has the advantage over a defamation that no defamatory meaning need be established in what has been broadcast or published. There just needs to be a contravention of the Act's requirements. Nor does the Act provide a defence equivalent to that of qualified privilege. And in contrast to a claim in malicious falsehood, the claimant is not required to plead or establish malice.

**7.98** Further, so far as damages are concerned, the somewhat technical rules in slander, libel, and malicious falsehood concerning aspects of general damage and the limited possibilities for recovering special damages are avoided. Under s 13, compensation for actual losses will always be recoverable, and the decision in *Vidal-Hall*

---

[230] Citing *Johnson* (n 217) [74] per Buxton LJ.

[231] But note that the judge's striking out of the claim in *Murray* was set aside on appeal: [2008] EWCA Civ 446, [2009] Ch 481 and see [62]–[63] in particular.

[232] See J Hartshorne, 'An Appropriate Remedy for the Publication of False Private Information' (2012) 4(1) J Media L 93–115, at 111–13 in particular.

[233] *Google Spain* (n 74).

[234] A comparison might be made with the test of 'responsible journalism' propounded in *Reynolds v Times Newspapers Ltd* [2001] 2 AC 127 and followed in subsequent decisions on the availability to the media of the defence of qualified privilege in defamation; see now the defence of publication on matter of public interest introduced by s 4 of the Defamation Act 2013, which formally abolished *Reynolds* but was said by the Bill's sponsors to be intended to enact the law as it had developed after *Reynolds*, culminating in *Flood v Times Newspapers Ltd* [2012] UKSC 11, [2012] 2 AC 273. See further the discussion at 11.173–11.189 (esp 11.182 and 11.188).

*v Google Inc*[235] has now disapplied the s 13(2) 'gateway' so that compensation for distress is recoverable (provided it is due) without the need to show that a complaint concerns the special purposes (or that pecuniary harm has also been caused). There is no guidance as to the quantum available for a claimant, or as to how it will relate to the corresponding levels of damages in defamation and malicious falsehood. But, the arbiter of quantum will be a judge, rather than the jury that has, to date, often determined defamation damages.[236]

All the above said, in *Quinton v Peirce*,[237] Eady J expressed some scepticism about **7.99** whether the DPA had established a fresh tort or set of remedies. He said that he was by no means persuaded that it was necessary or proportionate for him to interpret the scope of the Act to afford a set of parallel remedies when damaging information which is neither defamatory nor malicious has been published. He added that he was still less persuaded of the need to interpret the Act so as to give the court a power to order someone to publish a correction or apology when the person concerned does not believe he has published anything untrue.

*(b) Section 14—rectification, blocking, erasure, destruction*

Where a data subject satisfies the court that personal data of which he or she is sub- **7.100** ject are inaccurate the court may order the data controller to rectify, block, erase, or destroy those data and any other personal data in respect of which he or she is the data controller and which contain an expression of opinion which appears to the court

---

[235] (n 58).

[236] In *Campbell* (n 61) the total sum awarded at first instance for damages for breach of confidence and for compensation under the DPA was £3,500, which included £1,000 aggravated damages. The Court of Appeal however reversed Morland J's finding for the claimant on liability, therefore making the quantum of the award at first instance of historic interest only. However, the Court of Appeal did confirm, at [139], that it would have been open to the judge to consider an award of aggravated damages had his finding in her favour otherwise been valid. The award in *Douglas* (n 40) in relation to an established breach of the DPA was for nominal damages only in a case where there was a parallel claim for damage and distress suffered by reason of a breach of confidence. So far as the element of distress is concerned, the Court of Appeal decision in *Halliday v Creation Consumer Finance Ltd* [2013] EWCA Civ 333 to award £750 compensation for distress in the case of inaccurate credit data indicates that such awards may be only modest. That said, in *Grinyer v Plymouth Hospitals NHS Trust* (Plymouth County Court, 14 September 2011, HHJ Cotter QC) an award for £12,500 was made arising from the 'significant exacerbation' of an existing medical condition by the unauthorized disclosure of personal medical information. In *Weller v Associated Newspapers Ltd* [2014] EWHC 1163 (QB) it was common ground that the data protection claim stood or fell with that for the misuse of private information. An award of £10,000 compensation was made on the findings of the misuse of private information with no separate sum being awarded under the DPA. In *AB v Ministry of Justice* [2014] EWHC 1847 (QB) the claimant was awarded nominal damages of £1 in respect of delay by the defendant in complying with a series of data subject access requests by the claimant under s 7 DPA, to which the Court then added an award of compensation for distress of £2,250. In *CR19 v Chief Constable of the Police Service of Northern Ireland* [2014] NICA 54 the Court of Appeal in Northern Ireland recorded nominal damages of £1 to reflect an admitted breach of s 4 DPA, where in relation to a burglary by which the claimant's personal data had fallen into the hands of terrorists the trial judge had already awarded £20,000 in negligence for 'moderate psychiatric damage'.

[237] *Quinton* (n 51) [87]–[88]; see also 7.68 and ch 8 generally on the relationship between privacy and defamation.

to be based on the inaccurate data.[238] Where the data concerned accurately record information received from the data subject or a third party and the data controller has taken reasonable steps to ensure the accuracy of the data[239] the court may, instead of ordering rectification, blocking, erasure, or destruction, make an order requiring the data to be supplemented by such statement of the true facts as it may approve.[240] Where the data controller has not complied with the fourth Principle, the court may make such order as it thinks fit for securing compliance with that Principle, short of rectification, blocking, erasure, or destruction, and with or without a court-approved data supplement.[241] Where data is shown to have been inaccurate and has been, or has been ordered to be, rectified, blocked, erased, or destroyed the court may order the data controller to notify third parties accordingly. It will do so only where it considers such notification to be reasonably practicable having particular regard to the number of persons who would have to be notified.[242]

**7.101**   There is scope in principle here for something amounting to a court-ordered apology or correction, which until recently has been alien to English law and even now is treated with caution and only applied in limited prescribed circumstances.[243] However, the *obiter* comments in *Quinton v Peirce*,[244] noted at 7.99, would apparently challenge this conclusion, at least in a media case (as opposed perhaps to one brought over a private communication).

**7.102**   Additionally, where a data subject persuades a court that he or she has suffered damage by reason of any contravention of any of the requirements of the Act in respect of personal data in circumstances entitling him or her to compensation under s 13,[245] and that there is a substantial risk of further contravention in respect of those data in such circumstances, the court may order rectification, blocking, erasure, or destruction of any of those data. Again, subject to it being reasonably practicable having particular regard to the number of persons to be notified, the court may order the data controller to notify third parties to whom the data have been disclosed of the rectification, blocking, erasure, or destruction.[246]

---

[238]   s 14(1) DPA.
[239]   And has otherwise complied with his or her obligations under the fourth data protection Principle: see 7.67–7.68.
[240]   s 14(2)(a) DPA.
[241]   s 14(2)(b) DPA.
[242]   s 14(3) and (6) DPA.
[243]   Namely summary relief granted under the Defamation Act 1996, s 9 on an application for summary disposal of a defamation claim in the claimant's favour under s 8(1) of that Act; and the provisions for a summary of a court judgment to be published pursuant to s 12 of the Defamation Act 2013. The IPSO Editors' Code, cl 1 ('Accuracy'), requires a newspaper or magazine to correct promptly and with due prominence any 'significant inaccuracy, misleading statement or distortion' it has published, and to publish an apology 'where appropriate'.
[244]   *Quinton* (n 51).
[245]   See 7.92–7.99.
[246]   s 14(5)–(6) DPA.

*(c) Sections 42–4—request for assessment, information notices,
and special information notices*

**Request for assessment**[247]   In addition to their directly enforceable rights as **7.103**
against the data controller, those who are or believe themselves to be directly
affected by any processing of personal data may ask the Commissioner for an
assessment of whether it is likely or unlikely that the processing has been carried
out in compliance with the provisions of the Act.[248] It is notable that the person
concerned need not be the data subject who is the principal subject of processing,
but simply someone who as a minimum has a belief that some processing directly
affects him or her. This casts the net wide, and has the potential to generate requests
from individuals who may only have an incidental connection with processing that
a media organization is carrying out.[249]

The Commissioner is to make an assessment as he or she considers appropriate, **7.104**
and may have regard to the extent to which the request appears to raise a matter
of substance, the timing of the request, and whether or not the person making the
request is entitled under s 7 DPA to make an application in respect of the personal
data, that is whether or not he or she is a 'data subject'.[250]

**Information notice**   The Commissioner will notify the person making the **7.105**
request of any assessment that has been made as a result of it and of any view
formed or action taken as a result.[251] If the Commissioner requires information
from the data controller arising from the request (or, indeed, reasonably requires
any information from a data controller in order to determine whether the data
controller has complied or is complying with the data protection Principles) then
the Commissioner may serve an 'information notice' on the data controller.[252]
Subject to considerations of legal professional privilege and the possibility of self-
incrimination of an offence under the Act, the data controller must respond to the
Commissioner's notice within the timetable set by it, and in the case of an urgent
notice, within seven days.[253]

**Special information notice**   A similar mechanism is put in place by s 44, in rela- **7.106**
tion to processing for the special purposes.[254] Here, the Commissioner may serve a
'special information notice' arising either from a request for an assessment or of his
or her own volition—in the latter case if the Commissioner has reasonable grounds

---

[247] This should be distinguished from the procedures as to 'assessable processing', as to which
see 7.37–7.39.
[248] s 42(1) DPA.
[249] See the comments concerning the Information Commissioner's enforcement role under pt V
DPA in *Law Society v Kordowski* [2011] EWHC 3185 (QB), [2014] EMLR 2 [93]–[101].
[250] s 42(2)–(3) DPA.
[251] s 42(4) DPA.
[252] s 43(1) DPA.
[253] s 43(5) DPA.
[254] Journalism, art, literature: s 3 DPA.

for suspecting, in a case in which proceedings have been stayed under s 32,[255] that the personal data to which the proceedings relate are not in fact being processed for the special purposes or are not being processed with a view to the publication by any person of any journalistic, literary, or artistic material which has not previously been published by the data controller.[256] The Commissioner's special information notice will set a timetable for response. If the Commissioner is of the view that it requires an urgent response, and gives valid reasons for this view in the body of the notice, then a deadline of seven days for the information to be furnished can be set.[257] Protection for the data controller in relation to legal professional privilege and self-incrimination under the Act is again provided for.[258]

**7.107** **Determination as to the special purposes** Where at any time, whether as the result of the service of a special information notice or otherwise, it appears to the Commissioner that any personal data are not being processed for the special purposes or are not being processed with a view to first publication, the Commissioner may make a written determination to the data controller to this effect. However, the determination will not take effect until the end of the period within which an appeal can be brought or, if an appeal is brought, until it has been withdrawn or determined.[259]

**7.108** **Appeal** The rules for appeals[260] allow twenty-eight days for an appeal by a data controller against service of an enforcement notice, an information notice, or a special information notice to be notified to the tribunal.[261] There will then be a further twenty-one days, subject to extension, for the Commissioner to indicate his or her response to the appeal, before which the tribunal will proceed through various stages to give directions, summon witnesses, conduct a hearing or hearings and ultimately determine the appeal.[262] It is clear that even if the process begins with an urgent notice from the Commissioner, it is likely ultimately to become drawn out, and perhaps last months rather than weeks. There is a further right of appeal from the tribunal's determination to the High Court on a point of law.[263] A data controller who fails to comply with an enforcement notice, an information notice, or a special information notice is guilty of an offence under the Act and liable on summary conviction to a fine not exceeding the statutory maximum or on conviction on indictment to an unlimited fine. It will be a defence for the person charged to prove that he or she exercised all due diligence to comply with the notice in question.[264]

---

[255] See 7.116.
[256] s 44(1) DPA.
[257] s 44(6) DPA.
[258] s 44(7)–(9) DPA.
[259] s 45 DPA.
[260] Contained in the Data Protection Tribunal (Enforcement Appeals) Rules 2000, SI 2000/189.
[261] SI 2000/189, r 4.
[262] SI 2000/189.
[263] s 49(6)(a) DPA.
[264] ss 47 and 60(2) DPA.

## (5) Media Exemption

Satisfaction of the conditions for processing as appropriate, set out in 7.41–7.90, **7.109**
will protect a media organization from a complaint that it has breached the data
protection Principles or infringed the rights of a data subject. Of principal note for
the media in this context are the 'defences' of consent, legitimate interests, explicit
consent, and deliberately making information public discussed at 7.56–7.61.[265]
In addition, the Act provides a specific media exemption in the form of s 32, and
the Data Protection (Processing of Sensitive Personal Data) Order 2000[266] and
s 35(2) DPA provide further possible exemptions for the media. Each of these is
now considered in turn.

### (a) Section 32

As noted at 7.40, s 32 exempts personal data which are processed only for the **7.110**
'special purposes'[267] from any provision to which s 32(1) relates, which is likely to
impact upon a media organization's operations if: the processing is undertaken
with a view to the publication by any person of any journalistic, literary or artistic
material; the data controller reasonably believes that, having regard in particular to
the special importance of the public interest in freedom of expression, publication
would be in the public interest; and the data controller reasonably believes that,
in all the circumstances, compliance with *that provision* is incompatible with the
special purposes.[268]

The government's intention when the Bill was before Parliament was that the **7.111**
media should normally do the entirety of their job in conformity with the data
protection Principles and data subjects' rights. The s 32 exemption was introduced
to take account of the special difficulties that had arisen in the recent past, when
certain public figures had used their financial ability to stifle legitimate media
inquiries into their malpractices. Accordingly, government statements at the time
can be read as indicating that the exemption was only intended to apply before
publication,[269] effectively as a measure against prior restraint.

However, the Court of Appeal in *Campbell v MGN Ltd*[270] held that s 32(1)–(3) **7.112**
DPA apply to provide an exemption for the media both before and after

---

[265] See also 10.30–10.32.
[266] SI 2000/417. See Appendix F (available at <http://www.5rb.com/publication/the-law-of-privacy-and-the-media>).
[267] Defined by s 3 DPA.
[268] s 32(1)–(2) DPA.
[269] Lord Williams of Mostyn: *Hansard*, HL (5th Series), vol 586, col CWH95 (25 February 1998). Lord Williams also said, 'The key provision is Clause 31 [now s 32]. This ensures that provided that certain criteria are met, before publication—I stress "before"—there can be no challenge on data protection grounds to the processing of personal data for the special purposes', *Hansard*, HL (5th Series), vol 585, col 442 (2 February 1998). See also cols 462–3 (Lord Wakeham) and 477 (Lord Falconer).
[270] *Campbell* (n 14) [120], [121], and [128]–[131].

publication. The exemption applies in relation to data. Information which is published remains data as defined by the Act. On the facts, the Court of Appeal found that the s 32 exemption had been made out by the newspaper:

(1) It was conceded[271] that the processing in question had been undertaken with a view to the publication by the newspaper and its editor of journalistic material, which satisfied s 32(1)(a).

(2) The Court of Appeal held[272] that the publication was 'a journalistic package that it was reasonable to publish in the public interest'—the editor had given evidence of his belief to such effect to the trial judge, which the judge had accepted as truthful—and so s 32(1)(b) was satisfied. The reasons identified for the public interest were (i) it appeared that the claimant had been committing offences of possessing class A drugs, (ii) as a role model to young people, she had held herself out as someone who remained immune from drugs in an industry where drug abuse was notoriously common, and (iii) she had frequently made references to her private life in many interviews with the media. It had been conceded[273] that by mendaciously asserting to the media that she did not take drugs, she had rendered it legitimate for the media to put the record straight by publishing the bald fact that she was receiving treatment.

(3) Similarly, the Court of Appeal accepted[274] that the editor reasonably believed that in all the circumstances compliance with the Act was incompatible with the special purposes, which satisfied s 32(1)(c). On the facts, the newspaper had attempted to obtain the claimant's consent to its proposed publication (ie consent to processing) but the claimant had refused.[275] Thus, while the public interest justified publication by the newspaper, it knew it was unable to comply with the Act without the claimant's consent to publication. In these circumstances, its belief that compliance with the Act was incompatible with its journalistic pursuit was correct as well as reasonable.[276]

The House of Lords[277] did not give any separate or further consideration to Ms Campbell's data protection claim.

**7.113** **Reasonable belief that publication would be in the public interest** In considering whether the belief of a data controller that publication would be in the public interest was or is a reasonable one, regard may be had to his or her compliance with any code of practice which is relevant to the publication in

---

[271] *Campbell* (n 14) [133].
[272] *Campbell* (n 14) [132]–[133] and [137].
[273] *Campbell* (n 14) [36] and [38].
[274] *Campbell* (n 14) [137].
[275] *Campbell* (n 14) [133].
[276] *Campbell* (n 14) [137].
[277] *Campbell* (n 17).

question and is designated by the Secretary of State.[278] The IPSO Editors' Code and the Ofcom Broadcasting Code are designated, as are the BBC's Producers' Guidelines.[279]

While the language of the legislation appears advisory ('regard *may* be had...') as   **7.114** opposed to compulsory, in reality it is the codes (as designated) that a court will consider when looking at the reasonableness of a media organization's belief that it is acting in the public interest.[280]

**Reasonable belief that compliance with the provision relied on is incompat-**   **7.115**
**ible with the special purposes**   Even if, as was the position in *Campbell* just discussed, the court accepts the reasonableness of an editor's belief that publication would be in the public interest, it is possible to conceive of circumstances in which the editor could not satisfy the court of the further requirement that he or she have a reasonable belief that, in all the circumstances, compliance with the relevant particular provision of the Act was incompatible with the special purposes. As just noted, this situation did not arise in *Campbell*, since the claimant had been asked but refused to consent to the proposed publication. However, if the subject of a media publication were not notified of it in advance, and so became the subject of data processing deemed unfair by the first data protection Principle and the fair processing code,[281] the media data controller could have difficulty persuading a court that giving prior notice of publication to the subject was incompatible with the special purposes. Indeed, fair warning of intended publication and an opportunity to comment in advance are ordinarily regarded as consistent with proper and responsible journalism, and therefore the special purposes, in order, if nothing else, to allow the subject to give his or her side of the story. So, it may be that someone in the position of the claimant in *Mosley v News Group Newspapers Ltd*,[282] who was given no prior notice of publication and thus had no opportunity to seek to prevent it, could claim compensation under the Act for the distress caused to him by the unfairness deemed to have arisen.

---

[278] s 32(3) DPA.
[279] Where the media would seek to justify a publication on the basis that naming a wrongdoer will shame him or her into desisting from his or her wrongful conduct, similar concerns are likely to arise as those considered in *Ellis* (n 63): that publicity may make rehabilitation more difficult, and that family members may suffer adverse consequences.
[280] For the importance of the media codes, see *Douglas* (n 41) [94] where Brooke LJ stated that '[a] newspaper which flouts Section 3 of the [PCC] Code [*ie* the privacy provisions] is likely in those circumstances to have its claim to an entitlement to freedom of expression trumped by Art 10(2) considerations of privacy'. In *Douglas* (n 40), Lindsay J found at [231] that the s 32 exemption did not apply since there was no credible evidence that the *Hello!* defendants believed publication of the disputed photographs would be in the public interest and there was no room anyway for any conclusion that publication could reasonably be regarded as in the public interest.
[281] See 7.42–7.55.
[282] [2008] EWHC 1777 (QB), [2008] EMLR 20.

*(b) Section 32(4)–(5)—stay*

**7.116**   Where—at any time in any proceedings against a data controller in respect of a data subject's right of access, prevention, compensation and/or rectification, blocking, erasure, and destruction—the data controller claims, or it appears to the court, that any personal data to which the proceedings relate are being processed only for the special purposes and with a view to the publication by any person of any journalistic, literary, or artistic material which, at the time twenty-four hours immediately before the time of consideration, had not been published by the data controller, the court shall stay the proceedings until one of two conditions is met. These conditions are, either that (i) the Information Commissioner determines that the personal data are not being processed only for the special purposes or with a view to publication of new information, or (ii) the claim is withdrawn.[283] In *Campbell v MGN Ltd*[284] the Court of Appeal stated that s 32(4)–(5) DPA are purely procedural. Further, the stay is to subsist unless and until either the data controller's claim to a stay is withdrawn or the Information Commissioner determines the claim is not valid. It is to be inferred that if publication takes place before the Commissioner has ruled on the claim to a stay then the stay ceases to be effective. The practical effect of these provisions is that the DPA cannot be invoked to obtain an injunction to prevent the publication of 'news' in the form of material not previously published.

*(c) The Data Protection (Processing of Sensitive Personal Data) Order 2000*

**7.117**   **Does it protect the media?**   Article 2, para 3, of the schedule to the Data Protection (Processing of Sensitive Personal Data) Order 2000[285] sets out the circumstances in which it is permissible to disclose sensitive personal data for the special purposes. The circumstances required are that the disclosure of the data (a) is in the substantial public interest, (b) is in connection with one of a number of defined forms of wrongdoings, (c) 'is for the special purposes as defined in s 3 of the Act', and (d) 'is made with a view to the publication of those data by any person and the data controller reasonably believes that such publication would be in the public interest'.[286] These conditions are cumulative.[287]

**7.118**   It is not entirely clear whether this provision will protect the media if it publishes sensitive personal data in the circumstances given, or whether in fact the provision only exempts a media source from the data protection Principles in the event that he or she passes information of 'iniquity' to the media with a view to its exposure.

---

[283]  s 32(4)–(5) DPA. As to the assessment procedure see 7.103–7.108.
[284]  *Campbell* (n 14) [116].
[285]  SI 2000/417. See Appendix F (available at <http://www.5rb.com/publication/the-law-of-privacy-and-the-media>).
[286]  SI 2000/417, sch, art 2, para 3(1). See 7.113–7.114.
[287]  *Campbell* (n 61) [121].

However, there would be little purpose for the exemption if it protected only the source and not the journalist.

**Processing, or only disclosure?**    Paragraph 2 of the short statutory instrument   **7.119**
itself refers to its schedule as setting out circumstances in which sensitive personal data may be processed. If the designated circumstances exist, then such processing can proceed regardless of whether any of the conditions otherwise required for the processing of sensitive personal data[288] apply. However, para 3 of the schedule, which is the only paragraph to mention the 'special purposes',[289] begins with an explicit reference to the disclosure of personal data, as opposed to any wider reference to processing. So while the body of the statutory instrument is concerned to refer to designated circumstances in which processing of sensitive personal data may occur, the detail concerning those circumstances in the context of the special purposes immediately restricts that processing to disclosure.

**The substantial public interest**    The words 'substantial public interest' echo   **7.120**
Article 8(4) of the Directive. In the DPA itself freedom of expression is referred to as a public interest by virtue of the phrase 'the special importance of the public interest in freedom of expression' in s 32(1)(b). In *Campbell v MGN Ltd* disclosure of the claimant's therapy at Narcotics Anonymous was found at first instance not to be in the substantial public interest.[290]

**The defined forms of wrongdoing**    The 'defined forms of wrongdoing' are[291] the   **7.121**
commission by any person of any unlawful act (or failure to act) (whether alleged or established), or dishonesty, malpractice, or other seriously improper conduct by, or the unfitness or incompetence of, any person (whether alleged or established), or mismanagement in the administration of, or failures in services provided by, any body or association (whether alleged or established).

**'Disclosure…is for the special purposes'**    The language in the phrase   **7.122**
'Disclosure…is for the special purposes'[292] may suggest that the type of exempted processing under consideration is not merely 'private' disclosure between two parties, but in fact public disclosure in the sense of 'publication'. This is because the special purposes are journalism, art, and literature and if disclosure is in any meaningful sense to be 'for' those purposes, it must require publication. On the other hand, it is arguable that much more than publication goes into the pursuit of the special purposes, and the disclosure of information to, say, a media organization can be 'for' its journalistic purposes, even if that information itself, or at least some of it, does not survive in a final published piece of journalism.

---

[288] See 7.51.
[289] Journalism, art, literature: s 3 DPA.
[290] *Campbell* (n 61) [117].
[291] See SI 2000/417, sch, art 2, paras 3(1)(b) and (2).
[292] SI 2000/417, sch, art 2, para 3(1)(c).

**7.123** **Legislative background**   Whatever the scope of para 3 of the Data Protection (Processing of Sensitive Personal Data) Order 2000 is established to be, it does appear to represent a substantial change of position on the part of the government between the debate that took place in the context of the clause in the Bill that became s 32 of the Act, and the raft of statutory instruments that were issued on the date of the Act's enactment. On 2 February 1998, Lord Williams said:

> We have provided for exemptions for the media. We have done that as deliberate policy, not by way of Christmas accident, where they are necessary to reconcile privacy with freedom of expression. Following the meetings to which I referred, we have included in the Bill an exemption which I believe meets the legitimate expectations and requirements of those engaged in journalism, artistic and literary activity.[293]

**7.124** It may be doubtful whether the statutory instrument offers anything for the media in practical terms of exemption or defence beyond what is provided by the s 32 exemption. If, with reference to s 32, a media organization data controller establishes the reasonableness of its beliefs that a publication is in the public interest and that compliance with a relevant provision of the Act is incompatible with the special purposes then, without more, it will benefit from the s 32 exemption. If, on the other hand, the s 32 exemption is not available to it because those grounds are not satisfied, then it seems unlikely that the media organization would be able to engage para 2 of the statutory instrument, which requires to be established, amongst other things, that the disclosure of personal data *is* (objectively) in the substantial public interest.

*(d)  Data Protection Act 1998, s 35(2)*

**7.125** This provides (in the context of disclosures required by law or made in connection with legal proceedings) that personal data are exempt from the first to fifth data protection Principles, s 10 DPA (prevention of processing likely to cause damage or distress), and s 14(1)–(3) DPA (rectification, blocking, erasure, and destruction)[294] where the disclosure is necessary for the purposes of establishing, exercising, or defending legal rights. Whether the media would or could take advantage of this unhappy drafting (presumably the draftsman intended to refer to legal rights as between the parties in a case or to a transaction) is open to question. Were they to do so, the argument would be along the lines that disclosure in the course of publication is for the purpose of exercising the legal right of freedom of expression, with reference (now) of course to the HRA and Article 10 ECHR, although the HRA was not in force when the DPA was enacted.

---

[293] *Hansard*, HL (5th Series), vol 585, col 442 (2 February 1998).
[294] Collectively, the 'non-disclosure provisions', as identified in s 27(4) DPA.

# 8

## PRIVACY, DEFAMATION, AND FALSE FACTS

*Richard Parkes QC*

## A. Introduction

### (1) Relationship of Defamation with Privacy and Confidentiality

Many claims brought to protect privacy or confidentiality involve a publication **8.01** which is also defamatory. There are a number of tests that have traditionally been used to define defamatory words. Most commonly, perhaps, words have been taken to be defamatory if they tend to lower the claimant in the estimation of right-thinking members of society generally, or if they are likely to affect the claimant adversely in the estimation of reasonable people generally.[1] Another common

---

[1] *Skuse v Granada TV* [1996] EMLR 278, 286; *Gillick v BBC* [1996] EMLR 267, 275; *Jeynes v News Magazines Ltd* [2008] EWCA Civ 130; *Modi v Clarke* [2011] EWCA Civ 937.

formulation has defined as defamatory any words which expose the claimant to hatred, ridicule, or contempt. Some definitions have created a higher threshold for what is defamatory than others.

**8.02** The case of *Thornton*[2] shows the need for a threshold to exclude trivial claims and to accommodate the defendant's Article 10 rights and the principle of proportionality. In that case, the judge preferred a definition by which words are defamatory if they substantially affect in an adverse manner the attitude of other people towards the claimant, or have a tendency to do so. Parliament has now provided that a statement is not defamatory unless it has caused or is likely to cause serious harm to the claimant's reputation.[3] This has been held to oblige claimants to prove actual or likely damage to reputation,[4] and the court will have to take into account not only the seriousness of the charge in itself but other factors such as the mode and extent of publication. But on the face of it the central issue will remain the actual or likely impact of the statement on the attitude of others towards the claimant, and on any view those people must represent a reasonable mainstream viewpoint, not the viewpoint of (for example) criminal elements in society.

**8.03** To an extent, the law of privacy serves to protect reputation. Whether this is rightly seen as an incidental benefit (or disbenefit) of the introduction of a privacy law, or as an additional justification for a privacy law, is a moot point. Some areas of reputation are not protected by the law of defamation, but are likely to be protected by privacy law: for instance, it is not defamatory of a person to say that he votes for a particular mainstream political party, or that he holds particular religious beliefs (unless, perhaps, they are of an extreme or anti-social kind). But in either case the information could, if revealed, be damaging, because it could form the basis of discrimination against the person concerned. Disclosure of such information could not be prevented under defamation law, but it might well

---

[2] *Thornton v Telegraph Media Group Ltd* [2010] EWHC 1414 (QB), [2011] 1 WLR 1985. See also *Cammish v Hughes* [2012] EWCA Civ 1655, [2013] EMLR 13 [38]: 'The law does not provide remedies for inconsequential statements, that is, of trivial content or import. It is necessary that there should be some threshold test of seriousness to avoid normal social banter or discourtesy ending up in litigation and to avoid interfering with the right to freedom of expression conferred by Article 10 of the European Convention on Human Rights.'

[3] Defamation Act 2013, s 1:

> (1) A statement is not defamatory unless its publication has caused or is likely to cause serious harm to the reputation of the claimant.
>
> (2) For the purposes of this section, harm to the reputation of a body that trades for profit is not 'serious harm' unless it has caused or is likely to cause the body serious financial loss.

[4] It appears that the claimant must prove as a fact that serious harm to reputation has been or is likely to be caused. The legal presumption of damage seems to be a thing of the past: see *Lachaux v Independent Print Ltd* [2015] EWHC 2242 (QB); [2015] EMLR 28. For a case on bodies that trade for profit (s1(2)), see *Brett Wilson v Persons unknown* [2015] EWHC 2628 (QB).

be information in respect of which the claimant had a reasonable expectation of privacy.

Similarly, it is no longer defamatory of a woman to allege that she has been the vic- **8.04** tim of rape[5] or that she was not a virgin on marriage; but that information, which on any view is private, might, if disclosed, cause grave damage to a woman from a racial or religious background which values a reputation for virginity. Again, it is not defamatory to say that a person has reported a crime to police: most people would regard their action as proper. However, a minority would view the inform- ant with disfavour as a grass or a snitch, and the police go to great lengths to protect the identities of informants. In principle, that information is of the sort which merits the protection of privacy law.

While privacy law may serve to prevent the disclosure of information that is not **8.05** protected by the law of defamation, conversely, some defamation claims relate to and may incidentally serve to prevent the publication of private facts. Claims brought in confidentiality and defamation do not always overlap in this way. But there are many claims about publications relating to matters of health and sexual life, and some relating to religious and philosophical beliefs, which are, or may well be, both defamatory and a disclosure of private or confidential facts.[6] The ques- tion for the party making the claim in such cases is to decide which cause of action to plead. Whatever choice the claimant makes, the court is faced with the ques- tion: by what principles does it decide what information is to be protected? Another question is, does it matter whether the information is true or false? These questions are still not definitively resolved. Possible answers are discussed in this chapter.

Until recently the cause of action most commonly invoked to protect personal **8.06** information in this jurisdiction was defamation, which is available only when the relevant information is false (or cannot be proved to be true). The law of confi- dentiality was generally thought to require a pre-existing duty of confidential- ity, pre-supposing an existing relationship between claimant and defendant. The court therefore focused as much on the circumstances in which the information came into the defendant's hands as on the nature of the information. In defama- tion, by contrast, the court looks at the nature and content of the information in order to establish if it is published lawfully, and has never required any relationship between the parties.

To the extent of its focus on the nature of the information to be protected from **8.07** disclosure, rather than on the relationship of the parties, the law of defamation

---

[5] cf *Youssoupoff v Metro-Golden-Meyer* (1934) 50 TLR 581, CA.
[6] See *eg RST v UVW* [2009] EWHC 2448 (QB), where the claimant sought an injunction to restrain the publication of information that was arguably both private and defamatory, concern- ing his alleged encounters with a prostitute; *Terry v Persons Unknown* [2009] EWHC 2448 (QB), [2010] EMLR 10; *WER v REW* [2009] EWHC 1029 (QB), [2009] EMLR 17; *Hannon v News Group Newspapers Ltd* [2014] EWHC 1580 (Ch), [2015] EMLR 1. See the discussion at 8.77 *et seq.*

might have been thought to lend itself more naturally to the protection of privacy than the law of confidentiality. Moreover, the development of the law of defamation over centuries has tended to give priority to the principle of freedom of expression. Grafting a privacy right onto the root stock of other causes of action, such as confidentiality, in which this principle has not in the past been considered of major importance, has been argued to carry the risk that well-established safeguards will be 'jettisoned, disregarded or ignored'.[7]

### (2) Essential Features of Defamation and Malicious Falsehood

**8.08**   Defamation is a strict liability tort with potent presumptions as to falsity and (hitherto) damage that work in the claimant's favour.[8] By contrast, malicious falsehood[9] requires the claimant to prove falsity, malice, and either actual financial loss or statutory exemption from the need to prove actual loss.[10] Defamation protects personal, professional, and business reputation, whereas a cause of action in malicious falsehood posits no damage to reputation: it typically (but by no means exclusively)[11]

---

[7] W Prosser, 'Privacy' (1960) 48 Cal L Rev 383. Prosser also regarded informational privacy as protecting reputation. He said (at 398) that the development of the tort had 'no doubt gone far to remedy the deficiencies of the defamation actions, hampered as they are by technical rules inherited from ancient and long forgotten jurisdictional conflicts and to provide a remedy for few real and serious wrongs that were not previously actionable'.

[8] Libel and slander are the two facets of defamation, the former broadly embracing the written and broadcast word, including email and the internet, while slander covers spoken word and gesture. Libel is actionable without proof of actual damage; slander is not, except where it imputes commission of a criminal offence, or disparages the claimant in his office, business, trade, profession or calling. However, the legal presumption of damage may be no more: see *Lachaux*, n4. The primary defence to a claim in defamation is truth (formerly justification). Others include honest opinion (formerly fair comment), which protects opinion and comment based on true facts, and publication on a matter of public interest, which—very broadly—protects information published responsibly on a matter of general public interest (see n 21). Qualified privilege (which may be defeated by proof of malice) primarily protects communications made in accordance with a duty or interest to others who have a common and corresponding interest in the subject matter of the information. Absolute privilege, which prevails even in the face of malice, protects such communications as statements made in the course of judicial proceedings, including statements made by witnesses and complainants to the police. For a less flimsy exegesis, see A Mullis and R Parkes QC, *Gatley on Libel and Slander* (12th edn, Sweet and Maxwell 2013).

[9] Malicious falsehood was described by Stuart-Smith LJ in *Khodaparast v Shad* [2000] 1 WLR 618 [42] as a 'species of defamation'. In such unqualified terms that view may not command general acceptance. For a preferable analysis see *Ajinomoto Sweeteners Europe SAS v Asda Stores Ltd* [2010] EWCA Civ 609, [2011] QB 497 [28]. Sedley LJ regarded as realistic an 'approximation of the two torts... on the ground that both concern the protection of reputation, albeit one protects the reputation of persons and the other the reputation of property'.

[10] By Defamation Act 1952, s 3(1) it is not necessary to allege or prove special damage in a malicious falsehood case where the words complained of are calculated to cause pecuniary damage to the claimant and are published in writing or other permanent form, or if they are calculated to cause pecuniary damage to the claimant in respect of any office, profession, calling trade or business held or carried on by him or her at the time of the publication.

[11] Malicious falsehood claims have been brought in a number of non-commercial contexts: see eg *Kaye v Robertson* [1991] FSR 62 (a gross invasion of the plaintiff's privacy while a patient in hospital, when no right to protect privacy was recognized); *Joyce v Sengupta* [1993] 1 WLR 337 (defamatory allegations about the plaintiff's behaviour as a royal servant); *Khodaparast* (n 9) (publication

protects property interests, and in particular business goodwill,[12] and in those circumstances the scope for overlap with a claim to protect a privacy right is slight. Defamation and malicious falsehood are often employed as alternative causes of action in the same claim, but only where there is a good reason for doing so. Often that reason is founded on doubt as to whether the words complained of are in fact defamatory of the claimant; in the past, one reason was the availability of legal aid for malicious falsehood (never a possibility in defamation);[13] and more recently, it has been the apparent wish to circumvent the defamation offer-of-amends procedure.[14] Absent a good tactical reason, no litigant would choose to pursue a claim in malicious falsehood where a parallel claim in defamation was available.

In defamation (but not in malicious falsehood)[15] the words or images complained **8.09** of must refer to the claimant. It does not matter to what part of the claimant's life the publication complained of relates. It may relate to something deeply private, such as health or sexual life. It may relate to business or politics. But the subject of a libel action must always be information that is personal in the sense that it refers to an identifiable person who is the claimant.[16] Celebrity libel actions commonly do involve health, sex, and relationships.

There are two constituents of the tort of defamation which have inhibited the use **8.10** of defamation in the protection of personal information. The first is that the publication must be defamatory: it must tend to lower the claimant's reputation in the view of right-thinking members of society. A privacy claim may involve information which is defamatory of the claimant, but in many (perhaps most) cases it will not. Secondly, in defamation the information must be false. Or rather, it may be true, but there is a presumption of falsity, and it is for the defendant to prove that the information is true. This burden of proof is sometimes resented by journalists. They point to libel cases which have succeeded when there was good reason to believe the publication was true, but there was no legal proof available at the time of the trial. This supposed effect of the burden of proof in defamation can be seen as a crude and limited protection to the private life of claimants. But its effect can be exaggerated: it is very doubtful that a defamation action has ever turned on the burden of proof. Even if the claimant were obliged (as in malicious falsehood) to

---

of faked pornographic pictures of the claimant); and *Quinton v Peirce* [2009] EWHC 912 (QB), [2009] FSR 17 (publication of election communications).

[12] Malicious falsehood has been described as protecting 'interests in the disposability of a person's property, products or business': *Orion Pet Products v RSPCA* (2002) 120 FCR 191, 223 (Weinberg J). More recently, Sedley LJ described the cause of action as concerning 'the reputation of property, typically in the form of the goodwill of a business': *Ajinomoto Sweeteners* (n 9) [28].

[13] *Joyce v Sengupta* [1993] 1 WLR 337.

[14] *Tesco Stores Ltd v Guardian News and Media Ltd* [2009] EMLR 5.

[15] In malicious falsehood, the claimant need not be personally identifiable. A malicious falsehood need only identify a product, business or other economic interest: *Marathon Mutual Ltd v Waters* [2009] EWHC 1931 (QB), [2010] EMLR 3.

[16] The defamation claimant need not be an individual: it may, for instance, be a company or a partnership.

plead and prove falsity, the media defendant without evidence of truth would still be most unlikely to succeed.

**8.11**     The overriding principle in the law of defamation (and malicious falsehood) is that truth justifies any publication at all. If a publication can be proved true, then it does not matter how private the information may be, or how humiliating, or how lacking in public interest. In defamation and malicious falsehood, no publication of personal information can be unlawful provided it is proved to be true. This is a cardinal principle.[17] The priority given to truth in aid of the public interest in freedom of expression has inhibited the development of a law of privacy, and it has long been controversial.[18] It is therefore necessary to consider why English law has hitherto regarded truth as justifying publication of all defamatory personal information. This in turn requires examination of the values of freedom of expression and reputation which are protected both by defamation and by privacy and confidentiality laws.

**8.12**     The commonest defences to a claim in breach of confidence are that the supposedly confidential material is in the public domain, or that it is in the public interest for it to be disseminated. In defamation and malicious falsehood, by contrast, there is no defence of public domain: subject to the new statutory single publication rule,[19] it does not matter that the publication may have been made previously, however often or however widely.[20] There are public interest defences to defamation claims, in the shape of statutory and common law privilege, but since truth is a defence, these are not needed if truth can be proved.[21]

---

[17] See *eg Fraser v Evans* [1969] 1 QB 349, 360–1 (Lord Denning MR).

[18] As long ago as 1843, a Select Committee of the House of Lords recommended that truth should not be an absolute defence to a claim in defamation: in addition, publication would have to be for the benefit of the community. See 8.30. Before the introduction in 2006 of the Australian national uniform defamation laws, some states required the defendant to show not only truth but also public interest (New South Wales) or public benefit (Tasmania, Queensland, ACT). Resistance to change was partly founded on the belief that this requirement provided an indirect protection for privacy, although it is doubtful that it had that effect: see eg D Rolph, 'A critique of the national, uniform defamation laws' (2008) 16(3) Torts LJ 207, 228.

[19] Defamation Act 2013, s 8: where a person publishes defamatory material and then later republishes it, or material which is substantially the same, in a manner which is not materially different, the cause of action is treated as having accrued for limitation purposes on the date of the first publication.

[20] See *Associated Newspapers Ltd v Dingle* [1964] AC 371, which makes previous similar or even identical publications by other persons inadmissible in a defamation action even for the purpose of mitigating damages. However, s 12 of the Defamation Act 1952 enables the defendant to give evidence in mitigation of damages that the claimant has previously recovered damages (or has brought actions for damages, or has received or agreed to receive compensation) for publication of words to the same effect as those sued upon.

[21] Defamation law presumes the information complained of to be false. The established privilege defences are based on that presumption, and are therefore very narrowly defined. Unless the publication relates to certain defined subjects, such as proceedings in court or in Parliament, defendants must generally show that they were under a duty to make the publication and that the intended publishee had a corresponding interest in receiving the publication. The common law defence of *Reynolds* privilege (*Reynolds v Times Newspapers Ltd* [2001] 2 AC 127: in the process of being superseded, as to which see below) recognizes a duty to make disclosure to the public in general. Despite

## (3) The Value of Reputation

The need for the law of defamation was well stated by Lord Nicholls in *Reynolds v* **8.13**
*Times Newspapers Ltd.*[22] He said:

> Reputation is an integral and important part of the dignity of the individual. It also
> forms the basis of many decisions in a democratic society which are fundamental to
> its well-being: whom to employ or work for, whom to promote, whom to do busi-
> ness with or to vote for. Once besmirched by an unfounded allegation in a national
> newspaper, a reputation can be damaged for ever, especially if there is no oppor-
> tunity to vindicate one's reputation. When this happens, society as well as the
> individual is the loser. For it should not be supposed that protection of reputation
> is a matter of importance only to the affected individual and his family. Protection
> of reputation is conducive to the public good. It is in the public interest that the
> reputation of public figures should not be debased falsely. In the political field, in
> order to make an informed choice, the electorate needs to be able to identify the
> good as well as the bad. Consistently with these considerations, human rights con-
> ventions recognise that freedom of expression is not an absolute right. Its exercise
> may be subject to such restrictions as are prescribed by law and are necessary in a
> democratic society for the protection of the reputations of others.[23]

In summary, defamation protects a person against humiliation, and from discrim- **8.14**
ination based on false facts in personal and professional relationships. It also protects society from making political, professional, and personal choices on a factual
basis which is false.

## (4) The Value of Freedom of Expression

The value protected by freedom of expression is as easily explained. In *R v Secretary* **8.15**
*of State for the Home Dept, ex p Simms*[24] Lord Steyn has famously said that:

> In a democracy it is the primary right: without it an effective rule of law is not
> possible...it promotes the self-fulfilment of individuals in society...The free flow

---

later developments, it is still not an easy defence to make good, because of the need for the defendant
to prove that he or she has acted responsibly; but the House of Lords has urged a practical and flexible
approach to the question of responsible journalism with a degree of deference to editorial discretion
(*Jameel v Wall Street Journal Europe* [2006] UKHL 44, [2007] 1 AC 359), an approach echoed by the
Supreme Court in *Flood v Times Newspapers Ltd* [2012] UKSC 11, [2012] 2 AC 273. The common law
defence has now been abolished and replaced (for causes of action which accrue after 31 December
2013) by a statutory defence of publication on a matter of public interest. The defendant must show
that the statement complained of was, or formed part of, a statement on a matter of public interest,
and that he or she reasonably believed that it was in the public interest to publish the statement; and
in determining those questions, the court must have regard to all the circumstances of the case, and,
in considering the reasonableness of the defendant's belief, it must make such allowance for editorial
judgment as it thinks appropriate: Defamation Act 2013, s 4. It is perhaps unlikely that the new test
will produce very different analyses from those developed by the common law.

[22] *Reynolds* (n 21) 201.
[23] In *Jameel* (n 21) [91] Lord Hoffmann described reputation as a part of personality and as the
'immortal part' of the individual, language that goes some way to support the emergence of reputation as an Art 8 right, as to which see 8.69–8.70.
[24] [2000] 2 AC 115, 125–6.

of information and ideas informs political debate. It is a safety valve: people are more ready to accept decisions that go against them if they can in principle seek to influence them. It acts as a brake on the abuse of power by public officials. It facilitates the exposure of errors in the governance and administration of justice of the country.

**8.16** Lord Steyn was talking about public life. In private life the explanation is similar. Freedom of expression deters inappropriate behaviour[25] and encourages good behaviour. Being talked about in the media may bring people honour or shame. People modify their behaviour accordingly. If people do not modify their behaviour, then the public discussion of it can lead to the law being invoked, or to changes in the law.

**8.17** Both freedom of expression and protection of privacy are 'vitally important rights. Neither has precedence over the other. The importance of freedom of expression has been stressed often and eloquently, the importance of privacy less so. But it, too, lies at the heart of liberty in a modern state. A proper degree of privacy is essential for the well being and development of an individual.'[26]

**8.18** If defamation is necessary to protect the reputation that a person has in the minds of *right*-thinking members of society generally, then privacy can be said to be necessary to protect the reputation a person has in the minds of *wrong*-thinking members of society.[27] Privacy can protect the individual against unjust discrimination, and prevent society from making decisions on a factual basis which may be true (or for that matter false)[28] but irrelevant. Lord Nicholls said that it is in the public interest that the reputation of public figures should not be debased falsely. It is almost as much in the public interest that public figures should not be judged on information which is clearly irrelevant to their public lives, whether it is true or false.

## B. Protection of Privacy by Defamation Law

### (1) Right-thinking Members of Society

**8.19** One form of protection that defamation gives to privacy is in the test of what is defamatory. The test has long in principle been: do the words complained of lower the claimant's reputation in the minds of right-thinking members of society

---

[25] To borrow a phrase from *R v Legal Aid Board, ex p Kaim Todner* [1999] QB 966, 977; see also *Francome v Mirror Group Newspapers Ltd* [1984] 1 WLR 892, 898.

[26] *Campbell v MGN Ltd* [2004] UKHL 22, [2004] 2 AC 457 [12] (Lord Nicholls). The promotion of individual autonomy in the sense of the right to self-determination and the liberty to live life as one chooses is an important part of the rationale of protection of privacy: see 2.65–2.69.

[27] See the examples given at 8.03–8.04.

[28] See 8.71.

generally?[29] This test has been found satisfied even in cases where the only proper response of a right-thinking person to the publication complained of would in fact be not contempt or disapproval, but sympathy or indifference. The effect of stretching the definition of what is defamatory in this way has been to protect individuals against the publication of some private and personal material.

Another way of doing so is to construe a publication purportedly about the past **8.20** alone (as to which it is true) as referring also to the present (as to which it may be false). In the words of Lord Shaw of Dunfermline in *Sutherland v Stopes*:[30]

> [A] statement of fact or of opinion which consists in the raking up of a long-buried past may, without an explanation (and, in cases which are conceivable, even with an explanation), be libellous or slanderous if written or uttered in such circumstances as to suggest that a taint upon character or conduct still subsists, and that the plaintiff is accordingly held up to ridicule, reprobation or contempt.

### (2) Libel Cases where the Claimant's Reputation Should Not Have Been Lowered

In 1934 Princess Youssoupoff was awarded £28,000 (over £600,000 today) for **8.21** the suggestion in a film that she had been raped.[31] More recently Calcutt[32] told of a £1 million out-of-court libel settlement in the 1980s following stories in *The Sun* about Elton John's private life, involving allegations of rent boys, drugs, and removal of the larynxes of guard dogs to stop them barking. Calcutt also cited the observation of Sir Louis Blom-Cooper, then Chairman of the Press Council, on jury awards of damages. Sir Louis thought that large awards reflected jurors' disapproval of the improper disclosure by newspapers of intimate details of an individual's private life.[33] Elton John's case may have influenced Calcutt's proposal for the setting up of the Press Complaints Commission.

---

[29] See the discussion of tests for what is defamatory at 8.01–8.02. Another formulation is whether the words complained of bring the claimant into hatred, ridicule, or contempt. That test is more apt to cover privacy. In 1963 Leon Brittan suggested that privacy be protected in English law by developing the law of defamation: 'The Right of Privacy in England and the United States' (1963) 37 Tulane L Rev 235, 260–1. His suggestion was to extend the use of the 'ridicule' basis for defamation. That basis survives but is little used. In *Berkoff v Burchill* [1996] 4 All ER 1008, CA, the question whether the description of the claimant as 'hideously ugly' was defamatory in this way was left to the jury. Similarly, in 1992 Michael Jackson brought a defamation claim based on articles alleging that he had been hideously transformed by cosmetic surgery: *Jackson v MGN Ltd, The Times*, 20 March 1994, CA. The problem for defamation claimants in cases such as this is that, because truth is a complete defence, they may be subjected to the further offence and indignity of an inquiry into the truth of the allegation. For example, Jackson had to submit to a medical examination. His case settled shortly before trial.

[30] [1925] AC 47, 74.

[31] *Youssoupoff* (n 5).

[32] UK, *Report of the Committee on Privacy and Related Matters* (Cmnd 1102, 1990) (Chairman: David Calcutt, QC) para 1.5 and *The Times*, 21 April 2001, 3.

[33] *The Calcutt Report* (n 32) para 8.25. For a discussion of Calcutt, see 1.06.

**8.22** In 1991 the entertainer Jason Donovan was awarded £200,000 in an action against a magazine which had suggested that he was a liar and a hypocrite to deny that he was gay.[34] If information is personal or private, then, as the Rehabilitation of Offenders Act 1974 shows,[35] a proper legal response may be that the individual does not have to confirm or deny its truth. False denial may be hypocrisy, but failure to admit homosexuality surely is not. The reason the cases are pleaded to rely on a meaning of lying or hypocrisy is that the claimant is enabled to bring a claim in libel in respect of false and personal information, which, in other jurisdictions, would be regarded as a claim for false light.

**8.23** It may be preferable to recognize a separate tort of false light in English law—that is to say, to regard claimants such as these as having suffered an infringement of their privacy, not an injury to their reputation, notwithstanding the fact that the information is in fact false. Where false light exists as a tort it is categorized as part of the law of privacy. Thus a right of privacy can be infringed by a false allegation as well as by a true one.[36] This proposition is now accepted by the English courts, although it has not been expressed in terms of false light.[37]

### (3) Fair Comment on a Matter of Public Interest/Honest Opinion

**8.24** The right to privacy is recognized in defamation law also in the defence of fair comment on a matter of public interest, now replaced by the new statutory defence of honest opinion (which requires no public interest).[38] The defence has given rise to a number of cases where the courts have had to decide that certain matters relating to public figures are nevertheless part of their private lives, not matters of public interest.[39] So, for instance, the mere fact that a person was a Member of Parliament and a former minister did not make his private life a matter of public interest such as would justify defamatory comment about his behaviour towards his wife.[40] This defence, however, applies only to recognizable statements of opinion, not allegations of fact, and therefore has a narrow application. In many cases the information will be presented as factual, so that the fact that the information is of a personal and private nature will not assist the claimant. However, a series of decisions of the European Court of Human Rights has shown a tendency to categorize many media reports, which national authorities have regarded as statements of fact, as

---

[34] *The Times*, 4 April 1992.

[35] See 8.47.

[36] For false light torts in the US see 3.73–3.79 *et seq.*

[37] *McKennitt v Ash* [2006] EWCA Civ 1714, [2008] QB 73 [79], [86]; *PQR v Quigley* [2008] EWHC 1051 (QB).

[38] The common law defence has been abolished for causes of action arising after 31 December 2013: Defamation Act 2013, ss 3 and 16(5). The new defence of honest opinion is intended broadly to reflect the existing common law, except that the requirement of public interest no longer exists.

[39] P Milmo QC and H Rogers, *Gatley on Libel and Slander* (11th edn, Sweet and Maxwell 2008) para 12.29. This passage is not reproduced in the 12th edn (n 8), but see para 12.32 and n 181 of that work for a list of authorities.

[40] *Mutch v Sleeman* (1928) 29 NSWSR 125, 137.

expressions of opinion, the truth of which need not (indeed cannot) be proven.[41] This European trend, if such it is, may be having some effect on domestic jurisprudence under the Human Rights Act 1998.[42]

### (4) Defamation Damages and Invasion of Privacy

General damages for defamation include compensation for injury to feelings, including the distress, hurt and humiliation caused by the libel or slander. The injury to a claimant's feelings is likely to be particularly acute when the publication has intruded into his or her personal life, and will be compensated accordingly. In a proper case, a libel which has involved a particularly hurtful invasion of the claimant's private and personal affairs may merit an award of aggravated damages.[43] That appears to have been a factor in the awards in the cases of Elton John (by settlement) and Jason Donovan.[44] However, since truth constitutes a complete defence to a defamation claim, a claimant can obtain such damages, in effect for breach of his privacy, only if there is no defence of truth, or if the defence fails. A claimant complaining of the publication of private facts which can be proved to be true has no redress in defamation law, even though the publication of such information may be just as intrusive and hurtful as the publication of false allegations of a personal nature (sometimes more so). **8.25**

Historically, the law of defamation has offered partial protection for a claimant's privacy in the course of the litigation by limiting the evidence sought to be adduced in reduction of damages. Until relatively recently, any attempt to introduce evidence in mitigation of damages as to particular past acts of misconduct on the part of the claimant, tending to show his character and disposition, would have been rejected.[45] In *Plato Films Ltd v Speidel*[46] Lord Simonds said: **8.26**

> There may, in the result, be cases in which a rogue survives both evidence of general bad reputation and, where he has gone into the witness-box, a severe cross-examination nominally directed to credit, and recovers more damages than he should. But I would rather have it so than that the law should permit the injustice and, indeed, the cruelty of an attack upon a plaintiff for offences real or imaginary which, if they ever were committed, may have been known to few and by them have been forgotten.

---

[41] See *eg De Haes and Gisjels v Belgium* (1997) 25 EHRR 1; *Nilsen and Johnsen v Norway* (1999) 30 EHRR 878; *Jerusalem v Austria* App no 26958/95 (ECtHR, 27 February 2001); *Feldek v Slovakia* App no 29032/95 (ECtHR, 12 July 2001); and *Scharsach & News Verlagsgesellschaft v Austria* (2005) 40 EHRR 22. For recent decisions to the directly opposite effect, see *Pfeifer v Austria* (2007) 48 EHRR 175; *Petrina v Romania* App no 78060/01 (ECtHR, 14 October 2008); and *Petrenco v Moldova* App no 20928/05, [2011] EMLR 5.

[42] See *Branson v Bower* [2002] 2 QB 737; *Lowe v Associated Newspapers Ltd* [2006] EWHC 320 (QB), [2007] QB 580; *British Chiropractic Association v Singh* [2010] EWCA Civ 350, [2011] 1 WLR 133; *Joseph v Spiller* [2010] UKSC 53, [2011] 1 AC 852.

[43] *Gatley on Libel and Slander* (n 8) paras 9.4, 9.18.

[44] See 8.21 and 8.22.

[45] *Gatley on Libel and Slander* (n 8) para 33.30.

[46] [1961] AC 1090, 1125.

**8.27**  This rule has now been relaxed to the extent that evidence of specific acts of misconduct is admissible if the misconduct is background context directly relevant to the
assessment of the damage to reputation suffered in the sector of the claimant's life to
which the publication relates.[47] Nevertheless, inquiries into the claimant's past life for
the purposes of assessing damages remain limited to the subject matter of the defamation and the circumstances of its publication. When the defamatory imputation
refers to private matters about the claimant's life and the defendant seeks to prove their
truth, there is no such limitation on the investigation, no matter how intrusive and
damaging it might be, or how little public interest there is in it. Potential claimants
with good defamation claims are often deterred from suing at all by the likely level of
intrusion into their private affairs which litigation would entail.

**8.28**  So it is that despite the limited and incidental recognition of privacy rights that
defamation law affords, the availability of truth as a complete defence in defamation has the consequence that defamation claimants are little protected from intrusion into their personal affairs.

## C.  Conflict between Defamation and Privacy

### (1)  The Controversy over Truth as an Absolute Defence

#### (a)  The principle of freedom of expression

**8.29**  The rule that proof of the truth of the publication constitutes a complete defence
to a defamation claim has been seen as a factor limiting the protection of privacy
through the means of defamation, and as an obstacle to the development of a free-
standing right to privacy. It is the principal means by which English private law has
given effect to the right to freedom of expression.

#### (b)  Reports on the law of defamation

**8.30**  The rule has long been controversial. In 1843 the Select Committee of the House of
Lords on the Law of Defamation recommended a change in the law. They considered that there were many cases where truth should not be a complete defence to an
imputation relating to some personal defect or error of conduct long since atoned
for and forgotten, but that the defendant should be obliged to prove some element
of public interest in the publication in order to establish his or her defence. The
requirement to prove public interest was adopted only in respect of criminal libel.[48]

---

[47] *Burstein v Times Newspapers Ltd* [2001] 1 WLR 579; *Turner v News Group Newspapers Ltd*
[2006] EWCA Civ 540, [2006] 1 WLR 3469; *Warren v Random House Group Ltd* [2008] EWCA
Civ 834, [2009] QB 600.
[48] Until January 2006, some Australian jurisdictions confined the defence to cases of public benefit (ACT, Queensland, and Tasmania) or public interest (New South Wales). See n 18.

Cases involving essentially private matters such as *Youssoupoff*[49] (where the plaintiff **8.31** sued on an allegation that she had been raped) have troubled committees considering reform of the law of defamation. In 1948 the Porter Committee considered the hypothetical example of a woman who in her adolescence bore an illegitimate child.[50] Neither case would be likely to be thought defamatory today, but—more to the point—neither in the hypothetical example nor in *Youssoupoff* would the revelation of such private matters have engaged any conceivable public interest. The Porter Committee sympathized with the view that the defendant in such cases should show not just that the allegation was true but also that there was a public interest in publication, but rejected it on the ground that the task of the author or journalist would become impracticable. They did not address their minds to the more limited point that the defence of justification could be excluded where to allow it would be an unwarranted interference with a person's private life.

In 1975 the Faulks Committee[51] recognized that a requirement to show public **8.32** interest might deter people from resuscitating tales of crimes or misconduct happily long forgotten, but rejected the proposal on the grounds that such a provision would apply generally to all defamatory publications. They did not consider a limited qualification to the defence of justification excluding unwarranted interference with a person's private life. They were concerned about cases such as *Youssoupoff*[52] and others involving diseases for which there is no moral responsibility. Though recognizing such cases to be a problem, they suggested that 'these unfortunate people' resort to their claim in injurious falsehood if they had none in defamation: an impractical suggestion, given the impossibility of proving malice in most cases.

*(c) The policy in truth as an absolute defence*

The truth as an absolute defence rule has become so entrenched in English law that **8.33** the arguments against it have become lately overlooked. The law is said to be based on the principle stated in *McPherson v Daniels*:[53] 'For the law will not permit a man to recover damages in respect to an injury to a character which he either does not, or ought not, to possess.' But this principle does not justify refusing all defamation claimants a remedy because the information published about them is true. Not all

---

A requirement of public benefit would have halted the defendant in *KJO v XIM* [2011] EWHC 1768 (QB), who persistently informed the claimant's employers, potential employers, and public bodies of a long rehabilitated conviction.

[49] *Youssoupoff* (n 5).

[50] UK, *Report of the Committee on the Law of Defamation* (Cmd 7536, 1948) (Chairman: Lord Porter) paras 74–8, cited in the *Report of the Committee on the Law of Defamation* (Cmnd 5909, 1975) (Chairman: Mr Justice Faulks) para 139.

[51] Faulks Committee (n 50) paras 137–40.

[52] *Youssoupoff* (n 5).

[53] (1829) 10 B & C 263, 272, 109 ER 448, 451. Windeyer J put it this way: 'The law does not protect the reputation a man has, but only the reputation he deserves': *Uren v John Fairfax & Sons* (1966) 117 CLR 118, 150. In *Plato Films* (n 46) 1138 Lord Denning distinguished between a man's character (what he in fact is) and his reputation (what other people think he is).

true information about an individual is relevant to public reputation. Information about a person's private and personal life may not be relevant, especially if the person's reputation is based only on public acts.

**8.34**  It is not always clear why a prominent person's reputation for good works should be besmirched by reports of an adulterous affair. The difficulty is compounded when the published information does not impute any misconduct or immorality, but is deemed defamatory on other grounds, as in *Youssoupoff*, by virtue of the fact that it would lead people to shun, avoid, or ridicule the claimant. Is it relevant, for example, to the reputation of a prominent person that he has HIV or Aids?[54] In fact, the best expression of the reason behind the rule is not the *McPherson v Daniels* principle, but the public policy which has until recently considered the exposure of truth as the paramount interest, superior to the interest in protecting reputation.[55]

**8.35**  The rule permits the raking over of a person's past life even when he is a reformed character. It was this injustice that was recognized by the House of Lords Select Committee in 1843, and for which the Select Committee recommended that a remedy should be available.[56] Parliament has thought it right to assist those convicted of criminal offences to leave their mistakes behind them,[57] yet there is no equivalent protection against the exhumation of behaviour that is not criminal, or at least has not involved conviction. There is, however, some limitation on unjustified prying into past lives, for the reason stated by Lord Shaw of Dunfermline in *Sutherland v Stopes*,[58] namely in attributing to statements ostensibly about the past a meaning which refers to the present. The cruelty and injustice of raking up offences known to few and by them forgotten have given rise in French (and EU) law to the *droit à l'oubli* or the right to be forgotten.[59]

---

[54]  As long ago as 1847 this consideration led New South Wales to adopt a defence which required not only proof of truth but also proof that publication was in the public interest. Queensland, ACT, and Tasmania had a similar public benefit requirement. However, the public interest/public benefit requirements disappeared with the enactment of the national, uniform defamation laws in 2006: see n 48.

[55]  The view of Spencer Bower was that this policy was indefensible: 'The only tenable hypothesis on which immunity of this indefeasible character can be defended, is public policy, which means that the public good imperatively demands that any and every private disadvantage must yield to it, and yield so unconditionally that the individual shall not even be allowed to assert that he has been ruined by the publication of that which, though true, it did not in the least concern or benefit the public to know, and by a publication made, not with any eye to the interest of the community or of social morality, but with the sole and wicked object of inflicting private misery. *Is* it public policy that such a publication should be so protected? I contend that it is not.' S Bower, *A Code of the Law of Actionable Defamation* (2nd edn, Butterworth 1923) 336 cited in R Brown, *The Law of Defamation in Canada* (2nd edn, Carswell 1994) 504, para 10.2.

[56]  See 8.30.

[57]  Rehabilitation of Offenders Act 1974: see 8.47–8.49.

[58]  [1925] AC 47, 74.

[59]  P Kayser, *La Protection de la Vie Privée par le Droit* (3rd edn, Economica-PUAM 1995) 217, para 118; *Google Spain SL v AEPD* [2014] QB 1022, ECJ.

Where the publication of defamatory truths is motivated solely by malice, the  **8.36**
unqualified right to rely on truth may mean that the defendant can conceal his malice in publishing, because where truth is the defence, malice is immaterial. Absent a
conspiracy or a spent conviction,[60] an intention to injure the claimant is irrelevant if
the truth of the information is proved. It has been said that the rule that truth is an
absolute defence 'enshrines the scandalmonger as a favourite of the law'.[61]

### (d) Article 8 of the European Convention on Human Rights

By permitting the publication of truthful personal and private material, the rule  **8.37**
that proof of truth is a complete defence to a defamation claim may also bring
English law into conflict with Article 8, whether the publisher of the words complained of is a public authority or not.[62] This conflict becomes most apparent
when considering the principles governing prior restraint in freedom of expression
actions, which are considered at 8.50 *et seq*.

Any invasion of privacy, as an interference with a claimant's Article 8 rights, must  **8.38**
be prescribed by law and necessary in a democratic society in pursuit of one of the
legitimate aims set out in Article 8(2). Absent any requirement for interference
with private life to be proportionate to the aim pursued, the potential for tension
between Article 8 and truth as an absolute defence is clear. The same is true of other
established defamation defences, such as qualified or absolute privilege,[63] or honest opinion (the successor of the old common law defence of comment). However,
the potential for conflict has greatly increased now that it is firmly established that
Article 8 protects the right to reputation, as part of the right to respect for private
life.[64] In almost every defamation case a tension is likely to arise between, on the

---

[60] See Rehabilitation of Offenders Act 1974, s 8, and 8.47–8.49.

[61] B Harnett and J Thornton, 'The truth hurts: A critique of a defence to defamation' (1949) 35
Virginia L Rev 425, 444–45, cited in Brown (n 55) 503, para 10.2. The critique is summarized at
425 thus: 'it is at once clear that such a rule creates a wide operative area for the activities of those
who seek to destroy the reputations of fellow members of society. However malevolent the purpose
of the actor may be and however much he may depart from the community's standards of moral
behaviour in publishing statements concerning another, the actor is not civilly responsible for defamation so long as he keeps within the bounds of truth. All will readily admit that his action in
destroying another's reputation, unless required in some particular case by some overriding public
or private necessity, is morally reprehensible and socially undesirable. Yet no civil action for defamation will lie in such an instance.'

[62] The horizontal enforcement of Art 8 rights has been firmly established at least since the House
of Lords' decision in *Campbell* (n 26): see *eg* per Lord Nicholls [17]. The values embodied in Arts
8 and 10 are as much applicable in disputes between individuals or between individuals and non-
governmental bodies such as the news media as they are between individuals and public authorities.

[63] However, a challenge to the defence of absolute privilege failed in *A v UK* (2002) 36 EHRR
917, a case about words spoken in a Parliamentary debate. The European Court of Human Rights
held in that case that absolute privilege did not impose a disproportionate restriction on the right of
access to the Court under Art 6(1), and did not exceed the domestic margin of appreciation. That
reasoning applied also to the claimant's Art 8 rights.

[64] See *Radio France v France* (2005) EHRR 706; *Cumpana v Romania* (2005) 41 EHRR 41; *Pfeifer
v Austria* (2007) 48 EHRR 175; *Petrina v Romania* App no 78060/01 (ECtHR, 14 October 2008);

one hand, the Article 8 reputation right of the claimant and (if there is a reasonable expectation of privacy) his or her privacy right and, on the other hand, the Article 10 rights of the defendant. Neither Article 8 nor Article 10 has priority.[65]

**8.39**   The court's approach must now accord with the guidance of Lord Steyn in *Re S*:

> The interplay between articles 8 and 10 has been illuminated by the opinions in the House of Lords in *Campbell v MGN Ltd* [2004] 2 AC 457. For present purposes the decision of the House on the facts of *Campbell* and the differences between the majority and the minority are not material. What does, however, emerge clearly from the opinions are four propositions. First, neither article has *as such* precedence over the other. Secondly, where the values under the two articles are in conflict, an intense focus on the comparative importance of the specific rights being claimed in the individual case is necessary. Thirdly, the justifications for interfering with or restricting each right must be taken into account. Finally, the proportionality test must be applied to each. For convenience I will call this the ultimate balancing test.[66]

**8.40**   It remains unclear how the application of the 'ultimate balancing test' will affect the substantive law of defamation, but it appears likely that the established defences, and justification (truth) in particular, will have to adapt to reflect claimants' Article 8 rights (whether in reputation or privacy or both).[67] Whether that will entail the incorporation of a public benefit test, or simply the introduction of tests of legitimate aim and proportionality, it is too early to say.[68]

---

*Karakó v Hungary* (2011) 52 EHRR 36; *Europapress Holding DOO v Croatia* App no 25333/06, [2010] EMLR 10; *Petrenco v Moldova* App no 20928/05, [2011] EMLR 5; *Greene v Associated Newspapers Ltd* [2004] EWCA Civ 1462, [2005] QB 972; *Axel Springer AG v Germany* (2012) 55 EHRR 6; *Re Guardian News & Media Ltd, HM Treasury v Ahmed* [2010] UKSC 1, [2010] 2 AC 697.

[65]   See *Campbell* (n 26) [12] and [55]. Lord Hoffmann considered the relationship between the freedom of the press and the right of the individual to protect personal information. 'Both reflect important civilised values, but, as often happens, neither can be given effect in full measure without restricting the other. How are they to be reconciled in a particular case? There is in my view no question of automatic priority. Nor is there a presumption in favour of one rather than the other. The question is rather the extent to which it is *necessary* to qualify the one right in order to protect the underlying value which is protected by the other. And the extent of the qualification must be proportionate to the need: see Sedley LJ in *Douglas v Hello! Ltd* [2001] QB 967, 1005 [137].' Note, however, the words of Maurice Kay LJ in *Global Torch Ltd v Apex Global Management Ltd* [2013] EWCA Civ 819, [2013] 1 WLR 2993 [25]: 'the competing rights do not exist within a presumptive *legal* hierarchy but that does not mean that in given situations—for example, open justice versus reputational damage—one will not *generally* trump the other. What is important is that the judge approaches the balancing exercise in the right way in the circumstances of the particular case.' The use of the word 'trump' has unfortunate echoes of the old jurisprudence (Hoffmann LJ's 'freedom of speech . . . is a trump card which always wins': *R v Central ITV* [1994] Fam 192, 22). In context, in which the first instance judge is found not to have accorded open justice inherent superiority as a matter of law, the dictum is not as revisionist as it sounds.

[66]   *Re S (A Child) (Identification: Restrictions on Publication)* [2004] UKHL 47, [2005] 1 AC 593 [17].

[67]   It may well be that different consideration will apply to those defences that start from a statutory weighting in favour of free speech, as for instance the absolute privilege for reports of legal proceedings: see *eg Flood* (n 21) [45].

[68]   See the discussion in *Terry (previously 'LNS') v Persons Unknown* [2010] EWHC 119 (QB), [2010] EMLR 16 (Tugendhat J); *Hunt v Times Newspapers Ltd* [2012] EWHC 1220 (QB) [13];

*(e) The conflict between obligations of disclosure and the right to privacy*

One of the most powerful weapons in defamation defendants' armoury is **8.41** the right to have disclosed to them all the claimant's documents which support their case or adversely affect the claimant's case.[69] If it is necessary to do justice between the parties, the courts will usually order such disclosure even when the documents are confidential and/or private. In this way a disclosure order made against a person who is a party to litigation (or, in the case of a person ordered to produce documents under a witness summons, someone who has no interest in the litigation) may be an infringement of his or her Article 8 rights.[70]

Although this problem can arise in all kinds of claims, it is especially common **8.42** in defamation cases where the subject matter of the defamation is the claimant's private life. It is not unusual, for example, for a claimant to be required to produce private diaries or letters from the material time. It was this requirement which ultimately led to Lord Archer's undoing. The obligation to disclose relevant material regardless of its private nature is a consequence of the public policy that considers the exposure of truth to be the paramount good.

Now that the protection of private life is in principle recognized as having an **8.43** importance to society equal to that of Article 10 rights, the courts may become less ready to order disclosure of private materials. For example, if a media defendant seeks disclosure of a claimant's private letters or diaries in order to attempt to prove the truth of published allegations concerning the claimant's personal life, which lack any element of legitimate public interest, is there now an Article 8 argument for resisting the application? To take a more concrete example, would the court now order someone in the position in which the late singer Michael Jackson stood to submit to an intrusive medical examination so that a newspaper could seek to prove allegations about his personal medical history?[71] It is submitted that the

---

R Clayton QC and H Tomlinson QC, *The Law of Human Rights* (2nd edn, Oxford University Press 2009) para 12.19; *Gatley on Libel and Slander* (n 8) paras 1.14–1.15.

[69] CPR 31.6.

[70] P Matthews and H Malek, *Disclosure* (4th edn, Sweet & Maxwell 2012) paras 25.10 *et seq*. See also *Civil Procedure 2015* (Sweet & Maxwell) vol 1, para 31.3.36, which states that a party may be able to resist the disclosure of confidential information relating to a third party where the disclosure would involve a breach of the third party's Art 8 right to respect for private life: *Webster v Governors of Ridgway Foundation School* [2009] EWHC 1140 (QB). Disclosure may be justified under Art 8(2): *R v Secretary of State for the Home Dept, ex p Kingdom of Belgium* and *R v Secretary of State for the Home Dept, ex p Amnesty International* (DC, 15 February 2000). A party may also be able to resist disclosure of confidential information relating to another party to protect third party sources (*Gaskin v UK* (1990) 12 EHRR 36) or that party's mental or physical health (*R v Mid Glamorgan Family Health Services, ex p Martin* [1995] 1 WLR 110, CA). For disclosure of journalistic sources and Art 10 (freedom of expression) see *Goodwin v UK* (1996) 22 EHRR 123 and *Financial Times v UK* (2010) 50 EHRR 46.

[71] *Jackson* (n 29).

answers would not now depend solely on whether the disclosure was necessary to establish the truth of the issues in the case: the court would be bound to weigh the competing public interests between the exposure of truth, on the one hand, and the protection of private life, on the other.[72]

### (2) Recognition of the Potential Injustice of the Defence of Truth

#### (a) *Cases where truth is not an absolute defence*

**8.44**  The injustice that may be caused by the rule that truth is always a defence has been acknowledged by both case law and statute.[73] Causes of action in confidentiality and conspiracy have both been recognized as affording a limited means for avoiding this injustice of the law of defamation. Parliament has addressed the issue in relation to certain previous criminal convictions in the Rehabilitation of Offenders Act 1974,[74] and generally in the Data Protection Acts.[75]

**8.45**  Defamation was not an available cause of action in the early cases applying the law of confidentiality to disclosure of personal information, since the publications were not defamatory. But in 1967 the claim by the Duchess of Argyll for an injunction to prevent the disclosure proposed to be made by the duke clearly could have been brought in defamation, albeit with no prospect of obtaining an interim injunction,[76] because the information to be revealed was defamatory as well as personal. Although the duchess was in all likelihood seeking to protect her reputation as well as her privacy, the law of confidentiality was used in that case to avoid the possibility and potential injustice of permitting the purveyor of somebody else's secrets to defend himself by showing the secrets to be true. The law of contract has also been recognized as providing a remedy to this potential

---

[72]  Medical examinations are commonly ordered in personal injury cases where it is 'reasonable in the interests of justice so to order': *Lane v Willis* [1972] 1 WLR 326, 333. This is so despite the recognition that an order for a medical examination is an 'invasion of personal liberty': *ibid*, 333. The enactment of Art 8 may make little difference to the practice of ordering medical examinations in personal injury cases, where the state of the claimant's health is usually the primary question in the action. In a defamation action where, as in Michael Jackson's case, part of the claimant's complaint is the offence caused by the invasion by the media of his private life, it may be that the court will take a different view as to the balance between a claimant's Art 8 rights and the importance of establishing truth. In *Bennett v Compass Group UK and Ireland Ltd* [2002] EWCA Civ 642, [2002] ICR 1177 [41], [72], where an order was sought for disclosure of medical records, the Court stated that any such order must be clearly and carefully drafted and must ensure that no Convention rights are infringed. See also *OCS Group v Wells* [2008] EWHC 919 (QB), [2009] 1 WLR 1895.

[73]  In 2006, with the introduction of national uniform defamation laws, Australia abandoned any public benefit/public interest requirement and reasserted the absolute nature of the defence of truth: see n 18, and the discussion in Rolph (n 18), and the same author's 'Preparing for a full-scale invasion? Truth, privacy and defamation', Sydney Law School Legal Studies Research Paper No 07/85, November 2007.

[74]  See 8.47 *et seq*.

[75]  See ch 7.

[76]  *Argyll (Duchess) v Argyll (Duke)* [1967] Ch 302. See 8.50 *et seq*.

injustice, where the defendant is bound by a contractual confidentiality clause.[77] The tort of conspiracy can also be invoked in extreme cases.[78]

In such cases, the purpose of finding a cause of action other than defamation has **8.46** often been to obtain an interim injunction, generally unavailable in a defamation case because of the strict rule against prior restraint.[79] But of course a prior restraint will not necessarily be imposed merely because a cause of action other than defamation is relied on.[80] Moreover, there may be reasons, unrelated to prior restraint, for relying on another tort, such as the desire to avoid a defence of justification, or to evade the one-year limitation period that applies to defamation.[81] In the United States of America the tort of privacy developed in circumstances where no prior restraint could be obtained, even in a tort other than defamation.

### (b) The Rehabilitation of Offenders Act 1974

The Rehabilitation of Offenders Act 1974 'was intended to allow persons convicted **8.47** of the less serious offences to become, after a suitable period of time, rehabilitated. It was intended to allow the stain of the conviction to be wiped from the record.'[82] The Act provides that a person with a criminal conviction undergoes a specified period of rehabilitation running from the date of that conviction. At the end of the rehabilitation period the convicted person 'shall be treated for all purposes in law as a person who has not committed or been charged with or prosecuted for or convicted of or sentenced for the offence or offences which were the subject of the conviction'.[83] The period of rehabilitation is largely determined by the type of sentence passed. For instance, all offences for which an adult offender receives a sentence of more than six months and up to two and a half years will have a rehabilitation period of four years. There is no rehabilitation period for offences for which a sentence of four years and over is imposed. When a conviction is spent, the convicted person does not normally have to disclose his or her conviction. If questions are asked about previous convictions, they are treated as not relating to spent convictions.[84]

---

[77] *Attorney General v Barker* [1990] 3 All ER 257. Whether a contractual restraint is as effective as the Court there held is now open to question: *Vogt v Germany* (1996) 21 EHRR 205, paras 43–4. However, for a more recent example of an effective contractual restraint, see *Prince of Wales v Associated Newspapers Ltd* [2006] EWCA Civ 1776, [2008] Ch 57.

[78] *Gulf Oil (GB) v Page* [1987] Ch 327. Cf *Femis Bank (Anguilla) v Lazar* [1991] Ch 391. Conspiracy is tortious where two or more people agree to do an unlawful act, or to do a lawful act by unlawful means: damage is an essential ingredient.

[79] Set out in 8.51–8.52.

[80] See 8.57 *et seq.*

[81] See *Hannon* (n 6), where the defendant unsuccessfully applied to strike out claims brought in confidence and misuse of private information on the basis that they should have been brought in defamation, in which case they would have been statute-barred.

[82] *Thomas v Commissioner of Police for the Metropolis* [1997] QB 813, 823 (Sir Richard Scott V-C).

[83] Rehabilitation of Offenders Act 1974, s 4(1).

[84] Rehabilitation of Offenders Act 1974, s 4(2).

**8.48**  The Act does not impose any penalty for the publication of a spent conviction. However, it stipulates that where the subject of the spent conviction sues in defamation a defence of justification, which would normally succeed simply by proving the conviction,[85] will be defeated on proof of malice.[86] The defence of absolute privilege is also subject to a limitation; it will only be upheld if the spent conviction was referred to as part of court proceedings (which is normally all that is required) and if the spent conviction was ruled to be admissible evidence in those proceedings. So if the judge ruled during the course of a criminal trial that evidence of a spent conviction was inadmissible, publication of that information would not be protected by the defence of absolute privilege.[87] Spent convictions will generally be inadmissible in all but criminal trials unless their non-admission will mean that 'justice cannot be done'.[88]

**8.49**  Despite the apparent intention of the 1974 Act, it has been held that Article 8(1) is not engaged by the disclosure of a spent conviction, which is a matter of public record. The 1974 Act conferred certain privileges, but the continued disclosure of a conviction (in the case in question, by endorsement on a driving licence) did not constitute an interference with the claimant's private life within Article 8(1).[89] It has also been held that the 1974 Act does not render spent convictions confidential.[90]

### (3) The Conflict between the Rule against Prior Restraint and the Right to Privacy

#### (a) *The rule against prior restraint: priority for freedom of speech*

**8.50**  The conflict between truth as an absolute defence in defamation proceedings and the right to privacy is seen nowhere more clearly than in the question as to what

---

[85] Civil Evidence Act 1968, s 13(1) as amended by Defamation Act 1996, s 12.

[86] Rehabilitation of Offenders Act 1974, s 8(5). Malice was taken in *Herbage v Pressdram Ltd* [1984] 1 WLR 1160 to mean 'an irrelevant, spiteful or improper motive'. Malice is a familiar concept in defamation, but it is hard to find examples of it where the publication complained of is true. See generally *Horrocks v Lowe* [1975] AC 135; *Gatley on Libel and Slander* (n 8) para 18.17; and *Silkman v Heard* (QBD, 28 February 2001) (Eady J). But what is an improper motive in this context? In *KJO v XIM* [2011] EWHC 1768 (QB) [15], it was envisaged by Eady J, without deciding the point, to be the dominant purpose of injuring the claimant's reputation. Perhaps the matter should be assessed by reference to the public interest and the factors set out in Art 8(2). However, see 8.49.

[87] Rehabilitation of Offenders Act 1974, s 8(6). Additionally, if this fact were published in regard to a defendant or one of his or her witnesses prior to the giving of a verdict by the jury there would also be a viable action in contempt. Publication of a fair, accurate, and contemporaneous report of judicial proceedings is otherwise protected by absolute privilege, which also protects (in particular) words spoken in the course of judicial proceedings (including statements made out of court such as by witnesses in making witness statements or in making a complaint to the police), and in the course of proceedings in Parliament.

[88] Rehabilitation of Offenders Act 1974, s 7(2)–(3); *Thomas* (n 82).

[89] *R v DVLA, ex p Pearson* [2002] EWHC 2482 (Admin). See also the brief discussion by Eady J in *Silkman* (n 85), reproduced in *Gatley on Libel and Slander* (n 8) para 18.14, n 65, and in *KJO v XIM* [2011] EWHC 1768 (QB).

[90] *L v Law Society* [2008] EWCA Civ 811, as to which see also *KJO* (n 86) [17] *et seq.*

principles should govern the grant of interim injunctions in cases concerning the publication of personal information.

Since the Judicature Acts fused equity and law,[91] the rule in defamation cases has **8.51** long been clear and simple. The courts have always refused applications for interim injunctions where the defendant swears that he will seek to justify the defamatory imputation at trial, and the proposed defence cannot be shown to be a sham or have no chance of success.[92]

The rationale of this rule—which applies with equal force where the promised defence **8.52** is fair comment[93] or privilege,[94] or where there is a doubt as to whether the words complained of are defamatory[95]—has been twofold. First, there has been the need to avoid trespassing on the domain of the jury, whose function it has long been[96] to determine issues of meaning, justification, and fair comment. That element of the rationale is now moribund.[97] Second—the dominant factor in modern times, as use of the jury has declined—is the priority given to freedom of speech. As was said by the Court of Appeal as long ago as 1891: 'The right of free speech is one which it is for the public interest that individuals should possess, and, indeed, that they should exercise without impediment, as long as no wrongful act is done.'[98] No wrongful act is considered to be done if the words are true or fair comment, or if they are not found to have been defamatory. Those are issues for the judge (or jury) at trial, and '[t]he court will not prejudice the issue by granting an injunction in advance of publication'.[99] The same principle applies in malicious falsehood, even though there is no need for sensitivity to the role of the jury, since mode of trial has long been by judge alone.[100]

Historically, the priority accorded to freedom of speech has on occasion been **8.53** extended so as to trump the principles protected by other causes of action, but only where on the facts the other cause of action was closely linked to a claim in defamation. In *Sim v Heinz*,[101] for example, an actor applied for an injunction to restrain the appropriation of his voice for advertising. The decision prevented the development in England of what Americans call the tort of appropriation of

---

[91] There was no effective power of prior restraint in defamation before 1854, when the Common Law Procedure Act was passed. The new power was not used until after the reforms of the 1870s.

[92] *Coulson v Coulson* (1887) TLR 846; *Bonnard v Perryman* [1891] 2 Ch 269; *Khashoggi v IPC Magazines Ltd* [1986] 1 WLR 1412; *Holley v Smyth* [1998] 1 QB 726; *Greene* (n 64). But an injunction will be granted in an appropriate case: *ZAM v CFW* [2011] EWHC (QB) 476, [2013] EMLR 27 [23].

[93] *Fraser v Evans* [1969] QB 349.

[94] *Harakas v Baltic Mercantile & Shipping Exchange Ltd* [1982] 1 WLR 958.

[95] *Coulson* (n 92).

[96] By Fox's Libel Act of 1792 the question of 'libel or no libel' was reserved to the jury.

[97] The effect of Defamation Act 2013, s 11, which (by s 16(7)) applies to any action for defamation commenced after 31 December 2013, is that trial by jury will be as rare in defamation as it long has been in personal injury claims.

[98] *Bonnard* (n 92) 284.

[99] *Fraser* (n 93) 361 (Lord Denning MR).

[100] *Bestobell Paints Ltd v Bigg* [1975] FSR 421, considered in *Boehringer Ingleheim Ltd v Vetplus Ltd* [2007] EWCA Civ 583, [2007] FSR 29.

[101] [1959] 1 WLR 313.

image.[102] Because no prior restraint injunction was available in defamation, the claimant abandoned a libel claim, and relied only on passing off, in which interim injunctions are commonly granted. He argued that it did not matter if the damage in the passing-off action was the same as the damage in the libel action, as he was entitled to the injunction on the basis of his claim in respect of passing off. The Court of Appeal overruled his choice, holding that it would be inappropriate to grant an injunction in passing off, when it would be refused in respect of the same facts if the claim were pursued in libel.

**8.54** In *Woodward v Hutchins*,[103] perhaps the high-water mark of priority given to freedom of expression, four pop stars applied for an injunction to stop their former agent, who was bound by a confidential relationship of employment, disclosing to the public their discreditable behaviour. They put their claim in breach of confidence, breach of contract, and defamation, and Slynn J granted an injunction in confidence, but on appeal it was discharged. Lord Denning referred to the rule against prior restraint in defamation and applied it to confidentiality, saying: 'As there should be "truth in advertising," so there should be truth in publicity. The public should not be misled. So it seems to me that the breach of confidential information is not a ground for granting an injunction.' But the Court regarded the claim in confidence as interwoven with the defamation claim. As Lord Denning said, 'I cannot help feeling that the plaintiffs' real complaint here is that the words are defamatory: and as they cannot get an interlocutory injunction on that ground, nor should they on confidential information'. That was one of the grounds on which an injunction was refused in *Terry (previously 'LNS') v Persons Unknown*,[104] a claim brought in confidence and misuse of private information, where the judge concluded that the nub of the applicant's true complaint was the protection of his reputation, so that the rule in *Bonnard v Perryman* applied.[105]

---

[102] See 3.80 *et seq.*

[103] [1977] 1 WLR 760, 764. Similarly, Lord Brabourne failed to win an injunction in *Brabourne v Hough* [1981] FSR 79.

[104] [2010] EWHC 119 (QB), [2010] EMLR 16. See also *BKM Ltd v BBC* [2009] EWHC 3151 (Ch), where Mann J was concerned that protection of reputation was a 'significant underlying factor' in a claim brought to protect the privacy rights of the residents of a care home. In *Hannon* (n 6), the same judge rejected an application to strike out claims in confidence and misuse of private information, made on the basis that claims for damage to reputation could only properly be made in defamation. The judge found that the claims contained a heavy reputational element, but other causes of action were disclosed which were not *de minimis*, and the nub of the claims could not be said to have been damage to reputation only. The application was of great potential significance in an area of developing law, but was not suitable for determination on an application to strike out.

[105] By contrast, in *A v B plc* [2001] 1 WLR 2341, on the defendant's application to Jack J to set aside his order on the merits, the claimant sought an injunction restraining the publication in a newspaper of information (that was clearly defamatory of him) about an extramarital affair. He admitted that the gist of the information was true and brought proceedings in breach of confidence and/or privacy and breach of copyright. But for his admission that the information was true, the case could equally have been brought in libel. Granting the injunction in confidence (not in privacy), the judge took the claimant's choice of cause of action at face value and did not apply the *Bonnard v Perryman* rule, but instead applied *American Cyanamid* (as to which see 8.59). The Court

Notwithstanding the defamation rule, the courts have on occasion been prepared **8.55** to respect the claimant's choice not to sue in libel, even though the information is defamatory, but in another cause of action. The Duchess of Argyll obtained an injunction[106] framed in confidence but in respect of information which was plainly regarded as immoral and would have been defamatory by the standards of the day, despite the fact that the duke relied on truth.[107] The duchess conceded that she could not ask for interlocutory relief in respect of statements that were 'merely defamatory' and not confidential. Crucially, the confidentiality of the information arose out of the relationship of marriage, and the public interest in the institution of marriage prevailed over the principle that truth justifies any publication. There was no discussion in the judgment of the general principle as to when freedom of expression is overridden by the need to protect private life.

Similarly, the jockey John Francome's choice to sue in confidentiality was upheld, **8.56** notwithstanding that the information in question was also defamatory of him. The information had been derived from illegal bugging of his home, and that illegality was decisive.[108] In such pre-Human Rights Act cases, judges did not expressly recognize that respect for private life was a value upheld by English law. Where freedom of expression has not prevailed, the decision has been based on other values (such as the public interest in upholding the institution of marriage in *Argyll*, or unlawful behaviour by the defendant in *Francome*). Changes in society have made it increasingly difficult to identify such values,[109] which in any case have now been substantially supplanted by the modern focus on Convention rights.

The existence of the roadblock created by *Bonnard v Perryman* naturally leads claim- **8.57** ants to seek other routes to their goal of an interim injunction. Where the tactic is sufficiently transparent, the rule will still be applied. It is true, of course, that claimants may choose their cause of action, where more than one is available to them.[110] But their choice is not the determinant for the purpose of interim injunctions:

> The rule prohibiting the grant of an injunction where the claim is in defamation does not extend to claims based on other causes of action despite the fact that a

---

of Appeal ([2002] EWCA Civ 337, [2003] QB 195) allowed the newspaper defendant's appeal, but it did so because, on the facts, the injunction should not have been granted in confidence. The Court did not have to address the relationship between claims in confidence and claims in defamation.

[106] *Argyll* (n 76).

[107] *Argyll* (n 76) 309. There is no reference to the point in either the report of the defendant's argument or the judgment.

[108] *Francome v Mirror Group Newspapers Ltd* [1984] 1 WLR 892, 899.

[109] See *eg Stephens v Avery* [1988] Ch 449.

[110] *Joyce v Sengupta* [1993] 1 WLR 337, 342 (Sir Donald Nicholls V-C); *Ajinomoto Sweeteners Europe SAS v Asda Stores Ltd* [2010] EWCA Civ 609, [2011] QB 497 [28] (Sedley LJ): 'A great many fact situations are able to be litigated through more than one cause of action, and the choice of them is as often tactical as jurisprudential'. However, the demands of case management led Eady J to assert in *Tesco Stores Ltd v Guardian News and Media Ltd* [2009] EMLR 5 [48], that: 'There is no right to plead a cause of action just because it exists. The court is there to do justice and, especially nowadays under the CPR, to have regard to the overriding objective.' The judge held that on the

claim in defamation might also have been brought, but if the claim based on some other cause of action is in reality a claim brought to protect the plaintiffs' reputation and the reliance on the other cause of action is merely a device to circumvent the rule, the overriding need to protect freedom of speech means that the same rule be applied.[111]

**8.58** Parker LJ's warning in *Gulf Oil v Page*[112] that the court would scrutinize with the greatest care any case where a cause of action in conspiracy was joined to a cause of action in defamation, and would require to be satisfied that the joinder was not simply an attempt to circumvent the rule in defamation, must apply with equal force where the claim is in defamation and confidence, or defamation and misuse of private information, or defamation and harassment, or not (at least not expressly) in defamation at all.[113] Where a claim is brought in another cause of action to avoid the rule in defamation, objections of abuse of process might be raised.[114] Nor can the outcome depend on the label that the claimant happens to apply to his or her claim: it is a matter for the court to decide whether the principle of free speech applies or not.[115]

### (b) Prior restraint in non-defamation cases

**8.59** In the general run of confidence cases, where the claimant is concerned to prevent the imminent publication of confidential or secret information, the starting point

---

facts of that case there was no legitimate objective in pursuing a claim in malicious falsehood. See also *Ashley v Chief Constable of Sussex* [2008] UKHL 25, [2008] 1 AC 962.

[111] *Service Corp International plc v Channel Four TV* [1999] EMLR 83, 89–90 (Lightman J) (claim brought in confidence, copyright and trespass, following a letter before action which expressed concern for the plaintiff's reputation); *ZAM v CFW* [2013] EWHC 662 (QB), [2013] EMLR 27 [21]. Cf *Gulf Oil v Page* [1987] 1 Ch 327, 334 where an injunction was granted in conspiracy to injure, but Parker LJ warned that the Court would be alert to ensure that a cause of action in conspiracy was not used to get round the rule in *Bonnard v Perryman*; and *Microdata v Rivendale* [1991] FSR 681, where an injunction was granted on the ground of interference with contractual relations, but Griffiths LJ observed at 688 that if the Court were to conclude that though the plaintiff had framed his claim in a cause of action other than defamation but nevertheless his principal purpose was to seek damages for defamation, it would refuse interlocutory relief. If, on the other hand, the Court was satisfied that there was some other serious interest to be protected such as confidentiality, and that that outweighed considerations of free speech, then the Court would grant an injunction.

[112] *Gulf Oil* (n 111) 334.

[113] Speech or writing can amount to harassment: *Thomas v News Group Newspapers Ltd* [2001] EWCA Civ 1233, [2002] EMLR 4. 'Interim injunctions are increasingly granted to restrain harassment in the form of campaigns of vilification. Some of these campaigns involve the publication of defamatory allegations (others involve indecent images, or the publication of private or personal information). However, before granting an interim injunction on the basis of harassment, the court considers first whether reliance on the law of harassment is an attempt to by-pass the law on freedom of speech, and will only grant the injunction if satisfied that that is not the case': *ZAM* (n 111) [21]; see also *Howlett v Holding* [2006] EWHC 41 (QB) [10]–[15] and ch 6.

[114] As they were—unsuccessfully—on an application to strike out in *Hannon* (n 6). See in particular *McKennitt* (n 37) [79].

[115] *Terry* (n 68) [88]. See also *Hannon* (n 6).

has naturally been that the information is true, but freedom of speech has not been given priority over the need to protect confidentiality. Before the Human Rights Act 1998 (HRA), the test applied by the courts in considering interim relief in confidence cases was that prescribed by *American Cyanamid*,[116] which required the court first to determine whether there was a serious question to be tried, and next to consider whether the balance of convenience lay in favour of granting or refusing interlocutory relief, which was primarily a question of whether or not either party could be adequately compensated by an award of damages or by an undertaking as to damages.[117]

However, s 12 HRA introduced a new test which, by s 12(1), applies in all cases **8.60** where the court is considering whether to grant relief which, if granted, might affect the exercise of the Convention right to freedom of expression. By s 12(3), no such relief is to be granted so as to restrain publication before trial unless the court is satisfied that the applicant is likely to establish that publication should not be allowed.[118]

Initially, there were conflicting views of the effect of s 12(3). In *Douglas v Hello!* **8.61** *Ltd*[119] the Court of Appeal held that the test in freedom of expression cases was whether the court was satisfied that the applicant was likely to establish at trial that publication should not be allowed,[120] which presented a higher hurdle for

---

[116] *American Cyanamid Co v Ethicon Ltd* [1975] AC 396. There are dicta to the contrary, *eg* in *Schering Chemicals Ltd v Falkman Ltd* [1982] QB 1, a confidentiality case, where Lord Denning MR said at 16–17: 'The freedom of the press is extolled as one of the great bulwarks of liberty. It is entrenched in the constitutions of the world. But it is often misunderstood. I will first say what it does not mean. It does not mean that the press is free to ruin a reputation or to break a confidence, or to pollute the course of justice or to do anything that is unlawful. I will next say what it does mean. It means that there is to be no censorship. No restraint should be placed on the press as to what they should publish. Not by a licensing system. Nor by executive direction. Nor by court injunction. It means that the press is to be free from what Blackstone calls "previous restraint" or what our friends in the United States—co-heirs with us of Blackstone—call "prior restraint." The press is not to be restrained in advance from publishing whatever it thinks right to publish. It can publish whatever it chooses to publish. But it does so at its own risk. It can "publish and be damned." Afterwards—after the publication—if the press has done anything unlawful—it can be dealt with by the courts. If it should offend—by interfering with the course of justice—it can be punished in proceedings for contempt of court. If it should damage the reputation of innocent people, by telling untruths or making unfair comment, it may be made liable in damages. But always afterwards. Never beforehand. Never by previous restraint.'

[117] The rule in *Bonnard v Perryman* was not, of course, overtaken by *Cyanamid*: see *J Trevor & Sons v Solomon* (14 December 1977, CA (Civ Div) Transcript No 484C of 1977); *Herbage v Times Newspapers Ltd, The Times*, 30 April 1981, CA; *Herbage v Times Newspapers Ltd* [1984] 1 WLR 1160, CA.

[118] Additionally, s 12(4) obliges the court to have particular regard to the importance of the Convention right to freedom of expression and—where the proceedings relate to material which the respondent claims, or which appears to the court, to be journalistic, literary, or artistic material (or to conduct connected with such material)—to (a) the extent to which (i) the material has, or is about to, become available to the public; or (ii) it is, or would be, in the public interest for the material to be published; and (b) any relevant privacy code. See 12.09 *et seq* and 12.68 *et seq*.

[119] *Douglas v Hello! Ltd* [2001] QB 967.

[120] *Douglas* (n 119) [153].

the applicant to surmount than the *American Cyanamid* requirement to show merely that there was a serious question. By contrast, in *Imutran Ltd v Uncaged Campaigns Ltd* [121] the Vice-Chancellor perceived the difference between the tests to be slight: he considered the effect of s 12 on applications for prior restraint in confidence cases and concluded that 'the difference between the two [tests] is so small that I cannot believe that there will be many (if any) cases which would have succeeded under the *American Cyanamid* test but will now fail because of the terms of s 12(3)'.[122]

**8.62**  The matter was settled by the House of Lords in *Cream Holdings Ltd v Banerjee*.[123] The result is that the intention of s 12(3) has been held to impose a higher threshold than *American Cyanamid* in cases involving interim injunctions to restrain publication. However, there can be no single, rigid standard governing all applications for interim orders. On its proper construction, the effect of s 12(3) is to make the likelihood of success at the trial an essential element in the court's consideration of whether to make an interim order, so that:

> ...the court is not to make an interim restraint order unless satisfied the applicant's prospects of success at the trial are sufficiently favourable to justify such an order being made in the particular circumstances of the case. As to what degree of likelihood makes the prospects of success 'sufficiently favourable', the general approach should be that courts will be exceedingly slow to make interim restraint orders where the applicant has not satisfied the court he will probably ('more likely than not') succeed at the trial.[124]

**8.63**  The *Cream Holdings* test holds good for other cases which involve freedom of expression,[125] including of course misuse of private information.[126] However, it does not apply to defamation or malicious falsehood, where the rule in *Bonnard v Perryman* continues to apply. This was confirmed as recently as 2004 by the Court of Appeal in *Greene v Associated Newspapers Ltd*,[127] in which the rule in *Bonnard v Perryman* was directly challenged in the light of the HRA and the Strasbourg jurisprudence. The Court was prepared to accept that reputation was a right

---

[121] [2001] 2 All ER 385 [17].

[122] The Court of Appeal in *A v B plc* (n 105) [11(iii)] described the guidance provided by the Vice-Chancellor as 'useful'.

[123] [2004] UKHL 44, [2005] 1 AC 253.

[124] Which takes litigants back to a regime not dissimilar from the pre-*Cyanamid* rule that a plaintiff had to show a *prima facie* case, interpreted by Lord Diplock in *Cyanamid* as involving 'a rule of practice so well established as to constitute a rule of law that precluded [Graham J and the Court of Appeal] from granting any interim injunction unless, upon the evidence adduced by both the parties on the hearing of the application the applicant had satisfied the court that on the balance of probabilities the acts of the other party sought to be enjoined would, if committed, violate the applicant's legal rights': [1975] AC 396, 405.

[125] See *eg Boehringer Ingleheim Ltd v Vetplus Ltd* [2007] EWCA Civ 583, [2007] FSR 29 (trade mark infringement and passing off); *Georgallides v Etzin* [2005] EWHC 1790 (QB) (harassment).

[126] See *eg Lord Browne of Madingley v Associated Newspapers Ltd* [2007] EWCA Civ 295, [2008] QB 103.

[127] *Greene* (n 64).

protected by Article 8, and had the benefit of reading the opinions of the House of Lords in *Re S*,[128] but in effect continued to give presumptive priority to freedom of speech, concluding that the claimant's Article 8 reputation right (privacy rights seem not to have been in issue) could not be given great weight before the trial of the action, compared with the importance of the freedom of the press to report matters of public interest. That was in part because until it was established at trial whether the words were true, or comment, or privileged, it was not possible to say whether a wrong had been done at all; there is, after all, nothing tortious in publishing defamatory words—the wrong lies in publishing words that are defamatory and false (and not comment or not privileged). Thus the defamation rule survived s 12(3) HRA, a provision which the Court found not to be intended to 'whittle down' a defendant's right to freedom of expression before trial.

The courts therefore continue to refuse applications for interim injunctions where **8.64** the claim is brought in defamation or where, on analysis, the claimant's main concern is protection of reputation, whenever the defendant says or (when the application is made without notice), is likely to say,[129] that the defamatory imputation will be justified at trial (or privilege or fair comment will be pleaded), unless the proposed defence is shown to have no prospect of success. It is true, of course, that other arguments can be adduced in support of this approach. There is no doubt that in most cases it will be impossible for the judge hearing an interlocutory application, on paper, to decide whether or not the defendant will be able to prove the truth of the words complained of;[130] whereas it is generally easier to determine whether a claimant has a reasonable expectation of privacy, and then to weigh the competing Convention rights. There is also the public policy argument that—in defamation—damages are more likely to prove an adequate remedy, whereas in privacy cases they are not.

### (c) Can freedom of speech continue to receive priority?

However, it is very doubtful whether the survival of the common law prior- **8.65** ity for freedom of speech is compatible with the modern jurisprudence of

---

[128] [2004] UKHL 47, [2005] 1 AC 593. The speeches in *Re S* were delivered after argument in *Greene* but were read by the Court before judgment. That may explain why the Court appears not to have given full vent to the 'intense focus' on the conflicting rights that the House of Lords required in *Re S*.

[129] It is realistic to assume that the media will not publish defamatory material that they do not believe they can defend, so it is proper to make the assumption that, when served, they will rely on the rule in *Bonnard v Perryman*. That assumption was made by Tugendhat J in *Terry* (n 68).

[130] If an example were needed, it is provided by *Greene* (n 64) [34]–[41], where the Court of Appeal examined competing technical evidence. The central issue was whether emails attributed to the claimant had been forged. The Court concluded that the claimant's new evidence made it more likely than not that she would establish at trial that the emails were forgeries. But in the absence of 'knock-out' evidence they could not hold that the claimant would clearly succeed, so the judge's refusal of an injunction had to stand. However, there is a limit to the force of this argument, for the same difficulties should not arise where the defendant intends to rely on honest opinion or privilege, where in many cases the judge should be able to determine the issue at the interlocutory stage.

Convention rights. As Sedley LJ has said: 'The European Court of Human Rights has always recognised the high importance of free media of communication in a democracy, but its jurisprudence does not—and could not consistently with the Convention itself—give Article 10(1) the presumptive priority which is given, for example, to the First Amendment in the jurisprudence of the United States' courts.'[131] There is no bright-line rule against prior restraint in the Strasbourg jurisprudence: the position of the European Court of Human Rights has recently been stated to be that 'Article 10 does not prohibit prior restraints on publication or bans on distribution as such, [but]...the dangers which restrictions of that kind pose for a democratic society are such that they call for the most careful scrutiny'.[132]

**8.66** It is trite that Convention rights under Articles 8 and 10 are both important civilized values, but that neither can be given effect in full measure without restricting the other. There is no question of automatic or presumptive priority for one over the other. Considering in *Campbell v MGN Ltd* how the conflicting rights should be reconciled, Lord Hoffmann suggested that the question was the extent to which it was necessary to qualify the one right in order to protect the underlying value represented by the other, the extent of the qualification being proportionate to the need.[133]

**8.67** In *Re S*, a case involving a conflict between the Article 8 rights of a child liable to be identified in the reporting of a criminal trial to the detriment of his welfare, and the Article 10 rights of the media to report criminal proceedings freely, Lord Steyn declared that it was clear from *Campbell* that neither article had as such precedence over the other; that where the values under the two articles were in conflict—an intense focus on the comparative importance of the specific rights being claimed in the individual case was necessary—the justifications for interfering with or restricting each right must be taken into account; and that the proportionality test must be applied to each.[134]

**8.68** Two particular factors have brought to a head the conflict between the presumptive priority given to Article 10 freedom of speech rights by the rule in defamation, and the Strasbourg jurisprudence, by which neither right is to be accorded priority. One is the recognition that the right to reputation is protected by Article 8, and the other is the acceptance that a claim in misuse of private information may properly protect the publication of false as well as true information. These factors are discussed in the paragraphs which follow, and a possible resolution of this conflict is considered.

---

[131] *Douglas* (n 119) [135].
[132] *Obukhova v Russia* App no 34736/03 (ECtHR, 8 January 2009) para 22.
[133] [2004] UKHL 22, [2004] 2 AC 457 [12] and [55].
[134] *Re S* (n 128) [17]. See also *Re Attorney General's Reference (No 3 of 1999)* [2009] UKHL 34, [2009] 3 WLR 142.

*(d) Article 8 as a reputation right*

As to reputation, a series of Strasbourg decisions has established that the right to **8.69** reputation is one of the rights guaranteed by Article 8 of the Convention.[135] The reasoning appears to be that a person's reputation, even if he or she is criticized in the context of a public debate, forms part of the person's personal identity and psychological integrity, and therefore falls within the scope of private life.[136] The European Court of Human Rights has not been entirely consistent in this view,[137] and there has been a recent suggestion that a distinction should be drawn between the personal integrity rights falling within Article 8 which are unrelated to the external evaluation of the individual and matters affecting reputation only, where that evaluation is decisive: 'one may lose the esteem of society—perhaps rightly so—but not one's integrity'.[138] But the distinction is in practice not a clear one, for most libels of any gravity are likely to have a direct effect on the victim's private life, and it was not repeated by the Grand Chamber in *Axel Springer AG v Germany*, where it was stated that: 'In order for art.8 to come into play...an attack on a person's reputation must attain a certain level of seriousness and in a manner causing prejudice to personal enjoyment of the right to respect for private life.'[139] It may be significant that the Grand Chamber accepted that there may be a need to verify whether the domestic courts have struck a fair balance between Article 8 and Article 10 rights: the preferred approach in the past has been to respect the balance struck by the domestic courts as within the margin of appreciation.[140]

For domestic purposes, the question has been settled by the decision of the UK **8.70** Supreme Court in the *Guardian* case,[141] in which the Court concluded that where claimants complain that the impact of publication on their reputation as a member of their community and on their relationship with other members of

---

[135] See *Radio France v France* (n 64); *Cumpana v Romania* (n 64); *Pfeifer v Austria* (n 64); *Petrina v Romania* (n 64); *Karakó v Hungary* (n 64); *Europapress v Croatia* (n 64); *Petrenco v Moldova* (n 64); *Greene* (n 64); *Polanco Torres v Spain* App no 34147/06 (ECtHR, 21 September 2010); *Axel Springer v Germany* (n 64); *Re Guardian News & Media Ltd* (n 64); *Delfi AS v Estonia* App no 64569/09, [2015] EMLR 26, para 137.

[136] *Pfeifer v Austria* (n 64) para 35.

[137] As the Court itself observed in *Karakó v Hungary* (n 64) para 23: 'In the Court's case-law, reputation has only been deemed to be an independent right sporadically': see *Petrina v Romania* (n 64) and *Armoniene v Lithuania* App no 36919/02 (ECtHR, 25 November 2008).

[138] In *Karakó v Hungary* (n 64) para 23, the applicant could not show that the attack on his reputation had so seriously interfered with his private life as to undermine his personal integrity. There was therefore no breach of Art 8.

[139] *Axel Springer v Germany* (n 64) para 83, echoed by the Grand Chamber in *Delfi AS* (n 135).

[140] *Axel Springer v Germany* (n 64) para 84. In *Delfi AS* (n 135) para 139, the Grand Chamber stated that a wide margin of appreciation would usually be afforded where domestic courts struck a balance between competing Convention rights.

[141] *Re Guardian News & Media Ltd* (n 64). For a critical examination of the Supreme Court's analysis of the reputation right established in *Karakó v Hungary* (n 64), see A Mullis and A Scott, 'The Swing of the Pendulum: reputation, expression and the re-centring of English libel law' (2012) 63(1) NILQ 25–56. However, that critique was published before the decision in *Axel Springer AG v Germany* (n 64).

that community will seriously affect their private lives, the report will engage Article 8.[142]

### (e) Protection of false information

**8.71** As for the truth or falsity of the information which the claimant seeks to protect, in the old law of confidence it was a given that the information to be protected was true. Not so with the law of misuse of private information, which may (and very often does) extend to protect information that is false.[143] Whether or not information is confidential or private may now depend on the nature of the information, not whether it is true or false. In *McKennitt v Ash* it was nonetheless argued that there was no right to privacy in respect of false statements, for which the tort of defamation provided the appropriate remedy. At first instance, the claimant had described some of the defendant's evidence as untrue, distorted or misleading, and indeed the judge found some of the allegations made in the defendant's book to be untrue. The defendant responded by advancing what Eady J described as the 'somewhat simplistic' proposition that a reasonable expectation of privacy, or indeed a duty of confidence, could not arise in respect of false allegations. The judge observed that the protection of the law would be illusory if a claimant, in relation to a long and garbled story, was obliged to spell out which of the revelations were accepted as true, and which were said to be false or distorted.[144]

---

[142] For a discussion of the differences between an Art 8 right to reputation and the particular manner in which the English law of libel protects reputation, see *W v Westminster City Council (No 2)* [2005] EWHC 102 (QB), [2005] 4 All ER 96 [281]. That was a claim against a local authority in respect of defamatory words written by a social worker and published in a report to those attending a Child Protection Conference. The claimant brought a claim in libel and also under s 7 HRA alleging that the public authority had acted incompatibly with Art 8. The claim in libel failed on the application of established principles of libel law, because the words, though false, were published on an occasion of qualified privilege and without malice. However, on the same facts, the judge held that there had been an interference by the local authority with the claimant's rights under Art 8, giving rise to damage to reputation, distress, and humiliation.

[143] Or even entirely imaginary: *P, Q and R v Quigley* [2008] EWHC 1051 (QB), where the defendant threatened to publish on the internet what he called a 'novella', in which P and Q would appear, thinly disguised, engaging in what Eady J described as 'various unsavoury and fictitious sexual activities'. 'Damages for misuse of private information are to compensate for the damage, and injury to feelings and distress, caused by the publication of information which may be either true or false': *Cooper v Turrell* [2011] EWHC 3269 (QB) [102]. 'False facts' privacy cases are becoming increasingly common. For example, in July 2010 News Group Newspapers paid damages and costs to the film actors Brad Pitt and Angelina Jolie in respect of allegations which appear not to have been defamatory, but related to the couple's private family affairs, and were described in a unilateral statement in open court simply as 'false and intrusive'. Proceedings had been issued for misuse of personal information and breach of the Data Protection Act 1998.

[144] [2005] EWHC 3003 (QB), [2006] EMLR 10 [78], where the judge referred also to his decision in *Beckham v Gibson* (QBD, 29 April 2005) and to Tugendhat J's decision in *W v Westminster City Council* (n 142), where the claimant succeeded in his claim under s 7 HRA in respect of the disclosure of false information.

The submission was repeated in the Court of Appeal, where it was argued that the **8.72** falsity of some of the defendant's words was a complete answer to the claim. To that, Buxton LJ (with whom Latham and Longmore LJJ agreed) responded:[145]

> It would not reflect well on our law if that plea were to succeed. Ms McKennitt and her advisers cannot be criticised for choosing the wrong cause of action. They came to court to contest the truth of the book's allegations, and the Judge made his findings about those allegations, because the falsity undermined the public interest defence, and not because an allegation of falsity was inherent in the basic claim itself. If it could be shown that a claim in breach of confidence was brought where the nub of the case was a complaint of the falsity of the allegations, and that that was done in order to avoid the rules of the tort of defamation, then objections could be raised in terms of abuse of process. That might be so at the interlocutory stage in an attempt to avoid the rule in *Bonnard v Perryman*: a matter, it will be recalled, that exercised this court in *Woodward v Hutchins*...That however is not this case. I would hold that provided the matter complained of is by its nature such as to attract the law of breach of confidence, then the defendant cannot deprive the claimant of his article 8 protection simply by demonstrating that the matter is untrue. Some support is given to that approach by the European cases shown to us by Mr Browne that indicate that article 8 protects 'reputation', broadly understood; but it is not necessary to rely on those cases to reach the conclusion that I have indicated.

Longmore LJ added:[146]                                                                      **8.73**

> It was then said that there was no right of privacy in relation to false statements, in respect of which the tort of defamation was, in any event, available...This argument, in my judgment, is untenable. The question in a case of misuse of private information is whether the information is private, not whether it is true or false. The truth or falsity of the information is an irrelevant inquiry in deciding whether the information is entitled to be protected and judges should be chary of becoming side-tracked into that irrelevant inquiry...[T]he fact that it may be relevant to decide the truth or falsity of matters raised in support of an article 10 claim to freedom of expression does not mean that, if matters are shown to be false, the claim to misuse of private information disappears.

### (f) The problem stated

The problem is clear enough. If a claim in confidence or misuse of private infor-   **8.74** mation can be made even when the information is false, and if reputation is itself a right protected by Article 8, how is the court to determine an application for an interim injunction founded on false private or confidential material which is also defamatory of the claimant? In that situation, the facts presented to the

---

[145] *McKennitt* (n 37) [79]–[80].

[146] *McKennitt* (n 37) [85]–[87]. In *McKennitt* the claimant made clear in evidence which of the material which she sought to prevent from being published was true or false. However, the claimant will not necessarily be criticized for declining to state whether the information is true or false, even though the court is then placed in the invidious position of having to decide whether or not to grant an injunction without knowing the full facts of the case (*eg* if the facts were true, how far the information had reached the public domain): *WER v REW* [2009] EWHC 1029 (QB), [2009] EMLR 17.

court may be identical to those presented by a claimant who chooses to make his or her claim in defamation. The only difference is the label that the claimant chooses to apply to his or her cause of action. Indeed, the problem is still more stark when the information is true (and private, or confidential, and defamatory of the claimant), because in that case the court (faced with a claim in defamation), would reject an application for an injunction summarily on *Bonnard v Perryman* principles.

**8.75** Existing authority tends to suggest that the court will first attempt to determine whether the claimant is seeking, by employing a cause of action other than defamation, to circumvent the rule in *Bonnard v Perryman*[147] and will then, depending on the outcome of that determination, either dismiss the application in accordance with that rule, or apply s 12(3) HRA, as construed by the House of Lords in *Cream Holdings v Banerjee*.[148] Very different results are likely be reached in each case, and the outcome may turn on little more than impression.

**8.76** But even if the claim is brought in defamation, how can it be right that the court should give a presumptive priority to Article 10 rights where (*ex hypothesi*) the claimant's Article 8 reputation right is also engaged, without applying the 'intense focus' mandated by Lord Steyn in *Re S*[149] to the comparative importance of the rights in contention?

*(g) Discussion in recent authority*

**8.77** These issues were considered briefly on a without notice application by Tugendhat J in *RST v UVW*,[150] where the information was arguably both private and defamatory. The applicant was a person of some public reputation who about ten years previously had sexual relations for payment with a prostitute at his home. About two years later, the prostitute reminded him of the encounters and threatened to make them public if she was not paid additional money. In consequence, she and the applicant entered into an agreement for consideration whereby it was agreed that their encounters were confidential. Shortly before the application was made, someone representing the applicant received an email from a person whose name neither the applicant nor his agent recognized, the gist of which was that the writer had a story about the applicant. It emerged that the story concerned the sexual encounters and the subsequent agreement. The claimant/public figure's agent explained that legal issues arose, whereupon the

---

[147] See 8.51–8.52. For a case where it was argued unsuccessfully on an application to strike out that the claimant was seeking, by suing in confidence and misuse of private information, to get round the one-year limitation period in defamation, see *Hannon* (n 6).
[148] [2004] UKHL 44, [2005] 1 AC 253.
[149] [2004] UKHL 47, [2005] 1 AC 593.
[150] [2009] EWHC 2448 (QB), [2010] EMLR 13.

writer expressed himself in terms that were capable of being understood as a threat to publish in any event.

An application was made, but it was advanced in confidence and privacy, not defa- **8.78** mation. The judge was concerned whether the claim was properly to be regarded as a claim to protect the applicant's privacy, or a claim to protect his reputation, but that was not a question which could be resolved on an *ex parte* hearing. As the judge observed:

> At some point, the court will have to grapple again with the question of where the principle of *Bonnard v. Perryman* applies, and where it does not, when an application is made on the basis of privacy, but it is an application to restrain publication of material which is arguably defamatory. The court will have to decide how the rule in *Bonnard v. Perryman* is to be applied in the light of such authorities as are then available as to the status of reputation as an Article 8 right and, if it is an Article 8 right, how the exercise of the ultimate balancing test referred to in *Re S* is to be applied on an interlocutory application. Whether that was this case or not remains to be seen.[151]

In January 2010 it fell to Tugendhat J to grapple with the issue again in *Terry* **8.79** *(previously 'LNS') v Persons Unknown*.[152] *Terry* was another case in which the claim was brought in confidence and misuse of private information in respect of material which appeared to be largely, if not entirely, true, but also was probably defamatory of the applicant, in the sense that it was capable of lowering the claimant in the estimation of right-thinking members of society generally.[153] The judge was able to conclude on the evidence that the applicant's true complaint was the protection of his reputation rather than his private life, and dismissed the application on the basis, *inter alia*, of the rule in *Bonnard v Perryman*. In doing so, he followed the guidance of the Court of Appeal in *Gulf Oil v Page*[154] (where the need was stressed for the court to scrutinize with the greatest care any case where an attempt might have been made to circumvent *Bonnard v Perryman*) and in *McKennitt v Ash*[155] (where Buxton LJ suggested that it might be an abuse of process to bring a claim in confidence in order to avoid the defamation rule). The judge held[156] that it was a matter for the court to decide whether the principle of free speech applied or not, and that did not depend solely on the choice of the claimant as to his cause of action.[157]

---

[151] *RST* (n 150) [33]. *RST v UVW* was decided four months before the question of the status of reputation as an Art 8 right was determined by the UK Supreme Court in *Re Guardian News & Media Ltd* (n 64).

[152] *Terry* (n 68). The decision of the Supreme Court in the *Guardian* application (n 64) was not cited to the judge, because although he handed down his judgment two days after the Supreme Court decision was released, he heard arguments a week earlier.

[153] *Terry* (n 68) [9].

[154] [1987] Ch 327.

[155] *McKennitt* (n 37) [79].

[156] In reliance on *Gulf Oil* (n 154), in particular the judgment of Ralph Gibson LJ.

[157] *Terry* (n 68) [88].

**8.80** In *Terry*, the judge produced a careful analysis of the extent to which the law of privacy gives rise to an overlap with the law of defamation, and concluded that the cases could broadly be considered in at least four different groups:[158]

(1) The first group of cases, where there is no overlap, is where the information cannot be said to be defamatory (*eg Douglas v Hello!*, and *Murray*). It is the law of confidence, privacy and harassment that is likely to govern such cases.

(2) There is a second group of cases where there is an overlap, but where it is unlikely that it could be said that protection of reputation is the nub of the claim. These are cases where the information would in the past have been said to be defamatory even though it related to matters which were involuntary, *eg* disease. There was always a difficulty in fitting such cases into defamation, but it was done because of the absence of any alternative cause of action.

(3) There is a third group of cases where there is an overlap, but no inconsistency. These are cases where the information relates to conduct which is voluntary, and alleged to be seriously unlawful, even if it is personal (*eg* sexual or financial). The claimant is unlikely to succeed whether at an interim application or (if the allegation is proved) at trial, whether under the law of defamation or the law of privacy.

(4) The fourth group of cases, where it may make a difference which law governs, is where the information relates to conduct which is voluntary, discreditable, and personal (*eg* sexual or financial) but not unlawful (or not seriously so). In defamation, if the defendant can prove one of the libel defences, he will not have to establish any public interest (except in the case of *Reynolds* privilege, where the law does require consideration of the seriousness of the allegation, including from the point of view of the claimant).[159] But if it is the claimant's choice alone that determines that the only cause of action which the court may take into account is misuse of private information, then the defendant cannot succeed unless he establishes that it comes within the public interest exception (or, perhaps, that he believes that it comes within that exception).

**8.81** The cases in the first and second categories fall fairly plainly within s 12(3) HRA, but the question remains, which test should be applied in Tugendhat J's third and (particularly) his fourth category? Plainly, as the judge made clear,[160] it is not to be determined (or at least not solely determined) by the applicant's choice of cause of action. That is just as well, for to allow that choice to be the deciding factor would be to treat the question as to the appropriate principles governing interim injunctions in a superficial and unprincipled, and possibly unlawful, way. Suppose a claimant, complaining of the possible publication of personal, defamatory matters about him, gets it wrong and brings proceedings in defamation, not misuse of private information? Suppose a claimant who is a litigant in person sets out facts relevant to both causes of action but fails to specify which he or she relies on? It

---

[158] *Terry* (n 68) [96].

[159] Presumably the same will hold good for the public interest defence under Defamation Act 2013, s 4, which replaces *Reynolds* where the cause of action arises after 31 December 2013.

[160] *Terry* (n 68) [88].

would be curious if the result of an application for an injunction on identical facts depended entirely on a tactical choice by the claimant.

But is the appropriate test for interim relief to be determined on the basis of the **8.82** court's conclusion as to what the applicant's real complaint is? That approach would be no more principled, and almost certainly less consistent, than following the claimant's choice. The determination of the applicant's real complaint will not usually be as straightforward as it was in *Terry*, where the form and content of the evidence seem to have led the judge to a clear conclusion.[161] What if the drafting is less candid than it was in *Terry*, so that the applicant's true underlying concerns are less transparent? It will hardly encourage frankness and openness with the court, qualities that are essential on without notice applications, if the court's decision is to be determined, or at least substantially influenced, by the artfulness of the drafting of the application.

### (h) A possible resolution of the problem

If, where the factual situation gives rise to a claim both in defamation and in **8.83** confidentiality or privacy, the claimant's choice of cause of action is not conclusive, and if it is recognized that in most cases the court will not be able reliably to divine the true nature of the applicant's object in seeking an injunction, some other principled criterion must be developed to resolve these difficulties. Even if it were possible to determine with confidence whether or not in a given case the applicant's true motive is the protection of reputation, it would be difficult to justify continued application of a rule which gives an automatic or at least presumptive priority to one Convention right, to the detriment of another. Indeed, Tugendhat J has spoken of the 'necessity', consequential on the recognition of reputation as an Article 8 right, of applying to defamation cases the 'ultimate balancing test' of *Re S*.[162]

It may therefore well be that when *Greene v Associated Newspapers Ltd* is revisited in **8.84** the Supreme Court or in Strasbourg, the balance which *Bonnard v Perryman* has for so long struck between the protection of reputation and the right of free speech will be modified, at least to the extent that where the information to be protected is recognizably private or confidential, so as to engage the applicant's Article 8 rights, or is such as to engage the Article 8 right to reputation, the test to be applied on interim applications would be that prescribed by s 12(3), as explained by the House of Lords in *Cream Holdings*. Section 12(4) would then introduce a public interest

---

[161] In *Hannon* (n 6), the defendant applied to strike out for abuse two claims in confidence and misuse of private information which (so it was argued) should have been brought in defamation. Mann J considered the substance of the claims, which he accepted had a 'heavy reputational element', but their 'nub' or reality could not be described as being based on damage to reputation only: there were other elements to the claims which were not *de minimis*.

[162] *Flood v Times Newspapers Ltd* [2009] EWHC 2375 (QB); [2010] EMLR 8, [142]. He was speaking in the context of a substantive defence of *Reynolds* privilege, not of interim relief.

factor into applications for injunctions in defamation. Where no Article 8 rights were engaged, as for example where the claimant was a corporation, there would be no reason to modify the existing rule.

### (4) Impact of Article 8 Rights on Substantive Defences in Defamation

**8.85**　It must be recognized that any modification of the rule in *Bonnard v Perryman* will have implications not only for the defence of truth but also for fair comment and privilege, and there is no logical reason why those implications should not extend beyond the regime for interim applications to the substantive defences at trial as well. If a claimant sues in defamation on a matter that is not only defamatory but is also private and engages his or her Article 8 rights on that account, will the court not be bound to apply the 'intense focus' mandated by *Re S* to the substantive defences in defamation? It is significant that Laws LJ has twice noted 'the common law's increasing focus in this area on the balance to be struck between public interest and individual right: between free speech and private claims, rather than on reputation as akin to a right of property'.[163]

**8.86**　The requirement for Lord Steyn's 'intense focus' on competing rights has already been held to apply to *Reynolds* public interest privilege.[164] Lord Nicholls's opinion in *Reynolds*[165] that any lingering doubts should be resolved in favour of publication can

---

[163] *Waterson v Lloyd* [2013] EWCA Civ 136, [2013] EMLR 17 [67] (fair comment); *Lait v Evening Standard* [2011] EWCA Civ 859, [2011] 1 WLR 2973 [45] (fair comment, meaning, and summary judgment on the principle in *Jameel v Dow Jones* [2005] EWCA Civ 75, [2005] QB 946). Those observations were prompted by Lord Phillips' summary of the Strasbourg jurisprudence in *Joseph v Spiller* [2010] UKSC 53, [2011] EMLR 11 [74]–[79]. See also *Euromoney Institutional Investor plc v Aviation News Ltd* [2013] EWHC 1505 (QB) [24] (Tugendhat J: threshold of seriousness to be surmounted by corporate claimant).

[164] *Flood* (n 162) [148]–[149]. The Court of Appeal agreed: [2010] EWCA Civ 804, [2010] EMLR 26 [21]. The point was not directly addressed in the Supreme Court. Lord Phillips noted that the creation of *Reynolds* privilege reflected a recognition on the part of the House of Lords that the existing law of defamation did not cater adequately for the importance of freedom of expression, and made the point that the House had well in mind that Convention rights were about to be introduced into domestic law via the HRA, and that Lord Nicholls had stressed the importance of protection of reputation: [2012] UKSC 11, [2012] 2 AC 273 [44]–[48]. That is true, as far as it goes, but the House did not have in mind that a right to reputation would be developed as a facet of Art 8 protection, nor that Art 10 would lose the pre-eminence reflected in Lord Nicholls' words, nor that the conflicting rights would be subjected to the 'ultimate balancing test' of *Re S*. Those developments were given distinctly less weight by the Supreme Court than they had been by the Court of Appeal. Nonetheless, after hearing argument on the effect of the decision, Eady J felt able to observe that: 'What seems to be emerging clearly is that the "new methodology" sanctioned by the House of Lords in 2004, both in *Campbell v MGN Ltd* and in *Re S*, originally in the context of privacy, where we had little established jurisprudence of our own, is now finding its way inexorably into the application of our well known principles of defamation': *Hunt v Times Newspapers Ltd* [2012] EWHC 1220 (QB) [13]. Eady J felt that *Reynolds* privilege provided particularly fertile ground for that development, and he would no doubt have said the same of the new statutory public interest defence which replaces *Reynolds* for causes of action accruing after 31 December 2013: Defamation Act 2013, s 4.

[165] [2001] 2 AC 127, 205 *et seq*.

no longer stand.[166] In the different context of reporting restrictions,[167] Lord Hope, after concluding that Article 8 was engaged, set out the tests to be applied:

> The question then is whether publication of the facts that the BBC wish to publish in the exercise of their right of freedom of expression under article 10 can be justified under article 8(2). The tests that must be applied are well settled. They are whether publication of the material pursues a legitimate aim, and whether the benefits that will be achieved by its publication are proportionate to the harm that may be done by the interference with the right to privacy. Any restriction of the right of freedom of expression must be subjected to very close scrutiny. But so too must any restriction on the right to privacy. The protection of private life has to be balanced against the freedom of expression guaranteed by article 10: *von Hannover v Germany* 40 EHRR 1, para 58. One must start from the position that neither article 8 nor article 10 has any pre-eminence over the other. The values that each right seeks to protect are equally important. The question is how far, as article 8(2) puts it, it is 'necessary' for the one to be qualified in order to protect the values that the other seeks to protect.

It has been suggested that Lord Hope's formulation may be adapted to defama-  **8.87** tion, so as to serve as a summary of Lord Nicholls' ten non-exhaustive criteria for *Reynolds* privilege, and to require consideration of whether publication of the material pursues a legitimate aim, and of whether the benefits achieved by publication are proportionate to the harm that may be done by interference with the right to reputation. The result, in the light of the need to apply an 'intense focus' to competing Convention rights, is that Lord Nicholls' criteria now fall to be considered separately both as they relate to freedom of expression and as they relate to the right to reputation.[168]

---

[166] *Flood* (n 162) [148]–[149]; and see n 164.
[167] *Re Attorney General's Reference (No 3 of 1999)* [2009] UKHL 34, [2010] 1 AC 145 [23].
[168] *Flood* (n 162) [149]. See also *Clift v Slough Borough Council* [2010] EWCA Civ 1484, [2011] 1 WLR 1774.

# PART III

## COMMERCIAL RIGHTS AND INTRUSION

Part III

COMMENTARY, RIGHTS AND REMEDIES

# 9

## COPYRIGHT, MORAL RIGHTS, AND THE RIGHT TO ONE'S IMAGE

*Stephen Bate and Gervase de Wilde*

## A. Introduction

UK copyright is a right created by statute and is now contained in the Copyright, **9.01** Designs and Patents Act 1988 (CDPA).[1] Copyright is mainly regarded as a means of protecting the economic interests of creators of original works. However, it has a significant role to play in protecting privacy interests. Private correspondence and diaries are obvious examples of material that may attract copyright protection in the domestic sphere. In the commercial context, examples include corporate memoranda, other documents, and recordings containing confidential information. Copyright subsists in various descriptions of 'works', such as 'literary works', 'films' and 'sound recordings' and there may be more than one copyright work in any article. For example, a recording may include a 'literary work' as well as a

---

[1] Copyrights that came into existence prior to the commencement of the CDPA are governed both by the relevant prior law and the transitional provisions under the CDPA: sch 1 CDPA.

'sound recording' for copyright purposes.[2] A copyright work may contain private information or the work may be unpublished and therefore private in that sense.[3] Copyright is apt to protect privacy interests, because it gives the copyright owner the legal right to prohibit reproductions, *ie* copying, as well as other means of dissemination.

**9.02**  It has often been said that copyright protects the form of a work, not its content; or the way in which the ideas or facts contained in the work are expressed rather than the underlying facts or ideas themselves. There is some truth in this, but the boundary between idea and expression is sometimes difficult to identify.[4] To take the example of a 'literary work', the basic approach is that what is protectable by the law of copyright consists of the actual words used in the story or words colourably similar, rather than the underlying information.[5] So, for example, there is no monopoly in the facts in a news report.[6] In the case of a sound recording, it is only a reproduction of actual sounds in the recording that may infringe as opposed to, say, a written transcript of the words in the recording. However, the transcript may infringe the copyright in an underlying literary work. In the case of an audio-visual recording, which is defined as a 'film' for copyright purposes, a reproduction of any 'still' image would be sufficient to infringe the copyright in that film.[7]

**9.03**  The protection that copyright is able to offer to privacy interests arises from its status as a property right, infringement of which is actionable subject to certain statutory exceptions.[8] Copyright is territorial, which broadly means that domestic copyright laws relate to acts done within the jurisdiction of each territory. The laws of most other countries confer copyright protection on qualifying works. This chapter does not address the content of foreign copyright laws, though it is to be noted that foreign copyrights may be enforceable in the English courts.[9]

**9.04**  Copyright does affect exercise of the right of freedom of expression under the European Convention on Human Rights (ECHR).[10] It can create a significant

---

[2] Words once fixed in a material form, in this example recorded, can give rise to a separate 'literary work'. A good example of this is interviews. See the discussion at 9.67.

[3] This chapter assumes some familiarity with copyright principles, although some of the essential principles are identified for convenience. The interested reader is referred to the major works on the subject, namely K Garnett et al, *Copinger and Skone James on Copyright* (16th edn, Sweet and Maxwell 2013); and M Vitoria et al (eds), *Laddie, Prescott, and Vitoria on the Modern Law of Copyright and Designs* (4th edn, Lexis Nexis 2011).

[4] *Laddie, Prescott, and Vitoria* (n 3) paras 3.74–3.90.

[5] There are also other cases of so-called 'altered copying', *eg* where the original collection, selection, arrangement, and structure of the material has been taken (without consent): see *Baigent & Leigh v Random House Group Ltd* [2007] EWCA Civ 247, [2007] FSR 24 [145]–[146] (Mummery LJ).

[6] See *Express Newspapers plc v News (UK) Ltd* [1990] 1 WLR 1320, 1325.

[7] s 16(3)(a), 17(4) CDPA and see *Laddie, Prescott and Vitoria* (n 3) para 7.59. See generally 9.24.

[8] ss 1(1), 28 CDPA.

[9] Regulation (EC) 44/2001, Lugano Conventions 1988 and 2007; *Pearce v Ove Arup Partnership Ltd* [1999] FSR 525; *Lucasfilm Ltd v Ainsworth* [2011] UKSC 39, [2012] 1 AC 208.

[10] *Ashdown v Telegraph Group Ltd* [2001] EWCA Civ 1142, [2002] Ch 149.

restriction on the imparting of ideas or other information. An obvious example in the present context is the authenticity of journalistic accounts, where reproduction of a copyright work may be necessary to give or add credibility to a story.

However, one of the guiding principles in this area was eloquently expressed in a **9.05** Canadian case with reference to the Canadian Constitution:[11]

> The freedom guaranteed under the Charter is a freedom to express and communi-cate ideas without restraint...It is not a freedom to use someone else's property to do so. It gives no right to anyone to use someone else's land or platform to make a speech, or someone else's printing press to publish his ideas.

In other words, it is not necessary to infringe copyright to make one's point. The circumstances in which it may nonetheless be permissible to use copyright material to do so is one of the main topics addressed in this chapter.

Once a work has been published by or with the consent of the copyright owner, **9.06** there may be less of a reason to enforce the copyright to protect a privacy inter-est. However, the publication may have been limited and the copyright owner may object to further dissemination. The exclusive rights to control reproduc-tion and publication reserved to a copyright owner may enable the prevention of further dissemination. One example where such an attempt failed (albeit not in relation to private information) was in litigation between Time Warner and Channel Four concerning the film *A Clockwork Orange*. An injunction was discharged which had prohibited the broadcaster from showing clips from the film in a programme re-examining its social and artistic importance, in circumstances where no further exhibition rights in the film had been granted after 1974 on the instructions of Time Warner. The case also illustrates how the right to control publication may have to yield to those statutory exceptions (see 9.08), which broadly protect public interests associated with the dissemi-nation of information.[12]

Commercial exploitation of copyright can run contrary to the privacy interests **9.07** of those who are included in the work in question. For example, the copyright in a photograph may belong to a photographer but the subject may not want the photographs to be distributed commercially. In appropriate circumstances, the rights of the copyright owner or of those deriving title through him are required to give way to the privacy rights of the subject.[13] Another example is biography, where the subject may object to disclosures of his private life and relationships

---

[11] *Compagnie Generale des Etablissements Michelin—Michelin and Cie v National Automobile, Aerospace, Transportation and General Workers Union of Canada* [1997] 2 FC No T-825–94; noted at 'Limitations found outside copyright law', Guibault ALAI Study Days 1998, Australian Copyright Council.

[12] *Time Warner Entertainments Co LP v Channel Four Television Corp plc* [1994] EMLR 1, CA.

[13] See eg *Hellewell v Chief Constable of Derbyshire* [1995] 1 WLR 804 and s 85 CDPA.

in reliance on the tort of misuse of private information, so interfering with the commercial exploitation of copyright in the biography. Biography is an instance of the wider effect of privacy on the print and television media. Exploitation of the copyright in newspapers or television broadcasts may be affected by those asserting third-party privacy interests, usually through the actions for misuse of private information and breach of confidence.[14]

**9.08** As indicated, the exclusive rights capable of maintaining the private nature of copyright works are subject to statutory exceptions. Most of these are set out in ch III CDPA and identify situations where various public interests in the dissemination of information and ideas, education and other social or administrative purposes override the interests of the copyright owner. In the present context, the most important of these are the so-called 'fair dealing' provisions in s 30 relating to 'current events' and to a lesser extent, 'criticism or review'. Other relevant exceptions include restrictions on the use of copyright to control publication of interviews and other documents where fixation of the spoken word gives rise to a 'literary' copyright;[15] and privacy rights in certain photographs and films.[16]

**9.09** The other main exception of relevance is the so-called 'public interest' defence preserved by s 171(3) CDPA. The decision of the Court of Appeal in *Ashdown*[17] has breathed some fresh life into it as a result of the requirements of Article 10 ECHR and the approval by the Court of Appeal of the broader approach to public interest taken in *Lion Laboratories Ltd v Evans*.[18]

**9.10** The status of copyright as a property right also brings into play the rights provided for under Article 1 of the First Protocol of the ECHR, which provides:

> Every natural or legal person is entitled to the peaceful enjoyment of his posses-sions. No one shall be deprived of his possessions except in the public interest and subject to the conditions provided for by law and by the general principles of international law.

The preceding provisions shall not, however, in any way impair the right of a state to enforce such laws as it deems necessary to control the use of property in accord-ance with the general interest or to secure the payment of taxes or other contribu-tions or penalties.

**9.11** The relevant exceptions in ch III CDPA (and the exception under s 171(3) CDPA), in particular those relating to news reporting, criticism, review, and the public interest are properly analysed under that rule in Article 1 of the First Protocol

---

[14] Use of the civil wrongs of breach of confidence and misuse of private information for the pro-tection of privacy is considered in chs 4 and 5 respectively.
[15] s 58 CDPA.
[16] s 85 CDPA.
[17] *Ashdown* (n 10).
[18] [1985] QB 526, CA.

which relates to control of use of property.[19] Although copyright may restrict derivative expression, it is essential for the encouragement of creative expression. Inadequate protection for the fruits of the skill and labour put into original works would have a chilling effect on creative endeavour.[20] Copyright protection may help to preserve the private nature of an unpublished work. That said, the case law of the European Court of Human Rights under Article 10 establishes the vital importance of the press as a 'public watchdog', on whom it is incumbent to impart ideas and information of public interest.[21]

The relevant provisions of the ECHR incorporated into domestic law raise a num-  **9.12** ber of issues in the context of copyright, privacy, and the media. Their proper analysis depends on the interplay between Article 1 of the First Protocol and Articles 8 and 10 ECHR. First, where copyright does come into conflict with Article 10(1) on the facts of a particular case, are the various statutory and common law defences to an infringement claim adequate to protect those rights? Secondly, does the exclusive right of a copyright owner to prohibit first publication amount to an impermissible restriction of the freedom of expression of those who wish to publish the work without such authorization?

There may well be situations where all three rights are in play: those of the copy-  **9.13** right owner under Article 1 of the First Protocol, those of a third party under Article 8, and those of a media organization under Article 10. Thus, to what extent do statute and common law recognize circumstances in which the privacy rights of the subject of a work (or of other persons who may be featured in it) trump those of the copyright owner; and are those circumstances compatible with the rights of the copyright owner and those of the media? Does the traditional reconciliation of the competing rights under the CDPA require revision, and if so to what extent have the courts begun that process?

This chapter provides a brief restatement of some essential principles of copy-  **9.14** right law as relevant to the protection of privacy interests. It goes on to address the balance between copyright, privacy, and freedom of expression. In so doing, it examines how copyright can be used to further privacy interests in unpublished works and how the statutory and other limits to exploitation of copyright works operate in the context of news reporting and other publications. Section D of this chapter addresses the topic of 'Copyright and the Privacy of Third Parties'.

---

[19] *Sporrong and Lonnroth v Sweden* (1982) 5 EHRR 35, para 61.
[20] See the recognition of this in Council Directive 2001/29/EC on the Harmonisation of Certain Aspects of Copyright and Related Rights in the Information Society [2001] OJ L167/10. Paragraph (9) of the Preamble states: 'Any harmonisation of copyright and related rights must take as a basis a high level of protection, since such rights are crucial to intellectual creation. Their protection helps to ensure the maintenance and development of creativity in the interests of authors, performers, producers, consumers, culture, industry and the public at large.'
[21] *Observer and Guardian v UK* (1991) 14 EHRR 153, para 59.

**9.15**  This chapter also considers some of the more significant aspects of moral rights relevant to the protection of privacy interests.[22] These rights are mainly pertinent to published works. The moral rights given to authors of copyright works are the right of paternity in connection with published copies and the right to object to derogatory treatment.[23] Authors and others also have a statutory right to redress in relation to false attribution of authorship[24] which is relevant to some interviews. The latter two rights give some protection in respect of false light portrayals.[25] It should also be noted that performance rights under pt II CDPA may be used to protect privacy rights, albeit in rare circumstances. Finally, Section F examines the treatment of image/publicity rights under English law and discusses the extent to which a property-style image right as found in US law has developed.

## B. Privacy Interests and Copyright Subject Matter

### (1) Types of Subject Matter

**9.16**  The more important copyright works capable of protecting privacy interests are the following:

(1) 'original literary works' (*eg* letters, diaries, memoranda, interviews, test results, unpublished books, biographies, computer programs),[26]
(2) 'original artistic works'[27] (*eg* photographs and drawings), and
(3) sound recordings (*eg* tapes of private conversations) and films[28] (*ie* audio-visual or visual-only recordings, including recordings on security cameras, recordings on mobile phone cameras, video, and other film footage).

**9.17**  The requirement of originality in literary and artistic works refers to a degree of original skill and labour in the creation of the work, and not to any requirement of originality in the thought behind the work. Until recently, it was settled that originality regarding UK copyright referred to original skill and labour in the creation of the work, not to originality in the thought behind the work. This may now require some qualification in view of the concept of the 'author's own intellectual creation' and relevant EU Directives.[29] No such merit is needed for a film to attract copyright.

---

[22] ch IV CDPA is entitled 'Moral Rights'. These also include the right of privacy in connection with commissioned photographs under s 85. For convenience, that right is considered in 9.81–9.86.

[23] ss 77–83 CDPA.

[24] s 84 CDPA.

[25] W Prosser, 'Privacy' (1960) 48 Cal L Rev 383.

[26] ss 1(1)(a) and 3(1) CDPA. Section 3A covers databases. Note also the *sui generis* database right under the Copyright and Rights in Databases Regulations 1997, SI 1997/3032.

[27] ss 1(1)(a) and 4 CDPA. See *Painer v Standard Verlags GmbH & Ors* (Case C-145/10).

[28] ss 1(1)(b), 5A and 5B CDPA.

[29] *Newspaper Licensing Agency Ltd v Meltwater Holding BV* [2011] EWCA Civ 890, [2012] RPC 1. See also Case C-5/08 *Infopaq International A/S v Danske Dagblades Forening* [2010] FSR 495 and e.g. *Football Dataco Ltd & Ors v Yahoo! UK Ltd & Ors* (Case 604/10).

That said, copyright does not subsist in a film that is, or to the extent that it is, a copy of another film and the same principle applies to sound recordings.[30]

## (2) Conditions for Subsistence of Copyright and Duration of Copyright

In order for copyright to subsist in a work, certain conditions have to be met, and **9.18** if these are satisfied, the subsisting copyright is enforceable and may protect a privacy interest. There are two alternative criteria for copyright subsistence. A work can qualify either by reason of the place of its first publication or by the citizenship, domicile, or residence of the 'author';[31] and in the case of companies, place of incorporation.

Generally, if, when the author creates the work, he or she has a relevant associa- **9.19** tion with the United Kingdom or with a country identified in the Copyright and Performances (Application to Other Countries) Order 2013,[32] UK copyright will subsist in the work. So too if the (literary *etc*) work, film, or sound recording is first published in a country providing reciprocal protection to UK works, as specified in the Order. The general scheme is subject to numerous exceptions and transitional provisions for older works. The reader is referred to the main works on copyright for the detail.

Although some jurisdictions require certain formalities such as registration or the **9.20** use of the '©' symbol, nothing of the like is required under UK copyright law. Copyright springs into existence on the creation of a qualifying work.

Copyright is limited in duration. In the case of literary and artistic works, the **9.21** general rule is that the period of protection is seventy years from the end of the calendar year in which the author died.[33] For films, the general rule is seventy years; in that case, from the end of the calendar year in which the death occurs of the last to die of an identified list of persons connected with the making of the film.[34] The period of sound recordings is a period for fifty years if unpublished and not communicated to the public or played in public in that period and a period of seventy years now applies where a sound recording has been published, communicated to the public, or played in public.[35]

---

[30] ss 5B(4), 5A(2) CDPA.

[31] ss 153–62 CDPA.

[32] SI 2013/536 and Copyright and Performances (Application to other Countries) (Amendment) Order 2015, SI 2015/216. Copyrights already subsisting are unaffected (s 153(3) CDPA), so copyrights subsisting under earlier Orders in Council continue.

[33] s 12 CDPA. Enterprise and Regulatory Reform Act 2013, s 76 empowers the Secretary of State to reduce the copyright term of specified unpublished copyright works.

[34] s 13B CDPA.

[35] s 13A(2)(a), (b) and (c) CDPA; as amended. The duration of copyrights that came into existence prior to the commencement of the CDPA is governed by the transitional provisions of the CDPA: schs 1, 12, and 13 CDPA.

### (3) First Ownership of Copyright

**9.22**  The first owner of the copyright in a work is generally the person who creates it.[36] In the case of films, the author is the producer and principal director, and for sound recordings the author is the producer.[37] Thus, a film is treated as a work of joint authorship unless the producer and principal director is the same person.[38] A work of joint authorship is one produced by the collaboration of two or more authors in which the contribution of each author is not distinct from that of the other author or authors.[39] One co-author cannot lawfully exploit the copyright without the consent of the other, although one co-author may sue in respect of an infringement and obtain an injunction, and monetary compensation in respect of his share of the copyright.[40]

**9.23**  One of the more important exceptions to the general rule of first ownership relates to works created by employees, where the employer is the first owner of the copyright.[41] A person may be the first owner in equity in certain circumstances, such as where he or she has commissioned creation of the work and it is appropriate to conclude that the parties intended the commissioner to own the copyright. Likewise, a court will generally treat a company as the beneficial owner of copyright where the work has been created by a director (if not an employee) in the course of his or her duties.[42]

### (4) Exclusive Rights

**9.24**  The owner of the copyright has the exclusive right to do the following 'restricted acts' in the United Kingdom:[43]

(i)  Copy the work.
(ii)  Issue copies of the work to the public.
(iii)  Rent or lend the work to the public.
(iv)  Perform, show, or play the work in public.
(v)  Communicate the work to the public.
(vi)  Make an adaptation of the work (literary and artistic works) or do any of the above in relation to an adaptation.

---

[36]  ss 9–11 CDPA.
[37]  s 9(1)(aa), (ab), and 178 CDPA.
[38]  s 10(1A) CDPA.
[39]  s 10(1) CDPA.
[40]  *Prior v Lansdowne Press Pty Ltd* [1977] RPC 511. See *Copinger and Skone James* (n 3) paras 5-172–5-173.
[41]  s 11 (2) CDPA; subject to any agreement to the contrary.
[42]  See generally *Laddie, Prescott, and Vitoria* (n 3) paras 22.23–22.53.
[43]  s 16(1) CDPA. See also 9.02. The right to copy is not infringed by making a 'temporary copy' within s 28A; directed at web-browsing: see *Public Relations Consultants Association Ltd v Newspaper Licensing Agency* [2013] UKSC 18 and Case C-360/13 [2014] EMLR 28. There are other exceptions to the exclusive rights in s 16, *eg* s 72.

The Copyright and Related Rights Regulations 2003[44] amended the CDPA by **9.25** implementing Directive 2001/29/EC on the Harmonization of Certain Aspects of Copyright and Related Rights in the Information Society ('the Information Society Directive'). Communication to the public is stated to 'include the broadcasting of the work' and 'the making available to the public of the work by electronic transmission in such a way that members of the public may access it from a place and at a time individually chosen by them'.[45] The right of 'making available to the public' covers 'on-demand' and other specified internet services. For the purposes of UK copyright, the restricted act of communication to the public must take place in the United Kingdom. For example, it will take place in the United Kingdom if the website providing the service is located in another EU Member State, provided that the UK public is targeted.[46] Many transmissions over the internet are brought within the extended definition of 'broadcast' in s 16(2) CDPA. Other internet transmissions are caught by the right of making available.

The copyright in a work is infringed by a person who does, or authorizes another **9.26** to do, any restricted act in relation to the work without the licence of the copyright owner.[47] Copyright is infringed by the doing of any restricted act in relation to the whole or any substantial part of the work.[48] Acts of 'secondary infringement' are committed by a person who imports, possesses, or deals with (in various defined ways) 'infringing copies' of works with the relevant guilty knowledge.[49] Liability can arise also by joint tortfeasorship. The Court may also grant an injunction against a service provider, where that service provider has actual knowledge of another person using its service to infringe copyright.[50]

### (5) Transmission of Copyright and Licensing

Copyright is transmissible by assignment, testamentary disposition, or by opera- **9.27** tion of law, as personal or moveable property.[51] An assignment must be in writing and be signed by or on behalf of the assignor,[52] although other arrangements are

---

[44] SI 2003/2498.

[45] s 20(2) CDPA.

[46] See Case C-173/11 *Football Data Co Ltd v Sportradar AG* [2013] FSR 4; *EMI Records Ltd v British Sky Broadcasting Ltd* [2013] EWHC 379 (Ch), [2013] ECDR 8. As to the enforceability of foreign copyrights in the English courts, see *Lucasfilm* (n 9).

[47] s 16(2) CDPA. The principles were considered in *Paramount Home Entertainment Ltd v British Sky Broadcasting Ltd* [2013] EWHC 3479 (Ch), in which infringement on grounds of authorization and joint tortfeasorship was also found.

[48] s 16(3) CDPA. *Designers Guild Ltd v Russell Williams (Textiles) Ltd* [2000] UKHL 58, [2001] FSR 11.

[49] ss 22–3 and 27 CDPA.

[50] s 97A(1)-(3) CDPA. See *Twentieth Century Fox Film Corp v British Telecommunications plc* [2011] EWHC 1981 (Ch), [2012] Bus LR 1471 and its progeny; *eg Paramount Home Entertainment Ltd* (n 47).

[51] ss 1(1), 90(1) CDPA.

[52] s 90(3) CDPA.

enforceable in equity. An assignment or other transmission of copyright may be limited to one or more of the things the copyright owner has the right to do and to any part of the period for which copyright is to subsist.[53] Copyright passes under a will or on an intestacy. Thus, after the death of an author, the copyright (if still owned at that time by him or her) in private diaries or other unpublished works may be owned and enforced by the author's successors in title. An example is the recent reportedly unauthorized online publication of JD Salinger's works, *The Ocean Full of Bowling Balls, Paula,* and *Birthday Boy* in circumstances where the deceased author had embargoed publication of his unpublished work until 2060. In this type of example, the successors in title to an author may take legal action to prevent unauthorized commercial exploitation in the United Kingdom of previously unpublished works, or if the copyright is sold by the author's heirs, a purchaser of the copyright would be entitled to publish.

**9.28** The copyright owner can grant an 'exclusive licence' (in writing) which gives the licensee to the exclusion of all others, including the licensor, the right to exercise a right which would otherwise be exercisable exclusively by the copyright owner.[54] An exclusive licensee has, except against the copyright owner, the same rights and remedies in respect of infringement occurring after the grant of the licence as if the licence had been an assignment.[55]

**9.29** An 'exclusive licence' is a species of contractual licence. There are other types of contractual licence. Certain non-exclusive licensees are granted rights of action under the statute.[56] Where the extent of the licence is not made clear by its express terms, the starting point is that a licence is a derogation from the copyright owner's exclusive rights; and the court will only imply further terms to the extent that they are necessary to give effect to the transaction.

**9.30** The revocability of a licence depends on its terms and the events relied on as justifying a termination.[57] If a licensor purports to terminate the licence when he or she is not entitled to, an injunction may be granted to restrain him or her from acting in breach of an implied obligation not to revoke the licence; and thereby prevent the licensor from acting on the revocation.[58] Where the licensor is entitled to revoke the licence, he or she may be entitled to a 'packing up' period or reasonable notice. In principle, a bare licence may be revoked at any time because it is unsupported by consideration. However, the circumstances may require the licensor to give reasonable notice and may be such as to estop the licensor from revoking the licence

---

[53] s 90(2) CDPA.
[54] s 92(1) CDPA.
[55] s 101 CDPA.
[56] s 101A CDPA.
[57] *Grisbrook v MGN Ltd* [2009] EWHC 2520 (Ch); *Robin Ray v Classic FM plc* [1998] FSR 622.
[58] *Ocular Sciences Ltd v Aspect Vision Care Ltd* [1997] RPC 289, 433–4; *Hounslow LBC v Twickenham Garden Developments Ltd* [1971] 1 Ch 233; *Blair v Osborne and Tomkins* [1971] 2 QB 78.

at all.[59] A sub-licence does not necessarily come to an end on termination of the head licence.

### (6) Editing and Alteration

Subject to any contractual restrictions and the moral rights of the author,[60] the general rule is that an assignee of copyright is at liberty to carry out such editing of the copyright work as he or she wishes. An assignee seeking to carry out other alterations (*eg* an arrangement) of a copyright work would also have to ensure that he or she had taken an assignment of all relevant aspects of the copyright work and had cleared any underlying copyrights and other rights. **9.31**

A licensee is in a different position. All depends on the proper construction of the terms of the licence, express or implied. Before the introduction of moral rights under the CDPA, the law was that if the licence contained no relevant express or implied term, a licensee was free to make alterations.[61] Moral rights are considered in Section E. If an alteration would amount to 'derogatory treatment', an equitable title to the copyright (arising from a commissioning, for example) or an implied licence generally to use the work commercially would not be sufficient to defeat a claim for infringement of moral rights under s 80 CDPA.[62] **9.32**

## C. Exceptions and Limitations

The content of copyright works may be newsworthy or of great interest to the readership or audience of a media organization. In many cases, this will be due to some aspect of the work which the copyright owner wishes to keep private. Thus, there will be little chance of obtaining an assignment of the copyright or a licence to authorize publication. However, the ability of the copyright owner to control exploitation of a work is not absolute, the right to prevent publication of private or unpublished copyright works being qualified.[63] In most cases, the Article 10 rights at play will be satisfied by s 30,[64] which is discussed at 9.35–9.57. The extent to which the law has adapted or may be required to adapt further so as to accommodate the requirements of Article 10 is considered at 9.58–9.64. There have also been recent changes to s 30, of modest relevance to the issues under discussion.[65] **9.33**

---

[59] *Godfrey v Lees* [1995] EMLR 307.

[60] Moral rights are capable of being waived: s 87 CDPA.

[61] *Frisby v BBC* [1967] Ch 932. See *Copinger and Skone James* (n 3) paras 5-225–5-231.

[62] *Pasterfield v Denham* [1999] FSR 168, 183.

[63] The qualifications in ch III CDPA 'are all directed to achieving a proper balance between the protection of the rights of a creative author and the wider public interest': *Pro Sieben Media A-G v Carlton Television Ltd* [1999] FSR 610, 618.

[64] See *PCR Ltd v Dow Jones Telerate Ltd* [1998] FSR 172, 188, where the rights under s 30(2) were engaged.

[65] See the Copyright and Rights in Performances (Quotation and Parody) Regulations 2014, SI 2014/2350. The new qualified exemption for parody and caricature under the new s 30A CDPA is

**9.34** Publication of copyright works in the media sphere takes place in two main ways. The first involves publication of previously unpublished works; the second, publication of works that have been recently published in rival news media. Copyright may also be relevant to privacy and published works in a different context. An example is the right or liberty to carry out editing and alteration, which pertains to false light intrusions into privacy.

### (1) The 'Fair Dealing' Exceptions

**9.35** Chapter III CDPA sets out a series of permitted acts, the most important of which for present purposes are contained in s 30. This provides as follows:

> **30 Criticism, review, quotation and news reporting**
>
> (1) Fair dealing with a work for the purpose of criticism or review, of that or another work or of a performance of a work, does not infringe any copyright in the work provided that it is accompanied by a sufficient acknowledgement (unless this would be impossible for reasons of practicality or otherwise) and provided that the work has been made available to the public.
>
> (1ZA) Copyright in a work is not infringed by the use of a quotation from the work (whether for criticism or review or otherwise) provided that—
> (a) the work has been made available to the public,
> (b) the use of the quotation is fair dealing with the work,
> (c) the extent of the quotation is no more than is required for the specific purpose for which it is used, and
> (d) the quotation is accompanied by a sufficient acknowledgement (unless this would be impossible for reasons of practicality or otherwise).
>
> (1A) For the purposes of subsections (1) and (1ZA) a work has been made available to the public if it has been made available by any means, including—
> (a) the issue of copies to the public;
> (b) making the work available by means of an electronic retrieval system;
> (c) the rental or lending of copies of the work to the public;
> (d) the performance, exhibition, playing or showing of the work in public;
> (e) the communication to the public of the work,
> but in determining generally for the purposes of those subsections whether a work has been made available to the public no account shall be taken of any unauthorised act.
>
> (2) Fair dealing with a work (other than a photograph) for the purpose of reporting current events does not infringe any copyright in the work provided that (subject to subsection (3)) it is accompanied by a sufficient acknowledgement.
>
> (3) No acknowledgement is required in connection with the reporting of current events by means of a sound recording, film or broadcast where this would be impossible for reasons of practicality or otherwise.

---

not discussed here. In Case C-201/13 *Deckmyn v Vandersteen* [2014] Bus LR 1368 the European Court of Justice held that it was for national courts to strike a fair balance between the rights in a protected work and the freedom of expression of the user of that work who was relying on the exception for parody under Directive 2001/29/EC.

### (a) Sufficient acknowledgement

No 'fair dealing' defence under s 30(1) or (2) can succeed without the presence **9.36** of a 'sufficient acknowledgement', unless the provisions as to the impossibility of an acknowledgement apply. Subject to exceptions, an acknowledgement means an acknowledgement identifying the work in question by its title or other description and the author.[66] 'Sufficient acknowledgement' does not require that the acknowledgement be express rather than implied. It merely requires something which can properly be seen as an identification.[67]

### (b) The statutory purposes

The terms 'criticism or review' and 'reporting current events' are expressions of **9.37** wide and indefinite scope and any attempt to plot their boundaries is doomed to failure. They are expressions which should be interpreted liberally.[68] The term 'for the purpose of' is to be interpreted so as to exclude the mental element on the part of the user; in other words, objectively.[69]

**'Criticism or review'** Criticism of a work is not limited to criticisms of style. It **9.38** may extend to criticism of the ideas in the work and to the social or moral implications of the work.[70] Nor is it confined to criticism of the work being used. The 'work' in question is a copyright work, though not necessarily one in which copyright still subsists or a specific work.[71] The test is primarily objective and should focus on the impact on the audience of the infringing work and not the intentions or motives of the copyright user.[72] Suitable dictionary definitions are helpful in construing the terms 'criticism' and 'review',[73] but they only go so far and should be read subject to the cautionary words set out in the first two sentences of 9.37.[74] The court should be careful to prevent an attempt to dress up infringement of another's copyright in the guise of criticism.[75]

In *Pro Sieben Media AG v Carlton UK Television Ltd*[76] extracts from filmed **9.39** interviews and other footage concerning Mandy Allwood, who was expecting octuplets, were contained in a programme made by Carlton. It was held that the programme was made for the purpose of criticism of works of chequebook journalism in general and in particular the (then very recent) treatment by the

---

[66] See s 178 CDPA.
[67] See *Fraser-Woodward Ltd v BBC* [2005] EWHC 472 (Ch), [2005] EMLR 22 [71]–[72].
[68] *Pro Sieben* (n 63) 620.
[69] *Pro Sieben* (n 63) 620.
[70] *Time Warner Entertainments Co LP* (n 12); *Pro Sieben* (n 63) 621. See also *IPC Media Ltd v News Group Newspapers Ltd* [2005] EMLR 532 and *Fraser-Woodward* (n 67).
[71] *Fraser-Woodward* (n 67) [40]–[44].
[72] *Pro Sieben* (n 63) 620.
[73] See *Copinger and Skone James* (n 3) para 9-43.
[74] *Fraser-Woodward* (n 67) [36].
[75] *Time Warner* (n 12) 15.
[76] *Pro Sieben* (n 63).

media of the story of Ms Allwood's multiple pregnancy. In *Ashdown*[77] the defence under s 30 CDPA was dismissed because the criticism or review in the newspaper article complained of was of the acts of the Prime Minister, which were not relevant to those statutory purposes. In both these cases the defence was based on s 30(1) before the subsection was amended (by the Copyright and Related Rights Regulations 2003 in the light of Article 5.3 of the Information Society Directive) to require prior publication of the copyright work. In view of that amendment, the circumstances in which a defence under s 30(1) will succeed in a claim to enforce privacy will be very limited.

**9.40** **'Quotation'**   There is a qualified exemption for quotation under s 30(1ZA), to which the requirement of fair dealing (among others) applies. As the exemption is not available where the work has not been made available to the public, it is unlikely to be of much relevance in cases where copyright is used to enforce a privacy interest.

**9.41** **'Reporting current events'**   The present trend is towards a widening of the circumstances in which use of copyright material might properly be regarded as being for the purpose of reporting current events. Article 10 ECHR may serve to reinforce this development. Media coverage itself is capable of amounting to 'current events', *ie* the way the media has responded to a story can amount to 'current events'.[78] 'Current events' does not embrace all material that a news organization might wish to publish, although it is not restricted to news events less than 24 hours old.[79] Past events cannot be said to be 'current' because the media want to report some new facet of an old story.[80] However, simply because an event took place in the past does not mean that the 'current events' requirement cannot be met.

**9.42** The *Ashdown* case[81] concerned the unauthorized publication in the *Sunday Telegraph* in November 1999 of substantial verbatim extracts from a confidential minute made by the claimant, a former leader of the Liberal Democrats, of an important meeting he attended with the Prime Minister in October 1997. The Court of Appeal held that matters of 'current public interest' or matters representing a 'legitimate and continuing public interest' would satisfy the definition of 'current events'. On that basis, it was held arguable that the meeting in October 1997 to discuss possible future cooperation between the political parties in question

---

[77] *Ashdown* (n 10).
[78] *Pro Sieben* (n 63) 625 where the volume and intensity of media interest in Mandy Allwood and her octuplets was sufficient to bring the coverage within the ambit of current events; see also *Hyde Park Residence Ltd v Yelland* [2001] Ch 143 [32].
[79] *Pro Sieben* [1998] FSR 43, 54 (Laddie J).
[80] *Associated Newspapers Group plc v News Group Newspapers Ltd* [1986] RPC 515.
[81] *Ashdown* (n 10).

was likely to be of continuing public interest in November 1999 and therefore to amount to 'current events'.[82]

The central importance of politically related speech is at the heart of ECHR juris- **9.43** prudence on freedom of expression.[83] The approach taken in *Ashdown* may represent a real extension of the traditional boundaries of 'current events' for the purposes of the copyright, when compared to some earlier cases.[84] Even so, there are still limits to this exception where the use includes events that are current. In *HRH Prince of Wales v Associated Newspapers Ltd*,[85] which was decided after *Ashdown*, the Court of Appeal on an appeal against an order for summary judgment rejected a defence of the appellant newspaper publishers under s 30(2) in connection with the publication of extracts of the prince's diaries containing his reflections on various incidents relating to the handover of Hong Kong. The Court referred to the finding of the judge below that it was just arguable that part of the published articles related to current events, namely Prince Charles's failure to attend a banquet at Buckingham Palace to mark a Chinese state visit shortly before publication, and his role as heir. However, much of the piece had nothing to do with current events. The quotations from the diaries had been taken with a view to revealing the contents of the diaries as themselves an event of current interest, rather than for the purpose of reporting current events.[86] The Court also rejected a submission that once it was found that the articles were concerned with current events, however broadly, it should then go on to consider whether the dealing was fair, ignoring altogether the extent to which the articles were in fact concerned with reporting current events.[87]

### (c) 'Made available to the public'

As regards criticism, review, or quotation, circulation to chosen recipients will not **9.44** qualify as an 'issue of copies to the public' under s 30(1A)(a).[88]

---

[82] Lord Phillips MR stated at [64]: 'The defence provided by s 30(2) is clearly intended to protect the role of the media in informing the public about matters of current concern to the public…The meeting was undoubtedly an event, and while it might be said that by November 1999 it was not current solely in the sense of recent in time, it was arguably a matter of current interest to the public. In a democratic society, information about a meeting between the Prime Minister and an opposition party leader during the then current Parliament to discuss possible close co-operation between those parties is very likely to be of legitimate and continuing public interest. It might impinge on the way the public would vote at the next general election.'

[83] See *eg Castells v Spain* (1992) 14 EHRR 445, 476, para 42, and *Karhuvaara v Finland* (2005) 41 EHRR 51, 1154, para 52.

[84] *eg*, it is arguable that if this test had been applied to the Thalidomide case, *Distillers Co (Biochemicals) Ltd v Times Newspapers Ltd* [1975] QB 613, the result would have been different. See further *SAS Institute Inc v World Programming Ltd* [2010] EWHC 1829 (Ch), [2011] RPC 1 [325]; *Infopaq International* (n 29) and *Meltwater Holding* (n 29) [37]–[39].

[85] [2006] EWCA Civ 1776, [2008] Ch 57.

[86] *HRH Prince of Wales* (n 85) [78].

[87] *HRH Prince of Wales* (n 85) [79].

[88] In *HRH Prince of Wales* (n 85) circulation of up to 75 members of a selected class was held not to constitute publication for the purposes of s 30(1A)(a).

*(d) Fair dealing*

**9.45**   In *Ashdown* the Court of Appeal approved the test for fair dealing set out in *Laddie, Prescott, and Vitoria on the Modern Law of Copyright and Designs*,[89] in a passage from the 3rd edition, which stated:

> It is impossible to lay down any hard and fast definition of what is fair dealing, for it is a matter of fact, degree and impression. However, by far the most important factor is whether the alleged fair dealing is in fact commercially competing with the proprietor's exploitation of the copyright work, a substitute for the possible purchase of authorised copies, and the like. If it is, the fair dealing defence will almost certainly fail. If it is not and there is a moderate taking and there are no special adverse factors, the defence is likely to succeed, especially if the defendant's additional purpose is to right a wrong, to ventilate an honest grievance, to engage in political controversy, and so on. The second most important factor is whether the work has already been published or otherwise exposed to the public. If it has not, and especially if the material has been obtained by a breach of confidence or other mean or underhand dealing, the courts will be reluctant to say this is fair. This is not conclusive, because sometimes it is necessary for the purposes of legitimate public controversy to make use of leaked information. The third most important factor is the amount and importance of the work that has been taken. Although it is permissible to take a substantial part of the work (if not, there could be question of infringement in the first place), the taking of an excessive amount, or the taking of even a small amount if on a regular basis, may well negative fair dealing.

While approving this passage the Court of Appeal was of the view that the traditional tests must now be approached with Article 10 firmly in mind.[90] It has been said that the concept of fairness is a difficult one as it is highly sensitive to both context and contemporary mores.[91] Before turning to the effect of Article 10, it is worth considering in more detail the traditional criteria for fair dealing.

**9.46**   **Competition with the copyright owner**   The mere fact that the alleged infringer is a commercial competitor of the copyright owner does not of itself render any dealing with the copyright work unfair.[92] It is the effect of the use on the copyright owner's ability to exploit the work that is relevant.[93] However, the owner of an unpublished work may not want to publish it at all and the very fact of the publication may render the dealing unfair, albeit that all depends on the context.[94]

---

[89]   M Vitoria et al (eds), *Laddie, Prescott, and Vitoria on the Modern Law of Copyright and Designs* (3rd edn, LexisNexis 2000) para 20.16. The passage is reproduced in full in the 4th edn (n 3) para 21.47, although see the limited qualifications made by the authors at para 21.46.

[90]   *Ashdown* (n 10) [70]. See also *Fraser-Woodward* (n 67) [55] where Mann J also took into account the '3-step' test under Art 9(2) of the Berne Convention: that the use should not unreasonably prejudice the legitimate interests of the author or conflict with the author's normal exploitation of the work. See also Art 5.5 of the Information Society Directive.

[91]   *IPC Media Ltd v News Group* (n 70).

[92]   *BBC v British Satellite Broadcasting Ltd* [1992] Ch 141.

[93]   Thus, in *Ashdown* it was held that publication destroyed a part of the value of the memoirs which the claimant had intended to and did publish.

[94]   See *Ashdown* (n 10).

**Unpublished works** The statutory regime relating to the reporting of current **9.47** events under s 30(2) does not exclude unpublished works. However, if a work is unpublished this remains an important factor often pointing away from the application of the defence,[95] as is also the case if the copy of the work was obtained in breach of confidence.[96] The obvious point about publication of part of an unpublished work is that it may spoil the author's market.[97]

In *Ashdown* Lord Phillips MR stated:[98] **9.48**

> The fact that the minute was undoubtedly obtained in breach of confidence is a material consideration when considering the defence of fair dealing. The Vice-Chancellor rightly attached importance to the fact that the minute was secret and had been obtained by Telegraph Group without Mr Ashdown's knowledge or approval.

Much investigative reporting aimed at exposing matters of real public interest is by its very nature based on leaks, on the publication of unpublished documents in breach of confidence, and without the approval of the copyright owner. An unpublished work used for the purpose of criticism or review would fall outside under section 30(1). However, in rare cases the court might refuse an injunction on discretionary or Article 10 grounds or find the publication to be non-infringing on the basis of public interest: see 9.58.

It would be a significant restriction on the liberty to use substantial parts of copy- **9.49** right works for the reporting of current events if dealing with unpublished documents were ruled unfair simply because the documents had been leaked. However, the decision in *Ashdown* shows that concern about the unpublished nature of a copyright work and the circumstances in which it was obtained may give way to the public interest recognized by s 30(2) CDPA, informed by Article 10 considerations in appropriate circumstances, and provided that the use made of the unpublished material is proportionate and constitutes 'fair dealing'.[99]

**The amount and importance of the work taken** The amount of the work taken **9.50** and the importance of the extracts used are important guides to the fairness of the dealing, measured against the extent to which the rights conferred by Article 10

---

[95] Despite his rejection of the strict view of Romer J in *British Oxygen Co Ltd v Liquid Air Ltd* [1925] Ch 383, Ungoed-Thomas J expressed the view in *Beloff v Pressdram Ltd* [1973] 1 All ER 241, 263 that 'the law by bestowing a right of copyright on an unpublished work bestows a right to prevent it being published at all; and even though an unpublished work is not automatically excluded from the defence of fair dealing, it is yet a much more substantial breach of copyright than the publication of a published work'. See *Hyde Park Residence* (n 78) [37]: 'if the work had not been published or circulated to the public that is an important indication that the dealing was not fair', per Aldous LJ; and *Commonwealth of Australia v John Fairfax & Sons Ltd* (1980) 147 CLR 39.

[96] *HRH Prince of Wales* (n 85) [78].

[97] See *Hubbard v Vosper* [1972] 2 QB 84, 94 (limited publication to shareholders).

[98] *Ashdown* (n 10) [75].

[99] *Ashdown* (n 10) [76]–[82].

require the use made by the publisher. Thus, the key question in *Ashdown* was whether it was necessary to quote verbatim the passages of which Lord Ashdown was the author in order to convey to the readers of the *Sunday Telegraph* the authenticity of its reports of current events of public interest. If so, it was arguable that the dealing was fair.

**9.51** The facts were that accounts of the minuted meeting had already appeared in the press and the accuracy of these accounts had been challenged by the Prime Minister. The Court held that limited quotation of Lord Ashdown's own words was arguably justified so that the newspaper could demonstrate that it had obtained the minute and was in a position to give an authentic account of the meeting. However that did not justify the extensive reproduction of Lord Ashdown's words in the article complained of:

> The statement by the Sunday Telegraph that they had obtained a copy of the minute coupled with one or two short extracts from it would have sufficed . . . It appears to us that the minute was deliberately filleted in order to extract colourful passages that were most likely to add flavour to the article and thus to appeal to the readership of the newspaper. Mr Ashdown's work product was deployed in the way that it was for reasons that were essentially journalistic in furtherance of the commercial interests of the Telegraph Group.[100]

**9.52** The significance of the amount used may vary, depending on the context. The amount of a copyright work may be of less importance in the context of a television programme than if the exposure is in permanent form, as would be the case for publication of multiple copies in printed or other permanent form.[101] Any use of a photograph is likely to extend to most if not all the photograph, because otherwise it will not make much sense. In *Hyde Park Residence* the defendant newspaper publishers published extracts of film footage from security cameras at the Villa Windsor, a private residence of Mr Mohammed Al-Fayed in Paris. The publishers alleged that the so-called 'driveway stills' were used to refute falsehoods published by Mr Al Fayed after the deaths of his son and Princess Diana about the depth of their relationship and the circumstances of their deaths. However, the Court of Appeal held that publication of the still images was excessive and not justified on grounds of journalistic authenticity, because the newspaper could have reported the relevant information (the couple's arrival and departure times from the villa) and reported that it had taken the information from a copy of the video in its possession. The only relevance of the stills was the fact that the couple had stayed only 28 minutes in the villa, a fact that was known and did not establish that the couple were not to be married.[102] The obvious absurdity of Mr Al Fayed's allegations was an additional ground for rejecting the defence under s 30.[103]

---

[100] *Ashdown* (n 10) [82].
[101] See *Fraser-Woodward* (n 67) [56].
[102] *Hyde Park Residence* (n 78) [40].
[103] *Hyde Park Residence* (n 78) [78].

In each case it is necessary to ask whether the facts are such that the importance of **9.53** freedom of expression outweighs the conventional considerations relevant to fair dealing.[104] In so doing, it is necessary to recognize that considerations of public interest are paramount[105] as a result of the importance of Article 10.

In the European Court of Human Rights case of *Fressoz and Roire v France*[106] the **9.54** tax returns of the head of Peugeot had been published in a satirical magazine. The information was not confidential as it was open to inspection in public records. The journalists were convicted for making unlawful use of the documents. The Court observed:[107]

> If, as the Government accepted, the information about Mr Calvet's annual income was lawful and its disclosure permitted, the applicants' conviction merely for having published the documents in which that information was contained, namely the tax assessments, cannot be justified under Article 10. In essence, that Article leaves it open for journalists to decide whether or not it is necessary to reproduce such documents to ensure credibility. It protects journalists' rights to divulge information on issues of general interest provided that they are acting in good faith and on an accurate factual basis and provide 'reliable and precise' information in accordance with the ethics of journalism.

This may be compared with the approach of the House of Lords in *Campbell v* **9.55** *MGN Ltd*[108] in which the majority, while accepting that journalists should be accorded a reasonable margin of appreciation in taking decisions as to what needed to be included in an article to give it credibility, considered that the publication of a photograph of the claimant was not justified when balancing the Article 8 rights of the claimant with the Article 10 rights of the publishers.

In *Ashdown* the Court of Appeal acknowledged that *Fressoz* was not a copyright **9.56** case, but stated that it illustrated a general principle:[109]

> Freedom of expression protects the right both to publish information and to receive it. There will be occasions when it is in the public interest not merely that information should be published, but that the public should be told the very words used by a person, notwithstanding that the author enjoys copyright in them. On occasions, indeed, it is the form and not the content of a document which is of interest.

---

[104] *Ashdown* (n 10) [78]. The judgment of the Court of Appeal is couched in terms of whether or not the defendants had shown an arguable defence. The question was asked, 'Are the facts of this case such that, arguably, the importance of freedom of expression outweighs the conventional considerations . . . [relevant to fair dealing]?' However, the arguability appears to refer only to the factual basis of the defence, rather than the principles of law identified in the judgment.

[105] *Ashdown* (n 10) [71] (Lord Phillips).

[106] (1999) 31 EHRR 28.

[107] *Fressoz* (n 106) para 54. See also *Verlagsgruppe News GmbH v Austria* App no 10520/02, [2007] EMLR 13.

[108] [2004] 2 AC 457 [105]–[113], [152]–[156], [167]–[170].

[109] *Ashdown* (n 10) [43].

The emphasis on journalistic credibility shows that in rare circumstances it is no longer an answer for a copyright owner to say that it is not necessary to exploit a copyright in order to make one's point.[110]

**9.57**   Accordingly, journalistic considerations of the type identified in *Fressoz* and other case law of the Convention[111] (e.g. journalistic credibility) will be given due weight in connection with fair dealing defences based on current events.[112] However, that is not an end to the matter. A defendant seeking to rely on s 30(2) must show that the use made is proportionate to the requirements of public interest at play, being no more than is necessary to meet those requirements. The conclusions of the Court of Appeal in *Ashdown* are an example of this.

### (2) The Public Interest Exception

#### (a) *The residual cases where the public interest is still relevant*

**9.58**   The view that the balancing act between property rights on the one hand and freedom of expression on the other had already been carried out by the legislature in ch III CDPA cannot survive the decision of the Court of Appeal in *Ashdown*.[113]

**9.59**   It is now clear that there may still be cases, albeit rare, where the requirements of Article 10 will justify publication of copyright material in circumstances where a s 30 CDPA defence would not apply; where the public interest requires not only publication of the information embodied in a copyright work, but the very words or other copyright material. One example is where a media organization wishes to publish material of significant public interest such as a document produced in the past where publication would not meet the requirement of publication 'for the purpose of reporting current events'. The approach taken by the Court of Appeal in *Ashdown* was to say that the twin sources of s 30(2) CDPA and the public interest defence preserved by s 171(3) CDPA should be used to give full effect to the right to freedom of expression under Article 10.[114]

**9.60**   The fact that freedom of expression may require publication of a substantial part of a work does not mean that the copyright owner should forego compensation for the

---

[110]   Contrast *Hyde Park Residence* (n 78) [39]–[40]. See also *Ashdown* (n 10) [44]–[55].

[111]   *eg Goodwin v UK* (1996) 22 EHRR 123.

[112]   The same may well apply to defences based on criticism or review; particularly of the type exemplified by *Pro Sieben Media* (n 63).

[113]   *Ashdown* (n 10) [44]–[55]. In referring to freedom of expression, the Court was including the right to receive and impart information: see [43]–[45]. Although Art 5 of the Information Society Directive appears to prevent the survival of the public interest defence except in very limited cases, it probably survives in cases where freedom of expression is engaged in view of Art 10 ECHR and Art 11 of the Charter of Fundamental Rights of the EU, though even then there is a view that the exception will be extremely narrow: see *Laddie, Prescott and Vitoria* (n 3) paras 21.19–21.22.

[114]   *Ashdown* (n 10) [44]–[55]. In referring to freedom of expression the Court was including the rights to receive and to impart information: [43]–[45].

publication. Thus, the first question is whether an injunction should be refused on discretionary grounds, and in most cases refusal of an injunction will be sufficient to satisfy the requirements of Article 10.[115]

The rare cases where Article 10 will give rise to a substantive defence are those **9.61** where a defendant can show that the public interest justifies publication. Therefore, the 'public interest' defence is one where a defendant can show that the demands of Article 10 on the facts of a particular case should override the protection given to the copyright owner so as to not justify the grant of an injunction or in a rare case, to refuse relief altogether. Section 171(3) CDPA provides:

> Nothing in this Part affects any rule of law preventing or restricting the enforcement of copyright, on grounds of public interest or otherwise.[116]

The nature of the public interest defence is identified in *Lion Laboratories Ltd v Evans*,[117] where the principles were set out with respect to the laws of confidence and copyright.[118] Thus, there may be cases outside the sphere of iniquity where it is 'vital' in the public interest to publish the material.[119] Where Article 10 rights form the basis of the public interest defence, the principle of proportionality should be used to make a structured inquiry into whether or not publication is justified,[120] together with (it is suggested) the principles of fair dealing which arguably apply by analogy.

Accordingly, the circumstances in which a copyright will not be enforced on public **9.62** interest grounds are not to be understood solely by reference to the nature of the copyright work itself,[121] but on wider grounds connected to the public interest in the freedom of expression and dissemination of information and ideas required by Article 10.[122]

---

[115] *Ashdown* (n 10) [46]. The discretion would be exercised in accordance with the requirements of Arts 8 and 10, Art 1 of the First Protocol, and s 12 HRA. The court, as a public authority, has a duty to act compatibly with Convention rights under s 6 HRA.

[116] No equivalent provision appeared in the Copyright Act 1956. Note the explicit recognition of the possible impact of copyright on rights of confidentiality and privacy in s 171(1): 'Nothing in this Part affects—(e) the operation of any rule of equity relating to breaches of trust or confidence'; and 171(4): 'Nothing in this Part affects any right of action or other remedy, whether civil or criminal, available otherwise than under this Part in respect of acts infringing any of the rights conferred by Chapter IV (moral rights).'

[117] *Lion Laboratories* (n 18).

[118] *Ashdown* (n 10) [51]–[57].

[119] *Lion Laboratories* (n 18) 550.

[120] See *London Regional Transport Ltd v Mayor of London* [2001] EWCA Civ 1491, [2003] EMLR 4 [54]–[62].

[121] Such a formulation was adopted by Aldous LJ in *Hyde Park Residence* (n 78) but disapproved in *Ashdown* as being too limited: (n 10) [58]. It is suggested that the approach in *Ashdown* is correct.

[122] The right of the public to receive information even if it is 'clothed in copyright' is explored in J Griffiths, 'Copyright Law and the Public's Right to Information' in E Barendt and A Firth (eds), *The Yearbook of Copyright and Media Law 2001–02* (Oxford University Press 2002).

*(b) The public interest: copyright compared with confidential information*

**9.63** The principles applicable to the public interest and unauthorized publication of confidential information are considered in Chapters 11 and 4 respectively. However, a number of additional points are of note. Historically, the limits of the public interest justification for publication of confidential material have tended to be considered in copyright and confidence simultaneously, often without any useful exploration of any differences between the two regimes.[123]

**9.64** Copyright material and confidential information often lead to different conclusions for the purposes of a public interest defence, because of the nature of the rights at play. In particular, it is usually possible to convey information without infringing any associated copyright.[124] For this reason and because of the existence of the public interest exceptions in s 30 and elsewhere in ch III CDPA, it will generally be very difficult to establish a public interest defence to a claim for copyright infringement. English law currently recognizes no defence of parody to a claim of copyright infringement, which is statutory example of Article 10 rights being elevated above copyright as a property right: see fn 65.[125]

*(c) The public interest defence and photographs*

**9.65** Different considerations apply to photographs. Photographs are expressly excluded from the current events defence under s 30(2) CDPA. Under s 30(1), no unpublished photograph may be reproduced in connection with criticism or review. Whether or not Article 10 might justify publication of a photograph under the public interest defence would also require a proper consideration of relevant international Conventions (particularly the Berne Convention) together with applicable EC sources of law, including the Information Society Directive. Although news reporting is the obvious context of any defence based on the right to freedom of expression, there may well be other cases where a public interest defence grounded on Article 10 considerations might require refusal of an injunction[126] or allow a successful defence.

**9.66** A comparison with other European jurisprudence in this area is informative. In *Re Quotation of News Pictures*[127] an Austrian statute did not specifically recognize

---

[123] *Beloff* (n 95) 259: Ungoed-Thomas J said of the copyright claim over publication of a leaked memorandum that the key complaint concerned revelation of the facts in the memo and '[i]n that sense it is an action for breach of confidence but framed in breach of copyright'; see also *Lion Laboratories* (n 18) and *Times Newspapers Ltd v Mirror Group Newspapers Ltd* [1993] EMLR 445.

[124] *Hyde Park Residence* (n 78) [75]–[77]. In some cases, however, public interest considerations will give rise to defences to claims in both copyright and confidence; see *eg Lion Laboratories* (n 18).

[125] *Ian Richard Allen v Robert Redshaw* (2013) PCC 22/5/2013.

[126] An example of the type of case where this might be so was provided by the dispute over the unpublished work of the 18th-century poet John Clare. See J Griffiths, 'Copyright in English literature: Denying the public domain' [2000] EIPR 150. See also *SA Plan v Pierre Hugo* (30 January 2007, Cour de Cassation): Art 10 considerations given priority over the rights of the author's heirs to object to sequels.

[127] [2002] ECC 20 (Sup Ct, Austria).

a right to 'quote' photographs and this was held to be a lacuna contrary to freedom of speech which the Court would fill. A weekly newspaper published five miniaturized pages of the front page of the plaintiff's newspaper (including the photographs) in the context of an article about the plaintiff newspaper's attitude to a political group. There was reference in particular to an incident in which a photograph had been published of a youth suspected of arson where the claimant newspaper had not attempted to conceal the youth's identity. The newspaper owned the copyright in the photograph and sought an injunction. The Austrian Copyright statute recognized a right to quote text but was silent as to photographs. The Court held that the statute failed to recognize that it might be just as necessary in the interest of freedom of speech to quote a picture as to quote language. The use of the photographs was also held to be justified in the context of the matters reported.

### (3) Interviews and Copyright, Designs and Patents Act 1988, s 58

The third of the limitations on the exclusivity conferred by copyright con- **9.67** cerns interviews. Copyright will subsist in an interview or other spoken words as a 'literary work' once the spoken words are first recorded in writing or otherwise.[128] The first owner of that copyright will be the interviewee. A separate 'reporter's copyright' may also come into existence in respect of a published interview.[129]

A statutory restriction on exercise of the literary copyright is imposed by s 58 CDPA **9.68** in order to facilitate news reporting. It provides as follows:

(1) Where a record of spoken words is made, in writing or otherwise, for the purpose—
   (a) of reporting current events,[130] or
   (b) of communicating to the public the whole or part of the work
   it is not an infringement of any copyright in the words as a literary work to use the record or material taken from it (or to copy the record, or any such material, and use the copy) for that purpose, provided the following conditions are met.
(2) The conditions are that—
   (a) the record is a direct record of the spoken words and is not taken from a previous record or from a broadcast;
   (b) the making of the record was not prohibited by the speaker and, where copyright already subsisted in that work, did not infringe copyright;
   (c) the use made of the record or material taken from it is not of a kind prohibited by or on behalf of the speaker or copyright owner before the record was made; and

---

[128] s 3 CDPA.
[129] *Walter v Lane* [1900] AC 539; *Express Newspapers* (n 6).
[130] This is an important condition. It may prevent an author using notes of an interview significantly later than the date of the interview, *eg* for an unauthorized biography after the interviewee has died.

(d) the use is by or with the authority of a person who is lawfully in possession of the record.

This defence will be available in addition to any defence of fair dealing.[131]

**9.69** Section 58 is analysed in detail in the copyright textbooks.[132] It enables the speaker delivering a speech or granting an interview to require that his or her speech or interview is kept private, but only if the specified preconditions are met. Differing rules apply to governmental and non-governmental matters.[133] This provision goes some way towards protecting the confidentiality of expressly off-the-record press briefings.

**9.70** The main relevance of this section to privacy and the media is to the giving of interviews by celebrities, politicians, and others. Unless a prohibition on republication (or at any rate republication without prior approval) is stipulated before the interview commences, the interviewee will not be able to use copyright to prevent the broadcast of embarrassing slips or gaffes made in a recorded interview, insofar as the report is of a current event. This is because the exception in s 58 designed to restrict the effects of copyright on the use of interviews, will apply. The interviewee will, however, be able to prevent use which is not for the purpose of reporting current events, because the exception is not engaged. In cases where the interviewee sells his or her story to a media organization, exploitation of the story is often governed by the terms of a written agreement, which may contain an assignment of copyright.

## D. Copyright and the Privacy of Third Parties

**9.71** The privacy rights of third parties are capable of imposing significant restrictions on the exploitation of copyright. This occurs in the case of photographs, films, and books, where these rights are asserted against publishers and others seeking to exploit the written word or visual images. The reader is referred to Chapters 4 and 5 for a general discussion concerning rights of confidence and privacy. The basic problem is that the publisher finds that its exclusive right to engage in commercial exploitation of what is a copyright work may be affected by the rights of confidence or privacy of an individual to whom reference is made in that work. Thus, three Convention rights are engaged, under Articles 8 (privacy) and 10 (freedom of expression), and Article 1 of the First Protocol (property rights, *ie* copyright). To resolve the conflict between these rights, the guidance given by the House of

---

[131] ss 29–31 CDPA.

[132] *Copinger and Skone James* (n 3) paras 9-174–9-179 and *Laddie, Prescott and Vitoria* (n 3) paras 21.52–21.54. See also H MacQueen, '"My tongue is mine ain": Copyright, the spoken word and privacy' (2005) 68(3) MLR 349.

[133] *Attorney General v Jonathan Cape Ltd* [1976] 1 QB 752.

Lords in *Re S (A child) (Identification: Restriction on Publication)* will generally be apposite, with that guidance applicable to the three rights instead of the two (freedom of expression and privacy) there discussed.[134] This involves looking first at the comparative importance of the actual rights being claimed in the individual case; then at the justifications for interfering with or restricting each of those rights; and applying the proportionality test to each.

Photographs are a particular area where there has been case law and statute **9.72** affecting the exercise of copyrights in the context of privacy interests. Although pt III CDPA makes no express provision for a right of privacy in respect of non-consensual filming or photography, this does not preclude the existence of a right arising through the civil wrong of misuse of private information. Its existence may be treated as an instance of Article 8 rights taking precedence over rights under Article 1 of the First Protocol and Article 10. The consequence of rights of confidence or privacy trumping copyright interests is to create the possibility of stopping all exploitation of the copyright in cases where injunctive relief is granted.[135]

The line of authority relating to commissioned works goes back to the nineteenth- **9.73** century cases of *Tuck & Sons v Priester* and *Pollard v Photographic Co.*[136] In *Pollard* a photographer who had taken pictures of a woman in return for a fee was restrained by injunction from selling copies on the ground that sale or exhibition of the photographs would be a breach of confidence and also because of an implied term of the contract between the customer and the photographer that the prints taken from the negative were for the use of the customer only. If the photograph had been registered under the copyright legislation then in force, the copyright would have belonged to the person who commissioned it, namely the claimant, and she could have restrained further publication by the photographer on the basis of copyright infringement.[137]

For the greater part of the twentieth century such decisions were largely of aca- **9.74** demic interest because, under the Copyright Acts of 1911 and 1956, the commissioner of a photograph was automatically the owner of the copyright in it in circumstances where the commissioner paid, or agreed to pay, for the commission in money or money's worth.[138] Under the CDPA this statutory provision was

---

[134] [2004] UKHL 47 [17].
[135] For rights of confidentiality in images see 4.77.
[136] (1887)19 QBD 629, CA and (1889) 40 Ch D 345.
[137] Copyright Act 1911.
[138] See Copyright Act 1911, s 5 and Copyright Act 1956, s 4(3). The sections are not identically worded, but the differences are not material. Where the infringement of copyright was an invasion of privacy, vindictive (in the sense of exemplary) damages could be awarded: *Williams v Settle* [1960] 1 WLR 1072 where wedding photographs were sold to a newspaper by the photographer to illustrate a story about the murder of the bride's father.

removed and, subject to certain exceptions,[139] the author and first owner of the copyright in a photograph, whether commissioned or not, became the person who created it: that is, the photographer.[140] The statutory right of privacy in respect of commissioned works was embodied in s 85 CDPA, which therefore recognized the *Pollard* type of case.

**9.75** Part III CDPA creates a statutory right of privacy by s 85(1), which provides:

> A person who for private and domestic purposes commissions the taking of a photograph or the making of a film has, where copyright subsists in the resulting work, the right not to have—
> (a) copies of the work issued to the public;
> (b) the work exhibited or shown in public; or
> (c) the work communicated to the public.

There is a very limited range of exceptions to this right, as set out in s 85(2); incidental inclusions, parliamentary and judicial proceedings, Royal Commissions and statutory inquiries, acts done under statutory authority and certain exceptions with respect to anonymous or pseudonymous works.

**9.76** The statutory right of privacy only applies to a person who commissions[141] a photograph or film 'for private *and* domestic' purposes. It does not apply to commissions for commercial purposes, however private, nor to consensual photography short of a commission.

**9.77** The courts see no conceptual problem in privacy rights taking priority over copyrights: see, for example, *A v B, C and D*[142] where the claimant obtained a de facto exclusive right to prevent the commercial exploitation of her own image in circumstances where certain 'glamour' pictures of the claimant had been published with her consent but publication of other more sexually suggestive pictures was prohibited by injunction. Some European Convention countries, such as Spain, have expressly incorporated a right to one's own image in their domestic privacy codes.[143] Depending on the circumstances, children may have privacy rights in

---

[139] The exception is for employees in s 11(2). The commissioner can obtain ownership or control by taking an assignment or exclusive licence.

[140] See ss 9 and 11 CDPA.

[141] *Trimingham v Associated Newspapers Ltd* [2012] EWHC 1296 (QB), [2012] 4 All ER 717 [334]: commissioning means that there must be an obligation on the commissioned party to produce the work and an obligation on the commissioner to pay money or money's worth.

[142] (QBD, 2 March 2001) (Mackay J). The claimant was a former lap dancer. She visited a model agency and posed for photographs, which included pornographic and other nude shots. She said that she had told the photographer that the shots should only be shown within the industry and were not to be published without her consent. The photographer had assigned the copyright in them to an adult magazine, which in turn had granted a licence to a newspaper. An injunction was granted against the assignee and the licensee publishers.

[143] Art 18(1) of the 1978 Spanish Constitution provides: 'The rights of honour, family and individual privacy, and of one's own image are recognised.' See L Gimeno, 'Photographs, commercial exploitation of the image and copyright in Spain' [1998] Ent L Rev 131, 132. The author discussed the case of *Cristina B v Jose AM*, a Supreme Court decision of 29 March 1996, upholding an award

relation to the taking and exploitation of photographs featuring them based on the civil wrong of misuse of private information.[144]

There is a statutory regime applicable to consents and waivers of the right under **9.78** s 85.[145] However, the general principles of contract and estoppel are still applicable in s 85 cases.[146] By analogy with the tort of defamation, the court could require that a consent cover the specific publication complained of. In *Cook v Ward*[147] the defence of consent failed, because the defamatory publication was to a wider audience than the restricted publication to which the claimant had assented.[148] The court is likely to imply consent in certain circumstances, such as where the claimant has posed for a photograph with knowledge of the specific purpose for which it is to be used. If the claimant has been paid to pose for a photograph, this may well indicate unqualified consent to publication.[149]

If the consent is given gratuitously, then in theory it can be revoked at any time **9.79** before the invasion of privacy takes place. But if the copyright owner has been induced to change his or her position, he or she may be able to claim the existence of a licence by estoppel. If the consent is given for valuable consideration, then normally it would be irrevocable.[150] However, whether the copyright owner's right to publish is contractual or arises by estoppel, there will be circumstances in which the court will permit the owner of the privacy right to revoke the consent, although he or she may have to pay compensation to the copyright owner for so doing.[151]

As indicated at 9.71, whether or not a privacy right will prevail against a publisher **9.80** (of photographs, moving images, or the written word) generally depends on an appropriate weighing of the particular rights under Articles 8 and 10 and Article 1 of the First Protocol in accordance with the principles in *Re S*. In the case of the statutory privacy right and moral rights (see 9.81–9.92) under the CDPA, Parliament has already legislated for those rights to trump the rights of the copyright owner

---

of damages to a professional model who had consented to being photographed but who had not expressly consented to any publication of the photograph by the copyright owner.

[144] *Murray v Express Newspapers plc* [2008] EWCA Civ 446, [2009] Ch 481.

[145] ss 87(1)–(3) CDPA.

[146] s 87(4) CDPA.

[147] (1830) 6 Bing 409.

[148] *A v B, C and D* (n 142) is consistent with that approach.

[149] In Germany, approval for the public dissemination of a person's image appears to be deemed to have been granted if the person shown in the image received a consideration for its production: s 22 of the *Kunsturhebergesetz*. In *A v B, C and D* (n 142) the claimant was not paid for posing in the nude, and the Court regarded this as significant on the issue of whether she was to be treated as having consented to the publication of the photographs in the media.

[150] *Winter Garden Theatre (London) Ltd v Millennium Productions Ltd* [1948] AC 173.

[151] In *Nicholls v BBC* [1999] EMLR 791, CA, the claimant police informer agreed to participate in a film about his experiences on the condition that his new identity and location were concealed. He approved the film, but he changed his mind and obtained an injunction. The film significantly increased the risk of the claimant being identified, endangering the safety of himself and his family. The Court allowed him to revoke the consent.

if the person owning any such right is different to the copyright owner.[152] Where the individual whose privacy rights are engaged and the copyright owner are the same person, or where there is an assignment of the property right in favour of an applicant for a privacy injunction, the potential conflict will fall away.[153] A privacy right will often prevail over the exclusive right of the publisher. Where the privacy right does prevail, an injunction would not necessarily be granted. There may be separate considerations why this remedy should be refused on equitable or discretionary grounds and the balancing of Convention rights may confine the claimant to a monetary award.

# E. Moral Rights

**9.81** This section will address three of the moral rights arising under ch IV CDPA and their relevance to protection of privacy. In this context, the privacy interests protected are not concerned with unwanted dissemination of private information, but relate more to a person's right to control the integrity of his or her work and his or her association with it, and to prevent misappropriation of his or her name. For a fuller discussion of the general law, the reader is referred to the specialist textbooks.[154] The rights of an author to claim authorship of his or her work and to object to any distortion, mutilation, or other relevant treatment of it have found their most recent international expression in Article 6 *bis* of the Berne Copyright Convention.[155] These rights were introduced for the first time into English law in 1989, through the CDPA. The statutory right to redress in connection with false attribution of authorship is not to be found in the Berne Convention and was present in the Copyright Act 1956,[156] although English law appears to have long recognized a right to redress in connection with some aspects of false attribution.[157]

## (1) The Right of Paternity

**9.82** The paternity right is the right to be identified as the author of certain types of copyright work, including literary works; and in the case of a 'film' to be identified as its director.[158] The right lasts as long as copyright subsists in the work.[159] Subject to exceptions, the right is capable of being exercised against assignees of the copyright

---

[152] s 2(2) CDPA.

[153] See *eg Rocknroll v News Group Newspapers Ltd* [2013] EWHC 24 (Ch) where the applicant obtained an assignment of copyright in the photographs which were the subject of the application.

[154] *Copinger and Skone James* (n 3) ch 11 and *Laddie, Prescott and Vitoria* (n 3) ch 13.

[155] Berne Convention for the Protection of Literary and Artistic Works, Paris, Act of 24 July 1971, Misc 23 (1972), Cmnd 5002; as amended on 2 October 1979, TS 63 (1990), Cm 1212.

[156] s 43.

[157] *Lord Byron v Johnston* (1816) 2 Mer 29, 35 ER 851, referred to in Prosser, 'Privacy' (n 25).

[158] s 77(1) CDPA.

[159] s 86(1) CDPA.

and their successors in title. The right to be identified arises whenever the work has been published commercially in the case of literary works.[160] In connection with films the right of the director arises whenever the film is shown in public or if copies of it (*eg* DVDs) are issued to the public.[161] Where the right arises in relation to commercial publication or issue to the public, the identification must be clear and reasonably prominent and must be in or on each copy; or if not appropriate, in a manner likely to bring the identity of the author to the notice of the person acquiring the copy.[162] The right applies to the whole or any part of a work.[163]

The right has to be asserted in order to ground a right of action for infringement and **9.83** there are provisions relating to the way in which the right is to be asserted.[164] The right has characteristics of a property right, although it is not one. Thus, its assertion binds not only an assignee of the copyright but also those claiming through them, whether or not they have notice of the assertion.[165]

There are exceptions to the right. Among the more important are the following. **9.84** It does not bind the copyright owner where the first owner of the copyright in the work was the employer of the author or director.[166] Nor is it infringed by any use under s 30 in connection with the reporting of current events by means of a sound recording, film, or broadcast.[167] In addition, the right does not apply in relation to any work made for the purpose of reporting current events.[168] The right does not apply to publication of a literary work in a newspaper or magazine where the material was made available for the purpose of publication or with the consent of the author.[169] The right may be waived[170] but not assigned. The waiver may be conditional or unconditional and, unless the contrary is indicated, a written waiver will be presumed to extend to licensees and successors in title of the copyright owner.[171] Consent is a defence and the general law of contract and estoppel apply in connection with claims to enforce the right.[172]

### (2) The Integrity Right

The second of the moral rights arising under the Berne Convention is the right **9.85** not to have certain copyright works[173] subjected to 'derogatory treatment'. This is

---

[160] s 77(2) CDPA. Slightly different provision is made for lyrics: see s 77(3).
[161] s 77(6) CDPA.
[162] s 77(7)(a) CDPA.
[163] s 89(1) CDPA.
[164] s 78(1)–(2) CDPA.
[165] s 78(4)(a) CDPA.
[166] s 79(3)(a) CDPA.
[167] s 79(4)(a) CDPA.
[168] s 79(5) CDPA.
[169] s 79(6) CDPA.
[170] s 87(2) CDPA.
[171] s 87(3) CDPA.
[172] s 87(1) and (4) CDPA.
[173] The right lasts for so long as copyright subsists in the work: s 86(1) CDPA.

known as the 'integrity right'. The right is available to, among others, the author of a literary work and the director of a 'film'.[174] 'Treatment' is essentially any addition to, deletion, alteration, or adaptation of the work; and treatment is derogatory if it amounts to distortion or mutilation of the work or is otherwise prejudicial to the honour or reputation of the author or director.[175] It is not enough that the author is aggrieved.[176] The infringing acts are similar to the acts applicable to exercise of the paternity right, such as commercial publication and issue to the public.[177] The right extends to treatment of parts of a work resulting from previous treatment by a person other than the author or director, if those parts are attributed to or are likely to be regarded as the work of the author.[178] The right applies to the whole or any part of a work.[179]

**9.86**  The exceptions and qualifications to the right are similar to those applicable to the paternity right, with some differences.[180] Most notably, the current events exceptions do not apply and the right is restricted in relation to works the first copyright owner of which was an employer of the description mentioned above. The restriction is that the right to object to the derogatory treatment only arises where the author or director is identified at the time of the relevant act or has been previously identified in or on published copies of the work, unless there is a 'sufficient disclaimer'.[181] The provisions applying to waiver, consent, and estoppel mentioned at 9.84 also apply.

### (3) False Attribution of Authorship

**9.87**  The right to object to false attribution of authorship exists with respect to a range of copyright works, including literary works. Attribution means a statement, whether express or implied, as to the identity of the author.[182] Whether or not there has been an attribution is to be decided in accordance with the single-meaning rule applicable in the law of defamation; so the proper test is whether or not the reasonable reader would understand the material as containing a false attribution of authorship to the claimant.[183] It is not necessary for the claimant to be an author. Again, the right applies to the whole or any part of a work.[184]

---

[174] s 80(1) CDPA.
[175] s 80(2) CDPA.
[176] *Pasterfield* (n 62) 181–2 and cases there cited; *Morrison v Lightbond* [1993] EMLR 144; *Carlton v Coleman* [1911] 1 KB 771; *Huston v Turner Entertainment* IIC Vol 23, 702 (Cour de Cassation); *Snow v Eaton Centre Ltd* 70 CPR (2d) 105.
[177] s 80(4) and (6) CDPA.
[178] s 80(7) CDPA.
[179] s 89(2) CDPA.
[180] ss 81–2 CDPA.
[181] ss 82 and 178 CDPA.
[182] s 84(1) CDPA.
[183] *Clark v Associated Newspapers Ltd* [1998] 1 WLR 1558, 1568.
[184] s 89(2) CDPA.

The right is infringed by a person who, among other things, issues to the public **9.88** copies of the work bearing the attribution.[185] The right can only be asserted in respect of material that can be properly regarded as a 'work'.[186] Material added to what is the claimant's own work can render the whole of a work the subject of an attribution.[187] Publication of an article falsely attributing words spoken in an interview is actionable.[188] So too are spoof diaries.[189] The right is subject to a defence of consent[190] and the principles of waiver and estoppel also apply. The right continues to subsist until twenty years after a person's death.

## F. Publicity Rights

This section considers how domestic law has developed image or publicity rights **9.89** and whether the emergence of a US-style quasi-proprietary image right is likely in England and Wales.[191]

The exploitation of a person's image in the mass media of the twenty-first century **9.90** has become a valuable commercial commodity. The commonest applications are in marketing and product endorsement but there will be circumstances in which the mere reproduction of a particular person's image or identity will be of value. There may be several elements of a person's identity which may be worthy of commercial exploitation or safeguarding from unauthorized exploitation or use. Identity breaks down to physical appearance, name, signature, voice, and any other recognizable characteristic of that particular individual. The right to control the public exploitation of one's image or identity on an exclusive basis is known as the right of publicity. This enables the individual to prevent unauthorized commercial use of his or her image or identity, and, by the same token, exclusively to license the use of that image or identity. Recognition of the inherent commercial value of identity is central to the right of publicity.

---

[185] s 84(2)(a) CDPA. A second edition not updated by the original author may include a false attribution: *Harrison v Harrison* [2010] FSR 25.

[186] *Noah v Shuba* [1991] FSR 14, 33: two sentences on their own would not have constituted a 'work', the requisite amount or degree of information, instruction, or literary enjoyment being absent. See also *Infopaq International* (n 29).

[187] *Noah* (n 186) 32.

[188] *Moore v News of the World Ltd* [1972] 1 QB 441, CA. The appeal on this point was in respect of a direction to the jury given by the trial judge, a direction that Megaw LJ described at 451, as perfectly proper. For that reason he dismissed the appeal, but entertained doubts on the issue of attribution. Denning LJ at 449 had no doubt that it was a false attribution, and Stephenson LJ at 453 agreed for the reasons given that the appeal should be dismissed and stated that the direction to the jury contained no material misdirection.

[189] *Clark* (n 183).

[190] In *Moore* (n 188) a defence of consent had failed on the facts.

[191] A comprehensive survey of personality and image rights is outside the scope of this book. For more extensive analysis see S Smith, *Image, Persona and the Law* (2nd edn, Sweet and Maxwell 2008), and G Black, *Publicity Rights and Image* (Hart 2011).

**9.91**  The right of publicity is distinct from the core right to privacy. It is intended to shape and control the commercial aspects of image whereas the rationale of privacy rights is, at least in part, to protect and maintain secrecy.[192] Invariably the infringement of publicity rights involves damage to a personality-related commercial interest and damages will reflect a licence fee for authorized usage or any unjust enrichment by the defendant. Publicity rights need not engage Article 8 and are heritable, and capable of being licensed, sold, or managed by third parties.

**9.92**  English law lacks a recognized free-standing image or publicity right or tort with its own jurisprudential underpinning. Under the law of England and Wales the remedies against unjustified exploitation of a person's image that are available derive principally from recent developments in the law of passing off, privacy, and breach of confidence and, to a much lesser extent, from trade marks,[193] data protection, and defamation.[194] The right to publicity is an artificial, composite right and its precise ambit difficult to define. This contrasts starkly with the position under US law, where publicity rights have become much more developed over a hundred-year period. However, there is no doubt that in spite of authoritative judicial pronouncements set against the creation of image rights,[195] the tendency has been towards English law offering enhanced rights for the exploitation and control of one's image, especially via the development of the action for misuse of private information, breach of confidence, and passing off. The approach in trade mark law has been more restrictive. As a matter of commercial practice, the contracts of high profile sporting figures, particularly footballers, now frequently contain clauses referring to 'image rights'. The exploitation of such rights as an activity ancillary to another occupation is capable of protection under the doctrine of restraint of trade.[196]

**9.93**  The ruling on the availability of damages for the infringement of personality rights by the Court of Justice of the European Union in *eDate Advertising GmbH v X* has implications for online publishers within England and Wales whose content features individuals from jurisdictions where such rights are better established.[197] One of two joined cases before the Court in *eDate Advertising* was that of a claim by the French actor Olivier Martinez in France against the *Sunday Mirror*. The newspaper had published an article about Martinez's relationship with Kylie Minogue

---

[192] See the discussion on the difference between core privacy interests and privacy-related rights at 2.04–2.52.

[193] See 9.110–9.114.

[194] See *Tolley v Fry* [1931] AC 333. The protection provided by defamation is diminished by the limitation that the use or endorsement in question must objectively damage the reputation of the claimant.

[195] *Elvis Presley Enterprises Inc v Sid Shaw Elvisly Yours* [1999] RPC 567, 597–8 (Simon Brown LJ).

[196] *Proactive Sports Management Ltd v Rooney* [2011] EWCA Civ 1444, [2012] 2 All ER (Comm) 815 [93]–[94].

[197] Joined Cases C-509/09 and C-161/10 *eDate Advertising GmbH v X; Martinez v MGN Ltd* [2012] QB 654.

on its website, along with photographs of an encounter between them in Paris. It also attributed remarks to Robert Martinez, Olivier's father. Since the paper's website was available in France, Olivier and Robert Martinez brought a claim before the Tribunal de Grande Instance de Paris against the paper's owner, MGN Ltd. The national court referred a question about the scope of its jurisdiction to hear disputes about infringements of personality rights committed via the internet. In its determination, the European Court held that the holder of personality rights may bring proceedings for compensation for all of the damage arising from the infringement either before the courts of the Member State in which the publisher is established, or those of the Member State where the individual has his or her centre of interests.[198] However, the potential difficulties for publishers arising from this scenario are mitigated by the existence of Article 3 of Directive 2000/31/EC, which the Court in *eDate Advertising* noted precludes a Member State from making a provider of an electronic commerce service subject to stricter requirements than those provided for by the substantive law in force in the Member State in which the service provider was established.[199]

## (1) Publicity Rights in the United States

Publicity rights in the United States have been described as protecting 'the business value of popularity', and the cause of action related to them generally arises from damage to the commercial value of the relevant features of an individual's personality.[200] They are primarily a matter of state rather than federal law.[201] Although half of the states recognize rights of publicity either by statute or at common law, legal protection is not uniform.[202] Federal level protection for sports and screen personae is partially afforded by the Lanham Trade Mark Act 1946 which includes provisions that prevent unauthorized use of a celebrity's likeness or characteristics via misuse of a trade mark.[203] In this respect, it is the individual's likeness or distinctive characteristics that effectively operate as his or her personal mark. **9.94**

Common law rights of publicity (as distinct from approaches based on state statutes or trade marks) were recognized in the 2nd Circuit decision in *Haelan* **9.95**

---

[198] *eDate Advertising* (n 197) paras 48–9, 57.

[199] Council Directive 2000/31/EC of 8 June 2000 on certain legal aspects of information society services, in particular electronic commerce, in the Internal Market [2000] OJ L178/1; *eDate Advertising* (n 197) para 67.

[200] J Klink, '50 years of publicity rights in the United States and the never ending hassle with intellectual property and personality rights in Europe' [2003] IPQ 363.

[201] The first 'publicity right' in the US was enacted by the legislature of New York in 1903: see ss 50–1 of the New York Civil Rights Law: 'A person, firm or group that uses for advertising purposes, or for the purposes of trade, the name, portrait or picture of any living person without first having obtained the written consent of such person, or if a minor of his or her parent or guardian, is guilty of misdemeanor.'

[202] J Thomas McCarthy, *Rights of Publicity and Privacy* (Clark Boardman Callaghan 1987).

[203] s 43(a) Lanham Trade Mark Act 1946, 15 USCA 1125 (a) (1) (as amended by the Trade Mark Law Revision Act 1988).

*Laboratories v Topps Chewing Gum*, which prohibited a rival manufacturer's unauthorized use of pictures of baseball players marketed with chewing gum.[204] The decision cast publicity rights as a species of property right, a direction that federal law has broadly recognized in the half-century since. A claimant must prove ownership of the publicity right and establish that unauthorized use has led to damage to the commercial interest of the rights owner—essential elements confirmed by the US Supreme Court in *Zacchini v Scripps-Howard Broadcasting Co.*[205] In that case a television news report which showed the entirety of a human cannonball's act was held to be a publicity right. Along with the *Johnny Carson* case,[206] in which the claimant's catchphrase voiced on his television show was held to be a part of his image or identity, this example illustrates the generous scope afforded to publicity rights under federal law. The First Amendment is not a bar to recovery of damages for infringement of publicity rights, but is a consideration to be balanced against an individual's rights.[207] Likewise, intention to infringe has been regarded as irrelevant, the principal consideration being whether the claimant's identity is compromised by the infringing material.[208]

**9.96** US law is most marked by the differing common law and statutory approaches adopted by states. In some US jurisdictions the estates of deceased celebrities may continue as owners of the celebrity's publicity rights, in others they may not. Duration of protection varies widely. Unsurprisingly, given the importance of celebrity to the state's economy, California law provides strong protection for image rights in s 3344 of the Californian Civil Code along with suitable provision for duration of rights (lifetime plus seventy years) and exemptions for educational, incidental, and reporting news in the public interest.[209] Statutory protection is given to the voice of a dead celebrity.[210] The Californian Supreme Court laid down a test whereby the court first looks at the purpose and use of a celebrity's name or image and then considers whether or not the use of that image is 'transformative' enough to merit protection under the First Amendment.[211] The 9th Circuit affirmed this

---

[204] *Haelan Laboratories* (n 196).

[205] 433 US 562 (1977).

[206] *Carson v Here's Johnny Portable Toilets, Inc* 698 F 2d 831 (US Ct of Apps (6th Cir), 1983).

[207] *Zacchini v Scripps-Howard Broadcasting Co* (n 205).

[208] *Vanna White v Samsung Electronics America, Inc* 971 F 2d 1395 (US Ct of Apps (9th Cir), 1992).

[209] s 3344(a) states 'any person who knowingly uses another's name, voice, signature, photograph, or likeness in any manner, on or in products, merchandise, goods or services, without such person's prior consent, or in the case of a minor, the prior consent of his parent or legal guardian, shall be liable for damages sustained by the person or persons injured as a result thereof'.

[210] California Civil Code, s 990(b), as amended in 1985.

[211] In *Comedy III Productions Inc v Gary Saderup Inc* 25 Cal 4th 387, 29 Med L Rptr 1897 (2001), the owner of the publicity rights to The Three Stooges brought a claim against an artist who sold copies of his original drawing of the Stooges in the form of lithographs and T-shirts. The California Supreme Court stated that a work would be sufficiently transformative if its 'marketability and economic value' do not 'derive primarily from the fame of the celebrity depicted'. In that case, the Court did not find that the work contained any 'significant transformative or creative contribution'

test in obiter remarks in a case involving digitally manipulated images of Dustin Hoffman in the film *Tootsie*, holding that the elimination of the actor's body in the image in question would have been sufficiently transformative to satisfy the test.[212] The Court found that there was no commercial exploitation or speech where the image, which was of the actor wearing the latest fashions, did not use his image in an advertisement printed merely for the purpose of selling a particular product.[213]

## (2) Publicity Rights under English Law

In England and Wales, claimants wishing to control publicity about themselves **9.97** have been forced to improvise with the closest suitable legal doctrines for want of any formal legal provision by Parliament or the common law. The main causes of action that have been adapted to pursue that objective are considered below.

### (a) Passing off

Passing off may be used to prevent false (and unauthorized) celebrity endorse- **9.98** ments of goods and services. In *Irvine v Talksport* a photograph of the Formula 1 driver Eddie Irvine was doctored without his consent to show him holding a radio branded with the defendant's logo and then used in materials promoting the defendant's radio station.[214] The judge reasoned that the damage to the claimant's goodwill from false endorsement would 'reduce, blur or diminish' its exclusivity. The claimant's award of damages was increased to £25,000 on appeal, a figure representing the minimum value of an Irvine endorsement. No common field of activity or tendency that sales of products or services will diminish was necessary to establish the cause of action. A claimant will need to prove two facts:

> First that at the time of the acts complained of he had a significant reputation or goodwill. Second that the actions of the defendant gave rise to a false message which would be understood by a not insignificant section of his market that his goods have been endorsed, recommended or are approved by the claimant.[215]

The *Irvine* decision has met a perceived commercial need and has had the effect **9.99** of protecting the value of endorsements which by the early twenty-first century have come to provide substantial income for sports and entertainment people. Such cases are, however, explicitly not concerned with image (or publicity) rights, however much claimants wish they were.[216] Claims related to the unauthorized

---

but instead was made up of 'literal, conventional depictions of The Three Stooges' that derived their economic value primarily from the fame of the Stooges.

[212] *Hoffman v Capital Cities/ABC Inc* 255 F 3d 1180 (US Ct of Apps (9th Cir), 2001).

[213] *Hoffman* (n 212).

[214] *Irvine v Talksport Ltd* [2003] 2 All ER 881, CA.

[215] *Irvine* (n 214) [2002] 1 WLR 2355, per the analysis of Laddie J at first instance, approved by Jonathan Parker LJ on appeal.

[216] *Fenty v Arcadia Group Brands Ltd (t/a Topshop)* [2013] EWHC 2310 (Ch), the analysis of Birss J on this point, as on Rihanna's claim, being approved by Kitchin LJ on appeal ([2015] EWCA Civ 3, [2015] FSR 14).

use of a celebrity's image will remain rooted in establishing the classic ingredients of a passing off action, namely goodwill, misrepresentation, and damage, rather than trespassing into the territory of a free-standing general right to control reproduction of one's image, which would be more helpful to those concerned with privacy as well as commercial interests. In the context of passing off, merchandising raises different issues, although the legal principles in both endorsement and merchandising cases are the same.[217] Other aspects of personality may be protectable through the law of passing off, for example one's voice.[218]

### (b) Privacy

**9.100**   The development of the action for breach of confidence, to the point where a separate and distinct cause of action for misuse of personal information has evolved, has permitted a variety of publicity interests to be protected, although the requirements that there either be a breach of a contractual or equitable confidential duty or that a privacy interest is engaged are essential.

**9.101**   Information may be protected from disclosure which is not inherently a personal publicity right but consists of images or data that have commercial value based on their authenticity or novelty. For example, photographs taken without permission on the set of a high-profile horror film which disclosed the designs of the monster costumes and make-up were restrained pursuant to an equitable duty of confidence.[219]

**9.102**   The principal stimulus to the development of a right of publicity in England and Wales is the *Douglas v Hello!* litigation.[220] In spite of an exclusive agreement to publish selected photographs from their wedding in *OK!* magazine, rival magazine *Hello!* published lower-quality 'spoiler' photographs of the event obtained from an unauthorized paparazzo photographer who had evaded the tight security. The corporate claimant, OK! Ltd, joined the personal claimants, Catherine Zeta-Jones and Michael Douglas, in an attempt to prevent publication and subsequently sue for damages.

**9.103**   The Douglases' attempt to obtain a pre-publication injunction broke new ground, even if the ultimate balancing exercise of the competing Convention rights under Articles 8 and 10 did not favour restraining the defendant.[221] The photographs of

---

[217] *Fenty*, HC (n 216) [33].

[218] *Sim v Heinz* [1957] 1 WLR 313.

[219] *Shelley Films Ltd v Rex Features Ltd* [1994] EMLR 134. The film set of Mary Shelley's *Frankenstein* was secure, guarded by security personnel and notices forbade photography or unauthorized admission. In *Creation Records Ltd v News Group Newspapers Ltd* [1997] EMLR 444, disparate objects around a swimming pool were to be photographed for a band's album cover. The photographer was lawfully at the scene, although the purpose of shooting the album cover and the security measures taken allowed the claimants to show a seriously arguable claim in confidence to obtain an injunction.

[220] [2001] QB 967.

[221] The claim based on tortious interference with the contractual relationship between *OK!* and the Douglases was too speculative to justify the grant of an interim injunction. On the breach of

the event which disclosed personal appearances, were capable of protection as confidential information, and the claims made by the Douglases and *OK!* were described as 'an important and developing area of the law' in which 'it can be said with confidence that the law recognises and will appropriately protect a right of personal privacy'.[222]

Although an injunction was ultimately refused, the personal claims in breach of **9.104** confidence were successful at trial[223] and on appeal.[224] The relief afforded to the Douglases was founded on the unauthorized invasion of privacy that engaged their Article 8 rights but which could also be exploited as a personal commercial confidence against *Hello!*, although it did not constitute a transferable property right as might have been the case under US law. The Court recognized that the right to control publicity surrounding a private event gave rise to distress. It did not affect the result at trial that the couple had chosen to commercialize their rights in the images of their wedding by selling rights to *OK!*.

More pertinent from the perspective of publicity rights was the judgment of the **9.105** House of Lords in *Douglas v Hello!* which considered the rights of an exclusive licensee against unauthorized third-party interference with that licence.[225] The judge at first instance had held that the defendant had not induced the Douglases to breach their contract with *OK!* or caused tortious interference with *OK!*'s business. But *OK!*'s breach of confidence claim succeeded. The Court of Appeal ruled that all of *OK!*'s claims failed although the Douglases' breach of confidence claim succeeded. In the House of Lords a majority found for *OK!*, allowing English law to arrive at a position in which licensed publicity or image rights could be protected from third-party interference provided that the information making up the 'publicity' happened to be confidential and commercially valuable.

Lord Hoffmann, who gave the leading judgment of the majority, recognized that **9.106** *OK!*'s claim was to protect a commercial asset in the form of confidential information. Confidentiality stemmed from the obligation of confidence imposed on all those at the wedding and because the Douglases were in a position to control all photographic records of the event, which was both for their benefit and to protect *OK!*'s rights.[226] Privacy rights were a distraction as regards the corporate claimant's breach of confidence claim: what mattered was that it was information that a magazine was willing to pay for to print and a legitimate enterprise that the law should protect from interference.[227] The measure of damages would appear to be the value of the exclusivity which has been lost.

---

confidence claim, the official publicity surrounding the wedding tipped the balance in favour of allowing publication, damages being an adequate remedy.

[222] *Douglas* (n 220) [109]–[110] (Sedley LJ).
[223] [2003] EWHC 786 (Ch).
[224] [2005] EWCA Civ 595, [2006] QB 125.
[225] [2007] UKHL 21, [2008] 1 AC 1.
[226] *Douglas* (n 225) [113]–[117].
[227] *Douglas* (n 225) [118].

**9.107**    In *Douglas v Hello!* the defendants were aware of the commercial dimensions of their interference with *OK!*'s exclusive licence. *Hello!* had bid the same sum for the exclusivity. It remains to be seen what remedy will be available when commercially confidential information is published with no knowledge of exclusivity.

**9.108**    The majority did not consider that the publication of the authorized images in *OK!* undermined the confidentiality of the information from the point of the magazine's publication onwards. Lord Nicholls' dissenting judgment concluded that the simultaneous publication of the two sets of photographs in the respective magazines robbed *OK!* of any commercial confidence in the images because it placed them in the public domain.[228] The differences to be found in the unapproved photographs lay in terms of picture quality, posture, or facial expressions and were insufficient to constitute confidential information. Lord Walker (also in the minority) concluded that the confidentiality of information depends on its nature not its market value.[229] Both the majority and the minority were united in asserting that the case did not create a new intellectual property or image right. Lord Walker noted that the claimants had not claimed quasi-proprietary rights in the spectacle but non-proprietary rights of confidence in wedding photographs as a class.

**9.109**    The law in this area was further developed in *Murray v Express Newspapers plc* which concerned the publication of photographs taken at a distance of the infant son of author JK Rowling while in his pushchair in a public street. On a strike-out application at first instance, Patten J accepted that a legitimate expectation not to be photographed without consent when not engaged on official duties or public business created a quasi-image right.[230] The Court of Appeal distanced itself from the judge's acceptance that allowing the claimant to continue his claim would create a privacy shield for children of celebrities (and hence an exploitable image right as consent to publish would be required).[231] However, the right held arguable by the Court of Appeal (the case ultimately settled) bears comparison with an image right insofar as the law will prevent exploitation of images where there would be foreseeable objection and lack of consent but no distress or insult to dignity. In *AAA v Associated Newspapers Ltd.* an award of damages of £15,000 was made in favour of an infant claimant at trial in respect of the publication of photographs in a newspaper where there was no consent and no suggestion of distress.[232] Furthermore, in *Weller v Associated Newspapers Ltd*, the infant Weller twins, whose photographs had been published along with that of their teenage sister on *Mail Online* in circumstances where there was no embarrassment on their part, received damages of

---

[228] *Douglas* (n 225) 259. Lord Walker considered that *Hello!*'s publication did not destroy *OK!*'s licence but made it less valuable.

[229] *Douglas* (n 225) 299.

[230] *Murray v Express Newspapers plc* [2007] EWHC 908 (Ch), [2007] EMLR 583 [65].

[231] *Murray* (n 144) [54].

[232] [2012] EWHC 2103 (QB), [2013] EMLR 2 [121]–[127].

£2,500 each.[233] It seems likely that the reasoning of such cases is restricted to their circumstances, namely the protection of children from targeted media interest.

### (c) Trade marks

Domestic and Community trade marks may also provide some protection for image or publicity interests. As such, they may be one element in wider efforts to control the use of an individual's image, albeit in a way that is remote from privacy interests. An individual or a collective's image or name or a person's signature can be protected, in principle, although the law does not grant a monopoly in respect of such use, and protection falls considerably short of a right to publicity. A person who wishes to register a trade mark must specify the goods or class of goods in respect of which the trade mark is to be registered, show that the trade mark is capable of being represented graphically, and show that it is capable of distinguishing the goods or services of one undertaking from that of another.[234] Unlike passing off, the right is proprietary in nature and does not depend on establishing goodwill to enforce it, although proactive registration is essential. **9.110**

Registration of a famous name may be refused where the words are exclusively descriptive of a product but do not make it distinctive.[235] A unique name does not guarantee distinctiveness as it may serve to identify the subject matter or character of a good rather than as a badge of origin.[236] The name of a person or group is not indicative of trade origin in the contemporary world of unauthorized merchandising and the fact that registration in one particular class denotes official products will not enable registration for unconnected classes of goods.[237] References to famous names that are registered as trade marks in books and other media may constitute 'trade mark use', but are likely not to infringe the registered mark by virtue of denoting the characteristic of a product within s 11(2) of the Trade Marks Act 1994.[238] Where a sign is used which is not identical to a registered trade mark, for infringement to be shown the consumer must be deceived or there must be real risk of confusion.[239] **9.111**

The protection of celebrity merchandising or themed packaging of goods as trade marks is problematic. A mark based on a name is likely to describe goods or attribute quality based on association with a name, but is inherently incapable of distinguishing trade origin from similar goods, as the *Elvis Presley* case exemplified.[240] **9.112**

---

[233] [2014] EWHC 1163 (QB), [2014] EMLR 24; the subject of an appeal at the time of writing.

[234] Trade Marks Act 1994, s 1(1): if a name or image is found not to be inherently distinctive, the applicant will have to prove that it has acquired distinctiveness through extensive trading. See further, C Morcom, A Roughton, and S Malynicz, *The Modern Law of Trade Marks* (3rd edn, Lexis Nexis 2008).

[235] UK Patent Office, Practice Amendment Note 5/04.

[236] *Executrices of the Estate of Diana, Princess of Wales' Application* [2001] ETMR 25.

[237] *Linkin Park LLC's Trade Mark Application* [2006] ETMR 74.

[238] *Bravado Merchandising v Mainstream Publishing* [1996] FSR 205.

[239] *Wagamama Ltd v City Centre Restaurants plc* [1995] FSR 713.

[240] *Elvis Presley Enterprises* (n 195).

In that case the Court of Appeal rejected the notion of a general character right.[241] Merchandising practice is to sell a likeness: the presence of a name or image does not operate to guarantee any particular source. The public do not assume that products bearing a registered trade mark, name, or image emanate from a distinctive source.[242] The ubiquity of an image or commonplace quality of a name will fail to lend a mark requisite distinctiveness. The degree to which a name is famous or well known, the nature of the fame, and the extent of the souvenir trade built up around the name have been held to be relevant in respect of dead celebrities.[243]

**9.113** Physical likeness can be registered if distinctive of origin and instantly recognizable as a particular person, having become distinctive through use.[244] Registration of the name or image of a famous living person without consent may, however, amount to bad faith.[245] It seems that the registrability of a likeness favours association with the product and its source from the outset, or early on in the product history, as later inclusions of likenesses tend to merchandise the product rather than denote origin.

**9.114** A signature is capable of registration as a graphically represented design where it distinguishes the product and its provenance. The estate of Diana, Princess of Wales's attempt to register the princess's signature did not succeed because the mark was not indicative of the source of origin of goods bearing the signature and widespread use had been made prior to the application. For a signature to be registrable there must be something in its graphic style to make it unique; ordinary capitalized or cursive signed renderings of names are not distinctive.[246] Trade mark use of a signature must be probative of the connection between goods and the proprietor of the mark, not merely descriptive.[247]

---

[241] The *Report on the Law on Copyright and Designs* (Cmnd 6732, 1977) (Chairman: JNK Whitford) rejected arguments for a character right based on a title or a name of a character, taking the view that copyright protection in a literary or artistic form and the action for passing off afforded adequate legal protection.

[242] *Elvis Presley Enterprises* (n 195); *Halliwell v Panini* (Ch D, 6 June 2001).

[243] *Re Jane Austen Trade Mark* [2000] RPC 879.

[244] *Re Anderson* LR 26 Ch D 409.

[245] Notes on the Trade Marks Act 1994.

[246] *Elvis Presley Enterprises* (n 195).

[247] *Elvis Presley Enterprises* (n 195).

# 10

# INTRUSION INTO PHYSICAL PRIVACY

*N A Moreham*

## A. Introduction

It is possible to breach a person's privacy without disseminating any information **10.01** about him or her. Surreptitiously videoing people in their homes or offices, relentlessly pursuing them for an interview or photograph, hacking their voicemail messages, or using a bugging device to record their conversations all interfere with this non-informational aspect of their privacy.

Many theorists and judges have recognized this non-informational aspect of the **10.02** privacy interest, often labelling it 'intrusion' or physical privacy.[1] 'Intrusion' is defined in the *Oxford English Dictionary* as:

> ...the action of thrusting oneself in in an encroaching manner, or of introducing something inappropriately; uninvited or unwelcome entrance or appearance;

---

[1] See 2.29 *et seq.*

encroachment on something possessed or enjoyed by another *spec* in contexts of Journalism.[2]

And physical privacy was defined in Chapter 2 to mean:

> ...freedom from unwanted access to the physical self, rather than to private information about oneself. It includes, in particular, freedom from unwanted watching, listening, recording, photographing, and filming of one's private activities. Paradigmatic examples of interferences with physical privacy include individuals bugging their tenants; spying on people in toilets, showers or changing rooms; or intercepting people's telephone calls.[3]

**10.03**  Physical privacy interests will usually fall outside the scope of the disclosure-focused actions for misuse of private information and breach of confidence. And, in contrast to the United States, New Zealand, and Ontario, there is no tort of intrusion into seclusion in England and Wales. Protection of physical or non-informational privacy interests is instead provided by a piecemeal collection of common law actions and legislative measures. Included among them are the law of trespass, nuisance, intentional infliction of emotional harm, the Protection from Harassment Act 1997, the voyeurism provisions of the Sexual Offences Act 2003, and aspects of breach of confidence. This chapter will examine these and other protections of the physical privacy interest. It will also consider whether, and if so how, courts might extend physical privacy protection in the future.

# B.  Legislative Protection against Intrusion into Physical Privacy

## (1)  Protection from Harassment Act 1997

**10.04**  The most effective legislative protection against intrusion into physical privacy is conferred by the Protection from Harassment Act 1997 (PHA). The PHA was introduced to combat stalking, racial harassment, and disruption from neighbours[4] but 'harassment' is not defined in the Act and its reach is in fact much wider.[5] The PHA has the potential to catch a range of media activities including persistent photography, trailing, doorstepping, and, as discussed in Chapter 6, publication.

---

[2] J Simpson and E Weiner (eds), *The Oxford English Dictionary* (2nd edn, Oxford University Press 1989) 'intrusion *n.3*'.

[3] See 2.29. See also, N A Moreham, 'Beyond Information: Physical Privacy in English Law' (2014) 73 CLJ 350.

[4] See *Hansard*, HC (series 6) vol 287, cols 781, 783–4 (17 December 1996) and HL (series 6) vol 577, col 917 (24 January 1997).

[5] Tugendhat J has expressly recognized that the Act protects privacy and that regard should be had to Art 8 when interpreting it: see *Hipgrave v Jones* [2004] EWHC 2901 (QB) [21].

## (a) The prohibition of 'harassment'

Section 1(1) PHA provides that:

**10.05**

(1) A person must not pursue a course of conduct—
   (a) which amounts to harassment of another, and
   (b) which he knows or ought to know amounts to harassment of the other.[6]

## (b) Conduct which amounts to 'harassment'

Chapter 6 sets out in detail the requirements of criminal or civil harassment **10.06** claims.[7] These requirements are usefully summarized by Simon J in *Dowson v Chief Constable of Northumbria Police*. He says:

(1) There must be conduct which occurs on at least two occasions,
(2) which is targeted at the claimant [although the Court of Appeal has since held that conduct merely needs to have been targeted at *an* individual],[8]
(3) which is calculated in an objective sense to cause alarm or distress, and
(4) which is objectively judged to be oppressive and unacceptable.
(5) What is oppressive and unacceptable may depend on the social or working context in which the conduct occurs.
(6) A line is to be drawn between conduct which is unattractive and unreasonable, and conduct which has been described in various ways: 'torment' of the victim, 'of an order which would sustain criminal liability'.[9]

## (c) Physical privacy intrusions as harassment

Many types of intrusion into physical privacy are capable of contributing to a **10.07** course of harassing conduct. They include activities in which the media engage.

**Photography and other recording**   Courts have confirmed that taking photo- **10.08** graphs of a person can form part of a harassing course of conduct. For example, in *Crawford v CPS*, the Court held the defendant contributed to a harassing course of conduct (which also included surveillance and following) by surreptitiously taking photographs of his former wife and her new partner.[10] Videotaping a person can also form part of a campaign of harassment.[11]

**Interference with rubbish**   Rummaging through a victim's rubbish bags can **10.09** contribute to harassment.[12]

**Constant telephoning**   In *R v Hardy*, the Divisional Court confirmed that tel- **10.10** ephoning a small business ninety-five times in one and a half hours was harassing

---

[6] Harassment of more than one person is also prohibited: see s 1(1A) PHA and 6.03.
[7] See 6.05–6.26.
[8] See *Levi v Bates* [2015] EWCA Civ 206 [55] and 6.11–6.14.
[9] *Dowson v Chief Constable of Northumbria Police* [2010] EWHC 2612 (QB) [142].
[10] *Crawford v CPS* [2008] EWHC 148 (Admin).
[11] See *eg King v DPP* [2001] ACD 7.
[12] *King* (n 11).

behaviour.[13] Relentless telephone requests for information or an interview could therefore be harassment for the purposes of the PHA.

**10.11** **Gaining access to a person's home** Harassing activity has also been held to include gaining access to a person's home against his or her wishes. For example, in *DPP v Williams*, the Divisional Court confirmed that it was harassment to peep through the claimant's bedroom window and, on another occasion, to put his hand through an open bathroom window while she was having a shower.[14] The Divisional Court also held, in *Woolford v DPP*, that returning to the former matrimonial home was harassing behaviour even though the complainant was not living there at the time.[15]

**10.12** **Following, spying, or surveilling** Stalking or shadowing a person has always been regarded as the paradigmatic example of harassing behaviour.[16] As outlined below, stalking is now the subject of a separate offence under the PHA[17] but spying on a person and indicating to the victim that one is (or will be) following or watching him or her have also been found to constitute harassment under s 1 PHA. For example, in *R v Liddle*, the claimant's former partner was held to have harassed the claimant by visiting her house and sending her letters indicating intimate knowledge of her daily life (thereby suggesting that he had been watching her).[18] The Divisional Court also found harassment in *Crawford v CPS* after the defendant consistently observed the victim's house, photographed her and her new partner, and occasionally followed them.[19] Likewise, telling the claimant that he had had her watched on several occasions contributed to a harassing course of conduct in *Howlett v Holding*.[20]

**10.13** *Doorstepping and other forms of media hounding* The media practice of approaching and/or photographing a person in or around his or her home—often called 'doorstepping'—has also been the subject of orders under the PHA. For example, in *AM v News Group Newspapers Ltd and Persons Unknown*, a landlord, who was being overwhelmed with media inquiries about his terrorist-suspect tenant, obtained an order restraining defendants from harassing, pestering, threatening,

---

[13] See *eg DPP v Hardy* [2008] EWHC 2874 (Admin), (2009) 173 JP 10.
[14] *DPP v Williams* (DC, 27 July 1998).
[15] *Woolford v DPP* (HC, 9 May 2000).
[16] See *Howlett v Holding* [2006] EWHC 41 (QB) [24] and *Thomas v News Group Newspapers Ltd* [2001] EWCA Civ 1233 [16], [30].
[17] See 10.18–10.19.
[18] *R v Liddle* [1999] 3 All ER 816.
[19] *Crawford* (n 10).
[20] *Howlett* (n 16). Although compare *APW v WPA* [2012] EWHC 3151 (QB) in which Tugendhat J declined to award an injunction against the former boyfriend of a 'well to do [woman]...known to many members of the public'. The boyfriend had continued to send the claimant text messages and had turned up at restaurants where the claimant was dining although he had made no contact with her and left when requested.

or otherwise interfering with anyone within the claimant's house or garden; from approaching within 100 yards of the claimant's house; or communicating or attempting to communicate with him by any medium.[21] Similarly, in *Hong v XYZ*, the mother and baby of the actor, Hugh Grant, obtained a harassment injunction having had, in the months leading up to the injunction, groups of photographers parked outside their house (including some who approached them aggressively and/or followed them when they went out) and having received multiple voicemail and text messages, including one which was threatening in tone.[22]

In a similar vein, singer Harry Styles (who was nineteen years old at the time) **10.14** obtained an order preventing photographers from pursuing and/or placing him under surveillance, loitering, or stationing themselves outside his home or where he was staying, behaving in an intimidating or abusive manner, and/or taking photographs of him in such circumstances.[23] Prior to the order, photographers had been regularly loitering outside the claimant's house, monitoring his movements, chasing him from his house or pursuing him through the streets of London by car or motorbike, and employing driving tactics which were at best obstructive and at worst dangerous to the claimant and members of the public.[24] Nicola Davies J accepted that the photographers' conduct was causing the claimant anxiety and distress[25] and that he was very likely to establish at trial that the defendant's conduct was not allowed.[26]

In contrast though, Tugendhat J held in *Trimingham v Associated Newspapers Ltd* **10.15** that journalists did not harass the claimant by speaking or attempting to speak with people she mixes with in her private life: there can, he said, 'be little publicity without journalists conducting enquiries'.[27] Similarly in *Sharma v Jay*, Gray J struck out the claim of a research scientist who claimed that the defendants had harassed him by making 'unsolicited approaches to third parties, including

---

[21] *AM v News Group Newspapers and Persons Unknown* [2012] EWHC 308 (QB). See also *Kerner v WX and YZ (persons unknown responsible for pursuing and/or taking photographs of the claimant and her son at their home on 22 January 2015)* [2015] EWHC 128 (QB) and [2015] EWHC 1247 (QB).

[22] *Hong and KLM v XYZ and others (person or persons responsible for taking photographs of the claimants outside their home and in the street during November 2011)* [2011] EWHC 2995 (QB).

[23] *Styles v Paparazzi AAA* [2013] EWHC 4344 (QB) [1].

[24] *Styles* (n 23) [8].

[25] *Styles* (n 23) [9].

[26] *Styles* (n 23) [19]. The claimant stressed that he was not seeking to prevent publicity nor to stop fans from taking photographs of him [6] but felt that there was no justification for 'the level of pursuit, surveillance and general harassment that he ... [had been] forced to endure' [7]. See also *Stone and Williams v WXY* [2012] EWHC 3184 (QB) [3] (where reference is made to an interim injunction obtained by model, Lara Stone, and comedian, David Williams, aimed at preventing harassment by paparazzi around the time of their wedding). Singers Amy Winehouse, Lily Allen, and Cheryl Cole also obtained similar anti-harassment orders against the paparazzi in 2009 (Winehouse and Allen) and 2011 (Cole). For an early American paparazzi harassment case, see *Galella v Onassis* 353 F Supp 196 (DCNY 1972).

[27] *Trimingham v Associated Newspapers Ltd* [2012] EWHC 1296 (QB) [279].

funding organisations and pharmaceutical companies, seeking information about the claimant and his research work'.[28] Gray J said that the defendants had been right to concede that conduct of that nature could in principle amount to harassment[29] but held that there is a public interest in the exposure of wrong-doing in connection with clinical research and there was nothing oppressive or unreasonable about the conduct in question.[30]

**10.16** *Surreptitious surveillance*  A defendant cannot escape liability for stalking, spying or surveillance on the basis that his or her observation was conducted surreptitiously and therefore did not cause the subject 'alarm or distress' at the time. Arguments to the contrary were rejected by Eady J in *Howlett v Holding*. Having noted that the defendant had made the claimant aware he was having her watched, he said:

> Just because she does not know, in any given instance, that surveillance is taking place, it does not make it any the less distressing for her. What causes the distress is the awareness that secret surveillance is taking place, or is likely to take place at any moment. I see no reason why that form of besetting should fall outside either the spirit or the letter of the Act.[31]

The Divisional Court in *King v DPP* also upheld the view of the magistrates below that surreptitiously videoing the complainant was capable of contributing to a course of harassing conduct even though she did not find out about it until the police showed the video footage to her.[32]

**10.17** *Surveillance in public places*  It is also no defence to a harassment claim to show that the surveillance took place when the claimant was in public. As Eady J said in *Howlett v Holding*:

> ...it is not possible for those who wish to intrude upon the lives of individuals through surveillance, and associated photography, to rely upon a rigid distinction being drawn in their favour between what takes place in private and activities capable of being witnessed in a public place by other people.[33]

*(d) Harassment by stalking*

**10.18** A specific offence of stalking was added to the PHA by the Protection of Freedoms Act 2012. Section 2A(1) provides that a person is guilty of an offence if he or she pursues a course of conduct in breach of s 1(1) which amounts to stalking.

---

[28] *Sharma v Jay* (HC, 15 April 2003).
[29] *Sharma* (n 28) [28].
[30] *Sharma* (n 28) [37], [43].
[31] *Howlett* (n 16) [23]. This is consistent with Baroness Hale's observation in *Majrowski v Guy's and St Thomas's NHS Trust* [2006] UKHL 34, [2007] 1 AC 224 [66] that '[a]ll sorts of conduct may amount to harassment. It includes alarming a person or causing her distress: section 7(2). But conduct might be harassment even if no alarm or distress were in fact caused.'
[32] *King* (n 11).
[33] *Howlett* (n 16) [26].

A person's conduct will amount to stalking of another if it amounts to harassment of that other, the acts or omissions involved are ones associated with stalking, and the perpetrator knows or ought to know that the course of conduct amounts to harassment of the other person.[34] Section 2A(3) PHA provides a lists of examples of the types of acts and omissions which 'in particular circumstances, are...associated with stalking':

(a) following a person,
(b) contacting, or attempting to contact, a person by any means,
(c) publishing any statement or other material—
    (i) relating or purporting to relate to a person, or
    (ii) purporting to originate from a person,
(d) monitoring the use by a person of the internet, email or any other form of electronic communication,
(e) loitering in any place (whether public or private),
(f) interfering with any property in the possession of a person,
(g) watching or spying on a person.[35]

**10.19** Those guilty of stalking under s 2A are liable for a fine at level five of the standard scale or a term of imprisonment not exceeding fifty-one weeks.[36] Journalists, press photographers, and paparazzi could potentially fall foul of this provision. As the examples discussed at 10.13 attest, it is not unusual for media defendants to follow individuals, contact or attempt to contact them, watch or spy on them, or loiter outside their homes.

*(e) Limitations and defences*

**10.20** Although the PHA creates liability for media intrusion in a number of circumstances, its most obvious limitation is that it only applies where the claimant can show that the privacy interference was part of a course of conduct.[37] This means that a one-off interference—no matter how egregious—cannot satisfy the requirements of the Act. Those who engage in harassing conduct in the course of newsgathering activities could also potentially rely on the right to freedom of expression in Article 10 of the European Convention on Human Rights or one of the other defences discussed in Chapter 6.[38]

---

[34] s 2A(2) PHA. What the perpetrator 'ought to know' about the effects of his or her conduct on the victim is assessed by reference to what a reasonable person in possession of the same information would think (s 4A(2), (3)).

[35] s 2A(3) PHA. Section 4A PHA creates the further offence of 'stalking involving fear of violence or serious alarm or distress'. A person will be guilty of this offence if his or her course of conduct amounts to stalking and it either causes another to fear, on at least two occasions, that violence will be used against him or her, or causes a person serious alarm or distress which has a substantial adverse effect on his or her usual day-to-day activities, and the perpetrator knew or ought to have known that his or her conduct would have such an effect. The maximum penalty for stalking involving fear of violence or serious alarm or distress is five years' imprisonment (s 4A(5)).

[36] s 2A(4) PHA.

[37] See 6.08–6.10.

[38] See 6.27–6.35.

### (2) Harassment of a Person in the Home
### Criminal Justice and Police Act 2001

**10.21** Sections 42 and 42A of the Criminal Justice and Police Act 2001 (CJPA) target harassment of individuals in the home, protecting against the formation of 'media scrums' outside people's homes and harassment by so-called 'vigilante groups'.

**10.22** Section 42A makes it an offence to 'doorstep' a person in his or her home.[39] The offence will be established if the defendant is present outside the resident's dwelling; the defendant is there to represent to or persuade the resident or another individual (whether or not he or she uses the premises as his or her dwelling) either that 'he should not do something that he is entitled or required to do; or…that he should do something that he is not under any obligation to do'; the defendant intends his or her presence to harass or cause alarm or distress to the resident or knows or ought to know that his or her presence is likely to have this effect; and the defendant's presence does cause or is likely to cause the harassment of or alarm or distress to the resident, a person in the resident's dwelling, or another person in another dwelling in the vicinity.[40] The offence is punishable with a fine or prison term not exceeding fifty-one weeks.[41]

**10.23** Section 42 empowers a police constable who reasonably believes that an individual is present outside a person's house for the purposes just described, to do such things as the constable thinks necessary to prevent the person from harassing, alarming, or causing distress to the resident or other individual.[42] A constable's direction can include a requirement to leave the vicinity of the premises in question[43] and/or to leave and not to return within a specified time not exceeding three months.[44] The constable's direction can be made subject to conditions.[45]

**10.24** A person who knowingly fails to comply with an order to leave the premises is guilty of an offence punishable by a fine or a maximum of three months' imprisonment.[46] A person who is ordered not to return to the property within a certain time will be guilty of an offence punishable with a fine or a maximum of fifty-one weeks' imprisonment if he or she returns to the property within that time for the purposes of persuading the resident (or any other individual) that he or she should not do something that he or she is entitled or required to do; or 'that he should do something that he is not under any obligation to do'.[47]

---

[39] s 42A CJPA (as inserted by the Serious Organised Crime and Police Act 2005 (SOCPA), s 126).

[40] s 42A(1)–(2) CJPA.

[41] s 42A(5) CJPA.

[42] s 42 CJPA.

[43] s 42(4)(a) CJPA (as amended by s 127 SOCPA).

[44] s 42(4)(b) CJPA (as amended by s 127 SOCPA).

[45] s 42(5) CJPA.

[46] s 42(7) CJPA.

[47] s 42(7B) CJPA (as amended by s 127 SOCPA).

## (3) Data Protection Act 1998

The Data Protection Act 1998 (DPA) focuses on the protection of personal **10.25** information. However, because its key concept—'data'—is defined by reference to the manner in which information is obtained and stored, it has the potential to protect against a wide range of intrusions into physical privacy.[48]

As discussed in Chapter 7, 'data' in the DPA includes information which 'is being **10.26** processed by means of equipment operating automatically in response to instructions given for that purpose' (ie on a computer); is recorded with the intention that it should be processed by means of such equipment; or is recorded as part of a relevant filing system or with the intention that it should form part of the same.[49] 'Personal data' are those which relate to an identifiable living individual.[50] This means that the DPA applies to the use of any information about an identifiable person which is located on a computer[51] or in a manual filing system, or obtained for the purpose of uploading it to a computer or filing it. Clearly, in modern society, this captures a huge amount of material, including personal files stored on a computer and digitally-obtained photographs, films, or audio recordings.[52] The Act is relevant to any intrusion that involves these kinds of devices.

Numerous obligations are imposed on those who 'process' such personal data. The **10.27** concept of 'processing' includes organizing, adapting, or altering data; retrieving, consulting, or using them; disclosing them; aligning, combining, blocking, erasing, or destroying them.[53] People intruding on physical privacy will often be engaged in such processes. For example, a person who hacks another's computer will process any information he or she obtains from it and someone who takes a photograph with his or her mobile phone will process information by taking the photograph, uploading it, organizing it, storing it, looking at it, or deleting it. From the moment the computer is accessed or the image recorded on to the device, the hacker and photographer are therefore obliged to comply with the requirements of the DPA.

In order to meet the requirements of the DPA, the data controller must (unless **10.28** certain specified exceptions apply) comply with the 'data principles'.[54] The first,

---

[48] Much of the discussion in this section is drawn from N A Moreham, 'Protection against Intrusion in English Legislation' in N Witzleb, D Lindsay, M Paterson, and S Rodrick (eds), *Emerging Challenges in Privacy Law: Comparative Perspectives* (Cambridge University Press 2014).

[49] s 1(1) DPA.

[50] Specifically, a living individual who can be identified either from the data in question or from that data in combination with other information which is in, or is likely to come into, the possession of the data controller (s 1(1) DPA).

[51] See *eg Tchenguiz v Imerman* [2010] EWCA Civ 908, [2011] 2 WLR 592 [95]–[97].

[52] In *Douglas v Hello! Ltd* [2003] EWHC 786 (Ch), [2003] 3 All ER 996, Lindsay J held that the unauthorized photographs of the claimants' wedding were 'personal data' for the purposes of this provision [230]. See also *Douglas v Hello! Ltd* [2000] EWCA Civ 353, [2001] QB 967 [55]–[56].

[53] s 1(1) DPA.

[54] s 4 DPA which refers to sch 1, pts I and II DPA. The exemptions relate to national security (s 28); the prevention of crime, prosecution of offenders, and collection of taxation (s 29); health,

and most relevant, principle requires that personal data be processed 'fairly and lawfully'. Whether the process is 'fair' will depend on the method by which the data were obtained and whether any person from whom they were obtained was deceived or misled as to the purposes for which they were being processed.[55] The data controller must also meet one of a number of conditions by establishing, for example, that the subject consented to the processing[56] or that the processing was undertaken to further the 'legitimate interests' of the data controller, or a third party to whom the data was disclosed, and was not unwarranted by reason of prejudice to the rights and freedoms or legitimate interests of the data subject.[57] Data controllers who intrude into individuals' physical privacy will often fail to meet any of the conditions. Further conditions apply if, as is often the case, the processed information is deemed to be 'sensitive'.[58]

**10.29**  Breach of the DPA gives rise to both criminal and civil liability[59] and the remedies for the latter include damages.[60] Unless one of the exemptions applies, victims can require data controllers to cease or not to begin processing personal information about them, as long as they can show that it is causing, or is likely to cause, them substantial and unwarranted damage or distress.[61]

*(a) Defences and limitations*

**10.30**  Although at first glance the DPA appears to give significant rights of redress to those whose physical privacy is invaded by means of hacking, digital filming, or bugging, there are significant limitations on its scope. First, the Act provides no

---

education, and social work (s 30); regulatory activity (s 31); journalism, literature, and art (s 32); research, history, and statistics (s 33); publicly available information (s 34); disclosure required by law or made in connection with legal proceedings (s 35); and domestic purposes (s 36).

[55]  See s 4 and sch 1, pts I and II DPA.

[56]  sch 2(1) DPA.

[57]  sch 2(6) DPA. Courts have held that the business interests of a freelance photographer (*Murray v Express Newspapers plc* [2007] EWHC 1908 (Ch), [2007] EMLR 22 [76]) and the defendant's interest in covering a particular celebrity wedding (*Douglas* (n 52) [238]) could be regarded as 'legitimate purposes'. However, in *Douglas* the defendant's interest was outweighed by prejudice to the legal rights of the claimants (see [238]) and the conclusion in *Murray* that the claimant's legitimate business interest prevailed was undermined by the Court of Appeal's conclusion that Patten J had struck the wrong balance between the parties' competing interests (*Murray v Express Newspapers plc* [2008] EWCA Civ 446 [62]). For further discussion of these, and the other, conditions see 7.46–7.50.

[58]  sch 1, pt I(1)(b) DPA. 'Sensitive personal data' are defined in s 2 DPA and discussed at 7.24–7.27.

[59]  An offence is committed (for which the defendant can be fined) if, without the consent of the data subject, a person knowingly or recklessly obtains (or discloses) personal data or information contained therein (s 55(1)(a), (3) DPA). It is also an offence to procure such disclosure (s 55(1)(b)), to sell the data (s 55(4)), or to offer them for sale (s 55(5)). However, various defences apply (see s 55(2)).

[60]  See 7.92–7.99.

[61]  s 10(1) DPA which refers to sch 2(1)–(4). The exemptions apply if the data subject consented to the processing (sch 2(1)); if the processing was necessary for compliance with or entry into a contract with the data subject (sch 2(2)) or for compliance with another type of legal obligation (sch 2(3)); or if the processing was necessary to protect the subject's vital interests (sch 2(4)). See also discussion of the 'special purposes' at 10.31.

protection against surveillance or recording unless the intruder uses a digital device or intends to upload or manually to file non-digital recordings. A person who films a private activity with a non-digital camera (and does not then scan or systematically file the photograph or recording) will be beyond the Act's reach even though his or her act is indistinguishable in terms of impact and culpability from that of a person using a digital device. Use of a peep hole or other non-technological spying technique also falls outside the Act.

Secondly, the DPA exempts those processing personal data for the 'special purposes' of journalism, art, or literary purposes from, *inter alia*, the need to comply with the data principles[62] and from provisions allowing victims to prevent data processing causing damage or distress.[63] This exemption applies if the data processor intends to publish information contained in the data and reasonably believes that publication would be in the public interest (having particular regard to the public interest in freedom of expression),[64] and, in all the circumstances, compliance with the provision in question would be incompatible with the special purposes.[65] 'Journalism' has been held to involve the 'communication of information or ideas to the public at large in the public interest' meaning that 'anyone with access to the internet', not just those working for media organizations, can rely on the exception.[66] Thus, the Act's most significant obligations will not extend to those who photograph, film, or record the subject in order to obtain information which they reasonably believe is in the public interest and which they wish to publicize.  **10.31**

Finally, the DPA does not apply to personal data which an individual processes solely for the purposes of his or her 'personal, family or household affairs (including recreational purposes)'.[67] It is therefore not clear that it would apply to a person who, for his or her own purposes, videoed his or her neighbours' children in their bedrooms; installed a bugging device in a friend's car; examined his or her partner's former wife's bank account records (like the defendant in the Canadian case of *Jones v Tsige*); or videoed his or her flatmate in the shower (like the defendant in the New Zealand case of *C v Holland*).[68] The cumulative effect of these exemptions is that the DPA provides much less effective protection for physical privacy than first appearances would suggest.  **10.32**

---

[62] Except Principle 7 which relates to technical and organizational measures taken to protect the security of personal information.

[63] s 32(1), (2) DPA. They are also exempt from provisions relating to automated decision-making (s 32(2)(d)) and to rectification, blocking, erasure, and destruction (s 32(2)(e)). For discussion of media processing of sensitive personal data see the Data Protection (Processing of Sensitive Personal Data) Order 2000, SI 2000/417 and 7.117–7.124.

[64] s 32(1)(a), (b) DPA.

[65] s 32(1)(c) DPA. The Court of Appeal in *Campbell v MGN Ltd* [2002] EWCA Civ 1373, [2003] QB 633 confirmed that this exemption applies to all stages of the publication process ([107], [128]).

[66] *Law Society v Kordowski* [2011] EWHC 3185 (QB) [99].

[67] s 36 DPA.

[68] See *Jones v Tsige* 2012 ONCA 32, 108 OR (3d) 241 (discussed at 10.87); and *C v Holland* [2012] 3 NZLR 672 (discussed at 10.84).

### (4) Sexual Offences Act 2003—Voyeurism

**10.33**  Section 67 of the Sexual Offences Act 2003 provides protection against sexually motivated voyeurism and the facilitation of sexually motivated voyeurism. Under s 67, it is an offence punishable by a fine or imprisonment of up to six months (on summary conviction) or two years (on indictment):

> (1) to observe for sexual gratification a person doing a private act, knowing that that person does not consent to being observed for the observer's sexual gratification;
>
> (2) to operate equipment with the intention of enabling another person to observe another in the circumstances set out in (1);
>
> (3) to record a person doing a private act with the intention that the person doing the recording or a third party will obtain sexual gratification by looking at the image of that person doing that act and with the knowledge that the person does not consent to the act being recorded with that intention;
>
> (4) to install equipment or construct or adapt a structure to enable someone to commit the offence set out in (1).

A person will be 'doing a private act' if he or she is:

> ...in a place which, in the circumstances, would reasonably be expected to provide privacy, and...the person's genitals, buttocks or breasts are exposed or covered only with underwear,...the person is using a lavatory, or...the person is doing a sexual act that is not of a kind ordinarily done in public.[69]

A person can have a 'reasonable expectation of privacy' for the purposes of this provision 'without being wholly enclosed or wholly sheltered from the possibility of being seen'.[70]

**10.34**  The Explanatory Notes to the Sexual Offences Bill said that the offence is not designed to apply to journalists pursuing legitimate journalistic activity 'as in these circumstances the observing or taking of images will not be done for sexual gratification'.[71] However, photographers who obtain photographs of topless or partially naked celebrities could well be liable under s 67(3) if the complainant was in a private place at the time and the image was obtained so that others (the readers of a tabloid newspaper, magazine, or website, for example) could obtain sexual gratification by looking at it.

### (5) Interception of Communications

**10.35**  The news-gathering activities of the media are also affected by both criminal and civil liability for unlawful interception of communications. It is an offence under ss 83 and 84 of the Postal Services Act 2000 to delay or open a postal packet in

---

[69] Sexual Offences Act 2003, s 68.

[70] *R v Bassett* [2008] EWCA Crim 1174, [2009] 1 WLR 1032 [7] (liability found when a man and his young daughter were filmed in a doorless shower cubicle in a swimming pool changing room).

[71] Explanatory Notes to the Sexual Offences HL Bill (2002-03) 26, para 57.

the course of its transmission by post. Section 1 of the Regulation of Investigatory Powers Act 2000 (RIPA) also makes it an offence to intercept without lawful authority any communication in the course of its transmission by means of a public postal service or a public telecommunications system[72] or, subject to certain exceptions, intentionally to intercept a communication in the course of its transmission by means of a private telecommunications system.[73] It was for contravening, or conspiring to contravene, s 1(1) RIPA that private investigators and senior editors employed by the *News of the World* were tried and convicted in the telephone hacking scandal which came to light in 2011.[74]

'Telecommunication system' is widely defined in RIPA and includes any system **10.36** facilitating the transmission of communications 'by any means involving the use of electrical or electro-magnetic energy'.[75] It therefore includes emails, pagers, and, as the telephone hacking scandal demonstrated, mobile phone services. 'Public telecommunications system' means 'any such parts of a telecommunication system by means of which any public telecommunication service is provided as are located in the United Kingdom'.[76] This includes privately owned telephones, including an individual's home telephone, mobile, and personal email account.[77] A 'private

---

[72] s 1(1) Regulation of Investigatory Powers Act 2000 (RIPA).

[73] s 1(2) RIPA. RIPA applies to interception at any place in the United Kingdom and extends liability beyond that imposed by its predecessor, the Interception of Communications Act 1985. The legislation was required to meet the defects in the earlier legislation identified by the European Court of Human Rights in *Halford v UK* (1997) 24 EHRR 523, para 51, and generally to make UK legislation compatible with Art 8 of the Convention when the Human Rights Act 1998 came into force. RIPA was also designed to implement Art 5 of the European Parliament and Council's Directive 97/66/EC of 15 December 1997 which was aimed at safeguarding the confidentiality of communications. (The 1997 Directive was replaced by Directive 2002/58/EC of 12 July 2002 concerning the processing of personal data and the protection of privacy in the electronic communications sector.) The offences under the Wireless Telegraphy Act 2006, s 48 of (i) using wireless telegraphy apparatus to find out about messages, whether wireless or not; and (ii) disclosing information obtained in this way, remain intact: s 18(12) RIPA.

[74] By obtaining personal identification numbers and 'blagging' (pretending to be someone else in order to gain information or other benefit), private investigators obtained access to voicemails stored on the messaging systems of public relations consultants, victims of crime, members of the royal household, celebrities, politicians, and other newsworthy individuals (see *Bryant v Commissioner of Police of the Metropolis* [2011] EWHC 1314 (Admin) [11]–[13] for a description of the methods employed). The protagonists received sentences ranging from four to eighteen months. Systematic telephone hacking at Trinity Mirror has since come to light but has not yet been the subject of criminal proceedings.

[75] s 2(1) RIPA. The House of Lords held in *Morgans v DPP* [2001] 1 AC 315, 333 that, '[i]t is sufficient, to constitute a communication by means of a public telecommunication system for the purposes of the Act, for an electrical impulse or signal to be transmitted from the telephone number from which the impulse or signal is sent to the telephone number with which it has been connected. The sending of an electrical impulse or signal in either direction will do, irrespective of the response which it elicits from the recipient and the length or content of the message which it conveys.'

[76] s 2(1) RIPA.

[77] In *Halford* (n 73) both the UK government and the European Court of Human Rights proceeded on the basis that the applicant's home telephone was part of a public telecommunications network and was therefore covered by the 1985 Act: see in particular [52]. The *News of the World* telephone hacking prosecutions also make it clear that the mobile telephone network is a public telecommunications network for the purposes of RIPA: see *eg Coulson and Kuttner v R* [2013] EWCA Crim 1026.

telecommunications system' is a system which is not itself a public telecommunications system but is both attached to a public telecommunications system (either directly or indirectly and whether or not for the purposes of the communication in question) and has comprised within the system apparatus which is both located in the United Kingdom and which is used for making the attachment to the public telecommunication system.[78] This has been held to include the internal networks of hotels[79] and police stations[80] and would also include the internal telecommunication systems of newspapers and broadcasters.

**10.37**　In the case of a private telecommunications system, criminal liability is excluded if the person making the intercept had a right to control the operation or the use of the system or had been given express or implied consent to make the intercept by the controller of the system.[81] The Court of Appeal also held in respect of the 1985 Act that a call will still be intercepted on a 'private telecommunications system' even if it has come from outside that system and been connected via an internal switchboard.[82] Interception at the offices of a newspaper is therefore likely to be excluded from criminal liability as long as the person who carried it out had control of the system. 'Control' in this context means the ability to 'authorise and forbid'.[83] It is not enough that one had a 'right to operate or use the system'; he or she must exercise control over 'how the system is used and operated by others'.[84]

**10.38**　However, even if they avoid criminal liability, those who intercept communications on private telecommunications networks will still be civilly liable to the sender, recipient, or intended recipient of the communication unless they can establish that they had 'lawful authority' to make the interception.[85] A journalist wishing to establish lawful authority would have to show that the interception had, or was reasonably believed to have, been consented to by both the person who sent the communication and its intended recipient.[86] In other words, the parties to the conversation must be told in advance that the telephone call is being

---

[78] s 2(1) RIPA.

[79] See *R v Wright and McGregor* [2001] EWCA Crim 1394 and the example given in *Attorney General's Reference (No 5 of 2002)* [2003] EWCA Crim 1632, [2003] 1 WLR 2902 [92].

[80] The decision of the European Court of Human Rights in *Halford* (n 73) proceeded on the basis that the internal communication system at the Merseyside Police Headquarters was a private telecommunications network and therefore was not covered by the 1985 Act: para 52.

[81] s 1(2)(b), (6) RIPA.

[82] See *R v Wright and McGregor* (n 79) (telephone intercepts which had taken place in a hotel bedroom connected to the hotel's private system beyond the switchboard were held not to have been part of a public telecommunications system and therefore not to have breached the Interception of Communications Act 1985).

[83] *R v Stanford* [2006] EWCA Crim 258, [2006] 1 WLR 1554 [21]. It appears that voicemail interception at News Group Newspapers Ltd and MGN Ltd was usually conducted on pay-as-you-go mobile telephones not connected to the internal telephone network.

[84] *R v Stanford* (n 83) [22].

[85] s 1(3) RIPA.

[86] ss 1(5)(a), 3(1) RIPA.

recorded in a way that amounts to interception, and it must not be recorded unless they consent.[87]

No interception will take place for the purposes of RIPA unless the interceptor's **10.39** activities involve the telecommunication system itself. Section 2(2) RIPA provides that a person will only intercept a communication[88] if, in the course of its transmission by means of a telecommunication system, he or she (a) so modifies or interferes with the system, or its operation; (b) so monitors transmissions made by means of the system; or (c) so monitors transmissions made by wireless telegraphy to or from apparatus comprised in the system, as to make some or all of the contents of the communication available,[89] while being transmitted, to a person other than the sender or intended recipient of the communication.[90] This definition refers in each alternative to interference with 'the system' and therefore excludes a record of a conversation made by hand or by a sound recording made with an apparatus which is external to the system (such as a tape recorder held to the speaker of a telephone).[91] Thus, the Court of Appeal has held that there was no 'interception' when a listening device installed in an individual's car picked up his end of a conversation on a mobile telephone:

> In our view, the natural meaning of the expression 'interception' denotes some interference or abstraction of the signal, whether it is passing along wires or by wireless telegraphy, during the process of transmission. The recording of a person's voice, independently of the fact that at the time he is using a telephone, does not become interception simply because what he says goes not only into the recorder, but, by separate process, is transmitted by a telecommunications system.[92]

The Court of Appeal has also held that there is no 'interception' for the purposes of RIPA if one party to a telephone call records on a separate recording device the conversations that they have with the other participant.[93] Thus, it is unlikely that a journalist who tape recorded a conversation to which he or she is a party would have made an interception for the purposes of the Act.

Transmission does, however, continue if a public telecommunication system **10.40** is being used to store a communication in a manner that enables the intended

---

[87] The messages left by owners of voicemail services informing the caller that they are about to be recorded would presumably satisfy these requirements.

[88] That is, other than a broadcast for general reception: s 2(3) RIPA.

[89] Whether contemporaneously, or subsequently: s 2(8) RIPA.

[90] s 2(7) RIPA.

[91] *R v E* [2004] EWCA Crim 1243, [2004] 1 WLR 3279. See also *White v Withers LLP and Marcus Dearle* [2008] EWHC 2821 (QB) in which Eady J confirmed that there was no interception of a postal communication when the claimant's ex-wife took possession of a document which had already been delivered: [18].

[92] *R v E* (n 91) [20]. See also *R v Smart* [2002] EWCA Crim 772, [2002] Crim LR 684, where the Court reached the same conclusion under the 1985 Act, and *R v Allsop* [2005] EWCA Crim 703 [45].

[93] *R v Hardy* [2002] EWCA Crim 3012 [31]; *R v Hammond* [2002] EWCA Crim 1243, [2003] 1 Cr App R 30 and *R v McDonald* (Woolwich Crown Court, 23 April 2002).

recipient to collect it or otherwise to have access to it.[94] As the telephone hacking scandal has highlighted, this includes messages being stored on the voicemail facility of a public telecommunications system.[95] The Court of Appeal has also confirmed in that context that this is the case irrespective of whether the messages have previously been accessed by their intended recipient.[96]

**10.41**  Finally, unlike evidence intercepted by officers of the Crown and specified law enforcement officers,[97] RIPA does not exclude evidence intercepted by journalists from criminal trials. Journalists who plan their operations carefully therefore can, if they so wish, help assist the prosecuting authorities to obtain and rely on covertly acquired material without contravening RIPA.[98] In *Cruddas*, Tugendhat J reiterated that regulation in RIPA of the use of deception by the police and other officers of the state does not apply to journalists.[99] Further, he said that if a journalist uses deception with the intention of discovering something in the public interest, and the deception is proportionate to that interest, then he or she is unlikely to be held liable for the crime or civil wrong of 'dishonestly using deception'.[100]

### (6) Public Order Act 1986

**10.42**  Section 5 of the Public Order Act 1986 provides that:

> (1) A person is guilty of an offence if he—
>   (a) uses threatening or abusive words or behaviour, or disorderly behaviour, or
>   (b) displays any writing, sign or other visible representation which is threatening or abusive, within the hearing or sight of a person likely to be caused harassment, alarm or distress thereby.

**10.43**  Until the enactment of the Crimes and Courts Act 2013, the provision penalized words or behaviour which was 'threatening, abusive *or insulting*'. In *Vigon v DPP*[101] the Divisional Court upheld a magistrates' decision that the defendant was liable under s 5 for installing a video camera to film people trying on swimwear in the changing cubicle of his market stall. Smith J summarized the

---

[94]  s 2(7) RIPA.

[95]  *Coulson and Kuttner* (n 77). It seems unlikely that this provision would apply to messages stored on a physical answering machine but that would depend on the technological processes involved in storage and collection.

[96]  *Coulson and Kuttner* (n 77). The Court refers to Fulford LJ's suggestion (made in the course of the preparatory hearing for that case) that a different approach would be taken to emails because, unlike remotely-held voicemail messages, they are downloaded from the internet service provider's server to the computer of the subscriber: [22]–[24].

[97]  s 17(1) and (3) RIPA.

[98]  Any breach of RIPA by a journalist might, however, be relevant for the purposes of the Police and Criminal Evidence Act 1984, s 78 (which covers the exclusion of unfair evidence).

[99]  *Cruddas v Calvert* [2013] EWHC 2298 (QB) [43].

[100]  *Cruddas* (n 99) [43]. He continued that, in any event, the real legal risk for journalists is not that they be sued or prosecuted for deception but that they face a defamation suit: [43].

[101]  [1997] EWHC 947 (Admin), (1998) 162 JPR 115.

magistrates' decision (from which the Court could 'see no reason' to depart)[102]
as follows:

> The justices found that using a video camera to film customers in a state of undress
> was of itself insulting behaviour because, first, in its ordinary sense, insulting meant
> an affront to a person's dignity or modesty; and, second, filming of customers in a
> cubicle was insulting behaviour within that meaning. They found that the provi-
> sion of the changing room created an expectation of privacy and the installation
> of a camera was likely to cause harassment, alarm or distress to a customer because
> any right thinking person would have been insulted and customers would have
> been distressed by the knowledge that they were being filmed. The Magistrates
> found that the appellant was aware that his behaviour was insulting as evidenced,
> they said, by his efforts to conceal the camera and the absence of any warning
> notice to customers that they were being filmed.[103]

In the last edition of this book, we argued that:

> Section 5 could therefore impose liability on a defendant who photographed a
> claimant who had just been seriously injured in a car accident (at least in circum-
> stances where there was no public interest in the image) or videoed a claimant per-
> forming an intimate act (such as going to the toilet or engaging in sexual activity)
> in a remote public place or, as Smith J said in *Vigon* itself, if he or she 'peeped
> behind the curtains of the changing room and watched his customers undressing'.
> Thus, although it has not been widely used, the POA has the potential to cre-
> ate liability in a range of intrusion situations, including some in which the media
> might possibly be engaged.[104]

It is not clear, however, what weight *Vigon* now carries and, in particular, whether **10.44**
courts will regard surreptitious filming as 'threatening' or 'abusive' behaviour.
In *Gough v DPP*, the Divisional Court noted that the District Judge below
(having said that the terms in s 5 POA 'are not to be narrowly construed')[105]
had decided that '"[a]busive" meant extremely offensive and insulting'.[106] The
Divisional Court declined to say whether the judge's conclusion was correct
(since the defendant's naked walking was clearly 'disorderly') but it does suggest
that objectionable filming of the type at issue in *Vigon* could still fall within the
s 5 offence. Even if it does, however, s 5 does not apply if filming takes place
inside a dwelling or cannot be seen by 'a person likely to be caused harassment,
alarm or distress thereby'.[107] Thus, even if *Vigon* were followed, a landlord filming his tenant in her living areas or a neighbour filming the bedrooms of the
house next door could still escape liability.

---

[102]  *Vigon* (n 101) [16] (Kennedy LJ).
[103]  *Vigon* (n 101) [7]. In the course of reaching that decision, the Court rejected the argument
that filming a person in a state of undress was not 'behaviour' under the provision ([9]) and that it
only covered 'rowdy' behaviour such as shouting abuse or obscenities: [11].
[104]  M Warby, N Moreham, and I Christie (eds), *Tugendhat and Christie: The Law of Privacy and
the Media* (2nd edn, Oxford University Press 2011) para 10.81.
[105]  *Gough v DPP* [2013] EWHC 3267 (Admin) [10].
[106]  *Gough* (n 105) [10].
[107]  Public Order Act 1986, s 5(1), (2).

### (7) Computer Misuse Act 1990

**10.45**  It is an offence under the Computer Misuse Act 1990 to obtain unauthorized access to computer systems and the data and programmes stored thereon.[108] Section 1 stipulates that an offence will be committed if a person 'causes a computer to perform any function with intent to secure access to any programme or data held in any computer, or to enable any such access to be secured' in circumstances where the intended access is 'unauthorised' and the perpetrator knows that to be the case.[109] A person secures 'access' to a programme or data held in a computer if, by causing the computer to perform any function, he or she alters or erases the programme or data, copies or moves it, uses it, or 'has it output from the computer in which it is held (whether by having it displayed or in any other manner)'.[110] This section clearly covers computer hacking, regardless of whether it is designed to uncover private information.[111] The Computer Misuse Act 1990 would therefore catch conduct that falls within 'intrusion' torts in other jurisdictions, including in the Ontarian intrusion case of *Jones v Tsige* (where a bank clerk accessed the banking transactions of her partner's former wife on 174 separate occasions).[112]

## C. Protection against Intrusion in the Common Law

### (1) No General Intrusion Tort

**10.46**  The House of Lords has expressly declined to recognize a general right to privacy. In *Wainwright v Home Office*, it rejected the privacy complaint of Mrs Wainwright and her mentally and physically impaired son who were invasively strip searched during a visit to Mrs Wainwright's other son in prison. Lord Hoffmann, with whom the other Lordships concurred, said that although privacy values might underpin common law actions such as breach of confidence, there was no general tort of invasion of privacy: '[t]here seems to me a great difference between identifying privacy as a value which underlies the existence of a rule of law (and may point the direction in which the law should develop) and privacy as a principle of law in itself'.[113] Nor did Lord Hoffmann think that recognition of such a tort was desirable. He said that there was nothing in the jurisprudence of the European Court of Human Rights to suggest that 'the adoption of some high level principle of privacy' was necessary to comply with Article 8 of the Convention,[114] that no previous English decision had recognized the

---

[108]  Computer Misuse Act 1990, s 1.
[109]  Computer Misuse Act 1990, s 1.
[110]  Computer Misuse Act 1990, s 17(2).
[111]  See *eg R v Martin* [2013] EWCA Crim 1420. See also *Tchenguiz v Imerman* [2010] EWCA Civ 908, [2011] 2 WLR 592 [90] where Lord Neuberger MR said (speaking for the Court) that, 'where, as in this case, information is surreptitiously downloaded from a computer, there may also be criminal offences under the Computer Misuse Act 1990 and the Data Protection Act 1998'.
[112]  *Jones v Tsige* 2012 ONCA 32, 108 OR (3d) 241 (discussed at 10.87).
[113]  [2003] UKHL 53, [2004] 2 AC 406 [31].
[114]  *Wainwright* (n 113) [32].

existence of such a tort,[115] and that it was doubtful whether it would 'perform a useful function in enabling one to deduce the rule to be applied in a concrete case'.[116] It follows that there is no general tort of breach of privacy in English law.[117] A claimant therefore will not be able to recover for a privacy interference unless he or she can satisfy the requirements of the misuse of private information action or some other common law or legislative claim. This section will consider what those common law protections are.

### (2) Trespass—Protection against Interference with Land, Goods, or Corporeal Integrity

The law of trespass protects individuals against interference with their land, goods, **10.47** and person and incidentally, in some circumstances, the privacy of what occurs in those places. Journalists and reporters who obtain unauthorized access to an individual's land, goods, or person can therefore be the subject of a trespass claim.

### (a) Trespass to land

A person will be guilty of trespass to land if he or she unjustifiably intrudes into **10.48** land in the possession of another.[118] Trespass to land therefore protects individuals against unjustifiable intrusions into their homes and property. Of the three strands of the tort, trespass to land is the one most likely to be breached by journalists and reporters.

A person who enters another's land for an unlawful purpose or abuses the author- **10.49** ity under which he or she obtained entry will be regarded as a trespasser *ab initio*.[119] An action in trespass to land might therefore lie against a reporter who, against an occupant's express wishes, entered land to seek an interview or to film what was going on there. A reporter or photographer who used false pretences to obtain access to another's land could also be liable for trespass.[120] Media defendants who enter private property will often be able to rely on the implied licence to 'proceed

---

[115] *Wainwright* (n 113) [19]–[35].

[116] *Wainwright* (n 113) [18].

[117] This position was confirmed by the Court of Appeal in *McKennitt v Ash* [2006] EWCA Civ 1714, [2008] QB 73 [8] and by Nicola Davies J in *AAA v Associated Newspapers Ltd* [2012] EWHC 2103 (QB) [11]: '[i]t follows that any claim for physical intrusion into a person's life has to be made by reliance on existing and established torts such as harassment, assault, or in exceptional circumstances, intentional infliction of emotional harm'.

[118] See M A Jones et al (eds), *Clerk and Lindsell on Torts* (21st edn, Sweet & Maxwell 2014) para 19-01, and W E Peel and J Goudkamp, *Winfield and Jolowicz on Tort* (19th edn, Sweet & Maxwell 2014) para 14-001.

[119] Which means that his or her conduct 'relate[s] back so as to make his original entry tortious': *Clerk and Lindsell on Torts* (n 118) para 19-37. See also the *Six Carpenters' Case* (1610) 8 Co Rep 146a, 146b, 77 ER 695, 697.

[120] In a different context (an appeal against decision of the Broadcasting Standards Commission), Lord Woolf CJ has observed that 'although the public were invited to the premises the invitation was not in relation to secret filming' (*R v Broadcasting Standards Commission, ex p BBC* [2001] QB 885, CA [37]).

from the gate to the front door or back door, and to enquire whether [they] may be admitted and to conduct [their] lawful business'.[121] However, a visitor cannot rely on this licence if the occupier has made it clear that the visit is not welcome. A person who does not wish to speak to journalists could, for example, revoke the implied licence by erecting a sign to that effect at the entrance to his or her property. Trespass is actionable without proof of loss and a claimant can claim aggravated damages if the trespass is 'accompanied by infliction of injury on the claimant's proper pride and dignity'.[122] This could well include an award for any breach of privacy suffered.[123] The victim of trespass is also entitled to expel the trespasser.[124]

**10.50**   Trespass therefore provides protection against some forms of physical privacy intrusion but it has a number of significant limitations. First, only those in possession of the land on which the trespass occurs can bring an action for trespass. The tort offers no protection to visitors or family members with no proprietary interest in the land nor to people using public facilities such as toilets or changing rooms, nor to those staying in hotels, hostels, or hospitals. These limitations were starkly illustrated in *Kaye v Robertson* in which the claimant was held to have no action in trespass against two journalists who intruded into the hospital room where he was recovering from serious head injuries to 'interview' and take photographs of him.[125]

**10.51**   Further, an intruder will only be liable for trespass if he or she obtains actual physical access to the land. A person would not be liable for taking a photograph from adjoining land or from airspace (unless the activities in question are carried out at a sufficiently low height to interfere with the ordinary use and enjoyment of the land and structures upon it)[126] nor for tapping the claimant's telephone wire outside his or her property.[127] As Sir Robert Megarry VC said in *Malone v Metropolitan Police Commissioner*, '"the eye cannot by the laws of England be guilty of a trespass"; and, I would add, nor can the ear'.[128]

---

[121]   *Robson v Hallett* [1967] 2 QB 939, CA, 954 (Diplock LJ).

[122]   See *Clerk and Lindsell on Torts* (n 118) para 19-70. Exemplary damages are also available if, *inter alia*, 'the wrongdoer's conduct has been calculated to make a profit exceeding the compensation payable to the claimant': *ibid*.

[123]   See W Rogers, *Winfield and Jolowicz on Tort* (16th edn, Sweet & Maxwell 2002) para 12.75. The matter is not addressed in subsequent editions.

[124]   See *Hall v Davis* (1825) 2 Carrington & Payne 33, 172 ER 16 and *Halsbury's Laws of England* (5th edn, Lexis Nexis 2010) vol 97, para 586.

[125]   [1991] FSR 62, CA.

[126]   *Bernstein of Leigh (Baron) v Skyviews and General Ltd* [1978] QB 479, 488.

[127]   *Malone v Metropolitan Police Commissioner* [1979] 1 Ch 344, 369.

[128]   *Malone* (n 127) 369, citing Lord Camden in *Entick v Carrington* (1765) 19 St Tr 1029, 1066, 95 ER 807. However, in the earlier case of *Hickman v Maisey* [1900] 1 QB 752 the defendant, a racing tout, was held to have exceeded the ordinary and reasonable user of a highway and therefore to be guilty of trespass when he used a public way crossing the claimant's land to watch the trial of race horses on the claimant's land.

Finally, the claimant cannot use the law of trespass to prevent the defendant from using **10.52**
information or images obtained during the trespass. In *Service Corp International plc v*
*Channel Four Television Corp*, Lightman J held that even if the fact that the defendant
had gained entry to and filmed the claimant's funeral parlours by deception meant
that they were trespassers *ab initio*, the action could not confer upon the claimants the
right to prevent the defendants showing the film.[129]

### (b) Trespass to goods

Journalists and reporters can be liable for trespass to goods if they directly and imme- **10.53**
diately interfere with goods in the possession of another.[130] Actual damage to the
goods is not a requirement of the action[131] and so trespass can probably be established
if, without authorization, a person picks up and reads another's private diary or other
document, uplifts and copies a private photograph, or removes items from rubbish
bags which are still in the claimant's possession. However, the action would only avail
the claimant if the defendant obtained actual physical access to relevant goods. Also,
damages are usually only awarded to compensate for misappropriation of or damage
to the chattel[132] which means that damages for the privacy intrusion could only be
recovered under an award of exemplary damages.

### (c) Trespass to the person

In extreme cases, media intrusion could also lead to liability for trespass to the person. **10.54**
Trespass to the person involves a direct interference with a person's body or liberty,[133]
and recognizes '[t]he fundamental principle, plain and incontestable . . . that every person's body is inviolate'.[134] Trespass to the person can take three forms: battery (the
direct imposition of unwanted physical contact on another person),[135] assault (an act
which causes a person to apprehend the infliction of immediate, unlawful, force on his
or her person),[136] and false imprisonment (the unlawful imposition of constraint on

---

[129] [1999] EMLR 83, HC, 90.

[130] See *Winfield and Jolowicz on Tort* (n 118) para 18-008; and S Deakin, A Johnston, and
B Markesinis, *Markesinis and Deakin's Tort Law* (7th edn, Oxford University Press 2013) 401.

[131] See *Clerk and Lindsell on Torts* (n 118) para 17-128 and C Sappideen and P Vines (eds),
*Fleming's The Law of Torts* (10th edn, Thomson Reuters 2011) para 4-10 which both cite *Transco v*
*United Utilities* [2005] EWHC 2784 (QB) as authority.

[132] See H McGregor, *McGregor on Damages* (19th edn, Sweet & Maxwell 2014) para 36-084.

[133] See *Winfield and Jolowicz on Tort* (n 118) para 4-002; and *Clerk and Lindsell on Torts* (n 118)
para 15-01.

[134] *Collins v Wilcock* [1984] 1 WLR 1172, 1177.

[135] *Clerk and Lindsell on Torts* (n 118) para 15-09. See also R Heuston and R Buckley, *Salmond*
*and Heuston on the Law of Torts* (21st edn, Sweet & Maxwell 1996) 121; and *Markesinis and Deakin's*
*Tort Law* (n 130) 362.

[136] *Clerk and Lindsell on Torts* (n 118) para 15-12 (citing *Collins* (n 134) 1178). See also *Winfield*
*and Jolowicz on Tort* (n 118) para 4-018 and *Salmond and Heuston on the Law of Torts* (n 135) 122.
See also T Weir, *An Introduction to Tort Law* (2nd edn, Oxford University Press 2006) 136; and
*Markesinis and Deakin's Tort Law* (n 130) 361.

another's freedom of movement from a particular place).[137] A reporter or photographer who touched an individual or created the apprehension of such touching might therefore be guilty of a trespass. Cases of 'doorstepping' or 'media scrumming', which were sufficiently serious to confine or restrain the claimant, might also lead to liability for false imprisonment.[138] Damages for trespass to the person compensate both physical injury and non-corporeal injury including loss of dignity, mental suffering, disgrace, and humiliation.[139]

**10.55** It has been suggested in some privacy cases that trespass to the person might be extended to situations where there was no direct corporeal contact with the claimant, but such moves have had little support from judges or commentators. For example, Glidewell LJ's suggestion in *Kaye v Robertson* that deliberately shining a light in a person's eyes, and thereby injuring his or her sight or damaging him or her in some other way, might amount to a battery[140] has been criticized as ignoring the fact that injury is irrelevant to trespass.[141] Likewise, the Court of Appeal and House of Lords in *Wainwright v Home Office* overruled the conclusion of the judge below that trespass to the person could extend to situations where the defendant had caused the claimant to do something to him or herself (in that case, removing her clothes) which had led to a breach of her right to privacy and humiliation and distress.[142]

### (3) Intentional Infliction of Emotional Harm

**10.56** Previous editions of this work have argued that the tort of intentional infliction of emotional harm (also known as the principle in *Wilkinson v Downton*)[143] could provide some protection against non-informational privacy interferences.[144] This argument was made on the basis of authority stating that the *Wilkinson v Downton* requirement that the defendant's act was 'intended' or 'calculated' to cause physical harm could be satisfied if the defendant intended to do an act which could obviously or foreseeably lead to the harm suffered; in other words, that an intention to

---

[137] *Clerk and Lindsell on Torts* (n 118) para 15-23 (citing *Collins* (n 134) 1178). See also *Winfield and Jolowicz on Tort* (n 118) para 4-023; *Salmond and Heuston on the Law of Torts* (n 135) 123–24; Weir (n 136) 136; and *Markesinis and Deakin's Tort Law* (n 130) 370.

[138] An example of this kind of behaviour was provided by family members of the men who died in the Pike River mining disaster in New Zealand. They told researchers that on one occasion a crowd of reporters prevented them from alighting from a bus (which had taken them up to the mine site) until the police intervened: see N A Moreham and Y Tinsley, 'Grief Journalism, Physical Intrusion, and Loss: The Pike River Coal Mine Disaster' in A T Kenyon (ed), *Comparative Defamation and Privacy Law* (Cambridge University Press) (forthcoming).

[139] *McGregor on Damages* (n 132) paras 40-001 (referring specifically to assault) and 40.012 (referring specifically to false imprisonment).

[140] *Kaye* (n 125) 68.

[141] Weir (n 136) 136. See also *Winfield and Jolowicz on Tort* (n 118) para 4-005.

[142] *Wainwright v Home Office* [2001] EWCA Civ 2081, [2002] QB 1334 [64]–[72]; *Wainwright v Home Office*, HL (n 113) [18].

[143] *Wilkinson v Downton* [1897] 2 QB 57.

[144] *Tugendhat and Christie* (n 104) paras 10.29–10.43.

cause harm could be imputed as a matter of law.[145] It followed that the tort might have been committed if, for example, a media defendant caused a person physical or psychiatric harm by videoing her engaging in private activities, or by following and observing her for days.[146]

All that changed when the Supreme Court held, in the recent decision of *Rhodes v*     **10.57**
*OPO*, that imputation of an intention by operation of a rule of law 'has no proper role in the modern law of tort'.[147] Instead, a claimant in a *Wilkinson v Downton* action must now be able to show that the defendant 'intended to cause severe distress' to him or her.[148] Even though two of their Lordships inclined to the view that 'distressing the claimant' need not be the defendant's sole purpose,[149] it would be expected that such a requirement would rarely be met in cases involving unwanted recording, following or other physical privacy interferences by the media.

The tort's second requirement is that there were 'words or conduct directed towards     **10.58**
the claimant for which there is no justification or reasonable excuse' (with the burden of proof resting on the claimant).[150] The importance of the defendant's freedom of speech will, where relevant, have a significant bearing on the application of this requirement.[151] This again reduces the action's applicability to media defendants. The final requirement of the action is that the claimant suffered 'physical harm or recognized psychiatric illness'.[152] Three of their Lordships in *Rhodes* noted that, in spite of suggestions in earlier case law that this requirement should be relaxed, it was common ground amongst the parties to this case that it was still a requirement.[153] In contrast, Lords Neuberger and Wilson argued that there was 'a powerful case' that it is 'enough for the claimant to establish that he suffered significant distress as a result of the defendant's statement'.[154] Relaxation of the physical harm requirement would be a significant step but, given the difficulties claimants are likely to face in establishing the tort's other requirements, its impact in the context of physical privacy intrusions by the media is likely to be limited.

---

[145] See *eg Wainwright*, HL (n 113) [44]; *Wong v Parkside Health NHS Trust* [2001] EWCA Civ 1721, [2003] 3 All ER 932 [12]; and *OPO v MLA* [2014] EWCA Civ 1277 [77].

[146] *Tugendhat and Christie* (n 104) para 10.43.

[147] *Rhodes v OPO* [2015] UKSC 32, [2015] 2 WLR 1373 [81].

[148] *Rhodes* (n 147) [87] (referring to [83]) and [112]. For a further discussion of the degree of distress required, see [114].

[149] *Rhodes* (n 147) [114].

[150] *Rhodes* (n 147) [74]. Lords Neuberger and Wilson suggested that the tort should in fact be restricted to 'making distressing statements' ([101] *et seq*).

[151] *Rhodes* (n 147) [74]. The importance of freedom of expression was emphasized throughout the judgment (see *eg* [76]–[78] and [95]–[97]).

[152] *Rhodes* (n 147) [73]. See also *Wong v Parkside Health NHS Trust* (n 145) [11]–[12]; *Wainwright*, CA (n 142) [48] per Lord Woolf; and [80] per Buxton LJ; *Wainwright*, HL (n 113) [47].

[153] *Rhodes* (n 147) [73]. They noted that in *Wainwright* (n 113) [44]–[45], Lord Hoffmann had left open the question whether intentional causation of severe distress might be actionable but said that no one in this case had suggested that it is ([73]).

[154] *Rhodes* (n 147) [119].

### (4) Outraging Public Decency

**10.59** The requirements of the common-law offence of outraging public decency are, first, that the defendant did an act of such a lewd, obscene, or disgusting character as to outrage public decency[155] and, second, that the act was 'public' in the sense that it occurred in a place to which the public has access or where it was capable of public view, and there were at least two people actually present who could have seen it, even if they in fact did not.[156] The offence has led to the conviction of individuals who have obtained intimate images of others without their knowledge. For example, in *R v Hamilton*, the Court of Appeal upheld the conviction of a man who used a video recorder in a rucksack to film up the skirts of women in a supermarket[157] and in *R v Ching Choi* the Court of Appeal upheld the conviction of a man caught filming women using the female lavatories in a Chinese supermarket.[158] Although unlikely, it is possible to imagine circumstances where paparazzi or media photographers could be guilty of this offence for intrusions into physical privacy; if, for example, they filmed corpses or the victims of crime or tragedy in a way which was prurient or deeply disrespectful.

### (5) Nuisance and Harassment

**10.60** Before the enactment of the Protection from Harassment Act 1997 (PHA), courts had made some moves towards recognition of a tort of harassment based either on the law of nuisance or the tort of intentional infliction of emotional harm. However, in *Hunter v Canary Wharf*,[159] the House of Lords overruled the Court of Appeal's conclusion in *Khorasandjian v Bush* that a claimant could sue in nuisance for telephone harassment without a proprietary interest.[160] It also held that the subsequent enactment of the PHA made it unnecessary to consider how the common law might have developed.[161] Since that decision, the Court of Appeal in both *Wong v Parkside NHS Trust*[162] and *Wainwright*[163] have held that authority did not support previous suggestions that there had been a common law tort of harassment.

[155] *R v Hamilton* [2007] EWCA Crim 2062, [2008] QB 224 [30].
[156] *R v Hamilton* (n 155) [31].
[157] *R v Hamilton* (n 155). See also *R v Tinsley* [2003] EWCA Crim 3505 (a sentencing appeal by a man who had been filming up the skirts of women and girls in shops and on the public pavement).
[158] *R v Ching Choi* (CA, 7 May 1999).
[159] [1997] UKHL 14, [1997] AC 655, 691–92 per Lord Goff; and 698 per Lord Lloyd.
[160] [1993] QB 727. In *Khorasandjian*, the majority of the Court of Appeal held that the defendant was liable in nuisance (and could be restrained on a *quia timet* basis) for persistently telephoning the claimant, even though she had no proprietary interest in the premises to which the calls were made. See also *Burris v Azadani* [1995] 1 WLR 1372, CA and *Pidduck v Molloy* [1992] 2 FLR 202, CA.
[161] *Hunter* (n 159) 691–2 per Lord Goff and 707 per Lord Hoffmann.
[162] *Wong* (n 145) [28].
[163] *Wainwright*, CA (n 142) [104].

## (6) Access as a Breach of Confidence

As discussed in Chapter 4, the modern breach of confidence action has three **10.61** main requirements. They are first, that the information has the necessary quality of confidence about it; secondly, that the information has been imparted in circumstances importing an obligation of confidence; and thirdly, that there has been unauthorized use (or a misuse) of the information.[164] In the privacy context, breach of confidence is usually relied on to protect against the unwanted disclosure of private information.[165] The potential for breach of confidence to protect physical privacy—unwanted watching, listening, and recording without subsequent dissemination of the material—has, however, been greatly enhanced by the Court of Appeal's expansive interpretation, in *Tchenguiz v Imerman*, of the action's first requirement, namely that the information be 'misused' by the defendant.[166] The defendants in *Tchenguiz* were concerned that the claimant was hiding his assets from their sister, with whom he was engaged in matrimonial proceedings. To thwart these attempts, they accessed, copied, and passed on to their sister's solicitor, documents which the claimant kept on a computer server in their shared office. The Court of Appeal held that obtaining the information, without more, was enough to breach the confidence of the defendant. Speaking for the Court, Lord Neuberger MR said:

> ...intentionally obtaining such information, secretly and knowing that the claimant reasonably expects it to be private, is itself a breach of confidence. The notion that looking at documents which one knows to be confidential is itself capable of constituting an actionable wrong (albeit perhaps only in equity) is also consistent with the decision of the Strasbourg court that monitoring private telephone calls can infringe the Article 8 rights of the caller: see *Copland v United Kingdom*...In our view, it would be a breach of confidence for a defendant, without the authority of the claimant, to examine, or to make, retain, or supply copies to a third party of, a document whose contents are, and were (or ought to have been) appreciated by the defendant to be, confidential to the claimant.[167]

The Court said that *acquiring* private information about the claimant without his consent was unacceptable because:

> It is of the essence of the claimant's right to confidentiality that he can choose whether, and, if so, to whom and in what circumstances and on what terms, to reveal the information which has the protection of the confidence.[168]

---

[164] See *Coco v AN Clark (Engineers) Ltd* [1969] RPC 41, 47; and 4.14 *et seq.*

[165] T Aplin, L Bently, P Johnson and S Malynciz, *Gurry on Breach of Confidence: The Protection of Confidential Information* (2nd edn, Oxford University Press 2012) para 15.02.

[166] 'Misuse' has traditionally involved something more than access to confidential information, such as disclosure to a third party or unauthorized exploitation of trade secrets: see *Gurry on Breach of Confidence* (n 165) paras 15.02 and 15.18–15.23.

[167] *Tchenguiz v Imerman* [2010] EWCA Civ 908, [2011] 2 WLR 592 [68]–[69] citing *Copland v UK* (2007) 45 EHRR 37.

[168] *Tchenguiz* (n 167) [69].

The claimant was therefore able to restrain the defendants from *looking at* the documents again even though there was no evidence that they intended to reveal the contents to any third party.[169] This is because, 'given that the information is confidential, the defendant should not be seeing it' and 'whatever the defendant's intentions, there would be a risk of the information getting out'.[170]

**10.62** It is clear from *Tchenguiz* that the acts of acquiring the information and copying the documents were enough on their own to establish an obligation of confidence, even if no further use was made of the material. It follows that, in England and Wales, repeatedly accessing (but not disseminating) the banking records of one's partner's former wife, as the bank clerk did in the seminal Ontarian intrusion case of *Jones v Tsige*, would be a breach of confidence.[171] The implications for protection against other types of intrusion—against telephone hacking, spying, surreptitious filming, and such like—are also significant. As this author has argued in the Cambridge Law Journal:

> If a person can be liable for acquiring private information by looking at or copying confidential documents, then why not also for acquiring private information by other means? More particularly, if it is breach of confidence to obtain private information by reading a document, can it not also be a breach of confidence to obtain private information by watching, listening or recording people; by intercepting their telephone calls, bugging their private conversations or watching them in their homes, for example?[172]

This means, the article continues, that breach of confidence action could potentially be used to protect against other types of physical privacy intrusions:

> [C]ourts could legitimately decide that it is a breach of confidence to acquire private information through the use of the senses (by hacking a person's telephone calls, bugging a private dinner conversation or videoing an intimate encounter, for example) even if no further use is made of the material. It follows that limited redress for physical privacy breaches can be provided by breach of confidence: as long as confidential information is obtained in the course of the intrusion, liability could be imposed on those who eavesdrop, spy on or record others even if no dissemination or other misuse of the information results.[173]

**10.63** *Tchenguiz v Imerman* also has significant implications for the development of the misuse of private information action (discussed at 10.95).

---

[169] *Tchenguiz* (n 167) [72]. The fact that the documents were shown to the solicitor does not seem to have been material here.

[170] *Tchenguiz* (n 167) [72]. The defendant may change his or her mind or inadvertently reveal the information: [72].

[171] *Jones v Tsige* 2012 ONCA 32, 108 OR (3d) 241, discussed at 10.87.

[172] N A Moreham, 'Beyond Information: Physical Privacy in English Law' (2014) 73 CLJ 350, 370.

[173] Moreham (n 172) 371.

## (7) Intrusion in the Misuse of Private Information Action

As discussed above, there is no general tort of breach of privacy in English law. Like **10.64** breach of confidence, the misuse of private information action focuses on one particular aspect of the privacy right—the protection against dissemination of private information or images. There is, as yet, no action protecting specifically against unwanted watching, listening, or recording per se. Intrusive conduct on the part of the defendant can nonetheless have a significant bearing on the disposal of the claimant's misuse of private information claim. The intrusiveness of the acquisition of information is relevant to the application of the reasonable expectation of privacy test in misuse of private information and the balancing of Article 8 and 10 rights. There is also increasing recognition that intrusions into physical privacy should be actionable in themselves.

### (a) *Relevance of intrusive behaviour to the claimant's expectation of privacy*

As discussed in Chapter 5, the central question which determines liability for mis- **10.65** use of personal information is whether the claimant had a reasonable expectation of privacy in respect of the information or material published. Courts have made it clear that when addressing this question they will not only consider the nature of the information disclosed but also the way in which it was obtained. Thus, as Sir Anthony Clarke MR said in *Murray v Express Newspapers plc*, 'the nature and purpose of the intrusion' is one of the factors which will determine whether the claimant had a reasonable expectation of privacy.[174]

Courts considering the way in which the information was obtained have placed **10.66** particular emphasis on the fact that the claimant was targeted by photographers, either surreptitiously or openly. In *Murray*, the young son of the famous author, JK Rowling, appealed (through his parents as litigation friends) against a judgment striking out his claim that a professional photographic agency had breached his privacy by surreptitiously photographing him as he was being wheeled down an Edinburgh street in a pushchair. The fact that the claimant was targeted by the photographer had a significant bearing on the Court's conclusion that the claimant had a reasonable expectation of privacy. Sir Anthony Clarke MR (who delivered the judgment of the Court of Appeal) held that:

> ...the law should indeed protect children from intrusive media attention, at any rate to the extent of holding that a child has a reasonable expectation that he or she will not be targeted in order to obtain photographs in a public place for publication

---

[174] [2008] EWCA Civ 446, [2009] Ch 481 [36] (also known as *Murray v Big Pictures Ltd* in the Court of Appeal). See also *Campbell v MGN Ltd* [2004] UKHL 22, [2004] 2 AC 457 [75], where Lord Hoffmann said, citing *Hellewell v Chief Constable of Derbyshire* [1995] 1 WLR 804, 'the publication of a photograph taken by intrusion into their private place (for example, by a long distance lens) may in itself be such an infringement [of the privacy of the personal information], even if there is nothing embarrassing about the picture itself'.

which the person who took or procured the taking of the photographs knew would be objected to on behalf of the child.[175]

**10.67** He observed that, on the assumed facts, this was 'not an isolated case of a newspaper taking one photograph out of the blue' and subsequently publishing it but one where a number of media bodies had photographers camped outside the Murrays' house in the period before the publication.[176] The fact that the photographs were obtained surreptitiously was also important:

> This was not the taking of a single photograph of David in the street. On the claimant's case, which must be taken as true for present purposes, it was the clandestine taking and subsequent publication of the photograph in the context of a series of photographs which were taken for the purpose of their sale for publication, in circumstances in which BPL did not ask David's parents for their consent to the taking and publication of his photograph.[177]

Thus, although other factors (including the fact that the claimant was a child) were also considered, the intrusive way in which the photograph was obtained—surreptitiously and by targeting the claimant—bore directly on the Court's decision that the boy's claim for misuse of private information should not be struck out.

**10.68** Surreptitious targeting was also taken into account in *Campbell v MGN Ltd*,[178] in which a well-known fashion model was awarded damages for the publication of an article outlining the time, place, and frequency of treatment she was receiving for drug addiction and an accompanying photograph showing her outside one of her therapy meetings. Lord Hope held that the publication of the photograph of the claimant tipped the scales in his decision that the defendants had breached the claimant's reasonable expectation of privacy.[179] In reaching that conclusion, he considered not just the nature of the photograph and the effect of its publication but also the way in which it was taken. He stressed in particular that the photographs 'were taken deliberately, in secret and with a view to their publication in conjunction with the article. The zoom lens was directed at the doorway of the place where the meeting had been taking place.'[180] Baroness Hale also stressed that part of the harm caused by publication of the photograph was making the claimant 'think that she was being followed or betrayed, and deterring her from going back to the same place again'.[181]

---

[175] *Murray* (n 174) [57].

[176] *Murray* (n 174) [18].

[177] *Murray* (n 174) [17].

[178] *Campbell* (n 174).

[179] *Campbell* (n 174) [121].

[180] *Campbell* (n 174) [123].

[181] *Campbell* (n 174) [155]. Lord Nicholls took a different view, holding that the fact that the photographs were surreptitiously taken was irrelevant because the claimant was not complaining about the *taking* of the photographs but the dissemination of the information that they conveyed. He said that in this context they were therefore no different from the text communicating the same information: *Campbell* (n 174) [30]. English courts' disapproval of surreptitious recording has however also been made clear in other contexts: see *eg R v Broadcasting Standards Commission, ex p BBC* [2001]

Convention jurisprudence also supports the view that open targeting of a claimant **10.69** can bear on whether he or she had a reasonable expectation of privacy in respect of the information or images obtained. *von Hannover v Germany* [182] is the leading example. *von Hannover* was the climax of a ten-year campaign by Princess Caroline of Monaco to prevent publication of photographs taken without her consent as she went about her daily life. The photographs in question depicted her riding on horseback, shopping (either on her own or with a bodyguard), riding a bicycle, eating in a restaurant with a companion, skiing in Austria, leaving her Parisian residence (either alone or with her husband), playing tennis with her husband (and arriving by bicycle beforehand), and tripping over an obstacle at a beach club. The European Court of Human Rights unanimously held that by failing to provide the princess with a domestic remedy for publication of the photographs, Germany had breached its positive obligation under Article 8 of the European Convention for the Protection of Human Rights to respect her 'private life'. [183] In reaching that conclusion, the Court acknowledged that 'photos appearing in the tabloid press are often taken in a climate of continual harassment which induces in the person concerned a very strong sense of intrusion into their private life or even of persecution'. [184] As a result:

> ...even though, strictly speaking, the present application concerns only the publication of the photos and articles by various German magazines, the context in which these photos were taken—without the applicant's knowledge or consent—and the harassment endured by many public figures in their daily lives cannot be fully disregarded. [185]

The English Court of Appeal has also held that bright-line distinctions between the **10.70** acquisition and subsequent use of a photograph are artificial and unhelpful when trying to determine whether the Article 8 right to private life has been engaged. [186] In *Wood v Commissioner for Police of the Metropolis*, [187] the majority of the Court of Appeal upheld the claimant's complaint that the police breached his Article 8 right to respect for private life by openly following and photographing him on a public street outside a shareholders' meeting and then storing the photograph on a police

---

QB 885, CA [37], [44]; *R (Anna Ford) v Press Complaints Commission* [2001] EWHC 683 (Admin), [2002] EMLR 41 [30]; *R v Loveridge, Lee and Loveridge* [2001] EWCA Crim 973, [2001] 2 Cr App R 29 [30]; *Hellewell v Chief Constable of Derbyshire* (n 174) 807; and *Viagogo Ltd v Myles, Hardcash Productions Ltd and Channel Four Corp Ltd* [2012] EWHC 433 (Ch) [72]–[73].

[182] *von Hannover v Germany* (2005) 40 EHRR 1.

[183] *von Hannover* (n 182). For further discussion of Art 8 and the jurisprudence of the European Court of Human Rights see 3.13–3.39.

[184] *von Hannover* (n 182) para 59.

[185] *von Hannover* (n 182) para 68. Subsequent decisions have confirmed that the harassing conduct which the claimant was subjected to in *von Hannover* was not determinative in that case. See *McKennitt v Ash* [2006] EWCA Civ 1714, [2007] 3 WLR 194 [41] citing *Sciacca v Italy* (2006) 43 EHRR 20, paras 27, 29 and *Murray v Express Newspapers plc* (n 174) [59]–[60] citing *Reklos and Davourlis v Greece* [2009] ECHR 200.

[186] *Wood v Commissioner for Police of the Metropolis* [2009] EWCA Civ 414, [2009] 4 All ER 951 [39].

[187] *Wood* (n 186).

database. Laws LJ with whom the majority agreed on this point, held that when determining whether the claimant had a reasonable expectation of privacy (which he said was the touchstone for determining whether Article 8(1) was 'engaged') it was artificial and 'unhelpful' to distinguish between liability for the taking of the photograph and for its retention and use.[188] It was the police's conduct as a whole which should be taken into account when assessing whether Article 8(1) was engaged.[189]

**10.71** **The publisher's knowledge** So both the misuse of private information cases and Convention jurisprudence establish that courts will be more likely to find a reasonable expectation of privacy in respect of disclosure if the information in question is obtained intrusively. There is a question, however, about what knowledge the defendant must have of the circumstances in which the photograph was taken before he or she can be accountable for them. In *Weller v Associated Newspapers Ltd*, Dingemans J declined to consider the way that photographs were taken when determining the claimants' misuse of private information claim because the defendants were unaware of the particular circumstances of the photography. Dingemans J held, following *Murray*, that 'the absence of consent, and whether this was known or could be inferred' and the 'circumstances in which and the purposes for which the information came into the hands of the publisher' were both relevant to whether the claimants had a reasonable expectation of privacy.[190] He stressed, however, that although it was clear from the article that the *Mail Online* knew that the photographs of the infant twins and teenage daughter of musician Paul Weller had been taken without consent, it did not know that the photographer had harassed the daughter in a café nor that the photographer had said that the children's faces would be pixelated in any resulting publication.[191] These factors were therefore not mentioned as part of the judge's reasons for concluding that the claimants had a reasonable expectation of privacy in respect of the outing nor his conclusion that the balancing test favoured the claimants. The daughter's 'particular discomfort when cornered in the café' was also left out of account in the award of damages.[192]

**10.72** The judgment in *Weller* did not discuss, however, when a publisher might be expected to make inquiries about the circumstances in which a photograph was taken. Although Dingemans J said that the objective reasonable expectation of privacy test 'allows the Court to assess what the publishers knew, and what they *ought to have known*',[193] he did not address the second question expressly. He merely

---

[188] *Wood* (n 186) [39].

[189] *Wood* (n 186) [39].

[190] *Weller v Associated Newspapers Ltd* [2014] EWHC 1163 (QB) 37.

[191] *Weller* (n 190) [161]. It is not clear from the summary of the facts in *Weller* exactly what form this harassment took. It is clear that the photographer continued to follow and photograph the family despite being asked by the claimants' father to stop and that the daughter, Dylan, felt harassed by the photographer when at the café although it is not clear exactly what behaviour prompted those feelings.

[192] *Weller* (n 190) [196].

[193] *Weller* (n 190) [37] (emphasis added).

referred repeatedly to what the defendant *did* know about the photographer's conduct. This leaves open the question of what inquiries a publisher has to make when offered images or information by a third party; in other words, what they ought to know about the way an image or information was obtained.

### (b) Recognition of intrusion as a separate aspect of the privacy interest

The need to protect against 'intrusion' has been explicitly recognized in some cases   **10.73** as one of the aims of misuse of private information in English law. In *Goodwin v News Group Newspapers Ltd* (which concerned the continuation of an injunction restraining the defendant from disclosing the identity of a senior bank employee with whom the claimant, chief executive of RBS, had had an affair), Tugendhat J began his discussion of the reasonable expectation of privacy by citing the second edition of this book and saying:

> The right to respect for private life embraces more than one concept. Dr Moreham summarises what she calls the two core components of the rights to privacy: 'unwanted access to private information and unwanted access to [or intrusion into] one's... personal space'...I shall refer to the two components of the right as 'confidentiality' and 'intrusion'.[194]

He then went on to consider 'confidentiality' and 'intrusion' separately and, significantly, concluded that although publication of Goodwin's mistress's name would not be a breach of her reasonable expectation of 'confidentiality', it would be an actionable intrusion.[195] Eady J took a similar approach in *CTB v New Group Newspapers Ltd* to continued suppression of the name of an adulterous footballer who had been named on social networking sites. He said that '[i]t is important always to remember that the modern law of privacy is not concerned solely with information or "secrets": it is also concerned importantly with *intrusion*'.[196]

Both judges used the term 'intrusion' to refer to the effects of publication on the   **10.74** individuals concerned and not just interference with the physical privacy interests that are the subject of this chapter. Eady J was concerned about the 'intrusion', 'distress', and 'embarrassment' occasioned by 'wall-to-wall excoriation in national newspapers'.[197] Tugendhat J emphasized the 'distress' that publication was likely to cause and the relationship between 'intrusion' and harassment.[198] However, part of both judges' concern related at least in part to the physical intrusions associated

---

[194] *Goodwin v News Group Newspapers Ltd* [2011] EWHC 1437, QB [85] citing N A Moreham in *Tugendhat and Christie* (n 104) paras 2.07, 2.08, 2.16, and 12.71. Tugendhat J said that Parliament has recognized the importance of protection against intrusion by enacting the Protection from Harassment Act 1997 and the Human Rights Act 1998: [86].

[195] See particularly, *Goodwin* (n 194) [109], [111] and [120].

[196] *CTB v News Group Newspapers Ltd* [2011] EWHC 1326 (QB) [23].

[197] *CTB* (n 196) [24]. See also *CTB v News Group Newspapers Ltd* [2011] EWHC 1334 (QB) in which Tugendhat J declined a subsequent attempt to have the injunction lifted (following disclosure of the claimant's identity in Parliament) on similar grounds.

[198] See *Goodwin* (n 194) [114]–[118].

with the 'cruel and destructive media frenzy' which was likely to engulf the claimants and their families if the injunctions were lifted.[199]

*(c) Liability for merely taking a photograph or video recording*

**10.75** Although Lord Hope and Baroness Hale were willing to take account of the way in which a photograph was taken when determining liability for publication, none of the judges in *Campbell v MGN Ltd* went so far as to say that taking a photograph without more can satisfy the requirements of the misuse of private information action, at least not if the photograph was taken in a public place. As Lord Hoffmann said, '[t]he famous and even the not so famous who go out in public must accept that they may be photographed without their consent, just as they may be observed by others without their consent'.[200] Lord Hope agreed that '[t]he taking of photographs in a public street must…be taken to be one of the ordinary incidents of living in a free community'.[201]

**10.76** There has however been some judicial support for the opposite view. In *Murray v Express Newspapers plc*, Sir Anthony Clarke MR said that although the focus of the privacy action is on the *publication* and not the *taking* of photographs,[202] he did not rule out the possibility of redress for taking the photograph:

> It may well be that the mere taking of a photograph of a child in a public place when out with his or her parents, whether they are famous or not, would not engage Article 8 of the Convention. However, as we see it, it all depends upon the circumstances.[203]

**10.77** Laws LJ also held, in the Human Rights Act 1998 case of *Wood v Commissioner for Police of the Metropolis*, that the 'circumstances in which a photograph is taken in a public place may of themselves turn the event into one in which Article 8 is not merely engaged but grossly violated':[204]

> The act of taking the picture, or more likely pictures, may be intrusive or even violent, conducted by means of hot pursuit, face-to-face confrontation, pushing, shoving, bright lights, barging into the affected person's home. The subject of the photographers' interest—in the case I am contemplating, there will usually be a bevy of picture-takers—may be seriously harassed and perhaps assaulted. He or she may certainly feel frightened and distressed. Conduct of this kind is simply brutal. It may well attract other remedies, civil or criminal, under our domestic law. It would plainly violate Article 8(1), and I can see no public interest justification for it under Article 8(2).[205]

---

[199] See *CTB* (n 196) [24], [26]; *CTB v News Group Newspapers Ltd* [2011] EWHC 1334 (QB) [3]; and *Goodwin* (n 194) [120].

[200] *Campbell* (n 174) [73]. See also *Wood* (n 186) [33].

[201] *Campbell* (n 174) [122].

[202] *Murray* (n 174) [16].

[203] *Murray* (n 174) [17].

[204] *Wood* (n 186) [34].

[205] *Wood* (n 186) [34]. However, Laws LJ stressed that the situation he was describing bore no resemblance to the conduct of the police in that case.

In *Mosley v News Group Newspapers Ltd* (a case concerning the surreptitious taking   **10.78**
and dissemination of footage of the claimant engaged in sado-masochistic sexual
activities), Eady J went further and said that, '[n]aturally, the very fact of clandestine recording may be regarded as an intrusion and an unacceptable infringement
of Article 8 rights'.[206] But like Lord Nicholls in *Campbell*,[207] Eady J noted that the
pleaded claim was confined to publication of information and did not include the
intrusive method by which that information was acquired.[208]

Eady J's observation is echoed by Mann J in *BKM Ltd v BBC*, a case concer-   **10.79**
ning surreptitiously-obtained footage of elderly residents inside a care home.[209]
Mann J confirmed that, '[n]on-consensual filming is capable of being a very serious infringement of [the residents'] rights to privacy, whether it merely films them
in their home or whether it goes further and intrudes into their disabilities'.[210] Both
the filming and broadcast in *BKM* were, however, held to be justified by the public
interest in revealing possible lapses in the standard of care being provided.[211] It
is noteworthy that, in contrast to *Campbell*, both *BKM Ltd* and *Mosley* involved
recordings in private places.

**Strasbourg**   These domestic dicta are consistent with the European Court of   **10.80**
Human Right's decision in *Reklos v Greece* that the taking of a photograph, together
with retention of the negatives, can be a breach of an applicant's Article 8 right to
respect for private life. The Court there held that Greek domestic courts failed to
protect the private-life interests of a day-old child who was photographed without his
parents' consent while in a sterile unit at the hospital in which he was born. The Court
held that liability under Article 8 did not depend on publication of the photographs:

> A person's image constitutes one of the chief attributes of his or her personality, as
> it reveals the person's unique characteristics and distinguishes the person from his
> or her peers. The right to the protection of one's image is thus one of the essential
> components of personal development and presupposes the right to control of the
> use of that image. Whilst in most cases the right to control such use involves the
> possibility for an individual to refuse publication of his or her image, it also covers
> the individual's right to object to the recording, conversation and reproduction
> of the image by another person. As a person's image is one of the characteristics

---

[206] [2008] EWHC 1777 (QB), [2008] EMLR 20 [17].
[207] *Campbell* (n 174) [15], [30].
[208] *Mosley* (n 206) [17].
[209] *BKM Ltd v BBC* [2009] EWHC 3151 (Ch). No mention is made of a claim for breach of confidence or misuse of private information; the judge simply says that 'BKM brought this application
to restrain broadcast... in order to protect the right of the home's residents to privacy and family
life under the Human Rights Act': [7]. It is unclear whether the judge was applying Art 8 directly or
simply applying the requirements of the misuse of private information action (*ie* the need to balance
privacy and freedom of expression interests) without making explicit mention of the cause of action.
For further discussion of whether some media bodies can themselves regarded as public authorities
under s 6 HRA, see 1.57–1.65.
[210] *BKM* (n 209) [16]. See also [33].
[211] *BKM* (n 209) [35]–[37]. See also *Tillery Valley Foods v Channel Four Television* [2004] EWHC
1075 (Ch).

attached to his or her personality, its effective protection presupposes, in principle and in circumstances such as those of the present case...obtaining the consent of the person concerned at the time the picture is taken and not simply if and when it is published. Otherwise an essential attribute of personality would be retained in the hands of a third party and the person concerned would have no control over any subsequent use of the image.[212]

**10.81** The Court took the same approach to unwanted video surveillance in *Söderman v Sweden*. In that case, the Grand Chamber held that Sweden breached its positive obligations to a fourteen-year-old girl by failing to provide civil or criminal sanction against her step-father after he surreptitiously filmed her changing in the bathroom.[213]

## D. Developing an Intrusion into Physical Privacy Action

**10.82** Although English courts have so far declined to recognize either a specific action for intrusion into physical privacy or a broad privacy tort which could include non-informational privacy, there are indications that a specific action might be developed in the future. This section will consider recognition of the tort of intrusion into seclusion in other common law jurisdictions and set out arguments for development of a specific physical privacy action in England and Wales.

### (1) Intrusion in Other Common Law Jurisdictions

#### (a) United States

**10.83** As discussed in Chapter 3, US law has for many years recognized a tort of intrusion upon seclusion. As § 652B of the Restatement of the Law (Second) of Torts (1977) says:

> One who intentionally intrudes, physically or otherwise, upon the solitude or seclusion of another or his private affairs or concerns, is subject to liability to the other for invasion of his privacy, if the intrusion would be highly offensive to a reasonable person.

Intrusions can be effected physically (for example, by forcing one's way into another's home or hotel room) or by the use of the senses, either with or without mechanical aids.[214] Subsequent publication is not required.[215]

---

[212] *Reklos v Greece* App no 1234/05 (ECtHR, 15 January 2009), [2009] EMLR 16, para 40. The Court also took account of the fact that the photographs were taken in a place that was accessible only to the doctors and nurses of the clinic (para 37); that the baby's image was the sole subject of the photographs (para 37); there was no public interest in the baby (para 41); that the parents did not consent to the photography (para 41); and that the photographer retained the negatives (para 42).

[213] *Söderman v Sweden* [2013] ECHR 1128, para 117.

[214] See the commentary to § 652B Restatement of the Law (Second) of Torts (1977) (the 'Restatement').

[215] See commentary to § 652B of the Restatement.

### (b) New Zealand

The New Zealand High Court recognized a tort of intrusion into seclusion in **10.84** *C v Holland*. In that case, the defendant used a video camera to film his flatmate through a hole in the ceiling while she was having a shower. The claimant sued for damages and proceedings were brought to establish the preliminary issue of 'whether invasion of privacy of this type, without publicity or the prospect of publicity, is an actionable tort in New Zealand'.[216] Whata J held that it was, regarding the tort of intrusion into seclusion as:

> ... entirely compatible with, and a logical adjunct to, the *Hosking* tort of wrongful publication of private facts. They logically attack the same underlying wrong, namely unwanted intrusion into a reasonable expectation of privacy.[217]

The New Zealand tort of intrusion into seclusion has four main requirements: **10.85**

(a)  an intentional and unauthorised intrusion;
(b)  into seclusion (namely intimate personal activity, space or affairs);
(c)  involving infringement of a reasonable expectation of privacy; and
(d)  that is highly offensive to a reasonable person.[218]

Whata J also said that a legitimate public concern in the information may provide a defence to the privacy claim.[219] 'Information' in this context appears to refer to any material gathered in the course of the intrusion.

### (c)  Canada

As discussed at 3.119 *et seq*, four Canadian provinces have statutory privacy torts. In **10.86** these provinces, it is a 'tort, actionable without proof of damage, for a person wilfully and without claim of right, to violate the privacy of another person'.[220] These broad actions extend to situations where a defendant looks at, listens to, or records an individual in breach of his or her privacy, even if the material is not subsequently disseminated.[221]

---

[216]  *C v Holland* [2012] 3 NZLR 672 [1]. Helpfully discussed by T McKenzie, 'The New Intrusion Tort: The News Media Exposed?' (2014) 45 VUWLR 79.

[217]  *C v Holland* (n 216) [75]. The *Hosking* tort protects against highly offensive publication of private facts (see 3.98–3.100).

[218]  *C v Holland* (n 216) [94].

[219]  *C v Holland* (n 216) [96].

[220]  Privacy Act, RSBC 1996, c 373, s 1(1); Privacy Act, RSS 1978, c P-24, s 2; Privacy Act, RSNL 1990, c P-22, s 3(1). Manitoba's statute uses the language of 'substantially, unreasonably, and without claim of right': Privacy Act, CCSM, c P125, s 2(1).

[221]  See *eg Malcolm v Fleming*, 2000 Carswell BC 1316 (SC) in which a claimant was awarded both general and punitive damages ($15,000 and $35,000 respectively) after her landlord installed a video camera in her apartment and recorded her in various states of undress in her bathroom and bedroom; *LAM v JELI*, 2008 BCSC 1147, 170 ACWS (3d) 674 where an award of $50,000 ($20,000 of general damages, $5,000 for loss of income earning opportunity, and punitive damages of $35,000) was made against a defendant who filmed his former partner and her young daughter in the bathroom of his home; *Lee v Jacobson* (1992) 87 DLR (4th) 401, 31 ACWS (3d) 329 (BCSC) in which damages of $5,000 and $2,000 were awarded respectively to two claimants who had been observed by their landlord through a peep hole and two-way mirror in their bedroom; and *Watts v Klaemt* 2007 BCSC

**10.87** In addition, in *Jones v Tsige* the Ontarian Court of Appeal held that a bank clerk who accessed (but did not disseminate) the banking records of her partner's former wife on 174 separate occasions committed the common law tort of intrusion into seclusion for which she had to pay damages of $10,000. Having noted the vulnerability of personal information stored in electronic databases and that the 'facts cry out for a remedy', the Court recognized the existence of a tort based on the US tort of seclusion which applies when, an individual 'intentionally intrudes, physically or otherwise, upon the seclusion of another or his private affairs or concerns... [and] the invasion would be highly offensive to a reasonable person'.[222] Speaking for the Court, Sharpe JA continued that the key features of the cause of action are:

> ...first, that the defendant's conduct must be intentional, within which I would include reckless; second, that the defendant must have invaded, without lawful justification, the plaintiff's private affairs or concerns; and third, that a reasonable person would regard the invasion as highly offensive causing distress, humiliation or anguish. However, proof of harm to a recognized economic interest is not an element of the cause of action...[223]

### (2) Scope for Developing an English Tort of Intrusion into Physical Privacy

#### (a) Support for a tort of intrusion into physical privacy

**10.88** In spite of the House of Lords' decision in *Wainwright v Home Office* that there is no general tort of invasion of privacy,[224] courts in England and Wales have often recognized that there is more to the privacy interest than the protection of private information. For example, in *Campbell v MGN Ltd*, Lord Nicholls held that the wrongful disclosure of private information is just 'one aspect of invasion of privacy'.[225] He said:

> An individual's privacy can be invaded in ways not involving publication of information. Strip-searches are an example. The extent to which the common law as developed thus far in this country protects other forms of invasion of privacy is not a matter arising in the present case. It does not arise because, although pleaded more widely, Miss Campbell's common law claim was throughout presented in

---

662, [2007] BCWLD 4106 in which damages of $36,000 ($30,000 general, $5,000 punitive and $1,000 'out of pocket') were awarded against a defendant who recorded his neighbours' telephone conversations for a year and disclosed the contents of two conversations to her employer.

[222] *Jones v Tsige* 2012 ONCA 32, 108 OR (3d) 241 [70].

[223] *Jones* (n 222) [71]. The Court recognized that the interest at stake in *Jones* was informational privacy as opposed to personal privacy (which is grounded in the right to bodily integrity) or territorial privacy (which 'protects the home and other spaces where the individual enjoys a reasonable expectation of privacy'): [41]. However, it is clear that the Ontarian intrusion action would also apply to the non-informational intrusions under discussion in this chapter including situations where a person conducts surveillance, telephone hacking, or photography of a person in intimate circumstances. In England and Wales, the facts of *Jones v Tsige* would give rise to liability for breach of confidence (see 10.62).

[224] [2003] UKHL 53, [2004] 2 AC 406.

[225] [2004] UKHL 22, [2004] 2 AC 457 [12].

court exclusively on the basis of breach of confidence, that is, the wrongful publication by *The Mirror* of private information.[226]

Lord Mustill also defined privacy broadly in *R v Broadcasting Standards Commission,* **10.89**
*ex p BBC*, an appeal against a decision of the Broadcasting Standards Commission:

> To my mind the privacy of a human being denotes at the same time the personal 'space' in which the individual is free to be itself, and also the carapace, or shell, or umbrella, or whatever other metaphor is preferred, which protects that space from intrusion. An infringement of privacy is an affront to the personality, which is damaged both by the violation and by the demonstration that the personal space is not inviolate.[227]

And, as discussed at 10.75–10.79, some courts have suggested that the mere taking of a photograph might in some circumstances be enough to engage Article 8.[228]

### (b) Article 8

These broad interpretations of the privacy interest are consistent with both domes- **10.90**
tic and Strasbourg courts' interpretation of the private life interest in Article 8. The European Court of Human Rights has consistently observed that the right to respect for private life includes 'the physical and psychological integrity of a person' as well as the protection of private information. The physical and psychological integrity of a person includes the right to be free from intrusion into home or workplace, unwanted bodily exposure, physical assault, and unwanted surveillance (including a right to be free from non-consensual photography and video recording).[229] The right to respect for 'private life' also encompasses a right to personal autonomy and to develop relationships and identity.[230]

Domestic interpretations of Article 8 are similarly broad. In *Pretty v DPP*, Lord **10.91**
Bingham said that Article 8 'is directed to the protection of privacy, including the protection of physical and psychological integrity' and 'is expressed in terms directed to protection of personal autonomy while individuals are living their lives'.[231] Similarly in *R (Countryside Alliance) v Attorney General*, Lord Bingham said that Article 8 protects a 'private sphere within which individuals expect to

---

[226] *Campbell* (n 225) [15].

[227] [2001] QB 885, CA [48]. See also *Douglas v Hello! Ltd* [2001] QB 967, CA [126] where Sedley LJ said that a concept of privacy recognizes that 'the law has to protect not only those people whose trust has been abused but those who simply find themselves subjected to an unwanted intrusion into their personal lives'.

[228] See *eg Murray v Express Newspapers plc* [2008] EWCA Civ 446, [2009] Ch 481 [17]; *Mosley* (n 206) [17]; and *Wood v Commissioner for Police of the Metropolis* [2009] EWCA Civ 414, [2009] 4 All ER 951 [34]. For discussion of related issues in the context of harassment see 10.07–10.20.

[229] See *eg YF v Turkey* (2004) 39 EHRR 34, para 33 and *Pretty v UK* (2002) 35 EHRR 1, para 61. Other cases have referred to the 'physical and moral integrity of the person'; see *X and Y v Netherlands* (1986) 8 EHRR 235, para 22; *Costello-Roberts v UK* (1993) 19 EHRR 112, para 34; and *Stubbings v UK* (1996) 23 EHRR 213, para 61. See also 3.23–3.26 and 10.80–10.81.

[230] See further 3.31–3.36.

[231] [2001] UKHL 61 [23]. See also [100] per Lord Hope.

be left alone to conduct their personal affairs and live their personal lives as they choose'.[232] Baroness Hale held that Article 8 protects both 'private space' and 'the personal and psychological space within which each individual develops his or her own sense of self and relationships with other people'.[233] Lords Hope, Rodger, and Brown defined private life similarly broadly.[234] The United Kingdom has a positive obligation under Article 8 of the Convention to protect all aspects of the right to respect for private life effectively. That includes the non-informational aspects of the privacy interest identified in these judgments.

*(c) Extending misuse of private information*

**10.92**    It is clear from *Wainwright v Home Office* that it is not open to the courts simply to found a general cause of action on the basis of a breach of Article 8 (as distinct from the statutory cause of action against a public authority under s 7 of the Human Rights Act 1998). After discussing the scope of the invasion of privacy action recognized by Sedley LJ in *Douglas v Hello!*, Lord Hoffmann said:

> There seems to me a great difference between identifying privacy as a value which underlies the existence of a rule of law (and may point the direction in which the law should develop) and privacy as a principle of law in itself. The English common law is familiar with the notion of underlying values—principles only in the broadest sense—which direct its development. A famous example is *Derbyshire County Council v Times Newspapers Ltd* [1993] AC 534, in which freedom of speech was the underlying value which supported the decision to lay down the specific rule that a local authority could not sue for libel. But no one has suggested that freedom of speech is in itself a legal principle which is capable of sufficient definition to enable one to deduce specific rules to be applied in concrete cases. That is not the way the common law works.[235]

**10.93**    It follows that, as Eady J said in *White v Withers LLP and Marcus Dearle*, 'the enactment of the HRA 1998 has not given rise to a new directly enforceable tort of invasion of privacy in English law'.[236] Instead, as Gavin Phillipson and Alexander Williams put it, 'the courts must develop the common law compatibly with the Convention, but only where such development can be achieved by "incremental" development'.[237] In other words, courts need to identify another cause of action to act as a peg on which any liability for non-informational breaches of privacy can be hung. In the information context, this peg is breach of confidence. The question,

---

[232] [2007] UKHL 52, [2008] 1 AC 719 [10].

[233] *R (Countryside Alliance)* (n 232) [116].

[234] *R (Countryside Alliance)* (n 232) [54] per Lord Hope, [101] per Lord Rodger, and [139] per Lord Brown. See also *Wood* (n 228) [20]–[21].

[235] *Wainwright v Home Office* [2003] UKHL 53, [2004] 2 AC 406 [31].

[236] *White v Withers LLP and Marcus Dearle* [2008] EWHC 2821 (QB) [16].

[237] G Phillipson and A Williams, 'Horizontal Effect and the Constitutional Constraint' (2011) 74 MLR 878, 878–9. See also M Hunt, 'The Horizontal Effect of the Human Rights Act' [1998] PL 423, especially 441–2; A Lester and D Pannick, 'The Impact of the Human Rights Act on Private Law: The Knight's Move' (2000) 116 LQR 380.

then, is whether there is a cause of action which could be similarly extended to protect against physical privacy intrusions.

It is suggested that there is, since the misuse of private information action could **10.94** be extended to cover a wider range of privacy intrusions. More particularly, misuse of private information could be extended to situations where the claimant has a reasonable expectation of privacy, not in respect of the disclosure of private information, but in respect of his or her physical self, a private place, or a private activity. Such an action could provide protection against unjustified surveillance, spying, eavesdropping, and recording.

As this author has argued in the Cambridge Law Journal, three main arguments **10.95** support this proposed extension. The first argument is that the rationale for protecting against misuse of private information applies with equal force to the protection of physical privacy:

> ...in both physical and informational privacy cases the fundamental objection is the same: the defendant is obtaining unwanted access to a person by interfering with his or her reasonable expectation of privacy. And both physical and informational privacy breaches undermine the claimant's dignity, autonomy and relationships leading to feelings of distress, mistrust and violation.[238]

Second, courts developing 'applicable' common law principles—including misuse of private information—are bound to develop the law consistently with the Article 8 right to respect for private life.[239] Since the Article 8 right to respect for private life extends well beyond the protection of private information, it is defensible—indeed, some would say, necessary—for courts to extend the reasonable expectation of privacy to cover these wider private life interests including right to protection from, *inter alia*, visual and audio surveillance, bodily searches, and unwanted photography.[240] And third, the extension of the concept of 'misuse' in the breach of confidence case of *Tchenguiz v Imerman* supports the extension of the misuse of private information action:

> [I]n breach of confidence cases involving personal information, courts use the reasonable expectation of privacy test to determine whether confidence has been breached.[241] And, as the Court of Appeal said in *Tchenguiz*, 'the law should be developed and applied consistently and coherently in both privacy and 'old fashioned confidence' cases, even if they sometimes may have different features'.[242] It follows that if

---

[238] N A Moreham, 'Beyond Information: Physical Privacy in English Law' (2014) 73 CLJ 350, 373. See also *C v Holland* (n 216) [75] (discussed at 10.84–10.85) and R Wacks, *Privacy and Media Freedom* (Oxford University Press 2013) 246. Wacks asks: 'If 'privacy' is protected by Article 8–and [*Campbell v Mirror Group Newspapers Ltd* [2004] UKHL 22, [2004] 2 AC 457] bristles with sweeping pronouncements of its significance—why is 'intrusion' excluded?'

[239] See 3.37–3.39 and 5.03–5.12.

[240] Moreham (n 238). See 10.80–10.81.

[241] *Tchenguiz v Imerman* [2010] EWCA Civ 908, [2011] 2 WLR 592 [66]. See also 10.61–10.63.

[242] *Tchenguiz* (n 241) [67]. The Court was explaining why it should draw on misuse of private information cases in the breach of confidence context but the converse also applies.

the mere acquisition of private information can interfere with a claimant's reasonable expectations of privacy in breach of confidence, it will also breach the claimant's reasonable expectations in misuse of private information. Reading a person's diary, hacking his or her emails or copying his or her medical records is therefore highly likely to be an actionable breach of privacy. Once courts reach this conclusion, it is…a small step to conclude that it is also a misuse of private information to acquire information by other means; by spying on a person as he or she attends a medical appointment, by bugging a private dinner conversation, or installing a video in his or her home. It is suggested that courts should take this small step and go one further—they should drop the language of information altogether and recognise that unwanted watching, listening and recording are breaches of privacy in themselves.

**10.96** Finally, it is suggested that *Wainwright v Home Office* would not prevent courts from making this extension. This is because:

> Although Lord Hoffmann was opposed to recognition of a broad-ranging right to privacy, he did contemplate the incremental development of privacy protection.[243] Extension of misuse of private information would be such a development; no general right to privacy would be created. And to the extent that recognition of physical privacy is inconsistent with the specific conclusion reached in *Wainwright*—that there was no right of action available to prison visitors who were strip-searched in contravention of prison rules—things have moved on. Article 8 of the HRA would now provide the Wainwrights with a cause of action and Lord Hoffmann's doubts about whether the intrusive strip-search would have breached Article 8 were shown to be ill-founded in Strasbourg.[244] Protection of physical privacy is, then, a logical next step in the development of the right to privacy in private law.[245]

**10.98** Since those arguments were made, Mann J's decision of *Gulati v MGN Ltd* has provided further evidence of the courts' willingness to recognize a new physical privacy action from within the misuse of private information tort.[246] In that case, a claim to ascertain the damages payable for admitted telephone hacking, Mann J compensated the claimants not just for publication of the information obtained but also for the hacking itself. Substantial damages were therefore paid for hacking which did not result in articles:

> to reflect the fact that for a considerable period an individual's voicemail, and those of associates, were listened to and the private lives exposed there were studied by at least one journalist and probably more, on a frequent, sometimes daily, basis.[247]

Further development in the common law protection of physical privacy therefore seems likely.

---

[243] See *Wainwright* (n 235) [28]–[33].

[244] The European Court of Human Rights held that the guards' conduct breached the claimants' right to respect for private life in Art 8 of the Convention (*Wainwright v UK* (2007) 44 EHRR 40).

[245] Moreham (n 238) 375. The article goes on to discuss the form that such a physical privacy tort should take.

[246] *Gulati v MGN Ltd* [2015] EWHC 1482 (Ch). For further discussion, see N A Moreham 'Liability for Listening: Why Phone Hacking is an Actionable Breach of Privacy' (2015) 8 JML (forthcoming).

[247] *Gulati* (n 246) [230].

# Part IV

## JUSTIFICATIONS AND DEFENCES

# 11

## JUSTIFICATIONS AND DEFENCES

*Sir Mark Warby and Victoria Shore*

## A. Introduction

This chapter identifies and considers the answers available to claims for breach of privacy brought against the media. The aim is to provide a systematic description of the defences and justifications available to defendants. Some are of general application, whatever cause of action is invoked. These are considered in Section B. Otherwise, the approach adopted is to group the various causes of action by which privacy may be protected, and the defences and justifications that may be invoked, according to the different aspects of privacy for which protection may be sought. **11.01**

Section C therefore considers defences to claims for breach of informational privacy. Section D considers defences to claims for physical intrusions. Section E **11.02** examines defences to claims for protection from falsehood, and Section F considers the answers to publicity right claims. Section G considers limitation of actions.

## B. General Defences

**11.03**   The common feature of the first two defences dealt with in this section, consent and waiver, is that they depend on proof that the claimant's own conduct disentitles him or her to complain of what the defendant has published or done. In cases of consent that is because the claimant has willed the particular act. A defence of estoppel will be available where the claimant has, willingly or not, led the defendant into conduct which makes it unjust for the claimant to complain. The defence of change of position differs as it depends on the defendant's conduct rather than, or as well as, that of the claimant. Media privacy cases in which these defences or justifications have been successfully advanced are relatively rare, but they are nonetheless of importance.

### (1) Consent

#### *(a) Consent as a defence to privacy claims*

**11.04**   **A narrow doctrine**   It is well established that the consent, licence, or authority[1] of the alleged victim of an act will in general be a defence to, or negative a claim in tort[2] in respect of, that act. This is generally true also of the causes of action by which privacy claims may be advanced at law. However, in these contexts as in others, consent is in law a narrow doctrine. It is to be distinguished from acquiescence,[3] and from other defences based on the attitude which the claimant has displayed towards the conduct complained of.[4] Consent is generally a difficult defence to maintain. In the absence of written evidence the issue will fall to be decided on the oral evidence of the parties, the burden usually being on the defendant.[5] Even if the defendant has written consent, difficulties can arise.[6]

---

[1] Consent is the term used here, but this justification has been variously labelled in differing contexts. The maxim *volenti non fit injuria* has been used in tort law to cover both cases of consent and voluntary assumption of risk, though it is more apt to cover the latter: see M A Jones et al (eds), *Clerk and Lindsell on Torts* (21st edn, Sweet & Maxwell 2014) para 3-91. 'Leave and licence' has been used in cases of trespass to land: *ibid*, para 19-45. Both terms have been used to characterize the consent defence to libel claims. 'Licence' is the term used in copyright. 'Authority' has been used in breach of confidence.

[2] Consent is generally considered a defence: *Clerk and Lindsell on Torts* (n 1) para 3-92, n 364. But in some contexts the claimant may be required to prove the absence of consent. That is so in infringement of copyright (see 9.26) and trespass to the person: *Freeman v Home Office (No 2)* [1984] QB 524, 539.

[3] See *Bell v Alfred Franks & Bartlett Co Ltd* [1980] 1 WLR 340, 347 (Shaw LJ) affirming, albeit in a particular statutory context, that consent as opposed to acquiescence requires some affirmative step indicating acceptance.

[4] Such as waiver, discussed at 11.20–11.23.

[5] See n 2.

[6] The claimant may say that the document was signed under duress, or that consent was given for a different purpose, or that the act complained of falls outside its scope.

**Issues in media cases**    In cases concerned with media use or disclosure of personal    **11.05**
information the difficulties are likely to prove all the greater. Media publication
will be to a wide audience and the defendant will have to show that the claimant
consented to the extent of the publication.[7] Media publications also change in the
course of production and it will be necessary to demonstrate consent to the particular publication which occurs.[8] The need to comply with media privacy codes
can present additional hurdles.[9] The provisions of s 12(4) of the Human Rights Act
1998 (HRA) mean that failure to comply may lend support to a legal claim against
the media.[10]

## (b) *The underlying legal principle and its application in privacy*

There is one basic principle which can be seen to underlie all the variously named    **11.06**
versions of the defence of consent: it is 'good sense and justice [that] one who
has assented to an act being done towards him cannot, when he suffers from it,
complain of it as a wrong'.[11] Thus, consent is a defence to a contractual claim for
breach of confidence;[12] unauthorized use of information is an essential ingredient
of breach of confidence in equity;[13] the consent of the data subject to the processing
in question should generally suffice to avoid a breach of the Data Protection Act
1998 (DPA);[14] it is a defence to a libel action that the claimant consented to the
publication complained of by participating in or authorizing it;[15] and no breach
of copyright is committed by a person who acts with the licence of the copyright
owner.[16] Similarly, the 'leave and licence' of the landowner is a defence to a claim
for trespass to land.[17]

## (c) *How consent may be given*

**Express or implied**    In principle, consent may be given expressly or impliedly, by    **11.07**
words, written or oral, or by conduct.[18] In most contexts consent given by any of

---

[7]  See 11.11.

[8]  See 11.10.

[9]  For discussion of the codes see 11.18–11.19 and, generally, ch 14.

[10]  *Douglas v Hello! Ltd* [2000] EWCA Civ 353, [2001] QB 967 [92]–[95] (Brooke LJ); *Douglas v Hello! Ltd* [2003] EWHC 786 (Ch), [2003] 3 All ER 996 [186(vi)–(viii)], [202]–[205] (Lindsay J).

[11]  *Smith v Baker* [1891] AC 325, 360 (Lord Herschell). The words omitted from the citation in the text referred to one who has 'invited' an act. Inviting an act is a distinct concept.

[12]  *Tournier v National Provincial and Union Bank of England* [1924] 1 KB 461, 473 (Bankes LJ). See also *Nam Tai Electronics Inc v Pricewaterhouse Coopers Hong Kong* [2008] HKCFA 9, [2008] 1 HKLRD 666 [37]–[41].

[13]  *Coco v A N Clark (Engineers) Ltd* [1969] RPC 41, 47 (Megarry V-C); *Seager v Copydex Ltd* [1967] 1 WLR 923, 931 (Lord Denning MR). See also *Moorgate Tobacco Co Ltd v Philip Morris Ltd* (1984) 156 CLR 414.

[14]  sch 2 DPA; 7.56–7.57.

[15]  Prof A Mullis and R Parkes QC (eds), *Gatley on Libel and Slander* (12th edn, Oxford University Press 2013) para 19.10.

[16]  See n 2.

[17]  *Clerk and Lindsell on Torts* (n 1) para 19-46.

[18]  *Bell* (n 3) 347 (Shaw LJ).

these means would suffice to defeat or negative a privacy claim. This is so in trespass to land,[19] breach of confidence,[20] copyright,[21] and libel.[22] The court is likely, however, to be cautious before finding implied consent.[23] Besides, for obvious practical and evidential reasons it is always desirable where possible to obtain a clear, express written consent,[24] and keep it safe.[25]

**11.08** The DPA appears to recognize implied consent as sufficient to legitimize an otherwise lawful disclosure,[26] but the Directive requires it to be specific and informed.[27] Moreover, many media privacy claims will relate to personal information which is wholly or partly 'sensitive personal data' as defined in the Act.[28] In such a case the only consent which will suffice to legitimize processing is 'explicit consent'.[29] This would seem to exclude implicit consent.[30] The Commissioner has expressed the view that this statutory wording requires consent that is 'absolutely clear'.[31] It seems unlikely that explicit consent to the use or disclosure of sensitive personal data will be established in a media case unless the data subject has provided the information to the media in order to publicize his or her private life.

*(d) By and to whom consent must be given*

**11.09** Consent can only be operative if given by the claimant, or someone else duly authorized on his or her behalf, with legal capacity to consent. The consent of an adult incapable of giving consent, or of a child who is not 'Gillick competent', will be no answer to a claim.[32] Where the privacy of several individuals is engaged by the act or threatened act in question the consent of one will be no answer to a claim by another,[33] unless given on the other's behalf, as might be the position in the case

---

[19]  *Clerk and Lindsell on Torts* (n 1) para 19-46.

[20]  *Tournier* (n 12) 473 (Bankes LJ).

[21]  N Caddick et al, *Copinger and Skone James on Copyright* (16th edn, Sweet & Maxwell 2012) para 5-199 and see the discussion of implied licences in *Copinger* at paras 5-217–5-224.

[22]  *Moore v News of the World Ltd* [1972] 1 QB 441, 448 (Lord Denning MR).

[23]  See *eg R v Dept of Health, ex p Source Informatics Ltd* [2001] QB 424, CA [51]; *Theakston v MGN Ltd* [2002] EWHC 137 (QB), [2002] EMLR 22 [75].

[24]  In the case of copyright licences, for example, problems as to the scope of a licence are liable to arise when it has to be inferred from words or conduct.

[25]  A striking example of the desirability of not only making but keeping written records is provided, in a different context, by *Springsteen v Masquerade Music Ltd* [2001] EMLR 654, CA where it took eleven days in court to prove that consent had been given in a lost document.

[26]  sch 2, para 1 DPA speaks of the 'consent' of the data subject without qualification; the word 'consent' is undefined.

[27]  See 7.56.

[28]  s 2 DPA. See 7.24.

[29]  sch 3, para 1 DPA.

[30]  See *Source Informatics* (n 23) [51].

[31]  *Data Protection Act 1998: Legal Guidance* para 3.1.5. Further information is available at <http://www.ico.gov.uk>.

[32]  'Gillick competent' is shorthand for a minor who has the equivalent of adult capacity. For discussion of capacity in relation to children see 13.12. For adults see 13.09.

[33]  cf *Evans v Amicus Healthcare Ltd* [2004] EWCA Civ 727, [2005] Fam 1, where it was held that the use and storage of fertilized embryos required the consent of both partners.

of a parent-and-child relationship. Consent may be effective even if not communicated to the defendant, it is suggested. The principle under discussion does not depend upon the defendant's knowledge of or reliance on the consent but on the claimant's having assented to the act.[34]

*(e) What amounts to consent*

**Consent to the particular disclosure or act**    The consent given must be shown    **11.10**
to extend to the particular act complained of. The doctrine of informed consent is well established in relation to the disclosure of patient information; sufficient information must be given to the patient as to the purpose and extent of the procedure to be undertaken.[35] The position is similar as regards disclosure of information in the media, as most clearly illustrated in cases from the law of libel. The general rule is that consent will only be established where the claimant agreed to the publication of substantially the same matter as was in fact published.[36] In *Theakston v MGN Ltd* Ouseley J regarded the claimant's consent to 'this kind of material' being published in the past as a factor militating against the grant of an injunction.[37] This approach appears to be in line with that of the Court of Appeal in *A v B plc*.[38] However, it is unorthodox to regard it as an application of the doctrine of consent. Subsequent authority suggests that conduct of the kind discussed in *Theakston* should be taken into account when considering the extent and weight of an individual's reasonable expectation of privacy.[39]

**Consent to the extent of publication**    In a publication case, there must be con-    **11.11**
sent to the extent of publication that occurs. In *Cook v Ward* the plaintiff complained of a newspaper article telling a story which made him look ludicrous. The defendant's submission that there could be a claim in libel because he had told the story of himself was rejected, Tindal CJ remarking that 'there is a great difference between a man's telling a ludicrous story of himself to a circle of his own acquaintance, and a publication of it to all the world through the medium of a newspaper'.[40]

---

[34]  See text to n 11. The proposition in this sentence was accepted in the libel case of *Warren v Marsh* (QBD, 30 October 1992, Drake J) where, without D's knowledge, C had consented to the broadcast by L of defamatory statements which D had made about C in an interview.

[35]  See *eg Sidaway v Board of Governors of the Bethlem Royal Hospital and the Maudsley Hospital* [1985] AC 871.

[36]  *Moore* (n 22); *Mihaka v Wellington Publishing* [1975] NZLR 10; *Cornelius v de Taranto* [2001] EWCA Civ 1511, [2002] EMLR 112 [27]. In some circumstances however a person may contract in advance that another may publish the other's views about his conduct, whatever these may prove to be: *Cookson v Harewood* [1932] 2 KB 478; *Friend v Civil Aviation Authority* [1998] IRLR 253; and *Crossland v Wilkinson Hardware Stores Ltd* [2005] EWHC 481 (QB) [67]–[71], all concerned with written disciplinary codes.

[37]  *Theakston* (n 23) [66], [68]. The case concerned the claimant's visit to a brothel.

[38]  [2002] EWCA Civ 337, [2003] QB 195.

[39]  See 11.21–11.22.

[40]  *Cook v Ward* (1830) 6 Bing 409, 415; 130 ER 1338, 1341.

**11.12**  The same distinction was drawn at first instance in *A v B plc*, where the Court granted an injunction to prevent publication of details of a footballer's extramarital affairs. Accepting that the relationship had been conducted openly in public or semi-public places, the judge held that it had received no wider publicity than that and that there was a 'world of difference' between this and disclosure of details in a newspaper.[41] This distinction was also remarked upon by Sir Anthony Clarke MR in *Lord Browne v Associated Newspapers Ltd*.[42] It was decisive of an injunction application in another 2001 decision.[43] Lord Hoffmann also drew attention to it in *Campbell v MGN Ltd*.[44] Similarly, where a convicted murderer consented to disclosure of his medical records to an inquiry team, that consent did not justify disclosure of the same information to the public when it was later decided to publish the team's report.[45]

**11.13**  **Consent in data protection law**  Generally, consent will legitimize disclosure for data protection purposes only if it is 'freely given, specific and informed'.[46] The Commissioner has expressed the view that the 'explicit consent' required for the processing of sensitive personal data[47] should cover 'in appropriate cases...the specific detail of the processing...the purposes of the processing and any special aspects of the processing which may affect the individual, for example disclosures which may be made of the data'.[48] These views are not a source of law, but if correct they would suggest that the DPA imposes the strictest consent requirements of all in cases concerning personal information which is sensitive personal data. If that is so then defendants might find it difficult to escape a claim for compensation under the DPA, even if the evidence would sustain a consent defence to some other civil claim.[49] An alternative, and perhaps more likely, approach would be for the court

---

[41] (QBD, 30 April 2001) [12] (Jack J). The defendant said the number of people who knew was up to twenty-five. Jack J's later judgment in the same case is reported as *A v B plc* [2001] 1 WLR 2341. Both decisions were reversed by the Court of Appeal (n 38), without comment on this particular point.

[42] '... there is potentially an important distinction between information which is made available to a person's circle of friends or work colleagues and information which is widely published in a newspaper': [2007] EWCA Civ 295, [2008] QB 103 [61]. See also *R v Broadcasting Standards Commission, ex p BBC* [2001] QB 885 [44] (Hale LJ).

[43] *A v B and C* (QBD, 2 March 2001, Mackay J). The consent given by the claimant was held to be limited to photography for promotional purposes and subject to the grant of permission after seeing the pictures.

[44] [2004] UKHL 22, [2004] 2 AC 457 [73]–[75], referring to *Peck v UK* (2003) 36 EHRR 41.

[45] *Stone v South East Coast Strategic Health Authority* [2006] EWHC 1668 (Admin), [2007] UKHRR 137 [25].

[46] Art 2(h) of Council Directive 95/46/EC on the protection of individuals with regard to the processing of personal data and on the free movement of such data [1995] OJ L281/31 so defines 'consent' for the purposes of the Directive. This definition is not repeated in the DPA 1998, but it is suggested that the Act must be interpreted consistently with the Directive in this as in other respects.

[47] See 7.24, 7.56.

[48] *Data Protection Act 1998: Legal Guidance*, para 3.1.5.

[49] The impact would not, however, be the same as regards an injunction, as it is impossible to obtain an injunction to restrain a breach of the DPA if the subject material has not been published by the data controller: see 7.116.

to have regard to the DPA requirements when other causes of action are pursued and to tighten the relevant common law requirements, if necessary, to bring them into line.[50] The Court of Appeal has indicated that it will have regard to data protection law in considering issues of consent in the law of confidence.[51]

### (f) Validity of consent; vitiating factors

An adult will be presumed capable of consent unless it is proved otherwise,[52] but **11.14** it follows from general principles that even where actual consent is established, that consent may be vitiated by misrepresentation, mistake, undue influence, or other factors which would defeat a contractual or other consensual arrangement. Consent induced by fraud, where the misapprehension of the consenting party goes to the root of the whole transaction, will be vitiated[53] and consent will not afford a defence if the will of the consenting party was overcome by force or the fear of violence.[54]

### (g) Revocation of consent

**Principles**   There is no authority on the circumstances in which consent to media **11.15** use of personal information, once given, may effectively be revoked. However, there are some clear general principles established by authorities in other fields of law. In land law a gratuitous licence can be revoked by notice at any time, but a licence granted for consideration will be contractually binding, and can only be revoked in accordance with the terms of the contract.[55] The position in relation to copyright licences is similar.[56] Thus, in the case of materials voluntarily sent for publication there is an implied licence to publish such documents; the author is making an open offer to the publisher. Yet this can be revoked by notice, after which the publisher would have no right to publish the document.[57]

**Gratuitous consent**   Applying these principles to media privacy cases the start- **11.16** ing point would seem to be that consent given gratuitously can be revoked. If an individual who writes a letter to a newspaper containing details of her private life is able to withdraw her implied consent to publication, why should one who reveals similar information in an interview not revoke consent and sue, if necessary, to

---

[50] If *eg* an article relates to an individual's political opinion or religious beliefs, which are sensitive personal data under s 2 DPA, it could be argued by analogy with the Act that mere consent should not suffice and that any consent needs to be 'explicit'.

[51] *Source Informatics* (n 23) [51] citing para 8.2(a) of the Directive (n 46).

[52] Mental Capacity Act 2005; *E v Channel Four* [2005] EWHC 1144 (Fam), [2005] EMLR 30 [61].

[53] *Clerk and Lindsell on Torts* (n 1) para 15-96.

[54] *Clerk and Lindsell on Torts* (n 1) para 15-98.

[55] *Winter Garden Theatre (London) Ltd v Millennium Productions Ltd* [1948] AC 173; *Verrall v Great Yarmouth Borough Council* [1980] 1 All ER 839; *Clerk and Lindsell on Torts* (n 1) para 19-48.

[56] See *Copinger and Skone James* (n 21) para 5-231.

[57] *Bowden Brothers v Amalgamated Pictorial Ltd* [1911] 1 Ch 386 (supply of photographs); *Copinger and Skone James* (n 21) para 5-224.

prevent publication? The only answer would appear to be a defence of estoppel or change of position.[58]

**11.17** **Contract** If such an interview was given for consideration, consent to publication of the private matters could not be revoked unless there was provision for such revocation in the parties' agreement. A case could arise in which, due to a change of circumstances or change of mind, a person wished to revoke a contractual consent and prevent publication. The implication of a term or even the doctrine of frustration might come to the aid of such a claimant, but it is easy to envisage circumstances in which neither would avail—for instance, where unqualified contractual consent was followed by a belated appreciation that disclosure would expose the claimant to severe physical risk.[59] In such a case the court might decline to prohibit publication, leaving the media defendant to its remedy in damages.

*(h) Consent in the media privacy codes*

**11.18** Provisions in the media codes identify whose consent should be obtained, and how, if consent is to justify publication of particular material. The Ofcom Broadcasting Code on privacy expressly provides that consent means informed consent,[60] and lists six practices to be followed to ensure that informed consent is obtained.[61] Former broadcasting codes required that individual written consents should be sought in certain circumstances,[62] but this requirement does not appear in the Ofcom Code. The Independent Press Standards Organisation (IPSO) Code requires newspapers and magazines to ensure that they get full and proper consent when dealing with issues connected to the welfare of children,[63] and from the appropriate authorities when dealing with patients.[64] The Press Complaints Commission (PCC) Editors' Codebook recognized that consent could be given 'formally or by implication'.

**11.19** The codes recognize that consent given for one purpose is not valid if used for another purpose. Contributors should be made aware of 'any significant changes to the programme as it develops which might reasonably affect their original consent to participate, and cause material unfairness'.[65] The same issue arises in relation to 'set-up situations', where an individual consents to being recorded for a purpose different from that covertly intended by the programme makers. A court deciding whether to grant relief against the media is required to have regard to any

---

[58] See 11.24–11.30.

[59] This example is not far from the facts of *Nicholls v BBC* [1999] EMLR 791, CA. See 9.30 for the position in copyright law.

[60] Ofcom Broadcasting Code 2013, s 8.

[61] Ofcom Broadcasting Code 2013, cl 7.3 (fairness).

[62] ITC Code, cl 2.2(ii) required this, for filming in certain sensitive situations.

[63] IPSO Editors' Code, cl 6(iii) requires consent of 'a custodial parent or similarly responsible adult'. See also cl 6(ii) and 14.143.

[64] *Iain Hutchison and The News of the World*, 11 February 1996 (Report 37); *Mrs Rutherford and The Express on Sunday*, 10 June 1996 (Report 37).

[65] Ofcom Broadcasting Code 2013, cl 7.3.

relevant privacy code,[66] and a failure to comply is liable to weigh heavily against the media.[67]

### (2) Waiver of Rights

#### (a) Courting publicity not waiver

The laws of privacy in some other jurisdictions are to the effect that if individuals **11.20** choose to become public figures that may lead them to forfeit a measure of personal privacy, and limit their rights to pick and choose what items of information may be made public.[68] This is the position under US law, and the doctrinal bases for the principle include that of waiver:

> A person may waive or lose the right to privacy, in part at least, by becoming a public figure or personage, as, for example, by entering into a business or calling which gives the public a legitimate interest in his character, activities or affairs, or by reason of his accomplishments, fame or mode of life, or where likenesses, names and images are already in the public domain.[69]

A series of English Court of Appeal decisions from the 1970s and 1980s involving **11.21** interim injunctions can be analysed as treating the courting of publicity by the claimant as involving a waiver of confidentiality rights, even though earlier disclosures were of a different kind to that which it was sought to restrain.[70] But this approach has been the subject of academic criticism[71] and judicial reservations[72] and, while a similar approach can be detected in some of the early twenty-first century English jurisprudence,[73] it has since fallen out of favour. Instead, a claimant's previous disclosures are taken into account as an element in the assessment of whether there is a public interest defence,[74] or whether the claimant enjoys a reasonable expectation of confidentiality or privacy in respect of the particular

---

[66] s 12(4)(b) HRA.

[67] For a case where the consent provisions of the BBC's Producers' Guidelines were considered by the court, see *T (by her litigation friend the Official Solicitor) v BBC* [2007] EWHC 1683 (QB), [2008] 1 FLR 281.

[68] See eg 3.60 for the US approach.

[69] Corpus Juris Secundum, vol 77, 527 [30]. See also *Nam Tai* (n 12) analysing some consent cases as cases of waiver

[70] *Woodward v Hutchins* [1977] 1 WLR 760, 763–4 (Lord Denning MR), 765 (Bridge LJ); *Lennon v News Group Newspapers Ltd* [1978] FSR 573; *Khashoggi v Smith* (1980) 124 SJ 149. The cases are discussed in detail in earlier editions of this book.

[71] F Gurry, *Breach of Confidence* (Oxford University Press 1984) criticized *Woodward* and *Lennon* for applying too broad a brush; G Phillipson and H Fenwick, 'Breach of confidence as a privacy remedy in the human rights era' (2000) 63 MLR 660, 680 and *Media Freedom under the Human Rights Act* (Oxford University Press 2006) 777–8; R Toulson and C Phipps, *Confidentiality* (2nd edn, Sweet & Maxwell 2006) para 3-121.

[72] *Douglas*, CA (n 10) [96] (Brooke LJ); *Campbell v Frisbee* [2002] EMLR 656 [35] (Lightman J).

[73] *Theakston* (n 23) [68]; *Ashworth Hospital Authority v MGN Ltd* [2001] 1 WLR 515, CA [50] (Lord Phillips MR); [2002] 1 WLR 2033 [32] (Lord Woolf); *Campbell v Frisbee* [2003] EMLR 76 [34] (Lord Phillips MR);

[74] *A v B plc* (n 38) [11(xii)]; *Douglas* (n 10) [225] (Lindsay J); *Lady Archer v Williams* [2003] EWHC 1670 (QB), [2003] EMLR 38 [64]–[66] (Jackson J); *Campbell* (n 44) [57] (Lord Hoffmann).

information at issue,[75] or how the balancing test should be applied if there is such an expectation.[76]

**11.22** This approach appears to accord with principle. Waiver is a narrow doctrine; and while some Convention rights can be waived this will only be held to have occurred if it is done without undue compulsion, is established in an unequivocal manner, is attended by minimum safeguards commensurate with the importance of the right in question, and does not run counter to any important public interest.[77]

*(b) The reasonable expectations of self-publicists*

**11.23** The claimant's position, and his or her conduct, are clearly relevant circumstances when assessing whether any expectation of privacy he or she claims is a reasonable one and, or whether that expectation should be overridden by some other right or interest.[78] In *Axel Springer AG v Germany* the European Court of Human Rights analysed the impact of the applicant's prior conduct in revealing details about his private life via interviews and concluded that he had 'actively sought the limelight' and his 'legitimate expectation' that his private life would be effectively protected was reduced.[79] In *Trimingham v Associated Newspapers Ltd*[80] the claimant, a seasoned journalist and communications officer, was held to have no reasonable expectation of privacy in respect of certain information about, among other things, her sexuality and relationship history, as she was not a purely private person but the press agent and mistress of a cabinet minister who had campaigned on family values, had made her sexuality public, and had herself seen nothing wrong in disclosing similar information about others.

### (3) Estoppel

**11.24** There appears to be no reported English case in which a defence of estoppel has been raised in answer to a privacy complaint against the media. In principle, however, there seems to be no reason why defences of estoppel by representation, or by convention, or promissory estoppel, could not be raised in answer to such a complaint.[81] There would need to have been some form of communication between the

---

[75] *Jockey Club v Buffham* [2002] EWHC 1866 (QB), [2003] QB 462 [57(v)] (Gray J); *A v B* [2005] EWHC 1651 (QB), [2005] EMLR 851 [22]–[23] (Eady J) (referring to the discussion in 9.29–9.37 of the first edition of this book); *Douglas* (n 10) [210] (Lindsay J); *Douglas v Hello! Ltd* [2005] EWCA Civ 595, [2006] QB 125 [140]; *Ferdinand v MGN Ltd* [2011] EWHC 2454 (QB) [59] (Nicol J); *RocknRoll v News Group Newspapers Ltd* [2013] EWHC 24 (Ch) [19] (Briggs J).

[76] See *eg Campbell* (n 44) [66] (Lord Hoffmann).

[77] See *Pfeifer and Plankl v Austria* (1992) 14 EHRR 692, para 37; *Millar v Dickson* [2001] UKPC D4, [2002] 1 WLR 1615 [31] (Lord Bingham); R Clayton QC and H Tomlinson QC, *The Law of Human Rights* (2nd edn, Oxford University Press 2009) paras 6.266–6.280.

[78] See nn 74–76 and text thereto.

[79] (2012) 55 EHRR 6, para 101.

[80] [2012] EWHC 1296 (QB), [2012] 4 All ER 717.

[81] In US law the right to privacy 'may be lost by a course of conduct which estops the assertion': 'Right of privacy and publicity', Corpus Juris Secundum (n 69) vol 77, 527 [30], citing

claimant and media defendant prior to the publication or other act complained of. If the media defendant had relied to its detriment on such communication so as to make it inequitable for the claimant to complain, then a defence of estoppel could arise. In this way a media defendant might perhaps be able to hold an interviewee to a gratuitous agreement authorizing publication of personal information, despite the interviewee's second thoughts.[82]

Whether estoppel would run as a defence would of course depend on the particular **11.25** facts, including the degree to which the claimant had full information about the intended publication at the outset, the nature and gravity of the harm which publication had caused or might cause, the extent of the damage the defendant might suffer if prevented from publishing, and the means of the claimant. It is possible to imagine an estoppel defence succeeding if substantial sums had been irrecoverably spent before the claimant's change of mind, and the risk of damage to the claimant was not serious.

### (4) Change of Position

A third party who has received information disclosed by another in breach of confi- **11.26** dence may defeat a claim for breach of confidence if he or she has changed his or her position on or after receipt of the confidential information. The precise juridical basis of the defence is not settled. The defence will usually apply where the third party acquired the information innocently, and changed position in a material way before receiving notice of the confidentiality of the information, in the mistaken belief that he or she was free to use the information.

There are several judicial statements supporting the proposition that the equitable **11.27** doctrine of the purchaser for value without notice affords a complete defence to a claim for breach of confidence.[83] The application of that principle would create a defence if it is shown that the information has been bought for value without notice of its confidentiality. However, this defence runs into the conceptual difficulty of whether or not information should be treated as property for present purposes.[84] It is also capable of producing unjust results.[85]

Broader approaches to the problem have been suggested. Each solution takes into **11.28** account all the circumstances of the case in order to ascertain whether it would be just to allow the party to whom the duty of confidence is owed to enforce his or her rights. One analysis is to apply the defence of bona fide change of position

---

*Continental Optical Co v Reed* 86 NE 2d 306, 119 Ind App 643, rehearing denied 88 NE 2d 55, 119 Ind App 643.

[82]  See the example at 11.16.

[83]  *eg Morison v Moat* (1851) 9 Hare 241, 263–4.

[84]  C Mitchell et al, *Goff and Jones: The Law of Unjust Enrichment* (8th edn, Sweet & Maxwell 2011) paras 34-024 and 34-027.

[85]  G Jones, 'Restitution of benefits obtained in breach of another's confidence' (1970) 86 LQR 463, 478–83.

established in *Lipkin Gorman v Karpnale Ltd* [86] in the context of restitutionary claims.[87] In that case Lord Goff stated the principle broadly, saying that 'the defence is available to a person whose position has so changed that it would be inequitable in all the circumstances to require him to make restitution, or alternatively to make restitution in full'. [88] This defence is maintainable only if the defendant has acted in good faith.[89]

**11.29** Another approach is to treat the question as one essentially going to remedies. The authors of *Gurry on Breach of Confidence* have suggested that it is a question not of absolute defences such as bona fide purchaser or otherwise, but of factors which the court will take into account in determining what, if any, discretionary equitable remedies the court will grant.[90] The factors relevant on this discretionary analysis will often be the same as those relevant to a defence of bona fide change of position. One of these factors is expenditure before notice is received by the third party.[91] The fact that the third party has paid money for the information is not likely to be a matter of great weight as an answer to a damages claim, certainly where the third party has a claim against the confidant for damages.

**11.30** However, in the media field the real question at issue is likely to be whether or not the media organization is at liberty to publish. If the information is personal and was obtained without the claimant's consent then it will be difficult for the media to advance a case of innocent receipt and change of position. In the absence of other factors, once the media organization is put on notice of the claim[92] the claimant will be in a strong position to restrain publication, however much the media organization has spent beforehand.[93]

## C. Defences to Claims for Disclosure of Private Facts

**11.31** The principal causes of action of relevance where the complaint concerns the disclosure of private facts are misuse of private information and breach of confidence. Other causes of action which may be relied upon are breach of statutory duty under the DPA and copyright infringement. In all cases, the first question which may

---

[86] [1991] 2 AC 548, 577–81.

[87] See *Goff and Jones* (n 84) para 27.01.

[88] *Lipkin Gorman* (n 86) 580.

[89] To defeat the defence it is not necessary to prove dishonesty, merely that the defendant has not acted in good faith: *Niru Battery Manufacturing Co v Milestone Trading Ltd* [2003] EWCA Civ 1446, [2004] QB 985.

[90] T Aplin et al (eds), *Gurry on Breach of Confidence* (2nd edn, Oxford University Press 2012) paras 7-134–7-136.

[91] See *eg Jordan & Harrison Ltd v MacDonald and Evans* (1952) 69 RPC 10.

[92] Notice of an application for an interim injunction is generally necessary in any event: see 13.135–13.142.

[93] See *Prince Albert v Strange* (1849) 1 Mac & G 25, 41 ER 1171, CA; *Malone v Commissioner of Police for the Metropolis* [1979] Ch 344, 361; *Fraser v Evans* [1969] 1 QB 349, 361.

arise is whether ignorance or an innocent state of mind may be relied on to exclude liability. Otherwise, the main defences available may be viewed as based on the public interest in disclosure and/or the rights (and in particular the Convention rights) of others. Defamation does not provide a remedy for the disclosure of true but embarrassing private facts because its defences are based on the overriding public interest in the truth being made known.[94]

## (1) Innocent Publication

### (a) Common law

As noted in Chapter 4,[95] the limited authority to date suggests that the courts, in **11.32** applying the laws of breach of confidence and misuse of private information, will adopt the approach of the common law of defamation in attributing responsibility for publication to those who participate in, procure, or authorize it. At common law not only publishers, broadcasters, authors, and editors but also printers, news vendors, booksellers, and many other classes of person involved in the dissemination of published matter are held responsible for any libel it contains.[96] The common law of defamation mitigates the rigour of this approach by affording a defence of innocent dissemination to minor players, but this is of limited scope. Only those who perform a purely passive instrumental role in distributing defamatory matter are able to take advantage.[97]

### (b) Equity

The law of traditional breach of confidence is more generous to the ignorant than **11.33** the common law of defamation. The position of a third party that acquires and uses confidential information provided by another depends on his or her state of knowledge. An 'innocent' party, who uses information in ignorance of the fact that it is another's confidential information, may not be liable to pay damages,[98] although he or she may be liable to an injunction once on notice, subject to defences of bona fide purchase or change of position.[99] From an early stage in the development of the law of breach of confidence relating to private information, the imposition of a duty of confidence was held to depend on what the defendant knew or should have known about the claimant's reasonable expectations of confidentiality.[100] The law of misuse

---

[94] See further ch 8.

[95] See 4.157.

[96] See generally *Gatley on Libel and Slander* (n 15) para 6.23. But note the statutory defence referred to in 11.38.

[97] *Bunt v Tilley* [2006] EWHC 407 (QB), [2007] 1 WLR 1243 [23]. Even the passive participant may be liable if it continues to facilitate publication after notice that this is alleged to be unlawful: *Tamiz v Google Inc* [2013] EWCA Civ 68, [2013] 1 WLR 2151 [34].

[98] *Valeo Vision SA v Flexible Lamps Ltd* [1995] RPC 205.

[99] See the discussion in Toulson and Phipps (n 71) paras 3-056–3-064.

[100] See *A v B plc* (n 38); *Campbell* (n 44) [19]–[20] (Lord Nicholls), [92] (Lord Hope), [134], [137], [140] (Baroness Hale), [166]–[167] (Lord Carswell). The cases are considered in *Weller v Associated Newspapers Ltd* [2014] EWHC 1163 (QB), [2014] EMLR 24 [26]–[38].

of private information appears to be embracing the question of what is or should be known as an element of the circumstantial test.[101]

### (c) Misuse of private information and Convention jurisprudence

**11.34** In *Wainwright v Home Office* Lord Hoffmann suggested, obiter, that merely careless acts may not amount to actionable intrusions, or at least not give rise to a right to any monetary remedy.[102] However, the Strasbourg jurisprudence does not lay down lines as clear as these. It is generally unnecessary to establish any particular state of mind in respect of a breach of the Convention; the conduct of the parties as a whole, including whether the acts which are alleged to give rise to the violation were deliberate or accidental, may be taken into account in determining the gravity of the interference.[103] The current approach of English law is that what the publisher knew or should have known is one of the circumstances to be considered when determining whether the claimant enjoyed a reasonable expectation of privacy; but matters the publisher did not and could not have known may also be taken into account as negativing a reasonable expectation.[104]

### (d) Statute

**11.35** **Statutory defences for service providers**  The E-Commerce Directive of 2000[105] as transposed into English law[106] protects certain 'information society service providers' from liability for damages or other pecuniary remedy or any criminal sanction, although not against injunctive relief, in respect of the dissemination of information in respect of which they have neither knowledge nor control. The levels of protection vary according to whether the service provided is that of a mere conduit for transient messages (such as an email service) or a caching or a hosting service, each of which will involve some storing of information for the purposes of public access.

**11.36** A mere conduit will generally be unconditionally exempt from the forms of liability mentioned above even if put on notice of a claim,[107] and the defamation precedent suggests that injunctive relief is unlikely to be granted.[108] Exemption for those caching information depends on proof of an innocent, subsidiary role in its dissemination and expeditious action to remove or prevent access if notified that the source information has been removed or access to it disabled, or that a court or administrative authority has ordered this to be done.[109] The conditions for the hosting exemptions are

---

[101] See 11.34, n 104.
[102] *Wainwright v Home Office* [2003] UKHL 53, [2004] 2 AC 406 [51].
[103] For the overall approach to assessing whether conduct involves a breach of Art 8, see 3.18–3.21.
[104] *Weller* (n 100) [37]. See further 5.146–5.147.
[105] Council Directive 2000/31/EC on certain legal aspects of information society services, in particular electronic commerce, in the Internal Market [2000] OJ L178/1.
[106] Electronic Commerce (EC Directive) Regulations 2002, SI 2002/2013.
[107] SI 2002/2013 (n 106) reg 17; see 15.62.
[108] See *Bunt v Tilley* (n 97), where an injunction requiring an internet service provider to prevent its client from posting defamatory messages was refused.
[109] SI 2002/2013 (n 106) reg 18; see 15.63 *et seq.*

more demanding. Proof is required that the internet service provider did not know of unlawfulness or of facts or circumstances from which that would have been apparent, and expeditious taking down is required as soon as such knowledge is gained.[110]

**Statutory defences in defamation**   The legislature has stepped in to mitigate **11.37** the rigour of the common law of responsibility for publication by affording three separate statutory defences for those who are not directly responsible for a publication. These defences are specific to defamation, however, and will not avail in respect of other causes of action such as breach of confidence or misuse of private information.[111]

*Defendant not author, editor or commercial publisher*   Section 10 of the Defamation **11.38** Act 2013 provides that: 'A court does not have jurisdiction to hear and determine an action for defamation against a person who was not the author, editor or publisher of the statement complained of unless the court is satisfied that it is not reasonably practicable for an action to be brought against the author, editor or publisher.' These last words have the same meaning as in s 1 of the Defamation Act 1996, by which a publisher means a commercial publisher.

*Innocent publication*   Under s 1 of the Defamation Act 1996 a person is not respon- **11.39** sible for publication if he was not the author, editor, or publisher of an offending statement, and proves that, having taken reasonable care, he did not know and had no reason to believe that his acts involved or contributed to the publication of a statement defamatory of the claimant. This defence will be relevant to claims which the court has jurisdiction to hear despite s 10 of the 2013 Act.[112]

*Website operators*   Section 5 of the Defamation Act 2013 provides that a 'website **11.40** operator' has a defence to a defamation action brought in respect of a statement on a website if it shows that it was not the operator that posted the statement. Provision is made for the defence to be defeated by proof that the claimant cannot identify any other person responsible for the statement,[113] or that the website operator acted with malice in relation to the posting.[114] For those who fall within the undefined expression 'website operator' this special defence is likely to sit alongside the provisions of the E-Commerce Directive.

**Other statutes**   The statutory duty imposed on data controllers by s 4 DPA is a **11.41** duty to comply with the data protection principles, and no state of mind needs

---

[110] SI 2002/2013 (n 106) reg 19; see 15.66 *et seq.*
[111] Proposals in the late 1980s to enact an innocent publication defence for privacy claims came to nothing: see the Calcutt Report, *Report of the Committee on Privacy and Related Matters* (Cm 1102, 1990) App J cl 3(a) and App K cl 3(a).
[112] See 11.38.
[113] This is a summary of the broad effect of the complex provisions of Defamation Act 2013, s 5(3)–(8) and the Regulations made thereunder. See further J Price QC and F McMahon (eds), *Blackstone's Guide to the Defamation Act 2013* (Oxford University Press 2013) ch 6.
[114] Defamation Act 2013, s 5(11).

to be proved; but there is a public interest exemption which depends on state of mind,[115] and liability for compensation is qualified by a general defence of reasonable diligence.[116] Liability for secondary infringement of copyright is dependent on state of mind, but liability for primary infringement is strict.[117]

*(e) Summary*

11.42　The law is patchy. Those who participate in the dissemination of private information will have a defence to a damages claim for breach of confidence or misuse of private information if they (i) act in ignorance of the fact that they are causing or contributing to a wrongful disclosure of private facts; (ii) play a secondary and purely instrumental role in the disclosure; and (iii) are either information-society service providers within the scope of the E-Commerce Directive, or fall within the limited class of passive participants protected by the common law of innocent dissemination. It remains arguable that to escape monetary liability it would be enough, in a confidence case, to meet the first of these three conditions. Whether ignorance or innocence will afford any defence to a claim for misuse in cases where the other two conditions listed above are not satisfied remains to be decided. The same publisher would however have additional defences or answers to a claim brought in defamation even if, as might be, the claim arose from the self-same words. The law is plainly in need of harmonization.

## (2) Facts in the Public Domain

*(a) Introduction*

11.43　**Information in the public domain is not confidential**　It is a well-established principle of the law of confidence that there can be no claim to confidentiality in facts that are in the public domain. Inaccessibility has been described as a basic attribute of confidentiality,[118] and was the first limiting principle identified by Lord Goff in *Spycatcher*.[119] In this book, however, public domain is dealt with as a justification or defence.[120] It functions in that way in the tort of misuse of private information, and in confidentiality the burden of proof is likely in practice to fall on the defendant.

11.44　**Publicly known information can remain private**　The application of the public domain doctrine to misuse of private information differs from the position in confidence. The interests protected are different and hence, as explained by Lord Nicholls in *Douglas v Hello! Ltd*: 'In some instances... information may be in the

---

[115]　See 7.113–7.115.
[116]　See 7.92.
[117]　See 9.26.
[118]　*Attorney General v Observer Ltd* [1990] 1 AC 109, 214 (Bingham LJ).
[119]　*Attorney General v Observer Ltd* (n 118) 282 (Lord Goff).
[120]　See 4.65 (breach of confidence), 5.101 (misuse of private information).

public domain, and not qualify for protection as confidential, and yet qualify for protection on the grounds of privacy.'[121]

The focus in this section will be on breach of confidence and misuse of private **11.45** information, though some attention will be paid to data protection law. There is no public domain exception or defence which will avail as an answer to other causes of action which can be used to complain about disclosure of private facts, such as libel or copyright.

### (b) The public domain in the law of confidence

**A question of degree**   In *Spycatcher* Lord Goff said that the public domain doc-   **11.46** trine means 'no more than that the information is so generally accessible that, in all the circumstances, it cannot be regarded as confidential'.[122] As Cross J had pointed out, 'clearly a claim that disclosure of some information would be a breach of confidence is not defeated simply by proving that there are other people in the world who know the information'.[123] So the question whether particular information is not confidential because it is in the public domain is always a question of degree.[124] For media cases this principle is reflected in the requirements of s 12(4)(a)(i) HRA, that in considering whether to grant relief the court should have particular regard to the *extent* to which the material at issue has become available to the public.[125]

**A right to disclose is not enough**   It might be argued that information enters the   **11.47** public domain, and ceases to be confidential in nature, if it becomes known to a significant number of people under circumstances which impose on them no duty of confidence, leaving them free to disclose the information generally as they choose. This approach was taken by Lord Denning MR in *Woodward v Hutchins*,[126] but is heterodox[127] and has not received support from commentators[128] or been followed in subsequent authorities. In *Stephens v Avery*, Sir Nicholas Browne-Wilkinson V-C regarded as 'wholly misconceived' an argument that information about a sexual relationship was not confidential because one or other party *might*, in the sense of being entitled to, disclose details.[129] Subsequent authorities have consistently

---

[121]   *Douglas v Hello! Ltd* [2007] UKHL 21, [2008] AC 1 [255].
[122]   *Attorney General v Observer Ltd* (n 118) 282 (Lord Goff).
[123]   *Franchi v Franchi* [1967] RPC 149 (Ch).
[124]   *Franchi* (n 123) 152–3 (Cross J); *Attorney General v Observer Ltd* (n 118) 177 (Sir John Donaldson MR) and 259 (Lord Keith). Attempts to define further what degree of publication amounts to putting a matter into the public domain were abandoned in *Attorney General v Times Newspapers Ltd* [2001] EWCA Civ 97, [2001]1 WLR 885: see [18]–[23].
[125]   s 12(4)(a)(i) also requires the court to have particular regard to the extent to which the material 'is about to become available to the public'. For imminent disclosure see 11.50–11.52.
[126]   *Woodward* (n 70) 765.
[127]   cf Cross J's approach in *Franchi* (n 123).
[128]   See Toulson and Phipps (n 71) paras 3-118–3-124; *Campbell v Frisbee* (n 72) [35].
[129]   [1988] 1 Ch 449, 454–5. Also *CC v AB* [2006] EWHC 3083 (QB), [2007] EMLR 312 [49] (Eady J); *HRH Prince of Wales v Associated Newspapers Ltd* [2006] EWCA Civ 1776, [2008] Ch 57 (limited circulation of journal).

taken the view that limited disclosure, even in public places, is consistent with the continuation of confidentiality.[130]

**11.48** **Mere accessibility is not enough**   It seems, moreover, that it would be wrong to treat the word 'available',[131] or Lord Goff's reference to 'accessible',[132] too literally; material is only in the public domain if it is not only accessible but actually known,[133] so that library materials or information on a website may well not be in the public domain.[134]

**11.49** **All the facts must be public**   It is also a requirement, if the public domain doctrine is to defeat a claim to confidentiality, that all the facts in respect of which confidentiality is asserted are public property. This is firmly established in the context of commercial information.[135] It is also clear that 'within the law of confidence in its normal reach' the public domain doctrine is 'specific to the material in question'.[136] In *Lennon v News Group Newspapers Ltd*, where personal information was at issue, Lord Denning MR took a less discriminating, broader approach, asserting that because the parties to the marriage had engaged in 'making money by publishing the most intimate details about one another' the relationship between them has 'ceased to be their own private affair... It is all in the public domain.'[137] This approach was not favoured by academic writers[138] or by most other courts, which have generally sought to discriminate between particular items of information in assessing whether they are in the public domain.[139] As already noted, however,[140] subsequent authorities have taken a different approach, treating prior publicity about similar information as a factor going to the reasonableness of the claimant's expectations of privacy, or to the balancing of rights in the 'parallel analysis'.

**11.50** **Where general disclosure is imminent**   It would seem to follow from *Stephens v Avery*[141] that information will not cease to be confidential merely because it is about to be made public. It seems obvious that information which is about to be made public may, prior to its disclosure, be of the very highest degree of confidentiality.

---

[130]  See 11.54–11.55.

[131]  In s 12(4)(a)(i) HRA.

[132]  See 11.46.

[133]  *Stephens* (n 129) 454–5. The few cases where accessibility has been held to be sufficient to defeat confidentiality concern information disclosed in open court and are discussed at 11.71.

[134]  *Attorney General v Greater Manchester Newspapers* Ltd [2001] EWHC 451 (QB), [2001] TLR 668 [33]–[34]. Also *H (A Healthcare Worker) v Associated Newspapers Ltd, H v N (A Hospital Authority)* (QBD, 3 December 2001, Gross J) [33]; *CC v AB* (n 129) [49].

[135]  See *O Mustad and Son v Dosen (Note)* [1964] 1 WLR 109, 111; *Castrol Australia Pty Ltd v Emtech Associates Pty Ltd* (1980) 33 ALR 31.

[136]  *Theakston* (n 23) [66].

[137]  *Lennon* (n 70) 574–5; *Theakston* (n 23) [68].

[138]  *Gurry on Breach of Confidence* (n 90) paras 6.59–6.60.

[139]  *Barrymore v News Group Newspapers Ltd* [1997] FSR 600, 603 (Jacob J); *A v B plc* (n 41) [63] (Jack J).

[140]  See 11.21–11.23.

[141]  *Stephens* (n 129).

An example, given by Bingham LJ in *Spycatcher*, is the D-Day landing plans.[142] Another would be unpublished information about a public company's share prices.[143] Examples could be multiplied, in particular from commercial contexts. In line with this principle, injunctions have been granted in confidence to restrain disclosures of film costumes prior to the release of the film[144] and of photographs of a private wedding prior to their publication in a magazine under exclusive arrangements with the couple.[145]

A different approach, adopted by the Court of Appeal when refusing an urgent **11.51** application to enjoin unauthorized disclosure of information from Lady Thatcher's memoirs in *Times Newspapers Ltd v Mirror Group Newspapers Ltd*, has not taken root. Sir Thomas Bingham MR there doubted whether confidence could be said to attach to Lady Thatcher's memoirs in circumstances where they were about to be published.[146] In *Douglas v Hello! Ltd* the trial judge found that the fact that 'authorised publication is due in a moment ... may make it harder for the unauthorised publisher to justify his breach',[147] and held that the *Times Newspapers* decision was not authoritative in the post-HRA age.[148] The House of Lords affirmed the view of Lindsay J that personal information can be commercialized and still receive protection.[149]

Section 12(4)(a)(i) HRA requires the court, when considering whether to grant **11.52** any relief which may affect the Convention right to freedom of expression, to have regard to the extent to which material is 'or is about to be' in the public domain. It is suggested, however, that this provision directs attention to the question whether confidence *will* continue to subsist once information has entered the public domain, and does not support an argument that the prospect of future publication destroys present confidentiality.[150]

*(c) The impact of publicity on confidentiality in personal information*

**Public knowledge may destroy confidentiality** The public domain doctrine **11.53** clearly has some application to confidential personal information. In *Douglas v Hello! Ltd* the Court of Appeal observed that it 'may generally' be true of private information of a personal nature that once in the public domain it will no longer

---

[142] *Attorney General v Observer Ltd* (n 118) 214.

[143] *Exchange Telegraph v Gregory* [1896] QB 147.

[144] *Shelley Films Ltd v Rex Features Ltd* [1994] EMLR 134.

[145] *Douglas* (nn 10 and 121).

[146] [1993] EMLR 443, 446–7.

[147] *Douglas* (n 10) [186(viii)]. The Court of Appeal held that agreement that authorized photographs can be published will not provide a defence to a claim in confidence for the publication of unauthorized photographs: (n 75) [107].

[148] *Douglas* (n 10) [224].

[149] *Douglas* (n 121).

[150] In *Attorney General v Times Newspapers Ltd* (n 124) the fact that information relating to the security and intelligence services was about to be published in Russia did not destroy the confidentiality in that information until such time as publication took place: see [34]–[35].

be confidential, or entitled to the protection of the law: 'Once intimate personal information about a celebrity's private life has been widely published it may serve no useful purpose to prohibit further publication.'[151] A similar approach has been taken on several occasions by courts declining to grant injunctions to restrain further publicity after mass-media publication has occurred.[152]

**11.54** **Confidentiality can survive limited disclosure** The impact of the fact that allegedly confidential information is in the public domain to some degree will differ not only according to the extent of the publicity but also to the nature of the information. In the government or commercial context, even a limited degree of disclosure might serve to destroy any confidentiality in a secret for the simple reason that hostile governments or commercial competitors would be likely to gain swift access.[153] There is obviously a distinction to be drawn between such situations and cases concerning personal information.[154]

**11.55** It is clear that personal information may become known to a limited number of people and yet remain confidential. Thus, the fact that Prince Albert had given some of his etchings to friends, and Prince Charles had circulated his travel journals to dozens of friends and associates,[155] did not prevent either succeeding in their confidence claims against others. The difference between personal information being known to a very limited number of people and its general disclosure in a newspaper has been remarked on several times.[156] The conduct of the media body involved may itself offer evidence as to whether information is in the public domain for this purpose. If a story is labelled 'Exclusive' this will be powerful evidence that its contents are not known to a substantial number of people.[157]

**Confidentiality may survive substantial publication**

**11.56** *Generally* Even disclosure to a substantial number of people will not necessarily mean that the public domain doctrine defeats a claim in confidence. In *Spycatcher* Lord Keith observed that 'It is possible, I think, to envisage cases where, even in

---

[151] (n 75) [105].

[152] *eg* decisions of Eady J in *Beckham v Gibson* (QBD, 30 April 2005) and *Mosley v News Group Newspapers (No 1)* [2008] EWHC 687 (QB). Also *Green Corns Ltd v Claverley Group Ltd* [2005] EWHC 958 (QB), [2005] EMLR 748, [78] (Tugendhat J).

[153] *eg Attorney General v Times Newspapers Ltd* (n 124) where publication of a former SIS officer's memoirs was due to take place in Russia.

[154] See 11.62 and *Attorney General v Observer Ltd* (n 118) 260 (Lord Keith), 287 (Lord Goff). Also *R v BCC, ex p Granada Television Ltd* [1995] EMLR 163. For an illustration of the difference between commercial confidence and personal privacy in this context, see *BBC v HarperCollins Publishers Ltd* [2010] EWHC 2424 (Ch), [2011] EMLR 6, declining to grant an injunction to protect the true identity of 'The Stig', an anonymous character on the *Top Gear* TV programme, on the grounds that his identity had become so generally accessible that it was no longer confidential.

[155] See n 129.

[156] *A v B plc* (n 41) [60], [69] (Jack J); *CC v AB* (n 129) [40] (Eady J). Also *Lord Browne* (n 42) [61] (Sir Anthony Clarke MR); *K v News Group Newspapers* [2011] EWCA Civ 439, [2011] 1 WLR 1827 [10(3)], [11]. And cf the observations of Tindal CJ in *Cook v Ward*, quoted in 11.11.

[157] *Barrymore* (n 139) 603; *Attorney General v Parry* [2003] EWHC 3201 (Ch), [2004] EMLR 223 [15].

the light of widespread publication abroad of certain information, a person whom that information concerned might be entitled to restrain publication by a third party in this country', and went on to give examples concerning personal information.[158] Even large-scale domestic publicity may not defeat a claim in confidence.[159] As Eady J observed in *WB v H Bauer Publishing Ltd*, 'it may be more difficult to establish that confidentiality has gone for all purposes, in the context of personal information, by virtue of its having come to the attention of certain readers or categories of readers'.[160] Thus, in that case the Court was unwilling to conclude that any confidentiality in information concerning the claimant's role as the defendant in a rape case had been destroyed by publicity, although publication had taken place to hundreds of thousands if not more by publication in *The Times* newspaper.

Similarly, in *Venables v News Group Newspapers Ltd* the order made provided that **11.57** the prohibition on revealing the claimant's addresses would not be affected even if these were subsequently to be published abroad or on the internet.[161] Thus, information may be confidential even if some or all of it is or has been in the public domain. The position as regards personal information has been summarized in this way: 'the fact that information may be known to a limited number of members of the public does not of itself prevent it having and retaining the character of confidentiality, or even that it has previously been very widely available'.[162] Later decisions have adopted the same approach, focusing on the potential harm that republication could do.[163] This clearly has significant implications for media 'following-up' stories published by others.

*Combinations of information*   Even if information to be published is all publicly **11.58** available, the particular combination may not be. The bringing together of individual items of information available in the public domain can result in a novel, and confidential, combination. In *Re X and Y (Children)* an injunction was granted to protect against the risk that the piecing together of a jigsaw of public domain information 'will

---

[158] *Attorney General v Observer Ltd* (n 118) 260.

[159] In *Blair v Associated Newspapers Ltd* (QBD, 10 March 2000, Morland J) an injunction was granted in the early hours to stop publication in the *Mail on Sunday* despite widespread publication of the first edition and follow-ups in other papers. In *West v BBC* (QBD, 10 June 2002, Ouseley J) the Court held that confidentiality was available in principle as a remedy to prevent the broadcasting of the name of a convicted paedophile, notwithstanding that this information had recently been published in the national and local press.

[160] [2002] EMLR 145 [25]–[26].

[161] [2001] Fam 430, [105].

[162] *Mills v News Group Newspapers Ltd* [2001] EMLR 957 [25]. See also *Stephens* (n 129) 454; *ex p Granada Television* (n 154) 168; *Creation Records Ltd v News Group Newspapers Ltd* [1997] EMLR 444, 456; *R v Criminal Injuries Compensation Board, ex p A* [1992] COD 379.

[163] See eg *A v M (Family Proceedings: Publicity)* [2000] 1 FLR 562 (Charles J); *Re S (Publicity)* [2003] EWHC 254 (Ch) (Hedley J); *Re X and Y (Children)* [2004] EWHC 762 (Fam) [2004] EMLR 29 [49] (Munby J); *Douglas* (n 75) [105]. Public domain provisos were not included in the injunctions granted in these cases, or in *Green Corns* (n 152): see [81].

bring the story into the public domain in an entirely new way', harmful to children.[164] Similarly, in *Green Corns v Claverley*, it was held that the publication of addresses at which troubled children were to be housed, linked with other information, would 'together amount to new information which was previously accessible to the public only in a limited and theoretical sense'.[165]

**11.59**  *The 'fade factor'*  Over time, information once generally known or accessible may pass out of the public domain. The point was made by Balcombe J in 1995 that 'it is clear that the fact that a matter has once been in the public domain cannot prevent its resurrection, perhaps many years later, from being an infringement of privacy'.[166] That was said in the context of a true privacy complaint, under a media code, but later cases have lent support to the view that the same is true in respect of confidentiality. This is less likely to be the position since the advent of the internet which makes it impossible to see the public domain as something which has clear boundaries. Some information may be very well known, and some relatively obscure. Some may remain permanently public, other information may disappear from view.[167] If the public does not have the relevant information in mind at the time of the offending republication, the fact that it was once in the public domain may not matter. Thus, Lindsay J granted a permanent injunction to restrain publication of the photographs in the *Douglas* case, holding that confidentiality had not been irretrievably lost, because the look of the unauthorized photographs had, over time, passed out of the public mind.[168]

**11.60**  *Photographs*  It is clear that photographs conveying personal information are in any event likely to be treated differently from the same or similar information conveyed verbally or in other ways. In *Douglas v Hello! Ltd* both the trial judge and the Court of Appeal made this clear.[169] The *Douglas* decision suggests that the courts will be slow to accede to public domain arguments where photographs are concerned, unless the images are identical to those already in the public domain, or their disclosure could not reasonably be thought likely to cause significant distress, or both.[170]

*(d) The public domain and misuse of private information*

**11.61**  The authorities cited in the last few paragraphs are largely drawn from the early twenty-first century period in which breach of confidence was mutating, and before

---

[164]  *Re X and Y* (n 163) [66].
[165]  *Green Corns* (n 152) [81]. Also *R v Chief Constable of North Wales, ex p Thorpe* [1999] QB 396, 415 (Buxton LJ).
[166]  *ex p Granada Television* (n 154) 168.
[167]  *Re X and Y* (n 163) [66].
[168]  *Douglas* (n 10) [278].
[169]  See the decision of Lindsay J (n 10) [196], [209], [213], [217]–[221], [228] and the final Court of Appeal decision (n 75) [105]–[107].
[170]  Contrast the position in commercial confidence, where 'inaccessibility by the public is a particular touchstone': *Cray Valley v Deltech Europe Ltd* [2003] EWHC 728 (Ch) [52].

the recognition of misuse of private information as a separate cause of action.[171] The interest protected by the cause of action for misuse is privacy, and a person's interest in the protection of his or her privacy is not necessarily exhausted by mass publication, although secrecy may have gone.[172] Further publication could still cause further harm, in particular to a person's dignity and feelings.

Even before the HRA came into force domestic courts had expressed the view **11.62** that Article 8 could protect against the raking up of past events, even those which had been well publicized,[173] and the principle was successfully invoked in a 2001 application to restrain publication of photos of a celebrity taken before she became famous.[174] It will often be the case that privacy rights survive extensive publicity. Publicity may, indeed, increase the need for injunctive protection. In *CTB v News Group Newspapers Ltd* Tugendhat J observed that though the injunction in that case had not preserved a secret, it had not failed in so far as its purpose was to prevent intrusion or harassment.[175] In *Contostavlos v Mendahun*[176] it was held that 'in the case of intrusive and intimate photographs of the kind in question in this case there is no real prospect of a defence of public domain'.[177] Public speculation about the identity of an anonymized claimant is unlikely to destroy either confidentiality or privacy rights.[178]

### (e) *The public domain and data protection*

The public domain justification under the data protection legislation is very **11.63** restricted. Absent consent, disclosure of sensitive personal data may be legitimate if the information has been 'deliberately made public' by the individual concerned,[179] but there is no corresponding provision in respect of 'non-sensitive' personal data. The extent to which information is public knowledge will no doubt be taken into account in assessing whether disclosure is necessary for the purpose of a defendant's legitimate interests and not unduly prejudicial to the claimant.

## (3) Immunity and Privilege

### (a) *Introduction*

The common law has developed a range of privileges against claims for defamation, **11.64** giving absolute or qualified privilege, or immunity, to those who communicate information of particular kinds, under particular circumstances. These common

---

[171] By the House of Lords in *Douglas* (n 121).
[172] See the passage from *Douglas* (n 121), cited in 11.44.
[173] See *ex p Thorpe* (n 165) [416] (Buxton LJ).
[174] *A v B and C* (n 43).
[175] [2011] EWHC 1334 (QB) [3].
[176] [2012] EWHC 850 (QB).
[177] *Contostavlos* (n 176) [25].
[178] *WXY v Gewanter* [2012] EWHC 1601 (QB).
[179] sch 1, pt 1, para 1(b) and sch 3, para 4 DPA. See further 7.58–7.61.

law privileges have been extended and supplemented by statutory provisions. Thus, for example, statements made in Parliament or in court are absolutely immune from suit for libel; fair and accurate reports of proceedings in those places are given absolute privilege if contemporaneous; non-contemporaneous court reports, and reports of other proceedings, such as disciplinary findings by trade or sports bodies, are protected by qualified privilege.[180] The question arises of whether the English law of privacy provides, or should develop, similar privileges for the publication of private information and hence afford comparable predictability to those involved in, or the subject of, such publications.

### (b) Foreign common law

**11.65** Publication 'in circumstances which would render it a privileged communication according to the law of slander or libel' was the second of the limitations on the right to privacy suggested by Warren and Brandeis.[181] The existence of such a defence to a 'private facts' claim is established in US law,[182] and the analogy between privilege in defamation and the public interest justification for breach of confidence has also been recognized in South Africa.[183]

### (c) English law

**11.66** A defence that privilege would have applied had the action been brought in defamation was identified as a candidate defence by the Calcutt Committee in 1990,[184] and the first edition of this book suggested[185] that such a defence might be developed in English law. The analogy between privilege in libel and the public interest in confidence was relied on in argument before the Court of Appeal in *Campbell v MGN Ltd*[186] but the argument found no favour. The Court held[187] that the latitude given by defamation law to statements published on an occasion of qualified privilege should not be imported into the public interest defence to breach of confidence, which was said to be quite different. The media should have latitude, but on Article 10 grounds connected with journalistic credibility.

**11.67** Nevertheless, there are still grounds for suggesting that the analogy could be a useful one, and could help improve the predictability of outcomes in privacy cases, and increase harmony between defamation and privacy law. The defamation privileges

---

[180] For absolute and qualified privilege generally, see *Gatley on Libel and Slander* (n 15) chs 13–16.

[181] S Warren and L Brandeis, 'The right to privacy' (1890) 4 Harv L Rev 193, 216. (The first proposed limitation was matter of public or general interest, as to which see 11.74 *et seq.*)

[182] See Corpus Juris Secundum (n 69) vol 77, 528 [31].

[183] *Jansen van Vuuren NNO v Kruger* 1993 (4) SA 842 (A) 850, 851, where the defence of privilege was considered and applied.

[184] *Report of the Committee on Privacy and Related Matters* (Cm 1102, 1990) para 12.19(b); and see also the draft privacy bills at Appendix J, cl 3(e) and Appendix K, cl 3(d).

[185] At 9.108 and 9.118–9.120.

[186] [2002] EWCA Civ 1373, [2003] QB 658.

[187] *Campbell* (n 186) [59]–[62] (Lord Phillips MR).

are rooted in public policy doctrines about the desirability in the public interest of freedom of speech and discussion, which have similar force in respect of private information; and immunities are not, as such, inimical to the Convention. There is some case law, discussed in the paragraphs which follow, which can be analysed as recognizing the existence of privileges akin to those established in defamation.

**Parliamentary privilege**   The European Court of Human Rights has twice dis-   **11.68**
missed as inadmissible complaints against the United Kingdom about the doctrine of absolute immunity for parliamentarians, the complaints being made under Article 6(1) and Article 8.[188] In each of those cases the complaint related to defamatory statements that were alleged to be false. However, the immunity is based on a statute of general application and would surely mean that the same result would obtain both domestically and in Strasbourg if the complaint concerned the disclosure in Parliament of true but embarrassing private facts.[189]

**Immunity for statements made in or in connection with litigation**   A disclosure   **11.69**
of private information in court would surely be held immune from action in privacy, as the public policy in protecting free speech in court cannot be the less when it comes to private as opposed to defamatory information. It has been held that no claim for breach of confidence can be maintained for disclosures made by a party to litigation to his lawyers in connection with litigation.[190] The reason given was that the duty of disclosure and the right of the litigant to get advice upon it overrode the duty of confidence. In defamation, the case would be analysed as one involving an occasion of absolute immunity (due to its intimate connection with the giving of evidence) or alternatively qualified privilege based on duty and/or interest.

### Reporting privileges?

*Parliament*   It seems likely that if and when a case arises in which a privacy   **11.70**
complaint is made about a *report* of a statement in Parliament which is alleged unjustifiably to intrude into private life, the courts will hold that the media (and others) have immunity from suit in privacy for fair and accurate reports of such proceedings, to the same or a similar extent as that which has been long established in defamation, and for the same reasons.

*Legal proceedings*   Statute protects against defamation claims over fair and accu-   **11.71**
rate reporting of proceedings.[191] There is no comparable provision for confidence or privacy claims. But a complaint in privacy over newspaper reports of personal

---

[188]   *A v UK* (2003) 36 EHRR 51; *Zollmann v UK* App no 62902/00 (ECtHR, 27 November 2003).
[189]   The statute is the Bill of Rights 1688, prohibiting the questioning in any place outside Parliament of the freedom of speech within it. The DPA contains specific provisions to ensure no infringement of this privilege: s 35A, sch 2, para 5(aa) and sch 3, para 7(1)(aa). For reporting of Parliament, see 11.70.
[190]   *Mensah v Jones* [2004] EWHC 2699 (Ch) (Lightman J); *White v Withers LLP* [2009] EWCA Civ 1122, [2010] 1 FLR 859 [23] (Ward LJ).
[191]   Defamation Act 1996, ss 14, 15 and sch.

information disclosed in court provides no reasonable basis for a claim:[192] 'The basic rule is that anything said in open court may be reported: see e.g. *R v Arundel Justices, ex parte Westminster Press Ltd*'.[193] It may be that it is this rule which on a true analysis underlies the series of decisions in which claims to protect allegedly private or confidential information have foundered on the basis that the information has been disclosed in open court proceedings. The cases, discussed in Chapter 4,[194] have generally expressed the justification for refusing relief as being that the information is 'in the public domain', and hence not confidential. However, the public domain doctrine generally requires that information has actually become known to a substantial number of people,[195] yet the decisions treat prior disclosure in a public court as sufficient of itself to justify further disclosure; they proceed on an unstated assumption that such information becomes public property regardless of the actual extent of public knowledge. Putting the point another way, it could be said that a person ceases to have any reasonable expectation of privacy in respect of information made public in a courtroom.

**11.72** *Other matters of public record*   There is some authority to suggest that reporting of the contents of other public statements would attract protection from a claim in confidence or misuse.[196] There is authority that disclosing information which by law *should* be a matter of public record is no wrong.[197]

**11.73** *Responsible publication*   The authorities suggesting that there exists, in relation to the disclosure of private facts, a defence or justification analogous to the defence in defamation for a reasonable disclosure on a matter of public interest[198] are discussed later in this chapter.[199]

### (4) Overriding Public Interest in Disclosure

#### (a) Introduction

**11.74** The proposition that an overriding public interest in disclosure can defeat a claim in breach of confidence has been well established for many years. This section examines the public interest grounds recognized in equity for overriding a claim to confidentiality. The law's approach to breach of confidence has, however, changed significantly under the influence of the HRA. The emergence of the tort of misuse

---

[192] *Crossley v Newsquest (Midlands South) Ltd* [2008] EWHC 3054 (QB) [58] (Eady J).
[193] [1985] 1 WLR 708.
[194] See 4.96–4.100.
[195] See 11.55.
[196] See 4.101–4.102.
[197] *Initial Services v Putterill* [1968] 1 QB 396, 406 (Lord Denning MR). See 4.102 .
[198] The defence in libel is outlined at 11.174 *et seq.*
[199] See 11.173 *et seq.* In the US, newspapers and broadcasters have a qualified privilege to report on matters of public interest. See *Bichler v Union Bank and Trust Co of Grand Rapids* CA Mich, 745 F 2d 1006.

of private information has seen a 'new methodology' established for the resolution of conflicts between privacy and freedom of expression.

The new methodology requires the careful evaluation of all the Convention and **11.75** other rights which are in play in the specific circumstances of the particular case, and the application of a Convention-based proportionality assessment. As a result, the value of the particular rights of confidence or privacy which are being asserted come under closer scrutiny, while at the same time a wider range of matters falls to be considered as potentially justifying disclosure. The examination of the pre-HRA jurisprudence which follows[200] needs to be read in the light of these points. The application of the new methodology is considered separately at 11.106 *et seq.*

The possibility that a claim for copyright infringement can yield to a countervail- **11.76** ing public interest in freedom of expression has also been recognized in the post-HRA era. Data protection law is grounded in Convention rights and contains a number of exemptions, defences, and justifications giving effect to freedom of expression. The scope of these defences is examined in Sections E(2) and (3).

### (b) Breach of confidence

**The basic principle**   A conventional starting point on the topic of public interest **11.77** is the speech of Lord Goff in *Attorney General v Observer Ltd*,[201] where he stated:

> The third limiting principle is of far greater importance. It is that, although the basis of the law's protection of confidence is that confidences should be preserved and protected by the law, nevertheless that public interest may be outweighed by some other countervailing public interest which favours disclosure... [T]he principle extends to matters of which disclosure is required in the public interest.

Analytically, the impact of the public interest in disclosure on a breach of confi- **11.78** dence claim can be viewed in various ways. In some contexts it will limit the scope of the duty.[202] In others, the nature of the information may be such as to foreclose the creation of any duty. As Page-Wood V-C stated in *Gartside v Outram*,[203] 'there is no confidence as to the disclosure of iniquity'. The precise juridical status of the plea has been the subject of much analysis.[204] However, in modern times the public interest has largely been regarded as a defence to a claim for breach of confidence,[205] and as a species of a more general defence of 'just cause or excuse'.[206]

---

[200] See 11.77–11.104.

[201] *Attorney General v Observer Ltd* (n 118) 282–3.

[202] *Tournier* (n 12) 473.

[203] (1857) 26 LJ Ch (NS) 113, 114.

[204] *Gurry on Breach of Confidence* (n 90) ch 16, 326–8; *Toulson and Phipps* (n 71) ch 6; and Y Cripps, *The Legal Implications of Disclosure in the Public Interest* (2nd edn, Sweet & Maxwell 1994) ch 2.

[205] In some cases, a court may be inclined to refuse an interim injunction and leave the claimant to his or her monetary remedies.

[206] *Fraser v Evans* (n 93) 362. In the contractual context, see H Beale (ed), *Chitty on Contracts* (31st edn, Sweet & Maxwell 2014) para 16-005; *Gurry on Breach of Confidence* (n 90) paras 16.05–16.16; and *London Regional Transport Ltd v Mayor of London* [2001] EWCA Civ 1491, [2003] EMLR 4.

**11.79** **Overall scope** Before the HRA the circumstances in which this defence aided media defendants were limited. It was often said that there is a key distinction between what is interesting to the public and what it is in the public interest to make known.[207] The subjects on which a disclosure might be held to be of public interest were relatively limited. Sir John Donaldson MR observed in *Francome v Mirror Group Newspapers* that the media are prone to the error of confusing the public interest with their own interest.[208] It is possible, however, to trace the evolution of the public interest defence from the narrow grounds identified in *Gartside v Outram*[209] to a rather wider defence of public interest already recognized in more modern cases decided before the HRA.[210]

**11.80** **Disclosure of wrongdoing** This category is often subsumed, at least in part, under the proposition of Page Wood V-C in *Gartside v Outram*,[211] that a man cannot be made 'the confidant of a crime or a fraud'. The principle was applied in that case to accounting and business information tending to show that the claimant was defrauding its customers. Iniquity covers a range of conduct and subsequent cases have to some extent identified that conduct. However, as noted by Salmon LJ in *Initial Services v Putterill*[212] with reference to *Gartside v Outram*:

> The iniquity referred to in that case was quite dramatic, but what is the sort of iniquity that comes within that doctrine is certainly not easy to define. What was iniquity in 1856 may be too narrow or perhaps too wide for 1967.

**11.81** In the *Initial Services* case Lord Denning MR stated that:[213]

> The exception should extend to crimes, frauds, misdeeds, both those actually committed as well as those in contemplation, provided always—and this is essential—that the disclosure is justified in the public interest. The reason is because 'no private obligations can dispense with that universal one which lies on every member of society to discover every design which may be formed, contrary to the laws of the society, to destroy the public welfare': see *Annesley v Anglesea (Earl)*.[214]

**11.82** The 'misdeeds' in question include breach of statutory duty[215] and, generally, the proposed commission of civil wrongs.[216] Past civil wrongs are also included. However, commentators have warned that the circumstances of a disclosure of a

---

[207] eg *Francome v Mirror Group Newspapers* [1984] 1 WLR 892, 898 (Sir John Donaldson MR) and *Lion Laboratories v Evans* [1985] QB 526, 537 (Stephenson LJ).

[208] *Francome* (n 207) 898.

[209] *Gartside* (n 203).

[210] See the textbooks and decisions cited at n 206. The post-HRA position, including the impact on this aspect of the law of the IPSO Editors' Code and the DPA, is analysed later in this chapter.

[211] *Gartside* (n 203).

[212] *Initial Services* (n 197) 410.

[213] *Initial Services* (n 197) 405; approved in *British Steel Corp v Granada Television Ltd* [1981] AC 1096, 1201.

[214] (1743) LR 5 QB 317.

[215] *Beloff v Pressdram Ltd* [1973] 1 All ER 241, 260.

[216] *Weld-Blundell v Stephens* [1919] 1 KB 520, 527. See 7.121 for the definition of 'wrongdoing' in relation to data protection law.

past civil wrong must be carefully assessed to determine whether the disclosure really is in the public interest.[217] The fact that a set of circumstances is suspicious does not necessarily justify disclosure.[218]

The following are matters the disclosure of which has been held to be justified or **11.83** arguably so: price-fixing arrangements and consequent breaches of the Restrictive Trade Practices Act 1976; [219] the issue of false trade circulars;[220] breaches of the Rules of Racing issued by the Jockey Club;[221] fiscal irregularities and breaches of FIMBRA regulations made pursuant to the Financial Services Act 1976;[222] the antics of a pop group on an aeroplane; [223] criminal breach of statutory requirements to file accounts.[224]

Examples of disclosures which the court has found not to be justified on the basis of **11.84** iniquity are: disclosure to a customer's employer of banking information showing that the customer had a gambling habit and was overdrawn on his account;[225] disclosure of an adulterous lesbian relationship.[226] Immoral conduct is susceptible to a defence of public interest. However, the circumstances are limited.[227] A court may well ask how the information can be so morally shocking if a newspaper wishes to publish it.[228] In those circumstances, a defendant might seek to argue that the information would not satisfy the basic requirements necessary to establish a duty of confidence.[229]

**Other purposes beneficial to the community**    There are other cases where dis- **11.85** closure is required in order to further interests of the community. In the *Lion Laboratories* case[230] Griffiths LJ stated that although disclosure in the public interest would usually arise in the context of iniquity, it would extend to any situation where it would be vital in the public interest to publish confidential information.[231] The question of what publication would be vital has until recently received a very restricted answer.

---

[217] See n 71.
[218] *Kitson v Playfair, The Times*, 28 March 1896.
[219] *Initial Services* (n 197).
[220] *Initial Services* (n 197).
[221] *Francome* (n 207).
[222] *Re a Company's Application* [1989] Ch 477.
[223] *Woodward* (n 70); a decision that has been criticized (11.21) but may be right on its facts.
[224] *Abbey v Gilligan* [2012] EHWC 3217 (QB), [2013] EMLR 12 [104], where the failure could have put into question an individual's ability properly to carry out his public function.
[225] *Tournier* (n 12).
[226] *Stephens* (n 129).
[227] *Stephens* (n 129) 453. Browne-Wilkinson V-C stated in connection with sexual activities that 'there is no common view that sexual conduct of any kind between consenting adults is grossly immoral'. See also 5.45.
[228] *Stephens* (n 129).
[229] See in particular *Coco* (n 13) 47; *Shepherd v News Group Newspapers Ltd* (Ch, 20 March 1998) and *Theakston* (n 23).
[230] *Lion Laboratories* (n 207) 550.
[231] See also *Beloff* (n 215).

**11.86**  *Protecting public health or safety*  In *Hubbard v Vosper*[232] it was held that the public need to expose the practices of the Church of Scientology was such as to justify refusal of an interim injunction. Lord Denning noted that the claimant's own literature stated that course material could be dangerous in untrained hands and considered that its literature 'indicated medical quackeries of a sort which may be dangerous if practised behind closed doors'.[233] Disclosure of a psychiatric report on a paranoid schizophrenic to the appropriate authorities was considered appropriate for the purpose of allowing them to make an informed choice as to whether or not the claimant should be released; in other words, to protect members of society from possible violence.[234]

**11.87**  However, in *X v Y*[235] the Court refused to permit publication of the identities of doctors who had AIDS, on the basis that the public interest in the preservation of medical confidentiality should prevail. It may also be that the public interest in disclosure will no longer prevail once a perceived threat to the community has come to an end.[236] Even where there is an ongoing public interest in disclosure, that may be insufficient to outweigh other public interests in play.[237]

**11.88**  *Advancing other public welfare policies*  The case law discloses a variety of other countervailing public policies which may apply so as to create just cause or excuse for a disclosure. The following instances may be given. It will be noted that the majority concern limited rather than mass disclosures. Thus, reasonable use by the police of photographs of suspects was held justified in connection with the fight against crime.[238] It was legitimate for the police to disclose the identity and whereabouts of convicted paedophiles to owners of a caravan site to which the paedophiles had moved.[239] Compulsion of a solicitor to produce documents for inspection under the Solicitors' Account Rules has been held legitimate,[240] as has the disclosure of information by a bank which is reasonably necessary to protect

---

[232] [1972] 2 QB 84, CA.

[233] *Hubbard v Vosper* (n 232) 96. See also *Church of Scientology v Kaufman* [1973] RPC 635: refusal of an injunction at trial where the defendant established that the practices of the Scientologists were in fact dangerous.

[234] *W v Egdell* [1990] Ch 359, 416, 422, and 424.

[235] [1988] 2 All ER 648; also *Cornelius v de Taranto* [2001] EWCA Civ 1511, [2001] EMLR 329, 343; [2002] EMLR 112, CA.

[236] *Schering Chemicals Ltd v Falkman Ltd* [1982] 1 QB 1, CA. See, however, the dissenting judgment of Lord Denning MR.

[237] In *Distillers Co (Biochemicals) Ltd v Times Newspapers Ltd* [1975] 1 QB 613 it was unsuccessfully argued that the conduct of the manufacturers of the drug Thalidomide required publication in the media of documents disclosed in litigation over the drug. The European Court ultimately reversed this decision: *Sunday Times v UK* (1979) 2 EHRR 245.

[238] *Hellewell v Chief Constable of Derbyshire* [1995] 1 WLR 804, 811. See also *Swinney v Chief Constable of Northumbria Police (No 1)* [1997] QB 464 and *Swinney v Chief Constable of Northumbria Police (No 2)*, *The Times*, 26 May 1999, Jackson J.

[239] *ex p Thorpe* (n 165).

[240] *Parry-Jones v Law Society* [1969] 1 Ch 1, CA.

the bank or others against fraud, or other crime.[241] The public interest in protecting the administration of justice may override professional or other confidences.[242]

**Scrutiny of those exercising power**    The public interest in allowing those in public office to be held to account has been held to justify disclosure of otherwise confidential information in a number of circumstances. Disclosure by the BBC of the contents of a statement made to the police was justified by the public interest in examining whether or not the Serious Fraud Office had acted responsibly in connection with the two Maxwell criminal trials.[243] Disclosure of a minister's tax affairs was justified in connection with allegations of hypocrisy.[244] Disclosure of emails evidencing dealings between a businessman and the chairman of the London Organising Committee of the Olympic Games (LOCOG), Lord Coe, was held to be justified by the public interest in discussing the possibility that Lord Coe had failed to maintain separation between his private interests and his public duties, and in questioning his private and professional judgment.[245]    **11.89**

The media have failed to justify disclosure of information said to fall into this category in the following instances: the identity of a senior government minister who had given the claimant journalist information as to governmental matters, the identities of ministers who supported a possible replacement for the Prime Minister, and details of how the lobby system worked;[246] mismanagement of, and government intervention in, a nationalized industry.[247] It is open to argument whether on the present state of the law[248] a public interest defence would apply in either or both of these situations.    **11.90**

In *Lord Browne's* case[249] it was held that disclosure of his use of corporate facilities for the private purpose of conducting a personal relationship was justified by a public interest in scrutiny of the conduct of the chairman of a large and powerful public company.    **11.91**

**Correcting the record**    A further category of situation is where members of the public have been or are likely to be misled, illustrated by the issue of misleading trade circulars alleged in *Initial Services v Putterill*.[250] In *Woodward v Hutchins*[251] one ground for refusing the injunction was the public interest in correcting the    **11.92**

---

[241]  *Tournier* (n 12) 481 and 486.

[242]  *Attorney General v Mulholland, Attorney General v Foster* [1963] 2 QB 477, 489–90, CA.

[243]  *Bunn v BBC* [1998] 3 All ER 552.

[244]  *Lord Levy v Times Newspapers Ltd* (QBD, 23 June 2000).

[245]  *Abbey* (n 224).

[246]  *Beloff* (n 215) 261.

[247]  *British Steel* (n 213) 1169, where the issue arose in the context of an application to discover the source of a leak.

[248]  See 11.94 *et seq*.

[249]  *Lord Browne* (n 42) and see text to n 245.

[250]  *Initial Services* (n 197).

[251]  *Woodward* (n 70).

image which the claimant pop stars had created. In the *Lion Laboratories* case[252] it was held that information regarding faulty breathalyser machines could be disclosed, as it raised the possibility of wrong convictions for drink-driving; but that detailed technical information as to the operation of the machines should not be published. In *Abbey v Gilligan*,[253] there was held to be an overriding public interest in publication of private emails in order to show that, contrary to the impression created by his representatives, Lord Coe had an active role in a company established to exploit his services, image, and intellectual property rights.

**11.93** **Cautionary tales**  In one case it was held arguable that it was in the public interest to disclose, as a cautionary tale, that the notorious drug taking of a famous musician had led to him undertaking therapy.[254] It may be on this basis that it was conceded at the trial of *Campbell v MGN Ltd,* before the same judge, that it was legitimate to disclose the fact of Miss Campbell's therapy. However, this approach has not been developed in subsequent cases.

### Circumstances justifying disclosure to the public at large

**11.94** *Scrutiny of authority and correcting the record*  Where disclosure was held justified for these purposes, it followed that disclosure to the public was justified.[255]

**11.95** *Public welfare*  In *Lion Laboratories*[256] the public interest in appreciating the risk of unsafe convictions for drink-driving justified newspaper disclosure of information tending to show that Intoximeter breath-test machines were faulty. That interest had been fuelled by newspaper articles and there was, in the public arena, criticism of the machine which called for a reappraisal by the Home Office of its decision to use it. This lent further support to the plea of public interest.[257] The Court considered it to be no answer that the defendant publishers should have gone to the Home Office in the first instance. The Home Office was publicly committed to use of the machine and, however strongly it might oppose unjust convictions, the Home Office was associated with the machine in the public mind and the police use of it.[258]

**11.96** *Wrongdoing*  Several of the pre-HRA authorities emphasized, however, that the general public was not necessarily the group to whom disclosure of alleged wrongdoing should be made. 'The disclosure must be to one who has a proper interest to receive the information.'[259] This, at least in the first instance, might be a regulatory body. Thus, in *Francome v Mirror Group Newspapers*[260] it was held that

---

[252] *Lion Laboratories* (n 207).
[253] *Abbey* (n 224).
[254] *Gallagher v Dukes* (HC, 27 November 1997, Morland J).
[255] See the cases cited in 11.89–11.92.
[256] *Lion Laboratories* (n 207).
[257] *Lion Laboratories* (n 207) 541.
[258] *Lion Laboratories* (n 207) 544 and 553.
[259] *Initial Services* (n 197) 405–6 (Lord Denning MR).
[260] *Lion Laboratories* (n 207).

any public interest in the contents of the taped conversations would only warrant disclosure to the police or the Jockey Club disciplinary committee. In *Re a Company's Application*[261] it was recognized that disclosure of a financial adviser's alleged wrongdoing by its compliance officer to the Inland Revenue or to its regulator would be warranted, but not publication generally.[262]

### The degree of proof necessary to establish the public interest

*Wrongdoing*   If the public interest in disclosure arises from alleged wrongdoing, **11.97** and in some other instances, a question arises as to what level of proof is necessary in order for the defence to be sufficiently made out. Many of the authorities are decisions made on applications for interim injunctions or to strike out public interest defences. In *Lion Laboratories*, the test was said to be whether 'there is a serious defence of public interest which may succeed at trial' and, if so, to conduct a balancing exercise.[263] Section 12 HRA now mandates a different approach; a claimant must establish a probability that an injunction will be granted at trial.[264] That begs the question of the degree of proof necessary at that stage.

At one level the answer to that question is straightforward: the facts that are **11.98** alleged to justify disclosure must be sufficiently well established to justify the interference with confidentiality involved. The pre-HRA cases may nonetheless assist. In the *Spycatcher* case,[265] using words that could be seen as anticipating the *Reynolds* defence to libel, Lord Goff stated:[266]

> …a mere allegation of iniquity is not of itself sufficient to justify disclosure in the public interest. Such an allegation will only do so if, following such investigations as are reasonably open to the recipient, the allegation in question can reasonably be regarded as being a credible allegation from an apparently reliable source.

In that case Peter Wright's allegations of criminal activity on the part of the Security and Intelligence Services formed a very small part of the disclosures he had made in *Spycatcher*, and the defence of public interest failed. The two approaches may be capable of reconciliation on the basis that a defendant should have to prove the truth of his allegations where the nature of his case on public interest renders it feasible for him to do so.[267]

---

[261] *Re a Company's Application* (n 222).
[262] See also the Public Interest Disclosure Act 1998, s 43A and the definition of a 'protected disclosure' in the context of whistle-blowers. See 1.90.
[263] *Lion Laboratories* (n 207) 539.
[264] See 12.46–12.49.
[265] *Attorney General v Observer Ltd* (n 118).
[266] *Attorney General v Observer Ltd* (n 118) 283. Lord Keith also stated at 262, 'it is not sufficient to set up the defence merely to show that allegations of wrongdoing have been made. There must at least be a *prima facie* case that the allegations have substance.'
[267] See *Gurry on Breach of Confidence* (n 71) 341. This approach is taken in other areas of the law, *eg* in connection with damages.

**11.99** *Other justifications* There may be cases where the public interest which may justify disclosure does not require proof of the truth of the underlying facts. In *Malone v Commissioner of Police for the Metropolis*[268] Sir Robert Megarry V-C considered that whether police telephone-tapping was justified did not turn on whether there was a certainty that the conversation overheard would disclose iniquitous conduct; the question was whether there was just cause or excuse for the telephone-tapping and for the use made of material so obtained.[269] In such cases, the public interest could not be successfully invoked unless relevant safeguards were observed. In *Malone* Megarry V-C was concerned with criminal conduct.[270] In other contexts, the relevant confidential information might relate to some impending disaster. It would be surprising if a publisher invoking a public interest defence had to show that there was a certainty, rather than a significant risk, that the disaster would happen.[271]

### (c) The public interest in data protection law

**11.100** The DPA and subsidiary legislation contain one exemption and two public interest justifications potentially available in a media privacy case. The exemption is in s 32, which potentially exempts processing of any personal data from most of the data protection requirements where it is undertaken 'with a view to' the publication of journalistic material,[272] and there is a reasonable belief (a) that publication would be in the public interest and (b) that compliance with the relevant data protection provision would be incompatible with the 'special purpose' of journalism.

**11.101** The public interest justifications are in schs 2 and 3 to the Act. Schedule 2, para 6 provides for a balancing of rights, as has to be undertaken under the 'new methodology'.[273] Schedule 3 provides a somewhat similar, albeit more limited, justification for the processing of sensitive personal data. This applies where the processing is in 'the substantial public interest', is made 'with a view to' publication, is reasonably believed to be in the public interest, and is in connection with unlawful, dishonest, improper, or various other kinds of wrongful acts. The effect of these complex and somewhat unhappily worded provisions, and their interrelationship, is still not clear. They are considered in Chapter 7.[274] What can be said, however, is that it would be anomalous for a disparity to exist between the scope of these justifications and those available in the laws of confidence and misuse of private information.

---

[268] *Malone* (n 93).

[269] *Malone* (n 93) 377.

[270] He referred specifically to 'assault, theft or other crimes' as opposed to 'matters of national security': *Malone* (n 93) 377.

[271] See *Malone* (n 93) 362, and cf *GKR Karate v Yorkshire Post Newspapers Ltd* [2000] EMLR 410.

[272] A term which encompasses the act of publication itself: see 7.112.

[273] *Murray v Express Newspapers plc* [2007] EWHC 1908 (Ch), [2007] EMLR 583 [76] (Patten J) (not commented on by the Court of Appeal). For the 'new methodology', see 11.112 *et seq*.

[274] See 7.117–7.124.

*(d)  The public interest and copyright*

Copyright law contains two specific statutory public interest defences, in the form **11.102**
of the 'fair dealing' exceptions in s 30 which relate to 'reporting current events' and
'criticism or review'. An increasing range of circumstances has been recognized as
capable of satisfying these definitions, although the scope for the media to rely on
the fair dealing defence for criticism or review is curtailed by the fact that it is available only in respect of published works.[275]

In addition to fair dealing, the law of copyright recognizes a separate, non-statutory, **11.103**
defence of disclosure in the public interest. In *Ashdown v Telegraph Group Ltd*[276] the
Court of Appeal endorsed the approach taken in *Lion Laboratories*[277] and rejected
the narrow interpretation of the defence, which would have confined it to cases
where enforcement of copyright is refused because the work itself is injurious to
public life, or otherwise contrary to public interest. The public interest defence may,
in principle, extend to previously unpublished works. This broadens the scope of the
defences available for media publications. As a result of the decision in *Ashdown* the
public interest has also become highly material to the issue of fair dealing.

There is therefore some degree of convergence in the approach taken by the **11.104**
courts to public interest arguments in claims for breach of confidence cases and
copyright.[278] There are however significant remaining differences, partly due to
the differing juridical nature of the rights, and partly to the existence of a statutory
code for copyright but not for confidence (or misuse). The range of circumstances
in which a public interest defence will run in copyright is probably more limited
than in breach of confidence.

One reason for this is that a successful public interest defence in a copyright case **11.105**
allows the exploitation of a property right without compensation. Another reason is
that it is generally unnecessary to infringe copyright to make a point. A defendant will
need to show that the public interest requires the exploitation, and that it be free of
charge. The presence of express statutory exceptions has also been said to be highly relevant to the circumstances in which a wider defence of public interest might arise.[279]
It remains arguable, nonetheless, that the defences should be coextensive in copyright
and in confidence or privacy where the copyright owner's interest is not commercial,
and the claim is made solely to protect the privacy interest in an unpublished work.[280]

---

[275] See 9.35, 9.45–9.49. A defendant cannot rely on its own concurrent publication of a previously
unpublished work to found a comment or review defence: *HRH Prince of Wales* (n 129) [80]–[81].

[276] [2002] Ch 149, CA, rejecting the narrow interpretation suggested in *Hyde Park Residence Ltd
v Yelland* [2001] Ch 143, CA [64] (Aldous LJ).

[277] *Lion Laboratories* (n 207).

[278] See ch 9 for a more detailed treatment of the defences in copyright actions of 'fair dealing'
(9.35–9.57) and public interest (9.58–9.66).

[279] See *Hyde Park Residence* (n 276) [76] (Mance LJ).

[280] Such an argument was advanced in *HRH Prince of Wales* (n 129). It was described as 'novel
and interesting' but not ruled on by the Court of Appeal, as the public interest defence to the confidence claim was rejected: [82].

### (5) Overriding Rights

*(a) Introduction*

**11.106** **The rights-based approach**   The HRA requires a different, rights-based approach to the assessment of whether a disclosure of confidential or private information infringes a person's rights. Instead of, or as well as, asking whether the disclosure is justified in the public interest the court will now determine the outcome of the claim by a process in which all competing rights and interests are identified, weighed up, and balanced against one another, with the outcome depending on an assessment of proportionality. Chapter 5 examines one aspect of this process: the evaluation of claimants' rights.[281] This section looks at the other side of the scales: the matters which may serve to outweigh or override rights of confidence and privacy.

**11.107**   The overall scope of the available justifications is prescribed by Article 8(2). This provides that an interference with the right to respect for private life may be justified if it is in accordance with the law and necessary in a democratic society in the interests of national security, public safety, or the economic well-being of the country, for the prevention of disorder or crime, for the protection of health or morals, or for the protection of the rights and freedoms of others.

**The countervailing rights, freedoms, and interests**

**11.108**   *Article 10*   The primary countervailing factors in a media case will be the rights and freedoms guaranteed by Article 10(1) of the Convention, to impart and receive information and ideas. The values enshrined in Article 10 are part of the very content of the cause of action for misuse of private information.[282] The same appears to be true in cases where the law of traditional breach of confidence is applied to private and personal information.[283] Accordingly, in assessing the significance of Convention rights the courts are obliged to take into account the Strasbourg jurisprudence,[284] and the qualified rights under Article 10 will be the starting point for an analysis of whether disclosure may be justified.[285]

**11.109**   *Other rights, freedoms, and interests*   Other Convention rights may come into play, in particular those under Article 8 itself, freedom of conscience under Article 9, and fair-trial rights under Article 6. The available justifications for interfering with the Article 8 right to respect for private life are not, however, limited to Convention rights. Nor are they even confined to cases where legal rights are engaged. Article 8(2) provides that interference may also be justified by other considerations. Specific factors listed in Article 8(2) which are of potential importance in media

---

[281]   See 5.14–5.18 and 5.161–5.163. The application of the new methodology to media defences is outlined in 11.112 *et seq.*

[282]   *Campbell* (n 44) [17] (Lord Nicholls); *McKennitt v Ash* [2006] EWCA Civ 1714, [2008] QB 73 [11] (Buxton LJ).

[283]   The passages cited in the previous note spoke, in fact, of breach of confidence.

[284]   s 2 HRA; *McKennitt* (n 282) [11] (Buxton LJ).

[285]   *Douglas*, CA (n 10) [49], [136], and [137].

cases are the 'interests ... of public safety', 'the protection of health or morals', and the 'protection of the [Convention and other] rights and freedoms of others'. These rights and freedoms will include those of the media as provided for by the media codes of IPSO and Ofcom to which, in any event, the court must have regard under s 12(4)(b) HRA.

### Relationship with the public interest defence

*Terminology*   It may remain appropriate to speak of a public interest defence, **11.110** where the claim is brought in traditional breach of confidence,[286] but the label is potentially misleading in a misuse of private information claim. In such a case the court will have to conduct an evaluation of competing rights, neither of which has presumptive priority.[287]

*Substance*   In one of the early post-HRA cases, *London Regional Transport Ltd* **11.111** *v Mayor of London*,[288] it was suggested by Sedley LJ[289] that the application of the 'metwand' of the common law would be likely to lead to the same result as the use of the methodical concept of proportionality. That, however, was a case of commercial confidence. There is much that would be recognized as engaging Article 8 without attracting the protection of the law of confidence. At the same time the Strasbourg jurisprudence emphasizes, probably more than the common law authorities, the duty of the media to publish on matters of public interest or 'public concern'.[290] Under the influence of the Convention the English courts have moved away from the approach exemplified by such cases as *Francome*, in which,[291] where wrongdoing was alleged, the only proper recipient of information to that effect was considered to be the appropriate regulator, as opposed to the public at large.[292]

### (b) The methodology

**The ultimate balancing test and proportionality**   The rights protected under **11.112** Articles 8 and 10 are in principle of equal value, with neither having any presumptive priority over the other.[293] It must first be determined whether Article 8 is engaged at all. A balancing operation starts at the point where it is established that the person publishing the information knows or ought to know that there is a reasonable expectation that the information in question will be kept confidential.[294]

---

[286]   As in *Abbey* (n 224).

[287]   *Douglas* (n 10) [137].

[288]   *London Regional Transport* (n 206).

[289]   *London Regional Transport* (n 206) [56]–[62].

[290]   See 11.21–11.125.

[291]   As discussed in 11.96.

[292]   See the discussion in 11.96.

[293]   See *Douglas*, CA (n 10) [135] (Sedley LJ); *Campbell* (n 44) [12] (Lord Nicholls), [55] (Lord Hoffmann), [113] (Lord Hope, referring to Resolution 1165 of the Parliamentary Assembly of the Council of Europe); G Phillipson, 'Transforming breach of confidence? Towards a common law right of privacy under the Human Rights Act' (2003) 66 MLR 726, 748–58.

[294]   *Campbell* (n 44) [134] (Baroness Hale), approving dicta of Lord Woolf CJ in *A v B plc* (n 38) [11(ix)] and [11(x)]. See also *Weller* (n 100).

The methodology to be adopted was explained by Lord Steyn in *Re S (A Child)* where he said,[295] referring to the House's decision in Campbell:

> What does…emerge clearly from the opinions are four propositions. First, neither article has *as such* precedence over the other. Secondly, where the values under the two articles are in conflict, an intense focus on the comparative importance of the specific rights being claimed in the individual case is necessary. Thirdly, the justifications for interfering with or restricting each right must be taken into account. Finally, the proportionality test must be applied to each. For convenience I will call this the ultimate balancing test.

The same applies where other Convention rights, such as the right to a fair trial under Article 6, are in play.[296] The requirement for an intense focus on the specific rights being claimed means this 'is not a mechanical exercise to be decided upon the basis of rival generalities' but fact-dependent.[297]

**11.113** The approach to assessing the proportionality of an interference was well described by Sedley LJ in the *London Regional Transport* case. Discussing the interrelationship between the 'conscience test' for whether a disclosure would amount to a breach of confidence and the Convention methodology he concluded[298] that the right approach:

> …lies in the methodical concept of proportionality: Does the measure meet a recognised and pressing social need? Does it negate the primary right or restrict it more than is necessary? Are the reasons given for it logical?…So for my part I find it…helpful today to postulate a recipient who, being reasonable, runs through the proportionality checklist in order to anticipate what a court is likely to decide, and who adjusts his or her conscience accordingly.

### Human Rights Act 1998, s 12

**11.114** *Freedom of expression*   Section 12(4) HRA requires consideration whenever relief is sought that might affect the Convention right to freedom of expression. It requires the court to have 'particular regard' to the importance of the Convention right to freedom of expression. Although this does not afford that right any priority over competing Article 8 rights,[299] it does draw attention to the importance of freedom of expression in its own right, whether or not the particular form of expression serves a specific, identifiable, public interest purpose.[300]

**11.115** Where 'the proceedings relate to material which the respondent claims, or which appears to the court, to be journalistic,[301] literary or artistic material, or to conduct

---

[295] *Re S (A Child)* [2004] UKHL 47, [2005] 1 AC 593 [17]. The process has also been dubbed the 'parallel analysis'.

[296] As was the case in *Re S* itself.

[297] *A Local Authority v W* [2005] EWHC 1564 (Fam), [2006] 1 FLR 1 [53] (Sir Mark Potter P).

[298] *London Regional Transport* (n 206) [55]–[58].

[299] See 12.23, 12.49.

[300] For authority to this effect see 11.155. See also para 2 of the definition of public interest in the IPSO Editors' Code, quoted at 11.118.

[301] The scope and meaning of this term has been considered in detail by the Supreme Court in the context of the Freedom of Information Act 2000: see *BBC v Sugar* [2012] UKSC 4, [2012] 1 WLR 439.

connected with such material', s 12(4) requires the court to have 'particular regard' to three further matters. The first (the extent to which the material has, or is about to, become available to the public) is discussed above.[302] The other two are of particular relevance to this section of the chapter.

*The public interest* The court must have particular regard to 'the extent to **11.116** which . . . it is or would be in the public interest for the material to be published'.[303] This is old-fashioned terminology for a rights-based decision-making process,[304] but highlights the need to consider, in a media case, whether priority should be given to the rights of the media, its informants, and the public to impart and receive the information which is the subject of the proceedings.

*'Any relevant privacy code'* The requirement to have particular regard to such **11.117** codes[305] is unaccompanied by any definition of which codes are relevant; but the IPSO Editors' Code and the Ofcom code clearly count, as may others.[306] It has been held that the Editors' Code can have decisive effect, so that 'a newspaper which flouts section 3 of the code [privacy] is likely in those circumstances to have its claim to an entitlement to freedom of expression trumped by Article 10(2) considerations of privacy'.[307] The converse must, in principle, be correct: a privacy claim is unlikely to succeed where the media has acted in accordance with the relevant code.

The courts and the regulators are in broad agreement on some core points. The **11.118** IPSO Editors' Code, for example, provides protection for the privacy of individuals[308] but goes on to indicate that intrusion may be justified if the disclosure at issue can be demonstrated to be in the public interest, which is defined (non-exhaustively) as follows:[309]

1. The public interest includes, but is not confined to:
   (i) Detecting or exposing crime, or the threat of crime, or or serious impropriety.
   (ii) Protecting public health and safety
   (iii) Preventing the public from being misled by an action or statement of an individual or organisation
   (iv) Disclosing a person or organization's failure or likely failure to comply with any obligation to which they are subject
   (v) Disclosing a miscarriage of justice

---

[302] s 12(4)(a)(i) HRA, discussed at 11.46.
[303] s 12(4)(a)(ii) HRA.
[304] See 11.106.
[305] s 12(4)(b) HRA.
[306] Such as the BBC's Producers' Guidelines. See generally ch 14.
[307] *Douglas* (n 10) [94] (Brooke LJ), referring to the Code of the Press Complaints Commission. This reference to section 3 refers to material which is now found in section 3 of the IPSO Code.
[308] cl 3.
[309] The extract is from the 2016 version, set out in full in Appendix G (available at <http://www.5rb.com/publication/the-law-of-privacy-and-the-media>). The first three elements also appeared in the 2014 IPSO Code and the PCC Code. The categories are considered below, in conjunction with relevant case law.

> (vi) Raising or contributing to a matter of public debate, including cases of impropriety, unethical conduct or incompetence concerning the public
>
> (vii) Disclosing concealment, or likely concealment, of any of the above.

2. There is a public interest in freedom of expression itself.

**11.119**  **Journalistic latitude**  In assessing whether a particular publication is legitimate for reasons of 'public interest' the media must be afforded 'reasonable latitude' in their decision-making.[310] It has been suggested that a reasonable editorial belief that publication would be legitimate may, in principle, suffice to outweigh privacy rights.[311] In that context reference was made to para 3 of the public interest section of the PCC Code, making the editor's reasonable belief that publication was in the public interest a touchstone of the legitimacy of such publication:

> Whenever the public interest is invoked, the PCC will require editors to demonstrate fully that they reasonably believed that publication, or journalistic activity undertaken with a view to publication, would be in the public interest.

The IPSO Editors' Code contains similar provision. These issues are considered in more detail under the heading of 'Responsible Journalism' below.[312]

*(c) Article 10 rights*

**11.120**  The incorporation of the values enshrined in Article 10 into English law via the HRA and thence into misuse of private information means that its provisions are now part of the essence of these wrongs, where private information is concerned. The Strasbourg jurisprudence, to which the court must have regard, is 'incorporated' also.[313] Although the right to freedom of expression is not in every case the ace of trumps, it is a powerful card to which the courts of this country must always pay appropriate respect.[314]

**11.121**  **The jurisprudence of the European Court of Human Rights**  Although not an absolute right, the right to freedom of expression is accorded a high level of protection in the Convention jurisprudence, especially where it is exercised by the media.[315] The formulation adopted by the European Court in a number of cases is as follows:[316]

> The press plays an essential role in a democratic society. Although it must not overstep certain bounds, in particular in respect of the reputation and rights of others, its duty is to impart—in a manner consistent with its obligations and responsibilities—information and ideas on all matters of public interest. Not only does it have the task of imparting such information and ideas: the public also has a right to receive them. Were it otherwise, the press would be unable to play its vital role of 'public watchdog'.

---

[310] *Campbell* (n 44). This aspect of the decision is discussed in more detail in 11.176–11.179.

[311] By Tugendhat J in *Terry (formerly 'LNS') v Persons Unknown* [2010] EWHC 119, [2010] EMLR 400 [70]–[73].

[312] See 11.173, where the similarly-worded provisions of s 32 DPA are also considered.

[313] s 2 HRA; *McKennitt* (n 282) [11] (Buxton LJ).

[314] *Douglas* (n 10) [49] (Brooke LJ).

[315] *Jersild v Denmark* (1995) 19 EHRR 1; *Bladet Tromso and Stensas v Norway* (1999) 29 EHRR 125.

[316] See, amongst others, *Gaweda v Poland* App no 26229/95 (ECtHR, 14 March 2002) para 34.

Although formulated primarily with regard to the print media, these principles 'doubtless apply also to the audiovisual media'.[317] Although there is as yet no authority on the point, it seems that they must be equally applicable to 'new' media.

This approach goes beyond the pre-HRA English law, which was 'historically **11.122** based on freedoms, not rights'.[318] This formulation additionally emphasizes that the media not only have a right to freedom of expression but also a vital social duty to perform, a proposition which also goes further than pre-HRA English law. It also highlights the dual aspect of the Convention right, encompassing both a right to impart and a right to receive information and ideas.[319] Although this formulation, which is common, speaks of a duty to impart information on matters of 'public interest', some Strasbourg Article 10 decisions employ instead or in addition the term 'public concern',[320] which may be a notion of different scope.

The protection of confidentiality and of the rights and freedoms of others are **11.123** in principle legitimate grounds for interfering with freedom of expression.[321] Different weight will however attach to different claims to privacy or confidentiality, depending on the circumstances,[322] and it is clear and constant Strasbourg jurisprudence that any interference with freedom of expression must, if it is to be justified, not only serve one of the legitimate aims specified in Article 10(2) but also, whatever its purpose, be strictly necessary on the facts of the case and the need for it 'convincingly established'.[323]

Historically, the European Court made it clear that any 'balancing exercise' that has **11.124** to be carried out between the right to freedom of expression and the grounds for interfering with it under Article 10(2) does not necessarily start with the scales evenly balanced, and will always depend on the precise circumstances of the case. In *Sunday Times v UK*[324] the Court stated:

> The court is faced not with a choice between two conflicting principles, but with a principle of freedom of expression that is subject to a number of exceptions which must be strictly interpreted . . .: the court has to be satisfied that the interference was necessary having regard to the facts and circumstances prevailing in the specific case before it.

The Article 8 case law of the twenty-first century has however seen developments **11.125** in the jurisprudence. In *von Hannover v Germany (No 1)*[325] the European Court

---

[317] *Jersild* (n 315) [31].
[318] *Douglas* (n 10) [64] (Brooke LJ).
[319] These separate and distinct aspects of the right are further analysed at 11.126–11.132.
[320] eg *Couderc and Hachette Filipacchi Associes v France* App No 40454/07 (ECtHR, 12 June 2014) paras 42, 43.
[321] For discussion of these and other legitimate aims within the scope of Art 10(2) see also 5.164–5.171.
[322] As discussed at 5.161–5.163.
[323] *Autronic A-G v Switzerland* (1990) 12 EHRR 485.
[324] *Sunday Times* (n 238) [65].
[325] (2005) 40 EHRR 1.

expressed the view that where the justification for interfering with private life was under consideration the crucial question is whether the reporting of the facts in question is 'capable of contributing to a debate in a democratic society'[326] or of making a 'contribution ... to a debate of general interest'.[327] The Court held that on the facts of the case, details about the life of a member of a reigning family who carried out no official functions made no such contribution. The publication's 'sole purpose was to satisfy the curiosity of a particular readership regarding the details of the applicant's private life'.[328] The facts were not a matter of public concern, even if she appeared in public places and was well known to the public.[329] This approach has something in common with the way the English courts sought, before the HRA, to distinguish genuine public interest from matters that are of interest to the public,[330] though it is arguable that the English approach was less restrictive. Subsequent Strasbourg decisions have tended to move back towards an approach more protective of free speech rights.[331]

### The right to impart information

**11.126** *The media* Some post-HRA decisions have followed the approach of those pre-HRA cases in which disclosure to regulators was held sufficient to serve any public interest which was engaged.[332] The modern law has tended, however, to take a more generous approach to the right to communicate with the general public, particularly so in cases concerning the media.

**11.127** In *Imutran v Uncaged Campaigns Ltd*,[333] the issue was to what extent the defendant, a pressure group, could publish stolen confidential research information alleged to reveal cruelty to animals. Sir Andrew Morritt V-C held disclosure to the general public to be inappropriate, given the existence of a democratically established regulatory system for the supervision of animal experiments. The technical nature of many of the documents also made them suitable for inspection by specialists in the field rather than by the public. The injunction did not restrain publication to regulatory bodies.[334] Similarly, in *R v Shayler*[335] it was held that publication to the world at large will rarely be justified in the case of information subject to the Official Secrets Act 1989, s 1. It will generally be necessary for the person making the disclosure to have sought approval through the appropriate channels, and to have exercised the right to judicial review of any refusal of authorization to publish.

---

[326] *von Hannover* (n 325) [63].

[327] *von Hannover* (n 325) [76].

[328] *von Hannover* (n 325) [65].

[329] *von Hannover* (n 325) [77].

[330] See 11.79.

[331] See *Axel Springer AG v Germany* (2012) 55 EHRR 6; *von Hannover v Germany (No 2)* (2012) 55 EHRR 15.

[332] See 11.96.

[333] [2001] 2 All ER 385 [25]–[27].

[334] Nor to the RSPCA. The claimant consented to disclosure to the RSPCA without accepting that it was entitled to the information.

[335] [2002] UKHL 11, [2003] 1 AC 247.

Other decisions have adopted a more generous approach. In *Theakston v MGN Ltd*   **11.128**
Ouseley J refused to limit disclosure to the claimant's employers, the BBC, stating that 'the free press is not confined to the role of a confidential police force; it
is entitled to communicate directly with the public for the public to reach its own
conclusion'.[336] In *Jockey Club v Buffham*, where the effective defendant was the
BBC, Gray J, applying the proportionality test,[337] held that there were matters of
sufficient general interest concerning malpractice in horse racing to warrant the
broadcast of specified passages from the claimant's confidential documents.[338] In
*Cream Holdings v Banerjee* the House of Lords held that allegations of corrupt dealings between a company director and local authority official, based on confidential
information, were matters of 'serious public interest' which required disclosure
beyond the appropriate regulatory authorities.[339] Media disclosure was also held
legitimate in *Lord Browne v Associated Newspapers Ltd*, where it was unsuccessfully
argued that disclosure to the company, BP, whose resources had allegedly been
misused by the claimant, would suffice.[340]

*Informants: the right to tell one's story*   The rights of media informants to tell their   **11.129**
own story will also require consideration. The point appears to have been recognized first of all by the PCC, before the HRA came into force. In a decision of
January 2000[341] the Commission noted that the newspaper had not denied an
article about a TV soap star's relationship with her former fiancé was intrusive, or
sought to justify it on the grounds of consent or the public interest. Rather, its case
rested on the right of Ms Pirie's former fiancé to discuss their relationship publicly.
On this the Commission held that it must 'also have regard to freedom of expression and the public's right to be informed of matters of public interest. This may
include cases where one side in an otherwise private relationship between two parties gives an account of that relationship.'

A similar approach has been adopted in some decisions of the court. In *Theakston*[342]   **11.130**
Ouseley J said, 'I can see no reason why the question of confidentiality should be
judged solely from the point of view of one participant in the activities and relationship'. He went on to uphold the right to freedom of expression of the sex workers
who wanted to publish their account of the activities. This was also an important
factor in *A v B plc*, where the story of extramarital sexual adventures was voluntarily provided to the defendant newspaper by two women participants. Their rights
to tell their stories were a significant factor in the Court's decision to discharge the

---

[336]  *Theakston* (n 23) [69].
[337]  See 11.112.
[338]  *Jockey Club* (n 75) [46]–[51]. For other public interest factors taken into account by the judge
see [57].
[339]  [2004] UKHL 44, [2005] 1 AC 253 [24].
[340]  *Lord Browne* (n 42). See further 11.146.
[341]  *Jacqueline Pirie and the News of the World*, 23 January 2000 (Report 49).
[342]  *Theakston* (n 23) [64], [70]–[71], and [76].

injunction granted at first instance.[343] These Article 10 rights are accompanied by Article 8 rights to determine who should know about one's private life.[344] The right to speak about one's own experiences may have an added dimension where the speaker is the victim of exploitation.[345]

**11.131**  However, these rights have limits. As Eady J held in *McKennitt v Ash*, any revelation of intimate matters involving another should be 'crafted, so far as possible, to protect the other person's privacy', and 'it does not follow, because one can reveal one's own private life, that one can also expose confidential matters in respect of which others are entitled to protection if their consent is not forthcoming'.[346] Moreover, as the Court of Appeal emphasized in the same case, the weight to be accorded to any right to speak about shared experience must depend on the nature of the relationship in question, and does not extend to those who are merely the confidants of information about the experiences of another.[347]

**11.132**  **The right to receive information**  The Strasbourg jurisprudence makes it clear that the public has a right to information on matters of legitimate interest or concern.[348] The decisions in *Theakston*, *Buffham*, and *Cream Holdings*, discussed above,[349] can be readily analysed as giving effect to such a right, as well as to the rights of those proposing to make the communications in question. But there are still few English decisions which expressly analyse the legitimacy of disclosures from this perspective. Such an analysis was however undertaken in *SKA v CRH*[350] where Tugendhat J held that the claimant's children had rights under Articles 8 and 10 to be informed of the imminent birth of twin siblings that their father had conceived with a secret lover.

**11.133**  **The hierarchy of types of speech**  The jurisprudence of the European Court of Human Rights recognizes a hierarchy of kinds of speech, which will be important in conducting the proportionality assessment, and applying the ultimate balancing test. As Lady Hale observed in *Campbell v MGN Ltd*:[351]

> There are undoubtedly different types of speech, just as there are different types of private information, some of which are more deserving of protection in a democratic society than others. Top of the list is political speech. The free exchange of information and ideas on matters relevant to the organisation of the economic, social and political

---

[343]  *A v B plc* (n 38) [11(xi)], [43(iii)]. The position may be different if it is a third party who makes the disclosure without the consent of both parties (as in *Stephens v Avery*, n 129). Even then, it is necessary to ascertain whether or not the disclosure by the third party is a breach of confidence.

[344]  See 11.157–11.158.

[345]  *AVB v TDD* [2014] EWHC 1442 (QB), where a confidentiality agreement was held unenforceable on grounds of public policy as it purported to give up the sex worker's right to complain of exploitation.

[346]  [2005] EWHC 3003 (QB), [2006] EMLR 178 [77].

[347]  *McKennitt* (n 282) [28]–[32] (Buxton LJ).

[348]  See 11.121.

[349]  At 11.128.

[350]  [2012] EWHC 766 (QB) [76]–[77] (Tugendhat J).

[351]  *Campbell* (n 44) [148].

life of the country is crucial to any democracy. Without this, it can scarcely be called a democracy at all. This includes revealing information about public figures, especially those in elective office, which would otherwise be private but is relevant to their participation in public life. Intellectual and educational speech and expression are also important in a democracy, not least because they enable the development of individuals' potential to play a full part in society and in our democratic life. Artistic speech and expression is important for similar reasons, in fostering both individual originality and creativity and the free-thinking and dynamic society we so much value. No doubt there are other kinds of speech and expression for which similar claims can be made.

Other kinds of speech or expression that have been identified as having high value **11.134** in Convention terms are, in descending order of importance, speech by parliamentarians in Parliament on matters of public interest, [352] the making of allegations when instituting or conducting legal proceedings,[353] the deployment by a litigant of documents at trial,[354] speech on trade union matters,[355] and speech concerned with a person's identity and familial relationships.[356]

At the opposite end of the scale is speech of low societal value, such as 'vapid tittle- **11.135** tattle about the activities of footballers' wives and girlfriends'.[357] Lady Hale observed in *Campbell*[358] that '[t]he political and social life of the community, and the intellectual, artistic or personal development of individuals, are not obviously assisted by poring over the intimate details of a fashion model's private life'. Eady J summed up the position thus in *CC v AB*: 'The communication of material to the world at large in which there is a genuine public interest is naturally to be rated more highly than the right to sell what is mere "tittle-tattle".'[359] That is not to say that publication of personal information of this kind will never be legitimate; it may be, where the rival claim to privacy rights is not of sufficient weight, or where it represents an exercise of the 'right to criticize', or performs an educational function.[360]

**Topics** The fact-sensitive nature of the process of assessing whether privacy or **11.136** free speech should prevail has meant that there is yet to emerge a clear set of principles that enables a structured approach to issues of public interest. With that reservation, this section seeks to categorize more specifically the kinds of 'speech' which may, on the authorities, be accorded priority over claims to privacy rights.

---

[352] Speech of 'exceptionally high value': *R (Lord Carlile of Berriew QC) v Secretary of State for the Home Dept* [2013] EWCA Civ 199 [56]; aff'd [2014] UKSC 60, [2015] AC 945.

[353] 'There is a high public interest in litigants having their right under Art 6, which is also a right under Art 10, to commence proceedings in a tribunal unfettered by interventions from another person against whom the litigant is making allegations': *BUQ v HRE* [2012] EWHC 774 (QB) [74].

[354] 'a form of expression …which should attract a high degree of protection from the courts': *Commissioner of Police of the Metropolis v Times Newspapers Ltd* [2011] EWHC 2705 (QB), [2014] EMLR 1 [70].

[355] *Palomo Sanchez v Spain* [2011] IRLR 934 [56].

[356] *SKA* (n 350) [77].

[357] *Jameel (Mohammed) v Wall Street Journal (Europe) Sprl* [2006] UKHL 44, [2007] 1 AC 359, [147].

[358] *Campbell* (n 44) [149].

[359] *CC v AB* (n 129) [36].

[360] See 11.153.

**11.137**   *Contribution to debate of general interest*   The decision in *von Hannover (No 1)* identified the decisive factor in the balance between Articles 8 and 10 as whether the publication made a contribution to a debate of public interest, and this has been identified as the decisive factor in whether or not to grant an interim injunction.[361] The court must consider whether the disclosure in question can make a real contribution to 'the political and social life of the community'.[362] Issues of public interest or concern identified in the privacy cases include the question of whether it is proper for a chief executive, or other person holding public office or exercising official functions, to carry on a sexual relationship with an employee in the same organization,[363] the suitability of a footballer to be England Captain,[364] the pressures on young international sportspeople, which may lead them into drug use,[365] the illness of reigning sovereign of Monaco, and the conduct of members of his family during that illness,[366] the trend among celebrities of renting out their holiday homes,[367] and the merits of a family dispute conducted publicly by the parties.[368] The nature and extent of the influence exercised by the media itself is surely a matter of legitimate public concern.[369]

**11.138**   While the more serious the subject matter to which the disclosed information relates the more likely the court is to find its disclosure to be legitimate, the decisions cited above show that a relatively broad interpretation has been given to the notion of matters of public concern. And not every communication has to serve some lofty aim, or some higher public interest purpose, in order to be legitimate. As Tugendhat J said in *SKA*: 'It is a normal part of life, and an exercise in freedom of expression, that people talk to one another about each other's lives. The birth of babies is a normal topic of such conversations, and there is no reason why it should not be. So too with talk about who is in a relationship with whom.'[370] The nature of the expression used may however be a factor in assessing the balance; offensive cartoons and 'vexatious and injurious accusations' have been held to fall outside the scope of the protection afforded by a topic of public interest.[371]

---

[361] *K v News Group Newspapers Ltd* [2011] EWCA Civ 439, [2011] 1 WLR 1827 [10(5)], and see also [23].

[362] Lady Hale's words, quoted in 11.133.

[363] *Goodwin v News Group Newspapers Ltd (No 3)* [2011] EWHC 1437 (QB), [2011] EMLR 27 [101]–[103]

[364] *Ferdinand* (n 75) [64].

[365] *Spelman v Express Newspapers* [2012] EWHC 355 (QB) [72].

[366] *von Hannover v Germany (No 2)* 7 February 2012, [2012] EMLR 16.

[367] *von Hannover v Germany (No 3)* [2013] ECHR 835 [51].

[368] *Hutcheson v News Group Newspapers Ltd* [2011] EWCA Civ 808, [2012] EMLR 8 [45].

[369] This was one of the justifications given by the DPP in May 2012 for not prosecuting a *Guardian* journalist in connection with the alleged receipt of leaked information from a police officer relating to the phone hacking investigation. See <http://www.cps.gov.uk/news/latest_news/charging_decision_in_relation_to_allegations_that_a_police_officer_passed_confidential_information_to_a_journalist_about_operation_weeting/>.

[370] *SKA* (n 350) [89].

[371] *Palomo Sanchez* (n 355) [67].

*Exposure of wrongdoing*  This is a function which, in general terms, can be easily  **11.139**
recognized as serving a legitimate and important purpose. Confidentiality and
privacy will generally not be allowed to prevail over the need to uncover and act
against fraud or forgery, for example. So the court will require the disclosure of
confidential documents needed to investigate serious fraud,[372] and will not prevent the use in litigation of confidential documents which tend to support allegations of forgery and misleading evidence.[373] Similarly, disclosure of the identity
of a confidential journalistic source has been ordered to protect the integrity of
hospital records and to identify and punish the informant, who had breached a
duty of confidence by providing to a newspaper the medical records of a convicted
murderer.[374]

Different considerations may apply when it comes to publication to the world at  **11.140**
large, and it may be necessary to consider whether mass publication, as opposed
to some more limited disclosure, is proportionate.[375] However, the exposure of
crime or serious impropriety is one of the specific categories of legitimate disclosure identified in IPSO's public interest test,[376] and in *X v Persons Unknown* Eady J
gave as examples of public interest speech a disclosure 'for the purpose of revealing
(say) criminal misconduct or antisocial behaviour'.[377] Media publication of allegations of serious wrongdoing was approved in *Jockey Club v Buffham*[378] and *Cream
Holdings v Banerjee*.[379] In *Hyde Park Residence Ltd v Yelland*, Mance LJ said this
principle was of 'obvious significance' to any attempt by the claimants to enforce
an obligation of confidence so as to prevent publication of evidence showing statements made by Mr Mohammed Al Fayed and his employees to be false.[380] In
*Harrods Ltd v Times Newspapers Ltd*[381] the Court considered that proof of wrongdoing by a private company could form the basis for a public interest defence.

---

[372]  *Marlwood Commercial Inc v Kozeny* [2004] EWCA Civ 798, [2004] 3 All ER 648.
[373]  *Istil Group Inc v Zahoor* [2003] EWHC 165, [2003] 2 All ER 252, refusing an injunction to
prevent reliance on documents passing between the applicant and a witness.
[374]  *Ashworth Hospital Authority v MGN Ltd* [2002] UKHL 29, [2002] 1 WLR 2033 (although
the journalist was ultimately held not obliged to disclose: *Mersey Care NHS Trust v Ackroyd* [2003]
EWCA Civ 663, [2003] EMLR 36).
[375]  See 11.111. The injunction in *SKA* (n 350) was framed so as to permit disclosure to the claimant's wife and family but to prohibit media publication. Also *CC v AB* (n 129).
[376]  See 11.118.
[377]  [2006] EWHC 2783 (QB), [2007] EMLR 290 [25]. Note that the DPP's reasoning (n 369)
also included the fact that the articles in question 'were capable of disclosing the commission of
criminal offences'.
[378]  *Jockey Club* (n 75) and see 11.128.
[379]  *Cream Holdings* (n 339) and see also 11.128.
[380]  *Hyde Park Residence* (n 276). 'The events about which he put forward to the public a false
picture were public events. It seems to me therefore that we should approach the present application
on an assumption that Hyde Park can have no claim for, or for inducing or procuring, breach of
contract or for misuse of confidential information' [71]–[73].
[381]  [2006] EMLR 320 (Warren J). The issue did not need to be resolved on the subsequent
appeal: [2006] EWCA Civ 294.

**11.141**    The gravity of the misbehaviour in question will always be an important factor. In *McKennitt v Ash* it was accepted at first instance that 'a very high degree of misbehaviour' must be shown to trigger a public interest defence.[382] The Court of Appeal doubted whether so stringent a test is appropriate,[383] but did not provide an alternative criterion, and the approach that will be taken remains unclear. In *Mosley v News Group Newspapers Ltd* Eady J held that it was not for judges to impose morals, and suggested that even criminal misconduct may not warrant mass publication, if it was not significant, and would not be prosecuted.[384] But in *Terry v Persons Unknown* this part of his judgment was regarded as specific to the facts of that case. It is clear, however, that where there is an express duty of confidence the test of 'public interest' is more stringent; it must be shown that it is in the public interest that the confidence be broken.[385] It is also clear that even where disclosure as such is legitimate the nature and amount of detail provided must be proportionate.[386]

**11.142**    *Correcting the record*    'Preventing the public from being misled' is one limb of the definition of public interest in the IPSO Editors' Code,[387] and in *Campbell v MGN Ltd* the principle that correcting misleading public statements is a legitimate public interest function of the media was acknowledged. The claimant had conceded that the defendant newspaper could legitimately report her drug problem and correct her earlier lies to the media, claiming that she did not take drugs. The Court of Appeal recorded these concessions[388] and made clear that it regarded them as rightly made.[389] This approach was approved by the House of Lords.[390]

**11.143**    Disclosures about sexual infidelity have also been held justified on this ground. In *Campbell v Frisbee* the Court of Appeal held to be arguable a defence seeking to justify disclosure of an affair, on the basis that the claimant had painted a false picture of herself to the public, having (it was said) falsely 're-branded' herself as a reformed and stable individual, evidenced by the fact that she was engaged to be married.[391] In *Theakston*[392] it was held that BBC viewers had a right to know about the off-screen behaviour of the claimant who had sought to burnish his image, and the defendants should be at liberty to correct that false image by publicizing details of his visit to a brothel.[393] There was also held to be a public interest in showing

---

[382] *McKennitt* (n 346) [97] (Eady J).
[383] *McKennitt* (n 282) [69] (Buxton LJ).
[384] [2008] EWHC 1777 (QB), [2008] EMLR 20 [127].
[385] *Terry* (n 311) [97]–[100] (Tugendhat J). See [51] for the public interest test.
[386] See the discussion of the fact/detail issue at 11.169.
[387] See 11.118.
[388] *Campbell* (n 186) [35]–[36].
[389] *Campbell* (n 186) [43].
[390] *Campbell* (n 44) [24] (Lord Nicholls), [82] (Lord Hope). At [58] Lord Hoffmann stated that the claimant 'had specifically given publicity to the very question of whether she took drugs and has falsely stated that she did not'.
[391] *Campbell v Frisbee* (n 72).
[392] *Theakston* (n 23).
[393] Following *Woodward* (n 70).

that the claimant's conduct was inconsistent with the standards publicly set by the BBC for its presenters.[394] Applications for interim injunctions were refused in two 2005 cases after defendants argued that the disclosures to be made would serve to correct or re-balance false public images promoted by the claimants.[395] A central reason for the failure of the claim for misuse of private information in *Ferdinand v MGN Ltd*[396] was the fact that in interviews and his autobiography the claimant had portrayed himself as a reformed family man who had given up the ways of his past, including 'cheating' on his long-term partner. While that image persisted, there was a public interest in demonstrating it was false.

It is necessary to approach this line of argument with a degree of caution. The **11.144** decision in *Campbell v Frisbee* was based on the proposition that the defence there advanced might be supported by *Woodward v Hutchins*.[397] However, as discussed above,[398] that case is controversial, and in particular to the extent that it stands for a broad principle that the media is entitled to publish a wide class of material that shows a claimant in a poor light in order to rebut a favourable image fostered by the claimant. It is likely that the right to set the record straight goes no further than a journalist could consider justified for the purpose of rebutting the particular statements or other representations made. It appears from the House of Lords' decision in *Campbell* that it is not permissible when setting the record straight to add unnecessary intrusive circumstantial detail.[399]

*Scrutiny of authority* Holding public and other authorities to account is undoubtedly **11.145** an important function of the media, and one which can sometimes justify the use and disclosure of otherwise private or confidential information. So much is indicated by Lady Hale's observations in *Campbell* that: 'The free exchange of information and ideas on matters relevant to the organisation of the economic, social and political life of the country is crucial to any democracy.'[400] In *London Regional Transport Ltd v Mayor of London*,[401] the Court of Appeal upheld a decision to permit disclosure of a redacted report on funding arrangements for the London Underground system on grounds of public interest. The Court of Appeal agreed with Sullivan J,[402] who had identified the question of whether the government's Public-Private Partnership financing met a Value for Money test as 'a matter of vital concern to Londoners... the

---

[394] *Theakston* (n 23) [49]–[51], [68]–[69].
[395] *Beckham v News Group Newspapers* (HC, 24 April 2005) (where there was an express contractual confidentiality clause); *Wallace v News Group Newspapers* (HC, 9 May 2005).
[396] *Ferdinand* (n 75).
[397] *Woodward* (n 70).
[398] See 11.21.
[399] See further the discussion of the fact/detail distinction at 11.169.
[400] The full passage is quoted at 11.133. The DPP's May 2012 reasons for not prosecuting the *Guardian* journalist (n 369) also included the fact that the articles in question 'were intended to hold others to account, including the Metropolitan Police Service and the Crown Prosecution Service'.
[401] *London Regional Transport* (n 206).
[402] *London Regional Transport* (n 206) [207].

democratic process, if it is to be effective, must be informed by freedom of information'. Redaction of the report to exclude commercial secrets had protected those interests and any wider restriction on publishing the contents of the report was not necessary, given the substantial public interest in the funding of the Underground.[403] The public's interest in knowing the private thoughts of a member of the Royal Family on matters of political significance has however been held insufficient to outweigh the Prince of Wales' right to maintain privacy and confidentiality in respect of the content of private journals leaked in breach of an express duty of confidence.[404]

**11.146** The extent to which this category of legitimate interest, or public right to know, will justify media disclosure of private or confidential information about private organizations, or their senior executives, is unclear. However, in *Lord Browne v Associated Newspapers Ltd*[405] the Court of Appeal upheld the decision of Eady J to refuse injunctions to protect the privacy of information about alleged misuse of the corporate resources of BP by its then chairman, derived from disclosures made to a lover. The Court observed that 'BP is a large international public corporation with very large numbers of shareholders. This is in our view a relevant consideration in favour of publication of the information in the public interest.'[406] The Court held that the judge had been entitled to deploy the interests of BP, through its shareholders and directors, in support of his conclusion that the public interest in publication might prevail over the claimant's private interest under Article 8.

**11.147** *Public figures* Public figures are entitled to a private life, as most clearly established by the European Court's decision in *von Hannover*.[407] In *A v B plc*[408] the Court of Appeal, while acknowledging that public figures had private lives which would be 'respected in the appropriate circumstances', held that public figures should expect a lesser degree of protection for their privacy[409] and that the fact that the claimant was a well-known footballer and the captain of a Premiership football team created 'a modicum of public interest' in his off-field conduct.[410] The Court was careful to distinguish this principle from the public interest, strictly so-called, although it pointed out that in some situations there could be an overlap between the two principles.[411]

---

[403] The ECtHR has held that Art 10 applies to employment contracts, at least for those in government service: *Vogt v Germany* (1995) 21 EHRR 205, paras 43–4; *Grigoriades v Greece* (1997) 27 EHRR 464, para 45.

[404] *HRH Prince of Wales* (n 129).

[405] *Lord Browne* (n 42).

[406] *Lord Browne* (n 42) [55]. The Court rejected a submission that disclosure to BP itself would suffice. See also *Mosley* (n 384) [122], which can be read as suggesting that if the wrongdoing alleged against the claimant (president of the motorsport regulator the FIA) had been made out, the public would have had a right to know, so that it could judge his suitability for the role.

[407] *von Hannover* (n 325).

[408] *A v B plc* (n 38).

[409] See 5.114–5.120.

[410] *A v B plc* (n 38) [43].

[411] *A v B plc* (n 38) [11 (xii)].

This aspect of *A v B plc* was explained by the Court of Appeal in *Campbell v MGN*   **11.148**
*Ltd* which made clear that the mere fact that an individual has achieved prominence does not mean that his or her private life can be laid bare by the media.[412]
The House of Lords in the same case was clear that the claimant's celebrity and
long relationship with the media did not in themselves give rise to any right to
know about her private life. 'A person may attract or even seek publicity about some
aspects of his or her life without creating any public interest in the publication of
personal information about other matters.'[413]

Strasbourg authority underscores this point, while acknowledging that a public   **11.149**
role may impact upon an individual's privacy rights. In *Craxi v Italy (No 2)*[414]
the Court held that public figures are entitled to the enjoyment of the guarantees
set out in Article 8 of the Convention on the same basis as every other person.
The Court's decision in *von Hannover v Germany*[415] allowed, nonetheless, that the
right of the public to be informed can, 'in certain special circumstances ... extend
to the private life of public figures, particularly where politicians are concerned'.
The Court suggested however that this would only be so in the case of individuals
who performed some official or public role rather than those, like the applicant,
who were of interest because of their birth or relationships. Moreover, the Court
held that publication would only be legitimate if it could be said to contribute to a
debate on a matter of public concern. Strasbourg's approach to public figures has
since developed, however, so as to give greater freedom to reporters.

In *von Hannover v Germany (No 2)*,[416] the Court found that photographs of Princess   **11.150**
Caroline on a private holiday while her father was suffering from poor health could
be justified on the basis that to some degree they contributed to a debate of general
interest since the health of Prince Rainier was a matter of general interest and the
press was therefore free to report on 'the manner in which his children reconciled
their obligations of family solidarity with the legitimate needs of their private life,
among which was the desire to go on holiday'. The boundaries of what constitutes a
'debate of general interest' continued to expand with the decision in *von Hannover
v Germany (No 3)*,[417] ruling that there was no requirement for a link between the
subject matter of the photograph and the article it illustrated. The photograph of the
applicant on holiday, considered in light of the article, was found to contribute to a
debate of general interest, not because it supported and illustrated the information
conveyed, as in *von Hannover (No 2)*, but because it could not be said that the article
was a mere pretext for publishing the photograph. No explanation was offered as
to why the photograph showing the applicant and her husband at an unidentified

---

[412]   *Campbell* (n 186) [41].
[413]   *Campbell* (n 44) [57] (Lord Hoffmann). See also Lord Hope, [120].
[414]   (2004) 38 EHRR 995, para 65.
[415]   *von Hannover* (n 325).
[416]   *von Hannover (No 2)* (n 331).
[417]   App no 8772/10 (ECtHR, 19 September 2013).

location was sufficiently linked to an article which, in the Court's own words, focused mainly on the practical details relating to the villa in another country.

**11.151** *Associates of public figures* In some cases it may be legitimate to disclose information about a person who is not a public figure because of his or her association with someone who is. This was held to be so in *Trimingham v Associated Newspapers Ltd*,[418] where the claimant had been professionally employed by an MP, as well as forming a personal relationship with him. In *AAA v Associated Newspapers Ltd*[419] the public interest in the professional and private life of the claimant's father, a prominent politician, was held to favour disclosure of the fact that the claimant had been conceived as a result of an extra-marital affair. But the mere fact that a person has come to some public prominence as a result of a relationship with a famous person does not of itself put that person's private life into the public sphere.[420] The celebrity of a parent is no justification for disclosures about a child.[421]

**11.152** *Role models* An aspect of the Court of Appeal's judgment in *A v B plc* which deserves separate treatment is its suggestion that if a person is a role model, or 'sets the fashion', that can create a legitimate interest in the publication of private information about him or her.[422] This too was examined further by the Court of Appeal in *Campbell* which did not see[423] 'why it should necessarily be in the public interest that an individual who has been adopted as a role model, without seeking this distinction, should be demonstrated to have feet of clay'.[424] It may indeed seem paradoxical to argue that the public needs to know of the private vices of an outwardly virtuous individual, whose public conduct is treated as setting a socially valuable example. It could, however, be argued that the reason is the public interest in the truth, and that the conduct of others should not be guided, even beneficially, by a false public image, whether or not the individual is responsible for creating that image. The subsequent cases have however involved individuals who have volunteered for positions which make them role models.[425]

**11.153** *Educational value* An argument related to the one just outlined was identified by Lady Hale in *Campbell*, who observed[426] that in one way the article at issue

---

[418] *Trimingham* (n 80).
[419] [2012] EWHC 2103, [2013] EMLR 2.
[420] *RocknRoll v News Group Newspapers* [2013] EWHC 24 (Ch) [16].
[421] *Weller* (n 100) [182].
[422] *A v B plc* (n 38) [43(vi)].
[423] *Campbell* (n 186) [41].
[424] In *Lady Archer* (n 74) the defendant failed in an attempt to justify disclosure in reliance on the observations in *A v B plc* (n 38) about 'public figures' and 'role models'.
[425] The captain of England's football team, and its manager, have been held to be people from whom higher standards of behaviour are expected: see *Ferdinand* (n 75) [89]–[90] and *McClaren v News Group Newspapers Ltd* [2012] EWHC 2466 (QB) [34].
[426] *Campbell* (n 44) [149].

there 'could be said to be educational'. The editor had chosen to run a sympathetic piece 'still listing her faults and follies, but setting them in the context of her now-revealed addiction and her even more important efforts to overcome it'. Lady Hale observed that '[n]ewspapers and magazines often carry such pieces and they may well have a beneficial educational effect'. The argument bears comparison with the 'cautionary tale' justification upheld by Morland J in the pre-HRA case of *Gallagher v Dukes*.[427]

*The freedom to criticize*   The importance of this aspect of freedom of expression **11.154** was stressed by Tugendhat J in *Terry v Persons Unknown*,[428] where he identified it as a counterweight to the valuable freedom 'to live as one chooses'. In a passage quoted and discussed in more detail below,[429] the judge observed that the freedom to criticize the conduct of others as harmful or wrong could generate or contribute to public discussion and debate, and hence to the development of public opinion. His language reflects that of the European Court in *von Hannover*,[430] and the judge was plainly taking a broad view of the notion of matters of public interest or concern. The topic under discussion in *Terry* was an extramarital affair, and the judgment implies that the judge considered it at least arguable that disclosure of the facts could make a contribution to public debate over issues such as the morality or propriety of such conduct.

*The intrinsic value of the right to freedom of expression*   The IPSO Editors' Code **11.155** records[431] that there is a public interest in freedom of expression itself, and in *A v B plc* the Court of Appeal held[432] that the importance of freedom of expression is such that even if there is no specific, identifiable public interest in a particular publication, the fact that publication interferes with private life is not sufficient to outweigh the importance of a free press. The same point was made by Lady Hale in *Campbell,* where she observed[433] that: 'One reason why press freedom is so important is that we need newspapers to sell in order to ensure that we still have newspapers at all.' She added examples of items of personal information which would qualify as private but would have so little weight that the privacy interest would not be strong enough to justify restricting the press's freedom to report, even in the absence of any public interest.[434] It is important not to take as one's starting point that a disclosure always needs to be justified: 'individuals who wish to exercise their rights of freedom of expression do not have to demonstrate that they are

---

[427]   *Gallagher* (n 254).
[428]   *Terry* (n 311).
[429]   Under the heading of 'Responsible Journalism', at 11.173.
[430]   See 11.125.
[431]   At para 2 of the public interest test, quoted at 11.118.
[432]   *A v B plc* (n 38) [11(iv)].
[433]   *Campbell* (n 44) [143].
[434]   'The privacy interest in the fact that a public figure has a cold or a broken leg is unlikely to be strong enough to justify restricting the press's freedom to report it': *Campbell* (n 44) [157].

minding their own business. They can say what they choose, when, and to whom they choose, subject to the general law and the rights of others. In the present case it is only "none of their business" in the eyes of the law if it would interfere with the Art 8 rights of the claimants in a way that is unnecessary and disproportionate.'[435]

**11.156** **Purposes** As noted in Chapter 5,[436] the Court of Appeal has held[437] that the fact that information is obtained for the purpose of publication for profit can be a factor giving rise to or reinforcing a reasonable expectation of privacy. It has also been held that a wrongful purpose may weaken a claim to exercise the right to freedom of expression. In *CC v AB*,[438] Eady J analysed the reasons for the defendant's proposed disclosure of the claimant's adulterous affair with the defendant's wife, observing that he wished to expose and humiliate both participants, for revenge and financial profit.[439] The judge drew a distinction between communication for such purposes and communication to friends and relatives, doctors, or counsellors which would be accorded a high degree of protection.[440] By parity of reasoning, public disclosures which serve a valuable societal purpose will be given greater weight than those which are harmful or of no value.

### (d) Article 8 rights

**11.157** These will be the rights relied on by claimants but, as already noted, they can in principle also support a rival claim to freedom of expression. The right to personal autonomy guaranteed by Article 8 also encompasses a right to choose to impart information about oneself to the world at large, rather than keep it secret or private. Article 8 rights can therefore support a case in favour of media disclosure by an individual of his or her relationship or other dealings with the claimant.[441] Those rights may not carry great weight, however, if the source is unknown and paid for his or her story.[442] Article 8 rights can count in favour of disclosure for another reason: that disclosure facilitates the enjoyment of private or family life by people other than the claimant.[443]

**11.158** Since reputation is now recognized as a right protected by Article 8,[444] it is possible to imagine circumstances in which some justification for a publication that intrudes on another's privacy could be found in a need to protect the reputation of the media informant. Such could be the case, for example, where the claimant had

---

[435] *SKA* (n 350) [98].
[436] See 5.141–5.142.
[437] In *Murray v Express Newspapers plc* [2008] EWCA Civ 446, [2009] 1 Ch 481 [50].
[438] *CC v AB* (n 129).
[439] *CC v AB* (n 129) [28].
[440] Cf the approach in *SKA* (n 375).
[441] *Re Angela Roddy (A Minor)* [2003] EWHC 2927 (Fam), [2004] EMLR 8.
[442] See *Ferdinand* (n 75) [89].
[443] As in *SKA* (n 350), where the claimant had a secret second family: see the discussion at [76]–[77] of the family members' rights.
[444] See 8.38.

him or herself made statements about his or her relationship which the informant wished to correct, or place in a proper context.

### (e) Other Convention rights

**Article 6**  Expression for the purposes of legal proceedings deserves a high degree of protection.[445] Open justice has long been a strong rule of English legal policy, and one of the guarantees comprised in Article 6 of the Convention is the right to a fair and public hearing in criminal or civil proceedings. Open justice serves not only the interests of individual litigants but also the interest of the public in ensuring that the justice system is operated fairly and efficiently. Media reporting of legal proceedings supports that public interest, and the general rule is that everything said in a public court may be reported. These factors all serve as justifications for publication of court reports, even if these involve disclosures of private information.[446] These factors also militate strongly against the imposition of reporting restrictions on court hearings, even where private information will be disclosed that may cause substantial harm to others, and such restrictions will be exceptional.[447]  **11.159**

**Freedom of thought, conscience, and religion: Article 9**  Although this Convention right has not featured in media cases to date, it is easy to imagine circumstances in which a media defendant might wish to rely on it. The media frequently carry critical or otherwise controversial material about religious beliefs or practices, or sexual practices, which may run the risk of intruding into private life in ways that the subjects find objectionable. The important freedom to hold and express views on religious or ethical issues might, in the event of a claim in such circumstances, be a valuable counterweight.  **11.160**

### (f) Non-Convention rights, freedoms, and interests

This section considers rights, freedoms, and interests expressly mentioned in Article 8(2) as potential justifications for interference with the Article 8(1) right to respect for private life which may be pertinent to justifying media disclosures of private information. Few of these justifications have so far been litigated.  **11.161**

**The interests of public safety**  This justification could be relevant, for example, to a media disclosure using personal information to warn the public of some impending danger. Obvious examples include the presence in the community of a dangerous criminal (information about criminal activities being capable of coming within Article 8), or a case of the kind considered in 11.164.  **11.162**

**The prevention of crime**  This is a justification which could be resorted to in a case of the kind mentioned in the previous paragraph. It would also have an  **11.163**

---

[445] *BUQ* (n 353).
[446] See the discussion in 11.71.
[447] *Re S (A Child)* (n 295). For open justice see further ch 13, esp 13.93–13.94.

obvious relevance to the class of investigative journalism which involves under-cover engagement with criminal activities in the course of their performance, usu-ally in collaboration with the police or other authorities.

**11.164** **The protection of health**  On occasion, the media obtain information which may cast doubt on the fitness of health-care workers to carry out safely or competently their health-care duties. Examples include individuals said to be HIV positive, or to suffer from other medical conditions. In *H v Associated Newspapers Ltd*[448] an injunction restraining identification of a health-care worker with AIDS was modified so as to allow identification of the health authority for whom he worked in furtherance of an open debate on issues of public health. The specific legitimate purpose of protecting health identified in Article 8(2) would support a claim that publication of information of this kind is justified.

**11.165** **The protection of morals**  That this justification has not been explored in media cases so far appears somewhat odd on the face of it, given the many cases in which the media's ostensible purpose in publishing private information is to expose moral failings. The inclusion of this justification in Article 8(2) is probably best explained by the fact that Article 8(1), and the Convention as a whole, was origi-nally designed, and is expressed, to confer protection against interferences by the state. In that context, the need to provide that private life can be interfered with to protect morals can easily be understood. Nevertheless, now that the state's positive obligation to afford individuals protection from interference with privacy by other private persons has assumed such importance, this justification must surely be given a correspondingly broad ambit. Although not referred to by Tugendhat J in his remarks on the freedom to criticize in the adultery case of *Terry*,[449] it could be argued that this justification is pertinent to such a case.

**11.166** **Other rights and freedoms**  The 'rights and freedoms of others' referred to in Article 8(2) do not have to be rights which are positively and separately recognized in the Convention. In *Chassagnou v France*, however, the European Court held that 'in such a case only indisputable imperatives can justify interference with enjoyment of a Convention right'.[450] In *R (ProLife Alliance) v BBC*[451] the Court of Appeal recognized that where the rights of others are not themselves Convention rights they are 'less potent as a justification for interference with Convention rights than if they were', but questioned the usefulness of the phrase 'indisputable imper-atives', preferring instead the well-established concept of 'pressing social need', adding 'it is plain that in this sort of case pressing social need will not readily be found satisfied'.

---

[448] *H v Associated Newspapers* (n 134).
[449] See 11.184.
[450] (1999) 29 EHRR 615, para 113.
[451] [2002] EWCA Civ 297, [2002] 2 All ER 756 [52].

## (g) The degree of disclosure which is justified

**The court's approach**    If overriding rights are held to justify disclosure of private **11.167**
information, there may still be a question as to how much may legitimately be disclosed. The reasonable latitude allowed to journalists[452] must mean there is some
room for the media to reach a decision on what degree of disclosure is appropriate
with which the court, with the luxury of hindsight, might not agree. The decision
arrived at must, however, be one that the court can at least conclude was within the
permissible range of reasonable or rational editorial decisions, given the information which was or could have been available to the decision-maker. The right test
may be more stringent than this.[453] Whatever the extent of journalistic latitude
may be, the authorities discussed above[454] make clear that necessity and proportionality have vital roles to play in arriving at the correct or legitimate conclusion
as to the degree of disclosure which is justified. In this context, both considerations
cut both ways, of course. On the one hand, the interference with privacy that is
involved must be necessary and proportionate. On the other hand, as Lord Hope
observed in *Campbell*, it is not enough to say that the exclusion from an article of
certain details would have been reasonable; it has to be shown that the imposition
of liability for *not* excluding them is a necessary restriction on the defendant's
Article 10 rights.[455]

**Relevance**    It would seem important, first, to identify with some care the nature **11.168**
of the public interest which is said to justify disclosure, and then to determine
whether the disclosure at issue is relevant to the fulfilment of that interest. The
materiality of particular details to the requirements of a particular public interest
is highly relevant in the context of media defences to copyright claims.[456] Equally,
the public interest in the prevention of crime could not serve as a justification for
detailed disclosures of private information about a murder victim's family.

**Fact and detail**    It is usually the case that the greater the detail, the greater the **11.169**
degree of intrusion into a claimant's privacy. So, for example, in *Theakston* publication of photographs taken without consent was restrained, even though the
defendant was held to be at liberty to publish the fact and other details of the
claimant's visit to a brothel.[457] In *X and Y v News Group Newspapers and MGN
Ltd*, Butler-Sloss P held that there was no justification for disclosure of the present
names and addresses of the convicted murderer Mary Bell and her daughter, as
there was sufficient information in the public domain for the press and other parts
of the media to be able to comment freely on the relevant aspects of the case.[458]

---

[452]  See 11.66, and the discussion of 'responsible journalism' at 11.173 *et seq*.
[453]  See the remarks of Eady J cited in 11.180.
[454]  See esp 11.134–11.135.
[455]  *Campbell* (n 44) [115].
[456]  *Ashdown* (n 275).
[457]  *Theakston* (n 23) [40]–[41], [78].
[458]  [2003] EWHC 1101 (QB), [2003] EMLR 37 [39], [60(2)].

In *Campbell v MGN Ltd* disclosure that the claimant was a drug addict in receipt of therapy was justified, but not the details of her therapy or a photograph of her leaving a meeting of Narcotics Anonymous.[459] Lord Hope drew attention to the European Court's observation that the more intimate the aspects of private life which are being interfered with, the more serious must be the reasons for doing so before the interference can be legitimate. Lord Hoffmann stated that 'the addition of salacious details or intimate photographs is disproportionate and unacceptable. The latter, even if accompanying a legitimate disclosure of the sexual relationship, would be too intrusive and demeaning.'[460]

**11.170** **Context** In any individual case there may be other factors in play. The level of disclosure which is justifiable in the context of a public interest or overriding-rights defence may be heavily affected by issues of consent, or the extent to which the information is of a similar character to that which the claimant has himself published or authorized,[461] or is otherwise already in the public domain.[462]

*(h) The burden and standard of proof*

**11.171** At the interim stage s 12(3) HRA places the burden of proof on the claimant to show, in most cases, that he or she will probably win at trial. Put another way, this means that where a defendant raises a free-speech justification the claimant must normally show that it will probably fail. Whether this improves the position of the defendant as compared with the pre-HRA authorities[463] is probably a fruitless debate. At trial, it may be correct to say that the position is similar, though an alternative view is that the requirement to conduct a parallel analysis[464] means that neither side bears the burden of proof.

**11.172** At each stage, the question of what needs to be proved to justify disclosure will depend on whether the court's task is to determine objectively whether the disclosure was or would be in the public interest, or whether Article 10 requires a more flexible and media-friendly approach, as discussed in the following section.

**(6) Responsible Journalism**

**11.173** A series of twenty-first century privacy cases suggests that it may no longer be appropriate to consider the question of whether a disclosure is justified in the public interest, or by overriding rights or freedoms, as a hard-edged question admitting of only a single correct answer. A defence of reasonable journalism on a subject of public interest, akin to the defence in defamation, appears to be slowly emerging. Under this defence

---

[459] *Campbell* (n 44).
[460] For Lord Hope's remarks, see *Campbell* (n 44) [117] citing *Dudgeon v UK* (1981) 4 EHRR 149, para 52. For Lord Hoffmann's remarks see [58].
[461] See 11.04–11.30.
[462] *Jockey Club v Buffham* (n 75) [57(v)]; *Barrymore* (n 139) 603.
[463] See 11.97–11.99.
[464] See 11.112 *et seq.*

it would seem that a disclosure on a matter of public interest or concern may be justified as a legitimate exercise of editorial discretion even if the court, when making its own objective assessment, would reach a different conclusion. It is possible that the existence of a reasonable belief that the disclosure is legitimate may have a role to play, as it does in data protection law.[465]

### (a) The public interest defence in defamation

In *Reynolds v Times Newspapers Ltd*[466] the House of Lords recognized the existence of a common law privilege for the publication of defamatory statements which are not, or cannot be proved to be, true where the subject matter is of public interest or concern and the publisher has acted reasonably and responsibly. With effect from 1 January 2014 *Reynolds* privilege is replaced by a statutory public interest defence under s 4 of the Defamation Act 2013. But the common law defence is of relevance to the position in other causes of action for breach of privacy.  **11.174**

*Reynolds* privilege was grounded in the right to freedom of expression. Although the decision was made before the HRA came into force, the Act had been passed and the rights protected by Article 10 featured prominently in the reasoning of the House.[467] Under *Reynolds*, journalistic or other output[468] was protected on the grounds that information of public interest, disseminated responsibly, is information which the public has a right to know.[469] Whether the public had such a right depended on all the circumstances, including the subject matter, status, and sources of the information, its treatment by the publisher, and the extent to which the subject of the information had been afforded a right to comment or respond.[470] The application of these criteria was to be approached in a practical and flexible manner,[471] with due deference to editorial discretion. The defence developed so as to become more favourable to the media,[472] and was recognized as a special form of privilege for the dissemination to the public generally of information on a topic of real public interest or concern.[473] It was clearly capable in principle of applying to the publication of statements about a person's private life.  **11.175**

---

[465] See 11.100–11.101.

[466] [2001] 2 AC 127.

[467] '[The] starting point is now the right of freedom of expression, a right based on a constitutional or higher legal order foundation': per Lord Steyn, *Reynolds* (n 463) 207.

[468] The defence was available 'to anyone who publishes material of public interest in any medium': *Jameel* (n 357) [54] (Lord Hoffmann).

[469] *Reynolds* (n 463) 197 (Lord Nicholls).

[470] See *Gatley on Libel and Slander* (n 15) paras 15.2–15.20.

[471] *Jameel* (n 357) [56].

[472] *Jameel* (n 357) and *Flood v Times Newspapers Ltd* [2012] UKSC 11, [2012] 2 AC 273. Also *Al-Fagih v HH Saudi Research & Marketing (UK) Ltd* [2001] EWCA Civ 1634, [2002] EMLR 215, establishing a sub-species of *Reynolds* privilege for 'reportage'; *Roberts v Gable* [2006] EWHC 1025 (QB), [2008] 1 QB 502 and *Charman v Orion Publishing Ltd* [2007] EWCA Civ 972, [2008] 1 All ER 750, resolving certain issues about the reportage defence.

[473] *Loutchansky v Times Newspapers Ltd (Nos 2, 3, 4, 5)* [2001] EWCA Civ 536, [2002] QB 321, where it was also suggested that *Reynolds* privilege might in reality be an absolute privilege.

*(b) Responsible journalism as a defence in privacy*

**11.176** ***Campbell*: the first signs of a responsible journalism defence**  The first indication that a *Reynolds*-like defence might emerge in confidence or misuse cases can be
detected in the decisions of the Court of Appeal and House of Lords in *Campbell v
MGN Ltd*. The claimant complained of the disclosure of details of her drug addiction therapy, alleging this was a breach of confidence and a breach of duty under
the DPA. The trial judge's conclusion that publication did involve such breaches
was reversed by the Court of Appeal. It was then restored by the House of Lords,
but the reasoning applied at both appellate stages gave explicit recognition to the
need to allow journalists some latitude and discretion in determining whether
disclosure is legitimate.

**11.177** *Trial*  Morland J accorded some recognition to journalistic rights, holding that
since disclosure of the claimant's drug addiction was justified (to correct the record)
then 'clearly . . . balanced and positive journalism demanded that the public be told
that [she] was receiving therapy' for that condition.[474] But the judge dismissed a
submission that the editor's honest belief that he was entitled to publish afforded
a ground of defence, holding that it was 'for the court viewing the circumstances
objectively to determine whether the defendants were clothed in conscience with
the duty of confidentiality'.[475] The judge further rejected the defendant's reliance
on s 32 DPA, holding that the exemption it provides, which is partly dependent on
the defendant's reasonable belief that publication would be in the public interest,
was available only prior to, and not after publication.[476]

**11.178** *Court of Appeal*[477]  Reversing Morland J, the Court unanimously held that the
details of the claimant's therapy were not of any particular significance; journalists
had to be given a reasonable latitude as to the manner in which information which
was of public interest was conveyed; the details were a legitimate part of a journalistic package which it was reasonable to publish in the public interest; the exemption
under s 32 DPA extended to cover the process of publication; and the editor's belief
that publication was legitimate was reasonable, so that the exemption applied.

**11.179** *House of Lords*[478]  The Court of Appeal's decision was reversed by a 3:2 majority, on
the basis that it had adopted an erroneous test (of offensiveness to readers, rather
than to the subject) and underestimated the intrusion involved. However, while
reaching differing conclusions as to the result, the House unanimously agreed on
the need to allow journalistic latitude. It was common ground that the DPA claim
stood or fell with the claim for breach of confidence and, since the DPA defence

---

[474] [2002] EWHC 499 (QB), [2002] EMLR 617 [73]. The point was conceded.
[475] *Campbell* (n 474) [42]. See also [43].
[476] *Campbell* (n 474) [100].
[477] *Campbell* (n 186). See esp [53], [62]–[64], [107], [128], [131], [132]–[138].
[478] *Campbell* (n 44). See, esp on the degree of latitude, [28]–[29] (Lord Nicholls), [63]–[65] (Lord
Hoffmann), [107]–[108] (Lord Hope), [143] (Lady Hale), and [168] (Lord Carswell).

involved the issue of the editor's reasonable belief, the decision could be read as affirming that such belief is relevant to a defence in breach of confidence or misuse. The Court of Appeal's conclusions of principle on the scope and application of s 32 DPA were unchallenged and remain authoritative. The House may be taken to have reversed the Court of Appeal's conclusion of fact that the editor's belief in the legitimacy of publication was reasonable.

### *Mosley*: obiter, a narrow approach[479]

*Editorial latitude and beliefs*   In concluding that disclosure of the claimant's    **11.180**
sado-masochistic sex life was a misuse of private information Eady J considered the way in which the 'public interest' should be assessed, including the relevance or otherwise of a journalist's state of mind.[480] The judge asked himself whether, in the light of the authorities on journalistic latitude, including the House of Lords' decision in the defamation case of *Jameel*,[481] 'some allowance should be made for a different view on the matter'. He concluded that: 'The answer is probably in the negative, because it is only the court's decision which counts on the central issue of public interest.'[482] He acknowledged, however, that 'it could be argued as a matter of policy that allowance should be made for a decision reached which falls within a range of reasonably possible conclusions',[483] and said that against this background: 'There may be a case for saying, when "public interest" has to be considered in the field of privacy, that a judge should enquire whether the relevant journalist's decision prior to publication was reached as a result of carrying out enquiries and checks consistent with "responsible journalism".'[484] These remarks were *obiter*, because the point of law was not argued, the judge did not rule on it, and he held that even if such were the test it was not satisfied on the facts before him. Eady J also noted the remark of Lord Phillips MR in *Campbell v MGN Ltd* to the effect that the same test of public interest should *not* be applied to the 'two very different torts' of privacy and defamation.[485]

*Plurality of opinion*   The defendant argued that the public had a right to know of    **11.181**
the claimant's S&M activities, regardless of whether there was or was not a Nazi element.[486] Some reliance was placed on the adultery involved and it was argued, among other things, that in assessing the legitimacy of disclosure in a diverse society the court should hold that the right to impart and receive information extended to information which a substantial section of the public could reasonably regard as relevant to decision-making about an individual, even if the court's view differed.

---

[479] *Mosley* (n 384).
[480] *Mosley* (n 384) [131]–[141], headed 'Public interest: the journalists' perception'.
[481] *Jameel* (n 357).
[482] *Mosley* (n 384) [137]. See also [135].
[483] *Mosley* (n 384) [138].
[484] *Mosley* (n 384) [140]–[141].
[485] *Mosley* (n 384) [141]; *Campbell*, CA (n 186) [61].
[486] *Mosley* (n 384) [25].

The judge's response was that it was not for the state or for the media to expose sexual conduct which does not involve any significant breach of the criminal law. People might consider such conduct deplorable but 'that does not mean that they are entitled to hound those who practise them or to detract from their right to live life as they choose'.[487] He went on: 'It is important … to ensure that where breaches occur remedies are not refused because an individual journalist or judge finds the conduct distasteful or contrary to moral or religious teaching.'[488]

### *Terry:*[489] **a reconsideration**

**11.182** *Editorial latitude and beliefs* On an application to restrain disclosure about an alleged adulterous relationship of the England football team captain Tugendhat J referred to observations of Eady J in *Mosley*,[490] and cited para 3 of the PCC Code of Conduct and s 32 DPA[491] as sources 'relevant to an argument that the belief of a journalist may be relevant to a defence', remarking that it would be anomalous if the belief relevant to the s 32 exemption were irrelevant in misuse of private information. He found himself unable, on a without-notice application, to hold that such belief is irrelevant.[492]

**11.183** *Plurality of opinion and the freedom to criticize* It might be argued (as it was in *Mosley*) that the approach of Eady J cited above[493] involves a disproportionate restriction on freedom of expression. A different approach was taken by Tugendhat J in *Terry*. In a section of his judgment headed 'The social utility of the threatened speech' the judge declined to accept a submission that the speech was of low value because it revealed no criminality, and hence could not contribute to a debate in a democratic society. He held[494] that the issue was 'what the judge should prohibit one person from saying publicly about another'.

**11.184** Citing observations of Sir John Donaldson MR in *Francome v Mirror Group* to the effect that the media perform an invaluable role 'in exposing anti-social behaviour … and propagating the views of minorities',[495] Tugendhat J continued:[496]

> There is no suggestion that the conduct in question in the present case ought to be unlawful, or that any editor would ever suggest that it ought to be. But in a plural society there will be some who would suggest that it ought to be discouraged…. Freedom to live as one chooses is one of the most valuable freedoms. But so is the freedom to criticise (within the limits of the law) the conduct of other

---

[487] *Mosley* (n 384) [127].
[488] *Mosley* (n 384) [128].
[489] *Terry* (n 311).
[490] *Terry* (n 311) [71], citing *Mosley* (n 384) [135].
[491] See 11.100–11.101. The material in para 3 of the PCC Code is now contained in para 2 of the IPSO Code.
[492] *Terry* (n 311) [72]–[73].
[493] See 11.181.
[494] *Terry* (n 311) [101].
[495] *Terry* (n 311) [102], citing *Francome* (n 207) 989.
[496] *Terry* (n 311) [104].

members of society as being harmful, or wrong...It is as a result of public discussion and debate that public opinion develops.[497]

**Developments**   In *Hutcheson v News Group Newspapers Ltd* the Court of Appeal, **11.185** *obiter,* described this passage as 'powerful'.[498] In *Ferdinand v MGN Ltd* the issue was again the legitimacy of disclosures about infidelity, and other misconduct, on the part of the England football captain—John Terry's successor. Citing the Court of Appeal's characterization of Tugendhat J's observation, Nicol J said,

> I respectfully agree...pluralism has long been recognised by the Strasbourg Court as one of the essential ingredients of a democracy (see for example *Handyside v UK* (1979-80) 1 EHRR 737 at [49]). While I accept that the subjective perception of a journalist cannot convert an issue into one of public interest if it is not...the Court's objective assessment of whether there is a public interest in the publication must acknowledge that in a plural society there will be a range of views as to what matters or is of significance in particular in terms of a person's suitability for a high profile position.[499]

While the evidence of a journalist as to what he or she considered to be in the public **11.186** interest will be taken into account, it is only one factor.[500] The test is an objective one. In *Trimingham v Associated Newspapers,* a harassment case, it was held that information included in a story on a topic of public interest was not actionable, because 'the information was within the range of what an editor could in good faith regard as relevant to the story'.[501]

**Discussion**   It is clear law that a reasonable latitude or discretionary margin **11.187** should be allowed to journalists (and others) in assessing *how much* information it is legitimate, or 'in the public interest', to disclose on a particular topic. So much is established by the House of Lords' decision in *Campbell*.[502] In so ruling, the House relied on two principal sources. First, it was said that the proposition that it is unreasonable to expect that in matters of judgment newspapers will always get it absolutely right, which is the basis of the *Reynolds* privilege in defamation, 'is equally applicable to the publication of private personal information in the cases in which the essential part of that information can legitimately be published'.[503] Secondly, reliance was placed on the Strasbourg Article 10 jurisprudence, notably *Fressoz and Roire v France*, where journalists published tax returns of a prominent industrialist and the European Court held that: 'In essence, that article leaves it for journalists to decide whether or not it is necessary to reproduce such documents

---

[497]   For a critique of this aspect of the decision see P Wragg, 'A Freedom to Criticise—Evaluating the Public Interest in Celebrity Gossip after Mosley and Terry' (2010) 2(2) J Media L 295–320.

[498]   *Hutcheson* (n 368) [29].

[499]   *Ferdinand* (n 75) [64].

[500]   *Abbey* (n 224) [45].

[501]   *Trimingham* (n 80) [338(ii)].

[502]   See 11.179.

[503]   *Campbell* (n 42) [63] (Lord Hoffmann).

to ensure credibility.'[504] The existence of some form of 'responsible journalism' defence in privacy may thus be taken to be established.

**11.188**  In principle it would seem that the media should enjoy latitude in deciding whether it is legitimate to publish *at all* on a particular topic. *Reynolds* privilege permits such a freedom and, provided that the topic is one of legitimate 'public concern', and the information in question is capable of contributing to a public debate on that topic, even the more conservative of the Strasbourg decisions would appear to contemplate that a disclosure of private information may be lawful.[505] *Ferdinand* is authority for the adoption of this approach. The cases so far indicate that the state of mind of the publisher as to whether publication is legitimate may be a relevant factor, but that the test is an objective one, of whether a reasonable publisher in the position of the defendant could properly have taken that view.

**11.189**  The state of public opinion in the society, or section of it, which is to receive the information in question would seem to have some relevance to what a reasonable publisher could consider it legitimate to communicate. The mere fact that there are some in society who condemn particular kinds of behaviour, such as adultery, should not give publishers free rein to communicate to the public at large salacious stories which, in the name of the public interest, amount to 'hounding' those who practise such behaviour. But the law should make allowance for the facts that diverse opinions are sincerely held within society, and that the free flow of information is capable of enhancing the common good, both by reinforcing existing common values, and by contributing to change and development in public opinion. How the state of public opinion should be determined, and how the line should be drawn between 'hounding' and legitimate communication may be issues of interest in future litigation.

### (7) Other Defences

**11.190**  The laws of confidentiality and data protection make available a number of other lines of defence which could be of relevance in a media privacy case. It is suggested that, to the extent that any such defence would avail as an answer to a confidence or data protection claim, it could also be relied on as part of a defence seeking to justify an alleged misuse of private information. Although the causes of action differ in some respects the policy considerations underlying the defences discussed in this section would seem equally applicable to each. The position in copyright would be different, however, for reasons given above.

### (a) Compulsion of law

**11.191**  Disclosure by compulsion of law is an exception to the banker's duty of secrecy identified by the Court of Appeal in *Tournier v National Provincial and Union*

---

[504] (2001) 31 EHRR 2, cited *Campbell* (n 42) [64] (Lord Hoffmann).
[505] See *eg von Hannover* (n 325).

*Bank of England*,[506] and some statutory provisions require disclosure, regardless of any duty of confidence.[507] The DPA provides that disclosures are legitimate if required by law, otherwise than by contract.[508] It is not common for the media to be compelled by law to disclose personal information, but orders for disclosure of sources and the provisions of the Police and Criminal Evidence Act, Terrorism Act, and Official Secrets Act are examples of situations where this may occur.[509] Another is the duty of disclosure under the Civil Procedure Rules, which was a factor held to legitimize disclosure of another's confidential medical information in *Mensah v Jones*.[510] Disclosures under such circumstances could readily be analysed as justified under the exceptions to Article 8(2).

### (b) Lawful authority

A defence of lawful authority was envisaged by the Calcutt Committee, and pro- **11.192** vided for in the draft Bills mentioned above.[511] The exemptions and legitimizing conditions in the DPA contain several which could be categorized under this heading.[512] This aspect of the law has however so far been left unexplored in the laws of confidentiality and misuse of private information.

### (c) Protection of self or property

Disclosure where the disclosing party's interests require it is a further exception to **11.193** the banker's duty of secrecy identified in *Tournier*,[513] and is of general application in the law of confidence.[514] A defence to this effect was included in each of the draft Bills mentioned above.[515] Under the DPA processing which is 'necessary for the purposes of legitimate interests pursued by the data controller' satisfies one of the three requirements of the first data protection principle, except where 'unwarranted in any particular case'.[516] Such defences might be of relevance in a media case where, for example, a newspaper or broadcaster needed to use confidential or private information in order to mount a defence of truth to a libel claim against it.

---

[506] *Tournier* (n 12) 473. See also Toulson and Phipps (n 71) paras 3-168, 3-171.

[507] *eg* the Money Laundering Regulations 2007, SI 2007/2157.

[508] See, esp, s 35(1), sch 2, para 3 DPA.

[509] See 1.87–1.88.

[510] *Mensah* (n 190). The judge also held such disclosure 'necessary' within s 35(2) DPA and hence exempt from the non-disclosure provisions of the Act.

[511] See the Calcutt Report (n 186) para 12.19(e) and App J, cl 3(f), and App K, cl 3(e).

[512] See *eg* s 29 (criminal investigations), s 31 (regulatory proceedings), and sch 2, para 5 (processing necessary for the administration of justice).

[513] *Tournier* (n 12).

[514] See Toulson and Phipps (n 71) paras 3-173–3-181; *Nam Tai Electronics* (n 12) [51]–[61] per Ribeiro PJ. The principle does not, however, justify unauthorized access by one spouse to another's confidential information to ensure that assets are not concealed during financial remedy proceedings: *Imerman v Imerman* [2010] EWCA Civ 908, [2011] Fam 116.

[515] See the Calcutt Report (n 186) App J, cl 3(d) and App K, cl 3(c).

[516] sch 2, para 6(1) DPA.

## D. Defences to Claims for Intrusive Acts

**11.194** Where news-gathering activities by the media involve intrusion into seclusion (or physical privacy as it has been labelled in Chapters 2 and 10), this may give rise to claims for trespass, harassment, or other causes of action.[517] The established law applicable to such causes of action does not in general recognize that the media has any special position, or any special defences available. There is at least one exception to this, but the law appears to be in a patchy state in this respect.

### (1) Cases where the Media Have No Special Defences

#### (a) Trespass

**11.195** A journalist may have an express licence to enter property, and will in any event have an implied licence to enter property, approach, and knock on the front door.[518] Apart from licence or consent there are several recognized justifications for trespass, but none of these would seem to extend, or to be easily capable of being extended, to justification of entry on land by the media in pursuit of a story, whatever the extent of the public interest in the story. The available justifications include such matters as public or private rights of way, easements, entry to abate a nuisance, and necessity. The necessity defence is very narrowly construed, being limited to cases where entry is necessary to preserve life or property.[519] Necessity is no defence to trespass carried out to destroy genetically modified crops on the grounds that these were a threat to public safety.[520]

#### (b) Harassment

**11.196** **Detecting crime**    The prohibition on harassment does not apply where the person who pursued the course of conduct complained of shows that it was pursued for the purpose of preventing *or detecting* crime.[521] This is a public interest defence potentially applicable to some news-gathering activities by the media, but far more limited than the public interest justifications recognized in the IPSO Code[522] or, indeed, the law of confidence.[523]

**11.197** **Reasonableness**    It is a defence to prove that 'in the particular circumstances the pursuit of the course of conduct was reasonable'.[524] This enables a gap to be filled, by permitting the media to contend that it is reasonable in the circumstances to

---

[517] See ch 10 for a fuller discussion of the causes of action that might arise from such activities.
[518] See 10.48–10.52 *et seq* for detailed discussion of this case law.
[519] *Clerk and Lindsell on Torts* (n 1) para 19-57.
[520] *Monsanto plc v Tilly* [1999] EGCS 143.
[521] Protection from Harassment Act 1997, s 1(3)(a), considered in *Brand v Berki* [2014] EWHC 2979 (QB) [44(b)].
[522] See 'The Public Interest' clause of the IPSO Editors' Code.
[523] See 11.77 *et seq.*
[524] Protection from Harassment Act 1997, s 1(3)(c).

pursue or publish a particular story in the chosen way. The statutory provisions must be interpreted and applied with due regard for the Convention right to freedom of expression, and where Article 8 is relied on the tension between the competing rights must be addressed in the way described by the House of Lords in *Re S (A Child)*.[525] Accordingly, the statutory tort does not impose liability unless a legal sanction for the conduct in question is necessary and proportionate.[526] It is however no defence to a claim for harassment by publication, nor is it an answer to a claim for an injunction to prevent harassment, that the information is in the public domain.[527] Nor is truth a defence, if the conduct involves the unlimited imposition of public humiliation.[528] Matters capable of contributing to a debate on a public interest issue may yet amount to harassment[529]

**Criminal liability**    Harassment is one of a number of crimes involving intrusion that could give rise to criminal liability under a statute containing no media exception, and no public interest defence.[530] In such cases the authorities' decision under the second, public interest, limb of the prosecutors' test whether to prosecute should be informed by consideration of the human rights engaged, and whether prosecution is a proportionate response to the conduct alleged.[531] A prosecution pursued without such consideration may be vulnerable to challenge by way of judicial review, as may any resulting conviction.    **11.198**

### (2) Cases where Media Publication May Have Special Defences

There are three causes of action for intrusion where a form of public interest defence may be available: data protection, breach of confidence, and misuse of private information.    **11.199**

#### (a) Data protection

Where a claim is made under the DPA in respect of intrusive acquisition of data by someone engaged in 'journalism'[532] the exemption under s 32 of the Act may    **11.200**

---

[525] *Crossland* (n 36) [78]–[82] (Tugendhat J).

[526] *Trimingham* (n 80) [338(iv)]. Also *Merlin Entertainments plc v Cave* [2014] EWHC 3036 (QB), [2015] EMLR 3 (criticism not amounting to harassment).

[527] See *WXY* (n 178) [100].

[528] Nobody is entitled to impose this on another: *Law Society v Kordowski* [2011] EWHC 3185 (QB), [2014] EMLR 2 [133]. Also, *Brand v Berki* (n 521) [44(c)]. But claims that publication of matter that the defendant contends is true amounts to harassment need close scrutiny: *Merlin* (n 526).

[529] Contrast *Merlin* (n 526) with *Coulson v Wilby* [2014] EWHC 3404 (QB) [52]: 'if there is such a public interest it plainly does not extend to the deeply unpleasant personal abuse and vilification which has been levelled at these claimants'.

[530] See 10.35 *et seq* for other instances.

[531] Decisions are now taken by reference to guidelines issued by the DPP. For a decision not to prosecute a journalist for reports of leaked information about the phone-hacking scandal, relying on those guidelines, see n 369.

[532] 'Journalism' involves the 'communication of information or ideas to the public at large in the public interest' meaning that 'anyone with access to the internet', not just those working for media organizations, can rely on the exception: *Law Society v Kordowski* (n 528) [99], [155].

apply.[533] A publisher may, alternatively, be entitled to rely on the justification under sch 2, para 6, or, in the case of sensitive personal data, the justification under para 3 of the Data Protection (Processing of Sensitive Personal Data) Order 2000.[534] If prosecuted under s 55 DPA a defendant would have a defence under s 55(2)(d) if he or she proved that the obtaining or procuring was 'justified as being in the public interest'. This imposes an objective test, and thus falls short of the exemption under s 32, which requires proof of a reasonable belief that publication would be in the public interest. In consequence, a journalist could be criminally liable for an act which would be exempt from civil liability. Parliament has legislated to correct this anomaly, and to provide journalists with a defence corresponding to s 32,[535] but the amendment has not been brought into effect.[536] While this remains the position it is arguable that the law fails to provide journalists with the latitude that the House of Lords in *Campbell* held to be a necessary element of the correct balance between privacy and freedom of expression.[537]

### (b) Confidence or misuse

**11.201**  **Public interest**   Where the claim for intrusion is brought in breach of confidence or for misuse of private information, for instance in respect of the acquisition of information through surreptitious media surveillance of the claimant, it is arguable that the public interest defence which is established as an answer to claims for breach of confidence by disclosure will in principle be available. In *Malone v Commissioner of Police for the Metropolis*[538] authorized tapping by the police was held by Megarry V-C to be justified because its sole purpose was for the detection and prevention of serious crime. On appropriate facts, at least where the public interest element of a potential story was strong, a similar argument could be advanced in respect of media surveillance. 'Fishing' would be unlikely to be held justified, however.[539]

### Overriding rights

**11.202**  *Articles 10 and 11*   Reliance could also be placed on Article 10 of the Convention, and the important function of the media in a democratic society as a bloodhound as well as a watchdog.[540] Although Strasbourg was historically reluctant

---

[533] See 7.110 *et seq.*

[534] SI 2000/417. For discussion of these provisions see 7.117 *et seq.*

[535] s 55(2)(ca), enacted by s 78 of the Criminal Justice and Immigration Act 2008.

[536] Nor has another amendment to the DPA authorized by the Criminal Justice and Immigration Act 2008, s 77, an increase in the maximum sentence under s 55. In November 2012 the Leveson Inquiry recommended that 'the necessary steps should be taken to bring them into force': vol III, pt H, ch 5, paras 2.93–2.94. At the time of writing however that still has not been done.

[537] See 11.179 and 11.187.

[538] *Malone* (n 93). But see *Francome* (n 207).

[539] See *Mosley* (n 384) [141] where the claimant relied on the PCC Code in support of the argument that the intrusion involved in obtaining the published information was unjustifiable.

[540] *Reynolds* (n 463) 205 (Lord Nicholls).

to see Article 10 as encompassing a general right of access to information,[541] the Court now recognizes a relationship between Article 10 and access to information, such that blocking of access by a public authority may interfere with Article 10 rights.[542] Article 11 may also protect some forms of intrusive behaviour.[543] The Court has held that, in view of the important role of the media in bringing matters of general interest to public attention, undercover filming can represent a justifiable interference with Article 8 rights.[544]

*Article 8(2)*   In public law, surveillance of prisoners' mail has been held justified   **11.203** under Article 8(2) as a proportionate measure for the prevention of crime and the protection of the rights and freedoms and others.[545] This raises the possibility of such a line of argument being run by a media defendant accused of an intrusive wrong which interferes with Article 8 rights.

A potential problem with these arguments based on Convention rights could be,   **11.204** however, that interferences with the right to respect for private life, which surreptitious surveillance undoubtedly constitutes, must, under Article 8, be prescribed by law.[546]

## E.  Defences to False Light Claims

The English law causes of action which fall within the concept of what can loosely   **11.205** be called false light privacy claims are libel (and slander), malicious falsehood, aspects of data protection law,[547] and claims for false attribution of authorship and for breach of other moral rights. All these causes of action, and their limitations in protecting the false light type of invasions of privacy, have been separately considered elsewhere.[548] This section is confined to identifying some of the chief defences.

---

[541] See *eg Guerra v Italy* (1998) 26 EHRR 357; *Gaskin v UK* (1989) 12 EHRR 36.

[542] *Társaság a Szabadságjogokért v Hungary* (2011) 53 EHRR 3, paras 35–9; *Kenedi v Hungary* App no 31475/05 (ECtHR, 26 May 2009) 27 BHRC 335, paras 42–3; *Gillberg v Sweden* [2012] ECHR 569, para 93; *Youth Initiative for Human Rights v Serbia* [2013] ECHR 584, paras 22–4; *Österreichische Vereinigung zur Erhaltung v Austria* App no 39534/07 (ECtHR, 28 November 2013), 36 BHRC 697, para 33.

[543] See *Brega v Moldova* App no 52100/08 (ECtHR, 20 April 2010) (peaceful protest by journalist).

[544] *Haldimann v Switzerland* App no 21830/09 (ECtHR, 24 February 2015).

[545] *R (Szuluk) v Governor of Full Sutton Prison* [2004] EWCA Civ 1426, (2005) ACD 62.

[546] It was the lack of a clear legal basis for telephone-tapping which led the ECtHR to find a violation of Art 8 in *Malone v UK* (1984) 7 EHRR 14 and to the introduction of the Interception of Communications Act 1985; see also *R (Persey) v Secretary of State for Environment, Food and Rural Affairs* [2002] EWHC 371 (Admin), [2003] QB 794. For telephone-tapping by journalists see now the Regulation of Investigatory Powers Act 2000 (1.78–1.79).

[547] The processing of inaccurate personal data may be a breach of the fourth principle under the DPA: 'Personal data shall be accurate and, where necessary, kept up to date.' See 7.67–7.68.

[548] See chs 2 (Nature of the Privacy Interest), 7 (Data Protection), 8 (Defamation), and 9 (Copyright).

## (1) Defamation and Malicious Falsehood

### (a) *The requirement for the statement to be defamatory*

**11.206** **A limiting principle**   It is a cardinal principle of libel law that a statement is only actionable if it is defamatory of the claimant. This is not a defence, but a requirement of the cause of action. It does however function as a limiting principle, and hence a restriction on the utility of libel law as a vehicle for complaining of a false light statement. In US law, a false light claim may succeed if the statement is injurious to feelings even if it is not injurious to reputation. English libel law cannot generally be used in that way. An illustration is *Norman v Future Publishing Ltd*,[549] where the claimant was outraged by the false attribution to her of a joke which she considered racist, demeaning, and out of character. Her claim was struck out because the words complained of were not capable of being defamatory of her. The definition of what is defamatory was tightened by the Defamation Act 2013, s 1.[550]

**11.207** **Ridicule**   The common law recognizes that a statement may be defamatory because it exposes the claimant to ridicule, even if it does not damage reputation. The best known modern example is *Berkoff v Burchill*[551] where the description of the plaintiff as 'hideously ugly' was held defamatory. But such cases are rare,[552] and this aspect of the common law may not have survived the Defamation Act 2013, s 1.[553]

**11.208** **Malicious falsehood**   Occasionally, it might be possible to sue in this cause of action and thus circumvent the requirement to show a defamatory meaning, but the need to prove malice and probable financial loss will usually make this an impractical and unattractive proposition.

### (b) *Truth*

**11.209** In defamation substantial truth is a complete defence.[554] A malicious falsehood claim will likewise fail if the statement is true, even if malicious and financially damaging. Chapter 8 discusses whether rights of privacy may in future have the effect of qualifying the defence of truth in cases where the evidence relied on concerns private and personal matters.[555]

---

[549] [1999] EMLR 325, CA.

[550] Defamation Act 2013, s 1(1) provides that a statement is not defamatory unless it causes or is likely to cause serious harm to reputation.

[551] [1996] 4 All ER 1008, CA.

[552] The judgments in *Berkoff* identify and discuss most of the English, American, and Commonwealth ridicule cases to that date, which include *Cook v Ward* (n 40). Ridicule was also relied on, unsuccessfully, in *Norman* (n 549).

[553] See Price and McMahon (n 113) para 2.43.

[554] Defamation Act 2013, s 2, which applies to causes of action accruing after 31 December 2013 and abolishes the common law of 'justification'. Note that by virtue of Defamation Act 2013, s 2(3) the truth of one statement may be a defence to a claim in respect of another, false one. See generally *Gatley on Libel and Slander* (n 15) ch 11.

[555] See 8.85–8.86.

## (c) Honest opinion

Statute provides that it is a defence to a libel claim that the statement com-  **11.210**
plained of was a statement of opinion which indicated, whether in general or
specific terms, the basis of the opinion, and an honest person could have held
the opinion on the basis of (a) any fact which existed at the time the statement
was published, or (b) anything asserted to be a fact in a privileged statement
published before the statement complained of.[556] The defence is defeated if the
claimant shows that the defendant did not hold the opinion.[557] The common
law defence of fair comment is abolished[558] and, with it, the requirement that in
order to be defensible as comment a statement of opinion must relate to a matter
of public interest. Thus, it may be, the right to comment in defamatory terms on
a person's private life has been enlarged. It does not follow that the defendant
would be immune from liability for disclosing the private facts on which the
comment was made.

## (d) Public interest defences

**Absolute and qualified privilege**  These defences cater for cases where it is in  **11.211**
the public interest to excuse a publisher from liability for defamation even though
the statement complained of is not, or cannot be proved to be, true.[559] The law is
a mixture of common law and statutory provisions and is dealt with fully in the
standard text.[560]

**Publication on a matter of public interest**  The Defamation Act 2013 provides  **11.212**
for this defence, which is available in respect of a statement which was or formed
part of a statement on a matter of public interest, if the defendant reasonably
believed that publishing the statement was in the public interest.[561] In assessing whether such belief was reasonable the court must make such allowance for
editorial judgment as it considers appropriate.[562] The defence applies to statements of fact or opinion.[563] This is the successor to the *Reynolds* defence[564]
which is abolished.[565] The question of how far the law has gone and might go
in developing a similar defence to claims for misuse of private information is
discussed above.[566]

---

[556] Defamation Act 2013, s 3(1)–(4).
[557] Defamation Act 2013, s 3(5).
[558] Defamation Act 2013, s 3(8).
[559] The absolute defence of truth might also be considered to be a public interest defence in the
sense that there is a public interest in exposing the truth: see further 8.33.
[560] *Gatley on Libel and Slander* (n 15) chs 13 (absolute privilege), and 14 and 16 (qualified
privilege).
[561] Defamation Act 2013, s 4(1).
[562] Defamation Act 2013, s 4(5).
[563] Defamation Act 2013, s 4(4).
[564] *Reynolds* (n 463).
[565] Defamation Act 2013, s 4(6).
[566] See 11.173–11.189.

### (2) Data Protection

**11.213** The exemptions, defences, and justifications available to the media if complaint is made of publication without consent in breach of the accuracy requirement in the Fourth Data Protection Principle are for the most part public interest defences, though of a complex variety. They are discussed in Chapter 7.

### (3) False Attribution of Authorship, and Other Moral Rights

**11.214** Chapter IV of the Copyright, Designs and Patents Act 1988 (CDPA) identifies four types of moral right: (i) the right of an author to be identified on published copies of his work; the so-called 'paternity right';[567] (ii) the right of an author to object to 'derogatory treatment' of his work; the so-called 'integrity right';[568] (iii) the right, which is not confined to authors, to object to false attribution of authorship of a work;[569] (iv) the right of privacy in connection with commissioned photographs.[570] The CDPA makes express provision for defences of consent and waiver, although this does not affect the application of the general law of contract or the principles of estoppel.[571] Where relevant, the moral rights are also subject to particular exceptions and qualifications.[572]

## F. Defences to Appropriation of Name or Likeness Claims

**11.215** **Patchwork protection**    As noted in Chapter 3, American law recognizes 'publicity rights'—that is, rights to control unauthorized uses of the name, likeness, and other aspects of the identity of individuals,[573] though such rights are heavily qualified as regards the exploitation of those matters by the media as opposed, for example, to those who exploit the likeness of celebrities for advertising purposes.[574] In English law there are no established publicity rights as such. However, the image is considered to be part of a person's private life under Strasbourg Article 8 jurisprudence,[575] and a variety of English law causes of action may be pressed into service to carry out a similar function to that performed by publicity rights in other jurisdictions. These include contract,[576] hybrid breach of confidence,[577] misuse of

---

[567] s 77 CDPA.
[568] s 80 CDPA.
[569] s 84 CDPA.
[570] s 85 CDPA.
[571] s 87 CDPA.
[572] For a fuller discussion, see 9.81–9.88.
[573] See 3.81–3.84 and 2.47–2.52.
[574] See 3.83.
[575] See 3.23.
[576] *Pollard v Photographic Co* (1889) 40 Ch D 345 (contractual term of confidence).
[577] See 4.07 and 4.25.

private information,[578] data protection,[579] passing off, privacy, and trade marks.[580] Occasionally, libel law[581] or malicious falsehood[582] may provide a remedy. There is, however, no coherent set of principles as to when rights over publicity will be recognized.

**A patchwork of defences**    The defences available in those cases where English law **11.216** affords protection in the nature of publicity rights follow no clear pattern. Under current law the answers available to a claim the purpose of which is to control publicity or complain of the misuse of identity will depend on the nature of the causes of action relied on by the claimant in the particular case. Given that many privacy cases which reach the courts are brought by those with a commercial interest in controlling publicity about themselves[583] it will be necessary in due course to address the question of what defences should be available to protect the public interest in the free flow of information about them.

# G.  Limitation of Actions

Most privacy claims against the media are started promptly, the immediate objec- **11.217** tive being to obtain an interim injunction. But delayed complaints may occur, and there may be good reason for delay; the phone hacking claims of 2011 onwards[584] offer one example. What follows is a summary of the relevant limitation provisions. The primary limitation periods relevant to the various causes of action considered in this book are identified, as are some special rules which might apply. Provisions for the disapplication, extension, or exclusion of the primary periods under pt II of the Limitation Act 1980 are then considered, and the question of publication abroad discussed. For more detail on all these topics readers are directed to the relevant standard works, to which references are given in the notes.[585]

## (1)  Primary Limitation Periods

The following are the primary limitation periods which will apply, subject to the **11.218** special cases, extensions, disapplications, and exceptions identified in Sections (2), (3), and (4) below. In cases of continuing publication, such as in books or on the internet, or in cases of continuous internal 'processing' of personal data, limitation

---

[578] See 5.65, 5.85 *et seq.*
[579] See ch 7.
[580] See 9.97 *et seq.*
[581] See *eg Tolley v JS Fry & Sons Ltd* [1931] AC 333.
[582] *Kaye v Robertson* [1991] FSR 62.
[583] See *eg Douglas*, CA (n 10); *Terry* (n 311).
[584] See 5.97, 5.98.
[585] See generally A McGee, *Limitation Periods* (7th edn, Sweet & Maxwell 2014); *Clerk and Lindsell on Torts* (n 1) ch 32; *Chitty on Contracts* (n 206) vol 1, ch 28; and *Gatley on Libel and Slander* (n 15) paras 19.13–19.21.

will only afford a defence to some period of 'old' publication, save in defamation cases, to which a special rule applies.[586]

### (a) Traditional and hybrid breach of confidence

**11.219** **Contractual claims** Where the claim is based on contract the limitation period will normally be six years from the accrual of the cause of action.[587] The cause of action will usually accrue on the date of the breach.[588] This six-year period will apply unless, exceptionally, the contract is a 'specialty' within the meaning of s 8 of the Limitation Act 1980,[589] in which case a twelve-year period applies.

**11.220** **Non-contractual claims** There is no clear authority as to what limitation period applies. This is perhaps unsurprising, given the continuing debate as to the proper classification of the cause of action.[590] It is suggested, however, that the most likely conclusion is that a six-year period will generally apply. Traditional breach of confidence is not a tort[591] and the general view of textbook writers is that such claims are not directly subject to any of the statutory limitation periods.[592] It does not follow that there is no applicable limitation period. Non-contractual breach of confidence claims may appropriately be regarded as claims for 'an injunction or other equitable relief' within s 36(1) of the Limitation Act 1980. This provides that time limits specified elsewhere in the Act shall not apply to such claims 'except in so far as any such time limit may be applied by the court by analogy'.[593] The doctrine that equity will apply limitation periods by way of analogy is well established. It has been applied by treating a claim for breach of fiduciary duty as analogous to a claim in contract.[594] It is clearly apt to apply to claims for breach of confidence which are, depending on their nature, most closely analogous to claims in tort or contract or both. The alternative approach of not applying any limitation period is unlikely to commend itself to the court.[595]

---

[586] See 11.224.

[587] Limitation Act 1980, s 5.

[588] McGee (n 585) para 10.002; *Chitty on Contracts* (n 206) vol 1, para 28-032.

[589] Generally speaking, a deed. For discussion of the meaning of 'specialty' see McGee (n 585) paras 4.013, 4.036–4.039.

[590] See the discussion at 4.08–4.13.

[591] See 4.11, 13.62.

[592] See *Gurry on Breach of Confidence* (n 71) 357–9.

[593] s 36(1) goes on to speak of applying the statute by analogy 'in like manner as the corresponding time limit under any enactment repealed by the Limitation Act 1939 was applied before 1st July 1940'.

[594] Where concurrent remedies for breach of duty are available in law and in equity the court will apply to the equitable claim the analogous limitation period at law: *Knox v Gye* (1872) LR 5 HL 656, 674; *Paragon Finance plc v D B Thackerar & Co Ltd* [1999] 1 All ER 400, CA, 415–16; *Coulthard v Disco Mix Club Ltd* [2000] 1 WLR 707, 730. Where an equitable claim stands alone the same approach will be taken: *Cia de Seguros Imperio v Heath (REXB) Ltd* [2001] 1 WLR 112, CA, 120–1 and 124–6.

[595] The idea that there might be no limitation period does not appear to have occurred to anyone dealing with the belated confidence claim in *Christofi v Barclays Bank plc* [2000] 1 WLR 937. The Court assumed there was a limitation period and that it had expired: see 948 (Chadwick LJ).

The choice of analogous limitation period will, of course, depend on the nature **11.221** of the confidence claim at issue. The obvious candidates are the six-year periods for tort and contract under ss 2 and 5 of the Limitation Act 1980, though it can be argued that some types of privacy claim are most closely analogous to libel or, where the claim is against a public authority, to a claim under the HRA, both of which attract a one-year period.[596]

### (b) Misuse of private information

Misuse of private information has been held to be a cause of action in tort, sepa- **11.222** rate and distinct from breach of confidence.[597] If so, claims will be subject to the six-year primary limitation period provided for by s 2 of the Limitation Act 1980. If the cause of action were equitable in character, there would be an argument in at least some cases for applying by analogy the one-year limits which apply in libel and malicious falsehood, or the similar limit for HRA claims against public authorities.[598] It has not been decided whether misuse of private information is a tort actionable per se, akin to libel, or one which requires proof of damage of some kind. The correct classification would affect the time at which the cause of action accrues for limitation purposes.

### (c) Claims under the Data Protection Act 1998

The limitation period applicable to a claim for compensation for data processing in **11.223** breach of the data protection principles will be six years.[599]

### (d) Libel and malicious falsehood

The limitation period for both causes of action is one year from the date the cause of **11.224** action accrued.[600] In libel the cause of action accrues on the date of publication of the statement complained of, unless the statement is substantially the same as one that the defendant has previously published to the public; in that case the cause of action is treated as having accrued at the date of the first publication.[601] For those malicious falsehoods which are actionable without proof of special damage[602] the cause of

---

[596] s 7(5) HRA; the analogy was drawn in *Driza v Ministry of Justice* (Edmonton County Court, 19 April 2010, District Judge Silverman).

[597] *Vidal-Hall v Google Inc* [2014] EWHC 13 (QB), [2014] 1 WLR 4155. See 4.05 and 4.11.

[598] See n 596 and text thereto.

[599] Such claims, it is suggested, are for a statutory tort and hence subject to the six-year period provided for by the Limitation Act 1980, s 2: see 7.96. For the proper classification of a claim for breach of a statutory duty, or for compensation provided for by a statute, see McGee (n 585) paras 4.025–4.026.

[600] Limitation Act 1980, s 4A.

[601] Defamation Act 2013, s 8 ('the single publication rule'). The rule does not apply 'if the manner of [the subsequent] publication is materially different from the manner of the first publication': s 8(4). By s 16(6), no account is to be taken of any publication before commencement of the section. This was on 1 January 2014: Defamation Act 2013 (Commencement) (England and Wales) Order 2013, SI 2013/3027.

[602] That is, in cases within Defamation Act 1952, s 3.

action accrues on the date of publication. In other malicious falsehood cases it accrues when the special damage which is an essential ingredient of the cause of action was sustained.[603]

### (e) Copyright

**11.225** It is generally agreed that for the purposes of the law of limitation breach of copy-right is to be treated as a tort,[604] so that the normal tort limitation period of six years from the accrual of the cause of action applies.[605] The cause of action will accrue upon infringement. The CDPA provides for a six-year time limit for claims for delivery up of infringing copies, commencing on the date the copy was made. [606]

### (f) Harassment, trespass to land, nuisance, breach of statutory duty, and wrongful interference with goods

**11.226** A six-year limitation period will apply to each of these,[607] calculated from the date the cause of action accrued. Trespass to land being actionable without proof of damage,[608] time will start to run on the date of the trespass. In the case of nuisance and harassment,[609] damage is the gist of the cause of action so time will start to run when the damage is sustained.[610]

## (2) Special Cases

### (a) Personal injury or death

**11.227** Special time limits apply, under s 11 of the Limitation Act 1980, where personal injury or death is alleged to have resulted from conduct giving rise to a cause of action for 'negligence, nuisance or breach of duty (whether the duty exists by virtue of a contract or of provision made by or under a statute or independently of any contract or any such provision)'.[611] In cases within s 11, where the conduct complained of is alleged to have caused personal injuries, the limitation period is three years from accrual of the cause of action or the date of knowledge if later.[612] Where

---

[603] *Gatley on Libel and Slander* (n 15) para 19.13. The 'single publication rule' (n 601) does not apply, it would seem.

[604] See *Copinger and Skone James* (n 21) para 21-285.

[605] Limitation Act 1980, s 2.

[606] s 113 CDPA.

[607] Trespass and nuisance are unquestionably torts within the Limitation Act 1980, s 2. It is suggested that harassment is a statutory tort and hence within s 2.

[608] At the instance of the person in possession; see McGee (n 585) para 5.003.

[609] Under the Protection from Harassment Act 1997, s 3.

[610] Note that in Scotland a three-year period applies to a claim for damages for harassment, and runs from the later of the date on which the harassment ceased and the date on which the claimant gained actual or constructive knowledge that the defendant was a person responsible or the employer or principal of such a person: see Protection from Harassment Act 1997, s 10.

[611] Limitation Act 1980, s 11(1).

[612] Limitation Act 1980, s 11(4).

death is alleged to have resulted the period is three years from the date of death or the personal representative's knowledge.[613]

It is hard to envisage a media privacy case brought in negligence or nuisance, but there is plenty of scope for cases in which a 'breach of duty' by the media could cause personal injury. The House of Lords has held that 'breach of duty' has a broad meaning in the context of s 11.[614] The definition of personal injuries for the purposes of the Limitation Act 1980 is also broad; the term includes 'any disease and any impairment of a person's physical or mental condition'.[615] It is not hard to see how death or distress amounting to a recognized psychiatric illness might result from a data protection breach,[616] the breach of a contractual or equitable duty of confidence,[617] or the breach of a statutory duty to maintain anonymity.[618] Psychiatric harm could also be caused by misuse of private information, or defamation, and is an ingredient of the tort in *Wilkinson v Downton*.[619] The reasoning of the House in *A v Hoare*[620] would suggest that the shorter limitation period will apply to all personal injury claims save for harassment, which is expressly excluded from the scope of s 11.[621] **11.228**

The result is that with the exception of harassment a shorter limitation period applies to a breach of privacy which results in death or personal injury than applies if the only result is hurt to feelings. Where the special three-year period applies however it is subject to discretionary extension.[622] **11.229**

### (b) Latent damage

A second special regime applies to 'any action for damages for negligence' other than one for personal injuries or death, where facts relevant to the cause of action are not known at the date the cause of action accrues.[623] In such a case the limitation **11.230**

---

[613] Limitation Act 1980, s 11(5).

[614] *A v Hoare* [2008] UKHL 6, [2008] 1 AC 844 (trespass to the person by rape and sexual assault).

[615] Limitation Act 1980, s 38(1).

[616] In 2012 a British nurse committed suicide after Australian radio presenters duped her into providing personal data about the Duchess of Cambridge.

[617] As alleged in *Swinney* (n 238) (disclosure of claimant's identity as a police informer). For cases where injunctions have been granted to prevent such risks see *Nicholls v BBC* (n 59) (new identity of police supergrass); *Venables* (n 161) (new identities of child murderers); *CC v AB* (n 129) (risk of self-harm by wife of adulterer).

[618] Such as the Sexual Offences (Amendment) Act 1992, s 1: see 1.84 and 1.91.

[619] [1897] 2 QB 57, discussed at 10.56–10.58, where a condition which might now be regarded as post-traumatic stress disorder appears to have been caused by a malicious joke.

[620] *A v Hoare* (n 614). The House approved *Letang v Cooper* [1965] QB 232 where Lord Denning MR expressly held at 241 that the term 'breach of duty' in the predecessor statute encompassed 'any breach of any duty under the law of tort' including defamation, and Diplock LJ held at 345 that: 'In their ordinary meaning, the words "breach of duty" ... are wide enough to cover any cause of action which gives rise to a claim for damages for personal injuries...'

[621] Limitation Act 1980, s 11(1A). But not in Scotland: see n 610.

[622] Limitation Act 1980, s 33, as to which see 11.235.

[623] Limitation Act 1980, s 14A.

period is the later of six years from the date the cause of action accrues, or three years from the date of the claimant's knowledge,[624] subject to an overall limit of fifteen years from the date of the negligent act or omission or the damage caused.[625] This regime seems highly unlikely to be held to apply to privacy cases involving the media as in this context the term 'negligence' appears to refer only to the tort of negligence.[626]

### (3) Extension or Disapplication of Primary Periods

#### (a) Children and adults who lack capacity

**11.231**   Children[627] and adults who lack the capacity to conduct proceedings[628] are known for the purposes of limitation law as persons under a disability.[629] Subject to certain exceptions,[630] the rule is that if a cause of action accrues to a person when under such a disability, time does not begin to run until the person is no longer under the disability, or dies, whichever first occurs.[631] When time does begin to run, the limitation period will be the one otherwise applicable to the cause of action. The running of the limitation period is not suspended or interrupted by the onset of mental disability after the cause of action accrues, unless the tort causes immediate unsoundness of mind.[632]

#### (b) Fraud, deliberate concealment, and mistake

**11.232**   Section 32 of the Limitation Act 1980 provides that in cases within these categories the limitation period shall not begin to run 'until the [claimant] has discovered the fraud, concealment or mistake (as the case may be) or could with reasonable diligence have discovered it'. To the extent that it relates to cases of fraud this provision is of limited scope and unlikely to apply to privacy cases concerning the media. The exception is concerned only with cases 'based upon the fraud of the defendant',[633] typically only claims for fraudulent misrepresentation or deceit.[634] Likewise, privacy claims are unlikely to be actions 'for relief from the consequences of a mistake'.[635]

---

[624]   Limitation Act 1980, s 14A(3)–(10).
[625]   Limitation Act 1980, s 14B.
[626]   See *Clerk and Lindsell on Torts* (n 1) para 32-73.
[627]   The term used in the Limitation Act 1980 is 'infant': s 38(2). This means a person under the age of majority, which has been eighteen since the Family Law Reform Act 1969.
[628]   That is '(within the meaning of the Mental Capacity Act 2005)': Limitation Act 1980, s 38(2).
[629]   Limitation Act 1980, ss 28, 38(2).
[630]   For which see Limitation Act 1980, s 28(2)–(3) discussed in *Clerk and Lindsell on Torts* (n 1) para 32-21.
[631]   Limitation Act 1980, s 28(1).
[632]   *Clerk and Lindsell on Torts* (n 1) para 32-21 and cases there cited.
[633]   Limitation Act 1980, s 32(1)(a).
[634]   *Beaman v ARTS Ltd* [1949] 1 KB 550, 558, and 567.
[635]   Limitation Act 1980, s 32(1)(c). The predecessor of this section was held to apply only where the mistake is an essential ingredient of the cause of action: *Phillips-Higgins v Harper* [1954] 1 QB 411, CA. See, however, *Parkin v Alba Proteins Ltd* [2013] EWHC 2036 (QB).

The third exception under s 32 applies to cases where 'any fact relevant to the [claimant's] right of action has been deliberately concealed from him by the defendant'.[636] 'Deliberate concealment' includes cases where a deliberate breach of duty is committed in circumstances where it is unlikely to be discovered for some time.[637] If 'breach of duty' in this context bears the broad meaning attributed to it in *A v Hoare*,[638] s 32 would seem applicable to phone hacking, or other intrusive surveillance carried on surreptitiously by the media.[639]

**11.233**

### (c) Discretionary disapplication

**Defamation and malicious falsehood**   The court has a discretion under s 32A of the Limitation Act 1980 to disapply the one-year primary limitation period 'if it appears to the court that it would be equitable' to do so.[640]

**11.234**

**Personal injuries and death**   Where a breach of privacy causes personal injuries or death[641] the provisions of s 33 of the Limitation Act 1980 may apply. These are similar to the provisions of s 32A in providing a discretion to disapply the primary limitation period 'if it appears to the court that it would be equitable'. The list of factors to be taken into account by the court is, however, rather more extensive, and there is a much greater body of authority as to the exercise of the discretion.[642]

**11.235**

**Other cases**   Section 7(5)(b) HRA gives the court a discretion to extend time for a claim under s 6 where it is equitable to do so. However, apart from ss 32A and 33 of the 1980 Act, considered in the two previous paragraphs, there is at present no other provision permitting the court to disapply any primary limitation period of relevance to privacy claims against the media.

**11.236**

### (4) Breach of Privacy Committed Abroad

### (a) Cases where foreign law applies

Where the English court has jurisdiction to entertain a claim in respect of a breach of privacy committed by the media abroad[643] it is likely that the court will have to apply foreign law.[644] In any case where it does so the Foreign Limitation Periods

**11.237**

---

[636] Limitation Act 1980, s 32(1)(b). See *Cave v Robinson Jarvis and Rolf* [2002] UKHL 18, 2003] 1 AC 384.

[637] Limitation Act 1980, s 32(2).

[638] *A v Hoare* (nn 614, 620).

[639] See generally ch 10.

[640] For the proper approach to the exercise of the discretion see *Steedman v BBC* [2001] EWCA Civ 1534, [2002] EMLR 17, reaffirmed by the Court of Appeal in the teeth of a challenge to its correctness in *Brady v Norman* [2011] EWCA Civ 107, [2011] EMLR 16.

[641] See 11.227–11.228.

[642] For discussion of these authorities see *Clerk and Lindsell on Torts* (n 1) paras 32-54–32-67. In view of *A v Hoare* (n 614) it would seem that s 33 would permit discretionary extension of time for all privacy claims involving personal injury or death: see n 620.

[643] See 13.56–13.65.

[644] See 13.82–13.92.

Act 1984 requires the court to apply the law of limitation of the relevant foreign jurisdiction.

### (b) The general rule and the exceptions

**11.238**  The general rule provided for by s 1 of the Foreign Limitation Periods Act 1984 is that:

> ...where in any action or proceeding in a court in England and Wales the law of any other country falls...to be taken into account in the determination of any matter...the law of that country relating to limitation shall apply in respect of that matter...and...the law of England and Wales shall not so apply.

**11.239**  There are three exceptions. The rule does not apply to a matter in the determination of which both English law and foreign law fall to be taken into account.[645] Secondly, foreign limitation law will not be applied to the extent it conflicts with public policy.[646] Thirdly, any provision of the foreign law which provides for the extension or interruption of the limitation period on the grounds that a party is absent from a specified jurisdiction is to be disregarded.[647]

### (c) Application to media privacy claims: general

**11.240**  **The general position**   Most claims in respect of breaches of privacy committed abroad are likely to be determined by reference only to the relevant foreign law, for reasons explained in Chapter 13.[648] They will therefore be subject to the general rule stated above, and only the foreign limitation law will apply.

**Exceptions**

**11.241**  *Contract*   The law applicable to a contract is determined by the Rome I Regulation[649] by which the parties' choice of applicable law will generally be respected and, in the absence of a choice, the law applicable to the contract will be the law of the country of residence of the principal actor carrying out the contract.[650] The result of applying these rules may well be different from that which would be arrived at by applying the rules for torts.[651] The applicable limitation period will be governed by the proper law of the contract, determined by these rules.

**11.242**  *Defamation*   The common law 'double actionability' rule still applies to a defamation claim, a term which, for this purpose, includes malicious falsehood.[652]

---

[645] Foreign Limitation Periods Act 1984, s 1(1)(b) and (2). Defamation claims are such matters: see 13.85, text to n 253.

[646] Foreign Limitation Periods Act 1984, s 2(1). This will be so to the extent that the application of the foreign limitation law 'would cause undue hardship to a person who is, or might be made, a party to the action or proceedings': s 2(2).

[647] Foreign Limitation Periods Act 1984, s 2(3).

[648] See 13.82–13.92.

[649] Council Regulation (EC) 593/2008 on the law applicable to contractual obligations [2008] OJ L177/6.

[650] For further detail see 13.83.

[651] Though the application of the law identified in this way is subject to disapplication in certain circumstances: see 13.83.

[652] See 13.84–13.85.

The result is that an action for libel, slander, or malicious falsehood in respect of a foreign publication can be brought in England and Wales only if the publication is actionable both by English law and by the law of the place of publication.[653] The effect as regards limitation is that, subject to the exceptions identified above, a defamation claim in respect of foreign publication is barred if an action in the foreign country would be time barred under the foreign limitation law,[654] at least if the publication is in a jurisdiction not subject to the Brussels and Lugano Conventions[655] or the EC Judgments Regulation.[656]

---

[653] *Ibid*, and see 13.90. Note that the position may however differ in a case where the Electronic Commerce (EC Directive) Regulations 2002, SI 2002/2013 apply: Lord Collins et al (eds), *Dicey, Morris and Collins on the Conflict of Laws* (15th edn, Sweet & Maxwell 2014) paras 35-157–35-162.

[654] See *Dicey, Morris and Collins* (n 653) para 7-058. See also the discussion in *Metall und Rohstoff A-G v Donaldson Lufkin* [1990] 1 QB 391, CA, and McGee (n 585) para 25.003.

[655] Brussels Convention on the Jurisdiction and Enforcement of Judgments in Civil and Commercial Matters, 27 September 1968, TS 10 (1988), Cm 306; Lugano, 16 September 1988, TS 53 (1992), Cm 20013. See M Tugendhat, 'Media law and the Brussels Convention' (1997) 113 LQR 360 and A Briggs, 'Two undesirable side effects of the Brussels Convention' (1997) 113 LQR 364. The regime has been updated by the Lugano Convention of 2007, which came into force on 1 January 2010 and makes minor and technical changes, implemented in England and Wales by the Civil Jurisdiction and Judgments Regulations 2009, SI 2009/3131.

[656] Council Regulation 44/2001/EC, otherwise known as 'Brussels I'.

# Part V

## REMEDIES AND SANCTIONS

# 12

## REMEDIES AND SANCTIONS

*Matthew Nicklin QC and Chloe Strong*

## A. Introduction

This chapter considers the legal remedies that may be available to those who com- **12.01** plain that an invasion of their privacy has occurred or is threatened by the actions of the media, as well as touching briefly on the criminal sanctions that may be applicable. Regulatory remedies under the Data Protection Act are considered in Chapter 7 and the remedies available from the media regulators in Chapter 14. Whether a remedy is sought before or after publication, and whether the complaint relates to the content of an actual or proposed publication or the method by which personal information has been obtained,[1] it is likely that any relief granted will affect the exercise of the right to freedom of expression enshrined in Article 10 of the European Convention on Human Rights (ECHR).[2] In such circumstances

---

[1] For consideration of issues relating to methods of newsgathering which may infringe a privacy right see ch 10.

[2] European Convention for the Protection of Human Rights and Fundamental Freedoms (Rome, 4 November 1950, TS 71 (1953), Cmd 8969).

s 12 of the Human Rights Act 1998 (HRA) applies.[3] The interpretation given to this important statutory provision by the courts is considered in Section C, but this chapter begins by looking at Parliament's intention in enacting s 12. This is not necessarily to suggest that courts should have regard to such material as an aid to construction under the rule in *Pepper v Hart*[4] but rather to explain the legislative background to this highly relevant provision.

## B. Human Rights Act 1998, s 12

### (1) Background

**12.02**  Specific provision regarding freedom of expression was not included in the Human Rights Bill when it was introduced in the House of Lords in November 1997, so there is no material in the government's White Paper *Rights Brought Home*[5] or other consultation document on what was to become s 12. The section was introduced following concerns raised by Lord Wakeham, then chairman of the Press Complaints Commission (PCC), during the passage of the Bill through the Lords that, absent express provision to the contrary, the HRA would introduce a law of privacy and undermine the system of self-regulation favoured by the media. Following confirmation from the Lord Chancellor that, contrary to his earlier opinion, the PCC was likely to be considered a 'public authority' within the meaning of s 6,[6] a number of draft clauses were put forward to safeguard the media's position. One would have exempted the PCC from the scope of the Bill altogether; one would have required the court to make a report to Parliament whenever it was proposing to grant a remedy for breach of Article 8 for which there was no existing remedy; and another would have required the court normally to give precedence to rights under Article 10 whenever there was a conflict between it and Article 8. The government did not favour any of these proposals and instead promised to introduce its own clause to protect the interests of the media.[7]

**12.03**  The Home Secretary first set out the components of the intended new clause on Second Reading of the Bill in the House of Commons.[8] At that stage it was

---

[3] In addition, of course, to the other provisions of the HRA, including ss 2, 3, and 6.

[4] *Pepper (Inspector of Taxes) v Hart* [1993] AC 593, HL: the court may have regard to parliamentary material as an aid to statutory construction where: (i) legislation is ambiguous or obscure or leads to an absurdity; (ii) the material relied upon consists of one or more statements by a Minister or promoter of the Bill together if necessary with such other parliamentary material as is necessary to understand such statements and their effect; and (iii) the statements relied upon are clear.

[5] Home Office, *Rights Brought Home: The Human Rights Bill (1997)* (Cm 3782, 1997).

[6] For the implications of that see 14.159 *et seq*.

[7] An equivalent provision in respect of the right to freedom of thought, conscience, and religion was also introduced to protect the interests of religious organizations. This became s 13 HRA, consideration of which is outside the scope of this book.

[8] *Hansard*, HC, vol 306, col 775 (16 February 1998).

envisaged that the clause would relate specifically to the media (and the press in particular), would concern the relationship between Articles 8 and 10 and, in the case of journalistic, literary, or artistic material, would require the court to consider, amongst other things, whether a newspaper had acted fairly and reasonably.[9] 'Provisions along those lines' the Home Secretary said:

> ...would not be inconsistent with the Convention, but would send a powerful signal to the United Kingdom courts that they should be at least as circumspect as judgments of the European Court of Human Rights have been about any action that would give the Article 8 rights any supremacy over the freedom of expression rights in Article 10.

Asked whether that meant the clause would also ensure that Article 10 did not have supremacy over Article 8, the Home Secretary said that he could not confirm that 'because to do so would plainly make the safeguards entirely circular, and we do not want to do that'.[10] By the time the clause was introduced in Committee, however, all those aspects of the intended clause identified above had been dropped. The new clause related generally to the right to freedom of expression (and not only where that right is exercised by the media), did not mention Article 8 or any other limitations on the right to freedom of expression specifically, and did not require the court to consider whether a journalist had acted reasonably or fairly. There were no amendments to the clause prior to its enactment as s 12 HRA.

### (2)  Section 12(1)

Section 12(1) provides:                                                                                     **12.04**

> (1)  This section applies if a court is considering whether to grant any relief which, if granted, might affect the exercise of the Convention right to freedom of expression.

The Home Secretary explained that the section would apply in any case where a court[11] is considering granting relief—for example an injunction restraining a threatened breach of confidence or any relief apart from that relating to criminal proceedings[12]—which might affect the exercise of the Article 10 right to freedom of expression. He confirmed that it applies to the press, broadcasters, or anyone whose right to freedom of expression might be affected and that it is not limited to cases to which a public authority is a party. In that context he added 'we have taken the opportunity to enhance press freedom in a wider way than would arise simply from the incorporation of the Convention into our domestic law'.[13] Clearly this suggests that the section as a whole was intended to add something to the

---

[9] For a critique of the deficiencies of such an approach see R Singh, 'Privacy and the media after the Human Rights Act' [1998] EHRL Rev 712, 726–9.

[10] *Hansard* (n 8) cols 775–6.

[11] Court includes a tribunal by virtue of s 12(5).

[12] s 12(5) defines 'relief' as including any remedy or order (other than in criminal proceedings).

[13] *Hansard*, HC, vol 315, col 536 (2 July 1998).

protection of freedom of expression which the mere inclusion of Article 10 in the list of Convention rights did not achieve. It would seem that particular attention was being drawn to the protection of that right in actions between private parties, presumably beyond that which is occasioned by the inclusion of the courts within the definition of public authorities in s 6.[14]

### (3) Section 12(2)

**12.05** Section 12(2) provides:

> (2) If the person against whom the application for relief is made ('the respondent') is neither present nor represented, no such relief is to be granted unless the court is satisfied—
> (a) that the applicant has taken all practicable steps to notify the respondent;
> or
> (b) that there are compelling reasons why the respondent should not be notified.

While on the face of it this subsection is applicable to all stages of proceedings, it is clearly of most relevance to interim applications. The Home Secretary explained that this provision was intended overall to ensure that without notice injunctions are granted only in exceptional circumstances. He expressed the view that, even where both parties are represented, injunctions restraining free speech would continue to be rare. He envisaged that, in the case of broadcasting authorities and the press, rarely would an applicant not be able to serve notice of the proceedings on the respondent. As an example of compelling reasons why the respondent should not be notified he suggested a case raising issues of national security where the mere knowledge that an injunction was being sought might cause the respondent to publish the material immediately. He added that he did not anticipate that that limb would be used often. It was generally agreed that s 12(2) was aimed at restating and reinforcing the position under existing law and practice.[15]

### (4) Section 12(3)

**12.06** Section 12(3) provides:

> (3) No such relief is to be granted so as to restrain publication before trial unless the court is satisfied that the applicant is likely to establish that publication should not be allowed.[16]

---

[14] See also *Hansard* (n 13) col 553, where the Home Secretary insisted 'the new clause is [in] no sense a gesture. Anyone who reads it can see that it provides important *substantive* and procedural safeguards for those seeking to rely on Article 10 rights' (emphasis added).

[15] See eg the contribution of Edward Garnier QC MP in *Hansard* (n 13) cols 549–54 and the response of the Under Secretary of State for the Home Dept at col 561: 'The provisions in subsections (4) and, especially (2), offer safeguards. The honourable and learned Gentleman [Mr Garnier] says that those safeguards are acknowledged to some extent in the practice of the courts, but now they will be acknowledged in statute, and the added clarity in the law will give them substance.'

[16] On how the courts have interpreted 'likely', and the exercise to be carried out when a court is considering both Arts 8 and 10, see 12.46–12.52.

It is perhaps in relation to this subsection, which only relates to interim relief, that the clearest indication of its intended effect is discernible from the parliamentary debates. The Home Secretary said that this clause provided that no such relief is to be granted to restrain publication pending a full trial of the issues unless 'the court is satisfied that the applicant is likely to succeed at trial'.[17] Having referred to Strasbourg jurisprudence on prior restraint[18] he went on: 'we believe that the courts should consider the merits of an application when it is made and should not grant an interim injunction simply to preserve the *status quo ante* between the parties'.[19] After some discussion of the extent to which this changed the existing test for interim relief in freedom of expression cases, the Home Secretary said:

> The existing law in this area in Scotland is different from that in England and Wales. The Scottish courts, in considering whether to grant an interim order restraining publication, will take account of the relative strengths of the case put forward by each party. A Scottish court would be unlikely to grant an interim order unless it was already satisfied that the applicant was likely to establish his case. Therefore, subsection (3) is technically unnecessary in Scotland. It remains true, however, that media activities cross boundaries of the separate jurisdictions in the United Kingdom... For that reason, and because it is right in principle, we believe that the safeguards for freedom of expression contained in the new clause should apply throughout the United Kingdom.[20]

This is the clearest statement that the purpose of s 12(3) was to bring the law of **12.07** England and Wales on interim injunctions into line with the law in Scotland.[21] The best-known exposition of the law in Scotland prior to entry into force of the

---

[17] *Hansard* (n 13) col 536. In *Cream Holdings v Banerjee* [2003] EWCA Civ 103, [2003] Ch 650 the Court of Appeal had regard to parliamentary material which it requested of the parties after the conclusion of the hearing in order to interpret s 12(3) HRA. The Court was referred to the Home Secretary's remarks in HC Deb 2 July 1998, vol 315, col 536 but not to the passage from col 538 (cited in this paragraph) comparing the position in Scots law. Had it been so the Court might have had more difficulty in reconciling the lower threshold test which it ultimately held applies ('real prospect of success') with the words of Lord Fraser in *NWL Ltd v Woods* [1979] 3 All ER 614, HL, 628 cited in 12.07 (incorporated by reference in the Home Secretary's allusion to the pre-HRA 1998 position in Scotland) that a party had to be 'very likely' to succeed at trial if it was to obtain interim relief. In *Cream Holdings v Banerjee* [2004] UKHL 44, [2005] 1 AC 253 [15]–[20] various statements were made concerning the parliamentary intention which lay behind s 12(3) (without specific reference to any particular passages of *Hansard*) which led their Lordships to the conclusion that: 'The intention of Parliament must be taken to be that "likely" should have an extended meaning which sets as a normal prerequisite to the grant of an injunction before trial a likelihood of success at the trial higher than the commonplace *American Cyanamid* standard of "real prospect" but permits the court to dispense with this higher standard where particular circumstances make this necessary.'

[18] In particular the passage from the *Spycatcher* case: 'News is a perishable commodity and to delay its publication for even a short period may well deprive it of all its value and interest': *Observer and Guardian v UK* (1992) 14 EHRR 153, 191.

[19] *Hansard* (n 13) col 536.

[20] *Hansard* (n 13) col 538.

[21] Though it was not cited to the Court of Appeal in *Cream Holdings*, CA (n 17).

HRA is to be found in the judgment of Lord Fraser in *NWL Ltd v Woods*[22] where he said:

> The relevant difference between English law on interlocutory injunctions and Scots law on the very similar remedy of interim interdict can be appreciated by reference to the decision of this House in *American Cyanamid Co v Ethicon Ltd*,[23] a decision which does not apply to Scotland. In that case this House laid down that the court in exercising its discretion as to granting or refusing an interlocutory injunction ought not to weigh up the relative strengths of the parties' case on the evidence (necessarily incomplete) available at the interlocutory stage. Lord Diplock, with whose speech the other four noble and learned Lords agreed, said:[24]
>
>> 'the court no doubt must be satisfied that the claim is not frivolous or vexatious; in other words, that there is a serious question to be tried. It is no part of the court's function at this stage of the litigation to try to resolve conflicts of evidence on affidavit as to facts on which the claims of either party may ultimately depend nor to decide difficult questions of law which call for detailed argument and mature consideration. These are matters to be dealt with at the trial.'
>
> In Scotland the practice is otherwise, and the court is in use to have regard to the relative strength of the cases put forward in averment and argument by each party at the interlocutory stage as one of many factors that may go to make up the balance of convenience. That is certainly in accordance with my own experience as Lord Ordinary, and I believe the practice of other judges in the Court of Session was the same. Whether the likelihood of success should be regarded as one of the elements of the balance of convenience or as a separate matter seems to me an academic question of no real importance, but my inclination is in favour of the former alternative. It seems to make good sense; if the pursuer or petitioner appears very likely to succeed at the end of the day, it will tend to be convenient to grant interim interdict and thus prevent the defender or respondent from infringing his rights, but if the defender or respondent appears very likely to succeed at the end of the day it will tend to be convenient to refuse interim interdict because an interim interdict would probably only delay the exercise of the defender's legal rights.

**12.08**  As Lord Fraser went on to note, reported cases on this matter are not easy to find because applications for interim interdict are usually disposed of quickly without full opinions being giving, but the authorities he went on to cite[25] would appear to support his statement of the law. Reported Scottish cases since *NWL Ltd v Woods* are more mixed in their approach to the grant of injunctions.[26]

---

[22] *NWL Ltd* (n 17) 628.

[23] [1975] AC 396.

[24] *American Cyanamid* (n 23) 407.

[25] *General Assembly of the Free Church of Scotland v Johnston* (1905) 7 F (Ct of Sess) 517, 522; *Edinburgh Magistrates v Edinburgh etc Railway Co* (1847) 19 Scot Jur 421, 426; *Chill Foods (Scotland) Ltd v Cool Foods Ltd*, 1977 SLT 38, OH, 39.

[26] In *Fairburn v SNP* 1980 SLT 149, OH, for example, interim interdict was granted against an alleged defamatory statement which was about to be published because the defendant was unable to put forward a *prima facie* case of veritas (justification). See also *McMurdo v Ferguson* 1993 SLT 193, OH. In both cases the Court considered that the balance of convenience lay in favour of protecting the claimant's reputation and that damages would not be an adequate remedy. In *Kwik-Fit Euro Ltd v Scottish Daily Record* 1987 SLT 226, OH, on the other hand, interim interdict was refused even though it would have been difficult to calculate the claimant's exact loss. However, it was material

## (5) Section 12(4)

Section 12(4) provides: **12.09**

> (4) The court must have particular regard to the importance of the Convention right to freedom of expression and, where the proceedings relate to material which the respondent claims, or which appears to the court, to be journalistic, literary or artistic material (or to conduct connected with such material), to—
>   (a) the extent to which—
>     (i) the material has, or is about to, become available to the public; or
>     (ii) it is, or would be, in the public interest for the material to be published;
>   (b) any relevant privacy code.

The first part of this subsection has, perhaps, created the most uncertainty as to its precise meaning and it is unfortunate that no minister gave a clear statement of the intended effect of requiring the courts to have 'particular regard' to the importance of the right to freedom of expression. While at the same time asserting that the section as a whole added something of substance to the HRA,[27] the Home Secretary emphasized on more than one occasion that s 12(4) was intended to be consistent with Strasbourg jurisprudence.[28] Were this the case then it would not strictly be necessary given s 2 HRA which requires the courts to take into account any relevant Strasbourg jurisprudence in determining a question that has arisen in connection with a Convention right. Were it otherwise then s 3 HRA would require it to be read and given effect in a way which is compatible with Convention rights.

Perhaps the only proposition that can be stated with certainty from the par-  **12.10** liamentary debates is that the 'particular regard' provision was not intended to give precedence to freedom of expression over other competing rights. This comes from the government's rejection of an opposition amendment that would have provided that in a case where a court had to decide between a claim under Article 8 and a claim under Article 10, it should normally give precedence to the Article 10 rights. The Home Secretary said that the problem with that clause was that it went further than the terms of the Convention and Strasbourg case law: 'nothing in the Convention suggests that any one right should normally be given precedence over any other right'.[29] Preferring the government's formula he

---

that the same defamatory allegation had already been published and the defendant had held a press conference to rebut it. Since entry into force of the HRA, when considering whether to grant interim interdict Scottish courts have had regard to s 12(3) as interpreted by the House of Lords in *Cream Holdings*, HL (n 17) so that now one unified standard applies throughout the UK: see *X v BBC* 2005 SLT 796, OH; *Response Handling Ltd v BBC* 2008 SLT 51, OH; and 3.140–3.151.

[27]  See *Hansard* (n 14).
[28]  *eg Hansard*, HC, vol 306, cols 776–7 (16 February 1998).
[29]  *Hansard* (n 13) col 542. The requirement in s 3 HRA to read and give effect to legislation (including the HRA itself) in a way that is compatible with Convention rights might itself have prevented the new clause from having this effect.

went on: 'so far as we are able, in a manner consistent with the Convention and its jurisprudence, we are saying that whenever there is a clash between Article 8 rights and Article 10 rights, [the courts] must pay particular *attention* to the Article 10 rights' (emphasis added).[30]

**12.11** Clearer statements on the intended effect of the rest of s 12(4) were made in the course of the parliamentary debates. As regards s 12(4)(a)(i) the Home Secretary said that if the court and the parties to the proceedings knew that a story would shortly be published anyway, for example in another country or on the internet, that must affect the decision whether it is appropriate to restrain publication by the print or broadcast media in this country.[31] He cited the example of information being fully public in newspapers in Scotland making the notion of an injunction covering only England and Wales 'risible' but said that the fact that information was available 'across the globe in very narrow circumstances would not be weighed in the balance'.[32] He stressed that, ultimately, what weight to attach to any particular factors would be a matter for the courts to decide based on common sense and proportionality.

**12.12** Concerning s 12(4)(b) the Home Secretary identified the (then) relevant privacy codes as being, depending on the circumstances, the newspaper industry code operated by the PCC, the Broadcasting Standards Commission (BSC) code, the Independent Television Code (ITC), or a broadcaster's internal code such as that operated by the BBC.[33] He added that the fact that a newspaper had complied with the terms of the code operated by the PCC—or conversely, that it had breached the code—is one of the factors that the courts should take into account in considering whether to grant relief. What effect compliance with the code should have on the courts' attitude to granting relief is explained by his subsequent reference to a newspaper getting the 'benefit' of s 12(4)(b):[34]

> Plainly, the higher the conduct required, the better for the public and—this is why the provision creates a virtuous circle—the better the defence available under the new clause to a newspaper, should it be subject to an application for relief, for example, under Article 8.

**12.13** This is a clear indication that compliance with a strongly worded code is intended to discourage the courts from granting relief notwithstanding, it would seem, the fact that the media regulators cannot provide effective legal remedies for breach

---

[30] *Hansard* (n 13) col 543.
[31] *Hansard* (n 13) col 538.
[32] *Hansard* (n 13) col 540.
[33] The BSC and ITC codes (along with that of the Radio Authority) have since been replaced by Ofcom's Broadcasting Code. The PCC was replaced by the Independent Press Standards Organisation (IPSO) in September 2014, which now has responsibility for enforcing the Editors' Code of Practice. The BBC Editorial (formerly Producer's) Guidelines remain. See further ch 14, especially 14.14.
[34] *Hansard* (n 13) cols 539–40.

of Convention rights.[35] If further evidence of the government's intention in this regard were needed, the Home Secretary added:[36]

> On self-regulation, the new clause provides an important safeguard by emphasising the right to freedom of expression. Our intention is that that should underline the consequent need to preserve self-regulation. That effect is reinforced by highlighting in the amendment the significance of any relevant privacy code.

However, immediately following these remarks the Home Secretary concluded his explanation of s 12 by saying 'if, for any reason, it does not work as we envisage, and press freedom appears at risk, we shall certainly want to look again at the issue'.[37]

# C. Injunctions

## (1) Introduction

Section 12 applies where any relief affecting the Convention right to freedom of **12.14** expression is contemplated, but has its most significant impact on the grant of injunctions. It has a particular impact on interim injunctions, since a final injunction after a trial may be too late, and may offer little or no protection or comfort. For example, the final injunction granted at the end of the trial in *Mosley v News Group Newspapers Ltd*[38] contained a public domain exception[39] which permitted, *inter alia*, republication of the very *News of the World* feature that was the subject of the action, containing intrusive revelations about sexual activities including bondage, domination, sadism, and masochism on private premises. An interim injunction had been refused because the worldwide dissemination of the information and images that had already taken place was so enormous that the attempt to stem it would have involved the court 'slipping into playing the role of King Canute'.[40] On the other hand, in the *Douglas v Hello!* litigation Lindsay J accepted an undertaking, failing which he would have granted a final injunction, without a public domain exception.[41]

---

[35] At the very least a body must have power to award compensation and enforce its rulings to satisfy the requirements of Art 13 ECHR: *Peck v UK* (2003) 36 EHRR 41, paras 108–109. See further 14.171–14.186. This is likely to remain the position despite the power of Ofcom to fine a broadcaster or suspend its licence for a breach of the Code.

[36] *Hansard* (n 13) col 541.

[37] *Hansard* (n 13) col 541.

[38] [2008] EWHC 1777 (QB), [2008] EMLR 20.

[39] The public domain proviso in *Mosley* nevertheless excluded republication of the photographs and video recordings—see 12.78.

[40] [2008] EWHC 687 (QB) [34] (Eady J) (the interim injunction application).

[41] Reflecting the fact that even widespread previous publication of personal photographs does not necessarily have the effect that there may not be a fresh intrusion of privacy by further publication; see the Court of Appeal judgment on the appeal from the final judgment in *Douglas v Hello! Ltd* [2005] EWCA Civ 595, [2006] QB 125 [105] and *CTB v News Group Newspapers Ltd and Thomas* [2011] EWHC 1326 (QB). The cases are not entirely easy to reconcile. In breach of confidence, the issue turned on whether the material is 'so widely accessible that, in all the circumstances, it cannot be regarded as confidential': in the *Spycatcher* case, *Attorney General v Observer Ltd* [1990] 1 AC 109,

### (2) Interim Injunctions

**12.15** Particularly in cases involving personal information or pictures, it is well recognized that damages may be an ineffective remedy.[42] The interim injunction stage may therefore be all important. The tension between the competing principles of respect for privacy and freedom of expression is never more critical than at the interim stage. Two competing principles can be articulated as follows.

### (a) *The competing factors*

**12.16** **A requirement to provide an effective remedy**   Article 13 ECHR states:

> **Right to an effective remedy.** Everyone whose rights and freedoms are set forth in this Convention shall have an effective remedy before a national authority.

Where an interim injunction is the only effective remedy, that fact will inevitably be the dominant factor in the balance on the side of the grant of an injunction. The omission of Article 13 from the list of Convention rights incorporated by the HRA does not alter that fact. It is omitted because Article 13 guarantees the availability at national level of an effective remedy to enforce the rights, while the HRA provides the national mechanism for securing such a remedy in English law.[43] The aim of the HRA is that domestic courts rather than Strasbourg should remedy Convention violations,[44] which entails effective remedies.

**12.17** **A heavy burden of justifying prior restraint**   Against that, particular caution is required before prior restraint is enjoined in cases where the defendant's right of free expression is at issue.

### (b) *The jurisprudence*

**12.18** There are four main strands to the jurisprudence on prior restraint: statements in the European Court of Human Rights (ECtHR), judicial and other statements of general principle in England, the US approach, and the powerful and historic rule in defamation cases.

**12.19** **Strasbourg jurisprudence**   The best-known statement regarding prior restraint in the ECtHR is that:

> Article 10 of the Convention does not in terms prohibit the imposition of prior restraints on publication, as such... On the other hand, the dangers inherent in prior restraints are such that they call for the most careful scrutiny on the part of the court.

---

282 (Lord Goff). That led Eady J in *Mosley* (n 38) to conclude that there was nothing left to protect, and, in particular, that any injunction would be ineffective against foreign websites on which the images were, and would continue to be, accessible. The nature of the privacy right may not lead to the same conclusion: see 12.78.

[42] See 12.60–12.67.

[43] *Re S (Minors) (Care Order: Implementation of Care Plan)* [2002] UKHL 10, [2002] 2 AC 291 [61] (Lord Nicholls); *Brown v Stott* [2003] 1 AC 681 (Privy Council (Scotland)), 715 (Lord Hope).

[44] *Attorney General's Reference (No 2 of 2001)* [2003] UKHL 68, [2004] 2 AC 72 [175] (Lord Rodger).

This is especially so as far as the press is concerned, for news is a perishable commodity and to delay its publication, even for a short period, may well deprive it of all its value and interest.[45]

The burden of establishing the necessity of pre-publication measures is therefore a heavy one.

Against that should be set Resolution 1165 of the Parliamentary Assembly of the **12.20** Council of Europe of 26 June 1998, para 14 of which calls on governments to pass legislation containing guidelines, including:

> (vii) provision should be made for anyone who knows that information or images relating to his or her private life are about to be disseminated to initiate emergency judicial proceedings, such as summary applications for an interim order or an injunction postponing the dissemination of the information, subject to an assessment by the court as to the merits of the claim of an invasion of privacy.

The perishability of news may be a weighty consideration affecting the grant of an interim injunction, but it should be recognized that delay will not always deprive a story of its value. Whether it will is a question of fact in each case.[46]

**Statements of principle in England**   Blackstone's magisterial statement of **12.21** principle[47] has been influential (particularly in the United States):

> The liberty of the press is indeed essential to the nature of a free state; but this consists in laying no previous restraints upon publications and not in freedom from censure for criminal matter when published. Every freeman has an undoubted right to lay what sentiments he pleases before the public: to forbid this, is to destroy the freedom of the press; but if he publishes what is improper, mischievous or illegal, he must take the consequences of his own temerity.

So, in *R v Advertising Standards Authority Ltd, ex p Vernons Organisation Ltd*,[48] **12.22** Laws J said:[49]

> There is a general principle in our law that the expression of opinion and the conveyance of information will not be restrained by the courts save on pressing grounds. Freedom of expression is as much a sinew of the common law as it is of the European Convention.

The Court of Appeal said in *A v B plc*:[50]

> Any interference with the press has to be justified because it inevitably has some effect on the ability of the press to perform its role in society. This is the position

---

[45] *Observer and Guardian v UK* (n 18) para 60. See also *Sunday Times v UK (No 2)* (1992) 14 EHRR 229, para 51; *Wingrove v UK* (1997) 24 EHRR 1, para 58; *Editions Plon v France* [2006] 42 EHRR 36, para 42.

[46] See G Phillipson, 'Max Mosley goes to Strasbourg: Article 8, claimant notification and interim injunctions' [2009] 1 J Media L 73–96, 90.

[47] Blackstone, *Commentaries on the Laws of England* (Book IV, 17th edn, 1854) 182–3; quoted in *Holley v Smyth* [1998] QB 726, 737–8.

[48] [1992] 1 WLR 1289.

[49] *R v Advertising Standards Authority* (n 48) 1293.

[50] [2002] EWCA Civ 337, [2003] QB 195 [11(iv)–(v)].

irrespective of whether a particular publication is desirable in the public inter-est…Regardless of the quality of the material which it is intended to publish, *prima facie* the court should not interfere with its publication. Any interference with publication must be justified.

**12.23** The perhaps simplistic approach adopted in *A v B plc* to the concept of public interest and 'role-models' has been refined in later cases,[51] but these statements remain powerful, provided they are understood in light of the basic principle that neither Article 10 nor Article 8 has any presumptive priority or precedence over the other.[52] They are consistent with the Strasbourg jurisprudence that freedom of expression is applicable not only to information or ideas that are favourably received or regarded as inoffensive or as a matter of indifference, but also to those that offend, shock, or disturb.[53] Where a threatened publication engages the sub-ject's Article 8 right of privacy, the quality of the material will be decisive, in particular whether, on the one hand, it contributes to a debate of general interest in a democratic society[54] or, on the other, it falls into the category described by Baroness Hale as 'the most vapid tittle-tattle about the activities of footballers' wives and girlfriends'.[55]

**12.24** **The US approach**   The hostility in the United States to prior restraints is well-known and, particularly in cases involving American litigants or interests, sharp-ens the point made in the English and Strasbourg cases cited above. But the US approach derives from the First Amendment to the Constitution, which forbids Congress from making any law abridging the freedom of speech or of the press.[56] In England, the approach is of balancing rights of equal status without presump-tive priority.[57]

**12.25** **The defamation rule**   The rule applied in defamation cases is perhaps the strong-est example of a presumption against prior restraint where freedom of expression is at issue. It was settled in the late nineteenth century in *Bonnard v Perryman*,[58] and restated by the Court of Appeal in *Greene v Associated Newspapers Ltd*,[59] that a court will not impose prior restraint on publication, where the claim is based upon defamation, unless it is clear that no defence will succeed at trial. The rule is not applied in genuine cases of breach of confidence or privacy, in which interim

---

[51] *McKennitt v Ash* [2006] EWCA Civ 1714, [2008] QB 73 [62]–[63].
[52] *Re S (Minors)* (n 43) [17]; *Campbell v MGN Ltd* [2004] UKHL 22, [2004] 2 AC 457 [55].
[53] See *eg Lingens v Austria* (1986) 8 EHRR 407, para 41.
[54] *von Hannover v Germany* (2005) 40 EHRR 1, paras 60, 63, 76.
[55] *Jameel v Wall Street Journal Europe* [2006] UKHL 44, [2007] 1 AC 359 [147].
[56] And has not escaped criticism in the US: Prof Phillipson (n 46) notes that the analysis sup-porting it 'has been subject to sustained criticism', quoting J Jeffries in 'Rethinking prior restraint' (1983) Yale LJ 409, 429: 'In my view, a rule of special hostility to administrative pre-clearance is justified, but a rule of special hostility to injunctive relief is not.'
[57] *Re S (Minors)* (n 43) [17] (Lord Steyn).
[58] [1891] 2 Ch 269, CA.
[59] [2004] EWCA Civ 1462, [2005] QB 972.

injunctions are granted if s 12(3) HRA is satisfied and the balance favours the grant of an injunction.[60] Nevertheless, applicants for interim injunctions in privacy cases need to take care to avoid being caught by the defamation rule.[61]

### (c) Preliminary considerations

**Choice of cause of action**  The grant of an injunction is 'dependent on a pre-  **12.26**
existing cause of action against the defendant arising out of an invasion, actual or threatened by him, of a legal or equitable right of the plaintiff for the enforcement of which the defendant is amenable to the jurisdiction of the court'.[62] The following considerations are worth bearing in mind when deciding on the most appropriate basis or bases for an application for interim relief,[63] but the court will be alert to cause of action shopping, particularly where what is in substance regarded as a defamation claim is dressed up in another guise, to avoid the defamation rule for interim injunctions.[64]

(1) *Misuse of private information* This is now the natural candidate where protection is sought for private and personal information. The cause of action is not necessarily defeated if the information sought to be protected is false.[65]

(2) *Breach of confidence* The facts of an individual case may disclose a threatened traditional breach of confidence, as well as dissemination or threatened dissemination of information about private life.[66] If so, this will add substantial weight to the claim because of the importance in a democratic society of upholding duties of confidence. Where disclosure of information received in confidence is concerned, the test is not merely whether the information is a matter of public interest, but whether it is in the public interest that the duty of confidence should be breached.[67]

(3) *Breach of contract* Obligations of confidentiality or privacy are on occasion bolstered by contract. Conflicting views have been expressed as to whether

---

[60]  eg *Cream Holdings* (n 17); *Douglas* (n 41) [251]–[259]; *Greene* (n 59) [81].

[61]  See 12.45.

[62]  *The Siskina* [1979] AC 210, 256 (Lord Diplock). But caution is needed in applying Lord Diplock's statement, which is not an exhaustive statement of the court's powers to grant injunctions: *Broadmoor Special Hospital Authority v Robinson* [2000] 1 WLR 1590, CA [20]–[23] (Lord Woolf MR).

[63]  Where the claimant is an adult. Where a child's private and family life is concerned, the court's jurisdiction is now derived directly from Convention rights under the ECHR, so that it is not necessary to consider the earlier case law on the court's inherent jurisdiction relating to children. See *Re S (Minors)* (n 43).

[64]  See 12.45. The relationship between remedies for breach of privacy and defamation is also discussed at 12.107–12.108, 12.111.

[65]  *McKennitt* (n 51) [78]–[80] (Buxton LJ), [85]–[87] (Longmore LJ). But the falsity of the information might suggest that in substance the complaint is one of defamation. See further ch 8, especially 8.54–8.58 and 8.74–8.84.

[66]  *Campbell* (n 52) [53] (Lord Hoffmann).

[67]  *HRH Prince of Wales v Associated Newspapers Ltd* [2006] EWCA Civ 1776, [2008] Ch 57 [24]–[32], [65]–[69]. See also *McKennitt* (n 51) [15], [18].

the fact that there is an express contractual obligation of confidence affects the weight to be attached to the duty of confidentiality. This topic is considered below.[68]

(4) *Defamation* The extremely high threshold test for grant of an interim injunction makes this cause of action an unlikely candidate as a basis for preventing the publication of personal information.[69]

(5) *Malicious falsehood* The same difficulties apply as in defamation, with, in most cases, the additional problem of being able to demonstrate an almost unarguable case of malice (as an essential ingredient of the cause of action) at an interim stage.[70]

(6) *Data protection* The same advantages apply as in the case of invasions of privacy. However, s 32 of the Data Protection Act 1998 means that prior restraint is only available in limited circumstances, though secondary publication may be prevented.[71] In *Campbell v MGN Ltd*[72] the Court of Appeal held that the media exemption in s 32 applied not only to the period before publication, but is of general application.

(7) *Harassment* This covers a wider spectrum of objectionable intrusion than other causes of action, for example unsuccessful attempts at obtaining private information. However, it is a tort of rather uncertain ambit, particularly as regards the publication, as opposed to the gathering, of information by the media,[73] and requires a 'course of conduct',[74] as opposed to a single act such as a one-off publication. As the Protection from Harassment Act 1997 also creates a criminal offence, the conduct in question must also be serious enough to attract the sanction of the criminal law.[75] An apprehended harassment may be the subject of a claim in civil proceedings for an injunction by the person who may be the victim of the course of conduct in question.[76] In *Georgallides v Etzin*[77] an interim injunction was granted to restrain a protest by leafleting and placards outside a restaurant. The court took the view that the injunction was genuinely sought to prevent continuing harassment, not an attempt to evade the rule in *Bonnard v Perryman*.[78] To this end, the protest was allowed to continue, but subject to a fifty-yard exclusion zone.

---

[68] At 12.57–12.59.

[69] See 12.25.

[70] *Bestobell Paints Ltd v Bigg* [1975] FSR 421 (Ch).

[71] Data Protection Act 1998, s 10.

[72] [2002] EWCA Civ 1373, [2003] QB 633. See 7.112.

[73] See *Thomas v News Group Newspapers Ltd* [2001] EWCA Civ 1233, [2002] EMLR 78.

[74] Protection from Harassment Act 1997, ss 1 and 4. For a full discussion of the tort and how it relates to the area of privacy and the media, see ch 6 and 10.04–10.24.

[75] *APW v WPA* [2012] EWHC 3151 (QB) [12]. See also 6.21–6.23.

[76] Protection from Harassment Act 1997, s 3(1).

[77] [2005] EWHC 1790 (QB).

[78] *Bonnard* (n 58).

Indeed these types of injunctions appear to be increasingly popular with high profile figures trying to protect themselves from the paparazzi in particular.[79]

(8) *Trespass or nuisance* Similarly, although trespass and nuisance may cover a wider spectrum of objectionable intrusion in relation to the gathering (as opposed to the publication) of private information, they are likely to be of limited application[80] since injunctions will not generally be granted to prevent a threatened nuisance or trespass.

(9) *Copyright* Although sometimes regarded as a subsidiary or tangential form of protection for private information, the advantage of relying on the provisions of the Copyright, Designs and Patents Act 1988 (where they apply) is that once the subsistence and ownership of copyright is established, it is unlikely that proving infringement will be problematic. The court then has a solid property interest to protect, which is also less likely to be undermined by any public interest defence or other arguments based on freedom of expression.[81] A threatened infringement of copyright may form the basis for an application for an injunction at the suit of a person who would be entitled to sue for breach.[82]

**Sufficient threat**    Before applying for a *quia timet* injunction there must be a    **12.27** sufficient threat of injury to, or infringement of, the claimant's rights. The degree of probability of future injury that is required will obviously depend on the circumstances of the case, in particular the gravity of the injury that may follow.[83] However, the authorities suggest that an injunction will only be granted to restrain an apprehended or threatened injury where the injury is certain or very imminent,

---

[79] For examples of these types of injunction, see 10.13–10.15. Even non-celebrity claimants are increasingly bringing harassment claims alongside those for libel and/or a breach of privacy. This has been done where the defendants' actions in making those defamatory allegations, or in causing the breaches of privacy complained of, are claimed to have amounted to harassing conduct as well. See also *ZAM v CFW* [2013] EWHC 662 (QB), [2013] EMLR 27, where false allegations were made to the claimant's employer and family members that he had mismanaged and misappropriated family trusts, and was a paedophile, which resulted in damages of £100,000 being ordered in respect of the slanders and the libels, with a further £20,000 representing aggravated damages to compensate the claimant for the distress and harassment suffered. No separate award was made for the harassment element however as that consisted in the making of the defamatory publications themselves.

[80] The principle that 'an Englishman's home is his castle' has a strong basis in domestic law, but the requirement to show a proprietary interest and its inability to deal with the 'fruits of the intrusion' limit the effectiveness of this remedy to all but the most obvious cases. See further 10.50–10.52.

[81] *Ashdown v Telegraph Group Ltd* [2001] EWCA Civ 1142, [2002] Ch 149. See ch 9 for a full discussion of the protection afforded to privacy by the law of copyright.

[82] In *Rocknroll v News Group Newspapers Ltd* [2013] EWHC 24 (Ch) the claimant successfully obtained an interim injunction to restrain republication of private information contained within photographs taken of him, on the grounds of a threatened breach of privacy. However, he had also made the application for the injunction on the basis of an alleged breach of copyright. Although Briggs J did not analyse that separate claim in detail (because he was willing to grant the injunction solely on the basis of breach of privacy), he indicated that an injunction to restrain republication of the photographs themselves (as opposed to a description of the information contained within them) would also have been justified on the basis of the threatened breach of copyright.

[83] See I Spry, *Equitable Remedies* (9th edn, Thomson Reuters Australia 2013) 390–5.

or where the likely injury is extremely serious.[84] The court will need evidence or grounds to infer that the defendant threatens or intends to continue the publication complained of.[85] Any application for an injunction has to be based on facts; mere suspicion is not enough.[86]

**12.28**   *A v B, C and D*[87] well illustrates the strength of the rule that it is for the claimant to show a threat of publication of material which would infringe his or her legal rights. For this purpose, the claimant must be able to show what it is that the defendant is threatening to publish, in terms sufficiently precise to enable an enforceable injunction to be formulated.[88] Defendants do not have to assist by revealing anything about their plans beyond what they want to reveal. A defendant may be able to refute an allegation of intention by offering an undertaking not to publish without giving notice to the claimant.[89]

### (d) Preliminary procedural matters

**12.29**   **The injunction should be drafted in clear and precise terms**   The cardinal rule in all cases is that an injunction must be framed in such a way that the party affected can know with certainty what he or she is or is not allowed to do, especially since the penalty for non-compliance or breach is committal.[90] In *Times Newspapers Ltd v Mirror Group Newspapers Ltd*[91] the Court of Appeal held that no injunction could be granted to prevent premature publication of a pirated version of Lady Thatcher's memoirs on the basis of breach of confidence, because the plaintiffs had to concede that vital parts of the book would have to be excepted from the scope of any injunction and the drafting of such an exception could not be satisfactorily achieved.[92]

---

[84] 'But no one can obtain a *quia timet* order by merely saying "*timeo*"; he must aver and prove that what is going on is calculated to infringe his rights', *Attorney General for Dominion of Canada v Ritchie Contracting and Supply Co Ltd* [1919] AC 999 (Privy Council (Canada)) 1005 (Lord Dunedin). In *West v BBC* (QB, 10 June 2002, Ouseley J) the Court held that a claimant must establish 'the existence of a real and immediate risk' of infringement of his rights under Arts 2 or 3. See also *British Data Management plc v Boxer Commercial Removals plc* [1996] 3 All ER 707 where the Court of Appeal disapproved of an injunction that was too wide and unspecific because the precise words that the claimant was trying to prevent being published were unknown. Reasonable certainty as to the words sought to be restrained was necessary.

[85] *Quartz Hill Co v Beal* [1882] 20 Ch D 501, 508–9; *New Musical Express Ltd v Cardfont Publishers Ltd* [1956] RPC 211. Two cases in which the application failed on this basis are *D v L* [2003] EWCA Civ 1169, [2004] EMLR 1 [28]–[29] (Waller LJ) and *A v B, C and D* [2005] EWHC 1651 (QB), [2005] EMLR 36 [12]–[15] (Eady J).

[86] *Caterpillar Logistics Services (UK) Ltd v Huesca de Crean* [2011] EWHC 3154 (QB) [138] (upheld on appeal [2012] EWCA Civ 156, [2012] 3 All ER 129 [67]–[68] and applied in *CEF Holdings Ltd v Mundey* [2012] EWHC 1524 (QB) [255]).

[87] *A v B, C and D* (n 85).

[88] The injunction sought must specify which information is intended to be restrained from publication: *Caterpillar Logistics Services (UK) Ltd v Huesca de Crean*, CA (n 86) [68].

[89] This approach was adopted in *Fayed v The Observer, The Times*, 14 July 1986 (Mann J).

[90] Spry (n 83) 386–9.

[91] 1993 EMLR 442. The case has been criticized, but not on this point. See 4.89.

[92] Leggatt LJ said at 448: 'It is a matter of regret that because the plaintiffs are constrained to concede that vital parts of the book should be excepted from the scope of any injunction, and because

In privacy cases, there are also practical reasons for requiring precision: for exam- **12.30**
ple, there may be a need to ascertain the extent to which some of the personal
information sought to be protected is or is not in the public domain or whether a
public interest defence could succeed for part of the information. In *A v B, C and
D*[93] the claimant had severe, and ultimately fatal, difficulty in formulating a sufficiently precise injunction, because he did not know what his wife ('B') had said in
an interview, or what the magazine publishers ('C' and 'D') might publish.[94] But it
is unlikely that there will be many privacy cases where it would not be possible to
frame an injunction in terms clear enough to mark off the information which the
defendant is free to publish, with the result that no injunction can be granted at all.

**Injunctions against persons unknown** An action may be brought, and an **12.31**
injunction granted, against persons unknown, provided that the description used
for such persons is sufficiently certain, so as to identify both those who are included
and those who are not. In other words, the court must be confident that the order
is directed against particular wrongdoers, and the targets must understand that
the injunction is directed against them.[95] Such an order is known as a 'John Doe'
order.[96] It is effective if the targets are made aware of it, for example by the order
being posted in a place where it will come to the attention of the wrongdoers. There
are in any event many cases in which courts grant injunctions designed to bind parties not named on the order.[97] In privacy cases, this typically includes the media.

This form of action and order was not possible before the Civil Procedure Rules **12.32**
(CPR).[98] The jurisdiction to bring an action in this form, and the circumstances
in which it can properly be done, were fully examined by Sir Andrew Morritt V-C
in *Bloomsbury Publishing Group and JK Rowling v News Group Newspapers*.[99] The
facts of that case illustrate the circumstances in which the need to sue persons
unknown can arise. The fifth Harry Potter book was printed under conditions of
extreme secrecy and security, to ensure that confidentiality was maintained until
the launch date. Copies were illicitly removed from the publisher or the printing

---

the drafting of such an exception could not, in my judgment, be satisfactorily achieved, as the plaintiff's draft demonstrates, the continued pirating of passages from the book cannot be effectually
restrained by the plaintiffs, whatever prospects they may enjoy of eventually recovering damages.'

[93] *A v B, C and D* (n 85) [1], [5], [11], [24], [34]–[38].

[94] See also *British Data Management v Boxer Removals* (n 84).

[95] For discussion of some procedural issues arising see 12.29. In *Bloomsbury Publishing and JK
Rowling v News Group Newspapers Ltd* [2003] EWHC 1087 (Ch) the defendants were described as
'the person or persons who have offered the publishers of the *Sun*, the *Daily Mail*, and the *Daily
Mirror* newspapers a copy of the book "Harry Potter and the Order of the Phoenix" by JK Rowling,
or any part thereof, and the person or persons who has or have physical possession of a copy of the
said book or any part thereof without the consent of the claimants.'

[96] *Bloomsbury Publishing* (n 95) [11] (Laddie J).

[97] *Bloomsbury Publishing* (n 95) [22].

[98] The CPR were introduced on 26 April 1999.

[99] [2003] EWHC 1205 (Ch), [2003] 1 WLR 1633. The procedure was clearly approved by the
Court of Appeal in *South Cambridgeshire District Council v Persons Unknown* [2004] EWCA Civ
1280, [2004] 4 PLR 88 [9], [12].

works, and came into the possession of the *Sun* newspaper, which printed a story based on the lapse in security. Newspapers received telephone calls from someone offering for sale chapters from the book. Clearly, there was the basis and a need to injunct the wrongdoers, and to serve the injunction on the media.

**12.33**　However, there are traps for those seeking orders against persons unknown: the court will expect steps to be taken to bring the injunction to the notice of the defendants and to serve them, if necessary by alternative service.[100] Otherwise the procedure becomes one for obtaining an injunction, without opposition, without a return date, and without any prospect of progressing the action, for the purpose of binding the media generally, and indefinitely.[101] If one or more newspapers are the real target, they should be made defendants, and failure to notify the media in advance may result in the refusal of the injunction.[102]

**12.34**　**Injunctions *contra mundum***　Rarely, injunctions in privacy or confidentiality cases are made *contra mundum* (against the world). An example is *Venables and Thompson v News Group Newspapers*,[103] in which Dame Elizabeth Butler-Sloss P made orders against specific newspaper publishers and the whole world to protect the new identities and whereabouts of the James Bulger killers on their release from custody, to protect their rights of confidentiality and their rights to life and freedom from persecution and harassment. The injunction could not be based on the court's jurisdiction to protect minors, because the claimants were then of full age.[104] The injunction was granted to protect Convention rights but, while s 6(1) HRA makes it unlawful for a court to act in a way which is incompatible with a Convention right, it does not confer on the court any power which it does not otherwise have, either by statute or under its inherent jurisdiction.[105]

**12.35**　The power to make orders *contra mundum* does not exist at common law. See *Independent Publishing Co v Attorney General of Trinidad and Tobago*:[106]

> Their Lordships conclude that if the court is to have power to make orders against the public at large it must be conferred by legislation; it cannot be found in the common law.

In *Attorney General's Reference No 3 of 1999, Application by the BBC*,[107] Lord Brown identified the source of the power. The statutory basis for the grant by the High Court of injunctions against the whole world lies in s 6 HRA read together with s 37 of the Senior Courts Act 1981. The Senior Courts Act 1981 empowers the

---

[100] *X and Y v Persons Unknown* [2006] EWHC 2783 (QB), [2007] EMLR 10 [78]; *Terry v Persons Unknown* [2010] EWHC 119 (QB), [2010] EMLR 16 [20]–[22], [134]–[136], [143].

[101] Since the action can never be brought to trial, the interim injunction will remain in force, and bind third parties on whom it is served under the *Spycatcher* principle: see *Terry* (n 100) [20].

[102] See 12.36 on notifying third parties.

[103] [2001] Fam 430, Fam D.

[104] Another example is *X (Mary Bell) v O'Brien* [2003] EWHC 1101 (QB), [2003] EMLR 37.

[105] *Attorney General's Reference (No 3 of 1999), Application by the BBC* [2009] UKHL 34, [2010] 1 AC 145 [13] (Lord Hope).

[106] [2004] UKPC 26, [2005] 1 AC 190 [67].

[107] *Attorney General's Reference (No 3 of 1999)* (n 105) [57].

High Court to grant an injunction (interlocutory or final) 'in all cases in which it appears to the court to be just and convenient to do so'. The HRA obliges the court to act compatibly with Convention rights. *Contra mundum* orders are at the extremity of the court's power, and would not commonly be granted in aid of a private right, except where life or limb was at risk. In *OPQ v BJM and CJM*,[108] Eady J granted a final *contra mundum* order where the parties had settled their case on the basis of the defendant giving permanent undertakings not to publish the private information and where there was clear evidence that publication by a third party might have very serious consequences on the health, including the mental health, of the claimant.

**Whether to notify third parties on whom it is intended to serve the injunction** **12.36**
Often, a claimant will wish to serve third parties with an injunction once granted, the purpose being to put them on notice so that it will be a contempt of court for them to publish information covered by the interim injunction, under the *Spycatcher* principle.[109] Sometimes, the media are the real target of the application for the injunction, in the sense that the real object of the application is not so much to restrain the named defendant, but to silence the press by serving the injunction on them. In cases of these kinds, and others, a difficult issue may arise as to whether one or more representatives of the media ought to be given advance notice of the application, and the opportunity to oppose it. The decision is an important one. The court may, for example, find that without reasoned opposition from a party potentially affected it is unable to form a view on whether the claimant would be 'likely' to succeed at trial.[110] The rival considerations, and the authorities on how they ought to be reconciled are discussed in Chapter 13.[111]

**Whether the court should be told if the information is true or false**  In *WER v* **12.37**
*REW* the Court expressed concern about the fact that it was kept in ignorance of the truth or falsity of the information:[112]

> ...at first blush I found it troubling that a judge should be asked to grant an injunction restraining not just the defendant publication but a whole number of other media organisations from publishing certain information, in complete ignorance whether the information is true or false and in complete ignorance of the extent to which the information, true or false, had entered the public domain.

This did not prevent the judge from continuing the injunction, without opposition from the defendant, but he clearly remained unhappy about the position:[113]

> I remain unhappy about the invidious position in which the judge is placed in having to decide whether to grant an injunction when he is, in effect, blindfolded as regards the facts of the case before him.

---

[108] [2011] EWHC 1059 (QB), [2011] EMLR 23.
[109] *Attorney General v Newspaper Publishing* [1988] Ch 333, CA.
[110] *eg Terry* (n 100) [43]–[44], [101]–[103].
[111] At 13.140–13.142.
[112] [2009] EWHC 1029 (QB), [2009] EMLR 17 [8] (Sir Charles Gray).
[113] *WER* (n 112) [14].

Counsel's explanation for the claimant's reticence on this score was that, after serving the injunction on the media, the claimant's lawyers would on request have to supply to the media copies of the materials read by the judge.[114] The media would then learn of the extent to which the private information was true, if that was disclosed by the witness statements and other materials read by the judge, and would then 'naturally…make what they can of the information supplied to them'.

**12.38**  CPR 32.12(1) provides that witness statements may be used only for the purpose of the proceedings in which they are served, until put in evidence at a public hearing. This may not fully meet a claimant's concern. Tugendhat J noted in *Terry*:[115]

> There is an applicant's dilemma: if he gives notice to the media he reveals the very information which he is seeking to keep secret, none, or only some, of which may already be known to the newspaper to which notice is given, and he confirms as fact what may be already known only as rumour.

But claimants would be well advised to take note of the concern felt by the court, and in particular its entitlement to candour.[116] Falsity of private information does not deprive the claimant of the protection of the law of privacy: truth or falsity is strictly irrelevant to the question whether the information is entitled to protection as being private.[117] Eady J said in an address to the Intellectual Property Lawyers' Association:[118]

> …a claimant is not forced to go through an article about (say) his or her sex life or his or her state of health, in order to reveal that some aspects are true and others false. That would defeat the object of the exercise. Any speculation or factual assertions on private matters, whether true or false, can give rise to a cause of action.

**12.39**  There are, however, dangers in leaving the court blindfolded as regards the facts before it. Falsity is directly relevant to any issue of public interest: a public interest justification cannot be intelligently adjudicated upon without deciding whether the information is true or false.[119] There will often, also, be a difference between cases of private information which is a mixture of truth, half-truth, and falsity, and private information which is simply false. In a case of the second kind, the fact that it is false may be more significant than the fact that, if true, it would be

---

[114] CPR PD 25A para 9.2.

[115] *Terry* (n 100) [117].

[116] *Terry* (n 100) [11].

[117] *McKennitt* (n 51) [78]–[80] (Buxton LJ), [85]–[87] (Longmore LJ).

[118] Sir David Eady, The Intellectual Property Lawyers' Association, House of Lords, 18 February 2009, available at <http://www.publications.parliament.uk/pa/cm200809/cmselect/cmcumeds/memo/press/uc7502.htm>.

[119] *McKennitt* (n 51) [87] (Longmore LJ).

private, particularly if it is damaging to the claimant's reputation. Buxton LJ said in *McKennitt*:[120]

> If it could be shown that a claim in breach of confidence was brought where the nub of the case was a complaint of the falsity of the allegations, and that that was done in order to avoid the rules of the tort of defamation, then objections could be raised in terms of abuse of process. That might be so at the interlocutory stage in an attempt to avoid the rule in *Bonnard v Perryman*.

The way forward may be for the witness statements to deal with the facts fully and candidly, and for the order to make such provision as is strictly necessary under CPR PD 25A para 9.2 that the claimant need not provide copies of the witness statements to persons served with the order without being given undertakings regarding security of and access to the statements.[121]

**Other procedural considerations**   Issues such as hearings in private, limiting **12.40** access to the court file, anonymization of the parties, and orders to protect the hearing papers are dealt with in Chapter 13, but are important considerations on any injunction application.

**'Super-injunctions'**   On occasion, the question may arise of whether, in addi- **12.41** tion to anonymization and other measures to protect the claimant's identity, the injunction should also include a provision prohibiting, at least temporarily, the disclosure of the fact the order has been granted. Orders of this kind gained some notoriety in the British media in 2009, where they were dubbed 'super-injunctions', and were subsequently examined in detail in the May 2011 Report of the Committee on Super-Injunctions,[122] chaired by Lord Neuberger MR. The Committee of media law experts had been established amid concerns over the perceived increase in the use of super-injunctions and the associated lack of transparency in the court process when they were granted. Although the issue of super-injunctions came to a fore in 2011, these orders were not new; they already had quite a long ancestry in confidence and privacy cases. Such an order was made when the Liberal Democrat leader Paddy Ashdown obtained an injunction in the early 1990s to restrain revelation of an extramarital affair. The injunction was discharged on the claimant's application after a Scottish newspaper publicized the fact that it had been obtained by the claimant. Another well-known example was the order granted by Hoffmann J in 1989 in the case of *X Ltd v Morgan-Grampian (Publishers) Ltd* which prohibited the defendant not only from disclosing the information at issue (which consisted of the contents of a company's confidential

---

[120] *McKennitt* (n 51) [79].
[121] *Terry* (n 100) [117]. In the case of a newspaper, access might be restricted to the legal department.
[122] Report of the Committee on Super-Injunctions: 'Super-Injunctions, Anonymised Injunctions and Open Justice' (May 2011), available at <http://www.judiciary.gov.uk/wp-content/uploads/JCO/Documents/Reports/super-injunction-report-20052011.pdf>.

business plan) but also from 'disclosing to any person (other than for the purposes of obtaining legal advice in the present proceedings) the existence of the proceedings or of the plaintiffs' interest in such proceedings'.[123] The conclusion of the Report of the Committee on Super-Injunctions was that there had only been two examples of super-injunctions having been granted in recent years[124] and that, while such orders could (and should) still be obtained in the future where it was appropriate, they should be rare, and only where they were absolutely necessary (given the derogations from the principle of open justice that they necessarily involve).[125] As a result, Practice Guidance was issued by Lord Neuberger MR in August 2011,[126] setting out in detail the procedure to be adhered to when making an application for this kind of order, and highlighting the considerations that any court granting one ought to take into account. The Guidance emphasizes in particular that such orders should be rare, and only granted where 'strictly necessary'.

**12.42**   *Anti tipping-off*   One reason for such an order, as was emphasized in the Report,[127] is to prevent 'tipping-off' of third parties by the defendant before the claimant can serve it with the injunction or take other steps to prevent disclosure by it. This has been explained as follows:

> In the interval between learning of the intention of the Applicants to bring proceedings, and the receipt by the alleged wrongdoer of an injunction binding upon him or her, the alleged wrongdoer might consider that he or she could disclose the information, and hope to avoid the risk of being in contempt of court. Alternatively...the alleged wrongdoer may destroy any further evidence which may be needed in order to identify him or her. Tipping-off of the alleged wrongdoer can thus defeat the purpose of the order.[128]

It is a purpose that will normally be adequately served by a relatively short-term prohibition, expiring on service of the order on the respondent. It is unclear what justification there could be for a longer-running order of this kind.[129] CPR PD 25A contains a standard form of anti tipping-off order against a respondent.[130] Where

---

[123] [1991] 1 AC 1, HL 5.

[124] One of which was the super-injunction obtained by the family of Paul and Rachel Chandler, the British couple kidnapped by Somali pirates in 2009. This prohibited the reporting of matters concerning their kidnapping while they were being held so as to prevent any negative impact on the ongoing negotiations for their release. The super-injunction effectively 'expired' once they had left Somalia and were in the custody of Foreign Office officials.

[125] Report of the Committee on Super-Injunctions (n 122) iv–v.

[126] *Practice Guidance (HC: Interim Non-Disclosure Orders)* [2012] 1 WLR 1003.

[127] Report of the Committee on Super-Injunctions (n 122) 78, para 15.

[128] *G v Wikimedia Foundation Inc* [2009] EWHC 3148 (QB), [2010] EMLR 364 [41]; *Terry* (n 100) [138].

[129] *Terry* (n 100) [141]; *G v Wikimedia* (n 128) [42].

[130] 'Except for the purpose of obtaining legal advice, the Respondent must not directly or indirectly inform anyone of these proceedings or of the contents of this order, or warn anyone that proceedings have been or may be brought against him by the Applicant until 4.30 p.m. on the return date or further order of the court': CPR PD 25A, Annex, Model Search Order, para 20. See also *Practice Guidance (HC: Interim Non-Disclosure Orders)* (n 126) Model Order, para 7.

third parties are to be served with the order before the return date, this form may need adaptation so as to bind them for the same period of time.

*Other circumstances*   It is not altogether easy to conceive of any other circum- **12.43** stances in which a 'super-injunction' would be both necessary and proportionate, for the purpose of bolstering protection for the confidential or private information which is the object of the action. It will usually be enough that the proceedings are anonymized, and that the order provides proper protection against disclosure of the claimant's identity.

### (e) The jurisdiction of the court and the principles to be applied

**The court's jurisdiction**   Express power to grant interim injunctions is found in **12.44** s 37(1) of the Senior Courts Act 1981 and in CPR 25.1(1)(a). The jurisdiction thus conferred is effectively unlimited, though in all cases CPR 1.2 directs the court to seek to give effect to the overriding objective when exercising the power given to it by the rules, and in cases which engage the defendant's right of freedom of expression, s 12(3) HRA sets the threshold test for the exercise of the power.

**Relevance of the defamation rule**   The defamation rule precludes the grant of an **12.45** interim injunction unless it is clear that no defence to the action can succeed.[131] In *Greene v Associated Newspapers Ltd*,[132] the Court held that there is nothing in the Convention, or in s 12(3) HRA, which requires that the rule in *Bonnard v Perryman* be dispensed with or weakened. This naturally places a premium on a claimant stating his case in privacy instead of defamation, if he can. But there are evident potential problems about having overlapping causes of action subject to such radically different rules. A cause of action is simply a factual situation, the existence of which entitles one person to obtain a remedy against another.[133] Where torts overlap, the factual situation may be the same, and the remedy should respond to the factual situation, not the label the claimant chooses to put on it. This raises a question as to whether the rules regarding prior restraint should be aligned for the two causes of action, at least in cases where they overlap. It is now clear that reputation, as an aspect of personal integrity, in cases in which the publication impugns personal integrity, is part of private life protected by Article 8 ECHR,[134] which suggests clearly that the tests of necessity and proportionality should be applied in defamation cases just as in privacy ones. Hence it has been argued that the rule in *Bonnard v Perryman* needs to be revisited.[135] But it has not been suggested that the rule in privacy cases should be brought into line with *Bonnard v Perryman*.

---

[131]  See 12.25.

[132]  *Greene* (n 59).

[133]  *Letang v Cooper* [1965] 1 QB 232, CA, 242–3 (Diplock LJ).

[134]  *In re Guardian News and Media Ltd* [2010] UKSC 1, [2010] 2 AC 697 [37]–[42]; and (*eg*) *Cumpana and Mazare v Romania* (2005) 41 EHRR 14, para 91; *Pfeifer v Austria* (2009) 48 EHRR 8, paras 33, 35; *Karako v Hungary* App no 39311/05 (ECtHR, 28 April 2009). See also 3.23.

[135]  See 8.65 *et seq* and R Clayton QC and H Tomlinson QC, *The Law of Human Rights* (2nd edn, Oxford University Press 2009) para 15.28, and in two extra-judicial addresses: Sir David

**12.46**  **The threshold test**   Section 12(3) HRA provides:

> No such relief [*ie* relief which, if granted, might affect the exercise of the Convention right to freedom of expression][136] is to be granted so as to restrain publication before trial unless the court is satisfied that the applicant is likely to establish that publication should not be allowed.

This provision was authoritatively construed by the House of Lords in *Cream Holdings Ltd v Banerjee*.[137] The action was for breach of confidence against a chartered accountant who had worked as financial controller within the claimant group, and who had, upon leaving, taken with her documents that allegedly showed corruption involving a group director and a local council official. Plainly there was a possible public interest defence.

**12.47**  Lord Nicholls, with whom all of the other Lords of Appeal agreed, said that the principal purpose of s 12(3) was to buttress the protection afforded to freedom of speech at the interim stage by setting a higher threshold for the grant of interim injunctions against the media than the *American Cyanamid* guideline of a 'serious question to be tried' or a 'real prospect' of success at the trial.[138] But a threshold test of 'more likely than not' in every case would not be workable in practice, because in some cases an injunction would be necessary to preserve the position in the short interval before a full hearing of the application for interim relief could take place, or pending an appeal against the judge's order.[139] A lower test may also be required where the adverse consequences of disclosure of information would be extremely serious, such as a grave risk of personal injury to a particular person.[140]

**12.48**  Parliament must therefore be taken to have intended a higher standard than the usual 'real prospect' standard, but one which can be dispensed with where particular circumstances make it necessary.[141] On its proper construction, the effect of s 12(3) is that the court is not to make an interim restraint order unless satisfied that the applicant's prospects of success at the trial are sufficiently favourable to justify such an order being made in the particular circumstances of the case. The general approach should be that courts will be exceedingly slow to make such orders where the applicant has not satisfied the court that he or she will probably ('more likely

---

Eady, 'Speech at University of Hertfordshire' (10 November 2009), available at <webarchive. nationalarchives.gov.uk/20131202164909/http://judiciary.gov.uk/media/speeches/2009/speech-eady-j-11112009.htm?wbc_purpose=Basic> and Sir David Eady, 'Privacy and the Press: Where are we now?' (Justice Conference, 1 December 2009), available at <webarchive.nationalarchives.gov. uk/20131202164909/http://judiciary.gov.uk/media/speeches/2009/speech-eady-j-01122009. htm?wbc_purpose=Basic>. See also Tugendhat J's observations in *RST v UVW* [2009] EWHC 2448 (QB), [2010] EMLR 13; and his analysis in *Terry* (n 100) [74]–[96]; and 8.83–8.84.

[136] s 12(1) HRA.
[137] *Cream Holdings*, HL (n 17).
[138] *Cream Holdings*, HL (n 17) [15].
[139] *Cream Holdings*, HL (n 17) [16]–[18].
[140] *Cream Holdings*, HL (n 17) [19].
[141] *Cream Holdings*, HL (n 17) [20].

than not') succeed at the trial. A lesser degree of likelihood will only suffice where it is necessary for the court to depart from the standard, for reasons including those given above.[142]

Lord Nicholls added:                                                    **12.49**

> This approach gives effect to the Parliamentary intention that courts should have particular regard to the importance of the right to freedom of expression and at the same time it is sufficiently flexible in its application to give effect to countervailing Convention rights.

This sentence from Lord Nicholls' opinion is of importance in showing that their Lordships' construction of s 12(3) is designed also to satisfy the requirement in s 12(4) to have particular regard to the importance of the Convention right to freedom of expression. It appears that it will not usually be necessary to consider that part of s 12(4) as requiring any further or different test. Certainly, s 12(4) does not give presumptive priority to Article 10 over Article 8, or any other Convention right.[143]

In deciding, in a privacy case against the media, whether it is more likely than   **12.50** not the claimant will succeed at trial, the court has to consider how the conflict between Article 8 and Article 10 rights is likely to be resolved at trial. Where the claim is based on misuse of private information, this will involve the two-stage test set out in *Campbell v MGN Ltd*:[144] first whether, in respect of the information the disclosure of which is threatened, the claimant has a reasonable expectation of privacy, and secondly, whether the proportionality test comes down in favour of the claimant taking particular account of the degree of intrusion into private life, and the extent to which the publication is a matter of public concern. The critical propositions were stated in *Re S*[145] by Lord Steyn:

> The interplay between articles 8 and 10 has been illuminated by the opinions in the House of Lords in *Campbell v MGN Ltd* [2004] 2 AC 457. For present purposes the decision of the House on the facts of *Campbell* and the differences between the majority and the minority are not material. What does, however, emerge clearly from the opinions are four propositions. First, neither article has *as such* precedence over the other. Secondly, where the values under the two articles are in conflict, an intense focus on the comparative importance of the specific rights being claimed in the individual case is necessary. Thirdly, the justifications for interfering with or restricting each right must be taken into account. Finally, the proportionality test must be applied to each. For convenience I will call this the ultimate balancing test.

**Balance of convenience**   If the threshold test is met, the court will, as in other   **12.51** cases where the threshold test is lower, proceed to decide where the 'balance of

---

[142] *Cream Holdings*, HL (n 17) [22].
[143] See the quotation from Lord Steyn in 12.50. Also Lord Hoffmann in *Campbell* (n 52) [55]; *Douglas v Hello! Ltd* [2001] QB 967, 1005 (Sedley LJ).
[144] *Campbell* (n 52).
[145] *Re S* (n 43) [17].

convenience' lies. The fact the court has held that the claimant is more likely than not to establish, at trial, that publication should not be allowed, is not in itself enough. The critical factors have been considered above.[146] In many privacy cases the decisive factor will be the need to provide an effective remedy, as required by Article 13 ECHR. If the court is satisfied that the claimant is likely to establish at trial that publication should not be allowed, and if an injunction is the only effective remedy, it is not easy to envisage circumstances in which prior restraint should be denied, consistently with Article 13. This accords with authority, considered below.[147]

**12.52**   The balance between Article 8 and Article 10, or the proportionality test, enters into the decision on the grant or refusal of an interim injunction at two points:

(1)  *When the court is considering whether the threshold test is satisfied* For this purpose, the court has to assess how the balance between the two Convention rights will work out at trial, usually whether the public interest in publication, or the contribution made by the publication to a debate of general interest in a democratic society, is proportionate to the inroad on the right of privacy made by publication; and, conversely whether the extent to which it is necessary to qualify the right of free expression in order to protect the claimant's right of privacy is proportionate to the need for such protection.

(2)  *When the threshold test is satisfied, and the court is considering whether to grant an interim injunction* The court then has to consider the rather different question of whether prior restraint is justified by the need to protect the claimant's right of privacy. It may be possible to protect the claimant's right adequately, even if he or she is likely to win at trial, without the need to prevent the defendant from exercising his or her right of free expression at all.

**12.53**   It is not in every case involving privacy and the media that an injunction will be the only effective remedy. Sometimes confidence and privacy serve the ends of commerce, and damages may be an adequate remedy. This was, narrowly, the view of the Court of Appeal which heard the interim appeal in *Douglas v Hello!*[148] in which, as Sedley LJ observed,[149] 'the first two claimants [the Douglases] had sold most of the privacy they now seek to protect to the third claimant [*OK!*] for a handsome sum'. Even so, the Court of Appeal that heard the appeal from the final judgment considered, so far as the Douglases were concerned, that that decision was wrong, and the interim injunction should have been upheld.[150] If *OK!* had been the only claimant the decision to discharge the injunction could not have been criticized.

---

[146] At 12.15–12.25.
[147] At 12.60–12.67.
[148] *Douglas* (n 143).
[149] *Douglas* (n 143) 1006.
[150] See 12.66.

The grant or refusal of an interim injunction will not depend simply on whether the **12.54** case involves commerce or personal privacy. That would be too blunt an approach, as Sedley LJ pointed out in *Douglas v Hello!*:

> I do not suggest for a moment that there is a bright line between the personal and commercial and that everything on the commercial side, being about money, can be dealt with by an award of damages. Nor, equally, should it be thought that either Article 8 or our domestic law will never protect privacy which is being turned to commercial ends. Everything will depend on the infinite variety of facts thrown up case by case.[151]

So, even in some purely commercial cases, damages have not been regarded as an **12.55** adequate remedy. In *Shelley Films Ltd v Rex Features Ltd*[152] the Court regarded the potential damage caused to the plaintiff production company by the disclosure of commercially valuable, confidential information (in the form of photographs of the costumes, prostheses, and set of a forthcoming film) as being grounds favouring the grant of an injunction. Similarly, in *Creation Records Ltd v News Group Newspapers Ltd*[153] the Court accepted that damages would not be an adequate remedy since an offer to the defendant's readers of a poster showing the secret set used to photograph a pop group's album cover would have seriously impaired the ability of the plaintiff later to exploit the group's image through official marketing and merchandising, as well as sales of the forthcoming album, such loss being exceptionally difficult if not impossible to quantify. This case shows that an injunction may be appropriate to protect a publicity right or right of image.

Commerce is an obvious area in which damages may be an adequate remedy, but **12.56** it is not the only one. There may be an important distinction to be drawn between intimate or sensitive personal information or pictures, and information or pictures which are objectionable simply because they constitute unwanted attention, but are otherwise innocuous.[154] Cases in the latter category might include the pictures of JK Rowling's child in his buggy in an Edinburgh street with his parents,[155] 'out and about' pictures of Princess Caroline,[156] and a picture of Elton John standing outside the gate of his London home wearing a tracksuit and baseball cap.[157] In many of these cases, it is arguable that damages are an adequate remedy because the claimant's principal objection is not to the publication of the images themselves but the methods that were used to obtain them. The real impact on private

---

[151] *Douglas* (n 143) 1006. In commercial cases, the Convention right (if any) which is engaged is Art 1 of the First Protocol. See eg *Ajinomoto Sweeteners Europe SAS v Asda Stores Ltd* [2009] EWHC 1717 (QB), [2010] QB 204 [38] (Tugendhat J) (a point unaffected by the subsequent Court of Appeal decision [2010] EWCA Civ 609, [2011] QB 497).

[152] [1994] EMLR 134 (Ch).

[153] [1997] EMLR 444 (Ch) 445–6.

[154] See Phillipson (n 46) 94.

[155] *Murray v Express Newspapers plc* [2008] EWCA Civ 446, [2009] Ch 481.

[156] *von Hannover v Germany* (n 54).

[157] *John v Associated Newspapers* [2006] EWHC 1611 (QB), [2006] EMLR 27. The application failed because the claimant did not meet the threshold test of probability of success at trial.

life in this scenario arises from the targeting of individuals in a public place to obtain photographs for publication, leading to the constant fear of media intrusion, and an inhibition on their ability to engage freely in ordinary activities without unwanted attention.[158]

**12.57**  **Whether a contractual obligation adds weight to the case for an injunction**  In *Attorney General v Barker*,[159] Lord Donaldson MR, rejecting the submission that Article 10(2) ECHR suggested that publication abroad should not be restricted on the ground of breach of confidence, said:

> I would have thought that much more relevant was the question of whether a man's word is his bond and whether contractual obligations freely entered into shall be maintained.

However, in *London Regional Transport v Mayor of London*,[160] Robert Walker LJ rejected the submission that a contractual obligation carried greater weight:

> ...no authority has been cited to the court establishing that an apparent breach of a contractual duty of confidence is more serious, and is to be approached differently (as regards injunctive relief) than other apparent breaches...the court adopts the same approach to both.

On the other hand, in *Campbell v Frisbee*,[161] the Court of Appeal said:

> We consider that it is arguable that a duty of confidentiality that has been expressly assumed under contract carries more weight, when balanced against the restriction of the right of freedom of expression, than a duty of confidentiality that is not buttressed by express agreement.

In *HRH Prince of Wales v Associated Newspapers Ltd*,[162] the Court of Appeal, referring to this passage from *Campbell v Frisbee*, said:

> We adhere to this view. But the extent to which a contract adds to the weight of a duty of confidence arising out of a confidential relationship will depend upon the facts of the individual case.

**12.58**  What does this mean? Clearly the court was saying that there will be factual situations in which a contract *does* add weight to the duty that arises out of the confidential relationship between the parties, but that there will be others in which it makes little or no difference. Examples in which the existence of a contract would make no difference would be obligations of confidence owed by a doctor or lawyer: the obligation would be no less if the doctor treated the patient on the NHS rather than privately, or the lawyer advised pro bono instead of for a fee. Conversely, there may be circumstances in which a contract that seeks to impose an obligation of confidentiality,

---

158 *Murray* (n 155) [50], [55]–[57].
159 [1990] 3 All ER 257, CA 261.
160 [2001] EWCA Civ 1491, [2003] EMLR 4 [46].
161 [2002] EWCA Civ 1374, [2003] EMLR 3 [22].
162 *HRH Prince of Wales* (n 67) [69].

where none would exist apart from contract, adds nothing because it will not be enforced. An example might be an employment contract that sought to impose an obligation of confidentiality on the employee, after he or she ceased to be employed, in respect of information that the law would not classify as a trade secret.[163]

On the other hand, an express agreement may at the least constitute undeniable **12.59** notice to the confidant that particular classes of information are confidential and are imparted to him or her on the basis that the confidence must be respected. Express agreement that defined classes of information are to be treated as confidential may relieve the court of the necessity to decide whether, apart from agreement, the nature of the information would have supported an equitable obligation. Further, where the public interest is invoked to outweigh a private interest in confidentiality, the court is likely to add to the balance that 'there is a substantial public interest in requiring parties, who have with their eyes open and for valuable consideration contracted (most particularly in contracts of services or for services) not to disclose confidences, to comply with those obligations'.[164]

**Injunction as the only effective remedy**  This proposition may be thought to be **12.60** largely obvious, in cases concerning publication of personal and intrusive information or images, but its importance justifies some examination. The first point is that the underlying value the law is designed to protect in privacy cases focuses upon the protection of human autonomy and dignity—the right to control the dissemination of information about one's private life and the right to the esteem and respect of other people.[165] Refusal of an interim injunction denies the claimant the autonomous right to control the dissemination of information about his or her private life. Autonomy is meaningless if the defendant is permitted to disseminate the information against the subject's objection, at the price of paying some compensation, usually modest. Human dignity is neither preserved nor restored by an award of damages, but rather is monetized, which is entirely at odds with the value. The claimant whose concern is about loss of privacy and dignity will not normally proceed to a public trial if an interim injunction is refused, and if he or she does, the affront to human dignity is aggravated by the increased publicity resulting from the trial, and by the notion, which may be offensive, that he or she wants, or can be compensated, by money.

The second point is that, as Professor Gavin Phillipson says, in respect of the **12.61** interim injunction being the only effective remedy:[166]

> There is overwhelming agreement..., not only from leading academic authorities in the field of privacy but also from UK courts and other jurisdictions... There is thus

---

[163] *Faccenda Chicken v Fowler* [1987] Ch 117, CA, 137.

[164] *Campbell v Frisbee* [2002] EWHC 328 (Ch), [2002] EMLR 31 [30] (Lightman J). Note that Lightman J's decision was reversed on appeal (n 161).

[165] *Campbell* (n 52) [51] (Lord Hoffmann).

[166] Phillipson (n 46). But, for a contrary view, see A Scott, 'Prior notification in privacy cases: A reply to Professor Phillipson' [2010] 2(1) J Media L 49.

more or less universal agreement that in most cases involving unauthorized disclosure of sensitive personal information, an injunction is the only effective remedy.

The principal citations from the relevant authorities are given below.

**12.62**   *The European Court of Human Rights*   Notwithstanding the wide margin of appreciation allowed to national courts as regards the remedies afforded to individual complainants, the Court has repeatedly said that the Convention is intended to guarantee not rights that are theoretical or illusory but rights that are practical and effective.[167] *I v Finland*[168] shows that it may not be enough to satisfy either Article 8 or Article 13 to provide a remedy in damages for any breach of privacy which the complainant could prove: the domestic law may have to ensure that disclosure of the information is prevented from occurring in the first place. The Court said:[169]

> The domestic law must afford appropriate safeguards to prevent any such communication or disclosure of personal health data as may be inconsistent with the guarantees in Art. 8 of the Convention... The Court notes that the mere fact that the domestic legislation provided the applicant with an opportunity to claim compensation for damages caused by an alleged unlawful disclosure of personal data was not sufficient to protect her private life. What is required in this connection is practical and effective protection to exclude any possibility of unauthorized access occurring in the first place. Such protection was not given here.

In *Armoniene v Lithuania*, the Court accepted that the state enjoyed a margin of appreciation in deciding what 'respect' for private life requires in particular circumstances, and that limits could be imposed:

> However, such limits must not be such as to deprive the individual of his or her privacy and thereby empty the right of its effective content.[170]

**12.63**   In the *Spycatcher* case, the Court said,[171] rejecting a complaint by newspapers that interim injunctions preventing publication of excerpts from the book for over a year infringed rights of free expression:

> ...to refuse interlocutory injunctions would mean that [the press] would be free to publish the material immediately and before the substantive trial; this would effectively deprive the Attorney-General, if successful on the merits, of his right to be granted a permanent injunction, thereby irrevocably destroying the substance of his actions.

**12.64**   *English authority*   As long ago as 1849 in *Prince Albert v Strange*,[172] the Lord Chancellor, Lord Cottenham, said:

> ...but, even in the cases so referred to [cases where the injunction was for the protection of a legal title], I have always held, that it was for the discretion of the

---

[167] *von Hannover v Germany* (n 54) para 71; *Armoniene v Lithuania* (2009) 48 EHRR 53, para 38.
[168] (2009) 48 EHRR 31.
[169] *I v Finland* (n 168) [38], [47].
[170] *Armoniene* (n 167) [46].
[171] *Observer and Guardian v UK* (n 18) [62].
[172] 47 ER 1302, 1312. See also *Francome v Mirror Group Newspapers Ltd* [1984] 1 WLR 892, CA, 898, 900, 902.

court to consider whether the defendant might not sustain greater injury from an improper injunction, than the plaintiff from delay in granting it. In the present case, where privacy is the right invaded, the postponing of the injunction would be the equivalent to denying it altogether. The interposition of this court in these cases does not depend on any legal right; and to be effectual, it must be immediate.

This point has been often repeated. In *Attorney General v Newspaper Publishing*  **12.65**
*plc*,[173] Sir John Donaldson MR said:

> ...if, pending the trial, the court allows publication, there is no point in having a trial, since the cloak of confidentiality can never be restored. Confidential information is like an ice cube... Give it to the party who has no refrigerator or will not agree to keep it in one, and by the time of the trial you just have a pool of water.[174]

The Court of Appeal in *A v B plc* described an injunction, in a privacy case, as 'the only remedy which is of any value'.[175]

The strongest recent support for the proposition that in cases of infringement of  **12.66**
personal privacy, an interim injunction should be awarded, as the only effective remedy,[176] is provided by the Court of Appeal in the judgment on the final appeal in *Douglas v Hello! Ltd*.[177] The Court found that the Douglases had a virtually unanswerable case that their privacy was infringed, and that the fact that they could fairly be said to have traded their privacy to a substantial extent, by selling worldwide publication rights of a large number of authorized photographs, did not undermine the case.[178] The Court expressly did not imply that the award of damages (£14,500) should have been greater, but said:

> ...damages, particularly in that sum, cannot fairly be regarded as an adequate remedy...the Douglases would never have agreed to the publication of the unauthorised photographs. In those circumstances, bearing in mind the nature of the injury they suffered, namely mental distress, a modest sum by way of damages does not represent an adequate remedy.

> The sum is also small in the sense that it could not represent any real deterrent to a newspaper or magazine, with a large circulation, contemplating the publication of photographs which infringed an individual's privacy. Accordingly, particularly in the light of the state of competition in the newspaper and magazine industry, the refusal of an interlocutory injunction in a case such as this represents a strong potential disincentive to respect for aspects of private life, which the Convention intends should be respected.

---

[173] *Attorney General v Newspaper Publishing* (n 109) 358.
[174] A similar point was made by Lord Nicholls in *Cream Holdings*, HL (n 17) [18], and by the Court of Appeal in *Greene v Associated Newspapers* (n 59) [78].
[175] *A v B plc* (n 50) [11(ii)].
[176] See also *Contostavlos v Mendahun* [2012] EWHC 850 (QB), where an interim injunction had been granted to prevent the further dissemination of a sexually explicit videotape (or stills taken from it). The photographs were highly intrusive and intimate and there was no legal basis for resisting continuation of the order.
[177] *Douglas* (n 41).
[178] *Douglas* (n 41) [253]–[254].

...

Only by the grant of an interlocutory injunction could the Douglases' rights have been satisfactorily protected. Further, the interests of *Hello!* at the interlocutory stage, which were essentially only financial, could have been protected by an appropriate undertaking in damages by the Douglases.[179]

**12.67** In *Mosley v News Group Newspapers Ltd*,[180] Eady J said:

> Whereas reputation can be vindicated by an award of damages, in the sense that the claimant can be restored to the esteem in which he was previously held, that is not possible where embarrassing personal information has been released for general publication. As the media are well aware, once privacy has been infringed, the damage is done and pursuing a court action only augments the embarrassment. Claimants with the degree of resolve (and financial resources) of Mr Max Mosley are likely to be few and far between. Thus, if journalists can successfully avoid the grant of an interlocutory injunction, they can usually relax in the knowledge that intrusive coverage of someone's sex life will carry no adverse consequences for them and that the news agenda will move on.
>
> ...it has to be accepted that an infringement of privacy can never be effectively compensated by a monetary award. Judges cannot achieve what is, in the nature of things, impossible. That unpalatable fact cannot be mitigated by simply adding a few noughts to the number first thought of.

**12.68** **Section 12(4) HRA: public domain, public interest, and relevant privacy codes**   In cases where the material sought to be restrained is claimed by the defendant, or appears to the court, to be journalistic, literary, or artistic material (or conduct connected with such material), then s 12(4) requires particular regard to be had to: (a) the extent to which (i) the material has, or is about to, become available to the public or (ii) it is, or would be, in the public interest for the material to be published; and (b) any relevant privacy code. The nature and scope of the defences of 'public domain' and 'public interest' are considered in Chapter 11,[181] and the terms and relevance of the appropriate privacy codes are considered in Chapter 14.

**12.69** *Public domain*   While the fact that material has already been made public may be a defence, or a bar to injunctive relief, the scope of such a defence or bar is more limited in relation to personal information than it is in relation to commercial (or governmental) information.[182]

**12.70** *About to become available to the public*   The fact that information is about to become available to the public may mean that little material harm will be done to the defendant if there is an advancement of the date of a publication that will occur in any event. In other cases, the date of publication may be crucial to the value of

---

[179] *Douglas* (n 41) [256]–[257], [259].

[180] *Mosley* (n 38) [230]–[231].

[181] At 11.43–11.63 (public domain), 11.74–11.105 (public interest).

[182] This was first recognized by Lord Keith in the *Spycatcher* case (n 41) 260. As regards photographs, even widespread media publication is unlikely to justify repeat publications, unless the

the information, and call for protection of information in advance of publication. The classic examples are Budget secrets, and other price-sensitive information. The value of an exclusive interview or photo opportunity,[183] or of memoirs to be published in book form, or of the financial information of a profession, are all examples with direct financial implications for the individual concerned. In the case of Lady Thatcher's memoirs the Court of Appeal declined to grant an injunction on grounds including the imminence of publication, but the criticisms made of that decision appear well founded.[184]

*Privacy codes* 'Relevant privacy codes' are not further defined in the HRA. The **12.71** phrase could include the internal code of a newspaper or broadcaster.[185] The importance of these codes has been recognized by the courts following the observation of Brooke LJ in *Douglas v Hello!* that:

> A newspaper which flouts Section 3 of the [PCC] Code is likely in those circumstances to have its claim to an entitlement to freedom of expression trumped by Article 10(2) considerations of privacy... It follows that on the present occasion it is not necessary to go beyond section 12 of the 1998 Act and clause 3 of the Press Complaints Commission's code to find the ground rules by which we should weigh the competing considerations of freedom of expression on the one hand and privacy on the other.[186]

### (f) Equitable principles militating against the grant of an injunction

An injunction may be refused if the defendant can raise one of the general 'equi- **12.72** table defences' such as delay[187] or acquiescence, or that the claimant has unclean hands.[188] In *Douglas* the defendant's argument that no injunction should be granted on the grounds that the claimant company (its rival *OK!* magazine) had

---

attempt to stem the tide has passed the point of no return: contrast the Court of Appeal's approach in *Douglas* (n 41) [105] with *Mosley* (n 38) [33]–[36] (Eady J).

[183] *eg Attard v Greater Manchester Newspapers Ltd* (F, 14/15 June 2001, Bennett J).

[184] See *Douglas v Hello! Ltd* [2003] EWHC 786 (Ch), [2003] 3 All ER 996 [224] (Lindsay J), treating the Thatcher memoirs case as no longer binding. There are a number of commercial cases where the fact that information is about to be made public has been considered a reason why the date of publication should not be advanced by a third party: *Fraser v Thames Television Ltd* [1984] QB 44; *R v Broadcasting Complaints Commission, ex p Granada Ltd* [1995] EMLR 163, CA, 168; *Creation Records* (n 153) 456.

[185] *Hansard*, HC vol 315, col 536 (2 July 1988).

[186] *Douglas* (n 143) 994. These passages have been cited with approval, *eg* in *A v B plc* [2001] 1 WLR 2341, QB (Jack J) and *Mills v News Group Newspapers Ltd* [2001] EMLR 41, Ch (Lawrence Collins J). The provisions of cl 3 of the PCC Code were also considered in *A v B and C* (QB, 2 March 2001, Mackay J) and *Beckham v MGN Ltd* (QB, 28 June 2001, Eady J). Note that the PCC Code has now been superseded by the IPSO Editors' Code (n 33) and that the material from clause 3 of the PCC Code is contained in clause 2 of the IPSO Code.

[187] See *Bunn v BBC* [1998] 3 All ER 552, Ch; *Service Corp International plc v Channel 4 TV* [1999] EMLR 83, Ch.

[188] *Argyll (Duchess) v Argyll (Duke)* [1967] Ch 302. See also the Church of Scientology cases (*Hubbard v Vosper* [1972] 2 QB 84, 101 and *Church of Scientology of California v Miller, The Times*, 23 October 1987), where the Court held that evidence that the plaintiffs were protecting their secrets by deplorable means meant that they could not come to court asking it to protect those secrets by the equitable remedy of an injunction.

allegedly used similar 'spoiler' tactics in the past was not regarded, even if true, as being sufficient reason to refuse an injunction on equitable grounds.[189]

### (g) Failing to give notice to the subject of intended publication of private material

**12.73**  Mr Mosley[190] made an application to the ECtHR alleging a breach of the United Kingdom's positive duty under Articles 8 and 13 to provide protection for his private life, and an effective remedy. Mr Mosley succeeded at trial in England and was awarded £60,000 damages, but complained to the Strasbourg Court that he was denied the only effective protection, an interim injunction, because the newspaper defendant took steps to ensure that he was not alerted to the pending publication, for the purpose of avoiding a possible interim injunction. The United Kingdom's breach was alleged to lie in its failure to impose a duty on newspapers and other media, enforceable by criminal or regulatory sanctions, to give prior notification to a person of a publication which will infringe his Article 8 right by disclosing private information, so that he may seek an injunction.[191]

**12.74**  The ECtHR declared Mosley's claim admissible, finding that 'no sum of money awarded after disclosure of the impugned material could afford a remedy in respect of [his] complaint', [192] but on the facts of his case dismissed the complaint of breach of Article 8. Although the Court was satisfied that there had been a 'flagrant and unjustified invasion of the applicant's privacy',[193] the determination of the method of ensuring protection of Article 8 lay in the first instance with the relevant state and in doing so it enjoyed a significant margin of appreciation. The Court took the view that the award of damages (£60,000) and costs (£420,000) in the case was likely to have a 'salutary effect on journalistic practices'[194] and that *ex post facto* awards of damages could provide an adequate remedy for violations of Article 8.[195] The regime of pre-notification urged by Mosley would have wider implications beyond sensationalist reporting and might threaten political reporting and serious investigative journalism, thereby raising potential conflict with Article 10.[196]

> ...the Court has consistently emphasised the need to look beyond the facts of the present case and to consider the broader impact of a pre-notification requirement. The limited scope under Article 10 for restrictions on the freedom of the press to publish material which contributes to debate on matters of general public interest

---

[189]  *Douglas* (n 143) 974–975, 996 (Brooke LJ).
[190]  The claimant in *Mosley* (n 38).
[191]  The grounds of the application are explained and considered in a paper by Professor Gavin Phillipson (n 46).
[192]  *Mosley v UK* (2011) 53 EHRR 30, para 72.
[193]  *Mosley v UK* (n 192) para 104.
[194]  *Mosley v UK* (n 192) para 119.
[195]  *Mosley v UK* (n 192) para 120.
[196]  *Mosley v UK* (n 192) para 121. The Court was particularly concerned with the need for an effective sanction to underpin any notification requirement. The likely size of any *ex post facto* fine for non-compliance 'would run the risk of being incompatible with the requirements of Article 10' (para 129).

must be borne in mind. Thus, having regard to the chilling effect to which a pre-notification requirement risks giving rise, to the significant doubts as to the effectiveness of any pre-notification requirement and to the wide margin of appreciation in this area, the Court is of the view that Article 8 does not require a legally binding pre-notification requirement.

It cannot seriously be doubted that Mr Mosley's application draws attention to a **12.75** lacuna in effective protection for privacy rights. One solution might be the award of exemplary damages in the amount needed to supply the deterrent element that is presently recognized as lacking in damages for misuse of private information.[197] But that option has, for the moment, been closed by Eady J's decision in *Mosley*[198] that exemplary damages are not available for misuse of private information.

That ruling may receive reconsideration by the courts. If a newspaper can be shown **12.76** to have taken a deliberate decision to avoid alerting the subject of a story, in order to avoid the risk of an injunction (as was the case in *Mosley*[199]), the natural inference may be that it has sufficient knowledge that its action may unlawfully infringe the claimant's right, and that it has made the assessment that its own interest in publication is greater than the downside risk of adverse consequences, in the unlikely event that the claimant, having been deprived of the opportunity to obtain an interim injunction, decides to take the matter to trial.[200] If so, the case may fall within Lord Devlin's second category of cases in which exemplary damages may be awarded.[201] Exemplary damages have been criticized quite often as anomalous in the civil law. On the other hand, the Law Commission, following two consultation exercises, concluded that the central policy arguments for retaining them outweigh those against, which it characterized as either unfounded or surmountable, and that availability of exemplary damages should be placed on a principled basis and expanded to cover any tort or equitable wrong which is committed with outrageous disregard of the claimant's rights.[202] The government has stated that it does not propose to legislate, but considers the subject suitable for further judicial development.[203] It is also an area that is arguably better suited to regulatory intervention rather than the award of exemplary damages in civil litigation as a regulator can take the defendant publisher's conduct in previous cases into account when fixing any penalty. Were a UK broadcaster deliberately to ambush an individual

---

[197] *Douglas* (n 41) [257].

[198] *Mosely* (n 38) [172]–[197]. See the discussion of exemplary damages at 12.130–12.135.

[199] The editor accepted this in cross-examination: (n 38) [209].

[200] The ECtHR reached the clear view on the facts of *Mosley* that 'there is no doubt that one of the main reasons, if not the only reason, for failing to seek [Mr Mosley's] comments was to avoid the possibility of an injunction being sought and granted': (n 192) para 128.

[201] *Rookes v Barnard* [1964] AC 1129, HL. The second category was where the wrong involved oppressive, arbitrary or unconstitutional action by servants of the government.

[202] Law Commission, *Report on Aggravated, Exemplary and Restitutionary Damages* (Law Com No 247, 1997).

[203] Parliamentary answer 9 November 1999, referred to in *Kuddus v Chief Constable of Leicestershire* [2001] UKHL 29, [2002] 2 AC 122 [35].

with the publication of private information in circumstances similar to *Mosley*, it would risk sanction by the broadcasting regulator Ofcom. Regulatory action may be more effective in discouraging such conduct and avoids a number of the problems of exemplary damages. Any financial penalty would not represent an unjustified windfall to an individual claimant and, when fixed, could take into account the prior conduct of the relevant broadcaster. There is presently no equivalent regulatory sanction regime for the UK print media, leaving only the inapt tool of exemplary damages.

### (3) Final or Perpetual Injunctions

#### (a) Final injunction as a remedy

**12.77** If successful at trial, it would appear reasonable for a claimant to be granted an injunction to prevent any future publication or disclosure of the subject matter of the proceedings, provided there is a continuing threat. In *Tolstoy v UK*,[204] although the damages awarded by the jury in the applicant's libel action against Lord Aldington were considered by the ECtHR to be a disproportionate interference with his right to freedom of expression, the award of a permanent injunction preventing repetition of the allegation that Lord Aldington was a war criminal was considered 'the logical consequence' of the finding in that case.[205] Such reasoning would seem to apply with more force where the cause of action relates to publication of personal information that the court has found that the claimant was entitled to keep private.

#### (b) Public domain proviso

**12.78** A final injunction may contain a public domain proviso, as in *Mosley v News Group* in which Eady J held that the newspaper had failed to demonstrate a sufficient public interest to justify the substantial interference with the claimant's privacy interests.[206] However, if the trial concerned information that had already been published, a public domain proviso deprives the injunction of most or all of its effect, and requires careful consideration as to what if any proviso should be included. In *Bristol City Council v News Group Newspapers Ltd*[207] a public domain proviso was

---

[204] (1995) 20 EHRR 442.

[205] This principle was reaffirmed in *McVicar v UK* (2002) 35 EHRR 22. In that case the ECtHR found that even if a permanent injunction restraining the applicant from repeating allegations that athlete Linford Christie was a cheat who regularly used performance-enhancing drugs was 'capable of discouraging the participation of the applicant and other journalists in debates of legitimate public concern in the future', that restriction was necessary to protect Mr Christie's reputation (para 82). Similarly, in *Goodwin v UK* (1996) 22 EHRR 123, a fine for contempt of court for failing to comply with an order for disclosure of a journalist's source was found to be in breach of Art 10, whereas an injunction restraining publication of the confidential material which the source had disclosed was not.

[206] *Mosley* (n 38).

[207] [2012] EWHC 3748 (Fam), [2013] 1 FLR 1205.

also refused on the grounds that publication of the information would be intrusive and there was no evidence that any of the information was in the public domain. In *Mosley* descriptions of the claimant's sado-masochistic sexual activities were included within the public domain proviso because there had been enormous publication of these details. But the republication of personal or intrusive pictures or videos is still likely to represent interference with the claimant's privacy interests. In such cases a public domain proviso will therefore usually be inappropriate.[208] In *Mosley* the final injunction restrained publication of still and moving images and the sound recordings from the secret filming. These were not subject to the public domain proviso.

### (c) The effect on third parties?

A serious lacuna in the effectiveness of final injunctions to bind third parties was **12.79** identified in *Jockey Club v Buffham*,[209] in which it was held that the BBC, a third party to the proceedings which had been served with a final injunction preventing the publication of confidential information, would not be in contempt of court if it published that information (which came into its hands prior to the injunction being made). Gray J reasoned that this was because the essence of the contempt consisted in the interference by that third party with the course of justice in the proceedings in which the order was made.[210] The issue had been due to be considered by the Court of Appeal in a 2012 appeal, *Hutcheson (formerly WER) v Popdog Ltd (formerly REW)*,[211] but permission to appeal was refused when the issues concerned ultimately became academic. However, Lord Neuberger MR took the opportunity to hint that the decision in *Jockey Club* may be ripe for reconsideration in the Court of Appeal's reported decision on the permission to appeal application.[212]

## D. Damages

Damages are recoverable for all the civil wrongs considered in this book. The **12.80** approach in torts for intrusion into aspects of physical privacy, damage to reputation, breach of copyright, and harassment is considered elsewhere.[213] This section considers awards of damages for breach of confidence or misuse of private

---

[208] See *Douglas* (n 41) [105] and *CTB* (n 41) in which Tugendhat J observed at [24]: 'with each exposure of personal information or allegations, whether by way of visual images or verbally, there is a new intrusion and occasion for distress or embarrassment'.

[209] [2002] EWHC 1866 (QB), [2003] QB 462.

[210] *Jockey Club* (n 209) 469.

[211] [2011] EWCA Civ 1580, [2012] 1 WLR 782.

[212] *Hutcheson* (n 211) [26].

[213] See ch 10 (intrusion), 8.25 *et seq* (defamation), ch 9 (copyright), and 6.77–6.79 (harassment).

information, and damages under s 8 HRA in claims against public authorities for acting incompatibly with the Convention right to respect for private life. The key questions to be addressed are:

(1) Are damages available?
(2) If so, are damages available as of right or as a matter of discretion?
(3) Are damages available for actual pecuniary loss or damage to commercial interests and how should such damages be assessed?
(4) Are damages available for damage to non-commercial interests and how should such damages be assessed?
(5) Are aggravated or exemplary damages available?
(6) How can damage be mitigated?

### (1) The Availability of Damages in Principle

**12.81**   Historically, there was dispute about the availability of damages in principle as a remedy for a breach of confidence that had already taken place. By the 1990s the dispute had largely resolved itself *in favour* of the availability of damages. That dispute has not been imported into the law of misuse of private information, and there is no doubt that substantial damages may be awarded irrespective of any entitlement to an injunction.[214]

**12.82**   The historical dispute lay in the fact that the jurisdiction to award damages for breach of an equitable right of confidence (as opposed to a contractual right where recovery is uncontroversial) arose out of the Chancery Amendment Act 1858 (also known as Lord Cairns' Act) which gave the court the power to award damages 'in lieu or in addition to an injunction'. The argument ran that such recovery was not available where there were no grounds for an injunction, which would be likely if the breach had placed the information in the public domain. This interpretation led the Court of Appeal in *Proctor v Bayley* to hold that where there is no case for an injunction, damages cannot be given.[215] Sir Robert Megarry V-C reiterated this view (although with an acceptance that matters were developing) in *Malone v Commissioner of Police for the Metropolis*.[216]

**12.83**   However Lord Goff in *Spycatcher* stated that damages were available for past breaches of confidence on a 'beneficent interpretation' of Lord Cairns' Act.[217] This

---

[214] *Cornelius v de Taranto* [2001] EMLR 12; *Campbell v MGN Ltd* [2002] EWHC 499 (QB), [2002] EMLR 30, both Morland J.

[215] (1889) 42 Ch D 390, 401 (Cotton LJ).

[216] [1979] Ch 344, 360.

[217] *Attorney General v Observer* (n 41) 286. See the extensive discussion of this issue in R Toulson and C Phipps, *Confidentiality* (3rd edn, Sweet & Maxwell 2012) paras 9-037 *et seq*. The authors' conclusion accords with that of Cooke P in *Aquaculture Corp v New Zealand Green Mussel Co Ltd* [1990] 3 NZLR 299, 301 that for a claim based on a breach of a duty of confidence 'a full range of remedies should be available as appropriate, no matter whether they originated in common law, equity or statute'.

position has found express sympathy in the Canadian Supreme Court in *Cadbury Schweppes Inc v FBI Foods Ltd*:[218]

> Having regard to the evolution of equitable principles apparent in the case law, we should clearly affirm that, in this country, the authority to award financial compensation for breach of confidence is inherent in the exercise of general equitable jurisdiction and does not depend on the niceties of Lord Cairns' Act or its statutory successors. This conclusion is fed, as well, by the *sui generis* nature of the action. The objective in a breach of confidence case is to put the confider in as good a position as it would have been in but for the breach. To that end, the Court has ample jurisdiction to fashion appropriate relief out of the full gamut of available remedies, including appropriate financial compensation.

This is the position arrived at by the Supreme Court of Victoria Court of Appeal in **12.84** *Giller v Procopets*[219] in which the historical dispute was subjected to lengthy discussion. Maxwell P upheld Gillard J's decision that a claim for damages for distress resulting from intentional tortious conduct was cognizable in law:

> The purpose of the law of torts is to provide compensation where an injury has been caused by wrongful conduct of another. The facts of the present case demonstrate that if the defendant set out intentionally to cause harm and distress to the plaintiff by wrongfully showing or threatening to show the video film, which caused anger, humiliation, frustration, upset and distress, it is strongly arguable that the law would not be fulfilling its purpose if it did not permit compensatory damages for such mental distress and upset. The distribution and showing of the video is analogous to the publication of a defamatory imputation and the law should permit recovery for distress depending upon the gravity of the wrongful act and the effect upon the victim.

In *Spencer (Earl and Countess) v UK*[220] the applicant, in support of his position that **12.85** he had exhausted his domestic remedies, argued that damages were not available for previous publications (or for personal distress). The Commission, in ruling the complaint inadmissible, accepted there was some doubt as to the availability of damages where an injunction could not have been granted, but relied on Lord Goff in *Spycatcher* as showing 'the developing state of the law [of confidence] relating to the award of damages'. The availability of the remedy of an account of profits appears to have been the determinative factor in the ruling that 'the applicants have not demonstrated that [the remedy of breach of confidence] was insufficient or ineffective in the circumstances of their cases'.

In *Douglas v Hello!*[221] Sedley LJ placed substantial importance on *Spencer* thus: **12.86**

> ...of course neither Her Majesty's Government, which has the conduct of the United Kingdom's cases in Strasbourg, nor the Commission (during its lifetime), had power to determine what the law of England and Wales is; but the fact that

---

[218] [2000] FSR 491 (Ch), 516 (Binnie J).
[219] [2008] VSCA 236.
[220] (1998) 25 EHRR CD 105 (Commission Decision).
[221] *Douglas* (n 143) 1001.

this unanimous conclusion could emerge from a detailed consideration, after written and oral argument, of the state of the extant English authorities by a body of distinguished European jurists is of real persuasive force. It would not be a happy thing if the national courts were to go back without cogent reason on the United Kingdom's successful exegesis of its own law.

**12.87** In *Campbell v MGN Ltd* the House of Lords reimposed the judge's award of damages without comment on this issue.[222] In *Lady Archer v Williams*, a breach of confidence case, the claimant sought damages for the disclosure that she had undergone a facelift (with an injunction to restrain further disclosures by her former PA).[223] On the basis of *Cornelius* and *Campbell*, Jackson J accepted that where a breach of confidence causes injury to feelings the court has the power to award damages. He said that general damages for injury to feelings should be kept to a modest level, should be proportionate to the injury suffered, and should be well below the level of general damages for serious physical or psychiatric injury.[224] In *Douglas v Hello!* the award of damages for distress to the Douglases was said to be 'unassailable in principle'.[225]

**12.88** Damages are available against public authorities for breaches of Convention rights under s 8 HRA if the court which is asked to make such an award otherwise has the power, in civil proceedings, to award damages or order the payment of compensation. The court is entitled to consider all of the circumstances of the case including any other relief granted in relation to the breach, any other decisions made in relation to the breach in question and whether damages are necessary to afford just satisfaction to the claimant.[226]

## (2) Discretionary or as of Right?

### (a) Private law claims

**12.89** With some judicial trepidation, the action for misuse of private information came to be regarded as 'tantamount' to a tort from which damages flow as of right, albeit tinged by its provenance in equitable doctrine.[227] Whether damages are awarded as of right or one of a list of available discretionary remedies has not received direct

---

[222] The defendant's appeal on liability was successful in the Court of Appeal (n 72) as a result of which the damages were set aside, but the HL (n 52) found in favour of Ms Campbell on liability and reimposed the award.

[223] [2003] EWHC 1670 (QB), [2003] EMLR 38.

[224] Damages were assessed at £2,500. See *Cornelius* (n 214) and *Campbell* (n 72).

[225] *Douglas* (n 41) [259].

[226] s 8(3) HRA.

[227] *Mosley* (n 38) [8]–[10], [181] (Eady J) noting that textbooks on the law of torts included misuse of private information within their remit (P Milmo and W Rogers, *Gatley on Libel and Slander* (10th edn, Sweet & Maxwell 2004); A Dugdale and M Jones (eds), *Clerk and Lindsell on Torts* (19th edn, Sweet & Maxwell 2006)). The Court of Appeal has since held, in the context of permission to serve proceedings abroad, that misuse of private information is a tort: *Google Inc v Vidal-Hall* [2015] EWCA Civ 311, [2015] 3 WLR 409.

attention. The personal claimants in *Douglas v Hello!* and *McKennitt v Ash* were held to be 'entitled' to damages for distress.[228] In *Campbell v MGN Ltd* the order was set aside by the Court of Appeal on liability without comment on the size of the award of damages. The House of Lords did not consider the issue. The only comment on the size of the award was by Lord Nicholls who, in passing, described it as 'modest'.[229] In *Mosley* an adequate financial remedy was 'necessary'.[230] In *AAA v Associated Newspapers Ltd* damages of £15,000 were awarded for breach of the very young claimant's privacy right by repeated publication of an unpixelated photograph of her, with Nicola Davies J explaining that the level of award should serve as notice of 'how seriously the court regards infringements of a child's rights'.[231] The practice in out-of-court settlements, where details have been publicized, has been to include a compensatory element.[232]

### (b) The European Court of Human Rights' approach

The approach of the ECtHR to remedies does not invariably lead to an award of damages. Although the Article 13 ECHR right to an effective remedy is not a Convention right under the HRA, by s 2(1) HRA the court, when determining a question that has arisen in connection with a Convention right, must take into account Strasbourg jurisprudence. Article 41 ECHR provides that the court shall, if necessary, afford 'just satisfaction' to the injured party. The ECtHR often awards no damages on the basis that a finding of breach of the relevant right is itself just satisfaction.[233] In *Peck v UK* the applicant had suffered significant distress, embarrassment, and frustration that would not be sufficiently compensated by a finding of violation.[234] The applicant was awarded €11,800 in respect of non-pecuniary damage. **12.90**

### (c) Claims under the Human Rights Act 1998

The ECtHR's approach manifests itself in domestic law in the form of claims brought against public bodies under s 8 HRA. The discretionary, perhaps even residual nature of an award of damages is made explicit in s 8(3). This section provides that no award of damages is to be made unless, taking all the circumstances into account, including any other relief or remedy granted and the consequences of the decision of the court, the court is satisfied that damages are necessary for **12.91**

---

[228] *Douglas* (n 184); *McKennitt v Ash* [2005] EWHC 3003 (QB), [2006] EMLR 10 [162] (Eady J).
[229] *Campbell* (n 52) [10].
[230] *Mosley* (n 38) [235].
[231] *AAA v Associated Newspapers Ltd* [2012] EWHC 2103 (QB), [2013] EMLR 2 [127].
[232] See further 13.07.
[233] Although this is more likely in the case of a finding of a procedural rather than substantive breach. See D Shelton, *Remedies in International Human Rights Law* (2nd edn, Oxford University Press 2005) 260 and the discussion of just satisfaction in the Law Commission report: Law Commission, *Damages Under the Human Rights Act 1998* (Law Com No 266, 2000) paras 3.38–3.43.
[234] (2003) 36 EHRR 41.

just satisfaction. This provision, combined with s 2 HRA, which requires the court to take into account any relevant Strasbourg jurisprudence when determining matters that might affect Convention rights, imports directly into English law Convention jurisprudence on just satisfaction.

**12.92** In the context of claims under the HRA the courts have been keen to discourage the growth of a 'compensation culture'. Damages are not an automatic entitlement but an equitable remedy of last resort which must reflect the balance to be drawn between the interests of the individual and those of the public as a whole, not least where there has been no pecuniary loss or the complainant has contributed to what has occurred.[235] The approach is not comparable with awards for breaches of obligations under civil law. The House of Lords, in *R v Secretary of State of the Home Department, ex p Greenfield*, considered that where an infringement of a human right has occurred the primary concern is to bring the infringement to an end; any question of compensation is secondary, and findings of violations are likely to be sufficient to encourage Member State compliance with the Convention.[236] Domestic courts are entitled to take into account Strasbourg principles when deciding whether to award damages and the amount, and should not aim to be more or less generous.[237]

**12.93** In *R (Robertson) v City of Wakefield Metropolitan Council*[238] there was a claim for relief under s 8 HRA where a local authority lawfully exploited for commercial reasons its electoral register which contained aggregated private personal data, but did so without giving each individual concerned a right to object to their data being sold. The court held this to be a disproportionate way in which to give effect to the legitimate objective of retaining a commercially available register, and therefore a breach of the individual's Article 8 right. However, in *Wainwright v Home Office*, a case concerned with prison strip searches, Lord Hoffmann questioned whether the intrusive act should give rise to a remedy in damages irrespective of whether it was intentional, careless, or accidental.[239]

**12.94** In spite of the development of a 'compensation culture' many claims against public authorities under the HRA are primarily concerned with obtaining an explanation for

---

[235] *Anufrijeva v London Borough of Southwark* [2003] EWCA Civ 1406, [2004] QB 1124 [49]–[78], where the Court of Appeal considered the features of claims for compensation under the HRA.

[236] [2005] UKHL 14, [2005] 1 WLR 673 [9]. At [52] Lord Bingham, in a speech with which the rest of the House agreed, approved the view of the Court of Appeal in *Anufrijeva* (n 235).

[237] *ex p Greenfield* (n 236) [19].

[238] [2001] EWHC 915 (Admin), [2002] QB 1052.

[239] [2003] UKHL 53, [2004] 2 AC 406 [51]. The Court of Appeal had found that the claimants would have had a right to relief under s 7(1)(a) HRA had the events in question occurred after 2 October 2000, when the HRA came into force: [2001] EWCA Civ 2081, [2002] QB 1334. The ECtHR subsequently awarded the applicants €3,000 each for a breach of their rights under Arts 8 and 13: (2007) 44 EHRR 40, para 60.

a bureaucratic act or a declaration of infringement.[240] A prompt ameliorative response to the breach by the public authority may—like a declaration, an apology, or an investigation leading to a change in procedure or policy—constitute 'just satisfaction' for the claimant and no award of damages will be necessary.[241] The court should take into account whether the act causing the breach of Article 8 is continuing, the gravity of the breach (which may be the ambit of disclosure in a privacy claim), the degree of damage and distress suffered, and whether it was intentional.[242]

### (3) Pecuniary Loss

Where an infringement of privacy causes quantifiable pecuniary loss there is no **12.95** reason in principle why an award of damages to compensate for such loss should not be made in either a privacy claim or a s 8 HRA claim.[243] The central principle followed by the ECtHR in awarding damages is that of *restitutio in integrum*, seeking to return the applicant to the position in which he or she would have been had there not been a breach of Convention rights, which includes compensation for actual pecuniary loss.[244] This principle also runs through English law[245] and has been applied in the breach of confidence context,[246] in intellectual property claims,[247] and in passing off.[248] In *Douglas v Hello!* compensatory damages were awarded to *OK!* by the judge for the expected revenue which would have come from the editions carrying the authorized wedding exclusives as they

---

[240]  *R (Bernard) v London Borough of Enfield* [2002] EWHC 2282 (Admin), [2003] HRLR 4 [39] (Sullivan J).

[241]  *W v Westminster City Council (No 2)* [2005] EWHC 102 (QB), [2005] 4 All ER 96.

[242]  *W* (n 241) [247]–[252].

[243]  Shelton (n 233); Law Commission report (n 233). However, the Supreme Court of South Africa has held that special damages are not recoverable in libel unless the claimant proves falsity: *Media 24 Ltd v SA Taxi Securitisation (Pty) Ltd* [2011] ZASCA 117 (5 July 2011). The decision is discussed in an article by J Campbell, 'An Anomaly: Special Damages for Libel' (2011) 3(2) J Media L 193. Although such a principle is unlikely to be accepted in English defamation law, it might provide a basis on which to seek to limit recovery of special damages in privacy cases.

[244]  See *Barberà, Messegué and Jabardo v Spain* (1989) 11 EHRR 360, para 16 following *Ringeisen v Austria (No 2)* (1979-80) 1 EHRR 504, para 21 and the Law Commission report (n 233) paras 3.19–3.21, 3.23–3.25, 4.61–4.62.

[245]  See *General Tire & Rubber Co v Firestone Tyre & Rubber Co Ltd* [1975] 1 WLR 819, HL, 824–7 where Lord Wilberforce identified the normal categories at least in patent cases. They are the profit, or the royalty, which was or would have been achieved (*eg* where the defendant manufactures, or licenses the manufacture of, goods covered by the patent), and the licence fee that would reasonably have been charged (*eg* where it is not possible to assess the level of profit).

[246]  *Dowson & Mason Ltd v Potter* [1986] 1 WLR 1419, CA.

[247]  *General Tire* (n 245).

[248]  In *Irvine v Talksport* [2003] EWCA Civ 423, [2003] 2 All ER 881 [104], [106], [111] where the Court of Appeal held that the principles identified by Lord Wilberforce in the *General Tire* case (n 245) are applicable to the issue as to what would be a reasonable fee for the celebrity claimant's endorsement of the defendant's Talk Radio. A reasonable endorsement fee in the context of that case represented the fee that, on a balance of probabilities, the defendant would have had to pay in order to obtain lawfully that which it, in fact, obtained unlawfully, not the fee which the defendant could have afforded to pay.

were originally planned by the publisher.[249] The House of Lords restored the judge's award.[250]

**12.96** Various forms of consequential loss may form the basis of a claim. A claimant may incur financial loss in attempting to contain or retrieve the unauthorized information disclosure in question.[251] Additional costs caused to claimants by reasonable attempts to mitigate the effects of the intrusion or disclosure may be compensated for in damages.[252] The misuse of private information may lead to a loss of employment or opportunity, or deter third parties from dealing with the claimant. The courts are yet to consider a claim for damages in that form. Where the claimant is a sports or entertainment celebrity, substantial endorsement and sponsorship deals may be lost as a direct consequence of intentional disclosures of private or embarrassing information. The pecuniary loss here is akin to special damages in libel.

**12.97** Private information may be exploited commercially and be legitimately sold as a commodity by the subject of the rights in the same manner that a trade secret may be exploited.[253] The viability of any claim for pecuniary loss will depend on the circumstances. A claim for an account of profits may not succeed where no profit has been made. In a commercial publication, unauthorized private information may be disclosed as one article or feature within a more substantial newspaper or magazine thus an increase in sales may be difficult to pin to a particular article or feature.[254] Of course the unlawfully obtained private information may have been syndicated domestically or internationally for profit, although these profits may not outweigh the purchase price of unauthorized information or images, which are often priced to reflect market scarcity, risk, and the cost of obtaining it. In *Douglas* the rogue photographer's photographs were sold for £125,000.

**12.98** A notional licence fee may be an appropriate basis on which to arrive at a level of damages but may be incompatible with other bases on which loss may be claimed.[255] In *Douglas v Hello!* the Court of Appeal rejected the argument that a

---

[249] *Douglas v Hello! Ltd* [2003] EWHC 2629 (Ch), [2004] EMLR 2 [55]. Lindsay J set the award payable by *Hello!* to *OK!* at £1,026,706 plus costs occasioned by the interference with the exclusive licence. The Court found that newspaper republications of the unauthorized photographs had damaged *OK!*'s sales. As *Hello!* had not specifically prohibited republication by other media the additional damage thereby caused was not too remote for it to be held liable for, a finding of fact approved by the Court of Appeal ((n 41) [238]–[242]) and the House of Lords: *Douglas v Hello! Ltd* [2007] UKHL 21, [2008] 1 AC 1 [127]–[128].

[250] *Douglas*, HL (n 249).

[251] *Cornelius* (n 214). The claimant was entitled to damages in the sum of £750 representing her expenses of trying to retrieve an authorized psychiatric report from NHS systems.

[252] *Douglas*, Ch D [57]. The Douglases had to expedite the process for approving, selecting, and transporting photographs of their wedding so as to mitigate the commercial effect of the 'spoiler' edition, at a cost of some £7,000 awarded to them by Lindsay J.

[253] *Douglas*, HL (n 249). For further discussion of publicity rights see 9.89–9.114.

[254] Syndication profits may be more readily itemized.

[255] *Douglas* (n 184) [280]. At the trial the claimants' claims for purely compensatory damages (including pecuniary and non-pecuniary elements) and for a notional licence fee were held to be

claim for damages could be based on a notional licence fee for the unauthorized, lower-quality images of the wedding ceremony for a number of reasons: (i) the Douglases' primary complaint was of affront and distress for invasion of privacy; (ii) the Douglases would never have agreed to any of the unauthorized photographs being published; and (most importantly) (iii) having sold the exclusive rights to *OK!* the Douglases would not have been in a position to grant a licence to *Hello!*.

The notional licence fee basis may be applicable where no publicity deal has been **12.99** reached and the unauthorized images or information are of a quality that might foreseeably have been sold by the subject.[256] Unpublished official wedding photos of a celebrity are an example. The claimants in *Douglas* had an unusually wide array of remedies for pecuniary loss at their disposal. Besides the notional licence fee approach and quantification of compensatory damages returning the claimants to the position had the breach not occurred, an account of *Hello!*'s profits (if higher) was also on the table.[257] In *Attorney General v Blake* the House of Lords confirmed that a restitutionary financial remedy is available by way of an equitable discretion in exceptional cases where justice could not otherwise be done, the claimant having suffered no appreciable loss or disadvantage.[258]

The commercial licensee of private and confidential information has a right inde- **12.100** pendent of the personality or subject of the information to protect itself from unlawful interference with that licence.[259] In the *Douglas* case the Court of Appeal ruled that personal commercial interests in private information do not survive assignment to third parties as they would if they were proprietary.[260] In the House of Lords the majority reversed the Court of Appeal on the issue of *Hello!*'s liability (the personal privacy claims of the Douglases were not subject to an appeal) and provided a fillip to the market for the celebrity photo opportunity.[261] *OK!*'s claim

---

mutually exclusive; Lindsay J found that a claimant could not properly claim for loss caused by something which he is to be taken to have notionally authorized. The claimants were permitted to run alternative claims on the basis that the Court would make an award on whichever basis yielded the higher amount (with a warning of the costs consequences of so doing): *Douglas*, Ch D (n 249) [13]. The Court of Appeal rejected the notional licence fee approach, but the reasons for doing so were closely tied to the circumstances of that case.

[256] The subject of the information may lead evidence of what persons of similar status have been able to command for the exclusive licensing of information of a similar nature. There is an analogy with the concept of a notional licence fee in a copyright claim or an award of damages for wrongful interference with goods assessed at a reasonable price for their use. See the award made for the use of confidential information in the absence of any loss of profits in *Universal Thermosensors Ltd v Hibben* [1992] 1 WLR 840, Ch, 856. See also Torts (Interference with Goods) Act 1977, s 4 and *Jaggard v Sawyer* [1995] 1 WLR 269, CA, 282.

[257] *Douglas*, Ch D (n 249) [13].

[258] [2001] 1 AC 268, HL. Restitutionary damages by way of an account of profits are discussed at 12.139–12.152.

[259] *Douglas*, HL (n 249).

[260] *Douglas* (n 41).

[261] *Douglas*, HL (n 249) [299]. Lord Walker, in the minority, described the leading judgment of the majority, given by Lord Hoffmann, as 'an appeal to economic realities'.

was to protect a commercial asset that it had purchased in the normal operation of the market for celebrity tie-ins, a legitimate commercial activity in the United Kingdom which the law should protect from unlawful interference. Confidentiality in the information sprang from the control that the Douglases had over all images of their wedding, which was for their benefit and that of their exclusive licensee.[262]

**12.101** The majority (led by Lord Hoffmann) arrived at the view that many extrinsic circumstances of the case—the exclusivity of the deal with *OK!* and the measures to ensure exclusivity and *Hello!*'s knowledge of the position—determined the confidentiality of the information, rather than the nature of the information itself which was the focus of the minority dissent (Lord Nicholls and Lord Walker).[263] The decision of the House of Lords was influenced by the need to protect legitimate commercial interests. It remains to be seen whether a third-party purchaser of unauthorized private information without any knowledge of its bootlegged quality will be held liable. A claimant in misuse of private information will usually be able to decide between an account of profits and compensatory damages.

**12.102** An approach based on the market value of the information accords with the general approach in the United States to infringement of the publicity or personality aspect of the privacy right. Damages for the invasion of the property interests in the claimant's identity are calculated by reference to the commercial value of the personality.[264]

### (4) Non-pecuniary Loss

**12.103** Successful misuse of personal information claims are likely to result in an award compensating the claimant for non-pecuniary loss occasioned by the unlawful disclosure. Harm caused by disclosures of private information will vary with the circumstances of the disclosure itself. Some individuals will be aggrieved that *any* information was disclosed at all. Others will protest that information has been released in a manner that was not contemplated or that wrong or embarrassing information was disclosed.[265] Claims for damages ought to be advanced against

---

[262] *Douglas*, HL (n 249) [117].

[263] Lord Nicholls was not prepared to accept that the authorized photographs retained any confidentiality after the unauthorized images were published in *Hello!* for the reason that the essential information was common to both sets of photographs and the differences of presentation insufficiently significant: *Douglas*, HL (n 249) [259]. Lord Walker considered that *Hello!*'s publication did not destroy *OK!*'s licence but made it less valuable and that the confidentiality of information depends on its nature not its market value [298].

[264] *Hoffman v Capital Cities/ABC Inc* 33 F Supp 2d 867 (CD Cal 1999) rev'd on appeal, 255 F 3d 1180 (9th Cir 2001), and M Henry, *International Privacy, Publicity and Personality Laws* (Butterworths (Canada) Ltd 2001) 480. The tortious nature of privacy claims in the US avoids the theoretical complications that the equitable roots of the English cause of action may generate.

[265] *eg Douglas* (n 184). The claimants had gone to great lengths to select and approve a particular photographic record of the day for publication.

the appropriate defendant: the intruder or purloiner of private information may not be the same person who discloses it.[266]

It has become the practice of the courts to award damages for distress, hurt feel- **12.104** ings, and loss of dignity in privacy cases.[267] Damages for injury to feelings were awarded in *Cornelius v de Taranto*, a breach of confidence case, which although 'novel' were 'incremental rather than revolutionary'.[268] In *Campbell v MGN Ltd* the assumption that damages are available in principle for mental injury caused by breach of confidence was not challenged by the Court of Appeal and the House of Lords re-imposed the judge's award without further consideration of the issue. Awarding damages for distress in breach of confidence and misuse of private information is paralleled in a wide variety of instances. The House of Lords in *Farley v Skinner*[269] reaffirmed the availability of (and need for) damages for distress in claims for breach of contract where a major or important part of the contract was the provision of some amenity the loss of which causes the distress.[270]

Section 13 of the Data Protection Act 1998 provides for compensation for emo- **12.105** tional distress, pecuniary and non-pecuniary loss, and other forms of damage.[271] In the copyright context additional damages for the flagrancy of the infringement pursuant to s 97(2) of the Copyright Designs and Patents Act 1988 can include an element for damage to the claimant's feelings.[272] So far as concerns intrusion into seclusion or solitude, or prying into private affairs, the claimant may be able to assert a claim in trespass, in which damages for injury to pride and dignity are available.[273] In nuisance, the owner of the property may recover for loss of amenity and enjoyment of property.[274] Some privacy claims may also include an element of

---

[266] *Douglas*, Ch D (n 249) [57].

[267] *Cornelius* (n 214) (£3,000); *Campbell* (n 214) (£3,500, including an element for aggravation); *Lady Archer* (n 223) (£2,500); *Douglas*, Ch D (n 249) (£3,750); *Applause Store Productions Ltd v Raphael* [2008] EWHC 1781 (QB), [2008] Info TLR 318 (£2,000 in a claim brought in both privacy and defamation); *Mosley* (n 38) (£60,000).

[268] *Cornelius* (n 214) [77].

[269] [2001] UKHL 49, [2002] 2 AC 732.

[270] Lord Steyn reviewed the line of authorities and referred to research which showed that 'in the real life of our lower courts non-pecuniary damages are regularly awarded on the basis that the defendant's breach of contract deprived the plaintiff of the very object of the contract, viz pleasure, relaxation and peace of mind'. He was of the view 'that awards in this area should be restrained and modest. It is important that logical and beneficial developments in this corner of the law should not contribute to the creation of a society bent on litigation.' He thought that £10,000 for the situation in which a house owner was disturbed by aircraft noise although he had been advised by a surveyor that such noise was unlikely was high but open to the judge and should not be reduced. The other Law Lords took a similar approach.

[271] See 7.92–7.99. As to the ability to claim in respect of non-pecuniary loss as well as pecuniary loss under the Data Protection Act 1998, s 13, see *Vidal-Hall* (n 227).

[272] N Caddick et al, *Copinger and Skone James on Copyright* (16th edn, Sweet & Maxwell 2011) paras 22-201 *et seq* and cases cited therein.

[273] A Dugdale and M Jones, *Clerk and Lindsell on Torts* (20th edn, Sweet & Maxwell 2010) para 19-69; and see 10.47–10.53.

[274] *Farley* (n 269).

harassment. The Court of Appeal has given general guidance on damages for harassment in *Vento v Chief Constable of West Yorkshire Police*[275] and warned about the need to be alert to the risk of double recovery where there is more than one cause of action.[276] In *WXY v Gewanter*,[277] the defendant was found liable for harassment and misuse of private information arising from the publication of information about the claimant on a website together with threats to make further postings. The Court made a single award of damages for distress arising from both the harassment and misuse of private information. [278]

**12.106** In the American context the recovery of damages for emotional distress caused by invasion of privacy (without a need to plead or prove special damage) is well established.[279]

**12.107** An adequate remedy for the protection of *reputation* is an action in defamation:

> …because both libel and breach of privacy are concerned with compensating for infringements of Article 8, there is clearly some scope for analogy. However, it is important to remember that a claim for a breach of privacy is not concerned with compensating for, or vindicating, injury to *reputation*. The distinctive functions of a defamation claim do not arise. The purpose of damages in a breach of privacy claim, therefore, must be to address the specific public policy factors in play when there has been 'an old fashioned breach of confidence' and/or an unauthorised revelation of personal information. It would seem that the law is concerned to protect such matters as personal dignity, autonomy and integrity.[280]

**12.108** A sound strategy for a claimant where a publication infringes privacy and damages reputation may be to bring claims in defamation and misuse of private information, pleading separately the factual bases of remedies relevant to information disclosures and those relevant to allegations attacking reputation.[281] The remedy awarded by the court should also fully vindicate the infringement of the right to privacy to ensure

---

[275] [2002] EWCA Civ 1871, [2003] ICR 318 [65] *et seq.*

[276] *Vento* (n 275) [59].

[277] [2013] EWHC 589 (QB).

[278] *WXY* (n 277) [53], [59].

[279] R Sack, *Sack on Defamation: Libel, slander and related problems* (4th edn, Practising Law Institute 2010) para 12.4.11 and Henry (n 264) para 30.46. The German courts recognize that compensation for immaterial damages (*Geldentschädigung*) is the only sanction which can produce an effective protection of privacy: M Prinz, 'Remedies against an infringement of privacy: The effect of sanctions and compensation and their proportionality' in Council of Europe, *Freedom of Expression and the Right to Privacy* (Conference Reports: Strasbourg, 23 September 1999 (DH-MM 2000)) 7, 75.

[280] *Mosley* (n 38) [214]. Cf *Cumpana and Mazare v Romania* (n 134) in which the ECtHR held that reputation and honour are equally protected by Arts 8 and 10(2) ECHR. In that case the allegations were false in part, and the case came to the Court on the application of the publishers complaining of a breach of Art 14. It would appear to follow that damages for loss of reputation would be available under Art 8 for the unauthorized publication of private facts, whether true or false, in an appropriate case.

[281] Procedural issues in the bringing of privacy claims are considered in ch 13. In the context of this sentence, see in particular 13.81.

that it is met with an 'adequate remedy', and an award of compensatory damages may assist in fulfilling this purpose.[282] Distaste at niche and unconventional private acts will not result in nominal awards of damages, in order to protect plural and minority activities.[283] The act of intruding on a person's privacy may justify an award of damages in its own right, irrespective of whether any distress has been caused.

Some Strasbourg cases seem to suggest that intrusion into private life has an **12.109** intrinsic value that ought to be vindicated by an award of damages. In *Halford v UK*[284] the ECtHR found a violation of Article 8 by reason of the tapping of the applicant's office telephone by her employer, the police. She claimed compensation for the intrusion into her privacy and the distress it caused. The ECtHR found that the stress suffered by Ms Halford was not directly attributable to the interception of her calls but rather the broader conflict with her employers. Nevertheless, finding there had been 'a serious infringement of her rights by those concerned' the ECtHR awarded her £10,000 as a 'just and equitable amount of compensation'.

In many Convention cases the distinction between damages for the invasion itself **12.110** and damages for associated mental consequences is not so clearly made, but the reasoning of the ECtHR nevertheless suggests that an element of non-pecuniary compensation is being awarded for the fact of the invasion.[285] In *Hatton v UK*[286] £4,000 was awarded in non-pecuniary compensation for each applicant whose sleep had been disrupted by noise from night flights at Heathrow.[287]

In a seminal article in 1960, the American jurist William L Prosser argued that the **12.111** element of privacy that protects public disclosure of private facts (as opposed to intrusion into private life, presentation in a false light, or appropriation of name or likeness)[288] could be said to be aimed at the protection of reputation.[289] In relation

---

[282] *Ashley v Chief Constable of Sussex* [2008] UKHL 25, [2008] 1 AC 962 [21]–[22]; *Chester v Afshar* [2004] UKHL 41, [2005] 1 AC 134 [87].

[283] *Mosley* (n 38) [217].

[284] (1997) 24 EHRR 523.

[285] *eg Smith and Grady v UK* (2000) 29 EHRR 493 (judgment on just satisfaction): the ECtHR found a violation of Art 8 by reason of the investigations into the applicants' sexual orientation and their subsequent discharge from the armed services on the ground of homosexuality. The ECtHR awarded £19,000 for non-pecuniary damage to each applicant noting both that the interference was 'exceptionally grave' and that it had 'significant emotional and psychological impact'. However in noting also that 'it found the absolute and general character of the policy striking' there could be argued to be a punitive element in this award.

[286] (2002) 34 EHRR 1.

[287] See further the table of awards set out in J Simor and B Emmerson, *Human Rights Practice*, ch 21 (Sweet & Maxwell, R.26: August 2013), reproduced and updated from K Reid, *A Practitioner's Guide to the European Convention on Human Rights* (Sweet & Maxwell 1998).

[288] See 3.49–3.84 for consideration of these different aspects of the US right to privacy.

[289] W Prosser, 'Privacy' (1960) 48 Cal L Rev 383: 'The interest protected is that of reputation, with the same overtones of mental distress that are present in libel and slander. It is in reality an extension of defamation, into the field of publications that do not fall within the narrow limits of the old torts, with the elimination of the defense of truth. As such it has no doubt gone far to remedy

to the discussion of damages for misuse of private information there is some read-across of principles taken from the law of defamation, although the analogy must not be pressed too far.[290] The scope for analogy derives from the concern of both libel and privacy to compensate infringements of Article 8.

**12.112** In *AAA v Associated Newspapers Ltd*[291] damages for a breach of privacy were awarded for the publication of a photograph of the young claimant that had been taken from a distance, without her mother's knowledge (who was pushing the child's pram at the time). Similarly the claimant herself would not have had any knowledge of the photographs being taken either (even if she had been old enough to voice any distress suffered as a result).[292] In *Gulati v MGN Ltd*[293] several significant awards of damages were made to the claimants to compensate them for the misuse of their private information resulting from the defendant's phone hacking and subsequent conduct. Mann J explicitly recognized that damages were to be awarded in respect of both the infringements of the privacy rights themselves, as well as the distress caused by the defendant's activities.[294]

### (5) Quantum of Non-pecuniary Damages

#### (a) Principles of assessment

**12.113** Damages must be kept proportionate, and should not be open to the criticism of arbitrariness and it will be legitimate to pay some attention to the current level of personal injury awards.[295] However, as appears to have been confirmed by the judgment in *Gulati*,[296] there is every indication that future awards will be more significant than they have been in the past. In *Spelman v Express Newspapers*[297] Tugendhat J stated:

> If a remedy in damages is to be an effective remedy, then the amount that the court may award must not be subject to too severe a limitation. Recent settlements in the much publicised phone hacking cases have been reported to be in sums far exceeding what in the past might have been thought to be available to be awarded by the courts. The sums awarded in the early cases such as *Campbell* were very low. It can no longer be assumed that damages at those levels are the limits of the court's powers.

---

the deficiencies of the defamation actions, hampered as they are by technical rules inherited from ancient and long forgotten jurisdictional conflicts, and to provide a remedy for a few real and serious wrongs that were not previously actionable.'

[290] *Mosley* (n 38): see the discussion of the nature of compensatory damages in privacy cases [212]–[231] (Eady J).
[291] *AAA* (n 231).
[292] But see 12.119–12.120.
[293] *Gulati v MGN Ltd* [2015] EWHC 1482 (Ch).
[294] *Gulati* (n 293) [113], [132]–[133], [144].
[295] *Mosley* (n 38) [218]–[220].
[296] *Gulati* (n 293).
[297] [2012] EWHC 355 (QB) [114].

Compensatory damages reflecting deterrence, as in defamation, are inappropriate **12.114** in a civil law context and such an approach inherently conflicts with the notion that any damages awarded should be proportionate.[298] Compensatory damages will therefore tend to reflect the distress and indignity caused to the claimant. Any claim for damages will be limited to damages for injury caused within the jurisdiction of England and Wales, as in *Mosley*,[299] unless a claim for remedies in respect of publication abroad has been pleaded and proved.

All of the circumstances of the unlawful disclosure may be considered in relation **12.115** to quantum. The seriousness and scale of the intrusion and disclosure will be taken into account. A claim for damages may reflect the circumstances in which private information was obtained, possibly clandestinely or by subterfuge, as well as the nature of the information's onward disclosure. The character of the recipients of the information is a material factor, as is the defendant's knowledge of how a disclosure may harm a particular claimant.[300] The extent of the disclosure made by the defendant, whether it was deliberate or innocent and whether there was commercial exploitation are relevant.[301] Intrusions into privacy which are recorded photographically may affect the seriousness of the disclosure,[302] particularly so where the information in question is of sexual activity.[303]

In the *Mosley* case many of these elements were present together resulting in a **12.116** scale of distress and indignity 'difficult to comprehend' and 'unprecedented'.[304] Stills from secretly shot video footage concerning consensual sadomasochistic sexual behaviour were published in the largest circulation newspaper in the United Kingdom, while selected video footage was accessible on the newspaper's website resulting in traffic influxes of 600 per cent over normal volumes when it was posted. Eady J awarded compensatory damages of £60,000.

**Vindication?** An award of damages in defamation may properly be said to pro- **12.117** vide vindication by repairing and restoring a claimant's reputation whereas the harm inherent in the public disclosure of private information can never be wholly remedied—'Judges cannot achieve what is, in the nature of things, impossible. That unpalatable fact cannot be mitigated by simply adding a few noughts to the number first thought of.'[305] Therefore, damages for unlawful intrusions will aim

---

[298] *Mosley* (n 38) [227]–[229]. Any deterrent element can be supplied only by an award of exemplary damages if they are available.

[299] *Mosley* (n 38) [212].

[300] *Cornelius* (n 214).

[301] *Adenjii v London Borough of Newham* (QB, 16 October 2001, Garland J). A photo of a ten-year-old girl was used without consent by the local authority to illustrate HIV and youth-crime information leaflets, when she did not have any disease or history of youth crime. A £5,000 settlement was approved.

[302] *Douglas* (n 184) [84].

[303] *Mosley* (n 38) [23].

[304] *Mosley* (n 38) [216].

[305] *Mosley* (n 38) [230].

to afford some degree of *solatium* to the injured party, as the traditional object of *restitutio* is not available because the damage has been done.[306] Furthermore, damages in misuse of private information may be awarded in relation to disclosures of facts which were true, as, for example in *Mosley*, a case which (in large part) concerned the public disclosure of sexual information about the claimant which was true, or where the facts disclose wrongdoing[307] or expose the claimant to ridicule.[308]

12.118　A point that has arisen in recent cases is whether the award of damages should vindicate the wrong done to the claimant. The issue has arisen particularly in the context of privacy cases involving children who may not actually suffer any damage as a result of an admitted or proven breach of privacy. Should the award of damages nevertheless be substantial in such cases in order to vindicate the wrong or is the claimant limited to a nominal award?

12.119　In *Mosley*, Eady J remarked that vindication to mark the infringement of a right ought 'probably' to be taken into account in assessing damages.[309] Nicola Davies J followed this in *AAA v Associated Newspapers Ltd* when she awarded £15,000 damages to the one-year-old claimant who was covertly photographed in the street, and so suffered no identifiable distress or injury either by the taking of the photograph or its subsequent publication.[310]

12.120　However, the Supreme Court's decision in *Lumba v Secretary of State for the Home Dept* established that damages should not be awarded on the basis of a need to 'vindicate' a right. Disagreeing with the approach adopted by Eady J in *Mosley*, the Court held that if no loss is proved to have been caused by the wrong, the claimant is only entitled to nominal damages.[311] In *Weller v Associated Newspapers Ltd*, Dingemans J awarded £10,000 for the publication in a newspaper of photographs of Paul Weller's children. Following *Lumba*, the judge held that 'vindicatory damages' were not available in privacy claims:[312]

> Although it is right to say that the cause of action for misuse of private information does accommodate both articles 8 and 10 of the ECHR, the claim is for misuse of private information and not a direct claim for infringement of human rights or infringement of constitutional rights...I accept that...the effect of an award might be said in general terms to 'vindicate' the Claimant. However the use of the phrase 'vindicatory damages' in this area of law is in my judgment unhelpful

---

[306] *Mosley* (n 38) [231].
[307] *A v B plc* (n 186), injunction lifted on appeal (n 50). See also the facts of the US case relied on by Prosser (n 289): *Melvin v Reid* 112 Cal App 285, 297 Pac 91 (1931).
[308] In *A v B, C and D* (n 85).
[309] *Mosley* (n 38) [216].
[310] *AAA* (n 231).
[311] [2011] UKSC 12, [2012] 1 AC 245 [99]–[101].
[312] [2014] EWHC 1163 (QB), [2014] EMLR 24 [190]–[191]. See also *Gulati* (n 293) in which Mann J stated that an award of damages to reflect infringements of the privacy right itself would not amount to the wrongful reintroduction of vindicatory damages of the type ruled out in *Lumba* (n 311) and *Weller*; such damages would be truly compensatory [132].

and liable to mislead, by creating a consequential risk of either overcompensation because of double counting, or under-compensation because relevant features about the conduct are not considered.

It may yet be that, in a case where the court is constrained to award only nominal **12.121** damages for a flagrant breach of privacy, the issue of whether exemplary damages are available for breach of privacy could be reconsidered (whether or not the statutory provision for exemplary damages ever has any effect).[313]

### (b) Illustrative awards

By contrast with damages awarded in defamation cases, damages in privacy actions **12.122** had, prior to *Mosley*, been modest. In *Douglas v Hello!* the low award of damages for mental distress was considered by the Court not to be an adequate remedy for the injury suffered by the Douglases, a factor which led the Court to state that the Douglases' rights could only have been satisfactorily protected by the grant of an interlocutory injunction.[314] In *Campbell v MGN Ltd* Morland J awarded general damages for distress and injury to feelings of £2,500. He described the award as 'damages on a modest scale'.[315] Although the publication had been on the front page of a very large-circulation newspaper and the judge accepted, despite criticisms of her veracity, that the claimant had suffered genuine distress and injury to her feelings, he found that a significant part of that distress was caused by revelation of her drug addiction and the fact she was in therapy (publications about which she could not complain). The award was for the publication of the details of her therapy with Narcotics Anonymous only. The House of Lords re-imposed the award.

In *Lady Archer v Williams*[316] the claimant stated expressly in evidence that the **12.123** claim for damages was the least important part of the action, in which she sought the continuation of an injunction to restrain future breaches of confidentiality. The judge awarded £2,500. In *McKennitt v Ash*,[317] the claim featured a series of intrusions into private life in breach of trust, published in book rather than photographic form. Eady J awarded £5,000.

However, damages awards post-*Mosley* became markedly more substantial. In **12.124** *Cooper v Turrell*[318] a businessman was awarded £30,000 for a misuse of private medical information relating to him (some true, some false) which was disseminated on the internet by the defendant, and used to question the claimant's ability to perform the role he held within the company he worked for. The award for the breach of privacy was made alongside an award of £50,000 for libel, but Tugendhat J

---

[313] See 12.135.
[314] *Douglas* (n 41) [259].
[315] *Campbell* (n 214) [140].
[316] *Lady Archer* (n 223).
[317] *McKennitt* (n 228).
[318] *Cooper v Turrell* [2011] EWHC 3269 (QB).

explained that if the award for misuse of private information had been made in isolation it would have been £40,000.[319] In *AAA v Associated Newspapers Ltd* £15,000 was awarded by Nicola Davies J for the publication of an unpixelated photograph of a young child, with the judge emphasizing that the reward reflected how seriously the Court regarded infringements of children's rights.[320] In *WXY v Gewanter*[321] a wealthy female claimant with close connections to a foreign head of state and his family obtained £24,950 damages for a breach of privacy following the publication of private and confidential information about her online (including £5,000 by way of aggravated damages). The disclosures included details about her alleged sexual conduct and of private discussions between her and a third party in which it was claimed she had made sensitive disclosures about the head of state. In *Weller v Associated Newspapers Ltd* a total of £10,000 damages were awarded for the publication of unpixelated photographs of the claimants (who were acting through their father as their litigation friend). £5,000 damages were awarded in respect of the sixteen-year old claimant and £2,500 in respect of each of the ten-month old twins, where the misuse of private information was said to relate only to the children's facial features.[322] In *Gulati* damages of £1.2 million were awarded in total to the eight representative claimants.[323] Mann J cited the 'length, degree and frequency' of the defendant's conduct (which included publishing numerous newspaper articles as a result of information obtained by hacking in respect of seven of the claimants) as justifying damages that were so much larger than historical awards for breach of privacy had been.[324]

### (c) Reported settlements

**12.125** While many of the earlier settlements in privacy actions had been modest, there were examples of much higher sums being paid even pre-*Mosley* and *Gulati*. Film stars Michael Douglas and Catherine Zeta-Jones were reported to have obtained £25,000 each from MGN Ltd in early 2002 for publications in *The Sunday Mirror* of pictures of them together in a private swimming pool. The Radio 1 DJ Sara Cox reportedly received a settlement of £50,000 from *The People* newspaper and a photographer in June 2003 over the publication of pictures of her and her husband naked on their honeymoon. Hugh Grant, Liz Hurley, and Arun Nayur were said to have received £25,000 collectively from two picture agencies for the sale of photographs of the trio holidaying in the Maldives. In 2007, the actress Sienna Miller

---

[319] *Cooper* (n 318) [107].
[320] *AAA* (n 231) [127].
[321] *WXY* (n 277).
[322] *Weller* (n 312) [196].
[323] *Gulati* (n 293). The largest individual award of £260,250 was made to the actress and businesswoman Sadie Frost, who Mann J found had suffered a 'severe' impact as a result of the defendant's conduct [656], and in respect of whom thirty different articles had been published by the defendant on the basis of information obtained by hacking. The awards made to each of the other seven claimants ranged from £72,500 to £201,250.
[324] *Gulati* (n 293) [702].

was reported to have received compensation of £37,500 from a newspaper and photograph agency for publishing pictures of her naked, along with undertakings not to republish and to delete all copies. The same year Martin Sorrell, the chief executive of an advertising group, accepted £20,000 in a mid-trial settlement of a privacy claim in relation to an offensive image of Mr Sorrell with a female colleague. The female colleague co-claimant accepted £30,000 compensation in relation to the same subject matter. In 2010 Kate Middleton (as she was then known) won £5,000 in damages from a picture agency that syndicated photographs of her taken on a tennis court while on a Christmas break in Cornwall. In 2012 Times Newspapers Ltd settled a breach of confidence and privacy claim for £42,500 that had been brought over the unmasking of Richard Horton as the previously anonymous police office behind the 'Nightjack' blog, after a reporter allegedly unlawfully accessed his emails.[325] In 2013 it emerged that the pop-star Tulisa Contostavlos had accepted £42,500 damages from the news website TNT over its wrongful publication of a still from a sex tape which appeared on the internet.[326]

### (d) The claimant's conduct and causation of damage

In certain circumstances it may be right to take into account the claimant's own **12.126** conduct and ask whether his or her own choices have caused the distressing predicament giving rise to the claim.[327] In *Mosley*, the potential for the claimant's ongoing encounters with professional dominatrices being a relevant causal factor in bringing about some of the distress occasioned to himself and his family was recognized.[328] In *Campbell*, the supermodel's distress and injury to feelings were caused partly by two factual matters about which she could not complain: the fact that she had a drug addiction and was receiving therapy.[329]

## (6) Aggravated Damages

The conduct of a defendant may be taken into account in aggravation of dam- **12.127** ages.[330] As in defamation, the court is entitled to look at the circumstances of publication or disclosure (and the obtaining of the information if the claim for distress is pleaded in relation to it). Deliberate and sustained disclosures of private

---

[325] J Halliday, 'Nightjack blogger receives £42,500 payout from Times publisher' *The Guardian* (London, 8 October 2012), available at <http://www.theguardian.com/media/2012/oct/08/nightjack-blogger-payout-times-publisher>.

[326] The settlement figure emerged during a hearing on costs arising from the breach of privacy proceedings the claimant brought the year before: *Contostavlos v Mendahun* [2013] EWHC 4026 (QB).

[327] *Mosley* (n 38) [224].

[328] *Mosley* (n 38) [225]–[226].

[329] *Campbell* (n 214) [141] (Morland J).

[330] *Mosley* (n 38) [222]; *Campbell* (n 52) [35]. At the trial of *Douglas* (n 184) Lindsay J was invited to award aggravated damages. He assumed that an award of aggravated damages was available, but held the behaviour of *Hello!* not to be high-handed or oppressive or so flagrant or offensive as to justify an award of aggravated damages. There was no appeal against this aspect of the decision.

information may fall into the category of aggravating conduct. Further infringement of privacy in the conduct of litigation may be relevant to aggravation but collateral attacks on character and reputation, which would aggravate damages in a defamation context, will not.[331] Matters persisted in as justifications or as part of a public interest defence may run the risk of being taken into account on aggravation of damages where they serve to increase the sense of indignity to the claimant and are found to be unsustainable.[332] Journalistic comment accompanying the intrusion into privacy, whether a photographic intrusion or disclosure of private facts, may, in principle, aggravate damages if the allegations in question amount to dishonesty or misconduct.[333]

**12.128** An aggravated damages award of £1,000 was made in *Campbell v MGN Ltd* on account of the post-publication conduct of the newspaper. Morland J said:[334]

> A newspaper faced with litigation is entitled to assert and publish in articles that a claim against it should never have been made and that any complaint should have been made to the Press Complaints Commission. Articles making such assertions may be written in strong and colourful language. It is not for the Courts to censor bad taste.[335]
>
> However, if the newspaper conducts its defence or publishes articles which belittle the claimant in relation to her claim for breach of confidence or for breach of section 13 of the Data Protection Act 1998, insofar as that belittlement causes increased injury to [the claimant's] feelings it will sound in aggravated damages because the defendants are rubbing salt into the claimant's wounds.

**12.129** So too may the conduct and position of claimants be properly scrutinized in relation to damages. The extent to which a claimant's own conduct has contributed to the nature and scale of the distress might be a relevant factor on causation.[336]

---

[331] *Mosley* (n 38) [223].

[332] *Mosley* (n 38) [223]. Unfounded allegations that sexual role-play by the claimant involved a Nazi and concentration camp theme were sustained by the *News of the World* down to the end of the trial which Eady J recognized was 'therefore a legitimate element to take into account and to reflect in any award'.

[333] *Campbell* (n 72). The defendant argued that an award of aggravated damages in this context needed to be supported by a finding that the opinions expressed by the defendant's journalists were not honestly held. The Court of Appeal said that the terms of the articles relied on by the claimant justified the findings made by the judge and that it would have been open to him to award aggravated damages had his findings on liability been valid: [138]. These remarks were necessarily *obiter* because of the Court of Appeal's finding on liability. The House of Lords however reimposed the award of the judge. The only consideration of the issue of aggravated damages was by Lord Nicholls, who, although dissenting on the issue of liability, said that if there was a claim then the judge had 'rightly recognised that an award of aggravated damages was called for': *Campbell* (n 52) [35].

[334] *Campbell* (n 214) [165]–[166]. In *WXY* (n 277) the award of £24,950 included £5,000 in respect of aggravated damages, where one of the defendants had deliberately put pressure on the claimant (by making postings on his website containing the private information) for financial gain.

[335] Note the echo of Lord Woolf CJ in *A v B plc* (n 50) [11(xiii)]: 'In drawing up a balance sheet between the respective interests of the parties courts should not act as censors or arbiters of taste.'

[336] *Mosley* (n 38) [224].

## (7) Exemplary Damages

### (a) Common law principles

Exemplary damages awards traditionally will only be made in circumstances where  **12.130**
an element of punishment is thought appropriate by the court *and* the amount to
be awarded by way of compensation (including aggravated damages) is not sufficient to serve a punitive as well as a compensatory function. Exemplary damages
have been recognized as available in circumstances in which there was the knowing
commission of a tort *and* a calculation that more is to be gained through its commission than is liable to be paid in compensatory damages.[337] Until 2001 exemplary damages could only be awarded in claims based on causes of action in respect
of which exemplary damages had been awarded before 1964.[338] This restriction
alone would have ruled out exemplary damages for claims under s 8 HRA and
may well have pointed against the award of exemplary damages in causes of action
developing under s 6(1) HRA. In any event, breach of confidence was not a cause of
action in which exemplary damages had been awarded before 1964. The removal
of the pre-1964 requirement by the House of Lords in *Kuddus v Chief Constable of
Leicestershire*[339] opened up the question whether exemplary damages are available
either in private law claims for breach of confidence or misuse of private information or in claims under s 8 HRA against public bodies.[340]

### (b) Human Rights Act 1998 claims

In *Anufrijeva v London Borough of Southwark*[341] the Court of Appeal held that exem-  **12.131**
plary damages were not available under s 8 HRA. The Court of Appeal noted that
ss 6–8 HRA establish a code governing awards of damages to be applied with due
regard to Strasbourg jurisprudence.[342] The primary purpose of claims based on infringement of Convention rights is to bring the infringing action of the public authority to
an end. The approach to damages is distinct from that adopted in private law actions;
balance must be struck between the interests of the victim and public as a whole; they
are of a broad discretionary nature and a last resort rather than an entitlement.[343]

---

[337] *Rookes v Barnard* [1964] AC 1129, HL.
[338] *Rookes* (n 337); *Broome v Cassell & Co Ltd* [1972] AC 1027, HL; *A B v South West Water Services
Ltd* [1993] QB 507, CA.
[339] *Kuddus* (n 203).
[340] For principles applying to other causes of action that have privacy aspects, the reader is
referred to the main works on those areas. In particular it should be noted that statutory regimes for
copyright and data protection do not allow for exemplary damages, although by Copyright Designs
and Patents Act 1988, s 97(2) 'additional' damages can be awarded for the 'flagrancy' of infringement of copyright. See the comments in *Kuddus* (n 203) [46] (Lord Mackay): 'I add some further
considerations in respect of legislation such as the discrimination legislation and the data protection legislation. Exemplary damages would be available only if the legislation expressly authorises
exemplary damages in relation to any particular breach.'
[341] *Anufrijeva* (n 235).
[342] *Anufrijeva* (n 235) [52] (Lord Woolf CJ).
[343] *Anufrijeva* (n 235) [56].

*(c) Private law claims in confidence or misuse*

**12.132**  **The claim in *Douglas***   In *Douglas v Hello!*[344] Morritt V-C permitted the pleading of a claim for exemplary damages. At trial the claim failed.[345] Lindsay J drew three principles from *Kuddus*,[346] namely: (1) the question of whether to award exemplary damages should be determined by reference to the nature of the behaviour complained of rather than by reference to the specific cause of action; (2) a powerful case can be made that such damages should be considered where 'and perhaps only where' the behaviour complained of gives rise to a sense of outrage; and (3) a recognized category in which such damages may be awarded is where damages on an ordinary compensatory basis can be seen not to be sufficient to do justice. He was content to assume, without deciding, that exemplary damages 'or equity's equivalent' were available in breach of confidence. There was no need to decide the point because he held that the other two limbs of the test were not satisfied.

**12.133**  Lindsay J held that to describe the conduct of *Hello!* as outrageous would be to overstate the matter, particularly in an industry in which 'intrusion into privacy and little regard for each other's business rights have…been not unknown' and that he was not satisfied that equitable compensation would yield a figure such that *Hello!*'s profit would exceed the compensation due to the claimants, nor that *Hello!* had ever calculated that it might do so. On making the total award of £1,047,756 Lindsay J stated that although this substantial figure did not go beyond the compensatory into the penal it was such 'as may make *Hello!* alive to the unwisdom of acting as it did'.[347] There was no appeal against this aspect of the decision. However the (unprompted) finding by the Court of Appeal that the amount of compensatory damages awarded to the Douglases, although correct in principle, represented no real deterrent to a large media organization contemplating the publication of photographs which infringed an individual's privacy,[348] left the door open to further arguments concerning exemplary damages in future cases.

**12.134**  *Mosley*   It was however held in 2008 that exemplary damages are not available in claims for misuse of private information, at least not without the sanction of Parliament or the Supreme Court. In *Mosley v News Group Newspapers*[349] there was a claim for exemplary damages that the defendant attempted to strike out. Eady J held that it was 'somewhat uncertain' whether the law of misuse of private information was a tort,[350] and hesitated to extend the doctrine to the action in the absence of any clear

---

[344] *Douglas v Hello! Ltd* [2003] EWHC 55 (Ch), [2003] EMLR 29.
[345] *Douglas* (n 184) [272]–[274].
[346] *Kuddus* (n 203).
[347] *Douglas*, Ch D (n 249) [59].
[348] *Douglas* (n 41) [257].
[349] *Mosley* (n 38).
[350] Breach of confidence is not a tort: *Kitetechnology BV v Unicor GmbH Plastmaschinen* [1995] FSR 765, CA, 777–8. The Court of Appeal in *Douglas* (n 41) had accordingly suggested (*obiter* and reluctantly) that the cause of action pursued by the Douglases was not a tort [96]. But in

English authority, preferring to see the authorities as favouring a restrictive approach to extension.[351] On that basis, the extension of exemplary damages into an area of law fashioned by the interplay of Articles 8 and 10 could not be said to be 'prescribed by law' or necessary in a democratic society:[352]

> It was argued by [Counsel for the defendant], since a claim for invasion of privacy nowadays involves direct application of Convention values and of Strasbourg jurisprudence as part of English law, that it would be somewhat eccentric to graft on to this Convention jurisprudence an alien anomaly from the common law in the shape of exemplary damages—not apparently familiar in Strasbourg. I agree with that submission.

As against publishers of news-related material, there is the potential for a statutory **12.135** award of exemplary damages in certain circumstances. Section 34 of the Crime and Courts Act 2013 now provides for awards of exemplary damages to be made against publishers who could have been, but were not at the time of publication, a member of an 'approved regulator'. The section has no effect at the moment because there is no approved regulator and the reformed PCC, the Independent Press Standards Organisation, has no intention of applying for recognition as one.[353] It remains to be seen, also, whether the statutory exemplary damages regime in the Crime and Courts Act 2013 is itself compliant with Article 10.[354]

## (8) Mitigation of Damage

### (a) Claimant's status and conduct

In *Campbell* Morland J accepted that even 'self publicists...are entitled to some **12.136** space of privacy',[355] and the Court of Appeal approved the finding of the judge that those public figures who have seen themselves adopted as role models are not thereby liable to have their lives laid bare.[356] That said, if a claimant has consented to publication of other private facts about him or herself on a previous occasion that may perhaps be relied on in mitigation. However, this is probably better seen as a factor relevant to causation of damage. Previous consent to the publication of other

---

*Vestergaard Frandsen A/S v Bestnet Europe Ltd* [2009] EWHC 1456 (Ch), [2010] FSR 2 [19] Arnold J acknowledged that misuse of private information might not fall to be treated in the same way; and in *Vidal-Hall v Google Inc* [2014] EWHC 13 (QB), [2014] 1 WLR 4155 [70] Tugendhat J held that misuse of private information was a tort, and the Court of Appeal affirmed his decision: *Google Inc* (n 227).

[351] *Mosley* (n 38) [176]–[186]. The New Zealand Court of Appeal in *Aquaculture Corp* (n 217) 301 was prepared to extend the remedy into breach of confidence jurisprudence.

[352] *Mosley* (n 38) [196].

[353] Although the newly-formed group, IMPRESS: The Independent Monitor for the Press, announced in May 2015 that it will seek recognition as an approved regulator. For discussion of the regulatory regime see n 33 and ch 14.

[354] L O'Carroll, 'Tory and Leveson plans for exemplary privacy damages "may be unlawful"' *The Guardian* (London, 21 February 2013), available at <http://www.theguardian.com/media/2013/feb/21/tory-leveson-exemplary-privacy-damages>.

[355] *Campbell* (n 214) [71].

[356] *Campbell* (n 72) [41].

facts does not logically affect the seriousness of the invasion of privacy in itself, nor the hurt that it could cause. It may however show that the claimant is not the kind of person to be badly affected by publication of private facts.

### (b) Apology or other action by the defendant

**12.137** Once a private fact has been made public it is difficult for further action by the defendant to mitigate the damage caused to the claimant by the disclosure. Although contrition by a defendant may reduce the hurt to the claimant's feelings to some degree, an apology for the publication of the private information is not the same as an apology for a libel. Depending on the circumstances an apology in the former case may be incapable of providing anything approaching the consolation that an apology and retraction would afford in the case of a libel. A reputation can be vindicated, but once a private fact is known it cannot be removed from the public domain by further publication (although where the information is photographic or in the form of a film access to it can be prevented and the originals provided to the claimant). Gratuitous further reference to the disclosures might even make matters worse.[357]

## E. Other Remedies

### (1) Introduction

**12.138** Other remedies that may be available in respect of an infringement of privacy, depending on the cause of action, include restitutionary financial remedies, proprietary remedies, and orders for destruction of property. Where a restitutionary financial remedy is granted this will ordinarily be as an alternative to compensatory damages, as any other course would be liable to result in double recovery. Proprietary remedies, if available, and destruction orders, may be granted in addition to either compensation or restitution.

### (2) Restitutionary Remedies

### (a) An account of profits

**12.139** It is well established in relation to some of the causes of action by which a privacy claim may be pursued that a claimant may elect to seek an account of the profits made by the wrongdoer as a result of their wrongdoing, and if the claimant does so the court may so order. [358] There may be many privacy cases in which a claimant

---

[357] *Mosley* (n 38) [223]. See also *Gulati* (n 293) in which the misuse of private information resulting from the hacking of the claimants' mobile telephones was further compounded by the defendant publishing numerous articles based on the private information obtained by hacking in respect of all but one of the claimants.

[358] For discussion of the somewhat similar remedy of restitutionary damages see 12.154–12.156.

might see advantage in seeking an account of profits made by a newspaper or magazine from publication of a feature that infringed the claimant's rights.[359]

On current authority, however, the remedy is not one that is generally available in   **12.140**
all causes of action by which privacy rights may be protected. Further, where the remedy is in principle available, being an equitable one it is not available as of right but is always discretionary. The court may consider it inapt for the particular case before it. Moreover, the difficulties of taking an account have often been emphasized, perhaps never more vividly than by Lindley LJ in *Siddell v Vickers*,[360] in a passage which concludes: 'I believe in almost every case people get tired of it and get disgusted.'[361]

### For what wrongs may an account be available?

*Breach of confidence*   'An account of profits made through breach of confidence   **12.141**
is a recognized form of remedy available to a claimant.'[362] In *Spycatcher* Lord Goff said, 'an important section of the law of restitution is concerned with cases in which a defendant is required to make restitution in respect of benefits acquired through his own wrongful act'.[363] He then gave some examples and added 'and, of course of benefits acquired in breach of confidence. The plaintiff's claim to restitution is usually enforced by an account of profits made by the defendant through his wrong at the plaintiff's expense. This remedy of an account is alternative to the remedy of damages.'

*Copyright infringement*   Where, as for example in *HRH Prince of Wales v Associated*   **12.142**
*Newspapers Ltd*,[364] a breach of privacy involved infringement of copyright it is clear that an account of profits is an available remedy, as an alternative to damages.[365] An account was one of the remedies granted to the Prince of Wales in that case.

*Data protection claims*   The remedies available for breaches of the requirements   **12.143**
of the Data Protection Act 1998 would appear to be prescribed by the Act itself.

---

[359] See *eg* the facts of *Douglas* (n 184), or the case in which the proprietor of a gym obtained pictures of the Princess of Wales exercising by means of a hidden camera: J Darnton, 'Princess Wins a Court Ban on More Gym Photos' *The New York Times* (New York, 9 November 1993), available at <http://www.nytimes.com/1993/11/09/world/princess-wins-a-court-ban-on-more-gym-photos.html>.

[360] (1892) 9 RPC 152, CA, 162–3.

[361] One author has, for example, contended that gain-based remedies should be available in privacy cases in the same way as they are available in breach of confidence cases. In order to provide effective deterrence and protection against commercially motivated infringements, in particular by the media, he argues gain-based remedies should be available where the privacy invasion is deliberate and a particularly outrageous infringement of the claimant's rights—see N Witzleb, 'Justifying Gain-Based Remedies for Invasions of Privacy' (2009) 29(2) OJLS 325.

[362] *Spycatcher* case (n 41) 262 (Lord Keith).

[363] *Spycatcher* case (n 41) 286.

[364] *HRH Prince of Wales* (n 67).

[365] *Copinger and Skone James* (n 272) para 21-209.

They include compensation for damage, including distress, but not an account of profits.[366]

**12.144** *Misuse of private information*  It was not until 2007 that this civil wrong was recognized as a cause of action separate and distinct from breach of confidence,[367] and the cases since that recognition occurred have not discussed the availability of an account of profits.[368]

**12.145** *Other causes of action*  An account of profits is not generally available for common law torts, but in the cases of trespass to land and wrongful interference with goods, a restitutionary remedy may be available under the doctrine of 'waiver of tort', measured as the value of the benefit which the wrongdoer has received from the wrong,[369] though it appears that no restitutionary remedy can be given in cases of nuisance.[370]

### The discretion to order an account of profits

**12.146** *Personal privacy*  The principles by which the court should exercise its discretion as to whether to order an account of profits in a confidence case involving personal privacy have yet to be explored in any decided case. In *Campbell v MGN Ltd*[371] Morland J determined at a pre-trial hearing that an account was not an apt remedy for the wrong alleged in that case, but did not engage in any detailed analysis of the basis for so holding. In *Mosley* the claimant pleaded a claim for an account but after disclosure elected to seek damages.

**12.147** *Innocence*  The commercial breach of confidence cases suggest that the defendant's innocence will be a significant factor in exercising the discretion. In *Seager v Copydex Ltd*,[372] the Court of Appeal held that the defendants were 'quite innocent of any intention to take advantage of' the claimant, and declined to order an account of profits. The court then ordered that the damages should be assessed, by analogy with the law of conversion of goods, as the market value of the confidential information. On payment of the damages the right to exploit the device embodying the information should be regarded as belonging to the defendants.[373]

---

[366] See further the discussion at 12.155.

[367] See 5.02–5.13 for an account of the emergence of the new cause of action.

[368] See however 12.154–12.156.

[369] R Goff and G Jones, *Goff and Jones: The Law of Restitution* (7th edn, Sweet & Maxwell 2007) 801: 'Restitutionary claims based on another's tortious act'. (The issue of gain-based remedies for wrong-doing was excluded from the more recent edn of this title: R Goff and G Jones, *Goff and Jones: The Law of Unjust Enrichment (formerly The Law of Restitution)* (8th edn, Sweet & Maxwell 2011).)

[370] *Stoke on Trent City Council v W & J Wass Ltd* [1988] 1 WLR 1406, CA. See further 12.156.

[371] *Campbell* (n 214).

[372] [1967] 1 WLR 923, CA.

[373] See however 12.153 for criticism of this aspect of the decision.

In *Conran v Mean Fiddler Holdings Ltd*[374] Robert Walker J said that the court will **12.148** readily grant an account of profits where there has been deliberate deception.[375] On the facts of that case he did not regard it as one in which justice required that an account of profits should be ordered, principally because the infringement was innocent, and the claimant's business could not be regarded as being in competition with that of the defendant. It appears that the judge did not regard the defendant's profits as having been made on the back of the claimant's rights. The fact that an infringement may have been innocent does not, however, necessarily relieve the defendant of the obligation to account for profits.[376]

**The process of taking an account**   There is no case to be found in the books in **12.149** which the principles governing the taking of such an account are explained. So the view is expressed in *Goff and Jones*[377] that it is debatable whether the net profits made by *The Sunday Times* from the infringing serialization in the *Spycatcher* case were all the net profits made by the newspaper from the issue containing the extract, or only the percentage of profits attributable to the increased circulation of that issue in consequence of the serialization.

In copyright cases, where only part of the defendant's publication infringes the **12.150** claimant's rights, the court has to apportion the profits made by the defendant according to the relative value of the infringing and non-infringing material.[378] In *My Kinda Town Ltd v Soll*[379] Slade J said:

> The purpose of ordering an account of profits in favour of a successful plaintiff...is not to inflict punishment on the defendant. It is to prevent an unjust enrichment of the defendant by compelling him to surrender those profits, or those parts of the profits, actually made by him that were improperly made and nothing beyond this. Before specifying the form of the account, the court therefore should, I think, initially ask itself this question: What categories of the relevant profits or parts of such profits ought to be treated as having been improperly made by the Defendants? The facts of many particular cases may justify the conclusion that the whole of the relevant profits should be so treated. The facts of the present case, however, do not in my judgement justify such a conclusion.

It is therefore difficult to see how one could justify removing from the defend- **12.151** ant the whole of the profit from the offending issue of a newspaper or magazine, save perhaps exceptionally. An account of profits is an equitable remedy, which

---

[374] [1997] FSR 856, Ch D (a trade mark case). That Lord Keith was treating the remedy as discretionary is apparent from what he said in the *Spycatcher* case (n 41) 262: 'I can perceive no good ground why the remedy [of account of profits] should not be available to the Crown in the circumstances of this case'.

[375] *Conran* (n 374) 861.

[376] *Wienerworld Ltd v Vision Video Ltd* [1998] FSR 832, Ch D: a copyright case cited in *Copinger and Skone James* (n 272) para 21-209.

[377] *Goff and Jones* (7th edn) (n 369) para 34-021.

[378] *Copinger and Skone James* (n 272) para 21-211.

[379] [1983] RPC 15, Ch D, 55 (a passing-off case, reversed by the Court of Appeal [1983] RPC 407, on the ground that there was no passing-off).

should be moulded to meet the practicalities and justice of the case, in the light of its purpose, which is to prevent unjust enrichment. So, the choice will be to remove the whole cover price (less marginal production and distribution costs, if there are any of significance) of the increased circulation brought about by the offending material, or to apportion the whole of the profit derived from the issue in a pragmatic way, not measuring column inches, but assessing relative significance.

**12.152**  Defendants should not be permitted to answer that they would have made the same profit from the daily sale of their newspaper, or weekly sale of their magazine, even if the infringing material had not been included.[380] Moreover, in computing the profit, the defendant will not be permitted to deduct the cost of acquiring the infringing material.[381] If it becomes necessary to separate out profits made by the defendant from non-infringing material, for deduction from the amount payable to the claimant, it is for the defendant to prove the amount deductible.[382]

### (b) Quantum meruit

**12.153**  The approach to remedies adopted by the Court of Appeal in *Seager v Copydex*[383] has been criticized in *Goff and Jones*[384] who expressed the view that it would have been happier if the court had made a *quantum meruit* award (assessed on the same basis), and that the question whether the defendant should be permitted to continue to exploit the confidential information in the future, that is to say, the grant or refusal of an injunction, is independent of whether there should be a *quantum meruit* award. The authors further question whether it is right to take the view that information 'belongs' to the wrongdoer once its value has been paid;[385] this approach does appear especially odd when it comes to personal as opposed to commercial information.

### (c) Restitutionary damages

**12.154**  **Breach of contract**  In *Attorney General v Blake*[386] the House of Lords held that in a case of breach of contract the common law will in appropriate cases award damages measured by reference to the benefit gained by the wrongdoer from his breach, rather than by reference to the actual loss suffered by the claimant. In so holding, the House regarded itself as only modestly extending the scope of what it saw as a general principle, that 'where the circumstances require, damages are

---

[380] *Peter Pan Manufacturing Corp v Corsets Silhouette Ltd* [1964] 1 WLR 96, Ch D, 108.
[381] *Spycatcher* case (n 41) 262 (Lord Keith).
[382] *Copinger and Skone James* (n 272) para 21-211.
[383] Discussed at 12.147.
[384] *Goff and Jones* (7th edn) (n 369) para 34-022.
[385] *Goff and Jones* (n 369).
[386] *Attorney General v Blake* (n 258).

measured by reference to the benefit obtained by the wrongdoer'.[387] That rule had previously seen itself expressed in a limited range of cases concerned with property rights, and certain kinds of breach of contract such as contravention of a restrictive covenant.[388] In a case where this remedy is granted, the actual process of calculating the appropriate sum may involve taking an account of the profits gained by the wrongdoer, but it seems that in so doing the court is not exercising the equitable jurisdiction considered in the previous section but rather adopting an exceptional approach to the assessment of damages at common law. The profits are awarded as damages.[389]

**Data protection**  In *Murray v Express Newspapers plc* a claim for the market value  **12.155** of a photograph of JK Rowling's infant son was advanced in the context of a claim for 'compensation' for 'damage' under s 13 of the Data Protection Act 1998, the acquisition and publication of digital photographs being arguably caught by the Act.[390] It was accepted that the claimant child had not suffered any distress as a result of the taking and publication of the photograph. At the time it was considered that 'damage' in s 13(1) meant ordinary pecuniary loss,[391] and the claimant had not suffered any. Patten J held that s 13 did not allow the court to compensate a claimant for the loss of a bargaining opportunity or for the compulsory acquisition of his or her rights, holding that the Data Protection Act 1998 does not purport to give the data subject any property right in his or her personal data, but merely regulates the way in which it can be processed.[392]

**Non-proprietary torts**  When the *Murray* case reached the Court of Appeal the  **12.156** issue discussed in the previous paragraph was argued, but the Court did not pronounce on it, as it referred the issue back to the judge for trial.[393] However, in *Devenish Nutrition Ltd v Sanofi-Aventis SA (France)* the same Court affirmed[394] the decision of Lewison J at first instance,[395] that the *Blake* decision did not mean that an account of profits could be awarded on a claim for a non-proprietary tort such as breach of statutory duty.

---

[387] *Attorney General v Blake* (n 258) 285 (Lord Nicholls).
[388] eg *Wrotham Park Estate Co Ltd v Parkside Homes Ltd* [1974] 1 WLR 798, Ch D.
[389] This appears to be the proper interpretation of the language and reasoning of Lord Nicholls' speech in *Attorney General v Blake* (n 258).
[390] *Murray v Express Newspapers plc* [2007] EWHC 1908 (Ch), [2007] EMLR 22.
[391] *Johnson v Medical Defence Union* [2007] EWCA Civ 262, [2008] Bus LR 503 [74] (Buxton LJ); since held by the Court of Appeal to be *obiter* and wrong: *Google Inc v Vidal-Hall* (n 227) [68], [105].
[392] *Murray* (n 390) [89]–[92].
[393] *Murray* (n 155) [62]–[63].
[394] [2008] EWCA Civ 1086, [2009] Ch 390, applying *Stoke on Trent* (n 370).
[395] *Devenish Nutrition* (n 394) 398. Patten J's decision in *Murray* (n 390) was made between the decisions of Lewison J in *Devenish Nutrition* ([2007] EWHC 2394 (Ch), [2008] 2 WLR 637) and the Court of Appeal's decision in the same case. The issue was not directly addressed by the reasoning by which the Court of Appeal in *Google Inc* (n 227) concluded that Data Protection Act 1998, s 13 authorizes compensation for damage of all kinds.

### (3) Proprietary Remedies

**12.157** The possibility of a proprietary claim was discussed in the confidence case of *Satnam Investments Ltd v Dunlop Heywood & Co Ltd*[396] but rejected on the facts of that case. Although the Crown did not claim copyright in the *Spycatcher* case, the judgments suggest that Mr Wright might have held the copyright on constructive trust for the Crown.[397] However, for so long as confidential information is not regarded as property it seems unlikely that a court would grant a proprietary remedy in respect of its misuse.[398]

### (4) Delivery Up or Destruction of Materials or Property

**12.158** The court has a discretion to order delivery up or destruction of material embodying confidential information or derived from its misuse. This was done with the copies of the catalogue and the impressions of the etchings in *Prince Albert v Strange*.[399] Destruction, rather than delivery up, is the appropriate order where the physical material is the property of the defendant. The court will be reluctant to order the destruction of intrinsically valuable materials.[400]

### (5) Criminal Sanctions

**12.159** The common law and statutory offences most likely to be applicable to media activity are surveyed in Chapters 1, 10 and 15.[401] Some of the offences, such as the crime of obtaining access to personal data without the consent of the data controller,[402] attract only financial penalties at the time of writing.[403] However, the prosecution, conviction, and imprisonment of a number journalists in the second decade of the twenty-first century, in the wake of the phone-hacking scandal, demonstrates that criminal sanctions are not only available but also may be used in cases of media wrongdoing. The exercise of the discretion whether to prosecute is governed by Guidance issued by the Director of Public Prosecutions in 2012 on assessing the public interest in media cases.[404]

---

[396] [1999] 3 All ER 652, CA.

[397] *Spycatcher* case (n 41) 173 (Scott J), 211 (Dillon LJ), 263 (Lord Keith), 266 (Lord Brightman), 275–6 (Lord Griffiths), 288 (Lord Goff).

[398] G Virgo, *The Principles of the Law of Restitution* (2nd edn, Oxford University Press 2006) 529–30.

[399] (1849) 64 ER 293.

[400] *Saltman Engineering Co Ltd v Campbell Engineering Co Ltd* (1948) 65 RPC 203, CA, 219.

[401] See 1.36, 1.75–1.86, 10.04–10.45, and 15.17–15.24.

[402] Data Protection Act 1998, s 55.

[403] See also 7.39 (regarding carrying out assessable processing without completing the notice process) and 7.108 (regarding failing to comply with an enforcement notice).

[404] Issued 13 September 2012, available at <http://www.cps.gov.uk/legal/d_to_g/guidance_for_prosecutors_on_assessing_the_public_interest_in_cases_affecting_the_media_/>.

# PART VI

## THE ACTION

# 13

## PRACTICE AND PROCEDURE

*Sir Mark Warby, Richard Munden, and Julian Santos*

## A. Introduction

In privacy cases lawyers often need to advise at speed on a number of practical **13.01** and procedural issues. Claimants and defendants will need advice on whether to pursue regulatory or legal routes; if the latter, who can and should sue or be sued; in which court or courts; what causes of action can be relied on; what interim orders to seek and how; and a host of other issues. This chapter identifies and offers practical guidance on some important procedural issues in these areas. It seeks to provide, or show where in this work to find, answers to these simple questions: who, where, what, and how? The chapter does not set out to cover the entire procedural process, but focuses instead on issues most likely to be of interest in relation to privacy claims.

# B. Legal Action and the Alternatives

## (1) The Options

**13.02** Those complaining of actual or threatened privacy infringements have three ways to seek a remedy: self-help, regulatory proceedings,[1] and legal action. The factors influencing the choice will be the remedies available; the extent to which these meet the complainant's needs; the prospects of obtaining them; and the speed, ease, and cost of doing so. The routes are not necessarily mutually exclusive; a given case could involve the use of more than one, though media regulators may decline to entertain a complaint pursued concurrently with legal proceedings.[2]

## (2) Key Factors

### (a) Prior restraint

**13.03** The main concern of most complainants in media privacy cases is to stop publication. Self-help may suffice. Some publishers, notified of a complaint that is not plainly frivolous, will cease or refrain from publication[3] or at least modify what is published for fear of litigation. In the case of internet publication resort can be had to the simple expedient of giving the relevant internet service provider (ISP) notice of the complaint. ISPs based in Europe will usually remove offending matter promptly after such notice lest they lose the benefit of the exemptions afforded them by the E-Commerce Directive.[4] Many ISPs in other jurisdictions will do so also. Such incentives did not exist for the operators of search engines as a matter of common law,[5] but they are now considered to be data controllers in relation to data on web pages published by third parties for the purposes of the Data Protection Directive.[6] Further, removal of the offending matter from source sites will at some point result in its disappearance from a search engine's reports.

**13.04** If these methods are not apt to secure the claimant's objectives, an approach to a regulator is an option. The Press Complaints Commission (PCC) did on occasion persuade member publishers to refrain from publishing particular stories. The Independent Press Standards Organisation (IPSO) may continue this practice. However, media regulators have no power to grant restraining orders,[7] and the Information Commissioner's power to issue 'enforcement notices'[8] has never been

---

[1] See generally ch 14.

[2] See 14.33 *et seq.*

[3] *eg CC v AB* [2006] EWHC 3083 (QB), [2007] EMLR 11 [10].

[4] See 11.35–11.36 and 15.59–15.72. *Cassie Creations Ltd v Blackmore* [2014] EWHC 2941 (Ch) [49].

[5] See 15.50.

[6] Case C-131/12 *Google Spain SL v Agencia Española de Protección de Datos* [2014] QB 1022, discussed at 15.91.

[7] See 14.39.

[8] See 7.103–7.108.

used in a media case and seems inapt as a means of affording a swift and effective remedy. So resort to law is likely to be necessary. Claimants will however need to consider their prospects of obtaining injunctive relief, particularly where there has been widespread publication before it is possible to launch an application. The court may refuse relief on the basis that information is no longer confidential or, in a claim for misuse of private information, on the footing that it is too late to stem the tide.[9]

### (b) Vindication

If vindication of the claimant's rights, as opposed to restraint on publication, figures **13.05** high on the list of priorities then it may be appropriate, particularly where resources are limited, to pursue a regulatory complaint to Ofcom or the BBC (in the case of a broadcast), IPSO (in the case of a newspaper or magazine), or the Information Commissioner's Office.[10] Regulatory complaints have the advantages, compared to court proceedings, of relative speed and simplicity, lower cost, and a lower risk that a complaint will lead to further breaches of privacy. A successful regulatory complaint will usually lead to a published statement acknowledging the wrong done. Regulatory complaints are however not generally suitable for cases requiring detailed factual investigation, and unsuited to cases where either prior restraint or monetary remedies are sought.[11]

### (c) Compensation and other monetary remedies

Legal proceedings are the only means of obtaining monetary remedies. Damages **13.06** are widely considered to be an inherently unsatisfactory remedy for a breach of privacy involving the disclosure of confidential or private information, at least where this intrudes on a personal privacy interest as opposed to one of a more commercial character.[12] Awards for breach of confidence and misuse of private information are liable to be outweighed by the costs of proceedings, if the case merits serious argument or is fit for trial.[13] This, and the prospect that the bringing of a claim risks further publicity for private information, are considerable deterrents to the pursuit of a claim for monetary remedies.[14]

---

[9] For refusal of injunctive relief on the basis that the court will not act as King Canute see 12.14.
[10] For discussion of the regulatory remedies available and the applicable procedures see ch 14.
[11] For fuller discussion of the pros and cons of regulatory complaints see 14.32–14.37.
[12] See 12.60–12.67.
[13] The point is illustrated by the ratio between damages and costs in some of the high-profile privacy litigation of the early twenty-first century. Naomi Campbell's case involved a five-day trial and went to the House of Lords, where an award of £3,500 was upheld. Ms Campbell having been represented at that stage under a conditional fee agreement, the costs bill served on the defendants was for £1,086,296, held by the House of Lords not to be disproportionate: *Campbell v MGN Ltd* [2005] UKHL 61, [2005] 1 WLR 3394. *Douglas v Hello! Ltd* went three times to the Court of Appeal and once to the House of Lords, and involved several weeks of trial. At the end of it the Douglases recovered £14,600, although the award of £1m to their co-claimant, *OK!* magazine, was upheld by the House of Lords: [2007] UKHL 21, [2008] 1 AC 1.
[14] As observed by Eady J in *Mosley v News Group Newspapers Ltd* [2008] EWHC 1777 (QB), [2008] EMLR 20 [230]. The claimant was awarded £60,000 after a highly publicized trial. He then

**13.07** That said, twenty-first century privacy litigation has featured several well-resourced and determined claimants who have taken their claims as far as necessary to obtain relatively modest monetary remedies.[15] Further, in *Spelman v Express Newspapers*[16] Tugendhat J pointed out that the awards of damages in the early cases such as *Campbell* were very low, and that it could no longer be assumed that those awards were the limit of the court's powers. He also noted that settlements in the News Group Newspapers phone hacking litigation had been reported to be in 'sums far exceeding what in the past might have been thought to be available to be awarded by the courts'. It would be fair to say that there has been an upward trend in damage awards in recent years, albeit not a dramatic one.[17]

## C. Who? Parties

### (1) Who Can Sue and be Sued?

#### (a) Natural persons

**13.08** All living individuals can in principle sue and be sued for infringements of privacy rights.[18] They will ordinarily do so on their own behalf and, subject to any appropriate anonymity orders, in their own names.[19] Some issues arise, however.

**13.09** **Adults and capacity** The fact that an adult lacks capacity does not mean that he or she has lesser rights to privacy. Indeed, it is clear that some rights of privacy survive permanent loss of consciousness. In *Airedale NHS Trust v Bland*, Hoffmann LJ said: 'It is demeaning to the human spirit to say that, being unconscious, he can have no interest in his personal privacy and dignity, in how he lives or dies.'[20] The absence of relevant capacity means, however, that others must take decisions on behalf of the adult. Thus, those lacking relevant capacity are 'protected parties' under the Civil Procedure Rules (CPR)[21] and must claim or

---

complained to the ECtHR that the UK had violated his Convention rights by failing to impose a legal duty on the *News of the World* to give him advance notice of intended publication, enabling him to seek an injunction. The ECtHR held that damages were an adequate remedy and that there had not been a violation: *Mosley v UK* (2011) 53 EHRR 30.

[15] In addition to the cases cited in n 14, see *Murray v Express Newspapers plc* [2008] EWCA Civ 446, [2009] Ch 481. After a two-day appeal from a two-day hearing of the application to strike out the claim (brought by the author J K Rowling) the Court of Appeal ordered a payment of £150,000 on account of costs. The case was later settled.

[16] [2012] EWHC 355 (QB) [114].

[17] For discussion of quantum see 12.113–12.124.

[18] A claimant must however be within the jurisdiction of an ECHR Contracting State in order to benefit from the protection of Art 8: *OPO v MLA* [2014] EWCA Civ 1277, [2015] EMLR 4 [114].

[19] For the CPR provisions requiring use of parties' proper names, see 13.100. For anonymity orders, see 13.100 *et seq*.

[20] [1993] AC 789, 829.

[21] CPR 21.1.

defend proceedings by a litigation friend.[22] Until one is appointed, any step other than the issue and service of a claim form or an application to appoint a litigation friend will be of no effect unless the court otherwise orders.[23] There are special rules as to the service of applications and orders on protected parties and, where appointed, their litigation friends.[24] The Official Solicitor may act as litigation friend of a protected party.[25]

However, adults are presumed to have capacity unless the contrary is estab-  **13.10** lished, and the question of capacity is issue-specific.[26] Thus, in *E v Channel Four Television Corp*[27] Munby J rejected an application by the Official Solicitor to restrain broadcast of a documentary programme to protect what were alleged to be the best interests of Pamela, a thirty-two-year-old with a multiple personality disorder, said to lack capacity. She had participated in the making of the programme, explaining and analysing her condition. The Court was not satisfied that the Official Solicitor was likely to establish at trial that Pamela did not have the necessary capacity to consent to transmission (and, in any case, it was likely that the film would serve and promote Pamela's best interests). If an adult is found not to have capacity to consent to transmission, the court must then consider whether publication is in the adult's best interests and, if it is not, weigh the adult's Article 8 interests and the public interest in the protection of the privacy of the vulnerable and incapable against the private and public interests in freedom of expression under Article 10.[28]

**Children**   There is no doubt that children have privacy rights, but some issues  **13.11** peculiar to their status must be noted.

*Competence and procedure*   Children are 'protected parties' under the CPR, and  **13.12** claims must be brought or defended by them through a litigation friend unless the court orders otherwise.[29] It may order otherwise in respect of some older teenagers, who may be competent to assert or defend privacy claims on their own behalf.[30] The Article 8 rights of such individuals embrace the right to make their own decisions on whether or not to tell their personal story, and to have their choices in that

---

[22] CPR 21.2(1). For the appropriate way to entitle proceedings in such a case see CPR PD 21, para 1.1.

[23] CPR 21.3.

[24] CPR 6.25(2)–(6) and 21.8(1)–(2).

[25] As in *T (by her litigation friend the Official Solicitor) v BBC* [2007] EWHC 1683 (QB), [2008] 1 FLR 281. The claimant was a vulnerable young adult whose competence to consent to a proposed broadcast was in issue.

[26] Mental Capacity Act 2005, s 1; see *E v Channel Four Television Corp* [2005] EWHC 1144 (Fam), [2005] EMLR 30 [61], [104].

[27] *E v Channel Four* (n 26).

[28] *E v Channel Four* (n 26) [59].

[29] CPR 21.2(2)–(3). For the appropriate way to entitle the proceedings in such a case see CPR PD 21 para 1.2(1).

[30] For discussion of '*Gillick* competence' and an example see *Re Roddy (A Minor), Torbay Borough Council v Associated Newspapers Ltd* [2003] EWHC 2927 (Fam), [2004] EMLR 8.

regard respected.[31] Other children are very likely to be regarded as in need of a litigation friend,[32] and, if so, the position is as stated above.[33] Special rules govern the service of applications and orders on children, depending on whether they need and have a litigation friend.[34]

**13.13**  *Substantive rights*  The substantive privacy rights of children are at least as great as those of adults. In cases engaging s 1 of the Children Act 1989 their interests are paramount by statute. Otherwise, issues as to the privacy of children must be decided in accordance with the approach prescribed by the House of Lords in *In re S (A Child)*.[35] The House there held that since the Human Rights Act 1998 (HRA) the mass of case law as to the exercise of the court's inherent jurisdiction in relation to minors need not be considered:

> The foundation of the jurisdiction to restrain publicity in a case such as the present is now derived from [C]onvention rights under the ECHR. This is the simple and direct way to approach such cases.[36]

**13.14**  As Munby J explained in *Re Roddy*,[37]

> [The] exercise of the jurisdiction now requires the court first to decide whether the child's rights under Art 8 are engaged and, if so, then to conduct the necessary balancing exercise between the competing rights under Arts 8 and 10, considering the proportionality of the potential interference with each right considered independently.

The earlier case law may however remain relevant as a means of founding jurisdiction, where jurisdiction would have existed before *In re S*,[38] and 'in regard to the ultimate balancing exercise to be carried out under the ECHR provisions'.[39]

**13.15**  The evaluation of children's privacy rights can give rise to peculiar difficulties. The English authorities from before the HRA treated children as having rights no lesser but also no greater than those of adults. Hence, it was said that no child, simply by virtue of being a child, is entitled to an immediate right of privacy or

---

[31]  *Re Roddy* (n 30) [35]–[36]. Also *Re Stedman and Patten* [2009] EWHC 935 (Fam), [2009] 2 FLR 852, where a child's wishes as to disclosure of potentially private information had to be balanced with other competing rights.

[32]  In *Murray* (n 15) J K Rowling and her husband sued as litigation friends on behalf of their infant son.

[33]  Text to n 29.

[34]  CPR 6.25(2)–(6) and 21.8(1)–(2).

[35]  [2004] UKHL 47, [2005] 1 AC 593.

[36]  *Re S (A Child)* (n 35) [22].

[37]  *Re Roddy* (n 30) [14]–[16].

[38]  *Leeds City Council v Channel Four Television Corp* [2005] EWHC 3522 (Fam), [2007] 1 FLR 678.

[39]  *Re S (A Child)* (n 35) [23]. This approach was followed by Cobb J in *Z v News Group Newspapers Ltd* [2013] EWHC 1150 (Fam) [32]–[34].

confidentiality:[40] and that outside s 1 of the Children Act 1989 'the child is left to whatever remedies against the media the law would give an adult in comparable circumstances'.[41]

Consistently with this approach, the New Zealand Court of Appeal refused in **13.16** *Hosking v Runting*[42] to restrain the publication of photographs of an infant in his pushchair, when it saw no evidence that publication threatened to cause real harm. Likewise, the PCC in May 2001 dismissed a complaint by Alex Kingston about the publication of photographs of her children without her consent in *Hello!* magazine. The PCC ruled that there could be no expectation of privacy in a public place, and 'did not consider that the photographs could reasonably be held to have affected [the child's] welfare or to concern any aspect of her private life'. This was consistent with previous decisions of the Commission, that the mere publication of a child's image cannot breach the code when it is taken in a public place and is unaccompanied by any private details or material that might embarrass or inconvenience the child.

The court does recognize, however, the particular vulnerability of children and **13.17** young people, and the greater sensitivity they may have in respect of their privacy rights. This is reflected in *Re W*[43] and *X v BBC*,[44] decisions firmly based on the apprehended harm to the subjects in each case. In the latter case, a seventeen-year-old had provided a written consent to be filmed by the BBC but withdrawn it fearing that disclosure of private information might lead to physical harm. Although the Court concluded that she was not likely to succeed with her claim, an injunction was granted on the basis of Lord Nicholls's exceptional category in *Cream Holdings v Banerjee*.[45] Indeed, the protection now afforded to children's rights is such that a child's interests may be the deciding factor even where the child is not a party to the case. In *K v News Group Newspapers*,[46] considering an application for an interim injunction, the Court of Appeal cited several international human rights instruments[47] which establish the primacy of children's rights in all decisions concerning children and followed the approach

---

[40] *R v Central Independent Television plc* [1994] Fam 192, 207 (Waite LJ).

[41] *Kelly v BBC* [2000] EWHC 3 (Fam), [2001] Fam 59, 77.

[42] [2004] NZCA 34 at [165] (Gault P and Blanchard J). Keith J agreed: at [185].

[43] [2006] 1 FLR 1.

[44] [2005] CSOH 80.

[45] [2004] UKHL 44, [2005] 1 AC 253 [22]. The exceptional cases are those where (a) the potential adverse consequences of disclosure are particularly grave, or (b) a short-lived injunction is required in order to allow the court to hear and give proper consideration to the application.

[46] [2011] EWCA Civ 439, [2011] 1 WLR 1827.

[47] The second principle of the United Nations Declaration on the Rights of the Child 1959, Art 3.1 of the Convention on the Rights of the Child 1989, and Art 24 of the European Union's Charter of Fundamental Rights.

set out in Lord Kerr JSC's speech in *ZH (Tanzania) v Secretary of State for the Home Dept.*[48]

**13.18** The authorities in England and in Strasbourg also show that a focus on whether disclosure would cause identifiable harm is too narrow. The Court of Appeal's approach in *Murray v Express Newspapers plc*[49] makes this clear. Children do not benefit from a 'guarantee of privacy',[50] but 'the attributes of the claimant', including the fact that he was a child, were amongst the factors going into the balancing exercise to be performed.[51] The European Court of Human Rights (ECtHR) adopted a similar approach in *Reklos v Greece*.[52] Though the Court said that it could not address the general question of whether interference with 'the right to one's image' depends on the individual concerned being aware of it,[53] it implicitly answered that question in the negative. The more recent decisions of *AAA v Associated Newspapers Ltd*[54] and *Weller v Associated Newspapers Ltd*[55] confirm this approach, as well as applying the 'primacy' principle referred to at 13.17.

**13.19** **The right to disclose**  The ECtHR has, however, recognized that a child's Article 8 rights (in addition to his or her Article 10 rights) may also include the right, as part of a private life, to disclose facts. In *Re Roddy*[56] a local authority sought an injunction to prevent a seventeen-year-old girl from telling her story about life in care to a newspaper. Relying on *Pretty v UK*,[57] Munby J held that Roddy's Article 8 right was grounded in a right of autonomy and included a right to tell her story. Roddy's rights as a mature teenager were to be respected.

*(b) The deceased*

**13.20** **Dead at the time of the wrong**  In principle, it seems that a privacy claim which relies on a publicity right, or some proprietary or other economic right, may arise even if the individual is deceased at the time of the offending behaviour. A claim of that kind would need to be brought by the personal representatives of the deceased. An obvious example would be whether the estate of the late Princess of Wales could sue for breach of privacy in the exploitation of

---

[48] [2011] UKSC 4, [2011] 1 AC 166 [46]. See 5.168–5.170.

[49] *Murray* (n 15). See further 5.123.

[50] *Murray* (n 15) [58].

[51] *Murray* (n 15) [36].

[52] App no 1234/05 (ECtHR, 15 January 2009), [2009] EMLR 16. See also 5.123.

[53] *Reklos* (n 52) [34].

[54] [2012] EWHC 2103 (QB), [2013] EMLR 2.

[55] [2014] EWHC 1163 (QB), [2014] EMLR 24. Publishing photographs of ten-month old twins was a breach of their Art 8 rights, although they could not have been aware of the publication and would not have suffered any immediate embarrassment: [196]. See also 5.123.

[56] *Re Roddy* (n 30).

[57] (2002) 35 EHRR 1.

her image after her death. At common law, a right conferred by statute *prima facie* continues after death but otherwise purely personal rights lapse.[58] It is therefore well-established that there can be no claim in defamation on behalf of the deceased.[59] It may therefore be that a privacy claim on behalf of a person who was dead at the time of the alleged wrong will not be viable, if its aim is to vindicate personal rights related to individual dignity and hurt feelings. This was the opinion of the Law Commission in its 1981 report on breach of confidence.[60]

The weight of US authority is also against the view that a common law right to privacy survives after the individual has died.[61] The PCC took a similar approach when considering a complaint by the Tolkien family that articles published in a regional newspaper alleging that John Tolkien (deceased) was a paedophile were inaccurate in breach of clause 1 (Accuracy) and intrusive in breach of clause 3 (Privacy). The PCC rejected the complaints under clause 3 on the deceased's behalf, ruling that it was not possible to invade the privacy of someone who was dead.[62] Some statutory privacy protection is expressly limited to the individual's lifetime.[63]    **13.21**

The authors Toulson and Phipps have argued, however, that post-death disclosures should, and may in law, give rise to a cause of action for breach of confidence.[64] Citing these observations, an Information Tribunal has held that the duty of medical confidentiality is capable of surviving death,[65] and the High Court has held the proposition to be arguable.[66] Hence, the General Medical Council advises doctors that in addition to the 'obvious' ethical duty to maintain    **13.22**

---

[58] *Rickless v United Artists* [1988] QB 40, CA, 56. See also *Wilson v Wyatt* (1820), referred to in *Argyll (Duchess) v Argyll (Duke)* [1967] Ch 302, 319–20, where it was evidently assumed that a duty of medical confidentiality terminated on death.

[59] An attempt in the UK Parliament to enact statutory rights for the relatives of deceased persons to sue for defamation failed in the Committee stages of the Defamation Bill in the Commons, on 19 June 2012. For the draft amendment see <http://www.publications.parliament.uk/pa/bills/cbill/2012-2013/0005/amend/pbc0051906m.21-27.html>. A campaign on similar lines in Scotland resulted in a Consultation Paper of 11 January 2011: *Death of a Good Name—Defamation and the Deceased: A Consultation Paper* (<http://www.gov.scot/Resource/Doc/337251/0110660.pdf>), but the law has not since been amended.

[60] *Breach of Confidence* (Law Com No 100, Cmnd 8388 1981) paras 4.05–4.107.

[61] See *Lawson v Meconi* 2005 Del Ch LEXIS 74, 18–22; C Calvert, 'The privacy of death: An emergent jurisprudence and legal rebuke to media exploitation and a voyeuristic culture' (2006) 26 Loyola of Los Angeles Ent L Rev 133, 148–9; *Green v Chicago Tribune Co*, 675 NE 2d 249.

[62] 26 January 2003, Report 62. See further 14.71–14.73.

[63] Only the living enjoy data protection rights: Data Protection Act 1998, s 1(1). Similarly, statutory anonymity for the victims of sex crimes (discussed at 1.84) lasts only for the victim's lifetime.

[64] R Toulson and C Phipps, *Confidentiality* (2nd edn, Sweet & Maxwell 2012) para 11-051.

[65] *Bluck v Information Commissioner and Epsom and St Helier University NHS Trust* (2007) 98 BMLR 1.

[66] *Lewis v Secretary of State for Health* [2008] EWHC 2196 (QB), [2008] LS Law Medical 559 [18]–[30] (Foskett J).

confidentiality after a patient's death there may also be a legal duty.[67] It is notable, also, that the Freedom of Information (Scotland) Act 2002 includes, in the definition of personal information exempt from disclosure, a deceased person's medical records.[68]

**13.23** **Relatives of the deceased** Disclosure of personal information about a deceased person may amount to an interference with the privacy rights of the surviving family. Both the ECtHR[69] and the US courts (including the Supreme Court)[70] have made this clear. The PCC's *Tolkien* decision, while rejecting the relatives' own privacy complaint, upheld the further complaint of a breach of clause 5 of the Code (Intrusion into grief or shock).[71]

**13.24** **Death after cause of action accrues** The ECtHR appears to view a privacy claim as heritable. In *Craxi (No 2) v Italy*[72] the Court held that the deceased applicant's widow, son, and daughter had standing to continue the proceedings under Article 8 in the applicant's stead, and held that the award of €2,000 for non-pecuniary loss be paid to the applicant's heirs. In English law, although there is no authority on the point, it seems the better view is that the proceedings can continue, regardless of the nature of the claim.[73] Although at common law purely personal causes of action abate on the death of the claimant or defendant by the application of the maxim *actio personalis moritur cum persona*, statute provides as a general rule that causes of action survive death. Section 1 of the Law Reform (Miscellaneous Provisions) Act 1934 provides:

> Subject to the provisions of this section, on the death of any person after the commencement of this Act all causes of action subsisting against or vested in him shall survive against, or, as the case may be, for the benefit of, his estate.

---

[67] General Medical Council, *Confidentiality* (2009) para 70.

[68] s 38(2).

[69] In *Fairfield v UK* App no 24790/04 (ECtHR, 28 March 2005) the Court held an application under Art 8 inadmissible because the victim had died, and his relatives lacked standing. An application by relatives was however upheld in *Editions Plon v France* (2006) 42 EHRR 36 (medical confidences of President Mitterand). See also *Armoniene v Lithuania* (2009) 48 EHRR 53 where the ECtHR held that A's close relatives had an interest of their own to ensure that his right to privacy in respect of his HIV status was respected even if he died before the final domestic decision; and *Putistin v Ukraine* App no 16882/03 (ECtHR, 21 November 2013) where the Court stated that 'the reputation of a deceased member of a person's family may, in certain circumstances, affect that person's private life and identity, and thus come within the scope of Article 8'. It may therefore be possible, in certain circumstances, for relatives of a deceased person to bring a claim in the English and Welsh courts in respect of their own Art 8 rights.

[70] See eg *National Archives and Records Administration v Favish* 541 US 157 (2004), 167; *Reid v Pierce County* 961 P 2d 333 (Wash 1998), 342; *NY Times Co v City of NY Fire Dept* 829 NE 2d 266, (NY 2005), 269; and *Providence Journal Co v Town of Warwick* No 03-2697, 2004 RI Super LEXIS 136, (RI Super Court, 2004), 6–8.

[71] See n 62. The material from cl 5 of the PCC Code is now found in cl 4 of the IPSO Code. Ofcom takes a different view on privacy and the deceased: see eg Procedures for the consideration and adjudication of Fairness & Privacy complaints (1 June 2011) n 12.

[72] (2004) 38 EHRR 995, para 90.

[73] For the relevant procedure see 13.25.

Causes of action for defamation[74] were specifically excluded from this provision.[75] Hence, defamation proceedings abate on the death of either party.[76]

**Procedure**  If a privacy claim can be made on behalf of a person who was dead **13.25** at the time of the alleged wrong it would need to be brought by the personal representatives of the deceased. Likewise, in the case of a cause of action in privacy which accrues in a person's lifetime and survives his or her death. If the deceased sued during his or her lifetime the person(s) in whom the claim or liability then vests will need to apply to be substituted.[77]

### (c) Bankrupts

The fact that a person is bankrupt at the time of committing or being the victim of a **13.26** breach of privacy should not in principle affect the coming into existence of rights or liabilities, though it plainly may affect who can enforce the right, and how. As with the deceased, a distinction may be drawn between the different types of privacy rights. It seems that if claims of a commercial character are amongst those advanced the trustee will have a right to any proceeds of that claim.[78] There is good reason to believe that causes of action for breach of privacy which are of a personal rather than commercial character will remain with a bankrupt rather than his or her trustee.[79]

If a privacy claim of a personal nature remains with a bankrupt then any proceed- **13.27** ings in respect of it will be pursued by the bankrupt in his or her own name, in the ordinary way. A privacy claim of a commercial kind may require the trustee to be joined, or the proceeds held on trust for him, it seems.[80]

### (d) Companies

Companies can of course possess rights of confidentiality, but whether they have **13.28** any privacy rights is a different question. Other common law jurisdictions have declined to acknowledge the existence of corporate privacy rights. Both Strasbourg and domestic authority recognize, however, some limited rights under Article 8

---

[74] Meaning, it is suggested, libel and slander but not malicious falsehood, given *Hatchard v Mege* (1887) 18 QBD 771, 777.

[75] The position is different in Scotland. Section 2 of the Damages (Scotland) Act 2011 makes specific provision for the transmission to executors of an action for damages for defamation raised by the deceased before his or her death.

[76] *Smith v Dha* [2013] EWHC 838 (QB). See also *Hatchard* (n 74) 774. A good discussion of the historical context of abatement in defamation proceedings and its consequences can be found in *Stead v Foster* (NSW Supreme Court, 4 September 1998) as approved in *Kalejs v Minister for Justice and Customs* [2001] FCA 1769.

[77] CPR 19.2(4)(a), 19.8(1) and PD 19A paras 5.1–5.2.

[78] See *Re Kavanagh; ex p the Bankrupt v Jackson (The Trustee)* [1949] 2 All ER 264, CA, 268 (Jenkins LJ), suggesting that the bankrupt would keep compensation for breach of confidence but the other damages, for injury to the bankrupt's estate, would pass to the trustee.

[79] In *Haig v Aitken* [2001] Ch 110 Rattee J held that private letters in the possession of Jonathan Aitken, the disgraced former MP, did not form part of his estate that could be sold by his trustee in bankruptcy.

[80] *Haig* (n 79).

for corporations mainly, if not exclusively, founded on the aspects of that article which protect correspondence and the home or, in French, 'domicile' of a person, rather than his or her 'private life'.[81]

**Foreign common law**

**13.29** *The United States* The US courts have refused to allow companies to sue for breach of privacy:

> Unlike actions for defamation, suits for invasion of privacy can be brought only by individuals. Neither corporations, associations, nor partnerships have 'feelings' or a right to *personal* privacy, and they therefore may not recover damages...for such injury.[82]

**13.30** *Australia* A similar conclusion was reached by three members of the High Court in *Australian Broadcasting Corp v Lenah Game Meats*.[83] Gummow and Hayne JJ (with whom Gaudron J agreed)[84] concluded that although a tort of privacy might develop in Australia, it could only be for the benefit of individuals, not companies:[85] '[the company's] reliance upon an emergent tort of invasion of privacy is misplaced. Whatever development may take place in that field will be to the benefit of natural, not artificial persons.' Kirby J also expressed doubts as to whether a company had any privacy rights. Gleeson CJ did not express a final opinion[86] and Callinan J tentatively thought that there was no reason why a company could not enjoy privacy rights.[87]

**13.31** **England and Wales** Sometimes cited as a case supporting the proposition that a company can suffer infringement of its privacy is *R v Broadcasting Standards Commission, ex p BBC*.[88] However, upon analysis the case does not support the general proposition that English law protects the privacy of a company. Forbes J quashed a decision by the Broadcasting Standards Commission to uphold a complaint by Dixons Stores Ltd that covert filming in its shops by the BBC amounted to an unwarranted infringement of its privacy, holding that Article 8 of the European Convention on Human Rights was 'not designed or intended to protect corporations or companies' but 'to protect various aspects of human personality'.[89] The Court of Appeal reversed this decision, but did so by reference to the particular language of the Broadcasting Act 1996, rather than by reference to the scope of Article 8.

**13.32** Lord Mustill laid particular stress on the fact that the decision turned on the language and purpose of the statute, and made clear his substantial reservations

---

[81] See 13.36–13.38.
[82] R D Sack, *Sack on Defamation: Libel, Slander and Related Problems* (April 2014 update, 4th edn, Practising Law Institute 2010) para 12:3.5. See further 3.48.
[83] (2001) 185 ALR 1.
[84] *Lenah Game Meats* (n 83) [58].
[85] *Lenah Game Meats* (n 83) [116], [129]–[132].
[86] *Lenah Game Meats* (n 83) [43].
[87] *Lenah Game Meats* (n 83) [328].
[88] [2001] QB 885.
[89] See now, however, the Strasbourg jurisprudence mentioned at 13.36–13.38.

about the notion that a company could otherwise claim to have had its privacy infringed:[90]

> [I]n general I find the concept of a company's privacy hard to grasp. To my mind the privacy of a human being denotes at the same time the personal 'space' in which the individual is free to be itself, and also the carapace, or shell, or umbrella, or whatever other metaphor is preferred, which protects that space from intrusion. An infringement of privacy is an affront to the personality, which is damaged both by the violation and by the demonstration that the personal space is not inviolate. The concept is hard indeed to define, but if this gives something of its flavour I do not see how it can apply to an impersonal corporate body, which has no sensitivities to wound, and no selfhood to protect.

Lord Mustill acknowledged that there would be occasions where a company could **13.33** maintain a complaint on grounds which, in the case of an individual, could be presented as a breach of privacy. He gave the example of 'the clandestine copying of business documents'.[91] However, he emphasized that 'privacy and confidentiality are not the same', and that while 'a company can have secrets' and rights of confidentiality this was different from 'the essentially human and personal concept of privacy'.[92]

In *Tillery Valley Foods Ltd v Channel Four Television Corp*,[93] Mann J refused an **13.34** injunction sought by the claimant company on conventional breach of confidence grounds in relation to covert filming carried out on its premises.[94] The Court rejected the contention that mere filming on the claimant's premises by the undercover journalist rendered what was filmed confidential, holding that the activities filmed did not have a confidential quality and (relying on *Service Corp International plc v Channel Four Television Corp*[95]) that framing the claim in breach of confidence was an effort to escape the consequences of the rule in *Bonnard v Perryman*.[96]

Subsequent English cases have however recognized the possibility of reliance **13.35** by companies on Article 8 for some purposes. In *Office of Fair Trading v X*,[97] Morison J accepted that the issue of warrants against corporate defendants suspected of price-fixing could engage Article 8 rights if the complaint was of physical intrusion into the 'domicile' or of interference with correspondence, although the premises concerned were business places and not personal households. It also seems clear that corporations may sue to protect the rights of others in their care.[98]

---

[90] *R v Broadcasting Standards Commission* (n 88) 900.
[91] *R v Broadcasting Standards Commission* (n 88) 900.
[92] *R v Broadcasting Standards Commission* (n 88) 900.
[93] [2004] EWHC 1075 (Ch).
[94] *Tillery Valley Foods* (n 93) [2].
[95] [1999] EMLR 83, 89.
[96] [1891] 2 Ch 269, CA (no injunction in defamation unless claimant's case is so strong that a jury would be perverse to reject it). See further 8.50 *et seq*.
[97] [2004] ICR 105 [12].
[98] See *Green Corns Ltd v Claverley Group Ltd* [2005] EWHC 958 (QB), [2005] EMLR 31, where a company operating a care home for troubled children was allowed to bring an action to protect children in its care.

More recently, in *Ambrosiadou v Coward,*[99] Eady J said that each case is to be judged on its own facts. In *Viagogo v Myles*[100] it was agreed that Article 8 did not apply because the claimant was a body corporate. In *L H Bishop Electric Co Ltd v Commissioners for Her Majesty's Revenue & Customs* the First-Tier Tribunal held that:

> A company has human rights if and to the extent it is the alter ego of a person (or, potentially, a group of people). Therefore, it must be seen as being in the shoes of that person and must possess the same human rights because any other decision would deny that person his human rights. Therefore, while it is ludicrous to suggest a company has a private life or family, nevertheless a company which is the alter ego of a person can be a victim of a breach of [Article 8] (the right to private life) if, were it not so protected, that person's human rights would be breached....It is obvious that a company owned and controlled by a single person is in practice the alter ego of that person and to ensure full protection of such a person's human rights it may be necessary to treat those human rights as also pertaining to the company....Companies have a right to a private life where that private life is the private life of the alter ego of the company.[101]

Corporate claimants are likely to be more active in litigation where information capable of engaging the Article 8 rights of individuals, such as images of or information about celebrities, can be protected as commercially confidential information, whether owned or licensed.[102] *Cooper v Turrell*[103] is an example of a case of concurrent claims in breach of confidence (brought by a company) and misuse of private information (brought by an individual).

**13.36** **European Court of Human Rights** The principle that business premises and correspondence may be protected under Article 8 was established in 1993 in *Niemitz v Germany.*[104] In *Sociétés Colas Est v France*[105] the Court upheld an Article 8 complaint by companies whose offices had been raided by the French competition authorities. Noting that the word 'domicile' in the French text of Article 8 has a wider connotation than the word 'home' in the English text, the Court reasoned that a dynamic interpretation of the Convention required that in certain circumstances Article 8 rights could be interpreted as applying to a company's registered office, agencies, or other business premises.

**13.37** The Strasbourg jurisprudence was reviewed and restated in *Bernh Larsen Holding AS v Norway,*[106] where the applicant companies argued that their right to respect for private life had been infringed when representatives of the Norwegian tax

---

99 [2010] EWHC 1794 (QB) [33].
100 [2012] EWHC 433 (Ch) [34].
101 [2013] UKFTT 522 (TC) [556]–[562] (Judge Barbara Mosedale).
102 See eg *Douglas v Hello! Ltd* [2007] UKHL 21, [2008] 1 AC 1.
103 [2011] EWHC 3269 (QB).
104 (1993) 16 EHRR 97.
105 (2004) 39 EHRR 17, paras 41, 42, and 49.
106 (2014) 58 EHRR 8.

authorities took copies of all data on the companies' servers, including personal emails and correspondence of employees and other persons working for the companies. Given that none of the individuals concerned had complained of an interference with his or her private life, the Court did not find it necessary to examine the issue. The Court stated as follows:[107]

> The Court first reiterates that, as interpreted in its case-law, the word 'home', appearing in the English text of art.8—the word 'domicile' in the French text has a broader connotation—covers residential premises and may extend also to certain professional or business premises.[108] It includes not only the registered office of a company owned and run by a private individual[109] but also that of a legal person and its branches and other business premises.[110] Such an interpretation would not unduly hamper the Contracting States, for they would retain their entitlement to 'interfere' to the extent permitted by art.8(2); that entitlement might well be more far-reaching where professional or business activities or premises were involved than would otherwise be the case.[111]
>
> 105 The Court further reiterates that, in certain previous cases concerning complaints under art.8 related to the search of business premises and the search and seizure of electronic data, the Court found an interference with 'the right to respect for home'[112] and 'correspondence'.[113]

**13.38** It remains unclear whether this approach to Article 8 might be held to apply to interferences other than invasions of premises or interference with correspondence. Earlier decisions suggest not.[114]

**13.39** **Conclusions** It would appear that a company confronted with a publication, actual or threatened, that could be labelled as a breach of privacy will ordinarily need to rely on breach of confidence, defamation, passing off, breach of copyright, or trade mark infringement if it is to have a remedy in English law. It may be possible for a company to mount an Article 8-based claim if either (1) the complaint is of physical intrusion into the 'domicile', or interference with 'correspondence',[115] or (2) it is an 'alter ego' of an individual whose rights require the recognition of corporate privacy,[116] but purely corporate claims based on Article 8 in respect of other kinds of activity seem unlikely to be upheld.

**13.40** **Practice points** In any corporate claim it will be important to identify the confidential or private information and to identify correctly the corporate body which

---

[107] Para 107. Footnotes as in original, save for numbering.
[108] *Niemietz* (1993) 16 EHRR 97, para 30.
[109] *Buck* (2006) 42 EHRR 21, para 32.
[110] *Sallinen v Finland* (2007) 44 EHRR 18, para 70.
[111] *Niemietz* (n 108) para 31.
[112] *Niemietz* (n 108) para 71.
[113] *Niemietz* (n 108) para 71, and *Wieser* (2008) 46 EHRR 54, para 45.
[114] See *eg* the discussion of *Asselbourg v Luxembourg* App no 29121/95 (ECtHR, 26 June 1999) at 13.43.
[115] See 13.37.
[116] As in *LH Bishop* (n 101).

possesses the relevant right, especially in the case of groups.[117] Occasionally, anonymity orders will be appropriate to protect commercially sensitive information.[118]

*(e) Partnerships*

**13.41** There would seem no reason in principle why a partnership, limited or unlimited, should not sue or be sued in respect of a traditional or hybrid breach of confidence. Limited liability partnerships have a legal personality separate from that of the partners, and it would seem appropriate to apply the considerations relating to companies discussed at 13.28–13.40. While unlimited firms do not have separate legal personality they are recognized as having, collectively, legal rights and liabilities which can be asserted by or against them in the firm's name.[119] Whether rights in respect of particular information are owned by a partnership, or by individual members, may sometimes be a difficult question.[120]

**13.42** If a firm has a confidentiality or privacy right of its own, distinct from a right possessed by one or more of its partners, it will be entitled to protect or vindicate that right by suing in its own right, in the name under which it carried on business at the time the cause of action accrued.[121]

*(f) Unincorporated associations*

**13.43** Actions for breaches of privacy by and against unincorporated associations or their members would appear to raise issues similar to those concerning companies and firms, discussed above.[122] For example, in *Asselbourg v Luxembourg*[123] eighty applicants complained to the Strasbourg Court that their Article 8 rights had been infringed by the siting of a steelworks. Seventy-nine of the applicants were individuals, but the eightieth was Greenpeace-Luxembourg, an unincorporated association. Rejecting the case at the admissibility stage, the Court held that such an association could not be protected by Article 8 'merely because it has its registered office close to the steelworks that it is criticising', when the Article 8 infringement alleged was said to flow from 'nuisances or problems which can be encountered only by natural persons'. Greenpeace could act only as a representative of the members or employees whose interests were affected, and could not itself claim to be a victim of the violation.[124]

---

[117] For an illustration of how mistaken identification of a corporate claimant can have serious consequences see the libel action of *Adelson v Associated Newspapers Ltd* [2007] EWCA Civ 701, [2008] 1 WLR 585.

[118] See 13.100 *et seq*. See also the applicants' submission in *Bernh Larsen* (n 106) at para 97.

[119] See R Parkes et al, *Gatley on Libel and Slander* (12th edn, Sweet & Maxwell 2013) paras 8.26–8.27.

[120] See *eg Murray v Yorkshire Fund Managers Ltd* [1998] 1 WLR 951, CA.

[121] CPR PD 7A para 5A.3.

[122] See 13.28–13.42.

[123] App no 29121/95 (ECtHR, 26 June 1999).

[124] [1] of 'The Law' section. See also *Varec v Belgium* [2008] 2 CMLR 24 in which the European Court of Justice held at [48] that 'the notion of "private life" cannot be taken to mean that the professional or commercial activities of either natural or legal persons are excluded'.

Such actions also raise procedural issues, given that such associations are held to **13.44** lack legal personality separate from those of their members, and there appears to be no procedural mechanism to facilitate suit by or against the members in the association's name.[125] Whether representative proceedings could be pursued is unclear. Under the civil procedure regime in force until 1999 it was held that this was not a proper way for members of an unincorporated association to pursue a defamation case. Under the CPR, the threshold criterion for allowing a person to represent others in an action is that the persons to be represented must have 'the same interest in a claim'.[126] This may be so where the claimants and those represented are all solicitors seeking injunctions to restrain harassment and breach of the Data Protection Act 1998 by means of website publications, but not to the extent the claim is in libel.[127] The safer course would seem to be for individual claims to be advanced, where possible.

### (g) Public authorities

Public authorities may claim for breach of confidence but they are likely to have **13.45** to plead and prove that the disclosure was or would be contrary to the public interest,[128] and will also need to establish that the grant of relief that interferes with freedom of expression is, even if dictated by contract, necessary and proportionate in pursuit of a legitimate aim.[129] Public authorities have no rights under Article 8.[130] Moreover, the policy considerations which operate to disable public bodies from suing for defamation are likely to be applied to privacy.[131] Indeed, if companies cannot suffer hurt feelings from invasive breaches of privacy, then neither can government bodies. As with companies, public bodies may not therefore be able to rely on developments in the law that are based on protecting the privacy of the individual. This would accord with the position under the HRA whereby public authorities should not, in theory, be entitled to invoke Convention rights.[132]

---

[125]  See eg *EETPU v Times Newspapers Ltd* [1980] QB 585; *North London Central Mosque Trust v Policy Exchange* [2009] EWHC 3311 (QB).

[126]  CPR 19.6(1). The requirement is not met where a claimant purports to represent all victims of alleged price-fixing, who have different interests: *Emerald Supplies Ltd v British Airways plc* [2010] EWCA Civ 1284, [2011] Ch 345.

[127]  *Law Society v Kordowski* [2011] EWHC 3185 (QB), [2014] EMLR 2 [162]–[168].

[128]  See 4.41–4.42.

[129]  See 4.43.

[130]  *W v Westminster City Council (No 1)* [2004] EWHC 2866 (QB) [39] (Tugendhat J).

[131]  *Derbyshire County Council v Times Newspapers Ltd* [1993] AC 537.

[132]  See 1.58. Contrast the position under the Freedom of Information Act 2000 which permits government departments to protect the confidentiality of information that relates to the formulation or development of government policy (s 35) and allows all public authorities to exempt information the disclosure of which, in the reasonable opinion of a qualified person, would or would be likely to inhibit the free and frank provision of advice or exchange of views for the purposes of deliberation (s 36). This area of protection has been described as a 'space' which organizations need in order to operate effectively, which may be compared to the personal 'space' referred to by Lord Mustill where an individual can be 'free to be itself': see 13.32.

**13.46**  Conversely, public authorities are amenable to all forms of privacy claim, Article 8 being of course expressly designed to protect against state interference with private and family life, home, and correspondence. A public authority may as a defendant be entitled to rely on the right to impart and receive information and ideas under Article 10(1), where the rights engaged are those of the public to receive information imparted by the authority.[133]

*(h) Foreigners*[134]

**13.47**  **As claimants**  Foreign nationality, domicile, or residence, are no bar to the pursuit of a privacy claim in England and Wales. However, if the claim were based on minimal publication in the jurisdiction it might be vulnerable to dismissal as an abuse of process, on the ground that there was no real and substantial wrong; and such an argument would gain weight if the defendant were also foreign, with no or minimal links to this jurisdiction.[135]

**13.48**  **As defendants**  The English Court will exercise jurisdiction over persons of foreign nationality, domicile, or residence, and companies and firms domiciled abroad, in certain carefully prescribed circumstances, discussed at 13.56–13.65.

## (2) Claimants

**13.49**  Some kinds of privacy claim have the potential for numerous individual claimants. Examples include the targeting of staff of a medical research company by animal-rights campaigners for intrusive action; or media coverage of the conduct of care homes, said adversely to affect the lives of many residents. In such cases, it will often be impracticable for all affected individuals to be made claimants, but it seems doubtful that a representative action is permissible under the CPR.[136] However, the courts have so far permitted these situations to be dealt with by a company suing on behalf of and asserting the rights of the affected individuals, without those individuals being made parties or even providing direct evidence.

## (3) Defendants

*(a) Finding out wrongdoers' identities and roles*

**13.50**  **Generally**  It may sometimes be difficult to find out the identities of some or all of those causally responsible for a privacy breach. Even where identities are known,

---

[133]  *W v Westminster City Council (No 1)* (n 130); *London Regional Transport Ltd v Mayor of London* [2001] EWCA 1491, [2003] EMLR 4.

[134]  We refer here to any person firm or company that is a national of or domiciled in a country outside England and Wales, and to British citizens who are domiciled or resident abroad.

[135]  See *Jameel (Yousef) v Dow Jones Inc* [2005] EWCA Civ 75, [2005] QB 946. This doctrine applies even where the claim has no foreign element (see *Williams v MGN Ltd* [2009] EWHC 3150 (QB)), and to causes of action other than libel: see *Sullivan v Bristol Film Studios Ltd* [2012] EWCA Civ 570, [2012] EMLR 27 (copyright infringement). For further discussion see 13.56.

[136]  See 13.44.

there can be uncertainty about the roles played by those involved, and consequent doubt about their legal responsibility. In cases involving electronic communication in particular, it may be hard for a claimant to determine precisely who has done what. Because of the various exemptions afforded to ISPs under the E-Commerce Directive,[137] determination of their liability may require an assessment of their state of mind. Much of the relevant evidence in such cases may be in the possession of the defendant alone.

Where acts are performed or threatened by unknown persons via email, or on **13.51** the internet, or through some other service or medium afforded by an innocent third party, the would-be claimant may be well advised to seek an order that the service provider or other third party give pre-action disclosure either under CPR 31.17 or the *Norwich Pharmacal* principles.[138] The *Norwich Pharmacal* jurisdiction was subject to comprehensive consideration by the Supreme Court in *Rugby Football Union v Viagogo Ltd*[139] where the essential requirements were identified: the applicant must satisfy a court that (a) a wrong has been carried out, or arguably carried out, (b) an order is required to enable action to be brought against the wrongdoer, and (c) the respondent was mixed up in, or facilitated, the wrongdoing (even if innocently) and is able to provide the information necessary to enable the wrongdoer to be identified. The Court held that when considering whether to grant an order under this jurisdiction a court must take into account the applicant's ultimate aim in seeking disclosure and, where a respondent alleges that an order would interfere with the non-party's Article 8 ECHR rights, the court must apply the ultimate balancing test as set out in *In re S (A Child)*.[140]

**Journalistic privilege** Those considering any such application will need to bear **13.52** in mind the privilege from identifying sources which is enjoyed by those responsible for publications.[141] The main issues for consideration are likely to be: (a) whether the potential respondent is a person 'responsible' for a publication; if so, (b) whether the wrongdoer is a source of information contained in that publication; if so, (c) whether disclosure is necessary in the interests of justice. An ISP is unlikely to be considered 'responsible' for a third-party publication facilitated by its services, and is likely to be ordered to disclose the identity of its client wrongdoer, although the applicant will normally bear the innocent respondent's costs of dealing with the application and of making any disclosure ordered.[142]

---

[137] See 15.59–15.72.

[138] *Norwich Pharmacal Co v Customs and Excise Commissioners* [1974] AC 133.

[139] *Rugby Football Union v Viagogo Ltd* [2012] UKSC 55, [2012] 1 WLR 3333.

[140] *Re S (A Child)* (n 35).

[141] Contempt of Court Act 1981, s 10.

[142] See *eg Totalise plc v The Motley Fool Ltd* [2001] EWCA Civ 1897, [2002] 1 WLR 1233 (defamation); *Grant v Google (UK) Ltd* [2005] EWHC 3444 (Ch), [2006] All ER (D) 243 (copyright infringement); *G v Wikimedia Foundation Inc* [2009] EWHC 3148 (QB), [2010] EMLR 364 (breach of confidence and privacy).

*(b) Claims without naming defendants*

**13.53** A claimant may have good grounds to restrain a threatened wrong but be unable to identify the wrongdoer(s), or all of them. There may be no innocent third party amenable to a *Norwich Pharmacal* application, or no time to obtain such an order before the wrong is to be done. The range of potential wrongdoers may be so large that it is impossible to list all those against whom an order is justified. Or there may be insufficient evidence to establish against all the potential wrongdoers a threat or intention to do the wrongful act. Circumstances such as these may mean that there is simply not enough to justify any action, but there are, as explained in Chapter 12, two kinds of injunction which the court in principle has power to grant.

**13.54** **Orders against persons unknown: 'John Doe' orders**    Where the court exercises its power to grant an injunction against persons unknown,[143] the order will identify those against whom it is made by description.[144] This must be precise and apt, so as to cover adequately and only those against whom a legal right can be asserted, and to make it clear to them that they are its targets.[145] The court will need to be satisfied that the order can be brought to the notice of the 'John Doe' defendants, for it will be of no effect if not.[146] It may be that an extension of time for service of the claim form beyond the usual four-month time limit may be required, although indefinite extensions of time for service will not be granted.[147] Where a claimant seeking an interim non-disclosure order intends to serve it on, or give notice of it to, a non-party (particularly a media organization) the court will at the very least expect to see that the claimant has attempted to provide such parties with advance notice of the application if at all possible. Failure to do so can only be justified by compelling reasons (such as urgency or secrecy) and with clear and cogent evidence.[148]

**13.55** **Injunctions against the world ('*contra mundum*')**    The evidence will need to be strong to justify an order of this kind. That may be so where the threatened wrong poses risks to life and limb and the threat is widespread. Examples are given in Chapter 12.[149] In such a case, the order will be framed in terms which prohibit 'any person with notice of this order' from doing the enjoined acts.

---

[143] See 12.31–12.33.

[144] The guidance and Model Order in the *Practice Guidance (HC: Interim Non-Disclosure Orders) Senior Courts* [2012] 1 WLR 1003 should be followed. See also *Bloomsbury Publishing Group and JK Rowling v News Group Newspapers Ltd* [2003] EWHC 1205 (Ch), [2003] 1 WLR 1633.

[145] In the *Bloomsbury Publishing* case (n 144), the defendants were described as 'the person or persons who have offered the publishers of the *Sun*, the *Daily Mail*, and the *Daily Mirror* newspapers a copy of the book "Harry Potter and the Order of the Phoenix" by JK Rowling, or any part thereof, and the person or persons who has or have physical possession of a copy of the said book or any part thereof without the consent of the claimants'.

[146] *X and Y v Persons Unknown* [2006] EWHC 2783 (QB), [2007] EMLR 10 [77]–[78]; *Terry v Persons Unknown* [2010] EWHC 119 (QB), [2010] EMLR 16 [17], [136]–[137] and [143]. See further the discussion on service of such an order at 13.161.

[147] *Terry* (n 146) [143].

[148] Practice Guidance (n 144) paras 19–22. See eg *Kerner v XY and YZ* [2015] EWHC 128 (QB).

[149] See 12.34–12.35.

# D. Where? Jurisdiction and Venue

## (1) When does the English Court have Jurisdiction?

In the English common law of defamation each individual publication is a sep- **13.56** arate cause of action[150] and publication is considered to take place where the words are heard or read.[151] This approach has been adopted in privacy claims.[152] In privacy, as in defamation claims, the court will assume jurisdiction provided the tort committed within its territory is 'real and substantial'.[153] This need not involve mass publication, and the court will have jurisdiction even if publication elsewhere dwarfs that which occurs in England; the English courts have so far consistently rejected the 'single-publication' rule[154] applied in the United States.[155]

If, by application of these principles, publication within England and Wales is **13.57** enough to establish jurisdiction, a question may still arise of whether the courts of England and Wales are the right forum for the resolution of the dispute. This is particularly likely to be an issue where publication is made by and/or relates to a foreign individual or entity, and/or occurs in several jurisdictions. Such situations call for consideration of a variety of legal rules depending on the location of the different jurisdictions, the scale of the publication in each, the connections between them and the claimant and, in some instances, the legal rules that apply in each.

---

[150] *Duke of Brunswick v Harmer* (1849) 14 QB 185; *Berezovsky v Forbes Inc* [2000] 1 WLR 1004; *Loutchansky v Times Newspapers (Nos 2–5)* [2001] EWCA Civ 1805, [2002] QB 783 and *McLean v David Syme & Co Ltd* (1970) 92 WN (NSW) 611.

[151] *King v Lewis* [2004] EWCA Civ 1329, [2005] EMLR 4 [2]; *Bata v Bata* [1948] WN 366; *Lee v Wilson and Mackinnon* (1934) 51 CLR 276.

[152] *Douglas v Hello Ltd!* [2005] EWCA Civ 595, [2006] QB 125 [100]; *Vidal-Hall v Google Inc* [2014] EWHC 13 (QB), [2014] EMLR 14 [77]. See also *WXY v Gewanter* [2012] EWHC 1601 (QB) [103]–[107], where the Court considered publications of private information within England and Wales to be within its jurisdiction but not publications of the same matter elsewhere.

[153] See 13.47. For privacy cases in which the principles in *Jameel* (n 135) have been considered and applied see *White v Withers LLP* [2009] EWCA Civ 1122, [2010] 1 FLR 859; *Abbey v Gilligan* [2012] EWHC 3217 (QB), [2013] EMLR 12; *Price v Powell* [2012] EWHC 3527 (QB); *Vidal-Hall* (n 152).

[154] 'It is the prevailing American doctrine that the publication of a book, periodical or newspaper containing defamatory matter gives rise to but one cause of action for libel...It is no longer the law that every sale or delivery of a copy of the publication creates a new cause of action': *Ogden v Association of the United States Army* 177 FSupp 498, 502 (1959). The 'single publication rule' introduced by the Defamation Act 2013 (for which see 8.12) does not affect multi-jurisdiction publications but is instead a modification of limitation rules where statements are subsequently re-published.

[155] *Berezovsky* (n 150); *Loutchansky (Nos 2–5)* (n 150). The ECtHR rejected *The Times'* application challenging this aspect of the *Loutchansky* decision: *Times Newspapers Ltd v UK* App nos 3002/03 and 23676/03, [2009] EMLR 13. The 'single-publication' rule is also rejected in Australia: see *Gutnick v Dow Jones & Co Inc* (2002) 77 ALJR 255. The scale of publication elsewhere may be relevant to the exercise of the court's discretion, where this exists: see 13.57.

*(a) European civil jurisdiction*[156]

**13.58**  A person domiciled in England and Wales may be sued in the courts of England and Wales in respect of any civil wrong, regardless of where in the world the wrong was committed.[157] English proceedings may be served on a person domiciled abroad if they make claims in respect of which the court has jurisdiction under the Civil Jurisdiction and Judgments Act[158] or the Judgments Regulation.[159] Privacy claims will fall within this category if the case is in 'delict or quasi-delict' and England and Wales is a jurisdiction in which the harmful event occurred; or an injunction is sought to prevent a wrong there; or if another defendant is domiciled in the jurisdiction.[160]

**13.59**  In defamation, applying English law principles, the 'harmful event' occurs at the place where the offending words are read and the claimant's reputation is thereby harmed. Thus, where publication occurs in several jurisdictions the claimant may, as an alternative to suing in the defendant's domicile, sue in each place of publication.[161] This approach may be applicable to other causes of action that protect privacy, but it could be argued that the location of the harmful event depends on the interest protected. If the essence of the wrong is hurt to feelings it could be said that the harmful event occurs where the claimant is situated. This is the approach adopted in a number of US states.[162]

**13.60**  The effect of deeming the 'harmful event' in publication cases to occur at the place of publication is that an English-based claimant wishing to sue a defendant domiciled abroad in respect of publication in multiple jurisdictions has traditionally only been able to sue for the whole damage suffered in a single action in the courts of the defendant's domicile. In internet cases, however, claimants have another option. The Court of Justice of the European Union has interpreted Article 5(3) of the Judgments Regulation as permitting claimants complaining of infringement of their personality rights by internet publication to sue, in the alternative, in the courts for the place where the claimant's 'centre of interests' is located, in respect of damage sustained there and in other jurisdictions.[163] This would allow the claimant based in England or Wales, complaining of internet publication in multiple

---

[156] Governed by the Civil Jurisdiction and Judgments Act 1982 and the Judgments Regulation (Council Regulation (EC) 1215/2012). The Act of 1982 originally implemented the Brussels Convention 1968 and was amended in 2010 to reflect the Lugano Convention of 30 October 2007.

[157] Art 2 of the Brussels Convention and the Judgments Regulation.

[158] See n 156.

[159] See n 156.

[160] For further detail of the conditions, see *Civil Procedure 2015* (Sweet & Maxwell) paras 6.33.14 and 6.33.18.

[161] *Shevill v Presse Alliance* [1996] AC 959.

[162] *Sack on Defamation* (n 82) para 12:4.13; and see *Bernstein v National Broadcasting Co* 129 F Supp 817 (DDC, 1955); aff'd 232 F 2d 369 (DC Cir, 1955); cert denied 352 US 945 (1956); and *Pegler v Sullivan* 6 Ariz App 338; 432 P 2d 593 (1967).

[163] Case C-509/09 *E-Date Advertising GMBH v X; Martinez v MGN Ltd* [2012] EMLR 12. The place where the claimant's centre of interests is located may be his or her habitual place of residence, or the place where his or her professional activity is carried on.

jurisdictions, to sue in his or her 'home' court, and to serve proceedings in respect of such a claim on the defendant abroad.

Where a claim is to be served abroad pursuant to these provisions the court's per- **13.61** mission is not required, but a notice stating the grounds for so doing must be filed with, and a copy served with, the claim form.[164] In cases under the 1982 Act or Judgments Regulation the court has no power to decline jurisdiction on the grounds that another jurisdiction is more appropriate.[165]

### (b) Permission under Civil Procedure Rule 6.36

Where the claim does not fall within the scope of the 1982 Act or the Regulation **13.62** (generally, when the defendant is domiciled outside Europe) the court's permission to serve proceedings outside the jurisdiction will be required.[166] The provisions of CPR pt 6 most likely to apply to a privacy claim are similar but not identical to those which permit suit against European-domiciled defendants (see 13.58). Permission can be given if an injunction is sought ordering the defendant to do or refrain from an act within the jurisdiction;[167] or where the claim is in tort (such as for misuse of private information[168]), and damage was sustained in the jurisdiction or resulted from an act committed there;[169] or where the defendant is a 'necessary or proper party' to proceedings brought against another person on whom the claim form has been or will be served otherwise than in reliance on CPR 6.36 and PD 6B, para 3.1.[170] Permission may be granted to seek an injunction to restrain a breach of confidence but there may be an anomalous omission with regard to a claim for damages for that equitable wrong.[171]

**Procedure**   The application for permission must set out which ground is relied **13.63** on, state that the claimant believes the claim has a reasonable prospect of success, and give an address for the defendant.[172] In addition, where the defendant is sued on the third of the above-mentioned grounds, the application must state why there is a real issue between the parties which it is reasonable for the court to try.

---

[164] CPR 6.34 and PD 6B para 2.1 (requiring the use of practice form N150).

[165] In other words, the doctrine of *forum non conveniens* is inapplicable. Hence no such argument was available when a publisher domiciled in Belgium was sued by a Saudi bank for publication in England and Wales: see *Al Rahji Banking and Investment Corp v Wall Street Journal Europe SPRL* [2003] EWHC 1358 (QB) [1]–[4]. The position is different where the contest is with another UK jurisdiction: *Cumming v Scottish Daily Record and Sunday Mail Ltd* [1995] EMLR 538.

[166] See CPR 6.36 and, for the grounds on which permission can be granted, PD 6B para 3.1.

[167] CPR 6.36 and PD 6B para 3.1(2).

[168] *Google Inc v Vidal-Hall* [2015] EWCA Civ 311, [2015] 3 WLR 409.

[169] CPR PD 6B para 3.1(9). 'Damage' for this purpose includes distress: *Vidal-Hall* (n 152) [72]–[75] aff'd on different grounds *Google Inc v Vidal-Hall* (n 168).

[170] CPR PD 6B para 3.1(3). So, where D1 is a person unknown present in the UK who threatens to breach C's privacy, and D2 is a foreigner knowing D1's identity, C may be permitted to serve D2 abroad with a claim for *Norwich Pharmacal* relief: *Lockton Companies International v Persons Unknown and Google Inc* [2009] EWHC 3423 (QB).

[171] *Vidal-Hall* (n 152) [71].

[172] CPR 6.37(1).

**13.64** *Forum conveniens* The court will require to be satisfied that England and Wales is the appropriate forum, and may decline jurisdiction if not.[173] The *forum conveniens* principle, that a case should be tried in the forum which in all the circumstances of the case is the most appropriate,[174] might lead to a different outcome from the application of the rules of European civil jurisdiction discussed at 13.58 *et seq.* The principle has been considered in defamation cases falling outside the scope of the European rules and, in particular, cases involving US defendants. Although the starting point is that 'the jurisdiction in which a tort has been committed is *prima facie* the natural forum for the determination of the dispute',[175] this can in principle be displaced by other considerations.

**13.65** **Defamation** Libel and slander claims are now subject to a special statutory regime by which the court has no jurisdiction to hear and determine a defamation action against a person not domiciled in the United Kingdom, another EU Member State, or a Lugano Convention state unless it is satisfied that 'of all the places in which the statement complained of has been published, England and Wales is clearly the most appropriate place in which to bring an action in respect of the statement'.[176]

### (2) Allocation of Jurisdiction within England and Wales

#### (a) High Court or County Court

**13.66** The general rule is that proceedings in which both High Court and County Court have jurisdiction may be commenced in either court. However, claims for money within the County Court's subject-matter jurisdiction may only be issued in the High Court if they have a value of more than £100,000 (or for personal injury claims, £50,000).[177] The financial value of a privacy claim may be low, and the claim within the County Court's jurisdiction. Privacy claims in misuse of private information, data protection, harassment, and trespass may be apt for pursuit in the County Court. However, the County Court's jurisdiction in tort[178] excludes defamation,[179] and breach of confidence claims fall outside the County Court's limited equity jurisdiction,[180] as do most copyright claims.[181] For those cases that

---

[173] CPR 6.37(3). For the principles see *Civil Procedure 2015* (n 160) para 6.37.15.

[174] Applying the principles in *Spiliada Maritime Corp v Cansulex Ltd* [1987] AC 460.

[175] Per Ackner LJ in *Cordoba Shipping Co Ltd v National State Bank (The Albaforth)* [1984] 2 Lloyd's Rep 91, 94 as approved and applied in *Berezovsky* (n 150) 1031.

[176] Defamation Act 2013, s 9, enacted in response to concerns about 'libel tourism'.

[177] Under the High Court and County Court Jurisdiction (Amendment) Order 2014, SI 2014/821. But see n 182 and text thereto.

[178] County Courts Act 1984, s 15.

[179] Defamation claims, whatever their value, are expressly excluded from the tort jurisdiction by the County Courts Act 1984, s 15(2)(c).

[180] County Courts Act 1984, ss 23–4.

[181] The County Court's limited copyright jurisdiction is conferred by Art 2(1)(n) of the High Court and County Courts Jurisdiction Order 1991, SI 1991/724.

do fall within the jurisdiction of the County Court it might still be argued, at least in some instances, that there is sufficient reason[182] for issuing proceedings in the High Court even if there is a choice.

A defendant wishing to assert that High Court proceedings are inappropriate **13.67** may apply for transfer to the County Court.[183] The Northern Ireland Court of Appeal has held that a claim for invasion of privacy rights is one that can suitably be tried in the County Court if the level of damages likely to be awarded falls within the County Court jurisdiction,[184] although in another case it found that in such a developing area of law the complexity of the legal issues justified a High Court trial.[185]

### (b) High Court: Queen's Bench, Chancery, or Family Division

The allocation of media privacy disputes between these three divisions is, for the **13.68** most part, a matter of choice. The rules for distribution of High Court business between the divisions[186] touch only slightly on privacy-related claims. Hence, for example, while claims against the media aimed at protecting the privacy rights of children are often initiated in the Family Division[187] there are instances of such claims being issued and dealt with both in the Chancery[188] and Queen's Bench Divisions.[189] There appears to be no jurisdictional or rule-based reason why this should not be so, given that disputes are to be determined by weighing competing Convention rights rather than by reference to the court's inherent parental jurisdiction.[190]

Cases in which adults assert privacy rights have been brought in all three divisions. **13.69** The Family Division is usually resorted to where the claim is connected with family proceedings. The Chancery Division will be apt if the action involves a copyright claim of significance, copyright claims being assigned to that Division,[191] and Chancery judges having the greatest expertise in such matters. In the Queen's

---

[182] By County Courts Act 1984, s 19, costs are recoverable on the County Court scale only, if an action which could have been brought in the County Court is brought in the High Court, unless the court is satisfied that the defendant objected, or there was reasonable ground for supposing the sum recoverable would exceed that recoverable in the County Court, or that there was 'sufficient reason' to bring the action in the High Court.

[183] Under County Courts Act 1984, s 40 and CPR 30.2. CPR 30.3 sets out the matters to which the court must have regard on any such application. An alternative is to confer jurisdiction by agreement pursuant to County Courts Act 1984, s 18.

[184] *McGaughey v Sunday Newspapers Ltd* [2011] NICA 51. Also *Ames v Spamhaus Project Ltd* [2015] EWHC 127 (QB), [2015] 1 WLR 3409 [100].

[185] *King v Sunday Newspapers Ltd* [2012] NICA 24.

[186] Senior Courts Act 1981, sch 1.

[187] See *eg Re Roddy* (n 30).

[188] See *eg Murray* (n 15).

[189] See *eg T v BBC* (n 25).

[190] *Re S (A Child)* (n 35). Cases relating to the inherent jurisdiction are assigned to the Family Division: Senior Courts Act 1981, sch 1, para 3(b).

[191] Senior Courts Act 1981, sch 1, para 1(i).

Bench Division media privacy claims are generally placed in the Jury List,[192] where cases are heard by judges experienced in media law.

**13.70** Advisers to any party to a privacy claim will wish the case to be dealt with by a judge with experience and knowledge appropriate to the particular legal and factual issues arising. The two sides may have differing views on which division is most appropriate. It is however the claimant who makes the initial choice of venue, when issuing proceedings.

**13.71** **Transfer between divisions** A case may be transferred from one High Court division to another, or into or out of a 'specialist list'.[193] The rules and practice directions give no guidance on the criteria to be applied, and the meaning of 'specialist list' in this context is debatable.[194] There is some guidance in the case law, which indicates that the main criteria when considering an application for such transfer include (a) where and within what areas of judicial expertise the preponderance of the issues lies, and (b) whether transfer would enable the case to be dealt with significantly more quickly and cheaply.[195] It may, however, be difficult to establish that any division offers any clear advantage over another in either respect, so the prospects of persuading a court to exercise this power are likely to be uncertain. Absent some very cogent reasons, the cost risks involved in an application for transfer may be seen as disproportionate to the significance of the issue.

### (3) Proceedings Abroad

**13.72** Much media publication today is international. The fact that national substantive and procedural laws differ quite widely may mean there are juridical and other advantages to be gained by suing in a foreign court. If the person threatening or making a wrongful disclosure is domiciled abroad, the foreign court may be able to grant more effective remedies, regardless of any differences in the applicable laws. While practice and procedure in foreign courts are beyond the scope of this work, there are some points of domestic and European law that are worth noting.

### (a) Enforcement of foreign judgments

**13.73** In general terms, a wide range of foreign judgments may be enforced in this jurisdiction either by virtue of an international treaty or at common law.[196] It is to be noted in particular that, under the Brussels Convention and the Civil Jurisdiction and Judgments Act 1982, a judgment in a civil or commercial matter given in one

---

[192] For historic reasons only, and not because these cases are likely to be tried by jury. See the discussion of mode of trial at 13.183.

[193] CPR 30.5.

[194] *Civil Procedure 2015* (n 160) para 2.3.14.

[195] *National Amusements (UK) Ltd v White City (Shepherds Bush) LLP* [2009] EWHC 2524 (TCC), [2010] 1 WLR 1181.

[196] For detailed consideration of such issues, see A Layton QC and H Mercer (eds), *European Civil Practice* (2nd rev edn, Sweet & Maxwell 2004).

Convention country may, subject to certain formalities, be registered and enforced in another Convention country as if it were a judgment of the court of the registering jurisdiction. The grounds on which registration may be refused are limited. Hence if, say, a German court were at the instance of A, to grant an injunction to restrain publication by B, that judgment could in principle be registered in and enforced by the courts of England and Wales.

By these means, it might seem, a claimant with sufficient grounds to sue in another **13.74** European jurisdiction might be able to take advantage of more favourable substantive or procedural laws in that jurisdiction to obtain relief, enforceable in England and Wales, which might be harder or even impossible to obtain through a domestic action.[197] Indeed, it might appear possible in principle to obtain a foreign injunction effective in England against third parties to the claim.[198] Four important limitations on this prospect should be identified, however:

- First, only a judgment on the merits can be registered and enforced; an interim injunction granted without notice will not qualify.[199]
- Secondly, another European court will only have jurisdiction over a claim against an English-domiciled defendant to the extent that the European civil jurisdiction regime permits. In most cases this is likely to be restricted to jurisdiction over claims for 'harmful events' which occur or are threatened in the foreign jurisdiction, and will not extend to jurisdiction over what is done or threatened in England.[200]
- The third and related point is that all depends on the true scope and effect of the foreign judgment. Whereas there would be no obvious difficulties enforcing a judgment for damages or other financial relief which the foreign court had (under the Brussels Convention or Judgments Regulation) jurisdiction to grant, the situation regarding injunctions is not so straightforward. A foreign injunction, registered in England and Wales, would impact on actions taken in that jurisdiction if its terms prohibited such actions. On its proper interpretation, however, the foreign injunction might well be intended only to restrain conduct within the foreign court's territorial jurisdiction.[201] If so, it

---

[197] This is not just a hypothesis. In 1992, long-lens photographs were taken of intimate contact between the Duchess of York and her financial adviser, at a private holiday villa in France. He sought an injunction in England while both he and the duchess sought relief against *Paris Match* in France, with a view to its registration in England. The French court granted relief but as the English application was refused, and publication went ahead, registration of the French order was not pursued. In 2003 the then German chancellor sought to enforce in England a privacy injunction he had obtained in Germany. See also *Ambrosiadou v Coward* [2010] EWHC 1794 (QB), [2010] 2 FLR 1775 [22], [53]–[55].

[198] See 4.143 for the *Spycatcher* contempt doctrine.

[199] The French injunction mentioned in n 197 could not be registered in England, as it was granted without notice to the respondents. But if a defendant has had time to apply to discharge the position is different. See Layton and Mercer (n 196) paras 26-026–26-031.

[200] For the reasons discussed, in the context of the opposite situation, at 13.56–13.60.

[201] This may be unclear on the face of the foreign order, as was the case with the French injunction mentioned at n 197. If, however, the court's jurisdiction was limited as discussed in the second

must be doubtful at best that performance of the same acts in England would be a contempt of the English court, even if the injunction were registered. Certainly, on the current state of English law it would not be a contempt to make in England a disclosure which a final foreign judgment prohibited in, say, Germany.[202]

- Finally, the incorporation in English law of the Convention via the HRA and subsequent development of English law mean that disparities which previously existed between domestic and foreign privacy laws have greatly diminished.

### (b) Concurrent proceedings abroad

**13.75** English private international law[203] allows a claimant to sue the same defendant both in England and in one or more foreign jurisdictions in respect of the actual or threatened disclosure of the same information.[204] The laws against concurrent claims should be borne in mind, however.[205]

**13.76** **European law** In cases governed by the Brussels and Lugano Conventions and the Judgments Regulation,[206] concurrent pursuit in two jurisdictions of a claim in respect of the same cause of action is prohibited; the court 'first seized' has jurisdiction, and if another court is presented with a claim based on the same cause of action it must decline jurisdiction.[207] From the perspective of English law, which generally treats every individual publication as a separate cause of action,[208] it would seem that this need not present an obstacle to concurrent claims in two or more jurisdictions: so long as the English and foreign actions do not overlap, in the sense that they complain of the self-same publications, it can be said that the claims and causes of action differ.[209] On this analysis the prohibition on dual claims will not be violated by the issue of proceedings in England in respect of publication in England concurrently with the issue in, say, Germany of an action complaining of publication there.

---

bullet point it would be a matter of inference. Media reports suggested that the injunction relied on by Chancellor Schroeder (n 197) was probably confined to Germany.

[202] See 4.146 and 13.138 for the possible inapplicability of the contempt rule when it comes to final orders.

[203] See 13.90.

[204] A course of action followed by the FIA President Max Mosley in respect of disclosures made by the *News of the World* in 2008. He brought proceedings against the publisher in both France and England, as well as proceedings against others in Germany. See also 13.56–13.60.

[205] See further Layton and Mercer (n 196).

[206] See n 156.

[207] Brussels Convention, Art 21; EC Judgments Regulation, Art 27.

[208] See 13.56.

[209] As was the case in Max Mosley's litigation (n 204). The French action complained only of publication within the jurisdiction of the French courts. No objection to concurrent process was raised in the English action, nor did the French court, adjudicating after Eady J had refused an interim injunction ([2008] EWHC 687 (QB)), see this as any objection to its granting an injunction in respect of further publication in France.

These points cannot be said to be clearly established, however. 'Cause of action' in **13.77** this context has an autonomous meaning, not necessarily the same as its meaning as a term of art in English law. It would therefore be prudent for claimants to take steps to ensure that the court 'first seized' is the one that, if pressed, they would consider the better forum. This is not necessarily straightforward.[210] Moreover, many jurisdictions allow actions to be brought for a declaration of non-liability, so a foreign prospective defendant forewarned that he or she may face proceedings in England could seek to anticipate them by issuing proceedings for declaratory relief in his or her 'home' court, then asserting that this is the court 'first seized' of the cause of action.[211]

**Claims against defendants outside Europe**  In cases falling outside the **13.78** scope of the European provisions discussed above, the rules of English law that apply where concurrent actions are brought are those of the common law doctrine of *lis alibi pendens*.[212] This is an aspect of the *forum conveniens* doctrine[213] and, for reasons indicated above,[214] it is suggested that the English court would be unlikely to hold that it bars the pursuit in separate jurisdictions of concurrent but non-overlapping proceedings for invasion of privacy. Nor, it seems, is much weight likely to be placed on claims for negative declarations instituted abroad if the appropriate forum is being decided according to the common law.[215]

*(c) Foreign proceedings only*

Pursuit of a claim exclusively in a foreign court is most likely to be attrac- **13.79** tive where two conditions are satisfied. The first is that the court, by reason of the defendant's domicile[216] or on some other ground of its domestic law, will assume personal jurisdiction over the defendant, and hence jurisdiction to adjudicate upon and grant relief in respect of acts performed or threatened by it both within and outside that court's territorial jurisdiction. In such a case it is possible to envisage the grant of injunctive relief prohibiting that defendant from breaching the claimant's privacy in whatever place that might occur. The

---

[210] Art 30 of the Judgments Regulation (n 156) contains provisions as to when a court is seized of a case, but domestic procedural law can play a part in this. The facts may allow ample room for debate. See *eg Molins plc v GD SpA* [2000] 1 WLR 1741, CA.

[211] The effect of Art 30(1) is that whether a court has been 'seized' is a question of the relevant domestic law as to whether all of the necessary steps to effect service on the defendant have been taken: *SK Slavia Praha-Fotbal AS v Debt Collect London Ltd* [2010] EWCA Civ 1250, [2011] 1 WLR 866.

[212] Meaning 'proceedings pending elsewhere'.

[213] For discussion of the doctrine and its role in determining the convenient forum see Lord Collins of Mapesbury et al (eds), *Dicey, Morris and Collins: The Conflict of Laws* (15th edn, Sweet & Maxwell 2012) paras 12R-001–12-097. For *lis alibi pendens*, see *ibid* paras 12-042–12-046.

[214] See 13.75–13.77.

[215] *Dicey, Morris and Collins* (n 213) para 12-049.

[216] The basic criterion of jurisdiction in civil and commercial matters under the Brussels and Lugano Conventions.

second condition is that any judgment obtained could be enforced in England and Wales[217] or other jurisdictions foreign to the court granting the judgment.

## E.  What? Causes of Action and Applicable Law

### (1)  Causes of Action

**13.80**  Media intrusions into privacy may give rise to more than one concurrent cause of action. Undercover video or audio recording may give rise to trespass claims. Unauthorized access to personal information by these or other means, such as phone hacking, may be actionable as a breach of confidence, misuse of private information,[218] or a breach of statutory duty under the Data Protection Act 1998.[219] Its disclosure may give rise to causes of action in confidence, misuse, data protection, harassment, defamation,[220] or intentional infliction of emotional harm.[221] Where copyright works of the claimant containing private or confidential information are published, there may be copyright infringement claims.[222] The requirements of these various causes of action differ, as do the available defences and the remedies, though there are many overlaps. Analysis of the available causes of action their strengths and weaknesses, advantages and disadvantages, will be necessary.

**13.81**  If the primary remedy to be sought is an injunction then some causes of action have distinct advantages over others, as discussed in Chapter 12.[223] Other factors to be considered in selecting causes of action on which to rely include the following:

- Data protection law is technical and remains unfamiliar to many judges. Claims under this legislation will rarely offer tangible advantages over a claim for breach of confidence or misuse of private information.[224] In 2009 it was said that the paucity of current authority means that applications for summary judgment on such claims are 'for the moment at least, unlikely to find favour'.[225] However, this is a potential avenue in relation to personal data showing up on search engine results following the European Court of Justice's decision in *Google Spain*.[226]

---

[217] See 13.73–13.74.

[218] See *eg Various Claimants v News Group Newspapers Ltd (No 2)* [2013] EWHC 2119 (Ch), [2014] Ch 400; *Gulati v MGN Ltd* [2013] EWHC 3392 (Ch).

[219] As was alleged in *Murray* (n 15). Such conduct could, of course, also give rise to criminal proceedings.

[220] As in *Mosley* (n 14) where the claimant's sadomasochistic activities were alleged to be a 'sick Nazi orgy' in which he acted out the humiliation of Jewish prisoners: see [26]–[31].

[221] *Rhodes v OPO* [2015] UKSC 32, [2015] 2 WLR 1373, though such a case will be rare.

[222] As in *HRH Prince of Wales v Associated Newspapers Ltd* [2006] EWCA Civ 1776, [2008] Ch 57.

[223] See 12.26.

[224] Possibly the reason why no such claim was advanced in *Mosley* (n 14).

[225] *Imerman v Tchenguiz* [2009] EWHC 2024 (QB), [2010] 2 FLR 735 [62]. Also *KJO v XIM* [2011] EWHC 1768 (QB) [51].

[226] *Google Spain* (n 6). See the discussion at 15.16 and 15.91 *et seq.*

- The inclusion of a copyright claim, where available, may offer advantages. Evaluation of whether a publication infringes copyright in a literary work is generally not a complex task and summary judgment is a realistic option.[227] Although the value of copyright in unpublished private and personal works may sometimes be low, this will not always be so. Additional damages are available in cases of flagrant copyright infringements.[228] The inclusion of a copyright claim will affect venue, making the case apt for issue in the Chancery Division.[229]

- A libel claim, if combined with claims in breach of confidence or misuse of private information, may lead to a defence contention that the latter are being advanced to disguise what is in substance a claim to protect reputation, to which different rules and requirements apply.[230] The special rules about mode of trial that previously applied to libel claims are however a thing of the past for most claims.[231]

- Attempts to pursue separate proceedings for different causes of action arising from the same acts or the same series of acts are liable to attract applications alleging abuse of process,[232] whether the actions are concurrent or successive, unless good reason can be shown.

### (2) Applicable Law

Questions of applicable law commonly arise in relation to international publica-  **13.82**
tions. An internet publication accessed in several European territories, for example, may have harmful effects in each territory, in which case there is the potential for conflict-of-law issues.[233] Where legal action is envisaged in England in respect of acts abroad,[234] advisers will need to consider the extent to which foreign law applies or is relevant. The position is complicated by the fact that different rules apply to different causes of action, and remaining uncertainties as to the correct categorization of the causes of action for misuse of private information and breach of confidence.

### (a) Contract

The Rome I Regulation[235] determines the applicable law in respect of any contract  **13.83**
entered into after 17 December 2009. [236] The basic rules, so far as relevant, are as

---

[227] See *HRH Prince of Wales* (n 222).

[228] See 12.105.

[229] See 13.66, 13.69.

[230] See the discussion at 8.50 *et seq* and 12.45.

[231] See 13.183.

[232] Under the principle in *Henderson v Henderson* (1843) 67 ER 313, 3 Hare 100, as to which see *Johnson v Gore-Wood & Co (No 1)* [2002] 2 AC 1.

[233] Again, this huge topic is outside the scope of this work, but reference should be made to *Dicey, Morris and Collins* (n 213) and *Shevill* (n 161).

[234] Generally possible only where the defendant is present or domiciled in England and Wales or is one of several defendants: see 13.58.

[235] Council Regulation (EC) 593/2008 on the law applicable to contractual obligations [2008] OJ L177/6.

[236] The law applicable to earlier contracts is determined by the Contracts (Applicable Law) Act 1990, which gave effect to Convention 80/934/EC on the Law Applicable to Contractual

follows. The signatories to a contract may choose the law applicable to the whole or a part of the contract, and select the court that will have jurisdiction over disputes; and they may agree at any time to change the law applicable to the contract; if the law chosen is that of a country other than that relating most closely to the contract, the provisions of the latter law need to be respected. If the contract relates to one or more Member States, the applicable law chosen, other than that of a Member State, must not contradict the provisions of Community law. If the parties have not made an explicit choice of applicable law, the contract is governed by the law of the country of residence of the principal actor carrying out the contract unless the contract is related more closely to another country than provided by these rules, in which case the law of that country will be applied. The same applies when no applicable law can be determined.

*(b) Non-contractual claims*

**13.84**   **Common law**   At common law conduct in a foreign country is actionable in tort in England and Wales only if it is both tortious according to English law and civilly actionable by the law of the place it occurred (the 'double-actionability rule').[237]

**13.85**   **Statute**   The double-actionability rule was abolished for most torts by the Private International Law (Miscellaneous Provisions) Act 1995[238] which enacts these general rules: 'the applicable law is the law of the country in which the events constituting the tort…in question occur';[239] where elements of the tort take place in different countries the applicable law, so far as relevant, is in personal injury cases 'the law of the country where the individual was when he sustained the injury'[240] and otherwise 'the law of the country in which the most significant element or elements of those events occurred'.[241] The general rules may be displaced if, on a comparison of the factors which connect the case with the country whose law would be applicable under the general rule and those which connect it with another country, it is substantially more appropriate for the applicable law to be that of the other country.[242] The double-actionability rule was however preserved for defamation, a term which for these purposes includes malicious falsehood.[243]

**13.86**   **Equity**   Breach of confidence is not a tort, but an equitable cause of action.[244] In *Douglas v Hello! Ltd* the Court of Appeal found persuasive the reasoning of

---

Obligations and its Protocol and Accession Conventions. For cases falling under the Act of 1990 the general rule is that the parties can choose the applicable law, and absent an explicit choice of law the applicable law is that of the country most closely connected with the contract.

[237]   *Chaplin v Boys* [1971] AC 356.
[238]   Private International Law (Miscellaneous Provisions) Act 1995, s 10.
[239]   s 11(1).
[240]   s 11(2)(a). As noted at 11.228 privacy claims can involve personal injury.
[241]   s 11(2)(c).
[242]   s 12.
[243]   ss 9(3), 10, 13.
[244]   *Kitechnology BV v Unicor GmbH Plastmaschinen* [1995] FSR 765, 778; *Douglas* (n 152) [96]; *Vidal-Hall* (n 152) [52], [71].

*Dicey, Morris and Collins*[245] that a claim for breach of confidence falls to be categorized as restitutionary and therefore subject to the common law rules.[246] However, doubt has been cast on whether this is true as a general proposition,[247] and the view of the editors of *Dicey, Morris and Collins* is now that the 1995 Act will 'probably' apply to an action for breach of confidence 'insofar as it is designed to protect personal privacy'.[248]

**Rome II**    European law on the law applicable to non-contractual obligations in civil and commercial matters was harmonized by the Rome II Regulation.[249] The 1995 Act is disapplied in cases falling within the scope of Rome II.[250] However, among the matters expressly excluded from the scope of the Regulation are 'non-contractual obligations arising out of violations of privacy and rights relating to personality, including defamation'.[251] Matters falling within the scope of the exclusion will remain governed by the 1995 Act or, in the case of libel, slander, and malicious falsehood, the common law double-actionability rule.    **13.87**

**Discussion**    There is much force in the view advanced by *Dicey, Morris and Collins* that an action for breach of confidence which concerns private information and which is 'functionally equivalent to the separate privacy torts recognized in a number of legal systems outside England' is excluded from the scope of Rome II.[252] The reasons for concluding that a claim in misuse of private information falls out of scope are stronger still. The answer would not depend on the domestic characterization of these causes of action as torts or equitable wrongs. It is suggested that harassment and breaches of duty under data protection law will also fall within the scope of the exclusion. Defamation claims by individuals relating to private matters would seem clearly to fall within its scope, although there is room for debate about defamation claims brought in respect of business reputations by individuals, companies, or other business organizations. Accordingly, it is suggested, the law applicable to non-contractual    **13.88**

---

[245]  *Dicey, Morris and Collins* (n 213) para 34-091.

[246]  *Douglas* (n 152) [97]. See also the interim decision *Douglas v Hello! Ltd* [2003] EWCA Civ 139, [2003] EMLR 585 [23]–[26], [41].

[247]  *Ashton Investments Ltd v Rusal* [2006] EWHC 2545 (Comm), [2007] 1 Lloyd's Rep 311 [69]. See also *Vidal-Hall* (n 152) [141].

[248]  *Dicey, Morris and Collins* (n 213) paras 34-035, 34-091–34-092.

[249]  Council Regulation (EC) 864/2007 on the law applicable to non-contractual obligations [2007] OJ L199/40. The Regulation applies to events taking place after 20 August 2007.

[250]  Private International Law (Miscellaneous Provisions) Act 1995, s 15A.

[251]  Regulation (EC) 864/2007 (n 249) Art 1(2)(g). Provision was made (by Art 30(2)) for a study by the Commission into privacy rights across all Member States. The study was completed in February 2009 and proposed a harmonizing directive with a minimal material regulation of the minimum essential aspects (EU Charter and ECHR) and a self-limited rule based on the criteria of the country in which the publisher is established: see *Comparative Study on the Situation in the 27 Member States as regards the law applicable to non-contractual obligations arising out of violations of privacy and rights relating to personality*, February 2009, available at <ec.europa.eu/justice/civil/files/study_privacy_en.pdf>.

[252]  *Dicey, Morris and Collins* (n 213) para 34-092.

claims for infringement of privacy will in the majority of cases be determined by domestic law.[253]

**13.89** If the above suggestions are accepted, it is the 1995 Act[254] which contains the relevant choice of law rules for claims in harassment, data protection, and other causes of action recognized as torts in English law, apart from defamation.[255] The 1995 Act will also determine the choice of law for a claim in misuse of private information, held to be a tort[256] in *Google Inc v Vidal-Hall*.[257]

**13.90** The general rule of the common law in relation to torts involving communication of information is that the tort is complete where the communication is received and understood.[258] Accordingly, it would seem that the law of the place of publication will generally be applicable to claims in tort for wrongful publication to third parties. In defamation it will be one of the applicable laws; in other torts its application will be exclusive. In harassment and some other forms of privacy infringement[259] the most significant 'events constituting the tort' may involve communication to the claimant, rather than to third parties, with the consequence that the applicable law will be that of the place where the claimant is situated at the material time.

**13.91** **The 'presumption' as to foreign law**  Generally, in the absence of satisfactory evidence of foreign law an English court will apply English law; this has been referred to in the past as the presumption that foreign law is the same as English law.[260] However, this 'presumption' is controversial[261] and, and there are many examples of cases where it has been deemed inappropriate to apply it.[262] The Court of Appeal has held the presumption inapplicable to applications for interim injunctions in intellectual property cases,[263] but applied it to an application to enjoin a threatened intentional infliction of emotional harm.[264]

---

[253] Note however that in *OPO v MLA* (n 18) it was common ground that the choice of law applicable to an alleged intentional infliction of emotional harm was to be determined by the application of Rome II: see [95]–[96]. The judgments contain no discussion of the potential applicability of Art 1(2)(g).

[254] Private International Law (Miscellaneous Provisions) Act 1995.

[255] Including malicious falsehood: see (n 243) and text thereto.

[256] In the context of permission to serve outside the jurisdiction under CPR PD 6B para 3.1(9).

[257] n 168, affirming the decision of Tugendhat J in *Vidal-Hall v Google Inc* (n 152).

[258] *Gutnick* (n 155); *Berezovsky* (n 150); *The Albaforth* (n 175); and *King v Lewis* (n 151).

[259] See *eg Vidal-Hall* (n 152) [77].

[260] See *Dicey, Morris and Collins* (n 213) paras 9-025 *et seq.*

[261] As long ago as 1991 the presumption was described as 'quite unrealistic and curiously egocentric in the post-imperial age': Supreme Court Procedure Committee Report on Practice and Procedure in Defamation (July 1991).

[262] See *eg Global Multimedia v ARA Media Services* [2006] EWHC 3612 (Ch); *Tamil Nadu Electricity Board v ST-CMS Electric Co Private Ltd* [2007] EWHC 1713 (Comm); *Belhaj v Straw* [2013] EWHC 2672 (QB) [140].

[263] *Dunhill Ltd v Sunoptic SA* [1979] FSR 337, CA, a passing-off case.

[264] *OPO* (n 18) [108]–[111], which contains a valuable discussion. The decision of the Court of Appeal was reversed by the Supreme Court in *Rhodes* (n 221) but without affecting this point.

The prudent course, where foreign law does or may apply, will be to obtain expert **13.92** advice on that law in order to establish whether, if applied, it would require proof of more or fewer or different facts, or yield a different result from that which English law would produce. If the answers suggest that the foreign law would be more beneficial than English law to the adviser's client, or if an application is contemplated for an injunction to prevent some act abroad,[265] it will be necessary to obtain evidence of the foreign law, which will take the form of a statement from an appropriately qualified legal expert. An alternative, of course, is to proceed separately in the foreign jurisdiction concerned.[266]

## F. How? Conduct of the Action

### (1) Privacy and Open Justice

The conduct of any privacy action will by definition involve some ventilation of **13.93** private matters. Even where the case concerns information which has already received extensive publicity there will usually be good reason not to add to it. The facts disclosed and discussed in pleadings, evidence, and submissions are likely to go beyond what has been published. It is undesirable for the process of bringing a claim to vindicate privacy rights to result in further significant violations of privacy. These obvious points mean that privacy interests are liable to be opposed to the ordinary principles of open justice at every stage of an action. Means are available to mitigate the impact on privacy, but the principle of open justice is fundamental to the dispensation of justice in a modern, democratic society. This will be the court's starting point in considering any application for a derogation from open justice.[267]

The general rule is that all hearings, judgments, and orders will be public.[268] **13.94** Derogations from open justice can only be justified in exceptional circumstances, if and to the extent that they are strictly necessary to secure the proper administration of justice.[269] Cases concerning private or confidential information have long been recognized as one type of case in which such derogations may be necessary,[270] but there is no general exception to open justice merely because privacy or confidentiality are in issue.[271] The burden of establishing that any particular derogation from open justice is justified lies on the person

---

[265] See 13.82 *et seq.*
[266] See 13.72 *et seq.*
[267] *Bank Mellat v Her Majesty's Treasury* [2013] UKSC 38, [2014] AC 700 [2] (Lord Neuberger).
[268] See *eg* Art 6(1) ECHR, CPR 39.2 and *Scott v Scott* [1913] AC 417.
[269] Practice Guidance (n 144) para 9. See further 13.159.
[270] *Scott* (n 268) 437–8, 445, 447, 448 ('secret processes'); *Bank Mellat* (n 267) [2].
[271] Practice Guidance (n 144) para 12.

seeking it, and must be established by clear and cogent evidence.[272] When considering whether to grant a derogation, the court will have regard to the respective convention rights of the parties as well as the general public interest in open justice.[273] The grant of any derogation from open justice is not a question of discretion, but rather a matter of obligation and the court is under a duty either to grant or refuse the derogation sought.[274] A derogation from open justice will not be granted simply because the parties consent: the parties cannot waive the rights of the public.[275]

## (2) Initial Steps

### (a) *Third party access to court file*

**13.95** Ordinarily, statements of case, and judgments and orders made in public, are available for inspection by any non-party[276] as soon as the defendant has filed an acknowledgment of service or defence.[277] Those who report information drawn from documents on the court file may be able to claim immunity from suit.[278] Hence, the inclusion in the claim documents of private information about the claimant or others could lead to its public disclosure with no effective means of redress.

**13.96** Documents other than those mentioned in the previous paragraph may be inspected by a non-party with the court's permission.[279] Where such documents have been referred to in open court, then the court will generally favour disclosure where the applicant can show a legitimate interest in having access to the documents, although it will consider any damage that may be suffered as a result.[280] Where such documents have not been referred to in open court, the court will only permit access if there are strong grounds for thinking that it is necessary in the interests of justice to do so.[281]

---

[272] *Scott* (n 268) 438–9, 463, 477; *Lord Browne of Madingley v Associated Newspapers Ltd* [2007] EWCA Civ 295, [2008] QB 103 [2]–[3]; *JIH v News Group Newspapers Ltd* [2011] EWCA Civ 42, [2011] 1 WLR 1645 [21]; Practice Guidance (n 144) para 13.

[273] Practice Guidance (n 144) para 14.

[274] *AMM v HXW* [2010] EWHC 2457 (QB) [34]; Practice Guidance (n 144) para 11.

[275] *JIH* (n 271) [21(7)].

[276] CPR 5.4C(1).

[277] CPR 5.4C(3). In cases with multiple defendants the documents become open to inspection when each has filed an acknowledgment of service; or when at least one defendant has done so and the court has given permission; or a hearing has been listed; or when judgment has been given: *ibid*.

[278] See 11.64. The point was highlighted in early 2015 by reports of allegations of sexual misbehaviour against HRH Prince Andrew and a leading US lawyer in court papers filed in a Florida case to which neither was a party. The lawyer applied to intervene to strike the allegations from the record: 'US lawyer takes legal action in Prince Andrew sex case', available at <http://www.bbc.co.uk/news/uk-30692699>.

[279] CPR 5.4C(2).

[280] *Chan U Seek v Alvis Vehicles Ltd* [2004] EWHC 3092 (Ch), [2005] 1 WLR 2965 [30]–[44].

[281] *Dian AO v Davis Frankel & Mead* [2004] EWHC 2662 (Comm), [2005] 1 WLR 2951 [56]–[57]; *ABC Ltd v Y* [2010] EWHC 3176 (Ch), [2012] 1 WLR 532 [42]–[43].

### (b) Drafting of the claim documents

It will often be possible to draft the claim form and particulars of claim in a way **13.97** which does not disclose sensitive information. The CPR exclude from automatic public inspection 'any documents filed with or attached to the statement of case, or intended by the party whose statement it is to be served with it'.[282] The use of separate schedules is one way of providing the defendant with sufficient detail without simultaneously making public disclosure of confidential or private information. This will not always be apt, however, and does not cater for what the defendant may do. Failing agreement, in cases where the simple solution is inappropriate, the court may be asked to 'seal the file'.

### (c) 'Sealing the court file'

The court may be asked to make at the outset of proceedings an order colloqui- **13.98** ally known as 'sealing the court file', whereby public access to the statements of case and orders is barred, restricted, or made subject to conditions to protect the claimant's privacy. The court has power to prohibit non-party access to any such document, limit the classes of person who may gain access, allow access only to an edited version, or to make other orders.[283] A party wishing to inspect a document on a 'sealed' court file must apply for permission to do so.[284] It is common for the initial 'sealing' order to make provision for the amount of notice to be given to the claimant if any such application is made.

A party wishing to obtain a sealing order must normally file an application **13.99** notice.[285] Such orders are commonly made on application to a master, without notice to the defendant, at the time proceedings are issued. However, the claimant must put forward evidence and submissions sufficient to justify the order sought, tailored to what is necessary and proportionate in the circumstances.[286] There is a duty of full and frank disclosure on such an application.[287] Blanket orders are 'very rarely necessary' and it may be that no more than the 'sealing' of confidential schedules is warranted.[288] Where a sealing order has been made, a non-party wishing to obtain access to the documents must make an application. The court will only permit access if there are strong grounds for thinking that it is necessary in the interests of justice to do so.[289]

---

[282] CPR 5.4C(1).

[283] CPR 5.4C(4).

[284] CPR 5.4C(6).

[285] CPR 5.4C(5), but see *R (Corner House) v Director of the Serious Fraud Squad Office* [2008] EWHC 246 (Admin) where it was held that, in a judicial review claim, a request could be made, without issue of an application notice, upon filing the claim form or acknowledgement of service.

[286] *G v Wikimedia* (n 142) [17]–[20]. See further the principles set out at 13.94.

[287] See further 13.145.

[288] *Terry* (n 146) [6] and [23]. The application was to seal the entire file, but the court would have ordered the sealing of 'at most a confidential schedule': [147].

[289] *ABC Ltd* (n 281) [42]–[43].

*(d) Anonymizing the proceedings*

**13.100**  This can be appropriate in addition or in the alternative to the methods discussed in the previous two subsections.[290] The general rules are that the claim form and all other statements of case must give the full names of the parties;[291] the claim form must provide an address at which the claimant resides or carries on business, even if the address for service is his solicitor's business address;[292] and where the defendant is an individual the claim form should also include an address at which he resides or carries on business.[293] Any hearing in the case, even if in private,[294] is liable to result in a public judgment that reveals some information about the case which is of a private or confidential nature.[295] A claimant may have good reason not to wish his or her name linked to such information.

**13.101**  **Principles**  When considering an application for an anonymity order, the court will apply the principles applicable to all applications for derogations from open justice. Ultimately the question for the court is whether there is 'sufficient general, public interest in publishing a report of the proceedings which identifies a party and/or the normally reportable details to justify any resulting curtailment of his right and his family's right to respect for their private and family life'. No special treatment will be accorded to public figures or celebrities who are in principle entitled to the same protection as others. [296] The court should be wary of reliance on speculation,[297] but the decision whether to grant anonymity is always fact-sensitive.[298] Ordinarily the public interest in open justice will be better served by anonymizing the parties but otherwise allowing the facts of the case to be reported.[299] However, in certain circumstances it may be appropriate to refuse any anonymity order and name the parties, but ensure that details of the private information are not disclosed.[300]

**13.102**  **Claimants and family members**  The inclusion of the claimant's name or address in the claim form or other documents accessible to the public may on occasion

---

[290] In *G v Wikimedia* (n 142) the claimants were anonymized and a limited 'sealing the file' order was made, to maintain their anonymity: see [13]. Adequate protection of the information may require an injunction which prohibits the publication of information liable to identify the parties, or information about the case beyond what is contained in a public judgment of the court: *DFT v FTD* [2010] EWHC 2335 (QB), [41]; *AMM* (n 274) [7], [40], [41].

[291]  See CPR PD 7 para 4.1(3) and PD 16 para 2.6.

[292]  CPR PD 16 para 2.2.

[293]  CPR PD 16 para 2.3.

[294]  As to which see 13.159.

[295]  For the general rule in favour of public judgments and its limits see 13.188–13.189.

[296]  *JIH* (n 272) [21(5), (6)].

[297]  *Gray v UVW* [2010] EWHC 2387 (QB) [57], [63].

[298]  *XJA v News Group Newspapers Ltd* [2010] EWHC 3174 (QB) [6]–[7].

[299]  *JIH* (n 272) [33], [35].

[300]  As in *Hirschfeld v McGrath* [2011] EWHC 249 (QB) where information that the defendant was intending to publish in a book may have led to the parties being identified and therefore defeated the purpose of any anonymity order.

properly be said to be a disproportionate intrusion into privacy. If so, the claimant can ask for dispensation from these requirements, and invoke the court's power under the CPR to order 'that the identity of a party or witness must not be disclosed', which is available if the court 'considers non-disclosure necessary in order to protect the interests of the party or witness'.[301] As a public authority the court has a duty under the HRA not to act inconsistently with Convention rights, including Article 8.[302] In addition or in the alternative, reliance may be placed on the court's inherent jurisdiction to control its process in such a way as to avoid injustice.[303] In hearings to approve settlements involving children (or other protected parties) under CPR 21.10, an anonymity order prohibiting the publication of the name and address of the protected party and his or her family, and a restriction on access to court documents, will normally be made without the need for a formal application.[304]

**Defendants** 'There are some cases in which anonymity must be given to a **13.103** respondent, because if it is not, then the naming of the respondent may indirectly enable readers to identify the claimant or a third party whose interests require protection (sometimes referred to as jigsaw identification).'[305] Anonymization of the defendant may sometimes be justified in the defendant's own interests and has been granted on the grounds that it would be unjust to identify defendants accused of blackmail or other very serious wrongdoing before they have had an opportunity to state their case to the court.[306] Other possible instances would be where the case concerns a marital dispute, or alleged conduct by or towards a child, or other sensitive private aspects of life which engage the defendant's right to respect for privacy. Anonymity in such cases is authorized by CPR 39.2(4), cited at 13.102, and the power to make such orders is probably best viewed as stemming from the court's duties under the HRA.

---

[301] CPR 39.2(4), discussed at 13.105.

[302] The power, indeed duty, of courts and tribunals to protect anonymity where Art 8 so requires is now clearly established: see *Attorney General's Reference (No 3 of 1999), App by the BBC* [2009] UKHL 34, [2010] 1 AC 145 [53]–[55]; *Re Guardian News & Media Ltd* [2010] UKSC 1, [2010] 2 AC 697; *HM Treasury v Ahmed, App by Guardian News & Media Ltd* [2010] UKSC 1, [2010] 2 AC 697; *A v B* (EAT, 5 March 2010) [12]; *AMM* (n 274). Even before the HRA and CPR the Court of Appeal had held that the court has power to allow a person to sue under an alias where there is good reason: *McNab v Associated Newspapers Ltd* (CA, 17 May 1996) (libel action by pseudonymous author, former member of the SAS).

[303] This power has long been exercised by the criminal courts to protect the identity of blackmail victims, in the interests of convicting blackmailers; similar considerations support anonymity for blackmail victims in civil actions: *AMM* (n 274) [28]–[39].

[304] *JX MX v Dartford & Gravesham NHS Trust* [2015] EWCA Civ 96, [2015] EMLR 14, departing from the court's approach in other contexts, as set out in *JIH* (n 272).

[305] *G v Wikimedia* (n 142) [12]. For an example of pseudonymization of the defendant to protect a third party's privacy interests, see *Mattioli v XY* [2014] EWHC 269 (QB) [3]. See also *Gray* (n 297).

[306] *SKA v CRH* [2012] EWHC 766 (QB) [40]; *Gray* (n 297) [46]–[51].

**13.104** **Non-parties** CPR 39.2(4) empowers the court to anonymize witnesses, but makes no reference to other non-parties. There clearly may, however, be cases in which anonymity for non-parties who are not, or not yet, witnesses is required either to avoid jigsaw identification of a party or witness for whom anonymity is necessary, or to protect the rights or interests of the third party. Such might be the case, for instance, in relation to the spouse or child of an individual suing to protect his or her private and family life from the harm threatened by a disclosure of infidelity.[307] Again, it is now clear that there is power to confer anonymity in such cases, stemming from the court's duties under the HRA.[308]

### Procedure

**13.105** *Parties* These issues should be considered by claimants no later than the stage when proceedings are being drafted and issued. It is likely to be difficult to obtain anonymity later, particularly after a hearing in open court, even if the actual extent of publicity or knowledge about the case is negligible.[309] The claim documents should be drafted so to confer anonymity, or more correctly pseudonymity. Application should then be made for orders under CPR 39.2(4), and for dispensation from the requirements of CPR PD 16, to permit anonymization of the claim. An order may be sought simultaneously for the corresponding anonymization of such further documents in the case as is appropriate. A dispensation from CPR PD 16 is a permissive order rather than an injunction or relief granted 'against' any other party and accordingly there is no obligation on the applicant to give notice to any other party.[310] The practice has grown up of assigning anonymized parties a three-letter designation such as DBM. The true identity and address of any anonymized party will need to be recorded in a document retained on the court file but not open to public inspection. A defendant named or otherwise identified in claim documents who has good grounds for an application to be anonymized in his or her own interests will be well advised to apply promptly.[311]

**13.106** *Non-parties* The observations above about the need to act promptly apply equally to any witness or other non-party who wishes to invoke the court's jurisdiction to grant anonymity. The same would apply where a third person

---

[307] Both the wives involved in *CC v AB* (n 3) were anonymized. Neither was a party or a witness. See also *Mattioli* (n 305).

[308] See cases cited in n 290; *F v G* [2012] ICR 246 (Underhill J) [21].

[309] *Revenue and Customs Commissioners v Banerjee* [2009] EWHC 1229 (Ch), [2009] EMLR 24. As disclosed at [16]–[17], however, there are at least two instances in which post-hearing anonymity has been granted: *W v H* [2008] EWHC 399 (QB), [2009] EMLR 11 and *Wakefield v Ford* [2009] EWHC 122 (QB).

[310] *CVB v MGN Ltd* [2012] EWHC 1148 (QB), [2012] EMLR 29 [49]. Such an order can therefore be made by a Master: *ibid*; *ABC v Lit* [2013] EWHC 3020 (QB) [17].

[311] See n 309 and text thereto.

needs to be anonymized to protect a defendant's anonymity. At present, however, the CPR contain no requirement that any third party whose privacy rights are engaged by proceedings brought by others be given notice in order to consider whether to make such an application, a matter which arguably renders the rules non-compliant with Article 8. The potential drawbacks are discussed at 5.135–5.136.

### (3) Interim Non-disclosure Orders

A claimant forewarned of a threat to publish confidential or private information, or **13.107** of some other breach of privacy, may wish to seek an interim injunction (or 'interim non-disclosure order'[312]). The relevant substantive law, and the pros and cons of different causes of action, are discussed in Chapter 12, and in this chapter above.[313] This section identifies further procedural and practical issues, focusing on applications under the CPR.[314] The procedure is governed by CPR pt 25. Extensive guidance on recommended practice, including a Model Order, was issued by Lord Neuberger MR in 2011.[315]

#### (a) *Timing and documentation*

**Documentation** Ideally, any injunction application will be fully docu- **13.108** mented and served not less than three days before the hearing, in accordance with the primary rules of court.[316] However, time will often be short, with publication imminent, and applications are commonly made outside normal court hours. In such cases the injunction may be sought before proceedings can be issued. The court has power to grant an injunction in such a case but only if '(i) the matter is urgent, or (ii) it is otherwise necessary to do so in the interests of justice'.[317]

The essential document for any injunction application is a draft of the substantive **13.109** order sought.[318] Other documentation which should, if time permits, be prepared and put before the court in at least draft form is: an application notice,[319] a claim

---

[312] This is the term used in the Practice Guidance (n 144) and in many judgments thereafter for an interim injunction restraining publication of information.

[313] See 13.81 (causes of action).

[314] Applicable where (as is usual) the application is made in the Chancery or Queen's Bench Divisions or (less common) the County Court. Practice and procedure in the Family Division is regulated by the Family Procedure Rules.

[315] See n 144.

[316] See 13.135 *et seq*.

[317] CPR 25.2(2)(b). Unless one of these conditions is met the court has no jurisdiction. 'It is not simply a question of discretion': *Martin v Channel Four Television Corp* [2009] EWHC 2788 (QB) [2].

[318] 'Whenever possible a draft of the order sought should be filed with the application notice and a disk containing the draft should also be available to the court': CPR PD 25A para 2.4. The contents of the draft order are considered at 13.120–13.133.

[319] CPR PD 25A para 2.1.

form,[320] evidence by witness statement[321] (or, for a search order, affidavit),[322] a skeleton argument in support of the application, and an explanatory note.[323]

### (b) Undertakings

**13.110**  An applicant will need to be advised of the undertakings that will be required of him or her, and these will need to be incorporated in the draft order placed before the court. It is important that any addition or omission from the undertakings in the Model Order is brought to the court's attention.[324]

**13.111**  **To issue proceedings**   Where the injunction is sought before proceedings have been issued the applicant must undertake to issue and serve a claim form immediately.[325] It is good practice to draft a claim form so this can be issued promptly after the injunction hearing and served with the order.[326]

**To compensate for damage suffered**

**13.112**  *By respondents*   The undertaking of greatest significance is 'to pay any damages which the respondent sustains which the court considers the applicant should pay'.[327] Such an undertaking is required in almost every case where an interim injunction is sought.[328] The claimant is required to satisfy the court that he or she has the means to give effect to that undertaking, if necessary. Although lack of means is not a bar to an injunction in itself, it is 'a factor to be taken into consideration militating against the grant of the injunction sought'.[329] This undertaking could in some cases represent a significant financial exposure. This would be so if, for example, the injunction seeks to stop publication of a newspaper which has already gone to press.[330]

---

[320]  CPR PD 25A para 4.3.

[321]  CPR PD 25A para 3.2(1).

[322]  CPR PD 25A para 3.1.

[323]  Practice Guidance (n 144) paras 17, 33–5. Where an interim non-disclosure order restricts access to documents (seals the file), it must be accompanied by an explanatory note whenever served on a non-party not present at the hearing: [34].

[324]  *ABK v KDT* [2013] EWHC 1192 (QB) [12].

[325]  CPR PD 25A para 4.4(1); alternatively, the court will give directions for the commencement of the claim. See Practice Guidance (n 144) Model Order, sch B, para (3). And see further 13.167 as to the obligation to progress the claim.

[326]  As is required, where possible: CPR PD 25A para 4.4(2).

[327]  One of the undertakings which 'any order for an injunction . . . must contain' unless the court otherwise orders: CPR PD 25A para 5.1(1). The Model Order requires the claimant to undertake to 'comply with any order the Court may make', if it finds that the defendants should be compensated: Practice Guidance (n 144) Model Order, sch B, para (1).

[328]  The two exceptions are: first, the Crown will not be required to give an undertaking when acting to enforce the law: *F Hoffman La Roche and Co A-G v Secretary of State for Trade and Industry* [1975] AC 295; secondly, a legally aided claimant will not be denied an injunction merely because his cross-undertaking is valueless: *Allen v Jambo Holdings Ltd* [1980] 1 WLR 1252, CA.

[329]  *Bunn v BBC* [1998] EMLR 846, 855 (Lightman J).

[330]  As in *Blair v Associated Newspapers Ltd* (QBD, 10 March 2000) where Morland J granted an injunction, to restrain disclosures originating with a member of the Prime Minister's domestic staff, in the early hours of the morning.

Even if a perpetual injunction is refused at trial, the court still has a discretion[331]  **13.113**
whether or not to order an inquiry as to damages. *Universal Thermosensors Ltd v
Hibben* offers a salutary lesson.[332] The claimant established a breach of confidence
and obtained a finding that the defendants had acted dishonestly but, having
obtained an interim injunction in excessively wide terms which caused the col-
lapse of the defendants' business, the claimant had to pay the defendants damages
on its cross-undertaking.

*By those served or notified*  The applicant should identify to the court at the time  **13.114**
of making the application any third parties who have been given notice of the
application,[333] and those upon whom the injunction is intended to be served, as
the court will need to consider s 12(2) HRA in respect of each of them.[334] The
applicant will ordinarily be required to undertake to compensate *them* for any
damage they sustain which the court considers the applicant should pay.[335] This
undertaking also could be of considerable financial significance, especially where
the aim and potential effect of the injunction sought is to bind a number of media
organizations.

**To keep third parties informed of progress**  The applicant is required, and  **13.115**
should undertake, to inform the court on the return date of the identities of
any third parties served with or notified of the order, and thereafter to inform
those third parties of the progress of the action, at least in so far as it affects them.
This would include notification of any application that may affect the status of
the order. [336]

**To verify factual assertions relied on**  The normal rule is that an applicant  **13.116**
must place evidence before the court,[337] but where urgency justifies it the court
may act on the basis of a draft statement, other written materials not verified on
oath or by a statement of truth, or information provided orally by counsel. In
any such case the applicant will be expected to undertake to make, or procure
the making of, a witness statement or statements verifying what the court was
told.[338] If there are statements but not from the claimant or a non-party whose
rights are relied on the court may require undertakings that such statements
be made.[339]

---

[331] See *Cheltenham and Gloucester Building Society v Ricketts* [1993] 1 WLR 1545, 1551 (Neill LJ).
[332] [1992] 1 WLR 840.
[333] Practice Guidance (n 144) Model Order, sch C.
[334] Practice Guidance (n 144) para 20 and Model Order, sch D. And see further 13.136.
[335] The court 'should' consider, when it makes an order for an injunction, whether to require
undertakings to compensate anyone other than the respondent who may suffer loss: CPR PD 25A
para 5.1A. Such an undertaking is included in the Model Order: Practice Guidance (n 144) Model
Order, sch B, para (2).
[336] Practice Guidance (n 144) para 38 and Model Order, sch B, para (5).
[337] See 13.143–13.146.
[338] Practice Guidance (n 144) Model Order, sch B, para (3).
[339] *Terry* (n 146).

**To serve the application documents and order**

**13.117**  *On respondents*  In the rare case where a privacy injunction is made without notice to a respondent,[340] the applicant will ordinarily be required to undertake 'to serve on the respondent the application notice, evidence in support and any order made as soon as practicable' after the hearing.[341] This will include any evidence prepared pursuant to an undertaking given to, or order made by, the court at the hearing.[342] Also, 'where possible the claim form should be served with the order for the injunction'.[343] Where a 'John Doe' order is sought the court may require an undertaking to use reasonable endeavours to serve or notify the respondents.[344]

**13.118**  *On those served or notified*  Non-parties whom the applicant intends to serve with or notify of the order once obtained may well have a right to prior notice of the application.[345] Even where that is not so, such non-parties normally have a right to be supplied after the event with the materials relied on. Where an order 'will affect a person other than the applicant or respondent who... did not attend the hearing... and... is served with the order'[346] the applicant must comply promptly with any request by such a person for 'a copy of any materials read by the judge'[347] unless the court orders otherwise. In order to provide effective protection for private information, however, the material shall be supplied in return for an irrevocable undertaking to the court that the material and the information contained in it will only be used for the proceedings.[348] Third parties should be provided with an explanatory note to enable them to consider whether to give the undertaking.[349]

**13.119**  **To provide full notes of the hearing**  Where the application is made without any notice to a party or person on whom it is intended to serve any order obtained (as is only rarely justified[350]), or (as is common) urgently and on no, or short notice to any such person, who may be absent, then an undertaking should normally be given 'to provide full notes of the hearing with all expedition to any party that

---

[340]  For the requirement of notice and the limited exceptions see 13.135–13.139.
[341]  CPR PD 25A para 5.1(2).
[342]  See 13.116.
[343]  CPR PD 25A para 4.4(2).
[344]  *X & Y v Persons Unknown* (n 146) [79]; Practice Guidance (n 144) notes to para 5.
[345]  See the discussion at 13.140–13.142.
[346]  CPR PD 25A para 9.1.
[347]  CPR PD 25A para 9.2(1): 'including material prepared after the hearing at the direction of the judge or in compliance with the order'. It may be hard to persuade the court to 'order otherwise': see *Terry* (n 146) [16(5)], [19]–[20].
[348]  Practice Guidance (n 144) paras 24–8. A standard form of wording is set out in the notes to cl 13 of the Model Order. Such express provision is a legitimate protection for Art 8 rights: *TUV v Persons Unknown* [2010] EWHC 853 (QB), [2010] EMLR 19 [9]–[16] (Eady J). See also *Terry* (n 146) [16(5)] and [116]–[117].
[349]  Practice Guidance (n 144) para 24.
[350]  See 13.135–13.139.

would be affected by the relief sought'.[351] The undertaking may be limited to providing such a note on request where a person notified of the application indicates no opposition to the order.[352]

### (c) Form of order

A Model Order, including a penal notice, justification of lack of notice, anonymity, **13.120**
access to documents, service of the claim form on unknown defendants, reporting restrictions, the position of third parties, and other relevant provisions, along with explanatory notes, is appended to the Practice Guidance.[353] Any additions or omissions from this form of order should be brought to the court's attention.[354]

**Orders for hearing in private,[355] anonymity,[356] or sealing the file[357]** Where a hear- **13.121**
ing in private is sought the substantive order should be set out in the body of the draft order.[358] This paragraph should incorporate a statement of the grounds on which the order is made, whether by reference to the grounds given in CPR 39.2(3) or otherwise. Similar considerations apply to any orders for anonymity or 'sealing the court file'.[359]

### Main restraining order

*Precision* 'Any order for an injunction must set out clearly what the respondent **13.122**
must or must not do.'[360] This is of particular importance where an injunction affects the exercise of a Convention right, such as freedom of expression. 'An injunction to restrain the publication of confidential information must be specific as to the information which is said to be confidential.'[361] If the order is too broad, or too vague, the injunction may be refused on that ground.[362]

*Public domain proviso* Where the injunction restrains the disclosure of informa- **13.123**
tion consideration will need to be given to the inclusion of a proviso permitting the disclosure of information in the public domain. The court usually requires such a proviso.[363] It will usually be directed both to matters already in the public domain

---

[351] *Civil Procedure 2015* (n 160) para 25.3.10; *G v Wikimedia* (n 142) [28]–[31]. By CPR PD 25A para 9.2(2) such a note must be provided on request to third parties served or notified unless the court orders otherwise. The court will be reluctant so to order: see *Terry* (n 146) [16(5)], [19]–[20] and [116]–[117].

[352] *G v Wikimedia* (n 142) [32]. The right to have such a note supplied which is provided for by CPR PD 25A para 9.2(2) is confined to those persons served with the order who request such a note.

[353] See n 144.

[354] *ABK* (n 324) [12].

[355] For the justifications for this, see 13.159.

[356] See 13.100–13.106.

[357] See 13.98–13.99.

[358] As in the Model Order, cl 14.

[359] See the Model Order, cll 3 and 4 respectively.

[360] CPR PD 25A para 5.3, reflecting long-established common law principles.

[361] *Doncaster Metropolitan Borough Council v BBC* [2010] EWHC 53 (QB) [25].

[362] See *eg A v B, C, and D* [2005] EWHC 1651 (QB), [2005] EMLR 851 [11], [24], and [34]–[36]; *Caterpillar Logistics Services (UK) Ltd v Huesca de Crean* [2011] EWHC 3154 (QB) [87] aff'd [2012] EWCA Civ 156, [2012] 3 All ER 129 [68].

[363] Practice Guidance (n 144) Model Order, cl 15. See *X & Y* (n 146) [62]; *Doncaster* (n 361) [36].

at the time of the order and those which may later come into the public domain, other than as a result of breaches of the injunction.[364]

**13.124** *Return date* An order for an injunction 'in the presence of all parties to be bound by it' or 'at a hearing of which they have had notice' may 'state that it is effective until trial or further order'.[365] But these conditions are rarely met in respect of the initial injunction in a privacy matter. 'Any order for an injunction made without notice to any other party must unless the court otherwise orders contain a return date for a further hearing at which the other party can be present.'[366] The practice of seeking orders until trial or further order at a without-notice hearing has been deprecated.[367] A return date is particularly important where an order contains derogations from open justice, as it is the means by which the court ensures that those derogations are in place for no longer than strictly necessary.[368] Departure from this practice will need to be justified.[369] The court may refuse to make an order that does not provide adequate directions for progress of the action, even if agreed by the parties.[370]

**13.125** An injunction until trial may be justified if, for example, the application is 'without notice on notice'[371] or if it appears that there is unlikely to be a dispute as to the sensitive private nature of the information, publication of which is to be restrained. In such cases '[i]ncluding a return date has the disadvantage of putting the applicants to the cost of attending before the court a second time'.[372] But the general principle remains that whenever an application is made without notice or, which is similar, on short notice, any departure from standard practice must be drawn to the court's attention, explained, and justified.[373]

**13.126** **'Super-injunctions'** This is the name commonly given to an order restraining disclosure of the claimant's identity and the fact the claim has been brought. The circumstances in which such an order may be justified are considered in Chapter 12.[374]

**13.127** **Restraint on reporting of hearing** The disclosure of information about a hearing in private is only a contempt of court if made in breach of an express prohibition.[375]

---

[364] Practice Guidance (n 144) Model Order, cl 15. See *X & Y* (n 146) [62]–[67]. For further discussion of public domain provisos to injunctions see 12.78.

[365] CPR PD 25A para 5.2.

[366] CPR PD 25A para 5.1(3). The word 'must' was emphasized by the Court of Appeal in *Thane Investments Ltd v Tomlinson* [2003] EWCA Civ 1272 [21].

[367] *G v Wikimedia* (n 142) [26].

[368] Practice Guidance (n 144) para 40.

[369] Practice Guidance (n 144) para 25.

[370] *AVB v TDD* [2013] EWHC 1705 (QB) [6]–[8].

[371] That is where, although the notice required by the CPR has not been given, the respondent has in fact been notified and given the opportunity to be present, and does not appear or oppose the order: *AVB* (n 370) [27].

[372] *AVB* (n 370) [25].

[373] *Memory Corp v Sidhu (No 2)* [2000] 1 WLR 1443, CA, 1459–60.

[374] See 12.41–12.43. For the form of order, see Practice Guidance (n 144) Model Order, cl 7.

[375] *AF Noonan (Architectural Practice) Ltd v Bournemouth & Boscombe Athletic Community Football Club Ltd* [2007] EWCA Civ 848, [2007] 1 WLR 2614.

Often, the principal injunction sought will have that effect but not always, and if that injunction is refused there may nevertheless be other private information deployed at the hearing which deserves specific protection. The clause of the Model Order stating that the hearing will be in private therefore goes on 'and there shall be no reporting of the same'.[376]

### Ancillary orders

*Non-use of hearing papers*   An order prohibiting the use or disclosure of informa- **13.128** tion contained in the application documents may be appropriate. The principal injunction sought, or a reporting restriction, may cover much of this, but an applicant often has to reveal more private information than the defendant already has. It may be prudent to seek a privacy injunction in respect of the claimant's own evidence and submissions, even if the hearing is in private.[377]

*Disclosure*   A claimant may in some cases be well-advised to seek a disclosure **13.129** order.[378] In particular, where there is reason to believe that the information at issue has been provided by the defendant to one or more third parties the claimant will wish to discover where the information has gone and who is in possession of it, so that steps can be taken to prevent disclosure by them.[379] If such a disclosure order is apt, a 'super-injunction' to prevent tipping-off may deserve consideration.[380]

In considering whether to seek any, and if so what, disclosure order the claim- **13.130** ant's advisers in a media case will need to bear in mind the privilege of publishers in respect of sources; an order requiring immediate disclosure of such sources would need to be shown to be necessary in the interests of justice in order to override the privilege.[381] An alternative might be an order requiring the defendant to notify the order to third parties it knows to be in possession of the information in question, and to verify that it has done so, although the requirements for the grant of an interim mandatory injunction are exacting. It would seem hard to justify the grant of either of these kinds of order on an application made without notice.

*Preservation, delivery-up, and search orders*   An order for the preservation of docu- **13.131** ments or other items likely to be required as evidence may be justified if there is credible evidence suggesting that the defendant would otherwise take steps to cover his or her tracks by destroying or otherwise disposing of such evidential materials. An interim delivery-up order might, in a strong case, be warranted.[382]

---

[376] Practice Guidance (n 144) Model Order, cl 14.
[377] Practice Guidance (n 144) Model Order, cll 10–12. The CPR restrictions on collateral use of disclosure and witness statements are not likely to suffice, and see 13.100.
[378] Practice Guidance (n 144) Model Order, cll 8 and 9.
[379] See *eg WXY* (n 152) [103]–[107].
[380] See 12.42.
[381] Contempt of Court Act 1981, s 10.
[382] See *eg N v Ryan* [2013] EWHC 637 (QB), although the basis is not evident from the judgment.

It would normally have to be shown, however, that in the absence of such an order there was good reason to fear that the defendant would misuse the document or other item of which delivery up is sought, to the significant prejudice of the claimant. Appropriate provision would also need to be made for the clear identification of all items delivered up and the supply to or retention by the defendant or his or her legal representatives of copies of any such items, in order that the litigation can be fairly and efficiently conducted thereafter.

**13.132** In an extreme case a search order might be appropriate, but such orders are rare in privacy cases involving the media. Certainly, where the respondent is a substantial media organization it is unlikely that a claimant will be able to assemble evidence to show that it is likely to destroy evidence, sufficient to justify either delivery up or a search order. Search orders should follow the standard form in CPR PD 25A, unless departure is justified. Where an order, other than a search order, is made 'for delivery up or preservation of evidence or property where it is likely that such an order will be executed at the premises of the respondent or third party... the court shall'—and, it is submitted, the applicant should—'consider whether to include in the order for the benefit or protection of the parties similar provisions to' those specified in PD 25A in relation to injunctions and search orders.[383]

**13.133** **Penal notice**   The order should have a prominent penal notice, warning of the consequences of disobedience, and to use the prescribed form of words for this. Otherwise, the prospects for enforcement by motion for contempt will be prejudiced.[384]

*(d)  Notice of application*

**13.134** **To the court**   For non-urgent applications, notice will be given by the issue of the claim form and application notice, and the filing of these documents, together with the draft order and evidence in support. Where the application is urgent or made without notice 'the application notice, evidence in support and a draft order... should be filed with the court two hours before the hearing wherever possible'.[385] If no application notice has been issued by the time of the hearing the draft order should be produced then, and the application notice and evidence 'should be filed on the same or next working day as ordered by the court'.[386] If the hearing takes place by telephone[387] 'it is likely that the judge will require a draft order to be faxed to him'.[388] It may be possible to place other documents, such as

---

[383] CPR PD 25A paras 8.1 and 8.2.
[384] CPR 81.9 makes service of an order with a penal notice 'prominently displayed' a precondition to enforcement, although a breach may be overlooked if it does not affect the justice of the case: *Shadrokh-Cigari v Shadrokh-Cigari* [2010] EWCA Civ 21, [2010] 1 WLR 1311 [16].
[385] CPR PD 25A para 4.3(1).
[386] CPR PD 25A para 4.3(2).
[387] For telephone hearings see 13.160.
[388] CPR PD 25A para 4.5(3). Or email, if the judge so directs.

the application notice, evidence, and skeleton argument, before the court by the same means. In any event the application notice and evidence will need to be filed on the day of the application or next working day.[389]

**To defendants/respondents**

*The Civil Procedure Rules*  Any application to the court must normally be **13.135** made on notice to the respondent.[390] The general rule is that three clear days must elapse between service of the application notice and evidence and the hearing.[391] Time can be abridged. However, '[a]s a matter of principle no order should be made in civil or family proceedings without notice to the other side unless there is very good reason for departing from the general rule that notice should be given. Needless to say, the more intrusive the order the stronger must be the reasons for the departure.'[392] CPR pt 23 identifies circumstances in which an application may be made without notice.[393] These include 'exceptional urgency'[394] and 'where the overriding objective is best furthered by doing so',[395] but as a rule without notice applications should only be granted in very limited circumstances where to give notice would enable the defendant to take steps to defeat the purpose of the injunction, or where there was some exceptional urgency, which meant literally there was no time to give notice.[396]

*The Human Rights Act 1998*  An application for an order restraining publication **13.136** or any other form of expression falling within Article 10 is subject to s 12(2) HRA which prohibits the court from granting an injunction affecting freedom of expression where the 'person against whom the application is made is neither present nor represented', unless the court is satisfied that the applicant has 'taken all practicable steps to notify' the respondent of the application, or that 'there are compelling reasons why the respondent should not be notified'.[397]

*In practice*  In a privacy case, urgency, however exceptional, is highly unlikely of **13.137** itself to be a 'compelling reason' for not giving some notice. 'Examples which may amount to compelling reasons, depending on the facts of the case, are: that there is a real prospect that were a respondent or non-party to be notified they would

---

[389] CPR PD 25A para 4.5(4).

[390] CPR 23.4.

[391] CPR 23.7(1) and PD 23A para 4.1. The purpose of the three days' notice is to allow the respondents adequate time to consider the applicant's case on both factual and legal issues: *CEF Holdings v Mundey* [2012] EWHC 1524 (QB), [2012] FSR 35.

[392] *Moat Housing Group-South Ltd v Harris* [2005] EWCA Civ 287, [2006] QB 606 [63] (without notice orders restraining antisocial behaviour by tenant and ousting her from her home). See also [71]–[72] (emphasizing that the provision of notice is an 'elementary principle' of justice and departure from it warranted in 'exceptional circumstances' only).

[393] CPR 23.4(2) and PD 23A para 3.

[394] CPR PD 23A para 3(1).

[395] CPR PD 23A para 3(2).

[396] *CEF Holdings* (n 391) [255(a)]; *National Commercial Bank Jamaica Ltd v Olint Corp Ltd* [2009] UKPC 16, [2009] 1 WLR 1405.

[397] There must also be clear and cogent evidence: Practice Guidance (n 144) para 21.

take steps to defeat the order's purpose,[398] for instance, where there is convincing evidence that the respondent is seeking to blackmail the applicant.[399, 400] The court should be told of the absence of notice and the reason for it, and will need to be satisfied that the reason is a good one.[401]

**13.138** Where a respondent, or non-party, is a media organization it will be very rare that there will be compelling reasons why advance notification is not possible on grounds of urgency or secrecy. Only in truly exceptional circumstances will failure to give a media organization advance notice be justifiable on the ground that it would defeat the purpose of an interim non-disclosure order. Different considerations may arise where a respondent or non-party is an internet-based organization or individual, or where there are allegations of blackmail.[402]

**13.139** If the court is satisfied that the reasons given meet the standard set by s 12(2) HRA, it may further conclude that the 'overriding objective is best furthered' by dealing with the application without notice.[403] Otherwise the court must require the applicant to have given some notice to the respondent, even if it be short notice due to the urgency of the relief sought.[404] The court has repeatedly deplored the number of applications made without notice with no proper justification.[405]

**13.140** **To non-parties affected** Often, especially where the application is made against persons unknown, or *contra mundum*, the real targets of a privacy injunction are the media, the intention being to serve the injunction on them and thus bind them under the *Spycatcher* principle.[406] There are other situations in which media may have an interest in an application made against another. The defendant may be abroad, or otherwise not easily able, or not inclined, to attend to resist the application. The threat to publish in England may arise from the defendant having passed the private or confidential information to a foreign publisher. The object of the application may be to prevent the English media from recycling here information which is already or about to be published elsewhere. In such cases, the media have an obvious interest in being given advance

---

[398] *RST v UVW* [2010] EMLR 355 [7], [13].

[399] *ASG v GSA* [2009] EWCA Civ 1579 [3]; *DFT v FTD* (n 289) [7].

[400] Practice Guidance (n 144) para 21.

[401] *JIH* (n 272) [21(10)].

[402] Practice Guidance (n 144) para 22.

[403] See 13.136.

[404] This is the consequence of the bar on the grant of relief without notice in s 12(2) HRA. The CPR provide that 'except…where secrecy is essential, the applicant should take steps to notify the respondent informally of the application': PD 25A para 4.3(3). These points were re-emphasized in *Doncaster* (n 361) [31] where Tugendhat J held there was no good reason for failure to give notice, nor was the application 'so urgent that it could not have been dealt with in court the next day'.

[405] See eg *ND v KP* [2011] EWHC 457 (Fam); *O'Farrell v O'Farrell* [2012] EWHC 123 (QB) [66]; *Bristol City Council v News Group Newspapers Ltd* [2012] EWHC 3748 (Fam).

[406] That anyone knowing of an interim non-disclosure order who defeats its purpose is in contempt of court: *Attorney General v Newspaper Publishing plc* [1988] Ch 333, CA. See 4.146–4.147.

notice of the application so that a representative can, if desired, attend the hearing and argue against the grant of the injunction, or make representations on its wording.

Section 12(2) HRA identifies those to whom notice should be given as 'the person against whom the application for relief is made', which is not apt to include such non-parties. However, it is clear that their rights are potentially at issue. The authorities prior to the Practice Guidance of 2011 indicated that advance notice should be given to any non-party on whom the claimant intends to serve the order, unless: (1) the claimant has no reason to believe that the non-party has or may have an existing specific interest in the outcome of the application; (2) the claimant is unable to notify the non-party, having taken all practicable steps to do so; or (3) there are compelling reasons why the non-party should not be notified; or (4) giving notice to all who are to be served would in all the circumstances impose a disproportionate burden on the claimant.[407] This practice was said by Eady J in extrajudicial remarks to be 'working pretty well'.[408] **13.141**

The Practice Guidance states however that: **13.142**

> HRA s 12(2) applies in respect of both (a) respondents to the proceedings and (b) any non-parties who are to be served with or otherwise notified of the order, because they have an existing interest in the information which is to be protected by an injunction: *X and Y v Persons Unknown*.[409] Both respondents and any non-parties to be served with the order are therefore entitled to advance notice of the application hearing and should be served with a copy of the Application Notice and any supporting documentation before that hearing.[410]

### (e) Evidence

**Claimants**
*Evidence in support of the relief sought* 'An application for an interim remedy must be supported by evidence, unless the court orders otherwise.'[411] The evidence may be set out in a witness statement, or in a statement of case or application notice, provided these are verified by a statement of truth.[412] The evidence must 'set out the facts on which the applicant relies for the claim being made against the respondent'.[413] It is essential that this includes evidence of a sufficient threat to do the wrong which it is sought to restrain; absent such evidence the injunction will be **13.143**

---

[407] See *X and Y* (n 146) [11]–[12], [17]; *WER v REW* [2009] EWHC 1029 (QB), [2009] EMLR 17 [18]; *Terry* (n 146) [114], [118]–[119]; *TUV* (n 348) [24]–[26]. The cases are discussed in the second edition of this book at 14.115–14.122.

[408] Address to the Intellectual Property Lawyers' Association, 18 February 2009.

[409] *X and Y* (n 146) [10]–[12].

[410] Practice Guidance (n 144) para 19.

[411] CPR 25.3(2).

[412] CPR PD 25A para 3.2. Freezing and search orders require evidence by affidavit: CPR PD 25A para 3.1.

[413] CPR PD 25A para 3.3.

refused.[414] A bland statement that the defendant might do something if warned is unlikely to satisfy this requirement without some particulars in support.[415] Evidence should come from the claimant personally; if the applicant cannot make a statement for reasons of urgency then he or she should do so on the return date, or explain why he or she cannot.[416] If the applicant intends to rely on the rights of others he or she should consider what evidence from or about those others should be adduced.[417]

**13.144** *Evidence on procedural matters* The evidence must also explain why no notice or short notice was given if that is so.[418] The evidence should also set out the justification for any derogations from open justice, such as anonymity or sealing the court file. [419] The court has warned that in the preparation of injunction applications 'it is not uncommon for the legal representatives of claimants to focus their attention largely on the substantive application, and to omit to give the same degree of attention to subsidiary orders, including those providing for a derogation from the principle of open justice'.[420]

**13.145** *Full and frank disclosure* The CPR provide that on any interim injunction application, on notice or not, the applicant's evidence 'must set out … all material facts of which the court should be made aware'.[421] 'Every witness statement made in support of an application for an injunction made without any or any proper notice should contain a statement setting out the duty to give full and frank disclosure … and then indicating how that duty\ has been complied with.'[422]

**13.146** *Alternatives to formal evidence* Where the application is made urgently, either without notice, or on short notice, there may not be time to prepare formal evidence. The court may be asked to, and may agree to, act on the basis of less formal documentation or an oral account of the facts,[423] subject to an undertaking to file a witness statement as soon as practicable.[424]

**13.147** **Defendants/respondents** A media defendant or respondent is entitled to withhold the detail of any intended publication[425] and this is often done, making the claimant's task of establishing a threat to infringe rights that much harder. Evidence in opposition to an injunction application is likely to focus on what is in the public domain or proof of a public interest in disclosure, or of overriding rights. The court has however warned of 'a natural tendency on the part of

---

[414] See *eg Doncaster* (n 361) [26] and [39]. Mere suspicion is not enough: *Caterpillar Logistics* (n 362) [67]; *CEF Holdings* (n 391) [255(c)] and the discussion at 12.27–12.28.
[415] *CEF Holdings* (n 391) [255(b)].
[416] *Terry* (n 146) [36].
[417] See 13.148–13.151.
[418] CPR PD 25A para 3.4.
[419] Practice Guidance (n 144) [13].
[420] *G v Wikimedia* (n 142) [19]. Also *Terry* (n 146) [25]–[26].
[421] CPR PD 25A para 3.3.
[422] *CEF Holdings* (n 391) [255(d)].
[423] In other words, it may 'order otherwise', within CPR 25.3(2).
[424] See 13.116.
[425] *Re Roddy* (n 30) [88]; *BKM Ltd v BBC* [2009] EWHC 3151 (Ch) [29].

newspaper lawyers to dredge up' the contents of an electronic search in order to persuade the court that the claimant has 'become public property', and of the need for close scrutiny of each private revelation and how it came about.[426]

### Third parties

*The court's approach*   The English court's approach has been that, because the   **13.148**
HRA requires it not to act inconsistently with Convention rights, it is bound to take into account the Convention rights of third parties, even if not before the court.[427] As a result the court's decision may often depend heavily upon the rights and interests of persons not parties to the action before the court. The rights of others may in some cases be very important, even decisive.[428] Third party rights are very likely, therefore, to be invoked by the parties.

It may however be difficult for the court to make a reliable assessment of the wishes   **13.149**
and interests of a third party who is not present or represented, and does not give evidence,[429] and there is a risk that the court may be misled about such impacts by evidence and argument advanced by parties who are straining to bolster a claim for relief, or to resist it.[430] A procedural development that it is submitted would be appropriate would be to impose a duty on a party who intends to invoke a third person's rights in support of arguments for or against the grant of relief to give that third person formal notice of that intention, and to serve him or her with copies of relevant evidence and argument to be put before the court.

*Practical issues for claimants*   Where third persons' rights coincide with or tend   **13.150**
to support those of a claimant the options include encouraging the others to join as claimants, or to bring parallel proceedings, or to be heard by the court in some other capacity. Alternatively, a party may seek to bolster its case by merely adducing evidence from,[431] or about[432] the third persons, without joinder of or appearance from them. There may be justifications for third persons not being joined or giving evidence. They may be staff of a corporate claimant,[433] or persons for whom it has a responsibility,[434] so numerous that it is impracticable for them all to be joined.[435] Or there may be a reluctance to draw them too far into the proceedings, perhaps for reasons of personal sensitivity.[436] If a third person whose rights are relied on does not

---

[426]  *X and Y* (n 146) [46].

[427]  See *eg A v B plc* [2002] EWCA Civ 337, [2003] QB 195 [11(xi)] and [43(iii)]; *CC v AB* (n 3) [43]; *K v News Group* (n 46) [14].

[428]  See *eg K v News Group* (n 46) [14]–[22].

[429]  *Terry* (n 146) [66]–[67].

[430]  See cases cited at n 437.

[431]  As in *Ambrosiadou v Coward* [2011] EWCA Civ 409, [2011] EMLR 21 where a child's evidence was clearly highly important: see [41].

[432]  As in *Terry* (n 146).

[433]  See *eg Imutran v Uncaged Campaigns Ltd* [2001] 2 All ER 385.

[434]  See *eg Green Corns* (n 98) [31]; *BKM* (n 425) [7], [12]–[13].

[435]  For discussion of the difficulties with representative actions, see 13.44, 13.49.

[436]  As in *CC v AB* (n 3) where the impact of publication on the claimant's relatives was relied on, but they were not made parties.

become a party or give evidence this will need to be justified or explained, and the claimant may have to undertake to provide a statement after the hearing. Absent a cogent explanation of why the non-party is not speaking for him or herself the court may decline to place weight on the alleged rights.[437] The same must be true of third persons whose rights are relied on by defendants, and claimants will be alive to this, and mindful also that the right to tell one's story is not absolute, but qualified by the need to respect the privacy rights of those whom that story involves.[438]

**13.151** *Practical issues for defendants*  Defendants will wish to rely on the principle that claims to interfere with freedom of expression must be established convincingly by evidence.[439] They will urge a sceptical approach to reliance by a claimant on the rights of a third person who has not joined in the action or provided direct evidence.[440] They will want to ensure the court is alive to the risk that evidence adduced by a claimant about, rather than from, the third party is self-serving, or apt to conceal weaknesses in the claimant's own position.[441] The same may apply even where the claimant does adduce evidence from the third party, if it is someone, such as an employee, child or other relative, over whom there is reason to believe the claimant may be able to exert control or influence. Defendants will also want to be bear in mind the possibility of an approach to the third party by the defence. The court is likely to adopt a similar approach to reliance by defendants on the rights of third persons.

### (f) Submissions

**13.152** Written skeleton arguments are expected in support of injunction applications. The Practice Guidance refers to the preparation of a written skeleton argument as part of the advocate's duty.[442] Besides advancing the points of law and fact on which the applicant relies, the skeleton argument is a document which may, and often should, serve the purpose of fulfilling the applicant's duty of full and frank disclosure.[443]

### (g) The duty of full and frank disclosure

**13.153** **Nature and extent**  Applicants for injunctions without notice owe a duty to make 'full and frank disclosure' to the court of all material facts which are known, or

---

[437] See *Terry* (n 146) [12], [27]–[36], and [66]–[67]. Evidence about the key non-party was given by business partners of the claimant; the non-party gave no evidence. The Court carefully examined the evidence and the reasons it was adduced in this way, and found it wanting. See also *Hutcheson v News Group (No 1)* [2012] EWCA Civ 808, [2012] EMLR 2 [26], [47]; *SKA* (n 306) [82]–[85]; *BUQ v HRE* [2012] EWHC 774 (QB) [67].

[438] *McKennitt v Ash* [2005] EWHC 3003 (QB), [2006] EMLR 10 [77].

[439] See eg *Kelly* (n 41) 85 (Munby J).

[440] 'The judge should not, in our view, assume that it was in the interests of A's wife to be kept in ignorance of A's relationships': *A v B plc* (n 427) [43(v)].

[441] See eg *SKA* (n 306) [82]–[85]. For discussion of difficulties and doubts which may arise where a corporate claimant sues, ostensibly for the protection of the Art 8 rights of others, see the care home case of *BKM* (n 425) [7] and [12]–[13] (Mann J).

[442] Practice Guidance (n 144) para 30.

[443] See 13.153 *et seq.*

would on proper inquiry be known, to the applicant.[444] This is a 'high duty to make full, fair and accurate disclosure...and to draw the court's attention to significant factual, legal and procedural aspects of the case'.[445] The party applying must ask what it would be telling the judge if representing the defendant or a third party with a relevant interest and that is precisely what the judge should be told.[446] The duty applies whenever application is made on less than the three days' notice prescribed by the CPR, even where the opposing party is represented.[447]

The duty is owed not only by applicants but also by their lawyers, and is not discharged **13.154** by merely placing the facts before the court. 'The representatives of the applicant must specifically direct the court to passages in the evidence which disclose matters adverse to the application.'[448] They must identify the crucial points for and against the application, pointing out any which are to the applicant's disadvantage and which the judge should take into account in considering whether or not to grant the injunction.

Moreover: **13.155**

> It is the particular duty of the advocate to see that the correct legal procedures and forms are used; that a written skeleton argument and a properly drafted order are prepared by him personally and lodged with the court before the oral hearing; and that at the hearing the court's attention is drawn by him to unusual features of the evidence adduced, to the applicable law and to the formalities and procedure to be observed.[449]

**Consequences of non-observance** The court may refuse to grant or discharge an **13.156** injunction where the claimant has failed to give full and frank disclosure.[450] The risk of discharge is a valuable discipline, but discharge is not automatic[451] and there is a line of authority containing judicial criticism of a tendency among litigants against whom interim injunctions have been granted 'to allege non-material disclosure on rather slender grounds'.[452]

---

[444] See n 420 and, generally, *Brink's-MAT v Elcombe* [1988] 1 WLR 1350, CA, 1356–7; *Civil Procedure 2015* (n 160) para 25.3.5 and *Chancery Guide* (HM Courts & Tribunals Service, October 2013) para 5.22.

[445] *Memory Corp* (n 373) 1459–60.

[446] *CEF Holdings* (n 391) [75]–[78].

[447] The duty is released in respect of matters brought to the court's attention by the respondent but not otherwise: *CEF Holdings* (n 391) [179]–[184], [197].

[448] *Chancery Guide* (n 444) para 5.22.

[449] *Memory Corp* (n 373) 1459–60. This wording is included within the Practice Guidance (n 144) para 30, with the addition of the words 'including how, if at all, the order submitted departs from the model order'.

[450] See *eg Andresen v Lovell* [2009] EWHC 3397 (QB) [26]–[29], where a harassment injunction was discharged on account of evidence which was in parts positively misleading, and omitted important facts; *CEF Holdings* (n 391) [228], [256]; *YXB v TNO* [2015] EWHC 826 (QB) (misuse of private information).

[451] See *eg Brink's-MAT* (n 444) 1357, per Ralph Gibson LJ: 'whether the fact not disclosed is of sufficient materiality to justify or require immediate discharge of the order without examination of the merits depends on the importance of the act to the issues which were to be decided by the judge on the application'. See also *Behbehani v Salem* [1989] 1 WLR 723, 729. The question of non-disclosure was also raised in *A v B plc* (n 427).

[452] *Brink's-MAT* (n 444) 1359.

### Disclosures to be made in privacy cases

**13.157** *Generally*  It is impossible to catalogue the matters which an applicant may have a duty to disclose or draw to the court's attention when seeking an injunction in privacy, but it may be helpful to identify some points. Where the respondent is not present or represented then clearly the court's attention should be drawn to s 12(2) HRA[453] and to the requirements of s 12(3)–(4).[454] Further, where the respondent has had little or no advance notice, compliance with the obligation of full and frank disclosure will generally require a search for previous media publications of material concerning the claimant in the same category as the material the publication of which is sought to be prevented. The purpose is to inform the court of the extent to which material is already in the public domain, and of the extent to which the claimant has courted publicity for aspects of his or her personal life. This involves an internet search and, where practicable, a cuttings search.[455]

**13.158** *Truth or falsity*  It is a moot question whether, where it is sought to restrain disclosures about private life, the claimant is obliged to reveal whether and, if so, to what extent the information at issue is true or false. It is suggested that where the information is true, and its truth could reasonably be said to lend support to an argument that disclosure is justified in the public interest or otherwise as a legitimate exercise of freedom of expression, the applicant's duty of full and frank disclosure may require that they come clean on the issue. The issue is discussed more fully in Chapter 12.[456]

### (h) The hearing

**13.159** **Public or private**  'Open justice has been an essential principle of English law for centuries'[457] and, outside the Family Division, the general rule is that court hearings are in public.[458] However, the seven specified grounds on which the court may order that a hearing or part of it take place in private[459] include at least five which may be relevant to a privacy case. A hearing in private can be justified on the grounds that publicity would defeat the object of the hearing.[460] This may be because the object is to prevent disclosure, or because the hearing takes place without notice to avoid the defendant taking steps to forestall the relief sought, or both. Other grounds that may be applicable are that the hearing involves confidential information and publicity would damage that confidentiality,[461] that a private

---

[453] Though the failure to do so may not be fatal, see *Carr v News Group Newspapers* (HC, 14 May 2004).

[454] *Doncaster* (n 361) [34]–[35]; *Dar Al Arkan Real Estate Development Co v Al Refai* [2012] EWHC 3539 (Comm) [136]–[140].

[455] See *X & Y* (n 146) [41]–[52] and [57]–[58].

[456] See 12.37–12.39.

[457] *G v Wikimedia* (n 142) [16].

[458] CPR 39.2(1).

[459] CPR 39.2(3).

[460] CPR 39.2(3)(a).

[461] CPR 39.2(3)(c).

hearing is necessary to protect the interests of a child,[462] or that the hearing is without notice and it would be unjust to the respondent to hold it in public.[463] It should be borne in mind, however, that these grounds should not be read in isolation from, but rather as governed by, the further essential ground[464] that a private hearing is necessary in the interests of justice.[465] Hearings in private are derogations from the principle of open justice and therefore can only be justified in exceptional circumstances, when and in so far they are strictly necessary as measures to secure the proper administration of justice.[466]

**In person or by telephone**   Applications are normally dealt with by a court hear-   **13.160** ing but 'cases of extreme urgency may be dealt with by telephone'.[467] Where the relief needed is extremely urgent and a hearing cannot be arranged the High Court can be contacted by telephone between 10am and 5pm to hear an application by telephone.[468] Outside those hours a telephone hearing can be arranged by contacting the clerk to the duty judge[469] in the High Court or circuit equivalent.[470] Injunction applications will only be dealt with by telephone where the applicant is acting by counsel or solicitors.[471]

*(i) Service of order*

**On respondents**   The order will obviously need to be served on the respondent(s).   **13.161** This can cause difficulties in the case of 'John Doe' orders, which are made because the claimant is unable to identify the respondent. In such cases it may be that on some occasions it would be appropriate to request a newspaper editor or lawyer to notify a source, but routinely ordering this to be done would not be right; the court will usually require an undertaking by the claimant to use all reasonable endeavours to identify and serve the person(s) concerned.[472]

**On third parties**   Claimants will have had to consider in advance of the hearing   **13.162** which non-parties should be served or notified.[473] Service or notification provides a healthy disincentive to disclosure, due to the *Spycatcher* contempt principle.[474]

---

462 CPR 39.2(3)(d).
463 CPR 39.2(3)(e).
464 CPR 39.2(3)(g).
465 See 13.93–13.94.
466 For the principles applicable when derogations from open justice are sought see 13.93–13.94.
467 CPR PD 25A para 4.2.
468 CPR PD 25A para 4.5(1). Contact is made with the Royal Courts of Justice or the Urgent Court Business Officer of the appropriate circuit court.
469 An interim non-disclosure order cannot be granted by a Master: *ABC v Lit* (n 310) [17].
470 CPR PD 25A para 4.5(2). Outside London contact is made with the clerk to the appropriate area circuit judge, or to the Urgent Court Business Officer of the appropriate circuit who will contact the local duty judge. For details of Chancery Division practice see the *Chancery Guide* (n 444) para 5.23, and for the Queen's Bench Division see the *Queen's Bench Guide* (May 2014) paras 7.11.9–7.11.12.
471 CPR PD 25A para 4.5(5).
472 *X & Y* (n 146) [75]–[76] and [79]; Practice Guidance (n 144) Model Order, sch B, para (4).
473 See 13.140–13.142.
474 See 4.143.

In some cases there may be little or no disadvantage in making the fact of an order public or general knowledge. However, service or notification ordinarily generates a right to see the relevant evidence,[475] and may have the effect of bringing a 'story' to the attention of those served for the first time. Since anybody served or notified has a right to apply to discharge or vary an injunction, general distribution of the order has the potential to be counter-productive. Advisers will need carefully to balance the risks and potential rewards.

### (4) Summary Judgment and Striking Out

#### (a) Generally

**13.163** In a privacy claim, as in other kinds of action, either party may apply for summary judgment on the whole of a claim or on any particular issue; and the court may grant such an application if it considers that the other party has 'no real prospect' of success on the claim or issue and there is 'no other compelling reason why the case or issue should be disposed of at a trial'.[476] A party may additionally or in the alternative apply under CPR 3.4 for a claim or defence to be struck out as disclosing no reasonable grounds for bringing or defending a claim, or as an abuse of process.[477] There is a separate and additional regime for defamation cases, known as summary disposal, which is similar in some respects but specialized in its application. This is provided for by the Defamation Act 1996 and regulated procedurally by CPR PD 53.[478]

#### (b) Application to privacy cases

**13.164** Summary resolution of a privacy case may have attractions for a claimant or defendant. Either side may wish the claim to be brought to an end promptly for reasons of expense. Claimants will generally wish this also because of the risk that prolongation of the case will involve further disclosures and otherwise cause them distress or embarrassment. Whether summary judgment or an order striking out a claim or defence is likely to be granted will of course depend very much on the particular facts of the case, but is also liable to be influenced by the cause of action relied on.

**13.165** The court has a general self-denying ordinance against granting summary judgment or striking out a claim where the relevant law is in a state of development. This has been applied in claims under the Data Protection Act 1998.[479] The prospects of putting a swift end to a claim or defence are better if the cause of action relied on is one of those the parameters of which are more clearly established and well understood, such as copyright infringement. In general, it may be true to say

---

[475] See 13.118.
[476] CPR 24.2.
[477] Of particular relevance will be the *Jameel* doctrine (13.47 and n 153).
[478] CPR PD 53 paras 5.1–5.3.
[479] See *KJO* (n 225) [51] and 13.81.

that the need to apply an 'intense focus'[480] to the particular facts of the case will mean that attempts to obtain summary judgment for or against claims in claims for misuse of private information will face difficulties, whether or not that cause of action is still in a state of development. The argument is likely to be raised that the 'intense focus' cannot properly be applied without a full examination of the facts at a trial.[481] Where the application is made by the defence, the court may conclude that the claim is arguable,[482] leaving the parties to fight a trial at what may be disproportionate expense.

Nevertheless, there are examples of the court granting summary relief to claimants **13.166** in confidence and misuse of private information. Summary judgment was granted to HRH Prince of Wales in his misuse and confidence claim against Associated Newspapers.[483] The Court of Appeal held on the final appeal in the *Douglas v Hello! Ltd* litigation that on a proper application of the law the couple should have been granted summary judgment earlier on.[484] And in *Imerman v Tchenguiz*[485] Eady J granted final injunctive relief on a summary judgment application, the determination of that aspect of the matter not requiring a full application of the 'intense focus'.

### (5) Case Management

#### (a) Progressing the claim after an interim non-disclosure order

Because interim non-disclosure orders restrict the exercise of Article 10 rights of **13.167** respondents and, particularly, third parties (under the *Spycatcher* principle),[486] they require the court to take particular care to provide active case management.[487] A party who has obtained such an order is required to progress the claim towards trial, rather than 'sit on' the order. The court will not permit an applicant who fails to progress the claim to continue to benefit from the effect of the injunction as against third parties by effectively agreeing with the respondent that the injunction continues indefinitely. This has been described as an abuse of the process of the court.[488] In such circumstances the court will intervene of its own motion.[489]

---

[480] That is, the 'ultimate balancing test' prescribed in *Re S* (n 35). See 5.159–5.160.

[481] Such was the defendants' contention in *Imerman* (n 225): see [12]–[14]. The Court appears to have accepted that this argument has merit, where substantive defences are raised and difficulties arise about resolving the issues by summary judgment.

[482] As in *Murray* (n 15) where the application was to strike out under CPR 3.4, assuming the truth of all the facts alleged by the claimant. See also the Court of Appeal's decision setting aside summary judgment in *Campbell v Frisbee* [2002] EWCA Civ 1374, [2003] EMLR 3 [22]. In 2009 the claimant abandoned that action, saying it was disproportionately costly.

[483] *HRH Prince of Wales* (n 222).

[484] *Douglas v Hello! Ltd* [2003] EWHC 786 (Ch), [2003] 3 All ER 996 [259] (Lindsay J).

[485] *Imerman* (n 225). Similarly, *BUQ v HRE* [2015] EWHC 1272 (QB).

[486] See 12.36.

[487] Practice Guidance (n 144) para 37. Tugendhat J emphasized the need to protect the Art 10 rights of third parties in *Giggs v News Group Newspapers Ltd* [2012] EWHC 431 (QB), [2013] EMLR 5 [81].

[488] *Giggs* (n 487) [106].

[489] *JIH* (n 272) [36].

It may hold that the injunction has become permanent and so no longer applies to third parties;[490] or may impose a timetable with the sanction of dismissal of the action (or liberty to enter judgment) in default.[491] To avoid this scenario arising, the court now generally requires that non-disclosure orders are limited to a specified period (rather than 'until trial or further order').[492] The parties should amend the Model Order in this way, and draw the point to the attention of the judge.[493]

**13.168** The undertaking to issue a claim form must be complied with, unless the party applies to the court to be released from it. Breach of such an undertaking cannot be disregarded and an adequate explanation must be provided if sanctions are not to follow.[494] Particulars of claim should be served promptly, and normally within fourteen days.[495] This has long been recognized.[496] Any application for an extension of time will need to explain why the extension is necessary and proportionate in so far as it prolongs any interference with the Article 10 rights of third parties.[497] The same is true for an application for an extension of time in respect of any other step in the proceedings.[498]

**13.169** If return dates are adjourned, or it becomes apparent for whatever reason that the claim is unlikely to progress to trial, the court should proactively manage the claim and either dismiss the action, proceed to summary judgment, enter judgment by consent, substitute or add an alternative defendant or direct that the claim and trial proceed.[499]

### (b) Disclosure and inspection

**13.170** **By claimants**   Disclosure almost always involves some intrusion into confidentiality or privacy, but this is especially likely to be true of disclosure given by a claimant in a privacy action. A disclosed document which is especially sensitive may well be looked at in private only, and neither read nor referred to at a public hearing. The disclosing party will wish to seek orders or agreements to ensure this is so. In such a case the receiving party will remain bound by the prohibition on collateral

---

[490]  *WER* (n 407). The Court of Appeal dismissed an appeal as academic: *Hutcheson v Popdog Ltd* [2011] EWCA Civ 1580, [2012] 1 WLR 782. In doing so however it suggested that, contrary to *Jockey Club v Buffham* [2003] QB 462, a final injunction may also have *Spycatcher* effect (that is, it binds all with knowledge of it), which might prevent the court in future from adopting the course taken in *WER*.

[491]  *Giggs* (n 487) [31]–[32].

[492]  *SPA v TAS* [2014] EWHC 1512 (QB) [3]. Indeed the court may refuse to make an order that does not contain adequate provisions for progress of the claim: *AVB v TDD* (n 370) [6]–[8].

[493]  *JIH* (n 272) [37].

[494]  *Gray* (n 297) [36]–[37], [65]–[66].

[495]  *Giggs* (n 487) [110].

[496]  *Giggs* (n 487) [109], citing *Hytrac Conveyors Ltd v Conveyors International Ltd* [1983] 1 WLR 44, 47 and *RHM Foods Ltd v Bovril Ltd* [1982] 1 WLR 661, 665.

[497]  *Giggs* (n 487) [110].

[498]  *Giggs* (n 487) [111].

[499]  Practice Guidance (n 144) para 41; *XJA* (n 298) [13]; *Gray* (n 297) [37]; *Terry* (n 146) [134]–[136].

use which is contained in CPR 31.22(1). If, however, a disclosed document is read to or by the court, or referred to, at a hearing which has been held in public these restrictions will cease to bind[500] unless the receiving party undertakes otherwise or the court makes an order[501] prohibiting collateral use of the document despite reference being made to it in open court proceedings. In considering whether to make such an order prohibiting disclosure to third parties (or an order allowing disclosure of documents subject to the prohibition in CPR 31.22(1)) the court's approach is the same as when considering an application for disclosure of documents on the court file to a third party under CPR 5.4C(2) or (6).[502]

There may well be grounds in many privacy cases for seeking such undertakings **13.171** or orders. The circumstances in which a document will be considered to have been released from the ordinary prohibition on collateral use are extensive. Documents read by the judge outside court fall within the wording of the rule, for instance.[503] It follows that the prohibition in CPR 31.22(1) may cease to apply although little if anything about the contents of the document has actually been made public. So there may be much that remains worthy of protection by means of an order under CPR 31.22(2).

### By defendants

*Generally*   Disclosure by defendants in media privacy litigation is less likely to **13.172** engage the defendant's rights of confidence or personal privacy than disclosure by claimants, but where it does the considerations discussed at 13.170–13.171 will apply in the same way.

*Source protection*   An issue which often arises in relation to disclosure by media **13.173** defendants in privacy cases (as in other media litigation) is the privilege of publishers provided for by s 10 of the Contempt of Court Act 1981. The starting point is that documents containing information which may serve to identify the source of information of matter published or intended for publication are privileged from inspection. Except where, unusually, identification of the document would of itself tend to disclose a source, the existence of a document containing information tending to reveal sources must ordinarily be disclosed pursuant to pt 31. That is, it must be listed. However, privilege from inspection may be claimed[504] and that privilege may be exercised by giving inspection only of a version of the document redacted to conceal the identifying information. If the claimant wishes to assert an overriding right to inspect, he or she will have to apply to the court for a ruling on whether the claim to privilege should be upheld.[505]

---

[500]   CPR 31.22(1)(a).
[501]   CPR 31.22(2).
[502]   *NAB v Serco Ltd* [2014] EWHC 1225 (QB). For the approach on an application by a non-party under CPR 5.4C, see 13.95–13.96.
[503]   CPR 31.22(1)(a).
[504]   In the defendant's list, as provided for by CPR 31.19(3)–(4).
[505]   CPR 31.19(5).

**13.174** *Self-incrimination*   The effect of s 72(5) of the Senior Courts Act 1981 is that a party cannot rely on the privilege against self-incrimination to avoid giving further information about, or disclosure of documents containing, 'intellectual property', which includes technical or commercial information. Information about a person's private life does not fall within this definition, even if it could be disclosed to the media for financial gain. Nor is all confidential information necessarily 'technical or commercial'. To fall within that definition the information itself must be of a technical or commercial nature, and sufficiently confidential as to be capable of being the subject of a confidence claim.[506] The privilege can thus be relied on in the ordinary way where the information is purely private or is confidential information of a non-technical and non-commercial nature.

### The rights and interests of non-parties

**13.175** *Documents belonging to the non-party*   A party may be obliged to disclose documents belonging to another. An order prohibiting collateral use of such a document may be sought either by the disclosing party or 'by any person to whom the document belongs'.[507] Copies of private emails or photographs on a stolen computer, or obtained by hacking, are examples of classes of document that might belong to a non-party and be the subject of an application for an order prohibiting collateral use despite reference to them in court.[508]

**13.176** *Documents not belonging to the non-party*   CPR pt 31 offers no protection to a third party, private information about whom is contained in a document disclosed by a party, if the document does not 'belong' to the third party. The court does, however, have a statutory duty to protect all Article 8 rights from unjustified interference,[509] and third parties will have a sufficient interest to appear and make representations as to the disclosure by others of documents affecting their rights.[510] If the non-party is a witness he or she may be able to apply for an anonymity order under CPR 39.2(4).[511] Otherwise, the inherent jurisdiction might be invoked as a means of giving effect to the court's statutory duty. The effective invocation of either power will depend, however, on prior knowledge of a prospective disclosure. Although it is arguable that disclosure of such a document without prior notice to the non-party would be a misuse of private information or a breach of duty under the Data Protection Act 1998, there is no procedural rule requiring a party to litigation to give

---

[506] *Phillips v News Group Newspapers Ltd* [2012] UKSC 28, [2013] 1 AC 1 [24]–[27].
[507] CPR 31.22(3)(b).
[508] See 13.170.
[509] *ie* the duty under s 6 HRA not to act inconsistently with Convention rights.
[510] *Flood v Times Newspapers Ltd* [2009] EWHC 411 (QB), [2009] EMLR 18 [30]–[32].
[511] Discussed at 13.100.

such notice. The rules of procedure ought to be amended to provide such a requirement.

### (c) Witnesses and witness statements

Witness statements must ordinarily give the name and address of the witness,[512] **13.177** and witnesses are generally required to give their names when they give oral evidence. However, the CPR power to grant anonymity to a witness[513] can be used to permit his or her name and other identifying information to be withheld from the public.[514] Although the terms of CPR 39.2(4) are broad enough to allow this, it would seem that it would only be in a wholly exceptional case that it would be proper to permit one party to serve a witness statement while withholding the identity of a witness from the opposite party.[515]

The general rule is that collateral use of witness statements is prohibited,[516] but this **13.178** does not apply if and to the extent that the statement has been put in evidence at a public hearing.[517] In contrast to the rules about disclosure, CPR pt 32 contains no power for the court to prohibit collateral use after a witness statement has been put in evidence. Moreover, a witness statement which stands as evidence in chief is required to be available for inspection 'during the course of the trial' unless the court otherwise orders.[518]

The above is subject to the court's powers to grant a witness anonymity[519] or **13.179** to direct that a witness statement not be open to inspection because of (among other things) the nature of any confidential information it contains,[520] or to order that certain words or passages in the statement be excluded from inspection.[521] Although the rules do not say so in terms, it seems reasonable to suppose that to the extent that a witness's evidence is given in private to protect a privacy interest, the court will consider there are grounds for an order correspondingly prohibiting or limiting inspection of that witness's statement.

---

[512] CPR 32.8 and CPR PD 32 paras 17–18.

[513] CPR 39.2(4), discussed at 13.105.

[514] As was done, by consent, in respect of all the female witnesses who gave evidence at the *Mosley* trial (n 14), who were referred to as Woman A, Woman B, *etc*. For the approach to the exercise of this power, see *Ivereigh v Associated Newspapers Ltd* [2008] EWHC 339 (QB).

[515] The right to know the identity of one's accusers is an essential element of a fair trial that has been recognized by the common law for centuries: see *R v Davis* [2008] UKHL 36, [2008] EWCA 1128; *Al Rawi v Security Service* [2011] UKSC 34, [2012] 1 AC 531. The identities of some claimant's witnesses were initially withheld in *Mosley* (n 14) but after an application for their disclosure was made, they were identified to the defendant.

[516] CPR 32.12(1).

[517] CPR 32.12(2)(c).

[518] CPR 32.13(1).

[519] CPR 39.2(4) and 13.106.

[520] CPR 32.13(2) and (3)(d).

[521] CPR 32.13(4).

*(d) Order for speedy trial*

**13.180** On several occasions the Queen's Bench Division has directed the speedy trial of a privacy claim. Such orders were made in *McKennitt v Ash*[522] and in *Mosley.*[523]

**13.181** In general, orders for a speedy trial, which promote the interests of one case over those of others, are not common. They may be made at the instance of defendants against whom an interim injunction has been granted, if the resolution of the issue whether its grant is right or wrong is urgent. Such is the case, for example, where an interim injunction is granted to enforce a restrictive covenant of relatively short duration in an employment contract where the injunction decision may be decisive of the claim.

**13.182** Defendants in privacy actions who are made subject to interim injunctions may wish to bring the matter to trial swiftly, and the interests of any third parties whose Article 10 rights are interfered with by an injunction will also militate in favour of a speedy trial.[524] Those against whom no injunction is granted will wish to consider whether a trial prepared at ordinary speed is preferable. If disputes about disclosure are likely, or time is required to assemble defence evidence, this may be thought to be the case.

## (6) Trial

*(a) Mode of trial*

**13.183** Few claims for privacy infringement will be candidates for jury trial. Section 69 of the Senior Courts Act 1981 provides a strong statutory presumption that trial will be by judge alone. The main exception will be actions which include a claim for defamation, where the cause of action arose before 1 January 2014 but since the primary limitation period for defamation is one year,[525] very few such actions will now be brought.

*(b) Hearing in private*

**13.184** Whether the court's powers to sit in private[526] should be exercised in relation to the trial of an action will very much depend on the particular circumstances of the case. The entirety of the trial in *McKennitt v Ash* was in private,[527] though the appeal was heard partly in private and partly in public. Most of the trial in *Mosley*[528] was in public, with the court being cleared for sections of the cross-examination of the claimant and some of his witnesses.

---

[522] *McKennitt* (n 438).
[523] *Mosley* (n 14).
[524] See 13.167.
[525] See 11.224.
[526] See 13.159.
[527] *McKennitt* (n 438) [3].
[528] *Mosley* (n 14).

On an application under CPR 39.2 for witnesses to give evidence in private, the **13.185**
court must apply the principles applicable to any application for a derogation from
open justice.[529] The court must conduct a balancing exercise and consider the reasons and evidence given as to why such a measure is 'necessary, in the interests of
justice', such as a risk of harm to the interests of the witnesses, and consider whether
it is sufficient to justify the derogation that is sought.[530]

### (c) Anonymity and special measures

If the court grants a witness anonymity it may be necessary to devise special meas- **13.186**
ures to protect the witness's identity when they come to give evidence at the trial. In
the absence of such orders witnesses may not only be viewed and recognized when
in court, and depicted by court artists, but also filmed or photographed outside
court (even if the hearing is in private). Any order prohibiting identification would
require broadcasters and other publishers to pixelate or otherwise obscure identifying features, clothing, or the like.

Special measures could include secure means of entering and leaving the court **13.187**
premises and the courtroom without being viewed, filmed, or photographed; the
use of screens around the witness box; or the giving of evidence by video link.
In *Mosley*[531] there was discussion in pre-trial hearings of the possibility of such
measures being put in place for the female witnesses, but in the event none were
adopted. One wore wigs and other disguise when attending court. Pictures of them
arriving and leaving court were published but pixelated.

### (d) Judgment

Whether or not an anonymity order or an order restraining publication of nor- **13.188**
mally reportable details is made, a publicly available judgment should normally
be given, and a copy of the consequential court order made publicly available, if
necessary in an edited form.[532]

The considerations relevant to the terms in which to give a public judgment where **13.189**
private or confidential information is concerned have been discussed by the House
of Lords [533] and the Court of Appeal.[534] In *McKennitt v Ash* the judgment was public in its entirety, having been 'drafted so as to avoid intruding, so far as possible,

---

[529] See 13.94.
[530] See *eg Deripaska v Cherney* [2012] EWCA Civ 1235, where it was ruled not necessary in the
interests of justice for the evidence of witnesses said to fear reprisals to be heard in private. An alternative argument relying on the witnesses' Art 2 rights was also rejected.
[531] *Mosley* (n 14).
[532] *JIH* (n 272) [21(9)].
[533] *Cream Holdings* (n 45) [26].
[534] *Lord Browne* (n 272) [1]–[5]. For the general approach to public judgments after private hearings see *Dept of Economic Policy and Development of the City of Moscow v Bankers Trust Co* [2004]
EWCA Civ 314, [2005] QB 207 [39]–[41] and *Kazeminy v Siddiqi* [2010] EWHC 201 (Comm)
[41]–[45].

on any of the more intimate detail which the claimants wished to protect'.[535] So too, the whole judgment in *Mosley*.[536] 'Considerable discretion' had been shown by the defence 'in not referring, more than absolutely necessary, to embarrassing or intimate matters from the video recordings'.[537] Details of private information disclosed in open court which had not already been published were few and were kept to generalities in the judgment. If parties settle a case before judgment is delivered the court has a discretion to deliver judgment; in deciding whether to do so it will balance the parties' private interests against the public interests in making the judgment public.[538]

---

[535] *McKennitt* (n 438) [3].
[536] *Mosley* (n 14).
[537] *Mosley* (n 14) [233].
[538] *Prudential Assurance Co Ltd v McBains Cooper* [2000] 1 WLR 2000, CA; *Renaissance Capital Ltd v ENRC Africa Holdings Ltd* (QBD, 7 April 2011, Sir Robert Nelson).

# PART VII

PRIVACY REGULATION

# 14

## THE PRIVACY CODES

*Yuli Takatsuki and Nigel Abbas*

# A. Introduction

**14.01** Alongside the legal framework which regulates the media's activities, a system of regulation operates to uphold standards of journalism and programme-making and to provide at least a partial remedy for those whose privacy has been invaded by the media. Different bodies currently regulate different branches of the media. Ofcom (the Office of Communications) regulates the content of all television and radio programmes in the United Kingdom[1] except that the BBC retains sole jurisdiction in relation to certain matters broadcast on BBC channels funded by the licence fee.[2] The Independent Press Standards Organisation (IPSO) has recently taken over as principal regulator of the newspaper and magazine industry (although a new body, the Independent Monitor for the Press (Impress), has also recently been formed). IPSO replaced the Press Complaints Commission (PCC) in September 2014, with which has now ceased to exist, having regulated the print media industry since 1991. These bodies adjudicate upon complaints with reference to codes of practice which media falling within their regulatory remit are required to comply. The Ofcom Broadcasting Code, drawn up and regularly reviewed and revised by Ofcom, is the primary broadcasting code relating to the broadcast of television and radio programme content in the United Kingdom. IPSO, like the PCC before it, adjudicates on complaints with reference to the Editors' Code of Practice (Editors' Code), a code written, reviewed and revised by the Editors' Code Committee. Without exception, all the main codes of practice recognize and require the media to uphold the right to privacy and to justify any interference with it.[3]

**14.02** For many years there has been significant debate about whether the press regulatory regime[4] in particular provides an effective deterrent against, and remedies for, invasions of privacy. Most of the reviews in this area over the years have concluded that the system of self-regulation that applies to the press should be allowed to continue without the introduction of a statutory regime, although the debate on this subject has never been fiercer than in recent years.

## (1) The Leveson Inquiry

**14.03** In July 2011, Prime Minister David Cameron announced a public inquiry to investigate the culture, practices, and ethics of the press, in response to allegations of

---

[1] Ofcom replaced the previous regulators, the Broadcasting Standards Commission, the Independent Television Commission, and the Radio Authority in December 2003.

[2] In particular, the BBC retains sole jurisdiction over complaints relating to inaccuracy and impartiality, elections and referenda, sponsorship, and commercial arrangements.

[3] The Advertising Standards Authority regulates advertising across all media in the United Kingdom. It regulates both broadcast and non-broadcast advertising by applying codes written by the Committees of Advertising Practice: the Committee of Advertising Practice writes the UK Code of Non-broadcast Advertising, Sales Promotion and Direct Marketing; the Broadcast Committee of Advertising Practice writes the UK Code of Broadcasting Advertising. Sections 6 of both Codes deal directly with privacy matters.

[4] In particular, operated by the PCC and the Press Council before it.

widespread abuses by sections of the press, in particular phone hacking. Chaired by Lord Justice Leveson, the 'Leveson Inquiry' amounted to the most detailed analysis of the press and its workings in modern times. Evidence in relation to part 1 of the inquiry was completed in the summer of 2012, with Lord Justice Leveson publishing his 'Report on Part 1 of the Inquiry' on 29 November 2012. As regards the PCC, the press regulator at the time, Lord Justice Leveson concluded that, while it had been good at certain things, for example mediation and conciliation between complainants and the press, there had been so many serious failings over many years that it had lost the trust of both policy makers and the public. Rejecting the proposition that the PCC was even a 'regulator', as that term is commonly understood, he concluded that: 'It is difficult to avoid the conclusion that the self-regulatory system was run for the benefit of the press and not of the public.'[5] In his Report, Lord Justice Leveson set out in detail his recommendations for a voluntary, self-organized regulatory system 'that would provide an appropriate degree of independence from the industry, coupled with satisfactory powers to handle complaints, promote and enforce standards, and deal with dispute resolution'.[6] Such a system, he recommended, should be backed up by legislation, setting out the requirements of any new regulator and, importantly, providing a mechanism to recognize and certify that any new body met, and continued to meet, those requirements.

In March 2013, following cross-party talks on Lord Justice Leveson's recom-  **14.04** mendations about press regulation, the leaders of the three main political parties agreed to set up a new press watchdog underpinned by Royal Charter, not by statute. This 'Recognition Panel' would oversee, approve, and monitor any new press regulator, although it would have no powers to compel regulators to seek recognition. Strongly opposed by many in the press industry, which viewed the Royal Charter as 'state-sponsored regulation', giving politicians an unwelcome element of control, it was nevertheless approved by the Privy Council on 30 October 2013. As noted above, IPSO replaced the PCC in September 2014 and is now the principal regulator for the newspaper and magazine industry. Backed by most but not all of the industry,[7] its supporters claim that it will provide independent, tough, and effective regulation, in line with Lord Justice Leveson's recommendations, although its detractors dispute this. At the time of writing, IPSO shows no intention of seeking formal recognition by the Press Recognition Panel, which came into being on 3 November 2014.[8] An alternative

---

[5] *Report on Part 1 of the Inquiry* (Leveson LJ), vol IV, pt J, para 8.12.

[6] Leveson Inquiry (n 5) vol IV, pt K, para 7.12.

[7] At the time of writing a number of publishers including some national newspapers have decided not to become members of IPSO, preferring to operate their own system of complaints-handling and self-regulation.

[8] The Recognition Panel has no power to force IPSO, or any other press regulator, to seek recognition. However, failure to do so could potentially have serious consequences for the press. Signing up to regulation by a regulator formally recognized by the Recognition Panel now comes with benefits, or rather not being recognized by the Regulatory Panel comes with penalties, *eg* in relation to awards of exemplary and aggravated damages, as well as costs, when press

potential regulator, Impress, has also been set up, although at the time of writing no publishers have sought membership. Impress states that it intends to provide press regulation in full compliance with Lord Justice Leveson's criteria, and in May 2015 announced that it would be seeking recognition from the Press Recognition Panel.

**14.05** Lord Justice Leveson spent some time considering the Editors' Code, that is the code against which the PCC traditionally judged complaints, and that which IPSO now seeks to enforce. While acknowledging that the Code contained positive elements, Lord Justice Leveson's recommendation was that it be reviewed and improved upon.[9] In particular, he recommended that any press code should provide guidance on the interpretation of the public interest that justifies 'what would otherwise constitute a breach of the Code. This must be framed in the context of the different provisions of the Code relating to the public interest, so as to make it easier to justify what might otherwise be considered as contrary to standards of propriety.'[10] Accordingly, the Editors' Code of Practice Committee reviewed it. At the time of writing, IPSO applies and judges complaints against a version of the Code dated September 2014 but a new version of the Code comes into force on 1 January 2016. References to the Code in this chapter are therefore to the 2016 version.

### (2) Legal Significance of the Regulatory Codes

**14.06** While it is clearly in everyone's interests, not least editors', to have an industry code in place containing rules and guidance which are proportionate, practical, and unambiguous, which is likely to foster and support good regulatory compliance, any code has wider, legal significance as a result of the Human Rights Act 1998 (HRA). During the passage of the Human Rights Bill through Parliament, opponents of greater legal protection of privacy expressed serious concerns that the introduction of Article 8 of the European Convention on Human Rights (ECHR) into English law might usher in through the back door laws on privacy which they had successfully been resisting through the front door for many years. It was these concerns which led directly to the introduction of what was to become s 12 HRA.

---

organizations are involved in litigation resulting from the publication of news-related material: see ss 34–42 of the Crime and Courts Act 2013, which were enacted (although are not in force at the time of writing) in order to encourage press organizations to sign up to a formally recognized regulator.

[9] Leveson Inquiry (n 5) vol IV, pt K, para 2.3: 'There has been a lot of support for the current Editors' Code. However, issues have also been identified with it. I have made the points that in order to provide an ethical framework for editors and journalists to work within, it needs to set the ethical and legal context in which it applies, and that it must do so in a clear and practical way. I would not want to lose any of the positive elements of the existing Code, but . . . I recommend that a regulatory body should consider engaging in an early thorough review of the code with the aim of developing a clearer statement of the standards expected of editors and journalists. It is important that the public should be engaged in that review.'

[10] Leveson Inquiry (n 5) vol IV, pt K, para 2.10.

Section 12(4) HRA accords a special statutory significance to the regulatory **14.07**
codes of practice.[11] Under that section the court is obliged to have particular
regard to the terms of any relevant 'privacy code' when considering whether
to grant any relief which might affect the exercise of the right to freedom of
expression and the publication of any journalistic, literary, or artistic material.
The purpose of the provision was to signal to the courts that if the media act in
accordance with the applicable privacy code of conduct, the court should be slow
to intervene.

The statutory significance of the Editors' Code was judicially recognized shortly **14.08**
after entry into force of the HRA in *Douglas v Hello! Ltd.* Brooke LJ stated that:[12]

> A newspaper which flouts Section 3 of the [Editors'] Code is likely in those cir-
> cumstances to have its claim to an entitlement to freedom of expression trumped
> by Article 10(2) considerations of privacy... It follows that on the present occasion
> it is not necessary to go beyond Section 12 of the 1998 Act and Clause 3 of the
> Press Complaints Commission's code to find the ground rules by which we should
> weigh the competing considerations of freedom of expression on the one hand and
> privacy on the other.

Since then, the courts have repeatedly considered the Editors' Code and the **14.09**
Ofcom Broadcasting Code, and in particular their interpretation of the concept of 'public interest', in deciding whether to grant injunctions restraining
publication[13] or reporting restrictions[14] in light of the requirement under s 12(4)
HRA. Compliance with the media regulators' codes are also considered in claims
for misuse of private information following publication.[15]

The HRA, however, is not the only modern statute to recognize the regulators' **14.10**
privacy codes. The codes of practice are also relevant under s 32 of the Data
Protection Act 1998 (DPA), often referred to as the 'journalistic exemption'.
This provides that personal data processed only for the 'special purposes', which

---

[11] See 14.13 *et seq.*
[12] [2001] QB 967, CA [94]–[95]. Sedley LJ expressly agreed with these paragraphs in his judgment at [136]. These passages have been cited with approval in *A v B plc* [2002] 3 WLR 542 [11(xiv)]
and *Mills v News Group Newspapers Ltd* [2001] EMLR 41.
[13] *Spelman v Express Newspapers* [2012] EWHC 355 (QB) [35]; *Viagogo Ltd v Myles* [2012]
EWHC 433 (Ch) [14], [60]–[61]; *TSE v News Group Newspapers Ltd* [2011] EWHC 1308 (QB)
[21]–[22], [27], 'the HRA requires the court to have regard to the matters set out in sub-section (4)
whether they are raised by a defendant or not'; *Mosley v News Group Newspapers* [2008] EWHC
687 (QB) [31]; *X and Y v Persons Unknown* [2006] EWHC 2783 (QB), [2007] EMLR 10 [49], [51];
*Leeds City Council v Channel 4 Television Corp* [2005] EWHC 3522 (Fam) [25], [37]–[38], [40];
*McKennitt v Ash* [2005] EWHC 3003 (QB), [2006] EMLR 10 [94]–[96]; *Douglas v Hello! Ltd*
[2003] EWHC 786 (Ch), [2003] 3 All ER 996 [186]; and *Mills* (n 12) [31].
[14] *R v Marine A* [2013] EWCA Crim 2367, [2014] 1 WLR 3326 [57]–[58], [64] and [67]; *A (A
Child) (Application for Reporting Restrictions), Re* [2011] EWHC 1764 (Fam); *Re Stedman* [2009]
EWHC 935 (Fam), [2009] 2 FLR 852 [69].
[15] *Weller v Associated Newspapers Ltd* [2014] EWHC 1163 (QB); *AAA v Associated Newspapers Ltd* [2012] EWHC 2103 (QB) [53]–[54], [123]; *Ferdinand v MGN Ltd* [2011] EWHC
2454 (QB) [65].

is defined within the Act to include processing undertaken with a view to the publication of journalistic material, are exempt from certain provisions of the Act,[16] including s 10, which provides a means by which a data subject can seek an injunction to prevent processing in certain circumstances.[17] For the s 32 exemption to apply, one of the conditions that must be met is that the data controller 'must reasonably believe... that publication would be in the public interest'.[18] The section provides that when considering whether the belief of a data controller that publication would be in the public interest was or is a reasonable one, regard may be had to his or her compliance with any relevant code of practice. Accordingly, when considering applications for injunctions by data subjects under the DPA against media defendants, the courts are likely to consider the provisions of any relevant code of practice and whether the defendant has complied with those provisions.[19]

**14.11**  As a result of these two statutory provisions, the regulatory codes are now linked into the question of whether it is appropriate for a court to grant a legal remedy for alleged invasions of privacy by the media. In that sense it could be said that the codes have been given something approaching a legal status.[20] In any event, their provisions have become an important source material for lawyers and the courts.[21]

**14.12**  The main part of this chapter analyses those codes of practice which are most pertinent to the issue of privacy and the adjudications which have been made by the regulatory body relevant to the publication or broadcast complained of. Consideration is given first to legislation which governs their relevance, the HRA and the DPA, and then to the practical considerations which apply in deciding

---

[16] The provisions are: the data protection principles except the seventh data protection principle; s 7; s 10; s 12; and s 14(1)–(3).

[17] s 10 DPA.

[18] s 32(1)(b) DPA.

[19] *LNS v Persons Unknown* [2010] EWHC 119 (QB) [72]–[73], [129].

[20] While compliance or non-compliance with regulators' codes provisions on privacy is likely to be relevant to the determination of applications for prior restraint in privacy claims, reliance by an applicant on compliance or non-compliance with other provisions within the same codes, *eg* those regarding 'fairness', will be misconceived in privacy-related claims. See *Tillery Valley Foods Ltd v Channel Four Television Corp* [2004] EWHC 1075 (Ch).

[21] The Editors' Code has also provided important guidance in other areas of the law. The House of Lords considered the standards of the Editors' Code relevant in deciding the appropriate threshold for 'responsible journalism' to be applied to a *Reynolds* qualified-privilege defence in defamation: see *Jameel v Wall Street Journal Europe Sprl* [2006] UKHL 44, [2007] 1 AC 359 [55]. See also *Ewing v News International Ltd* [2008] EWHC 1390 (QB) where previous PCC rulings were relevant in deciding whether to allow a vexatious litigant to pursue further claims against the defendants under Senior Courts Act 1981, s 42(3). Note however that the common law defence known as the '*Reynolds* defence' has been abolished and replaced by a new statutory defence of 'Publication on a matter of public interest', by s 4 of the Defamation Act 2013, which came into force on 1 January 2014. Whether, and to what extent, 'responsible journalism', and the ten non-exhaustive factors identified by Lord Nicholls as being determinative of responsible journalism, will be relevant in deciding whether a media defendant can succeed in a s 4 defence remains to be seen; the matter is not yet entirely settled.

whether to pursue a complaint under them. The adjudications of the regulatory bodies are then analysed in detail along with any guiding principles that can be distilled from them. The chapter then summarizes the media regulators' remits with regard to 'new media' before finally considering how decisions of the media regulators can be challenged.

## B. The Human Rights Act 1998

Section 12 HRA applies where a court is considering whether to grant relief which, **14.13** if granted, might affect the exercise of the Convention right to freedom of expression (Article 10). Where a court is considering granting any relief which affects rights to freedom of expression in connection with journalistic, literary, or artistic material, it must have particular regard to any relevant privacy code. Section 12(4) states that:

> (4) The court must have particular regard to the importance of the Convention right to freedom of expression and, where the proceedings relate to material which the respondent claims, or which appears to the court, to be journalistic, literary or artistic material (or to conduct connected with such material), to—
> (a) the extent to which—
> (i) the material has, or is about to, become available to the public; or
> (ii) it is, or would be, in the public interest for the material to be published;
> (b) any relevant privacy code.

### (1) What is a 'Relevant Privacy Code'?

During the passage of the Human Rights Bill through Parliament the Home **14.14** Secretary told the House of Commons that the relevant privacy codes for the purposes of s 12(4) 'depending on the circumstances...could be the newspaper industry code of practice operated by the PCC, the Broadcasting Standards Commission code, the Independent Television Commission code, or a broadcaster's internal code such as that operated by the BBC'.[22] The codes of practice issued by the Broadcasting Standards Commission and the Independent Television Commission, along with the Radio Authority, were all replaced by a new Ofcom Broadcasting Code under statute[23] in July 2005,[24] which is now accepted (and later versions of it) as being the 'relevant privacy code' for the broadcasting industry.

The provisions of the Editors' Code (the code governing the newspaper and maga- **14.15** zine industry and applied by IPSO and the PCC before it) have been considered in

---

[22] *Hansard*, HC (6th series) vol 315, col 538 (2 July 1998).
[23] Communications Act 2003, s 327.
[24] The Ofcom Code is regularly updated, the latest version at the time of writing was published in July 2015.

a number of cases before the courts by reason of s 12(4).[25] For example, Eady J in *Mosley v News Group Newspapers Ltd*[26] had regard to the Editors' Code's interpretation of the 'public interest' in deciding whether to grant an interim injunction against the *News of the World* to restrain it from publishing a video on its website of the claimant engaging in sexual activities:

> I have well in mind, naturally, that one aspect of the public interest is the need to protect the public from being misled by a statement made by or on behalf of the relevant claimant. That is recognised expressly in the terms of the Code of Practice promulgated by the Press Complaints Commission (a factor to which it is appropriate to have regard, on an application of this kind, in the light of s. 12(4) of the 1998 Act).[27]

**14.16**  However, in *Campbell v Frisbee*,[28] an action for breach of confidence, the judge at first instance held that the Editors' Code was not a relevant privacy code in the circumstances of the case. Although s 12(4) HRA was relevant as the information provided to the *News of the World* by Miss Campbell's former assistant, Miss Frisbee, constituted 'journalistic material', Lightman J considered that the Code had no application to Miss Frisbee herself, who was only a source and not a media organization:

> I do not think that the Code is a relevant privacy code when considering a claim against an informant such as the Defendant. The Code is a code laid down by the press for the press establishing a benchmark in respect of the professional standards of the press enforced by the Press Complaints Commission ('the PCC'). The Code has no application to the Defendant: it does not lay down standards in respect of compliance or otherwise with obligations of confidence on her part; and the PCC has no jurisdiction in respect of her conduct.[29]

**14.17**  On appeal,[30] the defendant contended that there was good reason to treat a newspaper and its source of information on the same basis: the legitimacy of the publication of a story under the Code was relevant when considering the legitimacy of the act of the informant in providing the story to the media. While the Court of Appeal did not need to decide this issue, it held that the point was 'arguable'.[31] In *Trimingham v Associated Newspapers Ltd*,[32] proceedings which, *inter alia*, included a claim for misuse of private information, it was held that the discrimination section of the Editors' Code was not a relevant privacy code.[33] The claimant argued

---

[25]  See *eg* Lindsay J's consideration of the Editors' Code when considering s 12 HRA in *Douglas* (n 13) [205]. See also nn 13–15.

[26]  [2008] EWHC 687 (QB).

[27]  *Mosley* (n 26) [31].

[28]  [2002] EWHC 328 (Ch).

[29]  *Campbell v Frisbee* (n 28) [29].

[30]  [2002] EWCA Civ 1374, [2003] EMLR 3.

[31]  *Campbell v Frisbee* (n 31) [25].

[32]  [2012] EWHC 1296 (QB), [2012] 4 All ER 717.

[33]  The Editors' Code, in common with other media codes of practice, *eg* the Ofcom Code, contains rules on numerous matters wholly unrelated, or in some cases only loosely related, to privacy matters, *eg* accuracy, impartiality *etc.*

that Associated Newspapers had breached clause 12 of the Editors' Code, headed 'Discrimination' by making pejorative and irrelevant references to the claimant's sexual orientation (denied by the defendant) and that clause 12 is part of a relevant privacy code. However, Tugendhat J decided:

> Clause 12 of the Editors' Code may be about private life in the wide sense used in Art 8, but it is not a natural meaning of the words 'privacy code' in s.12(4)(b). Clause 12 is headed 'Discrimination'. It seems to me to be directed to matters which are within editorial independence. Whether there has been a breach of the Code is a matter for the PCC, and not for the courts.[34]

In other words the provisions relating to 'Discrimination' within the Editors' Code were not part of a 'relevant privacy code' and accordingly the court should not consider whether or not those provisions had been complied with, in determining a claim for misuse of private information.

### (2) Are the Adjudications Relevant?

Although merely of persuasive authority, the courts may consider not only the rel- **14.18** evant privacy code but also any adjudications made by the appropriate body insofar as they may shed light on the way in which the provisions of these codes have been interpreted and applied by those with experience in the particular area of print or broadcasting media. In the guidelines for judges hearing applications for interim relief laid down by the Court of Appeal in *A v B plc*[35] Lord Woolf warned against this approach, saying:

> . . . the court should discourage advocates seeking to rely on individual decisions of the Press Council [*sic*] which are at best no more than illustrative of how the Press Council [*sic*] performs its different responsibilities.

Three days after Lord Woolf made these remarks, a differently constituted Court **14.19** of Appeal in *R (ProLife Alliance) v BBC*[36] took a rather different view of the value of the adjudications made under the regulators' codes of practice. Simon Brown LJ found it 'instructive' to have regard to adjudications of the Broadcasting Standards Commission and Independent Television Commission (the broadcasting regulators at the time) on their attitude towards potentially disturbing material on television (the issue in the case being one of taste, decency, and offensiveness)[37] and Laws LJ indicated that, in the context of broadcast entertainment, the courts should 'pay a very high degree of respect' to the broadcasters' judgment, given the background of, amongst other things, the Broadcasting Standards Commission adjudications.[38]

---

[34] *Trimingham* (n 32) [74]. Note, the main 'privacy' provisions are contained within s 3 of the Editors' Code.

[35] [2002] EWCA Civ 337, [2003] QB 195 [11(xv)].

[36] [2002] EWCA Civ 297, [2002] 3 WLR 1080.

[37] *ProLife* (n 36) [61].

[38] *ProLife* (n 36) [37].

**14.20**  While courts are clearly not bound by such adjudications, it is difficult to see how any meaningful understanding of the codes' provisions can be arrived at without at least some regard to the body of decisions or 'case law' that has built up under them. Indeed, this may be of particular assistance where, on an application for an interim injunction, the judge may be unfamiliar both with the principles involved and with editorial and journalistic considerations relevant to their application. If the codes are to be regarded as the yardsticks by which to measure good and bad journalistic practice, it would seem to be necessary to see how the bodies with primary responsibility for implementing them interpret their provisions. Nevertheless, one important limitation must be recognized in reliance upon the adjudications. Despite judicial recognition of the expertise of the regulatory bodies,[39] their adjudications are often reported summarily, or without any full explanation of the reasoning process behind them, and are reached without the safeguards inherent in the judicial process (such as oral evidence from or cross-examination of witnesses or full legal argument).

## C. The Data Protection Act 1998

### (1) The Media Exemption

**14.21**  As we have seen in Chapter 7, data protection forms an increasingly important part of the law of privacy. The DPA obliges data controllers to comply with the data protection principles, gives a data subject certain rights of access to data held by others concerning him or her, and provides for compensation in certain circumstances, for example where an individual suffers damage by reason of contravention of the requirements of the Act.[40] Under s 32 DPA,[41] personal data which are processed only for 'special purposes' (that is journalistic, literary, or artistic purposes) are conditionally exempt from provisions of the Act relating to:

(a) the data protection principles (except for the requirement to keep data secure under the seventh principle);
(b) subject access;
(c) the right to prevent processing likely to cause damage or distress;
(d) prevention of automated decision-taking; or
(e) rights to rectification, blocking, erasure, and destruction.

**14.22**  The Act states that the exemption only applies to data processed 'with a view to publication...of any journalistic, literary of artistic material which, at the time 24 hours immediately before the relevant time, had not previously been published

---

[39] See *eg* Lord Woolf MR in *R v Broadcasting Standards Commission, ex p BBC* [2001] QB 885, CA; and *R v PCC, ex p Stewart-Brady* [1997] 9 Admin LR 274, 279; also Silber J in *R (Ford) v PCC* [2002] EMLR 95 [21]–[28].
[40]  s 13 DPA.
[41]  For a detailed discussion of s 32 DPA see ch 7.

by the data controller'.[42] In spite of the words 'with a view to publication', the exemption has been held to apply before, at the time of, and after publication.[43] However, it is conditional upon the newspaper or broadcaster reasonably believing that (i) publication would be in the public interest; and (ii) in all the circumstances, compliance with the rules in the Act is incompatible with the journalistic purposes. In considering whether the belief of the media organization that publication would be in the public interest is reasonable, regard may be had to its compliance with any relevant code of practice.[44]

Accordingly, proper compliance with a relevant code of practice may assist a **14.23** defendant in avoiding liability after publication in a data protection claim, as well as resisting an application for prior restraint. However, a lack of compliance will not necessarily mean that a defendant cannot avail itself of the s 32 exemption. In *Campbell*, the Court of Appeal held that MGN Ltd had satisfied the requirements for exemption under s 32 in publishing an article and accompanying photographs of the claimant emerging from Narcotics Anonymous, notwithstanding that the judge at first instance had found that the covert photography of the claimant was 'contrary to the letter and spirit' of the Editors' Code.[45]

## (2) Regulatory Action by the Information Commissioner

Both privacy complainants and media organizations should be aware that as well **14.24** as individuals being able to bring legal proceedings for compensation or another remedy for contraventions of the DPA, the Commissioner operates a system of regulation to encourage and enforce compliance with the Act.[46] The Commissioner has specific statutory powers to regulate compliance with the DPA, which include the ability to issue enforcement notices,[47] order an audit,[48] impose civil monetary penalties,[49] and commence criminal prosecutions for failure to comply with notices issued by the Commissioner.[50] The Commissioner may pursue regulatory action following a complaint or on his or her own volition. Requests may be made to the

---

[42] s 32(4)(b) DPA.

[43] *Campbell v MGN Ltd* [2002] EWCA Civ 1373, [2003] QB 633 [120]–[121], [128]–[131].

[44] s 32(3) DPA. The Data Protection (Designated Codes of Practice) (No 2) Order 2000, SI 2000/1864, provides that the relevant codes are those of the Broadcasting Standards Commission, Independent Television Commission and Radio Authority (now subsumed by Ofcom—the Ofcom Broadcasting Code), the BBC Producers' Guidelines (now replaced by the BBC Editorial Guidelines), and the Editors' Code.

[45] *Campbell* (n 43) [135].

[46] The Commissioner also ensures regulation with the Privacy and Electronic Communications (EC Directive) Regulations 2003, SI 2003/2426.

[47] s 40 DPA. An enforcement notice is a notice requiring a data controller to refrain from processing personal data, or to take certain steps, in order to comply with data protection principle(s) that the Commissioner considers the data controller has, or is, contravening.

[48] ss 41A–C DPA.

[49] ss 55A–E DPA.

[50] s 47 DPA.

Commissioner, by or on behalf of any person who is, or believes him or herself to be, directly affected by any processing of personal data, for an assessment as to whether it is likely that the processing has been, or is being, carried out in compliance with the provisions of the Act.[51]

**14.25**  Where the Commissioner is satisfied that a data controller has contravened or is contravening any of the data protection principles, he or she may serve an enforcement notice on the data controller 'requiring him . . . to do either or both of the following—(a) to take within such time as may be specified in the notice, or to refrain from taking after such time as may be so specified, such steps as are so specified, or (b) to refrain from processing any personal data, or any personal data of a description specified in the notice, or to refrain from processing them for a purpose so specified or in a manner so specified, after such time as may be so specified'.[52]

**14.26**  The Commissioner's powers to take regulatory action are restricted, however, where personal data are processed only for the special purposes with a view to publication, the Commissioner not having the power to serve an enforcement notice preventing the publication of journalistic, literary, or artistic material. Before serving an enforcement notice in connection with the processing of personal data for the special purposes, the Commissioner not only has to make a determination[53] that personal data are not being processed only for the special purposes, or are not being processed with a view to publication, but also must obtain leave from a court, which has to be satisfied that the contravention of the data protection principles is of substantial public importance.[54]

**14.27**  While regulatory action by the Commissioner against media organizations in respect of the processing of personal information for journalistic purposes is likely to be limited, because of the s 32 exemption and the Commissioner's limited powers with respect to enforcement notices in such cases, media organizations ought nevertheless to be mindful of the Commissioner's regulatory regime with respect to other processing of data, not least because of the Commissioner's powers to impose significant fines on data controllers for serious contraventions of the Act.

*(a) Monetary penalties*

**14.28**  By ss 55A—E DPA, introduced into the Act by the Criminal Justice and Immigration Act 2008,[55] the Commissioner has the power to serve monetary penalty

---

[51]  s 42 DPA.
[52]  s 40 DPA.
[53]  s 45 DPA.
[54]  s 46 DPA.
[55]  ss 55A–E DPA came into force on 6 April 2010. In addition, the same powers concerning monetary penalties were inserted into the Privacy and Electronic Communications (EC Directive) Regulations 2003 by the Privacy and Electronic Communications (EC Directive) (Amendment) Regulations 2011, SI 2011/1208.

notices on data controllers if he or she is satisfied that there has been a serious breach of the data protection principles, the breach was of a kind likely to cause 'substantial damage' or 'serious distress', and either the breach was deliberate, or the data controller knew or ought to have known that there was a risk that the breach would occur, and that such a breach would be of a kind likely to cause substantial damage or substantial distress, but failed to take reasonable steps to prevent the breach.[56] Notices are 'used as both a sanction and a deterrent against data controllers or persons who deliberately or negligently disregard the law'.[57] The Commissioner is required to publish guidance on how it exercises its powers to serve monetary penalty notices.[58] Such guidance sets out, amongst other things, the circumstances in which the Commissioner will consider it appropriate to serve a monetary penalty.

The Commissioner's powers to impose monetary penalties apply to all types of **14.29** data controllers in the private, public, and voluntary sectors with a small number of exceptions.[59] A media organization could, for example, find itself on the receiving end of a monetary penalty notice for a serious breach of the Act involving the accidental loss of personal data, whether or not associated with its journalistic activities.[60]

### (b) The size of monetary penalties imposed

Fines imposed by the Commissioner tend to be in the tens or hundreds of **14.30** thousands of pounds. The maximum monetary penalty the Commissioner can impose is £500,000.[61] In deciding what figure to impose, the Commissioner will look at the facts and circumstances of the particular case. At the time of writing, the Commissioner has imposed three monetary penalty notices in 2015: two in respect of contraventions of the DPA[62] and one for a breach of

---

[56] s 55A DPA.

[57] Data Protection Regulatory Action Policy, v 2, August 2013.

[58] s 55C(1) DPA: 'The Commissioner must prepare and issue guidance on how he proposes to exercise his functions under sections 55A and 55B.' The relevant guidance is entitled *The Information Commissioner's guidance about the issue of monetary penalties prepared and issued under section 55C(1) of the Data Protection Act 1998* and can be downloaded from the Information Commissioner's Office's website.

[59] By s 55(A) the Commissioner cannot impose a monetary penalty notice on the Crown Estate Commissioners or a person who is a data controller by virtue of s 63(3) of the Act, *ie* data controllers acting on behalf of the Royal Household, the Duchy of Lancaster, and Duchy of Cornwall.

[60] Data protection principle 7: 'Appropriate technical and organizational measures shall be taken against unauthorised or unlawful processing of personal data and against accidental loss or destruction of, or damage to, personal data.'

[61] s 55A(5) DPA, and Data Protection (Monetary Penalties) (Maximum Penalty and Notices) Regulations 2010, SI 2010/31, reg 2.

[62] In March 2015, the Information Commissioner's Office fined the Serious Fraud Office £180,000 after a witness in a fraud investigation was sent evidence relating to sixty-four other people involved in the case in error; and in April 2015, an online holiday insurance company was fined £175,000 after IT failings let hackers access customer records, leading to fraud on over 5,000 customers' credit cards.

the Privacy and Electronic Communications (EC Directive) Regulations 2003 (as amended).[63]

**14.31**  Monetary penalty notices are published on the Information Commissioner's Office's website. The penalty must be paid within the period specified in the notice which will be at least twenty-eight days after service of the monetary penalty notice. If the penalty is paid within twenty-eight days, the Commissioner reduces the penalty by twenty per cent. In the event a data controller does not pay, the penalty is recoverable by Order of the County Court or the High Court in England, Wales, and Northern Ireland.[64]

## D. Judicial Remedy or Regulatory Complaint?

**14.32**  The overlapping jurisdiction of the court and the media regulatory bodies in relation to protection of privacy means that a privacy complainant will need to consider not only whether he or she is able to make a complaint under the relevant regulator's rules and codes of practice as well as seek a legal remedy from the courts, but also consider the various advantages and disadvantages involved in taking either course of action.

### (1) Complaints which are also the Subject of Legal Proceedings

**14.33**  Ofcom will not consider or continue to consider complaints which are being pursued through the courts.[65] IPSO's Regulations state that it 'may, at its discretion, allow a complaint to be brought notwithstanding that legal proceedings (whether civil or criminal) may later be brought concerning the subject matter of the complaint'.[66] However, the Regulations are silent on whether it would entertain a complaint, or continue to entertain a complaint, where legal proceedings had already been initiated. Ofcom will also normally cease to consider a complaint that is being resolved through other channels, for example, through the broadcaster's own complaints procedures. The BBC Trust will not 'normally consider an appeal that is or has been the subject of legal correspondence with the BBC, or if legal proceedings have been issued . . .', however, there is no strict rule in this regard.[67]

---

[63] In February 2015, a personal injuries claims management company was issued with a monetary penalty for £80,000, for making direct marketing calls to people without their consent.

[64] In Scotland the penalty can be enforced in the same manner as an extract registered decree arbitral bearing a warrant for execution issued by the sheriff court or any sheriffdom in Scotland.

[65] See s 114(2) of the Broadcasting Act 1996 (as amended).

[66] IPSO Regulations, para 9. Note also that the IPSO Regulations state that it is 'not obliged' to consider complaints (para 8).

[67] *BBC Complaints Framework Procedure no.1: Editorial Complaints and Appeals Procedures* (October 2014) para 5.9.

## (2) Is there any Advantage in Making a Complaint to an Adjudicatory Body instead of Seeking a Judicial Remedy?

Although the remedies available to the complainant through the various regula- **14.34**
tory procedures are limited, there are three principal advantages of pursuing such
a course: first, a complaint does not cost anything and, if unsuccessful, will not
result in any award of costs against the complainant; secondly, the procedure is
easily accessible, informal, and non-legalistic; and thirdly, the complaint tends to
be resolved relatively quickly.

## (3) Is there any Disadvantage in Making a Complaint to an Adjudicatory Body instead of Seeking a Judicial Remedy?

One of the principal limitations to the powers of Ofcom and IPSO is that they **14.35**
have no powers to prevent broadcast or publication: the complainant must
apply through the courts for an injunction if he or she is seeking prior restraint.
Furthermore the regulators lack the legal power to award damages or a permanent injunction to complainants if their case is upheld.[68] Ofcom can impose a
fine on the relevant television or radio company licensee in appropriately serious
circumstances.[69] IPSO can also impose a fine, up to £1 million, in appropriate
circumstances.[70]

Another consideration is the short window of time in which complaints must be **14.36**
made to regulatory bodies, usually within a few months of broadcast or publication,[71] compared to the generally applied six-year limitation period for privacy
actions through the courts.[72]

---

[68] In *Peck v UK* (2003) 36 EHRR 41, paras 108–109, the European Court found that the lack of
legal power of the regulatory commissions to award damages to the complainant meant that those
bodies could not provide an effective remedy to him, within the meaning of Art 13 ECHR. The
Court noted that a regulator's power to impose a fine on the relevant television company did not
amount to an award of damages to the applicant.

[69] However, fines are rare, especially for privacy breaches. See 14.51.

[70] IPSO requires members to sign up to a regulatory regime which allows IPSO to issue fines
of up to £1m in suitably serious cases—see IPSO's *Financial Sanctions Guidance*, para 2.2 and the
*Scheme Membership Agreement*. This is marked contrast to the PCC which had no powers to fine
members. At the time of writing, in its first seven months of operation, IPSO has issued no fines to
members.

[71] Complaints to Ofcom about unwarranted infringements of privacy should be made within
twenty days—see *Procedures for the consideration and adjudication of Fairness and Privacy complaints*, para 1.11. IPSO's Regulations require complaints to be made within four months from the
date of conduct or first publication of the article complained of. However, if a complaint is received
after four months but within twelve months and the article remains accessible to the public on the
publisher's website, IPSO shall consider the complaint if it considers that it is still possible for it to
investigate and adjudicate fairly.

[72] On the applicable limitation periods in privacy type claims see 11.217 *et seq.*

### (4) Can a Complainant Pursue a Legal Remedy after an Adjudication Has Been Made?

**14.37** There is no reason in law why a complainant cannot pursue a legal remedy after an adjudication has been made by the relevant regulatory body, although the adjudication is not binding in any way in the legal proceedings. However, it may be of persuasive authority in view of the regard that the relevant legislation obliges the court to have to these codes of practice.[73] The risk for a complainant is that if his or her complaint is rejected by the adjudicatory body, then the court may be more reluctant to interfere with the regulator's decision. There is nothing however preventing a claimant from launching fresh proceedings in, for instance, misuse of private information, harassment, or even defamation if his or her complaint is rejected, if such a cause of action legitimately exists. If the complainant is minded to bring proceedings for defamation, it should be noted that the limitation period is one year in England and Wales.[74]

## E. The Regulatory Bodies

**14.38** There is a significant difference between the codes of conduct applicable to broadcasters and that applicable to the print media. The state has always retained control over the broadcast media, not least because broadcasting airwaves are limited. Radio and television broadcasters must be licensed[75] and the codes of conduct are part of this apparatus.[76] By contrast, despite frequent calls for statutory regulation, successive UK governments have preferred self-regulation of the print media, and indeed this position continues post the Leveson Inquiry. As noted above, in spite of the introduction of the Press Recognition Panel, created by Royal Charter, IPSO, currently the principal regulator of the newspaper and magazine industry, has no plans to seek recognition, and the Press Recognition Panel has no powers to compel it to do so. There being no limit to the volume of print media available, no licensing of the newspaper and magazine industry is required or permissible under Article 10, other than a formal system of registration or accreditation.

---

[73] See s 12(4) HRA and discussion of the authorities at 14.13–14.20. On the weight which the court will attach to the regulator's decision see 14.18–14.20.

[74] In *Hinks v Channel 4 Corp Ltd* (QBD, 3 March 2000, Morland J) the Court refused to extend the limitation period in circumstances where the claimants had awaited adjudications from the Broadcasting Standards Commission and Independent Television Commission before commencing proceedings, suggesting that an appropriate course of action would be to commence proceedings and then seek a stay from the court while the regulatory body considered a complaint.

[75] Art 10(1) ECHR makes clear that the right to freedom of expression does not prevent states from requiring the licensing of broadcasting, television, or cinema enterprises.

[76] It is a condition of a licence that a licensee has procedures in place for compliance with Ofcom's fairness and privacy code: Communications Act 2003, s 326.

One of the effects of this difference is that Ofcom has the power to revoke or **14.39** shorten the licences of commercial broadcasters,[77] whereas IPSO has no similar power over the print media. Ofcom can also require a broadcaster to publish a correction, or a statement of its findings.[78] While IPSO, under its Regulations, can require 'the Regulated Entity to publish a correction and/or an Adjudication', it has no real power to enforce such a remedy as membership is of course voluntary. The ultimate sanction for failing to comply with an adjudication, beyond a fine, would be expulsion from IPSO.

## (1) Broadcasters

### (a) Ofcom

Ofcom, which was established by the Office of Communications Act 2002 and con- **14.40** ferred its powers by the Communications Act 2003,[79] has regulatory responsibility across television, radio, telecommunications, and wireless communications services. Complaints and issues relating to cinema classifications, television and radio advertising, and video and video game rentals and sales fall outside Ofcom's remit and continue to be regulated by the British Board of Film Classification (BBFC), the Advertising Standards Authority, and the Video Standards Council respectively.

Ofcom has a very wide range of responsibilities. It regulates standards of harm **14.41** and offence, fairness, and privacy on all UK television and radio channels; licenses commercial television and radio; and oversees the telecommunications industry. Ofcom is statutorily committed to ensure that there is fair and effective competition in the media sector and, accordingly, the regulator has the power to rule on the public interest of media mergers and takeovers.

Ofcom is required under the Communications Act 2003 and the Broadcasting **14.42** Act 1996 (as amended) to draw up and implement a code for television and radio, covering standards in programmes, sponsorship, fairness, and privacy. This code is known as the Ofcom Broadcasting Code and applies to all radio and television content in services licensed by Ofcom,[80] or funded by the licence fee in the case of the BBC and S4C (the Welsh-language public service television channel), with certain exceptions in the case of the BBC.[81] The first Ofcom Code came into effect

---

[77] Communications Act 2003, s 238.
[78] Communications Act 2003, s 236(2).
[79] The Communications Act 2003 received Royal Assent in July 2003 and Ofcom began to fulfil its duties in December 2003.
[80] Broadcasters are required to observe the Code by the terms of their licences: see Communications Act 2003, s 325. Section 8 of the Ofcom Code relating to privacy and the guidance notes issued in conjunction with it are set out in Appendix G(i) (available at <http://www.5rb.com/publication/the-law-of-privacy-and-the-media>).
[81] Compliance by the BBC derives from an amendment to the BBC Agreement dated 4 December 2000, and in the case of S4C by statute (Communications Act 2003, s 203 and Broadcasting Act 1996, pt V).

on 25 July 2005 after a protracted period of consultation with broadcasters, consumers, and other interested parties.[82] Several updates to the Ofcom Code have since been published. The most recent version took effect in July 2015 and applies to all programmes broadcast on or after that date. Programmes broadcast prior to July 2015 are covered by the version of the Ofcom Code that was in force at the date of broadcast.

**14.43** The Ofcom Code was not intended simply to rewrite previous broadcasting regulatory codes but to usher in a new regulatory regime, rooted in the new parent broadcasting legislation, but also incorporating, where appropriate, the European Television without Frontiers Directive, the HRA, and the Audio Visual Media Services Directive.

**14.44** The Ofcom Code itself is divided into sections that represent the objectives set out in s 319(2) of the Communications Act 2003 and s 107(1) of the Broadcasting Act 1996. Those objectives have informed Ofcom's drafting of the Code which set out to provide adequate protection for under-eighteens in respect of programme content, to protect the public from harmful and offensive material, set standards for fairness and accuracy, ensure that content does not incite crime or lead to public disorder, secure impartial coverage of elections and referenda, and respect for religious views and beliefs, as well as ensuring that broadcasters avoid unwarranted infringements of privacy in the making of programmes.[83] In applying standards to television and radio services, Ofcom must have regard to the vulnerability of children and others whose circumstances appear to it to put them in need of special protection[84] as well as the need to guarantee an appropriate level of freedom of expression.[85] The Ofcom Code also includes provisions intended to regulate programmes for commercial and sponsorship interests and to safeguard editorial independence.[86] There are Guidance Notes published on each section of the Ofcom Code which, although non-binding, are provided to further assist broadcasters to interpret and apply the rules.

### (b) Ofcom complaints procedure

**14.45** Ofcom requires complaints about privacy to be made in writing and submitted through the completion of Ofcom's Fairness and Privacy Complaint Form, which

---

[82] Before 25 July 2005 the codes under which Ofcom adjudications on infringements of privacy were made were those of the legacy regulators, the Broadcasting Standards Commission Code on Fairness and Privacy, the Independent Television Commission Programme Code, and the Radio Authority's News and Current Affairs and Programme Code.

[83] See further Communications Act 2003, s 3(2) which states that Ofcom has a duty to apply standards that provide adequate protection to members of the public from the inclusion of offensive and harmful material (s 3(2)(e)), unfair treatment in programmes, and unwarranted infringements of privacy (s 3(2)(f)).

[84] Communications Act 2003, s 3(4)(h).

[85] Communications Act 2003, s 3(4)(g).

[86] See Ofcom Code, ss 9–10.

is available on its website. Broadcasters do not retain recordings of programmes indefinitely. As a consequence Ofcom may refuse to proceed with a privacy complaint received more than twenty working days after the relevant radio, satellite, cable, or terrestrial television broadcast.[87] If a complaint is submitted later than this date, Ofcom will weigh up all the relevant factors in deciding whether it is appropriate to consider the complaint.[88]

Once a fairness or privacy complaint is received, Ofcom will decide whether to **14.46** 'entertain' the complaint which involves assessing (i) whether the complainant falls under the definition of 'the person affected'; (ii) whether the matter is already the subject of legal proceedings in the United Kingdom; (iii) whether it is frivolous; and (iv) whether there is any other reason why it would be inappropriate to proceed.[89]

Once a complaint is entertained, Ofcom will ask the broadcaster to provide a state-  **14.47** ment in response to the complaint. Ofcom will then prepare its 'preliminary view' on the substance of the complaint, which is provisional only and subject to change in light of subsequent representations or material which are then invited from both sides.[90] Ofcom may decide to hold a hearing before reaching a decision if it considers that a hearing is appropriate, fair, and necessary to ensure that it can properly adjudicate on the complaint—for example, if there is a significant dispute of fact.[91] All such hearings are held in private. Ofcom aims to complete the consideration and adjudication of fairness and privacy complaints within ninety working days of the complaint being entertained.[92] Normally Ofcom will publish its final adjudication of the complaint in the Ofcom Broadcast Bulletin, an archive of which is maintained on the Ofcom website.

**Ofcom statutory sanctions**   When Ofcom finds a broadcaster in breach of the  **14.48** Code the matter may be referred to the Ofcom Executive for the determination of a sanction.[93] Ofcom is statutorily entitled to enforce a wide range of sanctions under s 392 of the Communications Act 2003. The sanctions available to Ofcom include directing the broadcaster not to repeat the offending item, or to broadcast

---

[87]  Ofcom's *Procedures for the consideration and adjudication of Fairness and Privacy complaints* (June 2011) paras 1.10–1.11. However, if a complainant pursues a privacy or fairness complaint directly with the broadcaster in the first instance then Ofcom may consider complaints after the relevant time period so long as he or she submits the complaint to Ofcom as soon as possible, and in any event within twenty working days of the final communication from the broadcaster: *ibid*, para 1.12.

[88]  Ofcom Fairness and Privacy Procedures (n 87) para 1.11.

[89]  Ofcom Fairness and Privacy Procedures (n 87): 'Entertainment Decision' box. An Entertainment Decision is usually made within twenty-five working days of receipt of a complaint: *ibid*, para 1.18.

[90]  Ofcom Fairness and Privacy Procedures (n 87) para 1.23.

[91]  Ofcom Fairness and Privacy Procedures (n 87) para 1.24 and pp 8–9.

[92]  Ofcom Fairness and Privacy Procedures (n 87) para 1.26.

[93]  Ofcom has published *Procedures for the consideration of statutory sanctions in breaches of broadcast licences.* The last updated version was published on 19 July 2013.

a correction or a summary of Ofcom's findings (the form and timing of which may be determined by Ofcom). The imposition of a fine is a further alternative sanction. The maximum fine Ofcom can impose is the greater of £250,000 or five per cent of the broadcaster's 'qualifying revenue'.[94] In the most extreme circumstances, a commercial broadcaster's licence may be shortened, suspended, or revoked but Ofcom does not have the power to shorten or revoke the licences of the BBC, S4C, or Channel 4. The imposition of a sanction is a serious matter and will only be considered where a broadcaster has seriously, deliberately, repeatedly, or recklessly breached the relevant requirement.[95]

**14.49** Although the revocation of a broadcasting licence is rare, since its inception in 2003, Ofcom has seen fit to revoke the licences of broadcasters on the basis of very serious, repeated breaches of the Ofcom Code. Ofcom terminated the cable auction channel Auctionworld's licence when it failed to remedy failures that Ofcom had already drawn to its attention in an earlier adjudication and Auctionworld's entering into administration suggested that it had materially misled Ofcom as to its financial position at the earlier adjudication.[96] Ofcom revoked the licences of a number of adult digital channels after they failed to remedy serious and repeated contraventions of the Code, including the transmission of highly explicit material without encryption.[97] In January 2012, Ofcom revoked the licence of Press TV Ltd when in the course of sanctions hearings in a privacy case (see 14.51), representations were made which suggested that editorial control of the channel rested with a media organization in Iran not licensed by Ofcom, which would amount to a breach of its licence conditions.[98]

**14.50** Otherwise Ofcom has imposed a range of fines from £500 (in the case of a regional radio station which failed to provide any radio service for nearly a month in breach of its licence conditions),[99] to the largest fine of £5,675,000 for ITV's failure to operate premium-rate phone lines on its television competitions fairly.[100]

**14.51** It is, however, relatively rare for a privacy or fairness case to merit the imposition of a heavy sanction. So far there have been three cases in which a breach of privacy has attracted a financial penalty from Ofcom. Two of the cases involved a prank call or 'wind-up' in which the broadcaster failed to seek consent from the participants prior to broadcast and the breaches were considered to be sufficiently

---

[94] Communications Act 2003, s 237(3). 'Qualifying revenue' is defined by the Broadcasting Act 1990, s 19 as all payments and financial benefits received by the broadcaster during the accounting year. In the case of the BBC, Ofcom can only levy fines of up to £250,000.

[95] Ofcom Statutory Sanctions Procedures (n 93) para 1.10.

[96] Adjudication in the case of Auctionworld Ltd (in administration), 17 December 2004.

[97] Adjudication in the case of Look4Love, 23 November 2006; also Adjudication in the case of Bang Media (London) Ltd and Bang Channels Ltd, 25 November 2010.

[98] Revocation Decision in respect of Press TV Ltd, 20 January 2012.

[99] Adjudication in the case of BBA Media Ltd (Westside Radio), 19 December 2011.

[100] See the Adjudications in the case of ITV2 Ltd, Granada Television Ltd and LWT (Holdings) Ltd, 8 May 2008.

serious and repeated to merit a significant fine.[101] In the third case, Press TV Ltd was fined £100,000 after a news item showed the complainant being held in an Iranian prison in circumstances where it was obvious that he was giving an interview under duress. Ofcom considered that because of the vulnerable position of the complainant, the broadcaster's failure to obtain his consent, and the effect which the broadcast had had on the complainant, the case represented a very serious and deliberate breach.[102]

### (c) The BBC

The BBC Trust is obliged, under the BBC's Charter, to ensure that there are in place guidelines designed to secure appropriate standards in the programmes it broadcasts as well as a framework within which the BBC should handle complaints.[103] It is required to observe certain aspects of the Ofcom Code including its provisions dealing with fairness and privacy. However, it is not subject to the sections of the Ofcom Code relating to accuracy and impartiality, elections and referenda, sponsorship, and commercial arrangements which remain the responsibility of the BBC Trust and can be addressed only by complaining to the BBC directly.[104] The BBC also has in place detailed and extensive provisions relating to privacy as part of its Editorial Guidelines, which are kept under review by the Editorial Policy team.[105]

**14.52**

Complaints should usually be made within thirty working days of the transmission of a programme.[106] At the first stage the complaint is considered by the BBC Executive. If the complainant is dissatisfied with this response, the second stage will be referral to the Editorial Complaint Unit, or a Senior Manager of the BBC Division responsible for the content, which will independently investigate the complaint. A further level of appeal ultimately lies with the BBC Trust.

**14.53**

The BBC will publish a public response to the complaint in the complaints section of its website along with any clarification, correction, or remedial action taken. The BBC will usually publish complaints on its website where the issue has attracted a high number of complaints. In addition, findings of the Editorial Complaints Unit are published on the BBC website as they arise and any subsequent appeals to the BBC Trust are published monthly.

**14.54**

---

[101] See Adjudication in the case of Kiss FM Radio Ltd, 20 June 2006, and Adjudication in the case of the BBC in respect of its service Radio 2, 3 April 2009. For further discussion, see 14.131–14.132.

[102] See the Decision of the Ofcom Broadcasting Sanctions Committee in respect of Press TV Ltd, 1 November 2012.

[103] BBC Charter (Cm 6925) (October 2006) s 24(2).

[104] Ofcom Code, preamble to ss 5, 6, 9, and 10.

[105] BBC Editorial Guidelines, Section 7, Privacy, is set out in Appendix G(ii) (available at <http://www.5rb.com/publication/the-law-of-privacy-and-the-media>).

[106] *BBC Editorial Complaints and Appeal Procedures* (26 June 2012) para 2.1.

### (2) Print Media

#### (a) Press Complaints Commission

**14.55** As noted above, the PCC no longer exists, and has been replaced by IPSO as the principal regulator for the newspaper and magazine industry. However, given IPSO's very recent introduction, and given that, at the time of writing, the Editors' Codebook,[107] that is the handbook which provides background to how the Editors' Code operates in practice, relies heavily on examples of PCC judgments, as indeed does this chapter (see Section F), it is instructive to consider briefly how the PCC operated and how it developed over the years, from its inception in the early nineties.

**14.56** The PCC was set up in 1991 as the response to government calls for regulation of press standards, replacing the former Press Council which the Calcutt Committee regarded as 'ineffective as an adjudicating body'.[108] It was a body to which members of the press voluntarily belonged, a system of self-regulation covering the majority of the newspaper and magazine industry both in print form and online.[109] The PCC, like IPSO does now, adjudged complaints with reference to the provisions of the Editors' Code.[110] Complaints raising possible breaches of the Editors' Code tended to be resolved swiftly by newspapers' editors, with the PCC adjudicating formally on the remainder, usually within forty days.

**14.57** The Editors' Code has evolved greatly from its introduction in 1991 to its present form often as a response to public concern about the press. For example, following the death of Princess Diana in 1997, the PCC recognized for the first time that 'everyone is entitled to respect for his or her private life' and incorporated Article 8(1) ECHR into its Code.[111] It placed limits on the publication of pictures of people in private places (without consent), along with the use of pictures taken as a result of persistent pursuit. In June 2004, the Editors' Code was amended again to reflect important advancements in technology, recognizing that the Privacy and Clandestine Devices sections needed to cover both mobile telephones and digital communications. The PCC also frequently issued public statements relating to

---

[107] I Beales, *The Editors' Codebook* (2014), available at <http://www.editorscode.org.uk/downloads/codebook/codebook-2014.pdf>.

[108] In 1993, Sir David Calcutt concluded that self-regulation of the print media by the PCC had failed and recommended the creation of a statutory body, the introduction of criminal offences, and for further consideration to be given to new civil remedies for invasion of privacy: see *Review of Press Self-Regulation* (Cm 2135, 1993) (Chairman: Sir David Calcutt, QC). None of these proposals was implemented.

[109] PCC Press Release, 25 September 1997: Speech of Lord Wakeham at a press conference in Parliament Chamber, Crown Office Row, Temple; also PCC Press Release, 8 February 2007 which extended the PCC's remit to include editorial audio-visual material on newspaper and magazine websites.

[110] The Editors' Code is often incorporated into editors' and journalists' contracts of employment.

[111] Although an oddity about the incorporation of Art 8(1) into the Code is that it adds 'health' as one of its protected matters.

the conduct of the press. For example, in September 2012, after the PCC received nearly 4,000 complaints concerning the publication by *The Sun* of photographs of Prince Harry taken in a Las Vegas hotel room, it issued a public statement stating that it would not open an investigation into the matter in the absence of a formal complaint by the Prince, but reiterating the Editors' Code's provisions on the photographing of individuals in private places without their consent.[112]

**14.58** The PCC only considered written complaints. Unlike Ofcom, the PCC did not hold hearings. The PCC would generally only accept complaints within two months of publication of the article or close of correspondence with the editor unless special circumstances applied. Unlike Ofcom, the PCC did not adjudicate on matters of taste and decency, or fairness, even where it affected other legitimate considerations under its Code.[113]

**14.59** Where a complaint was upheld against a publisher, the PCC could 'oblige' the newspaper or magazine to publish in full and with due prominence a critical adjudication of the article in question, but this was not a binding obligation.[114] If the breach was particularly serious, the PCC could refer the editor to his or her publisher to address the areas of concern, which could lead to further public rebuke.

### (b) The Independent Press Standards Organisation

**14.60** IPSO is now the principal regulator of editorial content within printed newspapers and magazines, as well as editorial content on electronic services operated by its members ('regulated entities'): such as websites, apps, and interactive content. Like the PCC, complaints are judged against the Editors' Code, and IPSO will not consider complaints about: (i) advertising, which will continue to be handled and adjudicated on by the Advertising Standards Authority; (ii) books; (iii) 'user generated content' posted on members' websites that has not been reviewed or moderated by the site's operators; and (iv) complaints about matters of taste and decency and due impartiality. Unlike the PCC, however, IPSO provides a confidential whistle-blowing hotline for individuals who have been requested by the organizations they work for to act in a way that is contrary to the Editors' Code.

**14.61** IPSO's Regulations state that it may, but is not obliged to, consider complaints '(a) from any person who has been personally and directly affected by the alleged breach of the Editors' Code; or (b) where an alleged breach of the Editors' Code is significant and there is substantial public interest in the Regulator considering the complaint, from a representative group affected by the alleged breach; or (c) from a

---

[112] 'PCC statement on Prince Harry photographs', 6 September 2012.

[113] In the complaint brought by Madeleine Moon MP against *The Sunday Times*, 25 May 2008 (Report 78) the PCC refused to consider whether a large picture of a noose was tasteless or offensive in the context of a story about suicide victims even though the complainant said it added to the intrusion into grief and shock under cl 5 of the Code.

[114] This is due to the self-regulation system of the press, which means that the PCC had no statutory powers of enforcement.

third party seeking to correct a significant inaccuracy of published information'.[115] Complaints must be made within four months (double the period required by its predecessor the PCC) from the date of the conduct, or first publication of the article complained of. However, if the article remains available to the public online or by other electronic means, IPSO will consider complaints within twelve months of first publication, as long as IPSO considers that it is still possible to investigate and adjudicate fairly in view of the passage of time.

**14.62**  Complaints which fall within IPSO's remit, disclose a possible breach of the Editors' Code, and are not rejected by IPSO after initial consideration, will be investigated by the Complaints Committee. After seeking comment from the regulated entity, IPSO will aim to find a satisfactory solution through mediation. Where mediation is unsuccessful, the Complaints Committee will make a determination as to whether or not the regulated entity has breached the Editors' Code. In cases of breach, the Complaints Committee will issue its adjudication, which may include a requirement that the regulated entity takes remedial action, which will normally be the publication of 'a correction and/or an Adjudication'. The nature, extent, and placement of such corrections and adjudications will be decided by IPSO. Complainants, unhappy with a determination of the Complaints Committee may request a review by the 'Complaints Reviewer' but only on the basis that the decision is 'substantially flawed'. Any such request must be made to IPSO within fourteen days of the original decision being made.

**14.63**  In certain circumstances, IPSO may decide to undertake a 'Standards Investigation', for example where IPSO 'reasonably considers that there may have been serious and systemic breaches of the Editors' Code (a Systemic Failure)'. The procedure for such investigations by an 'Investigation Panel' is set out in IPSO's Regulations.[116] Following such an investigation and decision by the Investigation Panel (or Review Panel), IPSO may impose one or more of the following sanctions: a requirement that the regulated entity publish the panel's findings (which may include a requirement to take remedial action); pay a fine;[117] pay the reasonable costs of the Standards Investigation; and in appropriate cases, terminate the regulated entity's membership of IPSO.

## F. The Codes and Adjudications

**14.64**  The main provisions in each of the codes concerning the right to privacy are set out in Appendix G. Section 8 of the Ofcom Broadcasting Code, which deals with privacy, and the Guidance Notes issued in conjunction with it, are reproduced in Appendix G(i). Channel 4's Producers Handbook provides a useful practical guide to the

---

[115] IPSO Regulations (27 November 2013) cl 8.

[116] See IPSO's website.

[117] Any fine will be determined in accordance with the Financial Sanctions Guidance—see IPSO's website.

Ofcom Code and the relevant law and procedure applying to the making and broadcast of television programmes.[118] The provisions of the BBC Editorial Guidelines (Section 7) regarding privacy are reproduced in Appendix G(ii). It contains the same wide-ranging provisions relating to privacy that programme-makers are obliged to adhere to, if presented in a more prescriptive form. All of the Appendices are available at <http://www.5rb.com/publication/the-law-of-privacy-and-the-media>.

A new version of the Editors' Code was ratified in late 2015 and comes into effect **14.65** on 1 January 2016. It replaces the 2014 version. Unless specified, references in this work are to the 2016 Code but both versions are reproduced in Appendix G(iii). For a detailed analysis of the Editors' Code and the most relevant adjudications, see *The Editors' Codebook*.[119]

The adjudications of the bodies are referred to where relevant below.[120] Since IPSO **14.66** only came into existence in September 2014, there are still at the time of writing very few reported privacy adjudications. However, both the 2014 and 2016 Editors' Codes share strong similarities with the Editors' Code that was applied by the PCC; indeed, the 2014 and PCC versions were almost identical. It is therefore likely that previous decisions of the PCC will continue to be of assistance in determining how IPSO is likely to approach matters. We therefore continue to refer below to relevant adjudications of the PCC.

## (1) The Right to Privacy

The Ofcom, BBC, and Editors' Codes all state that intrusions into an individual's **14.67** right to privacy without consent must be justified[121] although there is variation between the bodies as to what will constitute such justification. It is impossible to attempt a comprehensive definition of what is considered 'private' by the different bodies beyond the provisions of the codes, but clarification or elaboration is to some extent possible by reference to the adjudications examined below. Ofcom and the BBC provide guidance on the meaning of 'legitimate expectation of privacy' in their codes, describing the concept as varying according to the place and nature of the information or activity, the extent to which the information is in the public domain, and whether the individual concerned is already in the public eye.[122]

Both Ofcom and IPSO incorporate into their codes the text of Article 8(1) **14.68** ECHR.[123] The BBC Editorial Guidelines similarly refer to the 'right to privacy'

---

[118] The full guide is available at <http://www.channel4.com/producers-handbook/>.

[119] *The Editors' Codebook* (n 107).

[120] The adjudications are cited by referring to the complainant, the publication or programme complained of, the date of the publication or broadcast, and the report or bulletin in which the complaint is reported. References to PCC adjudications from 2010 onwards do not carry report numbers.

[121] *eg* by being outweighed by the public interest. See eg BBC Editorial Guidelines, para 7.2.3. Ofcom uses the term 'warranted' as opposed to 'justified'.

[122] See Ofcom Code, s 8 and BBC Editorial Guidelines, para 7.1.

[123] See Ofcom Code, App 3 and Editors' Code, cl 2(i). The Editors' Code includes 'health' as one of the rights protected by Art 8.

under the HRA.[124] Aside from the codes' explicit referral to the 'right to privacy', other aspects of individuals' private lives are covered by provisions in the codes dealing with topics such as doorstepping (the act of confronting someone unannounced outside his or her home for interview), harassment, and secret recording.

**14.69**   Examples of material that has been considered 'private' by Ofcom includes: identifiable footage of children broadcast without parental consent;[125] secretly recorded telephone calls;[126] footage of complainants in hospitals and prisons,[127] at work[128] (even in a public place),[129] at a private party,[130] and at a funeral;[131] footage of their home and car,[132] bedroom and personal possessions;[133] their email address,[134] telephone number,[135] sexual orientation,[136] marital problems,[137] and cosmetic surgery;[138]and photographs of a complainant in a bikini and shortly after giving birth.[139]

[124]  BBC Editorial Guidelines, para 18.5.

[125]  Mr and Mrs Hodgson, *Calendar News*, ITV Yorkshire, 22 July 2004 (Bulletin 65); Ms P, *Nurseries Undercover: The real story*, BBC1, 12 August 2004 (Bulletin 72); Ms V on behalf of her daughter (a Minor); *Dispatches*, Channel 4, 7 July 2004, (Bulletin 77); Mrs G and her daughter, *East Midlands Today*, BBC1 (East Midlands), 6 April 2006 (Bulletin 81); Ms K on behalf of her son, child K, *Child Chain Smoker*, C4, 28 June 2007 (Bulletin 106); Mrs D on behalf of daughter (a minor), *Daddy Daycare*, C4, 22 February 2012 (Bulletin 212); Mrs Janet Neal on behalf of grandchildren, *East Midlands Today*, BBC East Midlands, 16 November 2012 (Bulletin 230).

[126]  Mr Martin Payne, *Rogue Traders*, BBC1, 15 September 2005 (Bulletin 66); Ms Rebecca Gauld, *Katie and Peter: The baby diaries*, ITV2, 19 July 2007 (Bulletin 113).

[127]  On behalf of Morecambe Bay Hospitals NHS Trust, *Sky Report*, Sky News, 21 March 2006 (Bulletin 80); Ms Lisa Rodrigues on behalf of Sussex Partnership NHS Trust, *Dispatches: Britain's mental health scandal*, C4, 9 October 2006 (Bulletin 94); Mr A, *Strangeways*, ITV1, 23 May 2011 and Mr Timothy Hawley, *The Prison Restaurant*, BBC1, 26 April 2011 (Bulletin 189); Mr E, *Battle Scarred: Soldiers Behind Bars*, Channel 5, 8 April 2013 (Bulletin 240).

[128]  Mr W, *Terror in the Skies: A Tonight Special*, ITV1, 4 June 2007, (Bulletin 107); Mr Lennart Hane, *Insider*, TV3 (Sweden) 12 and15 October 2006 (Bulletin 113); Mr Christopher Hook, *Watchdog*, BBC1, 3 June 2010 (Bulletin 232); Complaints by Ms Rachel Gray, Mr Lynton Spence and Mr Lee Hollywood, *Exposure: The British Way of Death*, ITV1, 26 September 2012 (Bulletin 236). In Mariette McArdle, *Dispatches: Undercover Hospital*, C4, 11 April 2011 (Bulletin 231) the complainant's personal views about the workplace were held to be private given that she did not know she was being filmed.

[129]  Mr David Gamell, *Grimefighters*, ITV1, 12 April 2011 (Bulletin 191).

[130]  Glenn Swallow, *Weekend Nazis*, BBC1, 27 August 2007 (Bulletin 121); Ms D, *The Hotel*, C4, 20 January 2013 (Bulletin 236); cf Ms D, *Sunday Brunch*, C4, 27 January 2013 (Bulletin 236) where a complaint by the same complainant was not upheld as the footage was innocuous.

[131]  Miss Grace Nyesigire, *Swahili Diaries*, BEN TV, 10 January 2012 (Bulletin 207).

[132]  Mrs Susan Holland and Mr Marc Asquith, *Y Byd ar Bedwar*, S4C, 14 June 2005 (Bulletin 75).

[133]  Rebecca Gauld, *Katie and Peter: The baby diaries*, ITV2 19 July 2007 (Bulletin 113).

[134]  Mr Paul Anthony; *The James Whale Show*, talkSPORT, 26 April 2007 (Bulletin 103).

[135]  Dr Fazal Mahmood, Mr Gulam Robbani, and Mr Shah Hadi, *Bangladesh Protideen, News,* and *Friday Plus*, Bangla Television, various dates June—September 2007 (Bulletin 122); Mr David Edwards on behalf of Mrs Lisa Edwards, *Eastenders*, BBC1, 7 September 2009 (Issue 156); Mrs Alison Hewitt, *Panorama: Wills the Final Rip Off*, BBC1, 9 August 2010 (Bulletin 178).

[136]  Mr Jeremy Bamber, *Killing Mum and Dad: The Jeremy Bamber Story*, Sky Three, 14 September 2010 (Bulletin 190).

[137]  Mr David Johnson, *Soapbox with Chris Hossack*, Phoenix FM, 1 July 2011 (Bulletin 197).

[138]  Miss B, *The Ugly Face of Beauty*, C4, 20 July 2010 (Bulletin 191); Miss F, *Central News*, ITV1, 12 February 2012 (Bulletin 213).

[139]  Mrs Taryn Sherwood, *Hidden Lives: Middle aged mummy's boys*, Five, 17 October 2005 (Bulletin 78).

In the limited adjudications available, IPSO has so far held that a pixe- **14.70**
lated but identifiable photograph of an injured girl at an accident scene was
private.[140] It has further rejected complaints that the following information is
private: the general location of a Saudi princess's London home,[141] a ten-year-
old criminal conviction,[142] and details of a Tunisian man's relationship with a
British woman where the woman wished to tell her story.[143] As for prior adjudications by the PCC, 'private' material included information concerning a
complainant's rental payments;[144] health, disability, and medical condition;[145]
pregnancy;[146] mobile phone number;[147] emails and correspondence;[148] childhood abuse;[149] pictures taken of the inside of a complainant's home,[150] in the
workplace,[151] and on holiday topless (even where they had been published
previously).[152]

### (a) Who can complain?

Ofcom will normally only consider privacy complaints made by the 'person **14.71**
affected' by the programme or by a person authorized by him or her.[153] 'A
person' means an individual, association, or corporate body and 'the person
affected' is a person whose privacy may have been infringed in a programme
or in the making of a programme.[154] In exceptional cases, a member of the
family of the person affected, a personal representative, or someone closely
connected to that person (such as an employer or a body of which he or she
was a member) may make a complaint without having obtained the authority of the person affected: for example, if the person affected has died or is

---

[140] A woman v *Derby Telegraph*, 20 November 2014 (01866-4).
[141] HRH Sara bint Talal bin Abdulaziz v *Sunday Telegraph*, 21 September 2014 (0334-14).
[142] Adris v *Lancashire Telegraph*, 28 August 2014 (0205-14).
[143] Moueli v *The Sun*, 31 July 2014 (01328-14); Moueli v *Daily Star*, 31 July 2014 (01208-14); Moueli v *The Daily Mail*, 31 July 2014 (01327-14).
[144] Mrs Kim Noble and *Jersey Evening Post*, 6 December 2001 (Report 57).
[145] Mrs Judith Tonner and *News of the World*, 21 July 2002 (Report 60); A man and *Dorset Echo*, 17 January 2008 (Report 77); Mr and Mrs Addai-Twumasi and *MK News*, 8 November 2006 (Report 74); Mark and Jo-Ann Pitt v *Cambrian News*, 21 July 2011; A married couple and *Camberley News & Media*, 13 July 2012.
[146] In particular before the twelve-week scan: see Joanne Riding and *The Independent*, 8 March 2006 (Report 73); Charlotte Church and *The Sun*, 23 February 2007 (Report 75).
[147] A couple and *The Loughborough Echo*, 22 August 2008 (Report 78).
[148] Mrs Primrose Shipman and *The Mirror*, 9 July 2001 (Report 56); Brian McNicholl and *The News of the World*, 15 July 2007 (Report 75); A woman v *Sunday Life*, 25 June 2012; cf Ian Stewart Brady v *Daily Mirror*, 2 December 2011 (letters sent by the complainant, a convicted murderer, to a member of the public not private).
[149] A Woman v *Take A Break*, 17 February 2011.
[150] A woman and *Barking and Dagenham Recorder*, 15 May 2008 (Report 77); Carolyn Popple and *Scarborough Evening News*, 5 February 2008 (Report 77).
[151] Mark Kisby and *Loaded*, February 2006 (Report 73).
[152] Ms June McKibbin and *Sunday World*, 10 January 2014.
[153] Broadcasting Act 1996, s 111(1) (as amended).
[154] See Ofcom Fairness and Privacy Procedures (n 87) para 1.6 and 'Entertainment Decisions' box.

unable to give authority because he or she is vulnerable or under the age of sixteen.[155]

**14.72** Ofcom has adjudicated on a complaint by a couple who claimed that their privacy had been infringed by footage of their elderly mother being verbally abused in a care home even though they themselves did not feature in the programme. Ofcom held that 'the nature of the images, together with the close family connection of the complainants did give them a legitimate expectation of privacy'.[156] It gave a similar ruling in relation to the family members of an elderly man, who had been shown receiving medical treatment just before his death, holding that footage of him in a vulnerable state was private 'to him and his family'.[157]

**14.73** IPSO will accept complaints from a person 'directly affected' by the article or journalistic conduct or someone authorized on his or her behalf.[158] It can also take forward complaints from representative groups where the alleged breach of the Editors' Code is significant and there is a public interest in IPSO doing so.[159] In an adjudication, it has held that where private details relate only to a deceased person, this cannot establish a breach of privacy.[160]

**14.74** IPSO has claimed to possess the power to initiate its own investigations absent a complaint from a member of the public. For example, IPSO decided to initiate its own investigation into the *Sunday Mirror*'s news-gathering techniques after the newspaper published an article about a Tory Minister's sexual online communications with an undercover reporter. The newspaper cooperated with the investigation but maintained that IPSO did not possess such a power in the absence of a complaint. The Regulator did not accept this contention but did acknowledge that the power 'needs to be more explicitly stated in its regulations'.[161]

*(b) Are some people less entitled to privacy?*

**14.75** The BBC Editorial Guidelines state that those whose behaviour is 'criminal or seriously anti social' are less entitled to the right to privacy.[162] Similarly, Ofcom has held that 'where a person is filmed either committing or being arrested for an offence, that

---

[155] Ofcom Fairness and Privacy Procedures (n 87) para 1.6, n 12.

[156] Mr and Mrs R, *Look North*, BBC1, 30 August 2007 (Bulletin 111).

[157] Mrs Yvonne Charley Walsh on her behalf and on behalf of Mrs M A Mallender, Mr Johnnie Mallender and Mr David Mallender, *999 What's Your Emergency?*, C4, 22 October 2012 (Bulletin 234).

[158] See IPSO's website: 'Making a Complaint' section.

[159] IPSO's website: 'Making a Complaint' section.

[160] See Hart v *Swindon Advertiser*, 11 September 2014 (0122-14). This is consistent with the previous regulator's view—see *eg* the PCC's adjudication in Messrs Manches on behalf of the Tolkien family and *Sunday Mercury*, 26 January 2003 (Report 62).

[161] IPSO Ruling on 'Issues Arising from an Article in the Sunday Mirror on 28 September 2014'.

[162] BBC Editorial Guidelines, Section 7: Privacy, 'Introduction, Legitimate Expecations of Privacy'.

person's expectation of privacy is diminished in light of their actions'.[163] The previous press regulator, the PCC, had considered that its Code 'confers rights to privacy on everyone...no matter how horrendous their crimes',[164] a statement that had been designed to prevent the print media from reporting an infamous prisoner's every move with the claim that such reporting was 'in the public interest'.[165] IPSO has not yet clarified its position on the rights of privacy of criminals and prisoners—however, the Editors' Code provides that 'everyone' is entitled to respect for his or her private and family life, though there may be a public interest exception where journalists are 'detecting' or exposing crime or the threat of crime, or serious impropriety'.

The Editors' Code further states that in justifying any intrusions into an individu-  **14.76**
al's private life, '[a]ccount will be taken of the complainant's own public disclosures of information',[166] implying that those who have publicly revealed certain aspects of their personal life may have a diminished expectation of privacy.

### (2) The Public Interest

By far the most common justification for intruding upon someone's right to privacy  **14.77**
is that the information published or sought to be published is in the public interest. The Ofcom Code states that revealing or detecting crime, protecting public
health or safety, exposing misleading claims made by individuals or organizations,
or disclosing incompetence that affects the public are all examples of publications
in the public interest.

Examples of issues that Ofcom has so far considered to be in the public interest  **14.78**
include the standard of care in nurseries,[167] care homes,[168] and prisons;[169] showing
the work of the police and emergency services;[170] revealing concerns about aviation

---

[163] See Mr Kulwarn Cheema, *Road Wars*, Sky3, 20 August 2008 (Bulletin 129); also Howell Solicitors on behalf of Andrew Jones, *Shops, Robbers and Videotape*, BBC1, 17 May 2006 (Bulletin 89).

[164] Ian Stewart-Brady and *The Liverpool Echo*, 12 January 2000 (Report 49); also Rampton Hospital Authority and *The Sun*, 11 April 2000 (Report 50).

[165] It reiterated this position in 2007 when considering a complaint by a convicted murderer, stating that '[i]ndividuals do not forfeit their rights to privacy...if they have committed serious crimes': Peter Coonan (formerly Sutcliffe) and *News of the World*, 23 July 2006 (Report 74). Nonetheless the PCC acknowledged that the complainant in this case had committed extremely grave crimes which had 'earned' him the enduring scrutiny and interest of the press and the public.

[166] Editors' Code, cl 2(ii)

[167] Ms Rubina Khan and *Nurseries Undercover: The real story*, BBC1, 12 August 2004 (Bulletin 84); Mrs M on behalf of her child and *Whistleblower: Childcare*, BBC1, 5 March 2008 (Bulletin 116); Mrs Tabussum Ahmed, *Dispatches: How Safe is your Child's Nursery*, C4, 11 February 2013 (Bulletin 238).

[168] Mr and Mrs R, *Look North*, BBC1, 30 August 2007 (Bulletin 111); see also Mr Peter Houghton on behalf of South West London and St George's Mental Health NHS Trust, *Dispatches: Britain's mental health scandal*, Channel 4, 9 October 2006 (Bulletin 102) where it was held that there was a public interest in the level of care provided to patients in mental health wards.

[169] Mr Montgomery and *Prison Undercover: The real story*, BBC1, 9 March 2005 (Bulletin 65).

[170] Colin Hawkley, *Motorway Cops: Deadly Distractions*, BBC1, 11 January 2011 (Bulletin 194); Mr A, *999: What's Your Emergency?*, C4, 10 September 2012 (Bulletin 226);

security;[171] animal welfare;[172] Islamist extremism;[173] the investigation of unqualified tradesmen[174] and other questionable business practices;[175] and attitudes to homosexuality in professional football.[176]

**14.79**  Similarly, the 2014 Editors' Code stated that the public interest includes '(i) detecting or exposing crime or a serious impropriety; (ii) protecting public health and safety; (iii) preventing the public from being misled by some statement or action of an individual or organisation'. The 2016 Editors' Code adds four further categories: '(iv) Disclosing a person or organizations's failure or likely failure to comply with any obligation to which they are subject; (v) Disclosing a miscarriage of justice; (vi) Raising of contributing to a matter of public debate, including serious cases of impropriety, unethical conduct or incompetence concerning the public; (vii) Disclosing concealment, or likely concealment, of any of the above.' It also adds exposing the threat of crime to point (i). Further, unlike the other Codes, both the 2014 and 2016 versions of the Editors' Code recognize a public interest in 'freedom of expression itself'. In cases involving children under sixteen, an 'exceptional public interest' must be demonstrated. The 2016 Editors' Code requires editors relying on a public interest defence to show not only that they had good reason to believe the public interest would be served, but how that decision was established at the time.

**14.80**  The BBC's Editorial Guidelines provide wider examples of public interest, which include exposing or detecting crime, exposing significantly antisocial behaviour, exposing corruption or injustice, disclosing significant incompetence or negligence, protecting people's health and safety, preventing people being misled by some statement or action of an individual or organization, and disclosing information that allows people to make a significantly more informed decision about matters of public importance.

*(a) Detecting or exposing crime or serious impropriety*

**14.81**  The obtaining and broadcasting of secretly recorded material without an individual's consent may be justified where it is for the purpose of detecting or exposing crime or a serious impropriety. For example, a secretly recorded telephone call broadcast as part of an exposé of unqualified tradesmen was held by Ofcom to be warranted as it showed the complainant 'engaging in dangerous and illegal behaviour';[177] also, surreptitious filming of an individual at a private football event set up

---

Mrs Jacqueline Graham-Kevan on behalf of daughter, *Police Interceptors*, Channel 5, 11 February 2013 (Bulletin 239).

[171]  Mr W and *Terror in the Skies: A Tonight Special*, ITV1, 4 June 2007 (Bulletin 107).
[172]  Terence Millard, *Five News*, Five, 2 July 2008 (Bulletin 130).
[173]  Carter Ruck Solicitors on behalf of the Islamic Cultural Centre and the London Central Mosque, *Dispatches: Undercover mosque*, Channel 4, 15 January 2007 (Bulletin 97).
[174]  Mr Martin Payne and *Rogue Traders*, BBC1, 15 September 2005 (Bulletin 66).
[175]  Mr Zafer Mahmood and Meridian Foundation Ltd, *Dispatches: Landlords from Hell*, C4, 4 July 2011 (Bulletin 204); Christopher Hook, *Watchdog*, BBC1, 3 June 2010 (Bulletin 232).
[176]  Mr Tamika Mkandawire, *Britain's Gay Footballers*, BBC3, 30 January 2012 (Bulletin 214)
[177]  Mr Martin Payne and *Rogue Traders*, BBC1, 15 September 2005 (Bulletin 66).

for the purpose of enforcing outstanding arrest warrants has been held a matter of legitimate public interest.[178]

In July 2013, Ofcom conducted an investigation (uniquely on its own initiative) **14.82** into Sky's admission that it had authorized a journalist to intercept the email accounts of a couple later convicted of fraud-related offences in the well-known 'Canoe Man' case (so called because the man had faked his own death in a canoe accident to collect life insurance and pensions). Ofcom held, exceptionally, that the unauthorized access of emails was warranted in the particular circumstances as the case had attracted considerable media and public attention and the emails had been accessed with a view to detecting or revealing crime where there was a real prospect that the relevant evidence would otherwise go unnoticed.[179]

Programmes which follow the work of police officers or the emergency services **14.83** often give rise to difficult issues relating to the identification of individuals who are shown as they are arrested, questioned, detained, or charged, or otherwise engaging in antisocial or criminal behaviour. Ofcom has provided general guidance to programme makers on this issue, stating that:

> . . . [r]egard should be given to, for instance, the actions of the individual (including the relative seriousness of any antisocial or criminal behaviour on his/her part), what details about the individual are to be featured, and any public interest justification for breaching any expectation of privacy the individual may have. For example, there may be a difference between broadcasting the name and unobscured face of an individual who is subsequently found guilty of a criminal offence and broadcasting details of someone who is subsequently not charged with a criminal offence, or someone who is acquitted, or someone who is interviewed as a possible witness.[180]

In one of its few rulings so far on the public interest, IPSO investigated the *Sunday* **14.84** *Mirror* over a story that revealed that Conservative MP, Brooks Newmark, had exchanged sexually explicit images online with an undercover reporter posing as a young female Tory party activist. IPSO held that the use of subterfuge by the journalist was justified on the grounds that it exposed 'serious impropriety' on the part of an MP who had made public his commitment to promoting a positive role for women in politics and was subject to a duty to uphold the highest standards in public life.[181]

The previous press regulator, the PCC, published several adjudications on the issue **14.85** of whether photographs of a child seemingly engaging in criminal or antisocial behaviour could be published in the public interest. For example, it held that photographs of a fifteen-year-old boy throwing fire bombs at a freight train engaged the public interest in revealing serious and antisocial behaviour despite there being

---

[178] Gary Hall, *MacIntyre's Big Sting: Wembley*, Five, 22 February 2006 (Bulletin 91).

[179] 'Canoe Man' and news items relating to Mr John Darwin and Anne Darwin, Sky News channel and various broadcasts, July–December 2008 (Bulletin 233).

[180] Mr A, *999 What's Your Emergency?*, C4, 10 September 2012 (Bulletin 226); see also Mr Warren Skyers, *Traffic Cops: Running on Empty*, BBC1, 23 June 2011 (Bulletin 198).

[181] IPSO Ruling: '*Issues Arising from an Article in the Sunday Mirror on 28 September 2014*'.

no parental consent for publication.[182] However, where photographs of another complainant's son being handcuffed by officers in his bedroom were published without subsequent evidence of criminality, the PCC held that there was no public interest justification and a 'clear error of judgment' had been committed on the part of the newspaper.[183]

### (b) Protecting public health and safety

**14.86**  Ofcom has held that surreptitious filming in places as sensitive as the inside of a mental health ward was justified by the 'public interest in the safety of patients and staff'.[184] The Channel 4 documentary in this case had revealed the lack of resources and inadequate level of care in some hospitals around the country. It has also held that secretly filmed footage of a faith healer claiming to cure cancer through her methods was warranted by the public interest in exposing practices that might lead vulnerable and impressionable people to neglect or defer life-saving medical treatment.[185]

**14.87**  Ofcom has further found that the inclusion of secretly recorded footage of an airport security manager without his consent was justified where it was part of an exposé of aviation security problems. The programme alleged that security officers at the airport had been involved in a range of inappropriate behaviour including misuse of security procedures, drinking and sleeping while on duty, stealing, drug use, and drug smuggling. Ofcom's view was that the material broadcast 'had considerable public safety ramifications'.[186] It has also been held by Ofcom that surreptitious filming inside a mosque was warranted for the purposes of investigating whether Islamist extremism was being promoted or spread in Britain. In coming to its decision, Ofcom considered the legitimacy of the secret filming 'in the context of the recent terrorist attacks in Britain'.[187]

**14.88**  As yet, there have been no IPSO adjudications concerning the public interest in protecting public health and safety. However, there are a number of adjudications by the previous regulator, the PCC, on this issue. For example, there was held to be a considerable public interest justification in publishing photographs of a man making a delivery to a nursery school kitchen where he had previously been convicted for distributing, making, and possessing child pornography. The PCC

---

[182]  A man and *Northwich Guardian*, 14 and 18 July 2007 (Report 75).

[183]  A woman and *Barking and Dagenham Recorder*, 15 May 2008 (Report 77); see also Carolyn Popple and *Scarborough Evening News*, 5 February 2008 (Report 77) and Christopher Bourne and *Sunday Mercury*, 4 December 2005 (Report 72).

[184]  Lisa Rodrigues on behalf of Sussex Partnership NHS Trust, *Dispatches: Britain's mental health scandal*, Channel 4, 9 October 2006 (Bulletin 94); also Peter Houghton on behalf of South West London and St George's Mental Health NHS Trust, *Dispatches: Britain's mental health scandal*, Channel 4, 9 October 2006 (Bulletin 102).

[185]  Mrs Jennifer Johnstone, *Newsnight*, BBC2, 22 June 2011 (Bulletin 198).

[186]  Mr W, *Terror in the Skies: A Tonight Special*, ITV1, 4 June 2007 (Bulletin 107).

[187]  Carter Ruck on behalf of the Islamic Cultural Centre and the London Central Mosque, *Dispatches: Undercover mosque*, Channel 4, 15 January 2007 (Bulletin 97).

held that the newspaper was 'entitled to highlight, and comment robustly on, this situation'.[188] Conversely, the identification of a complainant's daughter as a sufferer of a rare brain condition, Creutzfeldt-Jakob Disease, in an article about the illness and its uncertain diagnosis was found by the PCC not to be in the public interest, as the identification itself was not necessary to inform the public about the illness.[189]

### (c) Exposing misleading claims

Another important aspect of the public interest is the need to protect the public **14.89** from being misled by a statement made by or on behalf of an individual, company, or organization. This aspect of the public interest has been acknowledged by the courts.[190] The courts have on many occasions taken account of the recognition of this aspect of the public interest in the Editors' Code when deciding whether to grant injunctions to restrain publication.[191]

There are few regulatory adjudications in which this issue has arisen. As noted at **14.90** 14.84, in one of the few adjudications that have so far been published by IPSO on the public interest, the regulator found that the subterfuge deployed by the *Sunday Mirror* in exposing an MP's sexual online exchanges was justified in the public interest. As well as revealing 'serious impropriety', IPSO held that it potentially prevented the public from being misled by the MP's purported commitment to the 'highest' standards of behaviour and his purported commitment to promoting an environment in which Conservative women could be appropriately encouraged in achieving political success.[192]

As for the PCC's previous decisions on this issue, in one case, the PCC held that **14.91** the use of subterfuge by a Sunday newspaper to obtain photographs of a Nazi shrine in the home of a policewoman was in the public interest as it prevented the public from 'being misled'.[193] The policewoman, who was married to a member of the British National Party, had specific responsibilities for investigating racially motivated crimes.[194] In another, the PCC rejected a complaint brought by Rupert Allason MP in respect of an article in the *Daily Mirror* entitled 'Tory MP and his mistress'.[195] The newspaper claimed that its publication of the six-page article alleging that the married MP was conducting an affair with a named woman was in the

---

[188] A woman and *The Sun*, 21 February 2007 (Report 77) although surreptitiously obtained footage of the same man working in a supermarket was not in the public interest.

[189] Mrs Janet Rutherford and *The Scottish Daily Mail*, 10 June 1996 (Report 37).

[190] See observations in *Campbell* (n 43) [24], [57], [80]–[83], [129], and [163] and *Ferdinand v MGN Ltd* [2011] EWHC 2454 (QB) [65]–[66], [85]–[86]; also *Woodward v Hutchins* [1977] 1 WLR 760, 764–5.

[191] See *eg Mosley* (n 13) [31]; *X and Y* (n 13) [49], [51]; *McKennitt* (n 13) [94]–[96]; *Douglas* (n 13) [186]; and *Mills* (n 12) [31].

[192] IPSO Ruling: '*Issues Arising from an Article in the Sunday Mirror on 28 September 2014*'.

[193] DC Linda Daniels and *The Sunday Telegraph*, 26 October 2003 (Report 65).

[194] See also Rupert Allason and *The Daily Mirror*, 9 May 1996 (Report 37).

[195] Rupert Allason and *The Daily Mirror*, 9 May 1996 (Report 37).

public interest, as he had not disabused the public of his previous proclamations in election literature that he was happily married—an argument which the PCC accepted.

### (d) Disclosing incompetence and failings

**14.92** The obtaining and subsequent broadcast of secretly recorded footage will often be warranted in the public interest where it reveals incompetence or systemic failings. For instance, Ofcom has found that secretly filmed footage of individuals in their workplaces is justified by the public interest in revealing serious failings in prisons,[196] nurseries,[197] care homes,[198] and the funeral industry.[199]

**14.93** However, there must be a 'sufficient' degree of public interest before such filming will be justified. Hence Ofcom held that there was a breach of its Code where footage secretly filmed inside a closed hospital ward was broadcast as part of a report on overspending in hospitals. There was no *prima facie* evidence that the story was in the public interest and the footage did not expose any wrongdoing or reveal any information which could not otherwise have been obtained by consent.[200] An unwarranted infringement of privacy was also found when covert footage of a lawyer in his office was broadcast where there was insufficient evidence that he had committed any malpractice or contravened professional standards.[201] Where surreptitiously obtained material does not in itself establish incompetence or failings, then it may be permissible in the public interest to record the footage but not subsequently to broadcast it.[202]

**14.94** In some cases, this category of public interest has been held to override the particular care that must be taken towards the privacy of children. Where a mother complained that her daughter's privacy had been infringed by covertly recorded footage of her behaving badly at school, Ofcom held that it was justified by the significant public interest in exposing failures in the secondary school system.[203] Similarly, the broadcast of surreptitiously filmed footage of a child at nursery was held by Ofcom to be warranted by the strong public interest

---

[196] Mr Montgomery, *Prison Undercover: The real story*, BBC1, 9 March 2005 (Bulletin 65).

[197] Ms Sheri Atherton, *Nurseries Undercover: The real story*, BBC1, 12 August 2004 (Bulletin 84); cf Ms Rubina Khan, *Nurseries Undercover: The real story*, BBC1, 12 August 2004 (Bulletin 84) where there was a breach in the same circumstances arising from insufficient obscuring of her identity.

[198] Mr and Mrs R, *Look North*, BBC1, 30 August 2007 (Bulletin 111).

[199] Ms Rachel Gray, Mr Lynton Spence and Mr Lee Hollywood, *Exposure: The British Way of Death*, ITV1, 26 September 2012 (Bulletin 236).

[200] Complaint on behalf of Morecambe Bay Hospitals NHS Trust, *Sky Report*, Sky News, 21 March 2006 (Bulletin 80).

[201] Mr Lennary Hane, *Insider*, TV3, 12 and 15 October 2006 (Bulletin 113).

[202] See Dr Christian Farthing, *Conning the Conmen*, BBC3, 29 March 2007 (Bulletin 127); also Dr Peter Proud, *Conning the Conmen*, BBC3, 29 March 2007 (Bulletin 127).

[203] Ms V on behalf of her daughter (a minor), *Dispatches*, Channel 4, 7 July 2004 (Bulletin 77).

in investigating the care of very young children.[204] However, in both these cases Ofcom's decision was heavily influenced by the fact that the child's face had been pixellated or heavily blurred; the level of intrusion was therefore held to be justified and proportionate.

### (3) Public Figures

The codes agree that people in the public eye, either through the position they hold **14.95** or the publicity they attract, are in a special position. Rule 8.1 of the Ofcom Code states that whether the individual concerned is already in the public eye is a factor to be considered when assessing whether he or she has a legitimate expectation of privacy. The BBC Editorial Guidelines state that people in the public eye may, in some circumstances, have a lower expectation of privacy but that the BBC will 'normally only report the private legal behaviour of public figures where broader public issues are raised either by the behaviour itself or by the consequences of its becoming widely known'.[205]

IPSO's ruling in the *Sunday Mirror* case (see 14.84 and 14.90) does suggest that **14.96** the private activities of those in the political sphere can legitimately be subject to closer scrutiny by the press than those of ordinary people—not least because there is greater potential for misleading the public through their public statements and political commitments.

The PCC also adopted this position in its adjudications. For example, it rejected **14.97** a complaint by Ruth Kelly MP (on behalf of her child) in respect of a *Daily Mail* article which reported how the Cabinet minister was sending one of her children to a private school for pupils with learning difficulties. The PCC held that the article highlighted a matter of considerable public interest in revealing that the MP had elected to remove her child from the state system and that the information about the child's learning difficulties was necessary in the context of the story.[206] The PCC did however take into account the steps which a public figure has previously taken to protect his or her privacy or that of his or her family in the past. This point is illustrated by the complaint brought by the author, JK Rowling, in respect of photographs of her daughter taken on a beach while on holiday. The PCC noted that Ms Rowling had gone to considerable lengths to protect her daughter's privacy in the past and upheld the complaint.[207] A similar complaint was made by the

---

[204] Mrs M on behalf of her child (a minor), *Whistleblower: Childcare*, BBC1, 5 March 2008 (Bulletin 116).

[205] BBC Editorial Guidelines, para 7.2.4 reproduced in Appendix G(ii) (available at <http://www.5rb.com/publication/the-law-of-privacy-and-the-media>).

[206] Ruth Kelly MP and *The Daily Mirror*, 8 January 2007 (Report 74); cf Blair and *The Mail on Sunday*, 24 January 1999 (Report 47) where there was no public interest in revealing that the Prime Minister's daughter had been admitted into a local Catholic school; and A man v *Hamilton Advertiser & Wishaw Press*, 3 November 2011, where the identification of the thirteen-year-old granddaughter of a politician was not necessary to the story.

[207] JK Rowling and *OK! Magazine*, 17 August 2001 (Report 56).

model, Elle Macpherson, against *Hello!* magazine in respect of photographs of her and her children on holiday in Mustique. In upholding the complaint, the PCC noted that Ms Macpherson had made a particular effort to choose a private holiday location, staying in a private villa on a secluded island.[208]

### (4) Information Already in the Public Domain

**14.98** Rule 8.1 of the Ofcom Code states that the extent to which material is in the public domain (if at all) is also a factor to be considered when assessing whether the information, activity, or condition in question is covered by a legitimate expectation of privacy.[209] The BBC Editorial Guidelines also 'take account of information already in the public domain or about to become available to the public' when considering what is in the public interest,[210] although the fact that other parts of the media bodies have published the information does not automatically justify the BBC in reporting it too.[211]

**14.99** Privacy complaints have been rejected by Ofcom where the footage complained of (in one case of Julian Assange dancing in a nightclub; in another of a woman working at a topless hair salon), although arguably private, had already appeared on the internet.[212] However, where the complainant had posted a Facebook comment containing private information about her breast implants to a closed group of 150 members, Ofcom found that the information was not in the public domain.[213]

**14.100** IPSO also adopts the principle that information already in the public domain is less likely to be considered 'private'. This is set out under the 'public interest' provision of its Code which states that: 'The Regulator will consider the extent to which material is already in the public domain, or will become so.' Where, for example, material had been posted by the complainant on the photograph-sharing app, Instagram, without applying privacy settings, IPSO concluded that it did not raise a breach under clause 3 of the Editors' Code.[214]

**14.101** The previous print regulator, the PCC, had published a specific guidance note—'Privacy and the Public Domain'—on the issue of material uploaded by individuals on the internet. It had stated that the publication of information on social networking sites such as Facebook, Twitter, and MySpace could blur the distinction between 'private' and 'public', particularly where the individual had not used privacy settings to restrict circulation of the information—nonetheless,

---

[208] Elle Macpherson and *Hello!*, 29 August 2006 (Report 74).
[209] On the relevance of public domain to confidence and privacy claims see 4.65 and 5.128 *et seq.*
[210] BBC Editorial Guidelines, para 7.1, 'The Public Interest'.
[211] BBC Editorial Guidelines, para 7.2.4.
[212] See *eg* Mr Julian Assange, *True Stories: Wikileaks—Secrets and Lies*, More 4, 29 November 2011 (Bulletin 213); also Ms Charlotte Allwood, *Anglia Tonight*, ITV1, 30 November and 1 December 2011 (Bulletin 209).
[213] Miss F, *Central News*, ITV1, 12 February 2012 (Bulletin 213).
[214] See *eg* Ward v *Daily Mail*, 24 November 2014 (02168-14).

the mere availability of material online did not in itself justify its republication to the public at large.

An example which illustrates this nuanced approach is a complaint about a 2009 **14.102** newspaper article claiming that several survivors of the Dunblane shooting in 1996—who at the time of publication were turning eighteen—had 'shamed' the memory of their schoolfellows by posting 'foul-mouthed boasts about sex, brawls, and drink fuelled antics' on social networking sites. The article was illustrated with photographs taken from these sites. The PCC had upheld the complaint, finding that although the images were freely available online, they appeared to have been taken out of context and presented in a way that was designed to humiliate and embarrass the authors. Their publication constituted a 'fundamental failure to respect their privacy', even though no specific steps such as the use of privacy settings had been taken to protect the material.[215] However, in another PCC case, a woman who had uploaded photographs of herself onto her Bebo site when she was fifteen found, three years later, they had been published in *Loaded* magazine with the heading 'The Epic Boobs Girl'. Although she was seemingly unaware that the images had been widely circulated on the internet, a Google search revealed 1,760,000 matches relating to her. The PCC expressed sympathy for the complainant but held that the information was so widely accessible that it did not raise a breach under the Editors' Code.[216]

*(a) The complainant's own public disclosures*

A related extension of the public domain principle is that adopted in the Editors' **14.103** Code that '[a]ccount will be taken of the complainant's own public disclosures of information'. This specific principle has not yet been explored by IPSO in its adjudications, however, there is a body of case law from the PCC era on this issue which is likely to be instructive. One of the earlier PCC decisions in which this principle was expressed related to a complaint brought by Julia Carling against *The Sun* in respect of an article reporting on her own relationships and that of her husband and the Princess of Wales.[217] In the view of the PCC, persons who put matters involving their private life into the public domain were less able to claim the protection of the Code when articles were published without their consent which sought to comment on, contrast, or clarify the impression given. The PCC took the view that Mrs Carling had clearly placed details of her past and current relationships into the public domain by virtue of articles and interviews designed, in part, to enhance her image and promote her career.

The principle of proportionality was also a key element of the PCC's application of **14.104** this principle. In a PCC complaint brought by a Scottish soap actress, Jacqueline

---

[215] Mullan, Weir and Campbell v *Scottish Sunday Express*, 22 June 2009 (Report 79).
[216] A woman v *Loaded*, 1 May 2010.
[217] Julia Carling and *The Sun*, 13 October 1995 (Report 32).

Pirie, against the *News of the World* about her relationship with a former fiancé,[218] the PCC emphasized that 'even when individuals do put matters concerning their private lives into the public domain... the press cannot reasonably justify thereafter publishing articles on any subject concerning them'. The PCC reviewed cuttings of interviews with Ms Pirie and could not find any examples of her discussing voluntarily such deeply personal matters as those which were contained in the newspaper's article. Noting the 'complete absence of proportionality between the subject matter of the article and the material that was already in the public domain about the relationship', the PCC considered that the complainant had not forfeited her right to privacy in the subject matter published and her complaint was upheld.[219]

### (5) Disclosure of Private Addresses

**14.105** Generally, disclosure of an individual's personal residential address will be a breach of the broadcasting codes unless such disclosure is justified. Rule 8.2 of the Ofcom Code states that 'information which discloses the location of a person's home or family should not be revealed without permission, unless it is warranted'. This clause is mirrored in the BBC Editorial Guidelines.[220] Business addresses, which are usually in the public domain, do not enjoy the same protection.[221] This principle has been extended to cases where the complainant has used his or her personal address for business purposes[222] or where the complainant has voluntarily put his or her home address and mobile phone number in a Yellow Pages advertisement.[223]

**14.106** If footage does not disclose the complainant's exact address or if it reveals only what can be seen of a house from a public highway, there will be no infringement of privacy.[224] The rationale for rejecting such complaints seems to be that such information could be obtained by any member of the public walking down the

---

[218] Granada Television on behalf of Jacqueline Pirie and *News of the World*, 23 January 2000 (Report 49).

[219] For an example of an adjudication where the subject matter of the article was considered proportionate to the information already in the public domain, and the complaint was not upheld, see Vanessa Feltz and *The Sunday Mirror*, 15 July 2001 (Report 56).

[220] BBC Editorial Guidelines, para 7.1, 'Legitimate Expectations of Privacy—Location'.

[221] See Sony Computer Entertainment UK Ltd, *Ian Wright's Unfit Kids*, Channel 4, 20 September 2006 (Bulletin 92) where Ofcom rejected a complaint by Sony that its privacy was infringed by the filming of the exterior of its offices; see also Maxwell Hodge Solicitors on behalf of Mr John Ball, *Old Dogs, New Tricks*, BBC1, 24 August 2006 (Bulletin 93).

[222] Kaiser Nisar, *News Bulletin*, Sunrise Radio, 23 March 2006 (Bulletin 98); Gary Segal and Hilary Segal, *NorthWest Tonight*, BBC1 North West, 3 and 11 April 2007 (Bulletin 107); Mrs Jennifer Johnstone, *Newsnight*, BBC2, 22 June 2011 (Bulletin 198); Mr Gareth Davies on behalf of himself and Apex Multiple Contractors, *The Ferret*, ITV1, 30 July 2012 (Bulletin 234).

[223] Jason Smith, *The Ferret*, ITV Wales, 19 November 2008 (Bulletin 139).

[224] See Makhtoor Hussain, *Sky News Report: Forced marriages*, BSkyB, 29 March 2006 (Bulletin 90); also Mr Harbinder Panesar on his own behalf and family, *X Ray*, BBC1 Wales, 13 and 20 February 2012 (Bulletin 216); John Barton Jayne, *Cowboy Traders*, Channel 5, 18 April 2012 (Bulletin 236).

complainant's street and is therefore effectively already in the public domain.[225] However, context is key—where similar information is included in the context of a light-hearted entertainment show, Ofcom's approach has been far stricter.[226]

Ofcom has also made a distinction between 'general footage' of a person's land and 'specific footage' of his or her house and car. The broadcast of the latter has been said to require an overriding public interest justification whereas the former may not infringe a person's privacy even if they are recorded and broadcast without consent.[227]

**14.107**

IPSO is yet to rule on the disclosure of actual addresses but where an article provided information about the general location and nature of a Saudi princess's London home, IPSO expressed concern but concluded on balance that the report did not include enough detail to constitute an intrusion into the complainant's private life.[228]

**14.108**

The PCC had developed a different approach to Ofcom and the BBC. It had expressly held that addresses were not intrinsically private and disclosure may be legitimate or in the public interest on some occasions.[229] For example, publication of a person's address in reports of criminal proceedings was usually permitted on the basis of the general public interest in the identification of individuals who had been charged with criminal offences.[230] Similarly, if the address was already a matter of public record or in the public domain, there was no infringement. In a complaint made by JK Rowling against the Scottish *Mail on Sunday*, *Daily Mirror*, and the *Daily Record*, the PCC held that restraining publication of the complainant's address served no further purpose as it was already revealed on the internet, the complainant's Wikipedia page, and other media reports.[231]

**14.109**

---

[225] See eg Lady Jane Ann Winterton MP, *North West Tonight*, BBC1 North West, 4 February 2008 (Bulletin 120); and Dr Fazal Mahmood and others, *Bangladesh Protideen*, *News*, and *Friday Plus*, Bangla Television, various dates June–September 2007 (Bulletin 122); and Tahmina Mahmood and others, *Friday Plus*, Bangla Television, various dates June–September 2007 (Bulletin 122).

[226] Mrs S, *On the Air*, BBC1 Northern Ireland, 27 October and 19 December 2006 (Bulletin 92) where even reference to the district in which the complainant lived was held to be unjustified.

[227] See Susan Holland and Marc Asquith, *Y Byd ar Bedwar*, S4C, 14 June 2005 (Bulletin 75); Miss Davies, *Homes Under the Hammer*, BBC1, 14 September 2012 (Bulletin 227).

[228] HRH Sara bint Talal bin Abdulaziz v *Sunday Telegraph*, 21 September 2014 (0334-14).

[229] JK Rowling and *The Mail on Sunday*, *Daily Mirror*, and the *Daily Record*, 21–2 October 2007 (Report 77). Compare *Green Corns v Claverly Group Ltd* [2005] EWHC 958 (QB), [2005] EMLR 31 [51] where the Court confirmed that the disclosure of a person's address was a matter quite properly protected by Art 8. This was so in spite of the fact that the individuals resident at the address were not named in the article. The Court held that it was appropriate to restrain the publication of addresses of unoccupied care homes (which were the subject of local opposition) rather than risk harm to as yet unidentifiable child residents and carers who would be there in the future. The protection afforded to individuals in the Editors' Code in relation to the disclosure of their addresses was noted by Tugendhat J at [61].

[230] Mr MJ Bretherick and *County Times*, 1 February 2007 (Report 75).

[231] JK Rowling and *Mail on Sunday*, *Daily Mirror*, and the *Daily Record*, 21–22 October 2007 (Report 77).

**14.110** However, identifying the addresses of high-profile celebrities or public figures with security problems was likely to be in breach of the Editors' Code.[232] For example, a *Mail on Sunday* article which revealed the district where Daniel Craig lived and showed a photograph of the actor's home was held to be in breach as publication was likely to attract overzealous fans or stalkers.[233]

### (6) Ordinary People in the News

#### (a) The identification of innocent people

**14.111** Several complaints have arisen in relation to the identification of friends or relatives of those accused or convicted of a crime. The Ofcom Code does not refer specifically to relatives or friends of those accused of a crime but has held that, where there is a major criminal trial of public concern, the attendance of family members in court would not attract an expectation of privacy. For example, there was no infringement of privacy where the complainant was filmed outside court in a news report about the conviction of her mother, Shirley Capp, during the Soham murder trials. Footage of the complainant's young children in the same context, however, was not warranted.[234] Where a complainant had taken particular steps to keep her relationship with a serial killer secret from her children and others, Ofcom held she had a legitimate expectation of privacy in respect of the family connection.[235]

**14.112** The Editors' Code states that the press must avoid identifying, without their consent, relatives or friends of persons convicted or accused of crime.[236] However, IPSO has held that a newspaper was justified in identifying a man who had accompanied a woman to court accused of running a local brothel. Although the complainant was not directly involved in the case itself, IPSO held that he had appeared with the accused in a public forum and the newspaper was entitled to publish information beyond that merely heard in the proceedings themselves.[237]

**14.113** The previous regulator, the PCC, had held that where the complainant was genuinely relevant to the story, his or her identification would be justified.[238] Decisions under this clause had regard to the tone and the extent to which the relative was

---

[232] See *eg* Ms Dynamite and *Islington Gazette*, 26 March 2003 (Report 63); JK Rowling and the *Daily Mirror*, 14 July 2005 (Report 72); cf Ms Helen Edmonds and the *Mail on Sunday*, 24 July 2005 (Report 72) where the complainant was not a celebrity and there was unlikely to be any heightened security risk.

[233] Premier PR on behalf of Daniel Craig and *Mail on Sunday*, 12 October 2008 (Report 78).

[234] Mr and Mrs Hodgson, *Calendar News*, ITV Yorkshire, 22 July 2004 (Bulletin 65). For more on the heightened protection given to children, see 14.139–14.147.

[235] Ms B, *The Sketchbook Killer*, Crime and Investigation Network, 7 July 2012 (Bulletin 227).

[236] Editors' Code, cl 9(i).

[237] McCaffrey v *The Impartial Reporter*, 6 November 2014 (01683-14).

[238] See Mrs Ann Gloag and *Scottish Sun*, 15 May 2007 (Report 75); cf A woman and *Daily Mirror*, 26 March 2012.

made the focus of the article[239] and the general level of public interest in the case itself. For example, a complaint under the PCC Editors' Code was brought against the *Daily Mail* by the first wife of Frederick West, the latter having committed suicide while awaiting trial for rape.[240] The newspaper had published an article which included family photographs and a reference to the complainant. While the PCC 'sympathised' with Mrs West, it considered that the public interest in the case was great and had become of sufficient magnitude to warrant the publication of personal family details.

### (b) Individuals in times of grief or shock

Individuals caught up in newsworthy events, or suffering from grief or shock, are **14.114** also given special protection under the codes. Clause 8.3 of the Ofcom Code makes clear that individuals caught up in events which are covered by the news still have a right to privacy unless it is warranted to infringe it. This applies both to the time when these events take place and in later programmes which revisit those events. The Ofcom Code also makes further provision for 'people caught up in emergencies, victims of accidents, or those suffering a personal tragedy'.[241] Such individuals should not be filmed even in public places where it results in an infringement of privacy, unless it is warranted or the individuals concerned have given consent.[242] Ofcom found a breach of the Code where the BBC broadcast footage of an individual caught up in a fatal accident in which her sister had died. The public interest in examining the work of ambulance crews could have been equally well served without the inclusion of such sensitive footage.[243] In dealing with such cases, however, Ofcom will take account of the particular pressure journalists may face in emergency situations of this kind and the difficulty in making complex judgement calls under such circumstances.[244]

The Editors' Code provides similar protection, stating that in cases involving personal grief or shock, inquiries and approaches should be made with 'sympathy and discretion' and publication handled sensitively.[245] Thus in one of the few privacy complaints so far upheld by IPSO, the regulator held that there had been a **14.115**

---

[239] See *eg* Bob Lacey OBE and *Eastbourne Gazette*, 8 July 1998 (Report 44); Mr J Gbonda and *Evening Standard*, 15 June 2004 (Report 67); A woman and *MK News*, 27 October 2004 (Report 68).

[240] West and *The Daily Mail*, 30 November 1996 (Report 37).

[241] Ofcom Code, cll 8.16–8.19.

[242] The BBC Editorial Guidelines also cover, in some detail, the reporting of death, suffering and distress: see paras 7.4.38–7.4.43.

[243] Claire Halliday, *Front Line*, BBC1, 5 May 2003 (Bulletin 16); see also Mrs Yvonne Charley Walsh on her behalf and on behalf of Mrs M A Mallender, Mr Johnnie Mallender and Mr David Mallender, *999: What's Your Emergency?*, C4, 22 October 2012 (Bulletin 234).

[244] See Foreword to Section 8 of the Ofcom Code.

[245] Editors' Code, cl 4. The previous regulator, the PCC, had stated in respect of this rule that the purpose of it was not to prohibit the publication of news about traumatic events, only to 'minimise the risk of gratuitously aggravating people's vulnerability at such times': see Deidre Manchanda and *The Independent*, 7 August 2008 (Report 78).

failure to handle a report with appropriate sensitivity where a photograph had been published showing an eleven-year-old girl lying on the pavement in the aftermath of an accident before the emergency services had arrived. Although the photograph was taken on a public street and pixelated, IPSO held that the injured child had a reasonable expectation of privacy and parental consent should have been sought prior to publication.[246] It required the newspaper to publish IPSO's ruling upholding the complaint.

**14.116** The previous regulator, the PCC, had interpreted this rule to apply in the 'immediate aftermath' of a bereavement or shocking incident. So where, for instance, a death had taken place some years before publication then the rule was not engaged,[247] unless the publication was particularly 'gratuitous', 'graphic', or 'out of proportion to what was already in the public domain'.[248] Similarly, Ofcom has upheld a complaint where a programme went into excessive and graphic detail about the cannibal murder of the complainant's son, although the details had been highly publicized at the time of the trial several years before.[249]

**14.117** The Ofcom Code provides that particular care should be taken not to reveal the identity of a person who has died or been seriously injured unless it is clear that the next of kin have been informed of the event or unless it is warranted.[250] IPSO, however, has held that a newspaper was entitled to report a man's cause of death where it was given at an inquest even though the family had not yet been informed. The regulator stated that although it was unfortunate that the family had learned the cause of death from the newspaper report, the terms of clause 5 of the Code made clear that the rule did not restrict the right to report legal proceedings and as the assistant coroner had announced the cause of death, the newspaper was entitled to report the information.[251]

**14.118** The Editors' Code has special guidelines that journalists or photographers should follow when making inquiries 'at hospitals or similar institutions', namely that they should identify themselves to a responsible executive and obtain permission before entering non-public areas.[252] IPSO is yet to rule on this issue—however, there are several adjudications on this point from the PCC. For example, where a

---

[246] A woman v *Derby Telegraph*, 20 November 2014 (01866-14).

[247] Deidre Manchanda and *The Independent*, 7 August 2008 (Report 78).

[248] See *eg* A man and *Chat Magazine*, 13 September 2007 (Report 76) where, notwithstanding the passage of time since the murder, the unnecessary inclusion of graphic details and images constituted a clear breach; also Stephanie Grady and *Evening Courier (Halifax)*, 2 April and 12 July 2006 (Report 73).

[249] Mrs P made on her own behalf and that of family members and her son, *Cutting Edge: My Daughter Grew Another Head and Other True Life Stories*, C4, 3 March and 6 June 2010 (Bulletin 180).

[250] See Ofcom Code, cl 8.18; see *eg* Ms Melanie Purdie, *News*, Forth 1 Radio, 25 February 2011 (Bulletin 189) where a radio news item named a victim of a suspected murder before the family had been informed.

[251] Warsop v *Nottingham Post*, 30 September 2014 (01396-14).

[252] Editors' Code, cl 8(i). The 2016 Editors' Code also includes specific provision on the reporting of suicide (cl 5).

journalist entered a hospital without identifying himself and questioned the complainant's dazed and injured father, the PCC found a serious breach of its Code 'which no action could effectively remedy'.[253] The PCC made clear that public interest exemptions to this rule were likely to be rare.[254]

### (c) 'Doorstepping for daily newsgathering'

The BBC has a provision on 'doorstepping for daily newsgathering'[255] which **14.119** applies when large numbers of media representatives gather in the street outside the home of someone who has suddenly become the focus of attention in the news.[256] The BBC points out that the resulting 'media scrum' can become intimidating and unreasonably intrusive and that 'pooling arrangements' with other media organizations may be appropriate.

### (d) CCTV recordings

The Ofcom Code does not make specific reference to CCTV recordings, but rule **14.120** 8.4 states that 'broadcasters should ensure that words, images, or actions filmed or recorded in, or broadcast from, a public place, are not so private that prior consent is required before broadcast from the individual or organisation concerned, unless broadcasting without their consent is warranted'.[257]

The BBC Editorial Guidelines make express reference to the use of CCTV record- **14.121** ings. BBC programme-makers are told that they should take special care over legal issues which may arise on the use of CCTV footage, particularly if they do not have an established relationship with the source of the footage.[258]

IPSO does not specifically mention CCTV footage in its Editors' Code, however **14.122** it has considered a complaint about the publication of CCTV images which had been included in a story accusing a postman of deliberately failing to deliver a parcel. IPSO rejected the complaint on the grounds that the images were not taken in a place where the postman had a reasonable expectation of privacy, nor did they reveal private information.[259] The previous regulator, the PCC, has made clear that it did not consider a CCTV camera to fall under the meaning of a 'hidden camera' under clause 10 (Clandestine devices and subterfuge).[260]

---

[253] Emily Jennings and *Eastbourne Gazette*, undated (Report 60).

[254] John Pope on behalf of Northwick Park Hospital and *Evening Standard*, 27 November 2001 (Report 57).

[255] See further ch 10 on instances where news-gathering techniques of the media may result in physical intrusion into an individual's private life.

[256] BBC Editorial Guidelines, para 7.4.35. See also the prohibitions on intimidation, harassment, and persistent pursuit in the IPSO Editors' Code, cl 4.

[257] See the discussion of *Peck v UK* (n 68), where publication of CCTV footage of the complainant on a public street before his attempted suicide was a disproportionate interference with Art 8.

[258] BBC Editorial Guidelines, para 7.4.27.

[259] Allen v *Worcester News*, 16 December 2014 (03105-14).

[260] Cornwall County Council and *The Packet (Falmouth)*, 1 November 2006 (Report 74).

### (7) Secret Filming or Recording, Bugging Devices, and 'Fishing Expeditions'

*(a) Secret filming or recording*

**14.123**  Ofcom's Broadcasting Code has stringent requirements for surreptitious filming or recording. It is an area of the Code where the balancing act between the public interest and the individual's right to privacy is particularly fine. Secret filming and recording undoubtedly forms the largest category of privacy complaints considered by Ofcom. It will only be warranted if there is *prima facie* evidence of a story in the public interest; there are reasonable grounds to suspect that further material evidence could be obtained; and it is necessary to the credibility and authenticity of the programme.[261]

**14.124**  Ofcom has made it clear that where a member of the public is inadvertently secretly recorded (for example where a camera is left on without knowledge), this amounts to a breach of the Ofcom Code regardless of whether the footage retrieved is in the public interest because there will have been no decision to record surreptitiously and therefore no pre-consideration of whether such recording was justified in the first place.[262]

**14.125**  The broadcast, as opposed to the recording, of surreptitiously obtained footage may be in breach of the Ofcom Code where the footage *itself* does not provide information in the public interest. Ofcom partly upheld a complaint by a chiropractor that the broadcast of surreptitiously recorded footage of him treating three 'bogus' patients (in fact, undercover BBC reporters) was in breach of the Code as the material did not establish any incompetence or malpractice.[263] Ofcom found that the decision taken by the BBC to surreptitiously record the material was justified but the decision to broadcast was not as the material itself did not provide information in the public interest.[264]

**14.126**  Much of the 'Privacy' chapter of the BBC's Editorial Guidelines is devoted to surreptitious recording in public and private places, covering the approval to be sought by programme-makers prior to surreptitious recording and the general

---

[261]  Ofcom Code, cl 8.13. A good example of Ofcom's application of this three-stage test is Lisa Rodrigues on behalf of Sussex Partnership NHS Trust, *Dispatches: Mental health scandal*, Channel 4, 9 October 2006 (Bulletin 94) where secret filming in a mental health ward was held to be proportionate and justified; also Mr Terence Millard, *Five News*, Five, 2 July 2008 (Bulletin 130) where secret filming on a private chicken farm was justified by the public interest in revealing contraventions of animal welfare standards.

[262]  See *eg* Mrs Gwen Weir made on her behalf and on behalf of Andy Weir, *BBC Spotlight*, BBC1 South West, 28 June 2010 (Bulletin 184).

[263]  Dr Christian Farthing, *Conning the Conmen*, BBC3, 29 March 2007 (Bulletin 127); also Dr Peter Proud, *Conning the Conmen*, BBC3, 29 March 2007 (Bulletin 127); see also Complaint on behalf of Morecambe Bay Hospitals NHS Trust, *Sky Report*, Sky News, 21 March 2006 (Bulletin 80) and Mr Lennary Hane, *Insider*, TV3, 12 and 15 October 2006 (Bulletin 113).

[264]  For more examples of Ofcom's application of the secret filming rules, see 14.81–14.94.

principles to be applied in deciding whether such recording is justified. The Guidelines have a specific provision on unattended recording devices: such devices must never be used on private property without permission of the owner, occupier, or their agent 'unless it is for the purpose of gaining evidence of serious crime'.[265] By contrast, the Ofcom Code does not make a distinction between unattended recording devices and other forms of surreptitious recording. BBC programme-makers are further told that they must not go on 'fishing expeditions', searching for crime or antisocial behaviour by identifiable individuals if there is no *prima facie* evidence against them.[266]

The Editors' Code states that journalists must not obtain or publish material **14.127** acquired by using hidden cameras or clandestine listening devices, intercepting private calls, mobile phones, messages or emails, accessing digitally held private information without consent, or removing documents or photographs without authority, although an exception applies if such behaviour can be shown to be in the public interest.[267]

IPSO is yet to rule on the application of this rule but guidance on the issue of **14.128** hidden and clandestine devices may be obtained from previous PCC adjudications. For example, this clause of the Editors' Code was breached when the *Daily Telegraph* used clandestine devices to record the comments of Liberal Democrat MPs in constituency surgeries. The newspaper's justification was that it had acted on information that the private views of Liberal Democrat MPs were at odds with their policies. It was held that the evidence on which the newspaper had acted was of too general a nature and not sufficiently specific to justify the very serious level of subterfuge. Although the investigation may have uncovered material in the public interest, this could not retrospectively justify the decision.[268] Conversely, in a rather surprising earlier adjudication,[269] the PCC held that the use of clandestine listening devices by the *News of the World* was 'clearly' justified by the public interest in revealing that an NHS ambulance technician was also a 'secret vice girl' who took part in group sex sessions.[270]

The Editors' Code further provides that '[e]ngaging in misrepresentation and **14.129** subterfuge ... can generally be justified only in the public interest and then only where the material cannot be obtained by other means'.[271] This rule was considered

---

[265] BBC Editorial Guidelines, para 7.4.15.

[266] BBC Editorial Guidelines, para 7.4.14.

[267] Editors' Code, cl 10.

[268] Liberal Democrat Party and *The Daily Telegraph*, 10 May 2011; see also Nicki McLellan and *Kent & Sussex Courier*, 22 February 2013, where there were insufficient grounds to justify the use of subterfuge.

[269] Sheree Chambers and *News of the World*, 23 November 2003 (Report 67).

[270] The PCC also held in relation to the group sex sessions that 'while the activities may have taken place in private places such as hotel rooms, by inviting strangers such as the newspaper's undercover reporter to take part in them, there was nothing especially private about them'.

[271] Editors' Code, cl 10(ii).

in detail during IPSO's investigation into the *Sunday Mirror* after journalists had used subterfuge to expose Tory MP, Brooks Newmark (see further 14.84 and 14.90). IPSO stated that in cases involving subterfuge, it would have regard to the strength of any evidence which would justify deploying the tactic in the first place; evidence that escalation of the deception was justified at every stage by the actions and reactions of the subject of the investigation; and evidence that at the outset and at all key stages of the subterfuge the newspaper, or its agents, reviewed and gave heed to whether or not it was reasonable to continue the subterfuge. IPSO concluded that the use of subterfuge by the journalist had been justified at each stage of the investigation.[272]

### (b) Recording telephone calls

**14.130**   Ofcom's provisions on the recording of telephone calls[273] state that broadcasters should normally identify themselves to telephone interviewees from the outset and explain the purpose of the call and that the call is being recorded for possible broadcast. If this is not explained to the other party at the time of the call then the broadcaster must obtain consent before broadcast. These requirements can only be waived if 'warranted' at which point the standard three-stage test for surreptitious recording (outlined above) must be satisfied.[274] The BBC's Editorial Guidelines state that those 'recording telephone calls . . . without asking permission' are subject to the same rules as those engaging in other forms of secret recording. [275]

### (c) Set-ups and 'wind-up' calls

**14.131**   Both the Ofcom Code and the BBC Editorial Guidelines cover set-up or 'wind-up' situations. The Ofcom Code states that 'wind-up' calls (*ie* prank calls) for entertainment purposes may be warranted if they are intrinsic to the entertainment and do not amount to a significant infringement of privacy such as to cause significant annoyance, distress, or embarrassment.[276] Even if such conditions are satisfied, the resulting material should not be broadcast without the consent of those involved unless the individual is not identifiable. The requirement of pre-broadcast consent does not apply to celebrities and public figures, although a public interest justification will be required if the material is likely to result in 'unjustified public ridicule or personal distress'.[277]

**14.132**   Ofcom has taken a particularly robust approach to 'wind-up' calls. Notably, the first two privacy cases in which Ofcom found the broadcaster's conduct merited a serious fine involved prank calls in which consent was not sought prior to broadcast. In June 2006, Kiss FM was fined a total of £175,000 (£75,000 in respect of the breach

---

[272]  IPSO Ruling: 'Issues arising from an article in the Sunday Mirror on 28 September 2014'.
[273]  Ofcom Code, cl 8.12.
[274]  See 14.123.
[275]  BBC Editorial Guidelines, para 7.4.9.
[276]  Ofcom Code, cl 8.15.
[277]  Ofcom Code, cl 7.14.

of privacy) for broadcasting a prank call to a member of the public who mistakenly believed he was speaking to his Human Resources manager following his redundancy. The complainant was told that he stood no chance of redeployment due to inadequate qualifications. Ofcom held it to be 'the most serious case of unwarranted infringement of privacy it had heard', devoid of any public interest justification.[278]

In October 2008, the BBC was fined £80,000[279] for breaching the privacy of the **14.133** actor Andrew Sachs and his granddaughter, Georgina Baillie, during the broadcast of the *Russell Brand Show* on BBC Radio 2. A number of telephone calls were made to Mr Sachs in which references were made to the presenter's sexual relationship with Ms Baillie. Ofcom found that the calls were 'exceptionally offensive, humiliating and demeaning' and there was no justification whatsoever for the inclusion of highly personal and sensitive information.[280]

Under the BBC's Editorial Guidelines, any proposal to feature people in a live **14.134** broadcast without their knowledge, or any secret recording or doorstepping for comedy or entertainment purposes, must be approved in advance. The general principle is that all individuals involved must have given their consent before the material is broadcast.[281]

### (8) Long-lens Photography and 'Private Places'

The Editors' Code says that it is 'unacceptable to photograph individuals, without **14.135** their consent, in public or private places where there is a reasonable expectation of privacy'.[282] Although IPSO has yet to rule on this particular principle, there exists an interesting body of PCC adjudications relating to the use of long-lens photography, which may be instructive in determining how the new regulator will deal with this issue.

The principle that someone on privately owned land is not in a 'private place' **14.136** if he or she can be seen by passers-by has been observed in many adjudications of the PCC.[283] The general approach taken consistently by the PCC was to consider whether the complainant 'would have been visible and identifiable from the street when the photograph was taken', regardless of where he or she was technically standing.[284] Hence, complainants photographed in their front

---

[278] Adjudication in the case of Kiss FM Radio Ltd, 20 June 2006, [61].

[279] The £80,000 related solely to the breach of privacy. The BBC was fined a further £70,000 for breaches of other parts of the Code.

[280] See Adjudication in the case of the BBC in respect of its service Radio 2, 3 April 2009.

[281] BBC Editorial Guidelines, paras 7.4.9, 7.4.10, 7.4.17–7.4.20, and 7.4.33.

[282] See cl 2(iii). The wording of this provision differs slightly from that used in the 2014 Code. The 2014 wording was identical to the PCC version of the Editors' Code.

[283] In Sean Connery and *The Sunday Mail*, 25 April 1999 (Report 47) the PCC explained that there are areas open to the public where people may be considered to have a reasonable expectation of privacy just as there are places which are privately owned where an individual would not have such an expectation.

[284] See Mr and Mrs C Entwistle and *Worksop Guardian*, undated (Report 77).

garden tended to have no reasonable expectation of privacy,[285] and back gardens were no safer if they were visible from a public street and if the individuals were not engaging in particularly private activity.[286] Individuals who complained about long-lens photographs taken of them while getting into their car, or when inside their car, were also unsuccessful.[287] Photographs of inmates walking in the grounds of prisons were similarly dismissed where they were visible from a public footpath.[288]

**14.137** However, in decisions which are difficult to reconcile with the above principles, the PCC has equally held that photographs taken of individuals in public places showed a lack of respect for their private life.[289] For instance, the PCC upheld a privacy complaint on the basis that customers of a quiet café could expect to sit inside without having to worry that surreptitious photographs would be taken of them and published in newspapers.[290] When the Aga Khan and his wife were photographed on the deck of their yacht, moored near a private island on which the general public was not allowed, the PCC considered that this was 'clearly a place where there was a reasonable expectation of privacy', despite the *Daily Mail*'s protestations that the decks of yachts were in full sight of casual observers, particularly in the Mediterranean in the height of summer.[291] The PCC also 'deplored' the publication of photographs of Sir Paul McCartney and his family in Nôtre Dame

---

[285] Beever and *The News of the World*, 23 November 1997 (Report 42); also Corinne Tindall and *The Sunday People*, 11 June 2000 (Report 52). Note however that the situation may be different if there is evidence that the complainant has been 'lured' into his or her front garden by the reporter: A Man and *The Observer*, 12 July 1998 (Report 44).

[286] Gail Sheridan and *Scottish Sun*, 11 October 2006 (Report 75). But cf Cilla Black and *The Sunday Sport*, 17 June 2001 (Report 55) where a topless picture of Cilla Black sunbathing on her terrace, published in the *Sunday Sport*, was found to be a breach of privacy on the grounds that she was relaxing in a place where she could not be observed by members of the public.

[287] Dr Khare and *The News of the World*, 1 February 1998 (Report 42); A woman and *Mail on Sunday*, 10 July 2005 (Report 72); Muddassar Arani and *Daily Express, The Sun, Daily Mail*, and *Daily Telegraph*, 22 April and 7 June 2008 (Report 78). The mere fact that a photograph is taken *from* the inside of a darkened or hidden car does not give the complainant a right to complain if he or she is photographed in a public place: Mr and Mrs C Entwistle and *Worksop Guardian*, undated (Report 77); Rachel Parkyn and *Mail on Sunday*, 7 December 2008 (Report 79).

[288] Alexandra and Georgia Pryce and *The Daily Telegraph*, 19 July 2013; Chris Huhne and *The Sun, The Daily Mirror, Daily Telegraph, Daily Mail and Sunday Mirror*, 18 July 2013.

[289] Such an approach was consistent with that taken by the courts. In *Campbell* (n 43) the House of Lords found that there had been an infringement of Naomi Campbell's right to privacy when she had been photographed by a long lens in a public street. The supermodel was captured outside a Narcotics Anonymous meeting that she was attending, in circumstances in which other attendees' faces caught in the photo were pixelated. The therapeutic and medical aspect, and the risk of disturbing the progress of the therapy, meant that the claimant had a reasonable expectation of privacy—an expectation that might not have been upheld had she merely been photographed 'going about her business in a public street' (at [154]). See also *Weller* (n 15) where photographs taken of the claimant children shopping in California and sitting in a public café were held to be an unjustified intrusion into their private lives. See generally, ch 5.

[290] Hugh Tunbridge and *Dorking Advertiser*, 23 May 2002 (Report 58). This 'firm view' was reiterated in A man and *Evening Times (Glasgow)*, 5 April 2012.

[291] Begum Aga Khan and His Highness the Aga Khan and *The Daily Mail*, 16 July 1998 (Report 46).

Cathedral in Paris, stating that a cathedral was a clear example of a place 'where there is a reasonable expectation of privacy' and it 'expects journalists to respect the sanctity of individuals' acts of worship'.[292]

The Ofcom Code makes clear in its definition of 'legitimate expectation of pri-  **14.138** vacy' that 'some activities and conditions may be of such a private nature that filming or recording, even in a public place, could involve an infringement of privacy'. Ofcom has taken a similar approach to the PCC in terms of rejecting complaints of footage taken of places visible from public highways.[293]

The BBC has a clause specifically relating to operating on private property,  **14.139** informing programme-makers that they should normally leave private property when asked to do so by the legal occupier.[294] If the recording is covert, the Guidelines make clear that such recording on private property can only be justified where there is reason to believe illegal or antisocial behaviour is being exposed. So far as recording in public places is concerned the BBC considers that people in public places or in semi-public places such as airports, railway stations, and shopping malls cannot expect the same degree of privacy as in their own homes. However there may be circumstances where people can reasonably expect privacy even in a public place, for example when someone is receiving medical treatment.[295]

## (9) Children

Both the Ofcom Code[296] and the BBC's Editorial Guidelines[297] offer compre-  **14.140** hensive guidance on the involvement of children as contributors in programmes. Particular care must be taken by broadcasters when dealing with children and the consent of a guardian must be sought for any infringement of privacy, or questioning 'about private matters', unless it is warranted to proceed without consent. Broadcasters are warned that children do not lose their rights to privacy because of, for example, the fame or notoriety of their parents, or because of events in their schools.

There have been several cases where Ofcom has upheld a breach of the Code in  **14.141** respect of a child, but not an adult in the same circumstances. For instance, where a complainant was filmed outside court with her two children during a highly publicized criminal trial, Ofcom found a breach in respect of the children but not of the

---

[292] Sir Paul McCartney and *Hello!*, 30 May 1998 (Report 43).
[293] See *eg* Lady Jane Ann Winterton MP, *North West Tonight*, BBC1 North West, 4 February 2008 (Bulletin 120); Dr Fazal Mahmood and others, *Bangladesh Protideen*, *News*, and *Friday Plus*, Bangla Television, various dates June–September 2007 (Bulletin 122); Miss Davies, *Homes Under the Hammer*, BBC1, 14 September 2012 (Bulletin 227).
[294] BBC Editorial Guidelines, para 7.4.5.
[295] BBC Editorial Guidelines, para 7.1, 'Legitimate Expectations of Privacy'.
[296] Ofcom Code, cll 8.20–8.22.
[297] BBC Editorial Guidelines, Section 9.

parents.[298] Where children are specifically singled out by the camera ('person specific' footage), their privacy may be infringed even if they are in a public place and not engaging in any activity of a private or sensitive nature,[299] but the same level of vigilance is unlikely to be required for adults. In a documentary which looked at the high levels of academic achievement amongst British Chinese children, footage taken in a restaurant of a child's birthday party included several close-up shots of the complainant's son, a friend of the birthday boy. Ofcom held that express consent should have been obtained prior to broadcast and found a breach of rule 8.20 of the Code. However, there was no breach in respect of his parents.[300]

**14.142**  The Editors' Code also offers clear guidance on the coverage of children in the print media.[301] Aside from the specific provision on children in sex cases,[302] the Editors' Code states that 'all pupils should be free to complete their time at school without unnecessary intrusion', that children under the age of sixteen must not be photographed or interviewed on subjects concerning their own or another child's welfare without the consent of a responsible adult, and makes clear that the fame, notoriety, or position of a child's parent or guardian cannot be the sole justification for publication of material about a child's private life.[303] The public interest clause in the Editors' Code states that 'an exceptional public interest would need to be demonstrated to over-ride the normally paramount interest of children under 16'.

**14.143**  Where parental consent is required, IPSO has held that the consent of one custodial parent is sufficient.[304] Where the child is photographed at school, clause 6(ii) of the Editors' Code suggests that it is the consent of the school, not that of the guardian, which is relevant.[305] The consent of the child appears in general to be irrelevant.[306]

**14.144**  Prior consent is generally only required for those pictures or interviews 'involving their own or another child's welfare'. Under the PCC, examples of matters concerning a child's 'welfare' included an interview with a fifteen-year old about

---

[298] Mr and Mrs Hodgson, *Calendar News*, ITV Yorkshire, 22 July 2004 (Bulletin 65); see also Mrs Janet Neal on her own behalf and on behalf of her husband and grandchildren, *East Midlands Today*, BBC East Midlands, 16 November 2012 (Bulletin 230).

[299] As in Mrs G and her daughter (a minor), *East Midlands Today*, BBC1 (East Midlands), 6 April 2006 (Bulletin 81).

[300] Mr C on his own behalf and on behalf of their son (a minor), *Meet Britain's Chinese Tiger Mothers*, BBC2, 5 January 2012.

[301] Editors' Code, cl 6.

[302] Editors' Code, cl 7.

[303] The Court of Appeal in *Murray v Express Newspapers plc* [2008] EWCA Civ 446, [2009] Ch 481 [45]–[46], adopted the PCC's approach in determining whether the claimant's privacy had been infringed only as a result of his mother's fame.

[304] See Holling v *Daily Mail*, 27 September 2014 (01227-14); Holling v *The Sun*, 27 September 2014 (01226-14); Holling v *Barnsley Chronicle*, 26 September 2014 (0661-14).

[305] See also the PCC adjudication in Colin Eves and *Brecon & Radnor Express*, 27 September 2001 (Report 57).

[306] See PCC adjudication in Mrs S Granton and *Daily Post*, 3 August 2002 (Report 59).

a serious road accident involving her friend,[307] an interview with a fifteen-year old boy about gang violence at his school,[308] contact with a fourteen-year old about the fatal stabbing of his school friend,[309] and the identification of a child as the son of a suicide bomber.[310] IPSO has held that parental consent was required prior to publishing a photograph of two young girls in the immediate aftermath of an accident, as the upsetting incident clearly related to the children's welfare.[311]

Under the PCC, innocuous pictures of children taken in public places with no accompanying private or personal details were not considered to be in breach of the Editors' Code.[312] Neither were pictures of children whose identities are already in the public domain in relation to a newsworthy incident.[313] However, the PCC did take into account how the photographs were obtained, whether the photographs embarrassed the child,[314] interrupted his or her schooling, or damaged his or her welfare in some other way.[315] For example, where an innocuous photograph of a school pupil was juxtaposed against the headline 'Pre-school children porn web shock', the PCC found a breach of clause 6 as the headline clearly had the potential to cause the child embarrassment and upset.[316]    **14.145**

The PCC was particularly careful where a child's sexual life had been engaged. In one case a photograph of a topless fourteen-year-old girl had been published in a gallery of mobile-phone snapshots submitted by magazine readers. The magazine argued that it received over 1,000 photographs for publication each week but the PCC considered that there had been a serious intrusion and it should have taken more care to establish the provenance of the photographs.[317]    **14.146**

In relation to the children of famous parents, where photographs of a politician's children were published without consent, the PCC found a breach of the equivalent clause of the Editors' Code. In a complaint brought by the Blairs,[318] the    **14.147**

---

[307] Mr Phil Adey and *Daily Post Wales*, undated (Report 78).

[308] A woman and *Sutton and Epsom Advertiser*, undated (Report 72).

[309] Keith Cousins and *The Sunday Times*, undated (Report 73).

[310] A woman and *Derby Evening Telegraph*, 29 November 2005 (Report 72).

[311] A woman v *Derby Telegraph*, 20 November 2014 (01866-14).

[312] Donald and *Hello!*, 18 July 2000 (Report 52); Kingston and *Hello!*, 1 May 2001 (Report 55). IPSO are likely to take a more nuanced approach to this issue, given the 2014 decision of *Weller* (n 15).

[313] Ian Cooper and *Cambridge News*, 23 October 2007 (Report 77).

[314] Although see Quigley and *Zoo Magazine*, 12–18 May 2006 (Report 73) where a ten-year-old girl was photographed with her father making embarrassing and offensive gestures at a football match. There was no breach of the Code as the photographs were taken in a public place; also Stewart Frazer and *the Scotsman* and *Edinburgh Evening News*, 10 July 2013 where embarrassing photographs of the complainant's four-year-old son had already been shared on Facebook.

[315] Blair and *The Daily Sport*, 21 December 1999 (Report 49).

[316] Mrs Rebecca Louise Elder and *Midhurst & Petworth Observer*, 21 November 2013.

[317] A married couple and *FHM*, April 2007 (Report 75).

[318] Blair and *The Daily Telegraph*, 8 December 2001 (Report 57).

Commission stated that the 'acid test' to be applied by newspapers in writing about the children of public figures who are not famous in their own right (unlike the royal princes), was whether a newspaper would write such a story if it was about an ordinary person.

**14.148**  In another complaint by the Blairs, the PCC noted the great lengths to which the Blairs had gone in order to avoid publicity for their children and took this factor into account in reaching their decision.[319] Accordingly, one might expect that the extent to which a parent has compromised the privacy of his or her child may be taken into account in deciding whether a child's privacy has been infringed. While the PCC did not expressly state this, it did suggest that children who had begun to acquire their own public persona may be less entitled to protection, stating in one case that 'it is much more difficult to protect any [child] where he or she begins to acquire a public profile in their own right, for instance by making public appearances. Privacy is best maintained when not compromised in any way.'[320]

## G. Application of the Codes to 'New Media'

### (1) The Editors' Code

**14.149**  Although the internet remains on the whole unregulated, IPSO regulates 'editorial content on electronic services operated by regulated entities such as websites and apps, including text, pictures, video, audio/visual and interactive content'.[321] Complaints about 'user generated content posted onto regulated entities' websites which has not been reviewed or moderated by the regulated entity' and about 'online material that is not on sites owned by or under the control of regulated entities' is not regulated.[322]

**14.150**  IPSO's complaints procedures apply to complaints about regulated online content in the same way as they do to complaints about content in hard copy newspapers and magazines, except that, in respect of online material, the four-month time limit does not apply: if a complaint is made after four months but within twelve months of the date of first publication, and relates to content which is still accessible to the public on a regulated entity's website, IPSO will consider the complaint if it judges that it is still possible to investigate and adjudicate fairly, bearing in mind the lapse of time since first publication.

---

[319]  Blair and *Mail on Sunday*, 24 January 1999 (Report 47).
[320]  Blair and *The Daily Telegraph*, 8 December 2001 (Report 57).
[321]  IPSO Regulations, para 1.2. See IPSO's website.
[322]  IPSO Regulations, para 3.6.

Although IPSO is not bound by the precedents or guidance of its predecessor, the **14.151**
PCC, it is worth noting guidance issued by the PCC concerning privacy in a note
entitled 'Privacy and the Public Domain'.[323] The note contains guidance on the use
by journalists of images and material taken from social networking sites such as
Facebook, as follows:

> The publication of information by individuals on social networking platforms such
> as Facebook, Twitter and MySpace can blur the distinction between 'private' and
> 'public', particularly where the individual has not used privacy settings to indicate an
> intention to restrict the circulation of the information. Nonetheless, the mere availa-
> bility of material online does not in itself justify its republication to the public at large.

> The Commission has previously acknowledged that it may be acceptable in some
> circumstances to publish information taken from social networking websites, even
> if the material was originally intended for a small group of acquaintances.[324] A
> decision to publish material protected by privacy settings will generally require an
> editor to demonstrate a sufficient public interest in publication, but even where no
> privacy settings are in place, editors should consider carefully whether publication
> is justified. For example, in a case of bereavement or serious injury, when the terms
> of Clause 5 (Intrusion into grief or shock) apply, editors should take particular
> account of the likely effect on close friends and family of the publication of images
> or material taken from such sites.

### (2) Ofcom's Broadcasting Code

Ofcom has not attempted to assert significant regulatory control over internet **14.152**
content. Ofcom's privacy remit is defined in the Communications Act 2003 to
include only television and radio services, however they are delivered. It does not
include non-broadcast services such as online news. The 2003 Act defines television licensable content services (TLCS) and radio licensable content services
(RLCS) as the subject of Ofcom's oversight and these concepts are defined at
ss 232–3 of the Act.

### (3) ATVOD 'Rules and Guidance'

Following the implementation of the Audiovisual Media Services Directive[325] **14.153**
in December 2009, online video-on-demand services such as the BBC
iPlayer, 4OD (Channel 4), ITV Player, and Demand Five, are now regulated.
The Communications Act 2003, as amended by the Audio Visual Services

---

[323] See PCC Guidance Note: Privacy and the Public Domain, 15 November 2012.

[324] The earlier guidance referred to was published following a ruling against the Scottish Sunday
Express in which it was found to have made a 'serious error of judgment' by publishing Facebook
photos of the survivors of the Dunblane massacre. See Ms Mullan, Mr Weir, and Ms Campbell and
*Scottish Sunday Express*, 8 March 2009 (Report 79).

[325] Council Directive 2007/65/EC of 11 December 2007 amending Council Directive 89/552/
EEC on the Coordination of Certain Provisions Laid Down by Law, Regulation or Administrative
Action in Member States Concerning the Pursuit of Television Broadcasting Activities.

Regulations 2009 and the Audiovisual Media Services Regulations 2010, conferred functions on Ofcom to regulate on-demand programme services, and gave Ofcom powers to delegate certain functions to an appropriate regulatory authority.[326] That body is the Authority for Television on Demand (ATVOD), the independent co-regulator for the editorial content of UK video-on-demand services falling within the statutory definition of 'on demand programme services'.[327] Providers of these services are required by law to notify ATVOD before the service begins, and to advise ATVOD if the service closes or undergoes significant changes.[328] Details of the statutory requirements that apply to on-demand programme services, information on whether a service requires notification, and how to make a notification can be found on ATVOD's website.

14.154  The rules which providers of on-demand programme services must comply with are contained within ATVOD's 'Rules and Guidance' which can found on its website. These mirror the statutory provisions.[329] While the rules are binding, the accompanying guidance provided by ATVOD is not. The rules relate to 'harmful material'; 'advertising';[330] 'sponsorship'; and 'product placement'. There are however no rules concerning privacy matters. Users can complain on ATVOD's website about content which they believe breaches the rules. Where ATVOD finds that a service provider has breached the rules, it will normally publish a 'determination' on its website, explaining why the content in question has been found to be in breach. If necessary, ATVOD may use its statutory powers to issue a 'statutory enforcement notification',[331] requiring the service provider to do certain things, including publishing a correction and/or a statement of its findings, in a form, place, and time specified in the notice.[332] Service providers served with a statutory enforcement notice are under a duty to comply.[333] Both ATVOD and Ofcom can enforce compliance with an enforcement notice by issuing civil proceedings. ATVOD may also refer breaches of the rules to Ofcom which can impose more serious sanctions, including fines[334] and suspension of the service. The maximum fine which may be imposed is the greater of five per cent of the service provider's 'applicable qualifying revenue'[335] or £250,000.

---

[326]  Communications Act 2003, s 368B.

[327]  Communications Act 2003, s 368A.

[328]  Communications Act 2003, s 368BA, 'Advance notification to appropriate regulatory authority'.

[329]  Communications Act 2003, s 368D–E.

[330]  The Advertising Standards Authority has been designated to regulate advertising in on-demand programme services.

[331]  Communications Act 2003, s 368I.

[332]  Communications Act 2003, s 368I(4).

[333]  Communications Act 2003, s 368I(7).

[334]  Communications Act 2003, s 368J.

[335]  Communications Act 2003, s 368J(3) and (4)—for a definition of 'applicable qualifying revenue'.

## H. Challenging the Media Regulators' Decisions

### (1) Independent Press Standards Organisation

Under IPSO's regulations, a complainant may seek review of a decision made by **14.155** IPSO's Complaints Committee, for example that a publisher has not breached the Editors' Code. Requests for such a review can only be made on the ground that the process by which the Complaints Committee reached its decisions was 'substantially flawed'. A request for a review must be made by a complainant in writing within fourteen days of the relevant decision. It is entirely within IPSO's discretion as to whether or not it refers the complaint to the Complaints Reviewer for review.

Where IPSO accepts a complainant's request for a review, the Complaints **14.156** Reviewer will review the process by which the Complaints Committee reached its decisions. The rules state that the Complaints Reviewer will refer back to the Complaints Committee within fourteen days of receiving the request, stating whether or not it considers the process was or was not substantially flawed. If the decision is that the process was substantially flawed, the Complaints Committee is required to review its original decision, taking into account the Complaints Reviewer's findings and to issue an adjudication outlining its findings (which may include a requirement for the regulated entity to take remedial action).[336] Beyond this process, there are no other avenues of appeal open to a complainant, other than potential legal challenge. It is notable that IPSO's Regulations do not provide for regulated entities (as opposed to complainants) to seek review of decisions of the Complaints Committee, although again a legal challenge may be possible.

### (2) Ofcom

Ofcom's complaints handling procedures do not provide any opportunity for a **14.157** review, or any other sort of appeal, of Ofcom's adjudications regarding privacy complaints (or indeed any other type of complaint).[337] If a privacy complaint is entertained by Ofcom, it will first come to a provisional decision, its 'preliminary view', and following representations on that, from both the complainant and broadcaster, will make its final adjudication. At this point, the only way of challenging the adjudication is through legal challenge.

---

[336] IPSO Regulations, paras 24–9.

[337] Ofcom Fairness and Privacy Procedures (n 87). This is in contrast with the position in respect of complaints about both non-broadcast and broadcast advertising to the Advertising Standards Authority, whose procedures provide the opportunity for both complainants and advertisers to seek independent review of Advertising Standards Authority rulings if certain grounds are made out: if extra evidence has become available; and/or it is alleged that there was a substantial flaw in the Advertising Standards Authority Council's ruling or in the process by which that ruling was made.

### (3) Legal Challenge

**14.158**  Where all other avenues of review (if any) or appeal with the regulators themselves have been exhausted, both complainants and media organizations have the option of seeking to challenge legally the decisions of the media regulators. Indeed, over the years, all the main media regulators have seen the legality of their decisions challenged and scrutinized by the courts in judicial review proceedings in some respects. An analysis of the law of judicial review is beyond the scope of this text,[338] although consideration is given at 14.159 *et seq* to the potential implications of the media regulators being 'public authorities' within the meaning of s 6(3) HRA, and to the ways in which any challenge might be brought.

## I. The Regulatory Bodies as Public Authorities

**14.159**  Under the HRA it is unlawful for a public authority to act in a way which is incompatible with a Convention right.[339] Thus, if the media regulators are public authorities, it would seem to be possible for an individual who claims that an adjudication has failed adequately to protect his or her Convention right to respect for private life under Article 8 to be able to bring proceedings against the regulator under s 7(1)(a) HRA. Conversely, it may be possible for a media organization which is aggrieved at an adverse adjudication to complain to the court that the regulator has acted incompatibly with its Convention right to freedom of expression under Article 10.

### (1) Are the Media Regulators 'Public Authorities' under the Human Rights Act 1998?

*(a) Independent Press Standards Organisation (and its predecessor, the Press Complaints Commission)*

**14.160**  There is, as yet, no case law considering whether or not IPSO is a public authority within the meaning of s 6(3) HRA. Perhaps more surprisingly, the question was not directly determined in respect of the PCC either. After initially expressing the contrary view, the Lord Chancellor stated in the course of the debates on the Human Rights Bill that the PCC would be considered to be a public authority.[340] That led directly to Lord Wakeham, then chairman of the PCC, seeking to introduce a specific safeguard for press freedom into the Bill which ultimately became s 12 HRA.[341]

---

[338]  For a detailed analysis of the substantive law and procedural issues involved in bringing and defending claims for judicial review, see J Auburn, J Moffett, A Sharland, and R McManus QC, *Judicial Review, Principles and Procedure* (Oxford University Press 2013).

[339]  s 6(1) HRA.

[340]  *Hansard*, HL (6th series), vol 583, col 784 (24 November 1997).

[341]  Lord Wakeham's first proposal was to exempt the PCC altogether from the provisions of the Bill. See further 12.02 *et seq.*

Unlike the Freedom of Information Act 2000, which contains a list of public **14.161** authorities to which its provisions apply, the HRA adopts a non-exhaustive approach to defining a public authority, relying on a two-part test. Section 6(3) HRA defines a public authority as *including* (a) a court or tribunal and (b) any person certain of whose functions are functions of a public nature. Section 6(5) provides, in relation to a particular act, that a person is not a public authority by virtue *only* of s 6(3)(b) if the nature of the act is private (emphasis added). Thus, it has been said that all the acts (whether public or private) of a body which is a 'core' or 'standard' public authority must be compatible with Convention rights as must be the public acts of a body which has a mixture of private and public functions ('functional' public authorities).[342]

There was no direct decision on whether the PCC was or was not a public **14.162** authority within the meaning of s 6(3) HRA. Given the attributes of core public authorities (such as government departments, local authorities, the police, and armed forces—which are required to act compatibly with Convention rights in everything they do) it is unlikely that the PCC would have been regarded as falling within the same category. The relevant factors in respect of such bodies include the possession of special powers, democratic accountability, public funding in whole or in part, an obligation to act only in the public interest, and a statutory constitution.[343] The PCC was not a statutory creation, was not publicly funded, nor did it have legal powers to enforce its adjudications. Rather its authority rested on the agreement of the press to submit to its jurisdiction and comply with its rulings precisely in order to avoid legal determinations and sanctions. The same is of course true of IPSO: the Royal Charter does not oblige press organizations to sign up to regulation.

There is scope for suggesting, however, that IPSO is (and the PCC was) a hybrid **14.163** body, some of whose functions are functions of a public nature. This is most likely in respect of IPSO's adjudicatory functions. There have been a number of decisions concerning s 6(3) which set out the relevant factors to which the court will have regard in determining whether a body has functions of a public nature and, if so, whether the particular act in question is public or private. Many of these cases concern privately run care homes to which local authorities have contracted out responsibility for the provision of services. Although this is a very different context to the regulation of the media, the authorities provide some guidance on how the section should be interpreted.

---

[342] See *Hansard*, HL (6th series), vol 583, col 811 (24 November 1997) and Home Secretary at HC (6th series), vol 314, cols 409–10 (17 June 1998); and R Clayton QC and H Tomlinson QC, *The Law of Human Rights* (2nd edn, Oxford University Press 2009) vol 1, para 5.08.
[343] *Aston Cantlow and Wilmcote with Billesley Parochial Church Council v Wallbank* [2003] UKHL 37, [2004] AC 546 [7].

**14.164**  The leading House of Lords' authority is *YL v Birmingham City Council* which resulted in a 'sharp difference of opinion' between their Lordships.[344] Lord Bingham and Baroness Hale, in the minority, focused on the original purpose of the HRA and the generously wide scope that should be given to the definition of public authorities. Relevant factors to determine whether a function was public or private included: the essential nature of the function; the role and responsibility of the state in respect of the subject matter in question; the nature and extent of any statutory power or duty in relation to the function; the extent to which the state regulates, supervises, or inspects the function in question; the extent to which the state pays for the function; and the extent of the risk that improper performance of the function might violate a Convention right.[345]

**14.165**  Factors which were wholly or largely irrelevant in deciding whether a function is of a public nature are: whether the body is amenable to judicial review;[346] whether another (core) public authority would be liable for a breach of Convention rights; and whether the act complained of as a breach of a Convention right would be criminal or tortious.[347] Baroness Hale in particular relied on the rationale behind the HRA as being to provide domestic remedies for those who would otherwise have to seek redress from the European Court of Humana Rights,[348] noting that there were in the Strasbourg case law several bases on which the state had to take responsibility for the acts of private bodies.[349] In her view, this was such a case. The majority (Lords Scott, Mance, and Neuberger) disagreed however and, by implication, held that the United Kingdom would bear no responsibility for the acts or omissions of the company concerned with the care of *YL* were an application to be made to the European Court.

**14.166**  The majority did however, adopt the previous guidance given by Lord Nicholls in *Aston Cantlow and Wilmcote with Billesley Parochial Church Council v Wallbank*[350] that factors to be taken into account in determining whether a function was public or private included the extent to which in carrying out the relevant function the

---

[344]  [2007] UKHL 27, [2008] 1 AC 95 [126] (Lord Neuberger).

[345]  *YL* (n 344) [6]–[11] Lord Bingham and [65]–[72] Baroness Hale. In respect of the last factor Lord Bingham referred in particular to the potentially greater impact on an individual's rights under Art 10 in relation to certain of the articles.

[346]  s 6(3)(b) HRA extends the definition of public authority to cover bodies which are not public authorities but certain of whose functions are of a public nature. It is therefore likely to include bodies that are not amenable to judicial review. See 11.146.

[347]  *YL* (n 344) [12].

[348]  *YL* (n 344) [54]–[55] referring to the extracts from *Hansard*.

[349]  Citing *Van der Mussele v Belgium* (1983) 6 EHRR 163; *Costello-Roberts v UK* (1993) 19 EHRR 112; and *Wos v Poland* App no 22860/02 (ECtHR, 1 March 2005) as examples of the state delegating responsibility or relying on a private body to fulfil its obligations under the Convention; and *X and Y v Netherlands* (1985) 8 EHRR 235 and *Z v UK* (2001) 34 EHRR 97 as examples of positive obligations which the state has to take to prevent or provide redress for breaches of Convention rights: *YL* (n 344) [56]–[57].

[350]  *Aston Cantlow* (n 343) [12].

body is publicly funded, is exercising statutory powers, is taking the place of central government or local authorities, or is providing a public service. In essence, is the function performed 'governmental' in nature? The body in question in *YL* was said to lack these necessary attributes because it was a 'privately-owned, profit-making enterprise' which had 'sectional or personally-motivated interests'.[351] It was also said to be 'common ground' that functions of a public nature include the exercise of the regulatory or coercive powers of the state.[352]

In respect of its adjudicatory functions at least, IPSO, like the PCC before it, is pro- **14.167** viding a public service which has a direct bearing on the application of Convention rights. It cannot in any sense be described as a privately-owned, profit-making enterprise and would not accept that it had sectional or personally motivated interests. Although the fact that a body performs an activity which would otherwise fall to a public body to perform does not necessarily mean that such performance is a public function, where the role of such a body is closely assimilated to that of a public authority (which includes a court or tribunal) the more likely its functions are to be of a public nature.[353] Accordingly, to the extent that IPSO fulfils a quasi-judicial function which a court or tribunal or other state regulator would otherwise have to perform, it may be considered to be a public authority with a duty to act compatibly with Convention rights under s 6 HRA. Moreover, IPSO may be more likely to be seen as a public authority than the PCC, given IPSO's increased powers of sanction, for example the imposition of substantial fines.

### (b) Ofcom

Different considerations apply to some of the other regulators, especially those which **14.168** regulate the broadcast media, which are created by statute, and which do fulfil statutory functions. It has been affirmatively held that Ofcom is a public authority under the HRA.[354] But rather like the media organizations themselves it would be somewhat unsatisfactory if a body's duty to act compatibly with Convention rights were to depend on how that body is created and financed rather than on the functions it performs. There would appear to be no difference in principle between the role fulfilled by IPSO in respect of its adjudicatory functions for the newspaper and magazine industry and the role fulfilled by Ofcom in the same regard for the broadcast media. There would be merit in an approach which required the same standards of all the regulators whether they are regulating the print or broadcast media. It should be noted that the Freedom of Information Act 2000 identifies Ofcom[355] and the BBC (for

---

[351] *YL* (n 344) [105] (Lord Mance).

[352] *YL* (n 344) [63] (Baroness Hale). See *R (A) v Partnerships in Care Ltd* [2002] EWHC 529 (Admin), [2002] 1 WLR 2610.

[353] *Poplar Housing and Regeneration Community Association Ltd v Donoghue* [2001] EWCA Civ 595, [2002] QB 48.

[354] *Gaunt v Ofcom* [2010] EWHC 1756 (Admin) [17].

[355] As it did with Ofcom's predecessors, the Broadcasting Standards Commission, the Independent Television Commission, and the Radio Authority.

purposes other than those of journalism, art, or literature) as public authorities; but not the PCC (or IPSO) or the Advertising Standards Authority.

### (c) The BBC

**14.169**  The position of the BBC as both broadcaster and regulator is considered briefly above in 14.52–14.54. In its capacity as regulator and adjudicator of the Editorial Guidelines, it is suggested that its status is that of a functional public authority for the same reasons advanced in respect of IPSO.

### (d) The relevance of judicial review

**14.170**  For the reasons given by Lord Bingham in *YL*, the position in respect of judicial review is 'instructive' but not 'determinative'.[356] Like the Advertising Standards Authority,[357] BBC,[358] Ofcom and its predecessors (the Independent Television Commission,[359] Broadcasting Standards Commission,[360] and Radio Authority[361]), the PCC has been subject to judicial review proceedings.[362] However, in the case of the PCC, the court was never asked to rule specifically on whether it was amenable to judicial review.[363] Whether proceedings may be brought by way of judicial review depends under CPR pt 54 on whether that body is exercising a 'public function'. However, a body which is not a core public authority for the purposes of s 6 HRA may nevertheless be amenable to judicial review in respect of certain procedural requirements.[364] Thus, although there is considerable overlap between

---

[356] See S Grosz, J Beatson, and P Duffy, *Human Rights, the 1998 Act and the European Convention* (Sweet & Maxwell 2000) 61 (cited with approval in *R (Heather) v Leonard Cheshire Foundation* [2002] EWCA Civ 366 [36]). It was confirmed in *Aston Cantlow* (n 343) [52] and *R (Beer) v Hampshire Farmers Markets Ltd* (2003) 31 EG 67 [27]–[28] that it is possible to conclude that a decision by a public authority is not amenable to judicial review and that a decision by a private body may be. The domestic case law on judicial review can be 'very helpful' but reliance on domestic cases must be tempered by and, sometimes yield to, relevant Strasbourg jurisprudence. That is because the scheme of the HRA is to replicate as far as possible the circumstances in which the UK's responsibility would be engaged before the ECtHR. Consequently, that jurisprudence is especially likely to be helpful in determining whether a body is a core public authority. It is likely to be less helpful in relation to the fact-sensitive question of whether in an individual case a hybrid body is exercising a public function.

[357] See eg *R v Advertising Standards Authority, ex p Insurance Services plc* [1990] 2 Admin LR 77.

[358] See eg *R v BBC and Independent Television Commission, ex p Referendum Party* [1997] EMLR 605.

[359] *R v BBC* (n 358).

[360] See eg *R v Broadcasting Standards Commission, ex p BBC* [2001] QB 885, CA.

[361] See eg *R v Radio Authority, ex p Bull* [1998] QB 294.

[362] See eg *R v PCC, ex p Stewart-Brady* [1997] EMLR 185.

[363] The PCC accepted for the purposes of the application in *R (Ford) v PCC* [2002] EMLR 95 that it was arguable that it was a public authority within the meaning of the HRA and amenable to judicial review.

[364] *R (Heather) v Leonard Cheshire Foundation* [2002] EWCA Civ 366 [38]. In that case the Court of Appeal upheld the judgment of Stanley Burnton J that a body which was in receipt of public funding, and provided services that would otherwise have to be provided by the state by which it was also regulated, was not a public authority within the meaning of s 6 HRA on the basis that its functions were not sufficiently 'governmental' in nature.

the two tests, they are not synonymous.[365] However, the distinction may not make a difference in some cases since where proceedings are before the court by way of judicial review or otherwise the victim may be able to rely on his or her Convention rights by virtue of s 7(1)(b) HRA, relying, if necessary, on the status of the court as a public authority.[366]

### (2) The Effect of Being a Public Authority

If the media regulators are public authorities within the meaning of the HRA, what effect does this have on the exercise of the court's powers to review their decisions? The early indications were that the courts would take a very restrictive view of their role in respect of reviewing the decisions of the media regulators even where Convention rights are in issue, but that has been ameliorated by more recent decisions in which the courts have shown themselves willing to intervene more directly in the decision-making process for which those bodies are responsible.  **14.171**

In theory the court could be required to consider whether any interference with a Convention right by a media regulator satisfies the requirements of the Convention, namely that it was prescribed by law and necessary to fulfil one of the legitimate aims set out in Article 8(2) or 10(2). This approach has been adopted by the Administrative Court in cases in which it held (i) that the British Codes of Advertising and Sales Promotion were sufficiently clear, precise, and accessible, and underpinned by statute to be 'prescribed by law', and (ii) that adjudications by the Advertising Standards Authority that that code had been breached were compatible with Article 10.[367] These decisions show that those who are regulated by the regulators can challenge their adjudications even if the codes are designed primarily to protect individual rights.  **14.172**

Such an analysis was not appropriate in the case of *R (Ford) v Press Complaints Commission*[368] because the PCC had rejected Ms Ford's complaint that the privacy provisions of the Editors' Code had been breached. There was thus no 'interference'  **14.173**

---

[365] Nor are the tests on standing. The concept of 'victim' under the HRA is narrower than the required interest to bring proceedings by way of judicial review and s 7(3) HRA purports to limit the ability of an applicant to raise a Convention point on judicial review to those who would also be victims.

[366] In this regard it should be noted that, at least in Strasbourg, a body cannot be both victim of and liable for a breach of the Convention. To the extent that s 6 HRA replicates the test that applies under the Convention, the regulatory bodies are more likely to be considered to owe duties rather than be owed them.

[367] *R v Advertising Standards Authority, ex p Matthias Rath BV* [2001] EMLR 22; *SmithKline Beecham v Advertising Standards Authority* [2001] EWHC Admin 6. The legitimate aim in each case was the protection of rights of others, namely consumers. See also *R (Debt Free Direct Ltd) v Advertising Standards Authority* [2007] EWHC 1337 (Admin), which held that it was not appropriate to grant an injunction restraining the regulator from publishing its adjudication pending a legal challenge.

[368] *Ford* (n 363).

to be complained of. Rather the Court considered, *obiter*, whether the decision of the PCC had failed to give adequate effect to Ms Ford's right to respect for her private life under the positive obligations of Article 8. This, it is submitted, is a similar approach to that which the courts would adopt in respect of litigation between private parties by virtue of the court's position as a public authority. The fact that the PCC conceded for the purposes of the application that it was a public authority therefore added little of substance. The Court applied the modified judicial review test which has been in place since the entry into force of the HRA,[369] according to the PCC a wide 'discretionary area of judgment' which it equated to the Strasbourg concept of 'margin of appreciation'. It thus restricted itself to considering whether the PCC had made any errors of law in rejecting Ms Ford's complaint and held that its decision to do so was compatible with Article 8.

**14.174** The justification for taking this restrictive view of its role was stated to be the fact that the court was poorly equipped to adjudicate on the matters before it. Where a body such as the PCC has expert membership and was used to adjudicating on matters concerning privacy and free speech, the court should, in most cases, defer to its judgment on where the balance should lie.[370] The validity of this reasoning following the HRA must now be open to question. At the heart of the Editors' Code is a requirement to strike a balance between the rights under Articles 8 and 10. This is a function which the courts have become increasingly accustomed to performing in respect of media activities.

**14.175** So too, in *R (ProLife Alliance) v BBC*[371] the House of Lords showed a much greater willingness than the Court of Appeal had done to defer to the BBC's assessment of what material was likely to be offensive to public feeling when it banned an anti-abortion election broadcast. The House held that the Court of Appeal, which had effectively 'decide[d] for itself whether this censorship was justified',[372] had asked itself the wrong question and 'in effect carried out its own balancing exercise between the requirements of freedom of political speech and the protection of the public from being unduly distressed in their own homes'.[373] Since Article 10 in this context does not confer a right on everyone to express his or her own opinion on television, but a right to 'fair consideration for being afforded the opportunity to do so' the real issue was 'whether the requirements of taste and decency are a discriminatory, arbitrary or unreasonable condition for allowing a political party free access at election time to a particular public medium'.[374]

---

[369] See *R (Daly) v Secretary of State for the Home Dept* [2001] 2 AC 532 [27]–[28].

[370] In this regard Silber J adopted the reasoning of Lord Woolf in *R v Broadcasting Standards Commission* (n 360). It did not seem to matter that, unlike the Broadcasting Standards Commission, the 'requirement' to adjudicate on such matters arises not by statute but by the consent of the media.

[371] [2003] UKHL 23, [2004] 1 AC 185.

[372] *ProLife* (n 36) [37] (Laws LJ).

[373] *ProLife* (n 371) [16].

[374] *ProLife* (n 371) [58]–[62].

Lord Hoffmann preferred not to see the exercise of identifying the limits of a **14.176** decision-maker's powers as a matter of 'courtesy or deference' but as a question of law.[375] It is submitted that that may be true as a matter of classification but it does not help to identify the relevant criteria needed to determine whether those limits have been exceeded. Such guidance as is given is not very helpful. As Lord Hoffmann said:[376]

> ... once one accepts that the broadcasters were entitled to apply generally accepted standards [of what is offensive], I do not see how it is possible for a court to say that they were wrong. Public opinion in these matters is often diverse, sometimes unexpected and in constant flux. Generally accepted standards on these questions are not a matter of intuition on the part of elderly male judges.

It would appear that nothing short of irrationality would have rendered the deci- **14.177** sion of the broadcaster (as regulator rather than programme-maker) unlawful. The fact that the BBC conceded for the purposes of the case that it would be unlawful for it to act incompatibly with Convention rights under s 6 HRA would appear to have made little difference. Lord Hoffmann attached 'some importance' to the fact that two of the decision-makers were women. This, apparently, gave them greater expertise than the court to assess the likely effect of the broadcast on the 200,000 women in the United Kingdom who have abortions every year. On this reasoning, the decision of a body entrusted with decision-making powers is more likely to be respected by the court if it comprises at least some members of the class of people most likely to be affected by its decision.

The situation in respect of Ofcom, however, would appear to be somewhat differ- **14.178** ent. In *Gaunt v Ofcom*[377] the Court had to consider whether the actions taken by the regulator in admonishing a broadcaster were a proportionate interference with the claimant's right to freedom of expression under Article 10. The proceedings were brought by way of judicial review in which Convention rights were relied on but the case reads as if it were a direct action against Ofcom as a public author-ity (which it was found to be) under s 6 HRA. There is little or no application of 'a discretionary area of judgment' or deference to the expertise of the regulator, though the Court ultimately found that the regulator had not breached the claim-ant's rights. The case deserves analysis as a way in which the courts in future might approach the question of whether individual rights have been breached (or not upheld) by a media regulator in all cases under Articles 8 and 10 as they become more accustomed to applying Convention rights directly rather than reviewing the actions of the original decision-maker.

The claimant was a presenter on the independent radio station talkSPORT, well- **14.179** known for his hard-hitting and outspoken presentation. During the course of a live

---

[375] *ProLife* (n 371) [75]–[76].
[376] *ProLife* (n 371) [79]–[80].
[377] [2010] EWHC 1756 (QB), [2011] 1 WLR 663.

interview with a local authority councillor who was speaking about the Council's controversial proposal to ban smokers from becoming foster parents because of the dangers posed by passive smoking, the claimant variously called the councillor a 'Nazi', an 'ignorant pig', and 'health fascist'. The interview degenerated into what the Court described as 'an unseemly slanging match' with the interviewer doing much of the talking, on occasion being gratuitously offensive and ranting. It emerged during the course of the interview that the claimant had himself been brought up by a foster carer who smoked, a fact about which he had written in *The Sun* newspaper the same day under the headline 'Fags didn't stop my foster mum caring for me'. Shortly after the interview concluded, the claimant apologized to the listeners on air and subsequently to the councillor, regretting that he had lost control because the subject matter was close to his heart. He was suspended with immediate effect and talkSPORT terminated his contract ten days later. Ofcom received fifty-three complaints about the broadcast and the broadcaster issued its own on-air apology.

**14.180** In its amended finding the regulator held that clauses 2.1 and 2.3 of the Broadcasting Code had been breached by failing to comply with generally accepted standards regarding harmful and offensive language and that the language of the presenter had not been justified in the context. The duties under the Broadcasting Code are placed on broadcasters so the finding by Ofcom was against talkSPORT which did not challenge it before the Court. Nevertheless, the Court entertained a claim by the presenter that the regulator's decision was a disproportionate interference with *his* right to freedom of expression under Article 10. On the issue of standing the Court merely said: 'the decision enunciates an inhibition capable of affecting his unrestrained freedom to conduct radio interviews in the way in which he did on this occasion. We need say no more about his standing.'[378]

**14.181** The Court considered its task to be 'to decide for itself whether the Amended Finding disproportionately infringed the claimant's right to freedom of expression'.[379] In doing so it implicitly rejected submissions from Ofcom that the Court should not place itself in the position of the decision-maker and engage in a merits-based review, urging that considerable weight should be given to Ofcom's expert judgment on what constitutes generally accepted standards on the inclusion of offensive material. Although the Court stated that it had 'due regard to the judgment of the statutory regulator who proceeded on correct legal principles' it is hard to find evidence in the judgment of it actually doing so. On the contrary, the Court stated that it regarded 'generally accepted standards' in this context as 'elusive' and that the concept of harmful and/or offensive material needed to be moderated in the light of Article 10 and the domestic and Strasbourg case law. Having conducted

---

[378] *Gaunt* (n 377) [13].
[379] *Gaunt* (n 377) [42] and [44] applying *R (SB) v Governors of Denbigh High School* [2006] UKHL 15, [2007] 1 AC 100; *Belfast City Council v Miss Behavin' Ltd* [2007] UKHL 19, [2007] 1 WLR 1420; and *R (Nasseri) v Secretary of State for the Home Dept* [2009] UKHL 23, [2010] 1 AC 1. The phrase is reminiscent of the Court of Appeal's approach in *ProLife* (n 371).

a thorough review of the Convention jurisprudence on political speech and value judgments it concluded that the decision of the regulator was a proportionate interference with the claimant's right to freedom of expression. It noted in particular that no sanction or penalty had been imposed on the broadcaster, let alone the claimant. The Court of Appeal, in upholding the High Court's decision and dismissing the claimant's appeal,[380] acknowledged that the question of whether the publication of Ofcom's finding constituted a permissible interference with a claimant's Article 10 rights demanded 'rigorous scrutiny'.

A tendency towards restraint by the courts in interfering with the judgments of **14.182** specialist media regulators can however be detected in a more recent judicial review challenge involving Ofcom. In *R (Traveller Movement) v Ofcom*,[381] a challenge by way of judicial review, brought by the Traveller Movement (a representative body of travellers and gypsies in the United Kingdom), to Ofcom's decision to reject its complaint about two Channel 4 series, *Big Fat Gypsy Weddings* and *Thelma's Gypsy Girls*, one of the grounds relied upon was that Ofcom had acted irrationally in coming to the decision that expert evidence of harm arising from the two series, submitted by the claimant to Ofcom as part of its complaint, had failed to make out a breach of the Ofcom Code. In rejecting this ground, while giving some consideration to the claimant's arguments, Ouseley J acknowledged that counsel for Channel 4, the Interested Party, had been right to submit that 'it would have to be a very clear case in order for the judgment of the specialist regulator, on a topic involving harm, context and freedom of expression, to be held irrational and so unlawful. This is nowhere near such a case.'[382]

The apparent divergence of approaches regarding the appropriate degree of scru- **14.183** tiny to be undertaken by the court of a regulator's decision results in some degree of continuing uncertainty for those who wish to challenge a decision before the courts. To the extent that the purpose of s 12(4) HRA was to preserve the system of self-regulation for the press, a decision like *Ford* would seem to show that the ambitions of the instigators of the section have been successful. The same cannot be said of the approach of the Court in *Gaunt*.

### (3) Bringing a Legal Challenge

A claim brought against a media regulator for acting incompatibly either with a **14.184** complainant's, or a regulated body's, Article 8/10 rights could be brought either by way of judicial review, or possibly by a private law action in the County Court or the High Court.[383] The particular route chosen would be likely to depend on a

---

[380] [2011] EWCA Civ 692.
[381] [2015] EWHC 406 (Admin).
[382] *Traveller Movement* (n 381) [93].
[383] Pursuant to s 6(1) HRA: 'It is unlawful for a public authority to act in such a way which is incompatible with a Convention Right.'

number of factors, including the remedies being sought and the degree to which factual issues may be in dispute.

**14.185** If the aim of a claimant is to obtain a remedy only available in judicial review, such as a mandatory, prohibiting, or quashing order, a claim by way of judicial review pursuant to CPR pt 54 would be the only option.[384] The judicial review procedure may also be used where a claimant is seeking a declaration or an injunction,[385] but where a claimant is also seeking a remedy listed in CPR 54.2, the judicial review procedure *must* be used.

**14.186** Claims for judicial review 'may include a claim for damages, restitution or the recovery of a sum due but may not seek such a remedy alone'.[386] Accordingly, if damages are all that a claimant is seeking, a judicial review claim would not be possible and any action brought would have to be by way of a private law action. If there are significant factual disputes, it may also not be advisable to proceed by way of judicial review. In addition, the one-year time limit for a claim brought under the HRA, compared to the rule of bringing claims 'promptly and…in any event not later than 3 months' in judicial review claims, may also be a factor which determines the way in which a claim is brought.

---

[384] CPR 54.2.
[385] CPR 54.3(1).
[386] CPR 54.3(2).

# Part VIII

## PRIVACY, THE INTERNET,
## AND SOCIAL MEDIA

# 15

## PRIVACY, THE INTERNET, AND SOCIAL MEDIA

*Godwin Busuttil, Felicity McMahon, and Gervase de Wilde*

## A. Introduction

The ascendancy of social media poses acute challenges for privacy. While Facebook, **15.01** Twitter, YouTube, LinkedIn, and other similar services can confer major advantages on users in terms of access to information, ease of communication, and opportunities for network-building,[1] the ordinary concomitant is a significant surrender

---

[1] 'The Internet's capacity to disseminate information has been described by this Court as "as one of the great innovations of the information age"': *Crookes v Newton* 2011 SCC 47, [2011] 3 SCR 269 [34], referring to *Society of Composers, Authors and Music Publishers of Canada v Canadian Association of Internet Providers* 2004 SCC 45, [2004] 2 SCR 427. See also, to like effect, *Times Newspapers Ltd v UK* App nos 3002/03 and 23676/03, [2009] EMLR 14 [27]. 'It is indisputable that social networking sites can be a force for good in society, a truly positive and valuable mechanism': *AB Ltd v Facebook Ireland Ltd* [2013] NIQB 14 [13] (McCloskey J).

of personal privacy. This is because participation generally entails the disclosure of, and the ceding of control over, one's personal data.[2] In order to join the community and enjoy the benefits of membership, a person must establish at a minimum an online contact point and identity (*eg* in the form of a Facebook account or Twitter profile), typically by transferring some version of his or her actual, real-world, identity to the internet. Many, of course, go much further than this, sharing online—arguably 'oversharing'[3]—any manner of private information concerning themselves, often with complete strangers. In most cases to do so will prove harmless, but from time to time individuals may make themselves a target. A person's online identity can easily become a reference or focal point for the unauthorized dissemination of sensitive information and intimate photographs, a lightning-rod for the activities of harassers, stalkers, bullies, and trolls,[4] particularly when combined with other information available about that individual elsewhere.[5] It is not unknown for harassment to cross from the online to the offline sphere.

**15.02**  The internet, and social media in particular, have created unprecedented opportunities for wrongdoing of this kind. And, given the distinctive characteristics of publication via social media—instantaneous, readily accessible by both recipient and onlookers (in particular via mobile phones and other hand-held devices), cumulative, persistent, viral,[6] potentially global in reach, continuous and, unless arrested, permanent[7]—such misconduct is apt to produce in its victims powerful

---

[2] Except in cases where the user has chosen to conceal his or her true identity, though to do so inevitably precludes full participation.

[3] See R Zuckerberg, *Dot Complicated* (Bantam Press 2013).

[4] In *AB Ltd* (n 1) McCloskey J at [13] refers to 'an evidently growing trend of a disturbing nature and proportions, involving the abuse of social networking sites … they are becoming increasingly misused as a medium through which to threaten, abuse, harass, intimidate and defame. They have become a source of fear and anxiety. So-called "trolling" appears to be increasingly commonplace. There is much contemporary debate about evils such as the bullying of schoolchildren and its potentially appalling consequences. Social networking sites belong to the "wild west" of modern broadcasting, publication and communication. They did not feature in the Leveson Inquiry and, in consequence, are not addressed in the ensuing report … The misuse of social networking sites and the abuse of the right to freedom of expression march together.' See also, in this connection, the remarks made by Advocate General Cruz Villalón at [48] in the Opinion he delivered to the ECJ in Case C-509/09 *eDate Advertising GmbH x X* [2012] QB 654.

[5] Part (b) of the definition of 'personal data' in s 1(1) of the Data Protection Act 1998 reflects the fact that data which does not itself identify a living individual, and so is not personal data, may become personal data by reason of being combined with other data available somewhere else: '"personal data" means data which relate to a living individual who can be identified— (a) from those data, or (b) *from those data and other information which is in the possession of, or is likely to come into the possession of, the data controller*' (emphasis added).

[6] See *Cairns v Modi* [2012] EWCA Civ 1382, [2013] 1 WLR 1015 [27]: 'we recognise that as a consequence of modern technology and communication systems any such stories will have the capacity to "go viral" more widely and more quickly than ever before … this percolation phenomenon is a legitimate factor to be taken into account in the assessment of damages'.

[7] See *Clarke v Bain* [2008] EWHC 2636 (QB) [55] (Tugendhat J): 'The long term effect of a libel has commonly been expressed in metaphorical terms, such as "the propensity to percolate through underground passages and contaminate hidden springs" (*eg Slipper v BBC* [1991] 1 QB 283, 300). The position today can be expressed more strongly, as it was in an article published in *The Guardian* (by Siobhain Butterworth, on 20 October 2008): "The consequences of putting information … into

feelings of humiliation and despair,[8] not least on account of the perception that their embarrassment is being served up for the gratification of thousands of others. It can result in grave and lasting damage for its victims; in several instances, it has been linked to suicide.[9] Its effect might be described as a unique fusion of the twin phenomena of disclosure (or, maybe, 'exposure') and intrusion discussed in *Goodwin v News Group Newspapers Ltd.*[10]

The potential for unwanted interference with privacy contingent upon engagement **15.03** with social media is so great that it has caused some observers to query whether participation is incompatible with the maintenance of personal privacy: as one US-based commentator put the point, the notion of 'privacy in social media is pretty close to [being] an oxymoron'.[11] In Dave Eggers' novel *The Circle*, a dystopian satire set in a near future in which a single social media corporation has achieved a monopoly over all online transactions, the author explores, among other things, the tensions between the competing social demands of transparency and privacy.[12] In a key scene, the book's protagonist, Mae, undergoes an epiphany. 'Privacy is theft', she pronounces to the general acclaim of her fellow *Circle* employees. The phrase is quickly adopted as a corporate slogan.

The English court, however, does not approach the issue in black and white. In **15.04** *Rocknroll v News Group Newspapers Ltd*, for example, it granted an interim injunction in misuse of private information to prevent the defendant newspaper from publishing photographs of the claimant partially undressed at a party.[13] The photographs had been obtained from a third party's Facebook account where they had, for a period of time, been accessible to that individual's 1,500 Facebook friends, and then, owing to a change in the account's privacy settings, to the public at large. It was nevertheless unlikely, Briggs J reasoned, that the defendant would be able to establish at trial that no useful purpose would be served by restraining the newspaper from publishing the photographs; there was no evidence that there had been widespread public inspection of the Facebook pages containing the photographs.

---

the public domain are more far-reaching in a world where things you say are linked to, easily passed around and can pop up if [the subject's] name is put into a search engine by, for example, a prospective employer. The web makes a lie of the old cliché that today's newspaper pages are tomorrow's fish and chip wrapping. Nowadays...the things...in a newspaper are more like tattoos—they can be extremely difficult to get rid of.'"

[8] For an account of social media's 'shaming culture', see J Ronson, *So You've Been Publicly Shamed* (Picador 2015).

[9] In the cases, for example, of Ryan Halligan, Megan Meier, Tyler Clementi, Hannah Smith, Daniel Terry, and Charlotte Dawson.

[10] [2011] EWHC 1437 (QB), [2011] EMLR 27 [85].

[11] M Sableman, 'Privacy in social media—is it really an oxymoron?' (JDSupra Law News, 25 November 2013), available at <http://www.jdsupra.com/legalnews/privacy-in-social-media-is-it-really-a-80315/>, discussing the case of *Chaney v Fayette County Public School District*, 2013 US Dist LEXIS 143030 (ND Ga 30 September 2013).

[12] D Eggers, *The Circle* (Hamish Hamilton 2013). See also the non-fiction work, A Taylor, *The People's Platform: Taking Back Power and Culture in the Digital Age* (Fourth Estate 2014).

[13] [2013] EWHC 24 (Ch) (Briggs J).

The claimant, the judge concluded, therefore had a substantially better than even chance of establishing a reasonable expectation of privacy at trial. The fact that the photographs had been posted on Facebook did not preclude either the operation of the claimant's Article 8 rights or the grant of an injunction to prevent their publication in the traditional, print-based press. It is suggested that the same decision would have been reached if the claimant had posted the photographs to Facebook himself: there is no reason to think that this additional factor would have led the judge to refuse the injunction.

**15.05** The *Rocknroll* case is typical of the approach that English courts take to privacy cases, whether they involve internet publication or not. The decision to grant or withhold remedies in privacy cases, especially injunctions, is always a question of fact, degree and proportionality, to be reached following detailed and penetrating scrutiny of all the circumstances and a balancing of competing rights and interests.[14] English law eschews hard and fast rules and mechanical solutions but, as discussed earlier in this work, the general principles which determine the balance to be struck between competing rights are now fairly well-settled.[15] The task of judges in relation to the 'enormous challenges' that have been thrown up by the internet was identified by Sir James Munby P in *Re J (A Child)*:[16]

> The law must develop and adapt, as it always has done down the years in response to other revolutionary technologies.[17] We must not simply throw up our hands in despair and moan that the internet is uncontrollable. Nor can we simply abandon basic legal principles. For example, and despite the highly objectionable nature of much of what is on the internet, we must, at least in the forensic context..., cleave to the fundamentally important principles referred to...above [that is to say, freedom of expression, and the axiom that it is not for judges to act as editors or censors].

Among these challenges, arriving at a good understanding of the complex and sometimes abstruse workings and properties of the technologies involved will feature prominently. As also will rapid technological change: the internet and social media are but in their infancy.

**15.06** The legal means by which the court seeks to protect individuals against unwarranted infringements of privacy online are the same as those it deploys in other situations: there is as yet no civil cause of action directed specifically to online wrongdoing. Misuse of private information, breach of confidence, harassment, data protection, defamation, copyright, and human rights and anti-discrimination

---

[14] *Re S (A Child) (Identification: Restrictions on Publication)* [2004] UKHL 47, [2005] 1 AC 593 [17] (Lord Steyn).

[15] See *Hutcheson (formerly 'KGM') v News Group Newspapers Ltd* [2011] EWCA Civ 808, [2012] EMLR 2 [17]–[35] for a summary of the principles.

[16] [2013] EWHC 2694 (Fam), [2014] EMLR 7 [43].

[17] This point is also made in *Dow Jones & Co Inc v Gutnick* [2002] HCA 56, (2002) 210 CLR 575 [38].

legislation all have a role to play. The tort of harassment under the Protection from Harassment Act 1997 (PHA) might be said, however, to have a special place in the armoury. The fact that in principle it confers on the court the power to grant injunctions to restrain any form of alarming or distressing behaviour, including speech,[18] means it is the most flexible and effective weapon in putting a stop to the activities of a persistent online wrongdoer, especially one who chooses to vary the mode and nature of his or her attack. As for the Data Protection Act 1998 (DPA), it remains doubtful whether it provides for any general power to grant an injunction to restrain unlawful processing of personal data. While Eady J granted an interim injunction on this basis in *Sunderland Housing Group Ltd v Baines*,[19] Mitting J in *Mahmood v Galloway*[20] concluded that '[the DPA] does not contain any provision for a court by injunction to short-circuit the statutory rights of those in respect of whom an infringement may have occurred'.[21] These are therefore conflicting first instance decisions, of which Mitting J's seems the more convincing. The landmark decision of the European Court of Justice in *Google Spain SL v Agencia Española de Protección de Datos*[22] has however breathed new life into ss 10 and 14 DPA as a means to obtain injunctive relief against internet service providers (ISPs).[23] Injunctions in misuse of private information and defamation need to be tailored to particular information or words, which can cause difficulties in the online sphere where the information and words may easily change. This highlights another advantage of the PHA, since injunctions in harassment are addressed directly to the objectionable *conduct*, regardless of the precise form it takes.[24] Such conduct may include the public disclosure of personal information, but it need not do so for a victim's Article 8 rights to be engaged.[25]

Some of the advantages of the tort of harassment in this field, and potential limitations of alternative causes of action, are illustrated by the judgment of Tugendhat J in *Law Society v Kordowski*.[26] The case concerned an application for **15.07**

---

[18] See *Thomas v News Group Newspapers Ltd* [2001] EWCA Civ 1233, [2002] EMLR 4; *ZAM v CFW* [2011] EWHC 476 (QB); *Trimingham v Associated Newspapers Ltd* [2012] EWHC 1296 (QB), [2012] 4 All ER 717; *Hayes v Willoughby* [2013] UKSC 13, [2013] 1 WLR 935; and *ZAM v CFW* [2013] EWHC 662 (QB), [2013] EMLR 27. For detailed discussion of the PHA 1997, see ch 6 and 10.04–10.20.

[19] [2006] EWHC 2359 (QB). See also Tugendhat J's observations in this connection in *Law Society v Kordowski* [2011] EWHC 3185 (QB), [2014] EMLR 2 [172], although *Mahmood v Galloway* [2006] EWHC 1286 (QB), [2006] EMLR 26 (concerning which, see further below) was not apparently cited to him.

[20] [2006] EWHC 1286 (QB), [2006] EMLR 26.

[21] *Mahmood* (n 20) [26].

[22] Case C-131/12 [2014] QB 1022.

[23] See *Mosley v Google Inc* [2015] EWHC 59 (QB), [2015] EMLR 11 (Mitting J).

[24] See *Merlin Entertainments plc v Cave* [2014] EWHC 3036 (QB), [2015] EMLR 3 (Elisabeth Laing J) [41]–[42].

[25] For discussion of the relationship between the PHA 1997 and Art 8, see *Law Society* (n 19) [59]; *Wainwright v Home Office* [2003] UKHL 53, [2004] 2 AC 406 [18]; and *Trimingham* (n 18) [48]–[49].

[26] See n 19.

a final injunction to restrain the defendant from continuing to publish a website ('Solicitors from Hell') on which members of the public were encouraged to post derogatory remarks about lawyers. Many availed themselves of the opportunity, often anonymously. In granting the injunction, Tugendhat J held that it was reasonable to infer that each individual listed on the website would have had his or her attention drawn to the website, either directly, via a search engine, or by third parties, on two or more occasions and thereby suffered such distress and alarm on at least two occasions. This was enough to satisfy the requirement imposed by s 1(1) of the PHA that the defendant must have engaged in a 'course of conduct'.[27] He also held that even if an allegation posted on the website happened to be true or honest comment, the defendant's harassment could not conceivably be justified by the defences in s 1(3):[28]

> Even if there were evidence that the allegations were true, the conduct of the Defendant could still not even arguably be brought within any of the defences recognised by the PHA. No individual is entitled to impose on any other person an unlimited punishment by public humiliation such as the Defendant has done, and claims the right to do. His conduct is a gross interference with the rights of the individuals he names.[29]

In principle, therefore, in order to become liable for harassment, a person need do no more than post offensive or distressing material online and decline to take it down when asked. Naturally enough, though, this may not be sufficient to ground a case in harassment: all will depend on the precise facts of the case. Furthermore, reliance on harassment may avoid the need for the court to debate the truth or falsity of the speech in question. These features of the tort may, in an appropriate case, enable a claimant to obtain the protection sought more expeditiously and cheaply than would otherwise be the case.

**15.08** While it is clear that the same governing principles of law will apply to infringements of privacy however and wherever they occur, there can be no question but that infringement of privacy on the internet[30] gives rise to a number of idiosyncratic legal issues. It is to these that this chapter now turns.[31]

---

[27] For all these matters, see *Law Society v Kordowski* (n 19) [60]–[75]. The decision was applied on similar facts in *QRS v Beach* [2014] EWHC 3057 (QB) (interim injunction) and [2014] EWHC 3319 (QB) (final injunction).

[28] Which provides that the defendant will have a defence if the course of conduct was pursued for the purpose of preventing or detecting crime, under any enactment or rule of law or to comply with any condition or requirement imposed by any person under any enactment, or was reasonable in the particular circumstances. See further 6.27 *et seq.*

[29] *Law Society v Kordowski* (n 19) [133].

[30] This chapter will not discuss privacy infringements by means of data collation by ISPs (the subject matter of the case of *Vidal-Hall v Google Inc* [2015] EWCA Civ 311, [2015] 3 WLR 409) or as a result of surveillance by state entities.

[31] This chapter focuses on the specific issues to which use of the internet and social media gives rise in the misuse of private information context. Issues which are not internet-specific (*eg* the defence of public domain) are discussed in detail elsewhere in this work, including any internet-related dimension.

## B. Liability Arising from Online Publication: Preliminary Considerations

The question of what a person should do when confronted with an intrusive or **15.09** harassing online publication is not always a straightforward one. In the most serious cases, it may be appropriate immediately to apply to the court for an interim injunction without pre-notifying any respondent.[32] However, it is usually advisable to try to resolve disputes informally and consensually before having recourse to the law. The first port of call in online privacy complaints should usually be the author of the offending content, or some other person with ostensible control over the relevant content, provided of course that he or she is contactable and that making contact will not risk making matters worse. Where these conditions are satisfied, a well-written email, making reasonable and proportionate demands (*eg* for take down, and an undertaking not to repeat), may yield a quick and inexpensive solution to the problem.

In tandem, or alternatively, an approach ought to be made to the operator of the **15.10** online platform (*eg* website, blog, forum, or message board) or of the social media service where the offending material has appeared.[33] Most operators who provide such 'hosting' services—certainly all the mainstream ones—possess, publish, and claim to enforce 'terms of use' rules and policies that proscribe the posting of abusive or offensive content. A letter complaining persuasively of a breach of those 'terms of use' may secure the voluntary removal of the material, whether by the operator itself or, following notification by the operator, by the author. In the case of a website, it might also prove fruitful to make contact with the domain name registrar.

Often, however, this will not work. Such approaches may be dismissed for any **15.11** number of reasons, including that they are unfounded in law or in fact, or

---

[32] But see s 12(2) HRA; the Master of the Rolls's *Practice Guidance (Interim Non-Disclosure Orders)* [2012] 1 WLR 1003 [18]–[28]; *National Commercial Bank of Jamaica Ltd v Olint Corp Ltd* [2009] UKPC 16, [2009] 1 WLR 1405 [13] (Lord Hoffmann); and *AB v Barristers Benevolent Association Ltd* [2011] EWHC 3413 (QB) [28] (Tugendhat J). Only in genuinely exceptional cases, *eg* where they involve blackmail or where the respondent might take steps to defeat the purpose of the application if he or she were notified of it in advance, will it be appropriate for an applicant not to give advance notice.

[33] '[F]or purely technical reasons it would appear disproportionate to put the onus of identification of the authors of defamatory comments on the injured person in a case like the present one. Keeping in mind the State's positive obligations under Article 8 that may involve the adoption of measures designed to secure respect for private life in the sphere of the relations of individuals between themselves…the Court is not convinced that measures allowing an injured party to bring a claim only against the authors of defamatory comments…would have, in the present case, guaranteed effective protection of the injured person's right to private life': *Delfi AS v Estonia* App no 64569/09 (ECtHR, 10 October 2013, First Section) para 91. (The decision has since been upheld by the Grand Chamber [2015] EMLR 26.)

that the complaints they comprise have been articulated with insufficient precision. But operators also sometimes reject such approaches on grounds which are unrelated to their intrinsic merits as a matter of English law.[34] The companies that operate the vast majority of the most popular platforms, *eg* Google Inc (YouTube, Blogger, and Google+), and Automattic Inc (WordPress), are incorporated and have their principal place of business in the United States, and have no established, real-world presence or corporate assets in any other jurisdiction.[35] Their amenability to civil suit in the United States is very limited. By s 230(c) of the Communications Act of 1934 (as amended),[36] providers of 'interactive computer services' are in general statutorily immune from civil suit in the United States in respect of the online publications they facilitate:

**230 (c) Protection for 'Good Samaritan' blocking and screening of offensive material**

**(1) Treatment of publisher or speaker**

No provider or user of an interactive computer service shall be treated as the publisher or speaker of any information provided by another information content provider.

**(2) Civil liability**

No provider or user of an interactive computer service shall be held liable on account of—

(A) any action voluntarily taken in good faith to restrict access to or availability of material that the provider or user considers to be obscene, lewd, lascivious, filthy, excessively violent, harassing, or otherwise objectionable, whether or not such material is constitutionally protected; or

(B) any action taken to enable or make available to information content providers or others the technical means to restrict access to material described in paragraph (1).

The only exceptions to this rule are civil claims based upon (domestic US) intellectual property rights and the 'Electronic Communications Privacy Act of 1986 or any of the amendments made by such Act, or any similar State law'.[37]

**15.12** It may be observed, furthermore, that US courts are bound not to enforce or to give effect to any judgment of a foreign court in a defamation case where, *inter alia*, the judgment appears to the American court to be inconsistent with the

---

[34] See further 15.15.
[35] The best known exceptions to this are Facebook and Twitter, whose terms of service specify that users outside the US (in the case of Twitter) or the US and Canada (in the case of Facebook) do business with and have their data controlled by their Republic of Ireland companies.
[36] Also known as the Communications Decency Act of 1996, codified at 47 USC § 230.
[37] See s 230(e)(2), (4).

First Amendment to the US Constitution.[38] The relevant measure is s 4102(a) of the SPEECH Act of 2010:[39]

**Recognition of foreign defamation judgments**

**(a) First Amendment considerations**

Notwithstanding any other provision of Federal or State law, a domestic court shall not recognize or enforce a foreign judgment for defamation whenever the party opposing recognition or enforcement of the judgment claims that the judgment is inconsistent with the First Amendment to the Constitution of the United States, unless the domestic court determines that the judgment is consistent with the First Amendment. The burden of establishing that the foreign judgment is consistent with the First Amendment shall lie with the party seeking recognition or enforcement of the judgment.

Section 4102(c) of the SPEECH Act makes specific provision in respect of foreign judgments for defamation against providers of interactive computer services. Its effect is that the US court will not recognize or enforce a foreign judgment that imposes civil liability for defamation on such an entity:

**(c) Judgment against provider of interactive computer service**

Notwithstanding any other provision of Federal or State law, a domestic court shall not recognize or enforce a foreign judgment for defamation against the provider of an interactive computer service, as defined in section 230 of the Communications Act of 1934 (47 U.S.C. 230), whenever the party opposing recognition or enforcement of the judgment claims that the judgment is inconsistent with such section 230, unless the domestic court determines that the judgment is consistent with such section 230. The burden of establishing that the foreign judgment is consistent with such section 230 shall lie with the party seeking recognition or enforcement of the judgment.

Since judgments of the English court in privacy or harassment cases would not **15.13** ordinarily be regarded as defamation judgments,[40] if one were to seek to enforce an English privacy judgment in the United States, it seems that s 4102 of the SPEECH Act would not apply. Nevertheless, where the defendant is the provider of an interactive computer service, s 230(c) of the Communications Act itself precludes the enforcement in the United States of any foreign court order that

---

[38] Although note Tugendhat J's *obiter* remarks in *Adelson v Anderson* [2011] EWHC 2497 (QB) [70]–[87] on the circumstances in which it might be possible to persuade a US court that an English court defamation judgment comports with the First Amendment and so ought to be enforced in that jurisdiction.

[39] Its full title is the Securing the Protection of our Enduring and Established Constitutional Heritage Act of 2010, codified at 28 USC §§ 4101–4105. See *Trout Point Lodge Ltd v Handshoe* 2013 WL 4766530 (5th Cir, 5 September 2013) for the first appellate opinion to consider the relevant provisions of the SPEECH Act.

[40] Although it is not clear how the US court would approach a judgment of the English court in a 'false privacy' case, the possibility of which was suggested by the Court of Appeal's judgments in *McKennitt v Ash* [2006] EWCA Civ 1714, [2008] QB 73.

imposes civil liability on such a person,[41] regardless of the legal basis of that liability. Furthermore, in relation to other types of defendant, even prior to the coming into effect of the SPEECH Act, US courts tended to decline to enforce foreign, including English, court decisions affecting free speech on First Amendment grounds.[42] There is as yet no reported instance of a US court having been asked to enforce an English court judgment based on misuse of private information. But by analogy with the defamation cases of *Bachchan* and *Matusevitch*,[43] and having regard to the legislative policy of the SPEECH Act, it seems likely that US judges would be reluctant to enforce such a judgment, particularly where the effect of the judgment was to curtail the speech of a US citizen or corporation. As one commentator has put the point: 'in the not too distant future, breach of privacy judgments against American publishers may become viewed as the . . . threat to American First Amendment rights, replacing foreign defamation judgments'.[44]

**15.14**  The upshot of all of this is a general climate of impunity, real and perceived, on the part of the US-based internet platform providers. They can act—or, more typically, fail to act—safe in the knowledge that their potential exposure to liability (whether in the form of adverse financial consequences following foreign civil suit or for sanctions for contempt of court for failing to comply with foreign court orders) is severely constrained, both in the US (as a matter of law) and elsewhere (because they have no directors or employees there to commit to prison,[45] nor assets to sequestrate or charge).

**15.15**  The fact that US-based ISPs are operating in such a climate has led to a tendency to be dismissive of complaints that arrive from outside their shores and which do not fall within one of the relatively narrow categories of complaint that US law recognizes as valid (*eg* an infringement of a US copyright or a breach of US criminal law)[46] irrespective of their merits, seriousness, or urgency.[47] Experience and

---

[41]  See *Global Royalties v Xcentric Ventures* No 07-956-PHX-FJM (D Az, 10 October 2007).

[42]  See *eg Bachchan v India Abroad Publications* 154 Misc 2d 228, 585 NYS 2d 661 (Sup Ct NY Co 1992) and *Matusevitch v Telnikoff* 347 Md 561, 702 A 2d 230 (Md 1997).

[43]  See n 42.

[44]  H Melkonian, *Defamation, Libel Tourism and the SPEECH Act of 2010: the First Amendment Colliding with the Common Law* (Cambria Press 2011) ch 5.

[45]  A foreign director of a foreign corporation which is already before the English court has been held to be susceptible to an application for committal for contempt of court: *Dar Al Arkan Real Estate Development Co v Al Refai* [2014] EWCA Civ 715, [2015] 1 WLR 135.

[46]  See in this regard s 230(e) of the Communications Act of 1934.

[47]  See, by way of illustration, the dilatory nature of Google's response to the claimant's complaint in *Tamiz v Google Inc* as described and considered in the first instance judgment of Eady J: [2012] EWHC 449 (QB), [2012] EMLR 24 [15]–[20] and [38]. See also Google's evidence before the Joint Parliamentary Committee on Privacy and Injunctions to the effect that it was reluctant on policy grounds to develop technology that would ensure the removal of links to unlawful material in search results generated by its proprietary search engine, and the Committee's response to that evidence in its Report: 'Google acknowledged that it was possible to develop the technology proactively to monitor websites for such material in order that the material does not appear in the results of searches. We find their objections in principle to developing

anecdotal evidence suggest that they will rarely agree to remove content voluntarily except with the consent of its author. They tend to insist upon the production of an English court order before they will contemplate taking action at all[48] and it is not unknown for them to demand the production of a US court order.[49] Given the statutory arrangements described above, unless on the particular facts of the case a US court can be persuaded to make an order which did not depend on the establishment of a civil cause of action, *ie* in the exercise of a US criminal jurisdiction, this is likely to be impossible to achieve.

Nevertheless, the decision of the European Court of Justice in *Google Spain*[50] in 2014 has changed radically the terms of engagement with US-based ISPs, for two central reasons: (i) it decided that search engine operators—and therefore possibly other types of ISPs—are 'data controllers' for the purposes of the EU Data Protection Directive (and by implication, domestically, the DPA), and (ii) it held that European subsidiaries of those corporations are amenable to suit in the courts of Europe in respect of such processing even if they carry on no part of the parent's 'publishing' business. Under the circumstances, whereas previously one might reasonably have queried whether there was any point in seeking to enlist the help of US-based service providers on a voluntary basis, *Google Spain* has significantly ameliorated the position. **15.16**

## C. Criminal Liability

An offensive, upsetting, or harassing online publication will in some circumstances **15.17** give rise to criminal as well as civil liability.[51] While the primary object of criminal proceedings is to punish rather than to injunct,[52] the instigation of a police

---

such technology totally unconvincing. Google and other search engines should take steps to ensure that their websites are not used as vehicles to breach the law and should actively develop and use such technology. We recommend that if legislation is necessary to require them to do so it should be introduced.' (HL Paper 273 HC 1443, 27 March 2012, paras 110–15, available at <http://www.publications.parliament.uk/pa/jt201012/jtselect/jtprivinj/273/273.pdf>). See also R Robertson and T Doble, 'Twitter still to grasp the nettle?' (Collyerbristow.com, 30 January 2014), available at <http://http://www.collyerbristow.com/media-centre/content/twitter-still-to-grasp-the-nettle>, and C Criado-Perez, '@Twitter: Optimised for Abuse' (Week Woman, 11 May 2014), available at <http://weekwoman.wordpress.com/2014/05/11/twitter-optimised-for-abuse/>.

[48] See *eg G v Wikimedia Foundation* [2009] EWHC 3148 (QB), [2010] EMLR 14; *Bacon v Automattic Inc* [2011] EWHC 1072 (QB), [2012] 1 WLR 75.

[49] *Bacon* (n 48) [13].

[50] *Google Spain* (n 22).

[51] See generally J Agate and J Ledward, 'Social Media: How the Net is Closing in on Cyber Bullies' [2013] 24(8) Ent LR 263–8.

[52] A criminal court does nonetheless have the power to impose a restraining order on a defendant convicted or *acquitted* of *any* offence (not just an offence of harassment or stalking under the PHA 1997): see PHA 1997, s 5, as amended by the Domestic Violence, Crime and Victims Act 2004, s 12, and *eg* the sentencing remarks of the judge in *R v Nimmo and Sorley* (24 January

inquiry will often cause a wrongdoer to desist. If he or she does not, persistence risks aggravating the situation, putting the wrongdoer at greater risk of crossing the line into criminality and, if convicted of an offence, of being sentenced more severely. Criminal proceedings do not preclude civil proceedings, and vice versa.[53] Indeed, evidence of a conviction, a prosecution, or a police inquiry will often help persuade a judge on an application for a civil injunction that the matter is (objectively) serious. Furthermore, there may be other advantages to making a criminal complaint in an appropriate case. The police have wider investigatory powers than ordinary citizens, they are better resourced than most, and their services are free, at the point of use at any rate.

**15.18** The question of whether a publication on social media will be deemed suitable to be prosecuted in a criminal court now falls to be considered in accordance with the Director of Public Prosecutions' *Guidelines on prosecuting cases involving communications sent via social media* (the Guidelines).[54]

**15.19** The initial assessment section of the Guidelines identifies four categories of communication capable of being effected online that may give rise to criminal liability:

    (i) credible threats of violence to the person or of damage to property;

    (ii) communications specifically targeting an individual or individuals and which may constitute harassment or stalking within the meaning of the PHA 1997;

    (iii) publications in breach of a court order; and

    (iv) grossly offensive, indecent, obscene, or false communications.[55]

The Guidelines provide that communications coming within the first three categories ought to be prosecuted robustly where they are seen to satisfy the two-limb test of evidential sufficiency and public interest set out in the Code for Crown Prosecutors. Publications in the fourth category, meanwhile, are said to be subject to a high exclusionary threshold: in most cases, prosecution is unlikely to be in

---

2014), available at <http://www.judiciary.gov.uk/judgments/r-v-nimmo-and-sorley-judgment/>, a prosecution under Communications Act 2003, s 127.

[53] See *eg* the parallel civil and criminal proceedings arising from phone-hacking at the *News of the World* newspaper: decisions arising in the civil litigation have been reported variously under the names *Phillips v News Group Newspapers Ltd* (eg [2012] UKSC 28, [2013] 1 AC 1) and *Mobile Phone Voicemail Interception Litigation, Re* (eg [2012] EWHC 397 (Ch), [2012] 1 WLR 2545) and *Various Claimants v News Group Newspapers Ltd* (eg [2013] EWHC 2119 (Ch), [2014] Ch 400). The criminal proceedings in *R v Coulson, Brooks and others* concluded at the Old Bailey in June 2014.

[54] The Guidelines were issued on 20 June 2013. They may be found at <http://www.cps.gov.uk/legal/a_to_c/communications_sent_via_social_media/>. When making a complaint to the police in respect of an online communication, it may be advisable to draw the Guidelines to their attention, in particular the statement at [11] that such cases 'are likely to benefit from early consultation between police and prosecutors, and the police are encouraged to contact the CPS at an early stage of the investigation'.

[55] Guidelines (n 54) para 12.

the public interest.[56] The Guidelines make clear that resending communications originally posted by someone else[57] may also incur criminal liability.[58]

In relation to the first category, that of credible threats of violence or damage to property, the Guidelines highlight two specific offences which are of particular relevance to social media users: that of sending an electronic communication which conveys a threat contrary to s 1 of the Malicious Communications Act 1988, and of sending a message of a menacing character by means of a public telecommunications network contrary to s 127 of the Communications Act 2003. It was decided by the Divisional Court in *Chambers v DPP*—known as the 'Twitter Joke' case[59]— that a Tweet is a message sent via a public electronic telecommunications network for the purposes of s 127 of the Communications Act 2003.[60] The Guidelines also make it clear, relying upon the decision in *Chambers*, that unless the message in question induces fear or apprehension in its recipients, it lacks the requisite element of menace and its publication cannot constitute an offence under s 127(i) (a).[61] Similarly, the threat must be credible if it is to warrant criminal prosecution. The offences of making threats to kill contrary to s 16 of the Offences Against the Person Act 1861 and of putting people in fear of violence contrary to s 4 of the PHA 1997 ought also to be borne in mind. **15.20**

As regards the second category, that of targeted or harassing communications, the Guidelines draw specific attention to the fact that, for the purpose of offences under the PHA 1997, the impugned conduct must consist of a sequence of events (a 'course of conduct') rather than two or more distinct and separate incidents.[62] **15.21**

In relation to the fourth category, grossly offensive, indecent, obscene, or false communications, the Guidelines indicate that the germane offences are also to be found in the provisions of s 1 of the Malicious Communications Act 1988 and s 127 of the Communications Act 2003. The statutory terms 'indecent or grossly offensive' have been held to be ordinary English words:[63] whether or not a communication is indecent or grossly offensive is an issue to be determined by the tribunal of fact. As already noted, the Guidelines emphasize in respect of this category the high threshold that must be met before the evidential requirements in the Code for **15.22**

---

[56] Guidelines (n 54) para 13.
[57] *eg* by Retweeting or Favouriting them, as to which see 15.30.
[58] Guidelines (n 54) para 2.
[59] See further <en.wikipedia.org/wiki/Twitter_Joke_Trial>.
[60] *Chambers v DPP* [2012] EWHC 2157 (Admin), [2013] 1 WLR 1833 [25].
[61] *Chambers* (n 60) [17]. For a case in which the element of menace was admitted to be present, see *R v Nimmo and Sorley* (n 52). The defendants were convicted of posting Tweets that were menacing to Caroline Criado-Perez and Stella Creasy MP. Nimmo and Sorley were sentenced respectively to eight weeks and twelve weeks in prison.
[62] Guidelines (n 54) para 23, citing *Lau v DPP* [2000] 1 FLR 799.
[63] *Connolly v DPP* [2007] EWHC 237 (Admin), [2008] 1 WLR 276 [10]; Guidelines (n 54) para 30.

Crown Prosecutors will be satisfied. The right to freedom of expression protected by Article 10 of the European Convention on Human Rights (ECHR) extends to speech which is offensive or distasteful. The statutes in question criminalize conduct which is grossly offensive: communications which are merely offensive or painful to the recipient will not attract liability.[64]

**15.23** In a separate development, by s 33 of the Criminal Justice and Courts Act 2015 (which received Royal Assent on 12 February 2015), Parliament has legislated to criminalize the publication of what is colloquially known as 'revenge porn'. The provision makes it an offence punishable by up to two years' imprisonment to disclose private sexual photographs and films without consent and with intent to cause distress.

**15.24** There are, of course, limitations on the role for the criminal law in this context. The police and prosecutors are only likely to intervene in fairly extreme and egregious cases. The public interest test will often not be passed even where there is a powerful private interest in action being taken. A private prosecution is liable to be uncertain in outcome and costly. The statutory provisions in question have no extra-territorial effect, so they are not applicable to the acts of UK citizens carried on outside the jurisdiction. Apart from the offence of making threats to kill and some of the more serious harassment offences (*eg* under s 4 of the PHA 1997), none of the relevant offences is extraditable.[65] As already mentioned, the principal object of criminal proceedings is not to stop misconduct, but to punish it. Accordingly, if a victim's aim is, as it usually is, to put a stop to online misconduct as quickly as possible, criminal proceedings can only be at most an adjunct to the principal means of achieving this result: the civil law.

## D. Civil Liability

### (1) Introduction

**15.25** Where an online posting infringes privacy, various persons with different roles in the publication process may in principle be responsible in law. The potentially broad scope of liability is significant in an environment in which the potential for

---

[64] Guidelines (n 54) para 39.

[65] Extradition Act 2003, s 148(1)(b) requires the conduct to be punishable under the laws of the relevant part of the UK with imprisonment or another form of detention for a term of at least twelve months or a greater punishment. While making threats to kill has a maximum penalty of ten years' imprisonment and putting people in fear of violence carries one of five years' imprisonment, none of the other offences mentioned in this section currently fits the bill. However, the new 'revenge porn' offence under s 33 of the Criminal Justice and Courts Act 2015 (which came into force on 13 April 2015) carries a maximum term of imprisonment of two years. Moreover, by s 32 of the same Act the maximum penalty for committing an offence under s 1 of the Malicious Communications Act 1988 was increased to two years' imprisonment.

interference with privacy is so great, and the challenges involved in tackling such conduct so numerous.

By analogy with defamation,[66] common law liability is joint and several: anyone **15.26** who causes or contributes to the act of publication to any extent can be held liable for that act and for all the losses suffered as a consequence. Accordingly, apart from the author or originator of the material in question, there are several other candidates for civil suit: the broadband provider which enables internet users to access the offending material; the operator of the website or blogging platform on which the material appears; the owner of the servers that store or cache it;[67] and the operator of the search engine which points readers in its direction. Such persons are often collectively referred to as internet service providers (ISPs). The extent to which each different type of ISP may be held responsible for publication of private material is at 15.45 *et seq*. ISPs are liable to have a key role to play in privacy cases, where the emphasis is on preventing further intrusion rather than vindicating a past slight (as it is in defamation): they have the power to put a stop to a continuing unlawful publication, and as such may be considered 'best placed' to provide claimants with the relief they seek.[68] Similar considerations apply in relation to data protection: under s 1(1) DPA 'any person who (either alone or jointly or in common with other persons) determines the purposes for which and the manner in which any personal data are, or are to be, processed' may be a data controller. In *Vidal-Hall v Google Inc*,[69] the US-incorporated defendant, in its capacity as operator of the Google search engine on Apple-based (Safari) browsers, did not dispute that it was a data controller for the purposes of the DPA. The European Court of Justice in *Google Spain*[70] found as a fact that Google Inc and its Spanish subsidiary were data controllers for the

---

[66] In *Douglas v Hello! Ltd* [2003] EWCA Civ 139, [2003] EMLR 585 [36] the Court of Appeal decided that the principles governing responsibility for publication in breach of confidence cases were arguably the same as those that applied in defamation. Furthermore, in *Vidal-Hall* (n 30) it was confirmed that misuse of private information, in contrast with breach of confidence, was a tort. On this footing, it is submitted that there is no sound basis for distinguishing between defamation and other publication torts in this regard.

[67] 'Caching' is defined in reg 18 of the Electronic Commerce (EC Directive) Regulations, SI 2002/2013, as the 'automatic, intermediate and temporary [storing of information] where that storage is for the sole purpose of making more efficient onward transmission of the information to other recipients of the service upon their request'.

[68] Recital (59) to the EU Information Society Directive (Directive 2001/29/EC of the European Parliament and of the Council of 22 May 2001 on the harmonisation of certain aspects of copyright and related rights in the information society [2001] OJ L167/10) provides in terms that: 'In the digital environment, in particular, the services of intermediaries may increasingly be used by third parties for infringing activities. In many cases such intermediaries are best placed to bring such infringing activities to an end.' See Arnold J's judgments in *Twentieth Century Fox Film Corp v British Telecommunications plc* [2011] EWHC 1981 (Ch), [2011] RPC 28 and [2011] EWHC 2714 (Ch), [2012] 1 All ER 806 in which the effect of Recital (59) is analysed (in the context of the first case to involve an application for a copyright blocking injunction under s 97A of the Copyright, Designs and Patents Act 1988).

[69] *Vidal-Hall* (n 30).

[70] *Google Spain* (n 22).

purposes of the EU Data Protection Directive[71] in their capacity as the operators of Google's proprietary search engine.

**15.27**  Nevertheless, common sense—in addition to current legislative policy in the shape of ss 5 and 10 of the Defamation Act 2013 and the accompanying Defamation (Operators of Websites) Regulations 2013—suggests that the person who ought to be regarded as primarily responsible for the unlawful conduct is the author or originator of the offending material. However, it may be difficult if not impossible to identify and track down the author of a publication, owing to widespread reliance on anonymity and pseudonymity on the internet, particularly by those who mean to do harm. The court may use its *Norwich Pharmacal* powers[72] to order an ISP or some other informed third party to give up details of an author's identity or other information if that would help a would-be claimant pursue a remedy. But the author will often have managed to cover his or her tracks, and the process of obtaining and enforcing *Norwich Pharmacal* relief will be a fruitless, but nonetheless costly, exercise. Problems may also arise where the author, even if identifiable, resides in a foreign country where practical or principled obstacles stand in the way of the enforcement of an English court-ordered remedy protecting privacy.[73]

**15.28**  Faced with such difficulties, a claimant may wish to proceed directly against persons who are partly responsible for the posting in question and more susceptible to suit, specifically the ISPs which enabled the publication to occur on the internet. But special common law and statutory defences shield ISPs—and in certain cases, give them complete immunity—from liability, especially where they act quickly to disable access to the offending material upon being notified of the problem.

**15.29**  A third possibility is the pursuit of an action against 'persons unknown'. Until now, the court has tended to view the initiation of privacy proceedings in this form as an inherently temporary arrangement, enabling the grant of an interim injunction that will bind, at pain of committal for contempt of court, any person served with notice of it, while giving the claimant a chance to try to track down the author. For reasons that will be explored below,[74] it is suggested that a claim in this form may come to be seen as an appropriate way to pursue a privacy claim all the way to judgment and thereby to obtain effective final relief in circumstances where, despite the claimant's best efforts, the author simply cannot be identified.

---

[71]  Council Directive 95/46/EC on the protection of individuals with regard to the processing of personal data and on the free movement of such data [1995] OJ L281/31.

[72]  *Norwich Pharmacal Co v Customs and Excise Commissioners* [1974] AC 133, HL; *Rugby Football Union v Viagogo Ltd* [2012] UKSC 55, [2012] 1 WLR 3333.

[73]  As regards the potential difficulties to which this aspect of things might give rise, see the discussion in *Re J (A Child)* [2013] EWHC 2694 (Fam), [2014] EMLR 7 [44]–[65].

[74]  See 15.115.

## (2) Responsibility for online publication: special considerations

One hallmark of the online model of publication, whether via websites, or through **15.30** the medium of social networks, is its inter-connectivity: its reliance on hyperlinks, references, footnotes and other forms of connectors such as Facebook 'Likes' and Twitter 'Retweets' and 'Favourites'.[75] This distinctive feature of internet-based communication is one which may be exploited by a determined publisher, disseminating the material via multiple interconnected web-based platforms.[76] It also raises specific issues for the assignment of legal responsibility between different persons involved in the publishing process.

The issues are broadly twofold. First, the original publisher may become liable for **15.31** very substantial online publication if the material he or she publishes goes viral: the world wide web and social media have immeasurably enhanced the capacity of stories and information to spread more widely and more quickly than ever before.[77] The originator of defamatory words, and so, it would appear to follow, of material that infringes privacy, may be held liable for all the damage that flows from such republication by others where such republication is a reasonably foreseeable consequence of the original publication.[78] Second, it may also lead to liability on the part of individuals who choose to republish the unlawful material, even if their engagement with the material is only of the most fleeting kind.[79]

There are numerous ways in which an internet user can republish material online **15.32** and thereby in principle become legally responsible for its publication. The issues that arise are, however, best exemplified by use of the best-known instrument of online inter-connectivity, the hyperlink.

By using a hyperlink, a user may direct his or her readers' attention to material **15.33** available elsewhere on the internet which has been posted in breach of someone's privacy. This raises the issue of whether a person who incorporates a hyperlink in this way thereby becomes responsible in law for publication of the linked content. No English court has yet found it necessary to determine the matter,[80] but it was considered directly by the Supreme Court of Canada in the case of *Crookes v Newton*.[81] The majority in that case held that using a hyperlink, of itself, should

---

[75] According to Twitter's own Glossary , a Retweet is 'A Tweet that you forward to your followers', and 'Favoriting a Tweet indicates that you liked a specific Tweet. You can find all of your favorite Tweets by clicking on the favorites link on your profile page' (see Twitter Glossary at <https://support.twitter.com/articles/166337>).

[76] *Brand v Berki* [2014] EWHC 2979 (QB); *QRS v Beach* (n 27).

[77] *Cairns* (n 6) [27].

[78] *McManus v Beckham* [2002] EWCA Civ 939, [2002] 1 WLR 2982 [44].

[79] See eg the nature of the Tweet for which the defendant was found liable in *Lord McAlpine of West Green v Bercow* [2013] EWHC 1342 (QB).

[80] Although in one instance in defamation proceedings it opted to proceed for the purpose of an application to strike out the claim on the footing that hyperlinked material was to be treated as part of the words complained of: *Tamiz v Guardian News and Media Ltd* [2013] EWHC 2339 (QB) [48].

[81] *Crookes* (n 1).

never be regarded as publishing the content to which the hyperlink is connected and refers for the purposes of the law of defamation.[82] The decisive reason for that conclusion was that the hyperlinker lacks control over the publication of the material to which he or she has created the link.[83]

**15.34** So far, this is the only common-law decision considering the point but it is questionable whether it will be followed elsewhere. It is submitted that English courts are more likely to follow the fact-dependent approach adopted in the two minority opinions. In their joint concurring judgment, McLachlin CJ and Fish J said that hyperlinking might in certain circumstances create responsibility for publication; where a hyperlink, when read contextually, constitutes an adoption or endorsement of some linked defamatory matter, it could give rise to liability on the part of the hyperlinker.[84] In the other minority opinion, Deschamps J suggested that the rule ought to be that where a deliberate act makes information readily available to a third party in comprehensible form, such an act might in principle result in liability.[85] The more flexible stance taken in these minority decisions seems more in keeping with the English courts' approach to questions of fact in publication cases than the dogmatic position embraced by the majority.

**15.35** While publication on Twitter has featured in a number of decided cases in England, the question of whether Retweeting or Favouriting someone else's Tweet constitutes republication has yet to be considered.[86] But applying general established principles, there is no reason why it should not, with the consequence that those who Retweet or Favourite unlawful material may become jointly and severally liable for its publication, or, alternatively, be viewed as party to a reasonably foreseeable trail of republications of the original Tweet for which the original publisher is responsible.

---

[82] *Crookes* (n 1) [14].

[83] *Crookes* (n 1) [27].

[84] *Crookes* (n 1) [50]. Such an approach is consistent with the approach taken in common law reportage cases where adoption or endorsement of the underlying material precluded a defence of neutral reportage: see *eg Roberts v Gable* [2007] EWCA Civ 721, [2008] QB 502 and *Charman v Orion Publishing Ltd* [2007] EWCA Civ 972, [2008] EMLR 16. The common law reportage defence was (*semble*) abolished by the Defamation Act 2013 which came into force on 1 January 2014. Now see s 4 (and specifically s 4(3)) of the Act for the new statutory iteration of the defence.

[85] *Crookes* (n 1) [59].

[86] To date, the most prominent cases of 'Twitter libel' have been *Cairns* (n 6) and *Lord McAlpine of West Green v Bercow* [2013] EWHC 981 (QB), [2014] EMLR 3 and at [2013] EWHC 1342 (QB). As regards Retweeting, it may be observed that the criminal prosecution in the case of *R v Nunn* (a case concerned with online threats to rape Stella Creasy MP after she expressed support for Caroline Criado-Perez's campaign to feature a woman on the British £10 banknote) appears to have been based, at least in part, on Retweets: see C Philby, 'Twitter troll "embarked on campaign of hatred against Labour MP Stella Creasy"' *The Independent* (19 May 2014), available at <http://www.independent.co.uk/news/uk/crime/twitter-troll-embarked-on-campaign-of-hatred-against-labour-mp-stella-creasy-9399533.html>.

Similarly, use of the Facebook 'Like' button, which enables users to share with **15.36** other users content available within Facebook and elsewhere on the web, has not been considered in a reported decision of the English court. The position has, however, been analysed in the United States. In *Bland v Roberts*, the plaintiffs claimed that they had been dismissed from their employment for supporting their employer's political rival. They had given their support by 'Liking' his rival's campaign page on Facebook. The Fourth US Circuit Court of Appeals held that posting a Facebook Like was a constitutionally protected form of speech under the First Amendment. Significantly, the Court was prepared to accept that conferring a Facebook Like upon other pre-existing material qualified as speech: clicking the Like button caused the publication on Facebook of a statement that the person clicking the button liked the material in question, which was to be regarded as a substantive statement.[87] Beyond this, the special facts and context of the decision limit its usefulness.

## E. Responsibility for Online Publication: the Search for an Author

Where the author is unknown, it may be appropriate for the person seeking to **15.37** establish his or her identity to apply to the court for a *Norwich Pharmacal* order against an ISP or other interested third party, or, alternatively, for an order for pre-action disclosure under Civil Procedure Rules (CPR) 31.17.[88]

An applicant making a *Norwich Pharmacal* application of this type will be **15.38** expected to establish, among other things, that disclosure of the relevant information is necessary and proportionate taking into account the rights of any individual whose identity and data are likely to be disclosed under Article 8 ECHR and under Article 8 of the Charter of Fundamental Rights of the European Union.[89] Article 8 of the Charter provides for a right to protection of personal data, while Article 52(1) permits exceptions to that right 'subject to the principle of proportionality'. Where the issue of proportionality falls to be considered in a *Norwich Pharmacal* context, the appropriate approach is the same as when Article 8 ECHR needs to be balanced against competing rights and interests,

---

[87] 730 F 3d 368 (4th Cir 2013). For more on the legal significance of 'Liking', see L E Gray, 'Thumb War: the Facebook "Like" Button and Free Speech in the era of Social Networking' [2013] 7 Charleston L Rev 447.

[88] *Norwich Pharmacal* (n 72); *Rugby Football Union* (n 72); *Various Claimants v News Group Newspapers Ltd* [2013] EWHC 2119 (Ch), [2014] Ch 400. In the specific internet context, see in particular *Golden Eye (International) Ltd v Telefónica UK Ltd* [2012] EWCA Civ 1740, [2013] EMLR 26.

[89] *Rugby Football Union* (n 72) [45] and *Golden Eye* (n 88) [19].

namely, the application of the 'ultimate balancing test' articulated initially by Lord Steyn in *Re S*.[90]

**15.39** In this context, the Court of Appeal in *Totalise plc v Motley Fool Ltd*[91] recognized the danger that granting an order for the disclosure of an anonymous user's identity may constitute an unjustifiable interference with that individual's right to respect for his or her private life, particularly when that individual is not before the court. It has been argued that this aspect of the Court's decision supports the view that anonymity is not to be regarded merely a mask for wrongdoing, but as having a positive social value in its own right.[92]

**15.40** Websites and discussion forums typically have privacy policies which play a part in determining the rights and interests of their users, and which may prove a further barrier to the identification of an anonymous author. In *Clift v Clarke*[93] the newspaper's website had a privacy policy which stated that users' personal information would not be disclosed to third parties without their consent. The judge held in that case that, even where the conditions for the exercise of the *Norwich Pharmacal* jurisdiction were satisfied, the court might nevertheless refuse the application as a matter of discretion, having regard to the rights and legitimate expectations of website users arising out of such a policy.[94]

**15.41** Close attention should therefore always be given to the specific circumstances affecting the individual whose personal data will be disclosed on the granting of a *Norwich Pharmacal* order.[95] Such considerations will be weighed against other potentially decisive factors such as the strength of the case contemplated by the applicant, the public interest in applicants vindicating their rights, and any deterrent effect that granting the order might have.[96]

**15.42** Even if a would-be claimant obtains an order against an ISP or other interested third party requiring it to provide details of an anonymous author's identity

---

[90] *Rugby Football Union* (n 72) [44]–[45].
[91] [2001] EWCA Civ 1897, [2002] 1 WLR 1233 [25].
[92] 'The Court is mindful . . . of the importance of the wishes of internet users not to disclose their identity in exercising their freedom of expression': *Delfi AS v Estonia* (n 33). On the same topic, see M Daly, 'Is there an entitlement to anonymity? A European and international analysis' [2013] EIPR 198, 202. In connection with blogger anonymity, see also *Author of a Blog v Times Newspapers Ltd* [2009] EWHC 1358 (QB), [2009] EMLR 22; E Barendt, 'Bad News for Bloggers' [2009] 2 J Media L 141–7; K Hughes, 'No Reasonable Expectation of Anonymity?' [2010] 2 J Media L 169–81, and Lord Neuberger, 'What's In A Name? Privacy and Anonymity on the Internet' (30 September 2014), available at <http://www.supremecourt.uk/docs/speech-140930.pdf>. For the approach of the US court, see *Music Group Macao Commercial Offshore Ltd v John Does, Defendant*, 2015 WL 930249 (US District Court for the Northern District of California).
[93] [2011] EWHC 1164 (QB).
[94] *Clift* (n 93) [40]–[41].
[95] *Rugby Football Union* (n 72) [46].
[96] *Rugby Football Union* (n 72) [17].

or other potentially germane information, if the respondent to the *Norwich Pharmacal* application is based outside the jurisdiction, enforcement questions remain. US-based ISPs' usual stated policy is that they will disclose users' details when legally required to do so. However, what this means in practice may vary. In *G v Wikimedia Foundation*, which specifically concerned a *Norwich Pharmacal* order, the lawyers for the publisher of the online encyclopedia, Wikipedia, stated in correspondence that they would be willing to comply with a 'properly issued court order narrowly limited to the material you ask for in your letter', albeit that they insisted that in doing so they were not waiving their client's right as a foreign corporation to argue that the English court had no jurisdiction over it.[97]

In the subsequent case of *Bacon v Automattic Inc*, three respondents (all of which **15.43** were American companies operating platforms that hosted websites where defamatory comments had been posted) responded differently to the claimant's claims.[98] The first respondent, Automattic Inc, the operator of the blogging platform WordPress, requested a court order issued by the English court. However, the second respondent, Wikimedia Foundation, on this occasion insisted upon an order issued by a US court before it would disclose any information that identified the user in question. It took the position that a foreign subpoena would not be complied with absent an immediate threat to life and limb.[99] The third respondent, the publisher of the *Denver Post* newspaper in print and online, did not respond to the claimant's correspondence. However, the unchallenged evidence was that the *Norwich Pharmacal* order the court was being asked to make could (as a form of discovery) be enforced without difficulty against Wikimedia Foundation in California under the Interstate and International Depositions and Discovery Act.[100] The fact that discovery was being sought in aid of English defamation proceedings apparently did not, according to the US law evidence presented to the court, affect the position.

Where a *Norwich Pharmacal* order is sought against a respondent based out- **15.44** side the jurisdiction, it may be appropriate for the applicant to seek to serve the claim form on the respondent by an alternative method in reliance on CPR 6.15.[101] The need to do so may arise because the information held by the respondent in relation to the alleged wrongdoer is only retained for a limited period of time.[102]

---

[97] [2009] EWHC 3148 (QB), [2010] EMLR 14 [38].
[98] *Bacon* (n 48).
[99] *Bacon* (n 48) [13].
[100] California Code of Civil Procedure, 2029.100 *et seq*. See *Bacon* (n 48) [14].
[101] It is not necessary to rely on CPR 6.15 if the method of service sought to be employed is permitted by the law of the country in which the claim form is to be served: *Bacon* (n 48) [53].
[102] *Bacon* (n 48) [17].

# F. Responsibility for Online Publication: Internet Service Providers

## (1) Liability of Internet Service Providers at Common Law

**15.45**  Most of the authorities on responsibility for publication on the internet have arisen in the defamation context. Since there appears to be no reason to distinguish between defamation and other publication torts including misuse of private information on this issue,[103] the courts in the latter context are likely to be guided by these developments.

### (a) Hosts and social media platforms

**15.46**  In *Godfrey v Demon Internet Ltd*[104] it was decided that the defendant ISP, which hosted on its server a Usenet newsgroup[105] and provided access to posts on the newsgroup at the request of users, was a publisher at common law. Morland J held that, since the defendant hosted, transmitted, and had the ability to delete the defamatory material in question, it was more than a mere conduit. It would therefore be liable in principle as a publisher unless it could establish a defence of innocent dissemination.

**15.47**  In *Tamiz v Google Inc*[106] the liability of ISPs was considered for the first time by the Court of Appeal. The claim related to allegedly defamatory material posted on a blogsite hosted on a platform operated by the defendant. The master had originally permitted the claimant to serve the claim form out of jurisdiction in California but, on the defendant's application, the judge set aside permission on the grounds (1) that the defendant was not a publisher at common law, (2) that even if it was a publisher it would have unassailable defences under s 1 of the Defamation Act 1996 and under reg 19 of the E-Commerce Regulations,[107] and (3) that in any event, owing to the short period of time between the defendant being notified of the existence of the material and its take-down, the claimant was unlikely to have sustained any meaningful damage to reputation, such that the principle in *Jameel (Yousef) v Dow Jones*[108] was engaged.

**15.48**  The Court of Appeal dismissed the claimant's appeal, upholding Eady J's conclusion that 'the game was not worth the candle', but in doing so it elucidated the applicable common law principles. The Court held that prior to notification, the defendant was not to be regarded as a 'primary publisher'[109] and nor could it even

---

[103]  See *Douglas* (n 66) [36].
[104]  [2001] QB 201.
[105]  A form of internet discussion group predating web forums.
[106]  [2013] EWCA Civ 68, [2013] 1 WLR 2151.
[107]  As to which, see 15.67.
[108]  [2005] EWCA Civ 75, [2005] QB 946.
[109]  *Tamiz* (n 106) [25].

be considered a 'secondary' or 'subordinate' publisher[110] since it neither knew nor ought by the exercise of reasonable care to have known that the material it was hosting was defamatory. However, once notified of the existence of the material, the defendant host arguably became a publisher at common law. By allowing the defamatory material to remain online after being notified of its presence and after a reasonable time had elapsed within which it might have acted to remove it, Google had associated itself sufficiently with the presence of that material on the blogsite so as to make it responsible for its ongoing publication.[111]

### (b) Broadband providers (mere conduits)

In *Bunt v Tilley*,[112] meanwhile, the Court considered the position of companies **15.49** providing access to internet users who posted defamatory statements on websites hosted by third parties (*ie* broadband providers). Eady J found that no liability attached to such ISPs as a matter of common law, as they had neither knowledge of, nor involvement in, the process of publication, nor any means of control over it. Their position was analogous to that of a telephone company.[113]

### (c) Search engine operators

In *Metropolitan International Schools Ltd v Designtechnica Corp*[114] Eady J consid- **15.50** ered the potential liability of operators of internet search engines for the publication of results and the snippets of material which are produced when a user carries out a search, when those results and snippets happen to be defamatory. Google Inc, a defendant in its capacity as the operator of its proprietary search engine, stated that in accordance with its 'notice and take down' policy, once it had been notified of the problem, it had taken such steps as it could to prevent the defamatory snippets from being displayed. The judge held that prior to notification the operator was not responsible, and had no liability, for publishing the snippets as it did not formulate the search terms and had no active input into the results: the relevant acts occurred automatically, without human intervention.[115] After notification, even if its notice and take-down procedure had not been put into effect as rapidly as it might have been, Google had not become liable as a publisher on the basis of authorship or acquiescence.[116] The broader question of whether the operator of a search engine could ever become liable after it had been notified of an offending search result was not decided.[117]

---

[110] *Tamiz* (n 106) [26] (by which the Court meant a facilitator analogous to a distributor, the type of situation considered by the Court in *Emmens v Pottle* (1885) 16 QBD 354).

[111] *Tamiz* (n 106) [33]–[36].

[112] [2006] EWHC 407 (QB), [2007] 1 WLR 1243.

[113] *Bunt* (n 112) [37].

[114] [2009] EWHC 1765 (QB), [2009] EMLR 27.

[115] *Metropolitan International Schools* (n 114) [11]–[13] and [50]–[53]. Contrast the findings of the European Court of Justice in *Google Spain* (n 22) in the data protection context.

[116] *Metropolitan International Schools* (n 114) [58] and [64].

[117] *Metropolitan International Schools* (n 114) [56]–[62].

**Other jurisdictions**

**15.51** *Northern Ireland*  In *CG v Facebook Ireland Ltd*[118] the High Court of Northern Ireland held that, along with the author of the pages, Facebook was liable as a publisher after it had been placed on notice of the unlawful character of the material in question. The claim was brought in harassment, misuse of private information, and under the Human Rights Act 1998 (HRA). The Court granted the plaintiff a final injunction and damages.

**15.52** *Hong Kong*  The courts of Hong Kong have interpreted common-law principles governing the responsibility of platform operators for the publication of defamatory material more strictly than the English court. In *Oriental Press Group Ltd v Fevaworks Solutions Ltd*,[119] the Hong Kong Final Court of Appeal considered the liability in defamation of an online forum provider. The case related to comments posted by users of the forum which, it was not disputed, were defamatory of the plaintiffs. The Court declined to follow the Court of Appeal's approach in *Tamiz* and distinguished *Byrne v Deane*[120] in deciding that the defendant was a 'subordinate publisher' *ab initio* (*ie* even without knowledge of the offending material it was publishing), subject to a defence of innocent dissemination at common law (which on the facts the Court found was made out). Meanwhile, with respect to search engines, the High Court of Hong Kong held in *Yeung v Google Inc*[121] that the plaintiff had a good arguable case that Google Inc was the publisher of the defamatory auto-complete search suggestions and search results complained of, and was liable for their publication.

**15.53** *Australia*  The Supreme Court of Victoria in *Trkulja v Google Inc (No 5)*[122] also took a different approach from that adopted in the analogous case in England (*Metropolitan International Schools Ltd*), holding that it had been open to the jury to find (as they had) that Google was a publisher of images and snippets generated by its search engine even before it had been notified of the offending material. The judge referred to the English case law, specifically the *Metropolitan Schools* judgment, and declined to follow it, holding that while search engine results were automatically generated and that therefore Google's role was a passive one, the process operated just as Google had designed and intended it to, with the consequence that it was liable for the product of that process.[123]

---

[118] [2015] NIQB 11, applying *XY v Facebook Ireland Ltd* [2012] NIQB 96.
[119] [2013] HKFCA 47, [2014] EMLR 11.
[120] *Oriental Press Group Ltd* (n 119) [50]–[52].
[121] [2014] HKCFI 1404.
[122] [2012] VSC 533. See also *Bleyer v Google Inc* [2014] NSWSC 897 (in which McCallum J acceded to a *Jameel v Dow Jones*-type argument in deciding to stay permanently a libel action based on the publication of search engine results to three people).
[123] *Trkulja* (n 122) [18].

*Ireland*   In *McKeogh v John Doe*,[124] an interlocutory decision in a defamation case   **15.54**
(which also raised privacy issues),[125] the Irish High Court proceeded on the basis
that Facebook Ireland Ltd and Google (both the US corporation and its Irish
subsidiary) were publishers when acting in their capacity as the operators of the
video-sharing service YouTube. Peart J granted a mandatory injunction against
them, ordering Facebook to disclose to the plaintiff an electronic copy of what
was alleged to be a fake Facebook profile, and ordering the defendants to send
their appointed experts to a meeting with the plaintiff's expert for the purpose of
assessing what technical measures could be taken to remove the offending material
from the internet. The judge also indicated readiness to grant a further mandatory
order for the removal of the material in the event that the parties could not reach
agreement as to this result between themselves.[126] Peart J acknowledged that there
might be a question as to whether the defendants could be properly regarded as
'publishers' and accepted that there was an arguable case that the defendants would
have a defence (including under the E-Commerce Directive),[127] but concluded that
these were matters for trial which did not prevent the grant of an injunction on an
interlocutory basis.[128]

*New Zealand*   The issue of whether the individual controller of a social media   **15.55**
page (*eg* of a Facebook profile or page) can be held responsible for the publication
of posts on that page authored by others arose in a case brought before the High
Court of New Zealand, *Wishart v Murray*.[129] After surveying pertinent case law
from around the common-law world, Courtney J found that such a person might
be liable in two situations: (1) where the person is aware of the unlawful material
and fails to remove it, or (2) where the person is not aware of the unlawful material
but, in all the circumstances, ought to know that posts made by others on the page
are likely to be defamatory.[130] On appeal, the Court of Appeal of New Zealand
concluded that only actual knowledge would do.[131]

### (d) Corporate social media accounts

Where a social media account, such as a Facebook profile or a Twitter feed,   **15.56**
belonging to a corporate entity is used by an employee to breach the privacy of
another employee or some other third party, or to harass such an individual,

---

[124] *McKeogh v John Doe*, Record No 2012/254P (Peart J), 16 March 2013. This decision is currently the subject of an appeal to the Irish Supreme Court.
[125] See Peart J's previous judgment in the case: [2012] IEHC 95.
[126] *McKeogh* (n 125) [23].
[127] As to which, see 15.61.
[128] *McKeogh* (n 124) [14].
[129] *Wishart v Murray* [2013] NZHC 540, [2013] 3 NZLR 246.
[130] *Wishart* (n 129) [17].
[131] *Murray v Wishart* [2014] NZCA 461. The Northern Irish court in *CG v Facebook Ireland Ltd* (n 118) held that such a person could be liable as a publisher, taking into account matters such as his or her power to delete posts and to block users.

the issue may arise of whether the corporation is answerable in law for the employee's misconduct. Certainly, a corporation may become liable if through an appropriate human agent it authorizes or approves the conduct in question including by failing to do something about it when the conduct comes to its attention. But a company may also be held vicariously liable for a misuse of private information perpetrated by its employees using social media in the course of their employment in the same way as it can in respect of other tortious activities.[132] An employer may be held vicariously liable under the PHA 1997.[133]

**15.57**  The limits of vicarious liability in the context of social media use are, however, unclear. Where an employee using a social media account is on a 'jaunt of their own',[134] *eg* posting personal details about an ex-partner who had nothing to do with the company, then it may be that the company will not be found vicariously liable, on the ground that the activity in question was not sufficiently closely connected to the employee's employment. But if, by contrast, part of a company's corporate social media strategy is to encourage employees to present a more 'personal' face to the world, then it may be unable to avoid liability when the employee does just that. All will turn on the specific facts and circumstances, but the existence of such slender distinctions and the risk of substantial liability make it all the more important that companies develop clear policies governing the use of social media at work.

**15.58**  Another question is who owns a corporate social media account. In *Whitmar Publications Ltd v Gamage*,[135] the High Court ordered certain former employees of the claimant company to convey to their former employer exclusive access and control (including passwords) of LinkedIn groups which had been maintained by those employees on the company's behalf as part of their job. The claimant alleged that the employees had used information gained from the social media accounts, together with other confidential information which had come into their possession as employees, to set up and develop a rival business. Meanwhile, in *Fairstar Heavy Transport NV v Adkins*[136] the Court of Appeal ordered the former CEO of the claimant company to permit his former employer to inspect and copy emails stored on his personal computer relating to the company's business. The court is liable to take a similar approach towards data of this nature stored on former employees' personal social media accounts where the employer needs to have access to that material.

---

[132] Misuse of private information has been authoritatively recognized to be a tort: *Vidal-Hall* (n 30). See also M A Jones et al (eds), *Clerk and Lindsell on Torts* (21st edn, Sweet & Maxwell 2014) ch 6. Where the act in question is a deliberate act, the test is that as set out in *Lister v Hesley Hall Ltd* [2001] UKHL 22, [2002] 1 AC 215: 'so closely connected with his employment that it would be fair and just to hold the [employer] vicariously liable' (Lord Steyn).

[133] *Majrowski v Guy's & St Thomas's NHS Trust* [2006] UKHL 34, [2007] 1 AC 224. See further 6.25–6.26.

[134] *Re Kay* [1967] 1 QB 140.

[135] [2013] EWHC 1881 (Ch).

[136] [2013] EWCA Civ 886, [2014] EMLR 12.

## G. Online Publication: Special Statutory Defences

The defences that apply generally to claims for breach of confidence and misuse of **15.59** private information are discussed in Chapter 11. Issues that arise specifically when one is considering the misuse of private information online are addressed in this section.

Where the defendant is not the author of the offending material but an entity **15.60** involved in the hosting, storage, or electronic transmission of that material, the first line of defence may be to deny responsibility for publication.[137] In the case of an ISP whose role in the publication process is merely that of a conduit or a cache, such a defence will almost certainly present a complete answer to any claim for liability. As regards hosts, however, following *Tamiz v Google Inc*,[138] liability is likely to turn on the defendant's knowledge of the offending material, whether it has taken steps to disable access to it, and, if so, how quickly.[139] As for operators of search engines, meanwhile, as the law stands in *Metropolitan Schools*,[140] the defendant is unlikely to have any liability.[141] It should be noted at the outset that there is no equivalent in privacy to the statutory innocent dissemination defence provided for in s 1 of the Defamation Act 1996 or to the new defence for operators of websites provided for in ss 5 and 10 of the Defamation Act 2013.

### (1) Defences under the E-Commerce Regulations 2002

The E-Commerce Regulations confer a number of different defences, with differ- **15.61** ent requirements on different types of ISP. The level of protection afforded by the defences varies according to the nature of the service provided and whether it is in the nature of a 'mere conduit' service (reg 17), caching (reg 18), or hosting (reg 19). The Regulations implement domestically Directive 2000/31/EC of the European Parliament and of the Council of 8 June 2000 on certain legal aspects of information society services, in particular electronic commerce, in the Internal Market, which is generally known as the E-Commerce Directive.

The E-Commerce Regulations apply to providers of what are termed 'informa- **15.62** tion society services'.[142] Recital (17) to the Directive explains that this means:

---

[137] See 15.45.

[138] See 15.47.

[139] A host will have a defence under reg 19(a)(ii) 'where upon obtaining knowledge or awareness' of the offending material 'it acts expeditiously to remove or to disable access' to it: see 15.67. The relationship between the time limit within which a host must achieve take-down if it is avoid liability at common law (see *Tamiz* (n 106) [33]–[36]) and the time limit stipulated in reg 19(a)(ii) is unclear (though it is possible that they are co-extensive). The Court of Appeal in *Tamiz* decided it was unnecessary for it to resolve any of the issues that arose in the case with reference to the E-Commerce Directive or Regulations: see [52] of the judgment.

[140] See 15.50.

[141] But contrast the position under the DPA following *Google Spain*: see 15.91.

[142] E-Commerce Regulations, regs 1(3) and 2.

'any service normally provided for remuneration, at a distance, by means of electronic equipment for the processing (including digital compression) and storage of data, and at the individual request of a recipient of a service'. 'Remuneration' has been held to include remuneration through advertising revenues.[143] Therefore the availability of the defences under the Regulations is not confined to those ISPs to which users pay a fee or to operators of websites which sit behind a paywall.

**15.63** The Regulations create defences against claims for pecuniary remedies or criminal sanctions, but contain no provision affecting the availability of injunctive relief.[144] Thus it is conceivable, in theory at least, that a claimant might have a good claim against a host for an injunction requiring it to take down material being published in breach of privacy even though the host has a complete defence under reg 19 to a claim for damages.[145]

### (a) Mere conduits (regulation 17)

**15.64** Regulation 17 confers a defence on 'mere conduits', that is to say, service providers that provide internet users with access to the internet and nothing more (*ie* broadband providers). The defence, where it applies, absolves the provider from civil and criminal liability. The conditions are that the provider did not (a) initiate the transmission of the information in question, (b) select the recipient of the transmission, or (c) modify the information contained in the transmission.[146] The defence will continue to apply where a provider carries out automatic, intermediate, and transient storage of the information, provided that such storage (a) occurs for the sole purpose of carrying out the transmission, and (b) goes on no longer than is reasonably necessary to achieve this purpose.

### (b) Caching (regulation 18)

**15.65** Where a provider's role in the publishing process is confined to the automatic, intermediate, and transient storage of the information for the purpose of making more efficient the onward transmission of the information to other recipients, it will have a complete defence under reg 18 to any claim 'for damages or for any

---

[143] See E-Commerce Directive, Recital (18); *Metropolitan Schools Ltd v Designtechnica Corp* [2009] EWHC 1765 (QB), [2009] EMLR 27 [82]–[85]. See also the discussion of the point in *Mulvaney v Sporting Exchange Ltd (trading as Betfair)* [2009] IEHC 133.

[144] See regs 17(1), 18(1), 19(1), and 20(1)(b).

[145] *ie* where the defendant host can show for the purposes of reg 19(a)(i) (see 15.67) that, at the time the claim for the injunction was made, it did not have actual knowledge of unlawful activity or information or was not aware of facts or circumstances from which it was apparent that the activity or information was unlawful. The availability of a defence under reg 19(a)(ii) by contrast is self-evidently incompatible with the continued publication of the offending material. But as regards the problems that may be involved in obtaining injunctive relief against a hosting ISP generally, see 15.106–15.113.

[146] See n 147.

other pecuniary remedy or for any criminal sanction', provided that the following conditions are met:

(1) it does not modify the information;[147]
(2) it complies with conditions on access to the information;[148]
(3) it complies with any rules regarding the updating of the information, specified in a manner widely recognized and used by industry;
(4) it does not interfere with the lawful use of technology, widely recognized and used by industry, to obtain data on the use of the information; and
(5) it acts expeditiously to remove or to disable access to the information it has stored upon obtaining actual knowledge of the fact that the information at the initial source of the transmission has been removed from the network, or access to it has been disabled, or that a court or an administrative authority has ordered such removal or disablement.

As can be seen, in common with reg 19(a)(ii) (hosts), it is a condition of the reg 18 **15.66** defence that, if a caching provider is notified of certain specified information, it must act expeditiously to remove or disable access to the offending material which it is caching. In practical terms, this represents an obligation on the provider to ensure, if it wishes to avoid liability for damages, that cached copies of the offending material within its control do not continue to circulate on the internet after it has been informed that the original material has been removed, or ordered to be removed, from the web.

### (c) Hosting (regulation 19)

Regulation 19 confers a defence on entities which host on their servers information **15.67** (such as web pages) consisting of information supplied by another. This defence arguably attaches to a wide range of hosting situations, from the mere passive hosting of data on a server, to the provision of platforms and associated publishing tools, to the operation of special areas on websites performing wider functions (*eg* journalistic, advisory) where users themselves generate the content.[149] There may, therefore, be more than one person hosting the offending material for the purposes of the Regulations. For example, where the material in question is user-generated comments on a news website, both the news organization which owns and operates the website and the ISP which hosts that website on its servers arguably fall within the definition of 'host' for the purposes of reg 19.[150]

---

[147] In *Mosley v Google Inc* (n 23) it was held at [41] that reducing the size and definition of images in order to produce a 'thumbnail' did not amount to modifying the image for the purpose of reg 18 (or, presumably, reg 17). Something more was needed, according to Mitting J, such as altering the image or adding something to it (*eg* text).

[148] 'Conditions' which are not specified anywhere in the Regulations or the accompanying Explanatory Note.

[149] *eg* 'under the line' reader comments in relation to an online news article: see *Karim v Newsquest Media Group Ltd* [2009] EWHC 3205 (QB).

[150] Though, in practical terms, a complainant in such circumstances is unlikely to direct his or her complaint to anyone other than the news organization.

**15.68** Regulation 19 provides that a hosting service provider 'shall not be liable for damages or for any other pecuniary remedy or for any criminal sanction' where:

  a) the service provider:
     (i) does not have actual knowledge of unlawful activity or information and, where a claim for damages is made, is not aware of facts or circumstances from which it would have been apparent to the service provider that the activity or information was unlawful (reg 19(a)(i)); or
     (ii) upon obtaining such knowledge or awareness, acts expeditiously to remove or to disable access to the information (reg 19(a)(ii)), and
  b) the recipient of the service—that is, the internet user who published the relevant information—was not acting under the authority or the control of the service provider.

**15.69** Regulation 22 makes further provision in respect of when a service provider may be said to have obtained 'actual knowledge' for the purposes of reg 18 or 19. In determining whether the ISP has actual knowledge a court must take into account all matters that appear relevant, including:

  a) whether a service provider has received a notice through a means of contact made available by the provider in accordance with reg 6(1)(c) (*ie* the email address and other contact details that a service provider is obliged to make available to enable internet users and relevant enforcement authorities to contact it rapidly and to communicate with it in a direct and effective manner); and
  b) the extent to which any notice includes –
     (i) the full name and address of the sender of the notice;
     (ii) details of the location of the information in question; and
     (iii) details of the unlawful nature of the activity or information in question.

**15.70** The question of when it will be deemed to have been 'apparent' to a host for the purposes of reg 19 that the activity or information in question was unlawful will depend on the facts of each case and the extent to which the provider exercises control over the material it hosts. In *L'Oréal SA v eBay International AG*[151] the European Court of Justice ruled that a host which did not confine itself to neutral, technical, processing of the material in question, but which instead provided assistance to users of its service, *eg* by promoting or 'optimizing' the material (in this case, the offers for sale on the eBay auction site), might be considered to have acquired a degree of knowledge of or control over the material which precluded reliance upon the hosting defence under Article 14 of the E-Commerce Directive.[152] While the *L'Oréal* case related to intellectual property, it seems reasonably clear that the court will extend the same degree of protection to hosts when the claim relates to private information or personal data.[153]

---

[151] Case C-324/09 *L'Oréal SA v eBay International AG* [2012] EMLR 6.
[152] *L'Oréal* (n 151) paras 112–16.
[153] *Mosley v Google Inc* (n 23) [53].

Another important question to which reg 19/Article 14 give rise is the degree of **15.71** specificity that is required when giving notice. Is it incumbent on a complainant to provide a host ISP with precise details of each and every offending post or page? Or is it possible to give a more general form of notification and expect the host to act to remove other similar material that may be available elsewhere on the platform? Although some platform hosts (including Google and Facebook) have policies which require a complainant to identify the individual URL where each piece of offending material appears,[154] the High Court of Northern Ireland in *CG v Facebook Ireland Ltd*[155] rejected this as unnecessary.[156] In this connection, although Article 15 of the E-Commerce Directive forbids the imposition of general monitoring obligations on an ISP, it should be noted that Recital (47) to the Directive states that this does not prohibit the imposition of monitoring 'in specific cases'. What is and is not allowed by the Directive in this regard is unclear. In *L'Oréal* the European Court of Justice said that measures 'cannot consist in an active monitoring of all the data of each of its customers in order to prevent future infringement'.[157] However, in the same case it was emphasized that injunctions against ISPs must be effective, proportionate, and dissuasive, and must both bring infringement to an end and prevent future infringement. In *Mosley v Google Inc*,[158] meanwhile, the Court held that the claimant had a real prospect of establishing that the imposition of an injunction requiring Google to remove all the offending images, without the need to specify each and every URL, would not offend against Article 15.

Concerns have been expressed[159] that a restrictive interpretation of the reg 19/ **15.72** Article 14 defence may discourage hosts from moderating user-generated content for fear of being found to have involved themselves in the publishing process 'too much'. The question of how much is too much for this purpose has not been considered by English courts. In this connection, however, it may be noted that the European Court of Human Rights decided in the case of *Delfi AS v Estonia*[160] that a ruling of the Estonian court, whereby it held that the operator of an online news portal could not avail itself of a defence under the domestic equivalent of reg 19

---

[154] Uniform Resource Locator, which is a reference to an online resource that specifies the location of the resource on a computer network and a mechanism for retrieving it. Each individual page on the world wide web has one.

[155] [2015] NIQB 11. See 15.51.

[156] As did the Supreme Court of British Columbia in *Equustek Solutions Inc v Jack* 2014 BCSC 1063 (Fenlon J). Now see also *Niemala v Malamas* 2015 BCSC 1024 (Fenlon J).

[157] *L'Oréal* (n 151) para 139.

[158] *Mosley v Google Inc* (n 23).

[159] *eg* in *Kaschke v Gray* [2010] EWHC 690 (QB), [2011] 1 WLR 452 [87]. Similar concerns were expressed during the course of the parliamentary debates relating to the new proposed defence to defamation claims for website operators, eventually enacted as s 5 of the Defamation Act 2013. In the event, s 5(12) expressly provides that a s 5 defence will not be defeated only by reason of the fact that the operator of a website moderates the statements posted on the website by others.

[160] *Delfi AS v Estonia* App no 64569/09 (ECtHR, 10 October 2013, First Section). The decision has since been confirmed by the Grand Chamber [2015] EMLR 26.

because it exercised too great a degree of control over the user-generated content in question, did not violate Article 10 ECHR.

## H. Online Publication: Relevant Causes of Action

### (1) Harassment

**15.73**  Section 1 of the PHA 1997 prohibits conduct which amounts to the harassment of another and which the person responsible for the conduct knows or ought to know amounts to harassment of another. The requirements of the PHA 1997 are discussed in Chapter 6. The Act is considered specifically here because it has played, and is likely to continue to play, an important role in tackling the modern phenomenon of harassing behaviour online.

**15.74**  Widespread internet and social media use has created new and previously undreamt of opportunities for the harassment of others. People's social media identities can provide a focal point for harassment, giving a wrongdoer an easy way to get directly in touch. For example, in *AMP v Persons Unknown*, a male individual contacted the female claimant via her Facebook page and told her that sexually explicit images of her would be published widely on the internet if she did not add him as a Facebook friend.[161] Alternatively, an individual with no pre-existing online presence may be targeted with a page or site set up specifically for the purpose of disclosing sensitive information about him or her, *eg* his or her status as a convicted sex offender.[162] Furthermore, an individual may find that another person has created a social media account pretending to be him or her.[163] The extent to which the establishment and operation of a fake profile of this kind will be found to constitute actionable harassment will depend on all the circumstances, including the type of content featured and the efforts put into maintaining it, but there is no question as a matter of law that it may do so.

**15.75**  One distinctive feature of online publication is that it is not a 'one-off' event, but continuous. For as long as a distressing or offensive publication remains online, the distress it causes is also liable to be continuous. As discussed at 15.07, it is at least likely to be a reasonable inference in such circumstances that the victim will experience alarm or distress on two or more occasions, which is all that is needed

---

[161]  [2011] EWHC 3454 (TCC), [2011] Info TLR 25 [6].

[162]  *XY v Facebook Ireland Ltd* [2012] NIQB 96; *CG v Facebook Ireland Ltd* [2015] NIQB 11.

[163]  In an effort to combat this phenomenon, Twitter has put in place a system of verification in which a blue badge is awarded as a mark of authenticity. The company states at <support.twitter.com/articles/119135> that '[v]erification is currently used to establish authenticity of identities of key individuals and brands on Twitter'. The defamation and privacy case of *Applause Store Productions Ltd v Raphael* [2008] EWHC 1781 (QB), [2008] Info TLR 318 centred on a fake Facebook profile which the Court held the defendant had created.

to ground a claim in harassment.[164] The prominence[165] and 'searchability'[166] of a website or webpage may also contribute to the distress and harassment the victim suffers.

Published material which alarms or distresses a person for the purposes of s 7(2) of **15.76** the PHA 1997 will not necessarily consist of or include private or confidential information. However, when it does, the alarm or distress caused by its dissemination is likely to be all the more acute. In such a situation a claim in harassment may prove a useful adjunct to a claim for misuse of confidential or private information.[167] The publication online of sexually explicit or otherwise intimate material relating to a particular individual, for instance, is likely to be deemed harassing.[168] Furthermore, applying the principles set forth in *Law Society v Kordowski*, if publication is effected by means of a website set up specifically for that purpose,[169] the website's creator is likely to be taken to have known that what he or she was doing amounted to harassment of the claimant. In the *AMP* case,[170] where private information in the form of sexually explicit photographs of the claimant was uploaded to a BitTorrent hosting site with the claimant's name appended to the relevant files, the Court had little hesitation in granting an interim injunction to restrain harassment under the PHA 1997.[171] The Court took a similar approach in a case that involved the emailing of intimate photographs of the claimant to the claimant's husband and friends coupled with threats to inflict pain and humiliation on her,[172] and in another which concerned the emailing of private information about the claimant to the claimant's wife and a number of his business associates.[173] At a high level of abstraction, it is submitted that any form of unsolicited publication on the internet about an individual of a personal nature may engage his or her Article 8 rights when the position is considered in the broad sense outlined by the House of Lords in *Campbell v MGN Ltd*, namely that the underlying value protected by

---

[164] *Law Society v Kordowski* (n 19) [64].

[165] *Law Society v Kordowski* (n 19) [67].

[166] See in this regard *Flannagan v Sperling* Civ 2012-090-986 (4 June 2013), a decision of Harvey DCJ sitting in the District Court of Waitakere, New Zealand. Judge Harvey is the author of a book on internet law in New Zealand: *internet.law.nz* (3rd edn, Lexis Nexis NZ Ltd 2011).

[167] Examples of such claims include: *AMP v Persons Unknown* [2011] EWHC 3454 (TCC), [2011] Info TLR 25; *WXY v Gewanter* [2012] EWHC 496 (QB); *ABK v KDT* [2013] EWHC 1192 (QB); and *EWQ v GFD* [2012] EWHC 2182 (QB).

[168] It may also amount to a criminal offence of disclosing private sexual photographs and films without consent and with intent to cause distress, under s 33 of the Criminal Justice and Courts Act 2015: see 15.23.

[169] As happened in *QRS v Beach* [2014] EWHC 3057 (QB); [2014] EWHC 3319 (QB).

[170] *AMP* (n 167). In relation to this case, see A Murray, 'New Approach to Privacy: AMP v Persons Unknown' *The IT Lawyer* (20 December 2011), available at <theitlawyer.blogspot.co.uk/2011/12/new-approach-to-privacy-amp-v-persons.html#!/2011/12/new-approach-to-privacy-amp-v-persons.html>.

[171] *AMP* (n 167) [45].

[172] *ABK* (n 167) [11].

[173] *EWQ* (n 167) [62].

the law is human autonomy and dignity—the right to control the dissemination of information about one's private life and the right to the esteem and respect of other people.[174]

**15.77**   As already mentioned, harassment may also occur by means of the appropriation and taking control of an individual's pre-existing social media profile, known colloquially (and somewhat infelicitously) as a 'frape'. While often intended humorously, this kind of appropriation may have serious consequences for its victim because the information in question will be published to people who have been granted privileged access to his or her social media pages (*ie* the victim's 'friends') and for this reason it is more likely to be believed. In *Otomewo v Carphone Warehouse*, for example, the applicant's Facebook profile was taken over by some of his work colleagues, who then altered the profile to include a statement to the effect that he had come out as being homosexual.[175] This was held by the Employment Tribunal to be an act of sexual orientation harassment under the Equality Act 2010 for which the respondent employer was vicariously liable. The act of harassment was aggravated by the fact that it was perpetrated using Facebook, a public forum, which resulted in the relevant information being displayed to the applicant's friends and family. Since a status hijack is likely to be ephemeral in nature (*ie* lasting only until the owner regains control of the profile), the 'course of conduct' requirement of the PHA 1997 may be difficult to satisfy. But considering the matter from a privacy law perspective, where, as in *Otomewo*, the modification of an online profile creates an untrue account of the nature of an individual's sexual orientation, a 'false privacy'[176] or defamation claim may also be supported by the offending publication.

**15.78**   The facts of the harassment case of *Trimingham v Associated Newspapers Ltd* have a particular resonance in the internet and social media context. The claimant complained that the defendant's newspaper had harassed her within the meaning of the PHA 1997 by repeatedly publishing details of her sexual orientation and making offensive and insulting remarks about her appearance. She alleged that this constituted oppressive and unreasonable conduct. Although the judge disagreed and dismissed the claim,[177] he found that repeated publication of personal information of this kind, if it became excessive, might amount to taunting, and therefore to harassment for the purposes of the Act. Taunting, as is well known, epitomizes the behaviour of the internet troll.

---

[174] [2004] UKHL 22, [2004] 2 AC 457 [51]. For a study of privacy as autonomy in the internet context, see P Bernal, *Internet Privacy Rights: Rights to Protect Autonomy* (Cambridge University Press 2014). See also *Gulati v MGN Ltd* [2015] EWHC 1482 (Ch).

[175] *Otomewo v Carphone Warehouse Ltd* [2012] EqLR 724; the words of the offending status update were 'Finally came out of the closet, I am gay and proud'.

[176] Discussed further in ch 7.

[177] *Trimingham* (n 18) [268].

## (2) Misuse of Private Information

The internet, as a medium of publication, is uniquely well-suited to the vivid pres- **15.79**
entation of private information, *eg* in the form of video footage or audio recordings. This contrasts with the conventional medium of newspapers, which can
only feature still images, illustrations, or textual descriptions. Furthermore, the
proliferation of material of a personal nature posted about individuals on social
media sites offers new and abundant opportunities for the unauthorized exploitation of such material, as happened in *Rocknroll v News Group Newspapers Ltd*.[178]

In *Mosley v News Group Newspapers Ltd*, possibly the best known privacy action **15.80**
and one of the few to have been tried,[179] the publication included video footage
posted on the defendant newspaper's website which depicted the claimant taking
part in a sado-masochistic orgy. The publication of the footage, which by the date
of the trial had been viewed hundreds of thousands of times (an application for an
interim injunction having been dismissed),[180] was ultimately held by the judge to
have caused considerable humiliation and distress to the claimant, for which he
was awarded £60,000 damages.[181]

The interim injunction application in *Contostavlos v Mendahun* also arose from **15.81**
the publication on the internet of video footage that featured the claimant pop
singer and television personality engaged in a sexual activity.[182] The footage
was published online including on a website for which the first defendant was
responsible. The judge, in granting the injunction, referred to the final decision of the Court of Appeal in the *Douglas v Hello!* litigation in support of the
proposition that a public domain defence was unlikely to be available where
the material in question consisted of intrusive and intimate photographs.[183]
In *Cooper v Turrell*, meanwhile, one particular aspect of the defendant's campaign of misuse of the individual claimant's private information, which led to
judgment being entered against him for substantial damages, was his uploading to a WordPress blog of an audio file recording private and confidential
information.[184]

### (a) Particular features of internet-based misuse of private information

There are a number of other features that distinguish disclosures of private infor- **15.82**
mation on the internet. The first is the potential extent of publication and the
rapidity with which extensive publication might occur, particularly if the original

---

[178] [2013] EWHC 24 (Ch).
[179] *Mosley v News Group Newspapers Ltd* [2008] EWHC 1777 (QB), [2008] EMLR 20.
[180] [2008] EWHC 687 (QB).
[181] *Mosley v News Group Newspapers* (n 179).
[182] [2012] EWHC 850 (QB). In Australia, substantial damages have been awarded for online
publication of such material, *Wilson v Ferguson* [2015] WASC 15.
[183] [2005] EWCA Civ 595, [2006] QB 125 [105]–[107]; *Contostavlos* (n 182) [25].
[184] [2011] EWHC 3269 (QB). In relation to the award of damages, see further 15.127.

posting 'goes viral'.[185] Digital information is almost infinitely reproducible at little or no additional cost. In the *Mosley* case,[186] in addition to the hundreds of thousands of views of the offending footage on the defendant's website, images taken from the footage were separately republished in many jurisdictions around the world.[187] Similarly, in *Contostavlos v Mendahun*, the video footage rapidly appeared on a number of websites run by third parties.[188] The judge noted, however, that the claimant's solicitors in that case had been so successful in their 'firefighting' activities that messages were appearing on the internet complaining that the footage in question could not be found.[189]

**15.83**  Quite apart from the problems associated with online anonymity (discussed at 15.37 *et seq*), the technological means by which data are processed, transferred, reproduced, and distributed on the internet can make it extremely difficult to identify the person or persons responsible for a particular action. In the *AMP* case[190] the claim was brought against 'persons unknown' to prevent unidentified BitTorrent users from distributing ('seeding') sexually explicit photographs of the claimant. The diffuse nature of BitTorrent technology, a protocol that allows a user to join a 'swarm' of other users in downloading and uploading data files from each other simultaneously, meant that the alleged wrongdoers could only be identified with reference to their shared characteristic: that of being a person in possession or control of any part or parts of the relevant files containing the relevant digital photographic images.[191]

**15.84**  Further distinctive aspects of publication on the internet are its permanence and its accessibility. In contrast with print newspapers and television broadcasts (which traditionally published information once and then filed it away in relatively inaccessibly places, eg in a library or a broadcaster's archive), information published on the internet remains there indefinitely until publication is deliberately stopped, readily searchable through the instrument of search engines.[192]

**15.85**  Another feature is that disclosures commonly form part of a broader publication-based campaign of harassment. Such campaigns often extend beyond misuse of private or confidential information to defamatory and harassing attacks on their target.[193] Even if there is an allegedly legitimate purpose behind the campaign (they typically claim to be exposing of dishonesty, hypocrisy, or some other form

---

[185] *Cairns* (n 6) [27] and n 6 generally.
[186] See 15.80.
[187] D Crossley, 'Google go down in Paris' *Inforrm's blog* (13 November 2013), available at <inforrm.wordpress.com/2013/11/13/google-go-down-in-paris-how-did-it-come-to-this-dominic-crossley/>.
[188] *Contostavlos* (n 182).
[189] *Contostavlos* (n 182) [28].
[190] *AMP* (n 167).
[191] *AMP* (n 167) [20].
[192] See further 15.02.
[193] *Thompson v James* [2013] EWHC 515 (QB) [406].

of 'iniquity' on the claimant's part), indiscriminate publication to the world at large is unlikely to be seen as proportionate if the disclosure merely raises only a possibility of wrongdoing on the claimant's part. If on true analysis there is only a suspicion or a possibility of wrongdoing, as was found to be the position in *WXY v Gewanter*, the only form of disclosure that is likely to be legitimate is to a relevant investigative authority.[194] Furthermore, it is not only the rights of the target of the campaign which may be engaged in such cases: where what is at stake is an ostensibly harassing campaign, the court has observed that the interests of the public at large may also support the need for an injunction.[195] It is recognized to be in the public interest that those who knowingly publish false and harmful information on the internet should be prevented from doing so.[196]

### (3) Data Protection and the Information Commissioner

#### (a) *The Data Protection Act 1998*

The DPA is of particular relevance to websites and social media.[197] It confers on living individuals a quasi-proprietary right in information held about them by others which enables them to obtain access to and control over that information, and entitles them to be compensated where their information is misused. The DPA can therefore be a useful weapon in the armoury in situations where misuse of personal or private information has occurred online. **15.86**

Section 1 DPA defines 'data' as information which is being processed by means of equipment operating automatically in response to instructions given for that purpose. The application of this provision to computer systems is self-evident and it has been held specifically to include storing and publishing information on a website.[198] It seems obvious that use of internet applications such as cloud computing would also be regarded as processing for the purposes of the Act. **15.87**

The DPA further provides that 'personal data' means data which relate to a living individual who can be identified either from those data or from those data and other information which is in the possession of, or is likely to come into the possession of, the data controller.[199] The definition of sensitive personal data set out in s 2 DPA includes categories of information in which an individual would conventionally have a reasonable expectation of privacy, such as information as to his or her physical or mental health condition and sexual life.[200] **15.88**

---

[194] *WXY v Gewanter* (n 167) [65]. But, in contrast, see *Merlin Entertainments plc v Cave* [2014] EWHC 3036 (QB), [2015] EMLR 3.

[195] *Law Society v Kordowski* (n 19) [175].

[196] *Cooper* (n 184) [105].

[197] For a fuller account of the role of the DPA in privacy cases, see ch 7.

[198] *Law Society v Kordowski* (n 19) [76]; Case C-101/01 *Criminal Proceedings against Lindqvist* [2004] QB 1014.

[199] s 1 DPA.

[200] s 2 (e), (f) DPA. See further ch 7.

**15.89**   The DPA defines the data controller as a person who (either alone or jointly or in common with other persons) determines the purposes for which and the manner in which any personal data are, or are to be, processed.[201] An individual who establishes and runs a website featuring the personal data of others, as the defendant did in *Kordowski*, is a paradigm of a data controller.[202]

**15.90**   The DPA provides that it shall be the duty of a data controller to comply with the data protection principles in relation to all personal data with respect to which he or she is the data controller. It ought to be borne in mind that the journalism, literature, and art exemption provided for in s 32 DPA is likely to be relevant in many internet and social media-based cases.[203]

**15.91**   The decision of the European Court of Justice in *Google Spain*[204] has had a revolutionary impact where data protection, the internet, and social media are concerned. In 1998 the claimant, Mr Costeja González, was named in a Spanish newspaper as the owner of a property which was to be forcibly sold in order to repay his social security debts. Twelve years later a search against his name on the Google Spain search engine was still generating results which referred to the matter. The claimant considered that this amounted to an infringement by Google of his rights as a data subject. He made a complaint to the Spanish Data Protection Agency, the object of which was to require Google to block the personal data in question and to desist from processing it. The Agency upheld the complaint against Google. Google brought proceedings in the Spanish court challenging the Agency's decision. The Spanish Court referred to the European Court of Justice for a preliminary ruling a series of questions related to the Agency's interpretation of the EU Data Protection Directive,[205] on which it had based its conclusions concerning Google. The European Court of Justice decided, significantly, that:

(1) the activity of a search engine amounted to the processing of personal data within the meaning of the Directive, and the operator of a search engine was the 'controller' in respect of those data;

(2) when a search engine operator established a branch or subsidiary in a EU Member State for the purpose of promoting and selling advertising space to residents of that Member State in connection with the search engine, the search engine's processing of personal data was carried out by that 'establishment' on the Member State's territory, with the consequence that the Directive was binding on the establishment;

---

[201]   s 1(1) DPA.
[202]   For the facts of *Kordowski*, see 15.07. It may also be noted that in *Vidal-Hall* (n 30), Google, in its capacity as the operator of its proprietary search engine on Apple-based (Safari) browsers, did not dispute that it was a data controller for the relevant purpose.
[203]   See 7.109 *et seq*.
[204]   *Google Spain* (n 22).
[205]   Directive 95/46/EC (n 71).

(3) when a data subject made a request to a controller under the Directive to end the processing of personal data, the controller was obliged to examine the merits of the request and accede to it where appropriate; and

(4) the rights of data subjects under Articles 7 and 8 of the Charter of Fundamental Rights of the European Union[206] generally overrode not only the economic interests of the search engine operator, but also the interest of the general public in having access to the information in question.

The consequences of the judgment are liable to be far-reaching. Most importantly, it makes it clear that data subjects will be able to enforce their data protection rights in European courts against the local European subsidiaries of search engine operators. Arguably, by parity of reasoning, the same might apply to other types of US-based ISPs which have subsidiaries in Europe, *eg* Google in the Blogger context. Google and other search engine operators have responded by introducing a new web form which allows data subjects to request the removal of specific search results that include their name (so-called 'right to be forgotten' requests).[207] The Article 29 Data Protection Working Party established under the Directive has issued guidelines on the implementation of the *Google Spain* ruling,[208] while the Information Commissioner's Office has published search result de-listing criteria of its own.[209]

Where a data controller is found to have acted in breach of its statutory obligations, **15.92** the data subject's rights to prevent processing likely to cause damage or distress under s 10 DPA,[210] to compensation under s 13 DPA,[211] to rectification, blocking, erasure, and destruction under s 14 DPA,[212] and to request an assessment by the Information Commissioner under s 42 DPA become relevant. The powers of the court under ss 10 and 14 may, where appropriate, be particularly effective privacy remedies in the online sphere. Sections 10 and 14 supply the route by which UK data subjects may take advantage of the rights against search engines described in *Google Spain*.[213]

The right of data subjects under s 42 to request an assessment by the Information **15.93** Commissioner of whether processing has been carried out in compliance with the

---

[206] Which provide for a right to respect for private and family life (Art 7) and a right of protection of personal data (Art 8).

[207] Google Inc, 'Search removal request under data protection law in Europe', available at <support.google.com/legal/contact/lr_eudpa?product=websearch>.

[208] Guidelines on the Implementation of the Court of Justice of the European Union judgment on 'Google Spain and inc v Agencia Española de Protección de Datos (AEPD) and Mario Costeja González' C-131/121, adopted on 26 November 2014.

[209] Information Commissioner's Office, 'Search result delisting criteria', available at <ico.org.uk/for-organisations/search-result-delisting-criteria/>.

[210] See 7.81 *et seq.*

[211] See 7.92 *et seq.*

[212] See 7.100 *et seq.*

[213] See *Hegglin v Persons Unknown* [2014] EWHC 2808 (QB) [16], [20]; *Mosley v Google Inc* (n 158) [24]–[25].

provisions of the DPA further enables individuals to seek to invoke the Information Commissioner's powers of enforcement. The Commissioner's approach to the exercise of its powers of enforcement was considered by the Court in *Law Society v Kordowski*.[214] The claimant Law Society had written to the Information Commissioner[215] to complain about the offending website, but the Commissioner in his reply referred to the domestic purposes exemption in s 36 DPA, and stated that the DPA was not designed to deal with the problems that it faced.[216] The judge criticized the Commissioner's approach. He expressed sympathy with the practical difficulties faced by the Commissioner, but said that he did not understand how s 36 applied[217] and that he was unable to reconcile the Commissioner's view with prior authoritative statements of law.[218] The judge also observed that if in a particular case there was no room for argument that the processing in question was unlawful, then it became more difficult for the Commissioner to say that the matter was not one which could conveniently be dealt with by means of his enforcement powers under pt V DPA.[219]

### (b) The Information Commissioner

**15.94** The Information Commissioner's Office has published guidance on the applicability of the DPA to social networking and online forums.[220] The Guidance draws attention to the s 36 domestic purposes exemption which provides that when personal data are processed by an individual only for the purposes of his or her personal, family, or household affairs (including recreational purposes), they are exempt from the data protection principles and the provisions of pts II and III of the Act.

**15.95** As the Guidance makes clear, the s 36 exemption is only available to individuals; it cannot be relied on by corporations or other organizations that process personal data. If corporate entities publish personal data on their own or a third party's website, if they download and use personal data from a third party website, or if they run a website which allows third parties to add comments or posts about living individuals, then they must adhere to their obligations as data controllers under the DPA.[221] Furthermore, where a group of individuals posts collectively as a group, the more formal the group is and the more it exists independently of its individual members, the less likely it is that the domestic purposes

---

[214] *Law Society v Kordowski* (n 19).
[215] Though not apparently, it should be noted, with express reference to s 42 of the Act.
[216] *Law Society v Kordowski* (n 19) [96].
[217] *Law Society v Kordowski* (n 19) [99].
[218] *Law Society v Kordowski* (n 19) [100].
[219] *Law Society v Kordowski* (n 19) [101].
[220] Information Commissioner, 'Social networking and online forums—when does the DPA apply?', available at <ico.org.uk/media/for-organisations/documents/1600/social-networking-and-online-forums-dpa-guidance.pdf>.
[221] Guidance (n 220) para 7.

exemption will apply.[222] The Guidance identifies a series of questions a group of individuals can ask themselves to decide whether the exemption applies to them or not. So far as individuals are concerned, the Guidance also draws attention to the fact that some people use social media for mixed purposes and emphasizes that where posts are not made for purely domestic or recreational purposes the poster is not exempt from complying with the requirements of the DPA.[223] The Guidance also outlines the considerations that need to be borne in mind in the data processing context by those who run online forums or social networking sites, including by explaining what they may have to do in order to comply with the obligation to take reasonable steps to ensure the accuracy of the data they publish.[224]

Significantly, the Guidance also describes the Information Commissioner's **15.96** Office's understanding of what its own role is when a complaint is made against a person running a social networking site, whether that person is an organization or an individual.[225] The Guidance states that the Information Commissioner's Office will entertain complaints about posts on social media where the posts have been made by businesses, organizations, or individuals acting for purposes other than domestic ones, subject to considerations of proportionality. It also indicates that the Information Commissioner's Office will only entertain a complaint about a website's failure to address a data processing issue where the person or organization the object of the complaint is a data controller.

In broad terms, the effect of the Guidance is that where a complaint to the **15.97** Information Commissioner's Office arising out of the use of internet-based social media is being contemplated, the identity of the data processor and the purposes for which the data in question were being processed should be carefully scrutinized before a complaint is made.

*(c) Data protection reform*

The DPA implemented in UK law the Data Protection Directive.[226] **15.98** Implementation of the Directive has been uneven as between EU Member States. Moreover, when the Directive was drafted and adopted, the internet was barely in its infancy.[227] Perhaps unsurprisingly, these matters among others have

---

[222] Guidance (n 220) para 18.
[223] Guidance (n 220) para 25.
[224] Guidance (n 220) para 38.
[225] Guidance (n 220) paras 40–4.
[226] Directive 95/46/EC (n 71).
[227] As Steve Peers put the matter in 'Google Spain and the EU's data protection Directive' *Law, Justice and Journalism* (13 May 2014), available at <blogs.city.ac.uk/cljj/2014/05/13/google-spain-and-the-eus-data-protection-directive/>: 'The EU's data protection Directive was adopted in 1995, when the Internet was in its infancy, and most or all Internet household names did not exist. In particular, the first version of the code for Google search engines was first written the following year, and the company was officially founded in September 1998—shortly before Member States' deadline to implement the Directive.'

prompted European legislators to query whether the Directive remains fit for purpose, and to call for reform.

**15.99** This process began formally with a communication from the EU Commission in 2010.[228] The communication made specific reference to social networking, cloud computing, and to increasingly elaborate ways to process and disseminate data, as motivating factors for the development of a new approach. The Commission drew attention to Article 8 of the Charter of Fundamental Rights of the European Union,[229] which recognizes a right to the protection of personal data, and suggested that in this way the Charter laid the ground for the establishment of new EU legislation protecting individuals' interests in their personal data, and in relation to the free movement of such data.

**15.100** The text of a draft Regulation on data protection was published in 2012.[230] A novel and controversial feature was the 'Right to be forgotten and to erasure' proposed at Article 17 of the draft Regulation. This suggested giving data subjects a new right to insist that data controllers erase and abstain from further dissemination of their personal data. The draft Regulation made provision for certain limited exceptions to the right, including, significantly for media purposes, an exception[231] to the right to erasure of data where its retention was necessary for exercising the right of freedom of expression in accordance with Article 80, where Article 80 posited a broad exemption in respect of the processing of personal data carried out solely for journalistic purposes or the purpose of artistic or literary expression.

**15.101** The European Parliament approved a version of the draft Regulation on 12 March 2014.[232] The text, including that of Article 17, is substantially different from the original draft. Although now described in rather more neutral terms as a 'Right to Erasure', in certain ways the instrument approved by the Parliament goes even further in favour of data protection. For example, under the reformulated Article 17, rather than merely being obliged to take all reasonable steps to inform third parties of a data subject's request for the erasure of data that has been made public, a controller in such circumstances is required to take all reasonable steps to ensure

---

[228] Communication from the Commission to the European Parliament, the Council, the Economic and Social Committee and the Committee of the Regions—*A comprehensive approach on personal data protection in the European Union*, EU: COM (2010) 609.

[229] As to which, see further 15.38.

[230] Proposal for a Regulation of the European Parliament and of the Council on the protection of individuals with regard to the processing of personal data and on the free movement of such data (General Data Protection Regulation), EU: COM (2012) 11. The discussion in the Preamble to the Regulation makes clear the intended breadth of the right, and its particular relevance to data processing to which the subject has given his or her consent as a child, when not fully aware of the risks involved: see at (53), (54).

[231] Proposal for a Regulation (n 230) Art 17(3)(a).

[232] See European Commission—Memo dated 12 March 2014, 'Progress on EU data protection reform now irreversible following European Parliament vote', available at <europa.eu/rapid/press-release_MEMO-14-186_en.htm>.

that the data is erased, including by third parties. Nevertheless, it remains to be seen where further intra-EU negotiations will lead, particularly in the light of the ruling in *Google Spain*.

# I. Online Publication: Remedies

Remedies in misuse of private information and harassment are discussed gener- **15.102** ally in Chapters 12 and 6. This section focuses specifically on issues that may arise where the unlawful or allegedly unlawful publication has occurred, or is taking place, online.

## (1) Injunctions

Injunctions are unquestionably the most important remedy for claimants in mis- **15.103** use of private information cases. The aim of protecting privacy will only truly be achieved by preventing publication in the first place or, where some publication has already occurred, by preventing more widespread publication. Unlike in defamation, damages are unlikely ever to be regarded as an adequate remedy. Although in *Mosley v UK*[233] the European Court of Human Rights rejected the argument that injunctive relief was the only remedy that was 'effective' in privacy cases for the purposes of Article 13 ECHR, there can be no question that it is the *most* effective. Given the propensity of information to spread widely and quickly across the internet, injunctions are likely to be particularly important in the online context, though this very feature is likely to militate against the grant of an interim injunction.[234]

### (a) Injunctions against authors and others

If the author[235] of the offending material is identifiable, an interim injunction may be **15.104** sought to prevent publication or further publication in the ordinary way.[236] It is when an author cannot be identified, or where authorship is unclear or appears excessively diffuse (in the sense that several persons may potentially be involved), that other options may need to be explored. Applying for an interim injunction against one or more of the following may, depending on the facts of the case, be a possibility:

(1) against a relevant ISP, *eg* the ISP providing the social media service or hosting the blogsite where the offending publication has occurred (a platform provider);

---

[233] (2011) 53 EHRR 30.

[234] See *Mosley v News Group Newspapers* (n 180) and *Re Stedman* [2009] EWHC 935 (Fam), [2009] 2 FLR 852.

[235] Or another person primarily responsible or vicariously liable for the publication in question, *eg* a newspaper publisher.

[236] See 12.15 for the general principles governing the grant or refusal of interim injunctions in privacy cases.

(2) against persons unknown;

(3) against one known defendant as a representative of other persons;

(4) *contra mundum* (*ie* against the world at large); and

(5) a blocking injunction.

Each of these is considered below.

**15.105** The important practical point to note at the outset, however, is that provided that the claimant is able to obtain an interim injunction that restrains *someone* from further disclosing or disseminating specified confidential or private information, anyone else who is notified of the injunction will also be bound by its terms, certainly until the trial of the action, at pain of contempt of court if the injunction is breached. This is the effect of what is generally known as the *Spycatcher* principle.[237] It has, furthermore, been held to be legitimate for the court to continue an interim injunction in privacy against one defendant where the primary purpose in doing so is to achieve *Spycatcher* relief against others.[238] It may also be that the *Spycatcher* effect survives the conclusion of the proceedings. In *Hutcheson v Popdog Ltd*[239] the Court of Appeal questioned the correctness of Gray J's decision in *Jockey Club v Buffham*[240] that the principle was only of effect in relation to interim injunctions.

### (b) Injunctions against platform providers

**15.106** In the absence of an identifiable author, and even where there is one,[241] it may be attractive to pursue the corporate platform provider hosting the website or social media service where the offending publication has occurred. Not only is the platform provider likely to be readily identifiable, contactable, and in a position to bring publication to an end, but in most cases it will be a substantial corporate entity from which costs might be recovered. Moreover, a platform provider, in contrast with the author, will have no personal stake in the subject matter of the publication in question, and would wish, one might think, all other things being equal, to take advantage of a defence under reg 19 of the E-Commerce Regulations[242] to any claim for civil liability arising from the publication by acting expeditiously to disable access to the offending material.

**15.107** Nevertheless, to apply for an interim injunction against a platform provider where, following a complaint, it has refused or failed to remove from its platform material of a private nature is liable to be fraught with difficulties.

---

[237] For a more detailed account of the *Spycatcher* principle, see 12.36.

[238] *Ambrosiadou v Coward* [2011] EWCA Civ 409, [2011] EMLR 21 [38]–[40].

[239] *Hutcheson (formerly WER) v Popdog Ltd (formerly REW)* [2011] EWCA Civ 1580, [2012] 1 WLR 782.

[240] [2002] EWHC 1866 (QB), [2003] QB 462.

[241] *eg* where the author is impecunious or is likely to prove difficult to deal with.

[242] As to which, see 15.67.

The first and most significant obstacle is jurisdictional. Before the court grants an **15.108**
injunction against a foreign platform provider, it will need to be satisfied not only
that the provider in question is amenable to the English court's jurisdiction, in the
sense that service can be effected on it, but also that any injunction, if granted,
would not be idle or ineffectual. Regarding the latter point, the court will require
evidence as to the applicable law and practice in the foreign court, including on
whether the foreign court would be likely to enforce the injunction and on the
foreign jurisdiction's approach to freedom of expression.[243]

But, as already noted,[244] most of the major ISPs are incorporated and have their **15.109**
principal place of business for publishing purposes in the United States, where
they have immunity from civil suit under s 230(c) of the Communications Act of
1934 (as amended). Although Sir James Munby P touched on the topic of the First
Amendment to the US Constitution in his judgment in *Re J (A Child)*,[245] the predi-
cate of his decision was that he did not have before him any detailed evidence on
the domestic law of the United States, including in relation to s 230(c).[246] Applying
Sir James's test in the light of that provision, it is hard to see how the English court
could reach a conclusion other than that a US court would not enforce a privacy
injunction granted in England against a platform provider incorporated there.[247]

However, even if the platform provider is located in a foreign jurisdiction other than **15.110**
the United States where there is no equivalent in the law of that state to s 230(c), it may
be difficult to persuade the court that the injunction, if granted, would not be idle or
ineffectual.

If, for example, the suggested order is intended to prevent the publication of pri- **15.111**
vate information only within England and Wales[248] (which as a matter of English

---

[243] *Re J (A Child)* [2013] EWHC 2694 (Fam), [2014] EMLR 7 [63]–[65] (Sir James Munby P).
In the subsequent case of *Re E (A Child)* [2014] EWHC 6 (Fam), [2014] Fam Law 425 the same
judge granted an injunction that restrained (or purported to restrain) the Slovakian media from
publishing on the internet, in English, any account by the child's mother of her experiences of the
family court proceedings in England which identified the child as the subject of those proceedings:
see at [55]–[59].

[244] See 15.11.

[245] *Re J (A Child)*(n 243) [63].

[246] See [68].

[247] Although note that in *Metropolitan Schools Ltd v Designtechnica Corp* [2009] EWHC 1765
(QB), [2009] EMLR 27 Eady J observed at [116] that the unenforceability of an English court order
in the US 'would not necessarily be a conclusive reason against allowing the proceedings to go on,
or even against the grant of an injunction at the end of a trial: see *In re Liddell's Settlement Trusts*
[1936] Ch 365, 374. Some litigants find it worthwhile to have a determination of rights or issues on
the record irrespective of enforceability.'

[248] Although note that in *eDate Advertising* (n 4), the European Court of Justice (Grand
Chamber) held (distinguishing Case C-68/93 *Shevill v Press Alliance SA* [1995] 2 AC 18) that
in internet-based privacy cases, where publication had occurred through the EU, a citizen of a
Member State was entitled to sue in respect of all the damage that had allegedly been caused in the
courts of the Member State 'in which the centre of his interests were based' as well as before the
courts of the Member State in which the publisher was established. In other words, provided that a
claimant has his or her centre of interests in England, he or she should (in principle) be able to sue

law it must be if the platform provider is based outside the European Union),[249] the court may need some persuasion that a foreign court would enforce such an order against a platform provider based in its own jurisdiction when giving effect to that order could mean requiring the platform provider either to block access to the offending material only in England and Wales (which, in the case of a platform provider, might be technically impossible) or to impose a restriction which is much wider in geographical terms than the original injunction (which is unlikely to be seen as necessary, proportionate, convenient, or desirable). Moreover, it may be hard to convince an English court that such an injunction, even if it were enforced by a foreign court, would not be futile. Under such circumstances, there would not, in any event, be any restriction on the information spreading freely outside of this jurisdiction, with the result that it would in all likelihood flow back into this jurisdiction (*eg* via social media) regardless of the injunction.[250] All of this, of course, is to say nothing, first, of the effort and expense that would be involved in adducing evidence of this nature, in circumstances where time is usually of the essence and where its efficacy was quite uncertain; second, of the need to satisfy the court in accordance with s 12(3) HRA that the claimant is more likely than not to establish at trial that publication in question 'should not be allowed';[251] and third, of the further problems that may be encountered by a claimant (*eg* further foreign litigation, a practical inability to enforce the order or to obtain sanctions for contempt of court) if any order that is granted by the English court is simply ignored.

**15.112** The second major problem is the form or terms of the injunction that it might be appropriate to grant against a platform provider. Eady J broached this issue in the *Metropolitan Schools* case,[252] remarking upon the seemingly insuperable practical and technical difficulties that an operator of a search engine would face in seeking to comply with a non-publication injunction granted in orthodox, time-hallowed form.[253] Platform providers, it is suggested, would face similar problems in complying with an order that was, to adapt Eady J's words, 'purely formulaic and not tailored in any way to the practical difficulties [they] confront'.[254] Since *Metropolitan Schools* was decided, it has, furthermore, become clear that in order to be amenable to civil suit in English law at all, a platform provider must first be notified of

---

a platform provider based in another EU Member State in England in respect of the publication of private material throughout the EU via the internet and the damage such publication is alleged to have caused.

[249] By analogy with defamation, see *Berezovsky v Michaels* [2000] 1 WLR 1004, 1012, HL.

[250] Although it is true to say that the court has shown itself reluctant hitherto to set aside privacy injunctions on such grounds: *CTB v News Group Newspapers Ltd* [2011] EWHC 1326 (QB).

[251] For a general discussion of s 12 HRA, see 12.02 *et seq*.

[252] *Metropolitan Schools* (n 247) [59]–[63]. As regards this authority more generally, see 15.50.

[253] *ie* along the following lines: 'that the defendant, whereby by itself, its directors, servants or agents or otherwise howsoever, is restrained from further publishing or causing or authorising to be published the same or any similar information of or concerning the claimant'.

[254] *Metropolitan Schools* (n 247) [59].

the existence on its platform of the specific words or material complained of.[255] Accordingly, it is submitted, where an injunction is intended to impose a restraint on a platform provider that goes beyond the instant publication of the offending material, *ie* from permitting the re-appearance of that material elsewhere on the platform on future occasions, if the order is to be fair, effective, and indeed lawful, it will need to take account of the requirement for the claimant to give notice. In other words, there would have to be built into any such order a mechanism whereby the claimant was obliged to notify the defendant of any republication alleged to be in breach of the order before the defendant could be expected to take action (failing which it might be in contempt of court): a platform provider cannot realistically be expected to monitor or patrol its platform for republications that might be said to be in breach of the order. Such considerations are only fortified by the existence of a prohibition in Article 15(1) of the E-Commerce Directive upon EU Member States imposing a general obligation on ISPs to monitor the information they transmit or store, or actively to seek out facts or circumstances indicating illegal activity.[256]

All these points will make it very difficult to frame a lawful and workable injunc- **15.113** tion that prevents a platform provider from permitting the republication of the offending material once the original publication has been taken down, if it is possible at all. This may explain in part why, so far as the authors of this chapter are aware, there is no reported example of such an order having been applied for or granted in the English court.[257] If this is to be done in a satisfactory way, it will almost certainly require the assistance and cooperation of the defendant platform provider in ascertaining what is technically feasible and in tailoring the terms of the injunction accordingly.

If what is at stake is personal data, ss 10 and 14 DPA may provide a convenient **15.114** alternative route to obtaining injunctive relief.[258] If this route is available, one of the main problems associated with obtaining injunctive relief against a US-based ISP will be avoided: the defendant will be English and there will be no need to obtain permission to serve out, with all that entails. Any order granted will of course also have the advantage of being enforceable in the English court, against the English defendant.

---

[255] *Tamiz v Google Inc* (n 106), as to which, see 15.47. As for the requirement that the platform provider be notified of the *specific* words or material in question, see *Bunt v Tilley* (n 112) [21]–[23] (discussed at 15.49).

[256] A provision which (somewhat curiously) finds no explicit expression in the domestic E-Commerce Regulations, as to which, see 15.61. For an authoritative interpretation of Art 15(1), see Case C-70/10 *Scarlet Extended SA v SABAM* [2012] ECDR 4 and Case C-360/10 *SABAM v Netlog NV* [2012] CMLR 18. Even though the prohibition in Art 15(1) only extends in terms to 'general obligations to monitor' and does not preclude the imposition of monitoring obligations in specific cases (see Recital (47) to the Directive), it is hard to see how in practical terms it could ever be reasonable for a court to impose such an obligation on a platform provider. Although see 15.71.

[257] For the position in Northern Ireland and Ireland by contrast, see 15.51 and 15.54.

[258] See 15.92.

*(c) Injunctions against persons unknown*

**15.115** In the light of the previous discussion, where the author is unknown, it may appear simpler and more convenient for a claimant to proceed against 'persons unknown' and to serve any such order granted on all persons whom it is believed may be involved in the publication of the offending material (including, where appropriate, internet platform providers) on a *Spycatcher* basis (on the footing that, prior to service of the order at any rate, they are not publishers of the material in question).[259] Once a platform provider has been notified by this means of the presence of the offending material on its platform, it becomes potentially liable for the continued publication of the material unless it acts promptly to disable access to it.[260] This may act as an incentive to take down the relevant material if it can. Anyone notified of such an order is at liberty to apply to the court at any time to vary it or to set it aside.[261] This arguably remedies or, at least, mitigates any potential injustice that might be thought to be caused to a platform provider by a claimant adopting this procedure. In this connection, it may also be noted that by this stage an approach will (certainly, should) already have been made to any relevant platform provider asking it to remove the offending material, which will have been declined or ignored.

**15.116** Certainly, injunctions against 'persons unknown' have become commonplace in privacy cases.[262] The problem is that they have generally been regarded by the court as inherently temporary measures,[263] designed to provide a claimant with injunctive relief on a short-term basis while he or she identifies the author or another person directly responsible for the publication in question who may then be served with proceedings. It is notorious that such inquiries may prove fruitless. Accordingly, the perceived risk in bringing proceedings against 'persons unknown' is that if no author or other appropriate defendant can be identified, the proceedings will have to be discontinued, with the consequent loss of injunctive relief and wasted costs that such would entail.

**15.117** Putative claimants, it is submitted, should not have to concern themselves with this problem. The identification and service of a named defendant will, of course, always be desirable. But in a case where, despite the claimant's best efforts, it has not proved possible to identify a specific wrongdoer, this should not be permitted to work injustice. What matters to a claimant faced with the publication of

---

[259] *Tamiz* (n 255), as to which see 15.47.

[260] *Tamiz* (n 255), and E-Commerce Regulations, reg 19, as to which see 15.67.

[261] See para 17 of the Model Order that accompanies the *Practice Guidance (Interim Non-disclosure Orders)* [2012] 1 WLR 1003.

[262] See *eg X v Persons Unknown* [2006] EWHC 2783 (QB), [2007] EMLR 29; *TUV v Persons Unknown* [2010] EWHC 853 (QB), [2010] EMLR 19; *Terry (formerly LNS) v Persons Unknown* [2010] EWHC 119 (QB), [2010] EMLR 16; *Contostavlos* (n 182); and *Hegglin* (n 213).

[263] See *Terry* (n 262) [134]–[136] and [143], and *Practice Guidance (Interim Non-disclosure Orders)* (n 261) [41] and the commentary in the Practice Guidance on para 5(a) of the Model Order attached thereto.

personal material concerning him or herself online is the prompt and permanent removal of that material from the internet, howsoever that is achieved, and regardless of the identity of the individual perpetrating the attack. In other words, while it may be relevant or useful for a claimant to know who the author of the attack was, this is, at most, a subsidiary issue in the context of achieving the claimant's immediate aims. It is the take-down of the material that is the priority, not knowing who put it up in the first place.

Accordingly, provided that the continuation of the proceedings in 'persons   **15.118**
unknown' form is apt to confer upon the claimant a valuable legal benefit, specifically in the form of ongoing injunctive protection against non-parties served with the order,[264] it is contended that the court ought to permit such proceedings to be continued in that form until trial and that there is no reason in principle why it should not. Conversely, the absence of a named defendant should never be permitted by the court to operate as a bar to the obtaining of injunctive relief in a privacy case, and thereby prevent the effective protection of a claimant's Article 8 ECHR rights, where the grant of such relief is otherwise appropriate. Furthermore, if the concerns expressed by the Court of Appeal in *Hutcheson v Popdog Ltd* about the correctness of *Jockey Club v Buffham* turn out to be well founded, it may come to be regarded as appropriate to grant final injunctive relief in privacy cases in 'persons unknown' form.[265]

There is authority for such a course being taken. In *AMP v Persons Unknown*, a   **15.119**
privacy and harassment claim brought to prevent unidentified BitTorrent users from distributing sexually explicit photographs of the claimant on the internet, Ramsey J indicated that he was content for the proceedings to continue to trial and presumably to judgment without a named defendant.[266] The judge accepted the claimant's submissions to the following effect: (i) that a procedure which required further applications to add additional defendants when they were identified would be cumbersome and lead to unnecessary costs and time being spent, which would be contrary to the overriding objective of the CPR; (ii) that identifying the class of persons unknown by reference to their shared characteristic, namely any person in possession or control of any part or parts of the relevant files containing the relevant digital photographic images, would be a sufficient description of the defendants to enable them to be served with any order which the court might make; and (iii) if at any stage it became necessary to proceed further against any particular defendant for failing to comply with an interim order, the particular defendant in question could then be specifically identified.

---

[264] See 15.105 and the reference there to the decision of the Court of Appeal in *Ambrosiadou v Coward* (n 238).

[265] For *Hutcheson v Popdog Ltd* and *Jockey Club v Buffham*, see 15.105 and the footnotes thereto.

[266] *AMP* (n 161) [19]–[21]. For an example of this in a defamation case, see *Brett Wilson LLP v Persons Unknown* [2015] EWHC 2628 (QB) (Warby J).

### (d) Injunctions against a representative defendant

**15.120**  This is a variant on applying for an order against 'persons unknown' where the identity of one person responsible for the publication of the offending material (*eg* via a particular website or blogsite) is known and it is believed that other persons are involved but their identity is unknown. CPR 19.6(1) provides that a claimant or a defendant may act as a representative party where more than one person has the same interest in the claim and the representative has the same interest in the claim as the represented parties. Considering the Court's final judgment in the case of *Law Society v Kordowski*[267] and the authorities concerning 'protester' harassment referred to in that judgment,[268] it seems that this may be a convenient way to proceed in an appropriate case.[269]

### (e) Injunctions contra mundum

**15.121**  Another variant on this theme is to make an application for an order *contra mundum*, that is to say, one that is made against the world at large rather than against specific defendants. Anyone that is put on notice of such an order is bound by it, at pain of sanctions for contempt of court if it is breached. Traditionally a feature of family proceedings to protect vulnerable children from unwanted publicity,[270] Eady J granted such an order on a final basis in the privacy case of *OPQ v BJM*.[271] He did so explicitly in order to meet the problem subsequently addressed by the Court of Appeal in *Hutcheson v Popdog Ltd*, namely, that *Spycatcher* relief, vital on the facts to the effective protection of the claimant's Article 8 ECHR rights, would come to an end upon the conclusion of the proceedings.[272] Since the advent of the HRA, the judge reasoned, the significance of historical distinctions between discrete jurisdictions had faded and, in *Re S*,[273] been replaced by a new methodology of weighing conflicting Convention rights. By that means, he held, the court had acquired a power derived from Convention rights to grant injunctions against the world in support of a private right to confidentiality where the claimant's physical and moral integrity was adversely imperilled. Moreover, on the facts, there was solid evidence as to the health, including the mental health, of the claimant and various other members of his family, whose rights had to be taken into account. It was clear from that evidence that publicity of the information that was the subject

---

[267] *Law Society v Kordowski* (n 19). For further details of this case, see 15.07.
[268] See *eg Edo MBM Technology v Campaign to Smash EDO* [2005] EWHC 837 (QB).
[269] See *eg QRS v Beach* [2014] EWHC 3057 (QB); [2014] EWHC 3319 (QB).
[270] *eg* the injunction granted by Morland J to protect while they remained children Thompson and Venables, the boys convicted of the murder of Jamie Bulger, which they then applied successfully to have continued into their adulthood: *Venables v News Group Newspapers Ltd* [2001] Fam 430. See also in this connection the President of the Family Division's *Practice Direction on Applications for Reporting Restrictions* (18 March 2005) [2005] 2 FLR 120.
[271] [2011] EWHC 1059 (QB), [2011] EMLR 23.
[272] See 15.105.
[273] *Re S (A Child) (Identification: Restrictions on Publication)* [2004] UKHL 47, [2005] 2 AC 593.

of the proceedings might have very serious consequences. None of the protected information was in the public domain; there was no public interest in its disclosure; there was no question of exposing or detecting crime; and the information would have made no contribution to a debate of general interest. In the circumstances, the judge held, the balance came down in favour of protecting the claimant's rights by granting an injunction *contra mundum*. Eady J observed significantly that there were no other means open to the court of fulfilling its obligations under the HRA effectively to protect the claimant's right to respect for his privacy under Article 8 ECHR.

Until the point raised by the Court of Appeal in *Hutcheson v Popdog Ltd* as to the **15.122** correctness of *Jockey Club v Buffham* is laid to rest, it may be prudent for a claimant in an appropriate case, where the continuation of *Spycatcher*-type relief against non-parties matters, to apply for an injunction *contra mundum* at the conclusion of the proceedings. Furthermore, if *Jockey Club v Buffham* is held to have been decided correctly, *OPQ v BJM* may come to be seen as an important precedent. Finally, there seems to be no reason in principle why a court should not grant an interim injunction *contra mundum*, if the evidence warrants it, and if to do so appears necessary and proportionate. Interim orders *contra mundum* are regularly made in the family courts to protect children.

### (f) Blocking injunctions

The court has a statutory jurisdiction under s 97A of the Copyright, Designs and **15.123** Patents Act 1988 to grant a blocking injunction against a broadband provider requiring it to block access to a specified website in order to prevent further breaches of a claimant's copyright (*eg* because the website is being used for the unauthorized uploading and downloading of the claimant's films in breach of its copyright in those films).[274] The injunction is not granted against a broadband provider on the footing that it is a wrongdoer but on the basis that it is in a good position to prevent the perpetuation of the proven wrongdoing of others. The nature and mode of operation of the s 97A jurisdiction in the copyright context is discussed in greater detail in Chapter 9.

The question that arises in the privacy context is whether, in a particularly egre- **15.124** gious case on the facts, where despite the claimant's best efforts it had proved impossible to bring to an end proven wrongdoing being effected through a

---

[274] See Arnold J's judgments in *Twentieth Century Fox Film Corp v British Telecommunications plc* [2011] EWHC 1981 (Ch), [2011] RPC 28 and [2011] EWHC 2714 (Ch), [2012] 1 All ER 806, the first case to have involved an application for a copyright blocking injunction under s 97A of the Copyright, Designs and Patents Act 1988. See also *Dramatico Entertainment Ltd v British Sky Broadcasting Ltd* [2012] EWHC 1152 (Ch), [2012] 3 CMLR 15; *EMI Records Ltd v British Sky Broadcasting Ltd* [2013] EWHC 379 (Ch), [2013] Bus LR 884; *Football Association Premier League Ltd v British Sky Broadcasting Ltd* [2013] EWHC 2058 (Ch), [2013] ECDR 14; and *Paramount Home Entertainment International Ltd v British Sky Broadcasting Ltd* [2013] EWHC 3479 (Ch), [2014] ECDR 7.

particular website in violation of the claimant's Article 8 rights (*eg* because the website and everyone involved in it was based in a foreign jurisdiction where there was no effective right of access to a court, or where there was no practical means to make those responsible answerable for their conduct), the court might be prepared to grant a blocking injunction albeit that it lacked express statutory authority to do so.

**15.125** Applying the same process of reasoning that led Eady J to conclude in *OPQ v BJM* that he had the power to grant an injunction *contra mundum* in a privacy case,[275] it is certainly arguable that the court has, and would decide that it had, the jurisdiction to grant a blocking order in such a case. Despite the absence of explicit statutory authority, it is submitted that the court's general power under s 37 of the Senior Courts Act 1981 to grant injunctions when just and convenient, coupled with its obligation under s 6 HRA to protect individuals' Convention rights, specifically in this context those conferred by Article 8 ECHR, and the common law's tendency to abhor a vacuum, constitutes a sufficient basis on which to ground jurisdiction.[276] Furthermore, it would exercise it if, as Eady J found in *OPQ*, it was necessary and proportionate for it to do so, and there was simply no other means open to the court of fulfilling its obligations under the HRA. In parenthesis, as one informed commentator has argued, it would be anomalous if intellectual property rights were capable of being protected if necessary by means of blocking orders, but other important rights, such as those to respect for privacy and protection of reputation, were not.[277]

### (2) Damages Awards in Cases of Online Publication

**15.126** The topic of damages in privacy and harassment cases is discussed in Chapter 12. In the specific context of the internet and social media, the court has acknowledged the potential for information posted online to 'go viral' and to cause increased damage thereby even if the information is published in the first instance only to a relatively small number of people: in a defamation case, the Court of Appeal upheld a very substantial award of damages which had been imposed, in part, in recognition of this phenomenon.[278]

---

[275] As to which, see 15.121.

[276] As regards this suggested interpretative approach, see Lord Brown in *In Re BBC* [2009] UKHL 39, [2010] 1 AC 145 [57] and Lord Rodger in *In Re Guardian News and Media Ltd* [2010] UKSC 1, [2010] 2 AC 697 [30].

[277] See D Mac Síthigh, 'The Fragmentation of Intermediary Liability in the UK' (2013) 8(7) JIPLP 521. It may be noted that similar reasoning persuaded Arnold J to grant a blocking order in a trade mark case notwithstanding the absence of specific statutory warrant to do so: see *Cartier International AG v British Sky Broadcasting Ltd* [2014] EWHC 3354 (Ch), [2015] EMLR 10. Notably, the judge held that the Court had jurisdiction to grant the order sought on a purely domestic interpretation of s 37(1) of the Senior Courts Act 1981.

[278] *Cairns* (n 6). The claimant was awarded £90,000 in respect of a libellous Tweet posted by the defendant, even though he only had sixty-five Twitter followers.

Damages have been awarded in a number of privacy cases based on online publi- **15.127** cation. The two described below may be regarded as illustrative:

(1) In *Cooper v Turrell*,[279] a claim brought in defamation and misuse of private information, Tugendhat J awarded the individual claimant £30,000 for misuse of private information, and indicated that he would have awarded £40,000 were it not for the fact that he was also awarding libel damages which would compensate the claimant for the distress he had suffered. The action was concerned with private information about the claimant's health, which the defendant recorded surreptitiously before disseminating it to a number of third parties.

(2) In *WXY v Gewanter*,[280] the same judge decided to make one award of damages in respect of misuse of private information/breach of confidence and harassment given that the claimant had sustained distress arising from a single course of harassing conduct which had involved the actual and threatened disclosure of his private information. The Court awarded the claimant £24,950 including £5,000 by way of aggravated damages to reflect the fact that the defendant, by his threats, had intended to benefit financially at the claimant's expense.

---

[279] *Cooper* (n 184).
[280] *WXY* (n 167).

# INDEX